QUEEN

COMPLETE WORKS

REVISED & UPDATED

Queen: Complete Works (Revised & Updated)
Print ISBN: 9781789090000
E-Book ISBN: 9781789090499

Published by
Titan Books
A division of Titan Publishing Group Ltd.
144 Southwark St.
London
SE1 0UP

First published in 2007. This revised and updated edition: October 2018
10 9 8 7 6 5 4 3 2 1

Did you enjoy this book? We love to hear from our readers. Please e-mail us at: **readerfeedback@titanemail.com** or write to Reader Feedback at the above address. To receive advance information, news, competitions, and exclusive offers online, please sign up for the Titan newsletter on our website: **www.titanbooks.com**

A CIP catalogue record for this book is available from the British Library.

Printed and bound by CPI Group (UK) Ltd.

QUEEN
COMPLETE WORKS
REVISED & UPDATED

GEORG PURVIS

TITAN BOOKS

This book is dedicated to
Donald Hartman Hawk, Bruce Hedrick,
and Roger Bennett.

"And then from all this gloom
Life can start anew
And there'll be no crying soon."

CONTENTS

FOREWORD
HEY, WHERE'S MY BACKSTAGE PASS...?

"I think that's one of the positive things a rock band can do, generate that feeling of being together ... We do have a lot of power. We just hope we can divert it in the right direction. I know it looks like a Nüremberg Rally, but our fans are sensible people, they're creating the situation as much as we are, it's not that we're leading them like sheep ... It's very simple really, you just play music which excites people, which interests them. It's rock'n'roll, there's no philosophical reason why we should be there."
– Brian May, *Melody Maker*, 1980

In the 1970s, once the hippie dream of Woodstock was shattered by the nightmare of Altamont within the short span of four months, the rock world took a drastic turn, splitting in several directions, all under the broad and bloated term of "rock music". Heavy and loud was the order of the day, with bands like Free, Led Zeppelin, and Deep Purple driving their point home with all of the subtlety of a jackhammer, while others skated that trend entirely by putting more stock into image, creation, and presentation – and so music suddenly became art. Quirky names became the new standard: Roxy Music, T. Rex, and the New York Dolls; and the boys looked like girls and the girls looked like boys and the general public who had grown up on "clean" music were outraged because they couldn't tell the difference. This wasn't music meant to shock and awe, but to make the audience reflect and visualize.

In the middle of all this, Pete Townshend of The Who wrote and then abandoned a concept album that would have had band and audience joining together to become one. Even with the failure of this concept a new philosophy was born: involve the audience in every aspect of the live show. This feeling of togetherness was to make the fans feel special and connected with their idols, and through this, the live show would take on a new energy.

To say that one man perfected this sounds hyperbolic, but one man did indeed pioneer this tactic, and became a legend in the process.

The word "legend" is hyperbole itself, and is a status that is both limiting and scary all at once. But ask a million people who is the best vocalist in the history of rock music, and the answer will almost overwhelmingly be Freddie Mercury; his status as a legend has transcended his eccentricities and human frailties, and he is held only with the highest regard nowadays. Unfortunately, it took his untimely death for the world to finally see him for who he actually was: a paradox of warmth and standoffishness, of power and shyness, of strength and romance. He was a tragic figure from the outset, destined for greatness but wanting only normality, acceptance, and love.

In the early days of Queen's heyday, Freddie rarely connected with the audience. He remained a public enigma, offering fickle quotes in the press, such as "I'm as gay as a daffodil!", and littering these Mercurial statements with "dears" and "darlings". Live, he exuded darkness, storming onstage dramatically and growling, "The nasty Queenies are back! What do you think of that?" Resplendent in black velvet and make-up, he insisted on enjoying the luxuries of a star but with the budget of a vagabond.

Then, a seismic shift took place in the mid-1970s; glam rock came to an end and, while Roxy Music and David Bowie consistently reinvented themselves to fit the trends, Queen combined their love of the grandiose with the style du jour: *News Of The World*, for example, was royal punk, nitty, gritty, and dignified all at once. And an amazing thing happened: Freddie Mercury finally found his confidence, and added a fourth quality to his hat-trick of singer, songwriter, and pianist: he became an entertainer, determined to involve the audience and ensure maximum enjoyment. Concerts weren't simply events to listen to music; they were now presentations, visual experiences that were designed to wow. In the middle of an overactive dry ice machine and flash bombs, Freddie stood tall and proud, ensconced not in velvet but leather, affectionately addressing the audience as "tarts" and "fuckers" and using his own powerful voice as a catalyst for the spectators to join in the singing. Some audiences needed encouragement, but most were thrilled to be a part of the show and entered in with gusto.

That's not to say that Queen was Freddie's backing band; each member was a cog in the well-oiled machine. Witness Brian May, with his homemade guitar, lovingly crafted by father and son in 1963 over the course of 18 months, that has become one of the most recognizable instruments in the rock world. But what good is a guitar without an amp? A little homemade device, fondly known as the Deakey Amp and named after its creator (more in a moment), that gives off a warm, orchestral sound, as if a quartet of violins was rocking away instead of a guitar. The shy guitarist found his voice after awhile, and even though he couldn't quite believe all of the hype that surrounded his band and fellow bandmates, he still bounced out onstage every night, determined to give his all. While Freddie entertained, Brian was the consummate perfectionist, refusing to hide his displeasure if he played a bum note – even if the audience was blissfully unaware that anything was amiss. His own high standards helped keep Queen on track, even when they lost their direction as success overshadowed creative invention.

On the opposite end of the spectrum is Roger Taylor, the archetypal drummer in search of fast cars, loose women, and good times. But to label him as just a drummer would be superficial; the man is outspoken, lovably gruff, and one talented musician, handling all of the instruments with remarkable adeptness and redefining the meaning of the word "solo" on his first two albums. While he may look onstage as if he is simply trying to get through the show for the inevitable afterparty debauchery, he's among the top drummers in the world: rock-steady and flashy at once, combining the lunacy of Keith Moon with the inventiveness of John Bonham. He suits the needs of the song without being heavy-handed or showing off too much. These days, his contentious views on politics, religion, and c-lebrities have gained notoriety

among the fan base, but he's as good for press fodder as Freddie was, throwing in a good-natured jab at his best friend Brian's obsession with perfection or his band's occasional lapses in judgment.

Then there's John Deacon, the underrated and understated bassist who, in keeping with the tradition of bass guitarists, rarely spoke. Only when he took the microphone at the Freddie Mercury tribute concert in April 1992 did fans actually realize he had a voice. But behind his silence (and a self-professed inability to sing) lay the secret weapon to Queen's success: while Freddie went off on several stylistic jaunts, and Brian and Roger were the eternal hard rockers, John's loyalties were in the pop world. His second-ever song was a wise choice as the follow-up to Queen's massive worldwide hit, and when he introduced funk to Queen's rock sensibilities, he was once again rewarded with the biggest-selling single in their American record company's history. Yet one look at this unassuming bassist and the feeling can't be hidden that he was a million miles away from it all; barely cracking a smile onstage, he played with inventive precision. Unlike his idols John Entwistle and Chris Squire, he wasn't a show-off, and, like his partner in rhythm, his playing suited the song instead of acting as a showcase for his abilities. However, under all of the trappings of success was a man who yearned for normalcy, and being the father of a half dozen kids was all the more reason to walk away from the spotlight. Not a peep has been heard from him since 1997, though Brian and Roger maintain that he's happier now than ever before.

Freddie's vision of audience participation started in the mid-1970s, but it came to fruition in 1985, at the legendary Live Aid concert. Amid a sea of 72,000 spectators, Freddie secured his position as the world's best showman by getting them all to sing along in a spontaneous moment of elation. The set was tightly structured so that Queen could get all of their hits in without running over their time allotment, but he still stopped the show briefly to engage in a bit of vocal banter. The audience – some Queen fans, most not – played along, singing back every word and phrase he threw at them. With a defiant grin and an enthusiastic shout of "All right!" (shouted back at him, of course), he helped Queen attain the position as the highlight among highlights.

And to think how they transformed from a wannabe, second-rate Led Zeppelin rock band into a barnstorming act that defied classification. Their albums were all over the stylistic map, shifting gears carefully without throwing the listener too violently into change. Each band member adapted to the others' needs while providing to each song a remarkably unique trademark; only through disagreements and tension did they discover their own limitations, but as a unit, they were an unstoppable force, a distinction that Brian and Roger had to face following Freddie's death and John's retirement. Though they were replaced, Brian and Roger discovered just how irreplaceable the other two were. The fans still ate it up, enjoying every morsel no matter who the singer or bassist was – just as long as the guitarist and drummer were there – but the magic of Queen was Freddie Mercury, Brian May, Roger Taylor, and John Deacon. It was a once-in-a-lifetime joining of forces, never to be repeated, and while each quarter was a giant in his own way, it was the combination that turned Queen into a legendary phenomenon.

HOW TO USE THIS BOOK

Part Three lists songs by Queen, and individual solo songs, in alphabetical rather than chronological order. This is advantageous since it discards the necessity for an index and also allows one entry for songs recorded in different versions, creating a more cohesive and understandable format.

Part Three uses the abbreviations listed below. Also included are single release dates (month/year) followed, where applicable, by the highest UK chart placing in [square brackets]. Instead of presenting both US and UK singles, only the UK singles are given since Queen statistically were always in the upper reaches of their home country's charts. An in-depth (but certainly not comprehensive) singles discography in Part Eight explores both UK and US releases. 'Compilation' listings are only given if this was the first official release of the track, or if the version in question was appearing for the first time and differs drastically from the standard version. Likewise, soundtrack albums are only cited in Part Two if they contain exclusive material (as in the case of Brian's *Furia* soundtrack) or if it was the first release of the song (as in Freddie's 'Love Kills' single). Note that Queen's *Flash Gordon* album is considered a band album and not a soundtrack. 'Bonus' listings refer to the extra tracks included on Hollywood Records' 1991 US CD reissue campaign, and, more recently, the 2011 Universal Records worldwide CD reissue campaign.

SAMPLE ENTRY

TOO MUCH LOVE WILL KILL YOU
(May/Musker/Lamers)
• A-side (Brian): 8/92 [5] • Album (Brian): *BTTL* • B-side (Brian): 6/93 [23] • Live (Brian): *Brixton* • Album (Queen): *Heaven* • A-side (Queen): 2/96 [15]

This indicates that 'Too Much Love Will Kill You' was released, in chronological order, as (i) a Brian May solo single in August 1992, reaching No. 5 in the chart; (ii) an album track on Brian's Back To The Light; (iii) the B-side of Brian's solo June 1993 single, reaching No. 23 in the UK chart; (iv) a live version on Brian's Live At The Brixton Academy; (v) an album track on Queen's Made In Heaven; (vi) a Queen UK single in February 1996, reaching No. 15 in the chart.

ABBREVIATIONS USED IN PART THREE

Studio Albums

Queen	*Queen*
Queen2	*Queen II*
SHA	*Sheer Heart Attack*
Opera	*A Night At The Opera*
Races	*A Day At The Races*
NOTW	*News Of The World*
Jazz	*Jazz*

Game	*The Game*
Flash	*Flash Gordon*
Space	*Hot Space*
Works	*The Works*
AKOM	*A Kind Of Magic*
Miracle	*The Miracle*
Innuendo	*Innuendo*
Heaven	*Made In Heaven*
Cosmos	*The Cosmos Rocks*

Compilation and Live Albums

Killers	*Live Killers*
Hits1	*Greatest Hits*
Magic	*Live Magic*
BBC	*Queen At The Beeb /*
	Queen At The BBC
Hits2	*Greatest Hits II*
Wembley	*Live At Wembley '86 / Live At*
	Wembley Stadium
Classic	*Classic Queen*
HitsUS	*Greatest Hits (1992 edition)*
Hits3	*Greatest Hits III*
WWRYHits	*We Will Rock You: Greatest Hits*
	(2004 edition)
On Fire	*Queen On Fire: Live At The Bowl*
Return	*Return Of The Champions*
Montreal	*Queen Rock Montreal*
Ukraine	*Live In Ukraine*
Budapest	*Hungarian Rhapsody: Queen Live*
	In Budapest
Rainbow	*Live At The Rainbow '74*
Odeon	*A Night At The Odeon*
On Air	*On Air*

Solo Albums – Roger Taylor

Fun	*Fun In Space*
Frontier	*Strange Frontier*
Happiness?	*Happiness?*
Electric	*Electric Fire*
Earth	*Fun On Earth*
Lot	*The Lot*

Solo Albums – Roger Taylor (with The Cross)

Shove	*Shove It*
MBADTK	*Mad: Bad: And Dangerous To Know*
Blue	*Blue Rock*

Solo Albums – Freddie Mercury

BadGuy	*Mr Bad Guy*
Barcelona	*Barcelona*
Pretender	*The Great Pretender*
FM Album	*The Freddie Mercury Album*
Box Set	*The Freddie Mercury Box Set*

Solo Albums – Brian May

Starfleet	*Star Fleet Project*
BTTL	*Back To The Light*
Brixton	*Live At The Brixton Academy*
Another	*Another World*
Furia	*Furia*
Acoustic	*Acoustic By Candlelight*
	(with Kerry Ellis)
Golden	*Golden Days* (with Kerry Ellis)

A NOTE ON THE TEXT

Where spelling and stylings of song and album titles vary over the years, I have favored the earliest official release: for instance, while 'Dreamer's Ball' may be grammatically correct, it is printed as 'Dreamers Ball', on *Jazz*. In the case of 'rock and roll' and its many variants, the same situation applies to the correct spellings of the Rock 'n' Roll Medley, 'Born To Rock 'N' Roll' and 'Modern Times Rock'n'Roll'.

Album variations are more of an exception than the rule. I have applied the title *On Air* as the 'official' title of their BBC releases: the first such instance, in 1989, was released as *Queen At The Beeb*, and its North American release in 1995 was released as *Queen At The BBC*, but in 2016, the whole kit'n'kaboodle of Queen's BBC sessions was universally released as *On Air: The Complete BBC Sessions*.

All quotes from news outlets, magazines and websites have been written as they appeared in their respective publications. While the text of the book adheres to US spelling, quotes may vary.

WHAT'S NEW IN THIS EDITION?

Since this book's second edition in 2011, Queen have finally opened up their archives for the fans to enjoy, though one might cast a cynical eye, insisting they more accurately cracked open the door and let a few goodies sneak out. This answers the question that everybody has asked me since I announced I was updating the book: "What more could possibly be updated about Queen?" Well, there's the Queen + Adam Lambert partnership, the Brian May and Kerry Ellis partnership, the various archival releases, *Bohemian Rhapsody...* the list goes on.

After publishing the first edition of this book in 2007 and figuring that was a good experience all around, I started talking with Pieter and Erin Cargill, webmasters of Queen Archives (www.queenarchives. com) and all around wonderful people, and we lamented the lack of an all-encompassing Queen website, with lyrics, quotes, song information, discographies, concertography, sessionography, and so forth. That site became Queenpedia (www.queenpedia. com), which is still going strong today.

And yet, there's something about the written, printed word that people love. You could try to curl up with a laptop and read a book, but it's just not the same. Oh sure, e-Books are all well and good, but you don't get the feel or the smell of a printed book; you can write in the margins of the book, correcting the author and adding your own notes and thoughts; you can pass it back and forth between friends, whereas with an electronic device, it would be like lending out $200 and hoping nothing goes wrong – if it's dropped even once, well, *forget about it.*

So. With this edition, I contacted Titan Books with the proposal to once again update my manuscript, to correct any errors that I had noted in the margins of my own copy, while consulting a "brain trust" of fans with whom I developed a reputation since the first edition was published. In the absence of any official word from the band, who remain tight-lipped on what's in the archives, this "brain trust" was the next best thing – better, in fact, because they were able to add discussions to the mix. Queen fans are loyal and intelligent, and in the virtual presence of these top collectors, I felt like I had finally become one of them.

Concerned with the possibility of being viewed as a turncoat – I was invited to this Mensa of Queen fans, and then suddenly am publishing a second edition with all the information I collected – I asked them what I should do: do I include all of the information we've been discussing, or do I include only what's "common knowledge"?

Their collective response couldn't have been more overwhelmingly positive, with the consensus being, "You *must* get the most accurate information out there!" While Queen Productions continues to sanction publication after publication of their history, the contents of their studio archives remains a scarcity. Imagine, if you will, a book much like Mark Lewisohn's *The Beatles Recording Sessions* or *The Beatles Chronicle.* Fans don't have access to that information, and yet they thirst for it constantly, much like they thirst for *Greatest Video Hits 3* or the fabled anthologies, first announced back in the late 1990s and still being pushed back.

Queen: Complete Works was my attempt at something similar, a printed collection of everything that's known, and everything that isn't common knowledge. At the time, it *was* complete, but the problem with having a book printed is that it's almost immediately obsolete. In the intervening dozen years since the first edition was published, so much new information has come to light that tackling the edits to this book became a massive undertaking. Happily, after spending seven years since the last edition was published perusing other interests, my interest in Queen was rekindled when Adam Lambert joined forces with Brian and Roger, and, it seems that since then, Queen has been more prevalent than ever.

So what can you find here that's different from the second edition? Well, with the new information and a lot of rewritten entries, this is practically a new book entirely. If you're feeling adventurous, you're more than welcome to hold up the two editions for a side-by-side comparison, but I urge you to instead put on your favorite Queen album and read up on it and the related songs.

Oh, and have a pencil ready – just in case you need to make some notes and send them my way.

- Georg Purvis

PART ONE
PRE-QUEEN

This section addresses known live (and occasional studio) performances by the multitude of bands featuring John Deacon, Brian May, Freddie Mercury and Roger Taylor before they came together as Queen, together with a postscript describing the formation of the band and their progress towards making the first Queen album.

In some cases, information is scarce: in lieu of set lists, only known songs performed at any given concert are provided. The itineraries, if they can be called such, are sadly incomplete, and it's unlikely that a full schedule of live performances will ever materialize.

EARLY PERFORMANCES (1957-1963)

Roger Meddows-Taylor was involved in a band at the tender age of eight. The Bubblingover Boys, with mutual friends from the Bosvigo Primary School, performed just one concert at a school dance during the summer of 1957 - instead of appearing on drums, Roger strummed a ukulele. Unsurprisingly, The Bubblingover Boys folded shortly after the dance, leaving Roger without a band until 1963, when he formed Beat Unlimited with Mike Dudley on guitar and David Dowding on bass. This time, Roger initially switched to guitar, though he would finally take the drummer's seat once the band changed their name to The Cousin Jacks. (They also went under the name of The Falcons.) Roger's new band would occasionally play at a local Liberal club, with one of their favorite songs being 'Wipe Out', giving Roger a chance to show off his skills. The Cousin Jacks disbanded in 1965, by which time Roger had decided that a career in music was for him.

Meanwhile, in Panchagni, India, Farookh Bulsara was attending St Peter's Boarding School and had befriended four other young musicians: Derrick Branche (who later appeared in the 1970s sitcom *Only When I Laugh*), Farang Irani, Bruce Murray and Victory Rana. In complete contrast to the persona he would later adopt as Freddie Mercury, Farookh was quite reserved and happy to bang away on a piano while Bruce took the role of front man and vocalist. The Hectics, as the band was called, formed in the spring of 1959 and would practice in a spare dormitory at St

Peter's, later becoming the unofficial school band and appearing at school dances and functions. Humble beginnings, yes, but it gave Farookh his first taste of being on stage; little did anyone know, least of all his band members, what was in store just a decade later.

1984 *(band)*
Autumn 1964-Winter 1968

Musicians: Dave Dilloway *(guitar)*, John 'Jag' Garnham *(rhythm guitar, vocals)*, Brian May *(guitar, vocals)*, John Sanger *(piano, vocals)*, Tim Staffell *(vocals, harmonica)*, Richard Thompson *(drums)*

Repertoire included: 'Go Now', 'Yesterday', 'I'm A Loser', 'Help!', 'Jack Of Diamonds', 'I Wish You Would', 'I Feel Fine', 'Little Egypt', 'Lucille', 'Too Much Monkey Business', 'I Got My Mojo Working', 'Walking The Dog', 'Heart Full Of Soul', 'Bright Lights, Big City', 'Chains', 'Little Rendezvous', 'I'm A Man', 'Bye Bye Bird', 'Dancing In The Street', 'Eight Days A Week', 'I'm Taking Her Home', 'My Generation', 'Cool Jerk', 'R-E-S-P-E-C-T', 'My Girl', 'Shake', '(I'm Not Your) Stepping Stone', 'You Keep Me Hangin' On', 'Whatcha Gonna Do 'Bout It?', 'Substitute', 'How Can It Be', 'Dream', 'Sha La La La Lee', 'So Sad (To Watch Good Love Go Bad)', 'Stone Free', 'She's Gone', 'Knock On Wood'

Known itinerary:
October 28, 1964: St Mary's Church Hall, Twickenham
November 4, 1964: Girl's School, Richmond

January 1965: Imperial College, London
January 15, 1966: Thames Rowing Club, Putney
January 29, 1966: Thames Rowing Club, Putney
February 5, 1966: Rowing Club, Shepperton
Spring 1966: Imperial College, London
Summer 1966: Boat Club, Molesey
Summer 1966: R&B Club, Putney
July 1/2, 1966: Boat Club, Henley-On-Thames
July 9, 1966: All Saints Church Hall, London
Autumn 1966: White Hart, Southhal
May 13, 1967: Imperial College, London
September 1967: School Of Medicine, London
September 1967: Top Rank Club, Croydon
December 23, 1967: Olympia Theatre, London

Brian Harold May had been inspired to start playing music after hearing the likes of Lonnie Donegan and Buddy Holly, and by the late 1950s had befriended Dave Dilloway from Hampton Grammar School, who also had aspirations to be a guitarist. Brian had wanted a Fender or a Gibson, then all the rage, but was unable to afford such a luxurious instrument. Instead, Brian and his father Harold spent 18 months, starting in the autumn of 1963, constructing a guitar that would become Brian's trademark for all his professional career.

The Red Special, as his axe was later dubbed, was a piecemeal construction formed from Brian's own design. The neck and body were carved from an aged mahogany fireplace, the tension of the strings was balanced by motorcycle valve springs, the tremolo arm was a discarded knitting needle, the fretboard markers were mother-of-pearl buttons borrowed from his mother's sewing box. Apart from three Burns pick-ups (which were modified by an epoxy resin), the guitar was entirely homemade and clearly a labor of love. Now all Brian needed was a band in which he could show off his accomplishment.

1984 was formed by Dave and Brian, with Bill Richards on vocals and guitar and John Sanger on piano. Bill left shortly after the band was formed because of his inferior guitar; Brian was chosen to diplomatically offer the ultimatum and Bill chose to leave since he couldn't afford a new instrument. Malcolm Childs replaced him for nearly a week before being canned due to his unreliable nature. Finally, John 'Jag' Garnham joined on rhythm guitar and vocals, and 1984 (named after George Orwell's novel and replacing earlier suggestions like Bod Chappie And The Beetles and The Mind Boggles) started the search for a drummer. An advertisement was placed in a music store window and answered by Richard

Thompson; the only missing ingredient now was a vocalist. Dave and Brian had found Tim Staffell in the audience of a dance at Murray Park Hall, jamming along on mouth organ, and asked him upfront if he would be interested in singing with them.

The band intended to write a futuristic mini-rock opera based loosely around Orwell's novel, but instead focused on honing their chops through favorite rock and R&B tunes. On 28 October 1964, the band made their live debut at St Mary's Church Hall in Twickenham, with the organizer, Chris Whittome-Knights, offering them a substantial (at the time) £10. From there, 1984 started building up their popularity by word of mouth and, soon enough, the band would be playing a gig a week. Sets usually included songs by The Yardbirds, The Rolling Stones, The Spencer Davis Group and The Beatles, among many others. Tim was the designated lead singer, but Brian would take over the mic on 'Yesterday' (which drove the girls wild) and assist on harmonies on 'Help!' and 'I'm A Loser'.

During the spring of 1966 at Imperial College London, where Brian had been a student since the previous October, the band were filmed on 8mm color film, albeit lacking sound. The film, lasting around four minutes, focused mainly on the party at which 1984 were performing, but Brian and his guitar can be clearly seen in the background. On 31 March 1967, the band appeared at Broom Lane Studios by courtesy of some friends of Dave's, performing 12 songs – 'Hold On, I'm Coming!', 'Knock On Wood', 'N.S.U.', 'How Can It Be', 'Step On Me', 'Purple Haze', 'Our Love Is Driftin'', 'Remember', 'Sweet Wine', 'Get Out Of My Life, Woman', '(I Can't Get No) Satisfaction' and 'My Girl' – with one of them, 'Step On Me', an original written by Brian and Tim that was subsequently recorded by Smile.

After Bill Richards left 1984, he formed The Left Handed Marriage, and in the spring of 1967 Bill asked Brian if he would contribute guitar to a few recording sessions as he wanted a fuller sound. The band, with Bill, Jenny Hill, Henry Deval and Terry Goulds, had recorded the album On The Right Side Of The Left Handed Marriage, released in January 1967. Dave was also asked to contribute to the sessions at Brian's request, and three sessions were recorded.

The first took place at Manor Road Studios in Twickenham on 4 April 1967, with four songs – 'Give Me Time', 'She Was Once My Friend', 'Yours Sincerely' and 'Sugar Lump Girl' – recorded. The second was at Abbey Road Studios in St John's Wood on 28 June, though, sadly, Brian would not run into any of The

Beatles, who had completed their latest single, 'All You Need Is Love', two days beforehand. At this session, 'I Need Time' (a retitled 'Give Me Time') and 'She Was Once My Friend' were re-recorded. The third and final session was held on 31 July at Regent Sound Studios, with 'I Need Time' and 'She Was Once My Friend' again re-recorded, along with a new song, 'Appointment'. The three songs from the final session were due to be issued on the band's sophomore album but it remained unreleased; they were, however, included as bonus tracks on the 1993 CD reissue of *On The Right Side Of The Left Handed Marriage*.

The last two (known) performances of 1984 during 1967 were the highest profile: in September, the band was entered into the Battle Of The Bands competition (later reported by *Melody Maker*, giving 1984 their first press coverage) and ended up winning with a 20-minute set that included 'Ain't That Peculiar' and 'Crying In The Rain'. As a result, the band were invited to participate in the Christmas On Earth charity showcase on 23 December, which was an all-star affair involving most of the London 'underground', including Jimi Hendrix, Traffic, Pink Floyd, Herd and Tyrannosaurus Rex (later to become T. Rex). Many years later, Brian recalled that Hendrix walked up to the band and asked, "Which way to the stage, man?"

Unfortunately, this would mark the end of Brian's interest in 1984, though he would fulfil his commitments with the band into the New Year. Finally, in February 1968 Brian announced he was leaving. The band continued with Tim taking over on lead guitar for eight months (though he too would soon jump ship and meet back up with Brian), continuing for a few more years with little success. 1984 remained a cover band through its final years, with a non-performing reunion in 1990 via the Queen International Fan Club when Brian, Dave, John and Richard met at Dave's home for a chat and photo opportunity.

THE OPPOSITION /
THE NEW OPPOSITION / THE ART
Spring 1965-Summer 1969

Musicians, The Opposition (spring 1965-spring 1966): Nigel Bullen *(drums)*, Clive Castledine *(bass guitar)*, John Deacon *(guitar)*, Richard Young *(vocals, guitar)*

Musicians, The New Opposition (spring 1966-winter 1967): Pete 'Pedro' Bartholomew *(vocals)*, Nigel Bullen *(drums)*, Ronald Chester *(guitar)*, John Deacon *(bass guitar)*, David Williams *(guitar, vocals)*, Richard Young *(vocals, guitar, keyboards)*

Musicians, The Opposition (winter 1967-spring 1968) / The Art (spring 1968-summer 1969): Nigel Bullen *(drums)*, Ronald Chester *(guitar)*, John Deacon *(bass guitar)*, David Williams *(vocals, guitar)*, Richard Young *(keyboards)*

Repertoire included: 'You Don't Know', 'Going To A Go-Go', 'Meeting Over Yonder', 'In The Midnight Hour', 'Heatwave', 'Knock On Wood', 'Hold On, I'm Coming', 'Something You Got', 'Something About You', 'I'll Be Doggone', 'Can't Help Myself', 'Dancing In The Street', 'Headline News', 'Ride Your Pony', 'Land Of 1,000 Dances'

Known itinerary, The Opposition:
September 25, 1965: Clive Castledine's house, Leicester
October 1965: Gartree School, Leicester
December 4, 1965: Co-operative Hall, Enderby
December 17, 1965: Gartree School, Leicester
December 31, 1965: Market Harborough Youth Club, Leicester
January 15, 1966: Cooperative Hall, Enderby
February 5, 1966: Village Institute, Countersthorpe
February 11, 1966: Youth Club, Narborough
March 5, 1966: Constitutional Hall, Wigston
March 11, 1966: Village Hall, Evington
April 30, 1966: Cooperative Hall, Enderby
January 1967: USAF Base, Molesworth
February 12, 1967: Boys Club, New Parks
February 25, 1967: Antiquity Club, Churchgate
March 10, 1967: Roundhills Youth Centre, Thurmaston, Leicester
March 18, 1967: Boys Club, New Parks
March 31, 1967: Kirby Lane Community Centre, Melton Mowbray
April 23, 1967: Beaumont Keys
April 30, 1967: Boys Club, New Parks
July 1, 1967: Royal Oak, Wigston
November 4, 1967: Club, Evington
November 10, 1967: Boys Club, Witterworth
November 11, 1967: Zodiac 67 Club, Leicester
December 21, 1967: Raven Youth Club, Thurby Lodge
January 6, 1968: Dog & Gun, Thurlaston
January 12, 1968: Casino Ballroom, Leicester
January 27, 1968: Country Arms, Blaby
February 9, 1968: Royal Oak, Wigston

February 16, 1968: Youth Club, Lutterworth
February 17, 1968: Dog & Gun, Thurlaston
February 23, 1968: Roundhills Youth Center, Thumaston
February 24, 1968: Youth Club Hall, Kibworth
March 1, 1968: Royal Oak, Wigston
March 2, 1968: Country Arms, Blaby

Known itinerary, The New Opposition:
June 14, 1966: Cooperative Hall, Enderby
August 1966: Cooperative Hall, Enderby
October 1966: Casino Ballroom, Leicester
November 6, 1966: Monsell Youth Club, Eyres
November 11, 1966: Monsell Youth Club, Eyres
December 31, 1966: Market Harbor Youth Club, Leicester
January 13, 1967: Tennis Club, Leicester

Known itinerary, The Art:
Spring 1968: venue unknown, St Neots
Spring 1968: venue unknown, Kettering
March 16, 1968: Gartree School, Oadby
March 29, 1968: Youth Club, Lutterworth
April 28, 1968: Village Hall, Billesden
May 11, 1968: Village Hall, Kibworth
Summer 1968: Kirby Lane Community Centre, Melton Mowbray
December 17, 1968: Gartree School, Leicester
January 11, 1969: West End Ballroom, Coalville
January 18, 1969: Rugby Club, Hinckley
January 25, 1969: Community Centre, Muxloe
February 1, 1969: Village Hall, Kibworth
February 8, 1969: Village Hall, Bedford
February 15, 1969: Rugby Club, Tyers
August 1969: Youth Club, Great Glen

John Richard Deacon and a handful of his classmates from Beauchamp Grammar School in Leicester had formed The Opposition in the spring of 1965, inspired by such acts as Herman's Hermits, Peter & Gordon, The Hollies, The Rockin' Berries, and, of course, The Beatles and The Rolling Stones. John wasn't even 14 by the time The Opposition became a semi-serious venture. Initially, John played guitar (having not even picked up a bass yet) alongside his best friend, drummer Nigel Bullen, and their friends Richard Young and Clive Castledine.

John had been playing guitar since the age of 12 and was already quite proficient when he joined The Opposition. Their first gig was at a party at Clive's house, followed by a dance at Gartree School, though

their first authentic, paying show was at the Enderby Co-operative Hall, soon becoming regulars at youth clubs around Oadby.

Clive was dismissed in the spring of 1966, and John took over on bass and local singer Peter 'Pedro' Bartholomew joined on vocals. The former bassist's firing was instigated by Peter, who had agreed to sing with them on condition they get a better bass guitarist. David Williams joined on guitar and Richard moved to keyboards. With the personnel change, the band also switched their name to The New Opposition and would remain under that moniker until the beginning of 1967. Their set was comprised mostly of The Yardbirds, The Animals and various Tamla Motown singles, though their repertoire had expanded to include The Zombies and The Spencer Davis Group in the summer of 1966.

Ronald Chester joined later in 1966 and David Williams became the band's full-time vocalist after the dismissal of Peter Bartholomew, and they reverted to their original name only to change it again in the spring of 1968, this time to The Art. (The logic behind this decision? "David Williams was arty.") John left in August 1969 to concentrate on his electronics degree; the band had been solely a local group and had no aspirations to go any further. With constant pressure from his mother to focus on his education and not waste his time on music, John hung up his bass guitar for the better part of a year and worked diligently at Leicester University, though the desire to perform would soon prove too strong.

JOHNNY QUALE AND THE REACTION
Spring 1965-Autumn 1965

Musicians: Jim Craven *(bass guitar)*, Mike Dudley *(keyboards, guitar)*, Johnny Quale *(vocals)*, Graham Hankins *(guitar)*, John 'Acker' Snell *(saxophone)*, Roger 'Splodge' Taylor *(drums)*

Repertoire included: 'Game Of Love', 'Hey Mama (Keep Your Big Mouth Shut)', 'Whatcha Gonna Do 'Bout It?', 'Slow Down', 'R-E-S-P-E-C-T', 'I Got You (I Feel Good)', 'It's Gonna Work Out Fine', 'Land Of 1,000 Dances'

Known itinerary:
March 15, 1965: City Hall, Truro
April 15, 1965: City Hall, Truro
Summer 1965: Blue Lagoon, Newquay
Summer 1965: Village Hall, St Just

Summer 1965: The Garden, Penzance
Summer 1965: Princess Pavilion, Falmouth

While he was in The Cousin Jacks, word had spread about young Roger Taylor's expertise on the drums and, early in 1965, Johnny Quale And The Reaction sent an invitation to him to join the band. (Mike Dudley, Roger's musical ally, came along too). Johnny Quale, whose real name was John Grose, was known around Cornwall as an Elvis Presley impersonator – sideburns and all – and preferred straight-up rock as opposed to the more adventurous music other garage bands were engrossed in at the time. After a few rehearsals, the band made their live debut on 15 March 1965 at the Rock and Rhythm Championship at Truro's City Hall. Among the 15 groups that entered, Johnny Quale And The Reaction placed fourth, a position that pleasantly surprised the band. Spurred on by this, the band played a series of shows throughout the spring and summer of 1965, but the musical split between Johnny and the others was starting to show. The lead vocalist was still insisting the band play Elvis covers, while the band wanted to expand their musical direction.

The solution was to perform two sets, the first simply as The Reaction (allowing them to play the music they wanted with various band members taking turns on lead vocals), the second featuring Johnny Quale putting on his showman routine. In October 1965, the band were presented the opportunity to record an EP, representing Johnny's musical preferences on one side and those of the others on the flip. At Sound Studios in Wadebridge, the band recorded 'Bona Serra', 'Just A Little Bit', 'What's On Your Mind' and 'I'll Go Crazy' as Johnny Quale And The Reaction, and 'In The Midnight Hour' and 'I Got You (I Feel Good)' as The Reaction, with Roger providing lead vocals.

However, the end was nigh for Johnny. Saturday nights were normally kept clear of bookings, but when the band agreed to perform a gig at short notice on the night that an Elvis Presley film was to be screened at the Plaza in Truro, Johnny had to make a decision. He ultimately performed the gig, but tendered his resignation afterwards. Now minus their eccentric frontman, the band became simply...

THE REACTION
Autumn 1965-Autumn 1968

Musicians, autumn 1965-1967: Roger 'Sandy' Brokenshaw *(vocals)*, Jim Craven *(bass guitar)*, Geoff Daniel *(guitar)*, Mike Dudley *(keyboards, guitar)*, Mike Grose *(guitar)*, John 'Acker' Snell *(saxophone)*, Roger 'Splodge' Taylor *(vocals, drums)*

Musicians, 1967-summer 1968: Mike Dudley *(keyboards, guitar)*, Mike Grose *(guitar)*, Richard Penrose *(bass guitar)*, Roger Taylor *(vocals, drums)*

Musicians, summer-autumn 1968: Jim Craven *(bass guitar)*, Mike Dudley *(keyboards, guitar)*, Mike Grose *(guitar)*, Roger Taylor *(vocals, drums)*

Known itinerary:
November 17, 1965: Methodist Hall, St Agnes
December 1965: Truro School, Truro
December 27, 1965: School's Christmas Dance, Truro
January 8, 1966: Princess Pavilion, Falmouth
March 7, 1966: City Hall, Truro
March 12, 1966: Princess Pavilion, Falmouth
March 17, 1966: Flamingo Ballroom, Redruth
July 17, 1966: City Hall, Truro
August 15, 1966: Dartmouth, Devon
August 16, 1966: Town Hall, Torquay
January 7, 1967: Flamingo Ballroom, Redruth
January 24, 1967: Penmare Hotel, Hayle
January 28, 1967: Guildhall, St Ives
March 3, 1967: Flamingo Ballroom, Redruth
March 4, 1967: Princess Pavilion, Falmouth
March 10, 1967: Penmare Hotel, Hayle
March 11, 1967: Blue Lagoon, Newquay
March 31, 1967: Penmare Hotel, Hayle
April 21, 1967: County Grammar School, Truro
April 29, 1967: Penmare Hotel, Hayle
May 4, 1967: Skating Rink, Camborne
May 6, 1967: Blue Lagoon, Newquay
May 27, 1967: Skating Rink, Camborne
July 29, 1967: Beach, Perranporth
July 31, 1967: Village Hall, St Just
August 4, 1967: Rugby Club, Hayle
November 10, 1967: Pennance Hotel, Hayle
December 21, 1967: Raven Youth Club, Thurnby Lodge
July 4, 1968: Beach, Perranporth
July 13, 1968: Princess Pavilion, Falmouth

It was an easy transition for The Reaction: they were used to performing sets without their erstwhile lead singer, but they still needed a vocalist. After a series of auditions, they hired Roger 'Sandy' Brokenshaw, who was later fired due to his penchant for upbeat soul and mainstream ballads. The band wanted to progress into heavier musical territories, but were without a lead singer again. It eventually dawned upon the band that Roger Taylor would be the best vocal substitute, but he still wanted to establish himself as a proficient drummer, a difficult task when coupled with singing. He was up to the challenge anyway, and The Reaction morphed into the power trio they had always wanted to be.

The band also landed a pair of roadies, Neil Battersby and Peter Gill-Carey. Roger, meanwhile, gradually evolved into the leader of the group, an inevitability, considering his status as the lead vocalist. When the band contacted a booking agency (BCD Entertainments) about performing some dates, Roger successfully argued that the band might as well find their own bookings and save the ten per cent fee the agency required. Roger also explored his creative side, already establishing himself as an eccentric, theatrical drummer - in a move that even Keith Moon never attempted, Roger doused his cymbals with gasoline and set them alight. After acquiring his family's piano, he removed the outer frame, painted the now-exposed interior and, during shows, would leave his drums to pound out random chords. When the set came to an end with 'Land Of 1,000 Dances', he would attack the piano with as much ferocity as he had his drums. Other times, the band would conclude their shows by spraying each other with foam.

In February 1967, a horrific road accident almost brought an end to The Reaction. Roger had just been granted his driver's license and offered to relieve Neil Battersby of his duties for a night. As the van and its occupants – including Roger, Michael Dudley, his girlfriend Marian Little, Richard Penrose, his girlfriend Valerie Burrows, Neil Battersby and Peter Gill-Carey – traveled along the A30, they encountered some serious fog. Without warning, the van somersaulted and landed on its roof, sliding along the road for several feet before coming to a halt. Roger was thrown clear and was unhurt, but his passengers weren't so lucky: Michael received a broken hand and nose, Marian suffered a cut chest and Valerie had internal stomach injuries. Richard and Neil were covered in cuts and glass, but the worst injured was Peter, who was lying unconscious in the middle of the road and bleeding profusely. The accident was so severe that Peter was left with a paralysed right arm and was unable to finish his medical degree. Unbeknown to Roger, he had slammed into an abandoned fish van; seven years were spent in legally exonerating him.

The accident affected Roger considerably and, while The Reaction continued throughout 1967, he was grateful when university started up in October. Studying for his dentistry degree, he moved to Shepherd's Bush to study at the Royal London Hospital. Roger returned throughout the year to perform with The Reaction, which had turned into a psychedelic, Hendrix-inspired group in Roger's absence, and while the band continued to perform sparsely throughout 1968, they drifted apart for good in the autumn. Roger's next musical path was to involve two former musicians from a band in Middlesex, who were determined to start their own power trio and had placed an ad at Imperial College seeking a Ginger Baker/Mitch Mitchell-type drummer.

SMILE
Summer 1968-Winter 1970

Musicians: Brian May *(guitar, vocals)*, Tim Staffell *(vocals, bass guitar)*, Roger Taylor *(drums, vocals)*, Chris Smith *(keyboards)*, Mike Grose *(bass guitar, vocals – April 17 & 18, 1970 only)*

Repertoire included: 'Toccata and Fugue in D Minor', 'Can't Be So Sad', 'If I Were A Carpenter', 'Earth', 'Mony Mony', 'See What A Fool I've Been', 'Rollin' Over'

Known itinerary:
Summer 1968: PJ's Club, Truro
Summer 1968: Flamingo Ballroom, Redruth
Summer 1968: Imperial College, London
October 26, 1968: Imperial College, London
October 31, 1968: Imperial College, London
February 27, 1969: Royal Albert Hall, London
February 28, 1969: Athletic Club, Richmond
March 15, 1969: Imperial College, London
March 28, 1969: PJ's Club, Truro
March 29, 1969: PJ's Club, Truro
April 18, 1969: PJ's Club, Truro
April 19, 1969: Revolution Club, London
July 19, 1969: PJ's Club, Truro
September 13, 1969: PJ's Club, Truro
September 14, 1969: PJ's Club, Truro
December 13, 1969: Marquee Club, London
January 31, 1970: Imperial College, London
April 17, 1970: PJ's Club, Truro
April 18, 1970: PJ's Club, Truro
April 1970, unknown venue
May 1970, unknown venue

Taking their cue from the myriad power trios and supergroups being formed in the late 1960s, Brian and Tim Staffell called their new band Smile and had a completely different philosophy from 1984 - instead of relying mostly on straight-up covers, the band would write their own songs. In the absence of enough original material, however, Smile also deconstructed more contemporary songs from bands like The Small Faces, The Beatles and so forth. In an age when progressive rock was still booming, Smile was bringing its own approach to the genre.

Tim and Brian journeyed to Shepherd's Bush to hold an audition for Roger, who had answered an advert placed in the local paper for a drummer. They turned up with acoustic guitars and, since Roger's drum set was back in Truro, their new drummer tapped at a pair of bongos. Realizing his immense talent (even on bongos), Tim and Brian immediately formed a friendship with Roger and Smile was born. The band played three gigs during the summer of 1968 that served chiefly as a means of integrating Roger into Tim and Brian's collective vision, landing their first proper gig supporting Pink Floyd at Imperial College on 26 October. Not surprisingly, given their penchant for jamming on one song for up to 20 minutes, Smile fitted in nicely with Pink Floyd's audience. The Floyd, who were now minus founding member Syd Barrett, were shedding the hippie acid rock that had characterized their early hits and were redesigning themselves as the forefathers of progressive stoner rock.

Given Brian's relationship with the faculty at Imperial College, Smile became the house band there and were given free reign to rehearse on campus and perform supporting slots for more established bands like Pink Floyd, Yes, Tyrannosaurus Rex (later T. Rex) and Family. The band was augmented by roadie Pete Edmunds and sound mixer John Harris (who also occasionally deputised on keyboards), though a constant presence at rehearsals was Freddie Bulsara, who would later rechristen himself Freddie Mercury. He had met Tim at Ealing College of Art and the two became friends; it was inevitable that Freddie's path would cross with Brian's and Roger's, which ultimately led to the formation of Queen.

Keyboardist Chris Smith was briefly introduced into the fold and played a few shows with the band, but was told that his services were no longer required in February 1969; the band felt that they had a full enough sound without him. A charity show was organized at the Royal Albert Hall on 27 February 1969, where Smile shared the bill with Joe Cocker, Spooky Tooth, The Bonzo Dog Doo-Dah Band and Free, whose lead singer was Paul Rodgers. Smile were the headliners and were introduced, like the other bands, by legendary DJ John Peel, but their set started inauspiciously. When Tim walked out on stage, his bass guitar lead was too short and popped out of the amplifier by the time he reached the microphone at the front of the stage. He had also neglected to wear shoes or socks and discovered all too quickly that the stage was littered with splinters. Their set was filmed, albeit without sound, and included 'If I Were A Carpenter', an original by Tim called 'Earth', 'Mony Mony' and 'See What A Fool I've Been', which was derived from a Sonny Terry and Brownie McGhee song called 'That's How I Feel'.

After a gig in April 1969 at the Revolution Club, Smile were approached by an impressed Lou Reizner, a talent scout for Mercury Records, and offered a recording contract; it was accepted almost immediately. After two sessions in the summer of 1969 which saw six compositions recorded, a single – 'Earth', backed with 'Step On Me' – was released, though only in North America, where Smile had no fanbase. The tactic had worked with Deep Purple's debut single, 'Hush', but the Smile single failed to chart and their contract wasn't renewed.

But Mercury hadn't completely given up on Smile yet: in December, they organized a showcase concert at the Marquee Club and had the band play as the main support to Kippington Lodge (featuring a young Nick Lowe). While Smile's set was tight, the audience wasn't as receptive as they would have hoped and the end was in sight nigh for Smile. Brian was still a committed scholar and started to research zodiacal light. At the beginning of 1970, he studied in Tenerife (where the necessary equipment had been moved from Switzerland) and had two papers published in the Monthly Notices of the Royal Astronomical Society. Brian's absence from Smile was a portent for Tim - he was unsure if Brian would still be dedicated to the band on his return, deciding therefore to leave Smile and form another band. With a handful of prior commitments still to fulfill, Brian and Roger turned to the drummer's bassist friend Mike Grose to help them out for two dates – coincidentally, at a PJ's Club, which Mike co-owned at the time – in April 1970, before coaxing Tim back for two more gigs later in April and May. But enough was enough for Tim, and his departure after that formally ended Smile; Tim went on to play in the bands No Joke! (also with Mike), Humpy Bong, and Morgan. With their future in the music industry still unsure, Brian and Roger turned to Freddie Bulsara, the unofficial fourth member of Smile, for assistance.

IBEX
Spring-Autumn 1969

Musicians: Mike Bersin *(guitar, vocals)*, Freddie Bulsara *(vocals)*, Geoff Higgins *(bass guitar)*, Mick 'Miffer' Smith *(drums)*, John 'Tupp' Taylor *(bass guitar, flute, vocals)*, Richard Thompson *(drums, 23 August)*

Repertoire included: 'Jailhouse Rock', 'I'm So Glad', 'Communication Breakdown', 'Rain', 'We're Going Wrong', 'Rock Me Baby', 'Stone Free', 'Crossroads', 'Vagabond Outcast', 'We're Going Home'

Known itinerary:
May 23, 1969: Honiton Hall, Penketh
Summer 1969: Wade Deacon Grammar School for Girls, Widness
August 1969: Technical College, St Helens
August 23, 1969: The Bolton's Octagon Theatre, Bolton
August 24, 1969: Open Air Festival, Queen's Park, Bolton
September 9, 1969: The Sink, Liverpool
September 19, 1969: College of Technology, St Helens

Freddie Bulsara and Tim Staffell had befriended each other while at Ealing College of Art and, though Freddie was a vocal supporter of Smile, he never considered imposing himself upon the others by asking to be their vocalist; instead, he focused mostly on his studies at Ealing. Graduating in the spring of 1969, he instantly thought of joining a band. Ibex were a power trio comprised of Mike Bersin on guitar, John 'Tupp' Taylor on bass, flute, and vocals, and Mick 'Miffer' Smith on drums; occasionally, when John was preoccupied with his flute duties, Geoff Higgins would step in on bass. The band had sent a tape to Apple Records (owned by The Beatles) but had received no response. Freddie met up with them at a birthday party of a mutual friend of Brian and Roger's and discussed music at length.

Much as he had with Smile, Freddie tagged along with Ibex and gave them ideas on how to work on their

stage presentation and song arrangements. Inevitably, the band members simply asked Freddie if he wanted to sing with them, and, after a brief audition, he was in. Ibex rehearsed at Imperial College throughout the spring of 1969, with their set running the gamut from The Beatles to Yes to Rod Stewart. The band played a handful of gigs throughout the spring and summer of 1969, and it was obvious that Freddie was a born showman. His bandmates would later comment that while they were initially hesitant about his flamboyant stage antics, they paid off in the end, winning them some much-needed word-of-mouth support and a growing fanbase.

However, Ibex were always considered a temporary band in London and therefore relocated to Liverpool, where a legendary September 1969 performance at The Sink featured Brian and Roger joining the band on stage for an unknown selection of songs. (One number from that night – a cover of The Beatles' 'Rain' – was released on *The Solo Collection* in 2000.) After this, 'Miffer' Smith was the first member to depart, for reasons of job security; the others, not wanting to give up music completely, recruited Mike Bersin's friend (and former 1984 drummer) Richard Thompson. Thus, Ibex became Wreckage.

WRECKAGE
Autumn 1969

Musicians: Mike Bersin *(guitar, vocals)*, Freddie Bulsara *(vocals)*, John 'Tupp' Taylor *(bass guitar, vocals)*, Richard Thompson *(drums)*

Repertoire included: 'Green', 'Without You', 'Blag-A-Blues', 'Cancer On My Mind', 'Vagabond Outcast', 'F.E.W.A.', 'One More Train', 'Lover', 'Jailhouse Rock', 'Crossroads', '1983 (A Merman I Should Turn To Be)', 'Rain', 'We're Going Wrong', 'Communication Breakdown', 'Boogie', 'Universal Theme', 'Rock Me Baby', 'Let Me Love You'

Known itinerary:
October 26, 1969: Ealing College of Art, London
October 31, 1969: Ealing College of Art, London
November 1969: College of St Martin & St John, London
November 1969: Ealing College of Art, London
November 1969: Fulham Hall, Fulham
November 5, 1969: Imperial College, London
November 12, 1969: Rugby Club, Richmond
November 14, 1969: venue unknown, Liverpool

November 24, 1969: Wade Deacon Grammar School
   for Girls, Widnes
November 26, 1969: Rugby Club, Twickenham

Freddie had never been a fan of the name Ibex, and
called up Mike, Richard and John to tell each of them
that the others wanted to change it and that Wreckage
was the name agreed upon. A cunning plan, though
it later transpired that nobody else in the band really
cared what they were called. Nevertheless, the band
was markedly different from Ibex, despite featuring
three-quarters of the same personnel. Freddie felt that
Wreckage should be more about presentation, so a
considerable amount of their nightly wages was spent
on lights, which surprised the others, who considered
themselves a small-time pub band.

At this time, Freddie had started to work on a series
of songs that, according to Mike Bersin, would later
evolve into early Queen songs like 'Liar' (indeed, this
song was originally titled 'Lover' and written by Freddie
and Mike), 'Seven Seas Of Rhye', 'Jesus' and 'Stone
Cold Crazy'. Original compositions, all written or co-
written by Freddie, like 'Green', 'Without You', 'Blag-
A-Blues', 'Cancer On My Mind', 'Vagabond Outcast',
'F.E.W.A.' (short for 'Feelings Ended, Worn Away', much
as Cream's 'Swlabr' stood for 'She Walks Like A Bearded
Rainbow'), 'One More Train', 'Lover' and 'Universal
Theme' would be introduced into a set primarily
comprised of Led Zeppelin and Jimi Hendrix covers.

But apart from a handful of shows in the latter
part of 1969, the band was fast disintegrating, and
Freddie, who had relocated from posh Ealing to blue-
collar Liverpool, was disappointed that success was
still out of reach. One of Wreckage's final shows, at
Wade Deacon Grammar School for Girls in November,
saw the birth of one of Freddie's trademarks. In a fit
of frustration at the venue's poor sound and faulty
equipment, the vocalist swung his microphone stand
around but didn't realize the weight of its base; the
stand broke free from its heavy bottom, and Freddie
was able to move more freely.

After a gig two days later at Twickenham Rugby
Club, Wreckage broke up and went their separate ways.
Freddie returned to London and applied for graphic
design jobs, desiring the limelight even more now.

SOUR MILK SEA
Winter-Spring 1970

Musicians: Freddie Bulsara *(vocals)*, Chris Dummett
(vocals, guitar), Jeremy 'Rubber' Gallop *(rhythm guitar)*,
Paul Milne *(bass guitar)*, Robert Tyrell *(drums)*

Known itinerary:
March 20, 1970: Highfield Parish Hall, Oxford
Spring 1970: Temple at Lower Wardour Street, London
Spring 1970: Randolph Hotel, Oxford

In late 1969, Freddie, not satisfied with his brief
tenure in bands, answered as many ads for singers as
he could. His audition for Sour Milk Sea was curious:
despite being a bundle of nerves, he strode in with
confidence, with Roger Taylor and Smile's roadie
John Harris along for moral support. Roger held the
van door open for Freddie as the vocalist swept out
resplendent in his finest clothes, while John carried
Freddie's microphone in a wooden box. The band
were practically intimidated into hiring him as their
vocalist.

Chris Dummett, Jeremy 'Rubber' Gallop, Paul
Milne and Boris Williams had formed Tomato City
(which was also the name of one of their songs) in
1968 but changed their name to that of a recent Jackie
Lomax hit, 'Sour Milk Sea', which had been written
by George Harrison. Boris left shortly before Freddie
joined and was replaced by Robert Tyrell. The group
were influenced by British blues bands like John
Mayall And The Bluesbreakers (which featured a young
Eric Clapton, whom Chris Dummett had met many
years before), Chicken Shack and Fleetwood Mac, and
had supported Deep Purple and P P Arnold at such
prestigious venues as the Civic Hall in Guildford.

Freddie hadn't been the first vocalist to audition,
but he was the one who made an impression: when
asked if he wanted the lyrics to their songs, the vocalist
declined and said that he had brought along his own.
Sour Milk Sea's live debut with Freddie came on 20
March 1970, and an instant rapport between Freddie
and Chris developed, the duo writing songs together
throughout the spring.

However, the band were living on borrowed time:
their musical direction was starting to change, which
alienated Jeremy, Paul and Robert, who felt that they
should have stayed a heavy blues band. Sour Milk
Sea split in the spring of 1970 and the planned group
that Freddie and Chris were to form was scrapped: the

band's equipment belonged to Jeremy, and he had asked for it to be returned when Sour Milk Sea was no more. Chris had no money to invest in a new guitar, and was disappointed that the new band would not come to fruition. Freddie had other plans: Smile was disintegrating, and the vocalist felt that it was time to move in and offer to start a band with Brian and Roger.

DEACON
Autumn 1970

Musicians: Don Carter *(drums)*, John Deacon *(bass guitar)*, Peter Stoddard *(guitar)*, Albert [surname unknown] *(guitar)*

Itinerary:
November 21, 1970: Chelsea College, London

Music was still in John Deacon's bones: despite wanting to focus on academia, he asked his mother to deliver his bass guitar and amplifier to him so that he could at least play live with his classmates. He started practicing again in the autumn of 1970 and jammed with his flatmates – Don Carter on drums and guitarists Peter Stoddard and Albert, whose surname is unrecorded. They landed a gig at Chelsea College, opening for two other bands, and performed primarily blues covers and contemporary hits. That they named themselves Deacon, not because John was the leader of the group but because time had run out and it was the only name they could think of, only confirms how seriously the band took their future. After their sole gig in November 1970, Deacon disbanded and John started answering ads in local newspapers before running into Brian May and Roger Taylor, who asked him to join their band...

QUEEN

The story of Queen's progress towards recording their debut album is a long and intricate one, but worth retelling. In 1970, after Smile dissolved, Brian and Roger were approached by Freddie, suggesting that they should combine forces in an endearingly forthright manner: "Why are you wasting your time doing this? You should do more original material. You should be more demonstrative in the way that you put the music across. If I was your singer," he coyly added, "that's what I'd be doing!"

Brian and Roger considered their options and seeing no better alternatives, decided that Freddie was an obvious choice. The three discussed their musical direction and, of more immediate importance, ideas for the band's name. Roger proposed The Rich Kids, while Brian offered Grand Dance as a candidate. Freddie listened with faux enthusiasm before announcing his own idea: Queen. Brian and Roger balked at the suggestion, dismayed by the camp overtones.

Freddie said of the name later, "I thought [it] up ... It's just a name, but it's very regal, obviously, and it sounds splendid. It's a strong name, very universal and immediate. It had a lot of visual potential and was open to all sorts of interpretations. I was certainly aware of the gay connotations, but that was just one facet of it."

"The idea of Queen was conceived by me whilst I was studying in college," Freddie told *Melody Maker* in 1973. "Brian, who was also at college, liked the idea and we joined forces. The very earliest traces of the band go back to a group called Smile who made a single which was released in the States. The group was plagued by bad luck and eventually split up. Queen has been going for about three years now, but until recently we've not had a suitable outlet for our music."

The next task at hand was to recruit a bassist. Tim Staffell was never considered, having parted ways amicably in order to pursue his own musical endeavours with bands like Humpy Bong and Morgan, before settling down in the late 1970s to start a family. Roger remembered his friend Mike Grose from his days with The Reaction and asked him to join. As was the case with a few bassists at the time (most notoriously Bill Wyman from The Rolling Stones), Mike was asked to join not only because he was talented but also because he owned a huge Marshall amplifier stack and a Volkswagen van, both crucial pieces of equipment for any fledgling band. Mike agreed, leaving the band he was currently with – Bent Cement – and coming to London.

The quartet hit it off right away, and the next goal was to develop a sufficient quantity of material. Both Brian and Freddie had written songs within their previous bands, and so they started to rehearse. 'Liar', previously known as 'Lover' and written by Freddie and Mike Bersin, quickly became a mainstay of the rehearsals, along with other material such as 'Stone Cold Crazy' (written by Freddie during his tenure with Wreckage), 'Son And Daughter' (written by Brian) and 'Hangman', which grew out of a jam session and continued to evolve over the course of several years.

Though the four were pleased with their prospects, they still kept side jobs – Freddie and Roger stayed at their Kensington clothes stall, while Brian continued to work on his astronomy thesis – in case the band didn't make it.

Their big break came in the summer of 1970, when Roger's mother, who had arranged a Red Cross charity event in their hometown of Truro, reminded her son that he had promised to appear with Smile at the concert. Unwilling to disappoint her, he told the others about the gig, and appearing as Smile, the embryonic version of Queen made their live debut on 27 June 1970.

The band kept up a somewhat steady pace of live performances throughout the remainder of the year, but the first disappointment came in August 1970, when Mike Grose left. He had been playing bass for nearly seven years and had grown tired of being penniless, deciding instead to return to Cornwall and get a 'proper job'. Enter Barry Mitchell, introduced to Roger by a mutual friend; although he was considered the new boy and he felt somewhat uneasy with the others since they had already developed a rapport, he was quickly recognized as a man of talent and humor, and soon became one of the band members. Unfortunately, in January 1971, he too decided to part ways with Queen.

Their next bassist was Doug Bogie, and a popular myth has been built up about his brief stint with the band: according to legend, he successfully upstaged the others by jumping around and showing off in an unbecoming manner, resulting in his prompt dismissal. John S Stuart, a Queen collector and expert, refutes the tale: "Unfortunately, the mythological story that he stole the limelight from the rest of the band is just not true. The real story is that he filled in for a few gigs (not just the one-off slot that some biographies would have us believe), and the genuine reason for his departure is that he had to sit university exams. Remember, 'rock 'n' roll' was a part-time lifestyle and Queen were no more than a pub band. Investing in his future, [Doug] decided to take his studies seriously and sit his finals. This caused a huge rift in the band: either he put the band first or his 'career'. He chose the latter.

"Dougie lives and works as a film/TV producer in the Lothian area, and with hindsight regrets his decision to leave the band, but as he explained, 'One must do what one believes to be the right thing at the time, and if with hindsight it was not the right thing to do, then you have to live the rest of your life with that decision. But you cannot live in the past, and you have to move forward with your life.'"

Still determined to find the perfect bass player, the band auditioned a series of candidates until Roger, Brian and their road manager, John Harris, were introduced to a young bassist named John Deacon in a Chelsea disco. After he had met Roger and Brian, they asked him if he would like to audition for the band; John duly showed up a few days into February 1971 at Imperial College, Queen's regular rehearsal locale and Brian's alma mater, and the others felt an instant connection with their new bassist. Said Roger later, "We thought he was great. We were all so used to each other, and were so over the top, we thought that because he was quiet he would fit in with us without too much upheaval. He was a great bass player, too – and the fact that he was a wizard with electronics was definitely a deciding factor!" John had brought along an amp of his own making, later dubbed the Deakey amp, which he initially used for his own bass but later gave to Brian to create the unique, warm sound present on most of Queen's recordings. "We just knew he was the right one, even though he was so quiet," Brian would say of John. "He hardly spoke to us at all."

Once John had been established as the fourth member of the group, the band began the task of trying to interest record companies in signing them to a label. Lack of funds prevented them from recording the few songs they had written in order to present them to prospective record companies, until in the winter of 1971 Brian met up with his friend Terry Yeadon, who was involved in setting up a new recording studio called De Lane Lea Music Centre, a new studio built for music recording – the actual De Lane Lea Studios was intended mostly for film dubbing. The management were looking for musicians to test out the equipment that had been installed, and Terry asked Brian if he was interested in helping. When the issue of cost arose, Brian was informed that De Lane Lea would record them for free as payment for being test musicians. It was an offer he quickly accepted.

In December 1971, Queen entered the recording studio for the first time to record five tracks: Brian's 'Keep Yourself Alive' and 'The Night Comes Down' and Freddie's 'Great King Rat', 'Liar' and 'Jesus'; Louis Austin recorded the band, while Martin Birch, who would later earn recognition as producer of Rainbow and Deep Purple, was the engineer. The band knew exactly how they wanted the material to be presented and, according to Austin, "were very fussy. The songs were done one by one. They would carry on until they thought it was right. It sometimes took a very long time. But they put up with so much shit too during that time."

Brian and John still worked diligently on their college courses while Roger and Freddie continued to maintain the Kensington clothes stall, though Roger had started to become restless there and tendered his resignation in the autumn of 1971. He, too, had college courses, though he wasn't a serious student and had chosen to major in dentistry merely on a whim (he later switched his major to biology for the grant money it offered). So, dividing his time between his studies and the band, he felt like he was well on the way to becoming a rock star, and wanted to start living like one.

The band were still working on their demo tape towards the end of 1971 when John Anthony visited the studio. He had previously worked with Brian and Roger when Smile held a recording session at Trident Studios, and he was surprised at how meticulous the two had become. John had accompanied producer Roy Thomas Baker (who had previously worked on John Entwistle's debut solo album, *Smash Your Head Against The Wall*) and both of them were given a copy of Queen's demo tape. After a few listens, they both arrived at the same conclusion: Queen were an impressive band – it was only a matter of convincing the right people. Those people would be Norman and Barry Sheffield, managers of Trident, who were intrigued but cautious. "I found that first tape interesting," Barry said later. "You could tell there was talent individually, and they could play, they were good musicians. But I was wary of making a full commitment at such an early stage."

Meanwhile, the band distributed the tape to other companies, but received few responses; those who did respond politely declined to sign them. It wasn't until Terry Ellis, head of Chrysalis Records (home of Jethro Tull), showed an interest that they received their first offer. After much deliberation, however, the band turned it down, feeling that it fell short of their financial expectations. It was a fortunate decision: on 24 March 1972, Barry Sheffield was finally able to see the band perform live, and made the spontaneous decision to offer them a record deal. Queen were overjoyed, and when negotiations finally started in May 1972, they capitalized on the offer by insisting that three separate agreements be drafted: the publishing rights, recording deal and management contracts were to be negotiated separately. The band were taking a risk, but Trident proceeded with the deal, and three separate agreements were drawn up but not yet signed.

In terms of management, Norman Sheffield had sworn to Queen that he would personally take care of them, but now realized that such an undertaking would be too time-consuming; he didn't feel confident enough to split his energy between two labor-intensive jobs: managing Queen and running Trident Studios. So he contacted Jack Nelson, who had been an advisor for the fledgling Trident Audio Productions. At that time, Jack had convinced Norman to set up a production company in the hope of turning it into a record company, and was therefore the first person Norman thought of when he needed managerial advice. Jack agreed to become involved with Trident based on the strength of Queen's demo tape, which he began to shop around to managers in London. Finding little interest, Jack was advised by his friend, Dee Anthony, to instead manage the group himself.

In the summer of 1972, Jack set about the task of drumming up interest in Queen among the record labels, though he had a secondary motive too: in addition to getting Queen signed to a record deal, he had devised a package plan in which he would also sell the talents of Eugene Wallace and of Mark Ashton and Headstone. When he took the three bands' demo tapes to EMI, the record company were interested only in Queen and not the other two. Jack argued that Trident would not compromise, that it was all or nothing, so EMI turned him down. As a consolation for Queen, who had been focusing separately on their studies during this period, Trident sent them to their recording studio to begin work on their debut album.

PART TWO

THE ALBUMS

A. QUEEN ALBUMS

The first part of this section concentrates on studio and live albums that Queen, as a band, have released. Catalog numbers are given in the order of original UK and US albums, followed by CD releases over the years. Overseas and specialist reissues are ignored.

QUEEN

EMI EMC 3006, July 1973 [24]
Elektra EKS 75064, September 1973 [83]
EMI CDP 7 46204 2, December 1986
Hollywood HR-610464-2, June 1991
Parlophone CDPCSD 139, 1994
Island Remasters 276 387, March 2011 [94]

'Keep Yourself Alive' (3'47), 'Doing All Right' (4'09), 'Great King Rat' (5'43), 'My Fairy King' (4'08), 'Liar' (6'25), 'The Night Comes Down' (4'23), 'Modern Times Rock'n'Roll' (1'48), 'Son And Daughter' (3'21), 'Jesus' (3'44), 'Seven Seas Of Rhye...' (1'15)

Bonus tracks on 1991 Hollywood Records reissue: 'Mad The Swine' (3'20), 'Keep Yourself Alive' *(long lost retake)* (4'03), 'Liar' *(remix by John Luongo and Gary Hellman)* (6'25)

Bonus tracks on 2011 Universal Records deluxe reissue: 'Keep Yourself Alive' *(De Lane Lea demo, December 1971)* (3'51), 'The Night Comes Down' *(De Lane Lea demo, December 1971)* (4'24), 'Great King Rat' *(De Lane Lea demo, December 1971)* (6'09), 'Jesus' *(De Lane Lea demo, December 1971)* (5'06), 'Liar' *(De Lane Lea demo, December 1971)* (7'54), 'Mad The Swine' (3'22)

Bonus videos, 2011 iTunes-only editions: 'Son And Daughter' *(live version, Hammersmith Odeon, December 1975)*, 'Liar' *(live version, Rainbow Theatre, November 1974)*, 'Keep Yourself Alive' *(promotional video)*

Musicians: John Deacon *(bass guitar)*, Brian May *(guitars, vocals, piano on 'Doing All Right')*, Freddie Mercury *(vocals, piano, percussion, organ on 'Liar')*, Roger Taylor *(drums, percussion, vocals, lead vocals on 'Modern Times Rock 'n' Roll')*, John Anthony *(additional vocals on 'Modern Times Rock 'n' Roll')*
Recorded: Trident Studios, London, January 1972 -January 1973 *('The Night Comes Down' recorded at De Lane Lea Studios, London, September–December 1971)*
Producers: Queen, Roy Thomas Baker, John Anthony *('The Night Comes Down' produced by Louis Austin)*

Among the luminaries at Trident Studios in 1972 were Elton John, David Bowie and Paul McCartney and Wings, all of whom received precedence over Queen, who were forced to work during 'down time'. When the aforementioned stars weren't in the studio, Queen would be able to nip in and work, usually during the late night and early morning hours; fortunately for the band, Paul McCartney would often block-book studio time for his *Red Rose Speedway* album and not show up, giving Queen the opportunity to work then instead.

It wasn't the preferred way to work, but the band took advantage of the opportunity. It was during one of these sessions that Freddie happened to run into producer Robin Geoffrey Cable, who was elsewhere in the complex working on a re-recording of The Beach Boys' 1969 single 'I Can Hear Music' (for more information, see that song's entry in Part Three). Also during this period, Roger contributed percussion to two tracks on Al Stewart's *Past, Present And Future* album, though he wasn't able to recall later which songs they were; 'Roads To Moscow' has recently been identified as one of them.

The band were enjoying the benefits of working in a creative environment, the results of which spilled over into their arrangements. While most debut albums are typically recorded in a short span of time, with the goal of recording a band's live repertoire on vinyl with as few takes or studio frills as possible, Queen had a different plan. Since they had no record deal yet, there was no urgency to finish an album; so they took their time, utilizing the studio and availing themselves of Roy Thomas Baker and John Anthony's talents as much as they could.

Even though rehearsals started in January 1972, the sessions proper didn't begin until later in the summer. By that time, Brian and Freddie had written an impressive set of songs and had refined existing compositions, retained from previous bands, that they felt were strong enough to record. Most of the songs were not new: 'Liar' started life as 'Lover' in Wreckage, written by Freddie and Mike Bersin, but the band saw potential in the song and encouraged Freddie to transform it into something stronger. 'Stone Cold Crazy', another track by Freddie from his Wreckage days, was also practiced during these sessions but would remain unreleased on a studio album until it was re-recorded in 1974 for *Sheer Heart Attack*. Brian and Freddie were writing at such a frantic pace that many of the songs would be written during the summer 1972 sessions but held back for the band's second album. Among these were 'White Queen (As It Began)', 'Ogre Battle', 'See What A Fool I've Been' and a vocal version of 'Seven Seas Of Rhye'. Three songs which have gone down in Queen history as being the most elusive unreleased studio tracks from the first album's sessions – 'Silver Salmon', 'Polar Bear' (previously recorded by Smile) and 'Hangman' – were long rumored to be unrecorded, though recent searches through the band's archives revealed that these tracks certainly were. The existence of 'Hangman' has been officially denied, but a private collector has recently revealed that a 10" acetate studio recording of the song exists in his collection.

From the start, it's surprising how articulate Freddie and Brian were, expressing so much more than the typical sex stories that bands of the day like The Rolling Stones prided themselves on. The lyric matter on Queen's eponymous album ranges from mythical or religious stories (most by Freddie: 'Great King Rat',

'My Fairy King' and 'Jesus'), to hopes for a rosy future (Brian's 'Keep Yourself Alive' and 'Doing All Right'), and pining for the idyllic days of an uncomplicated youth ('The Night Comes Down', also by Brian). In fact, the songs contain none of the pub-rock element that most debuts at the time favored, with the exception of two tracks: Brian's 'Son And Daughter' is the odd man out on the album and shows that, even at this early stage, blues was not Queen's forte, while the preceding track, Roger's manic 'Modern Times Rock'n'Roll', is little more than a sound-bite, lasting just under two minutes and aping the *Sturm und Drang* of Led Zeppelin's 'Communication Breakdown'.

A song that somehow slipped under the radar, even to keen-eyed collectors, was Freddie's 'Mad The Swine', yet another religion-themed song that was originally placed between 'Great King Rat' and 'My Fairy King' on the first side. It remained unreleased until its inclusion as a bonus track on the 1991 US CD reissue of *Queen*, starting the ongoing process of unearthing obscurities from the Queen vaults, a process which continues to this day. Had it appeared on the original release of *Queen*, 'Mad The Swine' would have pushed the debut album into the unintended realm of Christian rock. It seems that the lyric content hadn't been of concern to the band; the production of the track was the major issue. Freddie and Roger found fault in the mixing of the song's drums and percussion and voiced their opinion to producer Roy Thomas Baker. Insisting that the track should remain as it was, Baker refused to change anything and, with neither side budging, they diplomatically decided to drop the track altogether.

The production of *Queen* remained an issue throughout most of the recording sessions. Roger told *Sounds* in 1974, "There were lots of things on the first album I don't like, for example, the drum sound," but added, "there are parts of it which may sound contrived, but it is very varied and it has lots of energy." The drums sound as if Roger were pounding on an assortment of rubber balls, especially the last roll of 'Great King Rat'; there is a lack of clarity in the mixing, with each drum sounding similar to the next. Only on 'The Night Comes Down' do the drums actually sound like drums, which speaks volumes about the production quality of the session. It dated from Queen's original 1971 demo tape when Louis Austin was manning the controls; a Trident version was recorded but the band were so displeased with the result that the original version was substituted instead.

Most of *Queen* sounds muddy and turbid, with the

instruments mixed not to complement each other as they would on later albums, but instead to blend with each other, unfortunately obfuscating the results. This effect was certainly unintentional: as mentioned before, the band were recording during down-time, and the mixing table levels would often have to be reset after every recording, resulting in an uneven sound from song to song. In an anguished moment, it was discovered that 'Liar' had been overdubbed onto the wrong backing tape, necessitating a remix of the track. The band felt that the album would have benefited from additional mixing: the sessions initially concluded in November 1972 and Trident were pleased, but Roy and Brian were not and insisted that more time be allotted to bring the album up to standard. Between live gigs and further studies for university, the album was finally finished to the band's satisfaction in January 1973; now it was Trident's responsibility to get record and distribution deals for Queen.

Jack Nelson was despatched to sell the completed album to various companies, but met with little success. "It took me over a year to get Queen a deal," he recalled to Jacky Smith in *As It Began*, "and everyone turned them down – I mean *everyone*. I won't name names as some of those people turned out to be my best friends and I don't want to tarnish their reputations, but they know who they are, every one of them." While dealing with other matters that required his attention, Jack gave a copy of the tape to Ronnie Beck, a publisher and representative of Trident, who travelled to the MIDEM trade fair in Cannes in a last-ditch effort to secure a deal. He, in turn, passed the album along to Roy Featherstone, a top executive for the embryonic EMI label.

Featherstone recalled to Smith the moment he heard Queen's songs for the first time: "I had been played hundreds of tapes that week, from people's mothers to their howling dogs ... None of them grabbed me; I was bored. Then Ronnie Beck handed me this Queen tape, and I listened. I was knocked out. What stood out for me was the combination of Freddie's voice and Brian's guitar on a track called 'Liar'. I have wondered since if that tape would have been so much like a breath of fresh air had the whole atmosphere at MIDEM not been so awful."

Featherstone was interested in the band, and after reading the Trident-prepared biography, sent a telegram to Trident to hold off on any record deals until he came back. Jack was in the process of negotiating

an agreement with CBS, who were also interested, but he ultimately turned them down when EMI offered a far more lucrative deal. However, Queen were still part of Jack Nelson's three-band package, and EMI were still only interested in acquiring Queen. Trident were adamant, however, so EMI, realizing that Queen were too valuable an act to lose, finally relented. In March 1973, the band were officially signed with EMI Records, which covered the UK and Europe, with a pending North American distribution deal via Elektra Records still in negotiation. A showcase event was set up on 9 April 1973 at the Marquee Club, a location which worked to the band's advantage since it was a familiar venue that provided a comfortable environment for both audience and musicians. Jack Holsten, Elektra's managing director, had insisted that he see Queen live before he made his decision, and was flown to London from Tokyo. Bowled over by the performance, he agreed to sign the band.

With their future as a band improving, Queen started putting the finishing touches to their album and also began devising cover designs. While digging through scores of photographs that had been generated during the previous five years, Brian and Freddie (with assistance from Douglas Puddifoot, who had taken most of the pictures) assembled a collage of the band both at work and play. A selection of images from Queen's first photo session at Freddie's Kensington flat are prominently displayed, while photos of Brian and Freddie, both bearded, were buried among the more conventional live shots.

The most important visual, though, was the front cover, and the three spent many hours searching for just the right picture. Brian explained in the liner notes of the posthumous Freddie Mercury box set, "The artwork for our first album was coming on nicely – Freddie and I had been working on a collage of Doug's pictures for the back cover. But the front cover was still a problem. One night I was flicking through the photos and I suddenly realized what a striking image Freddie in the spotlight made. I cut him out (cutting off his leg!), pasted him (slightly reduced) back on the spotlight image, and suddenly it jumped out as a cover. I remember thinking very consciously, 'Freddie as a singer will be our figurehead: let's use him as such!'"

Queen – almost known as *Top Fax, Pix, and Info* (suggested by Roger) and *Deary Me* (a favorite saying of Roy Thomas Baker's) – was released in July 1973, a mere fortnight after the release of the single 'Keep Yourself Alive', and Brian breathed a sigh of relief:

"The album took ages and ages, two years in total, in the preparation, making, and then trying to get the thing released." Sales were slow, though reviews were positive for the most part. *Time Out* called it a "thrusting, dynamic, forceful, not to mention heavy" debut, while *Melody Maker* said, "Their first album is a series of amazingly different songs, from faster-than-fast rockers to soft ballads. Traces of Yes and Black Sabbath can also be found but structurally it seems to sound original," continuing that "a single, 'Keep Yourself Alive', has been released in hopes of giving the band some early chart success. Like the album, it's commercial in a progressive kind of way."

"Singles are important to us and to have a hit now would help the band," Freddie said. "We've more to offer than bands like The Sweet: we're not just pop, because our music covers a wide area." He continued, lamenting that "We're worried that the name Queen will give people the wrong impression. We want to be a good British regal rock band and we'll stick to that way of thinking. Our music should override the image, because we'll concentrate on putting out a good product the whole time. Teenyboppers will probably like us and we might get a bit of a 'pop' tag, but it won't last. At the moment we're just interested in creating a reaction among those who come to see us."

Meanwhile, *Rolling Stone* likened the result to a passing of the torch from Led Zeppelin to Queen: "There's no doubt that this funky, energetic English quartet has all the tools they'll need to lay claim to the Zep's abdicated heavy-metal throne, and beyond that to become a truly influential force in the rock world. Their debut album is superb." The reviewer also made special mention of the rhythm section of Roger and John, declaring it "explosive, a colossal sonic volcano whose eruption maketh the earth tremble." The notice concluded with "There's a song on the album (remarkably reminiscent of 'Communication Breakdown') called 'Modern Times Rock'n'Roll', and that's exactly what Queen's music is. They're the first of a whole new wave of English rockers, and you'd best learn to love 'em now 'cause they're here to stay. Regal bearings aside, *Queen* is a monster." Such glowing opinions from *Rolling Stone* would not last too much longer.

Brian was always displeased with the original mixes, telling BBC Radio Two in 1998 that "There was a classic case where everything got messed up on the first album, 'cause we did [it in] basically dark time." In 1991, the album was remastered as part of Hollywood Records' recent acquisitions, bringing the album up to aural standards of the early nineties. Additionally, three bonus tracks were included: a remix of 'Mad The Swine'; a 1975 retake of 'Keep Yourself Alive' (though it was erroneously believed to be an alternate studio take from 1972); and a remix of 'Liar', heralding the first of many superfluous remixes that would grace Queen's reissued albums that year. Happily, 20 years later, with the purchase of Queen's catalog by Universal Records, their discography was once again overhauled, with noted sound engineer Bob Ludwig remastering the original tapes yet again, for the ultimate experience in clarity. What drew the most criticism was the bonus discs from this run, each containing five or six tracks per disc; the fabled anthologies had been decided as "book-end" projects, to be released only when Brian and Roger had exhausted their need for the Queen name. But the "rarities" presented on these deluxe editions were hardly essential, and the liner notes were barely informative (though they replaced purely abysmal essays by noted comedian and Queen fan Rhys Thomas, later published on Queenonline.com and drawing well-deserved criticism). The first album fared the best, with the five demo tracks from De Lane Lea Studios remastered and released for the first time; though the inclusion of 'The Night Comes Down' is puzzling at first, considering it was released on the album proper, it's obvious that the band sweetened up some of the vocals at Trident, thus justifying its appearance as a truly rough mix as part of the bonus disc.

"*Queen* sold really well over a longish period and coincided with our breaking ground, concert-wise," Brian said in 1977. "So we really had matured as a group and had our audience before the press caught on to us. I think that actually gave us a better start because we were better prepared." The album finally entered the UK charts on 30 March 1974, mere days before their second album was released, but would peak at only No. 32 during its initial five-week run. It re-entered in January 1975, shortly after the success of *Sheer Heart Attack* and 'Killer Queen', this time reaching No. 49, but its second re-entry the following January would bring it to its top position of No. 24, assisted by 'Bohemian Rhapsody'.

In the US, the album had a much more turbulent run, landing in the charts at No. 195 before finally peaking at No. 83 in its fourteenth week; considering that the band wouldn't tour America until April 1974, its chart placement was a surprise. The success of the album, though, was not the band's primary concern. In addition to touring endlessly in the autumn of

1973, Queen also recorded their second album; the song ideas were flowing in quick succession.

"From the beginning the group has kept its original concept," Brian explained to *Melody Maker* shortly after the release of *Queen*. "This album is a way of getting all our frustrations out of our system which we have built up over the years. We were into glam rock before groups like The Sweet and [David] Bowie and we're worried now, because we might have come too late." If they were concerned they couldn't out-glam the original glam rockers, they didn't let it show on their next release.

QUEEN II

EMI EMA 767, March 1974 [5]
Elektra EKS 75082, April 1974 [49]
EMI CDP 7 46205 2, December 1986
Hollywood HR-61232-2, November 1991
Parlophone CDPCSD 140, 1994
Island Remasters 276 425 0, March 2011 [92]

'Procession' (1'13), 'Father To Son' (6'14), 'White Queen (As It Began)' (4'35), 'Some Day, One Day' (4'22), 'The Loser In The End' (4'02), 'Ogre Battle' (4'07), 'The Fairy Feller's Master-Stroke' (2'41), 'Nevermore' (1'18), 'The March Of The Black Queen' (6'33), 'Funny How Love Is' (2'50), 'Seven Seas Of Rhye' (2'49)

Bonus tracks on 1991 Hollywood Records reissue: 'See What A Fool I've Been' (4'32), 'Ogre Battle' *(remix by Nicholas Sansano)* (3'29), 'Seven Seas Of Rhye' *(remix by Freddy Bastone)* (6'32)

Bonus tracks on 2011 Universal Records deluxe reissue: 'See What A Fool I've Been' *(BBC version, July 1973 – 2011 remix)* (4'22), 'White Queen (As It Began)' *(live version, Hammersmith Odeon, December 1975)* (5'34), 'Seven Seas Of Rhye' *(instrumental mix)* (3'10), 'Nevermore' *(BBC version, April 1974)* (1'29), 'See What A Fool I've Been' (4'31)

Bonus videos, 2011 iTunes-only editions: 'White Queen (As It Began)' *(live version, Rainbow Theatre, November 1974)*, 'Seven Seas Of Rhye' *(live version, Wembley Stadium, July 1986)*, 'Ogre Battle' *(live version, Hammersmith Odeon, December 1975)*

Musicians: John Deacon *(bass guitar, acoustic guitar on 'Father To Son')*, Brian May *(guitars, piano on 'Father To Son', vocals, lead vocals on 'Some Day, One Day', tubular bells on 'The March Of The Black Queen')*, Freddie Mercury *(vocals, piano, harpsichord on 'The Fairy Feller's Master-Stroke')*, Roger Taylor *(drums, percussion, vocals, lead vocals and marimba on 'The Loser In The End')*, Roy Thomas Baker *(virtuoso castanets on 'The March Of The Black Queen')*

Recorded: August 1973 at Trident Studios, London
Producers: Queen and Robin Geoffrey Cable *('Nevermore' and 'Funny How Love Is')*, Queen, Robin Geoffrey Cable, and Roy Thomas Baker *('The March Of The Black Queen')*, Queen and Roy Thomas Baker *(all other tracks)*

"Considering the abuse we've had lately, I'm surprised that the new LP has done so well. I suppose it's basically because people like the band." These words were spoken by Roger Taylor to *Sounds* mere weeks after Queen's second album was released. Still considered something of a cult band – thanks in no small part to the virtual failure of their debut album and single – Queen had toured Britain relentlessly in the latter part of 1973, playing wherever they could and hoping to gain as much exposure as possible. They were even invited to perform on a few BBC radio specials: their September gig at the Golders Green Hippodrome was broadcast on *In Concert*, and in December they played again on John Peel's *Sounds Of The Seventies*, their third appearance on that show in 12 months.

All this publicity should have been beneficial to Queen but they were still receiving negative press, lambasting them for being too excessive and self-indulgent. Listening to their first album, it's difficult to agree with that criticism, but it certainly seems more justified after a run-through of their second release, unimaginatively titled *Queen II*. "To me, *Queen II* was the sort of emotional music we'd always wanted to be able to play," Brian said, "although we couldn't play most of it on stage because it was too complicated. We were trying to push studio techniques to a new limit for rock groups – it was fulfilling all our dreams because we didn't have much opportunity for that on the first album. It went through our minds to call the album *Over The Top*."

However, it is this album that has remained a fan favorite to this day. It shows Queen at their finest, producing music that was deliberately not tailored for the hit parade. *Queen II* is a superior collection of complex music awash in guitar layers, vocal overdubs and ambiguous lyrics. Some have even argued that it's the band's own version of a concept album, like The Beatles' *Sgt. Pepper's Lonely Hearts Club Band* of 1967, which every band since had attempted to imitate. Some were successful – Pink Floyd's *Dark Side Of The Moon*, The Who's *Tommy*, Genesis' *The Lamb Lies Down On Broadway* and even Yes' fascinating *Relayer*. But most were just extravagant, overproduced affairs straining towards a theme that was too muddled or so overwritten that the result seemed contrived and pompous. This was not the case with *Queen II*; not a concept album but a collection of songs with a loose theme running throughout. If *A Night At The Opera* was Queen's *Sgt. Pepper*, then this album was their *Revolver*.

Sessions for the album took place almost as soon as sessions for the debut had wrapped up. In August 1973, the band went back to Trident Studios with Roy Thomas Baker and Mike Stone, and demanded of the Sheffields the necessary studio time to complete this album instead of recording during down-time. The result of that meeting enabled Queen to complete the album within the month; the band had several ideas they wanted to explore, and were able to flesh them out fully with the additional time granted. Interestingly, several songs that had already appeared in concert but not on the debut album were recorded: 'Father To Son', 'Ogre Battle', 'White Queen (As It Began)' and 'Procession' had all been premiered as early as 1972, with some of the songs dating back to at least 1969. A notable omission from the sessions was 'Stone Cold Crazy', which had been in the set list for years; that song would be revisited for their *next* album, though in a more accelerated form. Several out-takes from the August sessions indicate that portions of 'The Prophet's Song' were also rehearsed; that song would finally appear on *A Night At The Opera* over two years later.

Clearly, the band were in a creative period: Brian and Freddie were both writing beautiful and innovative songs, emerging as a new kind of songwriting team. Although they wouldn't collaborate, per se, until 'Is This The World We Created...?' nearly a decade later, they were instinctively adept at synergistic teamwork. It's obvious that Freddie wrote 'The March Of The Black Queen' after hearing 'White Queen (As It Began)'; Freddie's new composition then inspired Brian to restructure 'Father To Son' as a powerful tour de force, leading Freddie to rethink his own 'Ogre Battle'. 'Nevermore' and 'Some Day, One Day' sound like cousins, both articulating a similar theme of abandoned love.

It was because of this kind of creativity, and the

distinctly loose yet interdependent lyrical theme running throughout the songs, that they decided to label the album sides 'Side White' (Brian's songs) and 'Side Black' (Freddie's songs). Notice the distinct light and shade in all the songs: Brian's forceful 'Father To Son' blends together several dark passages before light dawns towards the end with a singalong acoustic segment, and segues effortlessly into the more elegant and textural 'White Queen (As It Began)'. Freddie's comic-relief number 'The Fairy Feller's Master-Stroke' diminishes gradually into the mournful 'Nevermore', which in turn descends into the sinister 'The March Of The Black Queen', making the album a veritable panoply of sounds and sensations.

Roger was also adapting to the new songwriting approach. His first composition for Queen, 'Modern Times Rock 'n' Roll' wasn't the most promising and although most listeners regarded his second song 'The Loser In The End', as far worse, it ties in beautifully with 'Father To Son', a song which inspired Roger to write his paean to mothers everywhere. Only John didn't contribute any songs to the album; still regarding himself as "the new boy", it would take extenuating circumstances (Brian's hepatitis and ulcer the following year) for him to finally write his first song. Perhaps he just couldn't relate to the darker themes of the album and since he would later be known for writing strictly pop songs, it's impossible to imagine a lighthearted pop-rock ditty fitting anywhere within this seamless album.

Production duties were split between Roy Thomas Baker and the band, but John Anthony wasn't back on board. There was animosity between Freddie and Anthony, a clash of egos in a creative environment with neither side willing to compromise. The more amicable Baker was preferred and put in charge of identifying each member's creative forte and channeling it into something cohesive. Because of the range of musical experimentation in the album, Baker must have been overwhelmed by all the new and unfamiliar sounds, so it's not surprising that a second producer was invited to assist him. Initially, David Bowie was approached to produce the album (he had accepted this type of invitation for Lou Reed's *Transformer* in 1972); though flattered, Bowie declined because he was currently busy recording *Pin Ups* before commencing another new and ambitious project, eventually released as *Diamond Dogs*. So the band approached another familiar face and asked Robin Geoffrey Cable to help with some of the band's loftier ambitions.

Queen had certainly changed within a year: each band member was becoming more outspoken with his ideas, none more so than Freddie. It must have been a marked contrast to Cable, who had first met the vocalist when he was a timid, reserved person, and was suddenly confronted with a song like 'The March Of The Black Queen'. Since that song was co-produced by Cable, Baker and the band, he was asked to help with 'Nevermore' and 'Funny How Love Is', a song that he must have felt more at home with, as it resembled the 'wall of sound' technique made famous by Phil Spector in the 1960s. This was the technique used by Cable when recording 'I Can Hear Music' and 'Goin' Back' with Freddie, tracks released in mid-1973 under the pseudonym Larry Lurex.

Elsewhere on the album, the band strayed close to overproduction, but considering the times and the songs that were being submitted for recording, arrangements that may have been labeled then as contrived and self-indulgent are now considered classic. The best-produced song is undoubtedly 'The Fairy Feller's Master-Stroke', inspired by Hendrix. With the panning of sounds from side to side; it takes repeated listens to experience all that is going on and is best investigated using headphones. The drum sound had improved considerably, with Roger achieving a thunderous attack on his own composition, 'The Loser In The End'. On other songs, the instruments aren't very clear and can sometimes be difficult to differentiate, but it all adds to the mood and atmosphere of the album. While Queen would sound clearer and more accomplished on subsequent albums, they would never sound better.

"For some strange reason we seemed to get a rather different feel on the album," Brian observed to BBC's Radio One in 1983, "because of the way we were forced to record it, and even allowing for the problems we had none of us were really displeased with the result ... Led Zeppelin and The Who are probably in there somewhere because they were among our favourite groups, but what we are trying to do differently from either of those groups was this sort of layered sound. The Who had the open-chord guitar sound, and there's a bit of that in 'Father To Son', but our sound is more based on the overdriven guitar sound, which is used for the main bulk of the song, but I also wanted to build up textures behind the main melody lines."

The band all individually later admitted that they were like children let loose in the candy store, using the studio as an instrument and getting bogged down by production touches. John told the specialty

magazine release *Queen File* in 1974, "*Queen II*, like the other albums, is good because of the time we spent on the production. On *Queen II* we did all the guitar overdubs, the acoustics, bells, lots of piano; in other words, everything! We go to all the mixes, we don't just leave it to the producer. Even after the mixing we spent two weeks at Trident whilst the album was being cut." Freddie told *Sounds* in 1976, "I did discipline myself ... Take vocals, because they're my forté – especially harmonies and those kind of things. On *Queen II* [we went] berserk." Brian told *Sounds* in 1984, "When *Queen II* came out it didn't connect with everyone. A lot of people thought we'd forsaken rock music. They said, 'Why don't you play things like "Liar" and "Keep Yourself Alive"?', which were on the first album. All we could say was, 'Give it another listen, it's there, but it's all layered, it's a new approach.' Nowadays people say, 'Why don't you play like *Queen II*?' A lot of our close fans think that, and I still like that album a lot. It's not perfect, it has the imperfections of youth and the excesses of youth, but I think that was our biggest single step ever ... [It] did OK but we felt it had been misunderstood by a lot of people ... We were slated for that album by the critics; the critics unanimously hated it, wrote it off as worse than rubbish."

The album cover became an instant icon in the glam rock circle, and also launched Queen's foray into music videos the following year. "It was just one of those flashes of inspiration that happens sometimes," explained photographer Mick Rock, who had shown Freddie a photograph of Marlene Dietrich. "There was a feeling that [echoing the Dietrich pose] might be pretentious. To Freddie, that word was meaningless – 'but is it fabulous?' was all that mattered. Those were the days of androgyny, and Freddie was prepared to push it quite a way." Added Freddie, "It doesn't have any special meaning, but we were fascinated with this type of thing, and the wardrobe we used at the time described it perfectly well."

Freddie, at the six o'clock position, is flanked by John and Roger at either side while Brian, being the tallest, appears above Freddie. With hooded eyes and features white and waxen, the four unsmiling faces stare emotionlessly. Dressed in all black and set against a stark black backdrop, the only other color comes from Freddie's attenuated hands, crossed protectively over his chest. There wasn't any hidden meaning in the photograph, and it contrasted beautifully with the inner, which is the exact opposite of the front cover: the band are dressed in all white, Freddie hiding all but the top half of his face with a white fur blanket as the others stare at the camera in an almost bemused manner, mirroring their respective positions on the front (only Roger and John are switched). Still, it's moody and strangely dark, despite the overall use of white and light: both portraits are the aural equivalent of the light and shade present in the songs on the album.

The sessions concluded fairly quickly, with 11 complete songs ready plus 'See What A Fool I've Been', ultimately released as the B-side of 'Seven Seas Of Rhye' but not on the album itself. (The non-album B-side was later released on the 1991 remaster, along with two remixes of 'Ogre Battle' and 'Seven Seas Of Rhye', the latter receiving high praise from Freddie. Twenty years after its initial reissue, Universal Records once again remastered it and released a deluxe edition, with a bonus disc of largely arbitrary selections; all good separately, but as bonuses, they were minimal.) But the band already had another tour scheduled and decided it was too soon to release yet another album. Other circumstances, including minor errors in the mixes and artwork, resulted in further delays; John, quite reasonably, insisted he be credited correctly instead of as Deacon John. The album finally emerged in March 1974, a mere fortnight after the smash success of 'Seven Seas Of Rhye'. Reviews ranged from the good (*Sounds*: "this album captures them in their finest hour", *Disc*: "standards are very high") to the middling (*Melody Maker*: "there's no depth of sound or feeling") to the downright bad (*Record Mirror*: "the dregs of glam rock"). Surprisingly, *Rolling Stone* was relatively supportive (at least regarding the first side), gushing that it "is quite an improvement, containing many of the same muddled tendencies, but with the saving grace of timely and well-chosen power chords and some rather pretty tunes", while describing the second side as "a lyrically muddled fairy-tale world with none of Genesis's wit or sophistication. They've also appropriated the most irritating elements of Yes' style: histrionic vocals, abrupt and pointless compositional complexity, and a dearth of melody," ultimately concluding that it "remains a floundering and sadly unoriginal affair."

In the immediate aftermath, Roger voiced an opinion to *Sounds*, which is shared by the majority of Queen fans: "We took so much trouble over [*Queen II*]; possibly too much, but when we finished we felt really proud. Immediately it got really bad reviews, so I took it home to listen to and thought, 'Christ, are they right?' But after hearing it a few weeks later I still like

it. I think it's great. We'll stick by it."

SHEER HEART ATTACK

EMI EMC 3061 0C 062 96025, November 1974 [2]
Elektra 7E-1026, November 1974 [12]
EMI CDP 7 46206 2, December 1986
Hollywood HR-61036-2, March 1991
Parlophone CDPCSD 129, 1994
Island Remasters 276 441 1, March 2011 [82]

'Brighton Rock' (5'10), 'Killer Queen' (3'01), 'Tenement Funster' (2'47), 'Flick Of The Wrist' (3'17), 'Lily Of The Valley' (1'44), 'Now I'm Here' (4'14), 'In The Lap Of The Gods' (3'22), 'Stone Cold Crazy' (2'16), 'Dear Friends' (1'08), 'Misfire' (1'50), 'Bring Back That Leroy Brown' (2'15), 'She Makes Me (Stormtrooper In Stilettoes)' (4'09), 'In The Lap Of The Gods...Revisited' (3'45)

Bonus tracks on 1991 Hollywood Records reissue: 'Stone Cold Crazy' *(remix by Michael Wagener)* (2'16)

Bonus tracks on 2011 Universal Records deluxe reissue: 'Now I'm Here' *(live version, Hammersmith Odeon, December 1975)* (4'27), 'Flick Of The Wrist' *(BBC version, October 1974)* (3'26), 'Tenement Funster' *(BBC version, October 1974)* (2'59), 'Bring Back That Leroy Brown' *(a cappella mix)* (2'18), 'In The Lap Of The Gods...Revisited' *(live version, Wembley Stadium, July 1986)* (2'35)

Bonus videos, 2011 iTunes-only editions: 'Killer Queen' *(Top Of The Pops version 2, 1974)*, 'Stone Cold Crazy' *(live version, Rainbow Theatre, November 1974)*, 'Now I'm Here' *(live version, Montreal Forum, November 1981)*

Musicians: John Deacon *(bass guitar, upright bass on 'Bring Back That Leroy Brown', acoustic guitar on 'Tenement Funster', almost all guitars on 'Misfire')*, Brian May *(guitars, vocals, lead vocals on 'She Makes Me (Stormtrooper In Stilettoes)', piano on 'Now I'm Here' and 'Dear Friends', banjolele on 'Bring Back That Leroy Brown', guitar orchestrations)*, Freddie Mercury *(vocals, piano, jangle piano on 'Killer Queen' and 'Bring Back That Leroy Brown', organ on 'Now I'm Here', vocal extravaganzas)*, Roger Taylor *(drums, vocals, lead vocals on 'Tenement Funster', percussion, screams)*
Recorded: July-September 1974 at Trident and AIR Studios, London; Wessex Studios, Highbury; Rockfield, Monmouth
Producers: Queen and Roy Thomas Baker

In late January 1974, the band received vaccinations for their upcoming trip to Australia; unfortunately, Brian's needle hadn't been cleaned and he contracted an infection which developed into gangrene. (For a time, it was thought his arm would need to be amputated.) Unwisely, he continued working and the experience weakened his immune system. While on the road supporting Mott the Hoople in May, he contracted hepatitis, forcing Queen to cancel their remaining dates (they were replaced by Kansas) and fly home. Inoculations were hastily administered and Brian fell into a deep depression: the band had finally made their major breakthrough, and he was struck down with a serious illness that brought all activity to a standstill.

Well, not all activity. Freddie, Roger and John used Brian's recovery time wisely: while their ailing guitarist lay in a hospital bed, the trio started working on new songs for an unplanned second album of the year. Brian, too, started working on songs, and even felt well enough after nearly two months of rest to join his bandmates in the studio to work with them. Fate was to strike yet again, however, and, unfortunately, Brian was on the receiving end once more. This time, he collapsed at the studios with a duodenal ulcer and was quickly re-admitted to hospital. There were times when he felt well enough to visit the studios and a bed was made up so that he could lie down if he felt ill. (Most of the time, he did.) Reports of sessions regularly being interrupted by the guitarist running off to the bathroom to vomit weren't far from the truth.

It was the determination of the others that kept the band going during this rough patch. Despite having to cancel a planned tour in September, the band remained a household name, with 'Seven Seas Of Rhye' still keeping them fresh in the public's minds. The band remained optimistic, even with their dismayed guitarist worrying that the others would try to replace him; the thought hadn't even occurred to them. It was also during this time that the then-hot Island artists Sparks approached Brian, cockily stating that Queen were yesterday's news and asking if he would join their band. Brian politely declined; despite his illness, he was still loyal to the group, convinced that they were bound for bigger and better things.

John had finally started to gain faith in the band, especially after the trashing they received on their first two releases. "I've got more confidence in the group now than ever before," he said. "I was possibly the one person in the group who could look at it from the outside because I was the fourth person [to join] … I knew there was something there but I wasn't so convinced of it – until possibly this album." He later told *Record Mirror* in 1975, "I reckon I'll always be involved in music and recording from now on. Anyway, I like the world I'm in these days: the other day we met Paul McCartney and that was great. He even said hello to Roger and said he was doing fine. McCartney has been Brian's hero since teen days."

The band immersed themselves in studio work in the early summer of 1974, recording as much material as possible. Initial sessions started at Rockfield Studios in Monmouthshire, with backing tracks for 'Happy Little Fuck', 'You're Young And You're Crazy', 'Banana Blues', 'In The Lap Of The Gods Part 2' (those four working titles of 'Brighton Rock', 'Tenement Funster', 'Misfire', and 'In The Lap Of The Gods...Revisited', respectively), 'Flick Of The Wrist', and 'Stone Cold Crazy' laid down on 28 July. Time was divided between the Coach and Quadrangle studios, and by the end of the month, backing tracks for 10 of the 13 songs had been recorded. The band then moved on to Wessex Studios in August for two weeks to overdub vocals and percussion, while Brian, on the rebound from his illness, booked time at Associated Independent Recording (AIR) Studios in Westminster, and recorded the basic tracks of 'Dear Friends' and 'She Makes Me (Stormtrooper In Stilettoes)'. In September, with the sessions winding down, the band returned to Trident Studios to mix the tracks, and Brian submitted 'Now I'm Here', his final song for the sessions, which was recorded at this time; that track was later mixed at Sound and Recording Mobiles (SARM) Studios late in October, before the 13-track album was sent off to the Mastering Lab in Los Angeles.

It was a learning experience, not only for the band but also for Roy Thomas Baker, who became known as the Fifth Queenie. Seemingly by magic, he was able to piece together fragments of songs when only a basic rhythm track (generally consisting of piano, drums and bass, without guitar) had been recorded. Brian would then add his parts when he felt well enough to do so. Out of necessity there were substitutes for Brian when he was unable to record: John stepped into the role of rhythm guitarist in Brian's absence, and while his parts were later wiped and recorded by Brian, John's meticulous guitar work graced his first-ever composition, 'Misfire'.

Sheer Heart Attack saw Queen experimenting with studio trickery and instrumentation, more so than on their first two albums: the musician credits are a veritable laundry list of instruments. The double bass made its first appearance on 'Bring Back That Leroy Brown', albeit for only a few short seconds (it would later be used to greater effect on "39'), while the jangle piano, which sounds like a honky-tonk piano, was also used on 'Leroy Brown'. The band switched and matched instruments throughout recording, perhaps with the notion that if it was all to end after this album, at least they were going to have a good time recording it.

However, not everyone was having a good time. Brian was still in misery as he lay in his hospital bed, pondering his future with the group and contributing only four songs. (John and Roger each wrote one and Freddie wrote six: although all four received credit for 'Stone Cold Crazy', it was originally written solely by the vocalist.) Each of Brian's four contributions has a different underlying meaning, stemming from his then-fragile state of mind. 'She Makes Me (Stormtrooper In Stilettoes)' can be interpreted as Brian's desire to return to the metaphoric womb of Queen, while 'Now I'm Here' is a desperate assertion that he will indeed soon return. The title alone of 'Dear Friends' may well address the other three in the band, while the song itself might broach the possibility of him leaving the group. Of course, this is all hypothetical, but Brian's frail emotions soon turned to elation when he was well enough to return to the studios.

"I was able also to see the group from the outside, almost, and I was very excited by what I saw," Brian told BBC's Radio One in 1983. "We'd done a few things before I'd got ill, but when I came out they'd done a lot more things including a couple of backing tracks of songs that I hadn't heard from Freddie and I was really excited; 'Flick Of The Wrist' was one. It gave me a lot of inspiration to get back in there and do what I wanted to do. I did sort of get them to change a few things which I didn't feel were right and I also asked for a couple of things to be changed, which they said, 'No, you're wrong,' and they were probably right. It was good I wasn't negative at all; I just went back in there with a lot of energy and enthusiasm and did my bits and the whole thing got finished off quite quickly then. I also managed to do some writing, I think 'Now I'm Here' was done after that period which came out quite easily. I'd been wrestling with it before and never got anywhere but, after the illness, it just seemed to come out and it went down very easily in the studio ... We weren't going for hits, because we always thought

of ourselves as an album group, but we did think that perhaps we'd dished up a bit too much for people to swallow on *Queen II*."

Sheer Heart Attack flows far better than the previous album: Roger's dark and brooding 'Tenement Funster' segues into Freddie's vicious 'Flick Of The Wrist', which in turn flows into the delicate 'Lily Of The Valley'. These three songs form the central core, the nucleus, of the first side. The songwriting as a whole is stronger and more focused than previously, with Freddie tightening his lyrical subject matter and condensing his thoughts into more digestible frameworks. The longest songs on the album – 'Brighton Rock', 'Now I'm Here' and 'She Makes Me (Stormtrooper In Stilettoes)', all three by Brian – all run over four minutes, while the other ten songs average just over two and a half minutes in length, with all efforts to produce an epic à la 'Liar', 'Father To Son' or 'The March Of The Black Queen' having, apparently, been abandoned ... for the time being, at any rate.

The uncontested highlight is Freddie's moving 'In The Lap Of The Gods...Revisited', which not only closes the album but also became the set closer in the live setting for three years. There were many potential singles on the album, yet only 'Killer Queen' was seriously considered; it was due to the success of that single that the band eventually relented and issued a second single, 'Now I'm Here', a surprising choice considering the other, more obviously chart-friendly songs. "Not a collection of singles, dear, although we might draw another one off later for a single," Freddie told *NME* in November 1974. "I'm not absolutely sure about that, though. No, not all the numbers last for ages. There were just so many songs we wanted to do, and it's a change to have shorter numbers. It's so varied that we were able to go to extremes. I only had about two weeks to write my songs, so we've been working fucking hard."

The musical diversity is well in evidence and there are no songs that sound similar to any other; the band were more interested in expanding their experience and indulging their tastes (which may have been why critics called it self-indulgent) than conforming to the Led Zeppelin-esque image they had acquired. Indeed, it would have been easy to have recorded an album of rockers and ballads, but it's the quirky margins of the album that give *Sheer Heart Attack* its charm. Songs like 'Bring Back That Leroy Brown', 'Misfire', 'In The Lap Of The Gods' and even 'She Makes Me (Stormtrooper In Stilettoes)' cannot be considered rock 'n' roll; even

'Killer Queen' is difficult to categorize. It's too light to be considered rock, and Queen were certainly not a bubblegum pop band (it was kept off the top spot, significantly, by David Essex's 'I'm Gonna Make You A Star'). So what is it? It's a fun and disposable, yet complex and tuneful, slice of glam rock that only the likes of David Bowie and Marc Bolan had perfected.

At this point in their career, the band already had an eye firmly cast on what was considered popular in the singles chart, yet they weren't willing to sacrifice their artistic integrity and experimental natures to produce an album of generic, soulless rock. The ideas were coming in rapid succession, and Roy Thomas Baker was the only man considered ideal to mould those concepts into full-fledged songs while making them palatable as well. Despite the lack of togetherness during the sessions, Baker still managed to produce a crystal-clear and cohesive sound; his production is powerful on all 13 songs and the quality has improved significantly since the muddled sound on *Queen II*. However, as Baker was quick to note, people still found room to criticize: "People didn't like it at the time because they thought it was a bit over the top, which it was. It had every conceivable production idea that was available to us."

It comes as no surprise that there are no unreleased songs from the sessions. There exists an incomplete demo recording of the title track, written by Roger and originally intended for use on the album; instead, he worked on 'Tenement Funster' (originally titled 'Young And Crazy' and then 'Teen Dreams') and kept the other song for another album. It would be drastically reworked for the 1977 album *News Of The World* and achieve notoriety as Queen's answer to punk. Had it been finished for this album, it wouldn't have had quite the same effect, but it did provide the band with an appropriate album title.

The dearth of additional material was evident in 1991, when Hollywood Records reissued the album, and only a contemporary remix of 'Stone Cold Crazy' was released. (A far more exciting remix of that same song by Trent Reznor remained unreleased, apart from escaping on a promo disc called *Freakshow*.) The 2011 deluxe edition contained three useless additions (BBC run-throughs of 'Tenement Funster' and 'Flick Of The Wrist', and the July 1986 Wembley Stadium rendition of 'In The Lap Of The Gods...Revisited') and two gems (a live recording of 'Now I'm Here' from the 1975 Christmas Eve Hammersmith Odeon concert, and an a cappella mix of 'Bring Back That Leroy Brown').

"God, the agony we went through to have those pictures taken," Freddie exclaimed to *NME* in 1974 of the photo sessions for the album cover. "Can you imagine trying to convince the others to cover themselves in Vaseline and then have a hose of water turned on them? The end result is four members of the band looking decidedly unregal, tanned and healthy, and as drenched as if they've been sweating for a week … Everyone was expecting some sort of cover. A *Queen III* cover, really, but this is completely new. It's not that we're changing altogether – it's just a phase we are going through. We're still as poncy as ever. We're still the dandies we started out to be. We're just showing people we're not merely a load of poofs, that we are capable of other things."

Mick Rock's cover – certainly not as iconic as *Queen II* – shows the four band members lounging in close proximity to one another. Freddie is gazing off into the distance, seemingly transfixed by what lies ahead; Brian looks bemused, as if unable to take it all in; John rolls his eyes and smirks; Roger just looks stoned. Perhaps in an effort to share some of the spotlight with Freddie, Roger expressed displeasure with the way his hair looked and asked that hair extensions be provided. This is evident on out-takes of the cover shot, several of which also feature the band unable to keep straight faces. The final album cover, although decidedly rock 'n' roll, gives no real indication of the music within: the band have (temporarily) stepped out of their prog-rock exterior to deliver a photo that is very un-Queen-like and unpretentious. The back cover uses the same photograph, except that it's smashed or cut into shards; the visual equivalent of a sheer heart attack.

The album was released in November 1974 after the runaway success of 'Killer Queen' the month before. The week before *Sheer Heart Attack* appeared in the UK, the band made their return to the British touring circuit, their first live shows since Brian's health problems in May. The set list was restructured to accommodate the new album, prompting their audiences to rush out and buy it. The album rocketed to No. 2 in their home country, while the band made their first appearance in the US Top Twenty when the album peaked at No. 12, thanks, no doubt, to an extensive countrywide campaign in January 1975.

Reviews for the album were fairly complimentary, though there were the occasional ones in which jaded critics started to show their disdain for the band. In *Rolling Stone*, it was asserted that "Queen – on the record and on the jacket, too – makes no concessions to moderation ... If there's no meaning (there isn't), if nothing follows (it doesn't), if you can't dance to it (it would seem that you can't), *Sheer Heart Attack* is still, like its two predecessors, a handsomely glossy construction." 'Killer Queen' and 'Bring Back That Leroy Brown' were singled out as "surprisingly light showcases for Queen's wit and vocal dexterity, calculated – like everything this band has ever done – to turn heads in surprise and wonder." The review concluded with, "If it's hard to love, it's hard not to admire: this band is skilled, after all, and it dares."

The *NME* proclaimed, "A feast. No duffers, and four songs that will just run and run: 'Killer Queen', 'Flick Of The Wrist', 'Now I'm Here' and 'In The Lap Of The Gods...Revisited'. Even the track I don't like, 'Brighton Rock', includes May's Echoplex solo, still a vibrant, thrilling experience whether you hear it live or on record." A review that ran in the Associated Press in America declared, "This is a testament not only to Queen's immense talent, but to their versatility as well. Queen will be playing Madison Square Garden as headliners by the time their fourth album comes along." Not quite: the band wouldn't appear at that landmark venue until 5 February 1977, well after the release of *A Day At The Races*.

For Queen fans, the album marked the first in a series of unparalleled releases that were true to the band's experimental nature while providing chart-friendly singles, a streak that would end with *News Of The World* three albums later. While most fans prefer *Queen II* or *A Day At The Races*, citing those albums as Queen's finest, others consider *Sheer Heart Attack* to be the first time the band produced a completely flawless yet charming album from start to finish. It was a track record that would follow through to their next release as the band perfected the balance of pomp, circumstance and rock. And maybe a little opera for good measure.

A NIGHT AT THE OPERA

EMI EMTC 103, November 1975 [1]
Elektra 7E-1053, December 1975 [4]
EMI CDP 7 46207 2, December 1986
Hollywood HR 61065 2, September 1991
Parlophone CDPCSD 130, 1994
Hollywood 6 9286-01091-9, April 2002
Parlophone 7 24353 98309 3, August 2002
Parlophone 0 0946 3 38457 2 5, November 2005
Island Remasters 276 442 4, March 2011 [96]

'Death On Two Legs (Dedicated to......)' (3'43), 'Lazing On A Sunday Afternoon' (1'07), 'I'm In Love With My Car' (3'04), 'You're My Best Friend' (2'51), ''39' (3'30), 'Sweet Lady' (4'02), 'Seaside Rendezvous' (2'16), 'The Prophet's Song' (8'19), 'Love Of My Life' (3'38), 'Good Company' (3'23), 'Bohemian Rhapsody' (5'53), 'God Save The Queen' (1'13)

Bonus tracks on 1991 Hollywood Records reissue: 'I'm In Love With My Car' *(remix by Mike Shipley)* (3'26), 'You're My Best Friend' *(remix by Matt Wallace)* (2'50)

Bonus tracks on 2011 Universal Records deluxe reissue: 'Keep Yourself Alive' *(long-lost retake, July 1975)* (4'05), 'Bohemian Rhapsody' *(operatic section a cappella mix)* (1'04), 'You're My Best Friend' *(isolated backing track mix)* (2'58), 'I'm In Love With My Car' *(guitar and vocal mix)* (3'20), ''39' *(live version, Earl's Court, June 1977)* (3'47), 'Love Of My Life' *(live single edit, 1979)* (3'43)

Bonus videos, 2011 iTunes-only editions: 'Bohemian Rhapsody' *("no flames" promotional video)*, 'Seaside Rendezvous' *(30th anniversary collage)*, 'Love Of My Life' *(live version, Milton Keynes Bowl, June 1982)*

Musicians: John Deacon *(bass guitar, electric piano on 'You're My Best Friend', upright bass on '39')*, Brian May *(guitars, orchestral backdrops, vocals, lead vocals on ''39' and 'Good Company', toy koto on 'The Prophet's Song', orchestral harp on 'Love Of My Life', genuine 'aloha' ukulele (made in Japan) and guitar jazz band on 'Good Company', operatic vocals on 'Bohemian Rhapsody')*, Freddie Mercury *(vocals, vocals, Bechstein Debauchery, and more vocals, vocal orchestration of woodwinds on 'Seaside Rendezvous', operatic vocals on 'Bohemian Rhapsody')*, Roger Taylor *(drums, percussion, vocals, lead vocals on 'I'm In Love With My Car', bass drum and tambourine on ''39', vocal orchestration of brass on 'Seaside Rendezvous', operatic vocals on 'Bohemian Rhapsody', timpani on 'Bohemian Rhapsody' and 'God Save The Queen')*
Recorded: Sarm East Studios, Aldgate; Olympic Studios, Barnes; Rockfield Studios, Monmouth; Scorpio, Lansdowne and Roundhouse Studios, London, August-November 1975
Producers: Queen and Roy Thomas Baker

"I think we knew we had something special. We said, 'This can be our *Sgt. Pepper*.' Or whatever." A characteristically understated description of *A Night At The Opera* courtesy of Brian, from a 1991 interview with *Q*, yet still applicable to the album eventually released in November 1975. The success of *Sheer Heart Attack* hadn't been a fluke; Queen were content to stick to their guns and continue putting out the high calibre of material that comprised their first three albums.

"I do enjoy the studio, yes," Freddie told *Sounds* in 1976. "It's the most strenuous part of my career. It's so exhausting, mentally and physically. It drains you dry. I sometimes ask myself why I do it. After *Sheer Heart Attack* we were insane and said never again. And then look what happens! I think that is the basis of Queen actually. We were very, very meticulous. That has now become an obsession in a funny way, for want of a better word. It's subconscious now, but we feel that we have to better that past standard we've created. Otherwise they'll say, 'God, look at what they did on *Sheer Heart Attack* and look at what they're churning out now'. And you have to supersede it for your own satisfaction."

The album was born out of difficult situations, as most classics are: the band were hard up, despite their successes ("people thought we were driving around in limos," Brian lamented in the late 1970s), and at the mercy of their managers, Barry and Norman Sheffield. With the worldwide success of 'Killer Queen', the band felt they weren't being paid enough. When they first signed with Trident in 1972, they had each been given £20 a week, even though the Sheffields had originally insisted on only £15. It had increased a bit to £60 weekly by the time *Sheer Heart Attack* was released, but the band still wanted more of what they felt was rightfully theirs. The matter reached a head when John demanded a cash advance of £4000 so that he and his heavily pregnant wife Veronica (whom he had married in January 1975) could put a down-payment on a house. When he was coldly refused, the band started legal proceedings to sever all ties with Sheffield and Trident.

The first step was to abandon all recording at Trident. They also hired a lawyer, Jim Beach, in December 1974, who initiated negotiations with Trident in an attempt to void Queen's contractual obligations. Finally, after nearly nine months of lengthy parleys and arguments, deals were signed to free them from Trident absolutely. The band gained control of their back catalog and their former publishing company, Feldman, was taken over by EMI. They were now signed up directly with EMI and Elektra, effectively removing Trident from the position of liaison, and were given free rein to acquire new management.

The two drawbacks were that Queen had to pay £100,000 to buy out their contracts and give Trident one per cent of their royalties on the next six albums; unfortunately, these included *A Night At The Opera* through *The Game*, certainly the band's most successful run. Additionally, a tour of America originally scheduled for September 1975 had to be canceled because it had been organized by Jack Nelson (their US tour manager who was associated with Trident), despite the already booked venues and previously sold tickets. This was a major blow, given Roger's claim in *Record Mirror* some months before that "we spent an awful lot of money on the last American tour and now we've been offered a good deal to go back and tour for about a month in August. We really must do it to replenish our funds. We simply can't afford not to, so the album won't be completed until after we get back."

With funds running low, the band immediately started looking for new management, and three names were shortlisted: Led Zeppelin's manager Peter Grant, who was very interested in having Queen under his wing but wanted them to be signed to his own Swan Song record label, which the band weren't keen on; Peter Rudge, who was on tour with The Rolling Stones and couldn't be contacted in time; and John Reid, who was managing Elton John and initially didn't want to take on another band, but reconsidered when he learned it was Queen.

Don Arden, manager of Electric Light Orchestra, had met with the band during their early 1975 tour of America and offered them a very lucrative deal. They reluctantly declined because they were still in the process of negotiating their way out of Trident, but Arden spoke directly to Norman Sheffield and presented his offer to him. Trident agreed to his suggestions and the negotiations sped up, but by the time the band returned from Japan in May, these deals were scrapped by mutual agreement. Queen instead hired Reid.

Luckily, they managed to hold on to Roy Thomas Baker, and initial recording sessions took place at Rockfield Studios in August 1975, with the backing tracks for most of the songs recorded then. Unlike previous albums, the band started from scratch this time and had little new material to work with; only portions of 'The Prophet's Song', which had been started and subsequently abandoned during sessions for *Queen II*, had existed in some form prior to the sessions. However, it was difficult to deny that 1975 was a year of creativity for the band: inspired by their recent headlining tour to America (they were able to finish it this time) and Japan, they felt a sense of rejuvenation and excitement. They had passed the proverbial 'third album' litmus test, and were ready to prove to the world that they were going to be around for quite some time.

The ideas flowed abundantly as the band immersed themselves in the studios. Expanding on the previous two albums' creed of experimentation, instruments were hired and attempted by all band members, and if there was a sound they couldn't achieve without the aid of synthesizers or session musicians, Brian worked out ways to create it on his guitar. The song that was given the most attention was Freddie's 'Bohemian Rhapsody', which the others initially found to be both puzzling and amusing. Once they realized he was serious, they still had their reservations but, because Freddie was extremely confident about the song, they let him create whatever he wanted as they focused on their own songs. "We ran the tape through so many times it kept wearing out," Brian said about the rough mix for 'Bohemian Rhapsody', often believed to be a myth but, in reality, true. "We transferred it in a hurry. Strange business – holding on to this elusive sound signal which gradually disappeared as we created it. Every time Freddie decided to add a few more 'galileos' we lost something too."

The main sessions alternated between Rockfield and Sarm East Studios, with most of the backing tracks occurring at the former. The band had started recording there during basic sessions for *Sheer Heart Attack* the year before, but they found Sarm East on a par with Rockfield's capabilities. Vocal overdubs were held at Scorpio Studios, while further overdubs took place at Olympic Studios, where such luminaries as The Who, The Rolling Stones and Jimi Hendrix had recorded, and Lansdowne. (Trident, of course, was not used, though a recording from the studio did slip out: 'God Save The Queen' had been recorded there by Brian and Roger on 27 October 1974.) Incidentally, the day after the press premiere at Roundhouse Studios, during which Freddie angrily ordered the assembled journalists to stand during the playing of Brian's arrangment of the national anthem, the band stayed on at the studios to record overdubs; the next day, they went out on tour in support of the album.

It was this meticulous attention to detail that caught the press' collective eye, as well as the album's highly expensive cost (reportedly £40,000). Freddie addressed this issue in *Melody Maker* even before the album was released: "It's really taken the longest to do out of all the four albums. We didn't really cater for it. We just set upon it and said that we were going to do so many things. It's taken us about four months and now we've really gone over the deadline with the tour approaching. It's more important to get the album the way we want it, especially after we've spent so long on it."

"We don't want to be outrageous," he continued. "It's in us. There are so many things we want to do which we can't do all at the same time. It's impossible. At the moment we've made an album which, let's face it, is too much to take for most people. But it was what we wanted to do. We could have done a few things that are on *A Night At The Opera* on the first album but it would have been too much to take for certain people. Really. It just so happens that you can't cram everything on one album. It's a progression. After the third album, we thought, 'Now we've established ourselves and we can do certain things'. Like, vocally we can outdo any band. We just thought that we would go out, not restrict ourselves with any barriers, and just do exactly what we want to do. It just so happened that I had this operatic thing and I thought, 'Why don't we do it?' We went a bit overboard on every album, actually. But that's the way Queen is. In certain areas we always feel that we want to go overboard. It's what keeps us going really. If we were to come up with an album that people would say, 'It's just like *Sheer Heart Attack* but there are a few bits on *Sheer Heart Attack* that are better,' I'd give up. I really would. Wouldn't you?"

"Apart from 'Killer Queen', which was obviously catchy, I don't think of our singles as being immediately commercial," Roger had claimed to *Record Mirror* before 'Bohemian Rhapsody' was even conceived. "Quite honestly, I've no idea whether the next single will be a melodic thing like 'Killer Queen' or an out-and-out rocker, although I've got a feeling there will be plenty of rockers on the next album."

For all the praise 'Bohemian Rhapsody' received, there are certainly other tracks which garnered similar attention in the studios, most notably 'The Prophet's Song'. Freddie again noted their work ethic, and singled out the vocal overdubs on this song in particular: "There were a lot of things we needed to do on *Queen II* and *Sheer Heart Attack* but there wasn't enough space. This time there is. Guitar wise and on vocals we've done things we haven't done before. To finish the album we will work till we are legless. I'll sing until my throat is like a vulture's crotch. We haven't even reached the halfway stage yet but from the things I can hear we have surpassed everything we've done before musically."

Obviously, the band were eager to extend the boundaries they had previously set for themselves. From the opening piano strains of 'Death On Two Legs (Dedicated to...' to the closing timpani rolls of 'God Save The Queen', *A Night At The Opera* stands as Queen's finest 43 minutes on vinyl, exploring all sorts of musical styles, many of them experimented with on the previous record but expanded upon here. Staying true to Roger's reference to the rockers, they are in abundance on *A Night At The Opera*: 'Death On Two Legs (Dedicated to...', 'I'm In Love With My Car', 'Sweet Lady', 'The Prophet's Song' and 'Bohemian Rhapsody' all rock with the best of them, though certainly none are as raw or energetic as the earlier 'Liar', 'Great King Rat', 'Son And Daughter', 'Ogre Battle' or 'Stone Cold Crazy'. The band were more interested in creating an array of styles, and some of the more self-indulgent moments ('Lazing On A Sunday Afternoon', 'Seaside Rendezvous', 'Good Company') are reminiscent of many of The Kinks' mid- to late-1960s records, timeless and classic in their own right but for the most part, critically ignored.

The musicianship here is tight and more focused than on the previous three albums. "It's more extreme," Brian told Jonh (sic) Ingham in *Sounds*. "It's varied, but it goes further in its various directions. It has a couple of the heaviest things we've ever done and probably some of the lightest things as well. It's probably closer to *Sheer Heart Attack* than the others in that it does dart around and create lots of different moods, but we worked on it in the same way we worked on *Queen II*. A lot of it is very intense and very layered … On *A Night At The Opera* we got into the real big production; that was actually mapped out on the second album on which we did a couple of things that were more complex and operatic. *A Night At The Opera* and *A Day At The Races* were really

• the most-arranged period." Freddie summed it up rather succinctly in *Circus* in 1977, stating, "*A Night At The Opera* featured every sound from a tuba to a comb. Nothing is out of bounds."

As with *Sheer Heart Attack*, the band experimented with many new instruments that hadn't been attempted before. The biggest change introduced a third keyboardist into the fold: John, who had started his songwriting career with 'Misfire' in 1974, brought to the sessions a new song titled 'You're My Best Friend'. Because he had finally started learning how to play the piano, he wanted to experiment with more creative sounds instead of simply playing a traditional

piano. The instrumentation called for an electric piano with significant distortion, though Freddie didn't care for the sound and insisted that John play it on the standard piano instead; ultimately, however, John got his way. Brian also joked during a session that John should play double bass on "39', an acoustic busker's song; the next day, John amazed everyone by performing the part wonderfully. Admittedly, he had previously played the instrument on Freddie's 'Bring Back That Leroy Brown', but that was merely a few seconds as opposed to three and a half minutes.

Roger's role was restricted more to percussion, although he got a chance to perform vocalizations of the woodwinds on Freddie's music hall number 'Seaside Rendezvous'. Brian seemed the most interested in experimenting instrumentally: apart from arranging most of the complex guitar parts (as well as the guitar jazz band for 'Good Company'), he also contributed the ukulele, harp and toy koto, an instrument he picked up in Japan.

In fact, the band's recent touring schedule influenced their drive to return to the studios. "What really helped was the last tour," Freddie told *Melody Maker* at the album's press premiere. "We've done a really successful worldwide tour which we've never done before. It taught us a lot. It taught us how to behave on stage and come to grips with the music. We started off in Britain and by the time we took that same stage act across to America and then to Japan, we were a different band. All that experience was accumulating, and when we came to do this album there were certain things which we had done in the past which we can do much better now. Our playing ability was better. Backing tracks on this album are far superior … I think Queen has really got its own identity now. I don't care what the journalists say, we got that identity after *Queen II* … Of course, if we do something that's harmonized, we'll be The Beach Boys, and if we do something that's heavy, we'll be Led Zeppelin, or whatever. But the thing is that we have an identity of our own because we combine all those things which mean Queen."

The first signs of a new Queen product, their first since the re-release of 'Keep Yourself Alive' in the US in July 1975 (there hadn't been a UK single since 'Now I'm Here' in January), came in October 1975 in the form of 'Bohemian Rhapsody'. Freddie stated, quite casually, in *Melody Maker* that "We look upon our product as songs. We don't worry about singles or albums. All we do is pick the cream of the crop, then we look upon it as a whole to make sure the whole album works." The resulting collection is best listened to as a complete process, even though Queen were loath to record concept albums (the closest they got was with *Queen II*): each song complements its predecessor nicely, and most act as a kind of introduction or segue to the next song, as in the lengthy 'Tenement Funster', 'Flick Of The Wrist' and 'Lily Of The Valley' triptych on *Sheer Heart Attack*.

As Brian explained to BBC's Radio Two in 1999, "For *A Night At The Opera*, we sort of returned to the *Queen II* philosophy. We had our confidence, because we'd had a hit. We had a kind of almost desperation about us too, because we were totally bankrupt at that point. You know, we had made hit records but we hadn't had any of the money back and if *A Night At The Opera* hadn't been the huge success it was I think we would have just disappeared under the ocean someplace. So we were making this album knowing that it's live or die. A bit of a competitive edge as well, I think – we wanted it to be our *Sgt. Pepper* and we each individually wanted to realize our potential as writers and producers and everything."

The very title of the album suggests a more polished and refined Queen, as if they had honed their skills to become a more regal and adventurous unit than the underground rock outfit they had established themselves as on their first three releases. By contrast to *Sheer Heart Attack*, the title of which indicates a more balls-to-the-wall kind of rock album than the stadium rock Queen would perfect over the next few years, the albums' covers are almost night and day. Whereas on *Sheer Heart Attack* the band are represented as sweaty, exhausted rock stars, on *A Night At The Opera* the patriotic redesign of Queen's official insignia adorns an otherwise plain white sleeve, with the band's name and the album title regally splashed in a cursive font. The back sleeve reads almost like a programme or playbill, while the inside features full lyrics and four black and white photos of the band members.

"The title of the album came at the very end of recording," Freddie told *Melody Maker* in 1975. "We thought, 'Oh God, we've got all these songs, what are we going to call the album?' It was going to be called all sorts of things, and then I said, 'Look, it's got this sort of operatic content. Let's look upon it that way.' Then Roger and I thought of the title. It fitted, not only because of the high singing. It seemed that Queen were putting their necks on the line; we've always done that. We go through so many traumas, and we're so meticulous. There are literally tens and twenties of

songs that have been rejected for this album – some of them nice ones. If people don't like the songs we're doing at the moment, we couldn't give a fuck. We're probably the fussiest band in the world, to be honest. We take so much care with what we do because we feel so much about what we put across. And if we do an amazing album we make sure that album is packaged right, because we've put so much loving into it."

The critics were almost universal in their praise: *Melody Maker* wrote, "The overall impression is of musical range, power and consistently incisive lyrics. My hair is still standing on end – so if you like good music and don't mind looking silly, play this album." *Sounds* argued that "Queen have the ability to actualise and encompass the outer limits of their sense of self-importance," while American magazine *Grooves* opined, "Sharp operatic interludes, abrupt rhythmic changes, *A Night At The Opera* defies convention and places Queen in that rarefied circle of genuine superstars." "Don't get the idea that *A Night At The Opera* constitutes Queen's attempt at light opera," Winnipeg's *Free Press* wrote. "There's still plenty of the familiar firepower which fans have come to expect from the group, although the overall emphasis is on the quieter, more subdued side of the group's diverse musical framework." Tony Stewart in *NME* opined that "Already there's been a suggestion that this, Queen's fourth album, has cost more to make than any other recorded in British studios ... More than anything else, *A Night At The Opera* is a consolidation of the previous album's success, skillfully balancing artistry and effectology. Throughout the album, they display their individual songwriting abilities and musicianship to devastating effect – though there is one track, 'Sweet Lady', which is probably the most awful rock number they've ever recorded; it mars an otherwise excellent set ... If it's the most expensive album ever made in a British studio, it's also arguably the best. God save 'em."

A DAY AT THE RACES

EMI EMTC 104, December 1976 [1]
Elektra 6E-101, December 1976 [5]
EMI CDP 7 46208 2, December 1986
Hollywood HR 61035 2, March 1991
Parlophone CDPCSD 131, 1994
Island Remasters 276 441 6, March 2011 [104]

'Tie Your Mother Down' (4'49), 'You Take My Breath Away' (5'08), 'Long Away' (3'33), 'The Millionaire Waltz' (4'55), 'You And I' (3'26), 'Somebody To Love'

(4'57), 'White Man' (5'00), 'Good Old-Fashioned Lover Boy' (2'54), 'Drowse' (3'45), 'Teo Torriatte (Let Us Cling Together)' (5'53)

Bonus tracks on 1991 Hollywood Records reissue: 'Tie Your Mother Down' *(remix by Matt Wallace)* (3'44), 'Somebody To Love' *(remix by Randy Badazz)* (5'00)

Bonus tracks on 2011 Universal Records deluxe reissue: 'Tie Your Mother Down' *(backing track mix)* (3'48), 'Somebody To Love' *(live version, Milton Keynes Bowl, June 1982)* (7'57), 'You Take My Breath Away' *(live version, Hyde Park, September 1976)* (3'07), 'Good Old-Fashioned Lover Boy' *(Top Of The Pops version, July 1977)* (2'52), 'Teo Torriatte (Let Us Cling Together)' *(2005 HD remix)* (4'47)

Bonus videos, 2011 iTunes-only editions: 'You Take My Breath Away' *(live version, Earl's Court, June 1977)*, 'Tie Your Mother Down' *(live version, Milton Keynes Bowl, June 1982)*, 'Somebody To Love' *(promotional video)*

Musicians: John Deacon *(Fender bass, acoustic guitar on 'You And I'),* Brian May *(guitars, vocals, leader of the orchestra, harmonium, piano and Vox electric piano on 'Teo Torriatte', introduction on 'Tie Your Mother Down', slide guitar on 'Tie Your Mother Down' and 'Drowse', guitar orchestrations on 'The Millionaire Waltz', lead vocals on 'Long Away'),* Freddie Mercury *(vocals, piano, choir meister, tantrums),* Roger Taylor *(drums, vocals, percussion, pandemonium, lead vocals, rhythm guitar, and timpani on 'Drowse'),* Mike Stone *(backing vocals on 'Good Old-Fashioned Lover Boy')*
Recorded: July-November 1976 at The Manor, Oxfordshire; Wessex Studios, Highbury; and Sarm East Studios, Aldgate
Producers: Queen

"Each time we go into the studios, it gets that much more difficult," Freddie explained to *Circus* in 1977, "because we're trying to progress, to write songs that sound different from the past. The first album is easy, because you've always got a lot in your head that you're anxious to put down. As the albums go by, you think, 'They'll say I'm repeating a formula'. I'm very conscious of that."

A Day At The Races takes all the knowledge and experience Queen had accumulated from six years of studio work and wraps it up nicely in a ten-track, 40-minute album. Progressing, if it was possible,

from the studio trickery of *A Night At The Opera*, the album was superficially as blatant a follow-up as an album could be, featuring similar typesetting and a black cover, even sporting a title taken, again, from a classic Marx Brothers film. Still magnificently produced, the album featured all the trademarks of its predecessor: music hall ('Good Old-Fashioned Lover Boy'), a gorgeous ballad ('You Take My Breath Away'), pure, fun pop ('You And I') and heavy rock ('Tie Your Mother Down', 'White Man'), though the band also managed to break into different musical territories, most successfully with gospel on 'Somebody To Love', experimenting also with foreign languages on 'Teo Torriatte (Let Us Cling Together)' and testing the limits of studio technology on 'The Millionaire Waltz'.

However, it would be unfair to compare the two albums, as *A Night At The Opera* is more instantly recognizable, thanks to 'Bohemian Rhapsody' and 'You're My Best Friend'. Sitting uncomfortably in the shadow of its predecessor, *A Day At The Races* has still managed to become a fan favorite over the years, and is widely regarded, along with *Queen II*, as the band's crowning glory.

Roger said of the album in *Circus*, "The new songs are stronger, and the playing is quite possibly better (the writing's better, too!)," explaining further that the album represents "a step ahead of our previous work. We tried to avoid over-complicating. We tried to get a more basic feel in." Though none of the arrangements were as elaborate as those on 'Bohemian Rhapsody' or 'The Prophet's Song', the band were still ambitious in their own way. 'The Millionaire Waltz' and 'Somebody To Love' definitely rivaled the production values of the previous album, and the introduction (later reprised at the album's conclusion) constituted some of Brian's most challenging guitar work to date.

What's obvious is that the band had matured and were just about to find their 'voice'. As a result of their new eminence, it would also be the last album the band meticulously produced. Everything released after this would cater to a newer audience: the people who filled up the vast stadia they hadn't attempted to fill before the success of 'We Will Rock You', 'We Are The Champions' and all their early to mid-1980s achievements. *A Day At The Races* is a transitional album for Queen, and cynics would say that the band were merely repeating a well-worn formula. While there might be some semblance of truth in that criticism, Roger was correct in saying that the songs were more basic-sounding. There's a kind of roominess that washes over the ten songs, allowing the music to breathe more freely. Compare 'Sweet Lady' and 'White Man': whereas in the former the instruments are all very closely mic'd and pristinely recorded, there's a degree of rawness and roughness around the edges in the latter title. 'White Man' would have introduced an unrefined note to *A Night At The Opera*, while 'Sweet Lady' would have been too polished for *A Day At The Races*.

It's in that supposed drawback that *A Day At The Races* scores its greatest success. There isn't a weak song on the album, and while Freddie was still able to indulge himself with songs like 'Good Old-Fashioned Lover Boy' and 'The Millionaire Waltz' – both comparable to the slighter 'Lazing On A Sunday Afternoon' and 'Seaside Rendezvous' – the songwriting as a whole is decidedly stronger and more meticulous. Roger and John especially shine as songwriters: John's contribution, 'You And I', sounds like a follow-up to 'You're My Best Friend', but he was able to advance his writing and arranging abilities and succeed in writing a song that surpassed his prior contribution in every way. Roger, too, achieved unexpected prominence with 'Drowse', a song so superbly written and arranged that it's impossible to believe it came from the man who wrote 'Modern Times Rock 'n' Roll' and 'The Loser In The End'. While Brian had always been a strong songwriter, unfairly rated second to Freddie, he outdid himself this time by contributing four consistently strong songs. It would seem that Freddie was starting to let the others contribute equally, whereas previously he had dominated the albums with his songwriting. That's not to imply that he was attempting to assert himself as the sole songwriter in the group, or that his songwriting had deteriorated on this album, but the other three were finally comfortable enough to take on the responsibility of writing more.

Recording sessions for the album were initially held at The Manor in Wessex in the summer of 1976, nearly three months after their last group activity on a tour of Australia. There wasn't any great rush to get the album out, as there were, unusually, no tour dates until January 1977: normally, the band would tour for the first half of the year, record an album in the interim, then go back out on tour until the end of the year. However, they were now eager to put pleasure ahead of business. They had finally broken from their previous managers and had become more or less self-managed, meaning they could work at their leisure. On top of that, Brian finally married his fiancé, Chrissy

Mullen, on 29 May; it was a perfect excuse to take some time off, which also allowed John to spend time with his own wife, Veronica, and their son Robert.

When sessions finally started, the band used ideas and songs that had been first attempted during the *A Night At The Opera* sessions the previous summer, or even earlier: the riff for 'Tie Your Mother Down' had been written back in January 1971, while ideas for 'Teo Torriatte (Let Us Cling Together)' were started after Queen's first trip to Japan in May 1975. At the end of July, basic tracks for six songs had been started: 'Good Old-Fashioned Lover Boy', 'The Millionaire Waltz', 'You Take My Breath Away', 'Simple Man' (a working title of 'White Man'), 'Drowse', and 'Somebody To Love'. Recording progressed slowly, partly due to the intentional absence of Roy Thomas Baker. "We finally got that organized," Freddie explained to *Circus* in 1977. "We just felt that, for this one, we needed a bit of a change. We were quite confident in doing it ourselves. The other albums we really co-produced, although we always took a very keen interest."

"It was all very amicable," Roger told *Circus*. "Roy's been in and out of the country. He's heard some rough mixes. Who knows? Maybe he'll be back producing the next one! It's been tremendous pressure recording this album." Freddie agreed somewhat, but was more optimistic. "I think it turned out for the better," he told *Circus*. "Taking more responsibility has been good for us. Roy's been great, but it's a progression, really – another step in our career. We simply felt that it was now or never."

Surprisingly, John was the most candid on the subject. "We had a chat with Roy Baker, who's very well-known now, who did our first three albums," he said in a KLOS-FM radio interview in 1977. "And we needed him, 'cause he's like a really good super engineer, he knew all the technical ins and outs of the studio. So he was able to tell us how we could do this, sort of record our vocals over 50 times, or do this 'phasing'. The ideas that we wanted to do, just how he could actually, physically record them. But *A Night At The Opera* was the last album we did with him. We had done four albums with him, and we came to the position where we had taught ourselves what to do in the studio, and one didn't really need the services of the producer, because within the group, within the four of us, we had plenty of ideas. All we really needed was a good engineer. So that's what we did with the new album... we more or less produced it ourselves with an engineer [Mike Stone]."

"I mean, [on] *A Night At The Opera* and *Sheer Heart Attack*, we had co-production credits on it, so it was sort of a slow thing when you're first in the studio: you're new, you're beginners, you have to learn. And then it depends how long it takes. You have to get that confidence in the studio to know what to do in time, and then you can sort of perhaps take it over yourself. Whereas it depends on different people; some artists just don't know what goes on in the studio at all. But we've always been very interested in working in studios, how to get the best out of them. It's just been a natural extension really, to just produce our own."

Sessions were interrupted in August by preparations for what would become Queen's first British dates since December 1975. As with any up-and-coming young band, they had fallen prey to the lure of different territories and sadly started to neglect their their mother country; the band wanted to thank their English fans for their continued support and arranged two shows in Edinburgh and one show in Cardiff, with an all-day free gig at Hyde Park as the climax of the proceedings. Only two new songs were premiered during this mini-tour: 'Tie Your Mother Down', which wasn't performed at Hyde Park due to timing restraints, and 'You Take My Breath Away'. This marked one of the rare occasions when new material was performed before its actual release.

After the four dates, the band went back into the studio to finish up work on the album. "There are definitely different sounds and a few surprises on the album, but we've still maintained the basic Queen sound," Freddie told *Circus*. "A Day At The Races is definitely a follow-up to *A Night At The Opera*, hence the title." Brian, however, wanted to avoid the inevitable follow-up claims, saying, "I wish, in some ways, that we had put *A Night At The Opera* and *A Day At The Races* out together, because the material for both of them was more or less written at the same time, and it corresponds to an almost exactly similar period in our development. So I regard the two albums as completely parallel, and the fact that one came out after another is a shame, because it was looked on as a follow-up, whereas really it was sort of an extension of the first one."

John was keener on the technical side of things, and was pleased with the way the recording sessions went: "There's a lot of stuff on our records, you know. Especially when you get the headphones on ... I suppose our thing is fairly modern in a way, because we do use the studio a lot. I suppose it sounds more modern in a way because of all the various multi-tracking we do. That wasn't done five years ago because the facilities weren't around. When we recorded our first album, 16-track machines were the thing. And we just used the facilities that they could do ... But now working in the studio is an art in itself, because you can come up with sounds that you could never reproduce on stage."

In the normal round of publicity, and perhaps in lieu of any concert performances, the band appeared at Kempton Park (a specially designed horse-racing track) on 16 October in a special race called the Day At The Races Hurdle. Sponsored by EMI Records and suggested by John Reid, the four showed up initially uninterested in the spectacle, but eventually warmed to the event as it was a beautiful day and attendance was high. The press were there in order to ask questions and hear the completed product, while two bands – Marmalade and The Tremoloes – were commissioned to entertain between races. John, Brian, Freddie and Roger were each asked to place a bet on a horse, which they duly did; little did any of them suspect that they all coincidentally bet on the same horse (Lanzarote, ridden by John Francombe), which turned out to be the winning horse of the day.

The biggest event was supposed to take place on 1 December, when the band were slated to appear on ITV's early evening magazine show *Today With Bill Grundy* but pulled out at the last minute. EMI provided a replacement in the form of The Sex Pistols; it was this appearance that shot them to overnight notoriety and spelled the end of Grundy's primetime career. Instead, Freddie made a guest appearance on his friend Kenny Everett's radio programme *Be Bop Bonanza*, in which the pair very nearly drowned in champagne while 'reviewing' the new album. At one point, Kenny threw his clipboard into Freddie's lap and asked him to read the weather, which the vocalist reluctantly did – and still managed to get it wrong. This interview was finally released in 2016 on the all-encompassing BBC sessions box set, *Queen On Air*.

Because of all the publicity, *A Day At The Races* went on to become Queen's second Number One album in the UK upon its release in December. Additionally, EMI received the highest advance orders for the album of any they had released up to that point. In the States, the album reached No. 5, one position beneath its predecessor, but still a respectable showing. For the first time, a Queen album received mixed reviews. While the band were no strangers to incendiary (and often ludicrous) notices for their over-the-top live shows, their albums had all earned, at the minimum, respectful praise; by 1976, a sea change was taking over not only rock'n'roll but the rock press as well: so-called dinosaur acts like Pink Floyd and The Rolling Stones were cast aside in favor of new wave and punk upstarts like The Sex Pistols, The Clash, and The Ramones. These new bands stripped rock to its core, offering up basic three-chord rockers in lieu of the progressive, multi-layered leanings that Queen had been known for. Whether the critics were genuinely impressed with the new wave of musicians or they were keen on jumping on the bandwagon is a matter of debate, but the fact is that Queen were suddenly viewed as pariahs, despite being a relatively young band compared to other "legacy" groups; as a result, the band fell out of fashion with critics who had previously praised their adventurous albums, and while Queen would achieve great success as the decade wore on, they would never regain their status as critical darlings until well after Freddie's passing.

Dave Marsh offered a tepid review, more or less reviewing Queen's stage presence rather than the album itself. "In addition, to cement their 'seriousness', they use instrumental effects which hint at opera in the same way that bad movie music palely evokes the symphony," he wrote, also remarking that "*A Day At The Races* is probably meant to be the sequel to Queen's 1976 [sic] smash, *A Night At The Opera*, but nothing much has changed."

The *Washington Post* was cautious with its praise, calling out the obvious parallels between this album and its predecessor in a piece titled *Queen's Déjà Vu "At The Races"*. "When *A Night At The Opera*, released at about this time last year, turned into one of 1976's most popular albums, the four musicians in Queen … had a tough decision to make. For their next effort they could either stick their necks out and try something new – or play it safe and deliver more of the same. It takes only a glance at the cover of *A Day At The Races* to determine the choice they made … Once again, Queen … has come up with a judicious blend of heavy metal rockers and classically influenced, almost operatic, torch songs. It's the oddness of this combination that prevents Queen from being lumped together with all the other third-generation English heavy metal bands … The only new departure here is 'Teo Torriatte', the album's finale. The Beatles have sung in German and French, and Roxy Music in German, French, Italian and Latin, but never before has an English-speaking rock group attempted to sing a song in Japanese. Queen's rendition of this May composition, which apparently translates as 'Let Us Cling Together', is a charming novelty – so don't be surprised if it turns up again as the opening bars of next year's *Duck Soup*."

"It's important in rock to know when to move to new musical ground and when to stick with what you've got," Winnipeg's *Free Press* opined in a bizarre praise of creative arrested development. "By staying close to the perimeters of last year's hugely successful *A Night At The Opera*, Queen has another massive bestseller in *A Day At The Races*. David Bowie could benefit from Queen's counsel: *Low*, Bowie's latest change of direction, adds to the Englishman's colorful, elusive persona, but the album's icy disorienting Kraftwerk Meets Eno experimentalist rock leaves me wanting less persona and more music. Bowie's popularity will push *Low* into the Top 10 alongside *A Day At The Races*, but its stay there should be brief … While this reliance on familiar strains puts *Races* in the shadow of *Opera*, the band has approached the individual tracks with a care and skill that gives them their own personality and punch. More than simply a repeat of its last work, *Races* is a reconfirmation of Queen's position as the best of the third wave of English rock groups."

Circus damned the album the most with faint praise: "Let's not fault Mercury's fabrications for shrewd indulgence. Ostentation is the man's strategy, and Queen albums beg to be judged by their pomp. Grandeur is the other side of pretension. And Freddie Mercury is abrasive – but oh so knowing. These Limey lads are effete, flaky, and fey, but they're not blase. With *A Day At The Races*, they've deserted art-rock entirely. They're silly now. And wondrously shameless. Rule Britannia!" A review in *Sounds* hit a little too close to home: "It is too formulated, too smart ass, too reliant on trickery as a substitute for inspiration. Although I believe that Queen have produced some of the most impressive, majestic, sophisticated music of the decade over the last few years, there has to be a substance behind the frills. If I am wrong about this album, then apologies to anyone misled by premature opinion."

Whether it was calculated or unintentional, *A Day At The Races* would be Queen's final excursion in the grandiose pomp and glam they had perfected from their formation. From this point forward, they moved with the fashions, and while they would only occasionally acquiesce to trends, their sound would progress to keep up with the times, while still keeping an eye to their past so as not to totally alienate their loyal fanbase. As a result, they weren't so much pioneers anymore as they were followers, but this abdication was crucial in order for them to not only stay relevant, but to also fill seats and move product. There would still be flashes of brilliance on many of their subsequent albums, but *A Day At The Races* marks the last time that Queen would construct an album as a continued listening experience. Just as 1976 was a transitional period for rock'n'roll, it was similarly so for Queen, with *A Day At The Races* marking the end of their formative years, leading them into territories uncharted that would bring them some of their greatest worldwide successes.

NEWS OF THE WORLD

EMI EMA 784, October 1977 [4]
Elektra 6E-112, November 1977 [3]
EMI CDP 7 46209 2, December 1986
Hollywood HR-61037-2, March 1991
Parlophone CDPCSD 132, 1994
Island Records 277 174 8, June 2011 [105]
Virgin/EMI Records 00602557842678, November 2017

'We Will Rock You' (2'02), 'We Are The Champions' (3'02), 'Sheer Heart Attack' (3'27), 'All Dead, All Dead' (3'10), 'Spread Your Wings' (4'35), 'Fight From The Inside' (3'04), 'Get Down, Make Love' (3'51), 'Sleeping On The Sidewalk' (3'07), 'Who Needs You' (3'06), 'It's Late' (6'26), 'My Melancholy Blues' (3'26)

Bonus track on 1991 reissue: 'We Will Rock You' *(ruined by Rick Rubin remix)* (5'01)

Bonus tracks on 2011 Universal Records deluxe reissue: 'Feelings, Feelings' *(take 10, July 1977)* (1'54), 'Spread Your Wings' *(BBC version, October 1977)* (5'25), 'My Melancholy Blues' *(BBC version, October 1977)* (3'12), 'Sheer Heart Attack' *(live version, Paris, February 1979)* (3'34), 'We Will Rock You' *(fast live version, Tokyo, November 1982)* (2'54)

Bonus videos, 2011 iTunes-only editions: 'My Melancholy Blues' *(live version, The Summit, December 1977)*, 'Sheer Heart Attack' *(live version, Hammersmith Odeon, December 1979)*, 'We Will Rock You' *(Queen Rocks version)*

The Raw Sessions, 40th Anniversary Edition: 'We Will Rock You' *(alternative version)* (2'28), 'We Are The Champions' *(alternative version)* (4'37), 'Sheer Heart Attack' *(original rough mix)* (4'10), 'All Dead, All Dead' *(original rough mix)* (3'10), 'Spread Your Wings' *(alternative take)* (4'57), 'Fight From The Inside' *(demo vocal version)* (3'08), 'Get Down, Make Love' *(early take)* (4'03), 'Sleeping On The Sidewalk' *(live in the USA, 1977)* (3'51), 'Who Needs You' *(acoustic take)* (2'38), 'It's Late' *(alternative version)* (6'51), 'My Melancholy Blues' *(original rough mix)* (3'43)

Bonus Tracks on 40th Anniversary Edition: 'Feelings, Feelings *(take 10, July 1977)* (1'54), 'We Will Rock You *(BBC version, October 1977)* (1'35), 'We Will Rock You *(fast BBC version, October 1977)* (2'52), 'Spread Your Wings *(BBC version, October 1977)* (5'33), 'It's Late *(BBC version, October 1977)* (6'37), 'My Melancholy Blues *(BBC version, October 1977)* (3'11), 'We Will Rock You *(backing track)* (2'02), 'We Are The Champions *(backing track)* (2'58), 'Spread Your Wings *(instrumental)* (4'22), 'Fight From The Inside *(instrumental)* (3'02), 'Get Down, Make Love *(instrumental)* (3'49), 'It's Late *(USA radio edit, April 1978)* (3'52), 'Sheer Heart Attack *(live version, Paris, February 1979)* (3'35), 'We Will Rock You *(fast live version, Tokyo, November 1982)* (2'53), 'My Melancholy Blues *(live version, The Summit, December 1977)* (4'12), 'Get Down, Make Love *(live version, Montreal, November 1981)* (4'37), 'Spread Your Wings *(live version, Europe, January–March 1979)* (5'22), 'We Will Rock You *(live version, Milton Keynes, June 1982)* (2'11), 'We Are The Champions *(live version, Milton Keynes, June 1982)* (3'41)

Musicians: John Deacon *(bass guitar, footstomps and handclaps on 'We Will Rock You', acoustic guitar on 'Spread Your Wings' and 'Who Needs You')*, Brian May *(guitars, vocals, footstomps and handclaps on 'We Will Rock You', piano on 'All Dead, All Dead', lead vocals on 'All Dead, All Dead' and 'Sleeping On The Sidewalk', maracas on 'Who Needs You')*, Freddie Mercury *(vocals, piano, footstomps and handclaps on 'We Will Rock You', cowbell on 'Who Needs You')*, Roger Taylor *(drums, percussion, vocals, footstomps and handclaps on 'We Will Rock You', rhythm and bass guitars on 'Sheer Heart Attack' and 'Fight From The Inside', lead vocals on 'Fight From The Inside')*
Recorded: July-September 1977 at Basing Street Studios, London, and Wessex Studios, Highbury, London
Producers: Queen, assisted by Mike Stone

By 1977, with the seemingly overnight onslaught of punk rock, 'dinosaur' bands, as they were labelled, were forced to either adapt to the stylistic changes or, if they chose to remain set in their ways, be considered obsolete. Queen fell somewhere in between these two approaches: on the one hand, they weren't too concerned about their acceptance among punk fans, but on the other, they knew that something had to give. The regal pomp and circumstance that dominated Queen's first five releases established their sound and legacy, but they didn't want to be considered a one-trick pony, releasing album after album of decadence and grandeur while simultaneously trying to top 'Bohemian Rhapsody'.

So they compromised. After a stately jaunt through America in the early part of 1977, before returning to Europe and, finally, London in the spring, the band took some time off to rethink their future. Roger, almost bursting at the seams in his desire to record some material outside the Queen canon, took the plunge and tried his hand at a solo recording (in the very strictest sense of the word by playing every instrument and singing every vocal himself). He recorded at least four songs at his home studio in the summer of 1977 – 'Sheer Heart Attack', which had been written during the sessions for that album in 1974 but remained uncompleted, 'Fight From The Inside', 'Turn On The T.V.' and a revamped version of Parliament's 'I Wanna Testify' – and booked time to record them properly at Basing Street Studios whenever Queen weren't working there.

With Mike Stone assisting on production and engineering duties, the two songs he chose as ideally representative of his unique style were early forerunners of the style the band would adopt on their next album. Stripped back and with more emphasis on rhythm rather than lush overdubs, 'I Wanna Testify', backed with Roger's original 'Turn On The T.V.', was released in August 1977, making barely a blip on the radar. Nevertheless, it was the creative liberation he needed and, with that feeling temporarily assuaged, he was ready to resume his role in Queen.

Sessions for the album began in July 1977, with studio time alternating between Wessex, which had been first used on *Sheer Heart Attack* and again on *A Day At The Races*, and Basing Street, finally finishing up early in September, for a total of ten weeks. The alacrity with which they recorded was deliberate: a North American tour was scheduled for mid-November, which meant that they had to buckle down and record an album that not only progressed their sound, but could also be taken out on the road. Because of this

time crunch, this likely explains why Roger's two songs were glorified demos, while minor mistakes remained on 'Get Down, Make Love' and 'Sleeping On The Sidewalk'. Surprisingly, two out-takes are known to exist and have slipped out in the collectors' circle over the years: 'Feelings, Feelings' was an older composition by Brian from 1971 (this was later released on the 2011 reissue of the album, as well as the 2017 box set reappraisal), and 'Silver Salmon', written by Tim Staffell and dating from the Smile days, was given a cursory run-through.

The first batch of sessions began late in July at Basing Street, with five of the ultimately released tracks started and completed to satisfaction: 'It's Late', 'We Are The Champions', 'Who Needs You', 'Spread Your Wings', and 'All Dead, All Dead'. The band were still finalizing the arrangements during this time, with 'It's Late' containing some piano during the double-time jam section, while 'Who Needs You' was tried as a reggae number before being given its more Latin-tinged arrangement. The following month, sessions switched over to Wessex, where the final six tracks were recorded in a relatively quick manner.

It was during the second batch of sessions that Queen encountered the very band that had forced upon them their stylistic shift. The Sex Pistols had made a name for themselves as loud-mouthed, booze-fuelled upstarts, and had even been used as a replacement for Queen when they had to bow out of an appearance on Bill Grundy's *Today Show* in December 1976 (Freddie had scheduled a dentist appointment for that day, his first in 15 years). This was an unusually combative interview, with the Sex Pistols, their entourage, and Grundy himself inebriated beyond comprehension. Grundy couldn't imagine that a band like the Sex Pistols had any staying power, while Johnny Rotten spent most of his time muttering obscenities to himself. When challenged by Grundy to repeat what he had said, Rotten responded innocently, "Shit." "Go on, then," Grundy prodded, "say something outrageous." Steve Jones, taken aback by a lascivious comment toward their entourage, called Grundy a "dirty fucker … what a fucking rotter". With that, Grundy was seen as irrelevant and the Sex Pistols were the new biggest craze.

If Queen were worried about their sudden drop from favor, it didn't show. (One has to wonder what would have happened had Queen been able to keep their commitment, and if The Sex Pistols and punk in general would have had as much of an impact.) While recording at Wessex, the band finally met The

Sex Pistols, then recording their *Never Mind The Bollocks* album: "We used to bump into them in the corridors," Brian later told Mark Blake. "I had a few conversations with John Lydon [Johnny Rotten], who was always very respectful. We talked about music." Roger later told *Rolling Stone* in 1981, "It gave us a kick up the ass. It was so angry, so different, so outrageous. I mean, the first time I ever saw John Rotten, I was really shocked, 'cause I had never actually seen the whole thing in person. He sort of crystallized the whole punk attitude, and there's no doubt about it, the guy had amazing charisma."

The band weren't immune to the occasional prank from the punks, though. The Pistols' engineer, Bill Price, recalled that Rotten had seen Queen in concert and was desperate to meet the band. "I said, 'Oh, Johnny, that's not a good idea'. Sometime later Johnny came back and said, 'I've been to see Freddie'. I said, 'Oh, okay'. And as he said it, there was a tap on the door, Queen's producer said, 'Freddie was playing piano. One of the band members just crawled on all fours across our studio up to the side of the piano, said, 'Hello, Freddie', and left on all fours. Could you make sure he doesn't do it again?"

Not all of the Pistols were respectful, however, with bassist Sid Vicious bursting into Queen's control room and haranguing the band. Peter "Ratty" Hince remembered the interaction well, writing about it in his book, *Queen Unseen*: "One afternoon when Queen were working in the control room, Sid Vicious stumbled in, the worse for wear, and addressed Fred: 'Have you succeeded in bringing ballet to the masses yet?' (A reference to a quote Fred had made in the music press.) Fred casually got up, walked over to him and quipped: 'Aren't you Stanley Ferocious or something?', took him by the collar and threw him out. So much for the mean edge of punk." Freddie recalled later, "I called him Simon Ferocious or something, and he didn't like it at all. I said, 'What are you going to do about it?' He was very well-marked. I said, 'Make sure you scratch yourself in the mirror properly today, and tomorrow you're going to get something else.' He hated the fact that I could even speak like that. I think we survived that test."

The band regarded the album highly, and were mostly enthusiastic about the new stylistic shift. Brian explained to *Circus* in 1978, "It's a spontaneous album. I think we've managed to cut through to the spontaneity lacking in our other albums. I have no apologies to make for any of our previous albums. We're proud of them and wouldn't have let them out if we weren't.

But I now feel some may have been over-produced, so we wanted to go with a more spontaneous, rock and roll based album. It was nice to do something that didn't need such intensity. For example, with 'Sleeping On The Sidewalk', we did it in one take because it just seemed right the first time. We like to think of the album as a window on an unguarded moment, not a set-piece. Each cut seems to do that, from the participation songs ['We Will Rock You' and 'We Are The Champions'] to Freddie's mood pieces. Even his numbers on the album are different, from his heavy 'Get Down, Make Love' to 'My Melancholy Blues', which is just what it says."

Roger agreed with Brian's observation, saying in a Christmas Eve 1977 BBC Radio One interview, "It's really a new departure; it's a more spontaneous album," while Brian added that "Our separate identities do come to the fore on this album, on which every cut is completely different from the one before it and there's no concept at all. Apart from each having contributed two tracks to the album, Roger and John have been much more involved in the playing."

The first part of Brian's statement about no one song sounding like its predecessor is quite true: there are considerable stylistic changes apparent throughout the album, and in this respect it may well be Queen's most adventurous and experimental album to date. In addition to the proto-punk of 'Sheer Heart Attack', the band also dabbled in new wave with 'Fight From The Inside' and even tackled funk ('Get Down, Make Love') and Latin music ('Who Needs You'), genres that hadn't previously been explored on any Queen album but which would eventually become commonplace in their work.

There were the occasional throwbacks to some of the band's more extravagant works, especially with 'We Are The Champions', which revolutionized power ballads nearly a decade before such an approach became acceptable, while, surprisingly, the typical piano-oriented ballads ('All Dead, All Dead' and 'Spread Your Wings') were generated by Brian and John respectively. In fact, Freddie was eager to expand beyond the traditional rock approach; he had stated in a January 1977 interview with *Circus* that "I really feel that, on the next album, we're going to get it orchestrated by an orchestra. I think we've really done as much as we can with guitars." While it's not quite as shocking as Dick Rowe's assertion that "guitar groups are on the way out," Freddie may have merely been having fun at the expense of his interviewer.

However, apart from 'We Are The Champions', his two contributions were as far away from traditional rock music as possible, hinting at his eagerness to expand his ideas beyond the traditional power trio format.

Freddie continued with the assertion that "We always did it ourselves, and it was rewarding. But now we've done it, and it's time to move on." When asked if the next logical step was to introduce synthesizers, Freddie initially balked at the idea. "We've built up a terrible aversion to them, but you never know. To me, Brian always sounds better than a synthesizer." Brian confirmed in a 1983 *Guitar Player* interview that the spacey sounds in the middle of 'Get Down, Make Love' were the product of a harmonizer, not a synthesizer in the strictest sense. "That's a harmonizer thing, which I've really used as a noise more than a musical thing. It's controllable because I had a special little pedal made for it, which means I can change the interval at which the harmonizer comes back, and it's fed back on itself so it makes all swooping noises. It's just an exercise in using that together with noises from Freddie; a sort of erotic interlude." Additionally, creating dismay and criticism, the album was the band's first not to feature the legend "no synthesizers" on the sleeve, something that had been traditional on the first five albums.

It's in the experimentation, though, that Queen are most successful. 'We Will Rock You' is a powerful opener and still, after decades of exposure, remains one of the band's most famous songs. The lighter moments, especially John's 'Who Needs You' and Brian's throwaway, slaphappy blues number 'Sleeping On The Sidewalk', are refreshing bursts of breeziness which would have undoubtedly been dropped if the band were trying to create another *A Night At The Opera*. Roger had strengthened his songwriting, and was showing himself to be an adept and multi-talented instrumentalist: he handled both rhythm guitar and bass on 'Sheer Heart Attack' and 'Fight From The Inside', and the latter would have been a solo recording were it not for some rudimentary guitar riffs from Brian.

One complaint about the album may be the lack of coherence among the songs. Only five feature all four band members collectively: 'We Are The Champions', 'Spread Your Wings', 'Get Down, Make Love', 'Who Needs You' and 'It's Late'. Even though Freddie does harmonize with Brian on 'All Dead, All Dead', it's almost entirely the guitarist's show since the vocalist makes no other significant contribution. 'We Will Rock You' features foot stomps and handclaps, but

the only true instrumentals come from Brian's guitar, and 'Sleeping On The Sidewalk' is performed by a power trio comprising Brian, Roger and John. Indeed, the only band member who's consistently on every recording is Roger, and it's this jostling of instruments and personnel that gives *News Of The World* a disjointed feel, and because the band weren't recording with a producer (only Mike Stone, who assisted the band with their recording) and were working against a tight deadline, the result is rushed, with many of the tracks sounding like aggrandized demos.

In hindsight, with an additional month and better production, this album could have been as polished as the previous five, but this was the opposite desired effect: the band were deliberately pushing themselves out of their comfort zone to redefine their sound. More importantly, it worked: upon its release in October 1977, the album, boosted by 'We Are The Champions', raced to No. 4 in the UK. If this was a disappointment after the chart-topping *A Night At The Opera* and *A Day At The Races*, there was consolation from the USA, where it hit No. 3, making it the band's only studio album that did better in America than in Britain. No doubt the band's two American tours in 1977 contributed to that status.

"In many ways this is the most intriguing Queen album since their finest, *Sheer Heart Attack*," commented the *Daily Mirror*. "Whether all the obvious tension within the band will spur them on to greater things, or simply pull them apart, remains to be seen." *Record Mirror*, however, was indifferent: "This is Queen stripped down to almost basics. The track 'Sheer Heart Attack' is a Queen attempt at new wave, a classy version of the Sex Pistols with some very heavy lyrics. It's not a bad album by any means, but could have been better." And *Sounds* nitpicked over the little things: "Aw, Queen, why did you *do* this to us? Why doesn't this album say 'no synthesizers'? Side one is foreboding, side two much better after a disillusioning beginning with 'Get Down, Make Love' ... but how nice of [them] to finish so exquisitely with 'My Melancholy Blues'. Sweet fantasy."

The Valley News opined that their first four albums were there strongest, and picked out high points of the new album, but wasn't impressed overall: "Although *News* is a rockier disc than *Races*, it appears that Queen wants to focus on accessible styles that have wide appeal. As a result, the two latest albums are tamer, less exciting works that the band's first four LPs. But Queen still pulls off top honors with its colorful vocals (Mercury reigns supreme here), rich harmonies, May's guitar virtuosity and the band's sharp production work." Meanwhile, *The Washington Post* boiled the album's sound down to pure pop: "Queen's sixth album, *News Of The World*, reveals another facet of the group's musical identity. This album represents a departure from the usual Queen flamboyance and dynamism of musical effects which sustained, for example, *A Night At The Opera* or *Sheer Heart Attack*. Less flamboyance, less implicit drama, less operatic overtones characterize this album; more understatement (with one monumental exception – 'Get Down, Make Love'), more experimentation in the range between hard and soft rock, more intelligence and moderation of conception ... Because of Queen's liberal absorption of musical styles and themes over the last 10 years, it is difficult to pinpoint what individualizes their personal style. But if we can isolate their most distinguishing characteristic, it is a heavy metal bass line – heavy on guitar and drums – which both support and play against a multi-voiced melodic line. A case in point is the first cut of the album, 'We Will Rock You', which has a marvelously primitive, ritualistic, tribal quality to it ... 'It's Late', a plaintive rock song in typical Queen style about a failed relationship, is less successful than 'We Will Rock You', though it is still likable. It is flawed by the instrumental break and high-powered instrumental ending, both of which go off on a drum and guitar bonanza, interrupting the otherwise neat structure and undercutting the melodic poignancy. And this seems to be a major problem with Queen: they don't know when to end a song, they frequently succumb to excess in effects, and they tend to supply their songs with instrumental breaks that have little to do with anything. Still, 'We Will Rock You' is a song that both reflects and helps the criteria applicable to the best in rock music: energy, communal reveling, insistent percussion, celebrative rebelliousness against any norm. And, fortunately, there are additional rays of intelligence, talent and craft throughout the album."

Rolling Stone offered a backhanded compliment, noting that the album "makes Queen the first major band to attempt a demonstration of superiority over punk rock by marching onto its stylistic turf. It works, too, because the power trio behind vocalist Freddie Mercury is truly primitive. Once you've seen Queen on stage, away from the cut and paste of the studio, it's painfully clear that 'Sheer Heart Attack' is less a matter of slumming than of warfare among equals in incompetent musicianship." The review continued, calling the material "chilling stuff, but the coldness seems to befit Queen ... Late sons of the Empire though they may be, Queen has nothing to fear, or to do. In their moneyed superiority, they are indeed champions."

Perhaps predicting the critical japes, or as a result of the less-than-kind reviews they had been receiving lately, the band once again delivered an iconic album cover (it's no mistake that the album is titled after a supermarket tabloid keen on character assassination through slander). The *News Of The World* sleeve was adapted from a Frank Kelly Freas painting that adorned an October 1953 edition of *Astounding Science Fiction* magazine that Roger, an avid fan of sci-fi, had stumbled upon, depicting a robot with a lifeless body in his hand, underneath which is the caption, "Please... fix it, daddy?" Undoubtedly buoyed by the parallels to the drubbing Queen had received in the press as of late, the band contacted Freas to adapt and update the painting for their new album. "When they sent me their four earlier albums," Freas told Mel Vincent inn 1977, "I decided to do the drawing before listening to them, because I thought I might just hate them, and it would ruin my ideas." Replacing the lifeless body with that of Brian's, while Freddie drips from the robot's hand and the rhythm section falls to their doom to a cavernous void, *News Of The World* is a startling and somewhat creepy cover, vastly different from their earlier sleeves, but no less impactful or stunning. Freas, a classical music fan, finally listened to the albums after the painting was complete and was surprised to find he enjoyed what he heard: "They are firmly grounded in classical music, but they are inventive. It's like these guys have absorbed all the quality music they can and then put it all in a bucket and stirred it up."

From this point on, Queen were no longer innocent progressive rockers playing campy songs about call girls, faeries and ogres. They were now world-class champions with one eye focused on the charts and the other on world domination, and they couldn't have been happier. *News Of The World* was reassessed in 2017 with a massive box set, which offered not only a pure analog cut of the record on vinyl, but the 2011 Bob Ludwig remaster, a bonus disc of disparate associated versions of the album's tracks (instrumentals, backing tracks, live versions, 'Feelings, Feelings', and, enticingly, the US radio edit of 'It's Late'), and a disc labeled *The Raw Sessions*. This was the most intriguing of the bonuses: presented in the same running order as on the album, *The Raw Sessions* offered 11 alternative recordings of the familiar album, ranging from moderately interesting ('We Will Rock You', 'My Melancholy Blues') to revelatory ('All Dead, All Dead' with Freddie on vocals, an acoustic take of 'Who Needs You', and early takes of 'Get Down, Make Love' and 'It's Late'). The most tantalizing bonus was a live recording of 'Sleeping On The Sidewalk', recorded in the first week of the News Of The World tour (no specific date is given) with Freddie on lead vocals, which had long been rumored to exist. The disc contains many hidden gems, giving hope to fans worldwide that similar treatments would be administered for further box sets of future albums.

An extra bonus came by way of a DVD documentary, *The American Dream* (BBC4 had aired a slightly different cut on 4 November 2017, called *Queen: Rock The World*), which was culled from hundreds of hours of footage by BBC music presenter Bob Harris, who had been given full access to the recording sessions, soundchecks, and concerts on the News Of The World tour. Select scenes had been used in various documentaries over the years, but this was the first time that a linear documentary had been assembled from the footage Harris' team had shot. There are some priceless moments here, notably while Queen are performing a soundcheck, with Freddie reading lyrics from the inner sleeve of the album, and later an instrument swap has taken place, with Roger on The Red Special and Freddie on drums. There's also a visit to the studio, where the band run through performances of 'We Are The Champions' and 'My Melancholy Blues', though this footage had been seen, largely in full, on the 2011 documentary *Days Of Our Lives*. Elsewhere, the band contemporaneously discuss their immediate plans and their future, both separately and together, and while there's nothing particularly revealing – or at least nothing fans didn't already know – it's nice to finally have an idea of what Harris' vision would have been. Happily, there's no new footage (though the BBC documentary shoehorned in a passing mention of Brian and Roger performing with Adam Lambert), meaning the documentary is an as-it-happened capsule in time, with no journalists or musicians espousing just how great Queen and the album are – which we've already known for 40-plus years.

JAZZ

EMI EMA 788, November 1978 [2]
Elektra 6E-166, November 1978 [6]
EMI CDP 7 46210 2, December 1986
Hollywood HR-61062-2, June 1991
Parlophone CDPCSD 133, 1994
Island Records 277 176 8, June 2011 [128]

'Mustapha' (3'01), 'Fat Bottomed Girls' (4'17), 'Jealousy' (3'13), 'Bicycle Race' (3'03), 'If You Can't Beat Them' (4'15), 'Let Me Entertain You' (3'02), 'Dead On Time' (3'23), 'In Only Seven Days' (2'29), 'Dreamers Ball' (3'30), 'Fun It' (3'29), 'Leaving Home Ain't Easy' (3'15), 'Don't Stop Me Now' (3'29), 'More Of That Jazz' (4'15)

Bonus tracks on 1991 Hollywood Records reissue: 'Fat Bottomed Girls' *(remix by Brian Malouf)* (4'27), 'Bicycle Race' *(remix by Junior Vasquez)* (4'57)
Bonus tracks on 2011 Universal Records deluxe reissue: 'Fat Bottomed Girls' *(single version)* (3'23), 'Bicycle Race' *(instrumental mix)* (3'09), 'Don't Stop Me Now' *(long-lost guitar mix)* (3'34), 'Let Me Entertain You' *(live version, Montreal Forum, November 1981)* (2'48), 'Dreamers Ball' *(early acoustic take, August 1978)* (3'40)

Bonus videos, 2011 iTunes-only editions: 'Bicycle Race' *(promotional video)*, 'Fat Bottomed Girls' *(live version, Milton Keynes Bowl, June 1982)*, 'Let Me Entertain You' *(live version, Japan, April 1979)*

Musicians: John Deacon *(bass guitar, acoustic guitar on 'In Only Seven Days')*, Brian May *(guitars, vocals, lead vocals on 'Leaving Home Ain't Easy')*, Freddie Mercury *(vocals, piano, co-lead vocals on 'Fun It')*, Roger Taylor *(drums, percussion, vocals, electronic drums on 'Fun It', lead vocals, rhythm and bass guitars on 'Fun It' and 'More Of That Jazz')*
Recorded: July-October 1978 at Superbear Studios, Nice, and Mountain Studios, Montreux
Producers: Queen and Roy Thomas Baker

Punk had died a relatively quick death, once it was discovered that the poster boys for punk, The Sex Pistols, were nothing more than a marketing machine for disenchanted youth. Their sole output, *Never Mind The Bollocks*, had defined the genre, but they were a powderkeg ready to explode: by the end of 1978, The Sex Pistols would be no more, and two months into 1979, neither would Sid Vicious. That didn't stop 1978 from being a year of transition for rock, with disco and new wave battling for attention in the charts, but Queen were largely indifferent to the musical trends that had shifted their focus the previous year: they weren't keen on repeating the formula of *News Of The World*, but their sound had progressed so drastically that they didn't want to return to the pomp rock of their early chart successes. Overall, there was no specific direction for their next album, which would bring about a bigger problem: where did Queen see themselves in the pantheon of rock music in 1978?

In an attempt to bring some clarity to the situation, Queen once again called on their former mentor, Roy Thomas Baker, to oversee production on their next album. Fresh from his groundbreaking work with The Cars, Baker brought a stripped-back yet multi-layered approach that had found favor with the Boston new wave rockers, whose eponymous debut album would shift a million copies by the end of the year. "We proved our point that we can produce ourselves, so we decided to co-produce with Roy and take some of the weight off our shoulders," Roger told *Billboard* ahead of the album's release. "Now we can get on with the music in a creative atmosphere instead of worrying about the tape and the technical end of it." Indeed, the band recorded outside of England for the first time, relocating to France and Switzerland, where the new surroundings provided suitable creative atmosphere: Freddie wrote 'Bicycle Race' after watching the Tour de France pass by his Swiss hotel room, and Brian's 'Dreamers Ball' was inspired by the legion of jazz musicians performing at the Montreux Jazz Festival. (Of course, the entire reason wasn't just to get their creative juices flowing: in 1978, the band became tax exiles, and recording in England became prohibitively expensive. Queen would almost exclusively record abroad for the next decade.)

Due to the change of scenery, the band delivered another diverse album that recalled the stylistic jumps found on *Sheer Heart Attack*, but times had changed: Queen were no longer hungry for fame and fortune; they had achieved financial independence the previous year when they opted to manage themselves. Worse, the band had stagnated, creatively: there's no doubting that a great deal of the songs on *Jazz* are all top-notch, and the band deliver some truly outrageous and inventive arrangements, but the album was essentially Queen-by-numbers, with the occasional surprise thrown in for good measure. It didn't help that the band had all grown weary of each other: "Around the

Jazz album we were all getting into our own things and nobody much liked what the other guys were doing," Brian explained in 1989 to the *Chicago Tribune*. "To be honest, there were times when we couldn't tolerate each other off-stage."

While *News Of The World* was flawed, with some of the songwriting not as strong as on their first five albums, it at least had a cohesion to it, with the genre-hopping complementing each successive song. Not so on *Jazz*: 'Bicycle Race' and 'Fat Bottomed Girls' should have been placed side-by-side, while 'Let Me Entertain You' should have opened the album instead of being placed at the close of the first side. The album bounces back and forth between different styles and, with little regard to a prescribed sequence, results in an uneven and awkward listen. Interestingly, the band seemed uncertain of how the album should have been presented: on an early handwritten running order, the first side was proposed to be 'Dead On Time', 'Bicycle Race', 'Fat Bottomed Girls', 'Don't Stop Me Now', and 'Let Me Entertain You', with the second side being 'Mustapha', a track called 'Don't Say No', 'Jealousy', 'Dreamers Ball', 'Fun It', 'Leaving Home Ain't Easy', and 'More Of That Jazz'. (Note the absence of both 'In Only Seven Days' and 'If You Can't Beat Them'.) Another prospective running order placed more of the hard rockers on side one, with 'Mustapha', 'Fat Bottomed Girls', 'Bicycle Race', 'If You Can't Beat Them', 'Fun It', and 'Let Me Entertain You'.

For once, Roy Thomas Baker failed the band with his production. While *The Cars*, clearly used as a template for *Jazz*, had a fresh, airy feeling to it, there was still room for layers and layers of backing vocals (listen to 'Good Times Roll' for a perfect example of how Baker got the production so right). On *Jazz*, the band sound stuck in ember, aware that they needed to advance their sound, but not quite making the mark with the final result; Roger's drums, especially, are tinny and devoid of depth, while the bottom end is almost entirely lacking. (It took some bright spark at Queen Productions Ltd. until 2011 to notice that there was no bass drum on 'Jealousy'.) "*Jazz* suffered from having too much level in too short a space," Brian told *Guitar* magazine in 1991. "Some of our backing tracks on the *Jazz* album had become quite perfect but had lost the initial enthusiasm – our method was to do it and do it until it was right, because we had been told you couldn't drop in to a multi-track machine." Clearly, Queen and Baker were at odds with how a Queen album in 1978 should sound, leading one to wonder why, exactly, their former producer was brought back in the first place if they weren't going to listen to him. The band were in desperate need of a change, but it wouldn't be until the following year that they enacted upon it.

While the production suffered, the band were still bringing some quality songwriting to the table: Freddie's 'Jealousy' and John's 'In Only Seven Days' are two of the loveliest ballads the band would ever record, while Brian was on a creative roll, with each of his four songs firmly entrenching Queen as both heavy rockers ('Fat Bottomed Girls' and 'Dead On Time') and poignant balladeers ('Leaving Home Ain't Easy' and 'Dreamers Ball'). After taking a backseat on *News Of The World*, penning only three titles, Freddie re-emerged in full force this time around, with songs ranging from the comically absurd ('Mustapha', 'Bicycle Race') to the fun-loving showman he had become ('Don't Stop Me Now', 'Let Me Entertain You'). Only Roger couldn't quite deliver the goods: 'Fun It' is an unimpressive slice of disco, and the chunky 'More Of That Jazz' is nothing more than filler, certainly not capable of ending the album on an upstroke. Roger agreed in a 2008 *Mojo* interview: "My songs were very patchy. *Jazz* never thrilled me. It was an ambitious album that didn't live up to its ambition. The double A-side single was good, but I was never happy with the sound ... it never thrilled me."

Sessions for the album started in Montreux in July 1978, after a significant amount of time had been allowed for the band's recovery from the strenuous European tour. Mountain Studios was used first, after it was decided not to record in England; this new studio would start a healthy relationship with that city, one which lasted until the end of Queen's career. Though the band eventually purchased Mountain Studios in 1979 (when resident engineer David Richards asked what they planned to do with the facility, Freddie infamously replied, "Why, dump it in the lake, dear!"), it would for seven years become their secondary studio after Musicland Studios since Freddie preferred the nightlife that Munich offered. The sessions proved fruitful: in an October 1978 press release with *Billboard*, it was reported that "four or five [songs] were discarded, [and] the band could easily have made a double-pocket album", but Roger pooh-poohed the notion: "Doubles are too hard to assimilate. It's so much of yourself to throw at people in one go." One known castaway was the drummer's 'Coming Soon', which would be finished on the next album; 'Don't Say No', long-rumored to be a working

title of an existing song, may have been another reject, while Brian's solo song 'Let Me Out' has been rumored to have been flown by the band in the late 1970s.

Brian, especially, found it difficult to be torn away from the comforts of home: on 15 June, he and wife Chrissy became proud parents to James, but Brian was soon quickly summoned to the sessions, leaving behind his new family. This left Brian an emotional mess, and he channeled his frustrations into song, penning the beautiful and mournful 'Leaving Home Ain't Easy', a song so personal that Freddie was banned from singing it. John, too, had become a father once again, when Veronica gave birth to Michael on 3 February, and a distinct line was drawn between fathers (Brian and John) and fun-lovers (Roger and Freddie). Midway through the sessions, a birthday party was held for the 29-year-old drummer, and Freddie endeared himself to the partygoers by leaping onto a crystal chandelier. Elsewhere, in his private life, the singer became more interested in the gay world, cruising night clubs and developing lasting friendships with gay men, including Peter Straker, a theatre actor who made his album debut with *This One's On Me*, a forgettable amalgam of glam rock and show tunes. Freddie was confident enough in Straker's abilities that he invested £20,000 into the album, and asked Roy Thomas Baker to produce the sessions, and only confirmed that Freddie was starting to lose interest in the endless cycle of writing, recording, and touring.

The album was completed by October, with the lead-off single, the double A-sided 'Fat Bottomed Girls' / 'Bicycle Race', being released towards the end of the month, reaching only a modest No. 11 in the UK. The album, when issued in November, charted at No. 2 in their native country and a respectable No. 6 in America, significantly boosted by an extensive stage campaign throughout the last two months of 1978, a tour which would become their last in the US until June 1980.

The cover continued Queen's tradition of delivering a unique work of art that was more than simply a photograph of the band with some text slapped over it. (That tradition would begin with *The Game*.) While they were in Berlin on 28 April, the band visited the Berlin Wall, where Roger noticed a painted design of concentric circles; elsewhere, he saw the word "jazz" in fast letters, and put the two together to create the album's sleeve. Adapted for vinyl by the creative team Cream, the sleeve was a stark contrast to their predecessors, recalling the black-and-white simplicity of *Queen II*. The free poster contained within wasn't quite as facile: a full-color fold-out featured the 65 naked beauties from the 'Bicycle Race' video, shot at Wimbledon Stadium on 17 September 1978 (without, much to their chagrin, the band's participation). Unfortunately for their American fans, there was a tremendous public outcry and the poster was banned; those lucky enough to receive their parents' or spouse's approval could send away for it.

Reviews for the album were censorious – not new for Queen, but until now, mostly unjustified. *NME* said of the album, "If you have deaf relatives, buy this low-class replica of Gilbert and Sullivan as a Christmas present," while *Sounds* offered, "I'd love to care about Queen in the same way as I did in the beginning of the decade, but now, with an album like this, it seems impossible." *Creem* absolutely destroyed it: "Queen used to make enjoyably ludicrous records like 'Liar' and 'Bohemian Rhapsody', and Roy Thomas Baker gave their music an entertaining art-rock veneer that he adapted so successfully for The Cars. But now, even their best jokes – 'Let Me Entertain You', a parody of their own worthlessness; 'Dreamers Ball', an extravagantly condescending jazz-blues – are pummeled by the approach to the material. All four of Queen's writers seem to know what a song is (they've learned and stolen from the worst of The Beatles just as Cheap Trick have absorbed and adapted the best) and when to stop, qualities lacking in many of their progressive competitors, and stripped of their pretentious overlays, the tunes on *Jazz* turn out to be swipes from The Cowsills, 'Holly Holy', *Magical Mystery Tour*, *Disraeli Gears*, Mott The Who-ple. If only Queen could lock into the simplest formula without attaching dead weights, if Freddie Mercury weren't such a screeching bore (even his cock-rock, like 'Don't Stop Me Now', is flaccid), if their arrangements weren't on the basic level of Mel Brooks' 'Prisoners Of Love', then *Jazz* could be studied as a catalog of pop-rock sources … Maybe Queen thinks all this is funny, that their undisguised condescension ('rock'n'roll just pays the bills') and operatic mannerisms atop a beat more Rockette than rock is entertainment, but it's not my idea of a good time. For me, their snappiest one-liner is on the inner sleeve: 'Written, arranged and performed exclusively by Queen'. As if anyone else would want to step forward and take credit."

Dave Marsh, as ever, lambasted the album in *Rolling Stone*. "It's easy to ascribe too much ambition to Queen," he wrote. "'Fat Bottomed Girls' isn't sexist – it regards women not as sex objects but as objects, period (the way the band regards people in general). When Mercury chants, in 'Let Me Entertain You', about selling his body and his willingness to use any device to thrill an audience, he isn't talking about a sacrifice for his art. He's just confessing his shamelessness, mostly because he's too much of a boor to feel stupid about it. Whatever its claims, Queen isn't here just to entertain. This group has come to make it clear exactly who is superior and who is inferior. Its anthem, 'We Will Rock You', is a marching order: you *will not* rock us, *we* will rock *you*. Indeed, Queen may be the first truly fascist rock band. The whole thing makes me wonder why anyone would indulge these creeps and their polluting ideas."

Even the band weren't entirely pleased with the album. In 1984, John succinctly stated "This is an album that I dislike," while in 1982 Brian told *International Musician & Recording World*, "*Jazz* was a European-flavoured thing. It was a strange mixture and didn't click very well in America." As the guitarist explained in a 1983 BBC Radio One interview, "We thought it would be nice to try again with a producer [Baker] on whom we could put some of the responsibility. We'd found a few of our own methods, and so had he, and on top of what we'd collectively learned before, we thought that coming back together would mean that there would be some new stuff going on, and it worked pretty well."

As in previous years, the band went on tour after the album's release. The autumn of 1978 included lengthy stays in America, Europe and Japan, but curiously, involved no UK dates, and finally concluded in May 1979. The band had reached a level of musical tightness and many regarded the tour as their finest. Despite the rigors of the tour, they still had energy enough to host a lavish party: the launch premiere for *Jazz* was held on Hallowe'en night 1978 in a worthy city – New Orleans. Following that night's show, the band were chauffeured to the New Dreams Fairmount Hotel, where the festivities began. This night has gone down in Queen annals as being an evening of unprecedented decadence, perhaps the model for all Queen parties to follow.

The band personally paid for the entire evening (as opposed to sending the bill to the record companies) and they certainly spared no expense: 400 guests were invited, including executives from EMI and Elektra Records, and press reporters from England, South America and Japan as well as the US. At midnight, a local brass band marched into the hall to launch the party; from that point the diversions intensified. Naked female mud wrestlers, fire-eaters, jazz bands, steel bands, Zulu dancers, voodoo dancers, unicyclists, strippers and drag artists provided the main entertainment, while trays of cocaine were placed on the heads of little people and served to all who wished to partake. Record company executives were ushered into a back room, where groupies pleasured them individually throughout the evening.

The party was so eventful that the album was never even played. The next day, the band held a more restrained press conference at Brennan's Restaurant, where the press finally took the opportunity to ask the questions they'd been meaning to ask the night before (and, one would assume, finally heard the album they had been invited to hear). The band were criticized for the excess, to which Freddie quipped, "I guess some people don't like to look at nude ladies. It's naughty, but not lewd."

Thirty years later, Roger recalled the excess with amusement and pride. "I have to say that the stories from that night are not that exaggerated," he told *Mojo*. "What memories would I be willing to share? How extraordinarily ill I felt the next day. Most of the stories you heard are true. The one about the dwarves and the bald heads and cocaine is not true. Or, if it was, I never saw it." After a pause and a think, he relented: "Actually, it could have been true..." Brian, meanwhile, missed out on the festivities; despite becoming a father earlier that summer, he spent the night searching for the mystical Peaches, a girl he'd met and fallen for in New Orleans back in 1974. "I didn't find her," he recalled sadly, "but she found me later on."

LIVE KILLERS

EMI EMSP 330, June 1979 [3]
Elektra BB-702, June 1979 [16]
EMI CDS 7 46211 8, December 1986
Hollywood HR-62017-2, November 1991

'We Will Rock You' (3'16), 'Let Me Entertain You' (3'16), 'Death On Two Legs (Dedicated to......' (3'33), 'Killer Queen' (1'57), 'Bicycle Race' (1'29), 'I'm In Love With My Car' (2'01), 'Get Down, Make Love' (4'31), 'You're My Best Friend' (2'10), 'Now I'm Here' (8'42), 'Dreamers Ball' (3'42), 'Love Of My Life' (4'59), "39' (3'26), 'Keep Yourself Alive' (4'00), 'Don't Stop Me Now' (4'28), 'Spread Your Wings' (5'15), 'Brighton Rock' (12'16), 'Bohemian Rhapsody' (6'01), 'Tie Your Mother Down' (3'41), 'Sheer Heart Attack' (3'35), 'We Will Rock You' (2'48), 'We Are The Champions' (3'27), 'God Save The Queen' (1'32)

Musicians: John Deacon *(bass guitar)*, Brian May *(guitars, backing vocals)*, Freddie Mercury *(vocals, piano, maracas)*, Roger Taylor *(drums, percussion, backing vocals, lead vocals on 'I'm In Love With My Car')*
Recorded: January-March 1979 at various European dates
Producers: Queen and John Etchells

Queen were long overdue to release an audio representation of their live experience, and with there being no immediate hurry to work on a studio follow-up to *Jazz*, the band spent much of the spring of 1979 selecting and mixing performances from their expansive European tour to release as their first live album. Not everyone was happy about it, though, with Brian lamenting, "Live albums are inescapable, really. Everyone tells you you have to do them, and when you do, you find that they're very often not of mass appeal, and in the absence of a fluke condition you sell your live album to the converted, the people who already know your stuff and come to the concerts. So, if you add up the number of people who have seen you over the last few years, that's very roughly the number who will buy your live album unless you have a hit single on it, which we didn't."

Live Killers, as it was eventually titled in June 1979, was culled from their three-month odyssey across Europe, though they never documented which songs derived from which shows. Recently, it's been speculated that most of the recorded material came from the Frankfurt (2 February) and Lyon (17 February) performances, and that the segments from those shows were selected and spliced to create the perfect end-product. As a result, though there may not be many overdubs (Brian vehemently claims that there are absolutely none), most of the errors – and, let's face it, there isn't a single band that can perform perfectly night after night – were patched up with superior segments to the point that any one song may have originated from more than one show.

Live Killers is a mixed bag of a release: the song selection, for what it is, sums up exactly how a Queen show in 1979 sounded, though four songs that were played nearly every night – 'Somebody To Love', 'If You Can't Beat Them', 'Fat Bottomed Girls', and 'It's Late' – were omitted due to time restraints. (Queen might have been better advised releasing a triple album, though their reticence to do so is understandable.)

The opening salvo of 'We Will Rock You' (the recorded debut of the fast version) and 'Let Me Entertain You' is unparalleled, while the emotive performances of 'Don't Stop Me Now' and 'Spread Your Wings' are exemplary. Additionally, Roger provides a fine vocal delivery on his own 'I'm In Love With My Car', and the band's gift of improvisation – rare during their more structured shows – shines through on 'Now I'm Here' and 'Brighton Rock'. The acoustic segment is also a lot of fun, with the band truly having a blast on 'Dreamers Ball' and "39', while the lovely singalong of 'Love Of My Life' was considered so representative of the live Queen experience that it would be the only live single the band would release in their career.

On the other hand, the biggest drawback to *Live Killers* is the mixing, which was executed by David Richards at Mountain Studios: the band sounds muddled, some of the instruments are poorly mixed, and the audience levels are inconsistent. Brian was certainly unhappy with the final result: "I've never been completely satisfied. I'll be a nonconformist forever. I think *Live Killers* was a kind of evidence of what we were doing live late in the 1970s. In some ways, I'm unsatisfied. We had to work hard in every concert and there were serious sound problems. There were concerts when we had sounded great, but when we listened to the tapes, they sounded awful. We recorded ten or 15 shows, but we could only use three or four of them to work on. Anyway, live albums never sound good because there are noises and shouts that affect it. As it stands, *Live Killers* isn't my favourite album." Brian wasn't the only one who was dissatisfied with the record: Roger expressed displeasure about the album, saying it wasn't representative of a Queen live show (later quipping that the only instrument retained from the actual live shows was the bass drum), while Freddie and Brian were disappointed by both the mix and the inclusion of 'Bohemian Rhapsody', convinced that the song lost its power without the accompanying visuals and that adding the pre-taped operatic portion could be considered cheating.

Despite the band's criticism of the album, *Live Killers* nevertheless received positive notices, apart from a full-on drubbing by *Rolling Stone*: "Anyone who already owns a substantial Queen collection will find *Live Killers* a redundant exercise anyway. Half of the double LP's 22 tracks come from *Night At The Opera* and *News Of The World*, and four more were on last year's *Jazz*. There are also two versions of their Aryan command, 'We Will Rock You' ... If *Live Killers*

serves any purpose at all, it's to show that, stripped of their dazzling studio sound and Freddie Mercury's shimmering vocal harmonies, Queen is just another ersatz Led Zeppelin, combining cheap classical parody with heavy-metal bollocks." *Sounds* reluctantly opined, "I don't find the obligatory post-'77 groan rising to my lips at the mention of their name, and this package is a perfectly adequate retrospective on most of their best songs," while *Record Mirror* gushed, "Bring out the champagne and the roses, this is a triumph. This album enhances Queen's songs and isn't a mere fill-in until the next studio project [though of course it was]. Listen and you'll not be disappointed."

THE GAME
EMI EMA 795, June 1980 [1]
Elektra 5E-513, June 1980 [1]
EMI CDP 7 46213 2, December 1986
Hollywood HR 61063 2, June 1991
Parlophone CDPCSD 134, 1994
Hollywood HR 9286-01110-9 7, October 2003
Island Records 277 175 2, June 2011 [138]

'Play The Game' (3'32), 'Dragon Attack' (4'18), 'Another One Bites The Dust' (3'37), 'Need Your Loving Tonight' (2'49), 'Crazy Little Thing Called Love' (2'44), 'Rock It (Prime Jive)' (4'32), 'Don't Try Suicide' (3'52), 'Sail Away Sweet Sister' (3'32), 'Coming Soon' (2'50), 'Save Me' (3'48)

Bonus track on 1991 Hollywood Records reissue: 'Dragon Attack' *(remix by RAK and Jack Benson)* (4'20)

Bonus tracks on 2011 Universal Records deluxe reissue: 'Save Me' *(live version, Montreal Forum, November 1981)* (4'16), 'A Human Body' *(non-album B-side, May 1980)* (3'42), 'Sail Away Sweet Sister' *(take 1 with guide vocal, February 1980)* (2'32), 'It's A Beautiful Day' *(original spontaneous idea, April 1980)* (1'29), 'Dragon Attack' *(live version, Milton Keynes Bowl, June 1982)* (5'14)

Bonus videos, 2011 iTunes-only editions: 'Dragon Attack' *(live version, Morumbi Stadium, March 1981)*, 'Save Me' *(live version, Seibu Lions Stadium, November 1982)*, 'Crazy Little Thing Called Love' *(Saturday Night Live version, September 1982)*

Musicians: John Deacon *(bass guitar, rhythm guitar and piano on 'Another One Bites The Dust', acoustic rhythm guitar on 'Need Your Loving Tonight')*, Brian May *(guitars,*

vocals, synthesizer and lead vocals on 'Sail Away Sweet Sister', piano and synthesizer on 'Save Me'), Freddie Mercury (vocals, piano, synthesizer on 'Play The Game' and 'Coming Soon', acoustic rhythm guitar on 'Crazy Little Thing Called Love'), Roger Taylor (drums, percussion, vocals, co-lead vocals, synthesizer, and guitar on 'Rock It (Prime Jive)' and 'Coming Soon'), Mack (synthesizer)
Recorded: Musicland Studios, Munich, February-May 1980 ('Crazy Little Thing Called Love', 'Sail Away Sweet Sister', 'Coming Soon' and 'Save Me' recorded at Musicland Studios, Munich, June-July 1979)
Producers: Queen and Mack

The time between November 1978, when Jazz was released, and June 1980, when The Game finally emerged, was wisely spent. Queen had decided to take a break from the studios and focus instead on their live work. While the North American leg of the Jazz tour in 1978 was marred by Freddie's excesses, the European and Japanese shows in 1979 are regarded as Queen's shining moments on the tour. They surpassed even themselves with the aptly titled Crazy Tour in late 1979, climaxing with a thrilling appearance at the Paul McCartney-organized Concerts for the People of Kampuchea. If there had been even a hint that Queen were starting to lose their staying power, it quickly vanished.

However, there was still the necessity for the all-important hit record. The band had entered Musicland Studios in June 1979, their first session at the studios in Munich, to record some preliminary ideas for songs. Unlike previous sessions, they had no complete songs prepared, a deliberate choice designed to exercise their spontaneous creativity; by the end of July, four complete songs were recorded ('Crazy Little Thing Called Love', 'Save Me', 'Sail Away Sweet Sister', and 'Coming Soon') and several additional song sketches. As yet, there was no pressure to come up with any product for general release. Part of this change in attitude occurred when Queen were introduced to Musicland's resident producer, Reinhold Mack (known only by his surname to his friends). He had recorded with ELO in previous years and brought some of his best techniques from those sessions, one of which focused on using minimal microphones to achieve a larger drum sound. Though Brian later admitted the band virtually produced themselves, Mack's expertise was useful to the band, particularly in allowing them the freedom to splice together various portions to create a complete, cohesive-sounding take. Previously,

the band would painstakingly record the backing track in one attempt, and if this broke down they would be forced to start over from the beginning. Mack's new method saved the band substantial time, as well as their sanity.

"That was when we started trying to get outside what was normal for us," Brian explained to On The Record in 1982. "Plus, we had a new engineer in Mack and a new environment in Munich. Everything was different. We turned our whole studio technique around in a sense, because Mack had come from a different background from us. We thought there was only one way of doing things, like doing a backing track; we would just do it until we got it right. If there were some bits where it speeded up or slowed down, then we would do it again until it was right. We had done some of our old backing tracks so many times, they were too stiff. Mack's first contribution was to say, 'Well, you don't have to do that. I can drop the whole thing in. If it breaks down after half a minute, then we can edit in and carry on if you just play along with the tempo.' We laughed and said, 'Don't be silly! You can't do that!' But in fact, you can. What you gain is the freshness, because often a lot of the backing tracks are first time through. It really helped a lot."

"I was working in Los Angeles with Gary Moore at the time," Mack told iZotope.com in 2007. "One day I had lunch with Giorgio Moroder. He mentioned rumors that I was supposed to go to Munich to work with Queen. Which was news to me. After calling the studios in Munich I was in a dilemma. Nobody knew anything about the sessions. So I figured [I would] take the trip. Worst case – a week and a ticket lost – no pain, no gain. Luckily it worked out pretty good … The band came off a tour of Japan and had some time to spend before going back to England. So it just fell into the 'right time, right place' category. The project did not start out as an album. It was a bunch of one- and two-week sessions. The first track we attempted was 'Crazy Little Thing Called Love'. Freddie picked up an acoustic guitar and said, 'Quick, let's do this before Brian comes'. About six hours later the track was done. The guitar solo was an overdub later on. Brian still hates me for making him use a Telecaster for the part. It was released as a pre-album single and went to number one. That obviously helped a great deal to inspire confidence and the working relationship tremendously."

Though the initial sessions in June 1979 were merely an attempt to explore and understand their separate working methods, Queen's partnership with Mack would prove fruitful. He encouraged the band to record in a simplified fashion, manifest in 'Crazy Little Thing Called Love' and 'Coming Soon'. However, Brian continued to write songs that were still very much like the Queen of old and insisted that 'Save Me' and 'Sail Away Sweet Sister' return to the more powerful ballads of their early days. After a brief break and a return to the stage rounding out the year, the band took some time to flesh out additional ideas and create full-fledged songs.

Brian said of the recording sessions, "That was breaking ground for us because, for the first time, we went into a recording studio without a deadline, purely with the intention of putting some tracks down as they came out. 'Crazy Little Thing Called Love' was one of them; another was 'Save Me'. There was a wide variety of things, and we're left in the position of having something in the can that we don't have to release straight away, and which at some future date we can perhaps fashion into an album. The basic reason for doing it was to put ourselves in a totally different situation. It's a way of getting out of that rut of doing an album, touring Britain, touring America, etc. We thought we'd try and change and see what came out. You have to make your own excitement after a while."

In October, the band released 'Crazy Little Thing Called Love' as their first non-album single; assisted by an image-conscious video, the single shot to No. 2 in the UK, their highest-charting single in two years. The resulting tour introduced the new single as well as Brian's 'Save Me', already touted as the next 45 and destined to become one of those rare songs played on a tour before its release. Surprisingly, when 'Crazy Little Thing Called Love' was released in America in December, the public were so delighted with the style change that the song soared to No. 1, becoming one of the fastest-selling singles of the year, eclipsed only by 'Another One Bites The Dust' in August 1980.

When the tour concluded in December 1979, the band took a four-week break before returning to the recording studio, fresh with new material and ideas. In February, the band started work on what was provisionally titled *Play The Game*, Queen's eighth studio release. The sessions were so productive that 25 songs were submitted and worked on. "We took more time than usual because we wanted to get something fresher instead of just churning out another one," Roger told *Rolling Stone* in July 1980. "This is the most different album in relation to the one before

it. We wrote the whole album in the studio and then pared 25 songs down to 10. It's the first time we've cut more than we needed. Some of the tunes will be changed and re-recorded and some of them will get lost. Some of them *deserve* to get lost." Considering the only known out-take was Roger's 'A Human Body', which was rejected for album status due to it being too melodic, there's a likelihood that the band set aside any songs that were deemed too conventional and focused instead on the more stripped-back, rhythmic tracks that made up the resultant album.

Brian confirmed as much shortly after the release of the album: "Recently, we've become more selective, I think, and we try to make albums which don't go in so many directions at once. For example, *The Game* was really pruned, and the others refused to include a couple of things I wanted on, because they said they were too far outside the theme of the album, and that we should be trying to make slightly more coherent albums." As an aside, he remarked, "I'm into paradoxes. I wanted to make an album about them, but the group told me I was a pretentious fart. They were right."

For the first time, but certainly not the last, the band experimented with synthesizers. "Roger's really the guy who introduced us to synthesizers," Brian said. "You can now get polyphonic synths with a device for bending the notes which is much closer to the feel of a guitar than ever before, so now we use the synth, but sparingly, I think, particularly on *The Game*. There's very little there, and what there is merely complements what we'd used already, so there's no danger of the synth taking over, which I would never allow to happen. I get a good feeling from playing the guitar which you don't get with anything else: a feeling of power, and a type of expression."

John expanded on Brian's thoughts: "We wanted to experiment with all that new studio equipment. We had always been keen to try out anything new or different while recording. The synthesizers then were so good; they were very advanced compared to the early Moogs, which did little more than make a series of weird noises. The ones we were using could duplicate all sorts of sounds and instruments – you could get a whole orchestra out of them at the touch of a button. Amazing."

Additional departures which caused many fans to throw their collective hands into the air were the tighter structure of the songs and the lack of a general theme. "Most of the album is different from the epic sound," Roger told *Rolling Stone*. "It's punchier, harder-hitting and more to the point. It doesn't really sound like a Queen album in the old sense. We felt almost too much effort went into *Jazz* and we wanted to be more spontaneous this time." "Spontaneous" had been used to describe *News Of The World*, Queen's last deliberate revitalization, but while the stripped-back sound had worked on that album, they fell back into old habits with Roy Thomas Baker on its follow-up, resulting in a bloated, convoluted album. Brian was happier with Mack and the initial sessions, telling *International Musician & Recording World* in 1982, "*The Game* was a result of a new environment. Working in Munich with a new engineer produced a really different approach. We started to put a whole lot of importance on the backing track once again. The emphasis was on rhythm and clarity. We had to build each track up."

The emphasis was now on the rhythm, instead of on orchestrations and lavish productions. The prime mover in this new sound was John: one of his new songs, 'Another One Bites The Dust', was written and recorded as a deliberate reaction against Queen's previous excesses, stripping back the pomp and circumstance to reveal the rhythmic side of the band, with the drums and bass pushed to the front, and the guitar practically non-existent. Elsewhere, Roger championed the new wave sound, while Freddie's own songs were par for the course: two pastiches and a ballad. Only Brian was determined to maintain Queen's status as a rock band, with 'Dragon Attack' balancing that fine line between rock and rhythm, while his other two songs were touching, poignant piano-based ballads.

"I like (the guitar) to be rich and warm, but at the same time aggressive and with an edge to it," Brian told *Sounds* in 1984. "Getting back to Mack, our approach to the guitar differed because he wanted me to try different amps and I wasn't happy with that, but for certain things it worked out well. On 'Crazy Little Thing Called Love', where we were going for a period sound, I played a Telecaster through a Boogie amp and it worked out fine. It was different. I kicked against that, but in the end I saw it was the right thing to do. As far as recording my own guitar, he wanted to use more mikes and get the same approach as you would with the drums, that started to make it too distant for me. I wanted the guitar to be inside the speaker and the ambience to be created in the listener's environment. This all came from my resistance to putting echo on anything. I regarded ambience on the guitar as the same as echo and thus making it less immediate. I wanted to hear all the guts and the string stretch and the fingers."

The result was an unhappy compromise. With Brian firmly planted in the traditional Queen sound, and Freddie and John moving away from that sound, *The Game* finds the band pulling in opposite directions, and not necessarily succeeding, for the first time. The guitarist would never truly be happy with Queen's sea change, always regarding Mack's new methods with cautious praise, but maintaining his love of loud guitars and drums. "Everything we did on *The Game* was different from the way we'd done it before," Brian told *Sounds* in 1984. "It was a fusion of our methods and his methods. There was some conflict; I had a lot of disputes with him over how we should record guitars. I suppose by that time I wasn't even thinking about it, I just wanted to record it the way I always recorded it. But Mack said. 'Look, try my way.' Eventually we did compromise and got the best of both worlds."

The shift worked, however, and the singles that were chosen were undoubtedly the strongest songs from the album: 'Crazy Little Thing Called Love', a welcome shift in style, and 'Save Me', a traditional Queen ballad-cum-rocker, both came nine and six months, respectively, before the album was released, while 'Another One Bites The Dust', the band's most successful foray into funk, was released two months after *The Game*. 'Play The Game' was released as the forerunner to the album, and though it was the most traditional Queen-sounding song of the bunch, it also performed the worst in the UK. Not better was John's 'Need Your Loving Tonight', released in Elektra-only territories five months after the album was released, and so it performed miserably, peaking at No. 44 in the US; considering that their last single, 'Another One Bites The Dust', had reached No. 1 three months before, this was a major disappointment for the band.

The album, now retitled *The Game* after Roger complained about the original title's implications of conformity ("It was suggested that we call the album *Play The Game*," Roger later said, "and I don't like the idea of that; basically, that means, in English, let's go along with the Establishment. I don't particularly sympathize with that view."), was released in June 1980, just as Queen were about to embark on an extended North American tour. Reviews were generally positive. *Record Mirror* opened with "I LIKE QUEEN, I LIKE QUEEN, I LIKE QUEEN! So there you are, you bunch of jerks making your cute little sideswipes at one of Britain's leading attractions. Go and slap on the next Willie Nile record and leave me in peace," going on to say that "This album is a straight kick into the goal (Christ, what a pun). It's like winning the men's singles at Wimbledon. It's a pity, though, that Queen have seen fit to include two recent singles in the running order. Considering the price of albums these days would it not have been worthwhile to slap on some new material?" Incidentally, the most criticism in this review was reserved for 'Another One Bites The Dust': "What's all this then, eh? 'Bites The Dust' merely comes over as a bit of disco wrapping. Maybe the track isn't meant to be taken that seriously but I'm not sure. Sorry, but this is the weak point of side one plundering from a well flogged idea."

Sounds was typically caustic: "Of course, bands like Queen do *not* belong in the pages of the throwaway pop press! The many thousands of their faithful fans will declare *The Game* to be just what they wanted (or will they – the standard's dropped to an all-time low) but the journalists won't even recognize its existence. *The Game* is a colossal mountain of unmovable mediocrity. It is old and tired and bland and blinkered. It purrs with self-satisfaction," closing with, "In case it passed you by, Sham 69 also have a new album called *The Game*. Struggling beneath the usual Sham difficulties lies a message of protest, pleading and relevant 1980s comment. Queen's game is rather different. Cash from chaos? Cash from trash!"

"After five years of unchallenging, dismal albums, this was supposed to be Queen's comeback," the *Washington Post* wrote after lambasting the new directions. "But no such luck." *NME* wasn't any better, in a dual review of *The Game* and Kiss's *Unmasked*: "It would be nice to hope that these bands will one day recognize their creative bankruptcy and retire with dignity – nice, but unrealistic. Instead, we get two more utterly unnecessary albums full of a music which ran its course a good six years ago: lumbering slack-jawed, big-booted heavy rock; either in harmony syrup (Queen) or with cartoon crassness (Kiss). Both are slick, glossy and soulless. Neither mean a thing. Both have been joylessly conceived with cynical disregard for every value which ever made music genuinely important to life ... As a matter of fact, all the comparisons to be made here are immensely flattering to Queen. Like Kiss, they're flogging a dead pantomime horse, but it's at least one of their own design. You must strive to forget every Freddie Mercury song you hear, but at least you remember it in the first

place. And so on."

Meanwhile, *Rolling Stone* unleashed all its pent-up hatred for Queen. "Sad to say, Queen seemed more comfortable with the brazen hodgepodge of 'Bohemian Rhapsody', the martial madness of 'We Will Rock You', and the pointless frenzy of 'Bicycle Race'. Black leather jackets, echo chambers, funky handclaps, prominent bass lines and sparse instrumentation – these guys know how this music should sound and feel, but they can't bend enough to get with it. Which is probably why some of the current record consists of the same inflated ballads and metallic shuffles that have padded every previous Queen disc ... Certainly, *The Game* is less obnoxious than Queen's last few outings, simply because it's harder to get annoyed with a group that's plugging away at bad rockabilly than with one blasting out crypto-Nazi marching tunes. The future doesn't look bright, however. No matter how much Queen may try to hide it, they're still egomaniacs."

Egomaniacs or not, the band still had a hit record on their hands, even if it represented an uneasy truce for the first time. *The Game* quickly shot up to the top position in both the UK and the US, making it their first and only No. 1 record in America. (In the UK, it was their third, and certainly not their last.) With 'Crazy Little Thing Called Love' lodged high in the American charts, the band and their entourage stormed the US for their largest and longest tour ever; after being away from the States for nearly 18 months, it was exhilarating to them that they could still sell out venues like Madison Square Garden (four nights, which closed their campaign at the beginning of October) and have a high-profile album and single in the charts. The success was short-lived, though; these were their halcyon days, and after working so hard to finally break through, it would take only a few questionable flash decisions to dethrone them permanently.

FLASH GORDON

EMI EMC 3351, December 1980 [10]
Elektra 5E-518, January 1981 [23]
EMI CDP 7 46214 2, December 1986
Hollywood HR-61203-2, June 1991
Parlophone CDPCSD 137, 1994
Island Records 277 177 0, June 2011 [165]

'Flash's Theme' (3'30), 'In The Space Capsule (The Love Theme)' (2'43), 'Ming's Theme (In The Court Of Ming The Merciless)' (2'41), 'The Ring (Hypnotic

Seduction Of Dale)' (0'57), 'Football Fight' (1'29), 'In The Death Cell (Love Theme Reprise)' (2'25), 'Execution Of Flash' (1'06), 'The Kiss (Aura Resurrects Flash)' (1'45), 'Arboria (Planet Of The Tree Men)' (1'42), 'Escape From The Swamp' (1'43), 'Flash To The Rescue' (2'45), 'Vultan's Theme (Attack Of The Hawk Men)' (1'12), 'Battle Theme' (2'18), 'The Wedding March' (0'56), 'Marriage Of Dale And Ming (And Flash Approaching)' (2'04), 'Crash Dive On Mingo City' (1'00), 'Flash's Theme Reprise (Victory Celebrations)' (1'24), 'The Hero' (3'36)

Bonus track on 1991 Hollywood Records reissue: 'Flash's Theme' *(remix by Mista Lawnge)* (6'49)
Bonus tracks on 2011 Universal Records deluxe reissue: 'Flash' *(single version)* (2'48), 'The Hero' *(revisited, October 1980)* (2'55), 'The Kiss' *(early version, March 1980)* (1'11), 'Football Fight' *(early version, February 1980)* (1'55), 'Flash' *(live version, Montreal Forum, November 1981)* (2'12), 'The Hero' *(live version, Montreal Forum, November 1981)* (1'48)

Bonus videos, 2011 iTunes-only editions: 'Flash' / 'The Hero' *(live version, Morumbi Stadium, March 1981)*, 'Flash' *(alternate promotional video)*, 'Flash' *(Queen + Vanguard promotional video)*

Musicians: John Deacon *(bass guitar, synthesizer on 'Arboria (Planet Of The Tree Men)', guitar on 'In The Space Capsule (The Love Theme)', 'In The Death Cell (Love Theme Reprise)', and 'Execution Of Flash')*, Brian May *(guitars, vocals, piano, organ, synthesizer)*, Freddie Mercury *(vocals, synthesizer)*, Roger Taylor *(drums, percussion, vocals, synthesizer on 'In The Space Capsule (The Love Theme)', 'In The Death Cell (Love Theme Reprise)', 'Escape From The Swamp', and 'Marriage Of Dale And Ming (And Flash Approaching)', timpani on 'Flash's Theme', 'In The Death Cell (Love Theme Reprise)', 'Escape From The Swamp', and 'Flash To The Rescue')*, Howard Blake *(orchestral arrangements)*
Recorded: October-November 1980 at The Townhouse and Advision Studios, London; The Music Centre, Middlesex *('The Hero' recorded at Utopia Studios, London; orchestrations recorded at Anvil Studios, Denham)*
Producers: Brian May and Mack

1980 was proving to be a hectic year for Queen: with the international successes of 'Crazy Little Thing Called Love', *The Game* and 'Another One Bites The Dust', the band were now subject to a greater amount of exposure. Consequently, the demand for live shows increased greatly and they suddenly found themselves playing to larger audiences in more high-profile cities. The tours, too, stretched on far longer than before. The band's 1980 North American tour kicked off at the end of June and finally concluded in early October; after a short break, the band recommenced the tour in European cities and British territories between November and December, and then continued the tour in the first part of 1981 in Japan and South America.

Surprisingly, during their first break in October and November, the band were able to squeeze in final recording sessions for a film project they had started concurrently with *The Game* that spring. The year before, the band had been approached by director Dino de Laurentiis, who asked them if they would be interested in providing the main theme and incidental music for his film adaptation of *Flash Gordon*. Roger, an enthusiastic sci-fi and comic fan, jumped at the project, while the others were hesitant at first. Even de Laurentiis wasn't sure if he was making the right decision: when he learned of the band and how right they would be for the project, he innocently asked, "But who are the queens?" But all concerned quickly warmed to the idea. "We saw 20 minutes of the finished film and thought it was very good and over the top," Brian explained. "We wanted to do something that was a real soundtrack. It's a first in many ways, because a rock group hasn't done this type of thing before, or else it's been toned down and they've been asked to write pretty mushy background music, whereas we were given the license to do what we liked, as long as it complemented the picture."

Their initial reservations arose from a reluctance to work against a deadline, which they hadn't done willingly since *News Of The World* in 1977. Additionally, the band were suddenly forced to please the director, a marked change after spending years working only for themselves. "Unfortunately, we didn't have enough time," Brian told *On The Record* in 1982. "We were doing *The Game* and an American tour at the same time *Flash* was going on, so it was ridiculous. We put as much time as we could in. We would do a week here and a week there. I spent some time with the arranger and orchestra to try and get some coherence to it all. It was good experience, but next time I hope we have time to really pull the whole thing together as a unit ... The main challenge was working for a boss who wasn't yourself. We had the director in there the whole time. The only criterion for whether something was good was whether it helped the movie."

This album saw the band hopping from studio to studio almost as frequently as they had for *A Night At The Opera* in 1975: the bulk of the sessions took place at The Townhouse, which would later be used for the *A Kind Of Magic* and *The Miracle* albums, while overdubs occurred at The Music Centre and Advision Studios. Orchestrations, arranged by Howard Blake, were recorded at Anvil Studios, while Freddie quickly nipped into Utopia Studios to record a vocal on 'The Hero', which used a similar backing to an earlier song called 'Battle Theme'.

Blake wasn't the band's first choice to work with on the project: Paul Buckmaster, a meticuolous perfectionist who had long ago worked with David Bowie, The Rolling Stones, and Elton John, was drafted based on Queen's recommendation. After a few weeks on the project, the producers discovered to their horror that Buckmaster had written and recorded only a small fragment of the score; pressed for time, the producers opted to instead work with Blake, who had a mammoth task ahead of him: to write and record the soundtrack in 10 days, a task that he met admirably. Three days before the completion of his score, he collapsed due to exhaustion, exacerbated by bronchitis; additionally, he discovered to his annoyance that his score had merely been a skeleton, to be replaced later by synthesizers. The composer maintained that he got along well with the band: "[They] were always cordial," he later wrote on his website. "Brian May came over one day and hummed an idea for an overture. As he did so I jotted it down on some manuscript paper and then played it back on the piano, which really startled him. They all came along to the orchestral recordings and seemed fascinated. I remember Freddie Mercury singing the idea of 'Ride to Arboria' in his high falsetto and I showed him how I could expand it into the orchestral section now on the film, with which he seemed very pleased. Whilst scoring I had cassettes of guitar ideas from Brian, in particular the slow 'falling-chord' sequence. I wrote this out into my score at one point and surrounded it with big orchestral colour. When I came to the recording I had Brian's solo guitar on headphones and conducted the orchestra in synch. around it. Many months later Brian came over and we listened to the finished album."

It was a haphazard way of working but the results were far more impressive than most fans care to admit. Brian was characteristically proud of the album, while the others remained indifferent or even unaware that it was theirs. (One night in 1981, John and members of the road crew apparently got rip-roaring drunk, and someone decided to put on the soundtrack album; after a few minutes, John slurred to Crystal Taylor, Roger's (unrelated) assistant, "Who is this?") Ever the spokesman for Queen's works, the guitarist admitted to being wary of the film project at the beginning, but became very excited about it: "We'd been offered a few, but most of them were where the film is written around music, and that's been done to death – it's the cliché of 'movie star appears in movie about movie star', but this one was different in that it was a proper film and had a real story which wasn't based around music, and we would be writing a film score – we were writing to a discipline for the first time ever."

The album would mark the first – and only – time that a Queen album wasn't produced collectively between all the band members and a producer; instead, it's credited to May and Mack. "It was interesting to write music for that movie," Brian said in an off-the-cuff 1981 interview in South America. "Particularly I learned a completely new job because I had never composed any soundtrack before. And it gives the band a possibility to open a new market. Besides, for the first time we worked for someone else. We didn't create songs for our own pleasure, but for the film director. Anyway, we worked freely, I mean, nobody told us what we had to do. We wrote some of the songs quickly and easily because this record sounds like a typical Queen album."

The songs are given a stripped-back sound – only one or two musicians were together in the studio at any given time; this is certainly true on both John's and Roger's songs – but things do tend to get typically Queen in areas. The opening song, an inoffensively catchy main theme for the titular protagonist, is the only overblown moment on the first side, while things stray towards the meandering and pompous starting with the second side.

When asked whether the band went away to write specific songs for specific characters, Brian explained to *Rocks Off!* magazine, "It almost happened that way, actually, yes. After the first week – you know, almost everything came from that magical first week when we put all kinds of things down – we discovered we already had a lot of music that could be lined up with various characters and scenes. But, for instance, we didn't really have a Ming (the Merciless) theme which worked, so at that point Fred said, 'Okay, I'll write the Ming theme'. And he went home and came back the next day with the Ming theme written … John wrote the Arboria theme, which is something quite subtle, really, just a three-note theme played on flute synthesizer. That sets the atmosphere for Arboria, which is the planet of the Tree Men. John also wrote the stuff for the 'Execution Of Flash' scene, which is quite interesting. Roger did the piece we called 'Escape From The Swamp'. In the film, you hear that when Flash goes down the rope into the swamp and them climbs out to escape the creatures that are pursuing him. Roger also did a thing we initally called the 'Love Theme', and it stuck, really, but it turned out to be the scene early in the film when Flash and Dale are riding Zarkov's rocket from Earth through hyperspace to Mongo, where Ming rules, and recurs when Flash and Dale are in Ming's dungeon. That's called 'In The Death Cell'. Freddie did 'Vultan's Theme' – Vultan is king of the Hawkmen and allies with Flash to attack Ming, you see – and I wrote the battle theme, which carries on from that."

"We all started with the new LP, *Flash Gordon*," John explained in 1981, "but in the end it was Brian saying what is on the disk or not. That is a very unusual thing for us, and we got some trouble with it. Brian wanted to have a German producer, with whom he worked very closely in Munich, while we would have preferred an album from Queen. We did agree then, but were not very happy about it. But for the world it was another Queen album. People from outside do not have any idea how personal some songs are. For them it's a Queen song, even if it is a very personal [thing] of one member only."

Brian explained that his involvement as producer came about out of necessity: "That sort of happened, really, because everyone else was too busy when it came time to finishing the thing off. All this stuff was laid down and roughly mixed, but it needed reorganizing for the album, and I sort of took on that project because everyone was doing different things at that time. I suppose it was because I was interested in the process of getting it onto film as well."

Of course, it would be unfair to judge *Flash Gordon* as an actual album: the tracks were written to complement certain scenes in the movie, not to stand up as separate songs. However, the band insisted the album be marketed as a Queen album instead of a film soundtrack, which was a bad move on their part, as it has been consistently noted as the worst album they ever did. Again, this is unfair; David Bowie released several albums that brought synthesizers to the fore, and there are several songs on *Flash Gordon* that sound

straight out of his Berlin era (the trilogy of *Low*, *"Heroes"*, and *Lodger*). It's Queen's most avant-garde experiment in music; there's nothing exactly *bad* about it, just that it's not something that a casual fan could listen to on a regular basis. Brian defended the album in a 1983 BBC Radio One interview: "It's a Queen album with a difference but, we wouldn't have put it out with the name Queen on it if we didn't think it was musically up to scratch in that sense. So it was music written for a film but with the idea that it will stand up as an album even if you've never heard the film. Which is why I particularly wanted bits of the dialogue in it as well rather than just a dry music soundtrack album. I wanted to be able to put the album on and to be able to visualize the whole thing even if you hadn't seen it, virtually. So hopefully, it tells a story, you know, like those children's records you buy which I like very much. Where they tell the story and then they have the music and everything. You don't need anything else, it's just your own little world. You just get carried along by the story."

Surprisingly, the reviews were positive, for the most part. *Record Mirror* raved, "This is the sort of stuff I haven't heard since Charlton Heston won the chariot race in *Ben Hur*. An album of truly epic proportions that warrants an equally epic five out of five." *Sounds*, too, were impressed: "As a film soundtrack, *Flash Gordon* is something extraordinary." The album, upon its release in December 1980, coincided with the European and British legs of The Game tour, and led in nicely to the Japanese tour in February 1981. It gave Queen a Top Twenty album worldwide – impressive for a film soundtrack with only two actual songs – except in the US, where it peaked at No. 23, thus starting an unfortunate decline of the band's reign there. If releasing a film soundtrack as a main album wasn't a career destroyer, their next project would very nearly prove to be exactly that.

HOT SPACE

EMI EMA 797, May 1982 [4]
Elektra E1-60128, May 1982 [22]
EMI CDP 7 46215 2, December 1986
Hollywood HR-61038-2, March 1991
Parlophone CDPCSD 135, 1994
Island Records 277 175 8, June 2011 [154]

'Staying Power' (4'12), 'Dancer' (3'50), 'Back Chat' (4'36), 'Body Language' (4'32), 'Action This Day' (3'32), 'Put Out The Fire' (3'19), 'Life Is Real (Song For Lennon)' (3'33), 'Calling All Girls' (3'51), 'Las

Palabras De Amor (The Words Of Love)' (4'31), 'Cool Cat' (3'29), 'Under Pressure' (4'08)

Bonus track on 1991 Hollywood Records reissue: 'Body Language' *(remix by Susan Rogers)* (4'45)

Bonus tracks on 2011 Universal Records deluxe reissue: 'Staying Power' *(live version, Milton Keynes Bowl, June 1982)* (3'57), 'Soul Brother' *(non-album B-side)* (3'36), 'Back Chat' *(single remix)* (4'12), 'Action This Day' *(live version, Tokyo, November 1982)* (6'25), 'Calling All Girls' *(live version, Tokyo, November 1982)* (5'45)

Bonus videos, 2011 iTunes-only editions: 'Las Palabras De Amor (The Words Of Love)' *(Top Of The Pops version, June 1982),* 'Under Pressure' *("rah" remix promotional video),* 'Action This Day' *(live version, Milton Keynes Bowl, June 1982)*

Musicians: John Deacon *(bass and rhythm guitars, synthesizer, piano and drum programming on 'Cool Cat'),* Brian May *(guitars, vocals, synthesizer, synth bass on 'Dancer', piano),* Freddie Mercury *(vocals, piano, synthesizer, drum programming on 'Body Language' and 'Staying Power'),* Roger Taylor *(drums, percussion, vocals, rhythm guitar on 'Calling All Girls', synthesizer),* David Bowie *(vocals on 'Under Pressure'),* Dino Solera *(alto and tenor saxophones on 'Action This Day')*
Recorded: June-August 1981 at Mountain Studios, Montreux; December 1981-March 1982 at Musicland Studios, Munich
Producers: Queen and Mack ('Under Pressure' produced by Queen and David Bowie)

With the success of 'Crazy Little Thing Called Love' and 'Another One Bites The Dust', Queen were suddenly catapulted into a new realm. The stadium rock of *News Of The World* had been honed into a finely executed chart sound, and the band found themselves catering more to the hit parade than creating albums.

The more rhythmic side of *The Game* was explored in their next studio release, although they were certainly in no rush to start work on it. In what would become a trend for the remainder of their career, the band stayed out of the studios as much as possible so they could focus on their live shows. "In the studio it was difficult," Brian said in a 2005 Capital Gold radio interview, "because we were all pulling in different directions with our own ideas, our own dreams we wanted to fulfil, so yeah, we had some pretty difficult

times. The great thing which I think counts for us is that we never aired our dirty laundry in public. We never went out and slagged each other off in public. We settled our problems privately, and so we were able to move on."

When the band returned for a brief break between their first South American tour and their autumn tour of Mexico, there were several issues to settle before they focused on their new album. They had started discussions for their first greatest hits package, which had been planned for Christmas 1980, but it was canceled as it would have been their third album release that year, adversely flooding the market. It was decided that the compilation would be released instead in 1981, officially their tenth anniversary as a band.

They had also decided to film a series of shows and splice the best performances together for their first live video release. They had attempted this before with their November 1974 concerts at The Rainbow and again in June 1977 at Earl's Court Arena, but film from both of these (excellent) shows was scrapped for unknown reasons. After touring South America and Mexico in September, the band played their only North American shows in late November in Montreal for the film project, though the resulting footage wouldn't be used for nearly three years.

Remaining was the issue of the new album. Just as they had done in 1979, the band started recording sessions with Mack in the summer of 1981 with no specific tracks in mind, jamming until ideas developed. The sessions unfolded discontinuously between June 1981 and March 1982: the first round of sessions took place between June and August, before the band broke for rehearsals and a tour of Mexico; the second was a two week interval starting on 6 December; and the third commenced in the New Year, with Roger and John arriving on 18 January, and Freddie and Brian showing up five days later. This hinted at the band's preference to record at a comfortable pace. "We don't have a concept," Roger told *Popcorn* in June 1981. "Most of the songs are already there, but the different effects and details come to life step by step. When the album is finished, we will surely go on tour again. And it will be a completely new show."

"We moved out to Munich to isolate ourselves from normal life so we could focus on the music," Brian told *Uncut* magazine in 2005, "and we all ended up in a place that was rather unhealthy. A difficult period. We weren't getting along together. We all had different agendas. It was a difficult time for me, personally –

some dark moments." The band had indeed changed into traditional rock stars. Freddie was content to explore the licentious side of Munich, and frequented nightclubs almost every night of the week. Brian and Roger, too, would go out partying with their own circle of friends, while John preferred to be with his family or go on holiday during lulls in recording.

The sessions were fraught with disagreements, with each band member pulling violently in different directions while trying to maintain a unified sound. In the studio, Mack was expected to make sense of the songs that the band was individually bringing to the table, with directives from each band member over the sound and feel of the songs. It didn't help that Brian was digging his heels in to keep the band focused on their rock sound (indeed, of his three songs, only 'Dancer' dipped its toe into the dance/funk category) while John and Freddie desired the airiness of dance records. "As a group, we do not have a single direction," Brian admitted in a 1984 interview with *Faces*. "We're four very different people. I do feel we're more democratic than any group I've come across. But that means there's always compromise – no one ever gets his own way totally. We're always pushing four different directions, not quite sure where the equilibrium position is, for balance. We fought about arriving at a sensible format for *Hot Space*, then decided to push into a very rhythmic and sparse area, disciplining out all the indulgences we've been used to putting in. We felt our fans would take it as another experiment. But we found we'd stepped out – at last! – from the music people felt they could expect from us."

This signaled dark times for the guitarist, who found the distractions of Munich not entirely to his taste. "Emotionally, we all got into trouble [there]," he told *Mojo* in 2008. "'Hey, let's have a drink after the studio.' It was nice to start with ... We'd go out after the studio and then we weren't getting back until eight in the morning. So you don't get much work done the next day ... and then it's time to go out drinking again." After a particularly boisterous evening at a club, an inebriated Brian came back to the studio and demanded that Mack fire up the tape machines with a whole load of echo applied, and barely squeezed out a guitar solo for 'Put Out The Fire'.

Brian's guitar was almost entirely absent from John's and Freddie's dance songs, which Brian later complained about: "Fred's thing was: less is more, make it more sparse, and play less guitar." John, who had a more rhythmic feel on guitar, was recruited

to play on 'Staying Power', and insisted on playing on his own 'Back Chat'. Dissatisfied with the latter title, Brian suggested a fiery solo to complement the argumentative feel of the lyrics – which, incidentally, brought the bassist and guitarist to verbal blows. "I remember John saying I didn't play the type of guitar he wanted on his songs," Brian later told *Mojo* in 1999. "We struggled bitterly with each other."

Not that Freddie was entirely to blame for the guitarist's frustrations: Peter "Phoebe" Freestone, the singer's personal assistant, recalled an outburst that, while superficially full of frustration, was still laced with humor: "What the fucking hell do you want? A herd of wildebeest charging from one side to the other?!" Mack, who had the unenviable task of making sense of the songs, recalled, "Making *The Game* was the last time the four of them were in the studio together. After that, it felt like it was always two of them in one studio and two of them in another. You'd come in one day and say, 'Oh, where's Roger?' and someone would say, 'Oh, he's gone skiing' ... It's easier to conceive and give birth than it is to get this album finished." In March 1982, just as the sessions came to a close, Mack's wife Ingrid gave birth to their first child, John-Frederick.

Hot Space was finally finished in late March 1982, and the band flew off to Canada to film a video for 'Body Language' as well as to rehearse for their upcoming world tour. There's no doubt that recording had exhausted the band, and they hoped to find renewed energy in the live shows. "I enjoy the live stuff a lot more," Brian lamented to *Guitar Player* in 1983. "There are moments in the studio I enjoy, but most of the studio is sheer misery. The writing and the arranging of material is such a painstaking process these days for us. I can get in and play a solo anytime, but that's not the majority of the work that's done. The majority of it is real soul-searching and wondering whether a song is right. It's painful."

Wrapped in a startlingly bright and neon sleeve, devised from an idea by Freddie, *Hot Space* was bound to get attention on the shelves, and stood out among some of the more popular albums of the day. (In a nice nod to *Queen II*, the inner sleeve was a reverse of the front: the faces of the four band members are colored in their respective colors from the front, laid over a stark black background.) However, previous albums that featured band photos showed them all together, as a cohesive unit; here, each band member is boxed off into his own section, giving off the uncomfortable impression that the album was done separately from each other. Each band member was the driving force on his own song, with the others acting as backing musicians – or, if tensions were particularly high and the songwriter wouldn't budge, synthesizers or drum machines would be used instead. Indeed, there was no sense of togetherness on *Hot Space*; while *The Game* had been recorded piecemeal, it was still recorded as a collective group, but on *Hot Space*, the only songs it sounds like the band were in the same room together were on the more traditional Queen tracks like 'Put Out The Fire', 'Life Is Real (Song For Lennon)', 'Calling All Girls', and 'Las Palabras De Amor (The Words Of Love)'. The cover conveyed perfectly the band's creative and personal health at the time: they were pulling apart from each other in four different directions. Tensions would get so bad on the ensuing tour that there was discussion of breaking up the band.

The album was released in May 1982 after considerable delay (David Bowie, who guested on both 'Under Pressure' and 'Cool Cat', asked that his voice be removed from the latter, though he neglected to tell the band until the day before the album's release), nearly two months after 'Body Language' and almost two years after *The Game*. Sales were adequate, especially remarkable considering that the first single reached only No. 25 in the UK charts, and the album peaked at No. 4. It must have been disappointing for the band though, since *The Game* had reached the top slot in both England and America, but their fans across the pond hadn't embraced the new album as enthusiastically as had their British fans, and it reached only No. 22 in the US charts. This was the first proper Queen album since *Queen II* not to reach the Top Twenty, a steady decline in the band's US popularity beginning here and deepening over the next decade. Subsequent albums would never again reach the Top Twenty in America.

"I haven't found it that easy to accustom myself to the new stuff," Brian said in 1982. "A lot of the music which Freddie and John want to do is more R&B-oriented, and it's hard for me to do that because my playing is a reaction to that style, in a sense. I used to listen to people plucking away on Motown records, and I really didn't like it. I always thought to myself, 'That's the kind of thing I don't want to play. I want the guitar to be up there speaking'. So in a way the return to that was difficult to me. It was a discipline which I gradually worked into, but I find myself wanting to burst out of it all the time and make a lot of noise."

"[It] is an attempt to do funk properly," Brian cryptically explained in 1982. "It has a style of playing where you get in and get out quickly, hence the title." Brian, ever the defender of Queen's music, was himself unsure of the band's sudden departure in style. He updated his stance more clearly in 1989, saying, "I think *Hot Space* was a mistake, if only timing-wise. We got heavily into funk and it was quite similar to what Michael Jackson did on *Thriller* a couple of years ago, and the timing was wrong. Disco was a dirty word."

"Possibly Freddie was then getting interested in other things," Brian continued, "and a bit bored with being in the studio, because we did studios to death with the previous two albums, when we'd be in there for months on end, just working away, although we weren't particularly inefficient, it was just that there was a lot to be done. We all felt we'd done enough of that for the time being, and wanted to get back to basics and do something simpler, but Freddie got to the point where he could hardly stand being in a studio, and he'd want to do his bit and get out."

Reviews for the album were surprisingly positive: *Record Mirror* opined, "New styles, and a whole new sense of values. You'll love *Hot Space*, eventually." *Sounds* purred, "Queen have never made particularly blinding albums, but you'll have to agree that *Hot Space* shows more restraint and imagination than tripe like *Jazz*." Even *NME*, who normally reviled everything Queen released, was (relatively) glowing: "The production of the whole album is really a peach." *Rolling Stone* was mixed, praising 'Back Chat', 'Calling All Girls' and 'Cool Cat', though censuring the rest as "at best, routinely competent and, at times, downright offensive. 'Give me your body / Don't talk,' sings Mercury in 'Body Language', a piece of funk that isn't fun." It was a viewpoint shared by most fans.

At several points throughout the Hot Space world tour, when introducing particular tracks from the new album, Freddie categorically denied that the band had lost their traditional sound, and even said during the Milton Keynes performance, "It's only a bloody record! People get so excited about these things." Perhaps, but the rest of the band disagreed, and while most of the songs got a regular workout in the live setting in 1982 (only 'Dancer', 'Las Palabras De Amor (The Words Of Love)' and 'Cool Cat' remained unperformed), 'Under Pressure' was the only one to remain in the set list after 1984. ('Staying Power' was played for the first half of the Queen Works! tour in 1984, but was dropped and never reappeared after that.) There were no *Hot Space* tracks offered on the 1991 compilation *Greatest Hits II*, and only 'Las Palabras De Amor' was released on *Greatest Hits III* in 1999. 'Body Language' was issued on the 1992 US update of *Greatest Hits*, but the other singles have remained conspicuously absent from any compilation.

Brian was particularly critical of the album, while Roger, John and Freddie preferred to look on it as an experiment and nothing else. When asked if he was happy with the direction Queen were going in, Brian answered bluntly: "To be honest, no. I didn't feel that this tour [the 1982 Hot Space world tour] was making me very happy. I've often felt that in the studio, but that's the first time I felt it on tour. I didn't feel very happy until the last concert. The last night in Los Angeles, I felt quite cheered up. I was prepared to think, 'Well, I don't really want to do this any more'. Somehow, when it got to the last one, Freddie was really on form and giving a million percent, and I felt that I was going well. So the end of the tour finished on a good note for me. I felt like I did want to be out there doing it again sometime. But we are going to have a long rest."

THE WORKS
EMI WORK1 EMC 240014 1, February 1984 [2]
Capitol ST-12322, February 1984 [23]
Capitol CDP 7 46016 2, February 1984
EMI CDP 7 46016 2, December 1986
Hollywood HR-61233-2, November 1991
UK Cat No, September 2011 [113]

'Radio Ga Ga' (5'48), 'Tear It Up' (3'26), 'It's A Hard Life' (4'09), 'Man On The Prowl' (3'27), 'Machines (Or "Back To Humans")' (5'10), 'I Want To Break Free' (3'20), 'Keep Passing The Open Windows' (5'23), 'Hammer To Fall' (4'28), 'Is This The World We Created...?' (2'17)

Bonus tracks on 1991 Hollywood Records reissue: 'I Go Crazy' (3'42), 'Radio Ga Ga' *(extended version)* (6'53), 'I Want To Break Free' *(extended version)* (7'19)

Bonus tracks on 2011 Universal Records deluxe reissue: 'I Go Crazy' (3'43), 'I Want To Break Free' *(single remix)* (4'18), 'Hammer To Fall' *(Headbangers mix)* (5'18), 'Is This The World We Created...?' *(live version, Rock In Rio Festival, January 1985)* (3'02), 'It's A Hard Life' *(live version, Rock In Rio Festival, January 1985)* (4'25), 'Thank God It's Christmas' (4'21)

Bonus videos, 2011 iTunes-only editions: 'Tear It Up' *(live version, Wembley Stadium, 11 July 1986)*, 'I Want To Break Free' *(live version, Rock In Rio Festival, January 1985)*, 'Radio Ga Ga' *(promotional video)*

Musicians: John Deacon *(bass guitar, rhythm guitar and synthesizer on 'I Want To Break Free')*, Brian May *(guitars, vocals, synthesizer and harmony vocals on 'Machines (Or "Back To Humans")', acoustic guitar on 'Is This The World We Created...?')*, Freddie Mercury *(vocals, piano, synthesizer on 'Radio Ga Ga' and 'Keep Passing The Open Windows')*, Roger Taylor *(drums, percussion, vocals, synthesizer on 'Radio Ga Ga', vocoder and synthesizer on 'Machines (Or "Back To Humans")')*, Fred Mandel *(piano finale on 'Man On The Prowl', synthesizers on 'Radio Ga Ga', 'I Want To Break Free', and 'Hammer To Fall', programming on 'Radio Ga Ga')*, Mack *(Demolition Fairlight programming on 'Machines (Or "Back To Humans")')*
Recorded: August 1983-January 1984 at The Record Plant, Los Angeles, and Musicland Studios, Munich
Producers: Queen and Mack

The Hot Space World Tour had been a strain on the band; tensions were starting to mount on the road for musicians who, after all, could have retired, unworried about their financial future. Thankfully, Queen were still eager to express their collective creativity, even if it meant they'd be together, as Freddie put it, "until we fucking well die." They deserved a break, however, both from each other and from the music industry. So, following their final show at Seibu Lions Stadium on 3 November 1982, the band agreed on a year's hiatus, a well-deserved opportunity to relax and enjoy their success while they still had the chance.

"After the relatively unsuccessful *Hot Space* album," John said in 1984, "there was a little bit of dissatisfaction there, and we toured and didn't enjoy it so much, and we decided to take a long time off. It was quite a long time before we actually went into the studio, which gave us all a chance to get a break from each other and try new things as well. It has resulted in Brian doing some solo work, Roger doing another album, Freddie starting an album, and in the end I think it was good for us as well, and now that we're back together, we're more committed as a group."

While Brian, Roger and Freddie started separate solo projects during their time apart, John rested in the interim, though he did admit that the long, unproductive period often caused bouts of depression.

"We're not so much a group anymore," he told Martin Townsend in 1985. "We're four individuals that work together as Queen but our working together as Queen is now actually taking up less and less of our time. I mean basically I went spare, really, because we were doing so little. I got really bored and I actually got quite depressed because we had so much time on our hands…" Salvation came in July 1983 when he and Freddie flew to meet with director Tony Richardson in Los Angeles, where discussions were in progress for Queen to contribute music to the big screen adaptation of John Irving's 1981 novel *The Hotel New Hampshire*. While in the States, the two also decided to record the next album at the famous Record Plant studios. The following month, the band assembled for their first recording sessions together in almost 18 months.

As in previous group sessions, the time spent together was not without incident, as Brian explained to *Q's* Phil Sutcliffe in 1991: "We did hate each other for a while. Recording *The Works*, we got very angry with each other. I left the group a couple of times, just for the day, you know. 'I'm off and I'm not coming back!' We've all done that. You end up quibbling over one note." Despite their differences, which always seemed to produce interesting music, the sessions proved fruitful: nearly 20 songs were recorded for the album, comprising the nine that were selected for release (including the non-album track 'I Go Crazy'), as well as several songs which would remain unreleased. An early handwritten line-up for the album ran as following: 'Tear It Up', 'Whipping Boy', 'I Want To Break Free', 'Machines', 'Man On Fire', 'Take Another Little Piece Of My Heart', 'It's A Hard Life', 'Your Heart Again', 'Man On The Prowl', 'Radio Caca' (sic), 'Hammer To Fall', 'Keep Passing The Open Windows', and 'Man Made Paradise'. 'Whipping Boy', a song that originated during sessions for *Hot Space*, has been speculated to be 'I Go Crazy', while 'Your Heart Again' was recorded three years later by *EastEnder* actress Anita Dobson as 'Let Me In (Your Heart Again)'. 'Take Another Little Piece Of My Heart', meanwhile, was a jam with Rod Stewart and Jeff Beck, and surfaced in 1995 as 'Let Me Live'. 'Man On Fire' was saved for Roger's *Strange Frontier*, 'Man Made Paradise', which had started life as a *Hot Space* out-take, was finally released on Freddie's *Mr Bad Guy*, and 'Is This The World We Created...?' was a last-minute addition. Further out-takes include 'There Must Be More To Life Than This' and 'Love Kills', both of which were released as Freddie solo projects.

The vocalist explained the writing process of *The Works* in 1984: "Every album that's ever come out of Queen, we've come up with a batch of songs, and we really pick the best, and if I have songs that I feel are better than somebody else's – if I have five songs that are better than one of Roger's songs, I'll say we won't have his one song. I can remember that Roger actually wrote about three or four songs and, as far as I was concerned, [they] weren't good enough, so I said, 'Go back and write some more.' Then Roger will come up with something like 'Radio Ga Ga' and it's perfect!"

During the recording sessions, the band also concocted several songs for *The Hotel New Hampshire* but were disappointed when the producers decided to cut costs by using pre-recorded classical tracks instead, effectively nudging Queen off the project. The band didn't let the experience sour their attitude; instead, they incorporated at least one track, Freddie's epic 'Keep Passing The Open Windows', onto their new album.

The band spent eight weeks in Los Angeles, recording basic tracks and jamming with anyone who happened to stop by the studios. While out in the west coast city of excess, the band wracked up enormous bills hiring rental cars and partying after sessions, but the discouraging news of Richardson's soundtrack-killing decision forced them to recoup their losses and head back to Munich to finish up the album. It was there that their old demons returned: Freddie once again hit the nightclubs (not that he had behaved himself in Los Angeles: he met a biker known as Vince the Barman, who was always referred to by Freddie's friends with wistful sighs and earned the reputation of being "the one that got away") and Brian, Roger, and John all drank too much and missed their families. One day, the bassist, burned out on recording, went on an impromptu trip to Bali without telling the others.

The band were recording more as a band this time, though tensions were still frayed. Brian and John once again clashed over techniques, with John insisting that guest keyboardist Fred Mandel, who had accompanied the band on their 1982 Rock 'n' America and Japanese Hot Space tours, record the solo on the Roland synthesizer. Mandel was taken aback: "This was controversial, as no one did solos apart from Brian." Mack was convinced that the solo would remain a placeholder, but Freddie and John both insisted it remain; Brian relented, but not before adding a few touches on the Red Special to beef up the sound. The sour mood of Brian's insistence on a guitar solo on 'Back Chat' hadn't dissipated, and while all would maintain that contrasting viewpoints made for better results, it was still an uneasy compromise.

When sessions concluded in early January 1984, the band – particularly Brian – were pleased with the results. The guitarist explained, "I think our next album is damn good, much better than anything we've done for a while. It's going to be called *The Works*. And it really is! There's all the Queen trademarks: lots of production and arrangements and harmonies. We've experimented in the past and some of the experiments didn't work. Our last album was one big experiment and a lot of people totally hated it. And it didn't sell very well – not compared to earlier stuff, anyway.

"I always got the most enjoyment out of the harder material," he continued. "Actually, our new album is a lot harder, but I did fight to get it that way. We've done some fantastic over-the-top harmonies and a lot of heavy things that we haven't done for years. The pressure has always been against me, because not everybody in the band is into the same stuff as I am. I get the most pleasure out of things that I can hammer down and really get some excitement out of. Basically, I'm just like a little boy with the guitar, I just like the fat, loud sound of it. But that's not important to the others, and I agree with this, the songs come first. That's where the common ground ends and the arguments begin. The result is always a compromise."

Released in February 1984, *The Works*, adorned with a classy photo taken by George Hurrell, Hollywood's premier photographer during its golden age, in his Los Angeles studio. With the assistance of 'Radio Ga Ga', a UK No. 2 hit, the album entered the charts at a similar position, and stayed in the Top 10 for four consecutive weeks, returning later in April and again in August – thanks to the 'I Want To Break Free' single and the announcement of their UK tour, respectively. In the US, the album struggled into the charts at No. 58, and peaked at No. 23 – a disappointing result, considering the effort the band went to to make it more digestible to their fans. Brian was happy enough, telling *Faces*, "Now, *The Works* is doing very well, but I myself am starting to wonder: does that mean we played it too safe? I really do think you need to take the musical risks, to be comfortable with yourself."

The reviews, surprisingly, were generally positive; even the unsparing *Rolling Stone* gave the album three stars out of five, saying, "Granted, the messages have all been heard before and practically cancel each other out: love is all you need; let's get physical; machines have feelings, too; be an individual, stand your ground. Instead, the revelations are in the music ... *The Works* is a royal feast of hard rock without that awful metallic aftertaste; as such, it might turn out to be the *Led Zeppelin II* of the 1980s. Not such a depressing prospect at that." *Record Mirror* said of the album, "The comfortable yet demanding 'Radio Ga Ga' is brought down to earth by the hot and oily 'Tear It Up', with its cat scratch fever guitar. Another jewel in the crown." And *Sounds* uncharacteristically gushed, "It's all there, I can assure you: spurious social commentary in 'Machines', slight Fred ballad via 'Is This The World We Created...?', and even a nip of the old Brian May metal with the excellent 'Hammer To Fall'."

1984 also saw the band immerse themselves in producing videos for the album's singles, a project Roger disliked: "Now you've gotta make a mini-film! And often it's more expensive, and the record doesn't always suit the visual medium." When asked about the danger of video depriving the listener of their own imagination, Roger responded, "It can in a way. That was something that 'Radio Ga Ga' was about: you used to make your own pictures in your mind, but now there's a video, and you immediately think of those visual ideas that have already been thought of by somebody else." John was more optimistic: "It's a very important aspect of a group. And we've also all changed our looks over the years, but it's something that I don't tend to get involved with as much as the others."

The advent of MTV in August 1981 meant that videos could now capture a larger demographic audience, which should have worked to Queen's advantage in America. 'Radio Ga Ga' made the Top Twenty in the US, and 'I Want To Break Free' looked like it would follow its predecessor into the higher ranks of the charts. For years, it was assumed that the image of the band running around in drag (and Freddie cavorting with a group of spandex-clad ballet dancers) was a bit too much for Americans to tolerate, but, when inspected a little closer, invites scepticism. Both Culture Club, fronted by gender-bending vocalist Boy George, and Frankie Goes To Hollywood (their 1984 gay-themed hit 'Relax' topped the UK charts and prevented 'Radio Ga Ga' from hitting Number One) were extremely popular in America, as were their explicit videos. And let's not forget that this wasn't the first time that Freddie had worn spandex...

The success of the album in the UK was greeted with a sigh of relief, but more worrisome was the album's faltering in the US. Hopes were high for Capitol to deliver the goods after the disappointing promotion by Elektra of *Hot Space*. The record company had become a handicap to them; despite the band's lengthy live campaign across the States in the summer of 1982, record sales were poor. The band had been looking for a way out even before *Hot Space*, but that album was delivered to Elektra, who had contested that *Flash Gordon* wasn't a genuine Queen album. "We were trying to break from our old record company in America, which was important," Brian said the following year. "We didn't want to deliver another album in that situation. There was that feeling that we might just be making another Queen album and putting it back into the machine. We didn't want that, and it's all worked out very well. We agreed on Capitol, and signed a deal with them. Suddenly, we have a company in America that's really *excited* to be getting their first Queen album."

The early US success of 'Radio Ga Ga' gave Queen high hopes for a reconnection with their American audiences. However, several unfortunate factors came into play between 'Radio Ga Ga' in January and 'I Want To Break Free' in April 1984. The band's relationship with the radio networks was damaged by a breakdown in communication. In addition to this, as Brian explained to Q in 2005, there were record company problems. "We had spent a million dollars getting out of our deal with Warner-Elektra to get onto the Capitol label. And Capitol got themselves into trouble with a dispute that raged in the early 1980s over the alleged corruption of independent record promoters in the US. It was basically the ring of bribery that went on to get records played on US radio. There was a government enquiry into it, and everybody shut down very, very fast. Without going into it too deeply, Capitol got rid of all their 'independent' guys – and the reprisals from the whole network were aimed directly at all the artists who had records out at that time. We had 'Radio Ga Ga', which I think was Top Twenty and rising, but the week after that it disappeared from the charts."

As a result, Queen lost a substantial amount of airplay and coverage, and without those promoters to assist the band's newest singles with radio play and chart success, the band focused on other countries. This undoubtedly soured relations: the band must have felt bitter at the unfortunate timing, while Capitol must have been horrified – they had just signed Queen to a multimillion dollar record deal, and now the band refused to tour America. (They did agree to appear on a few music programmes to talk about the record, though that did very little to boost sales.) There was

little incentive, then, for the record company to market an album that the band wouldn't promote; as a result, the years with Capitol were discordant. Additionally, Freddie was becoming increasingly disenchanted with the longer tours, more comfortable with the brief European and British jaunts and the occasional excursions to other countries. If the band had followed their earlier touring cycles, there wouldn't have been a six-month gap between the release of *The Works* and the start of their European tour: it would have probably been filled with an extensive tour across America. Peter "Ratty" Hince, head of the band's road crew, later told Queenarchives.com that the band were considering it: "Yes, I believe some dates were planned in reserve. I think it was a huge mistake by Queen not to take that tour to America – it effectively killed the band there. The decision was because the singles from *The Works* had not done very well in the US, but were big hits everywhere else. Queen had just signed to Capitol Records and expected more I guess. The breaking point was the video for 'I Want To Break Free' – the 'drag' and comedy didn't go down well in America and Queen would not make an alternative video for the US market."

The video for 'I Want To Break Free' has often been singularly attributed with destroying Queen's relationship with North America. Brian later recalled to *Mojo*, "It was received in horror in most of America. They just didn't get it. To them it was boys dressing up as girls and that was unthinkable, especially for a rock band. I was in some of those US TV stations when they got the video, and a lot of them refused to play it. They were visibly embarrassed." Hince also remembered, "Queen were asked to do another promo for [the song]. They were told, 'This one isn't right for America. Will you do a performance video?' And they said no. They should have done it, because it killed them in the US." Freddie was exasperated at the sudden turn of events, and sighed to Simon Bates in 1985, "For the first time in our lives we were taking the mickey out of ourselves. But in America they said, 'What are our idols doing dressing up in frocks?!'"

Worse was still to come. Paul Prenter, Freddie's personal manager, was making enemies in the US. "I think America very much depends on the network of people who care about music, and a lot of that is the radio stations," Brian explained in *Q Classic* in 2005. "Radio stations are the connection between the artist and the community, and rightly so. Freddie had a personal manager [Paul Prenter] at the time who was very dismissive. And OK, Freddie needed a bit of protection, it was hard for him at that time. But I think this guy … well, I know for a fact this guy went around saying, 'No, Freddie doesn't want to talk to you. Why should he want to talk to you anyway?' And an enormous amount of damage was done to our relationship with the radio networks, who up to that point had been very close to us, very helpful." The result destroyed Queen's reputation in North America. "Freddie didn't want to go back and play smaller venues that we'd been before," Brian continued. "He was like, 'Let's just wait and we'll go out and do stadiums in America as well.' But it was one of those things that wasn't to be."

Instead, the band shifted their attention to the rest of the world, and while tours of Europe, South Africa, Australasia and Japan brought them to a wider audience, they ended the tour in lower spirits than before, and doubly exhausted. Not only were they suddenly pariahs in America (Brian would later lament that they couldn't even get arrested there), the trying ordeals of the year – including an ill-fated tour of apartheid Sun City, which had earned Queen a blacklisting on the Musician's Union, hefty fines and a ban on performing there as long as segregation dominated South Africa – had taken their toll on the band. Queen were looking forward to an indefinite, extended break at the conclusion of the Japanese tour in May 1985. They separately and emphatically maintained that breaking up was never an option: "It's not the money anymore," Roger told *Sounds* in 1984, "it's the thought of, 'Christ, what would we do if we ended it?' Obviously we could all have our solo careers and put new bands together, but that would be like climbing Mount Everest again … We'll only do it while the enthusiasm's there. The more interest that's shown in the band, the more enthusiasm is generated within the band." Little did they know that a well-polished, 20-minute set at Live Aid would generate more interest than they'd ever experienced before in their career.

A KIND OF MAGIC

EMI EU 3509, June 1986 [1]
EMI CDP 7 46267 2, June 1986 [1]
Capitol SMAS 512476, June 1986 [46]
Capitol CDP 7 46267 2, June 1986 [46]
Hollywood HR 61152 2, June 1991
UK Cat No, September 2011 [109]

'One Vision' (5'10), 'A Kind Of Magic' (4'24), 'One Year Of Love' (4'28), 'Pain Is So Close To Pleasure' (4'23), 'Friends Will Be Friends' (4'04), 'Who Wants To Live Forever' (5'16), 'Gimme The Prize (Kurgan's Theme)' (4'34), 'Don't Lose Your Head' (4'38), 'Princes Of The Universe' (3'37)

Bonus tracks on CD issue: 'A Kind Of "A Kind Of Magic"' (3'37), 'Friends Will Be Friends Will Be Friends…' (5'58), 'Forever' (3'20)

Bonus tracks on 1991 Hollywood Records reissue: 'Forever' (3'20), 'One Vision' (*Extended Vision*) (6'23)

Bonus tracks on 2011 Universal Records deluxe reissue: 'A Kind Of Magic' (*Highlander version*) (4'22), 'One Vision' (*single version*) (4'00), 'Pain Is So Close To Pleasure' (*single remix*) (3'57), 'Forever' (3'20), 'A Kind Of Vision' (*demo, August 1985*) (3'23), 'One Vision' (*live version, Wembley Stadium, 11 July 1986*) (5'12), 'Friends Will Be Friends Will Be Friends…' (5'59)

Bonus videos, 2011 iTunes-only editions: 'One Vision' (*extended promotional video*), 'Princes Of The Universe' (*promotional video*), 'A Kind Of Magic' (*live version, Wembley Stadium, 11 July 1986*)

Musicians: John Deacon (*bass guitar, keyboards on 'One Year Of Love' and 'Pain Is So Close To Pleasure', rhythm guitar on 'Pain Is So Close To Pleasure' and 'Don't Lose Your Head'*), Brian May (*guitars, vocals, keyboards on 'One Vision' and 'Who Wants To Live Forever'*), Freddie Mercury (*vocals, piano, keyboards on 'A Kind Of Magic', 'Friends Will Be Friends', and 'Princes Of The Universe'*), Roger Taylor (*drums, vocals, electronic drums on 'One Vision', keyboards on 'A Kind Of Magic' and 'Don't Lose Your Head'*), Spike Edney (*additional keyboards*), UMI & BBC B (*computer keyboards*), Lynton Naiff (*string arrangement on 'One Year Of Love'*), Steve Gregory (*saxophone on 'One Year Of Love'*), Michael Kamen (*orchestra arrangement on 'Who Wants To Live Forever'*), National Philharmonic Orchestra (*strings on 'Who Wants To Live Forever'*), Joan Armatrading (*incidental vocals on 'Don't Lose Your Head'*)
Recorded: September 1985-March 1986 at The Townhouse Studios, London; Musicland Studios, Munich; and Mountain Studios, Montreux
Producers: Queen and Mack (*'One Vision', 'One Year Of Love', 'Pain Is So Close To Pleasure', 'Friends Will Be Friends', 'Princes Of The Universe', 'Friends Will Be Friends Will Be Friends…', and 'One Vision (Extended Vision)'*), Queen and David Richards (*all other tracks*)

Live Aid had changed Queen. Before they agreed to the one-off appearance, there was discord once again within the band: not only had the tour supporting *The Works* been strenuous, tensions were mounting with Freddie's long-delayed solo album finally coming out in April 1985 and its success threatened to take his attention away from the band. (To his credit, Freddie consistently denied in interviews that he was ready to jump ship; he would often paper over any cracks of sincerity by claiming that the money generated from Queen's record sales was the main motivator for him not to leave.) The band were once again exhausted with the music business and with each other, and privately they agreed to take 1986 off and maybe reconvene in 1987 to work on another album.

But the reception they received following their flawless performance at Live Aid was universal and unanimous: Queen were the best act that day. The band – especially Freddie, who lately had to be coerced into recording – was so energized that they went back into the studios in September, with no material whatsoever, to work on a track in a collaborative environment and see what they could come up with. While in Montreux, the band were approached by Russell Mulcahy to contribute a song to his motion picture *Highlander*; they had been offered scripts before, and their last soundtrack work had been aborted by the film's producers midway through the sessions, so they approached the offer with some leeriness. Upon viewing a 20-minute rough-cut, however, the band walked away enthused, and offered to contribute the entire soundtrack.

"We had the scripts and we went to see quite a lot of the footage they'd got already," John said of the *Highlander* project, "and then we all went away and tried to write songs for various bits. I ended up writing a slow ballad in 6/8 which is called 'One Year Of Love'." Added Roger, "We found plenty of things in the plot to jump off on, to write songs around," noting also that the completed album was not a soundtrack in the strictest sense: "I think the idea of a complete soundtrack album puts quite a lot of people off. I think they're imagining all these orchestral links, which don't really do anything, and it's really sort of background music."

"We did all the music for the film first," John explained, "then when we came to do the album, we actually rearranged a lot of the tracks, made them longer, wrote more lyrics and tried to make them into full-fledged songs. So they stand up in their own right, without necessarily needing the film. You can actually hear them on the radio and [they] sound more like songs than incidental music."

Queen's involvement with the film was a natural fit, as Russell Mulcahy explained to denofgeek.com: "It was totally integral and it came about at a wonderfully early stage in the editing, in that I had cut together a twenty minute piece which was excerpts from a number of scenes ... I'd always been a fan of Queen and approached them. So, then they watched it and they said yes. So, the incredible thing that happened was that they came in early on the film and the composer was a guy called Michael Kamen, who passed away a number of years ago, and he also had a rock and roll background, but had been doing wonderful scores for Terry Gilliam's *Brazil*.

He was on board as composer, Queen came on board, they wrote some songs and then he would then take some of them and at the end, or halfway through, intercut the score. There was an extraordinary collaboration between the band. It wasn't just like we finished the film and asked for a song. They were very much involved in edit and during the months of post production.

There's a great advantage to having the film composer work with a band like Queen, as they also had that, as you know, that rock and roll but also operatic quality, which lends itself very much to the operatic quality of the movie."

By this point, the band and their preferred producers had split into two factions: Brian and Roger worked with David Richards on their songs, while John and Freddie worked with Mack. Richards, who had struck up a friendship with Roger in 1979 and helped the drummer record his two solo albums (even co-writing a handful of songs on *Strange Frontier*), was a familiar face to the band, and with Brian craving a change and a sympathetic ear to his own song ideas, the shift was natural. Freddie and John were more loyal to Mack, who saw his role decreasing greatly; he later lamented, "Everybody was doing their own thing now, in their own studios."

Indeed they were. The credits would include only three studios – Townhouse in Hammersmith, Musicland in Munich, and Mountain in Montreux – but a further four were used: Maison Rouge in Fulham, which had been used for 'One Vision'; Abbey Road in St. John's Wood, for orchestral overdubs with Michael Kamen; Sarm West in Kensington (only 10 minutes from Freddie's Garden Lodge mansion); and Milo Music in Hackney. Additionally, Freddie was committed to recording tracks for Dave Clark's musical *Time*, with sessions held at Abbey Road Studios in October 1985 and January 1986, thus interrupting progress on the album further. Roger was engrossed in production duties with David Richards, working on Magnum's *Vigilante* at Mountain Studios, while John formed an ad hoc band, The Immortals, to provide the main theme for the *Biggles* soundtrack. Brian engrossed himself in collaborations (writing, producing, and contributing guitar to 'Golden Days' and 'Crazy Nights', recorded by Japanese pop star Minako Honda and released the following year) and a silent fascination with Anita Dobson.

Work progressed steadily on the album by late winter 1985, with each band member working separately on his own songs before presenting them to the others. The enthusiasm that had resulted in 'One Vision' didn't carry over as much as the band might have hoped: much like *Flash Gordon* or, tellingly, *Hot Space*, the band were once again divided by their separate endeavours, and nowhere on the album does it sound like the four were in the same room together recording live. Instead, each song was pieced together from individual performances, built up from a basic framework and layered with adornments until it sounds like a reasonable facsimile of Queen.

Several outside musicians were brought in to help augment the tracks, whether it was a full orchestra on 'Who Wants To Live Forever' and 'One Year Of Love' (the latter also featured a saxophone solo), incidental backing vocals from Joan Armatrading on 'Don't Lose Your Head', or keyboard embellishments from Spike Edney on a handful of tracks. Long gone were the days of the band pouring over each note, devoting copious amounts of energy so that each song was performed solely by the four of them; instead, it was quicker and more efficient to hire the services of a session musician.

"We all have our own ideas of how a song should be done," Freddie explained of the writing processes, "because a song can be done in so many different ways depending on who's doing it. But sometimes I feel that it's not right, like in the case of Roger's track, which is 'Magic', he did it in a totally different way, which was quite good, but I just felt there was another commercial streak and I knew he was going away to LA for a week, and I got a hold of it and I changed it around completely and when he came back I said, 'Well, what do you think?' and he said, 'Oh, I like it!' It's a completely different song but sometimes you can see something else in other people's songs. I don't

mind that they do that to my songs as well. We sort of help each other.

"I don't know what Queen stand for," Freddie continued. "I know by now, it's four writers who write very different songs: John's been writing quite a lot now, and he writes in that one area that he likes, which is a sort of Tamla Motown [sound], and I love to sing songs like that. So he's very different; you could never call his songs heavy. I think Queen write just four very different types of songs. Brian writes from the guitar, so we have that element, and Roger writes from the drums, but he also crosses over a lot, so we have all kinds of things."

"I don't know where my motivation comes from," Brian pontificated, "except we're all trying to use this beast which Queen is as a vehicle to get our own ideas across. We all write very different kinds of songs, and it's quite a challenge to get them through this machine and get them out. It's hard to explain. For instance, myself: if I write a song which has a particular idea behind it and I can hear it in my head … when I take it to the other three, they'll see it totally differently and will want to do it in a different way. Some of their input will be very good and very necessary, and some of it will actually destroy the very meaning of the song. There's always interaction going on all the time, and the motivation, the challenge, is to get something across in the right way that moves people."

Released in June 1986, just as the band were about to embark on their epic Magic tour, *A Kind Of Magic* was adorned in a garish sleeve by Richard Gray, depicting the band members as genies in an illustration by Roger Chiasson. (The genie motif would be used to great effect on the Magic tour, with massive blow-up figures released to the sky during performances of the title track.) Curiously, there appears to have been some indecision whether to release the album as a soundtrack or a standalone Queen album; the band had certainly written enough material for the soundtrack, with one further unreleased track, 'Battle Scene', making its way to the collector's circles many years later, and had the band interspersed Michael Kamen's score with their own songs, it would have made for a fascinating listen. But it wouldn't have been a Queen album, and with only two non-soundtrack songs, 'Friends Will Be Friends' and 'Pain Is So Close To Pleasure', released on the album, and no desire to record any further tracks, the band stumbled upon the idea of making *A Kind Of Magic* a standalone Queen album with songs featured from *Highlander*, a detail they directly addressed in the liner notes: "Some songs on this album appear in different form in the film *Highlander*". Yet, at the end of the film's credits, the tag "Soundtrack Album Available On EMI Records And Tapes" was featured quite prominently, meaning that the producers likely were hoping a soundtrack would be released. Brian teased at the idea of revisiting the soundtrack idea in 2003 on the commentary track for *Greatest Video Hits 2*, indicating that it was still something that he had been thinking about; unfortunately, the passing of Michael Kamen meant that this idea was put on hold indefinitely.

The album was a quick seller in Europe and the UK, peaking at No. 1 in the latter. *Kerrang!* hit the nail right on the head, saying, "A potpourri of musical styles. And it's quite possibly only a band of Queen's stature and breadth of appeal who could put out an album of such diverse songs without disappointing a sizable portion of their fans." *Record Mirror* stated, "Queen have been plying their trade profitably for so long that there's really no point in becoming incensed at their one (lack of) vision. The only strong emotion Queen now evoke in me is a fervent wish that Brian May would cut his hair."

Issued a day after the UK release, the album peaked at No. 46 in the US; reviews were minimal, further cementing the notion that Queen had fallen from grace not only from fans, but from the critics, as well. Only *Rolling Stone* was typically caustic, saying that "the album, which might have been Queen's crowning moment, is absolutely bankrupt of gauche imagination," concluding that "dominated by barren slabs of synthscape and guitarist Brian May's orchestral fretwork, *A Kind Of Magic* sounds like hard rock with a hollow core: it's heavy plastic." Clearly, the magazine hadn't noticed the band's contributions to *Highlander*, taking 'Princes Of The Universe' out of context: "'We Are The Champions' still sounds as insistent as a jackboot compared to this album's boastful closer ... which veers into unintentional self-parody. The 'world-is-my-oyster' lyrics seem more lazy than arrogant, and the music is a mechanical thud rather than a metalized threat." *People Weekly* was just weary of Queen: "There's hardly a personal expression, let alone an intimate one, in this album, which includes a number of songs from the soundtracks of *Iron Eagle* and *Highlander* ... Just about everything is done in such loud, sweeping arrangements it's hard to listen to the LP without wanting to strike a noble pose for the close-up ... When Queen applies its mastery of electronics to songs that someone from this dimension can relate to – try 'I Want

to Be Free' *[sic]* from its album *The Works* – the group can be dazzling. In this case they're just overbearing."

If the reviews were less than ecstatic, it didn't bother the band; after nearly breaking up the year before, each member was particularly philosophical. In an interview with Mary Turner for *Off The Record*, they individually discussed arguments, but there was a degree of optimism in their comments: "The only thing that is hopefully good about us is after the arguments we can actually still face each other the next day or the day after and talk about something else and sort of get over it," John said. "The funny thing is I think we're now getting to that sort of point of maturity that we at least have that confidence that we are a successful band, which is obviously a desire in the beginning, that's why sometimes you want to be in a band and you want to be successful, so we now have that and now it's sort of a harder thing, of where you go from here, because we still have a few ambitions left."

"It's a survival test," Freddie countered. "Of course we could all just go away and say, 'Okay, we've had enough,' and live happily ever after, but that's not what we're in for ... we're in it to make music and [besides], what else could I do? This is the thing that interests me most. You don't know what it means when you write a song when people actually appreciate it and they say, 'It's a good song'. It's a wonderful feeling ... I've never let the press worry me. In the early days you think about it, you go out and buy the papers and make sure you're in it and all that, and now it's a completely different set-up because it's your music and basically what you worry about is the people that buy your product. That's what keeps us going."

LIVE MAGIC

EMI EMC 3519, December 1986 [3]
EMI CDP 7 4641 3 2, December 1986
Hollywood HR-61267-2, August 1996

'One Vision' (5'09), 'Tie Your Mother Down' (2'59), 'Seven Seas Of Rhye' (1'21), 'A Kind Of Magic' (5'29) *(Vinyl: 4'41)*, 'Under Pressure' (3'49), 'Another One Bites The Dust' (5'50) *(Vinyl: 3'36)*, 'I Want To Break Free' (2'41), 'Is This The World We Created...?' (1'31), 'Bohemian Rhapsody' (4'41), 'Hammer To Fall' (5'20) *(Vinyl: 4'18)*, 'Radio Ga Ga' (4'27), 'We Will Rock You' (1'33), 'Friends Will Be Friends' (1'09), 'We Are The Champions' (2'01), 'God Save The Queen' (1'19)

Musicians: John Deacon *(bass guitar)*, Brian May

(guitars, vocals, acoustic guitar on 'Is This The World We Created...?'), Freddie Mercury *(vocals, piano),* Roger Taylor *(drums, vocals, effects on 'A Kind Of Magic'),* Spike 'The Duke' Edney *(additional guitar on 'Hammer To Fall', vocals, keyboards)*
Recorded: 9 August 1986, Knebworth Park, Stevenage, Hertfordshire *(except 'Is This The World We Created...?' recorded at Wembley Stadium, London, 11 July 1986; 'Hammer To Fall' recorded at Wembley Stadium, London, 12 July 1986; 'A Kind Of Magic' (parts) and 'Under Pressure' recorded at Nepstadion, Budapest, Hungary, 27 July 1986)*
Producers: Queen and James 'Trip' Khalaf

With the Magic tour done and over with, the band once again went their separate ways, with no immediate plans for the future in place. There had been discussions to take the Magic tour to the Pacific Rim and maybe even America in 1987, but these ultimately amounted to nothing, with the band preferring to relax after such a lengthy traipse around Europe. (Secretly, Freddie was also aware that his energy levels were running low, though he feared confirmation that he might be HIV-positive, and so chose to ignore it for the time being.) Roger started work on a third solo album, which eventually morphed into the formation of a band, while Freddie finally enacted upon his desires to work with Montserrat Caballé. Brian held down the Queen fort towards the end of 1986, working with Mack on a remix of 'Pain Is So Close To Pleasure' for Capitol Records, as well as helping the producer mix the sound for the TV broadcast of Queen's second Wembley concert. The band finally reconvened on 10 November at Townhouse Studios, with Trip Khalaf as producer, spending 40 hours over the next three days to select and mix performances from the Magic tour to release as their second live album. (This time, instead of listening to every concert recorded on the tour, the band selected songs from four landmark dates: the two Wembley performances, the Budapest show, and the Knebworth gig.) Scheduled for a 1 December release, the band were so rushed to finish the final mixes that, at the conclusion of the session at 3:15am on 12 November, the tapes were sent immediately to EMI, who issued a test pressing to the band the next day.

It's no surprise, then, that *Live Magic* presents itself as a discombobulated mess. There's no doubting the band's performances, but with such a tight turnaround, and the band obviously in a different headspace than they were during the tour, some truly appalling

decisions were made, the most head-scratching one being the decision to heavily edit all but three – 'One Vision', 'Seven Seas Of Rhye', and 'Under Pressure' – of the 15 songs on the album. (The CD release had full versions of 'A Kind Of Magic', 'Another One Bites The Dust', and 'Hammer To Fall'.) The remaining 12 songs were either reduced to mere soundbites or edited so heavily that the basic structure of the song barely remained. One wonders why 'Bohemian Rhapsody', which the band had deemed uneditable for single release in 1975, was tampered with: the opera section was completely cut out, resulting in an unnerving jump from the soaring guitar solo to the heavy metal thrash. It should have been a case of all-or-nothing: if the song was worth including, surely it would have been more propitious to omit one of the shorter songs in order to present the full version of 'Bohemian Rhapsody'. If that wasn't feasible, why not just omit it altogether and substitute one of the other songs performed on the tour? Certainly, 'Crazy Little Thing Called Love' – a popular mainstay of the live set since November 1979 – would have been a worthy inclusion since it would have been the first time it was released on a live album.

Unsurprisingly, given the success of the tour, *Live Magic* was a huge seller, reaching No. 3 in the UK charts upon its release in December 1986 – certainly a lucrative strategy since the band hadn't been off the road for even four months when the album was issued. *Live Magic* wasn't even considered for release by Capitol in the States, angering the band's still-loyal fans, who were forced to import the album at great expense. It was finally issued on CD by Hollywood Records in August 1996, in an attempt to capitalise on the success that *Made In Heaven* afforded Queen, but it predictably failed to garner any attention.

Live Magic was superseded in 1992 by the release of *Live At Wembley '86*, which presented a full account of Queen's epic homecoming performance in Wembley Stadium on 12 July 1986; after that, few fans felt compelled to track down the edited 15-track original.

THE MIRACLE
Parlophone PCSD 107, May 1989 [1]
Parlophone CDPCSD 107, May 1989 [1]
Capitol C1-592357, June 1989 [24]
Capitol CDP 592357, June 1989 [24]
Hollywood HR 61234 2, October 1991
UK Cat No, September 2011 [143]

'Party' (2'24), 'Khashoggi's Ship' (2'48), 'The Miracle'

(5'02), 'I Want It All' (4'33), 'The Invisible Man' (3'56), 'Breakthru' (4'08), 'Rain Must Fall' (4'23), 'Scandal' (4'43), 'My Baby Does Me' (3'22), 'Was It All Worth It' (5'46)

Bonus tracks on CD issue: 'Hang On In There' (3'46), 'Chinese Torture' (1'45), 'The Invisible Man' *(extended version)* (5'28)

Bonus tracks on 1991 Hollywood Records reissue: 'Hang On In There' (3'46), 'Chinese Torture' (1'45), 'The Invisible Man' *(extended version)* (5'28), 'Scandal' *(extended version)* (6'34)

Bonus tracks on 2011 Universal Records deluxe reissue: 'I Want It All' *(single version)* (4'02), 'The Invisible Man' *(demo)* (5'02), 'Hang On In There' (3'46), 'Hijack My Heart' (4'11), 'Stealin'' (3'59), 'Chinese Torture' (1'44), 'The Invisible Man' *(extended version)* (5'30)

Bonus videos, 2011 iTunes-only editions: 'I Want It All' *(promotional video)*, Documentary: "The Making Of *The Miracle* Promo Videos", Documentary: "The Making Of *The Miracle* Album Cover"

Musicians: John Deacon *(bass guitar, rhythm guitar on 'Party' and 'Rain Must Fall', keyboards on 'Rain Must Fall' and 'My Baby Does Me')*, Brian May *(guitars, vocals, keyboards on 'I Want It All', 'Scandal', and 'Was It All Worth It')*, Freddie Mercury *(vocals, piano, keyboards on 'Party', 'Khashoggi's Ship', 'The Miracle', and 'Was It All Worth It')*, Roger Taylor *(drums, percussion, vocals, keyboards on 'The Invisible Man' and 'Breakthru', electronic drums on 'Rain Must Fall')*, David Richards *(programming, keyboards)*, Brian Zellis *(computer programming)*
Recorded: January 1988-February 1989, Olympic and The Townhouse Studios, London; Mountain Studio, Montreux
Producers: Queen and David Richards

The years between the conclusion of the Magic tour in August 1986 and the release of *The Miracle* in May 1989 were three of the most prolific for the band, and yet they only spent one-third of that time together as a collective unit. The Magic tour had been an exhausting trek, especially for Freddie. "At the end of [that tour], the biggest tour we'd ever done, Freddie said, 'I don't want to do this any more,'" Brian said. "It was kind of uncharacteristic because he was always up for everything and very strong, very optimistic. The fact

that he was quite definite about the fact that he didn't want to do it was something different. We thought maybe it was just a stage he's going through, or maybe there's something wrong. I remember having that thought in my head, but you push that thought aside."

Unfortunately, Brian had more immediate problems on his mind. The tour had been a particular strain on his marriage, and he found consolation by working with other musicians and artists, the least likely being *EastEnders* actress Anita Dobson. Brian had been approached by her manager about producing her debut record, eventually released as *Talking Of Love*; after an initial meeting with Anita, the two hit it off and romance flowered. Because Brian was still married, he attempted to keep the new relationship discreet for the sake of his children, though that didn't stop the press from publishing the rumors. John's marriage was also going through a rough patch: he and wife Veronica decided it would be best to work on the marriage and, in a move that would become characteristic of John, took extended ski-ing vacations to Biarritz.

According to Brian, "We said, 'Right, we're going to take a little break' – we didn't split up, but we needed space for ourselves – 'and when the time is right, we'll make the album, rather than somebody saying we've gotta make one.' So, we waited and we did various other things: Freddie and Roger both did solo projects, and I'm halfway through one, and I did a lot of producing."

The band finally reconvened at Olympic Studios in London to start preliminary work on their follow-up to *A Kind Of Magic*, though they had a different plan this time. As with previous albums, each member would work separately on his own songs and then present virtually completed demos, into which the others would introduce their own ideas. "We made the decision," Brian said in a 1991 Canadian radio interview, "that no matter who came up with the idea for the song, it would be credited to Queen, and not individuals, and I think it's the best single decision we ever made. I just wish we made it 20 years ago instead, because it makes such a difference to the creation process. I would recommend it to anyone, anyone who is actually a proper group."

"Co-writing every song was a big step for us," Brian told the *Chicago Tribune* in June 1989. "In the past, it got to the point where there'd only ever be one or two members of us in the studio at a time, so Queen wasn't really functioning as a group, as far as recording went. But this time, it was like the old days, with all of us there and plenty of arguments, but constructive ones.

There's still a lot of musical friction, because we've gone off in very different directions. But personally, we're getting on much, much better than we used to."

"We seem to work together better now than we did before," Roger said in 1989. "We're fairly up and down characters, and we're all very different with different tastes in many ways. And we used to have lots of arguments in the studio, but this time we decided to share all the songwriting, which was a very democratic and good idea. Then you get decisions made on artistic merit, rather than financial or ego grounds." Though it was a good idea to credit all the songs as Queen tracks, there were still clues as to who wrote what for careful listeners: Roger, still buzzing from fronting his own band, penned 'The Invisible Man' and most of 'Breakthru', while Brian contributed 'I Want It All' and 'Scandal'. John and Freddie cowrote 'My Baby Does Me' and 'Rain Must Fall', while Freddie stuck the opening of a work-in-progress to the beginning of 'Breakthru'. The rest – 'Party', 'Khashoggi's Ship', 'Was It All Worth It', and the title track – were true collaborations, musically initiated by Freddie but with all contributing lyrics. (The exception being 'Party', which was written and recorded without Roger.)

"It's basically the four of us," Brian said in 1989. "If we ever deviated from that, then we certainly came back to that. There's guitars, bass, drums and vocals, and nowadays there are a few synthesizers and samples and stuff thrown in. But we made a very conscious decision that the technology wasn't going to take us over, and we were going to keep the human element as far to the front as we could and use the technology to preserve and augment that. A lot of it's a very techno-aware album, but hopefully there's a lot of humanity in there as well – we think so, we think it's very exciting. We enjoy what we're doing, and the sounds reflect us as a group more so than the last few albums. It's not like, sit down with a drum-machine and a synthesizer. We played together and we evolved things that seemed to excite us, and then built everything around that."

Sessions kicked off in January 1988, meetings more devoted to planning and to creating demos than to the actual recording of songs. John explained of those initial sessions: "The first few weeks of recording, we did a lot of live material, a lot of songs ... Ideas came up, some jamming, we had a few ideas that were already prepared. 'I Want It All' was one of the few songs that was actually written before we went in." Roger continued, saying, "Yes, it is our first album since 1986 *(laughs)*. I think the reason for the delay

was that we wanted to sort of go away and recharge our batteries – quite logical, really – and just sort of generate some new energy and enthusiasm for being Queen. We [initially] went into the studio and enjoyed it very much, but we still didn't have any material. So we decided to go in for a longer time."

"We spent the whole of January in the studio and have been recording the first parts of the new album," Roger told University Radio Bath in March 1988, while on tour with The Cross. "So far there's 22 songs and it'll be the best album that Queen have done in ten years, easily. It's more back to the old style. I mean it's almost like echoes of Led Zeppelin and everything in there. It's great and it's all live in the studio, which is great. It gives it more spark and energy, I think. No machines – so far we haven't time to do overdubs anyway, so there's little synthesizer on it actually. It's basically bass, guitar and drums with some piano."

Sessions alternated between The Townhouse, which had been used previously on *A Kind Of Magic*, and the legendary Olympic Studios. Recording was frequently put aside for other endeavours: Freddie was still working on *Barcelona*, and Roger had a UK tour scheduled for February and March. On 14 April, Freddie appeared on stage in the *Time* musical at London's Dominion Theatre, despite his dislike of the medium. However, it was a special charity performance, and he was gently persuaded to do so by his friend Cliff Richard. Along with singing 'In My Defence' and the title track, which he had recorded years before, he performed two other numbers: the emotive 'It's In Every One Of Us' and the crowd-rousing chant of 'Born To Rock 'n' Roll'. It was shaping up to be a good year for the band.

On 2 June, Brian's father died, which hit the guitarist very hard. He and his father had been exceptionally close and, along with the disintegration of his marriage, this marked a low point in Brian's life. "The two worst things I ever did in his eyes were: one, give up my academic career to become a pop star," Brian recalled to *OK* magazine in 1998, "and two, live with a woman ... [He] was always trying to stop me going into the rock business but he built my guitar – the thing that propelled me into it." He went through several bouts of depression, and admitted years later that he entertained thoughts of suicide. He poured his emotions into a new composition, 'Too Much Love Will Kill You'.

After considerable time off, the band resumed sessions towards the end of that summer, this time recording at Mountain Studios; the album was completed by Christmas of 1988, though further overdubs and mixing meant that the sessions dragged on until February 1989. "After we did the tour in 1986, which was a very big European tour, we were all absolutely exhausted and shattered and we basically didn't want to work together or see each other for a while," John said. "Towards the end of the second year [off], we sort of met up and Freddie suggested, 'Perhaps we should try some time in the studio.' And then the third we spent making the album, so in a way it was a two-year gap for us rather than a three-year gap."

The band certainly do sound refreshed on the album, exhibiting a renewed enthusiasm not only for surviving personal rough patches, but also for expanding their creativity outside the group. While they may sound refreshed, that doesn't mean the album is a true return to form: sounding like a logical extension of *A Kind Of Magic*, *The Miracle* suffers from some spotty songwriting and an overall patchwork feel to several of the songs, with many of the tracks pieced together from various jams. Additionally, Roger's assessment that keyboards were going to be used minimally may have gotten fans' hopes up for a sound returning the band to their roots: instead, *The Miracle* is oversaturated with keyboards, sequencers, and programming, with many of the songs using technology as a crutch instead of as an enhancement.

What's good about the album is that there's a sense of collaboration on all of the tracks, something that had been missing from *A Kind Of Magic*. All four band members play on all the songs, and there are no outside musicians (apart from additional keyboards and programming by David Richards, and computer programming by Brian Zellis), meaning that this truly was a collaborative effort by the band. The band even score an anthemic classic with 'I Want It All', a loud rock song with all of the trademarks of the Queen of old, while the other four singles – 'Breakthru', 'The Invisible Man', 'Scandal', and 'The Miracle' – are all stellar, as is the epic finale, 'Was It All Worth It?'.

The margins of *The Miracle* are a bit spottier, with the opening one-two punch of 'Party' and 'Khashoggi's Ship' getting the album off to a rocky start, both literally and metaphorically: the two songs are certainly energetic and fresh, with plenty of crunching guitar work and soaring vocals, but are either awash in trendy programming ('Party') or unconvincing cock rock posturing ('Khashoggi's Ship'). Still, while the remaining songs weren't on the same tier as the aforementioned tracks, there's much to appreciate on

all of them, and there's nothing truly unlistenable or cringe-inducing as there had been on previous albums.

The problem is that the album is a bit too safe, which is all the more obvious when listening to the non-album B-sides or out-takes that have surfaced. 'Hijack My Heart', with lead vocals by Roger, would have been a nice change of pace (and would have given the drummer his first lead vocal on a Queen album in nearly a decade), while 'Hang On In There' and 'Stealin'' are so drastically different and atmospheric to anything the band had put out that they didn't deserve to be squirreled away on B-sides. Curiously, there isn't a traditional ballad, as there had been on *The Works* and *A Kind Of Magic*; 'Too Much Love Will Kill You' would have filled that role perfectly, as would have 'My Life Has Been Saved'. A proposed follow-up, to be titled *Another Miracle*, was to feature the extended remixes of three of the five singles, plus the non-album B-sides and a handful of new tracks, and was scheduled for a spring 1990 release, though this was scrapped in favor of a new studio album. (Intriguingly, in *The Lot*, a preliminary running order of *The Miracle* was included, along with a proposed title for the album, *Perpetual Craze*. The line-up ran: 'Party', 'Khashoggi's Ship', 'The Miracle', 'Too Much Love Will Kill You', 'Chinese Torture', 'I Want It All', and 'Breakthru' on side one, with 'All God's People', 'The Invisible Man', 'Scandal', 'Hang On In There', 'My Baby Does Me', 'Rain Must Fall', and 'Was It All Worth It?' on side two.)

It's easy to posit the "what ifs" decades after the album's release, but perhaps the band felt they had to play it safe not only to not alienate their fans after such a long hiatus, but to ensure that the album would be a commercial success. Brian especially was ready to throw his full weight behind the project, having endured a great deal of personal turmoil during the hiatus, and made sure that, no matter how commercial the song, the guitar wouldn't take a backseat to technology: "The way it came out very guitar oriented just happened, as far as I can see," he told *Hard 'n' Heavy*. "It's very strange. It may have come about because we were actually doing more playing together. There's a lot of live takes on there, so, you know, whereas we had got fairly machine oriented for a while, this isn't. There's a lot of technology, but it's kind of after the event. It's basically us playing as a band. So I guess it sounds like it. And no one's more happy than I am. Having decided that we were going to credit every track to the four of us, as opposed to just one, everybody argued over every note, which is very healthy, and it's much more of a cohesive group effort than we've done for a long time."

The cover was created by Richard Gray using a chromakey (known as bluescreening or greenscreening, as typically used for weather map presentations on TV) and an early variation of Adobe™ Photoshop (called Quantel graphic paintbox). It depicts an alarmingly creepy amalgamation of the four Queen faces to create a gigantic, one-headed, six-eyed creature. In a strange but subtle way, this was the band's way of graphically affirming that they were now a more cohesive unit than ever, a visual representation of the new, more democratic writing approach they so thoroughly enjoyed. "Two or three weeks before we finished," John said in 1989, "it was gonna be called *The Invisible Men*, but we changed it to *The Miracle*, which is a very heavy title in a way. It was from one song, and I think the sentiment is quite nice in a way, a bit naïve in some way, but it's reasonably genuine. Mainly it's entertainment, and if people get pleasure out of it and enjoy it, then that's the point."

Unfortunately, the band members explained from the beginning that no live dates would be forthcoming: "To get into the whole cycle of making an album, going on tour, then going home and making an album again – we want to get out of that," Roger said, which Freddie echoed almost verbatim in a separate interview: "I want to change the cycle of album, world tour, album, world tour. Maybe we will tour, but it will be for totally different reasons. I've personally had it with these bombastic lights and staging effects. I don't think a 42-year-old man should be running around in his leotard any more." It's strange for Freddie to have said something like that, a man who built his reputation as a showman upon the foundation of entertaining thousands and thousands of fans every night. Yet people accepted his explanation, though not wholly without accusations: rumors originated from the tabloids that Freddie was seriously ill, causing a backlash from the band members against such innuendoes. At the time, the band had no idea that Freddie *was* ill, but had been told by Freddie that something was definitely afoot and that he didn't foresee a tour in support of the album.

"I badly want to play live, with or without Queen," Brian proclaimed in 1989. "If we can't come to some kind of arrangement within the band, I'll get my own project together, but I can't stand it much longer. I want to go back on stage as fast as possible!" Brian would explain the next year that "We're at something of a crossroads at the moment. We're still very much alive in the studio – perhaps more so now than ever before – but this will be the first time we've released an album without promoting it with a tour. You see, at the moment Freddie just doesn't want to tour. He doesn't feel that he can, so the touring part of my life has come to a complete stop. It's a terrible shame because Roger, John and myself all love playing live and feel that part of the reason for making an album is to be able to take it out on the road and have fun. So, taking the touring side of things away messed up my life, really – without exaggeration. I feel it's taken the whole balance out of my life. If [Freddie] doesn't enjoy it or feel happy with it then I guess you can't do anything about it."

Released in May 1989, and preceded by 'I Want It All', *The Miracle* effortlessly soared to No. 1 in the UK, though it stalled at No. 24 in the US. While the demand – and desire – for Queen to play live had become feverish, few seemed thrilled with *The Miracle*. Kim Neely said in *Rolling Stone*, "If you're a fan who's been hankering for years to hear Queen get back to the bombast of its heyday, play your old copy of *A Night at the Opera* or *News of the World* instead. But don't give up hope. At least *The Miracle* offers little snippets of Queen's former majesty." She did offer praise for Freddie's vocals – "indeed, Mercury – especially on the title track – has never sounded better" – and for Brian's guitar, "when you can hear him. May's role on *The Miracle* is, for the most part, limited to a quick, typically brilliant solo here and there." *The Times* opined, "Musically, the synth-pop dabbling of 'Radio Ga Ga' and its ilk has been discarded in favor of the more familiar, grim amalgam of bubblegum metal power chords, mock symphonics and squiggly guitar solos. In its favor, it is difficult to imagine a collection more blithely out of step with the fashionably earnest Weltanschauung of contemporary rock. The miracles of which Freddie Mercury sings in the title track are everything from the longed-for Utopia of 'peace on earth' to the more mundane pleasures of 'Sunday mornings with a cup of tea'. Such is the extent of the social commentary."

Perversely, North American reviews were more positive. *The Dallas Morning News* wrote, "Queen's musicianship often has taken a back seat to Freddie Mercury's strutting histrionics. But Roger Taylor is one of rock's fastest and most accurate drummers, and guitarist Brian May is a major talent. These two move toward center stage this time, as Queen muscles through a song list that's remarkably varied for one album. Significantly, the music is all credited to the band as a whole, rather than to individuals members – with Mr. Mercury usually getting the lion's share of the credits. The payoff is a record that rocks you, with a few twists … Mr. Mercury, of course, does get to indulge his classical bent. The title song, a simple (perhaps simple-minded) celebration of life's little triumphs, is not quite operatic, but it does offer lush orchestrations and celestial harmonies that duel intriguingly with Mr. Taylor's rapid time-keeping. And with 'Was It All Worth It', Mr. Mercury takes a lofty look at the band's lengthy career, 'Living breathing rock 'n' roll'. The conclusion? Yes, it was worth it. But given the singer's rather fiendish chortle at the end, you're not sure if he means it." *Newsday* agreed: "Led by Freddie Mercury's raunchy vocals and Brian May's guitar slinging, the Queen machine rolls on with *The Miracle* … Mercury's voice is steady and solid, May's runs are as flashy and supple as ever. Most of the 10 songs, written collaboratively by the four members, stick pretty much to the band's formula of mini-suites: edgy pop with tempos that change half-way into the number and some delicious hooks." Astonishingly, the *Sun-Sentinel* lavished the album with praise: "Here's an album (like so many of Queen's others) that should be used as a pop music how-to for aspirants. Combining the forces of rock, pop, metal, clever melodies and cunning stylizations, *The Miracle* never lets down. From one track to the next there is, as usual, no telling which way this band will go, affording even the most jaded ear a challenge."

Roger summed up his thoughts on the album, and it's hard to disagree with him: "It's a very rounded album – I think it's quite mature, it's eclectic, and it's got a lot of hard-ass, great guitar on it." Considering the hardships the band had gone through before recording the album, it was a miracle that they were able to not only release an album as good as it was, but also that the creative juices were flowing so heavily that they jumped back into the studios almost immediately after they had finished to work on a follow-up. Only this time, the impetus was far more pressing, though only Freddie was aware of the gravity of the situation.

INNUENDO
Parlophone PCSD 115, February 1991 [1]
Parlophone CDPCSD 115, February 1991 [1]
Hollywood HR-61020-2, February 1991 [30]
UK Cat No, September 2011 [126]

CD: 'Innuendo' (6'31), 'I'm Going Slightly Mad' (4'22), 'Headlong' (4'38), 'I Can't Live With You' (4'33), 'Don't Try So Hard' (3'39), 'Ride The Wild Wind' (4'42), 'All God's People' (4'21), 'These Are The Days Of Our Lives' (4'15), 'Delilah' (3'35), 'The Hitman' (4'56), 'Bijou' (3'36), 'The Show Must Go On' (4'32)

Vinyl: 'Innuendo' (6'31), 'I'm Going Slightly Mad' (4'06), 'Headlong' (4'30), 'I Can't Live With You' (4'05), 'Ride The Wild Wind' (4'42), 'All God's People' (3'55), 'These Are The Days Of Our Lives' (3'55), 'Delilah' (3'35), 'Don't Try So Hard' (3'33), 'The Hitman' (3'43), 'Bijou' (1'19), 'The Show Must Go On' (4'27)

Bonus tracks on 2011 Universal Records deluxe reissue: 'I Can't Live With You' *(1997 retake)* (4'47), 'Lost Opportunity' (3'51), 'Ride The Wild Wind' *(early version with guide vocal)* (4'14), 'I'm Going Slightly Mad' *(Mad mix)* (4'35), 'Headlong' *(embryo with guide vocal)* (4'44)

Bonus videos, 2011 iTunes-only editions: 'Innuendo' *(alternate promotional video)*, 'These Are The Days Of Our Lives' *(Hollywood Records alternate promotional video)*, Documentary: "Mad In The Making: The Making Of The 'I'm Going Slightly Mad' Promo Video"

Musicians: John Deacon *(bass guitar, keyboards)*, Brian May *(guitars, vocals, harmonies, keyboards, drum programming on 'I Can't Live With You')*, Freddie Mercury *(vocals, piano, harmonies, keyboards, drum programming on 'Delilah')*, Roger Taylor *(drums, percussion, vocals, harmonies, keyboards, co-lead vocals on 'Ride The Wild Wind')*, David Richards *(programming, keyboards)*, Steve Howe *(wandering minstrel guitar on 'Innuendo', Somewhere In The Middle)*, Mike Moran *(piano and keyboards on 'All God's People')*
Recorded: March 1989-November 1990 at Metropolis Studios, London, and Mountain Studios, Montreux
Producers: Queen and David Richards

No sooner had sessions for *The Miracle* concluded in January 1989 than Freddie ushered the band back into the studios to begin work on a follow-up. Freddie had already demoed a delightful ditty, 'Delilah', dedicated to his favorite feline, and had several other ideas in mind that he wanted to get down on tape. For Brian and Roger, this meant that they not only had to promote the new album, but they had to put any aspirations for continued solo work on hold so as to accommodate their singer. The reasoning for Freddie's fervency wasn't made immediately known to the others, but, feeling rejuvenated by the collaborative nature of the *Miracle* sessions, it was certainly welcome.

As they had with *The Miracle*, the band spent the early days of the sessions jamming and getting reacquainted with each other. "We went to Switzerland, where we have our own little studio," Roger explained, "and worked there with co-producer Dave Richards for a couple of weeks just to see what came out. That's usually what we do. We often find it's very good to play together without too many fixed ideas to begin with. We very seldom have a lot of material when we go into the studio – there are ideas but they don't actually get formed until we get to work on it. We usually have two or three days just playing, finding sounds, getting the feel of each other again. We keep the multitrack running and seem to find that there's little bits that really seem to gel."

One of the jams that was deemed worthwhile became the title track and, although a jam suggests spontaneity, the resultant 'Innuendo' was polished up into an epic reminiscent of 'Bohemian Rhapsody' and 'The Prophet's Song'. 'The Show Must Go On' was created from a chord sequence that Roger and John were jamming to, inspiring Brian to take the sequence and develop a fully-fledged song from it. Other songs were more finalized, with Brian bringing two – 'Headlong' and 'I Can't Live With You' – he had intended for his solo album. The band also reached back to the previous album's sessions to revisit ideas they had deemed unworthy at the time, with several jams like 'Face It Alone', 'Affairs', and 'Grand Dame' worked on again, in addition to 'All God's People', a more fully-polished out-take from *The Miracle* that itself had started life as 'Africa By Night' during the *Barcelona* sessions. Further snippets of songs eventually leaked out to the collector's world, with 'Robbery' and 'My Secret Fantasy' being mere sketches, while 'Self-Made Man' would have been a stellar album track were it not for Brian's tentative rough vocal.

The sessions stretched out over more than a year, though, as Roger explained to *Rockline* syndicated radio in 1991, "What we'd do is we'd go into the studio, work for about three weeks and take two weeks off. The album was really a happy album to make – they're not all happy. It sort of wrote itself. We didn't have any problems with it at all, and I think it shows in the end result. The material has depth and maturity

to it, and it just runs well, I think, and in some ways it does remind us of the *A Night At The Opera* days."

Brian was also quick to compare *Innuendo* to *A Night At The Opera*. "It's quite a complex album," he said in 1991. "Some of the tracks are more along the lines of the mid-period stuff we did, like *A Night At The Opera*, where there's a lot of overdubs and complexity. It just takes a long time – you can't take short cuts … I think it's the best [album] for quite a long time. There's nothing I'm embarrassed about. Often you put out an album and you think, 'But I wish we'd done this.' This one I feel quite happy about, and I can listen to it without any problems. I like it a lot. I think it's nicely complex and nicely heavy, and there's a lot of invention on there."

"As much as possible, we've done it live in the studio, with three or four of us playing at one time," Brian told *Vox* in 1991. "There's a fair bit of new technology. Sometimes we would start off by programming something and working around it, but in almost every case we replaced original material with real stuff as we went along. With the digital [recording] gear you can allow yourself to do that more freely, because if you make copies you don't lose quality. What I've always said about digital is that you can preserve the 'liveness'. In the old days, you would say, 'That's very nice as a demo, but we'll now do it properly.' Now, you can say, 'That's great as a demo; we'll use this piece and incorporate it into the finished product.' So you use the first take of a vocal, for instance, and it's there, sparkling and clear on the final mix."

Midway through the sessions, it became apparent that something was not well with Freddie. Throughout the mid-1980s, the singer witnessed several of his friends suffering, and eventually dying, from AIDS; he was concerned enough to be tested in 1985, though the results came back negative. Following the Magic tour, Freddie became increasingly hounded by the British press, with *The Sun* running an exclusive that he'd had his blood tested at a Harley Street clinic, though, when cornered at Heathrow following a trip to Japan, Freddie denied he was ill. It wasn't until April 1987 that he was diagnosed with AIDS, which triggered his sudden outburst of creativity. However, due to the stigma surrounding homosexuality in the 1980s, and the lack of available treatment to AIDS patients, Freddie essentially went into hiding, finding solace in his music.

Instead of wallowing in grief, Freddie simply told his closest friends he was suffering, he was going to die, and that there was to be no further mention of it. (He also gave his partner, Jim Hutton, an out from their relationship, though, to his credit, Hutton never considered it.) He opted not to burden the band with his diagnosis, instead preferring to work on *The Miracle* (which, it should be noted, his doctors told him he wouldn't see the release of – that he was able to record a further album as well as a few disparate tracks before he couldn't work any further is a testament to his strength), though the band became increasingly aware that something was amiss during sessions for *Innuendo*. Brian later explained, "We didn't know actually what was wrong for a very long time. We never talked about it and it was a sort of unwritten law that we didn't, because Freddie didn't want to. He just told us that he wasn't up to doing tours, and that's as far as it went. Gradually, I suppose in the last year and a bit, it became obvious what the problem was, or at least fairly obvious. We didn't know for sure."

In 2011, Brian recalled that "Freddie found an amazing tranquility, and I never really heard him complain. I remember we went out one night, and he had horrible problems with his leg and I think Freddie saw me looking at it and he was like, 'Oh, Brian, do you want to see what it's like?' And he showed me, and he reacted to my face and said, 'I'm really sorry – I didn't mean to do that to you'. I never heard him go, 'This is really awful. My life is shit. I'm going to die'. Never, never, never. He was an amazingly strong person." Justin Shirley-Smith, who co-engineered the *Innuendo* sessions, was equally amazed by Freddie's strength: "This is hard to explain to people, but [the sessions weren't] sad, it was very happy. He was one of the funniest people I ever encountered. I was laughing most of the time, with him. Freddie was saying, 'I'm not going to think about it, I'm going to do this'."

Despite the black cloud surrounding Freddie's health, the album was still an enjoyable one to make, mostly because of the writing process ("I think, more than anything, *Innuendo* shows evidence of the four of us consciously trying to use each other to the maximum and writing together," Brian said) but also because of the renewed enthusiasm from their US record company. Queen's history with both Elektra and Capitol was not harmonious, starting off on a high note but quickly deteriorating into apathy (Elektra) or neglect (Capitol). The band negotiated their way out of their Capitol contract and started to shop around for a superior deal; in a neat bit of irony, Elektra made an offer, though Queen weren't willing

to play that game again. Rykodisc was also a prime candidate, though that record company specialized more in back catalog discographies (especially for the likes of David Bowie, Frank Zappa, and Jimi Hendrix) and not in new releases. While negotiations with Rykodisc were initially positive, in the end, the best and biggest offer came from Hollywood Records, a branch of the Walt Disney corporation, reportedly offering around £10,000,000 for the rights to Queen's back catalog and any new music. The band signed with them in September 1990, and plans were set in motion for a major campaign to signal the band's official 20th anniversary the next year.

"We're very, very happy to be with [Hollywood Records]," Brian said on *Rockline*, "and I don't think we've ever been so close to a record company in our lives. They have a very good attitude – very open – and it corresponds to our way of doing things. They always want to do things different, they don't want to do anything through the established channels. Up until now, I think we've benefited more in the last two or three months of being with Hollywood than the last five years anywhere else. It's a great relationship."

Whether this deal remained rosy in the end is a matter of opinion, but Hollywood did do a good job of reinstating Queen in the charts: when *Innuendo* was released in February 1991, it went gold in the US, a result that thrilled the band. To assist with sales, Hollywood threw a lavish party aboard the Queen Mary (Disney-owned and moored in concrete in Long Beach, California), attended only by Brian and Roger from Queen itself. Back home, the album peaked at No. 1, but Queen were now more focused on their status in the States. Instead of issuing 'Innuendo' as the first single, 'Headlong' became the premier single of the album, reaching an impressive No. 3 in the rock radio charts. 'Innuendo' followed in March, reaching No. 17, while 'I Can't Live With You' peaked at No. 28 in June. (It was clear that the band were once again in tune with their American audiences, though, for the record, none of the *Innuendo* singles charted at all in the *Billboard* Top 200.) To assist with promotion, Brian and, eventually, Roger travelled Stateside to conduct a series of radio interviews. These elicited great enthusiasm from fans, who called in to ask when the band would be back on the road. The party line remained that Freddie still didn't feel up to a tour, but Brian promised on *Rockline* that "the signs look good. But we still have to persuade Freddie that he actually wants to be here."

The reviews were typically caustic at home. *The Times* sneered, "In 20 years Queen have lost none of their appetite for music of the most grandiose banality. *Innuendo*, the album, is kitsch on a boggling scale. It recognizes few frontiers of style, let alone barriers of taste, as it sweeps from mock-flamenco interludes in the title track through Muppet-style heavy metal in 'Hitman' to the pseudo-spiritual lilt of 'All God's People' ... Only once does the burlesque pause long enough to reveal a human heart at work. 'These Are The Days Of Our Lives', a shamelessly soppy, middle-aged paean to the passing of youth, is a song which will touch a chord with the more mellow breed of Queen fan and possibly even beyond." *Vox* wasn't impressed either: "Queen have survived the changes since their debut in the days of glam better than any of their contemporaries. And, by and large, they survived by not giving a monkey's what anybody else was doing. However, their pop sensibility, quirkiness and sense of humor are largely missing here. After the title track you get 'I'm Going Slightly Mad', a pleasant enough refrain, and it's followed by 'Headlong', an ode to blasting down the highway with no particular place to go. But this is the sort of thing Dave Edmunds could do in his sleep; unfortunately, Queen sound like they are asleep. Even given the lush, chocolate-box production that drenches this album like syrup, you'd think they'd realize that rockabilly requires a bit of rough."

In North America, with so much riding on the album, the critics were equally unimpressed. *Rolling Stone* gave *Innuendo* a thrashing, calling it "so lightweight you'll forget it as soon as it's over – which, with this band, should go without saying", adding, however, that "there's nothing cynical about it" and "these old entertainers sound like they've decided to stop trying so hard, like they're finally satisfied with their lot in life." Baton Rouge's *The Advocate* seethed xenophobic: "What bombast. What vocals. What a bunch of pretentious twits ... The recording quality is fantastic. It should be nominated for next year's Grammys in the category of 'Best Engineered Recording By A Pretentious Bunch Of Twits'. English twits, at that." "Queen's third album since its albums stopped going gold (*The Works* being the last) is attracting the type of attention the band hasn't experienced in quite a while," *Dallas Morning News* wrote. "Unfortunately, *Innuendo* does little more than serve as a reminder of why interest waned. The theatrical pomposity of Freddie Mercury's over-tracked vocals, the metallic noodlings of Brian May's guitar, the operatically sprawling arrangements, the lyrical twaddle, all the signifying extravagances of the Queen sound remain intact and omnipresent through songs like the title track. At the center is the breathy cooing of Mr. Mercury. If he isn't singing a love song to his cat (highlighted by Mr. May's meowing, cat-scratch guitar), he is burbling on that 'I'm Going Slightly Mad'. The band can work up some undiluted momentum (as on 'The Hitman'), but the relentlessly anthemic grandiosity of Queen's approach generates all the passion and intensity of a *Flash Gordon* sequel."

Other reviews were more positive, with *People Weekly* opining, "Queen is to rock and roll what the comic-book Superman is to Nietzsche's Superman: one big rock 'em-sock 'em, colorful, way-larger-than-life, out-of-control exaggeration of an exaggeration. With its craving for overproduced musical bombast that crashes through your speakers like the Man of Steel bursting through a brick wall, Queen would never be called a subtle group. Still, as easy as it is to make fun of this sort of overbearing stuff, *Innuendo* is so over-the-top it's enjoyable. The album is a homecoming of sorts for Queen, a return to the mid-'70s glory days of such tunes as the infamous 'Bohemian Rhapsody'. The band's recent releases have pursued a more mainstream rock route with zero success, so it's nice to hear this reversion to the old exaggerated ways ... If this is cartoon rock and roll, at least it's good and brazenly cartoonish." "The boys are back with a lot less pomp this time," *The Cincinnati Post* proclaimed. "Freddie Mercury still has a taste for luridly melodramatic vocals, but rockers like 'Headlong' and 'Ride the Wild Wind' make up for it. For old fans, there are plenty of the group's trademark chorale vocals and headphone-mixed sounds, but Mercury's ballad *[sic]*, 'These Are The Days Of Our Lives', actually sounds restrained." The *LA Times* was less complimentary: "Given the bombast and harsh assault of Queen's biggest hits, it's a shock to find that the heart of the British quartet's 16th album, *Innuendo*, is made of soft, sweet, sticky, sentimental goo ... It's typical Queen, full of theatrical sound and fury with massed choruses of whooshing voices and treated guitars, all huff and puff. You know, the sort of bollocks the Sex Pistols quite rightly told us to never mind." *St. Petersburg Times* was more positive: "With Innuendo, the band's 12th studio album, Queen attempts to reacquaint itself with record buyers. Most of the songs have a 90s feel while maintaining that distinctive sound. 'I Can't Live With You', with its blaring four-part harmonies, could be an out-take from the classic album *Jazz*, but it still sounds fresh."

The band were so rejuvenated by the recording process that they went back into the studios to record non-album B-sides for the upcoming series of singles. The material was so strong that they decided to start work on a follow-up to *Innuendo*; while the band recorded for as long as they could, Freddie's staying power eventually began to wane as his condition worsened, and the remaining songs were abandoned as Brian and Roger focused on extracurricular activities to keep their minds off the inevitable. *Innuendo* was to remain Freddie's final statement to the world, 12 songs of passionately delivered emotion, with his exit line ringing like an epitaph: "I'll top the bill / I'll overkill / I've got to find the will to carry on with the show." A sublime end to a staggering career, and the perfect summation of one of rock's most irreplaceable front men.

LIVE AT WEMBLEY STADIUM

Parlophone PCSP 725, May 1992 [2]
Parlophone CDPCSP 725, May 1992 [2]
Hollywood HR-61104-2, June 1992 [53]
Parlophone 7 2435 9044 026, June 2003 [38]
Hollywood 2031-62422-2, June 2003

'One Vision' (5'49), 'Tie Your Mother Down' (4'06), 'In The Lap Of The Gods...Revisited' (2'29), 'Seven Seas Of Rhye' (1'18), 'Tear It Up' (2'12), 'A Kind Of Magic' (8'41), 'Under Pressure' (3'41), 'Another One Bites The Dust' (5'59), 'Who Wants To Live Forever' (4'07), 'I Want To Break Free' (3'34), 'Impromptu' (2'56), 'Brighton Rock Solo' (9'10), 'Now I'm Here' (6'20), 'Love Of My Life' (4'48), 'Is This The World We Created...?' (2'58), '(You're So Square) Baby I Don't Care' (1'36), 'Hello Mary Lou (Goodbye Heart)' (1'50), 'Tutti Frutti' (3'24), 'Gimme Some Lovin'' (0'55), 'Bohemian Rhapsody' (5'50), 'Hammer To Fall' (6'03), 'Crazy Little Thing Called Love' (5'58), 'Big Spender' (1'06), 'Radio Ga Ga' (5'57), 'We Will Rock You' (2'47), 'Friends Will Be Friends' (2'06), 'We Are The Champions' (4'04), 'God Save The Queen' (1'35)

Bonus tracks on 2003 reissue: 'A Kind Of Magic' (7'10), 'Another One Bites The Dust' (4'28), 'Crazy Little Thing Called Love' (5'55), 'Tavaszi Szél Vizet Áraszt' (1'53)

Musicians: John Deacon *(bass guitar)*, Brian May *(guitars, vocals, keyboards on 'Who Wants To Live Forever', acoustic guitar on 'Love Of My Life', 'Is This The World We Created...?', '(You're So Square) Baby I Don't Care', 'Hello Mary Lou (Goodbye Heart)', 'Tutti Frutti', and 'Crazy Little Thing Called Love')*, Freddie Mercury *(vocals, piano, rhythm guitar on 'Crazy Little Thing Called Love')*, Roger Taylor *(drums, vocals, effects on 'A Kind Of Magic', tambourine on '(You're So Square) Baby I Don't Care', 'Hello Mary Lou (Goodbye Heart)', and 'Tutti Frutti')*, Spike Edney *(keyboards, vocals, piano on 'Crazy Little Thing Called Love', rhythm guitar on 'Hammer To Fall')*
Recorded: 12 July 1986, at Wembley Stadium, London by Mack *('A Kind Of Magic', 'Another One Bites The Dust', and 'Crazy Little Thing Called Love' on 2003 reissue recorded 11 July 1986 at Wembley Stadium, London; 'Tavaszi Szél Vizet Áraszt' recorded 27 July 1986, at Nepstadion, Budapest)*
Producers: Queen

During the surge of Queen reissues between early 1991 and mid-1992 (which culminated in the special US-only compilations of *Classic Queen* and the restructured *Greatest Hits*), Queen's stand-out concert from Wembley Stadium was issued on CD for the first time, making it their first live album release in six years. Their last live album, *Live Magic*, was compiled of selections from a series of shows on the Magic tour; considering that this release also originated from that tour, the album could be viewed as a bit of a cop-out since *Live Magic* was still readily available (at least in the UK; it hadn't been released in the US). However, there are many differences between this release and *Live Magic*, not the least of which is that the Wembley Stadium concert is presented, for the most part, complete (inexplicably, the coda to 'Tutti Frutti' was removed), whereas *Live Magic* was a hodgepodge of shows, with the majority of the songs taken from their final performance at Knebworth Park.

Why this gig was selected for release instead of the Knebworth Park concert is simple: not only was this show filmed in its entirety (Knebworth wasn't), Wembley was their home territory and bands generally play better before a familiar audience; this is patently obvious upon first listen. Freddie is, as ever, larger than life, holding the audience in the palm of his hand and allowing John, Brian and Roger to focus on the instrumentals. Their performances are cohesive and tight, the band delivering two hours of hits, rarities and covers that are a joy to listen to.

Unlike their first live album, no single was forthcoming as a promotional gimmick (the band had learned their lesson with the failure of 'Love Of My Life' in 1979), although a promo-only release of 'We Will Rock You' and 'We Are The Champions' was issued in Holland. It was of little consequence anyway since *Live At Wembley '86* soared to No. 2 in the UK and No. 53 in the US; while the latter may be disappointing at first, for a six-year old live recording from a band who had hit their peak in America's charts in the early 1980s and hadn't toured there since 1982, that the album charted at all is an accomplishment, and a testament to the weight with which Hollywood Records treated Queen's back catalog.

In June 2003, the album was reissued and expanded (even further) as a counterpart to the DVD release of *Live At Wembley Stadium*, which finally featured the complete concert with previously unreleased footage. The album release added four songs to the end of the second disc: 'A Kind Of Magic', 'Another One Bites The Dust' and 'Crazy Little Thing Called Love' were all taken from the first night's concert on 11 July 1986 (the remainder of the show came from the following night), while 'Tavaszi Szél Vizet Áraszt' from their Budapest concert on 27 July was released for the first time on disc.

Most dramatically, the album was retitled *Live At Wembley Stadium* to coincide with the DVD release and given similar packaging, with the same cover photos and design as well as a booklet of images from the concert. Though the reissued album didn't chart in the US, it did achieve a decent No. 38 in the UK, yet only stayed in the charts for a fortnight as compared to the original's 15 weeks. Though the band had performed more dazzling shows during their career, *Live At Wembley Stadium* is far more exciting than *Live Killers* and *Live Magic* and serves as a stunning reminder that Queen were the biggest and best live band on the planet in 1986.

MADE IN HEAVEN

Parlophone PCSD 167, November 1995 [1]
Parlophone CDPCSD 167, November 1995 [1]
Hollywood HR-6201-7-1, November 1995 [58]
Hollywood HR-6201-7-2, November 1995 [58]
UK Cat No, September 2011 [144]

'It's A Beautiful Day' (2'32), 'Made In Heaven' (5'25), 'Let Me Live' (4'45), 'Mother Love' (4'49), 'My Life Has Been Saved' (3'15), 'I Was Born To Love You' (4'49), 'Heaven For Everyone' (5'36), 'Too Much Love Will Kill You' (4'20), 'You Don't Fool Me' (5'24), 'A Winter's Tale' (3'49), 'It's A Beautiful Day (Reprise)' (3'01)

Bonus tracks on CD issue: 'Yeah' (0'04), 'Track 13' (22'33)

Bonus tracks on 2011 Universal Records deluxe reissue: 'Heaven For Everyone' *(single version)* (4'39), 'It's A Beautiful Day' *(single version)* (3'58), 'My Life Has Been Saved' *(1989 B-side)* (3'16), 'I Was Born To Love You' *(vocal and piano version)* (2'55), 'Rock In Rio Blues' (4'33), 'A Winter's Tale' *(Cosy Fireside mix)* (3'49)

Bonus videos, 2011 iTunes-only editions: 'Heartache' ('Too Much Love Will Kill You') *(promotional video)*, 'Heaven For Everyone' *(promotional video)*, 'A Winter's Tale' *(alternate promotional video)*

Musicians: John Deacon *(bass guitar, keyboards on 'It's A Beautiful Day' and 'My Life Has Been Saved')*, Brian May *(guitars, vocals, keyboards, co-lead vocals on 'Let Me Live' and 'Mother Love', keyboards and drum programming on 'Mother Love')*, Freddie Mercury *(vocals, piano, keyboards)*, Roger Taylor *(drums, percussion, vocals, keyboards, co-lead vocals on 'Let Me Live')*, Rebecca Leigh-White, Gary Martin, Catherine Porter, and Miriam Stockley *(backing vocals on 'Let Me Live')*
Recorded: Mountain Studios, Montreux, January-May 1991; Allerton Hill and Cosford Mill Studios, Surrey; Metropolis Studios, London, October 1993-summer 1995
Producers: Queen, David Richards, Justin Shirley-Smith and Joshua J Macrae

Truly a labor of love for John, Roger and Brian, the posthumous *Made In Heaven* album started life in early 1991 when Freddie felt so energized and inspired by the *Innuendo* sessions that he wanted to record a few B-sides for the singles from that album. Those sessions proved so fruitful that the band decided to channel their intensity into another album instead. Sessions took place at the idyllic Mountain Studios in Montreux, a town where Freddie had found immense solace during the final years of his life, undisturbed by the locals and inspired by his magnificent surroundings.

Only three new songs were written for the album: 'Mother Love', 'You Don't Fool Me' and 'A Winter's Tale'. ('Lost Opportunity' was recorded during these sessions, but it was released on the CD single of 'I'm Going Slightly Mad', and was thus out of consideration for inclusion.) Sessions commenced in January 1991, with the band once again jamming to tap into their inspiration, though there was more of a sense of urgency to come equipped with full songs. "Right up until the end," Brian told Q in 1998, "Freddie asked me for lyrics and music that he could work on, and he was adamant that this material should be released."

The recording sessions continued intermittently between January and May 1991, with the band often working for two days a week, depending on Freddie's health. As recording progressed, Freddie's condition continued to deteriorate, and sessions came to a close on 22 May 1991, when he recorded his final vocal track on 'Mother Love'. Brian continued his *Innuendo* radio tour across America, visiting broadcast stations where he played accompaniments to songs from Queen's past, while Roger briefly toured with The Cross in support of their *Blue Rock* album. Finally, on 23 November 1991, an announcement was issued to the press: "Following the enormous conjecture in the press over the last two weeks, I wish to confirm that I have been tested HIV positive and have AIDS. I felt it correct to keep this information private to date in order to protect the privacy of those around me. However, the time has come for my friends and fans to know the truth, and I hope that everyone will join with me, my doctors and all those worldwide in the fight against this terrible disease." In response, the media's ink had barely had time to dry when on the very next day, 24 November, Freddie Mercury – attended by Jim Hutton, Peter Freestone and Dave Clark – succumbed to bronchial pneumonia at 6:48 pm.

As the news echoed around the world, Brian, John and Roger consulted with Jim Beach in order to plan the next step. The decision was made to stage a tribute concert in Freddie's name, but it wasn't yet finalized what form this would take; this was confirmed the week after Freddie's death when Brian and Roger appeared on early morning television to express their sorrow and propose a concert "to celebrate the life of Freddie Mercury." On 12 February 1992, at the British Music Industry Rock and Pop Awards, where the same duo received an award for Best Single of 1991 ('These Are The Days Of Our Lives'), Roger concluded an emotional acceptance speech by announcing "a concert that would be a tribute to Freddie's life at Wembley Stadium on 20 April."

The concert was an unqualified success, raising millions of pounds for AIDS awareness while providing a suitable send-off for Freddie (for more information, see Part Four). The rumor mill started turning shortly after the concert, at which George Michael's offering seemed to be the undisputed highlight: following

his duet with Lisa Stansfield on 'These Are The Days Of Our Lives', he presented an emotional reading of 'Somebody To Love', which was later extracted as a single and peaked at No. 1 in April 1993. Due to the success of the single, and Michael's obvious charisma and chemistry with the band, rumors abounded that he would become Queen's new lead vocalist, and when it was announced that there was enough additional material in the vaults for at least two more Queen albums, many speculated Michael would be present on those recordings.

However, this was not the case; the band had other intentions for the fruits of their final recording sessions. As far as they were concerned, anything without Freddie's voice or direct involvement could not be considered a Queen song. So it was apparent that fans would have to wait before receiving the long-promised follow-up to *Innuendo*.

Brian first mentioned the extant tracks in *Guitar World* in January 1993: "One of the things that we've agreed to do is finish off the tracks that Freddie sang after the end of the *Innuendo* album. There's two or three or four pieces there which we can finish, and they should be called the work of Queen. But after that, who knows? I don't think anybody knows." His comments indicated a deliberate shying away from the shadow of Queen, yet all the press wanted to know was about his past; this resulted in an almost blasé approach to interviewers. "There's a certain amount of material left which Freddie did the vocals for," Brian told *The Orange County Register* that April. "We and he knew what we were dealing with. We wrote as many lyrics as we could. Whenever he was strong enough, he'd go in [the studio] and do some stuff. I'd guess there will be one more piece of Queen product, but that'd probably be the end. I don't think any of us wants to go out dusting off the old out-takes and trying to stretch it out." On his relationship with John and Roger, he was even more nonchalant, telling *Guitarist* in 1994, "We are very conscious of each other and we have respect for each other. If we mess with each other's work we are very nervous about it. I think we can still communicate okay, but it's just that there isn't that kind of Queen machinery going on anymore. It's three people looking at what's left, and basically just trying to make something that is worthy of having the Queen name on it."

The first indication that wheels were in motion came in September 1993, shortly before John and Roger's involvement at the Cowdray Park charity concert, where they played with David Gilmour, Eric Clapton and Genesis. Jacky Smith, co-organizer of the Queen fan club, reported, "Roger and John have been discussing future projects, and Roger tells me that they both feel 'very positive about the future'." Indeed, Roger mentioned the activity in a BBC Radio One interview in May 1994: "I've seen quite a lot of John and a little bit of Brian. And we have started work on finishing some stuff that we started with Freddie. In due course of time I think that will appear as a complete album. And it sounds very good, although it's still in its reasonably early stages. We had started things ... and he'd done his parts on. He was working right up to the end, with the full intention of those works coming to fruition. So it's sort of a duty to finish them. And they're very good, it's some wonderful stuff." John, too, revealed in the winter 1994 issue of the fan club magazine, "Roger and I spent several weeks in the studio last year working on various Queen tracks. We played along with some of them, adding improved bass and drums to the songs."

Brian was put on edge by an increasingly persistent John and Roger, who decided to go ahead with recording sessions in his absence, with sessions starting on 13 October 1993. He masked this in his letter to the fan club in spring 1994: "For the past four months I've been delving into those last Queen tracks which we started with Freddie nearly three years ago. Of course, the remaining new material is very precious stuff, and in my mind the most important consideration is that this final collection must be worthy of the name Queen, so I've been delving very deep. I'm now very excited about how it's turning out, but only when I'm sure that Freddie is coming across in his full glory, in the way he would wish, will I begin to feel happy. Anyway, you can be sure that John, Roger and I will have put in the maximum amount of loving care (and the usual arguments!) by the time this thing hits the shops!"

"After [Freddie] died," Brian told Q in 1998, "my way of dealing with it was to go out on tour. But Roger and John became very impatient with me and started working on the tapes. I didn't want this stuff to go out without my involvement, so I took the tapes off them, felt that they'd done it wrong and spent months putting it all back together. Doing Made In Heaven was like assembling a jigsaw puzzle. But I wouldn't have put my seal of approval on it if I hadn't thought it was up to standard." He opened up in a 1998 interview with Guitar & Bass Magazine, venting his spleen at the rhythm section: "In fact, when I went on the Back To The Light tour, I heard that the other members of

Queen had already taken the decision to go ahead with this last album, without even asking my opinion. I was even more furious than before; I was not convinced that releasing this album was a good idea. As soon as I heard the news, I contacted Roger and John to make my disapproval known to them. To that they answered, that if it didn't suit me, they would go ahead without me! I was already fuming to have been treated that way, but even that was nothing compared to the anger I had after having listened to what they had put down on tape during my absence: it was truly catastrophic!"

With his mind now set on finishing the album to the standards he believed Queen's albums were held to, Brian perched himself in front of a computer for the next 18 months, working furiously on assembling suitable pieces of music comprised of existing vocals. Roger and John cooled off and met up with Brian throughout 1994, with the bassist reporting in the spring of 1995 that "the recording and mixing of Queen material is progressing and I hope we will be able to release the end results this year. I am sure that everybody will have varied and different comments and opinions on the finished work. It has not been easy as even Roger, Brian and myself see things differently and coming to an agreement between us takes time! Anyway, we will do our best as that is all we can do and I hope you feel that it was worth all the work to release a final Queen album!"

In the summer 1995 issue of the fan club magazine, Brian revealed, "As I write, we have only a few weeks to deliver all the finished mixed tracks, and all the artwork, if we are to meet the deadline for a Christmas onslaught! It feels a bit like the old days, but of course we're all very different in our ways now. I remember us working flat out in three studios simultaneously to deliver A Night At The Opera in 1975. At the moment work is going on in London, and at Roger's Mill, and at my own studio in sunny Surrey ... we may even make it! For me, I can hardly believe that most of the last 18 months or so of my life have gone into this – 'What, just for a few four-minute songs??!!!' Well, they're pretty precious songs, and I keep remembering this is really the last chance I'll ever have to work with Freddie's wonderful voice. Let's hope you all like this stuff."

"The time has come to put to bed this last studio album from Queen, a difficult child indeed!" Roger revealed in the autumn. "In content of songs, emotion, and, above all, in power and quality of performance from Freddie, the work is strong indeed. Boy, could that one sing. Some of the songs have never been heard before, including the last lyric and performance of our singer, others you might recognize but in totally different form and hopefully now improved."

The first signs of renewed Queen activity came in October 1995, when 'Heaven For Everyone' was issued as the band's first true single in nearly four years, and promptly went to No. 2 in the UK charts. Its parent album, *Made In Heaven*, was released two weeks later, immediately soaring to No. 1 in the UK and justifying the hard work the surviving members had put into the album. More importantly, they did Freddie justice, completing his final recordings without a trace of sentimentality or martyrship, allowing the three tracks to sit comfortably among the rest of Queen's discography.

In order to flesh the album out to a suitable running time – instead of simply throwing together a hits compilation and tacking the final recordings on at the end – the surviving members dove deep into their vaults to search for songs that would work contextually. This meant that known out-takes like 'Silver Salmon', 'Polar Bear', and 'Feelings, Feelings' wouldn't fit the bill, as they were far too rock-oriented and wouldn't have worked along the more introspective material. Instead, scraps of Freddie's vocals from out-takes over the years were structured into proper songs, with 'It's A Beautiful Day' coming from a tape where Freddie was doodling on the piano during the *Game* sessions and improvising a set of lyrics, while the roots of 'Let Me Live' came from the *Works* sessions, when Rod Stewart and Jeff Beck stopped by the band's sessions in Los Angeles to jam for a bit. Stewart's vocals were removed, and the song was adapted as a soulful, gospel-tinged ballad, with Brian and Roger writing their own verses to fill out the song.

Elsewhere, solo material was reworked heavily, with the band ably replacing Freddie's original arrangements of 'Made In Heaven' and 'I Was Born To Love You' with a typically bombastic Queen treatment (Brian was justifiably proud of the former, pointing out the pains and consideration he took to turn it into the epic it deserved to be), while 'Heaven For Everyone', featuring Freddie on vocals, was completely re-recorded, giving it a more somber arrangement with a truly astounding guitar solo. 'Too Much Love Will Kill You' was dusted off from the archives and released as-is, while 'My Life Has Been Saved' was plucked from obscurity and given a fresh lick of paint.

"We were trying to make an album up to the same performance and arranging and producing standards of the others, and I think we succeeded," Brian told *Classic Rock* in 1998. "It's definitely a kind of fantasy album. It's like what if Queen had still existed, because there was no such thing at that point. It had its moments of great joy and discovery, but a lot of hard slog and a lot of hard bits emotionally." Roger was more diplomatic on the recording process, and name-checked the album in a 1998 Radio Five interview as one of his favorites.

There was very little middle ground with the reviews; critics either loved it or hated it. Only *Rolling Stone* was mildly complimentary, calling the album "a strange, often discomfiting listening experience," while *Melody Maker* was disdainful: "*Made In Heaven* (I don't want to think about the nuances of that title) sounds exactly like every Queen record since *A Kind Of Magic* ... Some have called using the prerecorded voice of the late Mercury on this album necrophilia. Not me. I have no problem with Freddie making records while dead. No greater problem than I had with him making them while he was alive." *NME* was even more vicious, letting fly their hatred for the album: "*Made In Heaven* is consistent with the ongoing programme entitled *Freddie: The Remake*. He's now perceived as being warm, selfless and tragic – his physicality quite literally replaced on the cover by a bronze statue giving a straight-arm salute. Lovely ... Just what did the other band members feel they were gaining by bolstering up these fragments of Fred? Was it a satisfying mission – multi-tracking like mad, covering up for the missing lines and layering up a gigantic parody of the Queen sound to cover for the crappy material? At least the grave-robbing principle that launches The Beatles' latest venture ['Free As A Bird'] has some kind of historic, sentimental value. You'll not excuse this record in the same way ... *Made In Heaven* is vulgar, creepy, sickly, and in dubious taste. Freddie would have loved it."

The Times also mentioned the recent activity by The Beatles in a complimentary review: "Frankly, the impending battle of the bands with dead singers is not an alluring prospect. But while the regrouped Beatles have, by all accounts, been forced to work with some pretty scant contributions from the late John Lennon, the remaining members of Queen were bequeathed a generous album's worth of surprisingly full-blooded performances by Freddie Mercury ... Despite its overdue delivery, *Made In Heaven* stands up remarkably well as the closing chapter in a spectacular pop odyssey." *The Guardian*, too, was hesitant with its praise: "As usual with Queen, the lyrics, as opposed to the music, take centre stage. Musically, *Made In Heaven* simply takes up where *Innuendo* left off, with a dash of gospeloid chanting here, a creaky outburst from one-trick guitarist Brian May there ... [Freddie] poured out his heart, and his words have a throat-aching poignance. Even the record's opening verse, 'It's a beautiful day / The sun is shining / I feel good', which would have seemed banal at another time, assumes a painful significance."

Entertainment Weekly in the US called it "the perfect theatrical epitaph for a life dedicated to gorgeous artifice" and "a surprisingly organic work with no shortage of highlights." *Vox* proudly proclaimed, "Heaven's great!" and claimed that the album "contains some of the finest material of the band's career ... Queen have surpassed all expectations with *Made In Heaven*. This album will break your heart, shake your soul and, at the right volume, undermine the foundations of your house." *The Sunday Times* was also pleased with the album: "Aside from the dark, bluesy inflection of 'Mother Love' – a track Mercury recorded only weeks before the end – the mood here is upbeat and furiously triumphalist in the way that only Queen albums know how to be ... Vacuous lyrics, novelty effects and sonic bluster have their part to play here, too, of course, but by the rather routine standards of Queen's output up to and including 1991's *Innuendo*, this rates as a superior effort and a more-than-worthy epitaph to the great entertainer himself."

Indeed: Brian, Roger, and John assembled an album of fine material that not only sounded cohesive, but honored Freddie's last recordings without deluging them in sickly-sweet poignancy. *Made In Heaven* exhibits the right amount of humor and sadness, joy and pain, light and shade. While *Innuendo* was the quintessential conclusion to a varied and wonderful career, *Made In Heaven* was a fitting and perfect coda.

QUEEN ON FIRE: LIVE AT THE BOWL

Parlophone 863 211 2, October 2004 [20]
Hollywood 2061-62479-2, November 2004

'Flash' (1'54), 'The Hero' (1'44), 'We Will Rock You' (3'17), 'Action This Day' (4'52), 'Play The Game' (4'30), 'Staying Power' (4'03), 'Somebody To Love' (7'53), 'Now I'm Here' (6'18), 'Dragon Attack' (4'16), 'Now I'm Here (Reprise)' (2'20), 'Love Of My Life' (4'22), 'Save Me' (4'00), 'Back Chat' (5'00), 'Get Down Make Love' (3'39), 'Guitar Solo' (6'22), 'Under Pressure' (3'47), 'Fat Bottomed Girls' (5'25), 'Crazy

Little Thing Called Love' (4'15), 'Bohemian Rhapsody' (5'38), 'Tie Your Mother Down' (4'09), 'Another One Bites The Dust' (3'49), 'Sheer Heart Attack' (3'25), 'We Will Rock You' (2'08), 'We Are The Champions' (3'28), 'God Save The Queen' (1'24)

Musicians: John Deacon (*bass guitar, rhythm guitar on 'Staying Power'*), Brian May (*guitars, vocals, piano on 'Save Me'*), Freddie Mercury (*vocals, piano, acoustic rhythm guitar on 'Crazy Little Thing Called Love'*), Roger Taylor (*drums, vocals, Syn-drums*), Morgan Fischer (*piano, synthesizer, keyboards*)
Recorded: 5 June 1982 at Milton Keynes Bowl, Milton Keynes by Mack and Mick McKenna
Producers: Justin Shirley-Smith, Brian May and Roger Taylor

After the success of the *Live At The Wembley Stadium* DVD and CD releases in June 2003, rumors regarding the next live simultaneous release abounded. Some sources said the band's appearance in Budapest from July 1986 would be next, but to release a show from the same tour (the Magic tour) with an identical set list would have been a poor decision. Instead, *Greatest Video Hits 2* emerged that October, and the inclusion of 'Staying Power' from Milton Keynes set tongues wagging yet again.

The rumors were confirmed via Brian's website on 27 June 2004. Like the Wembley show before it, Milton Keynes had been filmed by Gavin Taylor and shown on television, albeit in a heavily edited form. Unlike Wembley, though, Milton Keynes remained unreleased to the general public, excepting those who had taped the original broadcast in 1983 (or those Americans who taped it from the showing it received on VH-1 in 1995). For years, it was assumed that the band had played an abbreviated set for television purposes, but when Greg Brooks' *Queen Live: A Concert Documentary* appeared in 1995, he enumerated all but 'Sheer Heart Attack' as having been performed that night.

Either way, this release would be a treat for casual fans to indulge in, and what emerged in October 2004 did not disappoint. There were only a handful of complaints, as there are with almost every release generated by any band. On the night of the original concert, Freddie's voice cracked during 'Fat Bottomed Girls'; for aesthetic reasons, this flaw was redubbed for the final release. Similarly, some of the dialog between songs was also edited, including the oft-repeated line from Freddie, "It's only a bloody record! I mean, people get so excited about these things." But these are only minor quibbles since the overall presentation is spectacular, and to own a virtually complete concert is certainly desirable. Considering that the last true live release was *Live At Wembley '86* in May 1992, *Queen On Fire: Live At The Bowl* is an excellent documentation of where the band were in their live career during what many have considered their creative nadir.

Reviews were favorable for the most part. The *Evening Standard*'s *Metro Life* magazine rated the DVD number four on the list of Top Five recent releases, glossing the title as "A vindaloo trauma, maybe? No, it's the Milton Keynes Bowl, the year is 1982 and Freddie Mercury and the guys are at the peak of their game. All the hits, done about as well as you could imagine. Even this non-Queen fan was impressed." *The Sun* completely missed the point: "Let's get one thing straight: Queen are one of the best, if not the best, live British bands ever. But do we really need *another* post-Mercury two-disc greatest hits album? There are some great live performances on here including 'We Are The Champions', 'Play The Game' and 'Love Of My Life', but you get the feeling they flogged something pretty similar last year. The Queen estate continues to coin it in – Freddie must be rolling in it in his grave."

Music Week said, "This double collection … captures perfectly one of the world's biggest rock acts at their performing peak – a full three years before their Live Aid masterstroke." *Mirror Ticket* gave the release three stars, saying that "this 1982 Milton Keynes show captures Queen in all their pomp and fury. Yet, despite Mercury's vaunted showmanship and their elevated reputation in the era of The Darkness, this double set isn't lost Britrock gold. For every gem they produced, Freddie's crew churned out an equal amount of padding." *On The Record* hit the nail squarely on the head: "Most Queen fans will admit that *Hot Space* wasn't one of the group's better albums. But the tour that followed the release of that album in 1982 was blistering hot. The concert from the Milton Keynes Bowl is released later this month as *Queen On Fire: Live At The Bowl* on DVD and CD. It's an incredible 110 minutes of classic Queen live, featuring loads of their biggest hits … It's hard to believe that the concert is 22 years old. Freddie and the boys sound so fresh."

The album is memorable for the ferocity with which the band launch into their rarer material. The opening salvo of 'The Hero' followed by the accelerated 'We Will Rock You' is a direct one-two punch, while more audience-friendly renditions of 'Staying Power',

'Action This Day' and 'Back Chat' completely transform those songs from the bland disco-funk of *Hot Space* into full-throttle rockers. The segment from 'Now I'm Here' until Brian's guitar solo flags, but it's redeemed by 'Under Pressure' and 'Fat Bottomed Girls', a song that was excised from the set list for the 1981 shows but enjoys a resurrection here. Overall, the release is a welcome and refreshing addition to the Queen discography, and a refreshing counterpart to the oversaturated representations of the Magic tour.

QUEEN ROCK MONTREAL
Parlophone 50999 5 04047 2 8, October 2007 [20]
Hollywood 000097302, October 2007

'Intro' (1'59), 'We Will Rock You' *(fast)* (3'06), 'Let Me Entertain You' (2'48), 'Play The Game' (3'57), 'Somebody To Love' (7'53), 'Killer Queen' (1'59), 'I'm In Love With My Car' (2'03), 'Get Down, Make Love' (4'45), 'Save Me' (4'14), 'Now I'm Here' (5'31), 'Dragon Attack' (3'11), 'Now I'm Here' (1'53), 'Love Of My Life' (3'56), 'Under Pressure' (3'49), 'Keep Yourself Alive' (3'29), Drum Solo (3'00), Guitar Solo (5'11), 'Flash' (2'11), 'The Hero' (1'51), 'Crazy Little Thing Called Love' (4'15), 'Jailhouse Rock' (2'32), 'Bohemian Rhapsody' (5'28), 'Tie Your Mother Down' (3'52), 'Another One Bites The Dust' (4'00), 'Sheer Heart Attack' (3'53), 'We Will Rock You' (2'09), 'We Are The Champions' (3'27), 'God Save The Queen' (1'27)

Musicians: John Deacon *(bass guitar)*, Brian May *(guitars, vocals, piano on 'Save Me')*, Freddie Mercury *(vocals, piano, acoustic rhythm guitar on 'Crazy Little Thing Called Love')*, Roger Taylor *(drums, vocals, lead vocals on 'I'm In Love With My Car')*
Recorded: 24 and 25 November 1981 at the Forum, Montreal, Quebec by Mack and Kooster McAllister
Producers: Justin Shirley-Smith, Kris Fredriksson, Joshua J Macrae, Brian May, and Roger Taylor

The farcical, endless releases of *We Will Rock You*, Queen's first theatrical concert presentation, is well-documented (see Part Six), so that makes its release in 2007 as *Queen Rock Montreal* all the more confounding, considering this marks the fifth time the video was released in some format. But, more substantial was the first release of the audio of this concert; while the spectacle of Queen's live show should be viewed in all its glory on DVD (indeed, despite its familiarity, *Queen Rock Montreal* is stunning in hi-def), hearing the interplay of the last time that Queen were a four-piece live band is a rare treat. Again, the songs are all familiar, but the performance is white-hot. There are some new treats, too: 'Flash' and 'The Hero' are performed in full here, with Brian on piano (and Roger's hilarious falsetto on "Oh Flash, I love you, I love you!") on the former, and a leisurely take on the latter, far different from the *Queen On Fire: Live At The Bowl* performance. Additionally, 'Jailhouse Rock' is released here for the first time; though it was performed as an encore number (just before 'Sheer Heart Attack'), it was edited to after 'Crazy Little Thing Called Love', due to Freddie's insistence on deliberately annoying the director, who had demanded that the band wear the same outfits on both nights. For the encores on the first night, Freddie wore white jeans, while on the second night, he wore the shortest shorts ever to have been produced, thus potentially screwing up the continuity of the film.

Beyond that, there's little else that's a particular revelation, except that the sound has been superbly remixed by Joshua J. Macrae, Justin Shirley-Smith, and Kris Fredriksson, making their already remarkable performance even better. As an album, it's a good documentation of their live finesse at the time, though it treads far too closely to the *Live Killers* and *Queen On Fire: Live At The Bowl* sets for comfort. (It continues the long line of cringe-inducing live album titles; was something like *Live In Montreal* too obvious, and didn't indicate just how much Queen rocked that night?) Considering Brian and Roger's mild indignation over the multiple *We Will Rock You* releases, that they were able to wrest back control of the project and release it to their own standards is exemplary; considering the fans' mild indignation over the multiple *We Will Rock You* releases, *Queen Rock Montreal* is the definitive version – until the next version, that is…

HUNGARIAN RHAPSODY: QUEEN LIVE IN BUDAPEST

Eagle Vision EVB334359 *(CD/Blu-Ray edition)*, November 2012
Island Records Group 0602537146239, Universal Music Group 0602537146239 *(box set edition)*, November 2012
Eagle Vision EV305269 *(DVD edition)*, November 2012
Eagle Vision EVB334229 *(Blu-Ray edition)*, November 2012

CD: 'One Vision' (5'36), 'Tie Your Mother Down' (4'42), 'In The Lap Of The Gods … Revisited' (2'17), 'Seven Seas Of Rhye' (1'41), 'Tear It Up' (1'47), 'A Kind Of Magic' (8'21), 'Under Pressure' (3'50), 'Another One Bites The Dust' (4'56), 'Who Wants To Live Forever' (3'59), 'I Want To Break Free' (3'33), 'Looks Like It's Gonna Be A Good Night' (3'38), 'Guitar Solo' (7'24), 'Now I'm Here' (5'58), 'Love Of My Life' (4'37), 'Tavaszi Szél Vizet Áraszt' (2'16), 'Is This The World We Created…?' (2'32), '(You're So Square) Baby I Don't Care' (1'29), 'Hello Mary Lou (Goodbye Heart)' (2'24), 'Tutti Frutti' (3'36), 'Bohemian Rhapsody' (5'30), 'Hammer To Fall' (5'07), 'Crazy Little Thing Called Love' (4'53), 'Radio Ga Ga' (6'12), 'We Will Rock You' (3'02), 'Friends Will Be Friends' (2'01), 'We Are The Champions' (3'52), 'God Save The Queen' (1'21)

Blu-Ray/DVD: 'One Vision' (5'36), 'Tie Your Mother Down' (4'42), 'In The Lap Of The Gods … Revisited' (2'17), 'Seven Seas Of Rhye' (1'41), 'Tear It Up' (1'47), 'A Kind Of Magic' (8'21), 'Under Pressure' (3'50), 'Who Wants To Live Forever' (3'59), 'I Want To Break Free' (3'33), 'Guitar Solo' (7'24), 'Now I'm Here' (5'58), 'Love Of My Life' (4'37), 'Tavaszi Szél Vizet Áraszt' (2'16), 'Is This The World We Created…?' (2'32), 'Tutti Frutti' (3'36), 'Bohemian Rhapsody' (5'30), 'Hammer To Fall' (5'07), 'Crazy Little Thing Called Love' (4'53), 'Radio Ga Ga' (6'12), 'We Will Rock You' (3'02), 'Friends Will Be Friends' (2'01), 'We Are The Champions' (3'52), 'God Save The Queen' (1'21), Documentary: *A Magic Year*

Musicians: John Deacon *(bass guitar)*, Brian May *(guitars, vocals, keyboards on 'Who Wants To Live Forever', acoustic guitar on 'Love Of My Life', 'Is This The World We Created…?', '(You're So Square) Baby I Don't Care', 'Hello Mary Lou (Goodbye Heart)', 'Tutti Frutti', and 'Crazy Little Thing Called Love')*, Freddie Mercury *(vocals, piano, rhythm guitar on 'Crazy Little Thing Called Love')*, Roger Taylor *(drums, vocals, effects on 'A Kind Of Magic', tambourine on '(You're So Square) Baby I Don't Care', 'Hello Mary Lou (Goodbye Heart)', and 'Tutti Frutti')*, Spike Edney *(keyboards, vocals, piano on 'Crazy Little Thing Called Love', rhythm guitar on 'Hammer To Fall')*
Recorded: 27 July 1986, at Nepstadion, Budapest by Mack
Producers: Justin Shirley-Smith, Joshua J Macrae, Kris Fredriksson, Brian May, Roger Taylor, Jim Beach

Queen Productions mined the seemingly endless supply of live shows recorded and filmed during the Magic Tour in 2012, with a beautifully restored edition of their Budapest concert, performed the day after Roger's 37th birthday. Previously released on VHS only as *Live In Budapest*, the awkwardly-titled *Hungarian Rhapsody: Queen Live In Budapest* (itself a nod to Hungarian composer Franz Liszt's 'Hungarian Rhapsody', as well as a reference to Queen's most famous song) is a fascinating document of the band at the height of their powers, bringing their massive set to a region of the world that few bands had been able to travel to during the Cold War.

The difference between the previous release and this release is, of course, the availability of the entirety of the concert on disc, with four previously unreleased tracks – 'Another One Bites The Dust', the improvisation 'Looks Like It's Gonna Be A Good Night' (here given an official title as opposed to the less imaginative 'Impromptu' on *Live At Wembley Stadium*), '(You're So Square) Baby I Don't Care', and 'Hello Mary Lou (Goodbye Heart)' – that had been excised from the VHS release. Unfortunately, film footage of these tracks didn't survive, having been discarded by the original film crew, MaFilm, as film was rather expensive in the Eastern Bloc in 1986.

The band are truly enjoying themselves here, and while they give off an air of little pretense with their performance – some of the songs are a little more ramshackle than usual, especially compared to the Wembley concert – they were still a bucket of nerves, with Brian later commenting, "It was the band's most challenging and exhilarating gig." There's a sense of camaraderie during the acoustic rock'n'roll medley, with the band engaging in a bit of light improvisational hijinx between 'Hello Mary Lou (Goodbye Heart)' and 'Tutti Frutti', with Freddie especially shining with some delightful scat vocalisations.

Released in November 2012, two months after the film was premiered in theatres worldwide, *Hungarian Rhapsody: Queen Live In Budapest* was packaged as a CD/DVD or CD/Blu-Ray release, with a deluxe edition box set and standalone DVD and Blu-Ray releases. The film featured a newly-constructed documentary by Simon Lupton, entitled *A Magic Year*, which followed the path from Queen's performance at Live Aid, which had rejuvenated their career, to the conclusion of the Magic Tour. *NME* was complimentary of the release: "Freddie Mercury once claimed that Queen were 'the Cecil B DeMille of rock and roll'. The only way to test that hypothesis was to project footage of the band onto the biggest screen possible to see if they

hold the attention of cinema-goers like the visionary film-maker once did. Which is exactly what *Hungarian Rhapsody* does, to great success. From opening number, 'One Vision', *Live In Budapest* reminds those that may have forgotten that Queen are, quite simply, one of the most important bands of the 20th Century and in Freddie Mercury, they lay claim to one of, if not, the greatest frontman of all time.

Watching Mercury capture and captivate the crowd conjures up the cocksure claim by Stillwater lead singer Jeff Bebe in *Almost Famous*; 'You know what I do? I connect. I get people off. I look for the guy who isn't getting off, and I make him get off'. Freddie got people off. You may have heard 'Bohemian Rhapsody' a million times before, just like the enthusiastic crowd here, but he delivers it with a freshness that makes you forget its overuse over 25 years on … Where *Hungarian Rhapsody* lets itself down is in its brief jaunts outside of the venue. 'See Roger Taylor Go-Karting! See Brian May in a hot-air balloon!' No thanks. This narrative choice offers nothing but rock stars looking bored. We're here to see Queen play music. This isn't a documentary, it's a concert movie and there are distinct differences, top of which is it should feel like you're at a concert. This behind the scenes bullshit, doesn't make us feel like VIPs, it just removes us from the atmosphere, like being forced to get up and go for a piddle every 20 minutes. And while this does detract – *Hungarian Rhapsody* lacks the flow of truly great concert movies like Talking Heads' *Stop Making Sense* or *The Last Waltz* – compared to recent cinema releases for the likes of Katy Perry and Justin Bieber, this, to use Freddie's own parlance, is "The Greatest Show On Earth."

"The intro section, with its TV news footage, lulls you into expecting the usual lo-fi visuals you get with live concert films," *The Guardian* wrote in a four-out-of-five star review. "But we soon realise that the Hungarian state film department employed dozens of film cameras to record Queen's momentous 1986 concert; what we get is very much *Queen: The Movie*. Still running on the momentum of Live Aid, Queen were at the height of their powers as a live act, and the roar of the 100,000-plus crowd becomes a component of the songs. This is a band who lived to be on stage, and this is the best document I've seen of that experience." *The Independent* was a little less complimentary: "Filmed in the aftermath of their Live Aid performance – arguably the highlight of their career – this is a humdrum account of Queen's Magic Tour and its climax in Budapest, the first stadium-rock concert to be staged behind what was then the Iron

Curtain. The build-up, featuring interviews with the band, looks very dated now, like an extended slot from Nationwide. The concert itself springs few surprises, confirming the band's studious professionalism, knack for a crowd-pleasing tune and, Mercury aside, utter lack of stage charisma. It didn't appear to do them any harm." *PopMatters* gave the package eight out of 10 stars: "Some day, when you're trying to explain to your grandchildren what stadium rock was all about, I recommend showing them *Hungarian Rhapsody: Queen Live in Budapest*, the concert film of Queen's 1986 performance in Budapest. It's not only a great concert film that captures the spirit of Queen at the height of their powers, but also documents an important moment in the history of Eastern Europe during the Cold War (something else you might have to explain to the grandkids) … The audience is with the band every step of the way. One reason Queen could play stadiums and fill them up was because they had the ability to make everyone in the audience feel like they were part of a great occasion. That ability was on full display in Budapest, where an estimated 80,000 fans packed Budapest's Népstadion ('people's stadium' – this was during the Cold War, remember?) to hear Queen perform, making it the largest concert ever performed in that stadium … As long as *Hungarian Rhapsody* sticks to presenting Queen's concert performance, it never sets a foot wrong. Unfortunately, the film includes some fairly lame material as well, of the type that might be used on a local television station to promote the idea that the members of Queen are ordinary folks just like you and I. So you get to see Roger Taylor go-karting and Freddie Mercury sampling a local distilled beverage, and you quickly understand why none of them went into acting (well, Mercury might have made a go of it, but not the others). Fortunately, there's not too much of this silly stuff in the main film. *Hungarian Rhapsody: Queen Live in Budapest* released in a set with two CDs that include all the songs in the film, plus a few more. Besides the illustrated liner notes, the only other extra is a 26-minute documentary which intends to chronicle Queen's "magic year" from Live Aid to the end of the Magic Tour, but feels cobbled together from grainy television footage and gushing endorsements from their contemporaries. None of that really matters though, because the concert film is so good that it can easily stand on its own."

LIVE AT THE RAINBOW '74

Virgin EMI Records 0602537910687 *(double-disc edition)*, September 2014 [11]
Hollywood Records D002044902 *(double-disc edition)*, September 2014 [66]
Virgin EMI Records 0602537910717 *(2-LP vinyl edition)*, September 2014 [11]
Hollywood Records D002083101 *(2-LP vinyl edition)*, September 2014 [66]
Virgin EMI Records 0602537910748 *(4-LP box set edition)*, September 2014 [11]
Virgin EMI Records 00602537910809 *(double-disc Blu-Ray and DVD edition)*, September 2014 [11]
Hollywood Records D002084700 *(double-disc Blu-Ray and DVD edition)*, September 2014 [66]

Double-disc and 4-LP vinyl box set edition: 'Procession', 'Father To Son', 'Ogre Battle', 'Son And Daughter', Guitar Solo, 'Son And Daughter' *(reprise)*, 'White Queen (As It Began)', 'Great King Rat', 'The Fairy Feller's Master-Stroke', 'Keep Yourself Alive', Drum Solo, 'Keep Yourself Alive' *(reprise)*, 'Seven Seas Of Rhye', 'Modern Times Rock 'n' Roll', 'Jailhouse Rock' / 'Stupid Cupid' / 'Be Bop A Lula', 'Liar', 'See What A Fool I've Been', 'Procession', 'Now I'm Here', 'Ogre Battle', 'Father To Son', 'White Queen (As It Began)', 'Flick Of The Wrist', 'In The Lap Of The Gods', 'Killer Queen', 'The March Of The Black Queen', 'Bring Back That Leroy Brown', 'Son And Daughter', Guitar Solo, 'Son And Daughter' *(reprise)*, 'Keep Yourself Alive', Drum Solo, 'Keep Yourself Alive' *(reprise)*, 'Seven Seas Of Rhye', 'Stone Cold Crazy', 'Liar', 'In The Lap Of The Gods…Revisited', 'Big Spender', 'Modern Times Rock 'n' Roll', 'Jailhouse Rock', 'God Save The Queen'

Standard DVD and SD Blu-Ray: 'Procession', 'Now I'm Here', 'Ogre Battle', 'Father To Son', 'White Queen (As It Began)', 'Flick Of The Wrist', 'In The Lap Of The Gods', 'Killer Queen', 'The March Of The Black Queen', 'Bring Back That Leroy Brown', 'Son And Daughter', Guitar Solo, 'Son And Daughter' *(reprise)*, 'Keep Yourself Alive', Drum Solo, 'Keep Yourself Alive' *(reprise)*, 'Seven Seas Of Rhye', 'Stone Cold Crazy', 'Liar', 'In The Lap Of The Gods…Revisited', 'Big Spender', 'Modern Times Rock 'n' Roll', 'Jailhouse Rock'. Bonus tracks: 'Son And Daughter', Guitar Solo, 'Son And Daughter' *(reprise)*, 'Modern Times Rock 'n' Roll'

2-LP vinyl edition: 'Procession', 'Father To Son', 'Ogre Battle', 'Son And Daughter', Guitar Solo, 'Son And

Daughter *(reprise)*, 'Keep Yourself Alive', Drum Solo, 'Keep Yourself Alive' *(reprise)*, 'Seven Seas Of Rhye', 'Modern Times Rock 'n' Roll', 'Liar', 'Procession', 'Now I'm Here', 'White Queen (As It Began)', 'Flick Of The Wrist', 'In The Lap Of The Gods', 'Killer Queen', 'The March Of The Black Queen', 'Bring Back That Leroy Brown', 'Stone Cold Crazy', 'In The Lap Of The Gods…Revisited'

Musicians: John Deacon *(bass guitar, vocals, triangle on 'Killer Queen')*, Brian May *(guitars, vocals, ukulele on 'Bring Back That Leroy Brown')*, Freddie Mercury *(vocals, piano, tambourine, janglebox on 'The Fairy Feller's Master-Stroke')*, Roger Taylor *(drums, percussion, vocals)*
Recorded: 31 March 1974 and 19 and 20 November 1974, The Rainbow Theatre, London by Roy Thomas Baker
Producers: Justin Shirley-Smith, Kris Fredriksson, Joshua J Macrae, Brian May, and Roger Taylor

It had been seven years since Queen Productions released any archival live material, which, considering the paucity of live material from other bands – contemporary mementos of the respective tours are better souvenirs for fans who were there – what Queen fans had gotten to that date is to be commended, though fans, subscribing to the chorus of 'I Want It All', demanded more. And even though it took some time, the live archives were opened up in September 2014, with the multi-format release of *Live At The Rainbow '74*. (Thankfully, the goofy, cringe-inducing album titles had been dropped, albeit temporarily.)

Originally slated to be Queen's third album – a multi-track reel-to-reel tape from Elektra was mastered on 27 January 1975, with appropriate overdubs administered by the band just prior to the mastering – the 31 March 1974 concert saw the band truly on top of their form, with none of the arena or stadium grandstanding that would eventually overshadow some of their subsequent live albums. The band is tight but loose, displaying the perfect amount of light and shade that their early shows thrived on; the energy is palpable, not only from the band, but from the audience, and it's clear that the fans are absolutely loving every moment of the show. There's very little patter between Freddie and the audience, but when he does talk, there's a theatrical level of menace that truly delights the crowd.

Unfortunately, Queen's first live album was to be delayed: Brian was stricken with hepatitis during their first North American tour, forcing the band's hand to adapt to the unexpected hiatus. And so the Rainbow gig was put on the backburner while the band wrote and recorded *Sheer Heart Attack*. By the time the Rainbow concert was ready to be released, Queen had moved on, and frustrations with their management resulted in an prolonged legal battle, meaning some of the more interesting diversions – *Live At The Rainbow* and a re-recorded 'Keep Yourself Alive' for the North American market – were canceled outright. (The March concert was eventually bootlegged in 1975 as *Sheetkickers*, becoming the first Queen bootleg on the market.)

That's not to say that there weren't plans anyway to release something. The band returned to the Rainbow Theatre in November 1974, where they performed their typical *Sheer Heart Attack* tour repertoire, with a film crew present in addition to the multi-track recorder. The band were less than pleased with the experience, as the film crew kept getting in the way, but that didn't prevent them from assembling a final film of the performance, which Brian later wrote in the spring 1975 Queen fan club magazine that was to be mixed and edited for *The Old Grey Whistle Test*, though this never panned out; a half-hour edit was shown before Led Zeppelin's *The Song Remains The Same* in 1976, *Jaws II* in 1978, and Pink Floyd's *Live At Pompeii* in 1979 and *The Wall* in 1982. A more expanded edit, running 52 minutes, was finally released on VHS in 1992 as part of the *Box Of Trix*.

While fans would have likely been content with an expanded, full concert of the November 1974 Rainbow gigs, Queen Productions threw in the bonus of the March 1974 concert, which wasn't filmed but was still of historical significance; to sweeten the pot, the full concert was presented, which contained for the first time a live recording of 'The Fairy Feller's Master-Stroke', long believed to have been performed live only a handful of times due to its complexity. (For the record, the band pull it off superbly, and it's a shame the song didn't last beyond the *Queen II* tour.) Released on CD, DVD, LP, and as an all-inclusive box set, *Live At The Rainbow* earned unparalleled praise from fans and critics alike, with Roger even noting how raw and raucous the band sounds, a far cry from the slick extravaganzas of their later tours. *PopMatters* gushed, "Holy shit, to have been there to see this. The Rainbow was a 3,000-seat venue, but from the majestic opening chords of 'Father To Son' on, Queen delivers a massive-sounding spectacle fit for Wembley. Brian May's guitars are upfront and gutsy, his effect-pedal mastery making them sound everywhere at once.

Roger Taylor is downright frenetic at times, his fills rolling like boulders. And of course, Freddie Mercury's voice towers above it all, soothing and cajoling like electrified silk.

Then comes the perennial live favorite 'Ogre Battle', a song that represents everything that makes *Queen II* one of the all-time slept-on classics – blazing, jittery blues riffage, operatic harmonies, and wild lines like 'the ogre men are still inside the two-way mirror mountain'. *Live At The Rainbow '74* gives us two chances to hear Queen play 'Ogre Battle' when it was fresh in their minds, and that alone makes it a treasure."

A NIGHT AT THE ODEON: HAMMERSMITH 1975

Virgin EMI Records 0602547500694, November 2015 [40]
Hollywood Records D002236102, November 2015
Virgin EMI Records 0602547578471 *(CD/DVD edition)*, November 2015 [40]
Eagle Vision EV307299 *(DVD edition)*, November 2015
Virgin EMI Records 0602547500717 *(Blu-Ray edition)*, November 2015
Eagle Vision EVSBD30980 *(Blu-Ray edition)*, November 2015
Virgin EMI Records 0602547500748 *(2-LP vinyl edition)*, November 2015 [40]
Virgin EMI Records 0602547500779, Virgin EMI Records D002262800 *(CD, Blu-Ray/DVD, and 12" vinyl box set edition)*, November 2015

CD and 2-LP editions: 'Now I'm Here' (4'43), 'Ogre Battle' (5'19), 'White Queen (As It Began)' (5'31), 'Bohemian Rhapsody' (2'28), 'Killer Queen' (2'08), 'The March Of The Black Queen' (1'30), "Bohemian Rhapsody' *(reprise)* (1'02), 'Bring Back That Leroy Brown' (1'32), 'Brighton Rock' (2'24), 'Guitar Solo' (6'37), 'Son And Daughter' (1'44), 'Keep Yourself Alive' (4'33), 'Liar' (8'45), 'In The Lap Of The Gods … Revisited' (5'24), 'Big Spender' (1'24), 'Jailhouse Rock' / 'Stupid Cupid' / 'Be Bop A Lula' / 'Shake, Rattle & Roll' / 'Jailhouse Rock' *(reprise)* (9'21), 'Seven Seas Of Rhye' (3'11), 'See What A Fool I've Been' (4'22), 'God Save The Queen' (1'23)

Blu-Ray and CD/DVD edition: 'Now I'm Here' (4'43), 'Ogre Battle' (5'19), 'White Queen (As It Began)' (5'31), 'Bohemian Rhapsody' (2'28), 'Killer Queen' (2'08), 'The March Of The Black Queen' (1'30), "Bohemian Rhapsody' (reprise) (1'02), 'Bring Back That Leroy Brown' (1'32), 'Brighton Rock' (2'24), 'Guitar Solo'

(6'37), 'Son And Daughter' (1'44), 'Keep Yourself Alive' (4'33), 'Liar' (8'45), 'In The Lap Of The Gods … Revisited' (5'24), 'Big Spender' (1'24), 'Jailhouse Rock' / 'Stupid Cupid' / 'Be Bop A Lula' / 'Shake, Rattle & Roll' / 'Jailhouse Rock' (reprise) (9'21), 'God Save The Queen' (1'23), 'Now I'm Here' *(recorded live at the Budokan, Toko, 1 May 1975)*, 'Killer Queen' *(recorded live at the Budokan, Toko, 1 May 1975)*, 'In The Lap Of The Gods … Revisited' *(recorded live at the Budokan, Toko, 1 May 1975)*, Documentary: *Looking Back At The Odeon*

DVD edition: 'Now I'm Here' (4'43), 'Ogre Battle' (5'19), 'White Queen (As It Began)' (5'31), 'Bohemian Rhapsody' (2'28), 'Killer Queen' (2'08), 'The March Of The Black Queen' (1'30), "Bohemian Rhapsody' (reprise) (1'02), 'Bring Back That Leroy Brown' (1'32), 'Brighton Rock' (2'24), 'Guitar Solo' (6'37), 'Son And Daughter' (1'44), 'Keep Yourself Alive' (4'33), 'Liar' (8'45), 'In The Lap Of The Gods … Revisited' (5'24), 'Big Spender' (1'24), 'Jailhouse Rock' / 'Stupid Cupid' / 'Be Bop A Lula' / 'Shake, Rattle & Roll' / 'Jailhouse Rock' (reprise) (9'21), 'God Save The Queen' (1'23), 'Now I'm Here' *(recorded live at the Budokan, Toko, 1 May 1975)*, 'Killer Queen' *(recorded live at the Budokan, Toko, 1 May 1975)*, 'In The Lap Of The Gods … Revisited' *(recorded live at the Budokan, Toko, 1 May 1975)*

12" vinyl in box set edition: 'Bohemian Rhapsody' (5'55), 'Now I'm Here' *(soundcheck, recorded 24 December 1975)* (5'03)

Musicians: John Deacon *(bass guitar, vocals, triangle on 'Killer Queen')*, Brian May *(guitars, vocals, ukulele on 'Bring Back That Leroy Brown')*, Freddie Mercury *(vocals, piano, tambourine)*, Roger Taylor *(drums, percussion, vocals)*
Recorded: 24 December 1975 at Hammersmith Odeon, London
Producers: Justin Shirley-Smith, Kris Fredriksson, Joshua J Macrae, Brian May, and Roger Taylor

Following the release of *Live At The Rainbow '74*, Queen's next archival release was predictably their landmark performance at the Hammersmith Odeon, which had been broadcast live on BBC2's *The Old Grey Whistle Test* (public demand dictated the show would be retransmitted the following year on 28 December). Radio One aired a nearly complete version on 28 February 1976, which allowed fans to record it properly for posterity; as a result, this became Queen's next biggest bootleg release, leaking out onto the black market under many guises: *Command Performance*, *There Ain't No Sanity Clause*, and *X-Mas 1975* being the most common.

This performance is no less electrifying than the Rainbow gigs, but with Queen's confidence growing exponentially following the success of 'Bohemian Rhapsody' and *A Night At The Opera*, there's a little less bite than there was to the tour supporting *Sheer Heart Attack*. Perhaps the band were exhausted from their massive live campaign *and* writing and recording their most successful album to date, but the main reason the performance is a little less frenetic was due to nerves: they were playing to their largest audience to date – not only within the Odeon, but to Britain itself on television, with tens of thousands of viewers witnessing the concert. Brian would later recall that "Freddie and I, though me particularly, had dreadful flu and could hardly walk, let alone play – so it wasn't one of our greatest performances. But it was still all very exciting. It was the adrenaline that kept us going." Roger later remembered that it was he who was feeling unwell, though this was more down to anxiety about losing momentum that had been built up during the British tour, as the Hammersmith gig was a week after the conclusion of their *A Night At The Opera* tour.

Regardless of nerves, influenza, and the imposing film crew, the band still turned in an electrifying performance, and while it wouldn't have worked as a contemporaneous live album (indeed, the band had abandoned any intentions of releasing a live album, for the time being), it's a startling artefact from a time before Queen became a grandstanding stadium act, with more focus being placed on presenting an act than a theatrical experience. The set list, too, reflected this: due to time constraints, the band had to restructure the set list, meaning 'Now I'm Here' became the opener (which worked very well for television, with Freddie appearing on both sides of the stage – a delightful trick of the light achieved by a stagehand dressing up in a spare Zandra Rhodes outfit) and 'Seven Seas Of Rhye' becoming an encore number. (This latter choice was likely a mistake, as Freddie noted to the audience that they had forgotten to play it.) The band are also on fire, running on all cylinders and turning in a truly spectacular show, once again subscribing to the tight but loose manifesto, with the most dazzling performance being the eight minute medley of hits, bookended by 'Bohemian Rhapsody' and with a semi-instrumental taster of 'Bring Back That Leroy Brown' to lighten the mood. The encore, which wasn't filmed as the film crew had packed up for the night, featured a particularly electrifying rendition of 'See What A Fool I've Been', long a concert favorite and a perfect conclusion to the night.

For years, the multitracks of the show were believed to have been lost until they were discovered in 2009 and suitably restored by Queen's sound engineers Justin Shirley-Smith, Joshua J Macrae, and Kris Fredriksson. A remastered, 50-minute version was televised on BBC2 that Christmas, leading to requests from fans that the concert be released properly; it took six more years before the show was released, once again in a variety of formats (CD, DVD, Blu-Ray, vinyl, and a deluxe box set containing memorabilia) and with such delightful bonuses as performances from their 1975 Japanese tour, a 22-minute documentary titled *Looking Back At The Odeon*, and a 12" vinyl single release containing 'Now I'm Here' from the day's soundcheck backing 'Bohemian Rhapsody'.

The remastered concert was premiered at the former Olympic Studios (now known as Olympic Studios Cinema), where, of course, some of *A Night At The Opera* had been recorded, on 8 October 2015; in attendance was Brian, who fielded questions later from *Rolling Stone*. He recalled with fondness, "It was very weird. It seems like watching another person, that young boy. I look so thin! I look very serious and the body language is so different now – I was quite shy in those days. There was a lot of noise and energy in the playing, but my body is different from the way I am now. These days I feel a channel in the body towards the noise that's coming out, but in those days it looks like it just comes from nowhere … It felt great at the time. There was a lot of adrenalin, a lot of joy because all our fans who'd followed us on the tour had all scrambled to get in there. Roger was really sick – he looks pretty good but he was feeling really bad. I think he threw up afterwards but you wouldn't know."

Released in November 2015, *A Night At The Odeon: Hammersmith 1975* earned rave reviews from critics and fans alike, and soared to No. 40 in the charts, no mean feat for an archival live release. "Eagle Rock Entertainment has unearthed an amazing trip back in time with the release of *A Night At The Odeon*," *Classic Rock Revisited* gushed. "We are talking the band Queen, live in 1975, in living color and great sound! The full set list is stellar, and features that now-four-decades-old classic 'Bohemian Rhapsody'. As epic as that tune is, the entire concert is what counts here … This era of Queen was much more than just a one hit song! … At the end of the day, this was a concert that is so good it will find its way back into your living room time after time after time. This was the real Queen, scratching and clawing their way to the top in an uncompromising and triumphant manner." *PopMatters* wrote, "It seemed not too long ago that Queen had just a couple of live albums. Plenty more have popped up over the years since frontman Freddie Mercury's passing, ones that conveniently give listeners glimpses of the Queen eras not documented on *Live Killers* and *Live At Wembley '86*. A new one has just been added to their canon, one that is trumpeted so proudly that it's a slight wonder that it hasn't been properly released before … This album captures the mighty glam-pop band playing to a packed house and a cluster of BBC cameras beaming their show into living rooms across the United Kingdom as its citizens hung their stockings with care. It must have come as a shock to some. When you combine the progressive musical leanings of the band's early sound with their taste for flamboyant theatrics while factoring in the fact that Queen could rock like crazy, the end concoction could have been terrifying to someone hoping for a relaxing evening in front of the television. Never having a chance to see Queen live, I tried to pester a friend of mine into telling me her experience of getting dragged by her older sister to see them some time in the late '70s. The most I can get out of her is 'I just remember I was scared' … There has been speculation on whether Queen were jesting their way through their career or if their appreciation for kitsch was reaching some profound new levels. *Melody Maker*'s Hammersmith Odeon show announcement of 'Britain's most regal band awaits your presence…'

certainly has a hammy ring all its own, as if the writing staff were gleefully awaiting for the band to fall flat on its face that night. But I wasn't there. One thing that is clear is that Queen were serious about their shows. True, *A Night At The Opera* once held the distinction of the most expensive album ever recorded due to the band's meticulous approach to perfection. At the same time, they wanted to make sure that the people sitting in the back of the balcony always got their money's worth. So, use this year's holiday season as an opportunity to turn the clock back to a simpler time. You know, a time when a six-minute mash-up of opera and rock could reach number one in the charts."

Queen fans *Record Collector* gave the album four stars: "Long a bootlegger favourite, the sumptuously remastered audio-visual feast of *A Night At The Odeon: Hammersmith 1975* finds Queen at the halfway house between what they were and what they became. Here, in its full glory, is the Christmas Eve show that was broadcast live on the BBC, promoting their new release, *A Night At The Opera*, just over a month old at the time. You simply can't take your eyes off Freddie Mercury; at the height of his knife'n'fork glam-mod haircut, jumpsuit and black nails era, he commands the performance. Brian May, John Deacon and Roger Taylor play as if their lives depend on it. 'Bohemian Rhapsody', then halfway through its run at the UK No. 1 spot, was at this point just another number in the set, starting and ending a medley of 'Killer Queen' and 'The March Of The Black Queen'. *RC* knows a lot of serious punks who absolutely worshipped the first three Queen albums (though, of course, they would never admit it at the time), and when you hear some of the spiky noise here, it is easy to see why."

B. SOLO ALBUMS

The second part of this section concentrates on studio, live and compilation albums that Roger Taylor, Freddie Mercury and Brian May have released. The albums are presented *chronologically instead of by band member, in order to present a broader overview of the solo work of Queen.*

ROGER TAYLOR
FUN IN SPACE

EMI EMC 3369, April 1981 [18]
Elektra 5E-522, April 1981 [121]
Parlophone CDPCS 7380, August 1996

'No Violins' (4'33), 'Laugh Or Cry' (3'06), 'Future Management (You Don't Need Nobody Else)' (3'03), 'Let's Get Crazy' (3'40), 'My Country I & II' (6'49), 'Good Times Are Now' (3'28), 'Magic Is Loose' (3'30), 'Interlude In Constantinople' (2'04), 'Airheads' (3'38), 'Fun In Space' (6'22)

Musicians: Roger Taylor *(vocals, drums, percussion, guitars, bass guitar, synthesizers)*, David Richards *(synthesizers)*
Recorded: Mountain Studios, Montreux, August 1979-January 1981
Producer: Roger Taylor

Towards the end of the initial sessions for *The Game* in July 1979, while the others returned to their families in England, Roger remained at Mountain Studios to work on ideas for his first solo album. 'I Wanna Testify', released back in August 1977, had whetted the drummer's appetite for solo success, though it was anything but: the single had failed and Roger was £5000 poorer from the experience, though he'd had a lot of fun along the way. During sessions for *Jazz* in 1978, he had started writing more and more songs, not so much intended for Queen use as his own.

"In the past, I have written so many songs," Roger said, "that it was impossible to put them on a Queen album. So a solo album was the only possibility ... There were certain things I wanted to do which weren't within the Queen format; in a way, it's like flushing out your system, and until you've done it you just don't feel fulfilled. If I get more ideas for songs I might eventually do another solo thing, but Queen would always get priority."

Hence the extended recording period for the album: he was able to lay down a few ideas in the summer of 1979, but had to cut work short in order to tour

with Queen. Sessions continued off and on during downtime while recording *The Game* in the winter of 1980 but band prorities meant that Roger had little time to focus on his own album until Queen worked on *Flash Gordon* in the autumn of 1980. Because most of the performances on the soundtrack were done separately, Roger was able to complete most of his album during those sessions, with the work stretching well into January 1981, in order to complete the album in time for an April deadline.

It's interesting, then, though hardly coincidental, that *Fun In Space* sounds so much like *Flash Gordon*. Borrowing the darker ambience of that soundtrack and incorporating synthesizers to an extreme, Roger wrote more sombre, atmospheric and downright moody songs that belie his rock 'n' roll roots. "Yes, [the diversity of the material is] probably the only weak point, where the critics might accuse me," he told *Popcorn* in 1981. "But on my first solo album I took the opportunity to show my whole spectrum. The second album will be more new wave." In fact, Roger explores that genre throughout this *first* album: 'Future Management' is decidedly cod-reggae, taking a cue from The Police, while a pair of songs on the second side – 'Good Times Are Now' and 'Airheads' – sound like an amalgamation of punk and new wave. Only on the two more ambitious numbers, 'My Country I & II' and the title track, does Roger consciously stray towards Queen territory, while 'No Violins' and 'Magic Is Loose' could easily be out-takes from *The Game*.

Carrying on the tradition of 'I Wanna Testify', Roger played all the instruments himself, with "50% of synthesizers by David Richards" according to the liner notes. Why? "There are different reasons," Roger explained to *Popcorn*. "First, I have my own ideas how the songs should sound. It's more important to show several abilities of my own. In the end I don't want to spend my life being behind the drums. There are lots of other drummers who show that solo albums are not only an affair of guitar-players, singers or keyboard-players." Roger was the band member who promoted the use of synthesizers, so it's no surprise that the album is abounding with them. Layer upon layer of keyboards were programmed and played by Roger, with some of the trickier synth work given to David Richards. The material and the mood is spacy enough for the synths to work well, especially on the two epics, though they also create atmospheric tones on songs like 'Magic Is Loose' and 'Laugh Or Cry', and are absolutely essential for 'Interlude In Constantinople'.

Reinforcing the tone of the sci-fi lyrics, the cover portrays an alien ("It's called Ernie and comes from an American Comic series," he explained to *Popcorn*. "I like the little beast that much, that I use it as a logo") reading a magazine with Roger on the cover, with the roles reversed for the back cover. "The title *Fun In Space* doesn't mean that the album should be regarded as *Son Of Flash Gordon*," Roger explained, "but in many ways it is nostalgic ... I've got some old sci-fi books and magazines which I browse through from time to time. Maybe there are things up there in space watching us. I wouldn't find that surprising at all." Incidentally, the alien creature was a model designed by Tim Staffell, who had no idea what project the monster was for or to whom it was connected. "In 1981, after I'd packed in music altogether," Tim told *Record Collector* in 1996, "I made a model for an album cover for the Hipgnosis design team. It was of a little alien head with glowing eyes. I didn't know what it was for, but it turned out – and I didn't discover this until years later – to be the front cover for Roger's *Fun In Space* album! I had no idea. That was peculiar."

Considering that Queen were at their busiest during the early 1980s, it was inevitable that the question of a solo tour would be raised. "No! Never!" the drummer exclaimed. "First of all, Queen is much more important than my solo career. Second, the band demands so much from me that I have no time for a solo tour." A shame, since *Fun In Space* remained Roger's most neglected album in his solo tours over the years, with 'Let's Get Crazy' being the only regular on The Cross' first tour in 1988, though 'Magic Is Loose' would finally be premiered in 2001. Roger was admittedly "so mentally exhausted [afterwards] that I couldn't even be trusted to select the single", so it was appropriate for EMI to do all the promotion work while he worked on the next Queen record.

The album, issued in April 1981 after the release of 'Future Management' the previous month, was a modest success, peaking at No. 18 in the UK, though it stalled at a disappointing No. 121 in the US. The reviews ranged from kind ("This is *Son Of Flash*

Gordon; it has similar comic book style characteristics. Listening to this is the most fun you'll have apart from playing Space Invaders." – *Record Mirror*) to caustic ("Revelling in bombastic arrogance, so redolent of Queen. A rich man's self-indulgence run riot over two sides of an album." – *Melody Maker*), but fan opinion of the album was whole-heartedly favorable. Although he would go on to bigger and better things over his next six albums (both as a solo artist and with The Cross), *Fun In Space* is a superb debut from a multitalented drummer.

BRIAN MAY & FRIENDS
STAR FLEET PROJECT
EMI SFLT 1078061, October 1983 [35]
Capitol MLP15014, November 1983 [125]

'Star Fleet' (8'06), 'Let Me Out' (7'13), 'Blues Breaker' (12'51)

Musicians: Brian May *(vocals, guitar)*, Edward Van Halen *(guitar)*, Alan Gratzer *(drums)*, Phil Chen *(bass guitar)*, Fred Mandel *(keyboards)*, Roger Taylor *(backing vocals on 'Star Fleet') Recorded:* The Record Plant, Los Angeles, 21/22 April 1983
Producer: Brian May

April 1983 found Brian with little to do. Queen had just taken a temporary leave of absence from both the studio and the live circuit, with Freddie and Roger focusing on solo projects. Reluctant to do the same, mostly because he didn't have a backlog of material he felt compelled to get out, Brian nevertheless booked time at Los Angeles' The Record Plant and flew from Paris to California in the middle of the month. After a minor dispute with the airline company – Brian refused to entrust his guitar to the luggage handlers and was forced to buy a seat for The Red Special since it was deemed too large for carry-on purposes – he arrived in the City of Angels and contributed guitar to Jeffrey Osborne's 'Stay With Me Tonight' and 'Two Wrongs Don't Make A Right'.

He then entered The Record Plant with the seed of a project in the back of his mind and called upon a group of musician friends to help him out, hoping that whatever they produced would be worthy of release. The first call was to Eddie Van Halen, guitarist of then megarockers Van Halen, soon to score international success with the release of *1984* and the single 'Jump'. Brian had admired Eddie for many years, and had even employed his two-handed tapping method on Queen's own 'It's Late' in 1977. REO Speedwagon drummer Alan Gratzer and Rod Stewart bassist Phil Chen made up the rhythm section, while Elton John keyboardist Fred Mandel, who had toured with Queen on the US and Japanese legs of their Hot Space tour the previous year, rounded out the group.

The initial idea was to jam for a few days and then maybe lay down a few songs, but those jams quickly produced two completed songs: 'Let Me Out', written by Brian many years before and initially intended for an undetermined Queen album, and 'Blues Breaker', inspired by original axe master Eric 'Slowhand' Clapton and influenced by his time with John Mayall. The only song brought to the sessions was 'Star Fleet', Brian's revised musical rendition of the popular Saturday morning Japanese cartoon, with lyrics originally written by Paul Bliss. The sessions proved fruitful but Brian was unsure if he wanted to release the results; regardless, he received permission from all involved, just in case.

That October, Queen signed a new record deal with Capitol Records for distribution in North America, and Brian signed a solo deal for what would become *Star Fleet Project* and for other future solo projects, which were never realized. He quickly began mixing the tapes and, because there wasn't enough material for a full-length album, decided that *Star Fleet Project* would be a three-track mini-album, or EP. Since it was essentially an all-star jam session, it was credited as "Brian May + Friends" and the results are a mixed bag of rock, sci-fi and blues, three genres which Brian adored.

The project was creatively liberating for the guitarist, who hadn't yet worked with other musicians while he was in control. Take, for instance, the running times of the songs: the shortest song just breaks seven minutes, while the longest comes close to 13 minutes, meaning that any and every good idea was used. For fans of blues and rock, *Star Fleet Project* was a treat; for fans of Brian, it was especially interesting to see what direction he was taking, and after the disappointing *Hot Space* album the year before, it was a relief to hear the guitarist let his curly locks down and have some fun.

The mini-album was released at the end of October 1983, and it reached No. 35 in the UK charts (No. 1 in the British Heavy Metal Charts), peaking at a less impressive No. 125 in the US. It has since become one of the more sought-after Queen-related solo projects, since it remains unreleased as a stand-alone CD.

In 1993, it was released as part of a two-part CD for Brian's 'Resurrection' single, but is long overdue for a proper re-release.

ROGER TAYLOR
STRANGE FRONTIER

EMI RTA 1, June 1984 [30]
Capitol SJ 12357, July 1984
Parlophone CDPCS 7381, August 1996

UK vinyl: 'Strange Frontier' (4'16), 'Beautiful Dreams' (4'23), 'Man On Fire' (4'04), 'Racing In The Street' (4'27), 'Masters Of War' (3'51), 'Abandonfire' (4'12), 'Killing Time' (4'57), 'Young Love' (3'21), 'It's An Illusion' (4'02), 'I Cry For You (Love, Hope And Confusion)' (4'20)

US vinyl: 'Man On Fire' (4'04), 'I Cry For You (Love, Hope And Confusion)' (4'20), 'It's An Illusion' (4'02), 'Racing In The Street' (4'27), 'Masters Of War' (3'51), 'Strange Frontier' (4'16), 'Beautiful Dreams' (4'23), 'Abandonfire' (4'12), 'Killing Time' (4'57), 'Young Love' (3'21)

Musicians: Roger Taylor *(vocals, drums, percussion, guitars, bass guitar, synthesizers, programming)*, David Richards *(synthesizers, programming)*, Rick Parfitt *(guitars on 'It's An Illusion')*, John Deacon *(bass guitar on 'It's An Illusion')*, Freddie Mercury *(backing vocals on 'Killing Time')*
Recorded: Mountain Studios, Montreux, and Musicland Studios, Munich, March 1983-May 1984
Producers: Roger Taylor, Mack, David Richards

Although *Fun In Space* hadn't been an overwhelming hit, Roger still enjoyed the process of writing and recording an entire album's worth of material. In early 1983, a brief hiatus saw Queen exploring their separate interests: John, once again, spent time with his family, and Roger flew to Scotland to ski. While there, he and his assistant Chris 'Crystal' Taylor (no relation) got into a bit of mischief by posing as vacuum cleaner salesmen; Roger's mind was on anything but recording. Still in a ski-ing mood, the two flew to Switzerland where they met up with Rick Parfitt of Status Quo; when Roger mentioned his intention to record another solo album, Parfitt expressed an interest in assisting him.

Roger booked time at Mountain Studios but it soon became evident that several of the proposed songs weren't working as well as he'd hoped, so he scrapped most of what he had recorded and started again. ("I'm *still* putting the final touches to my own effort, *Strange Frontier*, and hope it will be out sometime in April," Roger wrote in the spring 1984 issue of the Queen Fan Club magazine. "I've chucked out some and written some better ones. I hope you'll be surprised.") This time, he was determined to work at his own pace, instead of cramming time in between Queen activities. "[*Fun In Space*] was a bit of a rush job, actually," he told *Modern Drummer* in 1984. "I thought I'd run out of nerve if I didn't move on it quickly. And I did it much too fast. I spent most of last year when we weren't making *The Works*, making another solo album. It's in a much different class than the first one. It's a much, much better record ... I took a year making it. I made sure the songs were stronger and simply better. I threw out a lot of songs in the process. I also did two cover versions of other people's songs that I'm quite happy with."

As of 21 May 1983, a handwritten line-up of the new album indicated Roger was nearing completion: 'Love, Hope And Confusion', 'Beautiful Dreams', 'It's An Illusion', 'Masters Of War', 'Keep On Running', 'Strange Frontier', 'Young Love', 'I Wanna Take You Higher', 'Turn On The Power', 'Sun And Steel', 'Been To Spain', 'Two Sharp Pencils', 'All Your Dreams Will Come True', and 'Racing In The Street' made up his second album. 'Abandonfire' and 'Man On Fire' had yet to be written, but once the latter was recorded – and ultimately abandoned – during sessions for Queen's *The Works*, the band's loss was Roger's gain. With 14 songs ready to go, six were removed, and sessions continued to update the album to Roger's liking, with a more sociopolitical bent this time than on the futuristic, sci-fi sounds of *Fun In Space*.

Something else inspired Roger to rethink the material he had written. In the early 1980s, international relations were crumbling, with nuclear armaments falling into the wrong hands and incompetent world leaders fumbling their way through the chaos. "The idea of *Strange Frontier* – the whole title really – is supposed to be a point in time that we've supposed to have reached, that which is a point of self-annihilation that we've never been capable of before," Roger told Jim Ladd in 1984. "That's the idea. It's a part of 'temple frontier' really."

Roger was one of the less outspoken celebrities on the 'No Nukes' issue, though he was apparently a member of the UK's CND and spoke briefly about it in a 1984 interview; he even wore a 'No Nukes' T-shirt throughout the Queen Works! tour in 1984 and 1985. Other artists were putting out records on similar themes, but it wasn't until Bruce Springsteen's mega-successful *Born In The USA* that people would really start to take notice. That album was released only three weeks before Roger's *Strange Frontier*, yet the message is eerily similar. In an even stranger twist, Roger had recorded a cover version of Springsteen's 1978 track 'Racing In The Street', though the message there had little to do with the threat of nuclear war. It would be Roger's cover of Bob Dylan's 'Masters Of War' that made the most impact, strongly condemning those who advocated war; sadly, the message was still appropriate over two decades after the song had been written, and remains so another 20 years on.

Three of the remaining eight tracks featured a co-writer – 'Abandonfire' and 'I Cry For You (Love, Hope & Confusion)' were written with David Richards, and 'It's An Illusion' was written with Rick Parfitt – leaving half the tracks written solely by Roger. 'Strange Frontier' and 'Beautiful Dreams', which would provide a one-two power punch of an opener, are the strongest of the material, along with 'Killing Time' and 'It's An Illusion'. 'Man On Fire', itself an out-take from *The Works*, would never become the hit single it should have been, reaching only No. 66 in the charts.

Those anticipating a *Fun In Space II* would be sorely disappointed. Gone were the quirky, darker sci-fi songs; *Strange Frontier* was rife with world-weary – sometimes bleak, occasionally optimistic – messages, chock-full of synthesizers and programming, and devoid of humor. In most cases, Roger was taking himself a bit too seriously, sounding far too determined to make an impact and change the world. "There's all these different causes that really don't amount to anything," Roger explained to Ladd, who had just quoted – and praised – a verse from the title track about fallen freedom fighters. "Because if there's one religious fanatic, there's the terrible need to become fanatical about something ... There's a great new conservatism among young people that seems to be, and I can't understand it. Where's all the truth and rebellious spirits gone? It seems that people, a lot of teens today are incredibly conservative, and I find that a bit disappointing."

Though most of the songs are strong and each song shows Roger's impressive abilities as a multi-instrumentalist, the sound is sterile and over-produced, an issue that plagued most mid-1980s releases. Regardless, Roger had truly advanced as a songwriter, and seven of the originals could have easily rubbed elbows with any of the songs on *The Works*. The lyrics are consistent, with none of the tired jabs at politicians that would infect some of his later songs, and as a sophomore release, it's a decent follow-up to *Fun In Space*. Not everyone was convinced, however; *Sounds* was particularly caustic in its review of the album, saying that "He can write the songs, but he can't sing them like Freddie does. Which is why Queen get the hits."

Strange Frontier charted worse than its predecessor, peaking at No. 30 in the UK and not charting at all in the US, where its carefully-constructed running order was completely and randomly shuffled around by Capitol. The singles were well chosen but performed poorly – 'Man On Fire' stalled at No. 66, while the title track barely cracked the Top 100, peaking at a disappointing No. 98. It was inevitable, then, that no solo tour would be forthcoming, but with Queen busier than ever in 1984, going fully solo was the last thing on Roger's mind at that point.

FREDDIE MERCURY
MR BAD GUY

CBS 86312, April 1985 [6]
Columbia FC 40071, May 1985 [159]
Columbia CK 40071, May 1985 [159]

'Let's Turn It On' (3'42), 'Made In Heaven' (4'06), 'I Was Born To Love You' (3'39), 'Foolin' Around' (3'29), 'Your Kind Of Lover' (3'33), 'Mr Bad Guy' (4'10), 'Man Made Paradize' (4'09), 'There Must Be More To Life Than This' (3'01), 'Living On My Own' (3'23), 'My Love Is Dangerous' (3'43), 'Love Me Like There's No Tomorrow' (3'47)

Musicians: Freddie Mercury (*vocals, piano, synthesizer*), Fred Mandel (*piano, synthesizer, guitar*), Paul Vincent (*guitars*), Curt Cress (*drums*), Stephan Wissnet (*bass guitar, Fairlight, Kurzweil, and drum programming*), Jo Burt (*Fretless bass on 'Man Made Paradize'*), Rainer Pietsch (*arrangement on 'Mr Bad Guy'*), Mack (*Fairlight, Kurzweil, and drum programming*)
Recorded: 1983 to January 1985, Musicland Studios, Munich
Producers: Freddie Mercury and Mack

Freddie initially spent the first part of 1983 relaxing and enjoying his hiatus from the band and the road,

but he soon became interested in recording a few songs he felt weren't suitable for Queen's sound. After expressing this idea to Jim Beach, Queen's manager negotiated a one-time deal on Freddie's behalf with CBS Records in the UK and Columbia Records in the US. The contract appealed to Freddie because it was simple and wouldn't affect any of his work with the band. Freddie had no aspirations to become a solo star, explaining that it would be "silly to form a new band at 40."

Before sessions started in earnest, Freddie flew to Los Angeles to meet up with friend Michael Jackson, who was working on his *Thriller* album. (According to Brian, the King of Pop was inspired by the funkier moments on *Hot Space* to record his multi-platinum *Thriller*.) The two decided to record some material together. Three tracks – 'Victory', 'State Of Shock' and 'There Must Be More To Life Than This' – were recorded at Michael's home studio, and both of them were excited at the prospect of working together in the future. However, personal conflicts later cooled the relationship, though Freddie diplomatically stated that "Michael Jackson and I have grown apart a bit since his massive success with *Thriller*. He's simply retreated into a world of his own. Two years ago we used to have great fun going to clubs together but now he won't come out of his fortress. It's very sad. He's so worried that someone will do him in that he's paranoid about absolutely everything."

With the three Jackson-Mercury collaborations consigned to the vaults for the time being, Freddie continued working on songs for his own album but, before long, was contacted by Giorgio Moroder about the prospect of providing a song for the German producer's contemporary update of Fritz Lang's 1927 silent film *Metropolis*, which would use rock music to complement the scenes. Initially, Queen were approached, and Brian and Roger especially were interested in incorporating some of the visual element of Lang's sparse expressionist film into their live show, and a trade-off was suggested. 'Love Kills', which started life as a Queen track but was credited as a Freddie solo composition, was handed over to Moroder, and footage from the film was given to Queen.

Meanwhile, in mid-1983, Freddie started recording material in earnest for his solo album at Musicland Studios with producer Mack and an assembly of German musicians plus Fred Mandel. Working with a backlog of songs either rejected for Queen albums ('There Must Be More To Life Than This' and 'Man

Made Paradise' were written and recorded for both *Hot Space* and *The Works*, but rejected both times) or written specially for this project, Freddie took his time with the album, perfecting it until it met his rigorous standards. "I've put my heart and soul into this album," he explained to *Record Mirror* in January 1985. "It has some very moving ballads; things to do with sadness and pain, but at the same time they're frivolous and tongue-in-cheek, because that's my nature. I've wanted to do a solo album for a long time and the rest of the band have encouraged me to do it. I wanted to cover such things as reggae rhythms and I've done a couple of things with a symphony orchestra. It has a very rich sound and it's very beat-oriented. I think it's a very natural album, and I hope people will like my voice."

While the album is indeed rich and varied, it's perhaps a bit too much so. He explored a variety of styles, all with aplomb, which is one reason why it was so successful, but most of those styles are dated by today's standards, especially the synthesizer programming and drum-machines on nearly every track. It's no surprise that the most successful songs were the ballads, where Freddie wears his heart on his sleeve: 'Made In Heaven', 'There Must Be More To Life Than This' and 'Love Me Like There's No Tomorrow' are gorgeous and revealing, and were tastefully arranged with little of the excess Freddie prided himself on in Queen's canon.

Of the remaining eight experimentations – ranging from dance ('Your Kind Of Lover' and 'Living On My Own') to full-force disco ('Let's Turn It On' and 'Foolin' Around') – only the charming pop of 'I Was Born To Love You' and the grandiloquent title track stand out as superb. The former was considered so trifling by Freddie that it almost didn't make the cut, with the vocalist scoffing at the record company's idea that it would be a hit single. 'Mr Bad Guy' was full of the pomp and circumstance that summed up Freddie perfectly, making it the perfect album title. The unfortunate cod-reggae of 'My Love Is Dangerous' (complete with dub sounds and heavily echoed vocals) was a low point on the album, and the strange, almost new wave rock of 'Man Made Paradise' was rather unsettling, though the operatic vocal coda was pure Queen.

Nonetheless, Freddie was in fine voice throughout the album, redeeming some of the more lacklustre songs with an unquestionably powerful vocal performance, as if *Hot Space* and *The Works* had restricted him vocally and he seemed intent on breaking free. Without Roger and Brian to assist on the

harmonies, and instead of enlisting backing vocalists, Freddie did them all himself, creating lush vocal tones that sound simultaneously Queen-like yet entirely like Freddie in his own right. "I was pleased with [the album]," he told *The Sun* that July. "I was also pleased with my voice. I like it husky. It's all the smoking. That's why I smoke: to get that husky voice."

Comparisons with Queen were inevitable, which may explain why Freddie chose distinctive musicians with their own styles. Instrumentally, the shining star was Fred Mandel, who infused a fresh sound into the keyboards that enhanced many of the songs; the piano work on 'Your Kind Of Lover' and 'Living On My Own' was superb. The other musicians certainly added their own styles to the music, but it's difficult to listen to the album and not think how much Paul Vincent's guitar on 'Man Made Paradise' sounds like a carbon copy of Brian May, or how Curt Cress' live drums are reminiscent of Roger Taylor, and how much better the songs would have sounded as Queen songs.

Along with the two non-album B-sides, 'She Blows Hot And Cold' and 'Stop All The Fighting', a further five ideas were recorded, most of them frivolous. 'Gazelle' and 'God Is Heavy' were minor efforts and *Mr Bad Guy* was better off without them, although 'Money Can't Buy Happiness' and 'New York' were exquisite compositions that, if finished, would have made splendid additions. Sadly, one final song, 'Love Makin' Love', didn't make the cut and, though recorded again during sessions for *A Kind Of Magic* in 1985, it was fated to remain unreleased; only in 2000 on *The Solo Collection* did these five out-takes, along with several work-in-progress versions of the standard album tracks, finally get exposure. One of the original tracklistings for the album read: 'My Love Is Dangerous', 'Made In Heaven', 'Let's Turn It On', 'Living On My Own', 'Foolin' Around', 'There Must Be More To Life Than This', 'Mr Bad Guy', 'Your Kind Of Lover', 'Man Made Paradise', 'Love Makin' Love', 'Stop All The Fighting' and 'Love Me Like There's No Tomorrow'. Initially titled *Made In Heaven*, which Freddie revealed in interviews shortly before its release, the last-minute retitling to *Mr Bad Guy* (a far more apt title) and reshuffled order shows just how meticulous Freddie was.

"Yes, I would like it to be successful," Freddie revealed in 1985. "It matters to me a lot. I've made a piece of music which I want to be accepted in the biggest way possible. But I'm not worried about the fact that it might not be successful, because if it isn't,

I will just go out and make another one." Fortunately, the album reached No. 6 in the UK, while peaking at a dismal No. 121 in the US; the reviews weren't much better. *People Weekly* opined that Freddie "is not someone to take along on a sea cruise, since he can't seem to resist going overboard. For this record, his first solo, he piles on the flourishes: a simple dance riff in 'Let's Turn It On' is cluttered with overdubbing, echoes, and other studio tricks. Maybe he uses ornamentation because his songwriting is so vapid. The singles 'Foolin' Around' [sic] and 'Living On My Own' have some melodic merit, but much of this album sounds like an uninspired cabaret revue." *Rolling Stone* was, surprisingly, more complimentary: "On *Mr Bad Guy*, Freddie Mercury's first solo album, he puts his shamelessly angelic soprano to work on a group of swooping numbers that he describes as 'love songs, things to do with sadness and torture and pain, but at the same time they're frivolous and tongue in cheek'. Cheek and overbite being Freddie's operative mode, his trademark braggadocio and choirboy ebullience serve him well … The tracks run the gamut from slick and exuberant Eurodisco to slick and exuberant ballads and existential musings ('There Must Be More To Life Than This'). The record, co-produced and engineered by longtime Queen producer Mack, is meticulously gimmick-heavy, though lighthearted. *Mr Bad Guy* is unlikely to win Freddie many new converts, but Queen fans will eat it up."

The forerunner single, 'I Was Born To Love You', was a success, reaching No. 11 in the UK and even charting in the US, stalling at No. 76. Regrettably, the chart life of the other three singles – 'Made In Heaven' (No. 57), 'Living On My Own' (No. 50) and 'Love Me Like There's No Tomorrow' (No. 76) – was disappointing, though it did allow Freddie to return to work with Queen. "It's probably brought us closer together and will enhance our careers," he told *The Sun*. "It's like painting a picture. You have to step away from it to see what it's like. I'm stepping away from Queen and I think it's going to give everybody a shot in the arm. But I'll be working with Queen again. No doubt about that. Queen are gonna come back even bigger."

THE CROSS
SHOVE IT

Virgin V 2477, November 1987 [58]
Virgin-USA 7 90857 1, January 1988
Virgin CDV 2477, October 1987 [58]
Virgin-USA 7 90857 2, January 1988

UK tracklisting: 'Shove It' (3'28), 'Cowboys And Indians' (5'53), 'Contact' (4'54), 'Heaven For Everyone' (4'54), 'Stand Up For Love' (4'22), 'Love On A Tightrope (Like An Animal)' (4'49), 'Love Lies Bleeding (She Was A Wicked, Wily Waitress)' (4'25), 'Rough Justice' (3'22)

Bonus track on UK CD issue: 'The 2nd Shelf Mix' (5'49)

US tracklisting: 'Love Lies Bleeding (She Was A Wicked, Wily Waitress)' (4'23), 'Shove It' (3'26), 'Cowboys And Indians' (5'53), 'Contact' (4'50), 'Heaven For Everyone' (5'08), 'Feel The Force' (3'46), 'Stand Up For Love' (4'20), 'Love On A Tightrope (Like An Animal)' (4'48), 'Rough Justice' (4'13)

Musicians: Roger Taylor (*vocals, drums, percussion, programming, keyboards, guitars, bass guitar*), David Richards (*keyboards, programming*), Freddie Mercury (*lead vocals on 'Heaven For Everyone' (UK album version only), backing vocals on 'Heaven For Everyone' (US album version)*), Brian May (*guitar on 'Love Lies Bleeding (She Was A Wicked, Wily Waitress)'*), John Deacon (*bass guitar*), Spike Edney (*additional keyboards*), Jill O'Donovan and Susie O'List (*backing vocals*)
Recorded: Mountain Studios, Montreux; Townhouse and AIR Studios, London; Maison Rouge Studios, Fulham; Mediterraneo Studios, Siracusa, August-December 1987
Producers: Roger Taylor and David Richards

In May 1987, Roger started work on his third solo album, again playing all of the instruments, but was unsure of Queen's future as a live band. Eager to play live again, he conferred with the other three and proposed the idea of forming his own band as a side project. They agreed it was a good idea, with the proviso that Queen would always come first. Advertisements were therefore placed in all the top music papers, with the initial advert, "Drummer of a top rock band looking for musicians." Roger deliberately kept his name out of the ad since he didn't want to attract fanboys; however, he was a little too vague, and the replies were thin. He revised the ad to read, "If you think you're good enough and you want to be a star, call this number." This did the trick, and he was inundated with calls from young hopefuls, among them drummer Josh Macrae, guitarist Clayton Moss and bassist Peter Noone. These three were ultimately selected as Roger's new group after auditioning with 'Cowboys And Indians' and 'Love Lies Bleeding', two of Roger's new songs. Spike Edney was enlisted as keyboardist, while Roger naturally took over the role of vocalist and, in a drastic shift of personnel, rhythm guitarist.

Explaining his initial criteria for the band's applicants, Roger told *Sounds* in 1988, "I was actually looking, firstly, for musicianship; secondly, attitude; and for people that would make a great working unit together. We didn't want any session musicians getting paid by the note. We wanted a real group. U2 are a real group. They're all in it together. There's a lot of kinda half groups around these days; one or two people are getting money, the rest are on wages. Foreigner, for example; and Dire Straits. There are only two people in Dire Straits who are actually making the real money. I mean, it's none of my business, but most of these people are just hired hands. That's not a band. When you go to see a band, you don't go to see a particular person, you go to feel the spirit of the whole thing."

After suggesting a handful of names, none of which were taken seriously (or could be remembered), the new band settled on The Cross, which they reasoned would be easy to remember while being slightly controversial, though there were no implications of religious overtones. Although the album had been virtually completed by the time the band was formed, the new musicians added some finishing touches to a few tracks, as did Brian, John and Freddie. When Roger played them his new songs and asked for their opinions, he also extended the offer for guest spots (the specifics of John's bass contributions aren't known): Brian contributed guitar to the raucous 'Love Lies Bleeding' and Freddie performed an impassioned lead vocal on 'Heaven For Everyone' (a track Roger had written earlier in the decade; he had originally intended to give it to Joan Armatrading) while also providing backing vocals on Roger's own version, which was released only in the US.

The resulting album, titled *Shove It* and an appropriate gesture to the British press, who had become increasingly interested in salacious details and less in the music, is an interesting amalgamation of modern and classic rock. Comprised of only eight tracks (nine in the US), the album is acceptable though not extraordinary. The songs are typical of Roger's songwriting abilities, though there aren't really any standout tracks, except for 'Heaven For Everyone' and 'Feel The Force', which could have – and should have – been Queen tracks. The lyrics don't equal anything Roger wrote within Queen, and with the increased

popularity of rap, Roger took his turn on 'Cowboys And Indians', comprised of some of the most toe-curlingly awkward verses written.

The biggest problem is the album's production, resulting in a sound typical of mid-1980s fare. The drums are snappy and echoed, the bass sounds artificial throughout, and synthesizers and programmed instruments run rampant. Another mistake was the decision to include samples of Queen songs, notably in the title track. Almost like Robert Plant's 1988 piece 'Tall Cool One', which included samples of early Led Zeppelin tracks, Roger unnecessarily threw in bursts of Brian's guitar, backing vocals from a handful of Queen songs, and Freddie shouting "Yeah!" throughout.

The Cross' vinyl debut came in September 1987, when 'Cowboys And Indians' was released as the first single from the upcoming album. The band were disheartened when the single reached only No. 74 in the UK; the title track appeared as the follow-up in January 1988 and limped to a disappointing No. 82, while 'Heaven For Everyone', which should have been a surefire hit, peaked one position worse than its predecessor. Clearly, The Cross weren't aiming for the hit parade; they were geared more towards live shows, which they duly undertook in February 1988. The set list drew heavily from the debut, although several of Roger's earlier solo songs – 'Man On Fire', 'It's An Illusion', 'Strange Frontier', 'Laugh Or Cry' and 'Let's Get Crazy' – made appearances, and 'I'm In Love With My Car' was resurrected for the first time since 1981. The band focused on performing at small clubs throughout Europe, avoiding the Queen banner that undoubtedly flew over Roger's head (he insisted on not calling the band 'Roger Taylor and The Cross', much to the chagrin of greedy promoters, though he reluctantly relented when ticket sales were less than inspiring) while offering a decent show that enabled Roger to fulfil his desire to perform live again.

Overall, the album deserves a listen; while it certainly gives no indication as to what the band would achieve on their next two releases, the listener must remember that *Shove It* is essentially a Roger Taylor solo album in all but name. "*Shove It* is more of me than the next album will be," he clarified to *Sounds*. "Unfortunately, I had to go out and get a record deal first, so that we could fund this thing and get it all going. It was a case of the chicken before the egg, but it was the only way to do it."

FREDDIE MERCURY AND MONTSERRAT CABALLÉ
BARCELONA

Polydor POLH 44, October 1988 [25]
Polydor INT 837277 1Y, July 1992 [15]
Hollywood HR 61366 2, July 1992 [6; Classical Crossover]

'Barcelona' (5'39), 'La Japonaise' (4'49), 'The Fallen Priest' (5'46), 'Ensueño' (4'21), 'The Golden Boy' (6'04), 'Guide Me Home' (2'50), 'How Can I Go On' (3'51), 'Overture Picante' (6'39)

Musicians: Freddie Mercury *(vocals)*, Montserrat Caballé *(vocals)*, Mike Moran *(keyboards, programming, arrangements)*, John Deacon *(bass guitar on 'How Can I Go On')*, Homi Kanga *(violin on 'Barcelona')*, Laurie Lewis *(violin on 'Barcelona')*, Deborah Ann Johnston *(cello on 'Barcelona')*, Barry Castle *(horn on 'Barcelona')*, Frank Ricotti *(percussion on 'Barcelona')*, Madeline Bell, Debbie Bishop, Lance Ellington, Miriam Stockley, Peter Straker, Mark Williamson, and Carol Woods *(backing vocals on 'The Golden Boy')*
Recorded: January 1987-June 1988, Townhouse Studios, London, and Mountain Studios, Montreux
Producers: Freddie Mercury, Mike Moran, David Richards

During Queen's self-imposed hiatus following the Magic tour in August 1986, Freddie ultimately turned out to be the most prolific band member, writing and recording some of his most acclaimed solo material. After the tour concluded, he flew to Japan for an extended vacation, then returned to London in November where he recorded a demo version of 'The Great Pretender', the 1956 hit single by The Platters. The single proved to be unexpectedly popular, reaching No. 4 on its February 1987 release, and rumors circulated that Freddie was working on a covers album, which would include renditions of 'Smoke Gets In Your Eyes' and 'New York, New York'. That was merely wishful thinking – Freddie was instead focused on achieving a lifelong dream.

Freddie had admitted on Spanish television in August 1986 that his one ambition was to record with opera diva Montserrat Caballé. Someone from her camp had fortuitously tuned into that show and approached Caballé, who was flattered and overwhelmed at such a prospect: flattered that such a high-profile vocalist would want to record with her, but overwhelmed in that she wasn't as aware of his back catalog as he was of hers. Jim Beach contacted Spanish promoter Pino Sagliocco to set up a meeting between the two; when Freddie was informed, he became justifiably nervous, according to Mike Moran: "Freddie was in a lather of nerves. He wanted to take something to play to her that she would not have already heard via her children. So, finally, in she came, almost like the Queen of Sheba, Montserrat and entourage. It was a bit awkward at first, as no one knew each other, but Freddie plunged straight in – such a courageous man. He played her the track that he and I had written, which was his impression of her singing. She was amazed."

That track – 'Exercises In Free Love' – became the catalyst for the *Barcelona* album, which Freddie had started writing in January 1987, two months before their 24 March meeting at the Ritz Hotel in Barcelona. Initially, Freddie had intended to record only one song with her, but she became so excited that she asked to record an entire album. "I thought, 'My God, what am I going to do now?'" Freddie explained. "You just don't turn the super-diva down. I thought I'd better put my money where my mouth is."

Towards the end of January 1987, demo recording sessions began in earnest with 'Rachmaninov's Revenge', which eventually led to 'The Fallen Priest' with a new set of lyrics penned by Tim Rice (who also contributed words to 'The Golden Boy'); the sessions concluded with a fully developed musical statement in June 1988. Freddie focused on writing the lyrics while Mike Moran, who had previously collaborated with Freddie on his two contributions to the *Time* musical, arranged most of the music. The two worked side-by-side to create a sonic landscape that complemented the words and vocals well, meshing together many different styles instead of remaining exclusively operatic. 'La Japonaise' derived its influence from the Far East, while 'The Golden Boy' was Freddie's first excursion into gospel since 'Somebody To Love' over a decade before. Only on 'How Can I Go On' does he approach the archetypal Queen sound; elsewhere, his fusion of opera and rock is balanced in a manner that is appealing to lovers of both genres.

Instead of featuring other musicians or an orchestra to play the parts that Freddie and Mike were fashioning, Mike was constantly working with updated technology and the latest samplers to ensure that the music sounded as real as an orchestra. "We would start to slowly and meticulously track on the orchestral parts one instrument at a time," producer David Richards explained in the liner notes to *The Solo Collection*. "At this stage I remember working very hard to make the sampled and synthesized instruments sound as real as possible. This was frustrating sometimes, as I thought a real orchestra would sound better. Freddie maintained that he couldn't have the same control over the orchestration that way, and we could add real players after the parts had been finalized" – which they did on the title track. "And so, for weeks, the three of us sat in the studio doing this meticulous work until the day when finally it was perfect for Montserrat to come in and sing her parts. But this wasn't enough perfection. The studio itself had to be polished, cleaned and made ready, and Freddie made Townhouse Studios re-decorate the ladies' toilets just in case she wanted to use them."

Part of the reason the album took so long was, because of her busy work schedule, Caballé wasn't able to sing live in the studio with Freddie. Freddie, Mike and David therefore had to create completely finished backing tracks with Freddie providing falsetto vocalizations for Montserrat to follow (some of these tracks were released in 2000 on *The Solo Collection*). But because the process of constructing the backing tracks was so lengthy, most of the final vocal sessions didn't take place until the spring of 1988, by which time Freddie was back in the studios with Queen to work on *The Miracle*. Nevertheless, Montserrat's voice was captured on his songs, which left Freddie ecstatic. "That's it!" he exclaimed to Peter Freestone. "I've done it! I've got *her* voice on *my* music!"

Excluding the seven songs (plus the concluding sound collage, 'Overture Piccante'), only one true out-take exists, a song called 'Africa By Night' which was later heavily reworked as the *Innuendo* track 'All God's People'. Other working titles for the songs were 'Rachmaninov's Revenge' ('The Fallen Priest'), 'Vocal Exercises' ('Exercises In Free Love'), 'Freddie's Overture' ('Guide Me Home') and 'Japanese Song' ('La Japonaise'). Intriguingly, Freddie had spent a good deal of time before the *Barcelona* sessions commenced demoing tracks that he might have intended for a solo album. Four of these – 'Holding On', 'It's So You', 'I Can't Dance' and 'Yellow Breezes' – were recorded throughout February and March 1987, but once Caballé insisted she and Freddie work on an album together, these songs were discarded and forgotten.

The songs presented on *Barcelona* are exotic and unlike anything Freddie, or even Queen, had done

before. What's most surprising is Freddie's gorgeous voice: he was obviously a great vocalist, but hardly anyone realized the level of control he had over that voice until they heard this album. Even longtime co-producer David Richards expressed surprise at just how effectively Freddie could manage his voice. Freddie's vocals shine through on every song he sang on this album, but most impressively on 'La Japonaise' and 'The Fallen Priest', two of the more vocally demanding songs, yet sung almost as if they were throwaways. His pop voice returned on 'Guide Me Home' and 'How Can I Go On', which also featured a cameo appearance on bass guitar from John Deacon, and he allowed himself to exercise his cords a bit more freely on the opening title track and 'The Golden Boy'.

'Ensueño' was sung by Caballé with occasional vocalizations from Freddie, and took the basis of 'Exercises In Free Love' with lyrics written by Caballé herself. Elsewhere, Freddie wrote most of the lyrics, with help from Tim Rice on 'The Fallen Priest' and 'The Golden Boy'. (Freddie's association with Tim led to his consideration as the lead singer for Andrew Lloyd Webber's *The Phantom Of The Opera*, with demo versions of the title track and 'Music Of The Night' recorded but unreleased.) There are two extremes to the four Freddie-penned tracks: 'Barcelona' and 'La Japonaise' were written in celebration of Barcelona and Japan: the title track was composed specifically for Caballé's hometown and 'La Japonaise' was Freddie's dedication to the country of which he was fondest. 'Guide Me Home' and 'How Can I Go On' are more typical of Freddie, and it's hard to listen to them without thinking that Freddie knew his time on earth was limited. His words are poignant and pleading and they have little to do with the pursuit of love; they are more about a man who is searching for assistance and acceptance, while coming to terms with his place in life.

Barcelona was released in the UK in October 1988, where it reached No. 25 in the charts and received some conflicting reviews. *Kerrang!* called it "sensational. Quite extraordinary and the ultimate in high camp", while *Sounds* conceded that "This will appeal to real music lovers." Only *Record Mirror* was censorious, saying, "In the most curious matching of talents known to man, Freddie settles back in the armchair and whinges a bit while the weighty Montserrat woman leaps around the room, yodeling and warbling wildly. He's never been the same since 'Bohemian Rhapsody'."

It's easy to surmise that Freddie intended this album

as the finale to his solo career. Thereafter, he would abandon the auxiliary songs recorded during these sessions and concentrate on Queen; Peter Freestone once said that the only regret Freddie had was that he had so much music left in him. However, it would be difficult to top perfection, and *Barcelona* is as close to perfection as any Queen-related album would come.

THE CROSS
MAD: BAD: AND DANGEROUS TO KNOW
Parlophone PCS 7342, March 1990
Parlophone CDPCS 7342, March 1990

'Top Of The World, Ma' (3'55), 'Liar' (4'35), 'Closer To You' (3'18), 'Breakdown' (3'56), 'Penetration Guru' (3'48), 'Power To Love' (4'04), 'Sister Blue' (4'17), 'Foxy Lady *(CD only)*' (3'28), 'Better Things' (2'48), 'Passion For Trash' (2'37), 'Old Men (Lay Down)' (4'55), 'Final Destination' (3'35)

Musicians: Roger Taylor *(vocals, guitars)*, Spike Edney *(keyboards, vocals, mandolin on 'Better Things')*, Peter Noone *(bass guitar, vocals)*, Clayton Moss *(guitars, vocals, lead vocals on 'Better Things')*, Josh Macrae *(drums, percussion, vocals)*
Recorded: Mountain Studios, Montreux, September-November 1989
Producers: The Cross and Justin Shirley-Smith

With *The Miracle* finally completed and released, and with Brian out doing his own promotional work on the album, Roger took a short break before meeting up with Spike, Peter, Clayton and Josh in Montreux. While Roger had been busy with Queen, the others had started work on their own material for a potential second album, invigorated by the live shows and the (relative) success of *Shove It*. Since they hadn't written anything for the first album, let alone played on it, they were determined to become a more democratic unit.

Fortunately, Roger shared this desire and was eager to hear the demo tapes that the band presented to him. Impressed by what he heard, he started work on his own contributions; surprisingly, only two of his songs, 'Old Men (Lay Down)' and 'Final Destination', ended up on the album, with the remaining eight songs generated by the others (and with Jimi Hendrix's 'Foxy Lady' added for good measure). With Roger's songwriting now in the minority, it would be understandable to approach The Cross' sophomore album with trepidation since none of the other four

musicians were well-known songwriters, and it could be argued that Roger's desire to be only one-fifth of a fledgling rock band would affect the music adversely. Thankfully, *Mad: Bad: And Dangerous To Know* – an apt 19th century description of the disreputable poet Lord Byron, who had been imprisoned in Chillon Castle in Montreux, near Mountain Studios where the album was recorded – is a decent sophomore effort, and the songwriting is a vast improvement over the debut.

Whereas the production on *Shove It* had been so generically 1980s, the band was given an updated sound for this release, almost entirely eliminating the programming and synthesizers, and The Cross are revealed as what they had been from the beginning as evidenced by their live shows: a good old-fashioned rock band. Part of the success of the album's sound is attributable to Justin Shirley-Smith, an engineer who had cut his teeth working with Chris Rea on his 1987 album, *Dancing With Strangers*, and then progressed to two David Bowie projects: *Never Let Me Down* in 1987 (alongside David Richards), and Tin Machine's self-titled debut album in 1989. *Mad: Bad: And Dangerous To Know* was the first album he produced himself, and he would go on to become almost exclusively a Queen producer, also working closely with Brian on several of his solo recordings. The production on The Cross' second album is superb, a contrapuntal masterpiece that sounded as if the band were all playing in the same room together.

The songwriting on the album was surprisingly strong, with almost every track a potential single. Whereas Roger could take credit for only the final two songs, as well as a co-writer's credit on the opener, Peter Noone wrote three of the tracks ('Liar', 'Breakdown' and 'Sister Blue'), Clayton Moss wrote two ('Penetration Guru' and 'Better Things', the latter a self-sung ballad) and Spike Edney and Joshua J Macrae wrote one song each ('Closer To You' and 'Passion For Trash' respectively). The most chart-friendly song, 'Power To Love', was issued as the first single from the album in April 1990, but peaked at a disappointing No. 83 in the UK. 'Liar' was the next single, released only in Germany in August 1990 and deserving to be a hit just as much as the third single, 'Final Destination' – but neither charted. The band went on a short German tour in the spring of 1990 and, while sales in that country increased, Britain merely reacted with indifference. It was evident that, despite all the hard work The Cross had poured into their album, no one was paying attention.

THE CROSS
THE OFFICIAL BOOTLEG

Fan Club-only release, early 1991

'Piano Introduction' (2'19), 'Top Of The World, Ma' (4'16), 'Love Lies Bleeding' (4'38), 'Breakdown' (4'09), 'Penetration Guru' (4'09), 'Tear It Up (or "Bad Attitude")' (4'11), 'Liar' (5'24), 'Man On Fire' (4'59), 'Sister Blue' (4'28), 'Final Destination' (4'37), 'Foxy Lady' (5'22), 'I'm In Love With My Car' (3'09), 'Let Me Out' (7'54), 'Tie Your Mother Down' (3'55), 'Lucille' (6'29)

Musicians: Roger Taylor *(vocals, guitar, drums on 'Tie Your Mother Down')*, Peter Noone *(bass guitar, backing vocals)*, Clayton Moss *(guitar, backing vocals)*, Josh Macrae *(drums, backing vocals)*, Mike Moran *(piano, keyboards)*, Brian May *(guitar on 'I'm In Love With My Car', 'Let Me Out', 'Tie Your Mother Down', and 'Lucille', lead vocals on 'Let Me Out' and 'Tie Your Mother Down')*
Recorded: The Astoria Theatre, London, 7 December 1990
Producers: The Cross

Performed exclusively for The Official International Queen Fan Club Christmas Show in December 1990 at The Astoria Theatre, *The Official Bootleg* became the first exclusive release offered to fan club members and is an exciting and interesting insight into a much neglected area of Roger's solo career.

The recording is famous for featuring a guest appearance by Brian May, who joined The Cross on their encore (starting with 'I'm In Love With My Car') and even brought a few rarities with him. 'Let Me Out' was premiered for the first time and Little Richard's 'Lucille' was also given a run-through, while 'Tie Your Mother Down' featured Brian on lead vocals for the first time – which was obvious, as he both forgot crucial lines or simply focused more on his guitar work than singing. Only six of the 12 tracks from *Mad: Bad: And Dangerous To Know* were performed, a drastic reduction from the 11 usually featured, but the band did introduce 'Bad Attitude', which at this point was called 'Tear It Up', and would be recorded for the band's next album, *Blue Rock.*

Unfortunately, this rare insight into The Cross's strengths as a live band has slim to no chance of being released commercially; the best opportunity would have been to include the recording on *The Lot*, but it was passed over, and will likely remain an obscure rarity for fans to discover on their own terms.

THE CROSS
BLUE ROCK

EMI 1C 064 8 97624 1 (Germany only), September 1991
EMI 1C 064 8 97624 2 (Germany only), September 1991

'Bad Attitude' (4'45), 'New Dark Ages' (4'58), 'Dirty Mind' (3'30), 'Baby, It's Alright' (4'05), 'Ain't Put Nothin' Down' (4'30), 'The Also Rans' (5'27), 'Millionaire' (3'43), 'Put It All Down To Love' (3'34), 'Hand Of Fools (Out Of Control)' (4'30), 'Life Changes' (5'55)

Musicians: Roger Taylor *(vocals)*, Spike Edney *(keyboards, backing vocals)*, Peter Noone *(bass guitar, backing vocals)*, Clayton Moss *(guitars, backing vocals)*, Josh Macrae *(drums, percussion, backing vocals)*, Geoffrey Richardson *(violin and viola on 'Baby, It's Alright' and 'Life Changes')*, Helen Liebman *(cello on 'Baby, It's Alright' and 'Life Changes')*, Candy and Clare Yates *(backing vocals on 'Baby, It's Alright' and 'The Also Rans')*
Recorded: Real World Studios, Box, and Roundhouse Studios, London, February-August 1991
Producer: Mark Wallis

The time following the release of *Mad: Bad: And Dangerous To Know* was well spent by The Cross. They had toured most of Europe during 1990 but realized they were losing popularity in their home country. The second album didn't even chart, and Parlophone remained adamant in their refusal to finance a tour that was certain to lose money. Dismayed but not defeated, the band promptly dropped Parlophone, signed with German record company Electrola and flew to Peter Gabriel's Real World Studios in Box, renowned for its eclectic world music recordings. In a 1991 interview, Roger placated fans who were worried that The Cross would be travelling in a drastically different musical direction. "We picked [the studio] because we liked the look of it," he maintained. "Our music is like classic hard rock, and I like the idea of the world music thing, but no, that had nothing to do with it. It was a good studio, a good location, and a nice place and we liked it very much indeed."

The sessions started in February 1991, again without Roger, who was in Montreux recording new material for another Queen album. When Roger finally joined the others, the sessions were moved to the more central location of Roundhouse Studios, closer to Roger's home in Surrey; his girlfriend, Debbie Leng, was pregnant and he wanted to be near home when she went into labor. On 8 March 1991, she gave birth to a boy whom they named Rufus Tiger. After celebrating, the proud new father returned to the studios to continue work on The Cross' third album.

Blue Rock was released in September 1991, after nearly six months of sessions that produced (arguably) the best album recorded by The Cross. As with its predecessor, the album is democratic in its songwriting credits. Roger again wrote only two songs ('New Dark Ages', first submitted to Queen during the Innuendo sessions, and 'The Also Rans'), while Spike Edney wrote the bulk of the material, single-handedly – 'Dirty Mind', 'Baby, It's Alright' and 'Put It All Down To Love' – and in collaboration – 'Millionaire' and 'Life Changes', both with everyone but Roger; 'Bad Attitude', with everyone including Roger; and 'Hand Of Fools (Out Of Control)', with Peter Noone. Clayton Moss wrote only one song, 'Ain't Put Nothin' Down', while Peter Noone's 'Heartland', itself a Mad: Bad: And Dangerous To Know out-take, was relegated to B-side status.

The album is nicely unified and shows the band expanding upon the previous album, with even better results. When asked his opinion of the end product, Roger said, "If you want me to be honest, I think it's quite good. We have a producer this time," he added, referring to Mark Wallis, who began his career on the Starfighters' 1982 album In-Flight Movie, before working with such notables as Roger Daltrey, Tom Verlaine and Kirsty MacColl.

The songwriting on the album was even more mature than the previous one, with the exception of 'Bad Attitude' and 'Dirty Mind' which dealt with sex and lust in a callow manner, unrepresentative of Roger's normally subtle handling of these subjects. However, Roger's mind wasn't entirely focused on the album since 1991 would mark the final year of Queen as an active band, though no one (except Freddie) knew that for certain. Roger's preoccupation with Queen-related matters was inevitable; the brunt of the work was delegated to him and Brian, with Freddie's worsening condition and John Deacon's reclusive nature keeping both vocalist and bassist out of the spotlight. As a result, most of the backing tracks for Blue Rock were recorded without Roger, and he came in only to record his lead vocals (he didn't play any guitar on the album, his only solo album not featuring any

of his own guitar work) and to arrange his two songs.

The album was released only in Germany in September 1991, a fortnight after 'New Dark Ages' hit the stores, and although heralded by limited promotion except for the odd television appearance, the album performed moderately well. Rumors circulated that it was to be released in the UK in November 1991, an event canceled due to Freddie's death. Two singles – Roger's sublime 'New Dark Ages' and the gorgeous 'Life Changes' – were released to support the album, shortly before the band embarked on a brief tour in support of Magnum.

After the release of Blue Rock, Roger's attention returned to Queen, and with the death of Freddie, his energies were suddenly directed into organizing his tribute concert. On the first anniversary of Freddie's passing, in a letter to Queen fan club members, Roger wrote, "I would also like to point out that The Cross do not exist anymore, as it seems there is a little confusion about this. We are, however, still great friends and will be playing together – strictly for fun – in London at the Marquee Club on December 21st and 22nd. Could be good – will be fun!" Indeed, with Blue Rock remaining their swan song, and only a handful of gigs remaining, the chapter on The Cross was closed – prematurely, perhaps, but Roger's insistence that he was "just part of the band" was growing tiring. Almost immediately following the tribute concert in April, he went back to work on writing songs – this time as a solo artist for the first time since 1984.

THE CROSS
LIVE IN GERMANY

Fan Club-only release, early 1992

'Bad Attitude' (5'06), 'Millionaire' (3'20), 'Ain't Put Nothin' Down' (5'37), 'New Dark Ages' (6'01), 'Baby, It's Alright' (3'43), 'Dirty Mind' (3'26), 'Man On Fire' (5'33), 'Power To Love' (5'50), 'The Also Rans' (6'19), 'Top Of The World, Ma' (5'58)

Musicians: Roger Taylor (vocals, guitar), Spike Edney (keyboards, backing vocals), Peter Noone (bass guitar, backing vocals), Clayton Moss (guitars, backing vocals), Josh Macrae (drums, backing vocals)
Recorded: The Philipshalle, Düsseldorf, 22 October 1991
Producers: The Cross

Recorded on the fifth night of The Cross' brief tour of Germany during October 1991, *Live In Germany* is a fan club-only release, much like *The Official Bootleg*, and has been heard only by a lucky few (this author not among them). This 59-minute recording comes from The Cross' October 1991 concert in Düsseldorf, with a set list derived heavily from *Blue Rock*, and includes only three older songs – 'Man On Fire', 'Power To Love' and 'Top Of The World, Ma' – making it the first tour not to feature any of Roger's Queen compositions.

The cassette tape was released to the fan club in early 1992, and has eluded any official release since, making it one of the most obscure and little-heard Queen-related recordings.

BRIAN MAY
BACK TO THE LIGHT

Parlophone PCSD 123, September 1992 [6]
Parlophone CDPCSDX 123, September 1992 [6]
Hollywood HR 61404 2, February 1993 [159]

'The Dark' (2'20), 'Back To The Light' (4'59), 'Love Token' (6'04), 'Resurrection' (5'19), 'Too Much Love Will Kill You' (4'28), 'Driven By You' (4'10), 'Nothin' But Blue' (3'31), 'I'm Scared' (3'59), 'Last Horizon' (4'11), 'Let Your Heart Rule Your Head' (3'51), 'Just One Life' (3'38), 'Rollin' Over' (4'39)

Musicians: Brian May *(vocals, guitars, keyboards, programming, bass guitar, and anything else around)*, Cozy Powell *(drums)*, Gary Tibbs *(bass guitar on 'Back To The Light', 'Let Your Heart Rule Your Head', and 'Rollin' Over')*, Neil Murray *(bass guitar on 'Love Token' and 'I'm Scared')*, John Deacon *(bass guitar on 'Nothin' But Blue')*, Geoff Dugmore *(drums on 'Let Your Heart Rule Your Head' and 'Rollin' Over')*, Mike Moran *(piano on 'Love Token' and 'Rollin' Over', keyboards on 'Last Horizon')*, Don Airey *(extra keyboards on 'Resurrection' and 'Nothin' But Blue')*, Miriam Stockley and Maggie Ryder *(backing vocals on 'Back To The Light' and 'Rollin' Over')*, Suzie O'List and Gill O'Donovan *(backing vocals on 'Back To The Light' and 'Let Your Heart Rule Your Head')*, Chris Thompson *(co-lead vocals and backing vocals on 'Rollin' Over')*
Recorded: Allerton Hill, Surrey; Mountain Studios, Montreux; Sarm East Studios, Aldgate; Mono Valley, Monmouth; Marcus and Townhouse Studios, London, 1988-1992
Producers: Brian May and Justin Shirley-Smith

Rumors of a true solo record from Brian May had persisted ever since he stepped into The Record Plant in April 1983. Fans weren't satisfied with *Star Fleet Project*, and Brian had promised that he would start working on a solo album whenever Queen weren't the priority. Working with Bad News and Anita Dobson wasn't enough for the guitarist, though he enjoyed both projects immensely. So, in 1988, just before Queen went back into the studios to work on *The Miracle*, Brian started to demo a handful of songs that would ultimately end up on his first full-length project.

"Most of the time I've been working on my own," he told *Record Collector* in 1989. "The solo project is mainly about getting all the stuff I've had in my head onto tape, but I've found that some of my ideas ... have ended up on [*The Miracle*]. I think that the best ideas should really be concentrated towards the group, because it's still the best vehicle I can find – as the group is so good!" At least five songs were known to have been recorded in 1988: 'Back To The Light', 'I'm Scared', 'Let Your Heart Rule Your Head', a cover of The Small Faces' 'Rollin' Over' and 'Too Much Love Will Kill You', the latter written around 1986 and then recorded during sessions for *The Miracle*, though ultimately rejected.

Instead of an instrumental guitar album, one that might have been generated by, say, Jimmy Page or Brian's blues hero Jeff Beck, *Back To The Light* was an attempt to create a thematic album, showcasing a whole range of emotions Brian had been dealing with. "This isn't a 'guitar virtuoso' album," he told *Gold Compact Disc Magazine* in 1992. "It's an album of songs designed to feature a lot of guitar." The Red Special is in full force and Brian sounds more sure of his guitar-playing than on recent Queen albums, conveying the emotions not only through his singing but also through his strings. "For me, this album was a sort of divide, a crossroads," he explained to *RCD Magazine*. "In the beginning, I wanted to get back to basics and make an album on my own just to see what would happen. Now, in the end, I've put out something because I actually do have something to say, and it's worth saying. Over these five years, my life and feelings underwent a catastrophic change, and the music throughout this record reflects the entire process."

Lyrically, Brian was a confused man, which he even admitted in the liner notes for the album. "The song that begins the album," he explained to *Guitar World*, "'The Dark', has a lot of [guitars] built up like a wall. At the beginning, I'm trying to give the impression of a very frightened child faced with a very impossible wall. So there's a lot of guitars on there ... First, there's total blackness, and then there's light at the end of the tunnel, and points where you see inspiration in someone else's life. If the album is appreciated by people who are into what I'm into, then that will be enough. Everything else will be a bonus."

That blackness was spurred by a deep depression that started in 1987, following what turned out to be Queen's final tour. With the band off the road, his marriage in a shambles due to an increasing preoccupation with *EastEnders* star Anita Dobson, and his father dying of cancer in June 1988, Brian poured his struggles into song, enlisting the help of professional songwriters and friends to help him make some semblance of sense. The songs written during this period expressed a whole range of emotions, and dealt with the pain and difficulty of a failing relationship, and the sadness and emptiness of loss. Even the comedic, lighthearted numbers – 'Love Token' and 'Let Your Heart Rule Your Head' – betray the façade, and are tinged with traces of real-life experiences, be it domestic discord in the former or meaningful advice to trust emotions over logic in the latter.

"I'm a bit wary of explaining things, but throughout the whole album you can hear this person who is very confused, confronted by different situations as they roll past him," Brian attempted to clarify in *Guitarist Magazine*. "So I started off with the idea that there's this little baby in the cradle, he's completely in the dark and the dark is something really frightening. It was convenient that it was 'We Will Rock You' because here was this nursery rhyme and the version Queen did was very big and macho. Total opposites."

Songs for *Back To The Light* were tried out during sessions for *The Miracle* and *Innuendo*, and vice versa: Brian later revealed that 'Headlong' and 'I Can't Live With You' were intended for *Back To The Light*, while 'Too Much Love Will Kill You' was to be on *The Miracle*. In 1991, between sessions for what would ultimately become *Made In Heaven*, Brian continued work on his album, with 'Driven By You', 'Just One Life' and 'Love Token' recorded and completed by the end of the year. In November, it became evident that 'Driven By You' had the most potential to be a hit, and was duly released the day after Freddie's death, which Brian initially worried would be seen as a callous cash-in, but it in fact had the vocalist's blessing: "Tell him he must do it. What better publicity could he have?"

"It's a real strain doing solo projects," Brian lamented in 1989 to *Record Collector*, "because you are on your own. You can bring in other musicians, but it's not like being in a group situation where the responsibility is shared. At the end of the day, I'm left sitting in the studio with an engineer, saying, 'Is this worth it or not?', and it's very hard to make those judgments. Most of what I like is spontaneous, and most of the songs I write I like in a very rough form, so they don't sound as if they've been produced. So these solo tracks are difficult to take to record companies, because there is no obvious hit, and the material is not produced to sound like Queen records. Left to my own devices, I like to do things which are quite off the beaten track, then I wonder why they aren't hits! It's basically my own fault because I don't like the 'hit' format."

Nevertheless, *Back To The Light* and its five singles – 'Driven By You', 'Too Much Love Will Kill You', 'Back To The Light', 'Resurrection' and 'Last Horizon' – became hits, with four of the five singles reaching the Top 30. The album, released in September 1992 just before The Brian May Band went out on the road in its support, peaked at an impressive No. 6 in the UK, certainly the best showing any Queen-related solo album had received since *Mr Bad Guy* in 1985. Comparisons were made to the later Queen albums, and most were in Brian's favor: certainly, he was no Freddie, but the vocalist's influence was manifest. "[It was] very strange," he explained to *Guitarist Magazine*, of not recording with Freddie. "It was always a project which was in parallel with Queen, because we always had a positive attitude to people doing stuff outside the band, getting new experiences and bringing them back into the band. But it did become something very different at the end, when Freddie went. I started to realize that this was a kind of bridge towards the next part of life, whatever that may be.

"I always felt close to Freddie in the studio, whether he was there or not, because we worked together so intensively over the years. So I can still hear him talking to me when I'm doing some of this stuff, especially when I'm trying to sing – which has not been easy. But I wanted to do it, because I didn't want anyone else to be speaking my ideas when it was such a personal statement. So it was good for me to imagine Freddie sitting there."

Even though Brian had lost a collaborator in Freddie, he found a new working relationship with Cozy Powell. The drummer, who had a long and illustrious career, had been working with Black

Sabbath in the late 1980s when Brian was asked to contribute guitar to that band's *Headless Cross* album. The two, who had met in the mid-1970s and were appreciators of each others' work for as long, discovered an instant rapport, and in addition to Cozy playing drums on most of the *Back To The Light* tracks, Brian also contributed guitar to two tracks from Cozy's solo album *The Drums Are Back*. He liked the backing tracks for 'Ride To Win' and 'Somewhere In Time' so much that he added lyrics, creating 'Resurrection' and 'Nothin' But Blue' respectively, and Cozy became Brian's drummer of choice. It was a relationship that would last for most of the decade until the drummer's untimely death in April 1998.

Back To The Light is an interesting paradox: although it's Brian's most cohesive solo album it still sounds disjointed. While the songwriting was strong, the biggest disappointment was Brian's vocal performances, which he was quick to address in, of all places, *Guitarist Magazine*: "In the beginning, Freddie didn't have all the powers that he wanted to have as a vocalist; he just worked to achieve those and improved as he worked over the years. So I just took that as a good example. I thought, 'If I'm going to sing this album, I'm going to have to work at it', and I treated it rather like a weight-training program – I went in there, sang my guts out and tried to reach further every day. It's amazing what you can do if you really try. I was quite stunned, because in the beginning I was struggling with it – all those regions around top A – and in the end, in 'Resurrection', I got up to a top D above that, without going into falsetto, which was quite a little crusade for me. I was amazed that I could actually do that. It's another question as to whether I can do it on stage, but at least it happened, as least I know I can get there if I really try hard enough."

The lyrics were strong, the musical performances were consistent, and it wouldn't have been impossible to imagine most of the tracks becoming Queen songs. "I suppose [Queen comparisons are] inevitable," Brian observed in *Guitar World* in 1993. "There's bound to be similarities. I've got to carry some trademarks away from Queen, because I can't help being me. In my opinion, there are superficial similarities to Queen, but I think what is underneath on this album is actually pretty different. It's much more of a personal statement." The album it most closely resembled was *Innuendo*; indeed, it could be seen as a companion piece to that album, as if *Back To The Light* were Brian's own interpretation of the same circumstances. The only difference was

that it lacked the input of a four-way collaboration, with more emphasis on the guitar. "Yeah, I enjoy [the heavier stuff]," Brian said in *Guitar World*. "I have an outlet for that now, whereas sometimes the band had to be a bit more broad, stylistically. Now I can get more into the heavy stuff. And I do enjoy it, I must admit."

Unsurprisingly, the guitar work is exemplary; the Red Special could have done most of the singing (indeed, it did on special guitar-dominated versions of 'Nothin' But Blue', 'Just One Life' and 'Too Much Love Will Kill You'). "Ninety-five percent of [the songs were recorded with the Red Special]," Brian said in *Guitar World*. "On a couple of tracks, I also used this wonderful guitar that Joe Satriani gave me, which was a big departure for me. He gave it to me after we did the Guitar Legends concert in Seville, which I was lucky enough to be asked to put together. We all had a great time and I developed an even greater admiration for Satriani than I already had. He's such an amazingly dexterous player, you expect him to be technical and nothing else. But the fact is that he's got so much soul and feeling in what he does. He's really a guitarist's guitarist. Plus, he's a nice guy. Anyway, he sent me this guitar and I picked it up and was inspired. So I kicked in with it."

While Brian would record one further solo album, he would never again travel this path so successfully. It was touching to learn that Freddie was always a constant source of inspiration, no matter where he may have been. "There are many threads in the album," Brian explained. "And one of them is Freddie, obviously. It had to be. Because all through the making of this album I was becoming more and more aware that Freddie was facing the end of his life. So obviously I was aware as I finished off [these songs] that in some way it was going to relate to Freddie, too. And also to my dad and also to me. So there were a whole lot of link-ups there." It may have been the end for Queen, but a resurrection was just around the corner.

FREDDIE MERCURY
THE FREDDIE MERCURY ALBUM
Parlophone PCSD 124, November 1992 [4]
Parlophone CDPCSD 124, November 1992 [4]

'The Great Pretender' (3'25), 'Foolin' Around *(Steve Brown mix)'* (3'38), 'Time *(Niles Rodger mix)'* (3'49), 'Your Kind Of Lover *(Steve Brown mix)'* (3'59), 'Exercises In Free Love' (3'58), 'In My Defence *(Ron Nevison mix)'* (3'52), 'Mr Bad Guy *(Brian Malouf mix)'*

(3'55), 'Let's Turn It On *(Jeff Lord-Alge mix)'* (3'46), 'Living On My Own *(remix)'* (3'39), 'Love Kills' (4'29), 'Barcelona' (5'38)

FREDDIE MERCURY
THE GREAT PRETENDER

Hollywood HR 61402 2, November 1992

'The Great Pretender (Brian Malouf mix)' (3'39), 'Foolin' Around (Steve Brown mix)' (3'36), 'Time (Nile Rodgers mix)' (3'50), 'Your Kind Of Lover (Steve Brown mix)' (3'59), 'Exercises In Free Love' (3'57), 'In My Defence (Ron Nevison mix)' (3'52), 'Mr Bad Guy (Brian Malouf mix)' (4'01), 'Let's Turn It On (Jeff Lord-Alge mix)' (3'46), 'Living On My Own (remix)' (3'39), 'My Love Is Dangerous (Jeff Lord-Alge mix)' (3'40), 'Love Kills (Richard Wolf mix)' (3'28)

To commemorate Freddie, a compilation was inevitable and expected. What emerged has been the cause of controversy and debate ever since: instead of collecting Freddie's greatest hits onto a single disc compilation, a collection of ten of Freddie's songs from *Mr Bad Guy* and various singles was sent off to several producers to remix (and, in some cases, drastically restructure) the songs. The resulting albums – *The Freddie Mercury Album*, released in the UK, and its North American counterpart, *The Great Pretender* – are interesting blends of some of Freddie's finest material, though that didn't stop fans from crying foul: many believed that the original tracks were fine the way they were and should have been released unchanged. Roger agreed, writing in a contemporary letter to fan club members, "I'm not too keen on [the album] myself, and wish to point out that due to certain factors, one of which being Brian's solo commitments, none of the three remaining members of Queen have been involved in any way with the record." Nevertheless, the album was Freddie's most successful, peaking at No. 4 in the UK and charting respectably elsewhere.

The tracklistings were similar on both the UK and US issues, though there were some minor differences: the original versions of 'The Great Pretender', 'Love Kills' and 'Barcelona' were all present on the UK version, while remixed versions of the first two and 'My Love Is Dangerous' in lieu of the third were released on the US version. Thankfully, none of the *Barcelona* tracks were touched, leaving Freddie's magnum opus to be enjoyed in all its operatic glory, as it should be.

Whether or not the remixing was necessary is a matter of personal taste. However, all the songs sound fresh and lively, and even some of Freddie's dance-oriented material ('Foolin' Around', 'Your Kind Of Lover', 'My Love Is Dangerous') are transformed into interesting amalgamations of rock and dance that the original versions failed to achieve. 'The Great Pretender' is morphed into an epic rocker, and subtle remixes of 'Time' and 'In My Defence' enhance what were already powerful ballads. Even 'Mr Bad Guy' is transformed from a deliciously flamboyant orchestral piece into a snarling rocker. But considering the scarcity of *Mr Bad Guy*, a more conventional compilation would have been the preferred option; unfortunately, fans had to wait 14 years, and suffered endless remixes in the meantime.

FREDDIE MERCURY
REMIXES

TOCP 8151 (Japan), 1993

'Living On My Own (No More Brothers extended remix)' (5'13), 'Time (Niles Rodgers mix)' (3'50), 'Love Kills (Wolf Euro mix)' (3'25), 'The Great Pretender (Brian Malouf mix)' (3'39), 'My Love Is Dangerous (Jeff Lord-Alge mix)' (3'46), 'Living On My Own (Roger S mix)' (5'45)

Featuring six tracks – four of which were extracted from *The Great Pretender / The Freddie Mercury Album*, with the other two (bookending the album) an extended version of the popular No More Brothers 'Living On My Own' remix along with another remix of the same track – *Remixes* is largely superfluous but was worthwhile for having brought about a new wave of popularity for Freddie's back catalog. The album eluded UK and US releases, and was available only in Japan, Holland, Brazil, Italy and Bolivia. If you enjoyed the remixes immensely, this is for you; otherwise, stick to the superior compilations.

THE BRIAN MAY BAND
LIVE AT THE BRIXTON ACADEMY

Parlophone PCSD 150, February 1994 [20]
Parlophone CDPCSD 150, February 1994 [20]

'Back To The Light' (5'41), 'Driven By You' (4'17), 'Tie Your Mother Down' (4'39), 'Love Token' (3'05), 'Headlong' (6'08), 'Love Of My Life' (4'44), "39 / Let Your Heart Rule Your Head' (4'12), 'Too Much Love Will Kill You' (4'33), 'Since You've Been Gone' (3'41), 'Now I'm Here' (6'58), 'Guitar Extravagance' (6'06),

'Resurrection' (10'08), 'Last Horizon' (3'14), 'We Will Rock You' (3'54), 'Hammer To Fall' (5'31)

Musicians: Brian May *(vocals, guitars)*, Cozy Powell *(drums)*, Neil Murray *(bass guitar)*, Jamie Moses *(guitars, backing vocals)*, Spike Edney *(piano, keyboards, vocals)*, Cathy Porter *(backing vocals)*, Shelley Preston *(backing vocals)*
Recorded: Brixton Academy, London, 15 June 1993 by Justin Shirley-Smith
Producers: Brian May and Justin Shirley-Smith

Despite Brian's aversion to live albums (see his comments regarding Queen's *Live Killers*), it was inevitable that a souvenir of Brian's much-anticipated return to the stage would be released. With only 15 songs crammed onto one disc, *Live At The Brixton Academy* is half Queen, half *Back To The Light* material, with one cover ('Since You've Been Gone', originally recorded by Rainbow, featuring drummer Cozy Powell) thrown in for good measure. In the long run, it's a worthwhile purchase, with refreshing performances of Queen favorites and a much-needed shot in the arm to material from Brian's first solo album.

The album was conceived during the second leg of the Back To The Light world tour, though Brian cited three factors that almost prevented its release: first, the set list was edited, with only truncated versions of most songs appearing; second, a song had to be dropped for copyright reasons; and third, Brian encountered a multitude of technical issues throughout the night. The song that was lost was a reworked rendition of John Lennon's 'God (The Dream Is Over)', which featured a new set of lyrics about the break-up of Queen and Brian's desire to move on. Unfortunately, after Brian sent a version to Lennon's estate, Yoko Ono simply never responded, and the song had to be dropped.

These are minor complaints since *Live At The Brixton Academy* is a wholly rewarding listen, especially the never-before-performed 'Headlong', which went off in a new direction with Brian's vocals. It may not have been Queen, but it was the closest thing available to the magnificence and majesty of their shows, and Brian seemed the most willing to carry on the tradition of his former band's lavish production numbers. The 23 minutes that consist of 'Now I'm Here', 'Guitar Extravagance' and 'Resurrection' are unquestionably powerful, and Brian's ever-evolving guitar solo is impressive, no matter what your opinions of such a display may be. While the long-deleted video is

superior because of the added bonus of visuals, the album is a suitable showcase of the simple joy that Brian got out of performing live.

ROGER TAYLOR
HAPPINESS?

Parlophone PCSD 157, September 1994 [22]
Parlophone CDPCSD 157, September 1994 [22]

'Nazis 1994' (2'35), 'Happiness?' (3'17), 'Revelations' (3'44), 'Touch The Sky' (5'04), 'Foreign Sand' (6'53), 'Freedom Train' (6'12), '"You Had To Be There"' (2'55), 'The Key' (4'25), 'Everybody Hurts Sometime' (2'52), 'Loneliness...' (2'25), 'Dear Mr Murdoch' (4'19), 'Old Friends' (3'33)

Musicians: Roger Taylor *(vocals, drums, guitars, bass guitar, stuff)*, Jason Falloon *(guitars)*, Phil Spalding *(bass guitar on 'Revelations', 'The Key', and 'Old Friends')*, Mike Crossley *(piano and keyboards on 'Happiness?', 'Touch The Sky', 'Freedom Train', 'The Key', 'Dear Mr Murdoch', and 'Old Friends')*, Catherine Porter *(backing vocals on 'Everybody Hurts Sometime')*, Joshua J. Macrae *(programming)*, Yoshiki *(arrangement, drums, piano and synthesizer on 'Foreign Sand')*, Jim Cregan *(guitars on 'Foreign Sand')*, Phil Chen *(bass guitar on 'Foreign Sand')*, Dick Marx *(string arrangement on 'Foreign Sand')*, Brad Buxer and Geoff Grace *(programming on 'Foreign Sand')*
Recorded: Cosford Mill, Surrey, late 1993-mid 1994 *('Foreign Sand' recorded at One on One Recording, Los Angeles)*
Producers: Roger Taylor and Yoshiki *('Foreign Sand')*, Roger Taylor and Joshua J Macrae *(all other tracks)*

Following the Freddie Mercury Tribute Concert, Roger all but disappeared from the public eye. Still mourning his friend's death, he jumped back into writing music, much as Brian did, in order to find solace and begin the healing process. With The Cross no longer an active band, Roger started working on some new songs in mid-1992 for his first solo album since *Strange Frontier*.

However, there were other factors to deal with first. Roger and John returned to the studios in October 1993 to complete work on songs from the final Queen sessions two years prior, though progress was halted – and resumed slowly – when Brian got wind of the rhythm section's intents. Understandably livid that the pair would return to work without him, the guitarist finished his world tour and returned to the studios to join them in the recording process, beginning a lengthy,

18-month period of emotionally draining activity for all three. Intriguingly, Roger and John had formed an alliance, and most of the pair's letters to the fan club throughout the year made special mention of the two of them; their appearance at the Cowdray Ruins charity concert in September 1993 further hinted at their like-minded, almost bullish intentions.

During breaks from *Made In Heaven*, Roger continued working on his album, completing it by the beginning of the new year. Recorded entirely at his home studio, Cosford Mill – except for two tracks ('Foreign Sand' and a reworking of 'Final Destination') recorded with Japanese musician Yoshiki at One On One Recording in Los Angeles – the resulting album turned out to be Roger's strongest to date, certainly more personal than anything he had recorded either as a solo artist, with The Cross, or with Queen.

Although the arrangements and lyrics were more mature and evolved than those of *Strange Frontier* and *Fun In Space*, they did reflect some of his latterday Queen songs, and certainly his contributions to *Mad: Bad: And Dangerous To Know* and *Blue Rock*. Roger admitted this in a brief interview, saying, "There are a lot of optimistic sides, some other more tense atmospheres; in fact, lots of different feelings. The album is like that too because I'm maturing!" The songs encompassed a range of emotions: love, discovery, loneliness, pain and happiness. The odd man out was 'Nazis 1994', a scathing diatribe against the neo-Nazis who claim that the Holocaust never happened. This song gave voice to Roger's anger and horror when, during a tour with The Cross, he visited the concentration camp at Dachau.

Elsewhere, the album covered corrupt politicians and the rise of the far right. "Queen was always very apolitical," Roger told *The West Magazine* in May 1994. "Though some of our songs have been taken up as political anthems, I am not a politician. I am just interested in bringing this subject to peoples' attention. Nothing is wrong with a bit of froth, but it is important to write about things that matter." Roger was exceptionally bitter on 'Dear Mr Murdoch', a sarcastic diatribe against Rupert Murdoch whose tabloid, *The Sun*, had hounded Freddie in his final days, segueing neatly into the poignant 'Old Friends', suitably concluding the album in honor of Freddie. Otherwise, *Happiness?* is a fairly straightforward album, more honest and open than Brian's *Back To The Light*. "I hope that it's a good title," Roger mused in 1994. "I think that it's in harmony with the simple truths that I've tried to find. I really wanted to write a very personal album."

Perhaps the most important subject that Roger wrote about was Freddie. 'Old Friends' was a specific tribute to him, but references are made throughout the album, be they in terms of musical arrangement ('Foreign Sand' sounds like a cousin to Freddie's more ambitious compositions) or lyrics, which are sprinkled throughout nearly every song. In a way, *Happiness?* is Roger's way of distancing himself from the Leviathan that was Queen and applying a full-stop to the past 25 years of his life. If anything, it was a 50-minute therapy session.

The album was released four days after what would have been Freddie's 48th birthday, reaching an impressive No. 22 in the UK, the first time any of Roger's albums had achieved the UK Top Thirty since *Strange Frontier* over a decade before. The singles – 'Nazis 1994' in May, 'Foreign Sand' in September, and 'Happiness?' in November – all performed well, indicating that Roger had finally struck a chord with his audience, though the success was only brief – all the singles (and the album itself) remained in the charts for just two weeks each.

After his customary trip to the Gosport Festival in July 1994, Roger embarked on his first proper solo tour that September, starting off in Japan and winding his way back to England, France and Italy; the success of the latter shows was so great that a full tour of the country (which Queen visited only three times, in 1984) was booked for the beginning of January 1995. Roger enjoyed himself immensely and, with the ghost of The Cross finally laid to rest, was ready to move on and advance his solo career. It showed a lot of promise, and *Happiness?* was just the beginning.

BRIAN MAY
ANOTHER WORLD

Parlophone 4949731, June 1998 [23]
Parlophone 4949732, June 1998 [23]
Hollywood HR 62103 2, September 1998

'Space' (0'47), 'Business' (5'07), 'China Belle' (4'00), 'Why Don't We Try Again' (5'23), 'On My Way Up' (2'57), 'Cyborg' (3'53), 'The Guv'nor' (4'12), 'Wilderness' (4'52), 'Slow Down' (4'17), 'One Rainy Wish' (4'04), 'All The Way From Memphis' (5'16), 'Another World' (7'30)

Musicians: Brian May *(vocals, guitars, bass guitar, keyboards, programming, and arrangements)*, Cozy

Powell *(drums on 'Business', 'China Belle', 'Why Don't We Try Again', 'The Guv'nor', 'Slow Down', 'One Rainy Wish', and 'All The Way From Memphis', percussion on 'Why Don't We Try Again')*, Neil Murray *(bass guitar on 'China Belle', 'Slow Down', and 'One Rainy Wish')*, Taylor Hawkins *(drums on 'Cyborg')*, Jeff Beck *(guitar on 'The Guv'nor')*, Spike Edney *(keyboards on 'Slow Down')*, Jamie Moses *(guitar on 'Slow Down')*, Steve Ferrone *(drums and percussion on 'Another World')*, Ken Taylor *(bass guitar on 'Another World')*, Cathy Porter *(backing vocals on 'On My Way Up')*, Shelley Preston *(backing vocals on 'On My Way Up' and 'All The Way From Memphis')*, Nikki Love *(backing vocals on 'All The Way From Memphis')*, Becci Glover *(backing vocals on 'All The Way From Memphis')*, Ian Hunter *(special guest raconteur on 'All The Way From Memphis')*
Recorded: Allerton Hill, Surrey, and Metropolis Studios, London, 1995-1998
Producers: Brian May and Justin Shirley-Smith *(Eddie Kramer on 'One Rainy Wish')*

Following the release of *Back To The Light* and its subsequent tour, Brian finally felt confident enough to finish the final songs that Freddie had recorded before his death in 1991. The magnitude of the project, combined with continually hearing his dead friend's voice, was especially emotional for the guitarist but gave him an idea for a new project. Tentatively titled *Heroes*, the album would be a collection of his personal favorite tracks along with songs written especially for those he considered his heroes.

The first fruits of the idea were laid down in 1995: 'One Rainy Wish' and 'Hot Patootie (Bless My Soul)'. The first track, originally written and recorded by Jimi Hendrix in 1967, was later submitted to the Eddie Kramer tribute album to Hendrix, *In From The Storm*, while the second track, originally written for *The Rocky Horror Picture Show* in the 1970s, was submitted to the NSO Ensemble cast recording for their production of the cult classic stage show later in 1995. The following year, Brian laid down a series of covers, with only one of them given away for a side project. 'Slow Down', 'Only Make Believe' and 'Maybe Baby' – popularized by Larry Williams (and later The Beatles), Conway Twitty and Buddy Holly respectively – were all recorded with Brian's core band: Cozy Powell on drums, Neil Murray on bass, Spike Edney on keyboards and Jamie Moses on guitar.

Later that year, Brian was approached by Morgan Fisher, who had provided auxiliary keyboards on

Queen's 1982 Hot Space European tour; he was putting together a tribute album to Mott the Hoople, of which Fisher had previously been a member, and wanted Brian to participate. The song Brian recorded was 'All The Way From Memphis', a song destined for the *Heroes* album but first released in 1996 on the (anagrammatic) tribute album *Moth Poet Hotel*.

The final track submitted for the *Another World* album was The Shadows' 'F.B.I.', recorded with Francis Rossi and Rick Parfitt of Status Quo in 1997, though the song's first release came on *Twang!: A Tribute To Hank Marvin* that same year. Shortly after the Bejart Ballet concert in January 1997, which saw the three remaining members of Queen reunited on 'The Show Must Go On', with Elton John on vocals, Brian was so touched by the response to Queen's music that he wrote 'No-One But You (Only The Good Die Young)' as a tribute to Freddie, and it was at this point that the *Heroes* project was abandoned and the song was instead submitted to Roger and John as a potential Queen track. Since it was originally to have been the closing song on *Heroes*, Brian chose instead 'Another World' as the album's finale; that song was originally written and recorded for the film *Sliding Doors* but rejected (see the Part Three entry for 'Another World'). Brian decided "that, in order to have something worthwhile for the next Brian May album, I would have to rediscover who I was," as he put it in a 1998 interview with *Classic Rock*. "I decided to go out and do a lot of playing and open myself up for projects because I didn't want to make another introspective album. I thought I would go out into the world, experience things and rediscover my roots.

"The best thing was that it removed this last element of nostalgia from the project," Brian continued. "It reminded me that what this album is supposed to be about is my own journey. It's not about revisiting my heroes. That's a part of it, but there's a whole lot more going on ... There's a fine line between being very commercial and without any depth on one side, and being totally academic and not relating to people on the other ... I have a great interest in operating in this area which is almost art for art's sake, but you are speaking to people and you care whether they buy it or not. I want them to feel something. I want it to do something for them, which, thank God, it normally seems to."

Ultimately, however, *Another World* plays as a weak imitation of *Back To The Light*, with the guitarist still searching for the answers to all the questions posed on the first album. There are some great songs here –

'Business', 'Why Don't We Try Again' and 'All The Way From Memphis' are the highlights – but most of it is either half-baked or can be found on *Back To The Light*. 'Space' provides a similarly atmospheric introduction to its predecessor, while 'On My Way Up' is an even more light-hearted acoustic affair than 'Let Your Heart Rule Your Head'. Brian revisits the blues again, even inviting former Yardbird Jeff Beck to trade licks with him on 'The Guv'nor', but some truly dreadful moments are contained on 'Cyborg' and the schmaltzy title track. Whereas *Back To The Light* had taken many years to record, it sounded cohesive; *Another World* sounds pieced together with little forethought. It's hard to believe that it took Brian six years to generate this disappointing album, especially since he's a musician and songwriter who can write some truly inspired songs.

However, the advantages that *Another World* has over *Back To The Light* is six years of technological progress and the obvious improvement in Brian's voice. Whereas he sounds nervous and unsure of himself on his first effort (a deliciously unintentional auditory interpretation of the words, which are equally nervous and unsure), the intervening years found him performing lengthy tours with The Brian May Band, strengthening his approach and making his voice on a par with, if not Freddie, at least lead singers from several other top bands of the day. If anything, *Another World* is musically and vocally a stronger album, but the material hadn't progressed enough to make it superior to *Back To The Light*.

The album was released in June 1998 with an uncharacteristic amount of promotion, and Brian sat for interviews not only to discuss the album but also to talk about Cozy Powell, who had died in a car accident on 5 April (see Part Three entry for 'Business'). The promotion must have helped since the album charted at No. 23 in the UK; though not the No. 6 that *Back To The Light* had attained, nor the No. 20 that *Live At The Brixton Academy* had, it still broke the Top Thirty, which to Brian was the measurement of success. Two mini-albums – *Retro Rock Special* and *Red Special* – were released to attract more buyers in the US and Japan respectively, but when the album appeared in the US in September 1998 Hollywood Records gave it little promotion and it sank without trace. As a result, Brian refused to tour the US, though he did appear at the New World Music Theater in Chicago to perform a short promotional show; it would be another eight years before he performed a live show Stateside.

Guitarist magazine made special mention of Brian's voice, which "lends so much more emotion to the proceedings", and praised the versatility of the album, concluding that "Brian's made sure that there's something here for just about everyone." *Metal Hammer* singled out 'Business' and 'China Belle' as the highlights of the album, but said that "not all of *Another World* goes for the jugular like these two tracks, and wispy balladry like 'Why Don't We Try Again' and the title track are perhaps best consigned to the memory of the last Queen album." *Q* magazine, in its rambling review, started off with "The past inevitably follows Brian May around like a small black dog chained to his ankle. No choice but to pick it up and embrace it seems to be the pragmatic response", observing later that the album "might, in the vague half-light, just about pass for an anthem-free, Mercuryless tilt at former glories."

"Yes, I am pleased with it," Brian said in 1998. "It is more representative of my own journey and has something to say. I think I would feel bad if I went on the road again and I didn't have something to say that I thought was important." Shortly after the tour, Brian announced he was through with making solo albums; whether it was down to lacklustre sales or that he had finally found a worthy path to travel is open to interpretation.

ROGER TAYLOR
ELECTRIC FIRE
Parlophone 496 7241, September 1998 [53]
Parlophone 496 7240, September 1998 [53]

'Pressure On' (4'56), 'A Nation Of Haircuts' (3'32), 'Believe In Yourself' (5'00), 'Surrender' (3'36), 'People On Streets' (4'11), 'The Whispers' (6'05), 'Is It Me?' (3'23), 'No More Fun' (4'13), 'Tonight' (3'44), 'Where Are You Now?' (4'48), 'Working Class Hero' (4'41), 'London Town, C'mon Down' (7'11)

Musicians: Roger Taylor *(vocals, drums, percussion, guitars, bass guitar, keyboards)*, Keith Prior *(drums on 'Pressure On', 'A Nation of Haircuts', 'The Whisperers', 'Tonight', 'Working Class Hero', and 'London Town, C'mon Down')*, Steve Barnacle *(bass guitar on 'Pressure On', 'A Nation of Haircuts', 'Believe In Yourself', 'Surrender', 'Is It Me?', 'Where Are You Now?', 'Working Class Hero', and 'London Town, C'mon Down')*, Mike Crossley *(keyboards on 'Pressure On', 'A Nation of Haircuts', 'Believe In Yourself', 'Is It Me?', 'Where Are You Now?', 'Working*

Class Hero', and 'London Town, C'mon Down'), Jonathan Perkins *(keyboards on 'Surrender', 'People On Streets', and 'The Whisperers', keyboards and additional vocals on 'Surrender')*, Jason Falloon *(guitars on 'Pressure On', 'Believe In Yourself', 'Surrender', 'People On Streets', 'No More Fun', 'Where Are You Now?', and 'London Town, C'mon Down', acoustic guitar and bass on 'Tonight')*, Keith Airey *(guitars on 'A Nation of Haircuts' and 'Is It Me?')*, Matthew Exelby *(guitars on 'The Whisperers')*, Treana Morris *(additional vocals on 'Pressure On', 'Surrender', and 'London Town, C'mon Down')*, Arty *(additional vocals on 'People On Streets')*
Recorded: Cosford Mill, Surrey, early 1997-mid 1998
Producers: Roger Taylor, Joshua J Macrae

The four years between *Happiness?* and *Electric Fire* saw a resurgence of activity from Roger. As well as embarking on a major tour in support of the former album, which ran until early 1995, he also finished work on *Made In Heaven* with Brian and John. In between sitting down for promotional interviews as well as facing the camera again for the documentary *Champions Of The World*, he found time to squeeze in a few appearances with the SAS Band (formed by keyboardist Spike Edney, who had worked with Queen and with Roger in The Cross) as well as with Queen fanatics, Foo Fighters, at their Shepherd's Bush Empire gig, providing the drums on 'Sheer Heart Attack' – the first time he had played that song live in 13 years.

Roger still yearned to record new material. *Happiness?* had been a surprising and popular album, and another impetus was a performance with Elton John at the Bejart Ballet for Life in January 1997, which reunited Roger with Brian and John for one final concert. The show's finale, a shaky version of 'The Show Must Go On', didn't satiate Roger's desire for performance, and he quickly began recording a new album. While he had been recording demos throughout 1995 and 1996, sessions started proper in early 1997, shortly after the the Bejart Ballet, and proved to be exceptionally prolific: in addition to the 12 tracks released on the album, two further songs – an original titled 'One Night Stand' and a cover of Little Richard's 'Keep A Knockin'' – were also laid down. With an evolving roster of musicians, the sessions lasted until the middle of 1998, with familiar faces Jason Falloon and Mike Crossley from the *Happiness?* sessions and several new, younger musicians contributing instrumentally. "I spent quite a long time just coming up with the odd song here

and there," Roger said in a radio interview with SGR Colchester in March 1999, "and then all of a sudden, there it was – an album. And it is very diverse, I think, and of my solo work I think it's the best I've done so far."

The results were impressive, showing a revitalization and maturity both in lyrics and arrangements. For the first time on a solo record, Roger took a back seat to contributing instrumentally, allowing his team of backing musicians to do most of the work. Atypically, and to the chagrin of most of his fans, he provided drums on only seven of the 12 tracks, 'duetting' with his drummer of choice, Keith Prior, on 'Tonight'. Though his instrumental contributions are peppered throughout (most notably in 'People On Streets', which is almost entirely self-performed), he realized that he had a superior band and wanted to use their talents to the fullest.

The album moves through a variety of stylistic changes, though it features what Roger knows best: hard rock. 'A Nation Of Haircuts', 'Surrender', 'People On Streets', 'No More Fun' and the deconstruction of John Lennon's 'Working Class Hero' are all good, healthy rockers, something that had been seriously lacking on *Happiness?*, while Roger morphed into a balladeer on 'Believe In Yourself', 'The Whisperers', 'Is It Me?' and 'Where Are You Now?' Only the opening 'Pressure On' is a mid-tempo rocker, the perfect pop-rock single with a slight hint of Bowie influence, and the closing 'London Town, C'mon Down' is an uncompromising slice of funk, something that Roger had always loved to do.

The messages on the album are oblique and ambiguous, though they all deal with real-life issues and are mostly autobiographical: "Well, I like to think there is some meaning in some of [the songs], yeah!" Roger exclaimed to Colchester radio in 1999. "And I think if you do have an opinion, why not state it as long as you are not preaching at people or boring them? You are not a full, a whole person unless you have some points of view on life and what's around you."

Politicians were given a typical lambasting, though not quite as severely as one might have expected; Roger was particularly outspoken against domestic violence, chronicled in the song 'Surrender', which features a gorgeous lead vocal by newcomer Treana Morris. "Most people experience some kind of domestic violence," Roger said in 1998. "Without going any further, I do think it's something which is very prevalent in society. It's a very difficult issue to deal with as often incidents are kept within the family. It's really pretty foul."

Housed in a deep green cover (with an indistinct, original silkscreen and oil-on-canvas of 'Two-bar electric fire no. 1' by Tim Mara), the album was released in September 1998, almost four years to the day after *Happiness?*. The album's chart success wasn't as great as its predecessor's, peaking at only No. 53 in the UK, while the singles were only marginally more successful. 'Pressure On', released the same day as the album, reached No. 45, while 'Surrender' came in March 1999 and just missed the Top Thirty, peaking at No. 38.

The reviews this time were decidedly split, though most gave Roger a fair assessment. "Taylor sounds full of vim on this latest batch of clumpy ballads and gurning funk-rock," Q magazine said, "but 'London Town, C'mon Down's spoken word narrative and 'Believe In Yourself's rant against 'lawyers with fees ... and deciduous trees' are just two of the tracks hamstrung by our host's baffling lyrical conceits." *Metal Hammer* was a little more complimentary, calling the album "a varied selection of material" and saying that "Queen fans will lap it up." *Guitarist* said, "The material has a real David Bowie feel to it, most notably 'Pressure On', and there is a mixture of styles akin to a full-blown Queen album ... the dabbling in loops and electronics is enjoyable too." *Kerrang!* was exceptionally complimentary, calling it "an eclectic affair which should please both Queen fans and those with a taste for slightly more left-field sounds ... Taylor has managed to brew up some intoxicating songs on *Electric Fire*. 'Pressure On', for instance, is a tense experiment in atmospherics which contrasts nicely with the heavy guitars in 'A Nation Of Haircuts'." The review concluded, rather caustically, that it's "interesting stuff, for those with patience."

It seemed that Roger came out on top this time, yet he wasn't entirely certain he wanted to take the album out on the road; given its relative failure in the charts, it was surprising when he announced a short, UK-only tour that would commence in March 1999 and run for less than three weeks. Roger confirmed that after *Electric Fire*, fans shouldn't expect any more solo work from him. That was disappointing news; while Brian's two solo albums had been released with an eye on what was popular in the charts, Roger had always pushed the envelope and played whatever he felt like playing. While he wasn't always entirely progressive, he did reinvent his sound with each album, and it's for this reason many fans believe that *Electric Fire* is the strongest and finest solo album of his vast catalog. He would eventually go back on his word to not release another solo album, though it took quite a bit of time to rekindle the fire of inspiration.

BRIAN MAY
FURIA

Parlophone 7243 5 28321 2 5 PM 520 (France only), 1999

'Furia Theme (Opening Titles)' (4'40), 'First Glance (Solo Flute)' (1'35), 'Landscape' (1'14), 'Tango: "Cuesta Abajo"' (2'59), 'The Meeting (Solo Guitar)' (1'35), 'First Kiss' (2'03), 'Storm' (2'19), 'Phone' (1'07), 'Pursuit' (3'45), 'Diner' (1'18), 'Apparition' (1'36), 'Arrest' (1'28), 'Father And Son' (1'34), 'Aaron' (0'49), 'Fire' (0'55), 'Gun (Solo Violin)' (1'55), 'Reggae: "Bird In Hand"' (3'30), 'Killing' (1'13), 'Escape' (1'50), 'Go On' (2'20), 'Dream Of Thee' (4'36)

Bonus track on CD: 'Gun *(alternate version)*' (1'33)

Musicians: Brian May *(vocals, guitars, keyboard programming)*, Phillipa Davies *(flute)*, Rolf Wilson *(first violin)*, Dave Lee *(solo horn)*, Emily May *(vocal on 'Apparition')*, The London Musicians Orchestra *(strings)*, Michael Reed *(conductor, orchestrations)*
Recorded: Allerton Hill, Surrey, January-March 1999 *(orchestra recorded at CTS Studios, Watford)*
Producers: Brian May and Justin Shirley-Smith

Shortly after the Another World tour concluded in November 1998, Brian was approached by French film director Alexandre Aja, renowned for the 1997 indie film *Over The Rainbow* and at that time working on his second film. "Gilbert Marouani, a friend, asks if he can propose the film to Brian May," Aja wrote in the liner notes to the *Furia* soundtrack. "A joke? No, I think he's serious. Two months later, I meet Brian in a Paris hotel room, we speak of music, of George Orwell, and of the cinema. I am very tense; he has come to see a first edit. One and a half hours later, silence. I think he was moved. The next day, he calls me, worked all night through; he had written the main theme of the film."

Brian had never worked on a film soundtrack entirely by himself; there had been some confusion between the Queen guitarist and an Australian musician with the same name who wrote the soundtracks to nearly 50 films including *Mad Max* and *Dr Giggles*, but *Furia* became the first soundtrack credited to 'our' Brian.

Adapted from Julio Cortazar's story 'Graffiti' (the same author who had written 'Blow-Up', later turned into a film by Michelangelo Antonioni), the film tells a story of individual liberties being suppressed and young French rebels sneaking out into the night to challenge the patrols.

In a 2001 interview for the Fan Club Convention, Jacky Smith asked Brian about *Furia*. "Very happy to say that you will be able to see *Furia*, the film which I did the music for last year," he replied. "Be warned. It's a very serious film – a very heavy film, and not for those who have a weak stomach. I really mean that, you know, it is not a kind of happy movie, and there's some stuff in there which I still find very hard to watch. So don't bring your kids, folks, and don't come unless you've got a strong supply of optimism inside you, 'cause it takes some watching. It is a film about hope and freedom and a few other things besides but it's tough going in the middle. And I hope you enjoy the music! I certainly enjoyed doing it. It was a kind of formative period for me, but not an easy period, but I kind of poured my feelings into it. Quite proud of it as a soundtrack."

"Basically, I keep busy," Brian said in March 2001 in an interview with Launch.com. "I did a film soundtrack that went out in Europe and [is] just out in England called *Furia*, and it's kind of an artsy film. I doubt if it will see much general release in the States, because it's in the French language, but it's something that I'm very proud of. It's the first full soundtrack that I've done. I've done loads of bits and pieces for films, including *Highlander* and *Flash* and all those things, but this was a complete soundtrack."

As with the *Flash Gordon* soundtrack, the music for *Furia* serves as a backdrop to the film, except for the final track, a gorgeous, acoustic-based ballad titled 'Dream Of Thee'. Otherwise, the music features only minimal instrumentation, and is based almost entirely on the main theme (much as most of Brian's contributions to *Flash Gordon* featured repeated motifs from 'Flash's Theme'). It's not an album to listen to without some prior knowledge of the movie, but it does remain Brian's last true solo release, and therefore deserves a listen.

FREDDIE MERCURY
THE SOLO COLLECTION

Parlophone 5279640, October 2000

Disc One, Mr Bad Guy: 'Let's Turn It On' (3'42), 'Made In Heaven' (4'06), 'I Was Born To Love You' (3'39),

'Foolin' Around' (3'29), 'Your Kind Of Lover' (3'33), 'Mr Bad Guy' (4'10), 'Man Made Paradize' (4'09), 'There Must Be More To Life Than This' (3'01), 'Living On My Own' (3'23), 'My Love Is Dangerous' (3'43), 'Love Me Like There's No Tomorrow' (3'47)

Disc Two, Barcelona: 'Barcelona' (5'39), 'La Japonaise' (4'49), 'The Fallen Priest' (5'46), 'Ensueño' (4'21), 'The Golden Boy' (6'04), 'Guide Me Home' (2'50), 'How Can I Go On' (3'51), 'Overture Picante' (6'39)

Disc Three, The Great Pretender: 'The Great Pretender *(Brian Malouf mix)*' (3'39), 'Foolin' Around *(Steve Brown mix)*' (3'36), 'Time *(Nile Rodgers mix)*' (3'50), 'Your Kind Of Lover *(Steve Brown mix)*' (3'59), 'Exercises In Free Love' (3'57), 'In My Defence *(Ron Nevison mix)*' (3'52), 'Mr Bad Guy *(Brian Malouf mix)*' (4'01), 'Let's Turn It On *(Jeff Lord-Alge mix)*' (3'46), 'Living On My Own *(remix)*' (3'39), 'My Love Is Dangerous *(Jeff Lord-Alge mix)*' (3'40), 'Love Kills *(Richard Wolf mix)*' (3'28)

Disc Four, The Singles 1973-1985: 'I Can Hear Music' (3'30), 'Goin' Back' (3'34), 'Love Kills' (4'31), 'Love Kills *(extended version)*' (5'22), 'I Was Born To Love You *(extended version)*' (7'06), 'Stop All The Fighting' (3'19), 'Stop All The Fighting *(extended version)*' (6'37), 'Made In Heaven *(extended version)*' (4'50), 'She Blows Hot And Cold' (3'27), 'She Blows Hot And Cold *(extended version)*' (5'51), 'Living On My Own *(extended version)*' (6'39), 'My Love Is Dangerous *(extended version)*' (6'29), 'Love Me Like There's No Tomorrow *(extended version)*' (5'32), 'Let's Turn It On *(extended version)*' (5'09)

Disc Five, The Singles 1986-1993: 'Time' (3'59), 'Time *(extended version)*' (4'37), 'Time *(instrumental version)*' (3'23), 'In My Defence' (3'58), 'The Great Pretender' (3'29), 'The Great Pretender *(extended version)*' (5'55), 'Exercises In Free Love' (4'00), 'Barcelona *(edit)*' (4'28), 'Barcelona *(extended version)*' (7'08), 'How Can I Go On' (4'02), 'Living On My Own *(No More Brothers extended remix)*' (5'16), 'Living On My Own *(radio mix)*' (3'39), 'Living On My Own *(club mix)*' (4'27), 'Living On My Own *(Underground Solutions mix)*' (5'46)

Disc Six, Instrumentals: Barcelona' (4'27), 'La Japonaise' (4'47), 'The Fallen Priest' (5'50), 'Ensueño' (4'00), 'The Golden Boy' (6'05), 'Guide Me Home' (2'38), 'How Can I Go On' (3'59), 'Love Me Like There's No Tomorrow' (4'04), 'Made In Heaven' (4'17), 'Mr Bad Guy' (4'14), 'There Must Be More To Life Than This' (3'09), 'In My

Defence' (3'56), 'The Great Pretender' (3'27)

Disc Seven, Rarities (Mr Bad Guy sessions): Let's Turn It On *(a cappella)'* (3'05), 'Made In Heaven *(alternate)'* (4'28), 'I Was Born To Love You *(vocal & piano)'* (2'58), 'Foolin' Around *(early)'* (4'14), 'Foolin' Around *(unreleased extended version)'* (5'38), 'Foolin' Around *(instrumental)'* (3'40), 'Your Kind Of Lover *(early)'* (4'47), 'Your Kind Of Lover *(vocal & piano)'* (3'38), 'Mr Bad Guy *(orchestra out-takes)'* (0'36), 'Mr Bad Guy *(early)'* (3'29), 'There Must Be More To Life Than This *(piano out-takes)'* (2'49), 'Living On My Own *(early/ later)'* (4'30), 'Love Is Dangerous *(early)'* (2'12), 'Love Me Like There's No Tomorrow *(early)'* (2'18), 'Love Me Like There's No Tomorrow *(2nd early)'* (1'04), 'Love Me Like There's No Tomorrow *(3rd early)'* (3'26), 'Love Me Like There's No Tomorrow *(live take)'* (4'22), 'She Blows Hot And Cold *(alternate take featuring Brian May)'* (4'36), 'Gazelle *(demo)'* (1'21), 'Money Can't Buy Happiness *(demo)'* (2'37), 'Love Makin' Love *(demo)'* (3'36), 'God Is Heavy *(demo)'* (1'23), 'New York *(demo)'* (2'13)

Disc Eight, Rarities (Barcelona sessions): The Duet ("The Fallen Priest") *(extract from Garden Lodge)'* (3'04), 'Idea ("Barcelona") *(extract from Garden Lodge)'* (1'13), 'Idea ("Barcelona") *(2nd extract from Garden Lodge)'* (1'05), 'Barcelona *(early version)'* (4'22), 'Barcelona *(Freddie's vocal slave)'* (4'31), 'Barcelona *(later version)'* (4'26), 'La Japonaise *(demo vocal)'* (4'41), 'La Japonaise *(a cappella)'* (4'18), 'Rachmaninov's Revenge ("The Fallen Priest") *(early version)'* (4'47), 'Rachmaninov's Revenge ("The Fallen Priest") *(demo vocal)'* (5'52), 'Ensueño *(live takes)'* (5'36), 'The Golden Boy *(early version)'* (3'55), 'The Golden Boy *(2nd early version)'* (2'57), 'The Golden Boy *(a cappella)'* (5'12), 'Guide Me Home / How Can I Go On *(alternate version)'* (6'54), 'How Can I Go On *(out-take)'* (1'31), 'How Can I Go On *(alternate piano version)'* (3'46), '"When this old tired body wants to sing" *(late night jam)'* (2'42)

Disc Nine, Rarities (other sessions): 'Rain *(Wreckage)'* (3'52), 'Green *(Wreckage)'* (3'15), 'The Man From Manhattan *(Eddie Howell)'* (3'22), 'Love Is The Hero *(Billy Squier)'* (5'22), 'Lady With A Tenor Sax *(Billy Squier)'* (4'02), 'Hold On *(with Jo Dare)'* (3'39), 'Heaven For Everyone *(The Cross)'* (4'48), 'Love Kills *(rock mix)'* (4'28), 'Love Kills *(instrumental)'* (4'27), 'The Great Pretender *(demo)'* (3'05), 'Holding On *(demo)'* (4'12), 'It's So You *(demo)'* (2'40), 'I Can't Dance / Keep Smilin'

(demo)' (3'43), 'Horns Of Doom *(demo)'* (4'17), 'Yellow Breezes *(demo)'* (5'26), 'Have A Nice Day *(demo)'* (0'46)

Disc Ten, The David Wigg Interviews: London 1979 (The Crazy Tour) (8'08), Munich 1984 (Part 1: The Works Tour) (11'24), Munich 1984 (Part 2: Going Solo) (7'35), London 1985 (Week of Live Aid) (6'42), London 1986 (The Magic Tour) (10'33), Ibiza 1987 (Part 1: Freddie's 41st Birthday) (9'52), Ibiza 1987 (Part 2: Montserrat Caballé) (8'18), Ibiza 1987 (Part 3: The Great Pretender) (10'25)

Disc Eleven, The Video Collection (DVD): see Part Six

Disc Twelve, The Untold Story (DVD): see Part Six

Bonus disc (three disc set only): 'I Can Hear Music' (3'30), 'Love Kills' (4'31), 'The Great Pretender' (3'28), 'Living On My Own *(1993 radio mix)'* (3'39), 'In My Defence *(2000 remix)'* (3'55), 'Time *(2000 remix)'* (4'02), 'Love Kills *(rock mix)'* (4'27)

What better way to commemorate Freddie Mercury than with this gargantuan box set collecting a generous portion of his recorded material – both released and previously unreleased – and concentrating entirely on his brief solo career? Aimed at the diehard fans who have ample disposable income (initial prices averaged upwards of £150 in the UK, close to $200 in the US), *The Solo Collection* is not for the faint-hearted. With nearly ten hours of music and interviews divided among ten discs, as well as a further three hours on two DVDs, there is enough material here to keep listeners busy for a long time.

Rumors of a box set started to formulate around 1996, when it was reported that John Deacon had remixed 'There Must Be More To Life Than This' for a planned box set; ultimately, this might have been wishful thinking, for that song never surfaced, nor did confirmation of John's involvement. However, something was going on behind the scenes, and avid readers of *Record Collector* were given hints that that something would be spectacular. No one was ready, however, for *The Solo Collection*'s emergence in the autumn of 2000. Not only did it contain Freddie's two solo albums (*Mr Bad Guy* and *Barcelona*), but also the remix album *The Great Pretender*, a disc of instrumentals, two full discs of singles and their variations, two discs of rarities from his two solo albums, a third disc of miscellaneous rarities, and an interview disc with David Wigg (evidently the only journalist Freddie ever trusted).

Lovingly compiled by Justin Shirley-Smith and assembled, researched and copiously annotated by Greg Brooks, *The Solo Collection* was intended to be the final, definitive release of Freddie's solo career, with all the loose ends tied up. (It was this project that also sparked rumors, later confirmed, that a similar project was in store for Queen.) There's little to complain about here: each disc is uncluttered, with accompanying notes about each album, previously unreleased songs and variations to serve as an example of how meticulous Freddie was. A lengthy essay and beautiful images by a handful of Freddie's favorite photographers (including some early experimental sessions with Mick Rock), most accompanied by an explanation or anecdote by Brian May, make up the bulk of the extensive book, while the obligatory lyrics are also tucked neatly at the back.

It's inevitable that, in a collection of such uncompromising size, a few tracks would be missed or not included. Major criticism over the lack of any of Freddie's 1983 collaboration with Michael Jackson (which included 'State Of Shock', 'Victory' and 'There Must Be More To Life Than This') or his appearance at the *Time* musical in 1988 was aimed at the set, though the official reason is simple enough: the people who own those tracks were not willing to let them go. Additionally, why only 'Rain' from Wreckage's 1969 Liverpool gig was included instead of the full set is curious; again, the official reason is more of a deflection than anything concrete, with the vague explanation being that the sound quality for the remainder of the live set was below average. (As explained in the song entry for 'Rain', having heard the full set I can confirm that the quality is no worse than what is presented here.) Several auxiliary songs were also omitted, including single versions of 'Living On My Own', 'Mr Bad Guy', 'The Fallen Priest' and 'The Golden Boy', along with various reissue and extended variations of certain tracks, but these exclusions (or oversights) hardly detract from the listening experience.

Simply said, *The Solo Collection* is worth the price. For those more fiscally restricted, the three-disc *Solo* set is more affordable, containing *Mr Bad Guy*, *Barcelona* and a bonus disc running under a half hour of various songs from the many rarities discs on the ten-disc collection. But the more expansive (and expensive) set is recommended, and is the only place to go for everything that Freddie Mercury was and shall remain.

FREDDIE MERCURY
LOVER OF LIFE, SINGER OF SONGS: THE VERY BEST OF FREDDIE MERCURY

Parlophone 00946 367169 2 3 *(single disc edition)*, September 2006 [6]
Parlophone 00946 371824 2 0 *(double disc edition)*, September 2006 [6]
Hollywood Records D000007802, September 2006

Single disc edition: 'In My Defence' (3'55), 'The Great Pretender' (3'28), 'Living On My Own' *(1993 No More Brothers radio mix)* (3'39), 'Made In Heaven' (4'06), 'Love Kills' (4'30), 'There Must Be More To Life Than This' (3'01), 'Guide Me Home' (2'50), 'How Can I Go On' (3'52), 'Foolin' Around' (3'37), 'Time' (4'00), 'Barcelona' (5'40), 'Love Me Like There's No Tomorrow' (3'48), 'I Was Born To Love You' (3'40), 'The Golden Boy' (6'07), 'Mr Bad Guy' (4'12), 'The Great Pretender' *(1992 Brian Malouf remix)* (3'40), 'Love Kills' *(Star Rider remix)* (3'40), 'I Can Hear Music' (3'29), 'Goin' Back' (3'35), 'Guide Me Home' *(Thierry Lang piano version)* (4'19)

Double disc edition, second disc: 'Love Kills' *(Sunshine People radio mix)* (3'17), 'Made In Heaven' *(extended version)* (4'50), 'Living On My Own' *(The Egg remix)* (5'38), 'Love Kills' *(Rank 1 remix)* (7'19), 'Mr Bad Guy' *(Bad Circulation version)* (3'26), 'I Was Born To Love You *(George Demure Almost Vocal mix)* (4'02), 'My Love Is Dangerous' *(extended version)* (6'29), 'Love Makin' Love' *(demo)* (3'38), 'Love Kills' *(Pixel82 remix)* (6'14), 'I Was Born To Love You' *(extended version)* (7'06), 'Foolin' Around' *(early version)* (4'16), 'Living On My Own' *(No More Brothers extended mix)* (5'16), 'Love Kills' *(More Oder Rework by The Glimmers)* (6'53), 'Your Kind Of Lover' *(vocal & piano version)* (3'38), 'Let's Turn It On' *(a cappella)* (3'04)

With what would have been Freddie's 60th birthday looming, and the music-buying industry's appreciation of rounded numbers signifying important events, Freddie's estate and Queen Productions put together the first-ever single-disc compilation album of Freddie's untouched solo material. There had been *The Freddie Mercury Album* and *The Great Pretender* back in 1992, of course, but those discs were predominantly remixes, and weren't a true assessment of Freddie's output. *Solo*, the three-disc companion piece to *The Solo Collection*, was a step towards presenting his original visions, but that was designed as a catch-all for fans not willing – or able – to splurge on the more expansive box set.

Lover Of Life, Singer Of Songs comes closest to maintaining Freddie's original vision, mixing the best of his solo albums with the hit singles, and a few choice remixes thrown in for good measure. There's the odd misstep – two versions of 'The Great Pretender' on the same disc is overkill, as well as the superfluous remixes of 'Living On My Own' and 'Love Kills' – and the closing 'Guide Me Home', as performed by Thierry Lang, is a questionable inclusion on a disc that should feature Freddie's original songs, and not songs interpreted by others, no matter how good a performance it may be. But these are small, niggling complaints, and the disc is a superb cross-section of a solo career that Freddie only reluctantly agreed to, instead of bursting at the seams to assert his popularity outside of Queen.

The real problem comes on the double-disc editions, where a second disc of material is presented, with motives that are unclear. In a move similar to that right after Freddie died, the compilers packed the second disc full of remixes, all of them supremely uninteresting or insistently annoying, begging the question, why did anyone bother? Did the average – or even die-hard – Freddie fan really need *four* further remixes (in addition to the one on the first disc) of 'Love Kills', or two more 'Living On My Own' remixes – none of them, it must be said, the original extended remixes, but remixes of remixes? The selections from *The Solo Collection* – extended versions of 'Made In Heaven', 'My Love Is Dangerous', and 'I Was Born To Love You', the demo of 'Love Makin' Love', and the alternate versions of 'Foolin' Around', 'Your Kind Of Lover', and 'Let's Turn It On' – are nice, if superfluous, and the "Bad Circulation" remix of 'Mr. Bad Guy' features some alternate, unfinalized lyrics, making for pleasant but inessential listening. But when faced with the option of packing the second disc full of something interesting, what fans are instead offered is another crass attempt to further the notion that Freddie's dance-oriented excursions were his true passion, and that any of his songs from *Mr. Bad Guy* could be given anonymous club beats and be worthy of release on a related album.

That said, it didn't matter much; the compilation was a success, reaching No. 6 upon its release, while its similarly-titled companion DVD soared to the top of the charts for two weeks.

BARCELONA: SPECIAL EDITION

Island Records 371 141 4, September 2012
Island Records 371 140 6, September 2012
Island Records 371 184 4, September 2012

Disc One, Newly Orchestrated Album: 'Barcelona' (5'43), 'La Japonaise' (4'52), 'The Fallen Priest' (5'46), 'Ensueño' (4'22), 'The Golden Boy' (6'04), 'Guide Me Home' (2'50), 'How Can I Go On' (3'49), 'Exercises In Free Love' (3'57), 'Overture Picante' (6'47), 'How Can I Go On' *(bonus track, featuring David Garnett)* (3'56)

Disc Two, The Best Of The Rarities And Session Out-takes: 'Exercises In Free Love' *(1987 B-side)* (4'26), 'Barcelona' *(early version)* (4'21), 'La Japonaise' *(demo vocal)* (4'41), 'Rachmaninov's Revenge ("The Fallen Priest")' *(demo vocal)* (5'51), 'Ensueño' *(live takes)* (5'36), 'The Golden Boy' *(early version)* (3'54), 'Guide Me Home' / 'How Can I Go On' *(alternate version)* (6'54), 'How Can I Go On' *(alternate piano version)* (3'44)

Disc Three, DVD: Club Ibiza Performance ('Barcelona'); La Nit Barcelona Performance ('Barcelona', 'How Can I Go On', 'The Golden Boy'); 'Barcelona' *(promo video)*; *Barcelona: The Special Edition* mini-documentary; 'Barcelona' *(promo video, 2012 edit)*

Disc Four, Instrumental Orchestral Album: 'Barcelona' (5'39), 'La Japonaise' (4'51), 'The Fallen Priest' (5'47), 'Ensueño' (4'01), 'The Golden Boy' (6'03), 'Guide Me Home' (2'50), 'How Can I Go On' (3'37), 'Exercises In Free Love' (3'57), 'Overture Picante' (6'43)

Musicians: Freddie Mercury *(vocals)*, Montserrat Caballé *(vocals)*, Mike Moran *(piano, Hammond organ)*, John Deacon *(bass guitar on 'How Can I Go On')*, Rufus Taylor *(drums on 'The Golden Boy' and 'How Can I Go On')*, Naoko Kikuchi *(koto on 'La Japonaise')*, David Garrett *(additional violin on 'How Can I Go On', bonus track)*, FILMharmonic Orchestra: Adam Kelemns *(conductor)*, Stuart Morley *(piano on 'How Can I Go On', conductor on 'Exercises In Free Love', orchestrations)*, Lumír Van K, Svatopluk Ech *(bassoon)*, Jaromír Klepá *(celesta)*, Barbora Švýcarská, David Havelík, Helena P Íhodová, Jaroslav Mat Jka, Jaroslav Ondrá Ek, Martin Sedlák, Michaela Zelenková, Petr Houdek, Petr Malíšek, Petr Šporcl, Petra Malíšková, Roman Stehlík, Vladimír S Va *(cello)*, Aleš Hustoles, Jan Mach, Michal Kostiuk, Miroslav Plechatý, Vlastimil Mareš *(clarinet)*, František Havlín, Rita Epur Enko *(concertmaster)*, Jind Ich Schuchman, Marek

Lustig, Michal Mandel, Michal Novák, Ond Ej Balcar, Radomír Žalud, Roman Koudelka, Rudolf Andrš, Václav Hoskovec *(contrabass)*, Petr Pycha *(contractor)*, Mario Mesany, Martin Klimánek, Petra Ho Ánková, Robert Heger *(flute)*, Blanka Vojtíšková, František Langweil, Pavel Douba, Petr Hernych, Tomáš Kirschner, Zuzana Rzounková *(French horn)*, Hana Jouzová, Lucie Navrátilová *(harp)*, Jana Brožková, Jitka Tomší Ková, Lib Na Séquardtová, Radim Kocina *(oboe)*, Ivan Hoznedr, Ji Í Svoboda, Karel Fingl, Miroslav Kejmar Jn., Oleg Sokolov, Svatopluk Ech, Ml. *(percussion)*, František Zazvonil, Jan Triebenekl, Ji Í Novotný, Petr Ihák, Tomáš Ehák *(trombone)*, František Bílek, Luboš Jurní Ek, Marek Vajo, Svatopluk Zaal *(trumpet)*, Karel Malimánek *(tuba)*, Dominik Trávní, Eduard Vaní Ek, Jan Mare Ek, Jaromír Páví Ek, Ji Í Kabát, Ji Í Poslední, Martin Jirka, Old Ich Smola, Ml., Ond Ej Kameš, Pavel Ciprys, Pavel Ho Ejší, Radim Sedmidubský, Vladimír Bažant *(viola)*, Anna Va Ková, Antonín Burda, David Vorá, David Šroubek, Ester Kabátová, Eva Nykrýnová, Eva Rohanová, František Eret, František Havlín, Jan Dudek, Jan Jouza, Jan Ludvík, Jan Pet Ík, Jarslav Ko Án, Jiljí Teringer, Jind Ich Vácha, Ji Í Škoda, Josef Bauer, Josef Riedlbauch, Luboš Dudek, Lucie Sedláková H Lová, Marcel Kozánek, Marie Va Ková, Markéta Dobešová, Martin Pachner, Miroslav Vilímec, Otakar Bartoš, Pavel Herajn, Pavel Kutman, Petr Hlavá, Petr Novobilský, Rita Epur Enko, Vladimír Ku Era, Vlastimil Zeman, Václav Prudil, Zden K Starý, Zden K Zelba *(violin)*
Recorded: Recorded at Smecky Studio, Prague, Air Edel, Ripe Records, Radlett & Dean St Studios, London, and Wisseloord Studios, Hilversum, Netherlands
Producers: Kris Fredrikkson and Stuart Morley

To commemorate what would have been Freddie's 66th birthday, and to mark the 25th anniversary of the original 'Barcelona' single release, a completely updated and reorchestrated recording of *Barcelona* was issued, somewhat rather presumptively trumpeting it as "the version Mercury would have wanted to make at the time, had he felt able to work with a full symphony orchestra." There might be some truth to this, but Freddie remained adamant at the time that an orchestra not be used, as keyboards had developed so dramatically to the point that Freddie (and musical collaborator Mike Moran) had far better control over the music than they would have with an orchestra.

Regardless, *Barcelona: Special Edition* is a delightful curio, giving the arrangements more teeth, while reminding the listener just how startling Freddie's

arrangements could be. It was a tough line to balance, but arranger Stuart Morley treated the original recordings with kid gloves by "listening to the album over and over in short sections and noting down the harmonic structure, lead orchestral lines and instrumental voicings along with the vocal lines. I then proceeded to expand into making a full orchestral score (with a 2B pencil, ruler and eraser – the old fashioned way) working at the piano and constantly referring back to the original recordings to make sure the work I was doing remained faithful to Freddie and Mike Moran's original intentions." Morley also threw some of his own personal touches in, in order to make the orchestration more classically-minded, by referencing some of his influences: "[Nikolay] Rimsky-Korsakov's treatise on orchestration as well as various orchestral scores including Tchaikovsky's 4th symphony, Scheherzade and Dubussy's La Mer. It was important to me that the re-orchestration was constructed and voiced in an authentic classical style whilst remaining faithful to the sound world of the original album."

Once his arrangements were complete, Morley flew to Prague at Smecky Studios to oversee the recordings, undertaken by FILMharmonic Orchestra with conductor Adam Kelemns leading the charge. "I remember feeling a mixture of nerves and excitement when I made the short walk from the hotel to the studio," Morley recalled. "Hearing just over 80 people tune up before striking the first notes when the conductor gives their first downbeat is always slightly nerve racking for an arranger, but these feelings were amplified ten-fold because of my knowledge, respect and admiration of the original album and its creators. I'll never forget the wave of emotion that hit me later on that day when I was handed the headphones while we were recording one of the tutti sections from 'The Fallen Priest' (which was incidentally the biggest and most challenging orchestration to complete) and I felt the sheer power of the orchestra giving it their all, with Freddie and Montserrat soaring over the top of it. That was the moment I knew that we were a part of something really special."

Some other guest musicians made appearances: Naoko Kikuchi, one of the few koto players in the western world, was called in to provide her distinctive instrument to 'La Japonaise', while Roger's son, Rufus, provided drums on 'The Golden Boy' and 'How Can I Go On' (which are particularly jarring for those familiar with the original recording, and take some time to get used to). How much *Barcelona: Special Edition* works depends on how reverential the listener feels towards the original. Keep in mind this isn't replacing the 1988 release, but merely augmenting Freddie's vision. Additionally, the original recording mimics an orchestral so well that at times the re-recording becomes superfluous, but it's still a stunning, beautiful release, with the greatest of care taken to preserve the integrity of the original while not compromising Morley's own vision.

The album was released in a handful of formats: CD, CD/DVD, vinyl, and a limited edition box set from freddiemercury.com that added the original release of *Barcelona*, along with trinkets such as a t-shirt, the updated cover art prints (gorgeously painted by Matilda Beach), a black & white print of Freddie and Montserrat, a 7" red vinyl of 'Exercises In Free Love', and a certificate of authenticity. The reviews were minimal, with *Record Collector* taking the most umbrage: "For Queen fans, 'Bohemian Rhapsody' was the ultimate rock opera in miniature. But Freddie Mercury was never one to simply dip his toe in the water, and took a giant leap into the classical world with 1991's [sic] *Barcelona*, a collaborative album with mezzo-soprano Montserrat Caballé. This new edition sees 'third man' Mike Moran's synthesised keyboards erased and replaced by a full-blown Czech orchestra under the direction of Stuart Morley, the musical director of *We Will Rock You*. While the accompanying press release gushes that this is 'the version Mercury would have wanted to make at the time had he felt able to work with a full symphony orchestra', you wonder if his restless nature would have actually permitted him to return and tinker. The result is as sonically lush as would be expected, but the point of the exercise, gilding what was arguably a pastiche, remains debatable. While die-hard fans clamour for '70s Queen live shows to be issued, this is akin to colourising an old black-and-white movie – though, as it's not band material, there's unlikely to be an Adam Lambert-esque outcry. A triple-disc deluxe version offers the 'new' album, plus a rarities and out-takes disc and a DVD of five video clips, adding to the feeling of excess. As the man himself might say: if something's worth doing it's worth overdoing. Isn't it?"

BRIAN MAY + KERRY ELLIS
ACOUSTIC BY CANDLELIGHT: LIVE ON THE BORN FREE TOUR

Duck Productions Ltd. KECD003, June 2013
Duck Productions Ltd. KELP001, June 2013

'Born Free' (3'18), 'I Loved A Butterfly' (4'49), 'I Who Have Nothing' (3'45), 'Dust In The Wind' (4'21), 'The Kissing Me Song' (4'25), 'Nothing Really Has Changed' (4'56), 'Life Is Real (Song For Lennon)' (4'30), 'The Way We Were' (3'43), 'Something' (4'32), 'Love Of My Life' (4'37), 'I'm Not That Girl' (3'25), 'I Can't Be Your Friend' (4'32), 'In The Bleak Midwinter' (3'44), 'Crazy Little Thing Called Love' (3'47), 'No-One But You (Only The Good Die Young)' (6'04)

Musicians: Brian May *(guitars, vocals)*, Kerry Ellis *(vocals)*, Jeff Leach *(keyboards)*, Stuart Morley *(keyboards on 'Born Free')*
Recorded: 5 November 2012, The Apex, Bury St. Edmunds *('I Who Have Nothing', 'I'm Not That Girl', and 'No-One But You (Only The Good Die Young)')*; 6 November 2012, The Assembly Halls, Leamington Spa *('Love Of My Life' and 'Crazy Little Thing Called Love')*; 7 November 2012, Corby Cube, Corby *('Dust In The Wind', 'Life Is Real (Song For Lennon)', 'The Way We Were', and 'I Can't Be Your Friend')*; 11 November 2012, Union Chapel, London *('I Loved A Butterfly' and 'Something')*; 12 November 2012, Alban Arena, St. Albans *('The Kissing Me Song', 'Nothing Really Has Changed', and 'In The Bleak Midwinter')*; 17 November 2012, City Hall, Salisbury *('Born Free')*
Producer: Brian May

Shortly after recording a cover of 'Born Free' for Bill Travers and Virginia McKenna's Born Free Foundation, Brian and Kerry Ellis set out on an 11-date UK tour, where they performed a diverse set list of Queen hits and deep cuts, covers, and original recordings. The idea for the tour came about while the duo was recording material for a new album, with Brian explaining, "As on the *Anthems* album, some of the tracks have very big and splendid arrangements, but we have become more and more fascinated with the magic of great songs stripped down to their core and reinterpreted in an 'acoustic' way. We find there is a purity which makes the songs speak very clearly."

Acoustic By Candlelight: Live On The Born Free Tour was released six months after the tour's conclusion, and is a delightful, intimate, and beautiful recording that finds Brian, especially, looser and more relaxed than he normally is on stage with Queen + Adam Lambert. The set list is inspired, too, with the most welcome performance being 'Life Is Real (Song For Lennon)', which seems to be finally getting the recognition it deserves. Elsewhere, Kerry shows her vocal prowess on originals like 'I Loved A Butterfly', 'I Can't Be Your Friend', and the newly-written 'The Kissing Me Song', while giving a nod to her theatrical background on 'I'm Not That Girl'.

The album will certainly not be to everyone's tastes, especially those expecting an appearance from The Red Special, but for those who are fans of the Brian and Kerry partnership, this is an essential purchase.

ROGER TAYLOR
FUN ON EARTH

Virgin/EMI Records 0602537569984, November 2013 [69]
Virgin/EMI Records 0602537755196, April 2014

'One Night Stand!' (4'20), 'Fight Club' (3'02), 'Be With You' (3'09), 'Quality Street' (4'24), 'I Don't Care' (3'24), 'Sunny Day' (3'37), 'Be My Gal (My Brightest Spark)' (2'44), 'I Am The Drummer (In A Rock n' Roll Band)' (2'45), 'Small' (3'50), 'Say It's Not True' (4'58), 'The Unblinking Eye' (abridged version) (4'54), 'Up' (3'08), 'Smile' (3'00)

Bonus tracks on The Lot box set edition: 'Whole House Rockin'' (3'01), 'Dear Mr. Murdoch' (Nude mix) (3'49)

Vinyl edition: 'One Night Stand!' (4'20), 'Fight Club' (3'02), 'Be With You' (3'09), 'Quality Street' (4'24), 'Sunny Day' (3'37), 'Be My Gal (My Brightest Spark)' (2'44), 'Say It's Not True' (4'58), 'Small' (3'50), 'Up' (3'08), 'Smile' (3'00), 'I Don't Care' (3'24), 'Dear Mr. Murdoch' (Nude mix) (3'49), 'I Am The Drummer (In A Rock n' Roll Band)' (2'45), 'The Unblinking Eye' (abridged version) (4'54), 'Whole House Rockin'' (3'01)

Musicians: Roger Taylor (vocals, drums, percussion, keyboards, piano, bass guitar, guitars, stylophone on 'The Unblinking Eye'), Spike Edney (keyboards on 'Say It's Not True', 'Sunny Day', and 'Be My Gal (My Brightest Spark)'), Jason Falloon (guitars on 'Fight Club', 'I Don't Care', 'Be My Gal (My Brightest Spark)', 'I Am The Drummer (In A Rock n' Roll Band)', and 'Small'), Rufus Taylor (drums on 'Say It's Not True', piano on 'Be With You'), Kevin Jefferies (bass guitar on 'Fight Club',

'Be With You', 'Sunny Day', 'Be My Gal (My Brightest Spark)', 'I Am The Drummer (In A Rock n' Roll Band'), and 'Small'), Jonathan Perkins (organ, backing vocals on 'Sunny Day'), Steve Hamilton (saxophone on 'Fight Club', 'Quality Street', and 'I Don't Care'), Nicola Robins (violin on 'Sunny Day'), Steve Stroud (bass guitar on 'Say It's Not True'), Jeff Beck (guitar on 'Say It's Not True')
Recorded: 2007–2013 at The Priory, Surrey
Producers: Roger Taylor and Joshua J. Macrae

After the disappointing reception to Electric Fire, Roger privately – and then publicly – deemed his solo career to have reached its natural conclusion, and instead focused his energies on being more of a present father while enjoying the trappings that his success had afforded him. But the temptation to create never truly left him, and, rejuvenated by the partnership with Paul Rodgers, the drummer started to write again. The first tastes of his rebirth came in 2006, when he released 'Woman You're So Beautiful (But Still A Pain In The Ass)' as an Internet-only single. The following year, he tasked himself with contributing heavily to the new Queen + Paul Rodgers album, resulting in some of his finest songs to date.

His muse had clearly been resparked, thanks not only to the new creative partnership, but also to his blossoming relationship with Sarina Potgeiter, a South African ballet dancer, actress, and make-up artist. The two met in 2002, after the break-up of Roger's relationship with Debbie Leng, and tied the knot in September 2010, with a reception held in a black and red marquee in their garden. Emboldened by his new relationship, Roger continued to write over the period of several years, before he finally started to assemble what would be his first album in 15 years.

"I'm lucky enough to have a studio here where I live, and it was an accumulation of work," Roger later told Classic Rock magazine. "It wasn't fast; it was quite slow building up. It just sort of came together in the end, and I thought I'd collect it all into one album. Then, you try and make a coherent record. But it really was an accumulation over quite a long period." Several of the songs he had been working on leaked out in dribs and drabs over the course of six years: 'Say It's Not True', an obvious favorite of the drummer's, was a regular in the few set lists of concerts where Roger appeared, while 'Whole House Rockin'', released as 'Cosmos Rockin'' on The Cosmos Rocks, had also been premiered live in January 2009 at a SAS Band concert. The biggest surprise came in November 2009, when he released 'The Unblinking Eye (Everything Is Broken)' as a non-album single, while two further tracks, 'Smile' and 'I Am The Drummer (In A Rock n' Roll Band)', were premiered the following spring at that year's fan club convention.

While Roger would hint that the album was approaching completion regularly over the next two years, with a reported release for 2012, his proper follow-up to *Electric Fire* wouldn't see the light of day until November 2013. What emerged as *Fun On Earth* is a markedly different beast from his previous solo albums: instead of high-energy experimental rock tracks, Roger stripped back his sound considerably, writing and recording a reflective mood album with a few surprises thrown in along the way. Roger later described the album as being "rooted towards finding peace", and telling *Classic Rock* magazine that "I've come down to earth a bit, but there's still a bit of fun in there – some smiley tracks".

Indeed, *Fun On Earth* is a mixed bag of treasures, mostly dealing with Roger's advancement into middle age, though some of the "smiley" tracks he mentioned feature his tongue planted firmly in cheek, especially on the jazzy 'I Don't Care' and the humorous 'I Am The Drummer (In A Rock n' Roll Band)'. He also returned to several older songs, the most obvious being a more pastoral take on one of the highlights of *The Cosmos Rocks*, 'Small', while he updated the 1998 non-album track 'One Night Stand' to give it a more contemporary, organic sheen. Perhaps the least successful re-recording is 'Say It's Not True', recorded at a rehearsal for the SAS Band's appearance at Rock Against Cancer in May 2013; it's not that it's a bad performance, especially considering Jeff Beck appears on guitar, but it sits at odds with the more homespun-sounding material.

That more homespun material finds Roger performing the songs more or less on his own, though collaborators did jump in here and there to add some special touches to the material. The most successful tracks are those that Roger doesn't overthink, as is his wont to do: 'Fight Club' is a simmering, shimmering slow burn of a song, while 'Be With You' and 'Be My Gal (My Brightest Spark)' are two of the most affecting love songs Roger has written in years. 'Sunny Day' takes the base of 'Woman You're So Beautiful (But Still A Pain In The Ass)' and structures it into a gorgeous ballad, while 'Smile', an entirely self-performed track, closes out the album on an optimistic note. For the most part, *Fun On Earth* is exactly what it says on

the tin: a down-to-earth, pastoral album, completely at odds with anything else Roger has released in his career.

Liverpool Sound And Vision gave the album four stars, saying, "*Fun On Earth* is surely what Roger must have had in making this album, to have such musical icons as Jeff Beck, the very talented Spike Edney and Steve Hamilton, who provides one of the best saxophone backings on a track heard in years, on the record must have been a joy. The tracks that he has laid down for all too also have the feel of a man baring his soul, angry, full of bitterness, love and detraction for the audience." James Gaden, from *Rocktopia*, was pleased, too: "His most eclectic work yet, the album's title pays homage to where it all started and delivers rock fare such as 'One Night Stand!', 'Up' and the excellent tongue in cheek stomper 'I Am The Drummer (In A Rock n' Roll Band)' alongside gentle cuts like 'Be My Gal (My Brightest Spark)' and 'Smile'. Taylor adds his great rendition of the Queen + Paul Rodgers track 'Small' as well as revisiting 'Say It's Not True', now given a more bluesy feel by guest Jeff Beck. There's political fare in the form of 'The Unblinking Eye' as well as songs talking about soldier's struggles in 'Fight Club' and 'Quality Street', both of which make effective use of saxophone." "*Fun On Earth* is one of Taylor's most exciting, eclectic and accomplished pieces of work to date," *The Progressive Aspect* wrote. "Recorded at Priory Studios, Surrey, the 13 track album is a triumphant display of superior musicianship showcasing Taylor at his vocal best. Opening track 'One Night Stand' and 'I Am The Drummer (In A Rock n' Roll Band)' captures Roger's reckless, exhilarating side. The smooth refrains of 'Sunny Day' and 'Be With You' display Roger's talent as a lyricist and heartfelt vocalist. 'Say It's Not True' sees Taylor team up with Jeff Beck for the contemporary Queen favourite."

The album was released on the same day as *The Lot*, which featured two additional tracks not on the standalone release: a remix of 'Dear Mr. Murdoch' and the original vision of 'Cosmos Rockin'', here retitled 'Whole House Rockin''. *Fun On Earth* was given the Record Store Day treatment in April 2014, with Roger reconfiguring the running order of the *Lot* version to be spread across four sides, though this felt a little more disparate and random as opposed to the more considered running order of the original CD. While Roger has hinted that the muse hasn't left him entirely – the surprise release of 'Journey's End' in May 2017 confirmed this – he has said that the title of the album was deliberate: "My debut solo album was *Fun In Space* and this called *Fun On Earth*. I'm not sure if it'll be my last one but it does feel like the closing of a circle."

ROGER TAYLOR
THE LOT

Virgin/EMI Records 00602537537143, November 2013
Omnivore Recordings/Hollywood Records OVCD-110, November 2014

Disc One, Fun In Space: 'No Violins' (4'33), 'Laugh Or Cry' (3'07), 'Future Management' (2'58), 'Let's Get Crazy' (3'43), 'My Country I & II' (6'58), 'Good Times Are Now' (3'30), 'Magic Is Loose' (3'25), 'Interlude In Constantinople' (2'05), 'Airheads' (3'42), 'Fun In Space' (6'26)

Disc Two, Strange Frontier: 'Strange Frontier' (4'17), 'Beautiful Dreams' (4'25), 'Man On Fire' (4'06), 'Racing In The Street' (4'28), 'Masters Of War' (3'50), 'Killing Time' (4'59), 'Abandonfire' (4'14), 'Young Love' (3'23), 'It's An Illusion' (4'03), 'I Cry For You (love, hope and confusion)' (4'22)

Disc Three, Happiness?: 'Nazis 1994' (2'39), 'Happiness?' (3'26), 'Revelations' (3'53), 'Touch The Sky' (5'06), 'Foreign Sand' (6'53), 'Freedom Train' (6'17), "you had to be there" (2'58), 'The Key' (4'24), 'Everybody Hurts Sometime' (3'03), 'Loneliness...' (2'26), 'Dear Mr. Murdoch' (4'28), 'Old Friends' (3'34)

Disc Four, Electric Fire: 'Pressure On' (5'00), 'A Nation Of Haircuts' (3'34), 'Believe In Yourself' (5'09), 'Surrender' (3'40), 'The Whisperers' (6'09), 'Is It Me?' (3'29), 'People On Streets' (4'16), 'No More Fun' (4'22), 'Tonight' (3'48), 'Where Are You Now?' (4'52), 'Working Class Hero' (4'44), 'London Town, C'mon Down' (7'02)

Disc Five, Shove It: 'Shove It' (3'28), 'Cowboys And Indians' (5'55), 'Contact' (4'52), 'Heaven For Everyone' (4'55), 'Stand Up For Love' (4'23), 'Love On A Tightrope (Like An Animal)' (4'49), 'Love Lies Bleeding (She Was A Wicked Wily Waitress)' (4'26), 'Rough Justice' (3'20), 'The Second Shelf Mix' (5'52)

Disc Six, Mad: Bad: And Dangerous To Know: 'Top Of The World, Ma' (3'32), 'Liar' (4'29), 'Closer To You' (3'13), 'Breakdown' (3'54), 'Penetration Guru' (3'46), 'Power To Love' (4'02), 'Sister Blue' (4'16), 'Foxy Lady' (3'27),

'Better Things' (2'46), 'Passion For Trash' (2'35), 'Old Men (Lay Down)' (4'55), 'Final Destination' (3'35)

Disc Seven, Blue Rock: 'Bad Attitude' (4'46), 'New Dark Ages' (4'58), 'Dirty Mind' (3'31), 'Baby It's Alright' (4'06), 'Ain't Put Nothin' Down' (4'31), 'The Also Rans' (5'28), 'Millionaire' (3'43), 'Put It All Down To Love' (3'35), 'Hand Of Fools (Out Of Control)' (4'35), 'Life Changes' (5'55)

Disc Eight, Fun On Earth: 'One Night Stand!' (4'22), 'Fight Club' (3'02), 'Be With You' (3'10), 'Quality Street' (4'25), 'I Don't Care' (3'24), 'Sunny Day' (3'38), 'Be My Gal (My Brightest Spark)' (2'45), 'I Am The Drummer (In A Rock n' Roll Band)' (2'47), 'Small' (3'51), 'Say It's Not True' (4'58), 'The Unblinking Eye' (4'55), 'Up' (3'10), 'Smile' (3'02), 'Dear Mr. Murdoch' *(Nude mix, bonus track)* (3'17), 'Whole House Rockin'' *(bonus track)* (3'01)

Disc Nine, Solo Singles 1: 'I Wanna Testify' (3'48), 'Turn On The TV' (3'29), 'My Country' *(single edit)* (3'53), 'Man On Fire' *(extended version)* (6'09), 'I Cry For You (love, hope and confusion)' *(single remix)* (4'10), 'Strange Frontier' *(extended remix)* (8'37), 'I Cry For You (love, hope and confusion)' *(extended remix)* (6'27), 'Two Sharp Pencils (Get Bad)' (3'27), 'Nazis 1994' *(Radio Mix)* (3'27), 'Nazis 1994' *(Kick Mix)* (4'27), 'Nazis 1994' *(Schindlers Mix)* (4'23), 'Nazis 1994' *(Makita Mix)* (3'57), 'Nazis 1994' *(Big Science Mix)* (4'04), 'Foreign Sand' *(with Yoshiki)* (single version) (4'35), 'Final Destination' *(with Yoshiki)* (5'31), 'Everybody Hurts Sometimes' *(live at Shepherds Bush Empire)* (4'03), 'Old Friends' *(live at Shepherds Bush Empire)* (3'19)

Disc Ten, Solo Singles 2: 'Pressure On' *(single version)* (3'25), 'People On Streets' *(Mashed Mix)* (3'34), 'Tonight' *(Dub Sangria)* (3'51), 'Keep A Knockin'' (3'17), 'Surrender' *(radio mix)* (3'39), 'A Nation Of Haircuts' *(Club Cut)* (3'44), 'London Town, C'mon Down' *(single mix)* (3'24), 'Surrender' *(live at Cyberbarn)* (4'11), 'No More Fun' *(live at Cyberbarn)* (4'24), 'Tonight' *(live at Cyberbarn)* (4'23), 'One Night Stand' (3'54), 'Woman You're So Beautiful (But Still A Pain In The Ass)' *(Main Mix)* (3'57), 'Woman You're So Beautiful (But Still A Pain In The Ass)' *(Mad Mix)* (6'04), 'Woman You're So Beautiful (But Still A Pain In The Ass)' *(Dance Hall Mix)* (5'38), 'The Unblinking Eye (Everything Is Broken)' *(original single mix)* (6'14), 'The Unblinking Eye

(Everything Is Broken)' *(Almost Completely Nude Mix)* (6'12), 'Dear Mr. Murdoch' *(2011 recording)* (3'17)

Disc Eleven, The Cross Singles 1: 'Cowboys And Indians' *(single edit)* (4'34), 'Love Lies Bleeding (She Was A Wicked, Wily Waitress)' *(B-side version)* (4'16), 'Feel The Force' (3'48), 'Shove It' *(extended mix)* (5'54), 'Shove It' *(Metropolix)* (3'31), 'Shove It' *(Denis Pop remix)* (5'05), 'Heaven For Everyone' *(Roger vocal)* (5'06), 'Heaven For Everyone' *(Freddie vocal)* (4'55), 'Manipulator' *(extended mix)* (4'16), 'Manipulator' (3'59), 'Power To Love' *(extended mix)* (5'19), 'Power To Love' *(single edit)* (3'28), 'In Charge of My Heart' (2'18), 'Liar' *(extended mix)* (6'32), 'In Charge of My Heart' *(extended mix)* (4'44), 'Liar' *(single remix)* (3'19)

Disc Twelve, The Cross Singles 2: 'New Dark Ages' *(single edit)* (3'28), 'Ain't Put Nothin' Down' *(long version)* (4'55), 'Man On Fire' *(live)* (5'09), 'Life Changes' *(single edit)* (3'55), 'Heartland' (4'47), 'Celebration' *(Jam Studios session, previously unreleased)* (4'39), 'I Can Take You Higher' *(Jam Studios session, previously unreleased)* (3'31), 'I Can't Get You Out Of My Head' *(Jam Studios session, previously unreleased)* (3'38), 'Passion For Trash' *(Jam Studios session, previously unreleased)* (2'51), 'Top Of The World Ma' *(extended remix, previously unreleased)* (7'41), 'Shove It' *(US single version)* (3'10)

Name another drummer whose solo career has been so prolific that they can collect 12 discs worth of material in a compact box set. Of course there's Ringo Starr and Phil Collins, and undoubtedly those drummers' solo careers could easily fill 12, if not more, discs, but Roger Taylor was the first to do it for his own material. *The Lot* was announced in a spring 2013 issue of *Classic Rock* magazine, and the concept behind it was to collect everything the drummer had released, both as a solo artist and with The Cross. A daunting task, for sure, but one that made perfect sense: after declaring in 1998 that *Electric Fire* was to be his last solo album, Roger got the itch to create as far back as 2006, when he released 'Woman You're So Beautiful (But Still A Pain In The Ass)'. *The Cosmos Rocks* only fanned the flames even further, and by the start of 2009 he already had plans to work on (and eventually release) a new solo album. (Never mind the fact it took until November 2013 for *Fun On Earth* to finally materialize.)

Inevitably, Roger and Queen's archivists, Greg Brooks and Gary Taylor, trawled through the drummer's tapes and decided the time was right to issue an all-encompassing retrospective of Roger's vast solo discography. With five albums to his name, and a further three with The Cross, the box set was shaping up to be a hefty one already; four further discs were allotted for single mixes and variations, with a DVD containing all of his promotional videos. "I said, 'Let's have the lot in there'," Roger told *Classic Rock Magazine* in August 2013, "so I thought, 'Let's call it that.'"

It would be nice to call *The Lot* exactly what it is, but, inevitably, there were some omissions, the most glaring being the single edit of 'Happiness' and live single versions of 'I Want To Break Free' and 'Ride The Wild Wind' from 1994. (Gary Taylor later commented on the absence of the last two that Roger wanted his set to not contain any Queen material, which is understandable.) Furthermore, errors abounded: on 'Life Changes', the extended outro was rudely sliced with 30 seconds to spare, only to have the beginning of the single mix start, before it, too, was cut off. Timer markers on *Shove It* and *Happiness?* were incorrect; historical discrepancies ('Dear Mr. Murdoch' on *Electric Fire*? Not hardly, my dears!), and general typos and misspellings plague the otherwise beautiful booklet. Ironic that one of Roger's new songs was called 'Quality Street' and yet quality control flew straight out the window.

That being said, *The Lot* is an impressive summation of Roger's expansive solo career. ("Like anything, there are some things you regret," he shrugged to *Classic Rock Magazine*. "But my last solo album, *Electric Fire*, still sounds great.") Anyone expecting an archival exhumation like *The Freddie Mercury Collection* will be sorely disappointed: while there are five previously unreleased tracks ('Celebration', 'I Can Take You Higher', 'I Can't Get You Out Of My Head', and a Joshua J. Macrae-sung 'Passion For Trash', all from a December 1989 Jam Studios session, plus an extended remix of 'Top Of The World, Ma'), the four discs' worth of single edits and extended versions, all previously available but hard to come by, are a treat. The remastering is also splendid, giving the songs a new sheen and exposing some arrangements previously buried by contemporary mixing.

Despite the errors, some glaring omissions, and a relative dearth of previously unreleased material, *The Lot* lives up to the standard set by *The Freddie Mercury Collection*. One hopes a Brian May set will soon follow, though fans still live in hope that Queen will receive a similar treatment someday.

ROGER TAYLOR
BEST

Omnivore Recordings/Hollywood Records OVCD-105/816651016587, October 2014
Omnivore Recordings/Hollywood Records OVLP-105/816651016594 *(limited edition yellow vinyl)*, October 2014

'Future Management' (2'56), 'I Wanna Testify' (3'45), 'Let's Get Crazy' (3'42), 'Magic Is Loose' (3'24), 'Strange Frontier' (4'15), 'Man On Fire' (4'05), 'Beautiful Dreams' (4'24), 'Nazis 1994' (2'37), 'Foreign Sand' (6'52), 'Everybody Hurts Sometime' (3'02), 'Happiness' (3'26), 'Surrender' (3'39), 'Where Are You Now?' (4'51), 'A Nation Of Haircuts' (3'32), 'Tonight' (3'46), 'No More Fun' (4'20), 'The Unblinking Eye (Everything Is Broken)' (6'10), 'Sunny Day' (3'37)

Not so much released as slipped out unnoticed in the autumn of 2014, *Best* is a generous cross-section of Roger's solo discography, with the drummer hand-picking 18 tracks he felt were representative of his large body of work. (Tellingly, nothing from The Cross' three albums was selected.) As ever, some selections were undoubtedly questionable – 'Magic Is Loose', 'Everybody Hurts Sometime', 'Where Are You Now?', and 'No More Fun' were all included in lieu of legitimate singles ('My Country') or fan favorites ('Old Friends', 'Dear Mr. Murdoch') – 'Woman You're So Beautiful' was entirely absent, and *Fun On Earth* is represented only by 'Sunny Day', an entirely unrepresentative selection of that excellent album.

Regardless of each fan's personal preference, *Best* serves its purpose as a vital introduction to Roger's expansive solo career; for those not willing to splash out the dosh on *The Lot*, this is the next best alternative.

FREDDIE MERCURY
MESSENGER OF THE GODS: THE SINGLES

Mercury 00602547878700 *(13-disc vinyl)*, September 2016
Hollywood Records 002411521 *(13-disc vinyl)*, September 2016
Mercury 00602547879295 *(double-disc compilation)*, September 2016 [31]
Hollywood Records D002431302 ST01 *(double-disc compilation)*, September 2016

Disc One, The Singles: 'Living On My Own' (3'05), 'The Great Pretender' (3'27), 'In My Defence' (3'54), 'Love Kills' (4'30), 'Barcelona' (4'27), 'Made In Heaven' (4'10), 'Time' (4'02), 'Love Me Like There's No Tomorrow' (3'47), 'I Was Born To Love You' (3'39), 'The Golden Boy' (5'16), 'I Can Hear Music' (3'25), 'How Can I Go On' (4'02), 'Living on My Own' *(No More Brothers radio mix)* (3'41)

Disc Two, The B-Sides: 'Goin' Back' (3'33), 'Let's Turn It On' (3'43), 'My Love Is Dangerous' (3'40), 'She Blows Hot And Cold' (3'40), 'Living On My Own' *(Julian Raymond Mix)* (3'39), 'Stop All The Fighting' (3'20), 'Time' *(instrumental)* (3'23), 'Exercises In Free Love' *(Freddie vocal)* (4'00), 'Exercises In Free Love' *(Montserrat vocal)* (4'05), 'The Fallen Priest' (2:58), 'Overture Piccante' (6:41), 'Love Kills' *(Wolf Euro mix)* (3:27)

Vinyl, Disc One: 'I Can Hear Music' (3'25), 'Goin' Back' (3'33); *Disc Two:* 'Love Kills' (4'30); *Disc Three:* 'I Was Born To Love You' (3'39), 'Stop All The Fighting' (3'20); *Disc Four:* 'Made In Heaven' (4'10), 'She Blows Hot And Cold' (3'40); *Disc Five:* 'Living On My Own' (3'05), 'My Love Is Dangerous' (3'40); *Disc Six:* 'Love Me Like There's No Tomorrow' (3'47), 'Let's Turn It On' (3'43); *Disc Seven:* 'Time' (4'02), 'Time' *(instrumental)* (3'23); *Disc Eight:* 'The Great Pretender' (3'27), 'Exercises In Free Love' *(Freddie vocal)* (4'00); *Disc Nine:* 'Barcelona' (4'27), 'Exercises In Free Love' *(Montserrat vocal)* (4'05); *Disc Ten:* 'The Golden Boy' (5'16), 'The Fallen Priest' (2'58); *Disc Eleven:* 'How Can I Go On' (4'02), 'Overture Piccante' (6'41); *Disc Twelve:* 'In My Defence' (3'54), 'Love Kills' *(Wolf Euro mix)* (3'27); *Disc Thirteen:* 'Living On My Own' *(No More Brothers radio mix)* (3'41), 'Living On My Own' *(Julian Raymond mix)* (3'39)

Released to commemorate what would have been Freddie's 70th birthday, *Messenger Of The Gods: The Singles* appeared in two formats: a 13-disc box set containing repressings of all of Freddie's 7" vinyl singles, pressed on various colors, and a double-disc CD compilation of the same material. The decision to separate the A- and B-sides on the CD version is a baffling one, instead presenting the album more as a compilation with a disparate, random running order, as opposed to a chronological representation of Freddie's solo singles.

That being said, *Messenger Of The Gods: The Singles* is a lovingly compiled collection, with great care being taken to faithfully reproduce Freddie's solo output. (Of note is the absence of 'Rotwang's Party (Robot Dance)', the original B-side of 'Love Kills'; while this is an omission that no one missed, as it didn't contain any involvement from Freddie, perhaps an alternate B-side like the Freddie/Jo Dare collaboration 'Hold On', or a previously unreleased instrumental version of the A-side, would have been appreciated.) The liner notes are beautifully presented, with full annotations and images that may be familiar to most but are still lovely to see in context. One can only hope that, with the resurrgence in popularity of vinyl, Queen's singles output will get a similar treatment.

BRIAN MAY + KERRY ELLIS
GOLDEN DAYS
Sony 88985425362, April 2017 [27]

'Love In A Rainbow' (4'30), 'Roll With You' (3'55), 'Golden Days' (4'22), 'It's Gonna Be All Right (The Panic Attack Song)' (3'46), 'Amazing Grace' (2'48), 'One Voice' (3'22), 'If I Loved You' (3'33), 'Born Free' (3'11), 'Parisienne Walkways' (3'44), 'I Who Have Nothing' (4'08), 'The Kissing Me Song' (3'43), 'Story Of A Heart' (4'23), 'Can't Help Falling In Love' (3:13)

Musicians: Brian May *(guitars, vocals, keyboards, sitar, gayageum, bass guitar on 'Love In A Rainbow', 'One Voice', 'Born Free', and 'The Kissing Me Song')*, Kerry Ellis *(vocals)*, Neil Fairclough *(bass guitar)*, John Miceli *(drums)*, Rufus Taylor *(drums on 'Born Free' and 'The Kissing Me Song')*, Jeff Leach *(keyboards on 'Roll With You', 'Amazing Grace', 'Parisienne Walkways', 'The Kissing Me Song', and 'Story Of A Heart')*
Recorded: 2012–2016 at Allerton Hill, Surrey
Producers: Brian May and Kerry Ellis

While *Anthems* was a Kerry Ellis album, albeit with Brian's fingerprints all over it, thus necessitating classification as a "guest appearance", *Golden Days* is a full-fledged collaboration, with three newly-penned co-writes between the two artists. Featuring songs recorded as far back as 2012 ('Born Free' being the oldest), the album is a joyous combination of Kerry's theatrical rock vocals and Brian's bombastic arrangements, which will undoubtedly please those fans who find themselves at the center of such a unique musical Venn diagram.

There was evidently no immediate plan for a follow-up to *Anthems*, with Brian and Kerry writing and recording disparately after that album's release, but once the two got serious, the album started to flow much more naturally. "It's been a long time coming,"

Kerry stated in a press release for *Golden Days*. "We've spent the best part of a year recording it in bits and pieces but we are both very happy with it and it is an accurate reflection of where we are. It's got some new stuff, some old favourites and some songs we have been doing live but haven't recorded until now, so it's a real mixture of everything that we love and what excites us."

Brian later revealed that the album was initially going to be titled *Anthems II*, and *Golden Days* essentially follows the same template, combining showtunes ('If I Loved You'), cinematic classics ('Can't Help Falling In Love', 'Born Free'), favorites of Brian's ('Amazing Grace', 'Parisienne Walkways'), a little-known Brian-penned song ('Golden Days', written in 1986 and recorded by Minako Honda), and four songs written by Brian and Kerry. This album was especially notable in that it featured Kerry's debut as a songwriter: "It's the first time I have really sat down and written anything," Kerry later explained. "Basically it's taken me 15 years to pluck up the courage to write something. I am so proud with what we have produced and it did happen very organically. Brian was very encouraging and allowed me to develop the songs. The way we work is very collaborative. He comes up with a riff or part of a melody and has an idea for a lyric and from there we develop it together, ironing out the melody and writing the finished lyrics. Brian actually told me there's bits of me in the songs I didn't contribute to. He would pick up phrases I use and insert them into the songs. The whole experience has been so much fun and as a result the album has a good feel to it."

Indeed, *Golden Days* may not have been the direction that fans of Brian, the Red Special-toting guitar wizard, may have envisioned for him, but it's exactly what Brian prefers to be doing these days; while *The Cosmos Rocks* featured three songs by Brian, they were rote and rather unspectacular, with the exception of 'Some Things That Glitter'. Clearly, the guitarist was distracted by extramural activities, and songwriting wasn't at the forefront of his curly mind. But it took Kerry Ellis to drag the muse out of him, and the four songs he cowrote with Kerry are a delight, especially 'Love In A Rainbow' and 'Roll With You', two standouts on the album that easily could have been Queen tracks. The other originals don't quite reach the same heights as the one-two punch that opens the album, but 'The Kissing Me Song' is a cute if lightweight piece of fluff, while 'It's Gonna Be Alright (The Panic Attack

Song)' sheds some light on what, exactly, happens when suffering from a panic attack. (Trust me, it's not fun.) When measured up against the classics that Brian had written for Queen, the latter two songs aren't in the same league, but they're perfect for the project, and Kerry's vocals are an absolute treat.

Released in April 2017, complete with an unboxing video from Brian, who humorously fumbles with the plastic packaging (rock stars – they're just like us!), *Golden Days* was afforded a fair amount of promotion, including appearances by Brian and Kerry on *Good Morning Britain* and Radio 2, eventually peaking at a respectable No. 27 in the UK. (The album cover, which was roundly derided as low budget from more cynical fans, is actually a lovely homage to French Baroque painter Georges de La Tour, who used bright candlelight as a central focus in his paintings.) *Gay Times* could barely contain themselves in their review: "Brian May and Kerry Ellis return with a new album we've struggled to stop playing since the second we clicked play! We all know Kerry Ellis from her much-loved appearances on stage, but it's the vulnerability of her voice here that appeals so greatly through each track on *Golden Days*. It feels like a new sound, without being too different to what we already love. It's nice to hear a rock twang back in her tracks, and Brian's sure to have urged on such a thing. It's true that her stage music is a great success, and such theatricality comes soaring out in the likes of 'I Who Have Nothing'. If ever a diva rendition was to be sought for, this is it … The mixing of ballads to rock anthems falls well on the 13-track album; you'll find yourself back at the start rather quickly as you get caught listening to every one.

Standout coming from 'Love In A Rainbow', 'Amazing Grace', 'Born Free' and the stunning 'I Who Have Nothing'. Oh, and 'The Kissing Me Song' will be in your head for DAYS! Avoid at all costs as it's on 'Let It Go' levels of addictive! Once again, Brian May and Kerry Ellis' joining makes for a joyful album that'll keep to to the top of your playlist in 2017. Just be careful to not get caught singing along out-loud in public spaces like we did!" *The Reviews Hub* was a little more measured with its compliments: "Overall this is a pleasant and easy to listen to album that has a couple of outstanding cover tracks, nice album but not the most memorable." *Classic Rock Magazine* summed up what many Queen fans were likely feeling: "Soothing sitar weaves its way through 'Love In A Rainbow' and *Golden Days'* title song, one of five original compositions. Ellis's angelic vocals are the center point of several beautiful arrangements, including 'Amazing Grace' and 'Can't Help Falling In Love', which sit among a stellar, bilingual rendition of Jerry Leiber and Mike Stoller's 'I Who Have Nothing' and the hauntingly sublime take on Gary Moore's 'Parisienne Walkways'. 'It's Gonna Be Alright (The Panic Attack Song)' is optimistic despite explicit detail ('I can't get my breath, pain beating in my chest') and the upbeat tempo and sweeping chords smack of Journey's 'Never Walk Away'. The acoustic 'If I Loved You' and Benny 'ABBA' Andersson's 'Story Of A Heart' show that variation comes in spades on the self-produced *Golden Days*, providing a perfect showcase for May and Ellis's well-oiled working relationship. That said, there's not a single jot of satisfaction here for Wayne and Garth."

C. QUEEN + PAUL RODGERS ALBUMS
RETURN OF THE CHAMPIONS

Parlophone 3 36979 2, September 2005 [21]
Hollywood 7 2061-62526-2, November 2005

'Reaching Out' (1'06), 'Tie Your Mother Down' (4'30), 'I Want To Break Free' (3'59), 'Fat Bottomed Girls' (5'45), 'Wishing Well' (4'33), 'Another One Bites The Dust' (4'02), 'Crazy Little Thing Called Love' (4'35), 'Say It's Not True' (4'15), ''39' (4'38), 'Love Of My Life' (5'11), 'Hammer To Fall' (6'45), 'Feel Like Making Love' (6'20), 'Let There Be Drums' (3'42), 'I'm In Love With My Car' (3'36), 'Guitar Solo' (6'59), 'Last Horizon' (4'42), 'These Are The Days Of Our Lives' (4'38), 'Radio Ga Ga' (5'59), 'Can't Get Enough Of Your Love' (4'22), 'A Kind Of Magic' (6'07), 'I Want It All' (5'09), 'Bohemian Rhapsody' (6'18), 'The Show Must Go On' (4'33), 'All Right Now' (6'54), 'We Will Rock You' (2'35), 'We Are The Champions' (4'30), 'God Save The Queen' (1'33)

Musicians: Brian May *(guitars, vocals, acoustic guitar)*, Roger Taylor *(drums, vocals)*, Paul Rodgers *(vocals,*

acoustic guitar on 'Crazy Little Thing Called Love'), Spike Edney *(piano, keyboards, vocals),* Danny Miranda *(bass guitar, vocals, acoustic guitar on 'Say It's Not True'),* Jamie Moses *(guitars, vocals, acoustic guitar on 'Say It's Not True')*
Recorded: 9 May 2005 at Hallam FM Arena, Sheffield
Producer: Justin Shirley-Smith

Recorded on 9 May 2005 at Hallman FM Arena in Sheffield, *Return Of The Champions* is a largely complete show. 'Under Pressure' was played after 'Crazy Little Thing Called Love' but Brian explained, "This is actually something that we probably won't put on the DVD, so this is for you. This is like a bonus track!" The set draws heavily from Queen's expansive past, as well as throwing in several of Paul Rodgers' songs from Bad Company and Free, and the result is surprisingly listenable. While it doesn't stand up to Queen's heyday with *Live Killers, Live At Wembley Stadium* or *Queen On Fire: Live At The Bowl,* this is a new band out to have a good time, and it shows.

However, the audio release doesn't live up to its video equivalent, which is inevitable: Queen's shows were always about the theatrics, and this is no exception. Listening to the music does little justice to actually seeing the band, but for what it is, *Return Of The Champions* is a good celebration of Queen's past. Clearly, Roger is enjoying himself the most, and the few times he addresses the audience are great. Brian, meanwhile, was more reserved, allowing his excitement to come out in his charismatic playing, while Paul proved himself an adept frontman and unique interpreter of Queen's songs, though he obviously felt more at ease on his own songs.

The loss of John Deacon on bass was a heavy blow and, while Danny Miranda was a suitable substitute, it's not quite the same. One has to wonder, too, why Jamie Moses was brought on board; Brian had never needed a rhythm guitarist on previous Queen tours, and Jamie doesn't offer much in the way of expanding the sound. This may have something to do with the mix, though Brian did explain that Jamie was simply meant to provide rhythm while Brian tried some new things on lead.

The Independent called it "a knock-out CD", while the *Denver Post* said that "Purists can argue whether this is a revival of an iconic band's songs or a bastardization thereof, but the music is at least faithful to the spirit of Queen's 1970s glam-rock bravado, and in that it's a success." *Classic Rock Revisited* was perhaps

more justifiably critical, but gave particular praise to Paul's vocals on 'I Want It All' and 'Tie Your Mother Down' and the performances of Paul's own songs: "In fact, the crowd seems more surprised at the power of the Queen + Paul Rodgers combo on these tracks than they do on any of the Queen material." *The Sun* was impressed: "Whatever you make of Paul Rodgers stepping in to Freddie Mercury's shoes to front Queen on tour, you have to admit he's pretty good at it. And since Queen are still as popular as ever, despite the fact that frontman Freddie died nearly 14 years ago, there's still a huge market for shows like this ... The songs still sound just as fresh, the audience is just as captivated – and Brian May's hair hasn't changed."

Name disputes aside, Queen + Paul Rodgers' first proper album is a fine introduction to the *joie de vivre* their live shows exhibited on the 2005 tour. Having temporarily silenced the critics, the only question that remained was: how would they do as a studio band?

THE COSMOS ROCKS

Parlophone 50999 2 37025 2 3 *(CD)* [5]
COSMOS 001 *(limited edition)* [5]
Parlophone 50999 2 37025 1 6 *(LP)* [5]
Hollywood Records D000261502 *(CD)* [47]
Hollywood D000280801 *(LP/collector's edition)* [47]

'Cosmos Rockin'' (4'10), 'Time To Shine' (4'23), 'Still Burnin'' (4'04), 'Small' (4'39), 'Warboys *(A Prayer For Peace)*' (3'18), 'We Believe' (6'08), 'Call Me' (2'59), 'Voodoo' (4'27), 'Some Things That Glitter' (4'03), 'C-Lebrity' (3'38), 'Through The Night' (4'54), 'Say It's Not True' (4'00), 'Surf's Up . . . School's Out !' (5'38), 'Small (2'05)', 'Runaway' *(digital editions only)* (5'28)

Super Live In Japan – Highlights (Bonus DVD): 'Reaching Out', 'Tie Your Mother Down', 'Fat Bottomed Girls', 'Another One Bites The Dust', 'Fire And Water', 'Crazy Little Thing Called Love', 'Teo Torriatte (Let Us Cling Together)', 'These Are The Days Of Our Lives', 'Radio Ga Ga', 'Can't Get Enough', 'I Was Born To Love You', 'All Right Now', 'We Will Rock You', 'We Are The Champions', 'God Save The Queen'

Musicians: Brian May *(guitars, bass guitar, piano, keyboards, backing vocals, lead vocals on 'Say It's Not True'),* Roger Taylor *(drums, percussion, keyboards, backing vocals, lead vocals on 'Say It's Not True'),* Paul Rodgers *(lead and backing vocals, piano, keyboards, guitars, bass guitar),* Taylor Hawkins *(backing vocals on*

'C-Lebrity')
Recorded: June 2007 – August 2008 at The Priory, Surrey
Producers: Brian May, Roger Taylor, Paul Rodgers, Joshua J Macrae, Justin Shirley-Smith, Kris Fredriksson

Following the conclusion of the Queen + Paul Rodgers US tour in April 2006, the touring band went their separate ways to ponder the future of the partnership. While Paul had commitments as a solo artist, performing continuously from May until the end of October, and then again when his other commitments allowed it throughout 2007 and the early part of 2008, Brian and Roger had other plans, and not all of them were music-related. Roger was invigorated by the experience of playing to such large audiences again, and this sparked an interest in writing new material; indeed, he was the prime mover in getting Brian and Paul into the studio, and confirmed in 2006 that a new album from the trio would be inevitable. "There was no point in carrying on without new material," Roger told Australia's *Courier Mail.* "Otherwise you're not a potent, ongoing force. If you're just going to recycle old records, old songs, old hits, you sort of become your own tribute band." As if to prove he was still bursting with creativity, that August he released 'Woman You're So Beautiful (But Still A Pain In The Ass)', his first solo single since 1999.

Brian, however, was reluctant; despite the thrill of being on stage night after night, his fingers weren't moving as quickly as they had before, and he was in more physical pain throughout the lengthy world tours than he had been in years. Throughout the European tour in 2005, Brian wrote at length on his website about what a rush it was being in cities that had only recently witnessed their first Queen-related concert, but he also noted that the itinerary was rigorous and physically draining for him. (This was confirmed when Paul was stricken with vocal problems, forcing a last-minute rearrangement of vocal duties between Brian and Roger.) Such tours also meant extended time away from his family, and the process of getting back into a normal routine upon returning home was lengthy; Brian wasn't ready to relive this anytime soon, and so threw himself into other projects that involved *We Will Rock You: The Musical,* the completion of his thesis (titled *A Survey Of Radial Velocities In The Zodiacal Dust Cloud*) and his postgraduate degree, and a book titled *Bang!: The Complete History Of The Universe,* written with astrophysicist Chris Lintott and astronmer Sir Patrick Moore. The very last thing he wanted to do

was to pick up The Red Special and trot off around the world once again.

Owing to the persistence of Roger, however, and the undeniable feeling that the chemistry between the three primary musicians had indeed sparked a creative force, long believed to be missing in the dark days following Freddie's death, Brian conceded to work on new material once again, and sessions for an untitled studio album began in earnest in the summer of 2007. The recording location was at Roger's home studio (which only further confirmed his dedication to the project) in Surrey, allowing the band to feel at ease with their surroundings and with each other, and not struggle to meet deadlines or feel pressured into arrangements suggested by a hot-shot producer. This has its pros and cons, as can be expected: without a guiding force to overlook the sessions and offer an outsider's perspective, bands can fall into complacency; luckily, with three hard-headed musicians like Brian, Roger, and Paul, however, this wasn't ever the issue.

The goal of the sessions was to create something organic. Shortly after the sessions began in earnest, Paul spoke to *Billboard* about the progress so far: "We're letting it sort of develop itself naturally and not pushing it or giving it any pressure. We go in, just the three of us. Roger gets on the kit, Brian gets on othe guitar, I get on the acoustic guitar and piano, either/or, and then we share the bass line afterwards… I can hear the song line and then Brian can hear all the harmonies on top of it." The following year, in Australia's *Courier Mail,* Brian mirrored these sentiments, explaining how they played together everyday: "That's something I'm proud of. We didn't just go in there and fiddle with machines; we went in there and played our instruments and worked off each other – you can hear that on the album, I think. It's an organic album at its core."

"Organic" was the manifesto of the sessions, with the decision made early on not to employ session musicians to fill in the gaps – everything would be played by Brian, Roger, and Paul. Considering the chemistry that had developed, not only between the primary musicians but also Jamie Moses, Spike Edney, and newcomer Danny Miranda, on the 2005 and 2006 tours, it would have made sense to have had the touring band included on the sessions, as well. However, Brian, Roger, and Paul still felt they had something to prove – if not to their fans, then certainly to themselves – that the three of them could write and record an album of new material. While this may have worked in theory, in practice the result was a mixed bag: with no permanent bassist, those duties fell to Brian and Paul, and while they may be a brilliant guitarist and brilliant vocalist, respectively, they're certainly not bass guitarists, and John Deacon's inventive and fluid lines are sorely missing on the finished album.

Within the first three weeks, two complete songs – 'Voodoo' and 'Time To Shine', both by Paul – were submitted and finished to the band's satisfaction, with several other ideas started; by the end of the summer, nine tracks were ready to go, with five more still to come. The ideas flowed fast and free, and everybody learned something from each other: "Paul works in a completely different way to us," Roger told *Classic Rock Magazine*. "Brian and I go to incredible lengths to get things right. He'd never met two pickier, fussier individuals. We even ended up teaching him how to sing harmony vocals, which he'd never done before, but we learned from his spontaneity."

The first new Queen-related songs since the 46664 songs from 2003 was, incidentally, a re-recording of Roger's 'Say It's Not True', a live favorite on the 2005/2006 tours but drastically rearranged and overloaded with the pomp and grandeur of Queen's glory days: transformed from its simplistic, acoustic origins to an emotional, uplifting power ballad, it was a promising return to form, and allowed Paul a perfect opportunity to affirm himself as a vocalist on a par with Freddie. Released as a digital single for World AIDS Day on 1 December 2007, the song was released as a physical product later that month, but because of its previous availability, the single reached a disappointing No. 90 in the UK.

Recording on the album continued well into 2008, with promotion starting earlier than anticipated, when the touring band appeared on the second series finale of *Al Murray's Happy Hour* in April 2008. The new album title was announced, as such, in the loo, where Brian, Roger, and Paul were standing, having just graffitied the wall with "The Cosmos Rocks" and looking charmingly innocent, before they were introduced to perform the new single. But it wasn't 'Say It's Not True' that was performed; instead, Roger's 'C-Lebrity', a tired potshot at instant stardom, was announced as the lead single. The band delivered a rambunctious performance, with Paul and Roger clearly enjoying themselves, Brian less so, before finishing up with versions of 'All Right Now' and an unaired 'Bohemian Rhapsody'.

The next day, the online community exploded with activity, with equal amounts of venom from Queen purists and praise from open-minded fans.

Anticipation ran high, but the momentum ran out far too soon; considering the single wouldn't be released for another four months, and the album following two weeks after that, the promotional blitz was premature, and by the time 'C-Lebrity' was finally released, fans had either had it already by way of rips from YouTube, or had moved on to something else.

Work on the album finished for good on 1 August 2008, with Brian exclaiming on his website, "After many months, and much mountain climbing, and a degree of pain – we have an album!" He prophetically finished his update with, "And hey, can I have my life back now?! ... I need 5 months off! See ya..." The album was sent off to be mastered, and the touring band once again began rehearsals for the upcoming world tour, set to begin on 15 September in Kharkov, Russia – the same day that *The Cosmos Rocks* was released.

Reviews were cautiously hopeful, with most centering around the lack of Freddie and the almost-there-but-not-quite gelling of Paul's ramshackle blues-rock pedigree with Brian and Roger's background in histrionic bombast. *Uncut* was particularly venomous, frothing that "this ill-fitting rebirth, fronted by the defiantly ungay, unIndian and uneccentric Paul Rodgers, can be seen as an attempt to ditch the Mercury-inspired absurdity and bolster Queen's hard rawkin' credentials ... Only the funky military swagger of 'Warboys' and the beautifully-crafted Freddie tribute ballad 'Some Things That Glitter' (possibly Rodgers' finest vocal performance since his Free heyday) survive this faintly ridiculous project with any credit." *The Guardian* was also contemptuous: "All involved have underlined that Rodgers should in no sense be thought of as Freddie Mercury's replacement, but it's hard to stop yourself wondering what Mercury might have made of all this. The songs might have sounded less awful if they were delivered with a certain knowing camp, a grandiloquence that suggested a sense of the ridiculous. But Paul Rodgers' stock in trade is a kind of pained sincerity: not for nothing was he the favorite vocalist of our erstwhile PM. When he sings 'Once I loved a butterfly, don't wonder how, don't ask me why', he sounds as if he quite literally did love a butterfly, like one of those blokes you see on late-night Channel 4 documentaries trying to explain away his intimate relationship with a horse." *Virgin Media* simply hated the album: "At best, this sounds like Queen with a lifeless stand-in where their heart should be. At worst, it's not even that, sounding like a third-rate ZZ Top or just anonymously dull stadium rock. Hard to pick the nadir of such a dire selection, but 'C-Lebrity's galumphing satire particularly grates."

Two reviews, mostly mixed, brought up some valid points. Australia's undercover.com was a little more generous in its damning: "Had they gone to neutral ground and called it by another name other than Queen, we would be hailing it as one of the great rock releases on 2008. Unfortunately, it is so far removed from what Queen sounded like and not all that far removed from what the various Rodgers albums sounded like that it is difficult to accept *The Cosmos Rocks* as a follow-up to the Mercury legacy." *The Mail on Sunday*, too, nearly hit the nail on the head: "There are glimmers of May and Taylor's old skills – 'Time To Shine' is built on a wailing Arab motif, 'Call Me' contains hints of 'Crazy Little Thing Called Love', and 'We Believe' has a simplistic grandeur that could give them another Christmas No 1. But much of this album is pub-rock writ large."

The good notices approached the album with an open mind. Some, however, blew some truly hyperbolic smoke: "The new trio's first studio album has this seemingly unlikely coalition clicking together as a fine-tuned, cohesive unit," *Mojo* gushed. "Without Freddie's decorative flourishes, the onus is on straight shooting heavy rock, with bullish single 'C-Lebrity' the mission statement Queen/Bad Co hybrid. Elsewhere, 'Small' is a gentle throwback to Free, and 'We Believe' an '80s-spec stadium-rock anthem. Occasionally they stumble, as on the clunky 'Warboys', but with Rodgers imperious, Queen's second coming is vindicated." "Not only can *The Cosmos Rocks* sit proudly in the Queen canon," *Classic Rock* purred, "it can also do the same alongside Rodgers's work with Free and Bad Company ... As the album unfolds it rapidly becomes clear that all the components of classic Queen are here. It's a work of extraordinary confidence, taking the band's familiar blueprint and casually expanding it to encompass the organic blues and visceral soul of Paul Rodgers. Overall *The Cosmos Rocks* has more than enough power to take your breath away. Freddie's legacy is in safe hands."

Record Collector was cautious: "It's not until track 12 that the epic 'Say It's Not True' rekindles the pomp of Queen of old, followed by the harmony-rich 'Surf's Up . . . School's Out !'. Ending on a high note, then, but it may take some plays to get used to the idea that QPR is very much a meeting of equals." *The Pace Press* was more realistic: "[It] isn't a perfect album, but is well worth the 13-year wait. Brian May's guitar playing abilities, for someone as old as he is, haven't faded in the least. This album is full of tunes that will have fans rocking out and playing air guitar while walking city streets ... This album will take you up, down and all around Queentown. It's not perfect, but it's a step in the right direction."

"*The Cosmos Rocks* is undeniably patchy (as were all Queen albums, remember)," *Guitarist Magazine* opined, "but the band does rise to the occasion more than once, with 'Some Things That Glitter' offering a familiar piano-fueled arrangement and some lovely guitar from Brian May. Elsewhere 'Surf's Up . . . School's Out !' is far better than the toe-curling title would suggest and the lyrical pomposity of 'We Believe' is rescued by a wonderful lead vocal from Rodgers. All in all the album does exactly what it says on the tin." The BBC, too, had above-average marks for the album: "All in all, *The Cosmos Rocks* displays a band that seem to still be in love with rock. Why else would they be doing it? Surely not for money. May's guitar is in fine fettle throughout, and it's hard to begrudge such stalwarts their noisy fun. Fans of both sides will be happy, and that's just about as much as anyone could expect."

Stripped to its basic core, the album is indeed, as its creators had taken special care of noting, organic: the drums pop with a deep, resounding thud; the guitars are processed naturally and beautifully; and the band sounds as if they're in the same room together, instead of being pieced together bit by bit like so much of the music from the 1980s and 1990s. There's no studio trickery, no ProTools or Auto-Tune to sweeten what wasn't there initially; just three musicians getting together to record some music together. But once the other elements – melodies, hooks, and lyrics – are considered, the result isn't as pretty. The songs aren't *bad*; they're just spectacularly unremarkable. When taking into account some of the more adventurous songs from Roger's *Electric Fire*, or the softer compositions from Brian's *Another World* and *Furia* soundtrack, a lot of the songs on *The Cosmos Rocks* are shockingly generic; 'Still Burnin'', described in the press release as "a mission statement of why artists are compelled to create", is built upon a thundering blues/rock foundation, but when it's pulled apart and dissected, all that remains is gratuitous fluff. Roger is as committed as ever, and Paul, too, makes the best of the situation by establishing a vocal force on the songs, but the self-proclaimed bonhomie just isn't there.

Part of the problem is that the songs, while well-performed and musically interesting, struggle to match the stratospheric proportions of Queen's back catalog. This was a built-in pitfall with using Queen's name: nothing would ever compare to the halcyon days of *Queen II*, 'Bohemian Rhapsody', and 'We Are The Champions', and it would be impossible for a trio of 60-something rockers to reinvent the wheel. What works the best is the unconventional: 'Small', for instance, is a delicate acoustic rocker, while 'Voodoo' is a Santana-inspired Latin/blues pastiche that works as a mid-album throwaway. The most Queen-like song on the album, 'Some Things That Glitter', harks back to the gentler ballads that Brian contributed to their mid-career albums, while 'Surf's Up . . . School's Out !' married some much-needed humor with open power chords and an explosive, orotund arrangement. Other than that, the songs either tried but fizzled – for instance, 'Cosmos Rockin'', which rocks convincingly but comes off as forced; 'Time To Shine', an anthemic power ballad about mythical creatures (yes, really); and 'Call Me', a delightfully irritating ditty that goes on far too long – or failed to catch fire completely – the plodding blues rock of 'Warboys (A Prayer For Peace)', which equates soldiers to mindless automata; the overly preachy and labored 'We Believe'; and the faceless and unmemorable 'Through The Night'. After considerable build up, the let down was equally significant.

Another reason was that Brian was the one who had to be convinced the most to participate in the sessions, and a band is only as happy as the unhappiest member. "Brian is always the reluctant one," Roger told *Classic Rock Magazine*, "but when he gets there, he ends up loving it. With his astronomy and other commitments he has an awful lot in his life, whereas for me, everything else is peripheral to the music." This off-handed comment – much like the little digs in the press at John Deacon talking more to the accountants than he does to his former bandmates – hinted at something just bubbling under the surface. The songwriting details in the initial pressings credited everything to Queen + Paul Rodgers, but when the North American release came a month later, songs were credited to their three names, with the primary songwriter listed first. What was shocking was that Roger had written the bulk of the material, with Brian writing only three songs, with only 'Some Things That Glitter' remotely approaching his capabilities. Furthermore, as the year wore on, Brian became increasingly displeased with the tour, and militant changes to the set list stripped

away the most adventurous new material and replaced them with the old familiars.

So what happened along the way? The primary musicians refused to air any dirty laundry in public, but reports ("unnamed sources" usually being a lighting crew member who heard a story from a friend of a friend of a personal assistant to Jamie Moses' personal assistant) circulated that Paul and Roger were frustrated with Brian's reluctance to rehearse new material, while Brian and Roger were frustrated with Paul for detaching himself from the others as the tour wore on – though this may have had something to do with the constant comparisons to Freddie, and, when the tour reached South America, where Freddie is highly revered, Paul was practically ignored at press conferences. There may have been other forces at play, or it may have been as simple as the band agreeing that their time together ended naturally and amicably, but when a proposed North American tour for 2009 failed to materialize and Paul instead announced a solo tour, suspicions were confirmed: Queen + Paul Rodgers was no more.

LIVE IN UKRAINE

Parlophone 9 64603 2 0, June 2009
Hollywood Records D000453400, September 2009

'One Vision' (4'03), 'Tie Your Mother Down' (2'29), 'The Show Must Go On' (4'37), 'Fat Bottomed Girls' (5'00), 'Another One Bites The Dust' (3'35), 'Hammer To Fall' (3'42), 'I Want It All' (4'10), 'I Want To Break Free' (3'55), 'Seagull' (4'50), 'Love Of My Life' (5'45), '39' (4'37), Drum Solo (5'00), 'I'm In Love With My Car' (3'42), 'Say It's Not True' (4'02), 'Shooting Star' (6'21), 'Bad Company' (5'36), Guitar Solo (3'58), 'Bijou' (2'07), 'Last Horizon' (4'32), 'Crazy Little Thing Called Love' (4'04), 'C-lebrity' (3'52), 'Feel Like Makin' Love' (6'45), 'Bohemian Rhapsody' (5'53), 'Cosmos Rockin'' (4'28), 'All Right Now' (5'31), 'We Will Rock You' (2'19), 'We Are The Champions' (2'59), 'God Save The Queen' (2'05), 'A Kind Of Magic' *(digital download only)* (5'43), 'Radio Ga Ga' *(digital download only)* (6'15)

Musicians: Brian May *(guitars, vocals, acoustic guitar)*, Roger Taylor *(drums, vocals)*, Paul Rodgers *(vocals, acoustic guitar on 'Seagull')*, Spike Edney *(piano, keyboards, keytar, vocals)*, Danny Miranda *(bass guitar, vocals, upright electric bass on '39')*, Jamie Moses *(guitars, vocals)*

Recorded: 12 September 2008 at Freedom Square, Kharkov, Ukraine
Producer: Joshua J. Macrae, Justin Shirley-Smith, Peter Brandt

The first night of most tours is rarely filmed or recorded, for at least two very good reasons: the band is still blowing off the cobwebs from a lengthy period of rest, and the set list is often still in its infancy, with the band still trying to figure out a cohesive order based on audience reaction. It's surprising, then, that the first night of Queen + Paul Rodgers' Rock The Cosmos tour was filmed, recorded, and eventually released as the final album of the union. It was certainly all for a good cause, as explained in Section 7; with the sextet headlining the Don't Let AIDS Ruin Your Life free concert, the performance attracted 10 million worldwide viewers, and with old stalwart David Mallet returning to direct the show, the band felt more comfortable than they might have otherwise. But they were still in the process of working out the opening night jitters, which meant that some studio work had to be done to bring the performance up to the band's impossibly high standards.

It would be easy to focus on the glaring negative, that the set list remained too similar to the 2005/2006 tour, with only a handful of new songs ('One Vision', 'Shooting Star', 'Bijou', and three album tracks from *The Cosmos Rocks*) replacing old favorites. Indeed, the repertoire would progress throughout the tour, with more emphasis (eventually) placed on *The Cosmos Rocks*; there's no denying that the similarity in selections

between *Return Of The Champions* and *Live In Ukraine* is frustratingly strong. But there were some new elements that made this a more attractive purchase: Roger's drum solo was more visual this time, starting off with Roger and Danny Miranda goofing around on an upright bass, before Roger sat down in front of a snare and bass drum; roadies worked hurriedly around him to construct a more elaborate drum set that finally led the band into 'I'm In Love With My Car'. Brian's solo, too, varied a bit, and saw perhaps the biggest surprise of the tour: the live debut of 'Bijou', with Brian playing to Freddie's pre-recorded vocal. Even the three *Cosmos Rocks* tracks – 'C-lebrity', 'Cosmos Rockin'', and the power ballad rendition of 'Say It's Not True' – received a more muscular performance in the live setting.

All in all, it's difficult to escape the notion that *Live In Ukraine* was simply a way for the band to justify the elaborate cost of a film crew, and while the performance is genuine, its release six months after the cinematic release of *Let The Cosmos Rocks* smacks of afterthought. Furthermore, the CD wasn't released separately from the DVD (although a digital release was offered, with two bonus tracks – 'A Kind Of Magic' and 'Radio Ga Ga', though 'Wishing Well' remains inexplicably unreleased), which certainly didn't help sales. As a result, *Live In Ukraine* failed to chart in the UK, the first instance that a Queen-related product didn't chart. (Surprisingly, the package was released in the US, though predictably failed to chart.) By this point, Brian, Roger, and Paul were well past caring, and *Live In Ukraine*, for all its plusses, remains an undignified end to a union that deserved better treatment.

PART THREE
THE SONGS

This section covers songs written, recorded, covered or played live by John Deacon, Brian May, Freddie Mercury and Roger Taylor, either as solo artists, in early bands from the 1950s and 1960s, and as the collective unit known as Queen. Cover versions of Queen songs are only dealt with in rare cases (e.g., Bad News performing 'Bohemian Rhapsody' or Nine Inch Nails performing 'Get Down, Make Love'); renditions by obscure bands on numerous tribute albums have been ignored.

It should be remembered that Queen Productions are particularly guarded over the contents of the band's vaults, and that only a handful of songs marked as unreleased have actually been heard by collectors and fans, myself included.

AARON (May)
• Soundtrack (Brian): Furia

Yet another variation on the soundtrack's main theme, taken in a slightly lower key, 'Aaron' is a short and sweet performance by Dave Lee on the French horn, again with keyboards adding dimension to the piece.

ABANDONFIRE (Taylor/Richards)
• Album (Roger): Frontier

Taking the cold, electronic approach from 'Killing Time' even further, 'Abandonfire' strikes a bleak balance of conformity and nuclear war with masculinity ("Join our army and be a real man"). Cowritten by Roger and David Richards, the song is a product of its time, with an almost entirely synthesized backing (apart from some bright stabs of guitar), but is a decent mood piece on the second side of Strange Frontier.

ABSOLUTELY ANYTHING (Taylor)

Roger contributed the title track to Terry Jones' first film as director in over 20 years, and the first to feature all living members of Monty Python since The Meaning Of Life. Starring Simon Pegg, Kate Beckinsale, and the late, great Robin Williams, the film was released in the UK in August 2015 and garnered fairly harsh reviews – not surprising, given the plot of a man suddenly bestowed from power-hungry aliens (the aforementioned Pythons) the ability to do whatever he wants. Roger's contribution seemed to have gone largely unnoticed, which is a shame, as it's a lovely ballad that would have fit in perfectly on Fun On Earth. As of this writing (spring 2018), a soundtrack album has yet to be released, though 'Absolutely Anything' can be heard in low-fi quality on any number of Internet sites, the most common being YouTube. Hopefully, this track and Roger's contributions to Solitary will see the light of day soon.

ACTION THIS DAY (Taylor)
• Album: Space • Live: On Fire • Bonus: Space

Taking its title from a favorite expression of Winston Churchill, Roger's 'Action This Day' is perhaps the most successful fusion of rock and funk on Hot Space. Lyrically addressing the actions of love, the song is set to a pulsating drum-machine beat that tends to fall flat on record (live, it received a far more energetic treatment), but is notable as one of the last times Roger and Freddie shared lead vocals on a song.

'Action This Day' was performed at every Hot Space concert during 1982. For years, the definitive live version was that released on Queen On Fire: At The Bowl, but a second live version from a November 1982 performance in Tokyo was released on the 2011 reissue of Hot Space.

AFFAIRS

This jam was recorded during the Montreux sessions

for *Innuendo* in 1990, and leaked onto the Internet in November 2010 by way of producer David Richards, who premiered them at an appearance at the Italian Queen Community's fifth anniversary. Much like several other scraps of songs from this time ('My Secret Fantasy', 'I Guess We're Falling Out', and 'Robbery'), 'Affairs' has several good ideas and certainly deserved another look-in, but ultimately the right decisions were made. Still, this recording barely scratches the surface of what lurks in the archives, remaining to be unearthed and released to fans.

AIN'T PUT NOTHIN' DOWN *(Moss)*
• Album (The Cross): *Blue*

Written by Clayton Moss and released on *Blue Rock*, 'Ain't Put Nothin' Down' is a slight but enjoyable track that would have benefited from an additional remix to bring Roger's voice to the fore a bit more. The song is a plea to remain optimistic when all else fails but, unfortunately, the weak lyrics detract from the message considerably.

The song was performed live on the 1991 Blue Rock tour, usually as the third number, with a live version appearing on the Fan Club-only cassette release *Live In Germany*, and was included in the set lists for the remaining few shows between 1992 and 1993. 'Ain't Put Nothin' Down' was also released as the B-side of the 'New Dark Ages' single in 1991, with a unique single mix, extending the song by 30 seconds but adding very little except for a marginally longer intro and outro.

AIRHEADS *(Taylor)*
• Album (Roger): *Fun*

This "ain't too refined" new wave rocker sits mostly forgotten on the second side of *Fun In Space*, yet it's a masterful performance, with some chunky, distorted bass and guitars riffing manically over a breathless, tenacious drum pattern. It's by no means a classic song, but it certainly adds a bit of humor to Roger's debut solo album, which would be sorely lacking on subsequent albums.

ALL DEAD, ALL DEAD *(May)*
• Album: *NOTW* • Bonus: *NOTW*

Written about the death of Brian's childhood pet cat, 'All Dead, All Dead' is a mournful paean to lost friends,

with a childlike naïveté that illustrates the simpler view of death. "It was a song I had around for a while," Brian explained on an episode of *In The Studio With Redbeard*. "It was kind of about the passing of friends ... and I think the thing that started it off was my cat, losing my cat. My cat died when I was a kid, and I kind of never got over it. I think it was one of those things which surfaces now and again in different ways. I think I wrote the song for the album thinking that I was writing it about something completely different – but I think part of it was sort of getting it out of my system." Set to a grandiose piano backing track with lead vocals from Brian, and harmonies from Freddie on the choruses, the song is lovely in its restraint, with only the Red Special, approximating a church organ, offering any kind of embellishment.

"That's one of my favourites," Brian said in a 1983 interview with *Guitar Magazine*. "That was one of the ones which I thought came off best, and I was really pleased with the sound. It always gives me a surprise when I listen to it, because it was meant to really bring tears to your eyes. It almost does it to me."

Speaking of bringing tears to the eyes, a previously unreleased alternate take with Freddie on lead vocals (and singing the introductory lyrics that were printed on the inner sleeve but absent from the final recording) was released on the 2017 deluxe edition of *News Of The World*. A beautiful animated video, featuring a tuxedo cat (modeled after Brian's childhood pet cat, Pixie) roaming around the inside of Frank, the robot on the album's front sleeve, was unveiled shortly before the reissue's release in October 2017, and features a previously unavailable mix that combines Freddie's vocal version with the familiar album version.

ALL GOD'S PEOPLE *(Queen/Moran)*
• Album: *Innuendo* • B-side: 5/91 [14]

Fifteen years after first attempting gospel with 'Somebody To Love', Queen once again revisit the style with 'All God's People'. When asked about the song in an interview in *Guitar World*, conducted by Extreme guitarist Nuno Bettencourt, Brian said, "I love it too. I had less to do with that than I did with most of the stuff on the album. That was originally something Freddie was going to do on a solo album, and gradually we all played on it. I went in and played guitar and it seemed to work very well. John went in and played bass, Roger put the drums in, so it became a Queen track. I love it. Not many people have spoken to me about it, but I think it's great. It's got a lot of depth to it."

Written by Freddie and Mike Moran (who contributed keyboards to the recording) in 1987 and recorded as a demo during sessions for *Barcelona*, with the working title of 'Africa By Night', 'All God's People' was originally recorded – and considered – for *The Miracle*, but was dropped due to space limitations. The song was dusted off for inclusion on *Innuendo*, and its plea for peace and hope for the human race suited the tone of that album far better than the much-ballyhooed return to rock of *The Miracle*.

ALL RIGHT NOW *(Fraser/Rodgers)*
• Live (Q+PR): *Return, Ukraine*

An epic, swaggering blues rocker extolling the virtues of a one-night stand, 'All Right Now' became Free's biggest and best-known song, and still features in regular rotation across radio waves worldwide. Released on the 1970 album *Fire And Water*, the song was issued as a single in May 1970 and established Free as a top-class act. In fact, The Faces were so enamored with the band that they not only played several Free songs in their live sets, they also recorded their own response to 'All Right Now' in 1971, which was titled 'Stay With Me'.

The first performance of the song with a Queen-related member came on 19 October 1991, which was also the first time Paul Rodgers worked with a member of the band. Brian had organized the Guitar Legends Concert in Seville and asked several premier artists to contribute to the show. Paul Rodgers was one of those artists, and played a short set of Free and Bad Company songs towards the end of the concert: 'Can't Get Enough', 'Feel Like Making Love' and 'All Right Now', with Brian contributing guitar on all of them. In 1994, Brian guested on the number on three further occasions, but the first real sparks between guitarist and vocalist wouldn't ignite until over a decade later.

On 11 November 2004, Queen were inducted into the UK Hall of Fame. Since neither Brian nor Roger felt up to the challenge of singing the songs themselves, they asked Paul Rodgers to sing on 'We Will Rock You' and 'We Are The Champions', then decided to incorporate 'All Right Now' as the final performance. When the performance aired on television, the general vibe was positive, which Brian commented on shortly thereafter, and the wheels were set in motion for a full-scale tour, announced the following month. 'All Right Now' became a mainstay, was performed at every show

(allowing Brian to really get into an extended solo) and quickly became a crowd-pleaser.

ALL THE WAY FROM MEMPHIS *(Hunter)*
• Album (Brian): *World*

As with his previous solo album, Brian deconstructed a popular track by his peers and transformed it into a full-blown Queen treatment. Whereas before it had been 'Rollin' Over', a track previously written and recorded by the Small Faces (contemporaries of Smile), this time Brian rocked up Mott The Hoople's 1973 glam single 'All The Way From Memphis', based on an arrangement on their *Live* album. Brian played most of the instruments except for drums – done by Cozy Powell – and the backing vocals, provided by Shelley Preston, Nikki Love and Becci Glover. The stars of the show – Brian's Red Special and Cozy Powell's thundering drums – duel with each other magnificently as Brian howls Ian Hunter's words, while Hunter himself shows up in the middle of the song as a guest raconteur.

"The first proper gig we had as Queen," Brian explained in 1998, "we supported Mott The Hoople, which was a brilliant stroke – the best thing that could possibly have happened to us. We were doing a few small gigs around England, but really not getting incredibly far. I mean, there was a sort of reputation building up, but what we did was go out with [Mott] who had the proper audience already there. You know, they'd worked on their audience, they had it down, and anyone who was into state-of-the-art rock'n'roll at the time would have been there. So they saw us, which was just the best thing that could have happened. I saw Mott The Hoople play this song all round England and all round the States and it was a storm every night. It was something exemplary – to see an audience erupt and react that way to that song. I wish it was still possible to see [them] do that. But I'm gonna do it, which is why I put it on the album, 'cos I damn well wanna play that song live. I just love it so much. It's got all the right elements. Ian had it taped – you know, it's got light and shade, changes of pace, it's got suspense, and you think, 'When is it coming?' and he'd milk that for all it was worth, and [now] *I'm* gonna milk it!"

Indeed, Brian did just that, and 'All The Way From Memphis' – certainly the highlight of the three cover versions on *Another World* – became a concert favorite on his 1998 Another World tour. The studio version was also included on the cleverly titled *Moth Poet Hotel* (an anagram of Mott The Hoople) tribute album, on which Brian was by far the most well-known musician.

ALL THE YOUNG DUDES *(Bowie)*

Though Queen had just started out when David Bowie became a star, they took a cue from the artist by experimenting with different sounds, techniques and genres. It came as no surprise, then, that the band approached Bowie in mid-1973, asking him to produce their second album. He respectfully declined since he was tied up with another of Britain's glam rockers, Mott the Hoople. He provided them with 'All The Young Dudes', and it shot them back to the top of the charts.

In November 1973, Queen were asked to support Mott the Hoople on a countrywide UK tour; the band, eager to gain exposure, agreed, and backed a fast-rising Hoople to great success. On 1 December 1973, when Mott performed the encore of their biggest hit, 'All The Young Dudes', Brian, Roger and Freddie were asked to rejoin them and provide backing vocals for the song.

With Ian Hunter as a performer at the Concert For Life, instead of choosing a Queen song to tackle, he instead grouped with David Bowie and Mick Ronson following Bowie's performance of 'Under Pressure' to provide an electrifying version of 'All The Young Dudes'. Backed by Roger, Brian, John and Spike Edney, the song featured practically inaudible saxophone from Bowie, additional guitar from Ronson, and rhythm guitar and lead vocals from Hunter. The backing vocals were provided by Miriam Stockley, Maggie Bell, Chris Thompson, Peter Straker, and Gary Cherone and Nuno Bettencourt from Extreme. This version later appeared on Ronson's posthumous 1994 album, *Heaven And Hull*.

ALL THIS IS LOVE

In March 2017, the official Queen Twitter account tweeted a picture of a set of lyrics from a discarded song from the *Hot Space* sessions. Whether the song was actually recorded or not remains a mystery, but it's these tantalizing bits of information that keep Queen fans and collectors going.

THE ALSO RANS *(Taylor)*
• Album (The Cross): *Blue* • Live (The Cross): *Germany*

Opening the second side of *Blue Rock* is this superb composition by Roger, sounding like an update of his own 1974 composition, 'Tenement Funster'. The focus is on Roger's voice as he tells a tale of street misfits, struggling to fit into a society that shuns underachievers. There are callbacks aplenty to other artists, with an obvious nod to Bruce Springsteen's many lyrical woes of growing up as a working class hero. The opening line ("I was born on the 22nd floor of a bird cage") references two singles by The Rolling Stones: 'Get Off Of My Cloud' ("I live on the corner of the 99th floor of my block") and 'Jumpin' Jack Flash' ("I was born in a crossfire hurricane"), while the outro backing vocals, provided by Candy and Clare Yates, mirror almost exactly Lou Reed's 1972 single, 'Walk On The Wild Side'.

'The Also Rans' was performed live occasionally on the 1991 Blue Rock tour, usually as the penultimate number of the show, with a live version appearing on the 1992 fan club-only bootleg, *Live In Germany*.

AMANDLA *(May/Stewart/Anastacia/Louw/Bonsu)*
• Live: *46664*

Credited as a Queen track, 'Amandla' was written and recorded for the 46664 project in 2003. The song started off as a jam between Brian and Dave Stewart and then blossomed into something beyond Brian's original vision, making its credit as a Queen track all the more dubious. Featuring a prayer by Andrews Bonsu and vocals from Anastacia, the song is about as atypically Queen as a song can get, but Brian contributes the piano and the Red Special even makes an appearance towards the end.

AMAZING GRACE *(Newton)*
• Digital Download: 4/16 • Album (Brian & Kerry): *Golden*

This Christian hymn, penned by John Newton in 1779, has been covered by thousands of artists in the past few centuries, and so Brian and Kerry give it a bang on *Golden Days*. While The Red Special would have been perfect for an instrumental version, instead Brian and Kerry perform it acoustically, giving it a slightly different sound than would be expected. Brian had recently revealed he was rediscovering his love of acoustic guitar, hence the Acoustic By Candlelight tour, and his performance here is so deft and beautiful that it threatens to distract from Kerry's gorgeous vocal.

THE AMAZING SPIDER-MAN (May)

• CD single (Brian): 3/95 [37]

One of the more curious diversions in a Queen solo artist's history, 'The Amazing Spider-Man' was a BBC radio series that involved Brian's wife Anita Dobson in the role of Liz Allan, a high-school classmate of Peter Parker and a minor love interest in the original *Spider-Man* series. This would explain Brian's involvement in writing and recording the music for the series, which was titled *The Amazing Spider-Man* and credited to 'MC Spy-D + Friends'.

Following the successful radio series, the best bits of the music and dialog were edited into a CD single and released in March 1995, two months after the series had aired. In what can only be described as a ludicrous proliferation, several remixes were released as part of the CD single, with the main theme, the four-minute 'Mastermix', technically being the A-side. Additional remixes – including an eight-minute 'White Trouser Mix', a two-minute 'Sad Bit' and two dance remixes known as 'Solution Mix' and 'Solution Chilled Mix', as well as a short burst of guitar called 'The Amazing Spider Person (Brown Trouser Mix)' and a collection of sound effects titled 'The Amazing DJ Perk (MC Spy-D's Favourite Stings)' – were also issued, each more monotonous and puzzling than the last.

As it is, the original 'The Amazing Spider-Man' is a lot of fun, and Brian's music is well-arranged and performed, though depending far too heavily on the radio show to make any kind of sense on its own. Nevertheless, the success of the radio series translated into the single's sales, helping it reach No. 37 in the UK charts. Brian, however, had already moved well beyond the song, giving it little promotion and preferring to work on ideas for his next solo album and Queen's own posthumous *Made In Heaven*.

ANOTHER ONE BITES THE DUST (Deacon)

• Album: *Game* • A-side: 8/80 [7] • CD Single: 11/88
• Live: *Magic, Wembley, On Fire, Montreal, Budapest* •
Compilation: *Hits3* • Bonus: *Wembley* • Live (Q+PR):
Return, Ukraine

Queen were always keen on experimentation and pushing the limits of not only the studio and their creative team, but themselves as artists and musicians, and it was usually either Freddie or Brian who instigated the most memorable and adventurous departures from the norm. In early 1980, John – the quiet one who had been content writing strictly pop songs – opened up a whole new avenue for Queen by successfully introducing them to funk.

"I listened to a lot of soul music when I was in school, and I've always been interested in that sort of music," John modestly explained shortly after the release of the song. "I'd been wanting to do a track like 'Another One Bites The Dust' for a while, but originally all I had was the line and the bass riff. Gradually, I filled it in and the band added ideas. I could hear it as a song for dancing but had no idea it would become as big as it did. The song got picked up off our album and some of the black radio stations in the US started playing it, which we've never had before."

Brian's account of the song was a self-deprecatory one: "A lot of people have used 'Another One Bites The Dust' as a theme song – the Detroit Lions used it for their games, and they soon began to lose, so they bit the dust soon afterwards [laughs], but it was a help to the record. And, there's been a few cover versions of various kinds, notably 'Another One Rides The Bus', which is an extremely funny record by a bloke called Mad Al [sic – actually Weird Al Yankovic] or something in the States – it's hilarious. We like people covering our songs in any way, no matter what spirit it's done in, because it's great to have anyone use your music as a base, a big compliment."

Though the band's first attempts at funk had come with Freddie's 'Get Down, Make Love' in 1977 and Roger's 'Fun It' in 1978, those songs also contained other elements, rock in the former, disco in the latter. John's 'Another One Bites The Dust', however, was pure funk, and contained very few Queen-like elements: there was no guitar solo, the drums were crisp, tight and dry, and it featured a prominent bassline borrowed from Chic's 'Good Times'. Vocal harmonies were limited to occasional double-tracking on some verses and the choruses, and only Freddie's voice distinguished the song as being Queen.

It was this level of anonymity that allowed several US disc jockeys – specifically, in New York, Philadelphia, and Detroit – to label the song as a virtually unknown single from an obscure black R&B band. Once the song's success started to snowball, Elektra and EMI issued it as a single in August 1980, despite protests from Roger, where it reached a modest No. 7 in the UK but became Queen's second No. 1 single in the US, solidifying the band's popularity and making 1980 one of their most lucrative years, both in terms of ticket and record sales.

"This song was written 'cause I always wanted to do something in the direction of black music," John said in a contemporary interview. "It's not a typical Queen song and I do not know if we ever will do something similar again. We had disagreements about this song. Our company wanted this song as a single 'cause it was very successful at black radio stations. Roger tried to avoid that, because he said it's too disco-like and that is not good for the reputation of Queen."

As Brian explained in 1993, "John Deacon, being totally in his own world, came up with this thing, which was nothing like what we were doing. We were going for the big drum sound: you know, quite pompous in our usual way. And Deakey says, 'No, I want this to be totally different: it's going to be a very tight drum sound.' It was originally done to a drum loop – this was before the days of drum-machines. Roger did a loop, kind of under protest, because he didn't like the sound of the drums recorded that way. And then Deakey put this groove down. Immediately Freddie became violently enthusiastic and said, 'This is big! This is important! I'm going to spend a lot of time on this.' It was the beginning of something quite big for us, because it was the first time that one of our records crossed over to the black community. We had no control over that; it just happened. Suddenly we were forced to put out this single because so many stations in New York were playing it. It changed that album from being a million-seller to being a three-million seller in a matter of three weeks or so."

The song was recorded in the spring of 1980 at Musicland Studios, during the main sessions for *The Game*, and featured John playing bass and rhythm guitar, synthesizer, and backwards piano. Like 'Crazy Little Thing Called Love', though, the band were unsure of the song's commercial potential and initially opted to keep it as an album track. Though various stories persist, the most commonly known is that Michael Jackson, then hot on the heels of his 1979 *Off The Wall* album and building a (brief) friendship with Freddie, suggested that the band release the song as a single. Crystal Taylor, Roger's personal assistant, has said that it wasn't Michael who suggested it, but the road crew themselves: "The actual very first people to suggest 'Another One Bites The Dust' to be released as a single was The Royal Road Crew. We were lurking around at Musicland Studios while the fab ones were mixing, and I think it was Jobby [John's assistant] who said it would be a huge hit. When we told the band they just glared at us and told us to mix some more

cocktails. I suppose Mr Jackson saying it sounds more impressive than 'Our pissed road crew said...'"

"I can remember many times when Roger and I would be pulling in absolutely diametrically opposite directions," Brian said in 1998. "No chance of either of us budging. And Freddie would find a way through. He'd say, 'Well, you can do this and do this and it will all work.' That was one of Freddie's great talents. He was good at finding roads in the mist. But he would certainly fight for things he believed in. Like 'Another One Bites The Dust', which was a bit of a departure for Queen. Roger, at the time, certainly felt that it wasn't rock and roll and was quite angry at the way it was going. And Freddie said, 'Darling, leave it to me. I believe in this.' John had written the song. But it took Freddie's support to make it happen."

A video for the single was shot during a soundcheck on 9 August 1980 at The Reunion in Dallas, Texas. Directed by Daniella Green, the video shows the band running through the song as normal, with very few embellishments; only during the middle section, when Freddie prances around the stage with various multicolored baseball caps with devils' horns plastered to them, does the video actually get interesting.

Live, the song received very few airings during the first few performances in 1980. Only after its success in the charts did it finally become a mainstay in the set list, being performed during every tour between 1980 and 1986. The song remained an encore number until 1982, but was moved up earlier in the set list for the Queen Works! tour in 1984.

Inexplicably, a remix by Wyclef Jean was issued on the 1999 barrel-scraping *Greatest Hits III* album release. The song had been reissued in this format in September 1998 in support of the American film *Small Soldiers*, but is completely out of place among the other songs on the album.

ANOTHER WORLD (May)
• Album (Brian): *World*

Bringing Brian's second full-length solo album to an emotional close, 'Another World' is a typical ballad sung with such poignancy that it's hard not to be touched by the vocal performance. Unfortunately, schmaltzy string keyboards are added to the mix and the song is bathed in echo, reducing it to the level of such treacly MOR crooners like Barry Manilow and others of his ilk. Unflatteringly, the press release stated that it was a "ballad which would probably work for anyone from Axl Rose to Celine Dion."

Released as a Holland-only single after the album was issued, a more well-known version was issued on the Spanish-only album *Baladas 99*. Retitled as 'Otro Lugar', Brian sings the song in Spanish, approximating the phrasing of the English version, and it is indeed a beautiful rendition. The song was performed live with Brian standing at the front of the stage without a guitar (Jamie Moses played the acoustic guitar solo), and in this stripped-back arrangement was more effective than the album version.

The song took on a more poignant tone after Cozy Powell died in a car accident on 5 April 1998, though it had been completed before then with Ken Taylor on bass and Steve Ferrone on drums and percussion. When asked if Cozy (and, inevitably, Freddie) were in mind when Brian wrote the song, he explained, "As soon as you start working on an idea for a song, then all kinds of things come into your head, and you weave all the threads together. It's primarily a love song, really, and the first seed of the idea came from a film again, strangely enough. This guy [Peter Howitt] wrote a script for a film called *Sliding Doors* which has now come out, as a matter of fact. He was an old friend of mine, and he said, 'Please write me a song. I've always dreamed of asking you to write me a song, Bri.' So I wrote this 'Another World' track and was very pleased with it: took it straight round to him, and he loved it, jumped up and down, said 'This is it! This is the perfect thing for the film!' About four months later I'd never heard another word from him and he said, 'Oh, sorry Brian, politics, y'know, I got involved with a record company who is financing the film and we can't use your song.' So I was upset for a couple of days, but then I thought, 'Well, I have the song', and I started to weave into it the thoughts which go with my own life and my own feelings and I'm very ... actually, it's a shock. Every time I hear this song, it's a shock, because it's very different for me, and it really is another world in terms of technique and atmosphere in song writing and record making. It's a record which I didn't think I would make. I'm much more into excess, y'know *(laughs)*. This is a very grown-up kind of song, and it is another world for me."

APPARITION *(May)*
• Soundtrack (Brian): *Furia*

With vocalizations by Brian's daughter Emily (then only 12 years old), 'Apparition' is another variation of the main theme from *Furia*, although the ethereal rendition helps make this piece memorable.

APRIL LADY *(Lucas)*
• Compilation (Smile): *Ghost Of A Smile*

With Brian on lead vocals and acoustic guitar, 'April Lady' is one of the most delicate tracks recorded by Smile. Written by unknown songwriter Stanley Lucas, the song was suggested by producer Fritz Freyer, and was recorded in August 1969 at De Lane Lea Studios. "That was in 5/4 time, a bit clever," Tim Staffell remembered. "We responded to that, because we wanted to be seen to be capable. It had pretty meaningless words, but I quite liked it." Featuring some gorgeous harmony vocals from Tim and prominent chorus vocals by Roger, the song is a rare highlight of the sessions but, as with the other five tracks recorded that month, it snuck out on the 1982 bootleg *Gettin' Smile*, and then again in 1998 on *Ghost Of A Smile*.

ARBORIA (PLANET OF THE TREE MEN) *(Deacon)*
• Album: *Flash*

A sinister-sounding composition for *Flash Gordon*, John's atmospheric 'Arboria (Planet Of The Tree Men)' opens side two with a whirling synthesizer background, while a flute-like synth motif dominates the remainder of the piece.

ARREST *(May)*
• Soundtrack (Brian): *Furia*

Largely featuring programmed keyboards, 'Arrest' is a dark and brooding, albeit short, piece, ending with more dialog from the film.

ASSASSIN

'Assassin' has eluded collectors for years, and, according to legend, was the predecessor to 'Innuendo' but altered considerably due to its apparent similarity to Led Zeppelin's 'Kashmir'. This rumor has been disproved over the years, with Queen's archivist Greg Brooks confirming the song's existence, but that it wasn't an early version of 'Innuendo'; if anything, 'Assassin' is more likely to be a working title of 'The Hitman'.

BABY IT'S ALRIGHT *(Edney)*
• Album (The Cross): *Blue* • Live (The Cross): *Germany*

Coming after 'Dirty Mind' on *Blue Rock*, 'Baby It's Alright' is the best song written by Spike Edney, though that's not saying much. The song starts off as a delicate ballad before turning into a mid-tempo rocker, with Roger forgiving the object of his affection for the resulting heartache and blues. With a gorgeously understated guitar solo and subtle accompaniment by Geoffrey Richardson (violin and viola) and Helen Liebman (cello), the song also features some poignant backing vocals from Candy and Clare Yates, just a few of the many reasons why *Blue Rock* is regarded so highly by fans of The Cross.

The song was performed live on the 1991 tour in support of Magnum, with a live version appearing on the 1992 fan club-only release, *Live In Germany*.

BACK CHAT *(Deacon)*
• Album: *Space* • A-side: 8/82 [40] • Live: *On Fire*
• Bonus: *Space*

The song that instigated the *Hot Space* sessions led the band down an alley their fans weren't exactly prepared for. Written by John, this pseudo-funk rocker achieves a lot in its four-and-a-half-minute life; with a muscular backing track, 'Back Chat' chugs away as Freddie snarls the lyrics with malicious intent, the words depicting a sparring couple. Considering the strained relationships and drug- and alcohol-fueled recreations during the *Hot Space* sessions, the subject matter of 'Back Chat' hints at the ill feelings and frustrations of the period, with Brian later prophetically remarking that "We worked hard and played hard, but those later Munich days were lost in a haze of vodka ... You end up emotionally distracted, trying to keep your life together away from the studio. I was married with two children by then, and it was a continual life-and-death battle to keep everything going."

In its original state, the song lacked the scorching guitar solo; Brian recollected to *Guitar Magazine* in 1983, "We would experiment with the rhythm and the bass and drum track and get that sounding right, and then very cautiously piece the rest around it, which was an experimental way for us to do it. In [that song], there wasn't going to be a guitar solo, because John, who wrote the song, has gone perhaps more violently black than the rest of us. We had lots of arguments about it, and what he was heading for

in his tracks was a totally non-compromise situation, doing black stuff as R&B artists would do it with no concessions to our methods at all, and I was trying to edge him back toward the central path and get a bit of heaviness into it, and a bit of the anger of rock music. So one night I said I wanted to see what I could add to it – I felt that the song, as it stood, wasn't aggressive enough: it's [called] 'Back Chat', and it's supposed to be about people arguing and it should have some kind of guts to it. He agreed, and I went in and tried a few things."

'Back Chat', with rhythm guitars and synthesizers played by John and a now-dated electronic drum solo from Roger, was chosen as the fourth and final UK single from *Hot Space*. Upon its release in August 1982, expectations were high for a chart performance reminiscent of 'Another One Bites The Dust' only two years before. However, despite a punchier single mix by John, 'Back Chat' peaked at only No. 40 in the charts, their lowest British charting since the live rendition of 'Love Of My Life' in 1979.

The promotional video, filmed in Toronto during rehearsals for the Rock 'n' America US tour, was directed by Brian Grant and was a blatant rush job, with a glum-looking band positioned in a flooded warehouse, while Freddie attempts to instill some life into a lackluster performance by dancing around violently chugging pistons. The single mix remained unavailable on a compilation until 2009, when it finally showed up on *The Singles Collection – Volume 2*, while an extended remix, Queen's first of any kind, was created for the 12" release of the single. Remixed by John, it nearly doubles the length of the song and adds all sorts of percussion and instrumental segments, but was not included on *The 12" Collection*, released as part of the *Box of Trix* set in 1992. An ideal home for the extended mix would have been on the 2011 reissue of *Hot Space*, but this was overlooked in favor of the single mix.

Live, the song took a whole new direction, as with most of the *Hot Space* material, but was never given a fair chance in the live setting, only being performed a handful of times; it was dropped by the end of the 1982 Hot Space World tour.

BACK TO STORM

Initially known among collectors as 'Song 2', 'Back To Storm' was reportedly recorded during the 1985 sessions for *A Kind Of Magic*, though there's still speculation that it may have been an idea recorded by

Freddie during sessions for *Mr Bad Guy*. However, that is most definitely Roger on drums, with his distinctive hi-hat touches, long established as his signature sound, thus lending further weight to the *A Kind Of Magic* out-take theories. (An instrumental solo version of the song has leaked out as 'Little Boogie', and contains some lively piano work from Freddie.) Like most unfinished doodles, 'Back To Storm' is interesting enough upon first listen, but there's not much else here to sustain repeated listens.

BACK TO THE LIGHT *(May)*
• Album (Brian): *BTTL* • A-side (Brian): 11/92 [19]
• CD single (Brian): 6/93 [23] • Live (Brian): *Brixton*

Brian was in a confused state after the end of the Magic tour in August 1986. The video shoot for 'Who Wants To Live Forever' the following month would be the final unified spurt of activity the band embarked on for the next 18 months. That time would be spent focusing on solo projects, and Brian was certainly no exception. He had been itching to start work on his own album; *Star Fleet Project* was a one-off, a trio of loose jams with some of his musician friends, but hardly definitive of his capabilities as a songwriter. So, after some activity with other bands, including a brief stint helping Bad News produce and record their debut album, Brian finally set to work on his own project.

The title track of that album, *Back To The Light*, is an outpouring of emotion. Brian was clearly a troubled man during this period: his marriage was falling apart due to a scandalous attraction to *EastEnders* star Anita Dobson, and his father had passed away in June 1988, which hit him hardest. He was extremely close to his father, and dealt with his depression by rediscovering the instrument he had built with him back in 1963.

Segueing in from a short keyboard and guitar intro, 'The Dark', the song is a masterful display of light and shade, with Brian's voice distant and frail in the verses but powerful and commanding in the chorus. 'Back To The Light' was recorded in March 1988 at Allerton Hill, Brian's home studio, and was one of four songs initially set down at that session (the others were 'I'm Scared', 'Let Your Heart Rule Your Head', and 'Rollin' Over'), but this was clearly the strongest of the bunch. Brian certainly thought so and, as well as making it the first song performed during his 1992 and 1993 world tour, issued it as the third single from the album in November 1992. Backed with 'Nothin' But Blue' (the regular album version on the first CD

single, which also included 'Star Fleet' and 'Let Me Out', and with an instrumental guitar version on the second single, which included 'Bluesbreaker'), the single peaked at an impressive No. 19 in the UK, but was the first single from the album not to reach the Top Ten.

A live version, performed on *The Tonight Show* on 5 April 1993 and featuring a mock-Cockney introduction from host Jay Leno, was released on the CD single release of 'Resurrection', which also featured 'Tie Your Mother Down' (with Slash guesting on additional guitar) from the same performance. By this point, the Brian May Band had been on tour for six weeks, and Brian wasn't yet used to singing a two-hour show every night. As a result, his voice is tired and he tries but often fails to reach several of the higher notes from the song, dropping down an octave to prevent further vocal strain. A better live version can be found on *Live At The Brixton Academy*, by which time Brian had become accustomed to lengthy nightly performances.

BAD ATTITUDE *(The Cross)*
• Album (The Cross): *Blue* • Live (The Cross): *Germany*

The opening song on *Blue Rock* is a full-blown rocker allowing Roger to do his best Robert Plant impression as he squeals through a story of a misunderstood rebel, apathetic to society and downright confrontational toward authority. While the performance is muscular, with the guitars mixed roughly and Roger clearly relishing the occasion, the lyrics are downright laughable ("Only way to stay cool / Gotta break some rules / Systems made for fools" is just one particularly engaging triplet) and, with songwriting credit being split five ways among The Cross, it's hard to point specific blame at anyone. Nevertheless, it served as an appropriate set opener on the brief 1991 Blue Rock tour, and was even tried out onstage before it was recorded, with a ramshackle performance released on the 1991 bootleg *The Official Bootleg*, including an intriguing bit of information from Roger: "OK, here's a brand new song that we haven't finished writing yet, so the words are— aren't quite right. It's called 'Tear It Up' or 'Bad Attitude', we're not quite sure."

BAD COMPANY *(Rodgers/Kirke)*
• Live (Q+PR): *Ukraine*

Recorded by the band of the same name and released on their 1974 eponymous debut album, 'Bad

Company' is a timeless rock ballad and a staple of US radio. Therefore, it was expected that the song was to be included in the set lists of the 2005 and 2006 Queen + Paul Rodgers shows in North America, though the song actually debuted in Aruba and was also performed on the first date of the Japanese leg. For the 2006 shows, Paul played piano, with the instrument rising out of a pit in front of the stage, though on one occasion Brian evidently lost sight of where and when the piano was emerging and took a nasty tumble, falling into the pit. After the general confusion and a few minor bruises, the humbled guitarist was more cautious of his footing, with no further mishaps – especially the next night, thanks to the assistance of a flashlight-equipped tech.

BAMA LAMA BAMA LOO *(Richard)*

Little Richard's 1964 song was covered extensively by Queen in their live set, appearing in the Rock 'n' Roll Medley between 1970 and 1973.

BARCELONA *(Mercury/Moran)*
• A-side (Freddie): 10/87 [8] • Album (Freddie): *Barcelona* • A-side (Freddie): 7/92 [2] • Compilation (Freddie): *Solo Collection*

For one of the first times in his illustrious career, Freddie found himself writing to task. After meeting with Montserrat Caballé (see the separate entry in Part Two for *Barcelona*) and deciding to turn their collaborative efforts into a full album, Freddie was simultaneously elated and horrified by the fact that he would have to write 40 minutes of material. 'Exercises In Free Love' had already been written and recorded without Montserrat, and was therefore not in the running for inclusion, but the diva asked Freddie to write a paean to her hometown, Barcelona. The result was so inspired and majestic that it became the title track of their album.

Starting off with a Freddie-led chorus chanting the title over a subtly orchestrated backing, the song explodes with a clattering of piano, timpani and orchestration, and is certainly one of the most dramatic openings to any Queen-related album. After 90 seconds of the overture, the song slows down to a gorgeous piano-dominated segment, featuring Freddie and Montserrat duetting in English and Spanish, respectively. Unexpectedly, the song reprises the intro cries of the title, soaring to a completely new level with one of Freddie's most emotive vocal performances

guiding the way. Montserrat provides only occasional, though stunning, vocalizations; it wouldn't be until later in the album that their voices would truly mesh. For now, though, this is Freddie's show.

Atypically, outside musicians were used on the track, though most of the backing was painstakingly created on keyboards by Mike Moran and Freddie. Homi Kanga and Laurie Lewis contributed violins, with Deborah Ann Johnston on cello, Barry Castle on horn, and Frank Ricoffi on percussion. The instrumentation is cleverly arranged, and is a testament to Mike's talents (the instrumental version on *The Solo Collection* is a stunning revelation): the song twists and turns with astonishing ease, going from delicate keyboard passages to thunderous explosions of percussion and brass, and is a veritable rollercoaster of musicality that only hints at the diversity of the resulting album.

The song was aptly chosen as the debut single from the album, and anybody expecting Freddie's latest work to be an extension of the *Mr Bad Guy* singles, or even 'The Great Pretender' which predated the release of 'Barcelona' by eight months, was in for a surprise. Released in October 1987, the single, backed with 'Exercises In Free Love' (making its second appearance as the B-side of a single that year), reached No. 8 in the UK charts, making 1987 a year of triumph for Freddie: not only did he score his highest-charting single with 'The Great Pretender' in March, but the general public had responded well to his latest efforts.

An extended version, bringing the running time to seven minutes, was issued on the 12" version of the single, while the single version omitted the first 60 seconds of the track, starting with an introduction of chimes and piano. This version was later issued on Queen's *Greatest Hits III* in 1999, and the following year on *The Solo Collection*, which would also include three out-takes (not including 'Ideas' from the Garden Lodge tape) that were previously unheard, yet just as stunning. The first version, recorded on 28 April 1987 and dubbed 'Freddie's Demo Vocal', contained all of Freddie's own vocal parts, though the lyrics hadn't yet been finalized, as well as the falsetto vocalizations for Montserrat to follow. The second version, recorded later that same day, was a more polished rough mix and dubbed 'Freddie's Vocal Slave', with the vocalist's falsetto omitted and focusing only on his own parts. The most stunning out-take was recorded five days later on 3 May 1987 and is an isolated track of Freddie's vocals, revealing the awesome power and control he had over his voice.

Appropriately, the single was reissued in July

1992, in anticipation of the summer Olympics held in Barcelona, and peaked at No. 2 in the UK and becoming Freddie's highest-charting single to date, beaten only by 'Living On My Own' 12 months later. The song was submitted to the Olympics committee, and Freddie and Montserrat were slated to perform it as a duet at the opening ceremonies, but Freddie died eight months prior to the games; instead, the album version was performed over a video montage of the city.

He *was* able to perform the song twice with Montserrat, though both were mimed performances: the first was on 29 May 1987, shortly after the song had been completed, at the Ku Club in Ibiza, Spain, as the finale to the worldwide Ibiza 92 festival. The overwhelmingly positive reception to the song was the cue to continue work on the album. The second performance, and Freddie's last true performance in front of a live audience, was on 8 October 1988 and involved the duo miming to the track (as well as 'The Golden Boy' and 'How Can I Go On') at the La Nit event on the steps of Montjuic Castle in Barcelona. The pair were in the presence of the King and Queen of Spain and the event was commissioned to mark the arrival of the Olympic flag from Korea. The three-song set was filmed by Gavin Taylor (who had previously worked on Queen's 1986 Wembley show), employing no fewer than 18 cameras for the occasion, and was broadcast live worldwide. Unfortunately, the backing tracks for the songs were played at a slightly slower pace, causing Freddie to explode backstage, though hardly anybody could tell the tempo was off. This performance, along with the other two songs, were later released on the 2000 video compilation, *The Freddie Mercury Video Collection*.

'Barcelona' would also receive a video treatment, becoming the only officially commissioned video to emerge from the album, though the aforementioned mimed performances of 'The Golden Boy' and 'How Can I Go On' would later be used as promotional material for those songs. Filmed on 8 October 1987 at Pinewood Studios, Freddie and Montserrat performed the song in front of an audience of 300 fans. Freddie is dressed in a smart, dark blue suit while Montserrat is gowned in fine, flowing silk robes, and watching the two interact is profoundly moving.

BATTERIES NOT INCLUDED

Written and recorded during *News Of The World* sessions in 1977, little is known about this song,

except that it was written either by John or Brian. One collector has stated it could be the working title of another song from the sessions, but chances are it's a song in its own right.

BATTLE SCENE *(May)*

This stunning instrumental was the only incidental piece from the *Highlander* soundtrack to have been performed by Queen; all other pieces ('Under The Garden', 'Swordfight At 34th', 'The Quickening', 'Rachel's Surprise', and 'Highlander Theme') were composed by Michael Kamen. Written, according to the BMI website, by Brian, 'Battle Scene' is set to a droning synthesizer and otherworldly backing vocals, while the Red Special features significantly, thus justifying Brian's songwriting credit.

BATTLE THEME *(May)*
• Album: *Flash*

This powerful rocker, essentially an instrumental version of 'The Hero', chugs along nicely with the rest of *Flash Gordon* and provides an unexpected highlight on the second side of the soundtrack, which was bogged down with reprises of the main theme. Brian later recalled that the song was pieced together from out-takes of Roger's drums from 'The Hero' before he layered the remainder of the instrumentation. With typical guitar orchestrations and a triumphant synthesizer motif, the song enjoyed exposure in the 1980 European tour (and once in 1981 in Japan), but was dropped permanently after that.

BANANA BLUES

In a June 2002 issue of *Record Collector*, Greg Brooks listed this as the working title of one of Queen's songs, along with others: 'Under Dispute', 'Don't Say No' (see separate entry), 'Woolly Hat' (working title of 'Cool Cat') and 'You're Young And You're Crazy' (working title 'Tenement Funster'). As for 'Banana Blues'? In 2011, at the Stormtroopers In Stilettoes exhibition in celebration of Queen's 40th anniversary, tape boxes from sessions for Queen's first five albums were on display, and 'Banana Blues' is actually the appropriate working title of John's first-ever composition, 'Misfire'.

BE BOP A LULA *(Vincent/Davis)*

• Live: *Rainbow, Odeon*

Gene Vincent's 1956 hit single was presented as part of the Rock 'n' Roll Medley between 1973 and 1977, and was performed only rarely until the following year.

BE MY GAL (MY BRIGHTEST SPARK) *(Taylor)*

• Album (Roger): *Earth*

After the dissolution of Roger's relationship with Debbie Leng in late 2002, he met and fell in love with Sarina Potgieter; the two started dating in 2005, and five years later married at their Surrey home. It's no coincidence that as soon as Roger started a relationship with Sarina, his songwriting muse returned to him: the first fruits of his labors was 'Woman You're So Beautiful (But Still A Pain In The Ass)', a tongue-in-cheek nod to Sarina, while he would write some far more significant and meaningful songs inspired by her. 'Be My Gal (My Brightest Spark)' is a sprightly acoustic ballad, taken at a mid-pace tempo with an earnest Roger pouring his heart out to Sarina. Whereas 'I Don't Care' was a tongue-in-cheek admission of love, 'Be My Gal' is entirely sentimental, but not overbearingly so: the simple arrangement, with subtle keyboard and bass accompaniment, complement message, while a lovely guitar solo rounds things out. (And for anyone playing at home, the piano notes at the beginning of the song were lifted directly from 'Surf's Up . . . School's Out !')

BE WITH YOU *(Taylor/Taylor)*

• Album (Roger): *Earth*

Bleeding over from the downbeat 'Fight Club', 'Be With You' is a more upbeat acoustic rocker, simplistic in its message – Roger's in love, and he wants the world to know it – but effective in delivery. With a powerful rhythm section and some lovely guitar work from both Roger and the longstanding Jason Falloon, the song also features Roger's son Rufus on piano, with whom the song was cowritten.

BEAUTIFUL DREAMS *(Taylor)*

• Album (Roger): *Frontier*

Roger wasn't known for writing many ballads, preferring to write throwaway rockers about fast cars and pretty women. As his songwriting evolved, he penned a few slower songs, notably 'Laugh Or Cry' and

'Fun In Space' – though, in typical Roger fashion, these weren't typical ballads. Combining that latter song's sparse backing with a few layers of lush synthesizers, Roger created 'Beautiful Dreams' for his second solo album, *Strange Frontier*. Speaking with Jim Ladd in 1984, who commented that "what I got out of this was almost a song about going back to the children aspect," Roger agreed, saying that "it starts off as an innocent dream like you have as children. Just nice, innocent, uncoloured dreams. And then the second verse goes on to growing up a bit and, of course ... personal experience, going through some drug things and finding ... chemical dreams, you know, and then the third verse is back to the nuclear nightmare dreams. I used to have a lot of these. If I used to have a bad dream, it was usually about being involved in a holocaust and trying to grab everybody I cared about."

Ladd found the reference to chemical dreams particularly interesting, and brought it up later in the interview, to which Roger responded, "It's just to have a good time now, and it's a very different idea. I think it's a good point, actually. I don't know why, but I think something like the dream, like John Lennon said, 'The dream is over.' I mean he was referring to something else with The Beatles, but the dream is over. Everybody was sort of optimistic at that point and I think there was a sort of mass realisation that, 'Oh, we're never gonna change the world.' It's just not going to change like that, and it didn't and all the bad things came out of that, like Altamont [The Rolling Stones' infamous free concert in 1969 with security provided by the San Francisco Hell's Angels, which resulted in a bloodbath] and all that. Those things like Manson, I suppose. So people realized and rejected that optimistic philosophy. I dunno, that's what I think anyway."

Set to a gloomy synthesizer backing with a pulsating drum-machine keeping a steady rhythm, the song creates a nightmarish atmosphere of a nuclear holocaust, which, by the middle of the 1980s, was less a political threat and more a promise. The bridge strikes a particularly emotional nerve, basking in innocent optimism: "We'd like to find a cure for every known disease / There's no such thing you say / The answer is there to see." An undisputed highlight of *Strange Frontier*, 'Beautiful Dreams' nevertheless remained obscure among the other obvious chart-friendly material from that album, though it was issued as a Portugal-only single in 1984 with 'Young Love' on the B-side.

THE SONGS

BEING ON MY OWN (May)
• Bonus (Brian): *World*

The running time for 'Another World', an expansive 7'30, is misleading. The song actually ends at 4'08, but after almost a minute of silence Brian re-enters with an interesting piano and keyboard duet, much like 'Forever' from 1986. Striking a melancholy, minor key, the instrumental is based on the chords from 'Business' and was unofficially titled 'Being On My Own', extracted from that song's concluding line ("It's a hard business / Being on my own") and ending with a scrap of mumbled dialog from Brian: "That's about all I can do."

BELIEVE IN YOURSELF (Taylor)
• Album (Roger): *Electric*

In this, one of the first ballads on *Electric Fire*, never before has Roger sounded more like David Bowie than on 'Believe In Yourself. The song marks Roger's first appearance on drums on the album, but is more notable for its inspirational lyrics, imploring the downtrodden to remain positive despite adversity. 'Believe In Yourself' may not be a masterpiece, but it's an integral part of the album and showed maturity in Roger's songwriting abilities.

In the liner notes for *Electric Fire*, the lyrics are abridged, with the final few repeats of "I mean you" omitted, though each phrase is followed with a barely audible list of people and things to believe in (the liners instead say, "Here follows a rather odd list"). In case you were wondering, the list reads: bus conductors, people on trams, Welshmen and sheep, clamps, lepidopterists, collectors of stamps, leopards with spots on, tramps, space-wasting journalists, people in far-flung posts, unpleasant neighbours, ghosts, Duane Eddy, lawyers with fees, Elvis, deciduous trees, bosses, pets, nurses, vets, people with peepholes, you, Elsie, Stan, mother, and Desperate Dan.

BETTER THINGS (Moss)
• Album (The Cross): *MBADTK*

Written and sung by Clayton Moss, 'Better Things' is the first instance when Roger doesn't appear on lead vocals on a song by The Cross, though he does harmonize beautifully with Clayton at certain points during the song. 'Better Things' is a delicate, acoustic-driven song, slowing things down between 'Sister Blue' ('Foxy Lady'

on the CD version) and 'Passion For Trash' on *Mad: Bad: And Dangerous To Know*. The instrumentation is sparse, with a rattling of maracas and handclaps driving the rhythm along in the bridge, while a mandolin, plucked by Spike Edney, complements the melody. Despite some other questionable material on the album, 'Better Things' remains a lovely diversion.

BICYCLE RACE (Mercury)
• AA-side: 10/78 [11] • Album: *Jazz* • Live: *Killers* • Bonus: *Jazz* • CD Single: 6/96 [9]

Leave it to Freddie to get a paean to bicycles into the British Top 20. While 'Bicycle Race' may, superficially, be a throwaway and meaningless pop song, initial impressions can be deceiving: a closer listen reveals an intricately complex backing track, switching time signatures as effortlessly as 'Bohemian Rhapsody' or 'The Millionaire Waltz'. It just so happened that because the subject matter was something as trivial as riding a bicycle to escape life's problems that the song was written off as insubstantial. As with most of Queen's bigger hits, especially those that created controversy, a legend grew over the genesis of the song, that Freddie wrote it while watching the Tour de France pass by his hotel in the summer of 1978. However, the band were in Montreux that July, with sessions moving to the south of France in September, a far cry from the route the Tour would have taken anyway.

"Freddie wrote in strange keys," Brian said in 2000. "Most guitar bands play in A or E, and probably D and G, but beyond that there's not much. Most of our stuff, particularly Freddie's songs, was in oddball keys that his fingers naturally seemed to go to: E-flat, F, A-flat. They're the last things you want to be playing on a guitar, so as a guitarist you're forced to find new chords. Freddie's songs were so rich in chord-structures, you always found yourself making strange shapes with your fingers. Songs like 'Bicycle Race' have a billion chords in them."

Released as a double A-side with 'Fat Bottomed Girls', 'Bicycle Race' became a mainstay of the medley between 1978 and 1979, but was dropped for the Saarbrücken Festival in August 1979 and was never performed again. A video was shot in Dallas on 28 October 1978, the same day as the 'Fat Bottomed Girls' video, but remained unreleased in favor of a dodgy cut-and-paste video instead, interpolating still footage of the band throughout the years with obscured footage of the infamous naked bicycle race

155

at Wimbledon Stadium on 17 September 1978. For years, this censored video remained the official version, appearing on *Greatest Flix* in 1981, but the original, uncensored version was finally released in 2002 on *Greatest Video Hits 1*. An insipid remix was included on the 1991 *Jazz* reissue, extending the track to five minutes with an annoying dance-trance backing.

BIG SPENDER *(Coleman/Fields)*
• Live: *Wembley, Rainbow, Odeon*

A favorite of Freddie's was this steamy 1967 Shirley Bassey hit, and it was performed (usually before 'Jailhouse Rock') between 1973 and 1977, live versions of which were released on *Live At The Rainbow '74* and *A Night At The Odeon*. In addition to a brief recital on the final show of the Jazz European tour in 1979, it was also revived for a handful of Magic tour shows, an example of which was released on the *Live At Wembley Stadium* album.

BIJOU *(Queen)*
• B-side: 1/91 [1] • Album: *Innuendo* • Live (Q+PR): *Ukraine*

A lovely guitar and keyboards duet between Brian and Freddie, 'Bijou' is a moving love song, its brief lyrics summing up in four lines what other love songs from Queen failed to convey in four verses. Constructed around a soaring and mournful guitar showcase from Brian, the song is a gorgeous introduction to the mournful album closer, 'The Show Must Go On'. Brian later cited Jeff Beck's 1989 song 'Where Were You' as an influence for 'Bijou', and was designed as an 'inside out' song: The Red Special 'sings' the verses, while Freddie provides a short vocal where the guitar solo would be. Edited for vinyl release from 3'36 to 1'16, the full-length version also appeared as the UK B-side of 'Innuendo' in January 1991 and then the US B-side of 'These Are The Days Of Our Lives' later that September. Most notably, the song received its debut live airing in 2008 on the Queen + Paul Rodgers Rock the Cosmos tour, coming right after Brian's nightly guitar solo. To add further poignancy to this already heavy moment, images of Freddie and John flashed by on the screens behind the stage, prompting cheers from the audience.

BLAG *(Taylor)*
• Compilation (Smile): *Ghost Of A Smile*

Recalling Cream's 'N.S.U.' or Led Zeppelin's mighty 'Moby Dick', 'Blag' is a powerful semi-instrumental, written by Roger with the drums high in the mix. ("[That] was an instrumental written by Roger," Tim Staffell remembered. "It was a riff he'd had lying around for ages. That went down bloody well at gigs. It was a vehicle for us to blow. There were some three-part vocal harmonies on it, which supporter the rhythmic figure. It was a bit of a blaster.") The song twists through a series of instrumental changes before slowing down to allow Tim to sing the minimal lyric, which lasts only two verses; apart from the introductory "doo doo doo" vocals, the remainder of the song is made up of a guitar solo that would later be incorporated into 'Brighton Rock'.

Like the rest of the Smile material, the song was recorded in August 1969 at De Lane Lea Studios, produced by Fritz Freyer, and eventually released on the bootleg *Gettin' Smile* in 1982 and officially on *Ghost Of A Smile* in 1998.

BLAG-A-BLUES *(Bulsara)*

Written by a pre-Mercury Freddie, 'Blag-A-Blues' was performed by Wreckage on two known occasions at Ealing College Of Art on 26 and 31 October 1969.

BLUES BREAKER *(May/Van Halen/Gratzer/Chen/Mandel)*
• Album (Brian): *Starfleet* • CD single (Brian): 11/92 [19]

An epic improvised jam, 'Blues Breaker' is the perfect opportunity for Brian to match guitar wits with axe slinger Eddie Van Halen. The song sees the two of them trading licks like young boys trade baseball cards: the glee is apparent as both guitarists attempt to respectfully one-up each other. Kicking off with a rich piano riff from Fred Mandel, the duelling starts immediately while Phil Chen and Alan Gratzer provide a steady, burbling rhythm, embellishing only when the occasion demands (or when passion strikes). The song comes to a premature conclusion after 10 minutes, just before Fred Mandel leads the band in a piano-dominated coda while Brian's and Eddie's fingers take a break, and finally finishing up with a stray bit of indecipherable dialog and a whoop from someone. Overall, a swaggering and staggering conclusion to Brian's first solo effort.

In the liner notes for *Star Fleet Project*, Brian states that "...in 'Blues Breaker', which of course is purely spontaneous, you can hear a much more relaxed set of people, just laying back and enjoying the fresh inspiration of each other's playing," and going on to say that "you can hear us smiling as we search for answering phrases." Appropriately, the song was dedicated to legendary blues guitarist Eric Clapton. In a contemporary interview, Brian said, "Edward and I took a break from recording and started talking about how it was in the old days when Eric Clapton was doing his thing with John Mayall [and the Bluesbreakers]. We all found 'The Beano' album had been a big influence on us – remember, the one with Eric reading the comic on the cover? It was a classic collector's item for every guitarist. It sounded like they were having so much fun they couldn't stop ... 'Blues Breaker', which takes up all of side two on the album, is my favourite part of the record. It seemed very indulgent putting out a long jam, but, having listened to it, I think it's worthwhile ... it's rock blues with all the mistakes left in."

The "Beano" album to which Brian referred was *Bluesbreakers with Eric Clapton*, released in July 1966 and often considered Clapton's first fully developed album as a blues guitarist. Having just left The Yardbirds and only months away from forming Cream with Jack Bruce and Ginger Baker, the guitarist's stint with The Blues Breakers was short but sweet, and definitely influential. After *Star Fleet Project* was released, a copy of the mini-album was sent off to Clapton, who was reportedly less than impressed with the excessive noodling.

'Blues Breaker' remained a vinyl-only curiosity for nearly a decade, before it was issued on the second of two CD singles of 'Back To The Light' in November 1992 (the first CD single featured the other two *Star Fleet Project* songs), marking that song's first – and long overdue – appearance on CD.

BLURRED VISION (Queen)

• B-side: 11/85 [7] • Compilation: *Vision* • CD Single: 11/88

Essentially the programmed drum section from 'One Vision', this throwaway B-side contains little of substance and offers even less in the way of interest.

BODY LANGUAGE (Mercury)

• A-side: 4/82 [25] • Album: *Space* • CD Single: 11/88
• CD Single: 10/91 [16] • Bonus: *Space*

Written and performed exclusively by Freddie, save for a few guitar licks in the outro from Brian, 'Body Language' has divided fan opinion from the day of its release: how could the man who wrote 'Bohemian Rhapsody' come up with *this*? Containing little more in the way of lyrics than Freddie groaning "Give me your body", the song is set to a slinky, synth bass-driven and drum programming backing that was miles away from anything Queen had released before or since. Brian, for once, wasn't impressed, opining in 1982 that "there are some things on [*Hot Space*] which I felt came out too light, that's all. Like 'Body Language'. There's a lot of things where I felt that we became so obsessed with the rhythm side that we were afraid to turn up the guitars. Afraid to use the guitar as a force." Sixteen years later, he wasn't as diplomatic: "I can remember having a go at Freddie because some of the stuff he was writing was very definitely on the gay side. I remember saying, 'It would be nice if this stuff could be universally applicable, because we have friends out there of every persuasion'. It's nice to involve people. What it's not nice to do is rope people out. And I felt kind of roped out by something that was very overtly a gay anthem, like 'Body Language'. I thought it was very hard to take that in the other way." In 2003, Brian had softened his stance, saying, "This is very much a Freddie thing. He was immersed in the gay world. I think it's very well constructed, it's deliberately away from the Queen concept," while Roger also faintly praised it: "Not really us but not a bad record."

Bravely chosen as the first single from *Hot Space*, the song crept to No. 25 in the UK and No. 11 in the US and became a favorite in bars and dance clubs around the country. The promotional video, filmed in Toronto in April 1982 and directed by Brian Grant, features Freddie cavorting around a soundstage with half-naked men and women following him around before he meets up with the other band members for the finger-clicking interlude. The other three look out of place and uncomfortable, and Brian later unsympathetically attributed the video as a Freddie *tour de force*. In an attempt at being somewhat artistic – or perhaps Grant was just trying to instill a bit of humor into an otherwise unwatchable video – there is one humorous moment when, after Freddie dances with three large black ladies shaking maracas, the third and largest lady goes flying into a gigantic strawberry cake right before his eyes.

'Body Language' was performed in full on a few rare instances in the 1982 Hot Space European tour, but was only a semi-regular addition to the US set lists before it was dropped in time for the 1984 Works! tour. The track was chosen to receive a remix in 1991, with k.d. lang producer Susan Rogers selected for the task; the result was little better than the original, though the addition of piano was a welcome one. The *Hot Space* remaster would have been better off with the non-album 'Soul Brother' and the extended remixes of 'Staying Power' and 'Back Chat'.

BOHEMIAN RHAPSODY *(Mercury)*

• A-side: 10/75 [1] • Album: *Opera* • CD Single: 11/88
• AA-side: 12/91 [1] • B-side: 12/99 [6] • Live: *Killers, Magic, Wembley, 46664, On Fire, Montreal, Budapest, Odeon* • Live (Q+PR): *Return, Ukraine* • Bonus: *Opera*

So much has been said about 'Bohemian Rhapsody' over the course of three decades that it's impossible to unearth information that is new and shocking to the reader. And yet fans want, quite naturally, to know all they can about the song that has been called the Song of the Millennium. Many legends surround 'Bohemian Rhapsody', most of them true. However, the facts seem to get lost in the legend: Freddie, having written the bulk of his material for the *Sheer Heart Attack* album, started writing an operatic piece in the summer of 1975, originally titled 'Real Life'. "'Bohemian Rhapsody' didn't just come out of thin air," Freddie explained. "I did a bit of research, although it was tongue-in-cheek and it was a mock opera. Why not? I certainly wasn't saying I was an opera fanatic and I knew everything thing about it." He continued: "We wanted to experiment with sound. Sometimes we used three studios simultaneously. 'Bohemian Rhapsody' took bloody ages to record but we had all the freedom we wanted and we've been able to go to greater extremes."

Gary Lagan, assistant engineer for the album, said of the recording process, "The drums, the bass and maybe the guide guitar and piano from Freddie have got to be ten or 12 tracks and it only leaves you another 12 to fool around with, which isn't very much when you look at the amount of vocals that are going on. You had to keep bouncing things down, without losing the quality of everything, and we couldn't even go back a stage. Once you'd gone down a route then nine times out of ten it would destroy what you'd already done,

so you had to make sure that what you were doing was 100 per cent right, because there was no undo button in those days."

A legendary story made the rounds after the song had been released, which most attributed to sheer folklore, but Brian maintains its truth: "We were stretching the limits of technology in those days. Because 'Bohemian Rhapsody' was entirely done on 16-track, we had to do a lot of bouncing as we went along; the tape got very thin. This 'legendary' story, that people think we made up, is true: we held the tape up to the light one day – we'd been wondering where all the top end was going – and what we discovered was virtually a transparent piece of tape. All the oxide had been rubbed off. It was time to hurriedly make a copy and get on with it."

"I'm really pleased about the operatic thing," Freddie gushed in 1975. "I really wanted to be outrageous with vocals because we're always getting compared with other people, which is very stupid. If you really listen to the operatic bit there are no comparisons, which is what we want." Brian agreed, saying, "'Bohemian Rhapsody' was really Freddie's baby from the beginning: he came in and knew exactly what he wanted. The backing track was done with just piano, bass and drums, with a few spaces for other things to go in, like the tic-tic-tic on the hi-hat to keep the time, and Freddie sang a guide vocal at the time, but he had all his harmonies written out, and it was really just a question of doing it."

Many alternate meanings and claims about the song's lyrics have been put forth over the years, though its true story has died along with its author. (Roger once offhandedly mentioned that Freddie told him what it was about, but whether he was being deliberately coy or truthful is unknown. To many fans' frustration, he never even explained its meaning as told to him.) Freddie was always guarded when asked about his lyrics, preferring to let the listeners draw their own conclusions, but every possible interpretation has been posited over the years. Instead of offering his own opinions, this author will merely say that some ideas are more believable than others: whether the listener believes it's about Freddie coming to terms with his sexuality or something far more sinister is all down to what each fan concludes from the lyrics.

Roy Thomas Baker, producer of the sessions (and of Queen's first four albums), has claimed that Freddie used to come into the sessions with more and more ideas, expanding the operatic section until it became what it now is. However, Brian has maintained (as evident in the above quote) that Freddie knew where everything would go and that everything was constructed in his head before the song was recorded, and that the result is what Freddie had been hearing for months. "Freddie used to come into the studio armed with sheets and sheets of paper with notes scribbled all over them in his own particular fashion," Brian said. "It wasn't standard musical notation, but As and Bs and Cs and sharps in blocks – like buses zooming all over his bits of paper. He had the song all worked out when he came in. We played a backing track which left the gaps. And he would go, 'Bum bum bum bum, that's what happens here...'"

What was eventually released in October 1975 was a curious blend of rock, opera and balladry that was unlike anything ever attempted by a rock band before. The band were undoubtedly ambitious in their design and approach, but would it pay off in the end? "A lot of people slammed 'Bohemian Rhapsody'," Freddie grumbled, "but who can you compare that to? Name one group that's done an operatic single. We were adamant that 'Bohemian Rhapsody' could be a hit in its entirety. We have been forced to make compromises, but cutting up a song will never be one of them!"

While critical reviews were less than ecstatic, saying that Queen were just being pretentious, demand for the single was staggering, and it all started one weekend in late October, when Freddie and Roger visited their friend Kenny Everett, a DJ for the BBC, with a copy of the single in hand. "I got a call in 1975 – I was living in a beautiful honey-coloured Cotswold stone pub – from Freddie Mercury," Everett recalled many years later, "who said, 'Ken, I don't know what I've done. I was in the studio the other day and I finished off this single and it's about eight minutes long, and I don't know whether it's going to be a hit'. And I said, 'Oh, bring it over. We'll stick it on one of my tape machines in the studio and give it a listen. I doubt anyone'll ever play it, that length, because people are frightened of long records. They might think the DJ's gone to the loo and forgotten to come back!' So he brought it over and plonked it on the machine and of course this *glorious* operatic wonder came out, and I said, 'Oh, forget about this. It could be half an hour, it's still gonna be number one for centuries'. So I remember him being so unsure about this piece of genius. It was very odd, when you look at it in retrospect, because it was so great. I mean, it's like Mozart saying, 'Ohhh, I don't know whether my clarinet concerto's going to take off'.

Silly, really. I mean, it's got Number One written all over it from the first note."

Although sworn to not play the single on the radio, Kenny became so enamored with the song that he immediately played it the next day, gushing praise and cheekily remarking that he had promised not to play it. While the band may have been horrified that an as-yet-unreleased single reaching nearly six minutes was being transmitted across Britain, they were undoubtedly not prepared for the response it received. Listeners echoed Kenny's fascination for the song, and called the BBC asking where they could get a copy of the single. EMI rush-released the single on 31 October 1975, and the song instantly secured the top spot in the British charts.

Any trepidation about the single's success, as well as notions that it should be edited for release, were soon scrapped. The single sold millions of copies worldwide, and became Queen's first Top Ten hit in the US. Live, however, the song was a different beast altogether. "[It's] not a stage number," Brian explained. "A lot of people don't like us leaving the stage. But to be honest, I'd rather leave than have us playing to a backing tape. If you're out there and you've got backing tapes, it's a totally false situation. So we'd rather be up front about it and say, 'Look. This is not something you can play on stage. It was multi-layered in the studio. We'll play it because we think you want to hear it.'"

The solution to the problem was simple: the band had Kenny Everett construct a short intro piece on 13 November 1975 (the day before Queen's major British tour) that comprised a generic introduction before commencing with a snippet from 'Ogre Battle', and then merging into the operatic section, at the conclusion of which the band would bound onto the stage and perform the rock bit, which would then segue effortlessly into the next track. The band would then open the medley with the introductory ballad section (the multi-tracked intro chorus was never performed in any live setting), which would lead into the next number before the operatic bit; the medley would then conclude with the quieter "nothing really matters" section, and finally end with Roger bashing the gigantic gong behind his kit. The song was split up this way, with the introductory tape opening shows, for the 1975 and 1976 A Night At The Opera tours, as well as the Summer 1976 British dates.

For the Queen Lizzy tour in early 1977, the band rehearsed a full version of the song; knowing they would encounter difficulties with the operatic bit, the band instead had the album version blare from the PA system, allowing the stage lights and effects to do their work as the band took a short break, before re-entering the stage with the hard rock bit. The song was performed this way between 1977 and 1986, and while performances hardly deviated from one another from show to show, the song would always be received with unbridled enthusiasm from the audience and, regardless of their mother tongue, they would sing every word along with Freddie.

Intriguingly, Freddie was approached by the London Dance Centre in early October 1979, asking him if he would like to take part in a charity gala ballet performance to benefit the City of Westminster Society for Mentally Handicapped Children. The vocalist obliged, and rehearsed routines for 'Bohemian Rhapsody' and 'Crazy Little Thing Called Love', finally performing at the London Coliseum on 7 October 1979, wowing the audience (and Roger, who came along for moral support) and confirming Sid Vicious' snide comment that Freddie was "bringing ballet to the masses."

What has gone down in rock history about the song isn't so much its fusion of rock and opera, but the innovative tactic of making promotional videos more acceptable. Up until 1975, major rock acts had no way to promote singles unless they appeared on *Top Of The Pops* or any similar music television programme (the US had *American Bandstand*, as this was six years before MTV). While some films had been shot in the past, notably 'Happy Jack' by The Who in 1966 and 'Jumpin' Jack Flash' by The Rolling Stones in 1968, those were taped on film and commissioned primarily for *Top Of The Pops*. 'Bohemian Rhapsody', however, was taped on video and was used for a multitude of programmes; whereas, in the past, different TV shows would demand different performance clips, 'Bohemian Rhapsody' was a universal clip for all TV shows.

On 10 November 1975, Queen assembled at Elstree Studios with their director-of-choice Bruce Gowers and filmed a video for the single, bringing to life the *Queen II* album cover and immortalizing Mick Rock's iconic image. The video was completed in four hours, and cost a miniscule £4,000 – a princely sum in those days, but hardly anything now. Brian said of the video, "Everyone thought that the film was a huge production, but it was actually shot in only four hours. It was really easy to do, and since then we've spent a lot of time on films that probably weren't as good and certainly didn't get the exposure."

"People used to have clips before," John explained, "but they were often shot on film. It was quite accidental ... at the time, we were touring England, and we knew we wouldn't be able to get to record *Top Of The Pops* on the Wednesday. Our managers at the time had a mobile unit, so it was actually shot on video, in about four hours!" Roger explained it even further, saying, "Well, we didn't actually see it until it was actually on *Top Of The Pops*, because we were just doing it at the beginning of a tour. We were finishing rehearsals and we shot it on the last day in Elstree – and we just sort of got on a bus at the end at about 2 o'clock in the morning and drove to Liverpool, because we had a show there the next night – so we'd never seen the video until it was on *Top Of The Pops* the next week."

It would be impossible to list all the accolades and awards that 'Bohemian Rhapsody' has ever received; consistently voted Number One in music polls across the world, the song earned the high honor of being voted Song Of The Millennium in 1999, which certainly speaks volumes about the song's staying power and mass appeal. Perhaps the greatest honor, though, was when it was re-released in December 1991 with 'These Are The Days Of Our Lives' in the wake of Freddie's death, securing the Number One spot (again) in the UK and raising nearly £2 million for the Terrence Higgins AIDS Awareness organization.

Obviously, such a popular song would fall victim to parodies. The most famous one aired in 1987 – comedy act, The Young Ones, who formed a Spinal Tap-like group called Bad News, lampooned 'Bohemian Rhapsody' with an interesting blend of opera and metal. Queen fans were initially outraged, but were humbled to learn that not only did Brian produce the song, but that Freddie found it humorous as well (they really could have taken a lesson from the vocalist in terms of developing a sense of humor), thus receiving his stamp of approval. Special mention must also be made of Weird Al Yankovic's 'Bohemian Polka', in which he recreated the song to the accompaniment of an accordion.

However, the most humorous re-enactment was in the 1992 US movie *Wayne's World*, starring Mike Myers and Dana Carvey in a big screen version of the *Saturday Night Live* sketch. One of the sequences starts with Wayne (played by Myers), Garth (played by Carvey), and three friends sitting in a beat-up, blue AMC, driving down a major strip of their hometown and singing along to 'Bohemian Rhapsody'. When it came time for the rock section, the five started banging their heads and playing air guitar and drums. While it was common for such an occurrence to happen in metal acts, this was the first time that such a display had crossed over to rock (during a Queen song, no less).

A compilation video was structured, incorporating clips of Gowers' original 1975 video with segments of the movie, directed by Penelope Spheeris, and was included on the 1992 video compilation *Classic Queen*. The single was re-released in the US in February 1992, reaching an impressive No. 2 in May, due to both the movie and Freddie's death. Roger and Brian later said they loved the movie – as did Freddie, who watched a rough cut of it before his death – which calmed a nervous Myers, who had said in an interview that it was like "whizzing on a Picasso."

BOOGIE

Considering the obvious homage to Jeff Beck, it's likely that this song is actually 'Jeff's Boogie', originally recorded and released by The Yardbirds in 1967. If not, then authorship is unknown, but the song was performed by Wreckage on 31 October 1969 at Ealing College Of Art.

BORN FREE *(Barry/Black)*
• A-side: 11/12 • Live (Brian & Kerry): *Acoustic*
• Album (Brian & Kerry): *Golden*

Written by John Barry and Don Black, 'Born Free' featured in the film of the same name from 1966, and became a much-covered ballad over the years. Brian and Kerry take their turn at the song, turning in an astounding performance, dominated by piano and keyboards, with touches of The Red Special and cymbal swells leading into a full-on assault, offering some much-needed drama. The song was recorded as an anthem for Virginia McKenna's Born Free Foundation to save lions in South Africa: "It sounds impossible, but it seems there is a real possibility that in just a few years there will be no more lions in the World," he wrote. "There has been a growing awareness over the last few years, largely brought about by Born Free, that it is no longer cool to kill these wonderful creatures (of course it really never was – Ernest Hemingway has a lot to answer for, in my opinion) – it is OK to go on a shoot, but only if it is a camera shoot. But Lions and other wild African animals are STILL being poached, and still being killed by rich, brainless people. A lot

of these people come from Britain too. They are part of that old-style remnant of knuckleheadedness which needs to assert its power by killing defenceless animals and putting the heads of these wonderful creatures on their walls as trophies. I'm afraid it's same mentality as the fox-hunters, the deer-stalkers, the badger-baiters, etc ... who exhibit a depraved side of humanity that needs to be expunged. But at the moment many of these barbarians have the backing of our government – it's a grim time for animals indeed. So here we go ... in what may be a last-ditch attempt to turn things around in South Africa. There will be more details announced soon, but our contribution is an entirely new recording of the song 'Born Free', which I've arranged and produced for Kerry's magnificent vocal talents ... This is the beginning – a statement of intent – a photo-call in a London Hotel with Will Travers and executives of Born Free, and one of the Lion sculptures which will soon be gracing the streets of Cape Town. Hopefully so will we ! This project may take us on a long journey in many ways."

BORN ON THE BAYOU *(Fogerty)*

Creedence Clearwater Revival's 1969 hit was performed live by The Cross at the first fan club show in December 1992 at the Marquee, with Roger Daltrey providing lead vocals.

BORN TO ROCK 'N' ROLL

According to Dave Clark, he was so impressed with Freddie's two contributions to the *Time* musical soundtrack that he was going to give him a third; unfortunately, he had already promised 'Born To Rock 'N' Roll' to Cliff Richard, though he had Freddie record a demo anyway. That demo remains unreleased, as it was not available for *The Solo Collection*, but a live version from Freddie's 14 April 1988 performance at the Dominion Theatre eventually leaked onto the Internet, and what little can be heard of Freddie (over the occasional scream and cry of his name by fans) is impressive and enjoyable.

BREAKDOWN *(Noone)*
• Album (The Cross): *MBADTK*

Peter Noone's second of three songs submitted and recorded for *Mad: Bad: And Dangerous To Know* is a sombre, minor key power ballad, a description which makes the song sound worse than it actually is. 'Breakdown' isn't a highlight of the album, nor is it either the worst song, but it's standard, inconsequential fare, taking a swipe at the ubiquitous media and their sensationalist tactics. This tired subject matter, coupled with its generic arrangement, only confirms its status as filler material.

BREAKTHRU *(Queen)*
• Album: *Miracle* • A-side: 6/89 [7]

One of the standout tracks from *The Miracle*, 'Breakthru' starts off deceptively as a melancholy piano ballad, originally a separate song written by Freddie titled 'A New Life Is Born', before exploding into a ferocious rocker, propelled by a chugging bassline and heavy power chords. Written by Roger, the song received praise from Brian, who commented, "I very much like this track – it's a Roger track – full of energy. Of course the track is, speaking lyrically, about breaking through to the next part of your life. And on another level, it's just a nice bit of fun." Roger was a bit more critical, saying, "The song actually ended up more complicated than I wanted it. I think the others wanted to put a key change in – I really hate key changes usually, and that's not one of my favourite key changes – but I think this song should have been kept simpler and it was just slightly over-arranged in the end, but it kept everyone else happy."

Released as the second single from *The Miracle* in June 1989, 'Breakthru' was accompanied by an excellent video of the band performing the song atop a steam engine called The Miracle Express. "I suppose you imagine these things are done by trickery," Brian said in 2003, "but we actually were on top of this train, going about 40 or 50 mph, so you have to have incredible trust – if the driver had had to change speed even a tiny bit, we would have been off that thing and dead! So once we forgot that the train was moving and developed a sort of trust in the driver, we just behaved as normal." Roger agreed, saying, "It was quite fun, this, 'cause it was a steam train, but we kept getting smut in our eyes – I just remember it streaming into the eyes. It was a fun video, sort of gimmicky in a way, but just a nice idea: *The Miracle Express*. Sticky hot day, I remember." It's evident that the band are having a good time, especially Brian, who commented on the *Greatest Video Hits 2* DVD that his "personal life was starting to go to shit" and to be able to escape to the English countryside was a blessing. The entire affair was finished within two days, much to the relief of Freddie, who was appalled by the

local hotel's lack of air conditioning.

An extended remix of the track was created and is superior to the standard version since it includes several new segments: the song kicks off with an echoed Freddie chanting the title (the whole 'A New Life Is Born' intro is omitted altogether) before leading into an energetic, though brief, instrumental section, featuring some great power-chord work by Brian and with the bass mixed more prominently. This version, coming close to six minutes, was included on the 12" and CD versions of the single, and was released on *The 12" Collection* in 1992, but was kept off the reissue of *The Miracle*.

BRIGHT LIGHTS, BIG CITY *(Reed)*

This Jimmy Reed tune was played live by 1984.

BRIGHTON ROCK *(May)*
• Album: *SHA* • Live: *Killers*, *Wembley*, *On Fire*, *Montreal*, *Budapest*, *Rainbow*, *Odeon* • CD Single: 11/88 • Live (Brian): *Brixton* • Live (Q+PR): *Return*, *Ukraine*

Though the origin of 'Brighton Rock' dates all the way back to the Smile track 'Blag' from 1969, that was only the multi-tracked guitar solo which constitutes a majority of the song. With a set of lyrics that highlights a love-torn couple engaging in a holiday affair, the real star of the show here isn't Freddie or his singing (especially when he takes the role of the female, which makes for a jarring listen) but the excellent performance of the instrumentalists. Roger and John hold together a tremendous rhythm section, with the bass allowing plenty of improvisation and even mirroring sections of Brian's guitar extravaganza.

The spotlight is all on Brian, though, who turns in an engaging performance, showing just how versatile his homemade guitar is over any traditional build: employing custom pickups and delay, he is allowed complete freedom to move about his solo. For guitar enthusiasts, it is a real treat; for regular fans, it's a special bonus since it shows how unique a guitarist Brian is. "I'd gotten away from listening to Hendrix quite a bit by that time," Brian explained in a 1983 BBC Radio One interview, "and I'd like to think that that was more sort of developing my style really. Particularly the solo bit in the middle, which I'd been doing on the Mott The Hoople tour and sort of gradually expanded and has got more and more ever since. Although I keep trying to throw it out, it keeps creeping back in. That involves the repeat device actually using it in time, which I don't think, had been done before up to that time. It's a very nice device to work with because you can build up harmonies or cross rhythms and it's not a multiple repeat like Hendrix used or even The Shadows used, which is fairly indiscriminate, sort of makes a nice noise. But this is a single repeat, which comes back, and sometimes I'll add a second one too. So you can actually plan or else experiment and do a sort of 'phew' type effect. So that was at its very beginnings on 'Brighton Rock', and [it] became more developed after that."

As mentioned above, the solo started life five years before its transformation into a real song; when Brian brought the song to Queen, it found its way into 'Son And Daughter', an excellent example that can be found on the *Queen At The Beeb* album, which extends the song well past seven minutes. Originally submitted (but rejected) for the *Queen II* sessions in August 1973, the song was developed in concert over the following year before it became an actual song recorded for the *Sheer Heart Attack* album, with several different working titles attributed to it, among them 'Happy Little Fuck', 'Happy Little Day', 'Blackpool Rock', 'Bognor Ballad', 'Southend Sea Scout', 'Skiffle Rock' and 'Herne Bay'. Obviously, the band – and engineer Mike Stone, the culprit of these titles – were in a playful mood, but the song's eventual released title is a reference to a type of hard candy that is sold only on the front at Brighton Beach.

Of the officially released versions, the ultimate display of musical versatility was in 1979 on the *Live Killers* disc, which find the band blazing through a 12-minute interpretation, complete with additional, quieter guitar portions and an extended timpani solo from Roger. Though the guitar solo always became a nightly feature of any Queen show, the actual song was dropped from the set list occasionally; an example of this was on the *Live At Wembley Stadium* CD, which is retitled 'Brighton Rock Solo'. However, a decent live version is no good without visuals, which often showed Brian running around the stage as lighting rig would pulsate and swirl, creating a truly awesome spectacle. The song was first officially introduced to the set list during the A Night At The Opera UK tour in 1975 and remained until the final show on 9 August 1986. Never one to drop a good thing, Brian incorporated variations of the solo into the Brian May Band's set between 1992 and 1998, with the only officially released version on *Live At The Brixton Academy* in February 1994 under the title 'Guitar Extravagance'.

Inexplicably, the studio version was released on the CD single of 'Killer Queen' in November 1988; this marked the song's only release on a single anywhere in the world.

BRING BACK THAT LEROY BROWN *(Mercury)*
• Album: *SHA* • Bonus: *SHA* • Live: *Rainbow, Odeon*

Showing Queen's versatility in all kinds of musical styles, 'Bring Back That Leroy Brown' is a throwback to the 1920s music hall style that would be explored more in-depth with 'Seaside Rendezvous' on *A Night At The Opera*. Though this song was a hidden gem on *Sheer Heart Attack*, it would become a staple of the medley between 1974 and 1976, where an up-tempo version was performed with minimal vocals. Live versions were ultimately released on *Live At The Rainbow '74* and *A Night At The Odeon*.

Freddie's story of Leroy Brown (which alludes to Jim Croce's 1972 song 'Bad, Bad Leroy Brown') is accompanied by a terrific jangle piano and ukulele backing, and is an energetic performance which also features John's first attempts on a double bass; Brian even gets in a short but sweet banjo solo. While the results have divided Queen's fans for years, there's no denying the song is an excellent slice of Freddie's eccentricity and musical creativity. Further showcasing the amount of work that went into the vocals, a mostly *a cappella* mix was created for the 2011 reissue of *Sheer Heart Attack* that is a truly stunning example of the kind of creativity the band – and especially Freddie – exhibited in their early days.

BROTHER OF MINE

Reportedly written by Brian and dating from sessions for *The Miracle* in 1988, 'Brother Of Mine' has been a rumored track for years, recently revealed to be a slow ballad that may have evolved into an officially released track, either by Queen or on Brian's solo album. So far, the song has yet to surface, meaning 'Brother Of Mine' probably doesn't exist.

BUSINESS *(May)*
• A-side (Brian): 5/98 [51] • Album (Brian): *World*

One of Brian's hardest rockers, 'Business' features a great drum performance by the late Cozy Powell, and as the song chugs along at full throttle it allows Brian ample opportunities for guitar solos. The lyrics aren't the strongest that Brian ever wrote, but his voice has certainly matured since his first album six years previously and his performance is credible. The song had a rather convoluted birthing process: in 1993, Brian was asked to provide the theme music for *Frank Stubbs Promotes*, a British TV show about a down-on-his-luck promoter coming to terms with his lot in life. Shown on ITV, the show ran between 1993 and 1994 but was ultimately canceled due to poor ratings. 'Business', or 'Hard Business' as it was initially known, was provided as the theme music, and, listening to the original versions, it sounds as if little had changed between the first recorded version and the final version in 1998.

Released as the first single from *Another World* in May 1998, 'Business' peaked at No. 51 in the UK, despite considerable promotion and a special edition release featuring a pictorial and audio tribute to Cozy Powell, who died in a car accident on 5 April, merely weeks away before rehearsals for the upcoming Another World tour. Retitled 'The Business (Rock On Cozy Mix)', the single opened with Cozy's isolated drum parts before kicking into the normal version, albeit slightly edited, and concluding with a 30-second drum solo taken from *Live At The Brixton Academy*. Also included on the CD single was a track titled 'Brian Talks', which was Brian talking about Cozy, concluding with: "Cozy, if you're listening, you were the best, and we all know it, and God rest you, mate – we love you."

A specially enhanced section was also included on the single, which featured the song intercut with Brian talking about the genesis of the song and also Cozy's death. "'Business' started off as the theme for a TV series, and all they wanted was little bits, so I did little bits first, but there was a complete song in my head," Brian explained. "So eventually we put it all together, and Cozy was a big part of that. [He] would come in at a certain point, after I had programmed it and sorted it all out, you know, bits of arrangement, Cozy would come in and say, 'Ah, yeah, yeah, I see what you mean', and he would do his thing, and then suddenly the thing would start to come to life, because that's a human thing. You can programme until you're blue in the face, you know, but you never get that sort of thing that comes from real people interacting. Cozy would always be a great energy source, and I'm gonna miss him terribly, you know. He was a big part of most of the tracks on this album. It's something which stirs your guts in, in a particular way, and you know, to see Cozy hit those things, you felt something, you know, it

wasn't just hitting things in time, it was like everything had a certain menace to it and a certain joy. Cozy was very up, very funny."

BUTTERFLY

During the *In The Studio* segment of *The Magic Years*, Brian is seen (and heard) fiddling around on a piano, playing a variation on the chords from 'Save Me'. When asked later what the name of that song was, he vaguely recalled it was called 'Butterfly', but it's likely that a more complete version does not exist.

BYE BYE BIRD *(Dixon/Williamson)*

This Willie Dixon song, covered by The Moody Blues and Eric Clapton, was played live by 1984.

C-LEBRITY *(Taylor/May/Rodgers)*
• A-side (Q+PR): 9/08 [33] • Album (Q+PR): *Cosmos*
• Live (Q+PR): *Ukraine*

Queen gained the ire of critics in their formative years, having not only songs that aped the crunch-and-swagger of Led Zeppelin, but also rising quickly through the ranks with what appeared to be a minimum of effort. Instead of slogging around clubs and pubs 12 months a year, building a loyal following, and then finally getting their big break after years of hard work, the band's early shows were more infrequent, with at least Brian and John still uncertain that they would really "go" anywhere, while Freddie and Roger had more faith in their talents. Still, their collective focus wasn't on progressing the band but on securing their futures through academics, while occasionally performing a gig or two to test the waters. Once music became the primary focus, however, they had attracted the attentions of record labels and studios alike, and their big break with 'Seven Seas Of Rhye' was a fluke: David Bowie dropped out of a *Top Of The Pops* appearance, and Queen were drafted as a back-up. The rest, of course, is history.

Fast forward 35 years after the release of Queen's debut album, and the climate had changed drastically. Pop stars were created on television, their advancement determined by a panel of curmudgeonly record moguls and washed-up, drugged-out former musicians, and their success chosen by a call- or text-in campaign. Their 15 minutes of fame would be drawn out over a few months, with the aftershock lasting only until their first record arrived, by which time, a new series had begun and the world moved on to the next Big Thing.

Roger, ever the outspoken wag, channeled his disbelief of instant success and media manipulation into 'C-Lebrity', a bitter recrimination on these fame-hungered stars. "It's to do with the phenomenon of celebrity culture," Roger told *Classic Rock* magazine, "the desperation to get your face on the telly. The assumption that if somebody becomes famous they'll also be rich is so naïve. It annoys me that there are so many famous, useless people." Having once said his biggest fear was to become "old, rich, and useless", 'C-Lebrity' is a fitting diatribe from Roger, but his own status as a multi-millionaire who hadn't created anything of worth (subjectivity notwithstanding) since 1998 – the last time he released an album's worth of new songs – is more than a little hypocritical. Still, regardless of Queen's own quick rise to fame, they worked hard to maintain their status and commercial standing, whereas contemporary stars are a one-and-done deal, and that no matter how good their follow-up albums may be, the fickle nature of the general public assures their success is ephemeral. "I think it's an interesting lyrical idea, which came from Roger," Brian said on the Bob & Tom Show in 2008. "It was his kind of comment on the … yeah, the cult of personality, I suppose, and the cult of fame for its own sake, which to us is a very alien concept. I don't think it really makes people very happy but it's taken over the world for a little while."

With a gritty guitar riff, a thundering drum performance, and a stop-start rhythm, 'C-Lebrity' is a welcome return to the rock'n'roll sound so sorely lacking on latter-day Queen albums. Even Brian, who sounds like he's sleepwalking through a lot of *The Cosmos Rocks* (and probably didn't appreciate the less than subtle jab at the *We Will Rock You* musical), sounds convinced, his vocal harmonies just as prominent as Roger's, with Taylor Hawkins also helping out – the only outside musician to assist on the album. Paul, meanwhile, is committed enough, but his leonine roar is wasted on the trivial lyrics, which might have been better suited for Roger's voice. Despite its lyrical drawbacks, though, 'C-Lebrity' is a fine rocker, and rightly released as the lead single from the album in September 2008. While it reached No. 1 in the UK Rock Chart, it peaked at a respectable No. 33 in the UK singles charts, though it was inexplicably premiered five months before its release on the series two finale of *Al Murray's Happy Hour*. This remained the only heavy

promotion the single received, with its TV appearance serving as its promotional video – confirming that either the band had little confidence in the song to waste money on a video no one would watch (a drastic assumption), or that, more realistically, they believed success was a given in name recognition alone. Unfortunately, that wasn't the case, and the relative failure of 'C-Lebrity' was further ammunition for detractors and critics of the endeavor.

The song earned a well-deserved spot in the 2008 Rock The Cosmos tour, and, along with 'Cosmos Rockin'' and 'Say It's Not True', was performed at every show.

CALL ME *(Rodgers/May/Taylor)*
• Album (Q+PR): *Cosmos*

Harking back to the lighter margins of *Sheer Heart Attack* and *A Night At The Opera*, Paul's 'Call Me' was praised by Roger as having a "sort of spontaneous spontaneity about it". Laid down in one take, with Paul on acoustic guitar and Roger on drums, before Brian overdubbed a suitably over-the-top Red Special solo, the song serves as a refreshing chaser to the weightier 'We Believe', but just don't try to pull it apart for any deeper meanings.

Stuck for a third single to promote the album, both 'Call Me' and 'We Believe' were serious contenders, with promotional discs released to radio late in October 2008. Considering the other strong single-worthy material on the album, 'Call Me' was a surprising choice, but in the end it didn't matter; no single was released commercially, hinting at increasing tensions between the three primary musicians while on the 2008 Rock The Cosmos tour, and the world was deprived of a physical release of a song that contains little other than "Call me if you need my love" repeated 21 more times.

CALLING ALL GIRLS *(Taylor)*
• Album: *Space* • Bonus: *Space*

The second of Roger's songs for *Hot Space* is this energetic new wave rocker about the discovery of love. While 'Action This Day' was the sole song on *Hot Space* to successfully combine funk with rock and not make it sound totally removed from Queen's sound, 'Calling All Girls' proved that Roger had one ear to the current trends, and that new wave, while a passing fad, had kept his interest in faster songs alight. Not content with having played everything on his debut solo album, Roger played guitar on the song, which Brian confirmed in a 1982 *On The Record* interview: "I think Roger did the feedback tracks near the end of the break. You never know where things come from. Roger played a lot of guitar. He's always bursting to play guitar." Released as a US-only single in July 1982, two days before the band's North American tour started, the song peaked at an abysmal No. 60, despite being heavily featured in the set list. A live version from a November 1982 performance in Tokyo was released both on *Greatest Video Hits 2* in 2003 and again in 2011 on the reissue of *Hot Space*.

The song was accompanied by an interesting promotional video, directed by Brian Grant and filmed at the same time as 'Back Chat'. Taking a cue from George Lucas' first film, *THX-1138*, the video shows the band in a robot-dominated society as Freddie cavorts with his lover, an attractive young female, only to be thrown in a cell by the robots. It's up to Brian, Roger, and John to rescue their friend, and the humans band together to destroy the robots and save civilization. Roger, on viewing the video over 20 years after, was bewildered as to its meaning, wondering why such a complex idea was given to a simple song about love. Despite his criticisms, though, it really is a fine video, and is a welcome departure from the traditional performance videos the band usually filmed.

CAN'T BE SO SAD *(Miller/Stevenson)*

Moby Grape's 1968 obscurity was performed live by Smile.

CAN'T GET ENOUGH *(Ralphs)*
• Live (Q+PR): *Return*

Originally released on Bad Company's 1974 self-titled debut album, 'Can't Get Enough' was released as that band's first single and immediately became a hit. It's not surprising, then, that Brian, Roger, Paul Rodgers and the 2005 touring band performed the song in their set lists, giving a typical Queen-like treatment to Rodgers' distinctive vocals, turning Queen into a bar-room blues band if only for a few minutes.

CAN'T HELP FALLING IN LOVE
(Peretti/Creatore/Weiss)
• Album (Brian & Kerry): *Golden*

Performed solely by Brian and Kerry, this delicate take on Elvis Presley's well-known hit is a lovely closer to *Golden Days*, perfectly summing up the overarching message of love that the album pervades.

CANCER ON MY MIND *(Bulsara)*

Another track written by Freddie, the song was part of the set lists of Wreckage's live appearances, with two known performances on 26 and 31 October 1969 at Ealing College Of Art.

CELEBRATION *(Edney)*
• Compilation (Roger): *Lot*

Rumors of the origin of this song had bounced back and forth between it being an out-take from either *Strange Frontier* in 1983 or *Shove It* in 1987. Suspicion and rumors finally turned to fact in 2013 when the song was released on *The Lot*, dating the song to December 1989 when The Cross held preliminary *Mad: Bad: And Dangerous To Know* sessions at Jam Studios, with four songs of previously dubious origin recorded: 'Celebration', 'I Can Take You Higher', 'I Can't Get You Out Of My Head', and 'Passion For Trash'. 'Celebration' is undoubtedly the strongest of the bunch, and deserved an airing on *Mad: Bad: And Dangerous To Know*.

CHAINS *(Goffin/King)*

Originally performed by The Cookies, but later covered by The Beatles, this Gerry Goffin / Carole King song was played live by 1984.

CHINA BELLE *(May)*
• Album (Brian): *World*

Unlike *Back To The Light*, *Another World* featured more hard rock songs, and 'China Belle' is an interesting amalgamation of rock and humor that introduced a lighter quality to the loftier songs on Brian's second album. Starting off with a rollicking piano and guitar duet, the song kicks into high gear with some truly great drum and bass work from Cozy Powell and Neil Murray respectively. Brian's guitar work is inspired and detailed, as expected; with a hint of Far East sound and humorous lyrics, it was presumably about a Chinese 'lady of the night', though Brian wouldn't confirm this.

CHINESE TORTURE (Queen)

• Bonus: *Miracle*

Included as a bonus track on the CD version of *The Miracle*, 'Chinese Torture' started as a multi-tracked studio jam by Brian, and ended up as a released track thanks to Freddie's enthusiasm. The composition is essentially an instrumental showcase for The Red Special and a harmony pedal, and would have been an ideal solo piece (even a perfect, atmospheric concert opener) if the band had toured in 1989.

CLOSER TO YOU (Edney)

• Album (The Cross): *MBADTK*

Mad: Bad: And Dangerous To Know was the first democratic album to be released by The Cross, with each band member contributing at least one song, and Spike Edney's 'Closer To You' is an enjoyable, albeit ultimately forgettable, rocker. Considering that it's the keyboardist's songwriting debut within The Cross, there was obviously room for improvement, but it gives Roger a chance to stretch his vocal chords in the more ambitious moments. The song was performed live on the 1990 tour in support of the sophomore album, but wasn't invited back for the next tour. An acetate single was cut, with 'Top Of The World, Ma', as the B-side, though whether this was planned as a fourth single or as a replacement for either 'Liar' or 'Final Destination' isn't known. It does partly explain the previously unreleased extended remix of 'Top Of The World, Ma' that was released in 2013 on *The Lot*.

IL COLOSSO (May/Holdridge)

• Soundtrack (Brian): *The Adventures of Pinocchio*

The companion piece to 'What Are We Made Of', 'Il Colosso', with music by Brian and Lee Holdridge and a set of lyrics by Brian, is an ambitious, operatic, cinematic contribution to *The Adventures Of Pinocchio*, serving as an overture to the soundtrack of *Pinocchio*, though a more appropriate term would undoubtedly be 'mini-opera': the song shifts styles and moods ferociously, summing up the 90 minute film succinctly in seven and a half minutes.

"Over the last months in the studio we have been recording the vocals of the puppet characters in the Opera," Brian told the Official International Queen Fan Club in the summer of 1996. "A lovely Norwegian singer called Sissell for the Princess, a fantastic operatic tenor from the New York Met called Gerry Hadley as the King, our old friend Gary Martin (who sang with us on 'Let Me Live') as the Giant 'Il Colosso', and me as everyone else, including a cast of hundreds of peasants, soldiers, courtiers etc., and a cameo appearance as the Chamberlain!! Oh, and I nearly forgot – after many attempts we finally found a young boy to sing Pinocchio's part, who wishes only to be known as Just William [in actuality, an electronically-altered Brian], and he's made a fine debut as the rascal Pinocchio, himself playing the part of the Hero (for this is a play within a play). We recorded a full 75-piece orchestra in Seattle a few weeks ago, then mixed it all together for the film in L.A. The soundtrack album will include a full-length version of the opera and a duet of the main song 'What Are We Made Of', which I wrote specially for the project (but also for my album, hopefully!) Sissel sings the duet with me and she really has a beautiful voice. This is being talked about as a possible single, probably following the release of a Stevie Wonder song which forms part of the end titles."

COME TO YOUR SENSES

In 2009, Brian wrote this song for blues musician Troy Turner, who recorded it on his *Whole Lotta Blues* album, released the following May. This gritty blues grinder features accompaniment on guitar from Memphis session musician Steve Cropper, and is a highlight of Turner's album. Unsurprisingly, a demo recording was made, with Brian on vocals, guitar, and other programmed instruments, and was premiered at the 2010 Queen Fan Club convention. While the guitarist was presently infatuated with Kerry Ellis and recording and producing her long-player debut, *Anthems*, 'Come To Your Senses' proved that Brian still had the creative spark in him, and a blues album, with the Red Special featured prominently, would be a daring and welcome move from him.

COMING SOON (Taylor)

• Album: *Game*

The origins of Roger's first contribution to *The Game* were rocky: starting off as an out-take from the *Jazz* sessions in 1978, the song was re-recorded the following summer, originally intended to be the B-side of 'Play The Game' but instead promoted to album filler status when the alternative – the far superior 'A Human Body' – was deemed too melodic and became the B-side instead.

'Coming Soon' is a lyrically ambiguous new wave rocker, with Freddie and Roger duetting on lead vocals while Brian riffs along in the background and Roger and John create a tenacious rhythm section. Roger mentioned it in a 1980 'Innerview' with Jim Ladd: "Originally the idea was a sort of anti-advertising song, really: 'Coming soon to your neighborhood'. But in the end it was meant to be a modern pop song, that's all ... I certainly didn't have any intention of saving the world when I was writing it!" An alternate version, featuring different backing vocal and rhythm guitar parts, was included on the 2003 DVD-A release of *The Game* since the original master tape for the song went missing.

COMMUNICATION BREAKDOWN *(Bonham/Jones/Page)*

Performed by Ibex throughout most of their short career, a version of Led Zeppelin's 'Communication Breakdown' surfaced from the 9 September 1969 show at The Sink Club in Liverpool.

CONTACT *(Taylor)*
• Album (The Cross): *Shove* • B-side: 3/88 [83]

Sounding like a distant cousin of David Bowie's 'Let's Dance', 'Contact' is the nadir of *Shove It*, encompassing everything that sums up the 1980s in five minutes: dominant synthesizers, poppy drum-machines, and the obligatory squawking saxophone, all overshadowing a thinly veiled set of lyrics about sexual contact. From any other up-and-coming band forming around 1987, 'Contact' would be expected, but is just embarrassing from a man who should know better.

COOL CAT *(Deacon/Mercury)*
• Album: *Space* • B-side: 6/82 [17]

The first effective use of Freddie's falsetto is on 'Cool Cat', a delicious slice of cool funk from *Hot Space* that features John on bass and rhythm guitars, synthesizer and drum-machine (Roger and Brian are not present), thus justifying the first collaborative effort between vocalist and bassist. Recorded during the latter half of 1981 during preliminary sessions for *Hot Space*, 'Cool Cat' originally featured David Bowie on backing vocals and was slated to be the B-side of 'Under Pressure'. Bowie protested, however, much to the irritation of the band: "David just did a backing track," Brian explained in 1982. "I don't think anyone thought any more about it, except that it was a nice ornamentation.

We just sent him a courtesy note telling him that we had used it and he said, 'I want it taken off, because I'm not satisfied with it.' Unfortunately, he didn't tell us until about a day before the album was supposed to be released, so it really set us back. It delayed the album's release." A remixed version, without Bowie's vocals, was included on the album release in May 1982 and became the B-side to 'Las Palabras De Amor (The Words Of Love)' the next month.

COOL JERK *(Storball)*

Originally performed by The Capitols, 'Cool Jerk' was covered live by 1984.

COSMOS ROCKIN' *(Taylor/Rodgers/May)*
• Album (Q+PR): *Cosmos* • Live (Q+PR): *Ukraine*

The opening song to any album of new material after a significant hiatus is imperative for an artist. It can make or break fan and critical appreciation, and, no matter how good the other songs may be, it's going to be that first song that people remember the most, and if it falls below expectations, maintaining any interest in the rest of the album is going to be an uphill battle. Queen, for better or worse, always had opening songs that grabbed listeners by the lapels and shook them around, but they weren't always the best songs, or even all that easy to get into; more often than not, their album openers were always diversions from the norm, with gut-punching rock songs the exception rather than the rule. 'Cosmos Rockin'' follows in the trend of interesting and unconventional album openers, in that it's a true rock song.

With an intro reminiscent of 'One Vision' – a keyboard drone, a swoop of guitar feedback, the sound of an otherworldly deity awaking and demanding that there be rock'n'roll – and the main body of the song comparable to any Status Quo boogie rocker, this "fairly basic and jolly" song, as described by Brian, delivers a pure and simple message: the power of loud rock'n'roll pervades all. There's not much to dissect, no hidden meanings or philosophical questions left unanswered; at its core, 'Cosmos Rockin'' is a good-time rocker, an update of 'Rock It (Prime Jive)' – unsurprising, considering its songwriter. "Roger had this song called 'The Whole World's Rockin'' and it's on there now," Brian said on a 2008 Bob & Tom Show radio appearance. "It starts off with 'the whole house rockin'', and then 'the whole town rockin'', 'the whole world rockin", and then I went, 'Well, why don't we have "the whole universe rockin'"?' It's just for fun, you know. It's not a serious comment on cosmology, but it's just fun to think – you can get the whole cosmos rockin'. So that's kind of how the thing took shape and there's a few little allusions in there to the cosmos."

Is the song successful as an opener? It depends on the fan's expectations for *The Cosmos Rocks*; it follows in Queen tradition with an opener that grabs the listeners by the short and curlies, and, as a rock song, it's hard to listen to it and not feel the urge to at least tap a foot. But from a lyrical standpoint, it's a shambles, with a slapdash set of lyrics that, even for Roger's standards, are cringeworthy; it'd be nice to believe they're tongue-in-cheek, but there's no humor in Paul's delivery anywhere to suggest this, which isn't a condemnation of Paul as a vocalist, but his ability to sing the song with a glister of wit. It's certainly not fair to compare Paul to Freddie, but if Freddie had been handed these lyrics, and provided he found them acceptable enough to sing without a major rewrite, his vocal delivery would have bordered on the preposterous so that the listener knew he wasn't serious. As performed by Paul, however, one can't help but feel he truly believes that the cosmos really will rock.

Despite its drawbacks, 'Cosmos Rockin'' is an ebullient song, with the band clearly enjoying themselves and taking their own words to heart. It became a welcome addition to the 2008 Rock The Cosmos tour as an encore number, quickly earning a coveted place among the rest of the Queen + Paul Rodgers repertoire.

COWBOYS AND INDIANS (Taylor)
• A-side (The Cross): 9/87 [74] • Album (The Cross): *Shove* • CD single: 1/88 [84]

Shove It may have been a controversial release, but 'Cowboys And Indians' is the cause of much debate and discussion among Queen fans, with the general consensus that it is not among Roger's better songs, especially for The Cross. That statement may be too broad, as it is important to look at the song in the appropriate timeframe: the late 1980s were full of musical and stylistic changes, and many of the old wave found themselves stuck hopelessly in the middle. Roger was no exception, but he was willing to push the envelope and embrace new things; he may not have learned from the critical backlash from *Hot Space*, but he did know that the charts didn't lie.

That's not to say that the song is a masterpiece, but

it's also not the worst song Roger ever wrote. 'Cowboys And Indians' was simply designed and constructed to be a danceable, likable single to introduce the world to The Cross (even if it was still only Roger and, at times, Spike Edney), and, in that respect, it's a success. Clocking in at almost six minutes, the song is energetic and jubilant, telling a warped tale of Americana, updated for the 1980s, with the sights and sounds of the Old West now spread across the entire nation.

John Deacon is credited as playing bass on some of the tracks on *Shove It*, and, while unconfirmed, the bass on 'Cowboys And Indians' has his fingerprints all over it; unlike Roger's usual chunky sound, the style is fluid and more indicative of John's distinct trademark. Elsewhere, the song is constructed around a dodgy synth riff, percolating in a nervous way that lends the song a tense edge. The guitars are minimal, almost rudimentary in approach, but the main focus is on Roger's voice, and he doesn't disappoint, showing he's finally ready to front a band.

Released as the first single from *Shove It*, trimmed of nearly 90 seconds, the single didn't perform as well as expected, stalling at a disappointing No. 74 in the UK. A video was shot in September 1987, debuting The Cross in their finest acid-washed jeans and feathered mullets, while Roger's then-girlfriend, Debbie Leng, mimed backing vocals. Unsurprisingly, sales weren't improved drastically, and the video remained hardly seen until its release in 2013 on Roger's nearly all-encompassing box set *The Lot*.

The Cross, now with a permanent lineup, made their television premiere on Channel 4's *The Roxy* on 6 October 1987, with a performance of the song, and with three other specific performances on *No. 73* on 17 October, Germany's *WWF Club* late in 1987, and Japan's *Yoruno Hits* on 6 January 1988. 'Cowboys And Indians' received considerable attention as the second song performed on The Cross' appearance on *Meltdown* on 6 November 1987, and was featured extensively in the live setting throughout 1988 and 1990.

CRASH DIVE ON MINGO CITY (May)
• Album: *Flash*

This is yet another variation on the main theme from *Flash Gordon*, but featuring random guitar bursts from Brian and timpani rolls from Roger. The bulk of the song is comprised of dialog and serves more as incidental music than as an integral composition.

CRAZY LITTLE THING CALLED LOVE *(Mercury)*

• A-side: 10/79 [2] • Album: *Game* • CD Single: 11/88
• Live: *Wembley, On Fire, Montreal, Budapest* • Bonus: *Wembley* • Live (Q+PR): *Return, Ukraine* • Live (Brian & Kerry): *Acoustic* • Compilation: *On Air*

"I wrote it in the bath," Freddie told *Melody Maker* in 1981 of one of his most famous compositions. "I actually dragged an upright piano to my bedside once. I've been known to scribble lyrics in the middle of the night without putting the light on. [It] took me five or ten minutes [to write]. I did that on the guitar, which I can't play for nuts, and in one way it was quite a good thing because I was restricted, knowing only a few chords. It's a good discipline because I simply had to write within a small framework. I couldn't work through too many chords and, because of that restriction, I wrote a good song, I think."

The vocalist's description of his song indicates that it was intended from the beginning to be a simple, almost throwaway song. Times had definitely changed: Queen had entered a phase in the summer of 1979 which would later prove to be their most successful, and it was all due to this record. Deliberately stripping back their approach and recording style, the band started writing songs more focused on rhythm and 'feel', as opposed to presenting the expansive sonic scope that distinguished so many of their early songs.

The actual recording process didn't take long at all, as Brian explained: "The guys put down the backing track for that one when I was out doing something in Munich, where we were working ... I came back and thought, 'Oh my God, it's almost finished. Let me put some guitar on it before they stick it out.' Fred plays the rhythm acoustic guitar. All I really did was add a kind of ersatz rock and roll solo and some backing harmonies and it was done." Recorded with a sparse backing track of Freddie on acoustic guitar, John on bass and Roger on drums, the song was completed within a few takes; all Brian added was an appropriate solo on an old Fender Telecaster that belonged to Roger, and the song was completed.

"'Crazy Little Thing Called Love' was very untypical playing for me," explained Brian of his performance. "I'd never used a Telecaster on record before, and a Boogie amplifier, which I'd never have considered using. It's a very sparse record, and it was done with Elvis Presley in mind, obviously. I thought that Freddie sounded a bit like Elvis, but somebody's done a cover of it who sounds absolutely like Elvis, and the whole record sounds like a Jordanaires/Elvis recreation."

Freddie said of his first experience playing guitar on record: "I wrote 'Crazy Little Thing Called Love' on guitar and played rhythm on the record, and it works really well because Brian gets to play all those lead guitar fills as well as his usual solo. I'm somewhat limited by the number of chords I know. I'm really just learning, but I hope to play more guitar in the future."

Adopting an Elvis-style vocal as a tribute to The King, who had passed away two years before, Freddie's impression is so convincing that many thought it was a long-lost recording by Elvis himself – or, at the very least, that Queen were covering an old, forgotten song by The King. "It's not rockabilly exactly but it did have that early Elvis feel," Roger commented in a 1984 interview with *Sounds*, "and it was one of the first records to exploit that. In fact I read somewhere – in *Rolling Stone*, I think it was – that John Lennon heard it and it gave him the impetus to start recording again. If it's true – and listening to the last album [*Double Fantasy*] it certainly sounds as if he explored similar influences – that's wonderful."

'Crazy Little Thing Called Love' was released as a UK single with the fast live version of 'We Will Rock You' from *Live Killers* in October 1979, and peaked in the charts at No. 2, the band's highest placement there since 'We Are The Champions' in 1977. Originally, the band hadn't intended to release the song in the US, but radio stations started picking up the song as an import and demand for the single became massive. Elektra issued the song with 'Spread Your Wings' from *Live Killers* in December 1979, and by the next month, the single flew to the top of the charts, earning the band their first No. 1 there. "I remember we were working hard on [*The Game*] a couple of months later," Roger said in 2009, "to be told this had gone to Number One in America. It was quite weird; that was good news. We had a big celebration."

A video was shot on 22 September 1979 at Trillion Studios. Directed by Dennis DeVallance, the video shows Queen decked out in leather and performing the song as Freddie prances around, a gorgeous blonde in his arms as he hops onto a motorbike; he struts to the front, surrounded by four professional dancers (two females and two males; this was the first, but not last, time the band would use dancers in a video), and one of the females tears his shirt down the front. Freddie is clearly the star of the show here, and the band are pushed to the sidelines; however, it seemed most comfortable for them, even if the leather didn't appear so.

The song became a staple in the set list, and was performed at every show between November 1979 and August 1986, with Freddie always on acoustic rhythm (1979-1982) or electric rhythm (1984-1986) guitar. He would usually precede the song with a crack about his lack of guitar skill (though Brian would refute this in 2009: "It's worth mentioning … Freddie was really a good acoustic player. He was very modest about it, but he could really play the acoustic guitar very well in an inimitable style, very frenetic kind of style. I remember he wrote 'Ogre Battle' on the acoustic guitar.") before dedicating the song to "anybody's who crazy out there." The song offered the chance for extended improvisation, often stretching the song well beyond its original two and a half minute running time, and allowing the band – but especially Brian – free rein to jam. Live versions of the song appear on *Live At Wembley Stadium* (with one version from the complete gig from 12 July 1986, and a bonus track on the 2003 reissue from the night before), though it wasn't released on *Live Magic*, and a great version appears on the 2004 DVD and CD release of *Queen On Fire At The Bowl*. Robert Plant performed an appropriate version (in the style of his own song 'Darlene' from Led Zeppelin's 1982 album *Coda*) at the Concert For Life on 20 April 1992.

On 7 October 1979, Freddie appeared with the Royal Ballet at the London Colizeum to take part in a charity gala ballet, organized to benefit the City of Westminster Society for Mentally Handicapped Children. Rehearsing his parts with principal dancers Derek Dene and Wayne Eagling at the London Dance Centre earlier in the week, the visibly nervous vocalist appeared on stage, providing the encore with 'Bohemian Rhapsody' and 'Crazy Little Thing Called Love'. When he urged the audience to sing along with him on the latter number, it must have slipped his mind that the song had been in the shops for only two days, so it's doubtful that anyone except the few staunch Queen fans in attendance would have known the words. Roger, who came along for moral support, said afterwards, "I was more nervous than he was. I mean, I wouldn't do it – that's just not my scene. I'd like to see anyone else have the courage to do that, and carry it off as well as he did. He had a lot of balls to go on that stage. He loves all that stuff."

CROSSROADS *(Johnson)*

Undoubtedly Robert Johnson's best-known song, later famously covered by Cream, becoming Eric Clapton's signature tune for most of his early career, Ibex performed a version of the song at The Sink Club, Liverpool, on 9 September 1969.

CYBORG *(May)*
• Album (Brian): *World*

One of the most unorthodox songs to be written by Brian, 'Cyborg' "was a quick job I did for a computer game [*Rise Of The Robots*, though it wasn't used until the sequel, *Rise 2: Resurrection*]," Brian explained in 1998. "And it obviously cried out to be a proper guitar thing, so I went for it. These days I'm using my fingers to pick more. Because there are a lot of things you can do by plucking the strings in different directions. And it also links into tapping, because your right hand isn't holding a pick, so it's free to go up on the fret board. I'm not heavily into tapping, but there are certain things you can do where the [right hand] finger can also hit a fret and get little transition notes, which can be really nice."

The song was initially recorded in 1995 and boasts a set of lyrics taken from the cyborg's point of view; an update of 'Machines (Or "Back To Humans")' for the 1990s, the mechanized villain begs the protagonist to "come play with me", with the hero pleading, "I don't want to / I don't need to / But I must fight again." Brian later told *Music Scene Magazine*, "Right after I got asked for a song by this 'gang', I tried to think myself into the mind of this robot, thats a very interesting thing to do, because it triggers of something in yourself. At the beginning I wrote the song for the robot, at the end it was a song for me. I began to give the robot my emotions." His voice is electronically lowered to give it a more sinister quality for the cyborg's voice, and his thin, reedy voice for the hero's parts contrasts nicely with the menace of the villain. Several alternate versions, each sounding more disturbing than the previous one, would later surface as instrumentals on the *Director's Cut* edition of *Rise 2: Resurrection*. "I'm fascinated with sequencing and loops and all those things," Brian said. "But this is a romp as well. It's a science fiction thing, and I thought, 'Wouldn't it be fun to put the robot's point of view, for a change, you know, the robot's emotions,' and that's where it started. Again, you can find other stuff in there, because the robot's like the rest of us, you know? Well, this one is, anyway!"

Taylor Hawkins plays drums on the track, one of the few songs on *Another World* that didn't feature Cozy Powell. Brian explained, "Taylor was with Alanis Morrisette when Roger introduced me to him. He did a great job there, but he was kind of in the wrong place, and he's a totally explosive young guy, with incredible energy, and he found his proper place in the Foo Fighters. Well, we're Foo Fighters fans, we like them a lot, and been to see a couple of their gigs, and it turns out that they are big fans of us, and they say, 'Well, Queen's the Bible for us, you know, we learn a lot of our stuff from listening to you guys,' so I just said to Taylor, 'Would you like to come down here and do one?', and he went, 'Yeah!'"

Unfortunately, the song is completely out of place on *Another World*, thus reinforcing the slapdash manner in which the album was constructed, and would have been better off on a completely different project. It's hard to imagine how the song would help Brian find the "True Direction and freedom of the Spirit" (according to his liner notes for *Another World*), though it does fit the idea that "things are never *quite* what they seem."

DANCER *(May)*
• Album: *Space*

Centered around a pulsating drum-machine beat and bubbling synth bass (both provided by Brian), 'Dancer' is Brian's own attempt to keep up with the funk. "We were thinking about rhythm before anything else," Brian told the BBC in 1982, "so in some cases, like 'Dancer', the backing track was there a long time before the actual song was properly pieced together. We would experiment with the rhythm and the bass and drum track and get that sounding right, and then very cautiously piece the rest around it, which was an experimental way for us to do it." Lyrically, the guitarist addresses his own awkwardness with the genre, which is evident in the performance. Though not the best track on *Hot Space*, it nevertheless has several redeeming factors, namely Brian's guitar work and Freddie's impassioned vocal performance.

A supposed demo, titled 'Catfight For The Rest', surfaced on YouTube in August 2010, with the uploader claiming this version featured rhythm guitar and lyrics by Roger, though the uploaded recording was an instrumental. Needless to say, the song is a fake, and a poor one at that.

DANCING IN THE STREET *(Gaye/Hunter/Stevenson)*

Originally performed by Martha and the Vandellas, 'Dancing In The Street' was played live by 1984.

DANCING QUEEN *(Andersson/Andersson/Ulvaeus)*

A fitting song to play live, The Brian May Band included ABBA's incredibly popular 'Dancing Queen' as an encore during their concert in Stockholm in 1998, sung by Suzi Webb and Zoe Nicholas. Incidentally, when not on tour with Brian, the two women fronted an ABBA tribute band called FABBA.

THE DARK *(May)*
• Album (Brian): *BTTL* • Live (Brian): *Brixton*

Released on Brian's 1992 debut solo album, *Back To The Light*, as an atmospheric opener, 'The Dark' was recorded during sessions for *Flash Gordon* in 1980 at Anvil Studios with orchestrations from Howard Blake, and it's been rumored that Queen recorded their own version. If the song exists, it's not known in what capacity it would have been used since it doesn't fit the themes of the *Flash Gordon* album, but in the confines of *Back To The Light*, 'The Dark' couldn't be more appropriate.

DEAD ON TIME *(May)*
• Album: *Jazz*

This breathless rocker is an astounding yet sorely underrated song, with a pace that supports the lyrics about a man rushing through his life. "That was something I was quite pleased with, but really nobody else was," Brian said of the song in a 1982 *On The Record* interview. "It's something which nobody ever mentions very much. 'Fat Bottomed Girls' I thought was okay, but fairly banal. I thought people would be much more interested in 'Dead On Time', but it didn't really get that much airplay." Brian had every right to be proud of the song: it's one of Queen's finest studio performances, with the band firing on all cylinders and turning in a truly remarkable recording. And who can forget that gloriously over-the-top ending, provided by God Himself?

Sadly, 'Dead On Time' was never performed live, though Brian was certainly itching to do so and occasionally performed segments of the song in his guitar solo spotlight throughout 1978 and 1979.

DEAR FRIENDS *(May)*

• Album: *SHA* • EP: *Five Live* • B-side: 4/93 [1]

An exquisite and understated performance, Brian's brief 'Dear Friends' is a gorgeous piano ballad (played by Brian) that languished for years alongside the more experimental second side of *Sheer Heart Attack*, serving as a refreshing chaser between the frantic 'Stone Cold Crazy' and jaunty 'Misfire'. Although the song enjoyed wider exposure when it was released as the B-side of the live 'Somebody To Love' from the Concert for Life in 1993, 'Dear Friends' was never aired in the live setting.

DEAR MR MURDOCH *(Taylor)*

• Album (Roger): *Happiness?* • CD single (Roger): 9/98 [45] • Bonus (Roger): *Earth*

During the final years of Freddie's life, he was constantly hounded by the tabloid papers, whose representatives camped out on his lawn awaiting a photo opportunity of the ailing vocalist while printing ludicrous statements in the dailies about his health. Roger took particular exception to *The Sun*, a paper owned by Rupert Murdoch, the controversial media mogul who also possessed a stranglehold over Fox television. At the end of Freddie's life, the papers were still scrounging for outrageous and scandalous stories to print, forcing Roger to write an answer in the form of 'Dear Mr Murdoch'.

Not since the days of 'Death On Two Legs' has any member of Queen sounded so vitriolic – compared to 'Dear Mr Murdoch', Freddie's 1975 ode to their former managers sounds like a love song. The song was originally written for an aborted fourth album by The Cross, though a version was rumored to have been worked on during sessions for *Blue Rock* in 1991; thankfully, the song wasn't explored any further, causing Roger's emotions to fester until he couldn't take it any more. "I thought it was a gross intrusion on [Freddie's] privacy," Roger seethed at the time. "I felt outraged that his house was surrounded by these vultures when he was basically trying to die in peace." Considered too personal for a Cross album, the song was abandoned and later resurrected for *Happiness?*.

Set to a slow, dirge-like backing, particular emphasis is given to Roger's voice, which alternates between a slow, hissing calm and an angrier tone by means of a vocal processor (a similar effect was used on several songs from *Happiness?* in the live setting).

The lyrics read like an open letter, as Roger lists several of Murdoch's "accomplishments", concluding that he's polluting the world with his "jingoist lingo" and "nipples and bingo and sex crimes."

As with most of *Happiness?*, the song is performed almost exclusively by Roger, though the minimal guitar work is courtesy of Jason Falloon. 'Dear Mr Murdoch' featured live on early dates of the Happiness? tour in 1994, and was even more relevant in September 1998 when it was revealed that Murdoch was proposing a takeover of Manchester United by way of BSkyB. Roger not only supported the Independent Manchester Supporters Association by donating start-up funds of £10,000, he also released a special edition of 'Pressure On' with 'Dear Mr Murdoch' as part of the release.

Roger returned to the song in July 2011, stripping back the original recording to its basic structure and removing the verse about "vultures and carrion crow". The reason Roger revised the song? That month, Murdoch had been accused of hacking phones of celebrities, royalty, and public citizens in order to gain salacious or incriminating details to sell more papers. He was immediately questioned by police and government officials, which led to bribery and corruption allegations against the UK government and FBI investigations in the US. Needless to say, his downfall was swift: the following year, he resigned as director of News International, and three years after that, he resigned as the CEO of 21st Century Fox. Roger was obviously delighted in the downfall of the media mogul, and his subtitle of the remix, the 'Nude Mix', was a clever *double entendre* of not only the stripped-back arrangement but Murdoch's unseemly exploitations on Page 3.

DEATH ON TWO LEGS (DEDICATED TO...... *(Mercury)*

• Album: *Opera* • EP: *First EP* • Live: *Killers*
• CD Single: 11/88

Queen's legal troubles in the latter part of 1974 and most of 1975 were well publicized at the time. Unfortunately, as Brian put it, the band discovered that they were "virtually penniless" despite all those successful records and tours. Freddie was especially angry, and wrote the scathing 'Death On Two Legs (Dedicated to......' in the autumn of 1975 as a two-fingered salute to the Norman and Barry Sheffield, who had been depriving the band of their hard-earned money. "'Death On Two Legs' was the most vicious lyric I ever wrote," he told *Circus* magazine in 1977. "It's so vindictive that Brian felt bad singing it. I don't like to explain what I was thinking when I wrote a song. I think that's awful, just awful. When I'm dead, I want to be remembered as a musician of some worth and substance."

The track, originally titled 'Psycho Legs' (so named after the intro, which is reminiscent of Alfred Hitchcock's *Psycho*), was the cause of a lawsuit when Trident Productions saw red: despite no specific mention of Queen's management, the Sheffields concluded that it was about them, and a slanderous dedication at best. Queen were taken to court, tying up the band's intentions to work on their fourth album ("It affects your morale," Brian moaned to *Sounds* in 1975. "It dries you up completely ... We couldn't write at all that summer."), while a re-recording of 'Keep Yourself Alive' from July 1975, intended for a US-exclusie single release, got tied up in the legal issues, and was abandoned. The lawsuit was settled out of court, with a £100,000 severance and one percent royalties on Queen's subsequent six albums.

With some gorgeous harmonies and an acidic vocal performance from Freddie, 'Death On Two Legs (Dedicated to......' is an early highlight and gets the band's pivotal fourth album off to a gleefully vicious start. The song appeared on *Queen's First EP* in May 1977 and became a live favorite, played for the first time that same month, and becoming a regular part of the medley between late 1977 and 1981, but was dropped before the second leg of the Gluttons For Punishment tour – intriguingly, at the same time that the Sheffields' one percent deal as part of their severance ended.

DEEP RIDGE

In the summer of 2004, an alleged confidant of Brian 'revealed' that *Queen II* was originally meant to feature 13 songs instead of 11, and that the demo recordings of all the songs were to appear on the still-unreleased anthology box sets. The tipster named the two extra unreleased recordings as 'Deep Ridge', reportedly written by Brian, and 'Surrender To The City', written by Freddie. While the existence of these two songs is unlikely, it still paints an interesting image of Queen fans with little else to do but make up stories about tracks that don't exist. However, if 'Deep Ridge' and 'Surrender To The City' *do* exist, then I shall be the first in line to eat my hat.

DELILAH *(Queen)*
• Album: *Innuendo*

Freddie was living on borrowed time by the time sessions for *Innuendo* were underway, which made his outpouring of creativity all the more impressive. The sessions for *The Miracle* had barely finished before Freddie insisted the band work on material for their next album; in March 1989, he laid down a demo recording of 'Delilah', a playful ode to his favorite feline. When recording sessions proper began later that year, Freddie brought the song to the band, though Roger was reportedly less than enamored with the song, and only relented for its inclusion at Freddie's persuasion. Brian, meanwhile, got a lovely sound out of his guitar, with the solo played through a talkbox: "I finally succumbed and used one," he told Nuno Bettencourt in August 1991. "They wheeled it in and I said, 'Well, I suppose there's no other way I can make 'meow' noises'."

'Delilah' was released as a single in Thailand in December 1991, shortly after Freddie's passing, where it went to No. 1 in the charts.

DINER *(May)*
• Soundtrack (Brian): *Furia*

Another sombre keyboard piece from the *Furia* soundtrack, 'Diner' lasts just over one minute and, like some of the other shorter pieces on the album, serves merely as incidental music. It's also one of the few pieces to end with dialog from the film.

DIRTY MIND *(Edney)*
• Album (The Cross): *Blue* • Live (The Cross): *Germany*

'Dirty Mind' tackles the embarrassing topic of lust, which can be tolerable if handled right, but considering that Roger was just about to turn 42, with Spike not too far behind, the song is cringe-inducing as Roger screams, "I want a lover with a dirty mind!" One plus is that it returns the band to its rock roots, making it an acceptable addition to The Cross' set list in 1991, with a live version appearing on the 1992 fan club-only bootleg, *Live In Germany*.

DOES YOUR CHEWING GUM LOSE ITS FLAVOUR? *(Donegan)*

An interesting rendition by an apparently double-tracked Brian (though it may be a duet with an unknown musician), the recording origins of Lonnie Donegan's 'Does Your Chewing Gum Lose Its Flavour?' are uncertain, but the evidence – or what little there is of it – seems to point to the early 1990s.

DOG WITH A BONE *(Queen)*

Two versions of this interesting blues track exist, both recorded on 15 April 1988: the first is a "straightforward" recording, clocking in at under five minutes, while the second version is extended past six minutes and includes an in-song greeting from each band member to fan club members who attended the 1988 Fan Club convention. Though 'Dog With A Bone' was never intended for *The Miracle*, the preliminary sessions from which this song originates, it would have been a fun diversion as a B-side release, but its uniqueness to the Queen Fan Club remains special – so much so that it still has yet to surface on an official release.

DOING ALL RIGHT *(May/Staffell)*
• Album: *Queen* • Compilation: *BBC, On Air* • CD Single: 6/96 [9] • Compilation (Smile): *Ghost Of A Smile*

When Queen started work on their debut album in the summer of 1972, the Brian May/Tim Staffell co-write from Smile 'Doin' Alright' was a well-established live favorite by this time, and was deemed worthy enough to sit alongside newer compositions. ("It never struck me as a particularly brilliant song," Tim Staffell later said, "though the royalties did help out in a bind!") Set over a delicate piano introduction, played by Brian, and a gorgeous vocal from Freddie, 'Doing All Right' (as it was retitled) soon turns into a full-fledged rocker, with The Red Special in great form, reverting to a ballad for the conclusion. The harmonies are perfect, and the band performance is a major accomplishment considering their infancy.

A version for the BBC was recorded on 5 February 1973 and released on *Queen At The Beeb* in 1989, though the actual performance uses the album backing track with a re-recorded vocal. This performance is unique in that Roger sings the last verse, providing a stark, harsher contrast to Freddie's angelic tones.

DON'T LOSE YOUR HEAD *(Taylor)*
• Album: *AKOM*

This atmospheric synth-pop rocker was written specifically for the *Highlander* film (the title itself is a coy reference to the plot line that a highlander can only be killed through decapitation), though it was universal enough to relate to love-torn couples to keep cool in tense situations. While it's not a standout track on *A Kind Of Magic*, there are several redeeming factors: the multitude of layered drums and percussion are a treat; Freddie's vocals are absolutely stunning; and the Red Special delivers a scorching, searing guitar solo. Additionally, Joan Armatrading, then recording her *Sleight Of Hand* album, contributed incidental vocals (Roger was also planning on giving her 'Heaven For Everyone', a track he had written during this time but would end up keeping for himself), though her contribution was mixed well to the back.

Incidentally, the line "Don't drink and drive my car / Don't get breathalysed" was inspired by a drunk driving incident in 1985 involving the mild-mannered John and a Porsche. The bassist, who normally fancied Volvos, bought a Porsche for himself and visited Phil Collins at one of his London concerts. The two went out to celebrate afterwards, and when John was pulled over on the way home, the officer gave him a sobriety test, which he failed, earning John an expensive ticket. 'Don't Lose Your Head' was released as the B-side of the US issue of 'Pain Is So Close To Pleasure' in August 1986, and on the European 'One Year Of Love' single that October.

DON'T SAY NO

On early, handwritten running orders for the *Jazz* album, a mysterious track called 'Don't Say No' was listed as a second side track; conspicuously absent from the order was John's 'In Only Seven Days'. Queen archivist Greg Brooks had revealed 'Don't Say No' as a mystery song's working title in a 2002 *Record Collector* article; knowing now that the song was intended for *Jazz* has put the puzzle a bit closer toward completion, but it seems odd that 'In Only Seven Days' were to have such an out-of-place working title. Considering John's handwritten lyrics clearly indicated the title had been in place almost from the beginning, could 'Don't Say No' be an unreleased track from the *Jazz* sessions? Or was it just a nonsensical placeholder until the lyrics were finalized? Until Queen's archives are made public, we'll have to wait with bated breath.

DON'T STOP ME NOW (Mercury)
• Album: *Jazz* • A-side: 1/79 [9] • Live: *Killers*
• CD Single: 6/96 [9] • Bonus: *Jazz*

This joyous call to arms for fellow partygoers everywhere is a highlight of the *Jazz* album, and one of Freddie's most endearing, enduring, and underrated songs. Brian, for once, wasn't convinced: "It's very much Freddie's pop side and I remember thinking, 'I'm not quite sure if this is what we should be doing.' I think there was also a feeling that it lyrically represented something that was happening to Freddie which we kind of thought was threatening him, and probably it was in a sense. But having said that," he conceded, "it's full of joy and optimism..." It very well may also have been the decided lack of guitar that got under Brian's skin, though this was rectified with the emergence of a long-lost guitar mix from the sessions, duly released on the 2011 reissue of *Jazz*.

When issued as a single in January 1979 with John's 'In Only Seven Days' as the B-side, it became a Top Ten hit, peaking at No. 9 and charting higher than 'Fat Bottomed Girls' / 'Bicycle Race' had in October 1978. The American release, coming a month later with Roger's 'More Of That Jazz' as the flip, peaked at a disappointing No. 86. Accompanied by a standard performance video directed by Dennis DeVallance and shot during soundchecks in Brussels on 26 January 1979, the single became a fan and live favorite, and was performed at every date on the Jazz European and Japanese tours, as well as during the Crazy tour and Crazy tour of London in late 1979, but was dropped by the following year. In 2005, viewers of *Top Gear* voted 'Don't Stop Me Now' as "The Greatest Driving Song Ever", and co-host James May duly flew out to Sardinia to present Roger with an award ("The cheapest, nastiest trophy they could find").

DON'T TRY SO HARD (Queen)
• Album: *Innuendo*

A melancholy chaser to the joyful 'I Can't Live With You', 'Don't Try So Hard' is a fantastic and underrated ballad featuring a magnificent vocal from Freddie. For years, debate had raged over who wrote the song, with one of the first fan-run websites in the mid-1990s crediting it to John, but David Richards and, much later, Brian confirmed 'Don't Try So Hard' as Freddie's work, and a masterful piece of work is it, too.

The message of the song is not to reach too far for

success, as "it's only fools [who] make these rules." With an understated instrumental performance, atmospheric use of keyboards, and otherworldly vocal performance from Freddie, 'Don't Try So Hard' is a fantastic latter-day Queen song, truly one of the most outstanding non-single album tracks to have been written since the late 1970s, when the emphasis was on presenting an album as a cohesive piece instead of as a collection of songs. The UK vinyl release featured the song after 'Delilah' on the second side, with ten seconds inconsequentially edited out.

DON'T TRY SUICIDE (Mercury)
• Album: *Game*

Continuing the rockabilly themes explored on 'Need Your Loving Tonight' and 'Crazy Little Thing Called Love', 'Don't Try Suicide' is a song that takes the serious matter of suicide and turns it into a black comedy number, discounting suicide as a cry for attention instead of as a plea for help.

"'Don't Try Suicide' says just that," Roger told *Sounds* in 1980, "and I quite like that one, it's funny. You should never read the lyrics without listening to the album at the same time, you know. It isn't prose and they're not poems." With the instrumental backing of a lazy acoustic guitar and a great walking bassline, inspired by The Police's 'Walking On The Moon' (released as a single November 1979, just before Queen re-entered the studios to finish *The Game*), the song is a lighthearted throwaway, and is a welcome breath of fresh air among the loftier performances on *The Game*.

'Don't Try Suicide' appeared as the US B-side of 'Another One Bites The Dust' in August 1980, and gained considerable airplay on rock radio when DJs tired of playing its A-side.

A DOZEN RED ROSES FOR MY DARLING (Taylor)
• B-side: 3/86 [3] • CD Single: 11/88

Essentially the programmed drum sequence from 'Don't Lose Your Head' reconfigured as an instrumental with additional synthesizer and guitar segments, 'A Dozen Red Roses For My Darling' is far more interesting than its cousin, but is no more than an instrumental throwaway. The curiously titled song appeared as the B-side of 'A Kind Of Magic' in the UK in March 1986 and as the B-side of 'Princes Of The Universe' in the US the following month, while a superfluous extended remix appeared on 12" versions of 'A Kind Of Magic', extending the track by 45 seconds yet adding nothing substantial.

DRAGON ATTACK *(May)*
• Album: *Game* • B-side: 8/80 [7] • CD Single: 11/88
• Bonus: *Game* • Live: *On Fire, Montreal*
• Compilation: *On Air*

An interesting diversion into funk-rock, Brian's 'Dragon Attack' is the result of a drunken recording jam session in Munich in early 1980 ("It was put together in an unusual way," the guitarist later said. "We just jammed for awhile and put down the basic riff."), and can be seen as the catalyst for what would eventually become *Hot Space*. Roger and John swing convincingly, locking into an infectious groove that they adhere to throughout, allowing Brian full rein on some dirty guitar licks while Freddie sings the minimal lyrics, long rumored to be about his hard partying ways.

Issued as the B-side of 'Another One Bites The Dust' in the UK in August 1980, 'Dragon Attack' was also pressed as an edited South African acetate single (with 'Rock It (Prime Jive)' on the B-Side), reducing the running time by nearly two minutes and cutting out most of the bass and guitar solos - Sacrilege! The song was updated in 1991 with a remix by R.A.K., which replaced Roger's drums with a more urban drum-machine loop, while still retaining the bass work and Freddie's vocals, but almost completely omitting Brian's solo in lieu of an incomprehensible rap segment. Released as a bonus track on *The Game*, that reissue would have instead benefited far more from the non-album B-side 'A Human Body'. The song was played as a mid-song interlude during 'Now I'm Here', normally after Freddie's vocal interaction with the crowd; it was performed this way between 1980 and 1982, but in 1984 and 1985 was performed as a song in its own right, before 'Now I'm Here'. 'Dragon Attack' was brought out of mothballs for the 2006 US tour with Paul Rodgers, and was later revived for Queen's outings with Adam Lambert.

DREAM OF THEE *(May)*
• Soundtrack (Brian): *Furia*

The only true song on the *Furia* soundtrack, 'Dream Of Thee' is an achingly beautiful piece performed on acoustic guitar with haunting vocals by Brian. Concluding the soundtrack album in a sombre, downbeat style similar to the other pieces, the song's lyrics deal with the heartbreak of losing a loved one. This latter-day classic deserves more recognition than being tossed away at the end of a little-heard soundtrack.

DREAMERS BALL *(May)*
• Album: *Jazz* • Live: *Killers* • Bonus: *Jazz*

The song that nearly brought Brian and Roger to blows: the latter, being characteristically opinionated, didn't particularly care for the song, while the former, who wrote it, defended his own composition. Crystal Taylor, Roger's unrelated personal assistant, said, "Hated it on disc and hated it live, so there. I actually have a tape of Roger and Brian trying to record this in the studio, and shall we just say that tempers flared."

A shame, since 'Dreamers Ball' (sans possessive apostrophe) is a unique song on what turned out to be one of Queen's most diverse records. Recalling the boozy sounds of a New Orleans jazz bar, the song tells a story of the main character's magical night with her lover, and how the celebration will continue in her dreams. With Freddie adopting a drunken, slurred enunciation to his delivery, the rhythm of the song, well executed by John and Roger and featuring a prominent acoustic guitar, falls slightly behind the beat, as Brian lays down some gorgeous guitar harmonies. The backing vocals are exquisite as ever, and 'Dreamers Ball' is an unexpected highlight of *Jazz*. An early take from August 1978, performed more in the style of 'My Melancholy Blues' with subdued acoustic guitar and minimalist brushed drums, was released on the 2011 reissue of *Jazz*, and serves as an interesting alternate listen.

The song was performed live during the acoustic interlude in the 1978 and 1979 Jazz tours; in lieu of Brian's guitar solo, Roger and Brian would provide vocalizations, similar to 'Seaside Rendezvous'.

DRIVEN BY YOU *(May)*
• A-side (Brian): 11/91 [6] • CD single (Brian): 8/92 [5]
• Album (Brian): *BTTL* • Bonus (Brian): *BTTL*
• Live (Brian): *Brixton*

In early 1991, Brian was approached by the Ford Motor Company, who were interested in updating their image by using a more contemporary sound for their advertisements. Brian, who was near completion of his first solo album, agreed to work on a few ideas and, during early sessions for what would eventually become *Made In Heaven*, fleshed out a song that was enthusiastically received by the company. Three versions of 'Driven By You' were recorded, all sounding similar and lasting only 90 seconds each, but the response from the TV-viewing public was initially one of confusion, thinking that some no-name band was cashing in on Queen's distinctive sound. Thus, both the Queen and Ford offices were bombarded with irate calls, but once the confusion was cleared up, the next logical question became, "When can I get this single?"

"I thought advertising was a dirty word, and I didn't want much to do with it," Brian said in 1991. "But these ad guys threw some slogans at me and I thought, 'Well, I can do it if I relate to my own experiences and my own feelings'. And the phrase 'driven by you' immediately jumped out as a description of the way I saw the power struggle between two people in a relationship – it just poured out. I wrote a version for me, and I wrote a version for the ad people, and it worked out great. It was a good kick up the backside for me, too, because these people work quickly and do high-quality work. On English television, the adverts are a lot better than the programming!"

Brian's version was slated for release on 25 November 1991, such was the demand for the single. Freddie had informed the band and management that he was losing his battle to the AIDS virus, and when Jim Beach broached the subject of Brian's latest single, with the guitarist expressing concern that he wanted to pull it so as not to appear to be cashing in on Freddie's death, the ailing vocalist reportedly exclaimed, "Tell him he has to – what better publicity could he have?" Freddie died on 24 November and, the day after, 'Driven By You' appeared and raced up the charts the following week to No. 14 before peaking at No. 6 the second week, staying in the charts for an impressive nine-week run. When released as a single in the US in April 1993, the single charted for a further nine weeks in the *Billboard* Album Rock Tracks chart, peaking at an impressive No. 9.

The song is a sprightly rocker, with a heavy drum-machine chugging away beneath layers and layers of guitars. The guitar work on this track is impressive and typical of Brian's sound, but the most interesting aspect is the vocals, especially at the beginning. "The beginning of 'Driven By You' is just one voice, put through the Vocalist," Brian explained. "I did it live, but it's only one take – great machines!" The Vocalist, as Brian mentioned, is a machine that is able to do live multi-tracking of vocals, and is used on all of the chorus vocals throughout the song.

The song was an obvious candidate for the live setting, and was performed at every Brian May Band concert between 1992 and 1998, with a particularly touching acoustic version being recorded specially for a VH-1 special in May 1998. A live version was released on *Live At The Brixton Academy* in February 1994, and a video version of the song was taken from a live show on 19 October 1991 in Seville, Spain. This version was released on *Greatest Flix III* in 1999, though an early unique studio video, filmed during October 1991, has yet to surface.

Here's the tricky part: several alternate versions of the track were recorded, which is not surprising given the success of the single. The standard version was recorded in the summer of 1991 at Montreux Studios and was ultimately released as the single in November 1991 and later on *Back To The Light*. The advertisement version was the preliminary take submitted to the Ford Motor Company for their campaign starting in July 1991, and was released as part of the 12" version of the single. A rock radio version, remixed by Brian Malouf and featuring a rougher, more raw sound, was later issued on a US promotional CD, while a completely new retake with Cozy Powell on drums and Neil Murray on bass was issued on the CD single of 'Too Much Love Will Kill You' in August 1992 and later as a bonus track on the CD version of *Back To The Light*.

Three different edits for disc jockeys were also created, each one more humorous than the last. The first, subtitled "for DJs in a bit of a hurry", lopped off the first few seconds of the intro and some of the outro, with the running time now 3'38; the second was edited even further, subtitled "for DJs feeling under pressure", and ran only 3'23; while the third was only five seconds, subtitled "for DJs under extreme stress!", with a short burst of the chorus vocals and the concluding guitar riff. Phew!

DRIVEN BY YOU TWO *(May)*

• *CD single (Brian): 6/93 [23]*

An interesting alternative version of 'Driven By You', 'Driven By You Two' is a re-recording based on the style of its more complete sister recording. Although it lasts only 90 seconds, it's a surprisingly catchy instrumental, with Brian's guitar dueling with a hardworking drum-machine. The song was released as part of the second 'Resurrection' CD single in June 1993, and was recorded at the same preliminary sessions as 'Driven By You'.

DROWSE (TAYLOR)
• Album: *Races*

Roger had been proving himself more and more versatile as a songwriter since his debut on 'Modern Times Rock'n'Roll' in 1973. His glam-rock effort, 'The Loser In The End', hadn't been critically well received, but the dark and ominous 'Tenement Funster' was a step in the right direction, and 'I'm In Love With My Car' would prove its staying power as a live favorite for nearly five years. Instead of continuing in the hard rock vein, Roger instead turned introspective for his fifth song for Queen, harking back to the simple days of youth.

'Drowse' is an exquisite song, one of the finest Roger ever wrote, and certainly one of his finest vocal performances. It recalls Roger's adolescence, when he and his friends would "scuff up the sidewalk with endlessly restless feet" and broaden their minds "more in the pool hall than [they] did in the school hall." Essentially too young to enjoy what adults could but already past the border of childhood innocence, Roger finds himself bored to "rages of tears" with "the fantastic drowse of the afternoon Sundays." Musically, the song is an accomplishment since it features an almost Spector-like 'wall of sound' of acoustic and rhythm guitars, played by Brian and Roger, and one of Brian's first attempts on slide guitar, which soars effortlessly throughout the song.

Issued as the American B-side to 'Tie Your Mother Down' in March 1977, 'Drowse' eluded a placement in the live repertoire. The final words which Roger ultimately fades out upon, for years the cause of much speculation, were revealed in 1984: "I think I'll be Clint Eastwood / Jimi Hendrix, he was good / Let's try William the Conqueror / Now who else do I like?" And, if you turn up your volume loud enough, you can hear Roger's answer to his own question: "Brian May."

THE DUET (THE FALLEN PRIEST):
see EXTRACTS FROM GARDEN LODGE

EARLY MORNING BLUES (Blake)

This song was performed live by The Cross, with Brian on guitar and vocals and John on bass, during the band's 1988 Christmas party for the fan club.

EARTH (Staffell)
• Compilation (Smile): *Ghost Of A Smile*

One of the better tracks recorded by Smile to surface from the June 1969 Trident Studios sessions, 'Earth' is a laid-back, slightly spacey track reminiscent of Pink Floyd, with a suitably prominent Hammond organ high in the mix. "It had begun to become important to write your own material," Tim Staffell recalled in the liner notes to *Ghost Of A Smile*. "In the summer of 1968, I made a particular effort, and came up with two or three songs. 'Earth' was one of them, and ended up the strongest of the bunch. I wrote it because I was a bit of a science-fiction buff. In fact, all of the songs I knocked up that summer – and most of them were cobblers! – had science-fiction-based lyrics." The song predates ''39' and is about an astronaut lost in space, singing of the many worlds he sees, but lamenting that he'll never again see the planet Earth; heavy stuff, yet the song was chosen as the most chartworthy track from the sessions, and was released as Smile's first single in August 1969. Unusually, the single was a US-only release, and since Smile had no means of promotion in America, the single failed to chart, which brought a premature end to their deal with Mercury Records. "Everybody hedged their bets," Tim remembered of Mercury Records. "The record company wasn't willing to commit themselves to the single. I don't recall it being much of a big deal. None of us were over the moon about it, because there was no money in it. It didn't generate much interest." Shortly after their sessions in August 1969, Tim Staffell would jump ship, bringing an end to what could have been a promising career as a blues-based rock band.

In December 1992, at The Cross' Christmas concerts at The Marquee Club in London, a huge holiday present was in store for the fans: midway through the band's set on the first night, in strode Tim Staffell, who had been asked by Roger to perform on 'Earth' and 'If I Was A Carpenter'. The following night, in addition to Tim was Brian, thus becoming the first reunion of Smile in over 20 years.

The song was later issued on the 1982 bootleg *Gettin' Smile*, which prompted Brian and Roger to question the authenticity of the tracks. Apparently, they didn't remember recording as many as six tracks (presumably, 'Earth', its B-side 'Step On Me' and 'Doin' Alright' were the only ones to jog their memories as being legitimate), but they eventually recognized the remaining songs as their own. Only in 1998 were all six songs officially released on *Ghost Of A Smile*.

EIGHT DAYS A WEEK *(Lennon/McCartney)*

Originally by The Beatles, 'Eight Days A Week' was performed by 1984.

EL NOI DE LA MERE *(trad. arr. May)*

During Brian's nightly guitar solo on the Magic tour at the Monumental Plaza de Toros in Barcelona on 1 August 1986, he inserted a scrap of a traditional Catalan popular song.

ENSUEÑO *(Mercury/Moran/Caballé)*
• Album (Freddie): *Barcelona*
• Compilation (Freddie): *Solo Collection*

'Exercises In Free Love' had impressed Montserrat Caballé so greatly that she took the music of that song and added her own set of lyrics, making 'Ensueño' a standout track from the *Barcelona* album and a true showcase of Montserrat's vocal capabilities. The lyrics, written and sung exclusively in Spanish, are about a dream that a woman has of seeing her one true love, and are made all the more poignant with Freddie and Montserrat duetting effortlessly.

Apart from the standard album version, two alternate versions appeared on *The Solo Collection*: an instrumental version based on Mike Moran's piano abilities alone, which is simply beautiful, and an alternate vocal version recorded with only Montserrat on vocals, though three takes are presented, each breaking down due to Freddie's insatiable desire for absolute perfection.

ESCAPE *(May)*
• Soundtrack (Brian): *Furia*

Opening with a timpani roll and dominated by orchestrations, 'Escape' features The Red Special in full force – indeed, a rarity on the *Furia* soundtrack – but is, unfortunately, yet another variation on the main theme.

ESCAPE FROM THE SWAMP *(Taylor)*
• Album: *Flash*

Sounding curiously like Roger's nightly timpani solo from the 1979-1981 era, 'Escape From The Swamp' is an atmospheric, synthesizer-driven composition with some masterful percussion.

EVERYBODY HURTS SOMETIME *(Taylor)*
• Album (Roger): *Happiness?*
• B-side (Roger): 11/94 [32]

Like 'Loneliness...' and 'You Had To Be There', 'Everybody Hurts Sometime' is a shorter track, gracing the second side of *Happiness?* without much fanfare, yet is completely necessary to the album's concept of self-discovery. Displaying a surprisingly soulful vocal from Roger (he often introduced the song as an "optimistic blues" track), the song deals with pain and suffering, but points out that, without such elements in a person's life, "you ain't livin' at all." The song is performed nearly solely by Roger, with the ever-present Jason Falloon contributing a terrific guitar performance, and Cathy Porter backing up Roger beautifully.

A live version, released on the 12" version of the 'Happiness?' single, was taken from a performance at Shepherd's Bush, London, in 1994. While the album version is more emotive, the musical performance on the live version is clearly superior; the keyboards add to the emotions, and Jason Falloon's guitar work is stellar, as usual.

EVERYBODY NEEDS SOMEBODY

This title, along with 'Had To Believe Me' and 'In Search Of Love', was written by Freddie but left unrecorded during Queen's latter-day sessions in 1989.

EVERYBODY'S GOT TO LEARN SOMETIME *(Warren)*

A live cover version of The Korgis' No. 5 hit from 1980, 'Everybody's Got To Learn Sometime' was performed at the 46664 charity concert on 29 November 2003 by Brian, Roger, The Corrs violinist Shannon Corr, Italian rocker Zucchero on lead vocals, and the 46664 house band.

EXECUTION OF FLASH *(Deacon)*
• Album: *Flash*

John's first contribution to the *Flash Gordon* soundtrack consists of him doodling on a Fender Telecaster guitar as a synthesizer drones in the background. An effective atmospheric piece, the song leads into Freddie's vocal tour de force, 'The Kiss (Aura Resurrects Flash)', with an orchestration from Howard Blake.

EXERCISES IN FREE LOVE *(Mercury/Moran)*
• B-side (Freddie): 2/87 [4] • B-side (Freddie): 10/87 [8] • Compilation (Freddie): *Pretender, FM album, Solo Collection* • B-side (Freddie): 1/93 [29]

In late 1986, following sessions for 'The Great Pretender' and with the probability of a collaboration with Montserrat Caballé becoming a reality, Freddie recorded 'Exercises In Free Love' as his vocal approximation of the opera diva, with Mike Moran backing him up on the piano and orchestration. Largely improvised with no lyrics whatsoever, the vocalizations are stunning, and it was this track that Freddie would take to his first meeting with Montserrat, impressing her so much that she insisted the two record an album together. She also performed the track live on 29 March 1987 at Covent Garden, with Mike Moran accompanying her; so beautiful was the performance that the audience gave them a standing ovation.

And here it becomes complicated: Freddie's original version was released as the B-side of 'The Great Pretender', while a Montserrat vocal version, re-recorded during the *Barcelona* sessions, later became the B-side of 'Barcelona' in October 1987. Montserrat then took the music and wrote a special set of lyrics entirely in Spanish for inclusion on the *Barcelona* album yet, incredibly, Montserrat's vocal version wasn't included on *The Solo Collection*.

EXTRACTS FROM GARDEN LODGE

Several snippets of Freddie, Montserrat Caballé and Peter Straker, with Mike Moran fooling around on piano at the Garden Lodge on 29 February 1988, have been bootlegged as 'Extracts From Garden Lodge' or, alternatively, 'Garden Lodge Tapes'. Featuring such improvisations as 'The Duet' (which later turned into 'The Fallen Priest') and 'Idea' (later becoming 'Barcelona'), these insights into Montserrat becoming acquainted with Freddie's new material are fascinating; even at this early stage, he knew exactly what he wanted from his new collaborator.

Three additional 'songs' were recorded, without Montserrat but with Peter Straker instead: a lewd and profanity-laced version of 'Que Sera, Sera', 'Rock-A-Bye Dixie' and 'Girl From Ipanema', these are no doubt heavily influenced by liquor and the duo's spirits are clearly heightened. Understandably, these were not included on *The Solo Collection*, but have been in the traders' circuits for years.

FACE IT ALONE

Recorded during the *Miracle* sessions in November 1988 (the same week as 'Khashoggi's Ship' and 'Rain Must Fall') and revisited for the *Innuendo* sessions, 'Face It Alone' was name-checked by Greg Brooks at the 2000 Fan Club Convention as a stunning duet between Brian and Freddie on guitar and vocals, respectively, with a drum machine providing the beat. Unfortunately, no recording had leaked out following the convention, and 'Face It Alone' became the most sought-after unreleased recording in Queen's archives. Even more unfortunately, as with most demos and unreleased tracks, when the full version was finally leaked onto the Internet in 2010, expectations for an epic forgotten Queen classic were quickly dashed, when 'Face It Alone' was revealed as nothing more than Freddie "da-dee-dee"ing his way around some mournful guitar noodling.

THE FAIRY FELLER'S MASTER-STROKE *(Mercury)*
• Album: *Queen2* • Live: *Rainbow*

Falling between the manic 'Ogre Battle' and the sublime 'Nevermore' on Side Black of *Queen II*, Freddie's 'The Fairy Feller's Master-Stroke' is an accomplishment in studio trickery and creativity. "It was thoroughly inspired by a painting [of the same name] by Richard Dadd, which is in the Tate Gallery," Freddie explained in a Christmas Eve 1977 BBC Radio One broadcast. "I did a lot of research on it and it inspired me to write a song about the painting, depicting what I thought I saw in it. It was just because I'd come through art college and I basically like the artist and I like the painting, so I thought I'd like to write a song about it."

The song is a delightful excursion into fairies and mythical creatures, bringing to life Dadd's busy painting with poetic superlatives and tongue-tied verbosity. The band are in fine form here, adapting to the quick pace with ease, and adding a refreshing glimmer of lightness to the otherwise dark Side Black. A harpsichord – which, according to Brian, Freddie hadn't bothered to learn properly but fooled around with between takes – is the dominant instrument, only furthering the frivolous mood. With several layers of vocal harmonies and guitar orchestrations, the song is a true joy to listen to, and is a watershed composition in Freddie's advancement as a songwriter. For years it was assumed that, due to its complexity, 'The Fairy Feller's Master-Stroke' was never performed in the live setting, but the September 2014 release of *Live at the Rainbow '74* held a special surprise: a full live performance of the song. That the performance is so tight would suggest that the song featured in set lists on the band's spring 1974 UK tour, though very few tapes exist to confirm or deny that.

THE FALLEN PRIEST *(Mercury/Moran/Rice)*
• Album (Freddie): *Barcelona* • B-side (Freddie): 10/88 [83] • Compilation (Freddie): *Solo Collection*

As on 'The Golden Boy', Freddie and Mike Moran collaborated with Sir Tim Rice on 'The Fallen Priest', and the results are just as impressive. This is one of the more dramatic pieces on *Barcelona*, with Freddie's voice meshing perfectly with Montserrat Caballé's, creating six of the most moving minutes ever to be caught on tape. From a lyrical standpoint, Freddie and Mike are aided superbly by Rice, who adds a loquacious touch to an otherwise straightforward album: the title character proclaims that his "life of sacrifice" controls him, before admitting the inevitability of succumbing to temptations far too "mercurial, more wayward by the hour." Love, passion, and excess overpowers the priest as he ping-pongs between a life of celibacy and theological devotion, and giving into the seduction of the unknown, before God unfurls His wrath upon the priest and his forbidden lover. Heavy stuff indeed.

The arrangement is as impressive as the Greek tragedy, even more impressive that no other outside musicians were used; the music was painstakingly arranged and programmed by Freddie and Mike. With the equivalent of a full orchestra on synthesizers, the lush arrangements of 'The Fallen Priest' are fully appreciated by listening to the instrumental version included on *The Solo Collection*: as impressive as Freddie's and Montserrat's vocal performances are, the music itself is nothing short of a masterpiece.

The song was originally titled 'Rachmaninov's Revenge', which was for many years thought to be a genuine out-take from the *Barcelona* sessions. This working title is appropriate to the musical arrangement, and is a nod to Russian-American composer and pianist Sergei Vasilievich Rachmaninoff, a classical pianist whose style is alluded to in Mike's busy piano work. Two early versions were included on *The Solo Collection*: the first, initially titled 'Spanish Song' and recorded on 26 January 1987, contains a set of lyrics largely improvised by Freddie, with drum-machine programming, that turns it into a more contemporary late 1980s arrangement; fortunately, this was abandoned as the song was developed further. The second version, recorded nearly a month later on 19 February 1987, features a more muted instrumental performance suitable to the released version, though the lyrics still haven't been finalized, with Freddie providing appropriate falsetto vocalizations where he intended Montserrat would feature. Shortly after this basic run-through was recorded, he presented the work-in-progress to Sir Tim Rice, who wrote a set of lyrics; thus, the retitle to the more dramatic and ominous 'The Fallen Priest'.

'The Fallen Priest', a highlight of the *Barcelona* album, was also issued as the B-side of 'The Golden Boy' in October 1988, edited down to nearly half the length of the original. Surprisingly, this unique edit was not included on *The Solo Collection*, despite the copious room on the companion disc 'The Singles 1986-1993'; the edit was finally issued on *Messenger Of The Gods*:

FAT BOTTOMED GIRLS *(May)*
• AA-side: 10/78 [11] • Album: *Jazz* • CD Single: 11/88 • Bonus: *Jazz* • CD Single: 10/91 [16] • Compilation: *Hits1, HitsUS* • B-side: 6/96 [9] • Live: *On Fire* • Live (Q+PR): *Return, Ukraine*

For the first time in Queen's history, the lead-off single from their latest album blatantly tackled an issue that they'd previously avoided: sex. "We lost some of our audience with that," Brian said in 1982. "'How could you do it? It doesn't go with your spiritual side.' But my answer is that the physical side is just as much a part of a person as the spiritual or intellectual side. It's fun. I'll make no apologies. All music skirts around sex, sometimes very directly. Ours doesn't. In our music, sex is either implied or referred to semi-jokingly, but it's always there."

Centered round a memorable chorus with a slight country & western feel to it, 'Fat Bottomed Girls' features a jangly guitar line and some gloriously tubthumping drumming from Roger. It's clear that the band, but Freddie most of all, is having a good time, which Brian confirmed in a 2008 *Mojo* interview: "I wrote it with Fred in mind, as you do especially if you've got a great singer who likes fat bottomed girls ... or boys." The 1991 reissue of *Jazz* features a subtle remix by Brian Malouf, with a different intro and a more muted mix, but concludes with Freddie crying, "They getcha every time – them dirty ladies!", which was flown in from an alternate take.

The song was issued, in edited form, as a double A-sided single with 'Bicycle Race' in October 1978, as a precursor to *Jazz*. It peaked at a respectable No. 11 in the UK, but charted no higher than No. 24 in the US; that it failed to hit the UK Top Ten suggests that the world wasn't quite ready for 'Fat Bottomed Girls'. Regardless of its commercial failure, it still became a live favorite between 1978 and 1982, with a boisterous version appearing on *Queen On Fire: Live At the Bowl*. The song was resurrected in 1998 and was performed by The Brian May Band on his Another World tour, and was again reprised in Brian and Roger's live work with Paul Rodgers and Adam Lambert.

FATHER AND SON (May)

• Soundtrack (Brian): *Furia*

Unrelated to the similiarly-titled track from *Queen II*, 'Father And Son' is a dramatic, orchestral piece from the *Furia* soundtrack with a lovely flute showcase.

FATHER TO SON (May)

• Album: *Queen 2* • Live: *Rainbow*
• Compilation: *On Air*

Bleeding in seamlessly from the introductory instrumental 'Procession', Brian's epic 'Father To Son' kicks off the lyrical aspects of *Queen II* with the relationship between an elder and his offspring, from the perspective of the father handing down his kingdom – both in the literal sense and figuratively, with the passing-on of the family's legacy and honor – which is indirectly related to Brian and his relationship with his own father, Harold. The song moves along quickly through several rhythm changes, recalling Brian's earlier composition 'Son And Daughter', with a variation on that song's riff appearing later in the song. The acoustic conclusion strikes a warm note with a joyous sing-along that leads nicely into 'White Queen (As It Began)'.

"On *Queen II* there is a lot of stuff which I like," Brian said in a 1983 BBC Radio One interview, "because that was the beginning of doing guitar orchestrations, which I always wanted to do. 'Father To Son' starts off with an introduction. After it gets into the song and a few words are sung, it immediately goes into a six-parts orchestral kind of thing. It was really a big thrill for me to be able to do that, because I had never been allowed to spend that amount of time in the studio to construct

those things before then. That was the fulfilment of an ambition for me, to get started on that road of using the guitar as kind of an orchestral instrument."

He continued, saying, "Led Zeppelin and The Who are probably in there somewhere because they were among our favourite groups., but what we are trying to do differently from either of those groups was this sort of layered sound. The Who had the open chord guitar sound, and there's a bit of that in 'Father To Son', but our sound is more based on the over-driven guitar sound, which is used for the main bulk of the song, but I also wanted to build up textures behind the main melody lines."

'Father To Son' received plenty of exposure in the live setting, often performed as the first proper song in the set, following the pre-taped 'Procession' introduction, between 1972 and 1974, then played alongside 'Son And Daughter' later in the show, but was eliminated from the set list by the conclusion of the 1976 A Night At The Opera Japanese tour. Two stellar – and vastly different – versions were released on the excellent *Live At The Rainbow '74* live album in 2014, shedding some much-needed light on the power and majesty of Queen's live act before all the anthemic grandstanding became the norm.

F.B.I. (Marvin/Welch)

• CD single (Brian): 9/98

With Brian providing not only guitars but bass and drum programming, 'F.B.I' is a fairly standard run-through of a single originally released by The Shadows in February 1961. Francis Rossi and Rick Parfitt from Status Quo provide rhythm guitars, but if they hadn't been credited, it would have been impossible to know this. Indeed, as a cover, 'F.B.I' suffers the most from its production, reducing the drums to the loud-sounding noise typical of trick-shot programming that plagued so many otherwise decent songs in the 1980s. Yet 'F.B.I' was recorded in 1995 for inclusion on Brian's *Heroes* project and when that was abandoned, was later released on the CD single of 'Why Don't We Try Again' in September 1998.

FEEL LIKE

This song was what eventually grew into 'Under Pressure' when David Bowie showed up to a Queen recording session at Mountain Studios. A version with Bowie on piano has been leaked to bootleggers, and was played by Greg Brooks at a recent Fan Club convention, and it's not difficult to find the parallels between this song and 'Under Pressure', with its similar piano and guitar melodies; the pace is slower and Freddie's vocals are more reserved, indicating that he was mostly improvising the words. With some polishing and a finalized set of lyrics, 'Feel Like' would have been a worthy addition to *Hot Space*, but ultimately the right decision was made with working on 'Under Pressure' instead.

FEEL LIKE MAKIN' LOVE *(Ralphs/Rodgers)*
• Live (Q+PR): *Return, Ukraine*

From Bad Company's second album, *Straight Shooter*, released in 1975, 'Feel Like Makin' Love' was another big hit for that band, and was a surprising acoustic rocker with a hard-hitting chorus, unlike anything that any of Paul Rodgers' bands had released before. It was the success of this single which helped propel its sister album into the higher strata of the UK and US charts, making it an obvious choice for the set lists of the 2005 version of Queen with Paul Rodgers.

FEEL THE FORCE *(Taylor)*
• US B-side (The Cross): 1/88 • US album (The Cross): *Shove*

In the late 1980s, with the rising popularity of the compact disc, bands and record labels had to compensate by offering incentives for fans to purchase one format instead of another. This meant bonus tracks unavailable elsewhere, and Queen employed this tactic in 1986, with the CD version of *A Kind Of Magic* getting three extra "magical ingredients": two superfluous remixes of the title track and 'Friends Will Be Friends', and a gorgeous piano arrangement of 'Who Wants To Live Forever'. This practice was carried over into The Cross's first album, *Shove It*, with 'Feel The Force', an optimistic anthem chock full of synthesizers and programming, though there is some particularly strong guitar work throughout, courtesy of Roger. The song addresses sensory appreciation, with an additional sixth sense ("the force") with the power to "lift you up" and "make you sing and want to shout." Unlike most of the other tracks on *Shove It*, 'Feel The Force' is over just as it gets going, which is a shame since it's one of the stronger tracks to surface from the sessions for the album.

'Feel The Force' was shoehorned in on *Shove It*

before 'Stand Up For Love', and was released as the B-side to the title track in January 1988. The song was first performed live on 6 November 1987 on the TV programme *Meltdown*, then securing a position on the 1988 Shove It tour. The song earned its first worldwide release in 2013 on Roger's nearly all-encompassing box set, *The Lot*.

FEELINGS

This laborious blues rock song may be an early version of 'Feelings, Feelings', as it features a line that would show up in that song ("Gotta get rid of this feeling"), but the reality is that the band are jamming on a standard blues progression, with Brian delivering a squealing guitar riff while Freddie improvises incomprehensibly. Likely from the same session as 'Feelings, Feelings', 'Feelings' was rightly abandoned in its early stages.

FEELINGS, FEELINGS *(May)*
• Bonus: *NOTW*

After the underwhelming amount of bonus tracks on the first batch of the 2011 Universal reissues, *News Of The World* gets off to the right start with Brian's 'Feelings, Feelings', an out-take from the summer of 1977 sessions and premiered by Greg Brooks at a Fan Club Convention in 2000. What's especially wonderful about this is that the now officially-released version is Take 10, whereas what Brooks played to fans was Take 9. There isn't much difference in the two takes, except that the band sounds a little more confident in their playing; either pass wouldn't have been out of place on the album itself, though it also would have been an ideal non-album B-side.

F.E.W.A. *(Bulsara)*

With the full title being 'Feelings Ended, Worn Away' (the abbreviation a nod to Cream's 'Swlabr', short for 'She Walks Like A Bearded Rainbow'), 'F.E.W.A' was written by Freddie and performed by Wreckage on 31 October 1969 at Ealing College Of Art, with further (unconfirmed) performances throughout the rest of their brief career.

A FIDDLY JAM: see HANG ON IN THERE

FIGHT CLUB *(Taylor)*
• Album (Roger): *Earth*

Opening with a full minute of delicate acoustic guitar picking and saxophone from Steve Hamilton, 'Fight Club' is more representative of the down-to-earth, laid-back feel of *Fun On Earth*. The minimalist, almost simplistic lyrics belie the sinister truth of life: you're born, you grow up to work, and then you die. Roger sounds weary and resigned, sighing the words over an atmospheric bed of guitar feedback, before the song comes to an inconclusive end.

FIGHT FROM THE INSIDE *(Taylor)*
• Album: *NOTW* • Bonus: *NOTW*

With a chunky bass riff and layers of distorted rhythm guitars, Roger's 'Fight From The Inside' is an unexpected highlight nestled between John's 'Spread Your Wings' and Freddie's proto-funk 'Get Down, Make Love'. Addressing the unexpected rise of the punks, the song is also a thinly veiled attack on the press, which, by this time, was also receiving an influx of younger journalists intent on damning everything put out by so-called dinosaur rock acts. Like 'Sheer Heart Attack', Roger plays all the instruments himself, except for a few rhythm guitar parts by Brian, suggesting it may have originally been intended for his solo project that begat 'I Wanna Testify' and 'Turn On The TV'. An earlier version features alternate lyrics from Roger that weren't quite yet finalized, though the basic track seems to have already been in place by the time it was recorded. This version was released on the 40th anniversary edition of *News Of The World*.

FINAL DESTINATION *(Taylor)*
• Album (The Cross): *MBADTK* • German/French single (The Cross): 11/90 • Live (The Cross): *Bootleg*
• CD single (Roger): 9/94 [26]

If there's any one song that successfully displays Roger's progression as a songwriter and arranger, 'Final Destination' is it: starting slowly and quietly and gradually building in intensity, the song is a poignant and touching love song from Roger to his girlfriend Debbie Leng, with the drummer so enraptured that he feels "that I could ski right off the bridge of your pretty nose." Okay, so it may not be perfect, lyrically-speaking, but from a musical standpoint it's an accomplishment, and didn't deserve to be thrown away on The Cross's

sophomore album, where it languished unknown except for by the most die-hard of Roger Taylor fans.

Chosen as the third single from the album with 'Penetration Guru' on the flipside, but released only in Germany and Europe, 'Final Destination' failed to chart and, due to record label indifference, was deprived of a promotional video. It was a regular on The Cross' 1990 Mad: Bad: And Dangerous To Know tour, with a version from the 7 December 1990 Christmas Fan Club show at the Astoria Theatre in London released on the 1991 fan club-only release, *The Official Bootleg*.

Deservedly, the song was re-recorded during sessions for *Happiness?* in 1993, at One on One Studios in Los Angeles with Japanese star Yoshiki (see the 'Foreign Sand' entry for more information). Extending well beyond five minutes, the song is completely restructured (with the line "I would feel that I could ski right off the bridge of your pretty nose" replaced by "You would renovate my soul") and given a punchier arrangement by Yoshiki. The musicianship is stronger than The Cross' version, thanks in no small part to Yoshiki's masterful drumming and keyboard work. The re-recording was issued on the CD single of 'Foreign Sand' in September 1994 and as a Japanese-only bonus track on the *Happiness?* CD.

FIRE *(May)*
• Soundtrack (Brian): *Furia*

Not lasting even a minute, 'Fire' is a dark keyboard piece with appropriate accents from the orchestra, all climaxing quickly in a sudden finale.

FIRE AND WATER *(Fraser/Rodgers)*
• B-side (Q+PR): 9/08 [33]

The title track of Free's third album, 'Fire And Water' became an instant radio classic upon its release in 1970, overshadowed only (unfairly) by 'All Right Now'. The 2005 touring band of Queen with Paul Rodgers introduced the song into their set list on their penultimate night in Belfast on 13 May 2005. A live recording, from 27 October 2005 in Tokyo, was released as the B-side of 'C-Lebrity' three years later.

THE FIRE WITHIN *(May/Kamen)*

Written and arranged by Brian and composer Michael Kamen, 'The Fire Within' was Brian's chance to finally get a song performed for the Olympic Games. Lasting nearly nine minutes, the song was performed live at the opening ceremonies in Salt Lake City, Utah, on 8 February 2002, and was conducted by Kamen. Brian's guitar solo was prerecorded since he was unable to attend.

FIRST GLANCE (SOLO FLUTE) *(May)*
• Soundtrack (Brian): *Furia*

'First Glance' is the main theme of *Furia* performed on flute by Phillip Davies; though the preferable option would have been to keep the piece unadorned by keyboard drones, it still adds to the overall sombreness of the piece.

FIRST KISS *(May)*
• Soundtrack (Brian): *Furia*

A two-minute romantic interlude, 'First Glance' features prominent contributions from The London Musician's Orchestra conducted by Michael Reed, and apart from a few scattered keyboard drones, they are really the stars of this fine piece of music.

FLASH TO THE RESCUE *(May)*
• Album: *Flash*

Coming after Roger's 'Escape From The Swamp' on *Flash Gordon*, 'Flash To The Rescue' is a variation on the main theme comprised mostly of dialog with a repetitive piano riff chugging away in the background.

FLASH'S THEME *(May)*
• Album: *Flash* • A-side: 11/80 [10] • Compilation: *Hits1, HitsUS* • CD Single: 11/88 • Bonus: *Flash* • Live: *On Fire, Montreal* • A-side: 3/03 [15]

The main theme from the *Flash Gordon* album is this enjoyable piece of fluff, typically bombastic and over-the-top, as is Queen's wont. However, had *Flash Gordon* director Dino deLaurentiis had his way, the song very well may have never surfaced: "Mike Hodges really made it into a cult film by being very self-consciously kitsch, whereas Dino regarded it as an epic and not to be messed with," Brian recalled in 2001. "I'll never forget: [Dino] came to the studio, sat down and listened to our first demos and said, 'I think it's quite good, but the theme will not work in my movie. It is not right.' And Mike walked over and said, 'A chat with you, Dino. You don't understand where this film is going to be pitched...' But I had a

really nasty moment there: 'Oh no, he hates my 'Flash' ... aaaahhh-aaaaaahhh, and it's going to go on the cutting room floor.'"

Released as the only single from the album in November 1980, the song was edited down to under three minutes and retitled 'Flash', excising most of the album dialog except for just enough to sum up a two-hour movie in two minutes; the single reached No. 10 in the UK and No. 23 in the US. A video was filmed by Mike Hodges while the band were working on the song at Anvil Studios, showing them recording to film: specific scenes are projected onto a screen above the band, the method actual orchestras would use when recording music for a movie.

'Flash's Theme' was performed live as part of a *Flash Gordon* medley between late 1980 and 1981, but was dropped just after the *We Will Rock You* video shoot in November 1981. A live version, from the November 1981 concerts, was released on both *Queen Rock Montreal* and the 2011 reissue of *Flash Gordon*. The studio version was later used as the introduction for the 1982 Hot Space World tour, but was not played as a song in its own right. A remix by disc jockey Mista Lange was included on the 1991 remaster of *Flash Gordon*, extending the song to nearly seven painful minutes. Avoid at all costs.

FLASH'S THEME REPRISE (VICTORY CELEBRATIONS) *(May)*
• Album: *Flash*

The title says it all: coming at the end of the album, 'Flash's Theme Reprise (Victory Celebrations)' is made up mostly of movie dialog among Flash, Aura and Hans Zarkov. The song concludes in a gloriously over-the-top crescendo, with a final, echoed cry of "Flash!" and an orchestral outro before leading effortlessly into 'The Hero'.

FLICK OF THE WRIST *(Mercury)*
• AA-side: 10/74 [2] • Album: *SHA* • CD Single: 11/88 • Bonus: *SHA* • Live: *Rainbow* • Compilation: *On Air*

By late 1974 Queen were a hot live ticket, with respectable album and singles sales, yet they hadn't received the financial benefits they felt they were due. Freddie poured his frustrations into this acidic track which takes the stance of an unscrupulous manager manipulating a naïve entertainer with doublespeak and legal forms. The song spews venom from each line hissed by Freddie, and is an even more heated composition than 'Death On Two Legs (Dedicated to......', which expressed similar sentiments toward Queen's management.

The second song of the *Sheer Heart Attack* medley, 'Flick Of The Wrist' blends in effortlessly from Roger's 'Tenement Funster' and features a fine ensemble performance, complete with a tortured guitar solo and some breathless drumming from Roger. Somewhat bewilderingly chosen as the counterpart to 'Killer Queen', 'Flick Of The Wrist' became a double A-sided release with that single, issued in October 1974 and peaking at No. 2 in the UK and No. 12 in the US. Understandably, due to its quirky pop sensibilities, 'Killer Queen' received the most attention, and its counterpart fell into obscurity, eluding inclusion on any of the *Greatest Hits* packages, despite a special, single-only stand-alone edit (finally released in 2008 on *The Singles Collection – Volume 1*) and never receiving a promotional video.

'Flick Of The Wrist' was performed live between 1974 and 1976, with an electrifying version appearing on *Live At The Rainbow '74*. A remixed version of the album version, with a new lead vocal and guitar solo, was presented on the band's fourth BBC session on 16 October 1974, and subsequently released on the 2011 reissue of *Sheer Heart Attack* and again five years later on *On Air*.

FOOLIN' AROUND *(Mercury)*
• Soundtrack (Freddie): *Teachers* • Album (Freddie): *BadGuy* • Compilations (Freddie): *Pretender*, *FM Album*, *Solo Collection*

With a dominant, triumphant synthesizer motif, 'Foolin' Around' is another fine track from *Mr Bad Guy*, and neatly blends dance with rock – exactly what *Hot Space* should have sounded like. With the pulsating bass beat of Stephan Wissnet and random stabs of guitar from Paul Vincent, the song is otherwise bathed in synthesizers and drum programming, yet still sounds fresh and vital beyond its 1985 release date. As on 'I Want To Break Free', Fred Mandel provided a suitable synthesizer solo, with accompaniment from Vincent on Brian May-sounding guitar orchestrations, which later drew ire from Queen's guitarist, who questioned the point in hiring a soundalike when a quality song could have become a Queen song.

Interestingly, the song was proposed to be a single, with a 12" extended version prepared; while it did

feature in the 1984 Nick Nolte film *Teachers* (an earlier version appeared on the soundtrack album, with only subtle differences), the idea for single release was scrapped along the way. An instrumental mix was also prepared, and both of these versions were later released on *The Solo Collection*, but the most interesting find from the archives was an earlier version, recorded on 31 May 1984 at Musicland Studios. While some lines were later altered, it featured a completely new introductory verse as well as real drums (a drum-machine appears only on the album version), and is certainly essential listening. More mundanely, the song was remixed in 1992 by Steve Brown, with arrangements and instrumentation by Andrew Flashman and Andrew King. This version appeared on *The Great Pretender* in the US and *The Freddie Mercury Album* in the UK, and makes the song even more danceable than in its original incarnation.

FOOTBALL FIGHT *(Mercury)*
• Album: *Flash* • B-side: 11/80 [10] • Bonus: *Flash*

An energetic performance from the band, Freddie's 'Football Fight' is one of the few pieces from the *Flash Gordon* album featuring an ensemble performance. The song was included in the film in a humorous match between Ming's henchmen and Flash, throwing around a metallic football, the song is every bit as camp as the sequence it accompanies. An early take from February 1980 (titled 'Freddie's Theme No. 2' on the 24-track tape sheet) was released on the 2011 reissue of *Flash Gordon*, and is unique in that instead of synthesizer, the song is played on piano. Freddie can be heard guiding the band through the song, and while it wasn't intended as a finished recording, its roughness is charming and an interesting alternate to the polished, finished version.

FOREIGN SAND *(Taylor/Yoshiki)*
• Album (Roger): *Happiness?* • A-side (Roger): 9/94 [26]

Just to show that Freddie and Brian weren't the only ones who could produce mini-masterpieces, Roger outdid himself with 'Foreign Sand', clocking in just under seven minutes while trying to redefine the term 'magnum opus'. This also marked one of the more successful collaborations that Roger would undertake over the course of his vast solo career, this time recording with Japanese musician Yoshiki. Born Yoshiki Hayashi on 20 November 1965, he started playing piano at the age of four but later switched to the drums after his father bought him a set; it was this very instrument on which he released his anger and pain when his father committed suicide in 1975. In high school, he and some of his friends formed the band X, which later enjoyed success in the late 1980s with the singles 'Orgasm' and 'I'll Kill You'. "I was contacted by a man called Yoshiki," Roger explained in 1994. "We met, and we got on very well and we decided that we would do an 'east/west' collaboration. In the end, he wrote simply the music – this guy's an amazing concert pianist – and also an incredibly able rock drummer. So he sent me the music and I thought the music was great, and we talked about that a little bit, then we changed it a little, and I sent him some lyrics and the top nine back." Yoshiki explained, "When I was in London, Roger invited me to his house and we were talking about racial problems, discrimination, segregation ... I just told Roger, 'Can we do something about that?' and we decided to make some songs for singing about segregation."

With Yoshiki performing drums, piano, synthesizer and arrangements, Jim Cregan on guitars, Phil Chen (who had previously worked with Brian in 1983 on *Star Fleet Project*) on bass, Dick Marx on strings arrangement, and Brad Buxer and Geoff Grace on programming, the instrumental arrangement is a triumph: with tremendous degrees of light and shade, building up to glorious crescendoes and falling silent to barely perceptible whispers of piano. But an epic ballad is only as good as its words, and, tackling the futility and pointlessness of racial inequality, the song urges the world to be more accepting and loving of each other. In the post-Live Aid musical climate, and at a time when grunge rock was seen as the antithesis of pacifism and harmony, the message of 'Foreign Sand' is naïve yet simple, and, given the subject matter of 'Nazis 1994', a much-needed message.

The song was issued as the second single from *Happiness?* in September 1994, with 'You Had To Be There' as the B-side (12" and CD versions added the re-recording of 'Final Destination' with Yoshiki). Understandably, the song's running time was an issue, though Roger was willing to make a concession and edit the track to a more managable four and a half minutes, dropping and creating new musical sections. While the result isn't quite as dramatic, it's more digestible, and reached a well-earned No. 26 in the UK charts, becoming Roger's final Top 30 single as a solo artist. Because of Roger's involvement with Yoshiki, the

song was a hit in Japan, peaking at No. 13, with its success a catalyst for Roger's first solo dates there.

A video for the single, also featuring Yoshiki, was filmed in July 1994 in Los Angeles, but has rarely been seen outside of promotional viewings and an electronic press kit. Directed by Jeff Richter, the video portrays Roger standing with hands folded on a beach, as images of gruesome race riots and IRA car bombings pass by behind him, superimposed on screens within picture frames, with grand, sweeping shots Yoshiki either behind a drum set or looking like a mad professor at a concert piano at sunset.

FOREVER *(May)*
• 12" B-side: 9/86 [24] • Bonus: *AKOM*

Though no match for the superior 'Who Wants To Live Forever', Brian's melancholy 'Forever' is a gorgeous, instrumental piano version of the aforementioned epic. Performed exclusively by Brian, it shows his proficiency on piano, an instrument that, by 1986, was only rarely used for composition by the band. Included on the 12" issue of 'Who Wants To Live Forever' in September 1986, the song was also included as a bonus cut on the CD version of *A Kind Of Magic*.

46664 (THE CALL) *(Queen)*
• Live: *46664*

Credited to Queen but written by Brian, '46664 (The Call)' was submitted for Nelson Mandela's 46664 campaign, and recorded during the March 2003 Cape Town sessions. Imploring listeners to "make the call" to support AIDS research and charities, the message of the song is heartfelt and well-intentioned but is lost in approach: the arrangement is abrasive and confrontational, but in all the wrong ways, with Brian's voice, normally well-suited for ballads, completely at odds with its heavy arrangement. It's hard to fault Brian for this song and his message, but '46664 (The Call)' is plain dire, and the nadir of the Cape Town sessions. The song was premiered on Capitol Radio in 2003, but, as with the rest of the original recordings from those sessions, rightly remains unreleased. In 2007, in anticipation of Queen + Paul Rodgers' first studio album, a fan wrote to Brian's website and asked him of the fate of '46664 (The Call)', and if it would be on the new album; Brian responded that it would be something for him to consider, but, thankfully, the only 46664 song on *The Cosmos Rocks* was a rearranged

'Say It's Not True'.

FOXY LADY *(Hendrix)*

• CD (The Cross): *MBADTK* • Live (The Cross): *Bootleg*

A perfunctory run-through of Jimi Hendrix's 1967 classic, The Cross' version of 'Foxy Lady' hardly improves on the original, adding very little except for appropriate Hendrix-inspired guitar solos by Clayton Moss. The song was included only on CD versions of the album, as well as on a rare UK promo CD, but would have been fine as a non-album B-side if it meant including far superior original material like 'In Charge Of My Heart'.

Not surprisingly, given its live-sound approach, 'Foxy Lady' was included in the set lists around this time, with a live version cropping up on the 1991 fan club-only release *The Official Bootleg*, recorded on 7 December 1990 at the Astoria Theatre. Roger would later revive the song for his 1994 Happiness? tour. Nearly 30 years previously, Brian's band 1984 had played the song shortly before they dissolved.

FREEDOM TRAIN *(Taylor)*

• Album (Roger): *Happiness?*

Backed by a pulsating drum beat, deliberately designed to resemble the chugging of a train, Roger's terse 'Freedom Train' is an obvious highlight of the *Happiness?* album. Assisted by Jason Falloon on guitars and Mike Crossley on keyboards (Roger plays all the other instruments), the lyrics are delivered in a barely audible whisper as Roger sings of "troubled lands" and a "golden thread of circumstance", his voice raised only for the chorus. Coming after the lyrically heavy 'Foreign Sand', 'Freedom Train' follows in a similar vein, with the pleas of racial harmony on the previous track being attacked more viciously. Concluding dramatically with with some impressive snare drum work, 'Freedom Train' is truly a magnificent composition.

Interestingly, the song was attempted by Queen either during the *Innuendo* sessions or shortly following those sessions for what would be released as *Made In Heaven*. Unfortunately, little else is known about Queen's version except that Greg Brooks name-checked the song at the 2003 Fan Club Convention. If it indeed exists, it would undoubtedly be a gem and well worth the price of the anthologies no matter what form, embryonic or complete, it takes.

FRIENDS IN PAIN

Nothing is known of this unreleased track from the *A Kind Of Magic* sessions, except that it may be a John Deacon demo of either 'Friends Will Be Friends' or, less likely, 'Pain Is So Close To Pleasure' (or even a completely new song altogether).

FRIENDS WILL BE FRIENDS *(Mercury/Deacon)*

• Album: *AKOM* • A-side: 6/86 [14] • Live: *Magic, Wembley, Budapest*

Starting with a soaring guitar riff and melting into a poignant set of lyrics about friendship in tough times, this collaborative effort between John and Freddie produced an unforgettable anthem much in the style of 'We Are The Champions'. According to Peter 'Phoebe' Freestone, 'Friends Will Be Friends' was actually written by John but, with considerable input from Freddie, was co-credited as a Mercury/Deacon collaboration because of John's generous demeanour and the vocalist's final contribution – much like Roger's 'Radio Ga Ga' and 'A Kind Of Magic', both of which were changed drastically from their original visions.

"Freddie's written a song called 'Friends Will be Friends', and I think Freddie and John worked on it together," Brian said in a 1986 Capitol Radio interview. "It's something which I took to heart very much as well because it's kind of [a] traditional Queen sound. It has this ... if you can remember 'We Are The Champions' or 'Play The Game', it's in that kind of mould, it has all the Queen trademarks. And yet it's a new song and a new idea, and that's something I instantly related to. Very nice, very good track. It sounds very complete."

Released as the second single proper from *A Kind Of Magic*, 'Friends Will Be Friends', backed with 'Seven Seas Of Rhye' because of its upcoming inclusion in the Magic tour set list, peaked at a modest No. 14 in June 1986. The song was extended for the 12" release, opening with the chorus instead of the guitar introduction and lengthening the song well past six minutes. According to Roger, it wasn't the summer hit the band had hoped it would be, but the video, filmed on 15 May 1986 at JVC Studios in Wembley (during rehearsals for the Magic tour) and directed by David Mallet, is pleasant enough, showing the band on stage with legions of fan club members as an assembled audience. While it's clear from the expressions on the band members' faces that they're all having a good time, as a video, it's perfunctory, with the intent of getting something out there while the band is working on perfecting their live show.

The song was performed live between 'We Will Rock You' and 'We Are The Champions' on the Magic tour (though it wasn't performed on the first show in Stockholm), albeit in an abridged version; only on the first two dates in Leiden did the band perform full versions.

FRIENDS WILL BE FRIENDS WILL BE FRIENDS
(Mercury/Deacon)
• Bonus: AKOM

A pointless edit of the extended mix of 'Friends Will Be Friends', this was included on the European CD version of *A Kind Of Magic*; any fan would be well advised to stick to the original or the extended versions.

FUN IN SPACE *(Taylor)*
• Album (Roger): *Fun* • B-side (Roger): 6/81

A sparse and fitting conclusion to Roger's debut solo album, 'Fun In Space' is dominated by a relentless bass drum, representing the blips on a radar indicating signs of life, while a synthesizer swirls away (occasionally interrupted by drum beats and some twangy guitar licks) and Roger's disembodied, echoed voice unfolds what is, on the surface, a lament of a failed space mission, but is actually a celebratory tale ("Our structure is battered, but the corridors ring / With little green stories, of this and these things") and a plea for spacial jollification.

A rough mix of the song was premiered during a spring 1980 'Innerview' with Jim Ladd; even at that early stage, Roger had already decided that the album was to be titled *Fun In Space*. Clocking in at a lengthy 6'20, making it the second-longest track on the album, it ended up as the B-side of 'My Country' (the other epic from *Fun In Space*, though it was edited down for radio consumption; 'Fun In Space' remained unscathed as the single's flipside), but, like most of *Fun In Space*, received no live airing in any of Roger's solo tours.

FUN IT *(Taylor)*
• Album: *Jazz*

Forget 'Another One Bites The Dust' and *Hot Space*: 'Fun It' started Queen's fascination with funk and disco. Whether or not that's a good thing depends on your preference, but 'Fun It' is a brave if flawed

song, complete with a funky groove, a fat bass, and crunching rhythm guitars, while Freddie and Roger convey the simple message: when life's problems get you down, just dance them away. (If only it were that easy.) For once, Roger was unimpressed, telling *Mojo* magazine in 2008, "My songs were very patchy. In fact, if you want my honest opinion, *Jazz* never thrilled me. It was an ambitious album that didn't live up to its ambition."

Issued as the B-side of the US release of 'Jealousy' in April 1979, the "Don't shun it / Fun it" line would occasionally be used as an intro to 'Keep Yourself Alive' on several of the 1978 *Jazz* North American and 1979 *Jazz* European and Japanese dates.

FUN VISION: *see* ONE VISION

FUNNY HOW LOVE IS *(Mercury)*
• Album: *Queen2* • CD Single: 11/88

Serving as a light, refreshing dessert to the heavier main course of 'The March Of The Black Queen' (a tactic Freddie explored frequently, for example 'Lazing On A Sunday Afternoon' following 'Death On Two Legs (Dedicated to......)', 'Funny How Love Is' is a gleeful paean to free love striking in unexpected places and at unexpected times. Set to a bed of acoustic guitars played by Brian (not John, as previously believed; live group backing tracks were played at Fan Club conventions, with John on bass and Brian on acoustic guitar) and ringing percussion and drums from Roger, a youthful-sounding and double-tracked Freddie strains in the higher regions of his range, exuberantly extolling the virtues of love. It may have been a filler track compared to the other songs on Side Black, but it was at least a *good* filler track.

When sessions for the second album started in August 1973, a few of Freddie's newest songs needed Robin Geoffrey Cable's Phil Spector-inspired 'wall of sound' technique, and he was asked to assist with that approach. Cable had asked Freddie to contribute lead vocals to his reworkings of 'I Can Hear Music' and 'Goin' Back' (see separate entries); this time, it was Freddie who asked Cable to help him out by adding his distinctive touch to this song, 'Nevermore' and 'The March Of The Black Queen'.

Because of its complexity and dependence on atmosphere, 'Funny How Love Is' was never performed live. It was inexplicably included on the 1988 CD single version of 'Seven Seas Of Rhye' in a true stand-alone fashion: whereas the album version segues from 'The March Of The Black Queen', this version features a clean intro with strident acoustic guitar and piano chords.

FURIA THEME (OPENING TITLES) (May)
• Soundtrack (Brian): *Furia*

The first track on the soundtrack album to the French film *Furia*, 'Furia Theme' starts with a scrap of dialog before an ominous keyboard and orchestra sequence leads into the beautifully performed main theme. The Red Special makes a welcome appearance midway through the song, though the programmed drums and upbeat sequence are awkwardly out of place. Regardless, it's a fine overture, and serves as a fitting introduction to the little-seen film.

FUTURE MANAGEMENT (Taylor)
• A-side (Roger): 3/81 [49] • Album (Roger): *Fun*

A conspicuously jaunty reggae track sounding like a selection from the albums by new wave rockers The Police, Roger's ambiguous 'Future Management' alludes to an Orwellian future ("Recycle your thoughts / I'll rewire your mind") with offers of mind control and thought reprogramming. Conformity was an issue that Roger disliked, even going as far as protesting the working title of *Play The Game* for their eighth studio album, insisting it be abridged so as not to promote following convention. 'Future Management' addresses this in a mechanical manner, the lobotomized chant of "You won't need nobody else but me" as the song fades out chilling and spooky.

Released as the lead-off single from *Fun In Space*, 'Future Management' peaked at a disappointing No. 49 in the UK, but did mark Roger's first appearance on *Top Of The Pops* which featured him playing a guitar next to a soft sculpture of the alien from the album sleeve. Reviews for the single were mixed; *Sounds* said, "It's a reggaeish song which is bearable enough. A laudable attempt to step out of the shadow of the tooty one," while *NME* panned it: "Roger does a [Todd] Rundgren and plays everything apart from Scrabble. A plodding *regatta de blanc* that drags rather than just lays back."

THE GAME OF LOVE (Ballard)

Originally performed by Wayne Fontana and the Mindbenders, 'The Game Of Love' was played live by The Reaction.

GAZELLE (Mercury)
• Compilation (Freddie): *Solo Collection*

A short and strange drum-machine experimentation, featuring multi-tracked Freddies engaging in nonsensical vocalizations and repeated cries of the title. 'Gazelle' was recorded on 19 April 1984 at Musicland Studios, and was never a serious contender for inclusion on *Mr Bad Guy*, it was ultimately issued on *The Solo Collection*.

GET DOWN, MAKE LOVE (Mercury)
• Album: *NOTW* • Live: *Killers, On Fire, Montreal*
• Bonus: *NOTW*

By 1977, Freddie had become a self-proclaimed sex addict. Gone were the days of the vocalist timidly singing of faeries, ogres and other mythical creatures: this was a changed man, revelling in his leather phase. As he once said, "I quite like leather. I fancy myself as a black panther." However, he became more promiscuous in his sex life, as his 1977 proto-funk composition, 'Get Down, Make Love', celebrates. Set to a sleazy bass backing, Freddie moans and groans his way through the suggestive lyrics, crying "You say you're hungry / I give you meat!" and "I suck your mind / You blow my head" with unrestrained glee. Freddie's sexuality by this time was still a closely-guarded secret, though he was frank in interviews and all but confirmed his leanings with deliberately coy one-liners as "I'm as gay as a daffodil, darling!" It just didn't seem to matter much at the time, considering his early involvement in the blossoming glam-rock scene, where sexual ambiguity wasn't just promoted but embraced freely. Freddie simply evolved, and channeled his championing of carnal desires into song.

The middle portion of the song draws heavily from Led Zeppelin's 1969 classic 'Whole Lotta Love': whereas Robert Plant dueled against Jimmy Page's theremin on that recording, here Freddie squeals while Brian feeds The Red Special through a harmonizer. "I've used [that] really as a noise more than a musical thing," Brian explained in a 1983 BBC Radio One interview. "It's controllable because I had a special little pedal made for it, which means I can change the interval at which the harmonizer comes back, and it's fed back on itself so it makes all swooping noises. It's just an exercise in using that together with noises from Freddie – a sort of erotic interlude."

An early version finds the band recording an

attempt at a usable backing track, though they seem to lose their way quite a bit; the arrangement hasn't yet been finalized, and Brian and Roger especially are overbusy in their approach. Instead of the "erotic interlude", the band jam for a bit, and while this is a nice alternative to the familiar version, it tends to drag a bit. This was later released on the 40th anniversary edition of *News Of The World*.

Industrial band Nine Inch Nails recorded a deconstructed version of the song for their 1989 album, *Sin*, bringing the song to a much wider audience. Much like Nirvana's acoustic reading of David Bowie's 'The Man Who Sold The World', Nine Inch Nails' rendition has gained accolades and is considered a triumph by Trent Reznor and company. It was this recording that was brought to Queen Productions' attention, who asked him to remix 'Tie Your Mother Down', 'Stone Cold Crazy', and 'Spread Your Wings' for their respective reissues, although the third title remains unreleased.

Queen included the song in the set list between 1977 and 1982, allowing Freddie the opportunity to get lost within a blanket of darkness, dry ice, and flickering lights. Live versions can be found on *Live Killers* and *Queen On Fire: Live At The Bowl*, though something is definitely lost in translation without the assistance of the stunning visuals.

GIMME SOME LOVIN' *(Winwood/Winwood/Davis)*
• Live: *Wembley*

Queen performed a cover version of the 1965 Spencer Davis Group hit single a few times throughout the Magic tour in 1986, and the version released on *Live At Wembley Stadium* is a loose interpretation at best. That Freddie sings the wrong words is a further indication of the spontaneity.

GIMME THE PRIZE (KURGAN'S THEME) *(May)*
• Album: *AKOM* • CD Single: 1/98 [13]

The 1980s had been a difficult period, musically, for Brian: lost in a fog of funk and pop, the band members of Queen were pulling in different directions, and the guitarist was often on the losing end. He tried his best to keep the rock alive, but his songs were often passed over in favor of the chart-friendly ones, such as 'Another One Bites The Dust', 'I Want To Break Free', 'Radio Ga Ga', 'A Kind Of Magic'. 'Gimme The Prize (Kurgan's Theme)' channels the guitarist's frustrations into four minutes of neo-metal, showcasing The

Red Special more than it does Freddie. Structurally reminiscent of 'Brighton Rock' (which focuses more on instrumental prowess than its lyrical construction), the song is subtitled 'Kurgan's Theme', the villain from the *Highlander* movie, but the words aren't reliant to the plot, instead boasting of wartime pigheadedness and braggadocio: "Give me your kings, let me squeeze then in my hands / Your puny princes, your so called leaders of your land / I'll eat them whole before I'm done / The battle's fought and the game is won". The guitar solo is heavily inspired by the Scottish theme of the film, with Brian likening his sound to that of bagpipes.

Because of John's and Freddie's dislike for the track, which Brian revealed shortly after the album's release, 'Gimme The Prize (Kurgan's Theme)' wasn't a contender for inclusion on the Magic tour set list, despite its built-in guitar extravaganza. (The "bagpipe" guitar motif was interspersed into Brian's solo live performances of 'Fat Bottomed Girls', during the extended coda.) Due to its similarities with the stronger 'Princes Of The Universe', it was overlooked, too, as a single track, but was issued as the B-side to the US 'A Kind Of Magic' in June 1986. The track was remixed for the 1998 computer game *Queen: The eYe*, in which it was presented as a completely instrumental remix without dialog. This version was issued on the CD single of 'No-One But You (Only The Good Die Young)' in January 1998.

GIRL FROM IPANEMA:
see **EXTRACTS FROM GARDEN LODGE**

GO ON *(May)*
• Soundtrack (Brian): *Furia*

This coda to the *Furia* soundtrack features Emily May on vocalizations (as on 'Apparition') before the schmaltzy introduction of the orchestra with yet another variation on the main theme.

GOD (THE DREAM IS OVER) *(Lennon)*

During the first leg of Brian's Back To The Light European and UK tour in 1993, he introduced an updated rendition of John Lennon's 1970 solo track, 'God (The Dream Is Over)'. In its original form, the song is a powerful ode to the breakup of The Beatles, but in Brian's hands, it takes on a more poignant meaning for he changed the words to explain his emotional status at the time, both lambasting and proclaiming all that he believes – and doesn't believe – in. Tellingly, he concludes with "I don't believe in being Queen any more / I just believe in me." Following Freddie's death, he was attempting to escape the pall of Queen, and for those who still believed a reunion could happen, those dreams were categorically dashed by this song. At the time, he meant every word, though the story was different as the decade wore on.

Unfortunately, he wasn't able to acquire copyright permission from Yoko Ono, who objected to the altered lyrics, and the song remained unreleased, though it was originally intended to be on *Live At The Brixton Academy*, just before 'Hammer To Fall'.

GOD IS HEAVY *(Mercury)*
• Compilation (Freddie): *Solo Collection*

This curious composition was recorded in January 1984 during the *Mr Bad Guy* sessions and features minimal piano and drum-machine accompaniment as Freddie, apparently suffering from a bad cold, sings the equally slight lyrics.

GOD SAVE THE QUEEN *(trad. arr. May)*
• Album: *Opera* • Live: *Killers, Magic, Wembley, On Fire, Montreal, Budapest, Rainbow, Odeon* • Live (Q+PR): *Return, Ukraine* • Compilation: *On Air*

During the band's 1974 tour in support of *Queen II*, audiences would sing the national anthem while waiting for the band to take the stage. Brian was summarily inspired by this outpouring of support (or pre-showtime impatience) to record his own unique version, and, with the autumn 1974 Sheer Heart Attack tour looming, he booked time at Trident Studios on 27 October, laying down a charming if ham-fisted piano demo, rife with bum notes and missed chords. Using this as a guide, he overdubbed layers upon layers of guitar before drafting Roger to add snare drum, orchestral cymbals, and timpani. This then became the pre-recorded closing number to every show between October 1974 and August 1986, except for a few occasions in Dublin where it wasn't considered appropriate. Perhaps the most instantly recognizable Queen-related image – apart from Freddie strolling out on stage during the Magic tour in full glory, sporting a regal red crown and cape – was Brian's performance of the track in June 2002 at Party At The Palace, which kicked off the events with the guitarist playing the anthem on the roof of Buckingham Palace.

'God Save The Queen' was first issued as the double B-side of the July 1975 'Keep Yourself Alive' re-release, appearing only in North America, and with the drum introduction at full volume. When it was released four months later as the closing track on *A Night At The Opera*, the drums were reduced to a fade-in, but the recording is otherwise identical.

GOIN' BACK *(Goffin/King)*
• B-side (Larry Lurex): 6/73 • Compilation (Freddie): *Solo Collection*

'I Can Hear Music' was the more commercial track recorded during the summer 1972 sessions at Trident Studios, but 'Goin' Back' was the undisputed highlight, and its delegation as the B-side to 'I Can Hear Music' is a shame. Freddie turns in one of his finest vocal performances ever, and nowhere on *Queen* does he ever sound this young. The debut album had a dearth of ballads, and even the slower numbers like 'Doing All Right' and 'The Night Comes Down' were decidedly upbeat. 'Goin' Back' is a true ballad, and Freddie is the star of the show here. Indeed, he's the *only* star since Brian and Roger don't feature anywhere on this track; all the instrumentation is performed by unknown session musicians. A snippet of the song was later poignantly included in the outro of 'Mother Love', which turned out to be Freddie's final vocal performance, perfectly juxtaposed with this, one of the first songs he ever recorded.

THE GOLDEN BOY *(Mercury/Moran/Rice)*
• Album (Freddie): *Barcelona* • A-side (Freddie): 10/88 [83] • B-side (Freddie): 10/92 • Compilation (Freddie): *Solo Collection*

Inarguably not only one of the best tracks from *Barcelona* but also one of the best songs Freddie ever wrote, 'The Golden Boy' is an epic typical of Freddie's ambitious operatic style. Much like 'The Fallen Priest', which tells a similar dramatic Greek tragedy of love and temptation, 'The Golden Boy' is a classic story, again penned by Sir Tim Rice: outspoken and creative boy (yang) falls for quiet and reserved girl (yin), their passions intertwining until his ego inflates beyond redemption ("He started to believe that he was all they said and more"), and she, fuelled by the beauty of his art, falls heavily for him, only to be rejected outright by his rise to prominence. Ending in heartbreak, the poignant coda finds the inconsolable girl pining for her "hardened heart of yesterday", ruefully noting that "by changing for the better she had changed things for the worse".

Chosen as the second single from the album, 'The Golden Boy', backed with 'The Fallen Priest', was too much for the singles market and stalled at No. 83 in the UK. It was later released as the B-side of the October 1992 reissue of 'How Can I Go On'. The single edit reduced the running time by a minute, while a promotional edit cut the track down even further, to three and a half minutes but these unique version weren't included on *The Solo Collection*. A video was extracted from the La Nit performance on 8 October 1988 and was subsequently included on the 1989 *Barcelona* video EP as well as on *The Freddie Mercury Video Collection* in 2000.

An instrumental version was created for released on the 12″ vinyl and CD single release; while it's not purely instrumental, containing the entirety of the gospel vocals (provided by Madeline Bell, Debbie Bishop, Lance Ellington, Miriam Stockley, Peter Straker, Mark Williamson and Carol Woods), it does give a stunning insight into the construction of the track. Three alternate versions were also included on *The Solo Collection*: two early versions – the first recorded on 2 May 1987 and featuring the introduction which was already programmed and prepared for the song, along with Freddie singing the lyrics in his normal stage voice; the second, recorded on 9 November 1987, is another attempt at a demo vocal, and features only Freddie, but this time providing a completely different vocal delivery, as well as some superb falsetto; the third an a cappella version, recorded on 1 December 1987, which suggests that the final vocal was recorded on this day. To get a clear understanding of Freddie's amazing vocal control, the a cappella version is essential listening.

GOLDEN DAYS *(May)*

• Album (Brian & Kerry): *Golden*

Written by Brian for Minako Honda in 1986, who had her own hit with the single the following year, 'Golden Days' was an obvious favorite of Brian's. "I met her when she was already a star," he later wrote, "but still young enough to have to be chaperoned when she travelled to another country. Somehow the idea came up for me to write her two songs and record them in both English and Japanese. I wrote, very quickly, 'Golden Days' and 'Crazy Nights' (not the Kiss song which emerged a few years later). I sent her my demos, and it was arranged for her to come to London to record them. It was a time when we as Queen were going through a time

of 'being distant' with each other, and I plunged into different recording projects … And suddenly, there was little Minako, energetic, charming, and disarmingly professional for someone so young. We romped through the songs in Japanese – she had everything prepared and never put a foot wrong. The English versions were much more difficult. Minako came from a family that spoke no English, and she simply did not have the Western consonant sounds at her command. We had an interpreter, of course, but the more Minako applied herself to the rhythm of the English language the harder it seemed for her. Her manager was determined that she would shine as much in English as in Japanese, and I think poor Minako felt a lot of pressure. She would not give up, even though there were tears (which made me feel terrible!). In the end we stitched together pretty good English versions of both songs, but really, to hear Minako Honda at her cheeky ebullient best, you have to listen to the Japanese versions … The songs did quite well in Japan, but visibility in Britain, which had been the whole object of the project, was much more elusive. So, sadly, very few people in the UK are familiar with our work together. Only the devoted fans. Well, these days I have the good fortune to work with Kerry Ellis in the studio. From time to time, I open some of the old drawers and we look for material from the past that might have a new life. Kerry picked up on Golden Days a few weeks ago, and got attached to the song, so we determined to make a new version of it. It's taken shape quickly, and Kerry, of course, gives it a luminous new life. I've revisited the arrangement too, but a lot of the original feel is still there. So this will be one of the tracks on the album we're building. Right now it's sounding like a lovely tribute to dear Minako. We began by getting out the old multitrack, with Minako's voice clear and beautiful as the day we recorded her. It's great how music can make the years melt away."

Released in April 2017 as the title track of the first credited collaboration between Brian and Kerry Ellis, 'Golden Days' is a lovely reinterpretation of the song, with Kerry doing the song supreme justice (Brian later commented that Honda's voice appears on the recording; likely backing vocals).

GOOD COMPANY *(May)*

• Album: *Opera*

Nestled between 'Love Of My Life' and 'Bohemian Rhapsody' on the second side of *A Night At The Opera*, 'Good Company' is Brian's chance to indulge in music hall entertainment, sounding like a pastiche of The Kinks's more vaudevillian songs. Much like Ray Davies' character vignettes, Brian tells a tale of falling in love with Sally J, "the girl from Number 4", and as they grew up and their love intensifies, friends disappear into their own domestic bliss. Trying to juggle a marriage with work becomes a chore, and as his "reputation grew" as a tradesman, he "hardly noticed Sally as we parted company". This would become a recurring theme among Brian's self-sung songs on the next few Queen albums, with his discomfort of fame and fortune impeding on his familial priorities; compare 'Good Company' with 'Long Away', 'Sleeping On The Sidewalk', and 'Leaving Home Ain't Easy', and it's clear that Brian was most resistant to a life in the limelight glare. "I know I'm a very lucky person," Brian told *The Mail On Sunday* in 1999. "I've had the chance to fulfill so many dreams, and Queen was a wonderful vehicle. But I think it truly messed me up and I'm conscious that I have never really recovered. It's like you never grow up. We've all suffered. Freddie, obviously, went completely AWOL. He wasn't a bad person but he was out of control for a while. But in a way, all of us were out of control. Perhaps I shouldn't be speaking for Roger and John, but I think underneath it they'd agree with me – it screwed us up."

The skeleton of the song consists of a rock-steady rhythm section from John and Roger, with the primary stringed instrument here a charmingly strummed ukulele. The real star of the show is the guitar jazz band orchestra, which was performed exclusively by Brian. "It's all guitar, all those instruments," Brian explained in a 1983 BBC Radio One interview. "That was a little fetish of mine. I used to listen to traditional jazz quite a lot, in particular, the twenties revival stuff which wasn't actually traditional jazz but more arranged stuff like The Temperance Seven, who were recreating something which was popular in the twenties, sort of dance tunes, really. I was very impressed by the way those arrangements were done, you know, the nice smooth sound and those lovely changes between chords, because they were much more rich in chords than most modern songs are. So many chord changes in a short time, lots of intermingling parts.

"So I wanted to do one of those things and the song just happened to come out while I was plunking away at the ukulele and the song itself was no trouble to write at all. But actually doing the arrangements for the wind section, as it was supposed to be; there's a guitar trumpet and a guitar clarinet and a guitar

trombone and a sort of extra thing, I don't really know what it was supposed to be, on the top. I spent a lot of time doing those and to get the effect of the instruments I was doing one note at a time, with a pedal and building them up. So you can imagine how long it took. We experimented with the mikes and various little tiny amplifiers to get just the right sound. So I actually made a study of the kind of thing that those instruments could play so it would sound like those and get the authentic flavour. It was a bit of fun but it was a serious, serious bit of work in that a lot of time went into it."

Freddie said of the song in an interview with Kenny Everett in 1975, "[It's] a George Formby track with saxophones, trombone and clarinet sounds from [Brian's] guitar. We don't believe in having any session men, we do everything ourselves, from the high falsetto to the low bassy farts; it's all us."

GOOD TIMES ARE NOW *(Taylor)*
• Album (Roger): *Fun*

Driven by plodding drums and a funky bass line, Roger's 'Good Times Are Now' is a typical boy-meets-girl song and is lyrically a predecessor to 'Hijack My Heart'. Atypically, Roger sings to the object of his affection in tender verses instead of oblique asides, finally winning her heart and shooing away the "other pretty face" with the killer line: "Life in the future might never come to pass / You know, good times are now." Accentuated by short jabs of synthesizer, the backing track is built upon sparse bass and guitar lines, and sits at odds with the weightier, sci-fi-inspired atmosphere of *Fun In Space*; if it had been submitted for Queen, it probably would have been given a perfunctory run-through and either relegated to the cutting-room floor or, if lucky, a position as a non-album B-side.

GOOD OLD-FASHIONED LOVER BOY *(Mercury)*
• Album: *Races* • EP: *First EP* • CD Single: 11/88
• Bonus: *Races*

Freddie always had a wicked sense of humor, and insisted on injecting his songs with a tongue-in-cheek line or two. He once noted in an interview, "Our songs are utterly disposable. I don't want to change the world with our songs. People can discard them like a used tissue," though Brian wasn't convinced, telling *Mojo* magazine in 2008, "That's just Fred being clever. There was more to this than meets the eye ... The fact that he said his song was disposable dispelled any pretension and stopped him having to talk about it. I knew Fred pretty damn well and I know a lot of what was going on and there's a lot of depth in his songs. That false modesty shouldn't mislead anyone. Even the light stuff and the humour had an undercurrent." Starting with 'Funny How Love Is' in 1974, Freddie would begin a series of lighthearted contributions to Queen's albums, that culminated two years later with 'Good Old-Fashioned Lover Boy', his last comedic music hall-inspired song for nearly 15 years.

The song is an innocent slice of schoolboy romance, as Freddie serenades the object of his affection while offering a night of wining, dining, dancing and debauchery. He's clearly reveling in his lover boy charm, and, due to his romantic nature, hopes that the glitz and champagne won't wear off the morning after. "[It's] one of my vaudeville numbers," Freddie told Kenny Everett in 1977. "I always do a vaudeville track, though 'Lover Boy' is more straightforward than 'Seaside Rendezvous', for instance. It's quite simple, piano and vocals with a catchy beat; the album needs it to sort of ease off."

The song was issued as the lead track from the unimaginatively-titled *Queen's First EP* in May 1977, though only in the UK; the US received 'Long Away' the following month instead, while 'Good Old-Fashioned Lover Boy' was the Japanese B-side of 'Teo Torriatte (Let Us Cling Together)' in March 1977. The EP was a calculated move to rerelease three of Queen's lesser-known tracks from their heyday ('Death On Two Legs (Dedicated to......', 'Tenement Funster', and 'White Queen (As It Began)' were the others), but the press were cynical, citing the release as a ploy to milk the consumers of every penny, as all four tracks were widely available by the spring of 1977. Housed in a dull package and sold, at the band's insistence, for the price of a two-track single as opposed to a standard EP, the release peaked at a modest No. 17; considering that 'Tie Your Mother Down' didn't even scrape the Top 30 two months earlier, this placement caused a sigh of relief, yet was enough of a failure to force Queen to rethink their musical strategy for their next major release.

An official video was never made, though the band popped into the studios for an appearance on *Top Of The Pops* on 14 June 1977 (broadcast the next day), performing to a specially re-recorded backing track with a more aggressive sound. This version remained unreleased until 2002, when it appeared as a bonus

video on the *Greatest Video Hits 1* DVD release. Until then, a cut-and-paste version, butchered by Torpedo Twins Rudi Dolezal and Hannes Rossacher, which compiled footage from the June 1977 appearance at Earl's Court Arena, remained the 'official' promotional video. The song was performed live between 1977 and 1978 as part of the medley, but was out when Queen started to focus more on being a live rock band.

GRAND DAME

Premiered alongside 'Affairs' by David Richards in November 2010, 'Grand Dame' is a more basic instrumental jam, with heavy guitar work and a slight boogie feel that firmly instilled it as an enjoyable throwaway. While this kind of recording is a revelation and an indicator that the band were still creatively fertile, its staying power isn't as strong as 'Affairs' or other out-takes from the Montreux sessions for *Innuendo* in 1990.

GREAT KING RAT (Mercury)
• Album: *Queen* • Compilation: *BBC, On Air* • Bonus: *Queen* • Live: *Rainbow*

Kicking off a hat trick of Mercury-penned compositions on *Queen*, 'Great King Rat' is a stunning song, rife with oblique imagery and stunning prose that indicated early on Freddie's inventive gift of lyricism. While Brian's early songs were more straightforward, Freddie's goal was to cram his songs full of meaning to the point that they barely made any sense, and while he would dismiss his compositions as lyrical fluff, Brian maintains that this was simply to deflect having to explain his songs. "I don't like to explain what I was thinking when I wrote a song," Freddie said in a 1977 *Circus* magazine interview. "I think that's awful, just awful." And so, Freddie never explained 'Great King Rat', preferring to keep his fairytale story of the titular character's overindulgent death a mystery for listeners. As with his subsequent songs, which often contained tongue-in-cheek in-jokes or musical references to bygone days, Freddie threw in a reference to Mother Goose's 'Old King Cole', paraphrasing the rhyme as its lyrical hook: compare "Great King Rat was a dirty old man, and a dirty old man was he / Now what did I tell you / Would you like to see?" to "Old King Cole was a merry old soul, and a merry old soul was he / He called for his pipe in the middle of the night / And he called for his fiddlers three". Elsewhere, and in line with

Freddie's other early songs, are references to religion and the Bible, with Great King Rat painted as a joyful, fun-loving character, urging his followers to "put out the good and keep the bad".

This weighty composition was a live favorite in the band's formative years, and was often in and out of the set list throughout 1974 and 1975, before being resurrected for the 1984 Queen Works! tour. At least three studio versions are known to exist: the officially released studio version, complete with poorly mic'd and mixed drums; a demo version recorded between September and November 1971 at De Lane Lea Studios, with several improvised instrumental sections excised from the album version, bringing the running time to nearly eight minutes; and a recording for the BBC on 3 December 1973, which is given a fresher arrangement while still remaining close to the original. After countless bootleg appearances, the demo version was finally released in 2011 on the deluxe edition of *Queen*, while the BBC recording was issued in 1989 on the UK compilation *Queen At The Beeb*, and in the US in 1995 on *Queen At The BBC*.

THE GREAT PRETENDER *(Ram)*

• A-side (Freddie): 2/87 [4] • A-side (Freddie): 1/93 [29] • Compilations (Freddie): *Pretender, FM Album, Solo Collection* • Compilation (Queen): *GH3*

"Most of the stuff I do is like pretending, it's like acting: I go on stage and pretend to be a macho man. I think 'The Great Pretender' is a great title for what I do ... I've always had this [idea] in the back of my head – a cover version, and this song is the one I've always wanted to do. I went into the studio and tried a few trials, and I liked it. It suited my voice and it's a great song to sing."

Originally released by The Platters in 1956, 'The Great Pretender' was recorded in November 1986, mere months after the end of the Magic tour (in fact, a demo version was recorded three months to the day – 9 November 1986 – after Knebworth Park, Queen's last-ever gig), with Mike Moran and David Richards co-producing the sessions with Freddie. Moran, whom Freddie had met through his involvement with Dave Clark's soundtrack album of the musical *Time*, offered his own explanation of the sessions: "The mix saw our roles being somewhat reversed. David Richards, Queen's producer, came into London to mix the track at Townhouse. I was rather nervous and concerned about what was, after all, my co-production. The mix went on and on, and so did my neurotic attention

to every tiny teeny detail. On and on and on until Freddie could stand it no longer: 'For God's sake, leave it alone!' he demanded. 'Let's go home, dear. You're doing a me!'

"Freddie was in something of a quandary as to how to end the song," Mike continued. "I had a few ideas, but as I tested each one, he merely pronounced limply, 'Very good, dear'. I knew it wasn't up to scratch. The ending just got longer and longer and seemed never to reach an end. Freddie urged me to 'do a few flashy bits'. He loved anything technically virtuoso. It was then that he came up with Paganini, and that was the key to the problem. From that as a starting point, I went into a violin arrangement that eventually ended the record."

Although not credited on the single, the backing musicians were Harold Fisher on drums and Alan Jones on bass, with Mike Moran on keyboards and piano. With a superb and soaring lead vocal, 'The Great Pretender', backed with 'Exercises In Free Love', was released at the end of February 1987 and became the first Queen-related product to hit the shelves in the new year, though it would also mark the beginning of a frustratingly long hiatus. The single reached No. 4 in the UK, the highest chart position that any Queen-related solo single would reach until the re-release of 'Barcelona' in 1992, and later a remix of 'Living On My Own' in 1993 – all songs originally recorded and released by Freddie. An extended version, reaching nearly six minutes, was also created, and this would later be used as the soundtrack to the extended video version, which had rarely been seen until its inclusion on *The Freddie Mercury Video Collection* in 2000.

The song was reissued in January 1993, as it was featured in Irwin Winkler's film *Night And The City*, starring Robert DeNiro and Jessica Lange. The single peaked at No. 29 in the UK charts, though it had been remixed considerably for inclusion on the US compilation album *The Great Pretender*. Remixed by Brian Malouf, who had also provided the Headbangers mix of 'Hammer To Fall', the song's distinctive, percolating keyboard melody is replaced with a jangly guitar, lending it a more powerful, anthemic sound that adds a different feel to the emotion already provided in the original.

The success of the single also marked one of the few rare promotional appearances that Freddie made on television. In March 1987, right before sessions for *Barcelona* started in full, Freddie appeared on the *Vier Gegen Willy* show in Germany, wearing a white version of his pink suit while a video screen behind him flashed scenes from Freddie's past, including the memorable shot of the vocalist appearing at the conclusion of 'God Save The Queen' from the previous year's tour, resplendent in cape and crown.

Also in February, Freddie and director-of-choice David Mallet booked time to film a video for the single and, in line with their penchant for grandiose productions, the results were extraordinary. Freddie cavorts around the soundstage while revisiting many of his past glories (moments from 'I Want To Break Free', 'Crazy Little Thing Called Love', 'It's A Hard Life', 'I Was Born To Love You' and even 'Radio Ga Ga'), painstakingly reshot to synchronize with the lyrics, instead of merely using alternate takes. The originally planned conclusion, which would have seen Freddie on the white cliffs of Dover, was canned for two good reasons: cost, and because Freddie was reluctant to film on the English coast in the middle of winter. An equally extravagant, though far cheaper (and warmer!), alternative was proposed: Freddie descending a long staircase amid 100 life-size cardboard cut-outs of him in his pink-suited guise. "I wanted to show people that all these different roles I was creating in videos," Freddie said at the time, "was a kind of pretense – that I was pretending. I chose roles that I had done in the past, to bring back again, and then tried to marry them with the word 'pretender'. Basically, we had different mini-sets built around the studio, and recreated some of those things. Using my costumes, we sort of bridged all the elements together with lighting techniques and things."

For the contemporary footage, Freddie is dressed in a light pink suit, the creation of which wasn't without incident: the vocalist was less than pleased with the original suit, but liked the velvet piping it sported, and asked, quite innocently, if the suit could be made out of that material instead. Of course it was, though it wouldn't be the only wardrobe switch on the video: Freddie asked his two closest friends, Peter Straker and Roger Taylor, to join in the fun and provide mimed backing vocals for the video. Instead of appearing as themselves, though, it was suggested that the trio dress up in drag, costumed as garish whores hamming it up for the lenses. (This would fuel the rumor that Roger and Peter performed backing vocals on the song, perpetuated by the liner notes to *Lover Of Life, Singer Of Songs*; once and for all, the backing vocals were sung exclusively by Freddie, so there.) The video also marked another image modification for Freddie, marking the last appearance of Freddie's moustache,

a trademark that had been with him since 1980 and which had been the cause of much debate and, for some, consternation. Though he shaved it – briefly – for the 'I Want To Break Free' video in 1984, he stuck with the image-change this time since it looked more appropriate for his next endeavor: the *Barcelona* project. While facial hair would make a few more appearances in the last three years of his life, the video for 'The Great Pretender' marked the end of an era; in a way, it can be seen as Freddie's farewell to that portion of his life.

GREEN *(Bulsara)*
• Compilation (Freddie): *Solo Collection*

The earliest recorded Mercury-penned song is this pleasant song, laid down by Wreckage at Freddie's flat in Barnes during October 1969. Recorded in one take as a demo, the song features Mike Bersin on unplugged electric guitar, John Taylor on bass and Richard Thompson providing the rhythm by tapping on his legs with drum sticks. Only a month prior, Ibex had performed their last concert together, but Freddie convinced Mike and John to form a new group with him, and while Freddie did write new material, 'Green' remained the only song to be recorded by Wreckage.

THE GREEN PARADE

When asked by a fan in August 2006 what his favorite protest song was, Brian cheekily namechecked 'The Green Parade', coyly forgetting that such a song wasn't commonly available – not least because he had written it and decided not to release it! The history of the song goes back to the 1989 sessions with Ian Meeson and Belinda Gillet, who contributed vocals to a re-recording of 'Who Wants To Live Forever' for the British Bone Marrow Donor Appeal. According to Brian, the intent was for 'The Green Parade' to be issued as the B-side but, after a few takes (presumably with Roger on drums and John on bass, the same musicians who contributed to 'Who Wants To Live Forever'), time ran out and the song was never completed.

GUIDE ME HOME *(Mercury/Moran)*
• Album (Freddie): *Barcelona*
• Compilation (Freddie): *Solo Collection*

Recorded as a continuous piece with 'How Can I Go On', 'Guide Me Home' is one of Freddie's most underrated ballads, dominated largely by piano and Freddie's voice, with Montserrat Caballé adding her own touches. Lyrically dazzling and featuring some of Freddie's most beautiful couplets (especially "Where is my star in heaven's bough? / Where is my strength, I need it now"), the song is short and sweet, leading into the more musically upbeat, but lyrically similar, 'How Can I Go On'.

An instrumental mix was created for *The Solo Collection* and is absolutely breathtaking, while an alternate version was also featured. As it leads directly into 'How Can I Go On', the focus is more on that song, and only one verse was finalized for 'Guide Me Home', with vocal improvisations making up the majority of the remainder. A stand-alone single mix was created, ending with some finality (although the introductory keyboards of 'How Can I Go On' can be heard), but not included on *The Solo Collection*.

GUITAR EXTRAVAGANCE: *see* BRIGHTON ROCK

GUN (SOLO VIOLIN) *(May)*
• Soundtrack (Brian): *Furia* • Bonus (Brian): *Furia*

As with the other solo pieces from the *Furia* soundtrack, 'Gun' is a variation on the main theme, this time emotively performed by Rolf Wilson on first violin. An alternate version of this piece was included as a bonus track, though one would be hard pressed to distinguish the differences.

THE GUV'NOR *(May)*
• Album (Brian): *World*

Brian wasn't known for writing slinky, sexy blues songs, but 'The Guv'nor' is just that. It would have been a perfect addition to the aborted *Heroes* project since it was written specifically about Jeff Beck, guitar hero of The Yardbirds and later, a solo act. "I started to sort of sculpt the song," Brian explained, "and I thought, 'Wouldn't it be nice if it was kind of in some way about Jeff, who is the guv'nor in our area, and there's a sort of metaphor there, an analogy – there's always the kid in the area that everyone goes, 'Hmm ... don't go near him' kind of thing. So Jeff is that kind of guy, you know, don't even think of it. And I got Jeff in to play. I actually plucked up the courage to say, 'Jeff ... would you play on my track?' and he said, 'Yeah!', and he loved the track, which I was thrilled about, came down here and played, and did some great stuff, some

outrageous bits and pieces.

"But he said, 'Brian, I'm not really happy – I need to take it away and think about it, and do my stuff at home,' which tends to be what I do, so I said, 'Fine.' About a year later, I'm going 'Er ... Jeff? Anything happened to that track?', and he goes, 'Oh yeah, yeah ... no no no ... I'm really doing it, I really love it, but I haven't got around to it yet,' so I was crossing my fingers, and hoping he was gonna come back, and I think two days before we were due to deliver the album to EMI, finally, I got the stuff back from Jeff, and it was really, really great. He'd done some more stuff at home and pieced it all together. He's such a perfectionist, I couldn't believe that; you know, the image of Jeff Beck, which is true, is that he's unpredictable and he's spiky and spontaneous, you know. But there's another side to him which is very concerned, and very much a perfectionist. He didn't want that to go out unless it was something that was dead right. He rang up a few times and said, 'Are you sure it's okay?' and I said, 'Jeff? Okay? Are you kidding? It's unbelievable!'"

For the first time in 25 years, Brian is happy to abdicate the guitar throne to Beck, who absolutely scorches on the track. The rhythm section swings, with Brian on bass and Cozy Powell on drums, and the result is one of the better tracks from *Another World*, though it sits at odds among the more introspective songs.

HAD TO BELIEVE ME:
see EVERYBODY NEEDS SOMEBODY

HAMMER TO FALL *(May)*
• Album: *Works* • A-side: 9/84 [13] • CD Single: 11/88 • Live: *Magic, Wembley, Budapest* • Compilation: *Hits2, Classic* • Live (Brian): *Brixton* • Live (Q+PR): *Return, Ukraine*

A welcome return to hard rock is found in 'Hammer To Fall', a standout rocker from *The Works*, which addresses Brian's concern of living in a world dominated by trigger happy political leaders. Inspired by the 1953 play *Waiting For Godot* by Samuel Beckett, the song reaches a climax with the appearance of a mushroom cloud in the final verse, something that baby boomers had to live with as a real threat, with the line "What the hell we fighting for?" embodying Brian's pacifist nature by questioning the futility of war. The figurative hammer is a reference to the Soviet hammer and sickle, hinting at the worldwide fear of the U.S.S.R.'s rise in prominence during the Cold War era.

With a crunching guitar riff and an exuberant performance from the band, 'Hammer To Fall' recalls the early era Queen with an updated message for the 1980s. No wonder, then, that it was chosen as the fourth and final single from *The Works* in September 1984. By that time, however, the album had been in shops for nearly nine months, so the single peaked at a modest No. 13 in the UK (the first single from the album to miss the Top 10), not charting at all in the US. The original sleeve featured a dazzling photo of the band on stage, with their impressive lighting rig in full glory, but this was withdrawn and replaced with a dull red sleeve. Two reasons for this odd switcheroo have been posited, with the official gloss being due to objections from Brian, who complained it would give the impression that the single was a live release – a dubious justification, considering earlier sleeves (*Queen's First EP* and 'Don't Stop Me Now') featured impressive live shots. According to Paul Webb, avid Queen fan and collector, this was not the case, which he recalled on Queenmuseum.com: "...On Brian's 1998 Another World tour I won a QFC competition to meet the great man before the Royal Albert Hall show. I took my [12″ vinyl 'Hammer To Fall' picture] sleeve with me for Brian to sign, and inevitably I put the question to him, 'Why was this cover withdrawn?'. His reply was (and I remember it as if it were yesterday), 'Ah yes, I get the blame for this, don't I? Well, it's not true, it wasn't my fault that it got withdrawn. The man who took the picture was not an official Queen photographer. This meant that we would have had to pay vast sums of money to him for using this picture. This all came to light just in time and the live cover was taken off the shelves. I really like the picture, I think it's so much better than the red version.'"

There's no denying that the song was well-suited to the live setting, which the David Mallet-directed promotional video captured perfectly. The filming took place on 25 August 1984 at the Forêt Nationale in Brussels (the band had played a date at that venue, the first on the Queen Works! European tour, but had a day off on the day of shooting), and premiered the tour's impressive lighting rig, two mechanical cogs behind Roger, and dry ice galore. The video was also interspersed with crowd shots from the previous day's show, with the soundtrack overdubbed with the crowd screaming and clapping along.

'Hammer To Fall' was performed at every show between 1984 and 1986, including the Live Aid

performance at Wembley Stadium on 13 July 1985, and by Extreme vocalist Gary Cherone at the Concert For Life in 1992. Brian played the song live as the last song on his Back To The Light tour, but restructured the song for the 1998 Another World tour, slowing the song down as a shimmering ballad, before kicking the tempo up for the outro. A similar arrangement was used again on the first Queen + Paul Rodgers tour in 2005 and 2006, with Brian tackling the slower first verse and chorus, and Paul taking over for the double-time remainder.

Several remixes were produced shortly after its release; the 12″ mix, dubbed the Headbangers Mix, is essentially an extended remix of the track, with a pounding introductory drum solo and additional guitar work throughout. Brian Malouf remixed the song in 1991 for a Hollywood Records promotional release, giving the song a punchier mix and more prominent drum sound.

HAND OF FOOLS (OUT OF CONTROL)

(Edney/Noone)
• Album (The Cross): *Blue*

The penultimate track on *Blue Rock* is the gorgeous 'Hand Of Fools (Out Of Control)', addressing the topical conflict in the Gulf and pondering the eternal question of the validity and necessity of war. The line "While profit oils the big machine / And we're shortchanged the facts" rings eerily true to this day, with the world's dependency on oil a bane to advancing green technology. Set to a gentle bed of acoustic guitars and keyboards, the song was doomed to obscurity: it was never performed live nor featured on any single release.

HANG ON IN THERE *(Queen)*
• B-side: 5/89 [3] • Bonus: *Miracle*

Sessions for *The Miracle* proved to be fruitful, with the band writing songs based on collective jams while getting reacquainted with each others' company. One of the first songs recorded during the sessions was this acoustic rocker, originally titled 'A Fiddly Jam', which makes up the second half of the song, but finally given the more inspirational title of 'Hang On In There'.

Initiated by Freddie, the song hints at his own condition: by now suffering the effects of AIDS, it's not coincidental that he was writing more positive songs in order to keep his optimism high through the dark times ahead. Set to a dark acoustic backing, one of two songs from *The Miracle* sessions to be dominated by the instrument ('Stealin'' was the other; both, incidentally, were issued as non-album B-sides), the song quickly picks up pace, concluding with an upbeat jam. Due to time constraints, the song was left off the album proper, though it was issued as a bonus CD track and as the B-side of 'I Want It All'. Brian was remarkably candid about the song, telling *Sounds* in 1989, "Devotees of the band would get off on it, but it's not regular album material."

HANGMAN

One of the most sought-after Queen songs is 'Hangman', a track performed as a regular in the set list between 1970 and 1973, and only scarcely thereafter until 1976. Its origins remained shrouded in mystery for years until the early 1990s, when Brian confirmed in a personal letter to a collector that he wrote the music and Freddie penned the words. With a nod to Queen's early day Led Zeppelin-inspired crunch, 'Hangman' was derived from that band's 1970 rendition of Leadbelly's 'Gallows Pole'. The words were fluid and changed nightly, depending on Freddie's mood, with a curious line about pork pies and cups of tea thrown in for good measure. What was consistent was Freddie's cry of "Shag out!", just before an instrumental jam, which bootleggers erroneously divided into another track of that name. Given the abundance of material written for the first two albums, rumors circulated that a studio version was recorded for the debut album, although the official word was that no such recording exists. It turns out that the rumors were true: a 10" acetate from the 1972 Trident sessions contains a studio recording of 'Hangman', though this is now in Queen Productions' possession, and if it will ever be released is anyone's guess. Its absence from a proper Queen album is unsurprising: while it might have been suitable on the debut, their songwriting had progressed so vastly by the second album that this bluesy rocker would have been derivative and completely out of place.

HAPPINESS? *(Taylor)*
• Album (Roger): *Happiness?* • A-side (Roger): 11/94 [32]

The title track to Roger's third proper solo album is, uncharacteristically for Roger, an upbeat ballad with a set of introspective and philosophical lyrics of not only the need for happiness in everyone's life, but that the definition of happiness is based on the individual's needs and goals. Based on a delicate piano (performed by Mike Crossley) and acoustic guitar backing, the song kicks into high gear with a soaring guitar solo from Jason Falloon, leaving Roger as the other musician on understated drums, bass, and keyboards. Cleverly and beautifully arranged, 'Happiness?' is an early triumph, and was released as the third and final single from the album, peaking at No. 32.

A video was filmed for the single on 23 May 1994 in Vienna by the infamous Torpedo Twins, bringing to life the imagery of the album sleeve, with close-up shots of Roger's visage set against a colorful clouded sunset. Suitably, the song was a staple in Roger's 1994/1995 solo repertoire, but, in keeping with his desire to progress and incorporate newer material in lieu of older songs, wasn't revisited for the 1998/1999 Electric Fire solo tour.

HAPPY HENRIK'S POLKA

Adapted from the traditional Swedish folk song 'Lycklige Henrik's Polka', 'Happy Henrik's Polka' (erroneously titled in Jacky Smith's and Jim Jenkins' *As It Began* as 'Happy Hendrix Polka') was a hit for instrumental Swedish band The Spotnicks in 1962, and granted them international success. Given his admiration for instrumental rock band The Shadows, it's no surprise that Brian learned 'Happy Henrik's Polka' for a gig by 1984 at the Mosely Boat Club in the summer of 1966.

HAPPY X-MAS (WAR IS OVER) *(Lennon/Ono)*

John Lennon's 1969 single was performed live by The Cross at both fan club shows in December 1992 at the Marquee.

A HARD RAIN'S A-GONNA FALL *(Dylan)*

Bob Dylan's 1964 folk protest song was performed live by Roger Taylor during the early part of his 1994 Happiness? tour, but was dropped in favor of 'Man On Fire'.

HAVE A NICE DAY *(Mercury/Moran)*
• Compilation (Freddie): *Solo Collection*

On 18 April 1987, Freddie and Mike Moran were

hard at work recording 'Rachmaninov's Revenge' at Townhouse Studios when the vocalist took the opportunity to record a greeting for the upcoming fan club convention. Instead of providing a spoken greeting, he characteristically went over the top and recorded an improvised song. 'Have A Nice Day' (or 'Good Times' as it has alternately been called on bootlegs) gets the job done in its short, 46-second lifetime.

HEADLONG *(Queen)*
• Album: *Innuendo* • A-side: 5/91 [14] • Live (Brian): *Brixton*

While Queen went off into various musical dimensions in the 1980s, exploring the more attractive side of the pop-rock charts, Brian was the one to remain devoted to guitar-heavy rock. His contributions on Queen's mid-1980s albums were either tender ballads or balls-to-the-wall rockers, with no compromise; this kept Queen grounded in their roots, yet wasn't exactly hit parade material, with his songs either being relegated to album track status or as a throwaway final single. By 1990, though, the mission statement had changed: determined to make their newest album a callback to their glory days of the 1970s and not so reliant on synthesizers, the band introduced several new rock songs to the running order, finally giving Brian a chance to let loose on The Red Special.

"'Headlong' came from me, at our studio in Montreux, a home recording studio for us that's very state-of-the-art, lovely for creating," Brian told *Rip* magazine in 1991. "The ideas came in a couple of days. At first I thought about it as a song for my solo album [*Back To The Light*] but, as always, the band is the best vehicle. As soon as I heard Freddie sing it, I said, 'That's it!' Sometimes it's painful to give the baby away, but what you gain is much more. It became a Queen song."

The lyrics have baffled fans for years, with mostly nonsensical *non sequiturs* seemingly used simply because they sounded good. However, considering Brian's mental state in 1990, a deeper look may be in order: the "red hot lady" could be Anita; the "man with a stick in his hand" could be Brian, guitar in hand; "soup in the laundry bag" refers to dirty laundry and scandalous tabloid coverage (the original line, replacing "soup" with "shit", gets to the point more succinctly); and "a woman with a hot dog stand" is an archaic term for a dance club. The overarching message is simple: Brian is consumed with excitement for his new, blossoming

relationship, and 'Headlong' serves as a message to take a step back or risk rushing out of control.

A promotional video was shot on 23 November 1990 at Metropolis Studios, and was directed by The Torpedo Twins. Showing the band recording the song in the studio, it was interspersed with footage of the band goofing around in the control room and lying on bunk beds while singing the chorus. Freddie appears very perky during the performance, leaping around the sound stage and even doing push-ups at one point – certainly not giving the impression that he was on his deathbed. The video also features a unique guitar solo from Brian, extending the running time to just under five minutes (the audio of this version hasn't appeared anywhere on disc).

Released as the third single from *Innuendo* in May 1991 and backed by 'All God's People' (with the previously unreleased *Queen* out-take 'Mad The Swine' as a CD-only bonus track), 'Headlong' peaked at No. 14 in the UK. In the US, the single was backed by 'Under Pressure' and issued as the lead single in January 1991, and though it didn't appear in the *Billboard* charts, it did reach No. 3 in the rock charts. Brian performed the song on all of his solo tours, with a version from the Back To The Light tour released on his 1994 live album, *Live At The Brixton Academy*. An early version, with guide vocals by Brian, a more stripped-back arrangement, and some wild, wailing guitar work, was released as a bonus track on the 2011 reissue of *Innuendo*.

HEARTLAND *(Noone)*
• German CD single (The Cross): 10/91

A terse and uncompromising track of mental and emotional abandonment, 'Heartland' was recorded during sessions for *Blue Rock* but was deemed surplus to requirements and relegated to B-side status. It's no worse than anything else on the album and, with only ten tracks barely scraping 45 minutes, 'Heartland' would have been an ideal addition. As on 'Breakdown', Peter once again takes the lead vocal for the first half of the song before Roger takes over, their two voices harmonizing on the chorus, the former's nasally hum contrasting nicely with the latter's raspy squawk. The strength of the song lies in the band's performance, turning in a tight and remarkable effort showing instrumental maturity, with Clayton Moss especially showing little restraint on guitar.

Issued on the October 1991 CD single release of

'Life Changes', 'Heartland' deserved to be more widely heard but, out of respect for Freddie's death the following month, 'Life Changes' was withdrawn from release.

HEART FULL OF SOUL *(Gouldman)*

This revolutionary Yardbirds track was played live by 1984 and even, apparently, by The Art.

HEAVEN FOR EVERYONE *(Taylor)*
• Album (The Cross): *Shove* • A-side (The Cross): 3/88 [83] • A-side (Queen): 10/95 [2] • Album (Queen): *Heaven* • Compilation (Queen): *Hits3*

Crystal Taylor once labeled 'Heaven For Everyone' as the Queen single that never was, even suggesting that Roger save the song for a Queen project. Long rumored to have been recorded during sessions for *A Kind Of Magic*, the song was actually not submitted for the album (though a recent trawl through Roger's lyrics sheet indicate the song may have been written as early as 1983, for *Strange Frontier*); instead, it was one of the first songs recorded for *Shove It*, his first album with The Cross. Released as that album's third single in March 1988, it peaked at an abysmal No. 83 in the UK, despite the presence of Freddie on backing vocals.

The Cross did perform the song regularly throughout their career, but it was omitted from the set during the 1991 support tour to Magnum. The single was heavily promoted upon its release, with the band appearing on German television programs *Formel 1* on 23 April 1988 and on *ZDF*, around the same time, and was given further exposure when The Cross appeared at the Golden Rose festival in Montreux on 12 May 1988. A performance video, directed by Dieble and Myers, was also shot that year, with Roger languishing on a tropical beach (heaven) with a guitar as homeless people rise from beneath a decrepit building to join him, transformed from the unwashed masses to Hawaiian shirt-clad beach bums.

'Heaven For Everyone' was restructured by Brian, Roger and John in 1994 for inclusion on *Made In Heaven*. Freddie had recorded a lead vocal track for the song, which ended up on the UK release of *Shove It* and the German B-side of the same single, and the band took Freddie's original vocal and recorded fresh arrangements, including a scorching guitar solo from Brian but, unfortunately, dropping the spoken bits. While a case can be argued in favor of The Cross's

original, Queen's re-recording is vastly superior, and not only because of Freddie's ethereal vocal performance.

Chosen as the debut single from the album and the first "new" Queen single since 'The Show Must Go On' four years prior, 'Heaven For Everyone' was released in edited form in October 1995 with a unique mix of 'It's A Beautiful Day'. The single reached No. 2 in the UK, Queen's highest, new-chart entry since 'Innuendo' in 1991 ... and this was with an eight year-old song! David Mallet was recruited to make a film for the single; since there wasn't any footage of Freddie singing the song, a heavy dose of creativity was used to fashion an original video combining footage from the 1902 film *Le Voyage dans la lune* (*A Trip To The Moon*) with clips of the band, to remind you that this was a Queen video. The result was met with approval from the band (though Brian confided in a letter, dated 30 November 1995, that "I ... felt very let down by the execution of the videos for 'Heaven For Everyone'. Unfortunately, since this is a democracy of sorts, I was over-ruled, both in the choice of the single and how it was presented."), and inspired the band to commission independent directors from the British Film Institute to create unique videos for all the songs from *Made In Heaven*. The version directed by Simon Pummell, retitled 'Evolution', features performance artist STELARC. This was issued on the video compilation *Made In Heaven – The Films*, while Mallet's version was released on *Greatest Flix III*.

HELLO MARY LOU (GOODBYE HEART)
(Pitney/Manginaracina)
• Live: *Wembley, Budapest* • Compilation: *On Air*

First released by Ricky Nelson in 1961 as the US B-side to 'Travelin' Man', but released in the UK as an A-side, 'Hello Mary Lou (Goodbye Heart)' is a classic relic of the innocent, pre-British Invasion rock'n'roll, and was cited by Brian as a favorite single of his, not least because of the guitar solo. "And then you would find this wonderful solo in the middle of 'Hello Mary Lou', by Rick Nelson and that was *wow*, incredibly inspiring for me to find things like that," Brian gleefully told Richard Allinson in June 1998.

No surprise, then, that Brian was the prime mover in the song's inclusion in the set list for the 1986 Magic tour. Performed as the second song in the acoustic medley of influential 1950s and 1960s rock'n'roll songs (Elvis's '(You're So Square) Baby I Don't Care' and Little Richard's 'Tutti Frutti' were the other two songs), 'Hello Mary Lou (Goodbye Heart)' featured Brian on prominent vocals, almost overpowering Freddie and Roger at times. Though it lasted just over a minute in the live setting, it was pleasant enough to nearly justify the inclusion of the medley at the expense of 'Somebody To Love', 'It's A Hard Life', or 'Princes Of The Universe'.

HELP! *(Lennon/McCartney)*

This Beatles song was played live by 1984.

THE HERO *(May)*
• Album: *Flash* • Live: *On Fire, Montreal* • Bonus: *Flash*

Of the 18 compositions released on the *Flash Gordon* soundtrack album, only two have a set of lyrics: 'Flash's Theme', the lightweight main theme for the title character which also became the album's sole single, and 'The Hero', a more universal track reminiscent of Queen's heavier songs. Written by Brian, the song is essentially a vocal version of 'Battle Theme', constructed around film composer Howard Blake's melody of the same-titled orchestral piece. Stuck for an end credits composition, Brian and engineer Alan Douglas created a rough demo of 'The Hero' out of drum machine loops, before the rest of the band joined the session to commit to tape the raucous rocker. Completed in a day, the solo was overdubbed on an unknown guitar, as The Red Special was then back in Munich, and not at the Townhouse in London. Freddie reportedly cried to Brian, "You always write me these songs which fucking kill my beautiful voice!" Hearing his powerful but strained howl on 'The Hero', it's hard not to sympathize with him. An alternate take, with a slightly different vocal from Freddie, was heard during the end credits of the film, while a new mix by Justin Shirley-Smith and Joshua J. Macrae, prepared directly from the original multitrack tapes, was created for the 2011 deluxe edition of *Flash Gordon* and is worth the price of admission alone for Freddie's stunning double-tracked vocals.

'The Hero' was included in the set list late in the 1980 The Game European tour as part of a *Flash Gordon* medley. This was retained throughout 1981 in the Japanese, South American and Mexican tours, and was also played in Montreal for the *We Will Rock You* video shoot but dropped prior to its release. The song then became the opening number on the 1982 Hot Space European, UK and (occasionally) Japanese

tours before being dropped indefinitely. The song was brought out of mothballs for several shows of the Queen + Adam Lambert 2012 and 2016 shows, once again performed as the opening number following a taped introduction of 'Flash'.

"HEROES" *(Bowie/Eno)*

Instead of David Bowie tackling any other Queen tracks besides the obvious one, the chameleon rocker opted to perform two of his own songs, 'All The Young Dudes' and '"Heroes"', backed by Brian, Roger, John, Spike Edney on keyboards, and a host of backing vocalists. On '"Heroes"', Bowie's 1977 classic is transformed into an even more powerful anthem than on its original studio recording, and is undeniably one of the best performances of the concert.

HEY MAMA (KEEP YOUR BIG MOUTH SHUT) *(McDaniel)*

This little-known Bo Diddley track was performed live by The Reaction.

HIJACK MY HEART *(Queen)*
• B-side: 8/89 [12]

It had been nearly a decade since Roger sang lead vocals on a Queen song, but those yearning for the drummer's raspy, high-pitched voice would be pleasantly surprised by 'Hijack My Heart', an out-take from *The Miracle* sessions issued as the B-side of 'The Invisible Man'.

With the unspoken rule persisting throughout the 1980s albums that Freddie should be the main vocalist, it's unsurprising that 'Hijack My Heart' wasn't a serious contender for *The Miracle*, but one wishes that a concession had been made, as it's a particularly strong track and would have offered a bit of diversity, not only in the vocal department, but also in terms of lyrics: the song is very 'Roger', as he sings about beautiful women and fast cars. The faded outro contains some delicious funk bass lines, though a demo version which leaked out in 2006 contains some beautiful piano playing absent from the finished version. The song eluded release on retrospective compilations until the fourth installment of *The Singles Collection*, and was duly added as a bonus track on the 2011 reissue of *The Miracle*.

THE HITMAN *(Queen)*
• Album: *Innuendo* • B-side: 3/91 [22]

This vicious rocker is a welcome return to such early Queen anthems as 'Tie Your Mother Down' and 'Sweet Lady', and provided *Innuendo* with a fresh balance of hard rock songs with the more introspective ballads. The initiator this time was Freddie, who originally wrote the song on keyboards but gave it to John, who restructured the arrangement. "[The] finished version had very little to do with the original idea," Brian told *Rip* magazine in 1991. "Most of the riff came from Freddie. I wasn't even in the room when they wrote it. I changed the key and some of the notes to make it playable on the guitar. We finished the backing track, but it seemed to ramble. John sat down and decided to reconstruct the track. He changed the order. He changed everything. I went back and played on that. Then we filled in the gaps on the lyrics, did the harmonies and generally tidied up."

The song features a roaring ensemble performance and some truly inspired guitar work from Brian, but is marred by its forgettable lyrics and a thin, tinny mix. A minute-long demo version with Brian on lead vocals was released on the *Hints Of Innuendo* promo tape, and perpetuated the rumor that he was not only the prime mover behind the song, but that it was intended for *Back To The Light*. At this point in their career, the band were working on each others' songs with the rule that all songwriting credits were to the collective whole, so Brian may have been simply offering up his own lyrical ideas for consideration – and with lines like "Don't gimme no shit, man" watered down to "I'm just it, man", it was a blessing that the others intervened.

'The Hitman' was issued as the B-side of 'I'm Going Slightly Mad' in March 1991.

HOLD ON *(Mercury/Mack)*
• Soundtrack (Freddie): *Zabou*
• Compilation (Freddie): *Solo Collection*

Just before Mack started working with Queen again on 'One Vision', he had been in the studios with American singer/guitarist Jo Dare, recording material for an unspecified project. Dare, formerly of Chicago punk band The ODD, hadn't made much of her musical career up until that point, though she had an unbelievably powerful voice, which Mack casually mentioned to Freddie in passing one day. Intrigued, Freddie visited the session, and he and Dare quickly developed a rapport, ultimately leading to a recording collaboration. (Dare also later attended Freddie's 39th birthday extravaganza; consequentially, she duly appeared in the music video for 'Living On My Own', dressed as a cat.) 'Hold On' was eventually submitted for the 1986 German film *Zabou*, with lyrics by Freddie and music by Mack, marking the only known songwriting collaboration between the two. The song has a pleasant, Carribbean feel to it, while the lyrics recall the stiff-upper-lip optimism of 'Friends Will Be Friends', but the true stars of the show are the vocalists, who match each other superbly.

Released as a German-only single with Tina Turner's contribution to the soundtrack, 'A Change Is Gonna Come', as the flip-side, 'Hold On' failed to chart, and for years remained a curiosity, until its release on *The Solo Collection* box set in 2000.

HOLDING ON *(Mercury)*
• Compilation (Freddie): *Solo Collection*

This powerful song was recorded on 9 March 1987 at Townhouse Studios during the *Barcelona* sessions (but not intended for that album), with Erdal Kizilkay on bass guitar, David Richards on drum programming and Mike Moran on keyboards. Kizilkay, a multi-talented musician who had just contributed a slew of instruments to David Bowie's *Never Let Me Down* (also produced by David Richards at Mountain Studios), contributed the funky bassline, and Freddie was so inspired by Kizilkay that he delivered the spirited, improvised vocals. Unfortunately, the track was never completed, and forgotten in favor of stronger material when Queen reconvened the following year to record *The Miracle*. 'Holding On' was finally released in 2000 on *The Solo Collection*.

HONKY TONK WOMEN *(Jagger/Richards)*

This 1969 Rolling Stones classic was performed live by The Cross, with Bob Geldof on vocals, at the Gosport Festival on 30 July 1992.

HOOCHIE COOCHIE MAN *(Dixon)*

Due to a technical difficulty during The Brian May Band's September 1998 show in Warsaw, Jamie Moses took over on guitar and vocals and played this version of Willie Dixon's 'Hoochie Coochie Man' until Brian's technicians were able to fix the problem.

HORNS OF DOOM *(Richards)*
• Compilation (Freddie): *Solo Collection*

Recorded entirely by David Richards, without any contribution whatsoever from Freddie, on 11 February 1987 (during sessions for *Barcelona* in London), 'Horns Of Doom' is a compelling and sinister song, with synthesized horns, drum-machine, keyboards and percussion, but why it was released on *The Solo Collection* is anyone's guess. Even Greg Brooks' liner notes fail to mention the logic of its inclusion.

HOT PATOOTIE: *see* WHATEVER HAPPENED TO SATURDAY NIGHT?

HOW CAN I GO ON *(Mercury/Moran)*
• Album (Freddie): *Barcelona* • A-side (Freddie): 1/89 [95] • A-side (Freddie): 10/92 • Compilation (Freddie): *Solo Collection*

Undoubtedly one of Freddie's most gorgeous songs, 'How Can I Go On' is a highlight, not only of *Barcelona*, but of his entire latter-day oeuvre. Segueing from 'Guide Me Home', the song expresses similar sentiments, of a man searching for inspiration and guidance in the midst of emotional uncertainty: "Is anybody there to believe in me / To hear my plea and take care of me?" At a time when Freddie was thrown into inner turmoil and having to face his mortality, 'How Can I Go On' is especially poignant.

Several versions of the song were recorded during the *Barcelona* sessions and ultimately released on *The Solo Collection*. With an alternate recorded on 2 March 1988, this was an attempt to create a passable take, with Freddie ad-libbing vocals, indicating the lyrics had yet to be finalized, and vocalizing (like most of the other *Barcelona* out-takes) where Montserrat was to fill in. Two early takes were also captured – the first, on 9 April 1987, is stunning, with piano accompaniment for the first half before diverting to an orchestrated tangent that would be omitted in the released version; the second, on 24 June 1987, finds the recording starting halfway through the song already in progress, much to the audible disappointment of Freddie when told by David Richards that not all his vocal performance was recorded. An instrumental version was also created for the box set, and shows just how complex and breathtaking the original backing track really was.

Released as the third and final single from *Barcelona* in January 1989, and attracting a bit of attention from

Queen fans due to the presence of John Deacon on bass, 'How Can I Go On', backed with 'Overture Piccante', charted at a disappointing No. 95 in the UK. Because the song was recorded without a break from 'Guide Me Home', a special single mix was created, with the ultimate piano notes of the preceding track serving as the introduction. The song was remixed and re-released in October 1992, this time with 'The Golden Boy', to capitalize on the success of the summer 1992 Olympic Games, and the consequential re-release of 'Barcelona'. Unfortunately, the single performed even worse the second time, not charting at all in the UK.

A video was filmed on 8 October 1988 at La Nit, Barcelona, during one of the few promotional 'concerts' performed for the album (Freddie never performed any of the *Barcelona* material live, only miming to the album versions), this time at a celebration of Spain, who had just earned a contract to host the 1992 Olympic Games. The versions of 'The Golden Boy' and 'How Can I Go On' from this performance became the official promotional videos for the songs, and would later be issued on both a video EP in 1989 and *The Freddie Mercury Video Collection* in 2000.

HOW CAN IT BE

It's unknown whether 'How Can It Be' is a cover or an original tune (or even an alternate title for a completely different song altogether), but it was reportedly played live by 1984.

A HUMAN BODY *(Taylor)*
• B-side: 5/80 [14] • Compilation: *Vision* • Bonus: *Game*

According to co-producer Mack, Roger's 'A Human Body' was originally intended to appear on *The Game* in place of 'Coming Soon': "I remember Roger wrote three tracks for *The Game*, and the three caused problems in the band: there was a song called 'Coming Soon' which Roger, at first, thought would be on the single, leaving a place on the album for another one of his, 'A Human Body'. But Brian and Freddie objected that if 'A Human Body' was included, the album would be too melodic, since they had already written three songs for it. Finally, they convinced Roger, who was especially proud of 'A Human Body', and opted for 'Coming Soon'." Queen may have been guilty of some minor blunders in the past, but this was inexcusable: 'A Human Body' is a fine song and one of Roger's most accomplished compositions, with a strong ensemble performance and lyrics inspired by Captain Robert Falcon Scott's failed explorations in Antarctica. Roger takes the lead vocal on this mid-tempo, acoustic-driven rocker, performing most of the instruments (indicating it may have been originally intended for *Fun In Space*), with prominent backing vocals by Roger, Freddie and Brian.

Unfortunately, the song was neglected, due to its non-album status, appearing as the B-side of 'Play The Game' in May 1980, and included on the rarities album *The Complete Vision*, available only on the 1985 box set *The Complete Works*. The song eluded release on the CD format for years, glaringly overlooked for inclusion on the 1991 reissue of *The Game*, but was finally released in 2009 on *The Singles Collection – Volume Two* and two years later on the reissue of *The Game*.

I AM THE DRUMMER (IN A ROCK N' ROLL BAND)
(Taylor)
• Album (Roger): *Earth*

First premiered at the 2011 Queen Fan Club convention, this tongue-in-cheek rocker, with a terse, synth-based backing and a sturdy rhythm, is one of a handful of up-tempo songs to make an appearance on the otherwise laid-back *Fun On Earth*. A delicate bridge, dominated by piano, finds Roger affecting an upper-crust, almost Keith Moon-inspired vocal, as he channels the legendary Who drummer by rattling off a list of his likes and even addressing his status as "the butt of a thousand jokes / From far less-talented blokes". While it might be a bit out of place among the more introspective songs on the album, 'I Am The Drummer (In a Rock n' Roll Band)' is a welcome return to the loud, aggressive Roger of years past.

(I BELIEVE I'LL) DUST MY BROOM *(Johnson)*

This song was performed live by The Cross, with Brian on guitar and vocals and John on bass, at the band's 1988 Christmas party for the fan club.

I CAN HEAR MUSIC *(Greenwich/Spector/Barry)*
• A-side (Larry Lurex): 6/73 • Compilation (Freddie): *Solo Collection*

Queen had finally been given the chance to record their first album, though under restricted circumstances, and it was during this time that producer Robin Geoffrey Cable ran into Freddie in the corridors of Trident Studios in the summer of 1972. Cable had overheard Freddie singing a Queen track and, impressed with his voice, asked the vocalist to contribute lead vocals to a re-recording of the 1969 Beach Boys track, 'I Can Hear Music'. Cable considered himself a visionary producer, going for the lavish 'wall of sound' that Phil Spector had pioneered in the 1960s, and successfully recreated that sound on 'I Can Hear Music'. Even at this early stage of Freddie's career, he pierces through the din of ringing acoustic guitars and thunderous percussion, with an exuberantly youthful delivery that's still stunning all these years later.

Incidentally, during one take, Cable was heard grumbling about the sound of the synthesizer, which was providing a solo where a guitar might normally be; Freddie jumped at the opportunity, and suggested Brian provide a solo on The Red Special instead. Roger, too, was hanging around the studios and was duly recruited to perform the rollicking claves, maracas and tambourines that are densely layered throughout. Since the song wasn't technically a Queen track (the drums, bass, acoustic guitars and strings were all performed by unknown session musicians, and John Deacon didn't feature at all), it was initially fated to remain unreleased, but Cable loved the recording (and the other song, 'Goin' Back', also recorded during the sessions) so much that he insisted they be released. Through negotiations with Trident, a one-time deal was struck with EMI, and 'I Can Hear Music' was released in June 1973; 'Keep Yourself Alive' would be released as Queen's debut single two weeks later. For this reason, the song was not billed as Queen, but instead as Larry Lurex and The Voles From Venus, a lighthearted jab at two contemporary, separate acts: Gary Glitter and The Spiders From Mars, though The Voles From Venus was eventually dropped. Receiving little promotion, apart from a brief mention in *Record Mirror* ("It may sink without a trace, but the arrangement of this old Spector-inspired piece and the high-pitched voice going like the clappers ... well, it could click"), the single simply disappeared and remained unreleased on any official compilation until 2000, appearing on *The Solo Collection*, and again six years later on *Lover Of Life, Singer Of Songs*.

I CAN TAKE YOU HIGHER *(Taylor)*
• Compilation (Roger): *Lot*

For years, only a 40-second snippet of 'I Can Take You Higher' circulated among collectors, but from the short clip that exists, the strengths of the track are obvious, proving that it wouldn't have been out of place on *Strange Frontier*, for which the song was originally recorded. The song was returned to in December 1989, when The Cross ran through four tracks at Jam Studios, and while the more finalized version still would remain unreleased, it finally found a home on the 2013 box set *The Lot*.

I CAN'T DANCE / KEEP SMILIN' (*Mercury*)

• Compilation (Freddie): *Solo Collection*

Inspired by an anonymous ballet dancer friend of Freddie's, 'I Can't Dance' was recorded on 17 February 1987 (also the birth date of Brian's second daughter, Emily) at Townhouse Studios and actually featured the anonymous friend on additional backing vocals, though the released recording on the 2000 box set is an alternate version without the vocals (Freddie harmonizes with himself).

The song changes pace about two minutes in, with Freddie singing an upbeat song titled 'Keep Smilin''. Freddie had been approached by the parents of Colin Preston, who asked the vocalist to visit their son in hospital. Colin was a life-long Queen fan, and bore more than a passing resemblance to Freddie, and was involved in a car accident and sunk into a coma. Freddie went one better and took the studio time to record a personal song for the fan, then sent the tape to Colin's family. Freddie kept in contact with Colin's parents and heard that, while he rallied initially, he died shortly afterwards, but that the song had made a difference. Colin's family promised that the tape would be buried with him so that it would be a song just for him, and so it would seem in bad taste to include such a recording on any wider release, but it was included anyway on *The Solo Collection*, carrying a dedication to Colin.

I CAN'T GET YOU OUT OF MY HEAD (*Moss*)

• Compilation (Roger): *Lot*

Long believed to be an out-take from Roger's *Strange Frontier* album, 'I Can't Get You Out Of My Head' was recently discovered to be a Clayton Moss out-take from the *Mad: Bad: And Dangerous To Know* sessions – as confirmed by the songwriter itself on his YouTube channel page. (This, however, sits at odds with an acetate from the *Strange Frontier* sessions, purchased by a renowned collector in 1986, which has both

this song and 'Celebration' on it. The plot thickens!) With ringing acoustic guitars and tasteful saxophone, and a set of lyrics of being utterly smitten with a past love while lamenting the loss of the relationship, the song would have been a pleasant addition to its parent album, but was dropped in favor of Moss's other songs, 'Penetration Guru' and 'Better Things'. The song was finally released in 2013 on *The Lot*.

I CAN'T EXPLAIN (*Townshend*)

The Who's first single was performed live by The Cross at the first fan club show in December 1992 at the Marquee, with Roger Daltrey on lead vocals.

I CAN'T LIVE WITH YOU (*Queen*)

• Album: *Innuendo* • Compilation: *Rocks* • Bonus: *Innuendo*

Unlike the raucous 'Headlong' and 'The Hitman', 'I Can't Live With You' is a more controlled rocker on *Innuendo*, a track that Brian had originally written for a solo project. "I was in the studio for a couple of days to get some things out of my system," Brian told Extreme guitarist Nuno Bettencourt in a 1991 interview in *Guitar World*. "I thought that maybe I'd be left with a solo album, maybe with a Queen album – I just didn't know – and I came up with 'Headlong' and 'I Can't Live With You', and the guys liked them."

Not one of the standout tracks on the album, 'I Can't Live With You' sounds like a *Miracle*-era reject, especially with its tinny-sounding backing track. Freddie's vocal performance, as always, is superb, and Brian redeems the track with several soaring guitar solos, but in lieu of real dreams are programmed drums, and John's bass was pushed to the background, almost to the point of silence. "For some reason," Brian continued in *Guitar World*, "['I Can't Live With You'] was almost impossible to mix. It was one of those things where you put all the faders up and it sounds pretty good, and you think, 'We'll work on this for a couple of hours.' Then it gets worse and worse and worse. We kept going back to the rough mix. It's got an atmosphere to it. I think it sounds so special because we kept a lot of the demo stuff on it. Usually it all gets replaced."

The song was remixed for promotional single purposes in the US by Brian Malouf, indicating it may have been in the running for a Stateside-only release, but even that couldn't save it from being more than an average track with poor production. It was finally salvaged in 1997 with a completely new and more muscular backing track replacing the original, much as Brian originally intended it. The live drums and aggressive guitar turn it into the rocker it deserves to be, but, incidentally, it would have been out of place on *Innuendo*; thus, its placement was appropriate on *Queen Rocks*, a Brian-heavy compilation of rock songs from the band's catalog. In addition to its placement on the now-deleted *Queen Rocks*, the re-take was also issued as a bonus track on the 2011 reissue of *Innuendo*.

I CRY FOR YOU (LOVE, HOPE AND CONFUSION)
(Taylor/Richards)
• Album (Roger): *Frontier* • B-side (Roger): 7/84

Concluding Roger's *Strange Frontier* in a typically overblown manner, 'I Cry For You (Love, Hope And Confusion)' has split fan appreciation neatly down the middle, but, love it or loathe it, it's an optimistic rock anthem with percolating synths, programmed drums, and soaring guitars, with production values dating it firmly to 1984. Rife with cliche lyrics ("I cry for you", "love me tender", "give 'em hell", "hope springs eternal") meant to inspire, the song is nevertheless a superb finish to Roger's second solo album.

Released as the B-side of 'Strange Frontier' in July 1984, 'I Cry For You (Love, Hope And Confusion)' was remixed by John Deacon, slowing down the song to half-time, removing most of the drums – which revealed Roger's vocals more clearly – and adding his own flourishes on bass. This remix was then extended for the 12" vinyl version of 'Strange Frontier', this time by both John and Mack, bringing the running time to just over six minutes and adding further guitar work and programmed drums. Both single and extended mixes were finally released on Roger's nearly all-encompassing box set *The Lot*.

I DON'T CARE *(Taylor)*
• Album (Roger): *Earth*

Fun On Earth is a largely reflective, mostly laid-back affair, with Roger clearly in love with his wife and muse, Sarina. From a songwriting perspective, the album is hardly challenging, with a lot of the songs dealing with love and emotions – as he said in an interview, the album was titled as such because he's felt a lot more down to earth as he grew older – but he still threw in a treat or two for fans. 'I Don't Care' is the biggest surprise: a cool and sleek jazz tune, with Roger taking

the role of a big band drummer (incidentally, the drum pattern is reminiscent of his Queen + Paul Rodgers tour solo, 'Let There Be Drums') while assuring his muse that whatever she does is fine with him, so long as they can be together. (A classic case of toe-curling lyrics can be found on this song: "If love is blood / I got hemophilia".) With upright bass, saxophone, and vibraphones littering the musical arrangement, as well as some gritty guitar here and there, 'I Don't Care' is a welcome breath of fresh air from Roger's standard repertoire of political and theological jabs.

(I DON'T WANT NOBODY) TEASIN' AROUND (WITH ME) *(Emerson)*

Brian was asked to contribute a recording to *Good Rockin' Tonight: The Legacy Of Sun Records*, released in 2001 and also featuring luminaries such as Paul McCartney, Van Morrison, and Jimmy Page and Robert Plant. The absolute highlight was the one song that didn't appear on the album: Brian's recording of Billy 'The Kid' Emerson's 1954 blues track '(I Don't Want Nobody) Teasin' Around (With Me)' is deconstructed to a mournful slow burn, with the guitarist squeezing every last bit of emotion out of his weeping guitar. The true surprise was Brian's voice: long suited only for tender ballads and not loud rock songs, his voice is especially powerful on this recording, bouncing between a barely-restrained whisper and an anguished howl. When asked about the difference between singing rock and slower numbers in 2001, Brian said, "Actually, I've been playing some blues lately. I've done a couple of tracks and I usually end up singing and not screaming; it's in the range where I can put some passion into it. The funny thing is, I actually can scream. I just did this track for Scotty Moore on a Sun Records tribute. It starts off very quiet and then the guy screams because he's totally pissed off ... I did a version of that and I screamed it; the problem is that I can't do it all night." Despite not being released on the album, Brian gave it its one and only live performance on 7 July 2001 at the Montreux Jazz Festival in Stravinski Hall, Montreux.

I DON'T WANT TO BE A ROLLING STONE

During a Reddit AMA (Ask Me Anything) session in August 2012, a user asked Rhys Thomas if he unearthed any Queen out-takes while compiling *The Great Pretender*. "I haven't really," he responded. "Well, apart from another song by Bowie and Queen called 'I Don't Want To Be A Rolling Stone'. It's stunning. It was later reworked to become 'I Go Crazy'. It's [as] good as 'Under Pressure'. It would have been a great follow up single."

Furthermore, that same year, an anthology book called *The Complete Illustrated Lyrics* was published, which contained scanned replicas of handwritten (or typewritten) lyrics alongside other memorabilia and ephemera. Contained within was an early, potentially untitled draft for 'I Go Crazy', which fans have speculated may have gone under the 'Rolling Stone' title. However, considering some of the vitriolic anti-Bowie lyrics Brian penned ("We had a little party with the man who stole the blow / I played a little song 'n' said you can play along / He said that's NOT how it should go", "I wouldn't mind the milkman, I wouldn't mind the dude / And if the cleaner came along and wiped the tape it wouldn't put me in a bad mood"), it would be hard to imagine how Queen and David Bowie could have ever recorded this song.

I DREAM OF CHRISTMAS *(May)*

Written in July 1984 during sessions for 'Thank God It's Christmas', Brian's offering for a one-off holiday single turned out to be far superior to Roger's plodding contribution, which was chosen instead. Later recorded by Brian's girlfriend Anita Dobson in 1987, that version features a soaring guitar solo, prominent backing vocals from Mr May himself, and a children's choir, recalling John Lennon's 'Happy X-Mas (War Is Over)'. Unfortunately, it seems that Queen never recorded the track – certainly if they had, it would have snuck out as the B-side to 'Thank God It's Christmas' – and that a demo version from Brian may be all that exists.

I FEEL FINE *(Lennon/McCartney)*

Another Beatles song played live by 1984, Brian revisited it in 1978, during the Rock 'N' Roll Medley, and in 1986, throwing in the riff during his customary guitar solo.

I GO CRAZY *(May)*

• B-side: 1/84 [2] • Compilation: *Vision* • CD Single: 11/88 • Bonus: *Works*

Recorded during sessions for *The Works* in 1983, Brian's 'I Go Crazy' is one of the band's finest rockers and deserved a place on the album as much as 'Man

On The Prowl' or 'Tear It Up'. During the collective cherry-picking of songs for the album, though, 'I Go Crazy' was voted off, as Brian explained to *Faces* magazine in 1984: "As [Queen] is a democracy, [the others] don't get their own way, either. With this last album, now, I wrote a single, you might call it one of my heavy indulgences. It was very rough and raw, but I really liked the sound. The other three hated it so much they were ashamed to play it. So, it wound up as the B-side on 'Radio Ga Ga', which is good as it gives the fans a song they didn't receive on the album, more for their money. But you see, it was kept off the album by the majority."

Telling a heartbreaking story about a star-struck girl leaving her "normal" boyfriend for an unnamed famous rock singer, while he maintains a stiff upper lip attitude, 'I Go Crazy' is set to a muscular and exuberant backing track, which would have helped reaffirm Queen's status as a rock band, so sorely needed after the poor reaction to *Hot Space*. Incidentally, the song was first recorded during sessions for *Hot Space* in the autumn of 1981, which Greg Brooks confirmed 25 years later by premiering an early run-through recording at a Fan Club convention, though this version lacks vocals. Brian clearly enjoyed his song, and would occasionally play the riff in his nightly guitar solo throughout 1981 and 1982.

Oh, and the main character needn't have worried about seeing The Rolling Stones in 1984; they weren't touring that year.

I GOT MY MOJO WORKING *(Waters)*

This Muddy Waters blues tune was played live by 1984.

I GOT YOU (I FEEL GOOD) *(Brown)*

James Brown's famous hit single from 1966 was performed live by The Reaction.

I GUESS WE'RE FALLING OUT

Starting off with the same drum machine pattern used for 'My Baby Does Me', 'I Guess We're Falling Out' is a Brian-based ballad recorded during *The Miracle* sessions, and has often been deemed by fans as Queen's greatest unreleased song. Quite a hefty statement for a song that features only one complete verse, but there are the makings of a strong performance here, with gorgeous vocal harmonies and some fine guitar work, and it would have been a nice addition to *The Miracle* if only the band had finished it.

I LOVED A BUTTERFLY:
see **SOME THINGS THAT GLITTER**

I (WHO HAVE NOTHING)
(Donida/Mogol/Leiber/Stoller)
• Live (Brian & Kerry): *Acoustic* • Album (Brian & Kerry): *Golden*

This orchestral tour-de-force is the centerpiece of *Golden Days*, and had been an obvious favorite of Brian and Kerry's for several years. Based on the Italian song 'Uno Dei Tanti', 'I (Who Have Nothing)' was translated into English by Jerry Leiber and Mike Stoller and was recorded by Ben E. King, who had a hit with the song in 1963. On this recording, which turns into a glorious dance track midway through, features Zucchero's daughter Irene Fornaciari on Italian vocals; a more sedate acoustic version was released on *Acoustic By Candlelight*.

I WANNA HOLD YOUR HAND *(Lennon/McCartney)*

This 1964 Beatles single was played live by the Brian May Band on only one occasion: 12 December 1993 in Liverpool, a fitting location.

I WANNA TAKE YOU HIGHER

This isn't Roger's attempt at covering Sly & The Family Stone's 1969 single, but is instead a completely unrelated song from the fruitful preliminary sessions for *Strange Frontier* in 1983. With a jerky rhythm and layers of raw guitars, the song addresses Roger's fascination of fast cars and women, but was deemed superfluous and remains unreleased. The song was later incorporated into 'I Can Take You Higher', recorded in December 1989 with The Cross and finally released in 2013 on Roger's all-encompassing box set, *The Lot*.

I WANNA TESTIFY *(Clinton/Taylor/Taylor)*
• A-side (Roger): 8/77 • Compilation (Roger): *Lot*, *Best*

The summer of 1977 was a season of change for most bands, with the new generation of confrontational musicians raising a tuneless ruckus. Unlike the rest of Queen, who were deeply rooted in their own musical preferences of the past – vaudeville, music hall, gospel, funk, R&B, blues, and good old-fashioned rock'n'roll – Roger embraced the new sound and, while the rest of the band was resting after a strenuous year of touring, he immediately started to record home demos of several new songs.

This time, though, the ideas flowed faster than ever, and in no time he had three completed songs: 'Fight From The Inside', 'Turn On The TV' and 'I Wanna Testify'. Along with an upgraded version of 'Sheer Heart Attack' from the autumn 1974 sessions, Roger reserved 'Fight From The Inside' for the next Queen project but decided that the other two tracks were too good to leave unreleased. Before long, he had his first solo single ready for release.

'I Wanna Testify' is the stronger of the two tracks, and was rightly given top billing upon its release. The official explanation for the song was that Roger simply re-recorded The Parliaments' 1967 '(I Wanna) Testify' (which had already been upgraded in 1974 by the relaunched Parliaments), but a close listen to the original recordings and Roger's "cover" reveal that these are two completely different songs, sharing only a similar melody and chorus. Roger, giving credit where credit was due, credits George Clinton and Daron Taylor, the original songwriters, and rightly credited himself for the arrangements.

Written in the style of many other R&B classics of the 1950s and 1960s, the song finds a hapless, stressed father in the midst of personal conflict with his wife and son before overworking himself into alcohol addiction and losing not only his job but his family, too. It's a touching story, striking a rueful tone with the concluding verse, acknowledging his fault and urging others to do the same: "Please pay attention to the words that I mention / And listen to the moral of this song". Set to a chunky backing, with all instruments performed and all vocals sung by Roger – not taking the term "solo record" lightly at all – 'I Wanna Testify' is a strong single debut, showcasing not only Roger's clever arrangement but his adeptness at instrument swapping.

Unfortunately, all the effort that went into the single, with the drummer spending £5000 of his own money to record the song, didn't pay off in the end: released at the end of August 1977, the single sank without a trace. Roger wrote in the autumn 1977 issue of the fan club magazine, "About my own recent single – you know, the one you didn't hear on the radio – well, it was merely a pleasant excursion and will not be a regular thing. People have asked me if I'm going solo – well, certainly not, nothing could be further from the truth. I think it's vitally important right now that Queen keeps its strong group identity, as that is one of our main strengths. So many groups seem to break up at the wrong time or just prematurely; it won't happen with us." Promotion was minimal, despite a great performance on Marc Bolan's television show *Marc* in September 1977, mere days before the glam rocker's untimely death.

The song remained unreleased on CD for 36 years, when it appeared on Roger's nearly all-encompassing *The Lot* box set, and was released the following year on his *Best* compilation.

I WANT IT ALL *(Queen)*

• A-side: 5/89 [3] • Album: *Miracle* • Compilation: *Hits2*, *Classic* • Live: *46664* • Live (Q+PR): *Return*, *Ukraine*

Praised as a welcome return to Queen's classic rock sound, 'I Want It All' was written by Brian in 1988 and submitted to the sessions for *The Miracle* as one of the first completed songs for the album. Focusing on a world-weary society of oppressed youths, the song is a call-to-arms to adolescents yearning for more in life, with a powerful, anthemic rallying cry at the heart of the song. "We were heading into the period where we decided to share the credit for all the songs," Brian explained in 2003, "and John has said that [it] was pretty much a finished song when we went into the studios – that's true, it was just this riff that I was obsessed with for months. The actual title was a favorite phrase of Anita's, a very ambitious girl: 'I want it all, and I want it *now*'."

Rightly released as the forerunner to Queen's first studio album in three years, the song reached No. 3 in the UK upon its release in May 1989, and also became a minor US hit, peaking at No. 50. The single version is superior, with a punchier mix and omitting the instrumental intro, replacing it with the hard-hitting chorus, and editing out part of the instrumental section after the bridge. (Hollywood Records issued the wrong version of the song on the 1991 re-release of *The Miracle*, instead putting out a version that excised the first chorus and cut the song back a few seconds.) "'I Want It All' re-establishes our old image in a way," Brian said in 1989. "It's nice to come back with something strong. Something that reminds people we're a live group. I don't think we're a singles band, really. Just before we put the single out I started listening to what's on the radio, and the kind of stuff

that becomes a hit these days bears no resemblance to what we do. People only remember the hits, but I suppose we have done okay."

A video was shot for the single on 22 April 1989, with David Mallet directing (the last time he would direct a video with Queen while Freddie was still alive, though he would go on to direct the Concert For Life and 'Heaven For Everyone' from *Made In Heaven*). The video was an attempt to prove that Queen could still be considered a live band without actually touring; it didn't work. "Of course now we're in an era, making this video, where Freddie's already very ill," Brian said, "and he's finding it harder to actually find the energy to do things like this. You wouldn't think so seeing him in this video, because he just squeezes so much out of himself, but a lot of the time, in this period, he was pretty sick. So it's an amazing effort of will that he managed to do this at all." Shot at Elstree Sound Studios, the band are placed on a small stage in the center of a gigantic warehouse. The stage was chosen to create intimacy, yet they appear ill-at-ease – Freddie, especially – and remain mostly static during the video. Not one of the more memorable videos, it was nevertheless issued on *Greatest Flix II* and *Greatest Video Hits 2*, the latter featuring some memorably humorous out-takes of the band attempting to get the introductory sequence right. Roger explained the video in 2003, saying, "It's not the most interesting video, but it's so simple in terms of approach and ideas. It's just 'big': big lenses, big spotlights – a performance video. I think we got so sick of the concept things and stories and people pretending to act and dressing up and huge film sets and everything at the time was sort of trying to look like *Blade Runner*. I [thought] we'd make it very simple with a sort of live-ish performance."

Due to Freddie's ill health and his inability to tour, the song was never performed live by Queen in the singer's lifetime. "We were never able to perform this song live," Brian explained. "It would have become something of the staple core of the Queen show, I'm sure, very participatory. It was designed for the audience to sing along to, very anthemic." The song was, however, performed by Who vocalist Roger Daltrey and Queen during the Concert For Life on 20 April 1992, which suited Daltrey's voice just fine. In fact, Brian commented in 2003 that the bridge of the song was a Pete Townshend tactic he put to good use: "Interesting, I wrote myself a bit in the middle. I can't remember quite why that was, it's a very sort of Pete Townshend thing to do, isn't it? But it made a nice little kind of duet in the middle, a bit of sparring between me and Freddie, and I know he enjoyed that." The song became a live favorite of both the Queen + Paul Rodgers and Queen + Adam Lambert tours, becoming one of the few latter-day Queen singles to have been performed live.

I WANT TO BREAK FREE *(Deacon)*
• Album: *Works* • A-side: 4/84 [3] • CD Single: 11/88
• Live: *Magic, Wembley, 46664, Budapest* • Compilation: *Hits2, HitsUS* • Bonus: *Works* • B-side (Roger): 11/94 [32] • Live (Q+PR): *Return, Ukraine*

"One of our biggest hits," Brian said of 'I Want To Break Free' in 2003. "[John] didn't write many songs, but most of them sure counted." This understatement is an accurate evaluation of John Deacon's songwriting abilities: of the 15 studio albums released in Queen's career, eight of John's 21 compositions became singles, most of them major hits, but none more prominently than 'I Want To Break Free'.

Released as the second single from *The Works* in April 1984, the song became a major hit worldwide, peaking at No. 3 in the UK and becoming an anthem along the same lines as 'We Will Rock You' and 'We Are The Champions'. The song expresses the main character's desire to get away from his hectic life, though some have interpreted it as a gay anthem – which Freddie was asked about by a South American reporter in 1985, responding that he wasn't the writer of the song and that it wasn't about the gay world.

Musically simplistic, with a clean acoustic guitar played by John neatly filling in the spaces in the rhythm section performed by himself and Roger (whose drumming is very economical here, but well-suited to the song), the only downside of the song is the lack of a guitar solo. In lieu of such is a synthesizer solo played by Fred Mandel (who also contributed synthesizer work to 'Radio Ga Ga' and 'Hammer To Fall'), sounding remarkably like the Red Special and therefore begging the question as to why Brian's guitar wasn't used in the first place. (Mandel later explained that this was a deliberate choice on John's part; the keyboardist was horrified that he had edged out Brian, but John was adamant. This gives some insight that not all was rosy after such an extended break from recording and touring.) The single version, extended to just over four minutes with an atmospheric synthesizer intro (and this time with some additional guitar work from Brian), has appeared on *Greatest Hits II* and the

1992 US reissue of *Greatest Hits*, while an extended remix, running just over seven minutes, appeared on 12" versions of the single and featured snippets of other songs from *The Works* à la 'More Of That Jazz' from 1978. This version was also released as a bonus track on *The Works*.

A video for the single was made in March 1984, and went on to achieve far more notoriety than anything Queen had done in the past. Suggested by Roger's then-girlfriend Dominique, the video shows the four members spoofing the popular UK television soap opera *Coronation Street*, dressing up in drag and looking fairly convincing in the process. However, the drag section of the video lasts for only the first and last verses and choruses, with the remainder being made up of some truly baffling (yet very Mallet) sequences in which the band are surrounded by coal miners, made up of members of the fan club, in an abandoned warehouse. ("And bang – there's the Royal Ballet in a box," Roger quipped in the commentary for the song on the 2003 *Greatest Video Hits 2* DVD.) Typical of Freddie, it was the combination of this sequence with the drag that would be the final nail in the coffin of Queen's relationship with America: the single fared no better than No. 45 in the charts, and Queen never toured there again. However, "We had more fun making this video than we did any other," Roger said, though he regarded the offensive ballet sequence as "art with a capital 'f' ... there's not much more I can say to that."

The single became a beloved anthem for impoverished nations, and was always well received when performed live between 1984 and 1986. When the band performed the song on the Works! tours, Freddie would appear with a pair of false breasts, revealing them to a delighted crowd (and usually thrusting them in John's face) at the conclusion of the song. However, when the band appeared at the Rock In Rio Festival in January 1985, reports trickled back that this cross-dressing move wasn't so well received: "Pop star Freddie Mercury ... received a royal pelting when he appeared onstage in Rio de Janeiro wearing women's clothes, huge plastic falsies and a black wig," *People* magazine reported. "A near riot erupted when the crowd of 350,000 began tossing stones, beer cans and other missiles at him as he started to sing Queen's 'I Want To Break Free'. Why the violent reaction, especially when fans obviously knew they weren't paying to see Lawrence Welk? Explains Maria Caetano, who worked as an interpreter at the concert: 'The song is sacred in South America because we consider it a political message about the evils of dictatorships.'" *Record Mirror* reported: "There's a spot of trouble when Freddie decides to dress up in his best Bet Lynch gear for 'I Want To Break Free'. Some outraged Brazilians decide this just isn't on and get very nasty. Instead of throwing beer cans at the stage in time honoured tradition, they decide that pebbles and bits of concrete are far more effective. Fred does a sprint to safety and it's all forgotten quickly." The truth is that the audience did boo and react negatively, but nothing was flung at Freddie, as shown in the uncut video. Just to be safe, the following week Freddie opted to go flat-chested. Fortunately (or unfortunately, depending on your preference), the falsies were kept in the closet when the song was performed live by both Queen + Paul Rodgers and Queen + Adam Lambert.

I WAS BORN TO LOVE YOU (*Mercury*)

• Album (Freddie): *BadGuy* • A-side (Freddie): 4/85 [11] • Album (Queen): *Heaven* • Bonus (Queen): *Heaven*

Written by Freddie for his 1985 solo album *Mr Bad Guy*, 'I Was Born To Love You' is a joyous and ebullient admission of love. Set to a pulsating synth beat, with some raucous piano work, the song is an early highlight of *Mr Bad Guy* and was rightly chosen as the first single from the album. Released in April 1985, the single peaked at No. 11, surprising even Freddie, who didn't think much of it to begin with and had no choice but to capitulate to CBS's demands that it be finished and released. (In Japan, the song became a minor sensation, appearing in a commercial to promote cosmetics company Noevia, and peaking at No. 55 in the charts.) An extended remix, doubling the original running time to seven minutes, is a gruelling test of endurance and patience, throwing in just about everything that a remix can handle, including trick-shot drum programming and several vocal interludes. An early version, recorded on 25 May 1984, features only Freddie on vocals and piano and is a fascinating insight into his underrated capabilities on that instrument. This version, first released on the 2000 box set *The Solo Collection*, was later released as a bonus track on the 2011 reissue of *Made In Heaven*.

One of Freddie's more endearing videos was created for the single at Limehouse Studios on 2 and 4 April 1985 and directed by old stalwart David Mallet. Showing Freddie and a female lover cavorting

through several rooms of a luxurious home, with Freddie serenading her as she gleefully runs away from him, the video strikes a saccharine and poignant tone – though the following scenes of hundreds of Amazonian women goose-stepping in a large arena is baffling. Interspersed are shots of Freddie in a room full of mirrors, dancing and twirling around as his white leather jacket increasingly dislodges itself from his upper torso.

Revisited for the *Made In Heaven* project and given the typical Queen treatment, the song is an undoubted highlight of the album. The most rock-oriented track on the album, 'I Was Born To Love You' features an exuberant vocal performance from Freddie and a delightful instrumental backing painstakingly arranged by Brian. In Japan, it was used in a 1996 Kirin Ichiban Shibori liquor advert, and was released as a single in March 1996, peaking at No. 45. Six years later, based on its use as the theme to the TV show *Pride*, it was re-released, and peaked at No. 40. Recognizing the emotional connection that Japan had to the song, it received its live debut in 2005 during the Japanese leg of the Queen + Paul Rodgers tour, when Brian and Roger performed an acoustic version as part of the final encore; a rendition of this touching duet was later released on the *Super Live In Japan* DVD. Queen + Adam Lambert duly performed the song live at Japanese dates on their tours between 2012 and 2016, with a stellar version appearing on the *Live In Japan* Blu-Ray.

I WISH YOU WOULD (*Arnold*)

This Yardbirds song was played live by 1984.

I'M A LOSER (*Lennon/McCartney*)

This Beatles song was played live by 1984.

I'M GOING SLIGHTLY MAD (*Queen*)

• Album: *Innuendo* • A-side: 3/91 [22]
• Bonus: *Innuendo*

Written by Freddie with his tongue planted firmly in cheek, 'I'm Going Slightly Mad' is a welcome return to the camp, vaudeville songs that had peppered early Queen albums but ended abruptly in 1977 once the band's increasing success dictated their musical direction. Following the humor-impaired 1980s, this exasperated outburst of comic insanity was a refreshing reminder of Freddie's wicked sense of humor. A nice wordplay song, the lighthearted lyrics betray a serious side effect – states of dementia – of AIDS victims, which Freddie was indeed going through. While on a radio promotional tour for *Innuendo* in 1991, during which Brian was inundated with questions about the band touring the US again, he candidly – and off-handedly – mentioned that Freddie was prone to black outs, and "you don't want the singer blacking out in the middle of the song."

Jim Hutton, Freddie's partner during the last years of his life, said of the song in his book *Mercury And Me*, "When Freddie penned the song 'I'm Going Slightly Mad', it was after another through-the-night session with [friend] Peter Straker. Freddie explained he had the phrase 'I'm going slightly mad' on his brain and told Peter what sort of thing he wanted to say in the song. The inspiration for it was the master of camp one-liners, Noël Coward. Freddie set about with Peter trying to come up with a succession of goofy lyrics, each funnier than the last. He screamed when they came up with things like 'I'm knitting with only one needle' and 'I'm driving only three wheels these days'. But the masterstroke was 'I think I'm a banana tree'. Once that came out there was no stopping Freddie and Straker – they were then in full flow. I went to bed to fall asleep listening to their laughter wafting upstairs."

"That was very much a Freddie track and you tend to want to give the author his head," Brian told *Guitarist* in 1994. "Even though we said that everything is by Queen, there was still somebody who was basically the original author and everyone else worked on it. It was a good idea as it produced a lot of input, but in the end it was Freddie's baby so it was natural that he would want to get certain things right."

The promotional video, filmed on 15 and 16 February 1991 at Wembley Studios, and directed by Rudi Dolezal and Hannes Rossacher, ranks as one of Queen's finest and was also one of Freddie's final appearances in front of a camera, his illness starting to show. Despite wearing a layer of padding, two layers of clothes, and a wild, matted wig, he still appears gaunt but, adapting that old adage "the show must go on", he performed as if he was the paragon of health. During filming, Freddie was heard to comment, "I wanted to make the video as memorable as possible. I've always wanted to co-star in a video with a gorilla and a group of penguins. A little bit of Queen madness." At one point during filming, one of the penguins, Cleo, decided to mark her territory – unfortunately, it happened to be on the black leather couch where she was seated between Roger and Freddie, but both leapt out of the way in time. (Life imitating art, perhaps; witness one particular line of lyrics from 'Delilah'.)

The song was picked as the second single from *Innuendo* and was released in March 1991, peaking at a disappointing No. 22, though it reached No. 1 in Hong Kong. A version of the song stripped back the standard instrumentation and highlighted the various sound effects and vocal interjections that had long been buried in the mix and mostly unheard; suitably subtitled the "Mad Mix", this was released on the 2011 reissue of *Innuendo* and is a delightful listen.

I'M IN LOVE WITH MY CAR (Taylor)
• B-side: 10/75 [1] • Album: *Opera* • Live: *Killers, Montreal* • CD Single: 11/88 • Bonus: *Opera* • Compilation: *WWRYHits*, Compilation: *On Air* • Live (The Cross): *Bootleg* • Live (Q+PR): *Return, Ukraine*

Roger's paean to four-wheeled beauties became a cult favorite upon its release in 1975, before receiving widespread attention in the live setting two years later. Full of double entendres and sexual innuendo, the song's tongue-in-cheek demeanor may not have won Roger any points with the fairer sex: "Cars don't talk back / They're just four-wheeled friends now." Featuring a raucous guitar line from Brian and some masterful drumming, the song became a perfect showcase for Roger when played live, appearing as part of the medley between 1977 and 1981, and was brought out of mothballs in 2005 for the Queen + Paul Rodgers tour.

"I remember my car at the time," Roger said in a 1997 BBC interview, "because I think we've got the exhaust on the record, and that was a little Alfa Romeo. But I think it was more about people in general, for instance boy racers. In particular we had a sound guy/ roadie at the time called Jonathan Harris, who was so in love with his car, and that inspired that. I think he had a Triumph TR4."

When 'Bohemian Rhapsody' was selected as the first single from *A Night At The Opera*, Roger fought ardently for his song to be released as the B-side, though this was initially met with resistance. (Reportedly, the drummer locked himself in a cupboard until he got his way.) Roger told the *Detroit Free Press* in 1982 that "I wish that would've been a single in its time. Of course, I made just as much money on it. It was the backside of 'Bohemian Rhapsody', so I probably made more money that way." Sixteen years after its initial release, the scars still had yet to heal, with Brian grumbling to Q magazine, "We always rowed about money. A lot of terrible injustices take place over songwriting. The major one is B-sides. Like, 'Bohemian Rhapsody' sells a million and Roger gets the same writing royalties as Freddie because he did 'I'm in Love With My Car'. There was contention about that for years." Considering one of Roger's songs wouldn't be released as an A-side until 1982, and even then as a US-only single, having 'I'm In Love With My Car' as a B-side was a small concession – though his bandmates were less than amused when he purchased a Surrey mansion in 1978, while the others were still residing in modest city homes.

(I'M NOT YOUR) STEPPING STONE *(Boyce/Hart)*

Although Jimi Hendrix later wrote a song called 'Stepping Stone', it's likely that it was The Monkees' 1966 hit that was covered live by 1984.

I'M SCARED *(May)*
• Album (Brian): *BTTL* • B-side (Brian): 8/92 [5]

"I kept doing different versions of ['I'm Scared']," Brian told *Guitar World* in 1993, "as I kept finding out that I was scared of more and more things. And I figured that most of us are. We just keep it inside. I think it's good to let all that stuff out sometimes, do a bit of screaming." In the years following Queen's retirement from touring, Brian catapulted himself into more and more projects in order to keep himself busy, but privately he was suffering from depression. With his personal life in a shambles – his marriage was falling apart because of an unstoppable attraction to *EastEnder* Anita Dobson – and his father dying in June 1988, Brian went through an increasingly difficult period, even contemplating suicide, an admission he was only able to make several years later in hindsight.

Music was his only solace amid the turmoil and, in 1988, he prepared a tape of demos that he circulated to a select group of friends, giving them an indication of what he'd been up to and what his first solo album would contain. Two of those songs – 'The Dark' and 'My Boy' – dated back to 1980 and 1982 respectively, but the third song was a more recently-written hard rocker that fashioned Brian's fears into a self-deprecating story of public embarrassment and emotional anxiety.

First released as the B-side of 'Too Much Love Will Kill You' in August 1992, 'I'm Scared' was later remixed

for inclusion on *Back To The Light*, fattening up Brian's weaker vocal, making a few choice lyric changes, stripping away some fussy guitar work in the verses, and adding what was dubbed the 'Chaos Karaoke', a litany of fears collected into a jumbled chattering of semi-decipherable lines. Of what can be made out, Brian enumerates his fear of losing control, pain, being unknown, being ugly, dying, deformed, dull, the dark, being found out and, most importantly, being scared of Stephen Berkoff. (Known for his villainous character in *Beverly Hills Cop*, he also portrayed Adolf Hitler in the 1988 ABC miniseries *War And Remembrance*.)

I'M TAKING HER HOME

Originally performed by The Others, 'I'm Taking Her Home', the B-side of their breakthrough single 'Oh Yeah', was performed by 1984. Authorship is unknown.

IDEA (BARCELONA): *see* EXTRACTS FROM GARDEN LODGE

IF I WERE A CARPENTER *(Hardin)*

Tim Hardin's 'If I Were A Carpenter' was performed live by Smile in 1969, and was one of two tracks performed at The Cross' Marquee Club Christmas concert in 1992, which saw a reunion of Smile for the first time in over 20 years.

IF I LOVED YOU *(Rodgers/Hammerstein)*
• Album (Brian & Kerry): *Golden*

Written by Rodgers and Hammerstein and featured in *Carousel* from 1945, 'If I Loved You' is the requisite show tune on *Golden Days*, though Brian wisely scaled back the arrangement to just acoustic guitar and the occasional keyboard swell, leaving much of the focus on Kerry's voice.

IF YOU CAN'T BEAT THEM *(Deacon)*
• Album: *Jazz*

This snarling rocker falls victim to a cliché set of lyrics, and is a rare fall from grace from the normally dependable John Deacon. The band's recorded performance is superb, but after such classics as 'You're My Best Friend', 'You And I', and 'Spread Your Wings', which challenged Freddie's and Brian's own songwriting abilities, 'If You Can't Beat Them' is surprisingly rote, its melody akin to the MOR pap by Journey, Boston, or REO Speedwagon that was then clogging up the airwaves.

Live, however, the song was a different beast altogether, and became one of the standout tracks of the 1978 North American Jazz tour, where it was performed nightly. The song was retained for most of the following year's shows, but was dropped in 1980 in favor of stronger material. Despite its weaknesses as a studio song, its transformation on stage was astonishing, and would have made for better listening on *Live Killers* than some of the other songs released in its stead.

IMAGINE *(Lennon)*

The night after John Lennon's assassination, the band were so devastated by this senseless act of insanity that they quickly learned the former Beatle's 1971 plea for peace and performed it that night at Wembley Arena. Originally intended as a one-off, the band threw the song into their set list for a few more dates as a tribute, the most commonly bootlegged version being from Frankfurt on 14 December 1980. The song was revived by Queen + Paul Rodgers at the Hyde Park concert on 15 July 2005, as a panegyric to the innocent civilians killed in the suicide bombings in Tavistock Square and on the London Underground the week before, and was included as the sole bonus feature on the DVD version of *Return Of The Champions*.

IMMIGRANT SONG *(Page/Plant)*

A one-off performance from Berlin on the Magic tour in 1986 of the classic Led Zeppelin rocker, this song was recorded for their third album, released in 1970.

IMPROMPTU *(Queen)*
• Live: *Wembley, Budapest*

Ever since 1977, the band would perform a nightly improvised jam that would often go under different titles: 'Instrumental Inferno' was the most popular one, while 'Tokyo Blues' and 'Rock In Rio Blues' were not uncommon. The most widely known version exists on the *Live At Wembley Stadium* album and DVD releases, and comes right before Brian's guitar solo, and was based on Freddie's 1985 solo song, 'Foolin' Around'.

IN CHARGE OF MY HEART *(Taylor)*
• German B-side (The Cross): 8/90 • Compilation (Roger): *Lot*

One of the more curious non-album tracks to surface from the *Mad: Bad: And Dangerous to Know* sessions is this Roger-penned track, released as the B-side of 'Liar' in August 1990 and a concert favorite, serving as the set opener on the 1990 tour. The original version lasts barely more than two minutes, but the extended version is the one to seek out, with a suitably atmospheric opening of keyboards and pounding drums. The song eluded digital release for 23 years, before finally surfacing, both in its original and extended incarnations, on Roger's nearly all-encompassing box set, *The Lot*.

It was rumored that Queen recorded their own version of 'In Charge Of My Heart' during sessions for *The Miracle* – indeed, Freddie interpolates the line into his own composition 'Stealin'' – but these rumors are unfounded, and remain unconfirmed by any official source.

IN MY DEFENCE *(Clark/Soames/Daniels)*
• Soundtrack (Freddie): *Time* • Compilations (Freddie): *Pretender, FM Album, The Solo Collection*
• A-side: 11/92 [8]

In the summer of 1985, Dave Clark – formerly the drummer and leader of The Dave Clark Five – asked Freddie to take part in a charity soundtrack album for the then-popular West End musical *Time*. He agreed, but on condition that John, Roger and Brian be involved in the sessions. As Dave had already booked studio time with his own group of session musicians, he convinced Freddie with the caveat that, if he was displeased with the results, Dave would finance a re-recording of the song as a Queen performance. As it turned out, Freddie was satisfied, and, unfortunately, no Queen versions of any material for *Time* were attempted. As Freddie was preparing for the *A Kind Of Magic* album in London with the others, he would occasionally nip off to Abbey Road Studios to provide the vocals for both this song and the title track. While both performances were stellar and tested the limits of Freddie's vocal power, it was on the latter track that he shone, capturing the definitive take, according to Dave, in one pass.

The song was the first to be recorded in October 1985, with Mike Moran on piano, Paul Vincent (who had worked with Freddie on *Mr Bad Guy*) on guitars, Andy Pask on bass, Graham Jarvis on drums, and Peter Banks (not related to the former Yes guitarist of the same name) on keyboards. Despite his initial reluctance, the prearranged session proved fortunate in the end when Freddie met keyboardist Mike Moran, who would collaborate with Freddie on his next major project in 1987. Mike became a session musician following his graduation from the Royal College of Music in London, and provided music for films such as *Time Bandits* and *The Missionary*, though he gained his first major taste of fame with 'Rock Bottom', featured on the Eurovision Song Contest in 1977.

Unfortunately for Mike, the first day of recording would prove to be ominous since he was involved in a major traffic accident, breaking four ribs and bruising both wrists. Nevertheless, he soldiered on, asking Dave Clark not to mention to Freddie what had happened since they hadn't yet met each other. When he arrived at Abbey Road, Freddie strode up to him and, noting his physical appearance, offered him a glass of Stolichnaya vodka, which must have gone nicely with the painkillers Mike had taken earlier in the day, and a usable backing track was produced. Further work, including synths, guitars and additional Freddie overdubs, would be done in Munich at Musicland Studios.

The song became a highlight of the soundtrack for *Time*, among other contributions from Sir Laurence Olivier, Cliff Richard, Julian Lennon, Dionne Warwick and Burt Bacharach, Ashford and Simpson, Murray Head, Leo Sayer, Jimmy Helms, and John Christie and Stevie Wonder. It was remixed by Ron Nevison and issued posthumously as the sole single from *The Great Pretender / The Freddie Mercury Album* in November 1992, reaching a much-deserved No. 8 in the UK. Eight years later, Dave Clark himself remixed the track for inclusion on the three-disc *Solo* box set, giving the song a crisper feel while remaining mostly faithful to the original recording. Freddie performed the song only once on 14 April 1988 at London's Dominion Theatre, when he appeared at a special gala charity performance, dubbed Give Time For AIDS, with all proceeds donated to the Terence Higgins Trust. His four song set that night was 'Born To Rock 'n' Roll', 'Time', 'In My Defence' and 'It's In Every One Of Us', all with Cliff Richard and Sir Laurence Olivier, but the clear highlight of Freddie's final live performance remains 'In My Defence'.

IN ONLY SEVEN DAYS (*Deacon*)
• Album: *Jazz* • B-side: 1/79 [9]

John's second contribution to *Jazz* is this simple, upbeat piano track, with some sublime acoustic guitar work from John himself. At a time when it was more accepted that a major rock band write songs about one night stands and eschewing the subject of a fleeting holiday romance, John refused to adapt to custom and delivered this sweet ballad, with lyrics that drift toward the gratingly naïve. With one of Freddie's most understated piano contributions and a lovely orchestrated guitar solo, 'In Only Seven Days' was released as the flipside of 'Don't Stop Me Now' in the UK, but was understandably omitted from the live setting.

IN SEARCH OF LOVE:
see EVERYBODY NEEDS SOMEBODY

IN THE DEATH CELL
(LOVE THEME REPRISE) (*Taylor*)
• Album: *Flash*

A variation on Roger's earlier *Flash Gordon* composition, 'In The Space Capsule (Love Theme Reprise)', this piece features the same droning synthesizer with additional dialog between Flash and Dale.

IN THE LAP OF THE GODS (*Mercury*)
• Album: *SHA* • Live: *Rainbow*

Completely different from the similarly-titled conclusion of *Sheer Heart Attack*, 'In The Lap Of The Gods' starts the second side of the album off with a cacophonous introduction, complete with astounding screams from Roger, before mellowing out with a distorted lead vocal from Freddie. With an arrangement more akin to the grandiose prog-rock of *Queen II*, this song was the most adventurous piece on the third album, which Freddie confirmed in a December 1977 interview on BBC Radio One: "I was beginning to learn a lot on *Sheer Heart Attack*. We were doing a lot of things which was to be used on future albums. Songs like 'In The Lap Of The Gods', yes, I suppose. Working out the harmonies and song structure did help on say something like 'Bo Rhap'. Somebody said this sounds like Cecil B. De Mille meets Walt Disney or something. More to the point than The Beach Boys!"

'In The Lap Of The Gods' was performed live as part

of the medley between late 1974 and early 1975, but was omitted later that year in favor of newer material.

IN THE LAP OF THE GODS ... REVISITED *(Mercury)*
• Album: *SHA* • Live: *Wembley, Budapest, Rainbow, Odeon* • Bonus: *SHA*

This touching power ballad is a direct precursor to 'We Are The Champions', and became a fitting conclusion to not only *Sheer Heart Attack* but Queen's live shows, starting on the tour in support of that album. Freddie takes to task his critics' charges of delusional grandeur, who were humor-impaired even in the early 1970s, not realizing that the vocalist's act was exactly that: "There's no meaning in my pretending". The crass reference to finances notwithstanding (the band's maxim of the day was to give off the impression that they were far richer than their bank accounts would have them believe), 'In The Lap Of The Gods ... Revisited' is a superb example of Freddie's ability to craft an anthem, even when he's on the defensive.

By the time 'We Are The Champions' became a hit single, 'In The Lap Of The Gods ... Revisited' was deemed obsolete, and dropped from the set list, only to return in 1986 at Brian's insistence that the repertoire needed more light and shade. The song was rescued once again from obscurity when it was performed live by Queen + Adam Lambert starting in 2014.

IN THE SPACE CAPSULE (THE LOVE THEME)
(Taylor)
• Album: *Flash*

Written by Roger for the *Flash Gordon* album, this composition features John on Telecaster guitar and Roger on synthesizer and timpani. Written to accompany Flash's ascent to Ming's palace, the song also includes appropriate dialog leading into Freddie's 'Ming's Theme (In The Court Of Ming The Merciless)'.

INNUENDO *(Queen)*
• A-side: 1/91 [1] • Album: *Innuendo*

Going by its title alone, 'Innuendo' promises to be a grandiose epic, unlike anything Queen had done before and guaranteeing an exploration of musical territories not previously navigated. But by 1991, did Queen really need to reinvent themselves? Was it necessary to go into uncharted areas of music? They had done it all before – it would have been easier

to just stick with the pop-rock excursions from their albums of the 1980s.

In fact, the band had been channeling their separate creative energies into solo projects throughout the 1980s, and while Queen's albums all had been commercially successful, from a creative standpoint, they were unchallenging, by-numbers radio-friendly material, with the occasional diversion thrown in for good measure. Compare the worst of *Barcelona* to the worst of *A Kind Of Magic* or *The Miracle*, and the result is staggering: Freddie was invigorated enough to experiment with an unconventional (to average rock enthusiasts) genre, and yet appeared complacent with his own contributions to the mid-1980s albums. Shaken of their ennui, and jolted back into action by the vocalist's ailing health, the band knew they were running out of time and made a conscious decision to abandon the trends of the day and deliver an album that could stand up against their earlier albums.

While some songs were carefully calculated, others were spontaneous and developed through jamming, such is the case of the title track: during a jam session at Mountain Studios between Brian, Roger and John, Freddie, perched in the control booth with producer David Richards, suddenly felt inspired and rushed into the studio to take part, improvising lyrics as quickly as he could. With the basic germ of an idea in hand, the song was then fleshed out, with Roger taking control of the lyrics as Freddie became the arranger. "It was a group collaboration, but I wrote the lyrics," Roger explained in 2002, while Brian told *Guitarist* magazine in 1994 that the song "started off as most things do, with us just messing around and finding a groove that sounded nice. All of us worked on the arrangement. Freddie started off the theme of the words as he was singing along, then Roger worked on the rest of them. I worked on some of the arrangement, particularly the middle bit, then there was an extra part that Freddie did for the middle as well. It basically came together like a jigsaw puzzle."

"It's got the bolero-type rhythm, a very strange track," Brian said in a 1991 interview with *Guitar World*. "That's going to be the first single here. It's a bit of a risk, but it's different, and you either win it all or you lose it all. It had a nice sound and feel, and we stuck with that. The Spanish motif is suggested from the start: those little riffs at the beginning are sort of Bolero-esque. It seemed like the natural thing to explore those ideas on an acoustic guitar, and it just gradually evolved. Steve Howe helped out and did a fantastic job. We love all that stuff – it's like a little fantasy land adventure."

Yes guitarist Steve Howe was in Mountain Studios, producing Paul Sutin's *Voyagers* album, while Queen were recording the track, and ran into Martin Groves, who had worked with Yes in the past and was now Queen's equipment supervisor. Freddie recognized Steve in the hallways and invited him to listen, before Brian asked him to contribute some flamenco guitar to the track. "They played me 'Innuendo' and I go, 'Yeah, heavy metal flamenco!'" Steve recalled on his website. "And then Brian says, 'Look, I'd like you play on this,' and I said, 'You're joking, it sounds great, leave it like it is,' and he said, 'No no no, I want you to play on it, I want you to play really fast, I want you to run around the guitar a lot.' So I got up and running, we did a few takes, we edited it a little bit, we fixed up a few things, then we went and had dinner. So we went back to the studio and they said we really really like this and I said fine, let's go with it. So I left very happy ... A funny thing happened a little while later, I was on a ferry going to Holland and on this ferry, which takes a long time, five hours, were the Queen fan club, all going to Rotterdam to a Queen event, and a couple of them saw me and they came racing over and they said, 'You're Steve Howe! You're on 'Innuendo'!' ... My memories of Queen will always be emotional because they were a great band and it was just great, it really was a thrill to be part of that, and thanks for asking me."

"'Innuendo' was an improvisation type song where they actually recorded it here in the big concert hall ... and we set up like a live performance," David Richards said in 2001, "and they just started playing, and sort of got into a nice rhythm and a groove, and some chords and then Freddie said, 'Oh, I like that,' and rushed downstairs into the concert hall and started singing along with it. Obviously then, once that initial idea was down on tape, then there was a lot of rearranging and putting extra things on, but the actual beginning of it was like a live thing. It just happened. It was wonderful. [Freddie] played a strong role in the writing of ['Innuendo']. Steve just happened to drop in one day to say hello to me. He had been recording at Mountain some ten years before with the group Yes [*Going For The One*, 1977]. As soon as he popped his head round the door Freddie recognized him and said, 'Come on in and play some guitar!' He had no guitar with him so he used Brian's Dan Armstrong acoustic guitar with a direct output and tone control. Brian played the rhythm guitar and then echoed the solo afterwards on the Red Special."

The song was deservedly issued as the first single from *Innuendo* in January 1991, when it received mixed reviews but crashed into the charts at No. 1, albeit for only a week, thus becoming Queen's third No. 1 single in their career. Backed with 'Bijou', the single was expectedly compared to 'Bohemian Rhapsody', but broke Queen's previous record of scoring a No. 1 single with a song lasting just under six minutes: 'Innuendo' clocked in at 6'31, thus becoming Queen's longest number one single ever. Though it shouldn't be considered as such, an extended version of the single appeared on 12" and CD versions: adding on a mere 17 seconds, the song ends not as a fade-out, but with an explosion that swells into an ultimate full-force gale (appropriately, this was dubbed the 'Explosive Version').

"I think 'Innuendo' was one of those things which could either be big – or nothing," Brian told *Vox* in 1991. "We had the same feelings about 'Bohemian Rhapsody'. It's a risk, because a lot of people say, 'It's too long, it's too involved, and we don't want to play it on the radio.' I think that could be a problem in which case it will die. Or it could happen that people say, 'This is interesting and new and different and we'll take a chance'." Roger agreed with Brian's sentiment, saying in *Rip* magazine, "Big, long and pretentious! It goes through a lot of changes."

A video was assembled for the single in November 1990, but since the band were still working on the album, and a regular performance video wasn't considered good enough for the single, the band drafted The Torpedo Twins and Disney animator Jerry Hibbert to construct a video using animation and claymation, innovative for its time and even winning an award for best video of 1991. The video uses pre-existing photos of the band, redrawn in the style of different artists: Freddie was modelled after Leonardo daVinci; John after Pablo Picasso; Roger after Jackson Pollock; and Brian after old Victorian etchings. Unfortunately, the video hasn't been widely seen since it has yet to be released on the *Greatest Video Hits* collection, with the third instalment still unrealized.

The only live airing the song received was at the Concert For Life on 20 April 1992, with ex-Led Zeppelin vocalist Robert Plant singing lead vocals. ("Freddie had told me that they wrote the lyrics as a tribute to Led Zeppelin," Plant said in 2002.) The result is far from inspired, with Plant apparently absent from rehearsals the day he was supposed to learn the lyrics, but acknowledged the nod to Led Zeppelin's similar-sounding 'Kashmir' by throwing in a verse from that song. Because of his sub-par performance, Plant asked that the song not be included on the 1993 VHS and 2003 DVD releases.

INSTRUMENTAL INFERNO: *see* IMPROMPTU

INTERLUDE IN CONSTANTINOPLE *(Taylor)*
• Album (Roger): *Fun*

This short musical link on the second side of Roger's *Fun In Space*, placed between 'Magic Is Loose' and 'Airheads', would have fit in perfectly on *Flash Gordon* with its opening synthesizer drone and anthemic motif. The sound effects – a knock on a door, the sound of a glass breaking, a man belching, a crowd cheering and footsteps up and down a hallway – conjur up images of an intergalactic rock concert, with the flatulent rock star being introduced onstage by an overexcited emcee: "Good evening, Constantinople! The best audience in the world we've been told!" The song made for an appropriate taped introduction to Roger's 1999 Electric Fire UK tour.

INVINCIBLE HOPE *(Queen/Mandela)*
• Live: *46664* • Download: 1/05

Credited to Queen and Nelson Mandela, 'Invincible Hope' was written by Roger for the 46664 project and was performed at the Cape Town concert on 29 November 2003 as a short snippet after Mandela's speech. The superior studio version, recorded in March 2003 in Cape Town, South Africa, features Treanna Morris and Roger sharing lead vocals, with Nelson Mandela providing inspirational quotes throughout. Sounding like something from his *Happiness?* or *Electric Fire* albums, 'Invincible Hope' tackles the AIDS issue with a typical message imploring the impoverished and downtrodden to remain positive in the face of adversity.

The song was remixed slightly and released as part of an Internet-only download EP on the iTunes music store. Titled *46664: 1 Year On* and released in January 2005, 'Invincible Hope' was the lead-off track of the release, which also featured 'Whole Life' by Paul McCartney and Dave Stewart, 'People' by Jimmy Cliff featuring Sting and Tony Rebel, and 'Freedom's Coming' by Da Universal Playaz. This EP marked the first official release of Brian's and Roger's contributions to the 46664 project.

THE INVISIBLE MAN *(Queen)*
• Album: *Miracle* • A-side: 8/89 [12] • Bonus: *Miracle*

Inspired by H G Wells' novel of the same name, this slick disco rocker, with more than a passing resemblance to Huey Lewis and The News' 'I Want A New Drug' (and with lyrics reminiscent of Ray Parker Jr's 'Ghostbusters'), brought back horrific memories of the *Hot Space* debacle, but the fusion of synthesized and real instruments by 1989 was more authentic, and the finished song isn't as bad as it could have been. "I'm to blame for that one, sort of," Roger said in a 1989 BBC Radio One interview with Mike Read, "but then everybody came in, and that went through quite a few changes due to everybody else putting in different bits and restructuring it, etc., etc. I don't quite remember where the idea did come from. I think it came from a book I was reading, and it just seemed to fit in with a rhythmic pattern I had in mind and it sort of came from nowhere."

The lyrics are painfully simplistic (rhyming "head" with "bed"), and one of the more interesting lines ("Was it the shyness of my soul that made me lonely just like you? / No one noticed I was there, when I walked into the room"), though present on the demo with a more pronounced synthesizer backing, was inexplicably excised on the final version. For the first (and only) time in a Queen song, each band member is mentioned by name just before their respective instrumental solos, with Brian's contribution being a masterful and downright superhuman guitar solo. Virtuosos and bedroom air guitarists alike, eat your hearts out.

Released as the third single from *The Miracle* in August 1989, a video was directed by Rudi Dolezal and Hannes Rossacher at Pinewood Studios on 26 July 1989 – Roger's 40th birthday, thus explaining Freddie's ludicrous sunglasses, necessary amidst the copious amounts of alcohol and bright lights. The band appear as characters in a computer game called *The Invisible Man*, and during one gaming session the young lad presses the wrong button, and the band are transferred from screen to real life, wreaking havoc on the boy's bedroom and, gradually, family. (The actress portaying the teenage daughter is Danniella Westbrook, familiar to Britons as Samantha Mitchell on *EastEnders*.) A 12" mix was constructed, with a unique introduction of synthesized flute and bringing the running time to just under six minutes. This mix was also issued as a bonus track on the 1989 CD version (and 1991 and

2011 reissues), while a unique hybrid mix from August 1988, combining Roger's self-sung demo (and the aforementioned "shyness of my soul" bridge) with elements of the standard Queen version, also turned up as a bonus track on the 2011 reissue of *The Miracle*.

IS IT ME? *(Taylor)*
• Album (Roger): *Electric*

Like most other songs on *Electric Fire*, the subject matter of 'Is It Me?' is of romantic discord, but while it's addressed violently on 'Surrender', here it's the typical disagreements that lovers endure at any stage in a relationship. Structurally similar to 'Breakthru', with a slow, piano-based introduction giving way to an upbeat body, the song is yet another in a long line of songs that Roger felt needed a horrid "singing down the telephone" effect implemented on his voice, ruining an otherwise pleasant and lovely song. An alternate version, which extended the running time by a minute, was present on the CD master, but ultimately withdrawn and remains unheard.

IS THIS THE WORLD WE CREATED...?
(Mercury/May)
• Album: *Works* • B-side: 7/84 [6] • Live: *Magic, Wembley, 46664, Budapest* • Compilation: *On Air*

"We were looking at all the songs we had and we just thought the one thing we didn't have was one of those 'Love Of My Life' type of things," Freddie told Rudi Dolezal in 1984. "That song just evolved in about two days; [Brian] just got on acoustic and I just sat next to him, we just worked it together. I came up with the lyrical side and then he came up with the chords, and something just happened..." Written late in 1983 during sessions for *The Works* as a replacement for 'There Must Be More To Life Than This', 'Is This The World We Created...?' is one of Queen's simplest songs, with only acoustic guitar and Freddie's single-tracked baritone serving as its structure. (Additional piano, following Freddie's vocal melody, was recorded but later wiped.) Because of the minimalist approach to the arrangement, the impact of the potent lyrics of a first-world rock star viewing the injustices inflicted upon an impoverished Africa is heavy, dealing a blow to the heartstrings as the bemused performer ponders what kind of deity would allow His people to suffer so horrifically.

'Is This The World We Created...?' was performed alongside 'Love Of My Life' during the acoustic set between 1984 and 1986, and was also performed at Live Aid on 13 July 1985, separate from Queen's appearance: at approximately 9.44 pm, Brian and Freddie came back on stage and performed the song to rapturous applause. Brian revisited the song at the Dian Fossey Gorilla Fund concert in October 2002, and played the song with Andrea Corr on vocals at the 46664 concert on 29 November 2003.

IT'S A BEAUTIFUL DAY *(Queen)*
• CD Single: 10/95 [2] • Album: *Heaven* • Bonus: *Game*

Opening *Made In Heaven* is this atmospheric piece, first recorded as 'Beautiful Day' in April 1980 by Freddie doodling around on piano and singing a snatch of uplifting, optimistic lyrics. This improvisation was discovered while trawling the archives for material for *Made In Heaven*, and John fleshed it out into a full song by orchestrating a lovely keyboard segment, before Brian added some tasteful guitar work. The original "spontaneous idea" was finally released on the 2011 reissue of *The Game*.

An interesting yet marginally different version was issued on the 'Heaven For Everyone' CD single in October 1995, which is an amalgamation of this version and the reprise. More significantly, the song was remixed in 2005 by Ross Robertson and Russian disc jockey Koma, incorporating bits from all permutations of the song: the original, the reprise, the single version, and the 1998 *eYe* remix. Queen Productions was so impressed with this mix that it was sanctioned as an official release and sold on iTunes, as well as being used as the taped intro music to the Queen + Paul Rodgers world tour of 2005 and 2006.

IT'S A BEAUTIFUL DAY (REPRISE) *(Queen)*
• Album: *Heaven*

Fleshing out the simpler, laid-back opener of *Made In Heaven* with a chugging bass, soaring guitar, and thunderous drums, as well as clips of past Queen songs (notably, the intro to 'Seven Seas Of Rhye'), this reprise is a suitable closer to the coda of Queen's album discography.

IT'S A HARD LIFE *(Mercury)*
• Album: *Works* • A-side: 7/84 [6] • CD Single: 11/88

This heartfelt ballad is an undisputed highlight of the patchy *The Works* album, the first time since 'Jealousy' in 1978 that Freddie let down his good-time partying façade and laid bare to the world that he was a true romantic in search of something meaningful. (Shortly after this song was released, Freddie finally got what he wanted when he met Jim Hutton, who became his long-term partner until Freddie's death.) With an introduction borrowed from 'Vesti la giubba', a piece from the opera *Pagliacci*, the song is vocally rich and instrumentally lush, with lavish guitar orchestrations and a sumptuous piano melody, and is a harbinger to the *Barcelona* project that would commence three years later. Brian was especially proud of the song, saying in 2003, "To my mind this is one of the most beautiful songs that Freddie ever wrote. It's straight from the heart, and he really opened up during the creation of it. I sat with him for hours and hours and hours just trying to pull it away and get the most out of it. It's one of his loveliest songs."

Released as the third single from the album in July 1984, with Brian's and Freddie's 'Is This The World We Created...?' on the B-side, the song peaked at a modest No. 6. For 12" versions of the single, an extended remix was included which remained mostly faithful to the original, only adding an a cappella vocal section and repeat of the guitar solo. While the trend of the day was to drastically rearrange a single until it either barely represented its original recording, or to saturate it with effects and superfluous noises, this extended version is tasteful and subtle.

The music video, directed by Tim Pope in June 1984 (who also directed Roger's 'Man On Fire' video the previous month) at Arri Film Studios in Munich, has been met with derision and scorn by three of the four band members; only Freddie was pleased with the video, which isn't surprising, considering his prominent role. Brian, as ever, diplomatically reasoned that it was an indulgence of Freddie's and they were happy to humor him, but one look at John and Roger grumbling at each other and rolling their eyes suggest that some band members were more willing to mollify than others. That's not to say they didn't get their shots in at the singer, who, upon appearing on set in a ridiculous wig and a red skin-tight leotard covered in large eyes, was immediately labeled a giant prawn. Regardless of ridiculous costuming, the video is a fine adaptation of the lyrics, with Freddie starring as the tortured protagonist, desperately in search of love while surrounded by meaningless material possessions. Brian, clearly relishing his role as a sinister messenger of doom, wields a skull guitar, which later

led to wild rumors of the instrument being played on the record. Brian addressed this in a 1997 *Pop Of The Line* interview: "It's more of a prop than anything else. You can just about play it, but it was made especially for the video. But it was made more for the looks than anything else. Yes, I have played it, but you won't find it on any record, I'm afraid."

The song was performed live, sans skull guitar, on the 1984/1985 Queen Works! World tour, but wouldn't return for the 1986 Magic tour.

IT'S AN ILLUSION *(Taylor/Parfitt)*
• Album (Roger): *Frontier*

One of the few songs on that album to not be entirely about a nuclear holocaust or an uncertain future, 'It's An Illusion' is a simple lament of the loss of the American dream, which, in the Cold War era, became a standard of living to justify conspicuous consumption and sexual reproduction. While the baby boomer generation pushed for civil, political, and women's rights movements in the 1960s and 1970s, the liberal progressives had, by the 1980s, stagnated; with kids of their own and a responsibility to provide for their family, the young conservatives took over, heralding a decade of prosperity and excess, with socialism giving way to capitalism. Back in 1984, the phenomenon was just beginning, which Roger witnessed while traveling across the States on the 1982 Hot Space tour.

Written with Status Quo's Rick Parfitt, who also provides guitar and response vocals, the song is a highlight of the *Strange Frontier* album, with a muscular, exuberant rhythm section that also included John Deacon on bass. Of all the songs on the album, 'It's An Illusion' practically begged to be performed live, and when Roger formed his own touring band three years later, it became a mainstay of their 1988 and 1990 repertoires.

IT'S GONNA BE ALRIGHT (THE PANIC ATTACK SONG) *(May)*
• Album (Brian & Kerry): *Golden* • Digital Download: 6/17

A panic attack is no fun, and Brian penned this rockin' ode to those who suffer from them regularly. "This track is straight from the heart and is designed to bring light to your darkest moments," Brian later said, and in these tumultuous times of uncertainty, thanks to trigger-happy world leaders inciting fear and hatred among their people, a song such as this is sorely needed. "It works like a mood-altering drug," Kerry explained, before adding that she hopes the song "can light a fire in people's hearts." This joyous reminder to take a breath and look to the future is just the message that we need in these awful times.

IT'S GONNA WORK OUT FINE (McCoy/McKinney)

Originally performed by Ike and Tina Turner, The Reaction played 'It's Gonna Work Out Fine' live.

IT'S IN EVERY ONE OF US

On the *Time* musical soundtrack, 'It's In Every One Of Us' is performed by Cliff Richard, but when Freddie appeared at the Dominion Theatre on 14 April 1988 to take part in a four-song set, he was asked to duet with Cliff on this track, and was more suited for Freddie's voice.

IT'S LATE (May)
• Album: *NOTW* • Compilation: *On Air* • Bonus: *NOTW*

The sex and drugs and rock'n'roll lifestyle of rock stars is romanticized to the point that the reality is lost in a murky haze of nondescript hotel rooms and endless soundchecks. Brian's displeasure with being on the road constantly while trying to maintain a homelife was the subject of many of his greater songs throughout the 1970s, and even though the band rarely wrote while out on tour, their road-weary songs channeled the frustrations and trappings of success, painting a very lonely and isolated picture. In 1974, while on Queen's first North American tour in New Orleans, Brian became infatuated with a woman known only to legend as Peaches, and he struggled with the morality of this temptress while his long-term girlfriend, Chrissy, waited patiently for his return back home. He alluded briefly to the encounter in 'Now I'm Here', and when Queen returned to Louisiana for the album launch for *Jazz* in 1978, the guitarist abandoned the hedonism of the party and drove around the city in search of Peaches: "I didn't find her, but she found me later on," he recalled in a 2008 *Mojo* magazine interview. "God, I still feel a little tug on the heartstrings when I go to that city."

It's difficult to say what other Peaches-inspired songs Brian wrote, but most of his traveling songs allude to forbidden temptation, with 'It's Late' an admission

of guilt in the form of an epic Greek tragedy. "It's another one of those story-of-your-life songs," Brian said in a 1989 *In The Studio With Redbeard* interview. "I think it's about all sorts of experiences that I had, and experiences that I thought other people had, but I guess it was very personal, and it's written in three parts; it's like the first part of the story is at home, the guy is with his woman. The second part is in a room somewhere, the guy is with some other woman that he loves and can't help loving, and the last part is he's back with his woman."

The song was played only a handful of times between 1977 and 1979, and was out of the set list by the conclusion of the Jazz Japanese tour. The middle section, preceding the third scene, was a launching pad for improvisation and would take the band into strange and wonderful territories. The guitar solo also included a tactic which Eddie Van Halen would later make popular: tapping. "That was actually hammering on the fingerboard with both hands," Brian told *Guitar Player* in 1983. "I stole it from a guy who said that he stole it from Billy Gibbons in ZZ Top. He was playing in some club in Texas, doing hammering stuff. I was so intrigued by it, I went home and played around with it for ages and put it on 'It's Late'. It was a sort of a double hammer. I was fretting with my left hand, hammering with another finger of the left hand, and then hammering with the right hand as well. It was a problem to do onstage; I found it was a bit too stiff. It's okay if you're sitting down with the guitar. If I persevered with it, it would probably become second nature, but it wasn't an alleyway which led very far, to my way of thinking. It's a bit gimmicky." A version was also recorded on 28 October 1977 at Queen's final session for the BBC, with the middle section replaced by a bizarre interpretation of the 'seduction sequence' from 'Get Down, Make Love', complete with distorted vocalizations and harmonizer effects.

Overlooked for single release in the UK, since it was considered too weighty for the hit parade, it was released in April 1978, in lieu of 'Spread Your Wings' and with 'Sheer Heart Attack' as the B-side, in the US and Japan. The US release featured the full six-minute-plus cut, while the Japanese release received a unique three-minute edit, excising the second "scene" and most of the middle instrumental section. The single charted at No. 74 in the US, which accounts for its exclusion from any *Greatest Hits* package; it was finally issued on the 40th anniversary box set edition of *News Of The World* in 2017. An earlier take was issued on the same set, featuring a tentative lead vocal with slightly different lyrics over a similar backing track to the released version, though the real draw is some piano from Freddie during the instrumental jam.

The song, absent from the Queen + Paul Rodgers set list, despite crying out for an interpretation by the legendary vocalist, was finally performed live by Queen + Adam Lambert on their 2017 live campaign, though it remained for only a handful of performances before being unceremoniously dropped.

IT'S SO YOU *(Mercury)*
• Compilation (Freddie): *Solo Collection*

Another soulful track recorded on 3 February 1987 at Townhouse Studios (like many of the other tracks recorded during this period, including 'Holding On', 'I Can't Dance / Keep Smilin'', 'Horns Of Doom' and 'Yellow Breezes', this track was not intended for *Barcelona*), 'It's So You' was revisited later in February and again in March, but ultimately remained unreleased until *The Solo Collection* in 2000. A shame, since it features a gorgeous and soaring vocal performance, as well as some R&B piano playing from Freddie.

JACK OF DIAMONDS *(Donegan)*

This Lonnie Donegan song was played live by 1984.

JAILHOUSE ROCK *(Stoller)*
• Live: *Montreal, Rainbow, Odeon* • Compilation: *On Air*

Elvis Presley's 1957 hit single became a live favorite of Queen's, and was played from virtually the very first concert (Freddie even played it in his pre-Queen bands). Receiving about 350 performances between 1970 and 1985, though certainly not performed every night, 'Jailhouse Rock' would usually be placed in the list as an encore number, although it did become the show opener during the Crazy tour of 1979 and the Game tour in 1980. Live versions later surfaced on *Live At The Rainbow '74*, *A Night At The Odeon*, and *On Air*. The song was recorded during sessions for *Queen* in 1972, with a 10" acetate cut and prepared for release, but remains unreleased.

JEALOUSY *(Mercury)*
• Album: *Jazz*

Separating 'Fat Bottomed Girls' and 'Bicycle Race'

is this delicate, understated ballad from Freddie, a gorgeous confessional of a broken man, shattered by jealousy and begging for forgiveness, if only the pain would go away. With one of the simplest backings on *Jazz* of bass, drums, and piano, and an acoustic guitar solo for good measure, 'Jealousy' is a superb ballad, and, with the exception of 'It's A Hard Life', one of the last truly love-torn ballads that Freddie would submit for a Queen album.

An instrumental version was played by Greg Brooks at a Fan Club convention, with an additional 45 second bridge that was later excised and shoehorned into 'Play The Game' two years later. 'Jealousy' was issued in April 1979 as a the third and final single from *Jazz* in the US, with 'Fun It' as the B-side, but promotion was minimal and the single failed to chart. More mundanely, when the song was remastered in 2011, Roger's bass drum was reinstated, having been absent on the recording since 1978.

JESUS *(Mercury)*
• Album: *Queen* • Bonus: *Queen*

Written from the perspective of an astonished bystander witnessing the Lord's power as an elderly leper pleads for healing, 'Jesus' is a prime example of Freddie's early fascination with religion, which would be either written directly about or alluded to in his songs on the debut album; one other especially religious song, 'Mad The Swine', was originally planned for inclusion but was dropped – not because of subject matter, but because of drum sound disputes. As befits its title, though, 'Jesus' is the most overly religious song that Freddie would write, but he would focus instead on fantasy tales for the next album and abandon any thoughts on theology, only occasionally mentioning it in song here or there afterwards. The bulk of the song consists of a raucous instrumental section with a piercing guitar orchestration from Brian, before calming down for the conclusion of the track, fading out in an echo-drenched choir and leading nicely into the instrumental closer, 'Seven Seas Of Rhye...'.

A five-minute demo version, which omits the acoustic guitar and piano in favor of a more aggressive electric guitar, is taken at a slower pace, though it features a more hurried instrumental improvisation, and was recorded at De Lane Lea Studios between September and November 1971. After appearing on countless bootleg albums, the demo recording was finally released on the 2011 deluxe edition of *Queen*.

'Jesus' was included in the set list between 1971 and 1972, though no tapes of the song's performance exist, and was out of the set list by the following year. One intrepid fan attempted to resurrect the song in November 1978 during Freddie's customary audience request segment of the show, which the singer momentarily considered before dismissing it with, "That's from the first album. We've forgotten that. We wanna do something new!"

JOURNEY'S END *(Taylor)*
• Digital Release (Roger): 5/17 • A-side: 11/17 • B-side: 11/17

Since the last publication of this book in mid-2011, a lot of the guest artists and collaborators in these pages now have the modifier "the late" added: Amy Winehouse, Gary Moore, Jon Lord, Joe Cocker, Lemmy, B.B. King, Geoff Nicholls, George Michael, David Bowie, Keith Emerson, Rick Parfitt, David Richards … the list goes on. Realizing that life can be a fickle beast, and inspired by David Bowie's final statement, *Blackstar*, released three days before the legend's death, Roger wrote and recorded 'Journey's End' as a rumination on mortality. "Everybody's leaving at some point, and as you get older you think about it more," Roger explained. "I don't think anyone in their twenties thinks about that kind of thing, but of course, inevitably, one is forced to confront the fact. As I think David Bowie said, 'I embrace age'. I am not sure he meant it, but then he did say, 'The only drawback is the dying bit that is shit!'"

With the concept of mortality in mind, Roger spent some time in his studio towards the end of 2016, laying down a new song that didn't have a specific home in mind. Considering he'd dabbled in soundtrack recording lately – *Solitary* was very much a friends-and-family affair, starring, among others, Anita Dobson, Sarina Taylor, and Felix Taylor, and featured atmospheric mood pieces penned by Roger and a handful of his children, while *Absolutely Anything* featured a title track by Roger that featured in the opening sequence – the jump to create something a bit more abstract was a logical progression. "It's a 'piece'," Roger said in a press release for the single, "which is why there is a long [guitar] solo in it. I've just let it take its own course. I just didn't want to make it quick, edit it. I wanted it to be fairly contemplative, fairly dreamlike, a mood piece." He took further inspiration from Frank Capra's 1937 film *Lost Horizon*, based on

James Hilton's book of the same name: "A plane goes down and the survivors are lost in the Himalayas," Roger explained, "and they find this city of Shangri-La where there is a kind of Utopian perfection. It's a great mood piece, and I had that sort of atmosphere in my head when I was writing the song."

With the piece vaguely structured in his head, Roger took to the studio to lay down a basic track, playing all instruments initially, with additional keyboards from Joshua J. Macrae (who also co-produced the track with Roger), and an ethereal guitar solo provided by Jason Falloon. Roger explained that the song was written around a "rather lovely chord sequence, slightly in the mode of some of the turn of the century composers. It has a quite whimsical, rather fatalistic atmosphere. It's basically about thoughts of mortality. It is a sort of acceptance of the fact that this a journey, and that journey will come to an end. Even the bass sequence, which is almost random, is a plodding footstep kind of thing. A journey towards the tail end, the September of one's years."

The release of the single also featured a short-form video, directed by Stuart Brennan, an indie director known for *Plan Z* and *The Necromancer*, though his claim to fame was winning a BAFTA in 2011 for his performance in *Risen*, becoming the youngest-ever recipient of the award. The mini-epic features Roger only minimally, and rarely showing his face, as he walks through an autumnal scene that was filmed around his home in Truro; elsewhere, flashes of Roger's past (rowdy crowds in a concert setting and gorgeous overhead shots of his guitar collection) are interjected into some more cerebral moments of Roger's wife, Sarina, performing a gothic devil/angel *danse macabre* (filmed in Truro Cathedral), as well as aerial footage of Chinese mountains (thus furthering the *Lost Horizon* inspiration).

Initially released only as a digital video on iTunes, 'Journey's End' topped the UK digital video charts and peaked at No. 14 in the US, in addition to hitting the Top 10 in several other countries. Due to high demand, the song was available for download in June 2017, and earned a vinyl release that November for North America's Black Friday's Record Store Day, pressed on limited edition sunset gold vinyl. The 10" vinyl featured remixes of 'Tonight' and 'Revelations', as well as an instrumental version of the A-side, while a UK Record Store Day exclusive followed in April 2018, featuring both the regular and instrumental versions.

'Journey's End' is a beautiful, mesmerizing, and

cathartic experience, that should be experienced in its full cinematic glory, as opposed to a standalone track. Considering the lengths that contemporary musicians have gone to provide more bang for the listener's buck – consider Janelle Monáe's *Dirty Computer*, an album and "emotion picture" experience, or Beyoncé's self-titled 2013 album and its follow-up, *Lemonade*, both audio-visual albums released unexpectedly – this is a relatively progressive idea from Roger, and one that paid off in dividends. Roger was certainly pleased with his indulgence: "This piece is a journey, a sort of realization of coming up to the end of that journey. This has been an incredible journey – our career, our band Queen, which we thought was over with the death of Freddie, it just seems to continue, almost with a life of its own. And as long as people want to see us, we will be happy to indulge them."

JUST ONE LIFE *(May)*
• CD single (Brian): 11/91 [6] • Album (Brian): *BTTL*

This emotive ballad, recorded for Brian's *Back To The Light* album in 1990, might be construed as a tribute to Freddie but was actually written for actor Philip Sayer. "I wrote that after going to a memorial concert for an actor [Sayer], a friend of my lady friend whom I'd never met," Brian explained in *Guitar World* magazine in 1993. "I'd never even seen his work, though he was pretty well-known in England. But by the end of the evening, I felt that I knew the guy. I wrote the song around that and realized that it related very closely to the stuff I was searching for in my solo work. So it became another germ which grew into a piece of the album."

Sayer was a West End actor who appeared in adaptations of *A Midsummer Night's Dream*, *Deahtrap*, and *Rocky Horror Picture Show* before transitioning to the small (and later big) screen with *Crown Court* in 1976. He starred later in *Xtro*, *The Hunger*, and *Shanghai Surprise* (as well as a 1983 TV series titled, incidentally, *Dead On Time*), before he died on 19 September 1989 of lung cancer. 'Just One Life' was written shortly thereafter, and is a poignant panegyric for an actor who possessed so much potential but was so rudely cut down in his prime.

The song was released on the CD single of 'Driven By You' in November 1991, albeit in an altered version: Brian's shimmering vocals were instead replaced by The Red Special, and has suitably been labeled the 'Guitar Version'.

KALINKA *(trad.)*

This traditional Russian folk song was inserted into Brian's nightly guitar solo while in Moscow, in November 1998.

KANSAS CITY *(Leiber/Stoller)*

Jerry Leiber and Mike Stoller's 'Kansas City', covered by The Beatles in 1964, was performed by The Cross at their final concert (with Roger Taylor) at the Gosport Festival on 29 July 1993.

KASHMIR *(Page/Plant/Bonham)*

During Robert Plant's performance of 'Innuendo' at the Concert For Life on 20 April 1992, the vocalist threw in a verse from Led Zeppelin's classic 'Kashmir', an appropriate gesture since 'Innuendo' was partly inspired by the epic 1975 *Physical Graffiti* track.

KEEP A-KNOCKIN' *(Penniman/Williams/Mays)*
• CD single (Roger): 9/98 [45]

Recorded during sessions for Roger's *Electric Fire*, this version of Little Richard's 'Keep A-Knockin'' (which inspired Led Zeppelin's 'Rock And Roll', a favorite of Roger's) is enjoyable but clearly intended as a fun throwaway. Because of its scarcity, there aren't any personnel listings, leaving the mystery of the great saxophone accompaniment unsolved – for the time being. This jolly recording was released as part of the 'Pressure On' CD single in September 1998.

KEEP ON RUNNING *(Edwards)*

Recorded during sessions for Roger's original vision of *Strange Frontier* in 1983, 'Keep On Running', first recorded by The Spencer Davis Group in 1965, is a great rendition that deserved to be released in some form. Roger already covered Bruce Springsteen's 'Racing In The Street' and Bob Dylan's 'Masters Of War' as a pointed message of the withering American dream in the face of the Cold War, and, with two cover songs already on *Strange Frontier*, a third would have been overkill, but based on the outstanding vocal performance alone, 'Keep On Running' would have made a fine non-album B-side.

KEEP PASSING THE OPEN WINDOWS *(Mercury)*
• Album: *Works* • B-side: 11/84 [21]

A standout track from *The Works*, Freddie's 'Keep Passing The Open Windows' was originally written for the film *The Hotel New Hampshire*, the soundtrack of which the band had been working on simultaneously with *The Works* but eventually pulled out from when the producers opted to use a pre-recorded orchestral soundtrack to cut costs. While working simultaneously on two projects had kept the band's creative juices charged in 1980, this time the inspiration hadn't returned, so Queen were happy to focus instead on their next studio album. As Freddie told Rudi Dolezal in 1984, "When I write a song, I have in my head what the others can do and it's used as reference. But sometimes I do it knowing that it'll be difficult for everyone. It's my challenge. For example, I had written 'Keep Passing The Open Windows' for the film *Hotel New Hampshire* but it was finally refused so I had to change it completely so it could be adapted to *The Works*."

Updating Freddie's earlier stance on suicide (see 'Don't Try Suicide'), the song chugs along at a rapid pace as Freddie implores the listeners to keep their heads held high, since everybody faces tough times and suicide is not the answer. The band turn in a truly fantastic performance, driven by a percolating bass line that would be used to greater effect on 'A Kind Of Magic'. Everything melds together neatly, though the outro (with Freddie singing the title over and over again) drags on a bit. With some subtle synthesizer touches and a rock-steady rhythm, the song is a forgotten highlight on the second side of *The Works*.

'Keep Passing The Open Windows' was released as the B-side of the withdrawn 'Man On The Prowl' single in November 1984, before those two songs were used as the double B-side to 'Thank God It's Christmas'. An extended version, with a running time of just under seven minutes, was issued on 12" editions of that single, adding very little of substance to the original.

KEEP YOURSELF ALIVE *(May)*
• A-side: 7/73 • Album: *Queen* • Bonus: *Queen, Opera*
• B-side: 10/91 [16] • CD Single: 10/91 [16]
• CD Single: 10/95 [2] • Live: *Killers, Montreal, Rainbow, Odeon* • Compilation: *On Air*

Bearing the distinction of being the first song Brian played to Freddie and Roger in 1970, 'Keep Yourself Alive' is a milestone in the formative years of Queen, and a true 'sleeper' hit: at the time of its original release it was a flop, but because of increased exposure in the live set, its momentum grew until it became an undeniable powerhouse, an early indicator of the sound that Queen would develop over their next few albums, even if the rest of *Queen* wasn't as focused. With its startling use of tape phasing and a mouthful of lyrics about an underachieving, fun-loving fella, 'Keep Yourself Alive' is a prime example of the perfectionism that became the trademark of Queen's future sessions: despite its live, off-the-cuff feeling, every note is considered and deliberately placed, with just enough calculated spontaneity to keep it fresh and exciting.

The song was first recorded in September 1971, along with 'Great King Rat', 'Jesus', 'Liar' and 'The Night Comes Down', at De Lane Lea Studios as part of Queen's first recording session. Initially, the multi-tracked guitar intro was performed on an acoustic guitar, with the main riff overdubbed on electric, mirroring a similar tactic used on The Who's 'Pinball Wizard' from 1969. This rawer version is a revelation, with a more tentative vocal from Freddie and a busier drum arrangement; Brian certainly preferred it over the re-recorded studio version, telling BBC Radio One in 1983, "The first recording of it ever was in De Lane Lea when we did it ourselves and I've still got that recording and I think it's very good and has something which the single never had. But THEY pressurized us very strongly to redo all the tracks and we redid 'Keep Yourself Alive' with Roy and it was pretty awful, actually. I thought it was terrible and I was very unhappy about it and I thought the De Lane Lea one was better and I eventually managed to persuade Roy that it was better as well. So, we went back in and did it again in a way that was a bit more true to the original. But there is no way that you can ever really repeat something. I have this great belief that the magic of the moment can never be recaptured and, although we ended up with something that was technically in the playing and perhaps even in the recording a bit better than the De Lane Lea thing, I still think that the De Lane Lea one had that certain sort of magic, so I was never really happy. As it turned out no one else was ever really happy either and we kept remixing it. We thought that it's the mix that's wrong, we kept remixing and there must have been, at least, seven or eight different mixes by different groups of people. Eventually we went in and did a mix with Mike Stone, our engineer, and that's the one that we were in the end happiest with. That's the one we put out. But, to my mind 'Keep

Yourself Alive' was never really satisfactory. Never had that magic that it should have had."

The song was re-recorded properly in 1972, with a stricter and more conservative arrangement including all the elements that would become trademarks of the band: complex vocal harmonies, intricate guitar arrangements, a sturdy rhythm section and an eccentric lead vocal performance. Brian explained further in 1998, "As far as arranging the guitar harmonies, it wasn't that difficult – I was always able to hear in my head what was going to work. As a result, my guitar orchestrations were mostly intuitive and worked out on the spot, such as the harmonized solos on 'Keep Yourself Alive'. It was afterwards that I actually analyzed why a certain arrangement I came up with worked."

"That was real tape phasing," Brian told *Guitar Player* in 1983. "This was in the days when you took the tape off the synch head, put it though a couple of other tape delays, and then brought it back with the play head. There is no processing whatsoever on the solo in that tune, as far as I remember. I used John Deacon's small amplifier and the Vox AC-30 to do that little three-part chorus thing behind, as well as the fingerboard pickup on the guitar. There is a bit more tape phasing on the end of that track."

The song marks the first and only instance of Brian, Roger and Freddie singing lead vocals together on a Queen song until 1995's 'Let Me Live'. While Freddie sings the majority of the song, Roger and Brian engage in a bit of call-and-response in the bridge, with the drummer asking, "Do you think you're better every day?", answered by the guitarist, "No, I just think I'm two steps nearer to my grave." This would mark the first lead vocal appearance of Brian on a Queen song, though he wouldn't sing a complete song on the first album, finally tackling 'Some Day, One Day' on *Queen II*. Roger sang 'Modern Times Rock 'n' Roll', which appeared later on the debut album.

The final version was released as a predecessor to *Queen* in July 1973, two weeks before the album hit the shops. With Brian's suggestive 'Son And Daughter' on the B-side, the single was considered too long to get going (with a 20 second guitar-only intro, and a further 15 seconds of instrumental jamming before the verse finally starts) and flopped in the charts, becoming the first and only UK Queen single not to reach the charts. The song was rejected by BBC's Radio One disc jockeys five times, though the song actually achieved 'hit' status in parts of New England (Connecticut, Massachusetts, etc) and Japan.

For promotional reasons, Trident Productions set up a video shoot for this song and 'Liar', which was intended to be hawked to *Top of the Pops* and other music television programmes. Two versions were shot: the first, on 9 August 1973 at Brewer Street Studios, was directed by Mike Mansfield but was rejected by the band, since they felt it portrayed them falsely and had lighting which wasn't moody enough. The second version, filmed on 1 October at St John's Wood Studios, right before the band commenced an extensive British tour supporting Mott the Hoople, was directed by Queen and Barry Sheffield (the manager of Trident Productions) and showed the band in a more dramatic light, earning their approval. Despite all the trouble that went into the videos, they were never shown; instead, BBC TV compiled a collage video in July 1973 for the programme *The Old Grey Whistle Test*, which contained no Queen involvement whatsoever. In their stead is old black and white footage from television broadcasts over the years, which was originally created for US President Franklin Delano Roosevelt's campaigns from the late 1930s. This footage, along with interpolations from the above two video shoots, was recompiled in 1992 by the Torpedo Twins for inclusion on the US video compilation *Greatest Hits*. The second video version remained unreleased until *Greatest Video Hits Volume 1* in 2002.

'Keep Yourself Alive' would become an oft-performed track in the live setting, where it became a staple of the set list between 1970 and 1981. (It was dropped from the 1982 set list, but was revived in 1984 and 1985.) The song would undergo several tempo and mood changes over the years, and was often the base for extended improvisation. Two versions were recorded for the BBC: both were essentially remixes of the standard album version with re-recorded lead vocal tracks. The first was overdubbed on 5 February 1973 at Langham 1 Studio and was produced by Bernie Andrews (this version later appeared on the 1989 UK compilation, *Queen at the Beeb*, which was released in America in 1995 as *Queen at the BBC*), while the second was taped on 25 July, also at Langham 1 but produced by Jeff Griffin.

In the summer of 1975, Elektra Records approached Queen with the idea of re-releasing 'Keep Yourself Alive' as a single. By that point, the band had become more popular in the States, and, with sessions planned to commence on their fourth album shortly, this was met with a surprising amount of positivity. On 2 July, the band entered SARM Studios to record a completely revamped recording of the song, with a fresh, new arrangement more akin to its live renditions than the original. Unfortunately, shortly after the sessions ended, issues that had been building with Trident Productions and Norman and Barry Sheffield came to a head, and a moratorium was placed on all new recordings while the legal squabbles were worked out. 'Keep Yourself Alive' was lost in the mire of litigation, and, with Elektra at a loss, the original 1972 recording was released instead, albeit edited slightly. This re-recording would remain unreleased until 1991, when it was unearthed by Hollywood Records' archivists and included as a bonus track on the CD reissue of *Queen*. Twenty years later, the song once again appeared as part of a comprehensive archival release, this time being released – chronologically correctly – as a bonus track on deluxe editions of *A Night At The Opera*.

THE KEY *(Taylor)*
• Album (Roger): *Happiness?*

When compact disc took over vinyl as the leading format for album releases, musicians suddenly had the opportunity to fill up 74 minutes of space. This meant that a lot of albums were weighed down with songs that would have otherwise been cut, reducing a potentially great album to a decent album with too much filler. While most of *Happiness?* was strong, there was inevitably going to be a song that was deemed filler, and 'The Key' is that song: it's not necessarily a bad song, with a slinky, funky rhythm and falsetto vocals, but when stacked up against the other material, it pales in comparison. The production places it firmly in the early 1990s, with keyboards closer to a new age musician than a rock drummer, and the overly verbose lyrics don't say a whole lot, apart from the expected slams against politicians and theology. 'The Key' is simply Roger by numbers, and a blemish on his finest solo album to date.

KHASHOGGI'S SHIP *(Queen)*
• Album: *Miracle*

Adnan Khashoggi is a Saudi entrepreneur and arms dealer who formed the large Swiss property company Triad and became a multimillionaire virtually overnight. He hit some snags in his long string of successes: in 1975, the US accused him of receiving bribes to secure military contracts in Arab countries, and 11 years later he found his fortune withering

away due to the slump in oil prices and political problems in Sudan. But the man was notorious for his parties, with 'Khashoggi's Ship' being an homage to both his parties and his private yacht, the Kingdom 5KR. Though not taking the side of the infamously flamboyant mogul, the song is a defiant cry against party poopers everywhere, and Freddie howls about the good times to be had at his parties over a crunching guitar riff. Freddie's line "He pulled out a gun / Wanted to arrest me / I said 'uh-uh-uh, baby!'" is an eerie portent of what would actually happen to Adnan in April 1989, when he was arrested in connection with illegal property deals.

Bleeding over from the previous track, 'Party', the song is a welcome return to hard rock that would, unfortunately, be in a minority on *The Miracle*. An early version, recorded in November 1988, was premiered in 2001 at a Fan Club Convention, and featured most of the same instrumentation but a guide vocal from Freddie, with significantly different lyrics ("This big bad fucker", "I said, 'Go get laid'"). More mundanely, a standalone version, with a thundering drum intro, was released on the third volume of *Deep Cuts* in 2011.

KILLER QUEEN *(Mercury)*
• AA-side: 10/74 [2] • Album: *SHA* • B-side: 9/86 [24] • CD Single: 11/88 • CD Single: 10/95 [2] • Live: *Killers, Montreal, Rainbow, Odeon*

This paean to a high-class call girl combines witty lyrics with a jaunty melody, creating a fusion of sounds unheard of on the radio at the time: with Roxy Music and David Bowie cornering the glam rock market, and Pink Floyd and Yes going off on extended progressive rock journeys, the pure pop charts were in danger of being muddled by flash-in-the-pan, expendable drones like Gary Glitter, David Essex, Disco-Tex and the Sex-O-Lettes, and The Osmonds cluttering up prime real estate. (Essex's 'Gonna Make You A Star' was the No. 1 single in November 1974, keeping 'Killer Queen' from achieving an all-important top spot.) Brian was concerned that the song would be *too* commercial, telling *Guitar For The Practicing Musician* in 1993, "When we put out 'Killer Queen', everybody thought it was the most commercial. I was worried that people would put us in a category where they thought we were doing something light. *Sheer Heart Attack* was, in my mind, quite heavy and dirty, and 'Killer Queen' was the lightest and cleanest track, and I was worried about putting it out. But when I heard it on the radio

I thought, 'It's a well-made record and I'm proud of it, so it doesn't really matter.' Plus, it was a hit, so fuck it. A hit is a hit is a hit." A few years later, he wasn't as worried: "'Killer Queen' was the turning point. It was the song that best summed up our kind of music, and a big hit, and we desperately needed it as a mark of something successful happening for us."

Meanwhile, its songwriter didn't even consider it single-worthy: "We're very proud of that number," Freddie told *Record Mirror* in 1976. "It's done me a lot of proud. It's just one of the tracks I wrote for the album, to be honest. It wasn't written as a single. I just wrote a batch of songs for the *Sheer Heart Attack* album and when I finished writing it, and when we recorded it, we found it was a very, very strong single. It really was. At that time it was very, very unlike Queen. They all said: 'Awwwwwww.' It was another risk that we took, you know. Every risk we've taken so far has paid off." Freddie's modesty of it doing him a lot of proud wasn't unfounded: in 1975, it was awarded four individual plaudits, with one each from *Record Mirror* (second best single) and *NME* (top single), a Belgian Golden Lion Award, and, most prestigiously, an Ivor Novello Award, the first of six the band would receive over the years.

Freddie told *Melody Maker* in December 1974, "Well, 'Killer Queen' I wrote in one night. I'm not being conceited or anything, but it just fell into place. Certain songs do. Now, 'The March Of The Black Queen', that took ages. I had to give it everything, to be self indulgent or whatever. But with 'Killer Queen', I scribbled down the words in the dark one Saturday night and the next morning I got them all together and I worked all day Sunday and that was it. I'd got it. It gelled. It was great."

Even at an early stage in the sessions, the band knew it was a special song, with Roger recalling that particular attention was paid to it with its excessive takes and tracking. Despite his illness, Brian remembered fondly the recording of his suitable and cheeky solo, though he was more rueful of his indisposition and his inability to contribute to the productive initial sessions. "The first time I heard Freddie playing that song, I was lying in my room in Rockfield [Studios], feeling very sick," Brian recalled. "After Queen's first American tour I had hepatitis, and then I had very bad stomach problems and I had to be operated on. So I remember just lying there, hearing Freddie play this really great song and feeling sad, because I thought, 'I can't even get out of bed to participate in this. Maybe the group will have to

go on without me.' No one could figure out what was wrong with me. But then I did go into the hospital and I got fixed up, thank God. And when I came out again, we were able to finish off 'Killer Queen'. They left some space for me and I did the solo. I had strong feelings about one of the harmony bits in the chorus, so we had another go at that too." The song rightfully gained praise from the band, with Brian telling *Guitar For The Practicing Musician*, "There's nothing cluttered about 'Killer Queen'. There's a fantastic amount going on, but nothing ever gets in the way of anything else. I was pleased that the solo went along with that. Everything is crystal clear. And when the three voices of guitars are all doing little tunes of their own, it feels almost accidental that they go together. I was pleased with how it came out."

"People are used to hard rock, energy music from Queen," Freddie explained to the *NME* in 1974, "yet with this single, you almost expect Noël Coward to sing it. It's one of those bowler hat, black suspender numbers – not that Noël Coward would wear that. It's about a high-class call girl. I'm trying to say that classy people can be whores as well. That's what the song is about, though I'd prefer people to put their own interpretation upon it – to read what they like into it."

'Killer Queen' was the first single released from *Sheer Heart Attack* in October 1974, coupled with Freddie's vicious 'Flick Of The Wrist' as a double A-side. However, it was this song that received the most attention, being performed on the Dutch TV show *Top Pop* on 9 December 1974, a performance broadcast in the UK on Boxing Day (26 December) and now recognized as the song's 'default' performance video. The single peaked at No. 2 in the UK and No. 12 in the US, becoming a mainstay in the medley portion of the band's show, performed at every concert between 1974 and 1980, and then only on a few dates in 1981 before being dropped for the 1982 tour, but brought back in 1984 and 1985. The song was released as the B-side on the 'Who Wants To Live Forever' and 'Heaven For Everyone' singles in 1986 and 1995, respectively, and the title has recently been given the honor of being applied to the villain in the *We Will Rock You* musical.

KILLING (May)
• Soundtrack (Brian): *Furia*

Another piece lasting just over a minute, 'Killing' distinguishes itself from the other pieces on the *Furia* soundtrack with a pulsating programmed bass drum and ends with a startling snippet of action from the film.

KILLING TIME *(Taylor)*
• B-side (Roger): 6/84 [66] • Album (Roger): *Frontier*

Opening the more experimental second side of *Strange Frontier* is this synthesized confection, envisioning a post-apocalyptic future devoid of the luxuries of the present: with the world bathed in a nuclear soup, and society just getting back on track, all its denizens can do is wait. Songs of boredom are typically uninteresting in themselves, the songwriter's ennui seeping through in the lyrics and melody, but Roger keeps 'Killing Time' engaging, with scores of electronic drums and synthetic blasts of noise punctuating the abstract lyrics. An orchestral interlude has led to the unfounded rumor that Freddie cowrote the song, perpetuated by Queen websites from the early 1990s, when such gossip was taken as substantiated fact. Additionally, rumor ran rampant that Freddie provided backing vocals on the song; this remained unconfirmed for nearly 30 years, until the release of Roger's nearly all-encompassing box set *The Lot*, when the rumor was confirmed as fact.

In addition to its prime spot as second side opener, 'Killing Time' was also released as the B-side of 'Man On Fire' in June 1984.

A KIND OF MAGIC *(Taylor)*
• A-side: 3/86 [3] • Album: *AKOM* • CD Single: 11/88
• Live: *Magic, Wembley, Budapest* • Bonus: *Wembley*
• Live (Q+PR): *Return* • Compilation: *On Air*

In its original form, the title track for Queen's 12th studio album as written by Roger was described by Brian as being "quite lugubrious and heavy," but was restructured to be more chart-friendly: "Freddie totally lightened it up to make it a commercially accessible kind of thing, putting in this [bass] kind of thing and making little sort of mantras out of it." Roger agreed, saying, "Originally, it was much more filmic; in fact, it was used at the end of the movie [*Highlander*] as the closing credits, and it was much less sort of 'bounce'-oriented, it had a much more broken-up tempo and it was a sort of grander concept. We then reworked it, and I know Freddie took an interest in the song; and we reworked it into a single, really."

From its concept to the finished product, 'A Kind Of Magic' was destined to be a hit. With a universal lyric about the wonders of mankind, the song adheres to the theme of *Highlander* – mortality and existence – and even looks back to the earlier lyric of 'One Vision', also written by Roger. "Basically," the drummer explained, "the song is an actual line from the movie, and that was where the song came from. It's just sort of about an immortal, I suppose: 'This rage that lasts a thousand years, Will soon be gone,' and all that. It was written for the movie and it became very popular on stage, and I remember when we played it on the 1986 tour, it used to go down incredibly well."

The track's embryonic form, an edited version (3'23) which was played over the credits of *Highlander* (a fuller, but still incomplete version, running to 4'08, later featured on the *Live At Wembley Stadium* DVD as background music for the photo gallery section, while the full take was released as a bonus track on the 2011 reissue of *A Kind Of Magic*), is taken at a slower tempo and lacks the distinctive bassline, though the synthesizer effects and guitar work are intact. Freddie, sensing a great song buried within a good idea, took control of the song, borrowing a variation of the bassline from 'Keep Passing The Open Windows' and quickening the pace, turning the song into a poppy, chart-friendly single. When issued as a forerunner to the album in March 1986, three months ahead of the album, the single was a resounding success, peaking at No. 3 in the UK. Backed by Roger's instrumental 'A Dozen Red Roses For My Darling', the single was housed in a sombre, blue-tinted sleeve accompanied by the image of Kurgan, the villain from *Highlander*. The single was released in the US in June 1986, peaking at No. 42 and becoming the last single to chart in America until 'I Want It All' in 1989. Legend has it that the single reached No. 1 in no less than 35 countries, but there hasn't been any proof of the single reaching No. 1 anywhere in the world, though it did make the Top 10 in seven countries: UK, Ireland, Switzerland, the Netherlands, France, Germany, and Australia.

A striking video for the single was filmed by Russell Mulcahy in March 1986 at the Playhouse Theatre. ("At that time, it was pretty much derelict, it wasn't in use, and I think there was a question mark over its future," Brian commented in 2003, "so it was a perfect time for us to go in and make it look even *more* derelict.") With Freddie dressed as a magician and the others as vagabonds, the video is one of Queen's more inventive, and used animation for the first time since the 'Save Me' video in 1980, with the characters from the *A Kind Of Magic* album sleeve brought to life. "We all thought it was a neat idea for Freddie to be a wizard and for us to be the guys he transforms from tramps into glamorous rock stars," Brian explained in 2003. Glamorous rock stars they may be, but even fame and fortune couldn't allow base comforts such as central heating, meaning that when the band look miserable and cold in the intro and outro shots, that's not acting. "I remember discussing it with Russell Mulcahy in the Groucho Club," Roger said in 2003, "and just saying how we want strange little things to happen. I remember saying that I wanted gargoyles winking and things like that and having this magic stuff flying all over the place. I think it worked nicely; it's unpretentious." The video was included on an innovative video single release late in 1986. Backed by 'Who Wants To Live Forever', the format was a world-first, but was rendered obsolete shortly after its release. The video remained otherwise unreleased until 1991, when it was issued on *Greatest Flix II*; the US release was a year later on *Classic Queen*, and it wasn't until 2003 that the video received a major overhaul in terms of sound and vision on the *Greatest Video Hits 2* DVD.

The song was performed in the live setting for the Magic tour only. Placed between the first medley and 'Under Pressure', 'A Kind Of Magic' would regularly be extended well past its normal four-minute mark, allowing plenty of instrumental improvisation that was lacking from most other numbers, before ending in a typically big fashion. The first live version to be issued (taken from Queen's Budapest concert on 27 July 1986) was in December 1986 on *Live Magic*: for the vinyl release, the song was edited down to 4'47, but on the CD release, the full-length version was included, bringing the running time up to 5'29. When the 12 July Wembley concert was issued in May 1992, that version became the definitive one, running at an epic 8'42, with the last two minutes consumed by Freddie's vocal interplay with the crowd, while a second version from the previous night's concert was issued as a bonus track on the June 2003 CD reissue of *Live At Wembley Stadium*.

Roger has remained partial to the song, including it in most of his set lists. Its first solo live airing was actually performed by The Cross at the Gossport Festival on 29 July 1993, and again at the following year's performance, later being included in the set list for the Cowdray Ruins Concert on 18 September 1993, where the song was performed by Roger and John. Since then, it has become an integral inclusion in all of Roger's live shows, and has often been performed by Brian and Roger at special occasions and one-

offs. 'A Kind Of Magic' was originally supposed to be performed by Roger and Chris Thompson at the Concert For Life on 20 April 1992, but was dropped due to time constraints. Unsurprisingly, the song became a concert staple when Brian and Roger returned to the stage as Queen with Paul Rodgers between 2005 and 2008, and again with Adam Lambert starting in 2012.

A KIND OF 'A KIND OF MAGIC' *(Taylor)*
• Bonus: *Magic*

A pointless edit of the instrumental sections from the extended version of 'A Kind Of Magic', the only redeeming factor about this track is the emergence of a unique alternate guitar solo.

THE KISS (AURA RESURRECTS FLASH) *(Mercury)*
• Album: *Flash* • Bonus: *Flash*

Leading in from John's atmospheric 'Execution Of Flash', Freddie's 'The Kiss (Aura Resurrects Flash)' is a multi-tracked tour de force showcasing his beautifully controlled vocalizations. With a snippet of orchestration from Howard Blake (from a piece called 'Rocket Ship Flight', which had been arranged by Blake prior to Queen's involvement with the project), this song concludes the first side of *Flash Gordon* in a sublime fashion. An early demo, recorded during sessions for *The Game*, features Freddie on piano and vocals, and even captures a snippet of the melody of 'Football Fight' toward the end.

THE KISSING ME SONG *(May/Ellis)*
• A-side: 4/13 • Live (Brian & Kerry): *Acoustic* • Album (Brian & Kerry): *Golden*

This gorgeous song, a simple rock ballad extolling the virtues of love, was the first cowrite between Brian and Kerry Ellis. Recorded at Roger's The Priory in 2013, 'The Kissing Me Song' was first released as a Record Store Day exclusive, though the album version was slightly remixed and more of a studio creation. "'Kissing Me' is our Pop Art," Brian explained. "It's art mirroring life mirroring art. Maybe it will catch on!" Kerry agreed: "It's a feel-good song, youthful dreams, innocence, that imagined first kiss." A delightful music video featured fans from all over the world doing exactly as the song asked.

KNOCK ON WOOD *(Cropper/Floyd)*

Eddie Floyd's soul standard was performed live by 1984.

LA JAPONAISE *(Mercury/Moran)*
• Album (Freddie): *Barcelona* • Compilation (Freddie): *Solo Collection*

Japan was one of Freddie's most beloved countries, and he spent a considerable amount of time there in the last years of his life. 'La Japonaise' is a stunning ode to the country, constructed with prominent Eastern sounds, and even containing alternating lines in Japanese.

Two alternate versions were recorded: the first on 1 September 1987, credited as Freddie's demo vocal version and featuring largely improvised lyrics since the words had yet to be written; and the second, an a cappella version of the finished vocal, recorded on 9 November, is stunning upon first listen. An instrumental version was also created and included on *The Solo Collection*.

LANDSCAPE *(May)*
• Soundtrack (Brian): *Furia*

Introduced by the wail of a police siren and the sounds of the street, 'Landscape' is largely a keyboard atmosphere soundtrack piece, lasting a little over a minute and adding to the sombre ambience of the film.

LAND OF 1,000 DANCES *(Kenner)*

Originally performed by Wilson Pickett, 'Land Of 1,000 Dances' was performed live by The Reaction.

LAS PALABRAS DE AMOR
(THE WORDS OF LOVE) *(May)*
• Album: *Space* • A-side: 6/82 [17] • CD Single: 11/88
• CD Single: 10/91 [16]

Much as Queen's 1975 concerts in Japan had inspired Brian to write the gorgeous 'Teo Torriatte (Let Us Cling Together)', the guitarist's admiration for new cultures was channeled into 'Las Palabras De Amor (The Words Of Love)', written after the band's first-ever concerts in South America in 1981. Written and recorded for the *Hot Space* album in the winter of 1981, the song is a plea for love and hope in all societies around the world. Set to a lavish acoustic guitar backing, the song erupts into a traditional Queen anthem, and the hypnotic synthesizer woven throughout is perhaps the first successful integration of that instrument into a Queen song. "The minimalist era of Queen, liked by some but not by others, but this particular track was un-minimalist, it's really rather romantic," Brian said in 2003. "I was playing keyboards in this one, Freddie seemed to be less inclined to play keyboards, and many ideas came from keyboards rather than guitar. I like the track, painted with a very light brush."

"I write best when I'm not on guitar; maybe a few riffs or the basis, but strangely enough, you usually get the most perspective on a song when you're on an instrument that you're not accustomed to," Brian told *International Musician & Recording World* in 1982. "I'm not accustomed to playing the piano and I find that quite inspiring, because your fingers fall on different patterns. Whereas on a guitar, I pick it up and know where my fingers are going to fall. Mostly I sit alone someplace and think about it. That's the best way. I don't think my songwriting has changed as much as the others in the group. I tend to write more traditional Queen material like 'Las Palabras De Amor'. I still tend to write melodies and that certain sort of heaviness, which the group does well at its best; the guitar and piano which have that sort of thick sound. I really enjoy that, although these days it's used a little bit more sparingly."

A demo version of the song exists, with considerably altered lead vocals and a rougher arrangement, while a second version of the song was mixed but left unreleased. This version places more emphasis on the guitars, vocals and drums, while pushing the synthesizer further back into the mix.

Released as a UK single in June 1982 as the third single from the album, 'Las Palabras De Amor (The Words Of Love)' went on to reach No. 17 in the charts, which was described as disappointing, but considering the chart performances of the other recent singles – 'Under Pressure' reached No. 1, 'Body Language' peaked at No. 25 and 'Back Chat' charted at No. 40 – its placement in the singles chart was relatively impressive. Given that it was the only single taken directly from the album ('Under Pressure' was thrown on as a last-minute addition) to reach the Top 20, its exclusion from *Greatest Hits II* in 1991 is peculiar. Even more astonishing is the song's lack of inclusion in the live setting; though the band rehearsed a version in Leeds on 31 May 1982, and Brian played a snippet of the song before 'Love Of My Life' at the Milton Keynes Bowl on 5 June (he explained to the audience, "Well, it seems that we're not playing our song of peace tonight"), the first live airing the song would receive would be at the Concert For Life on 20 April 1992, where it was performed with Italian rocker Zucchero on lead vocals. More significantly, the song was performed on the South American leg of the 2008 Queen + Paul Rodgers Rock The Cosmos tour, with Brian on lead vocals, and received a rapturous response from the audience. Appropriately, the song was resurrected in September 2015 on the Queen + Adam Lambert Don't Stop Them Now tour of South America, again with Brian on lead vocals.

Though a video wasn't specially prepared for the single, the band did appear on *Top Of The Pops* for the first time in five years, performing the song on 10 June 1982, the broadcast going out the next day. The result leaves a lot to be desired: coming at the end of a grueling European tour, with less than receptive audiences to the new material, the band are clearly uninterested in being on the programme and give an uninspired performance. Nevertheless, it remains the only official performance of the song to have been attempted, and was duly released on the 1999 video *Greatest Flix III* (while the song was issued on its similarly titled counterpart, *Greatest Hits III*) and the 2003 DVD *Greatest Video Hits 2*.

LAST HORIZON (May)
• Album (Brian): *BTTL* • A-side (Brian): 12/93 [51]
• Live (Brian): *Brixton* • Live (Q+PR): *Return, Ukraine*

Recorded at Allerton Studios in 1988, Brian's 'Last Horizon' was released on his 1992 debut solo album, *Back To The Light*. Namechecked as one of Brian's favorite songs, he performed it on both of his Brian May Band tours in 1992/1993 and 1998, and even offered a remixed backing track, which 'erased' his guitar piece, as a download on his website for his birthday in 2004, for aspiring guitarists to play along to.

The song was performed by Queen + Paul Rodgers, which was unusual considering that prior tours hadn't featured any solo material (except for the vocal improvisations in 1984 and 1985, which loosely resembled Freddie's 'Foolin' Around'), but given Brian's appreciation for the song, its inclusion wasn't entirely unsurprising. The song was once again in the set list on the Queen + Adam Lambert tours starting in 2012, serving as an introduction to Brian's guitar solo.

LAUGH OR CRY (Taylor)
• Album (Roger): *Fun*

Roger's songwriting subjects were usually restricted to songs of chauvinistic love or politics (and, in the case of *Fun In Space*, science-fiction and aliens). Rarely did he write a tender love song, but he has been known to surprise his listeners, and 'Laugh Or Cry' is one of those surprises. Starting with a sparse acoustic guitar, piano and bass guitar introduction, the song is a beautiful excursion into a territory Roger rarely explored during the earlier part of his solo career.

The song was released as the B-side of the Japanese and American single, 'Let's Get Crazy', and was performed live by The Cross on their 1988 tour.

LAZING ON A SUNDAY AFTERNOON (Mercury)
• Album: *Opera*

Coming as the second track on *A Night At The Opera* is this quirky music hall-inspired number. Sung in a delightfully camp style by Freddie and ending with an over-the-top guitar solo, 'Lazing On A Sunday Afternoon' chronicles the busy schedule of the protagonist's week, with a day of respite planned before it begins all over again. In keeping with the experimental nature of *A Night At The Opera*, the vocals were recorded in an unconventional manner, with the signal from Freddie's microphone being fed into headphones placed in a metal can, thus giving it a megaphone effect.

"That's the way the mood takes me," Freddie lucidly told the *Record Mirror* in 1976. "Y'know... that's just one aspect of me, and I can really change. Everything on 'Sunday Afternoon' is something that... I'm really, I'm really sort of, I really... well, I love doing the vaudeville side of things. It's quite a sort of test... I love writing things like that and I'm sure I'm going to do more than that... It's quite a challenge."

'Lazing On A Sunday Afternoon' was performed live throughout 1976, but was dropped just before the Hyde Park concert that September.

LEAVING HOME AIN'T EASY (May)
• Album: *Jazz*

Brian's mournful, self-sung 'Leaving Home Ain't Easy' is a melancholy reflection on leaving his family once again, and expresses his disillusionment with stardom and the lifestyle it demands, a subject that Brian had first addressed in 'Good Company' back in 1975, and would reference at least once on subsequent albums. Just prior to sessions for *Jazz*, Brian became a father on 15 June, with the birth of his son, Jimmy, making going out on the road and being away from his blossoming young family all the more difficult. This dichotomy of staying to be with his family and leaving to support them is addressed, with its author reluctantly accepting that leaving is the only way.

Driven by a gorgeous acoustic riff, the song is an exquisite diversion from the slighter tracks on *Jazz*, and features some tasteful guitar orchestrations, sounding unmistakably like violins, while the bridge is Brian playing the part of his wife, begging him to stay. "The lady's part? It's me," Brian explained in 2002. "We slowed down the tape to record it so it comes out speeded up. I think Wheetus just did the same thing on 'Dirtbag'!"

LET ME ENTERTAIN YOU *(Mercury)*
• Album: *Jazz* • B-side: 1/80 [11] • Live: *Killers, Montreal*
• Bonus: *Jazz* • Compilation: *On Air*

By 1978, Freddie had transformed himself from a flamboyant yet mild-mannered vocalist into a defiant, outspoken and often lewd singer of songs and lover of life. Above all, though, he was an entertainer, a salesman hell-bent on giving the audience its full concert experience by whatever means. Never before had Freddie's attitude to his 'job' been more perfectly documented than on 'Let Me Entertain You', a bawdy slice of good-natured rock'n'roll written as a deliberate hard sell to audiences worldwide. Borrowing its title from a song written by Jule Styne and Stephen Sondheim in *Gypsy: A Musical Fable*, 'Let Me Entertain You' finds Freddie as a barker, ramping up the audience participation gimmick he had perfected on the 1977/1978 News Of The World tour. Given its concert-friendly atmosphere, the song would suitably become a live favorite between 1978 and 1981, securing a prime position as the second song in the set, though it was promoted to concert opener on a few dates on the 1979 Crazy tour.

A recording from *Live Killers* was issued as the US B-side of the fast live 'We Will Rock You' in August 1979, and then as the UK B-side of 'Save Me' in January 1980. A different version from the November 1981 Montreal concert was released as a bonus track on the 2011 reissue of *Jazz*. In 2007, Greg Brooks debuted an alternate version of the song at a Fan Club convention,

with the song's spoken outro replaced by a studio singalong of 'We Are The Champions' – a fun novelty upon first listen, and reminiscent of the self-referential 'I Do Like To Be Beside The Seaside' outro on *Queen II* and intro on *Sheer Heart Attack*.

LET ME IN YOUR HEART AGAIN *(May)*
Compilation: *Forever*

Written by Brian in 1983 and recorded during sessions for *The Works*, 'Let Me In Your Heart Again' was ultimately discarded, despite several lyrical rewrites to make the song work. Unwilling to let a good track go to waste, Brian brought the song out of mothballs in 1988 while recording Anita Dobson's *Talking Of Love* album. And so the song was forgotten for over two decades, until Queen archivist Greg Brooks discovered the unfinished Queen recording in the band's archives. In a conversation on QueenOnline, he assured fans that it was better than anything on *The Works*. Certainly a hyperbolic statement, but fans had to wait until November 2014 before having to decide for themselves, when 'Let Me In Your Heart Again' was finally released on the *Queen Forever* compilation.

So did Brooks' assurance stand up? Well, it's certainly the best of the three new songs on the new compilation album, but as is often the case with previously unheard songs, the excitement of hearing a new song with Freddie on vocals clouded the effect somewhat. It's certainly a fine track and would have augmented *The Works* spectacularly, but it definitely wasn't better than anything on that album. Constructed out of bits that worked and given a lick of paint to make it sound contemporary to 2014 (as opposed to a period piece), 'Let Me In Your Heart Again' is a beautiful ballad that would have sat well opposite 'It's A Hard Life', but whether the band were justified in leaving it off *The Works* is up to the listener.

The song was premiered on Chris Evans' BBC show in September 2014, with a promotional disc sent out for radio play, before a rather jarring William Orbit remix, prepared specially for Product Red, was released on World AIDS Day in December 2014. This version, included on the vinyl version of *Queen Forever* as well as on a promotional CD single, was augmented by Orbit on keyboards and programming and removed everything charming and endearing about the original version.

LET ME LIVE *(Queen)*
• Album: *Heaven* • A-side: 6/96 [9]

This welcome return to gospel started life in 1976 as an untitled impromptu jam with Rod Stewart, before it was revisited seven years later in Los Angeles – again with Stewart and his one-time bandmate, Jeff Beck – fleshed out more fully and given the working title of 'Take Another Little Piece Of My Heart'. Originally intended as the sixth track on *The Works*, according to an early "ideas" cassette, there's no proof to indicate that the song was finished; indeed, when Brian, Roger, and John returned to it a decade later, there was only 90 seconds of Freddie's voice with which to work – that an entire song was constructed around this snippet is not only a testament to the advances of technology, but to the tenacity of the others to create a complete song.

The song is a cry for help, pleading for life, love, and acceptance from the world, and features the distinction of having Freddie, Roger and Brian sing a verse each. They're assisted by an assembled group of backing vocalists, with three-quarters having worked with at least one band member in the past: Gary Martin contributed vocals to 'The Amazing Spider-Man'; Catherine Porter was a backing vocalist on Brian's 1992/1993 Back To The Light tour, and also sang on Roger's 'Everybody Hurts Sometime' and 'Old Friends'; and Miriam Stockley sang on Freddie's and Montserrat Caballé's 'The Golden Boy', one of the last gospel songs Freddie wrote in his lifetime. Only Rebecca Leigh-White was a newcomer, but was familiar to Pink Floyd fans as a backing vocalist on their most recent studio album, *The Division Bell*.

Chosen as the fourth single from *Made In Heaven*, 'Let Me Live' was initially banned from UK's Radio One on the grounds that it was too 'classic' (whatever that means), but that didn't harm sales at all, since it peaked at No. 9 in June 1996. Two CD singles were issued: the first featured *Jazz* album tracks 'Bicycle Race', 'Fat Bottomed Girls' and 'Don't Stop Me Now' (which was the B-side on the standard, 7" vinyl version), while the second featured 'My Fairy King', 'Doing All Right', and 'Liar' from the *Queen At The Beeb* album. A sticker on the second CD proudly boasted "featuring tracks from the upcoming *BBC Sessions* release", which sadly never materialized.

A video for the song was created in late 1995 by the British Film Institute. Directed by Bernard Rudden, the video shows a couple in the middle of a breakdown and unable to communicate with or relate to each other. This video was issued on both the 1996 video compilation, *Made In Heaven: The Films*, and on *Greatest Flix III*.

LET ME LOVE YOU *(Jeffrey Rod)*

Written by Jeff Beck and Rod Stewart (hence the credit to "Jeffrey Rod"), 'Let Me Love You' was originally performed by The Jeff Beck Group and released on their 1968 debut album, *Truth*. Wreckage performed the song as their set closer on 31 October 1969 at Ealing College Of Art.

LET ME OUT *(May)*
• Album (Brian): *Starfleet* • Live (The Cross): *Bootleg*
• CD single (Brian): 11/92 [19]

According to the liner notes of *Starfleet Project*, 'Let Me Out' was an older, unrecorded song brought out of mothballs for the April 1983 sessions in Los Angeles. (Rumor has it that the song was first floated by the *News Of The World* sessions, and was then revisited for the *Jazz* sessions.) The first three minutes are dominated by Brian on vocals, singing about a constraining relationship, followed by a lengthy guitar duel between Eddie Van Halen and Brian which becomes the focal point of the next three minutes. The remainder is a lyrical coda, with Brian bringing the song to a close. The song received its first live performance on 7 December 1990 at the Astoria Theatre, when Brian guest-starred on guitar for the last four numbers of The Cross' fan club gig. After 'I'm In Love With My Car', and as Roger walked off stage to rest, an epic eight-minute version followed, with Clayton Moss acting as a fine foil to Brian's guitar antics. It was ultimately issued on the fan club-only release, *The Official Bootleg*.

Apart from a few rare performances on the Back To The Light world tour, the song received one additional airing on 7 July 2001 at Stravinski Hall (as part of the Montreux Jazz Festival), with Brian on guitars and vocals, Jon Clearly on piano, Chris Spedding on guitar, John Hatton on bass, Bernie Dresel on drums and Emily, Jimmy and Anita May providing backing vocals. The studio version received its first (and, to date, only) appearance on CD when it was issued as a bonus track on the 'Back To The Light' CD single in November 1992.

LET THERE BE DRUMS (Nelson/Podolar)
• Live (Q+PR): *Return*

A top ten hit for The Ventures in 1961, 'Let There Be Drums' was originally performed by session drummer Sandy Nelson on that record and earned him respect as one of the first drummers to bring that instrument to the forefront. Essentially an extended drum solo with a 1960s surf riff in the background, the song was performed on the 2005 tour as an introduction to 'I'm In Love With My Car', and showed that Roger could still deliver the goods, despite being particularly outspoken against drum solos.

LET YOUR HEART RULE YOUR HEAD (May)
• Album (Brian): *BTTL* • B-side (Brian): 12/93 [51]
• Live (Brian): *Brixton*

Brian tapped into his past influences – namely his skiffle hero, Lonnie Donegan – to write this uplifting, upbeat song that served as a lighthearted chaser between the heavy 'I'm Scared' and the weighty 'Just One Life' on *Back To The Light*. Brian even produced a version of 'Let Your Heart Rule Your Head' for an unreleased Donegan album recorded in 1988, that featured its songwriter on backing vocals.

The song became a live favorite on the 1992/1993 Back To The Light tour, where it was preceded by an a cappella version of "39', and was resurrected for three dates (Hamburg, Offenbach and Tokyo) on the 1998 Another World tour. A live version was included on the *Live At The Brixton Academy* album, and was also released as the B-side of the 'Last Horizon' single in December 1993.

LET'S GET CRAZY (Taylor)
• Album (Roger): *Fun*

Kick-started with a raucous drum workout, 'Let's Get Crazy' is a highlight of *Fun In Space*, with a joyous vocal performance from Roger accentuated by a truly inspired and groovy bass line. Roger is really on fine form here, both vocally and instrumentally, but the outstanding feature is his drum work: this was one of the few songs in his extensive solo discography that featured the drums so prominently.

Chosen as a Japanese and American-only single in August 1981, 'Let's Get Crazy', backed with 'Laugh Or Cry', didn't chart, but remains one of the few songs from *Fun In Space* to be performed live. It was

a regular in The Cross' live set on their British and European tour between February and April 1988, but was bumped out of the set list once they acquired additional original material.

LET'S GET DRUNK

Not much is known about this song except that it was performed live by The Cross, with Peter Noone on vocals, during their inaugural 1988 tour – and suitably summed up the mood of the concerts.

LET'S MAKE LOVE (Mercury)

In the early days of the *Queen Forever* compilation, there were plans to include not only the three Freddie and Michael Jackson collaborations ('State Of Shock', 'Victory', and 'There Must Be More To Life Than This'), but a handful of other Queen songs Brian and Roger had been beefing up over the years. 'Let's Make Love', written by Freddie and recorded during the A Kind Of Magic sessions in 1986, was also planned to be released, but was pulled at the last minute. In June 2018, a 50-second recording of extremely low quality leaked online, and while it's difficult to hear exactly what Freddie is singing, it definitely is him; most intriguingly, the chorus harks back to the music hall style that Freddie so favored in his early songwriting days. Whether this song will ever be released can be answered with a big ol' question mark.

LET'S TURN IT ON (Mercury)
• Album (Freddie): *BadGuy* • Compilations (Freddie): *Pretender, FM Album, The Solo Collection*

Opening up *Mr Bad Guy* is this jaunty dance song, sounding like an update of 'Staying Power'. 'Let's Turn It On' is a lightweight though energetic track, a perfect candidate to introduce the listener to Freddie's first solo record, with an optimistic set of lyrics and busy instrumentation. With hints of Brian's guitar work (most noticeable during the guitar solo, in which Paul Vincent makes his guitar sound almost exactly like The Red Special, orchestration and all), the song would have worked well as a Queen track – provided *Hot Space* had been better received, of course.

In 1992, the song was remixed by Jeff Lord-Alge, with additional production by Julian Raymond, for inclusion on *The Great Pretender* and *The Freddie Mercury Album*, two mediocre attempts to update

Freddie's solo work to varying degrees of success. The 'Let's Turn It On' remix certainly wasn't a highlight, replacing the joyful backing with an anonymous dance track that dates the song to the early 1990s – much like the original dated it to the 1980s.

LET'S TURN IT ON WITH SIDEBURNS

Mixed, or mashed up, much like 'New York At Last' (see that entry), 'Let's Turn It On With Sideburns' (if ever there was an awkward song title, this is it!) was created some time after 2001, blending Freddie's 1985 track 'Let's Turn It On' with a track called 'Sideburns'. The latter title was released in November 2001 as part of *Guitarist* magazine's free CD and features Brian on guitar and Justin Shirley-Smith on programming. 'Sideburns' is an unofficial title and was more or less a demonstration by Brian, showing purchasers of the Burns guitar, the latest manufacturer to create a Red Special lookalike, what they could potentially do with their guitars. The mash-up transforms 'Let's Turn It On' from an upbeat disco track into a mid-tempo, thrashing rock song and the result is surprisingly effective, although it's far too short (just under three minutes), so that by the time the listener really gets into the song, it has already ended. Still, if one can find it, the track is more than worth it and warrants repeated listens.

LIAR *(Mercury)*

• Album: *Queen* • Compilation: *BBC, On Air* • Bonus: *Queen* • CD Single: 6/96 [9] • Live: *Rainbow, Odeon*

The songs on the band's first record were a collection of new material and old songs written in various incarnations by previous bands. The most well known was 'Doing All Right', which had actually been recorded by Smile with Brian, Roger and Tim Staffell; what's not as well known is that 'Liar' started life as a song called 'Lover' in Freddie's band, Ibex, and had been co-written with band mate Mike Bersin. Queen was especially impressed with the song, and incorporated a restructured version of it, now retitled 'Liar', into their repertoire.

The song is an early example of Freddie's use of oblique lyrical matter combined with his fascination of religion and theology. Reading less like a song and more like a confessional, 'Liar' is set to one of Queen's most raucous and hard-rocking backings, complete with several pounding guitar solos and an extended percussion introduction. Clocking in at over six minutes, it was the longest song the band had recorded at that time, and features an uncharacteristic (and uncredited) appearance by a Hammond organ, thus adding to the religious textures Freddie was musically weaving.

Brian said of the song in 1992, "I had heard Wreckage play this track in a rehearsal, and particularly liked one riff, but the rest of the song was changed drastically by the four of us, using some of my own riffs and Freddie's words. There is actually an interesting aside to this. 'Liar' was one of the first songs that we worked on together, and there was a moment when we discussed if we should all be credited in such cases. Freddie said, 'As far as I'm concerned, the person who wrote the words has effectively written the song.' It may not have been the most logical solution, but it was a workable rule which we used virtually unchanged right up to the last two albums, when we decided to share everything regardless of origin. The rule almost certainly discouraged us from co-operating on lyrics for a long time, and started a trend toward separateness in song-producing in general, which was acute at the time of the Munich records."

Of the writing process, John explained the genesis of 'Liar': "The biggest factor of our music being lighter than in the early days is that Freddie has developed more interest in the piano ... 'Liar', from the first album, was written on guitar, and naturally goes into the hard rock extreme, as opposed to 'Killer Queen'. Freddie is now surrounded by Japanese furniture and a grand piano, so the songs are written there. Simple, isn't it? But I doubt Roger writes songs on the drums."

"There was a classic case where everything got messed up on the first album," Brian explained of the first album's recording process in a June 1998 BBC Radio 2 interview, "'cos we did the first Queen album on basically dark time, in Trident Studios. In other words, you know, 'Somebody's just finished, boys. It's 4 o'clock in the morning and you've got till 5.' ... We'd done a backing for 'Liar', and [Trident] said, 'Oh, that's alright boys, just overdub on this tape,' which they pulled out. And it was the wrong tape. We only discovered weeks later and all the way through we were thinking, 'This doesn't sound right! What's happened to this tape?' So eventually we got to redo it again after a big fuss."

The song was first recorded in September 1971 at De Lane Lea Studios during Queen's first demo session, where it extends to nearly eight minutes and features several more improvised sections that were later excised from the final recorded version. (This demo recording was finally officially released in 2011, on the deluxe edition of the debut album.) In its original album form, the song is a whirlwind tour de force of powerful rock'n'roll but, lacking foresight, Elektra issued 'Liar' as a US-only single in February 1974, editing the song down to three minutes and cutting most of the important bits out. More of a butchering than an edit, this version has eluded a CD release and was consistently labeled the worst record ever issued by Queen (certainly through no fault of their own; even the band disowned the release), at least until the multiple releases in 1996 of the 'You Don't Fool Me' remixes. Speaking of remixes, a remix of 'Liar' appeared as a bonus track on the 1991 remaster of the debut album featuring more pronounced percussion but changing little else.

'Liar' was also played extensively in the set list from 1970 on, and was often shifted around in the repertoire; it was effective as both an opening and closing number, though by the mid-1970s it became an encore number. Dropped from the set in late 1978, it was reprised on a few one-off occasions (most notably during every April 1982 show), but was reintroduced into the set list in a medley with other early hits in 1984 and 1985, and was then used as an introduction to 'Tear It Up' during the Magic tour.

LIAR (Noone)
• Album (The Cross): *MBADTK* • European A-side (The Cross): 7/90 • Live (The Cross): *Bootleg*

The Cross had a habit of using titles already used by Queen in years past: 'Bad Attitude', released on *Blue Rock* in 1991, was originally titled 'Tear It Up', while The Cross' version of 'Liar' bears no relation whatsoever to the original version released in 1973. Unbelievably, the song drew no comparison to Freddie's masterpiece in contemporary reviews (probably because those who did actually review *Mad: Bad: And Dangerous To Know* didn't give the album more than a cursory listen), and while it's easy to say that The Cross' song is inferior, it should be remembered that they are very different compositions. This version is somewhat danceable, with a scratchy guitar motif throughout which suggests that there's an underlying reggae rhythm; the fashion in which Roger sings the song, however, is anything but.

Overall, 'Liar' is enjoyable, with a lyrical theme calling out the protagonist's lover for indiscretion,

and was deemed commercial enough to be the second single extracted from the album in July 1990. However, by this point, The Cross had no audience in the UK; their last single, 'Power To Love', only charted at No. 85, so 'Liar' was given a European-only release. Backed with the non-album 'In Charge Of My Heart', the single failed to chart, despite an edited single mix and an extended remix. Even the assistance of a promotional video, directed by German team Schultze, with a slightly altered backing track, helped little in pushing the single.

LIFE CHANGES (Moss/Edney/Noone/Macrae)
• Album (The Cross): *Blue* • German CD single (The Cross): 10/91

Closing what is generally regarded as The Cross' finest album is 'Life Changes', an optimistically naïve song of entering a new phase in a relationship. Set to a pleasant acoustic rock backing with an impassioned vocal from Roger, the song is a fine swan song to Roger's most commercially contentious side project: while he had plans to record a fourth album, or at least issue one further album with The Cross (only 11 songs recorded during *Blue Rock* sessions were released, leaving 14 further unreleased songs), the message within 'Life Changes' was as apt a career closer as any.

'Life Changes' was released as a German single in October 1991, shorn to a more compact three and a half minutes, excising much of the extraneous bits, the emotive outro, and Spike Edney's tinkling runs up and down the keyboards. This edit was available only as a CD single, with Spike's 'Put It All Down To Love', the album version of 'Life Changes', and Peter Noone's non-album song, 'Heartland', as the other tracks. Unfortunately, the words struck a poignant and difficult chord for Roger: Freddie passed away on 24 November 1991, and the single was withdrawn from release and all solo projects put on the back-burner.

LIFE IS REAL (SONG FOR LENNON) (Mercury)
• B-side: 4/82 [25] • Album: *Space* • Live (Brian & Kerry): *Acoustic*

The death of John Lennon on 8 December 1980 shook the music world. Queen had often cited him, and The Beatles, as their main influences, and when they learned of Lennon's assassination the morning after, they incorporated his 1971 single 'Imagine' into the set list at London's Wembley Arena that night.

Therefore, it was inevitable that a tribute to Lennon in some form would be written. 'Life Is Real (Song For Lennon)' is that tribute, and recalls many of Lennon's earlier piano works (the song borrows heavily from his 1970 confessional, 'Mother') while incorporating the oblique imagery that Lennon favored in his latter-day Beatles works.

Written by Freddie in late 1981 during a well-documented transatlantic plane ride to New York, the original opening lines were sexually graphic, but Freddie's assistant, Peter 'Phoebe' Freestone tactfully suggested that he make it something a little less offensive; thus, the opening line was altered to "Guilt stains on my pillow."

Driven by an ostentatious piano line and accentuated by a lovely acoustic guitar solo, the song is unfortunately dated with synthesizer flourishes, firmly placing the song to a specific time in 1982. Nevertheless, 'Life Is Real (Song For Lennon)' is an unrecognized highlight of *Hot Space*, and was issued as the B-side of 'Body Language' in 1982. The song was introduced into the 1982 Hot Space tour set list, but only for a half dozen dates that August, before being dropped for good. More significantly, the song was shortlisted for inclusion in the 1984 Queen Works! tour repertoire, and was rehearsed but dropped before the tour commenced. The song was brought out of mothballs for the Queen + Adam Lambert Once In A Lifetime tour in 2012, where it was performed once in Moscow with Zemfira on vocals, inspiring Brian to return to it the following year with Kerry Ellis on their Acoustic By Candlelight tour.

LILY OF THE VALLEY (*Mercury*)
• Album: *SHA* • B-side: 1/75 [11]

Freddie's gorgeous conclusion to the *Sheer Heart Attack* medley is 'Lily Of The Valley', a sombre plea for love set to a dulcet piano backing, with drums, bass, and guitar used sparingly. "Freddie's stuff was so heavily cloaked, lyrically," Brian told *Mojo* magazine in 1999. "But you could find out, just from little insights, that a lot of his private thoughts were in there, although a lot of the more meaningful stuff was not very accessible. 'Lily Of The Valley' was utterly heartfelt. It's about looking at his girlfriend and realizing that his body needed to be somewhere else. It's a great piece of art, but it's the last song that would ever be a hit." Indeed, the song was released as the B-side of both the UK 'Now I'm Here' single, and the US reissue of 'Keep Yourself Alive',

both with unique single edits: the first starts with the last guitar chord from 'Flick Of The Wrist', while the second is a true standalone edit, without any segue from the preceding song.

A LITTLE BIT OF LOVE (*Fraser/Kirke/Kossoff/Rodgers*)

Taken from Free's 1972 album *Free At Last* and released as a single, reaching No. 13 in the UK, 'A Little Bit Of Love' was performed live by Queen + Paul Rodgers.

LITTLE BOOGIE: *see* 'BACK TO STORM'

LITTLE EGYPT (*Leiber/Stoller*)

Originally by The Coasters, 'Little Egypt' was played live by 1984.

LIVING ON MY OWN (*Mercury*)
• Album (Freddie): *BadGuy* • A-side: 9/85 [50]
• A-side: 7/93 [1] • Compilations (Freddie): *Pretender, FM Album, The Solo Collection* • Compilation (Queen): *GH3*

"Basically," Freddie said in 1985, "if you listen to 'Living On My Own', that is very me: it's living on my own but having fun … It can be a very lonely life, but I choose it and so, that song, it's not dealing with people who are living on their own in sort of basement flats or things like that. It's me living on my own, and … I'm not complaining. I'm just saying I'm living on my own and I'm having a bogey time. Does that make sense, honey?"

It sounded like even Freddie had no clue what he was talking about, but there's no denying that, despite all his fame and fortune, he found the rock star lifestyle a solitary one. While John and Brian attempted to juggle a family life on top of jet-setting around the world, Roger and Freddie were more the archetypal rock stars – party all night, sleep all day, and get some work done whenever the mood strikes. Deep within Freddie's convoluted explanation lies a veiled sense of despair, as if he wanted to just give it all up and enjoy the rest of his life with someone, but that, for now, he was happy enough living on his own. It's no surprise that shortly after *Mr Bad Guy* was released in April 1985, he began a happy relationship with Jim Hutton, who was with Freddie and his only partner until the end of his life.

The album version of 'Living On My Own' is

certainly a fun slice of rock-disco (notable for its joyous scat vocalizations, which appeared during Freddie's vocal improvisations as early as the 1982 Rock 'n America tour, and piano 'freak out' by Fred Mandel), but upon its original release as the third single from the album in September 1985, it would only reach No. 50 in the UK charts, peaking at No. 85 in the US. However, it was remixed in April 1993 by the No More Brothers team (Serge Ramaekers, Colin Peter and Carl Ward), transforming it from a disco record into a decent techno remix. Eight versions – Album Remix, Radio Mix, Extended Mix, Club Mix, Dub Mix, L.A. Mix, Underground Solutions / Roger S Mix, and Techno Mix – were produced, and the results were so strong that it was released as a single in July 1993, giving Freddie his first and only (albeit posthumous) No. 1 single. A hybrid mix, combining an early take (recorded 6 April 1984) with a later take (recorded 29 May), was included on *The Solo Collection* and features some interesting lyrical alterations, but the preferred presentation would have been for these two different takes to have remained separate.

A video was produced and directed by Rudi Dolezal and Hannes Rossacher – better known as both DoRo and The Torpedo Twins (see the entry for 'One Vision' for more information) – at Henderson's nightclub in Munich on 5 September 1985. The occasion, more importantly, marked Freddie's 39th birthday, and the theme of the party was black and white, with the guests instructed to 'dress to kill' – and in drag; the only person dressed 'normally' was the birthday boy. The video for the single shows Freddie and his guests – over 300 flown in from various corners of the world, including all of Queen and their entourage – partaking in the excesses provided. (The next day, a sobered-up Freddie returned to shoot the singing scenes.) Unbeknown to the guests, though, cameras were secretly placed in various locations throughout the club, which got Freddie in a bit of hot water when CBS Records banned the video from American television since they didn't want to promote promiscuity. The video was re-edited in 1999 to match up with the 1993 remix for inclusion on the *Greatest Flix III* video.

LONDON TOWN, C'MON DOWN *(Taylor)*
• Album (Roger): *Electric* • B-side (Roger): 3/99 [38]

A funky, beat-dominated rocker concluding *Electric Fire*, 'London Town, C'mon Down' is a lengthy epic championing the perks of modern-day London, superbly sung by Roger and Treana Morris. While it remains largely bubbly and upbeat throughout, about halfway through the song cuts to half-speed for a reading of an excerpt from a Mervyn Peake article, 'London Fantasy'. The liner notes credit the voice to Peake himself, who died in 1968; the voice actually sounds more like Roger, fed through distortion.

An edited version, running just over three minutes and cutting out the extended finale, appeared as the B-side of 'Surrender' in March 1999. The song was performed during the 1999 Electric Fire tour, featuring Treana Morris on more prominent vocals, and served as a fine way for Roger to introduce the band.

LONELINESS... *(Taylor)*
• Album (Roger): *Happiness?*

A short but sweet track languishing on the second side of *Happiness?*, 'Loneliness...' is an underrated composition, serving as a therapy session for Roger following the death of Freddie: despite having so many people around him, having to face his friend's death alone was "the greatest curse." The song was performed live on the first few dates of the 1994/199 Happiness? tour, but was replaced by 'Man On Fire' early on.

LONG AWAY *(May)*
• Album: *Races*

Of the four members of Queen, Brian was the most ill at ease with stardom. The guitarist was never comfortable with the trappings of a rock lifestyle, and strove to balance his domestic and professional lives. He had first addressed this on 'Good Company', a jovial coming-of-age story, but by 1976, Queen's popularity had only increased, and Brian found himself longing for the days of obscurity. He often channeled his frustrations and insecurities with stardom into song, but it's on 'Long Away' that he's able to obliquely do so; as he often strove for universality in Queen songs, he wrote 'Long Away' so that his discomfort was masked by introspection, with a well-used astronomical allegory thrown in for good measure.

For the first (but not last) time on a Queen recording, Brian's main guitar of choice wasn't his trusty Red Special, but was a Burns 12-string guitar, used to achieve the jangly, Byrds-esque sound. However, a Burns guitar wasn't his first choice. "I couldn't play Rickenbackers because the necks are too thin," Brian told *Guitar World* in 1998. "I like a very fat and wide neck. My fingers only work in that situation. I always wanted to play a Rickenbacker, because John Lennon did. Roger collects extremely fucking rare guitars, and he has a Rickenbacker. But I can't play it."

In the US, the song was released as a single with 'You And I' on the B-side, making it the first (and only, until 'No-One But You (Only The Good Die Young)' in 1997) Queen single in any territory to feature a lead vocal by anyone other than Freddie; it failed to chart. The band reportedly rehearsed the song for the UK leg of the A Day At The Races tour in January 1977, but it was ultimately kept out of the set list. Surprisingly, Brian threw in a snippet of the song before 'Love Of My Life' on the 2005 Queen + Paul Rodgers European tour, in Pesaro, Italy, with a further five appearances tossed in sporadically. It received its first full live performance in May 2010, when Roger and Brian appeared as guests at a Taylor Hawkins and The Coattail Riders gig in London.

LOOKS LIKE IT'S GONNA BE A GOOD NIGHT: *see* 'IMPROMPTU'

THE LOSER IN THE END *(Taylor)*
• Album: *Queen2*

One of the numerous lyrical themes on *Queen II* is the passing of a legacy from generation to generation, which is addressed full-on in Brian's opening salvo, 'Father To Son', but is more loosely applied to Roger's sole contribution to the album. A less-than-heartfelt ode to maternal figures worldwide, 'The Loser In The End' is a raucous, almost Who-like composition that splits fan opinion. Some love it, others hate it, but there's no denying that the song is a much-needed shot in the arm after the relatively downbeat 'White Queen (As It Began)' and 'Some Day, One Day'.

Sung by Roger (as all his compositions in the early days were), the song opens with a tricky drum pattern in the style of Led Zeppelin's John Bonham, while an organ quivers in the background among wild guitars and a chunky bass. *Record Mirror* wasn't impressed with the song, reporting in a contemporary review, "['The Loser In The End'] must be the worst piece of dross ever committed to plastic – like 'She's Leaving Home' meets Black Sabbath?"

'The Loser In The End' was never performed live, but was released as the B-side of the Japanese issuing of 'Seven Seas Of Rhye'.

LOST IN SOUL

Much like 'Catfight For The Rest' (see 'Dancer'), 'Lost In Soul' is a fake recording uploaded to YouTube in 2007, but the faker at least attempted to make it sound semi-legit, using elements of the live instrumental take of 'Love Me Like There's No Tomorrow' from Freddie's *The Solo Collection*, sampled drums from Roger, and unsourced vocal ad-libs – not to mention the irritating but by-now familiar to die-hard fans intonation of Greg Brooks' pronouncing "Property of Queen Productions" repeatedly.

LOST OPPORTUNITY *(Queen)*
• CD Single: 3/91 [22] • Bonus: *Innuendo*

This swaggering blues workout was written and sung by Brian, marking the guitarist's final full lead vocal on a Queen song. Recorded in January 1991 in one take, after Freddie insisted that the band return to the studio to record some B-sides for the *Innuendo* singles, 'Lost Opportunity' deals with Brian's post-depression state of mind; having survived the late 1980s despite personal turmoil (his divorce from wife Chrissy, the death of his father, and unconfirmed rumors that all was not well with Freddie, hence Queen's retirement from the road), Brian was still finding it a struggle to remain positive, and the lyrics of 'Lost Opportunity' aptly sum up an average day in the life.

'Lost Opportunity' was the only song recorded in January 1991 to actually end up as originally intended, appearing as a bonus track on the CD single and 12" vinyl releases of 'I'm Going Slightly Mad' two months later. While it wasn't released on *The Singles Collection – Volume 4* in 2010, on the grounds that it wasn't originally released on 7" vinyl, it was released as a bonus track on the 2011 deluxe reissue of *Innuendo*.

LOVE IN A RAINBOW *(May/Ellis)*
• Album (Brian & Kerry): *Golden*

This gorgeous mid-tempo ballad opens *Golden Days* and finds Kerry Ellis in beautiful voice, with Brian helping her out on backing vocals, guitar, sitar, and gayageum. The vaguely psychedelic bent works extremely well, and it's a shame that a track like this likely won't get more exposure, as it could have been a perfect addition to the Queen + Adam Lambert repertoire.

LOVE KILLS *(Mercury/Moroder)*
• A-side (Freddie): 9/84 [10] • Soundtrack (Freddie): *Metropolis* • Compilations (Freddie): *Pretender, The Solo Collection* • B-side (Freddie): 11/92 [8]

Famed German producer Giorgio Moroder had established Musicland Studios late in the 1960s, where he recorded most of his own albums, nestled in the basement of the Arabella High-Rise Building. Throughout the 1970s, Moroder became an in-demand producer, co-writing and producing Donna Summer's smash disco single, 'I Feel Love', in 1977. While disco had been worked up from funk and R&B throughout the early 1970s, it was this crossover which inarguably launched the genre, and Moroder was at the forefront. While Queen would never record with Moroder himself, instead preferring the affable nature of Moroder's engineer, Reinhold Mack, Musicland became the band's studio of choice throughout the early and mid-1980s.

A noted film buff, Moroder became interested in restoring the controversial film *Metropolis*, released in 1927 by Fritz Lang and the brunt of criticism due to its Communist overtones. After its premiere, the film was trimmed substantially (the original running time was an excessive 153 minutes), with many key scenes either discarded entirely or stored improperly. When Moroder became involved, he was able to restore up to 83 minutes of the original film; additionally, he added subtitles instead of intertitles of character dialog, and, perhaps most controversially, opted to record a contemporary soundtrack instead of the original, minimalist score composed by Gottfried Huppertz.

Moroder approached each of the vocalists separately, with the intent of cowriting the entirety of the soundtrack along with his lyricist partner Pete Bellotte; while musicians like Bonnie Tyler, Jon Anderson, Loverboy, and Adam Ant all seemed fine with this, Freddie was more hesitant to concede to Moroder, which led to a bit of friction between the two. Regardless, Moroder was highly complimentary of Freddie, and, after the two met on 18 January 1983, Freddie agreed to work on the soundtrack, with the caveat that 'Love Kills' be released as a Queen song. Later in the year, when Queen were preparing to release their first single in almost two years, 'Radio Ga Ga', they wanted to use footage from *Metropolis* in the accompanying music video; Moroder gained the upper hand, requesting that, in exchange for the footage, 'Love Kills' would then become a solo song by Freddie,

with a co-credit to Moroder. (Peter Freestone, Freddie's personal assistant, later revealed that Freddie would play the song to Moroder on the phone, and that Moroder did contribute considerably to the recording, justifying his co-credit.)

The single was recorded early in sessions for *The Works* in the summer of 1983, and is, essentially, a Queen recording: the drum programming was done by Roger, with a suitable guitar solo from Brian and additional rhythm guitar by John. (The bass was performed on synthesizer.) Due to the agreed-upon trade-off, the band lost out on an excellent song (though they more than made up for it with the equally excellent 'Radio Ga Ga' video); thus, 'Love Kills' was released as Freddie's debut single in September 1984, where it reached an impressive No. 10 in the UK charts (three positions higher than Queen's current single, 'Hammer To Fall'), with an extended version issued on 12".

For the 1992 compilation *The Great Pretender*, a remix was created by Richard Wolf with a completely new backing, also being issued as the B-side of 'In My Defence' in November 1992. A rock remix was also created for inclusion on the 2000 box set, and while it's an interesting creation, there certainly must have been other material that would have been more beneficial. As if it couldn't get any more ludicrous, four remixes were included on the 2006 *Lover Of Life, Singer Of Songs: The Very Best Of Freddie Mercury* compilation, each of them less essential than its predecessor. Stick with the original.

In an attempt to regain the track as a Queen song, Brian rearranged 'Love Kills' for the *Forever* compilation, stripping away the familiar backing track, save for some sequencers and John's original rhythm guitar. Brian then overdubbed layers of guitar and bass, with Roger providing live drums, turning the song from a peppy, upbeat disco track into a scorcing slow burn of a ballad. Justifiably proud of the rearrangement, Brian plumped for the song to be performed live on the Queen + Adam Lambert 2014 North American tour, though it was inexplicably replaced by 'Dragon Attack' on the final two nights, never to return.

LOVE LIES BLEEDING (SHE WAS A WICKED, WILY WAITRESS) *(Taylor)*
• B-side (The Cross): 9/87 [74] • Album (The Cross): *Shove* • Live (The Cross): *Bootleg*

An underrated rocker from The Cross' debut album, 'Love Lies Bleeding (She Was A Wicked, Wily Waitress)' is a sleazy, slinky, sex-fueled song in which Roger recalls the sordid events of a chance meeting with a lady of the night – and furthering the rumor of his lyrical decay with the precious line, "I could see she had for me / A burger with my fries on". Certainly not the best track on the album, but one of the few songs to actually call back to Roger's rock roots, thanks to some terrific guitar work from Brian May, 'Love Lies Bleeding' was used as The Cross' introductory number for their 1988 tour. A significantly different version was released on the UK version of *Shove It* and as the B-side of 'Cowboys And Indians', stripping away the busier guitar riffs, but is inferior to the US version.

LOVE MAKIN' LOVE *(Mercury)*
• Compilation (Freddie): *Solo Collection*

Originally recorded for *Mr Bad Guy* on 9 December 1984 at Musicland Studios, 'Love Makin' Love' was submitted as a Queen track for the *A Kind Of Magic* sessions but, sadly, remained unfinished. If Freddie's solo version, available on *The Solo Collection*, is any kind of preview for the unreleased band version, *A Kind Of Magic* would have improved significantly with its inclusion.

LOVE ME LIKE THERE'S NO TOMORROW *(Mercury)*
• Album (Freddie): *BadGuy* • Compilation (Freddie): *Solo Collection*

Sounding like a counterpart of 'It's A Hard Life' from *The Works*, 'Love Me Like There's No Tomorrow' contains some of Freddie's most gorgeous lyrics and melodies and is a poignant conclusion to his debut solo album. With a title inspired partly by Freddie's then-partner Barbara Valentin, a German actress who starred in the film *Kiss Me Like There's No Tomorrow*, the song explores the heartbreaking sentiments of a romantic struggling to accept his lover's departure. (The song may indeed be about Valentin, for their relationship ended during the making of *Mr Bad Guy*.) It was around this time that Freddie's personal life started to slow down, as the desire for a long-term relationship began to sound increasingly attractive. Having lived a promiscuous lifestyle for so long, Freddie pours his emotions out on this song, deliberately doing a poor job of masking his emotions through a more universal narrator. Happily, Freddie's love life would improve drastically after the release of the album, when he met hair stylist Jim Hutton, and the two would embark on a long-lasting

relationship until the end of Freddie's life.

Released as the fourth and final single from *Mr Bad Guy* in November 1985, the song hardly troubled the charts, peaking at a disappointing No. 76; it would be the only single from the album that didn't receive a promotional video. An extended remix was issued on 12" vinyl releases of the single, and was notable for running over five minutes and featuring additional synthesizer enhancements. A handful of additional versions were released on *The Solo Collection*, along with an instrumental rendition, created specially for the set and mixed by David Richards and Kris Fredriksson, while four interesting early takes were included on the rarities disc. The first, recorded on 29 May 1984, features only Freddie and bassist Stephan Wissnet and is a fascinating glimpse into the framework of the backing track; the second, recorded on three days later, is dominated largely by drum-machine while Freddie is clearly still working his way through the lyrics; and the third, revisited in January 1985, is an attempt to produce a final cut. A live take, which features no vocals whatsoever, was recorded at some point in June 1984, with an upbeat finale not used on the final version.

LOVE OF MY LIFE *(Mercury)*
• Album: *Opera* • A-side: 6/79 [63] • Live: *Killers, Wembley, On Fire, Montreal, Budapest* • Live (Brian): *Brixton* • Live (Q+PR): *Return, Ukraine* • Bonus: *Opera* • Live (Brian & Kerry): *Acoustic* • Compilation: *On Air*

There are many highlights on *A Night At The Opera*, but none is quite as perfect as Freddie's 'Love Of My Life'. Blending nicely with the outro from 'The Prophet's Song', the track is a mournful ballad that many sources have indicated was written about Mary Austin, Freddie's longtime companion and girlfriend between 1970 and 1977. In several of Freddie's early songs, the underlying message indicated that he was emotionally confused, which Brian suggested was the inspiration for 'Lily Of The Valley'; if so, then 'Love Of My Life' can be seen as a poignant romantic send-off to Mary. Indeed, Freddie maintained that Mary was the love of his life, and the two remained best friends until his death in 1991, with the bulk of his estate bequeathed to her.

The band turn in a gorgeous, understated performance, with bass and percussion flourishes from John and Roger. The song's main focus is not only Freddie's classical piano, but the orchestral harp that accentuates Freddie's more dominating instrument. "There's also a lovely little ballad; my classical influence comes into it," Freddie explained to the *New Musical Express* in September 1975, well before the album was finished. "Brian is going to attempt to use harp, real life-size harp. I'm going to force him to play till his fingers drop off."

"I did it chord by chord," Brian told *Guitar Player* in 1983. "Actually, it took longer to tune the thing than to play it. It was a nightmare because every time someone opened the door, the temperature would change and the whole thing would go out. I would hate to have to play a harp on stage. I just figured out how it worked – the pedals and everything – and did it bit by bit."

The song became a live favorite over the years, and was reworked as a duet between Freddie and Brian. "It's adapted on stage for guitar," the vocalist told *Melody Maker* in 1981, "but it was written on the piano. I've totally forgotten the original and if you asked me to play that now, I couldn't. Sometimes, I have to go back to the music sheet, and I can't read that well either." The song was introduced on the 1977 News Of The World tour and remained an integral part of the acoustic segment until Queen's last tour in 1986, though it was omitted for the 1982 Rock 'n America tour. While the legend remains that the song was a natural for audiences to sing along to from its first performance, audience recordings indicate that this wasn't so; it wouldn't be until 1978 that UK audiences would participate, and it was on the 1979 Jazz European tour that the tradition really took off, hence its belated single release. The song was brought out of mothballs for Brian's 1992/1993 Back To The Light tour, and was performed as a tribute to the recently deceased Freddie. The reception made it almost impossible to remove from the set, and so it remained on the 1998 Another World tour, again on the 2005/2006 and 2008 Queen + Paul Rodgers tours, and later on the Queen + Adam Lambert tours.

A live recording from *Live Killers* was released as a UK single in June 1979, where it became the poorest-selling single in Queen's history, peaking at a dismal No. 63. The song struck a chord in South America, and it was only after the single was in the charts there for over a year that Queen finally took notice and booked a tour there in February 1981. "There are certain songs which are more popular in different countries," Roger said in 1991, "and we used to vary the songs that we played. For instance, in South America, there was a song that was a major hit, called 'Love Of My Life', which was never a hit anywhere else. So we'd always include that, and that became a major part of the show there."

LOVE ON A TIGHTROPE (LIKE AN ANIMAL) *(Taylor)*
• Album (The Cross): *Shove*

Dominated entirely by trick-shot drum effects, percolating sequencers, cheesy synthesizer effects and lacklustre lyrics, 'Love On A Tightrope (Like An Animal)' is a good example of what's wrong with *Shove It*, in danger of being overcome by its own arrangement. Programming, when used properly, can achieve beautiful results; this is not one of them.

For reasons known to no one, the song was issued on a promotional disc, along with one track each from Phil Collins, China Crisis and Donny Osmond (of all people). The song was performed live by The Cross in 1988, and, with a slightly refined arrangement, became a halfway decent song – but not enough to save its reputation.

LOVE TOKEN *(May)*
• Album (Brian): *BTTL* • B-side (Brian): 6/93 [23]
• Live (Brian): *Brixton*

Despite being one of the more upbeat rockers on *Back To The Light*, it would be in the listener's best interest not to pay too much attention to the lyrics. Relating the tale of a son watching his parents' marriage dissolve (a method of dealing with his own marital strife with wife Chrissy), the words border on the embarrassing, with Brian using questionable euphemisms and metaphors that would have benefited from some careful editing. Perhaps the most humorous moment comes about two and a half minutes in, when Brian takes on the roles of both mother and father in the middle of a 'colourful' fight. In keeping with his quieter demeanor, what could have been an interesting diversion was cleaned up for general release, though an early vocal track, included on a promotional disc for *RCD Magazine*, gets a little dirtier: "Meat for brains" becomes "Shit for brains", and "That's a shame" becomes a blunt "Fuck you".

Beyond the lyrics, though, 'Love Token' is a well-constructed track, with Cozy Powell the dominant force – his thunderous drums give the song its catchy rhythm, while Brian merely focuses on the rhythm until he delivers a scorching guitar solo after the fight. The song concludes with some bluesy piano from Mike Moran before leading into 'Resurrection'.

The song was performed live on the Back To The Light tour, usually after 'Back To The Light' (on the 1992 leg) or 'Tie Your Mother Down' (during the first part of 1993), before becoming an abridged intro to 'Headlong', as evident on the live album *Live At The Brixton Academy*. The song was slightly edited for release as the B-side of 'Resurrection' in June 1993, fading out just before the extended piano outro kicked in.

LOVER: *see* LIAR

LUCILLE *(Richard)*
• Live (The Cross): *Bootleg*

Little Richard's 1957 single was played by the band as an encore number at Earl's Court on 7 June 1977. The song was reprised by The Cross on their 1990 tour, with a live version on the fan club-only release *The Official Bootleg*.

MACBETH

In the spring of 1990, Brian was approached by theatre director Jane L'Epine Smith, who was about to undertake a stage production of William Shakespeare's *Macbeth*. Keen to bring a younger crowd to the shows by adding music, she wanted a contemporary composer to record incidental music for the production. Brian agreed and promptly set about laying down some ideas on a computer at his newly installed home studio, Allerton Hill. Those tracks were later copied onto a cassette to be played over the PA system during live performances. Three different versions exist: the floppy disk version, the cassette version, and a 'live' version of the music being performed over the PA.

In all, the performance is interesting though somewhat tedious, and becomes downright vexing at times, which Brian addressed at the time: "I'm very aware that the music could be irritating if not done well, and that a lot of people might feel that rock does not fit in with Shakespeare. But [he] was into making direct contact with his audience, the way Queen has always done." The music is worth listening to since it is adventurous, but the listener would need to have a high tolerance for computerized music in order to actively appreciate it.

MACHINES (OR 'BACK TO HUMANS') *(May/Taylor)*
• Album: *Works* • B-side: 4/84 [3] • CD Single: 11/88

As Brian explained of *The Works* in 1984, "A lot of the new album is a synthesis of the two kinds, almost a battle between machines and humans." On no other track is this more evident than on 'Machines (Or 'Back To Humans')' – originally titled 'Machine's World' – the second collaborative effort between Brian and Roger, and certainly their most successful. "It's a subject that's been much sort of tried, but I mean it's a sort of obvious thing," Roger told Jim Ladd in 1984. "Brian wanted to make it a battle between the human side by using the real drums and guitars, etc., and a totally synthetic side – the machines, you know; the drum machines and the synthesizers and the Fairlights. So the thing is meant to be a battle between the two, with the idea of basically going back to humans."

Roger was the prime mover behind the song, with the basic construct reminiscent of 'Radio Ga Ga', and both 'I Cry For You (Love, Hope And Confusion)' and 'Killing Time' from his *Strange Frontier* album. The drummer tended to embrace technology more freely than the others, and the song is largely his (including several questionable lyrics: "It's self-perpetuating a parahumanoidarianised"), though the song was heavily worked on by Brian, with the guitarist adding his own touches and constructing the song into something tangible. Whereas a lot of *Strange Frontier* rambled, the tight focus on Roger's songs on this album indicated that he was coming up with worthwhile ideas, but with just a little bit of assistance, those ideas became great songs. Despite its reputation as an of-its-time song, 'Machines (Or "Back To Humans")' is one of the few experimental songs on an album where Queen was playing it safe after the disappointing reception to *Hot Space*.

A superb instrumental version, mixed by Brian for the occasion, was issued as the B-side of the American release of 'I Want To Break Free' (other countries got the standard album version), incorporating instrumental bits from 'Ogre Battle' and 'Flash', plus parts of Freddie's vocal from the 1972 recording of 'Goin' Back'. This unique mix was issued on the long-deleted UK-only *12" Collection* companion disc as part of the 1992 *Box Of Trix*, and should have been an obvious candidate for inclusion on *The Singles Collection – Volume 2*, but so far eludes any further release. The song was used as an intro for the 1984 and 1985 Queen Works! tours, and formed the basis for a synthesizer-dominated improvisational jam before Brian's solo, but the song was never performed live in its entirety.

MAD THE SWINE *(Mercury)*

• CD Single: 5/91 [14] • Bonus: *Queen*

Discovered when Hollywood Records archivists raided Queen's vaults in search of bonus tracks for the impending US CD reissues, Freddie's 'Mad The Swine' was recorded during sessions for the debut album in 1972, and was preliminarily placed between 'Great King Rat' and 'My Fairy King' before it was removed for reasons that have been hotly debated for years. The official reason is that there were disputes between band and producer over the drum sound and additional percussion, but an equally plausible counter-argument may be that it was a tad too religious for everyone's liking, and, with an album already chock-full of songs with religious overtones ('Great King Rat', 'Liar', and 'Jesus'), this was one song too many. Despite a superb band performance and the sweetly-sung lyrics, with Freddie already showing signs of the power his voice could possess, the song was cast aside. Upon its discovery, the song was remixed by David Richards and duly released on the CD single of 'Headlong' in May 1991, and then as a bonus track on *Queen* that same year – and again a decade later, on the deluxe edition of the debut album.

Intriguingly, former Queen archive assistant, Gary Taylor, revealed that 'Mad The Swine' was performed live a handful of times in 1971 and 1972, and was even performed live once in North America in 1974.

MADE IN HEAVEN *(Mercury)*

• Album (Freddie): *BadGuy* • A-side (Freddie): 7/85 [57] • Album (Queen): *Heaven*

This centerpiece of Freddie's debut solo album is a terse, doom-laden ballad, with moments of light and shade that sits at odds with the rest of the dance-oriented material on *Mr Bad Guy*. The song is more heartfelt and profound than the more frivolous songs, with Freddie accepting his natural-born status as a true romantic, despite the pain and misery it brings upon him. Released as the second single from the album with 'She Blows Hot And Cold' as the B-side, and an extended remix of the A-side on 12" vinyl versions, 'Made In Heaven' peaked at a disappointing No. 57 in the UK. The video is more well-known for displaying the extravagance Freddie was willing to expend on his solo career. Set in a North London warehouse to replicate the stage of The London Opera House, it was based on Stravinsky's *The Rite Of Spring* and Dante's

Inferno. According to David Mallet, who directed the video in July 1985, "This was in the days before major special effects, so Freddie really was standing up there, and in fact he was very unhappy about it. He was standing on a disc about five feet round, and 60 feet up in the air. In the end, we put a harness on him; a very thin wire, because it became very obvious that he was getting serious vertigo up there."

Much like Queen's reworking of 'I Was Born To Love You', 'Made In Heaven' was rescued from Freddie's 1985 solo album, *Mr Bad Guy*, and drastically reworked to give it a genuine Queen treatment. Brian's goal with *Made In Heaven* was to make it sound as if the band had actually recorded all the songs together in the studio, which, at this late stage in their career, was hardly the case. He achieved that effect most successfully with this song, and so pleased were John, Roger and Brian with the results that it became a fitting title for their final album. The song explodes into life with Roger's thundering drums and then takes on a menacing pace, adding a sense of atmosphere with the introduction of keyboards and effects, the like of which wouldn't have been an option back in 1985. The finest moment comes with the guitar solo. Brian redeemed several mediocre Queen tracks with his trademark Red Special, but he gives one of his most emotive performances here with a haunting slide guitar solo, a technique he used very rarely but to good effect, transcending the song to new emotional heights. In 2004, Brian wrote on his website that he was pleased with the album as a whole, but he was proudest of the title track, "which I think is possibly the best-sounding Queen song *ever*."

Though not released as a single, Virgin Radio ran a promotional campaign on 25 November 1996 in which all the songs from *Made In Heaven* were pressed as promotional singles. To commemorate the fifth anniversary of Freddie's death, Virgin Radio held a 'Queen Day' and ran a competition by asking fans to call in and nominate their favorite track from the new album. One random caller per hour, for 12 hours, was selected to receive a 12" copy of their chosen song, thus making these among the rarest Queen singles ever. Unfortunately, the one caller who asked for 'Made In Heaven' was given a misprint of 'Heaven For Everyone'; EMI had printed five copies of Roger's song and none of Freddie's, so 'The Magnificent Seven', as these discs ('Heaven For Everyone' [VIRGIN2], 'A Winter's Tale' [VIRGIN3], 'Mother Love' [VIRGIN4], 'Let Me Live' [VIRGIN5], 'You Don't Fool Me' [VIRGIN6], 'It's A

Beautiful Day' [VIRGIN7], and 'I Was Born To Love You' [VIRGIN8]) were collectively known, came and went without the standout title track.

MAGIC IS LOOSE *(Taylor)*
• Album (Roger): *Fun*

Buried deep on side two of *Fun In Space* is this lovely gem of a song, a prime example of the light and shade methodology that Queen employed on their early albums. With a sparse introduction of glockenspiel and Roger's disembodied vocals, the song kicks into high gear with a ringing acoustic guitar melody and an upbeat backing of a thunderous drum beat and a quivering, swirling synthesizer. Magic would be a recurring theme throughout Roger's subsequent songs, and it would remain an intangible, inexplicable thing in almost all cases; what the magic is referring to here is anyone's guess. Even Roger seems unsure himself.

Unfounded rumors persist that the song was originally submitted during sessions for *The Game* in 1980, and that Freddie was particularly keen on the song, but it remained unreleased – or very possibly unrecorded. A sad but understandable loss: Roger was proving to be a prolific writer at the end of the 1970s, and it was inevitable that certain songs, no matter how high their calibre, would be tossed away in favor of other songs. While this would have made a superb Queen song, their loss was Roger's gain, and made *Fun In Space* that much stronger a debut solo album.

The song received its first-ever live airing on 19 February 2000, at a gig by the SAS Band (fronted by former Queen and The Cross keyboardist, Spike Edney) at the Shepherd's Bush Empire in London.

MAN MADE PARADISE *(Mercury)*
• Album (Freddie): *BadGuy*

Not one of the better tracks from *Mr Bad Guy*, 'Man Made Paradise' was first worked on by Queen in 1982 for *Hot Space*, and then became an even likelier candidate for release on *The Works*, even appearing as the closing track on an early running list of the album. Queen's version has been promised on the eventual release of their archival box set, though it's hardly likely to deviate much from the officially released version. As it is, the song – originally titled 'Paradise For Man' ("or something", as Freddie scribbled on the handwritten lyric sheet) – sounds much like an unreleased Queen song, with Paul Vincent providing

a solo reminiscent of Brian May, who later expressed annoyance that Freddie had instructed Paul to perform the solo in his style. Closing with some impressive a cappella vocalizations from Freddie, the song isn't a highlight of the album, but fits in nicely with the other dance-oriented material.

MAN ON FIRE *(Taylor)*
• A-side (Roger): 6/84 [66] • Album (Roger): *Frontier* • German CD single (The Cross): 11/90 • Live (The Cross): *Bootleg, Germany* • German CD single (The Cross): 8/91

Most of *Strange Frontier* was mired in sociopolitical posturing, undoubtedly well-intentioned at the time, but for fans used to the usually apolitical Queen, Roger's second solo album was off-putting at first. There are certain songs that balance out the politics, though, and 'Man On Fire' finds Roger back on familiar ground: written about a downtrodden, unemployed man searching for a solution to his financial strife, the song strikes a romantic, poignant tone in the bridge, where the narrator reveals the power of love is his main motivator.

Chosen as the first single in June 1984, a fortnight before *Strange Frontier* was released, the single charted at a miserable No. 66 in the UK and didn't chart at all in the US. Backed by 'Killing Time', a 12" extended version was also created, which opened with 90 seconds of additional drum work missing from the standard version. It was considered strong enough to be played live by The Cross (with live versions appearing on the 1991 and 1992 fan club-only bootlegs, *The Official Bootleg* and *Live In Germany*), and became a regular in the set lists for all their tours, as well as Roger's 1994/1995 Happiness? tour. Rumors circulated for years that 'Man On Fire' was submitted to sessions for *The Works*; indeed, in promotional interviews for that album, Freddie spoke of four or five songs that Roger wrote being rejected in favor of 'Radio Ga Ga', but it wasn't until 2010 that these rumors were confirmed with a preliminary running order for *The Works* placing the song as the fifth track on the album. A tape box from 22 September 1983, when Queen were still at The Record Plant, contained mixes for the likes of 'I Want To Break Free', 'Tear It Up', and 'Keep Passing The Open Windows', and was posted on Queen's official Facebook page as a lead-up to the release of *Queen Forever*, which contained another song also on the track sheet, 'Let Me In Your Heart Again', but scribbled at the bottom – and crossed out – was 'I Feel Like A Man On Fire', indicating at that early stage that the song was destined to be a Roger Taylor solo song.

'Man On Fire' also became Roger's debut solo video. Filmed in May 1984 and directed by Tim Pope, who also directed 'It's A Hard Life', the video depicts Roger taking out his aggression in his garage, hitting oil drums and dramatically pounding his fist into the palm of his hand. Unfortunately, a little girl was shown inside a building that ultimately exploded; hence, the video was banned by MTV and, apart from a few other showings worldwide, remains largely unseen.

MAN ON THE PROWL (Mercury)
• Album: Works • B-side: 11/84 [21]

In an attempt to recapture the good-time rockabilly of 'Crazy Little Thing Called Love' and 'Don't Try Suicide', Freddie submitted 'Man On The Prowl' to sessions for The Works, a song that's neither stellar nor offensive but merely fills up three and a half minutes. The elements are all there: rollicking piano (mostly by Freddie, though Fred Mandel provided the rip-roaring conclusion), a hiccuping doo-wop vocal from Freddie, and a devil-may-care set of lyrics of a swingin' bachelor in pursuit of a fun time. Considering the personal nature of other songs written around this time ('It's A Hard Life', 'Love Me Like There's No Tomorrow', and 'Man Made Paradise'), which find Freddie yearning for a lasting relationship, 'Man On The Prowl' sits hollow, despite its lighthearted disposition.

Inexplicably planned as the fifth and final single from The Works, 'Man On The Prowl' was withdrawn and issued instead as the B-side of 'Thank God It's Christmas'. An extended mix for the B-side was created for the 12" release of the single, prolonging the running time to over six minutes and well past the point of tolerability.

MANIPULATOR (Taylor/Edney/Strange)
• A-side (The Cross): 6/88

Stemming from a writing collaboration with the late Steven Strange, former frontman and vocalist for the band Visage, 'Manipulator' was technically a recording by The Cross, marking the first time the band recorded together. In the timeline of The Cross' history, the song was recorded shortly after sessions for Shove It, though it would have been an ideal addition to Mad: Bad: And Dangerous To Know since it possesses none of the

'qualities' of the first Cross album. With an uplifting melody, thanks to an airy production (courtesy of Roger, with engineering by Steve Chase and Peter Jones) that allows the music to breathe, and adopting the less-is-more attitude that was noticeably absent from Shove It, the song is an underrated composition that deserved more attention. The song was finally released in 2013 on Roger's nearly all-encompassing box set The Lot.

Released as a non-album single in June 1988, well after the release of The Cross' debut, 'Manipulator' failed to set the charts alight, despite considerable promotion in the set list at the time and a coveted performance (along with 'Heaven For Everyone') at the Montreux Golden Rose Festival on 12 May 1988. Considering the expense the band had incurred in shooting music videos for their first three singles, it comes as no surprise that, given the lack of success they had achieved previously, no video was shot for 'Manipulator'.

MANNISH BOY (Morganfield/London/McDaniel)

Queen performed Bo Diddley's 'I'm A Man' on a few dates of their 1977 A Day At The Races European tour, though bootleggers erroneously mislabeled it as Muddy Waters' 'Mannish Boy'. This confusion was understandable: Waters reworked 'I'm A Man' as 'Mannish Boy' a month after the release of the former, which itself was an "answer song" (a common practice among blues musicians, and seen as an honor instead of cause for a lawsuit) to Waters' 'Hoochie Coochie Man'. It's known that Queen performed 'I'm A Man' on this tour, but whether they performed 'Mannish Boy' is unconfirmed.

THE MARCH OF THE BLACK QUEEN (Mercury)
• Album: Queen2 • Compilation: Deep Cuts 1
• Live: Rainbow, Odeon

Opening regally with an atmospheric piano sequence, 'The March Of The Black Queen' is the centerpiece of Side Black of Queen II, running well over six minutes and capturing Freddie's love of oblique lyricism and storytelling. All of his songs on the band's sophomore album were convoluted fairytales, devoid of superficial meaning but holding a deeper meaning known only to its songwriter. It's a true production number, with several sections interwoven, stopping and starting with perceived ease, though John later revealed "we spent ages and ages rehearsing this one – not very easy at all, I can assure you!" Indeed, session out-takes reveal that the band needed a great deal of concentration to record the backing track, and despite Brian's later assertion that Mack introduced them to the method of pasting together various takes to achieve a cohesive result, this was an early example of the band recording the sections separately before collating them into a finished product. The result is a stunning insight into the complexity of Freddie's songwriting, though it does tend to meander aimlessly here and there, a complaint that befell most of the second album.

In a 1977 group interview, Freddie and Roger revealed that they almost lost the song due to overproduction. "Those were the days of the 16-track studios," the vocalist said. "Before, when we did so many overdubs on 16 track, it was like we just kept piling it on and on. The tape went transparent because it just couldn't take any more. I think it snapped in two places, as well." Roger confirmed this: "We lasted recording that one until the tape went transparent. Genuinely!" Robin Geoffrey Cable, who had helped produce 'Nevermore' and 'Funny How Love Is' with Queen, joined the band and Roy Thomas Baker on production duties, giving it the necessary air that it required. Unfortunately, much like the desultory arrangement, the production is murky at times, with a lot of the subtle nuances buried under the weight of guitar orchestrations and chorus vocals. The 2011 remaster is a revelation, with the right mood finally given to separate the elements and offer some much-needed clarity.

Because of its complexity, 'The March Of The Black Queen' was never performed live in full (starting with the "I reign with left hand / I rule with my right" section and concluding with an extended guitar solo), and served as a return to the 'Bohemian Rhapsody' coda of the medley between October 1974 and September 1976. Live versions were later released on *Live At The Rainbow '74* and *A Night At The Odeon*. Freddie obviously held some affection for the song, for he would reference its melody periodically on the 1984/1985 Queen Works! tour, often as a medley with 'My Fairy King'.

(MARIE'S THE NAME) HIS LATEST FLAME *(Pomus/Shuman)*

Originally recorded by Elvis Presley and reaching No. 1 upon its release in August 1961, '(Marie's The Name) His Latest Flame' was a song that took collectors by surprise when it leaked onto the Internet in the summer of 2006. Recorded by Brian and Cozy Powell, the song was reportedly intended for a Cozy Powell solo album in the late 1980s, but Brian later explained that it was recorded for his unreleased *Heroes* solo project. The song is enjoyable, with a thunderous drum performance from Cozy, but is unusual in that the Red Special is not used at all; only an ominous bed of acoustic guitars and subtle keyboards form the instrumentation. Otherwise, Brian's vocals – arguably some of his strongest, which helps to date the recording to sessions for *Heroes* and not the late 1980s, a time when his voice was questionable at best – are the centerpiece of the song. As with any new, previously unheard treasure, it would be easy to rank this song higher than any of the covers on *Another World*, but, once cooler heads prevail, its omission is understandable, though had it been finished, it would have been a worthy inclusion.

MARRIAGE OF DALE AND MING (AND FLASH APPROACHING) *(May/Taylor)*
• Album: *Flash*

This two-minute instrumental featured occasional blasts of the main theme but was mostly dominated by a repetitive piano motif beneath film dialog from *Flash Gordon*.

MASTERS OF WAR *(Dylan)*
• Album (Roger): *Frontier*

The often politically-outspoken Roger rarely instilled his beliefs into Queen songs out of fear of alienating their fan base, but he would take potshots at impotent politicians and their dehumanizing morals throughout his solo career, usually with mixed results. For *Strange Frontier*, recorded at a time when the Cold War was still a valid threat and world leaders were threatening each other with nuclear arms, Roger finally dipped his toe into the sociopolitical pool and found its waters welcoming; yet he was unable to better Bob Dylan's 'Masters Of War', a pacifistic song against war written after watching President Dwight Eisenhower's 1961 farewell address from the Oval Office.

"The other cover tune is a very old Dylan protest song which I did sort of electronically," Roger told Jim Ladd in 1984. "Strangely enough, a lot of the lyrics hold up quite well today. This one is done slower than

'Racing In The Street', but it's very electronic. I use a Linn [drum-machine] on it. It works quite nicely." Twenty-plus years later, its words still rang true, and Roger suitably deconstructed the original from its terse acoustic backing, rearranging it into a synthesized, mechanical onslaught, depicting a cold, lifeless society that the current world leaders were creating. Interestingly, Roger dropped three verses from his recording, more out of time constraints than because of the message conveyed.

MAYBE BABY *(Petty/Hardin)*
• B-side (Brian): 5/98 [61]

Originally recorded by Buddy Holly and The Crickets in 1958 – and released in March of that year, going on to reach No. 4 in the charts – Brian's version of 'Maybe Baby' is a joyful and faithful recording of the classic rock song, with the Brian May Band (Cozy Powell, drums; Jamie Moses, guitar; Spike Edney, keyboards; Neil Murray, bass) backing several nicely harmonizing Brians. Because of Brian's commitment to the original, the cover isn't unique, yet it's still a fun and short rendition.

The song was released on the North American send-away CD Retro Rock and was also released as the B-side of 'The Business' in May 1998, as well as on the Dutch release of 'On My Way Up' the same month. Intended first for the ultimately abandoned Heroes project, 'Maybe Baby' eluded live performance until November 2004, when Brian sang lead vocals on the song, backed by the original Crickets and Albert Lee at the 50th Anniversary of the Fender Stratocaster concert.

THE MEETING (SOLO GUITAR) *(May)*
• Soundtrack (Brian): *Furia*

Performed almost entirely on The Red Special, 'The Meeting (Solo Guitar)', as with 'First Glance (Solo Flute)', also features a keyboard droning away in the background to help pad out the musical structure.

MILLIONAIRE *(Moss/Edney/Macrae/Noone)*
• Album (The Cross): *Blue* • Live (The Cross): *Germany*

While Roger was away recording tracks for a post-*Innuendo* album with Queen, the other members of The Cross were feverishly writing songs for *Blue Rock*, resulting in the band's finest, albeit unappreciated, hour. 'Millionaire' was a four-way collaboration

among Clayton, Spike, Joshua and Peter, and the results are mixed. While there's a self-deprecating tone to the lyrics, the music is generic rock, and could be the low point of *Blue Rock* (although what may have been the low point in 1991 is still miles above the best from *Shove It* in 1987). Roger delivers the lyrics with an uncharacteristic sneer, cutting the song short with the humorous sendoff, "We have to stop now, guys, we can't afford any more."

The song was performed live on the tour supporting Magnum in the autumn of 1991, with a live version appearing on the 1992 fan club-only bootleg, *Live In Germany*.

THE MILLIONAIRE WALTZ *(Mercury)*
• Album: *Races*

A delightful excursion into the camp music that graced the early Queen albums, Freddie's 'The Millionaire Waltz' portrays the vocalist revelling in his riches and luxuries, but makes sure to stress that having everything in the world means nothing without love. "It's all about John Reid, actually," Freddie told Kenny Everett in 1976. "It's very out of the Queen format, really and we thought we'd like to do that on every album. I think I went a bid mad on this one. But it's turned out alright I think, it makes people laugh sometimes." Performed as a waltz, its unusual structure is dominated mostly by Freddie – on vocals and piano – and John turning in a superb bass performance, which has been praised both by fans and band members alike. The song finally accelerates into a Queen tour de force, but this outburst is brief, lasting barely 30 seconds, before Brian delivers a campy, orchestrated solo. "Brian has orchestrated it fully with guitars like he's never done before," Freddie told *Circus* magazine in 1977. "He goes from tubas to piccolos to cellos. It's taken weeks. Brian's very finicky." Brian later told *Guitar Player*, "I think that holds the record. There's one bit in there which is sort of a fairground effect in the background. I think there are three octaves for each part, and six parts. I'm not sure but there must be about 18 or 20 guitar tracks. It's a funny sound. It makes a peculiarly sort of rigid sound. I was really surprised. It sounded like a fairground organ."

In terms of arrangement and overall pomp and circumstance, 'The Millionaire Waltz' was the logical successor to 'Bohemian Rhapsody', which Roger stated in *Circus*: "[It's] an arranged, intricate number. There are several time-signature changes, though not quite so many vocal overdubs." Freddie was proud of the song, telling Kenny Everett, "I think it's good and we're patting ourselves on the back again. I really think it's worked out well especially from the orchestration point of view. Because [Brian] really used his guitar in a different sort of way; I know he's done lots of orchestrations before."

'The Millionaire Waltz' was played live in the medley between 1977 and 1978, always segueing into 'You're My Best Friend' following the "my fine friend" line.

MING'S THEME (IN THE COURT OF MING THE MERCILESS) *(Mercury)*
• Album: *Flash*

Written around a droning synthesizer motif with timpani explosions from Roger, Freddie's 'Ming's Theme (In The Court Of Ming The Merciless)' consists mostly of dialog between Ming and a representative from the people of Ardentia. Though the actual composition lasts less than 40 seconds, it's padded out for two further minutes with incidental dialog and synthesizer drones.

THE MIRACLE *(Queen)*
• Album: *Miracle* • A-side: 11/89 [21] • Compilation: *Hits2, Classic*

The title track of Queen's 13th studio album is another world-weary anthem, which had been tackled far more successfully earlier, and comes off sounding ham-fisted and overly saccharine. However, there's a certain optimistic sentimentality in the performance that transcends earlier Queen anthems; whereas something like 'We Are The Champions' dances that fine line between serious and tongue-in-cheek, 'The Miracle', like 'Friends Will Be Friends', was designed to be taken seriously, and, if Freddie had been well enough at this point to tour behind the album, would have marked that dreadful moment in the show when the audience would wave their arms and lighters.

Opening with a delicate keyboard sequence, there's a lot going on within the arrangement, as Brian explained: "It was very complex what we were doing – dozens of tracks, it was very carefully built up. It sounds very airy and light, but there's a hell of a lot going on in it. It has these two transitions in the end, it goes into this sort of rock bit, then into the floaty, 'that day will come' mantra bit." Roger concurred, saying, "It was an incredibly complex song, I loved the

textures, and I know Freddie was particularly fond of this song – again, not my favourite song, but I love the textures and changes; they're very clever. Very naïve lyric, in a rather sort of innocent, optimistic way. Not cynical enough for me, really."

While Freddie was the main instigator behind the musical arrangement, the lyrics were decided by committee. "Actually I think that was one of the songs where we all contributed," Freddie explained in a 1989 BBC Radio interview. "But lyrically, going back to 'The Miracle', I think the four of us really put everything into it because I mean somebody would come in with one line and say, 'Oh, that's terrible, I'll change it.' So in fact, in one way I hate it because I have to keep singing different lyrics every day until we sort of agree on the final one, but I'd say lyrically 'The Miracle' is a definite four-way split."

"I've always loved this track," Brian said in 2003. "I think it's one of Freddie's most magical compositions, and I remember the joy we had in the studio: it was one of those moments where we really did work together, all four of us, on the ideas, building it up, painting the picture, as if we all had brushes in our hands with different colours. But Freddie's concept – and a very brave concept, because you're talking about a man who knows he's got a death sentence hanging over him, and he's writing a song called 'The Miracle' – is very light, very joyful. I think it's part of Freddie's genius; it's always been one of my favourites of his creations."

Chosen as the fifth and final single from the album, 'The Miracle' was released in November 1989 and peaked at a disappointing No. 21 in the charts. "We got pasted to the wall for this in England," Brian told MTV's *Video Magazine*. "Everybody hated it, for some reason. It's very uncool to be idealistic in Britain, I suppose, at the moment, and they said, 'How can they talk about peace?' and all that sort of stuff. Then, of course, China [Tiananmen Square] happened and everything. It seems very relevant to us." Roger agreed: "In England, 'idealism' is 'naivety', which is wrong, it's not. There's nothing wrong with idealism. Nick Lowe wrote that great song, great title - '(What's So Bad 'Bout) Peace, Love and Understanding?' *[sic]*. Yeah, and what *is* so bad about it?"

Although the full version was released in the UK, the single was not even considered for the hit parade in America, though that country did receive a unique edit of the song for the 1992 compilation *Classic Queen*, in which there are numerous edits, including the superfluous rock coda, making for a more concise and leaner listen.

A video was made for the single at Elstree Studios on 23 November 1989, directed by the Torpedo Twins yet again. Based on a concept by Freddie, the video shows four young look-alikes performing the song in Queen's stead, with the star of the show, Ross McCall (who would later star in the US mini-series *Band of Brothers*), portraying an energetic Freddie, and perfecting his every move to such an extent that, when the band do appear at the start of the rock coda, Freddie himself was copying the copyist. "He certainly could strut," Roger said of young McCall, while Brian elaborated further on the video: "This was a joy to make because of the kids, who put so much talent and effort into being us. We were knocked out by how great they were. We had such a laugh doing it, we were just smiling the whole time."

MISFIRE *(Deacon)*
• Album: *SHA*

Clocking in at less than two minutes, 'Misfire' holds the distinction of being John's first composition for Queen. Although the words are ambiguous, and may contain a thinly veiled reference to sex – or perhaps, just as graphically, equating love to Russian roulette – it's set to an upbeat Caribbean backing (thus its original title, 'Banana Blues') that would set the pattern for many of John's chart-friendly compositions through the years.

Written and recorded during the *Sheer Heart Attack* sessions, the song features its author on almost all guitars, suggesting that Brian was too ill to record any of the guitar parts except for a tasteful solo that concludes the song. 'Misfire' was never performed live.

MR BAD GUY *(Mercury)*
• Album (Freddie): *BadGuy* • Compilations (Freddie): *Pretender, FM Album, The Solo Collection*

This self-deprecating, tongue-in-cheek title track to Freddie's debut solo album is a gloriously ambitious song, with the vocalist making light of his perceived tough guy image with an invitation to chase rainbows and trip on his ecstasy. While it reveled in the bombast of his earlier compositions, it made use of an element Freddie had wanted to do for a while: live orchestrations. "There are a lot of musical territories I wanted to explore," Freddie told *Record Mirror* in 1984, "which I really couldn't do with Queen. I wanted to

cover such things as reggae rhythms and I've done a couple of tracks with an orchestra. It will have a very rich sound."

In 1992, Brian Malouf remixed the song and, considering some of the remixes he had done for Queen in the past – 'Fat Bottomed Girls' and the Headbanger's mix of 'Hammer To Fall' – it comes as no surprise that the song was completely restructured and given a more rock sound, unfortunately mixing the orchestration into the background. The main riff is instead played on guitar, and sounds like something that Queen would have turned the song into, especially if Brian were given the chance. While it's not as strong as the original, the remix is definitely worth a listen.

An earlier version, recorded in May 1984 at Musicland Studios, was released on *The Solo Collection*, and finds Freddie using alternate lines that would be omitted from the final version. (One further early version, subtitled the "Bad Circulation mix", was released on *Lover Of Life, Singer Of Songs: The Very Best Of Freddie Mercury*, and is largely redundant except for a completely new first verse and the replacement of "bad communication" with – you guessed it – "bad circulation".) An instrumental version was also released on the box set, exposing the intricate orchestrations by Rainer Pietsch, as well as some previously obscured French horn arrangements during the choruses. A snippet of the orchestral out-takes was also issued, though it's hardly essential listening.

MR TAMBOURINE MAN *(Dylan)*

First recorded by Bob Dylan on his 1965 *Bringing It All Back Home* album, 'Mr Tambourine Man' was performed by The Cross at the Gosport Festival on 30 July 1992 and later at the 1992 Christmas shows for the fan club.

MODERN TIMES ROCK'N'ROLL *(Taylor)*
• Album: *Queen* • Compilation: *BBC, On Air*
• Live: *Rainbow*

Noted by *Rolling Stone* in a December 1973 review of Queen as "remarkably reminiscent of 'Communication Breakdown'", Roger's first contribution to the Queen canon gave little indication of what he would eventually write in years to come, but, for what it is, 'Modern Times Rock'n'Roll' is an enjoyable, though lightweight, composition heralding the arrival of a new kind of rock sound. It wasn't 'Roll Over Beethoven', but it carried a similar message.

Set to a frantic backing track, Roger takes the lead in his first-ever vocal performance on record. The song would normally feature as an encore number with Freddie singing instead of Roger, generally as the show closer (until 'In The Lap Of The Gods ... Revisited' became the conclusion in late 1974), between 1972 and 1975.

Two BBC recordings exist. The first, from 3 December 1973, is a fairly straightforward rendition of the song, with Roger's added line, "It's not that I'm bright, just happy-go-lucky", distinguishing it from the original. The second was recorded on 3 April the following year, and was slowed down and extended to nearly three minutes, featuring some fun vocal interplay between Roger and Freddie, and the addition of a slide whistle. The first version was issued on *Queen At The Beeb* in the UK in 1989 (the US issue, *Queen At The BBC*, didn't come out until 1995), while the second version was finally released in 2016 on the *On Air* BBC compilation.

MONEY (THAT'S WHAT I WANT) *(Berry/Gordy)*

First recorded by Barrett Strong in 1959 and later covered by The Beatles on their second album, *With The Beatles*, 'Money (That's What I Want)' was performed live by The Cross at the Gosport Festival on 30 July 1992.

MONEY CAN'T BUY HAPPINESS *(Mercury)*
• Compilation (Freddie): *Solo Collection*

An upbeat, reggae-inspired lament about the evils of money, 'Money Can't Buy Happiness' was recorded on 10 February 1984 at Musicland Studios and was, at one point, shortlisted for inclusion on *Mr Bad Guy*, but remained uncompleted. Featuring little additional instrumentation other than a drum-machine and occasional synthesizer blasts, the song would have been a terrific addition to the album had it been finished; as it was, it remained in the vaults until the release of *The Solo Collection* in 2000.

MONY MONY *(Bloom/Cordell/Gentry/James)*

Originally performed by Tommy James and the Shondells, 'Mony Mony' was later covered to greater success by Billy Idol, though it was also performed live by Smile in 1969.

MORE OF THAT JAZZ *(Taylor)*
• Album: *Jazz*

The second of Roger's contributions to *Jazz* wasn't much better than 'Fun It', suffering from a plodding, knee-jerk rhythm and boring, uninspiring lyrics about being ... bored and uninspired. Paeans to ennui are rarely successful, and 'More Of That Jazz' is no exception; dragging on for over four minutes with a repetitive guitar riff (likely performed by Roger, though the absence of personnel credits on the album make it difficult to know for certain) and a thudding drum performance that holds the song back instead of propelling it, the only saving grace is Roger's singing, which is inspired, and helps make the song only barely listenable. Its placement as the album closer, as a tie-in to the album title (and the awkward inclusion of clips of other album songs), brings *Jazz* to an undignified conclusion.

MOTHER LOVE *(Mercury/May)*
• Album: *Heaven*

If there was ever a song that combined the passion and driving force that Freddie demanded, 'Mother Love' was undoubtedly it. Written mostly by Brian and arranged by Freddie, the song is a highlight of *Made In Heaven*: centered around a sombre melody and propeled by a shuffling drum machine, the song is a vehicle for Freddie's emotional vocal performance. Recorded between 13 and 22 May 1991 (as confirmed by Justin Shirley-Smith on queenzone.com in 2014, who also stated that no further recording sessions were held after 22 May until October 1993), the song finds its shattered and broken narrator, his life draining from his body, pleading for the comfort and familiarity of mother. "Freddie, as normal, got to some point and said, 'No, no, no, no, no, this isn't good enough! I have to go higher here, I have to put more into this, have to get more power in,'" Brian recalled in 1995. "So he downs a couple of vodkas, stands up and goes for it, and you can hear the middle eight of 'Mother Love' just soars to incredible heights, and this is a man who can't really stand any more without incredible pain and is very weak, you know, has no flesh on his bones, and you can hear the power, the will that he's still got."

Brian later remarked with poignant fondness that this was the most significant collaboration he'd ever had with Freddie, and that the lyrics were more or less made up on the spot as the vocalist sat on and nodded approvingly. The song was left in a half-finished state for the rest of 1991, before Brian, Roger, and John returned to it in 1993. The guitarist recorded an emotional solo, not on his Red Special, surprisingly, but on a Parker Fly. ("It was probably lying around in Montreux," he recalled vaguely.) The song was then built up, with Brian adding the final verse and singing it himself. "It was never finished," he remembered in 1999. "He never came back to do the final verse, but to the end, even when he couldn't even stand, without propping himself up, he was just giving it his all. You can hear the incredible strength of his voice in that track, and the passion that he's putting into it. And we're making it up as we go along, you know, I'm scribbling words on pieces of paper and he's grabbing them and saying, 'Roll the tape. I'll do this one.' He knew that it might be the last time he was ever able to sing and, in that case, it was."

"In the last few weeks of his life, [Freddie] would say, 'Get me doing stuff. Write me more words, more words, more words. Give me stuff to sing, because when I've gone, you guys can finish it off,'" Brian told Virgin Radio in 2004. "Well, this song was almost finished. He said, 'Look, that's about as much as I can do.' He'd had a couple of vodkas. He'd gone totally for the middle eight, which you'll hear on this, which is phenomenal, and then he said, 'Look. It's okay, I'll come back in a few days and finish it off.' Well, that was the last time he was ever there, and so in the end I sang the last verse, because I didn't want to mess with the format of it at all. I just wanted it to be as it was. And this was something which I sort of carried in my pocket for a couple of years – actually, probably more than that – until the time when we were able to make the *Made In Heaven* album. And it's a long story. I mean there's more than 2 years of my life certainly in trying to assemble that material around the vocals that he'd left, and we all worked very hard on it. But what I wanted was to preserve that moment the best way I could and tell the story, and that's what you hear. There's a piece in the middle which to me represents, you know, looking back on your life and stuff like that. But there was no morbidity in singing it. It was a kind of joyful thing – that's all I can say. It's a fairly serious song but it was – there was great joy in Fred finding these notes, finding this performance. I think it's superb."

The song concludes with a reverse timeline of Freddie's life: the ending segment starts with a vocal impromptu from Wembley Stadium in 1986, then moves onto a brief clip of every officially released Queen

song compressed into ten seconds, and concludes with one of Freddie's first vocal performances from 'Goin' Back' in 1972. And what a fitting conclusion it is: "I think I'm going back, to the things I loved so well in my youth."

MUSTAPHA *(Mercury)*
• Album: *Jazz*

Despite *Jazz* being an album of compact, seemingly straightforward songs, Freddie contributed two of the most bizarre and complicated tracks the band would record, superficially nonsensical but, upon closer inspection, masterfully complex and superbly arranged. While 'Bicycle Race' was considered commercial enough for single release, 'Mustapha' featured only a marginal amount of English in its lyrics, yet that hardly stopped it from becoming a fan favorite. Audiophiles will also swoon at the neat production: the first half of the song was recorded and mixed in mono, but once Brian's guitars kick in, the song is suddenly in stereo, creating a startling and unexpected effect.

While rumors have persisted for years that the song was written for a Bombay classmate of Freddie's, the vocalist explained its true meaning in an interview shortly after the album's release: "It is complete gibberish. It isn't any language at all except in a few spots." Then again, this may have been a classic case of Freddie deflecting compositional dissection by dismissing the song outright, as he was wont to do.

'Mustapha' was performed live between 1978 and 1980, usually as the medley opener, but mostly as an introduction to other songs, while on the 1980 tour, as well as during some 1981 shows, the song was performed in its entirety. It created a minor sensation when it was issued in 1979 as a single from *Jazz* in Bolivia, Germany, Spain and Yugoslavia.

MY BABY DOES ME *(Queen)*
• Album: *Miracle*

Serving as a laidback chaser between 'Scandal' and 'Was It All Worth It?', this collaboration between John and Freddie recalls the slick funk of 'Cool Cat', with a bubbling bass and an emotional, soaring guitar performance from Brian. More of an atmospheric mood setter than an actual song, 'My Baby Does Me' is a nice reprieve from the other tracks on *The Miracle*, and would be the last time on a Queen album that the band explored the funk genre. More mundanely, the song was originally recorded as 'My Baby Loves Me', with a demo slipping out in recent years featuring – yes – the word "does" instead of "loves". Interestingly, the drum machine pattern used on this song was also used for the unreleased 'I Guess We're Falling Out'; when Queen archivist Greg Brooks played that song at a fan club convention in the early 2000s, it had segued from the aforementioned 'My Baby Loves Me' demo.

"That song stemmed from John and myself," Freddie said in a 1989 BBC Radio One interview. "I wanted something a little more relaxed, and the way the other songs were going, I thought we were getting so involved and they were very heavy. There was a lot of guitar input in some songs, and I felt that we didn't have something that was little bit more pristine, a little bit more clearheaded and not too involved, and so I thought, 'Let's just go for something quite straightforward and something that we hadn't got in the batch' … So we decided that we should have something with just a very easy backbeat, and something very listenable, and I don't think it was going to go on the album at first, we just decided that that would be a nice breather at the end of the second side."

MY BOY (May)
• Compilation (Brian): *Lullabies For A Difference*

Originally recorded by Brian in 1980 as part of a trio of demos ('The Dark' and 'I'm Scared' were the other two), this delicate ballad, written for Brian's then-two-year-old son Jimmy, was recorded during the *Hot Space* sessions but left unreleased; considering the direction Queen took with that album, the omission is unsurprising, if not disappointing. The original 1980 demo was later issued on the 1998 compilation album *Lullabies For A Difference*, compiled by Joan Armatrading.

MY COUNTRY I & II (Taylor)
• Album (Roger): *Fun* • A-side (Roger): 6/81

While Roger would shy away from denigrating politicians and lambasting jingoism on Queen records, his solo albums were fair game. His first, *Fun In Space*, was largely apolitical, but the major saga on it was 'My Country I & II', an epic, seven minute rocker that decries the futility of war and politicians' plight to further a winning ticket instead of enriching their constituents' lives. The song was well timed given the outbreak of war between Britain and Argentina over control of the Falkland Islands. Because 'Under Pressure' was topping the Argentinean charts at the time, the government there concluded that the song was British propaganda cooked up for the event and promptly banned the record from the airwaves. Roger seethed, "In Argentina, we were Number One when that stupid war was going on and we had a fantastic time there, and that can only be for the good. Music is totally international."

The first part of the song is a leisurely stroll, with Roger and some sweetly-sung chorus vocals proclaiming his conscientous objection. The second part, however, is an impressive display of power chords and clattering drums, as Roger all but howls his beliefs. The concluding coda, where Roger croons "You don't get me" repeatedly, fades out then back in before finishing abruptly. Truly a masterpiece.

'My Country I & II' was chosen as the second single from *Fun In Space* in June 1981, but unfortunately fell victim to the record company's decision to edit the track to a more radio-friendly running time. Clocking in at just under four minutes, the song is disjointed and almost immediately kicks into the second, drum-oriented part of the song; unsurprisingly, the song failed to chart. For over 30 years, the single edit remained unreleased only compact disc, but finally gained exposure on Roger's nearly all-encompassing box set *The Lot*.

MY FAIRY KING (Mercury)
• Album: *Queen* • Compilation: *BBC*, *On Air*
• CD Single: 6/96 [9]

Concluding the first side of *Queen* is Freddie's exquisite 'My Fairy King', a song which revealed the vocalist's fascination with mythical (and mystical) creatures and stories, subjects he would explore deeper on subsequent songs. Written later in original Queen bassist Barry Mitchell's waning days as a band member, the song was inspired by Robert Browning's poem 'The Pied Piper', even borrowing directly the lines "And their dogs outran our fallow deer / And honey-bees had lost their stings / And horses were born with eagles' wings". More significantly, the reference to Mother Mercury inspired Freddie to finally change his name from Bulsara, thus completing the first stage of his metamorphosis.

Driven by Freddie's piano, 'My Fairy King' marked the first time that the band even knew of his mastery of the instrument. "He's virtually a self-taught pianist," Brian later recalled, "and he was making vast strides at the time, although we didn't have a piano on stage at that point because it would have been impossible to fix up. So in the studio was the first chance Freddie had to do his piano things and we actually got that sound of the piano and the guitar working for the first time, which was very exciting. 'My Fairy King' was the first of these sort of epics where there were lots of voice overdubs and harmonies. Freddie got into this, and that led to 'The March Of The Black Queen' on the second album and then 'Bohemian Rhapsody' later on."

"'My Fairy King' was a number Freddie wrote," John said in 1976, "which ... was built up in the studio. Whereas there are other numbers which are essentially live songs, basically just the track and then just a few backing vocals and guitar solos over the top and that was it." The complexity of this song made it impossible to perform live, though Freddie obviously held some affection for it: he would occasionally slip the melody into improvisations on the 1982 Hot Space and 1984/1985 Queen Works! tours. It was presented, however, on the first BBC broadcast by Queen, albeit in a rougher fashion. Even though the BBC version merely takes the master track of the song from the Trident album sessions, the vocals were recorded on 5 February 1973; this version was released on the 1989 UK compilation Queen at the Beeb, and again six years later on the US equivalent, retitled Queen at the BBC.

MY GENERATION (Townshend)

The Who's 1965 power anthem was played live by 1984.

MY GIRL (Robinson)

Originally performed by The Temptations, 'My Girl' was also covered live by 1984.

MY LIFE HAS BEEN SAVED (Queen)
• B-side: 10/89 [25] • Album: Heaven

Written by John and recorded during sessions for The Miracle in 1988, 'My Life Has Been Saved' was unfairly relegated to B-side status as the flip-side of 'Scandal' in October 1989. With some beautiful keyboard work and a hardworking Brian on slide guitar, the song is a moody, atmospheric appreciation for life and taking things in stride in a world of disarray and confusion.

In the context of Freddie's passing, this seems like an odd choice to have revisited for the Made In Heaven album, but it provided an optimistic glimmer of hope to an album of downbeat, sombre ballads. Unfortunately, the reworked version is more keyboard-dominated, with Brian's guitar buried in the mix, and the touching vocal coda ("I made it up / I'm blind / I don't know what's coming to me") removed.

MY LOVE IS DANGEROUS (Mercury)
• Album (Freddie): BadGuy • B-side (Freddie): 9/85 [50] • Compilations (Freddie): Pretender, FM Album, The Solo Collection

The penultimate track from Mr Bad Guy is probably the least inspiring: Freddie's vocals are drenched in echo and set to a vague reggae-dub rhythm. Freddie, however, held some affection for it, feeling it accurately summed up his position as a lover. "I haven't actually analyzed myself and said, 'OK, my love is dangerous'," he said in 1985. "I think after all these years I just feel I'm not a very good partner for anybody and I just think that's what my love is. I think my love is dangerous. Who wants their love to be safe? Can you imagine writing a song called 'My Love Is Safe'? It would never sell!"

An early version, going under the name of 'Love Is Dangerous', was recorded on 29 May 1984 and deviates little from the released version, while an extended remix, running just over six minutes and bordering on the tedious, was created for inclusion on the 12" single version of 'Living On My Own'. Thankfully, it was remixed in 1992 for inclusion on the compilation album The Great Pretender, giving new life to an otherwise unremarkable track. Remixed by Jeff Lord-Alge and produced by Julian Raymond, the song is turned into a muscular hard rocker and benefits greatly.

MY MELANCHOLY BLUES (Mercury)
• Album: NOTW • CD Single: 11/89 [21] • Bonus: NOTW • Compilation: On Air

What better way to close News Of The World than with this slick jazz-lounge track? After the final bars of the raucous 'It's Late' have finished ringing, Freddie's dulcet piano heralds the intro to one of his most sublime compositions, and showed that, despite the base carnal desires of 'Get Down, Make Love', he could still come up with something surprising instead of shocking. Written from the viewpoint of an inveterate barfly, the narrator is drowning his sorrows in the bottom of a glass, lamenting the loss of his lover but certain he'll bounce back in time for the next party. Featuring an understated performance from Roger on brushed drums and John on bass, 'My Melancholy Blues' (originally demoed as 'My Melancholy Baby') is one of the few Queen tracks with no guitar contribution whatsoever. Instead, Freddie takes the initiative, turning in two gorgeous and tasteful piano solos.

The song became a regular in the 1977/1978 News Of The World tour, but was dropped from the Jazz tour in favor of 'Dreamers Ball'. An outstanding live version from December 1977 in Houston was released on the CD single of 'The Miracle' in November 1989, which had also featured on the cut-and-paste video anthology *Rare Live: A Concert Through Time And Space*. The BBC version, recorded on 28 October 1977, was finally released in 2011 on the double-disc edition of *News Of The World*, and five years later on *On Air*. Adding in a splendid guitar solo courtesy of Brian, the song concludes with a spine-tingling laugh from Freddie and is undoubtedly a highlight of the sixth BBC session. A rough mix, which doesn't offer much in variation apart from a slightly different vocal performance and studio chatter, was released on the 40th anniversary box set edition of *News Of The World*.

MY SECRET FANTASY

From the same batch of demos as 'Self-Made Man' and 'Robbery', 'My Secret Fantasy' is an alluring though lyrically sparse song, structured around a mesmerizing keyboard sequence. Rumored to have been written by John, it's very likely that Freddie had a hand in the writing of the song too.

A NATION OF HAIRCUTS *(Taylor)*
• Album (Roger): *Electric* • B-side (Roger): 3/99 [38]

Attacking the fashionistas of the world, Roger's 'A Nation Of Haircuts' is a fine, driving rocker on *Electric Fire*, buried among songs that deal with far weightier subjects like domestic discord and success stories. A nice complement to 'London Town, C'mon Down', the song rolls along at a decent clip, with Roger's diatribe (distorted by the "shouting down the telephone" effect he prefers on much of his latter-day material) cutting down a peg the moody heroin chic models more concerned with their coif than with anything of substance.

Believing that the very poseurs that he was lambasting wouldn't appreciate the grittier album version, Roger deconstructed the song into a sleek,

sexy "club dub" remix, removing the backing track completely and adding faceless programmed drums and percolating synths. Released as the B-side of 'Surrender' in 1999, this rendition is worth a cursory listen or two, but isn't a match for the less image-conscious original.

NAZIS 1994 *(Taylor)*
• A-side (Roger): 5/94 [22] • Album (Roger): *Happiness?*

It had been just over a decade since Roger's last true solo album, so imagine the response when faithful listeners purchased *Happiness?* and were greeted with the opening kick-march strains of 'Nazis 1994', the first song on the album. Set to a dirge-like rhythm, with little embellishment, the song expresses the drummer's outrage over the recent uprising of neo-Nazism and its proponents' ridiculous claim that the Holocaust never happened.

When asked about the song in 1994, Roger exclaimed, "You want to talk about 'Nazis', eh?! I believe that it is a real problem ... one of the main dangers that exist in today's society and particularly in Europe, of all places. I wanted to write something simple and direct which gives the main idea, one which repeats throughout the whole song. In my opinion the repetition fixes firmly the idea in people's heads. This sentence that continually comes back is, 'They say that it never happened'. To think that of the Holocaust is purely and simply outrageous. How can they be stupid enough to think that? The general atmosphere of 'Nazis' is cold and without feeling. That's at least what I wanted to create. The only emotions that we can set against these people are the strongest emotions. That's all there is which can stand against them."

Set to a terse backing of goose-stepping drums and Roger's hushed vocals, the song positively seethes anger and outrage. Originally, the repeated line was "We've gotta kick these fucking Nazis" instead of "stinking Nazis", but after careful consideration Roger altered the line to make it more accessible. Released as the first single from *Happiness?*, it created quite a controversy when radio stations refused to air it and record stores wouldn't stock it. Roger was surprised, telling the *Independent On Sunday*, "For me it is not political. It is a case of fundamental right and wrong. Peddling hatred through ignorance is wrong. The record is fairly outspoken but it doesn't make any political statements in my view. I find it odd that it is a successful record but the media seems shy of it." Music journalist and one-time bad boy Allan Jones weighed in for no particular reason: "I'm sure his heart is in the right place. But it is just not a very good record. Let's face it: he's an ageing rock star and they just don't want to play his record. Pop station audiences want little boys that they can look at and fancy or dance records. This song, as well as being controversial lyrically, is not a good tune." As with most good examples of controversy, the single still fared well, reaching No. 22 in the UK and becoming Roger's first Top 30 (and highest-charting) single.

The CD single featured several alternate remixes, each marginally less interesting than the previous one. The 'Big Science Mix' features Matt Hillier on additional analog synthesizers and was remixed by Joshua J Macrae, explaining its percussion-dominated backing, with excerpts from news reports and what sound like samples from Pink Floyd's *The Wall*. The 'Kick Mix', produced by Serge Ramackers, Dominic Sas and Remo Martuf for No More Productions, is an attempt at a dance remix, using the original banned version but adding a generic dance beat, and really starts to grate on the listener within the first 60 seconds. (However, it does feature an additional verse not heard on any other version.) The 'Radio Mix' is the most interesting of the bunch, restructuring Roger's drum beat to feature a droning synthesizer background and additional percussion. Again produced by No More Productions, the song was extended by nearly a minute yet still loses a verse. The 'Makita Mix Extended' and 'Schindler's Mix Extended', both produced by Danny Saber, are the most extreme, featuring excerpts from an actual Nazi rally.

The song was performed throughout Roger's 1994/1995 Happiness? tour, but was dropped in favor of more recent material on his Electric Fire tour. A video was made in the spring of 1994, directed by David Mallet in London. Two versions were produced: one featuring the normal album version, which was the most widely seen, and another of the banned version. Both versions feature intercut scenes of World War II Nazi footage, making for an unsettling viewing experience.

NEED YOUR LOVING TONIGHT *(Deacon)*
• Album: *Game*

Written by John for *The Game* album in 1980, 'Need Your Loving Tonight' is a joyous pop romp that recalls the bubblegum days of The Beatles, even deriving its title from 'Eight Days A Week', perhaps that band's finest pop song ever. Lyrically speaking, the song gives a false optimistic slant to the end of a relationship, with the narrator taking the higher road by insisting the break-up was a mutual decision. Released in the US as the fourth and final single from *The Game* in November 1980, 'Need Your Loving Tonight', backed with Roger's 'Rock It (Prime Jive)', reached a disappointing No. 44 and never appeared on any compilation. The song was performed on and off between 1980 and 1981, but wasn't a mainstay in the set list and was out just as quickly as it was in.

NEVERMORE *(Mercury)*
• Album: *Queen2* • Bonus: *Queen2* • Compilation: *On Air*

Slipping in unnoticed between the adventurous 'The Fairy Feller's Master-Stroke' and the epic 'The March Of The Black Queen' on the Black Side of *Queen II* is this gorgeous ballad by Freddie, which is rumored to have been written about his then-girlfriend, Mary Austin. Brian later attributed this and 'Lily Of The Valley', on the surface lyrically simple songs, to Freddie's realization "that his body needed to be somewhere else".

A BBC version, recorded on 3 April 1974, features a rougher arrangement, and more pronounced bass and drums (which are lacking on the album version). Other than this airing, 'Nevermore' was never performed live.

NEW DARK AGES *(Taylor)*
• Album (The Cross): *Blue* • German single (The Cross): 8/91 • Live (The Cross): *Germany*

Roger's exquisite 'New Dark Ages' is an emotive plea for safe sex ("Stop / Take care / Think / Is this real love?") and AIDS awareness. Set to a terse backing, dominated mostly by keyboards and bass, The Cross is in fine form here, and 'New Dark Ages' is arguably one of their finest performances captured in the studio. Released as the first single from *Blue Rock* in August 1991 with Clayton Moss' 'Ain't Put Nothin' Down' on the B-side, the single made no significant dent in the German charts, despite considerable promotion provided by The Cross as well as a fine video directed by Paul Voss. It's a 'Body Language' for the 1990s, with an oiled-up man and woman cavorting across the stage as the fully-clothed band perform the song. Presenting the *Hot Space* imagery from another angle, the single sleeve featured the same wide-eyed child from the 'Las Palabras De Amor (The Words Of Love)' single from

June 1982 with a pattern of birds as an overlay.

The song was performed live on the European tour supporting Magnum, with a live version appearing on the 1992 fan club-only bootleg *Live In Germany*. Intriguingly, it was revealed by Greg Brooks that the song was recorded during sessions for *Innuendo*, but remained unfinished due to objections from John.

A NEW LIFE IS BORN

Dating from *The Miracle* sessions, this (partly) unreleased track written by Freddie was featured as the intro to Roger's 'Breakthru' (the a cappella "when love breaks up" segment), but instead of the "somehow I have to make this final breakthru" line, Freddie continues into a gorgeous, improvised piano ballad. A second, more atmospheric, mostly instrumental version was also recorded, and both sound like pieces from Freddie's 1988 *Barcelona* sessions.

NEW YORK *(Mercury)*
• Compilation (Freddie): *Solo Collection*

Recorded on 6 July 1984 at Musicland Studios (a home demo was also recorded, though it remains unreleased), this short yet charming piano piece was the last thing to be recorded by Freddie before embarking on the upcoming Queen Works! world tour. Unfortunately, he didn't complete this piece upon returning to the sessions in December, and it languished unreleased for over 15 years before appearing on *The Solo Collection* in 2000.

NEW YORK AT LAST

An interesting fan mix (or 'mash up') featuring an almost club-style synthesized beat, 'New York At Last' was created in 2003 by a fan named Smash – real name Scott Akister – who programmed and produced the synthesizer and drum beats, and added Freddie's vocal from the unreleased song 'New York', originally recorded by Freddie during the *Mr Bad Guy* sessions in 1984. Mixing in guitar parts by Brian from 'Spread Your Wings' and 'Save Me', the mash was such a huge success on the Internet and among Queen fans that an online petition was started to get the song issued as a single. Unfortunately, the powers that be either decided against it, or simply didn't listen.

NEW YORK, NEW YORK *(Ebb/Kander)*

A snippet of Frank Sinatra's 'New York, New York' appears in the *Highlander* film during Kurgan's carjacked joyride into New York City, before merging effortlessly with 'A Dozen Red Roses For My Darling'. For years, Queen fans have hoped that a full version exists, but it has recently been revealed that the 30-second clip is all that was recorded.

THE NIGHT COMES DOWN *(May)*
• Album: *Queen* • Bonus: *Queen*

One of the earliest lyrics written by any member of Queen, Brian's elegiac 'The Night Comes Down' recalls the simpler days of his youth, and laments growing old and having to take on responsibility. Set to a gorgeous acoustic backing, driven by a subtle rhythm section that doesn't overpower the words, Freddie recalls a fling from the Summer of Love: "Lucy was high, and so was I / Dazzling!" That line, of course, harks back to The Beatles' controversial 1967 song 'Lucy In The Sky With Diamonds', which was presumed to be about LSD but was revealed by its author, John Lennon, as a lyrical depiction of a painting his son, Julian, had made of a classmate.

'The Night Comes Down' is a stunning excursion into acoustic territory the band would rarely explore again. Seemingly influenced by many of The Kinks' late 1960s singles, the song is a bright and cheery ballad, certainly a rarity among most other Brian-penned ballads. Performed live in 1971 and 1972 (recordings of which have not surfaced), its only post-*Queen* performance may have come on 1 March 1974, Greg Brooks reporting in his book, *Queen Live: A Concert Documentary*, that the song was rumored to have been played that day along with 'The Fairy Fellers Master-Stroke'. Considering the release of *Live at the Rainbow '74*, which featured 'The Fairy Fellers Master-Stroke', the likelihood of 'The Night Comes Down' having been performed more frequently than reported is pretty good.

Two versions of the song exist: the first is a demo, recorded in September 1971 at De Lane Lea Studios and produced by Louis Austin, while the second version hails from the Trident sessions in 1972. When the band listened to a playback of the re-recorded 1972 version, they decided that the original demo captured the mood they wanted to portray, so the new version was discarded and the old one was used instead. To date, the re-recording has yet to surface, and one can only wonder if it's possible for the unreleased version to surpass the beauty of the demo.

1983... (A MERMAN I SHOULD TURN TO BE)
(Hendrix)

Originally released on Jimi Hendrix's *Electric Ladyland* album in 1968, '1983... (A Merman I Should Turn To Be)' merely served as an introduction to Wreckage's rendition of The Beatles' 'Rain'.

NO MORE FUN *(Taylor)*
• Album (Roger): *Electric* • CD single (Roger): 3/99 [38]

A fast-paced, self-referential rock song (in the first verse, Roger makes note of Led Zeppelin, David Bowie and Mott the Hoople) that bemoans the loss of good times in the world, nostalgic for the golden days of rock'n'roll, 'No More Fun' is a more characteristic song from *Electric Fire*. Set to a menacing backing, and performed entirely by Roger except for some wilder lead guitar from the ever-present Jason Falloon (interestingly, 'No More Fun' marks the only appearance Roger would make on guitar), the song secured a rightful position in the 1998/1999 Electric Fire tour set list. A version from the Cyberbarn gig on 24 September 1998 was released on the second CD single of 'Surrender' in March 1999.

NO-ONE BUT YOU (ONLY THE GOOD DIE YOUNG)
(May)
• Compilation: *Rocks, Hits3* • A-side: 1/98 [13]
• Live (Brian & Kerry): *Acoustic*

The years following Brian's 1992 *Back To The Light* album, his first proper solo release pulling together songs written between 1988 and 1991, were spent touring that album as well as writing new songs. When rumors surfaced in 1997 that he was working on a follow-up, fans started to get excited, since it was the first new material from any Queen member since *Made In Heaven* in 1995. Even more exciting for fans was the one-off performance of Brian, Roger and John with Elton John at the Théâtre National de Chaillot at the premiere of the Bejart Ballet Lausanne (see Part Three), which was the first integration of Queen's music with ballet since Freddie's 1979 excursion with the Royal Dancers. The press predictably covered the appearance, which saw the pianist/vocalist performing 'The Show

Must Go On', and rumors started to circulate that Elton would front Queen on a world tour.

Brian wasn't interested in any reunion at this point, despite Elton's assertion that the band should re-form: "It must be like keeping a fabulous Ferrari in the garage and not being able to drive," Elton later quipped. However, shortly after the performance in Paris, Brian was so moved by the celebration of Queen's music and Freddie's life that he wrote 'No-One But You (Only The Good Die Young)' as a tribute to the late vocalist.

Originally, he intended to release the song on his solo album, which ultimately surfaced in June 1998 as *Another World*, but he sensed that it needed something that session musicians couldn't recreate. "It was written as a sort of tribute to Freddie and before long I became aware I was trying to make it sound very Queen-like," Brian told *Guitarist* in 1998. "There are some musical and verbal quotes in there and I thought, 'If it's going to sound like Queen, maybe it ought to be Queen.' I sent the track to Roger and he loved it and said we had to do it. Although I lost that track from my album, it worked out alright in the end; it was the final thing that made me realize I was on the wrong track for my album anyway." With Roger on board ("He put it away in a drawer somewhere,"

Brian explained in 1998, "'cause he was busy or whatever, and it was months later when Roger phoned up suddenly, excited and said, 'I just listened to the track and it's amazing, and we have to do it as a Queen song!'"), the duo asked John to help them out with it. Sessions took place in the spring of 1997 at Allerton Studios, Brian's home studio, and the song was completed in time for inclusion on a future compilation. The initial intent was for it to appear on a simultaneous compilation of ballads and love songs, but when this fell by the wayside, it secured a position as the final track on *Queen Rocks*.

Lyrically, the song draws inspiration from the unveiling of Freddie's statue, which overlooks Lake Geneva in Montreux ("A hand above the water/ An angel reaching for the sky") and is majestically featured on the sleeve of *Made In Heaven*. The theme of the song comes from the subtitle, and is unofficially dedicated to those who die too soon. This became more sentimental in August 1997, when Lady Diana Spencer was killed in a car crash after a flock of French paparazzi gave chase to her car. It was an indirect yet appreciated tribute, and it became appropriate to dedicate the song not only to Freddie but to everyone who lives on in spirit and memory.

Set to a melancholy piano backing (played by Brian in the style of Freddie), the song is a typical Brian ballad, sung emotionally by its author, with an occasional duet with Roger. Featuring only Brian, Roger and John, the song's success is due to its simplicity; with a basic arrangement, the song isn't bogged down with excessive instrumentation or backing vocalists. 'No-One But You (Only The Good Die Young)' wouldn't have sounded out of place on *Made In Heaven*, though it certainly doesn't belong on *Queen Rocks*, especially following the raucous 'It's Late'. The best plan for the song would have been to issue it is a non-album single, which was originally intended in November 1997, to coincide with its sister compilation; Parlophone pulled out at the last minute and were besieged by complaints from fans worldwide. Thanks to an Internet petition (proving that, sometimes, petitions on the web *can* make a difference), the record company released the single in January 1998 as a double-A single with 'Tie Your Mother Down'. Housed in a gorgeous yellow slipcase, with a rendering of Icarus on the front ("They're only flying too close to the sun"), the single brought Queen back into the UK Top Twenty, where it peaked at a respectable No. 13, closing the final chapter in the band's career almost indefinitely.

A video for the song was filmed on 29 November 1997 at Bray Studios by The Torpedo Twins, and is arguably the duo's finest. A tasteful black and white presentation of the three remaining members performing the song, three versions were constructed: the original, which was used as a promo only; a new edit interspersed, in traditional DoRo fashion, with shots of Freddie; and a making-of version that goes behind the scenes. The last two versions were issued on the *Queen Rocks* video in 1998, while the original has yet to be released on an official compilation.

Brian included the song in his 1998 Another World tour, where it sadly earned another dedication: Cozy Powell, former drummer of 1970s rock group Rainbow and a dear friend of Brian's who recorded with the guitarist on his two solo albums, died in a car accident on 5 April 1998, right before The Brian May Band was due to go on the road in support of *Another World*. Brian and Roger also performed the song in several shows of the Queen reincarnation, most notably at the pre-*We Will Rock You: The Musical* gig in Amsterdam.

NO TURNING BACK (Deacon/Ahwai)
• Soundtrack (The Immortals): *Biggles* • A-side (The Immortals): 5/86

Though it may not be an exceptional track, 'No Turning Back' is notable for being the only solo venture by John Deacon. Shortly after Live Aid in 1985, John was asked by director John Hough to provide a theme song for the movie *Biggles: Adventures In Time*, from the pre-war stories about true-blue air ace Major James Bigglesworth. With nothing better to do while waiting for the sessions for the next Queen album to start, John agreed, and promptly formed a new band, with friends Robert Ahwai on lead guitar and Lenny Zakatek on rhythm guitar and vocals, called The Immortals.

Written by John and Robert, 'No Turning Back' is an infectiously catchy slice of pop, the likes of which were dominating the charts in the mid-1980s (indeed, there's more than a hint of Phil Collins' 'Sussudio' with the programmed horns) and to which Queen themselves would contribute with the 'A Kind Of Magic' single. While 'No Turning Back' may be utterly disposable, inconsequential, and forgettable, it's still a fun, bouncy track, predating the summery vibes of 'Rain Must Fall' by three years; it would have been interesting to have heard Freddie's take on the song, though Lenny's silky, soulful voice has a different charm to it altogether.

Recorded during sessions for *A Kind Of Magic* at Townhouse Studios, produced by John and Robert, and mixed by Bert Bevans, 'No Turning Back' was released as a single to promote the film in May 1986. Understandably, The Immortals had no name recognition whatsoever, and the film itself failed to attract positive notices, meaning John's only foray into a solo career ended before it ever really began. Regardless, a lavish amount of attention was devoted to remixing the song to make it interesting for collectors, with three versions available: the standard version running nearly four minutes; a semi-instrumental mix dubbed the 'Chocks Away Mix'; and an extended version dubbed the 'Joystick Mix', with neither of the new mixes offering anything revelatory – if you've heard one, you've heard them all. A video was filmed shortly before the single's release, with the three musicians wearing the famous Biggles headgear and goggles plus a guest appearance from the film's septuagenarian star Peter Cushing.

NO VIOLINS *(Taylor)*
• Album (Roger): *Fun*

This paean to nostalgia served as a fine introduction to *Fun In Space*, with a deceptively slow intro kicking into high gear with a thundering roll around the drum set and chugging guitar riffs. There are the requisite sci-fi references ("security complex" and "monochrome duplex" lend it a futuristic bent, though these could just as easily be a call-back to the Cold War conception of the future) but otherwise the song is a touching rememberance of the past. Coming from the typically sex and drugs and rock'n'roll attitude of the drummer, this is a superficially surprising subject matter, but when viewed in the context of earlier songs like 'Tenement Funster' or 'Drowse', which have a guarded wistfulness to them, 'No Violins' is in good company.

NOT FADE AWAY *(Holly/Allison)*

Buddy Holly's terrific 1957 single, covered by The Rolling Stones in 1964, was performed as an acoustic guitar intro to 'Crazy Little Thing Called Love' on just two occasions: in Stockholm on 10 April 1982 and, in more complete form, on 4 September 1984 at Wembley Arena.

NOTHIN' BUT BLUE *(May/Powell/Nicholls/Makin)*
• Album (Brian): *BTTL* • B-side (Brian): 11/92 [19]

Blues wasn't a style that Brian often explored, despite the obvious influence of Jeff Beck and Eric Clapton (indeed, his 1983 composition, 'Blues Breaker', was dedicated to the latter). The early 1990s, however, saw a rush of blues compositions from Brian. 'Lost Opportunity', which was released on the CD single of 'I'm Going Slightly Mad' and was recorded just after sessions for *Innuendo*, was essentially a solo track from Brian with accompaniment by Roger and John. More sublime was 'Nothin' But Blue', a track initially recorded as 'Somewhere In Time' on Cozy Powell's 1992 solo album, *The Drums Are Back*, and with John on bass. For his own solo album, Brian took the instrumental backing from that session and added his own lyrics to create a new version.

Surprisingly, Brian strayed from his trusty guitar on this song. "Ninety-five percent of [the guitar tracks were done on The Red Special]," Brian told *Guitar World* in 1993. "On a couple of tracks, I also used this wonderful guitar that Joe Satriani gave me, which was a

big departure for me. He gave it to me after we did the Guitar Legends concert in Seville, which I was lucky enough to be asked to put together. We all had a great time and I developed an even greater admiration for Satriani than I already had. He's such an amazingly dexterous player, you expect him to be technical and nothing else. But the fact is that he's got so much soul and feeling in what he does. He's really a guitarist's guitarist. Plus, he's a nice guy. Anyway, he sent me this guitar and I picked it up and was inspired. So I kicked in with it … It's his special model, and he had one made for me. It's wonderful. I'll be taking that out on tour with me, I hope." With a set of lyrics about the breakup of a relationship and the sadness of its aftermath, the song took on a deeper meaning when Brian told *The Orange County Register* in 1993 that it was written "the night before Freddie died. I had this strong feeling that it was going to happen. It flowed out very quickly. I could just hear the song in my head."

NOW I'M HERE *(May)*
• Album: *SHA* • A-side: 1/75 [11] • CD Single: 10/91 [16] • CD Single: 12/95 [6] • Live: *Killers, Wembley, On Fire, Montreal, Budapest, Rainbow, Odeon* • Live (Brian): *Brixton* • Bonus: *SHA* • Compilation: *On Air*

One of the contenders for the most performed Queen song in their career, 'Now I'm Here', in its original recorded form, is a slow, Stones-like rocker chronicling a rock band touring the moonlight mile: America. Inspired by Queen's own journeys on the road, the song was actually started during their first North American tour in support of Mott the Hoople (March-May 1974), but the words came later that year, before being the last song recorded for the album that September. One of the few Queen songs written about the road, it was also unusual in that it was written *on* the road. The words take on a different meaning in the context of the events that transpired while on tour with Mott the Hoople (see Parts Two and Four for more information).

Because of Brian's illnesses during the year (gangrene in January, hepatitis in May, and a duodenal ulcer during the summer), he fell into a deep depression and constantly worried whether the band would replace him. Instead, their support of the guitarist grew stronger, and they worked on recording new songs for their third album in his absence. Brian, too, would feverishly write when he felt well enough, and all his songs from *Sheer Heart Attack* indirectly relate to his time away from the group. None more so than 'Now I'm Here' (originally titled 'Peaches', itself an oblique reference to an American girl Brian fell for and would subsequently lust after), the title of which can be seen as a reassurance to the others, or maybe as a sarcastic twist.

Mainly, the song's rhythmic and lyrical inspiration is drawn from America: "We'd done a few things before I was ill," Brian said of the sessions, "but when I came back they'd done a load more, including a couple of backing tracks of songs by Freddie which I hadn't heard, like 'Flick Of The Wrist', which excited me and gave me a lot of inspiration to get back in there and do some writing – 'Now I'm Here' was done in that period. That song's about experiences on the American tour, which really blew me away. I was bowled over by the amazing aura rock music has in America."

The riff recalls any number of classics recorded by The Rolling Stones, with a guitar solo similar to many Chuck Berry songs; during the outro, Freddie shouts, "Go, go, go little Queenie!", a clever reference to Berry's 1959 song, as well as the band's namesake. But the performance is unmistakably Queen. The star here is clearly Brian, who has not only found his voice as a songwriter but has also grown far more confident in guitar arrangements. The song is cleverly written and designed, and starts off with a raw guitar riff over Freddie's echo-laden vocals. It then explodes into life, and is chock full of vocal harmonies, crunching guitars and a steady rhythm section. The subtle use of piano and organ, played by Brian and Freddie respectively, adds texture to the song and leads into the guitar solo nicely.

The song was selected as the second and final single from *Sheer Heart Attack*. Released only in the UK, the single, with a stand-alone version of 'Lily Of The Valley' as the B-side, reached a respectable No. 11 in the charts, but was too weighty to be considered a serious chart blockbuster.. The song received a television performance on Christmas Day 1974, when the band appeared on Granada TV's programme *45*; unfortunately, this tape has not yet surfaced.

A promotional video wasn't made for the single ('Killer Queen' didn't receive one either, but its 'official' video has become the one shot for *Top Of The Pops*), but the song did receive further BBC treatment on 16 October 1974, when the band nipped into Maida Vale 4 Studios to record a session with Jeff Griffins producing, to be used on Bob Harris' show on 4 November. Because the band were preparing for the upcoming British tour, they didn't have enough

time to record new versions of the songs ('Stone Cold Crazy', 'Flick Of The Wrist' and 'Tenement Funster' were the other three recorded), so the backing tracks from the *Sheer Heart Attack* sessions were used instead, with new lead vocals on each track by Freddie (and Roger, in the case of the final song).

Understandably, the song found a welcome home in the live setting, where it debuted as the stage opener on 31 October 1974 in Manchester (after the pre-recorded 'Procession' concluded); it was then shuffled throughout the live set until 9 August 1986, but was played at every concert in that almost 12-year span with the exception of Hyde Park in 1976 and Live Aid in 1985. The song took on a different shape starting in 1978, when Freddie would inject a vocal improvisation that incorporated the crowd (a good example of this is on *Live Killers*). Between 1980 and 1982, the band would often divide the song into several sections: the main part of the song, followed by Freddie's improvisation, went into an instrumental improvisation, followed by the introduction of a new song ('Dragon Attack' normally, though 'Put Out The Fire' would also be performed on the 1982 Japanese tour), and then a short reprise of the main 'Now I'm Here' riff. The song could last anywhere up to 15 minutes, though it reverted back to its original structure, albeit taken at a faster pace, for the 1984, 1985 and 1986 tours.

The song was performed at the Concert for Life by Def Leppard, but with Brian providing lead guitar; he had also appeared at a Def Leppard concert on 9 September 1987, where he jammed with them on the song. The guitarist also incorporated the song into his 1992 and 1993 Back To The Light tours, but did not include it on his 1998 Another World tours. During Brian's self-organized Expo '92 Guitar Festival in Seville, the song was performed with Gary Cherone and Paul Rodgers on lead vocals, and with additional guitar from Joe Satriani, Steve Vai, Nuno Bettencourt and Joe Walsh. It was also performed on 25 November 1999 with Foo Fighters, during a concert in which Brian and Roger both guested. While 'Now I'm Here' wasn't performed during Brian and Roger's tenure with Paul Rodgers (the drummer reportedly wasn't thrilled with performing it, as it required a great amount of energy from him), it was brought out of mothballs for the Queen + Adam Lambert 2014 tour, performed as the opening number after the prerecorded 'Procession' – a nice nod to the song's humble beginnings on the Sheer Heart Attack tour.

OGRE BATTLE (Mercury)
• Album: Queen2 • Compilation: BBC, Deep Cuts 1, On Air • Bonus: Queen2 • Live: Rainbow, Odeon

Opening the 'black side' of Queen II is 'Ogre Battle', a suitably dark and foreboding track set to a manic guitar riff. Despite fitting in almost perfectly with the themes on the second album, 'Ogre Battle' was actually written as early as 1972 and was originally destined for the first album, but remained unrecorded since it was considered too heavy lyrically. Granted, it would be difficult to imagine this song on the first album among Freddie's other contributions, but it adds a sense of mysticism to Queen II that makes the song a standout.

"Freddie also wrote 'Ogre Battle' which is a very heavy metal guitar riff," Brian explained to Guitar World in 1998. "It's strange that he should have done that. But when Freddie used to pick up a guitar, he'd have a great frenetic energy. It was kind of like a very nervy animal playing the guitar. He was a very impatient person and was very impatient with his own technique. He didn't have a great technical ability on the guitar but had it in his head. And you could feel this stuff bursting to get out. His right hand would move incredibly fast. He wrote a lot of good stuff for the guitar, a lot of it was stuff which I would not have thought of, because it would be in weird keys. He had this penchant for playing in E flat and A flat and F, and these are not places that your hand naturally falls on when playing the guitar, so he forced me into finding ways of doing things which made unusual sounds. It was really good."

Those "unusual sounds" – a whooshing sound effect used to fade into distorted (and backwards) guitars and drums – indicated an early sign of Queen's desire to experiment in the studio. "That was a bit of a miracle, actually," Brian told Guitar Player in 2008. "They had this massive gong in the studio that Roger hit. When we turned the tape over, the gong sounded great backwards and that sound was going to be at the beginning of the track. That got us wondering what the rest of the track would sound like backwards. Well, it sounded very similar. The riff is palindromic; it sounds the same forwards and backwards. So we decided to run the entire track backwards in the intro and then we seamlessly crossfaded it with the forwards track. I don't think it's even a crossfade; I think it's a butt edit and you can't even tell. I used my fingerboard pickup and bridge pickup out of phase for that tone."

'Ogre Battle' was performed live as early as 1972,

and remained in the set list until June 1977 at Earl's Court, though a one-off performance followed in Philadelphia on 23 November 1977. Two scorching renditions were released on the 2014 archival live set, Live At The Rainbow '74, and again the following year on A Night At The Odeon. A BBC version was recorded on 3 December 1973 and is a completely new recording, though the versions released on Queen At The Beeb and Queen At The BBC were both edited. Somehow, the master tape was damaged, and the first minute or so of the song, basically consisting of sound effects and guitar loops, had to be excised from the albums since it was considered to be of sub-par quality. A rougher quality recording was found in time to be released in 2016 on the BBC retrospective On Air. A remix was released on the 1991 reissue of Queen II and was presented in the style of its BBC counterpart; what's most interesting about the remix is the addition of wah-wah guitar in the intro, along with other guitar effects, plus the splendid use of a slide guitar during the solo.

Bizarrely, the title was used for a Nintendo 64 video game in 1997; titled Ogre Battle 64: Person Of Lordly Caliber, a follow-up was planned to be called Ogre Battle 2: The March Of The Black Queen.

OLD FRIENDS (Taylor)
• Album (Roger): Happiness? • B-side (Roger): 11/94 [32]

Featuring the only full-band performance on Happiness?, Roger's 'Old Friends', like the rest of the album, is dedicated to Freddie. With poignant lyrics written specifically for his friend, 'Old Friends' glides along at a mid-tempo pace, with programmed conga drums providing most of the rhythm. The song even features a Brian May-type solo courtesy of Jason Falloon, though it wouldn't be difficult to imagine Brian providing his own take on the song. A perfect counterpart to Brian's numerous tributes to Freddie, the song touchingly concludes with "The best thing I can say after all this time/You were a real friend of mine."

The song was rumored to have been chosen as Roger's solo vocal performance for the 1992 Concert For Life, but was cut, along with rendition of 'A Kind Of Magic', due to timing constraints. Regardless, the song was performed exclusively on Roger's 1994 and 1995 Happiness? tour. A live version appeared on the 12" version of 'Happiness?', recorded at Shepherd's Bush in London, but the charm and magic of the song is best experienced with the studio rendition.

OLD MEN (LAY DOWN) *(Taylor)*
• Album (The Cross): *MBADTK*

Opening with a nearly two-minute keyboard introduction, Roger's epic 'Old Men (Lay Down)' is one of the highlights on *Mad: Bad: And Dangerous To Know* and certainly packs a punch. While the title may sound like a poke at the older generation, the lyrics target politicians and their misuse of power, as well as the senselessness of war. Roger lampoons the dusty old men, calling into question their fashion sense, closed-mindedness and even their hygiene. The lyrics are juvenile at times, though the line "They own newspapers/And they own me" is chilling; unsurprising, however, given that Roger would write a similar diatribe the following year in 'Dear Mr Murdoch'. The power of the song, however, comes not from the lyrics but from the instrumental performance. Set to a terse backing, the guitar and bass take a back seat as the drums gallop like a marching crowd, coming to an abrupt conclusion mid-beat. That Roger was able to keep a song of this quality for his solo project only speaks of the calibre of the material he was submitting to Queen at the time.

OLYMPIC THEME

In 1988, both Roger and Brian were individually approached by Thames Television, each of them being asked to compose the theme music for the company's coverage of the Olympic Games. Roger's track, which lasts four minutes and features John Deacon on bass, is the stronger of the two compositions, sounding like a cross between 'Killing Time' and 'Vultan's Theme', with driving drums, triumphant timpanis, and a savage synthesizer motif.

Brian's composition is more well-known and was leaked recently, with keyboards and drums (surprisingly) dominating as the guitar takes a back seat. Both would have been appropriate, but Thames Television ultimately went with a theme composed by Eric Clapton, leaving Roger's and Brian's efforts to languish unreleased.

ON MY WAY UP *(May)*
• Album (Brian): *World*

An enjoyable acoustic rocker released on *Another World* in June 1998, 'On My Way Up' was originally recorded in 1994 for the second season of *Frank Stubbs Promotes* (see the entry for 'Business'), a programme shown on ITV and starring Timothy Spall. When asked by the producers if he would provide the themes for the show, Brian responded with both 'Business' (then titled 'Hard Business') in the first season and 'On My Way Up' in the second. At the time, these were short clips of the songs, but Brian had also recorded full versions since he no doubt felt they were good enough for future use.

The songs were given a final mix in 1997 and ultimately issued on *Another World*. 'On My Way Up' is optimistic, though fairly uncharacteristic of Brian. Judging from his explanation, however, he found parallels between Frank Stubbs and himself: "The central character of this song is someone who is basically a loser, you know, but he has total belief, and a kind of insane optimism, and he's going somewhere. 'Man, I'm on my way,' and that's what this song is. And again, it became imbued with different things once I got going on the song, so it could be a few other things as well." The instrumental performance is jaunty, with Brian providing all the instruments, including a rare appearance on bass, while the drums are merely programmed.

The song was included on Brian's 1998 Another World tour, and was released as a Holland-only single in June 1998. A live version was included on the Japanese-only mini-album, *Red Special*.

ONE MORE TRAIN

This song's authorship is unknown, but it's likely an original number from Wreckage, and was performed on 31 October 1969 at Ealing College Of Art.

ONE NIGHT STAND! *(Taylor)*
• Download (Roger): 9/98 • Album (Roger): *Earth*

Upon the release of *Electric Fire* in September 1998, a campaign ran on Roger's official website: listeners who entered the final words heard on the album would get a special Internet-only download. The resulting song, 'One Night Stand', was an out-take from the *Electric Fire* sessions and chugs along with a heavy emphasis on the guitars and bass. The lyrics, those which can be deciphered, deviate little from "I wanna one-night stand". Individual tracks of the song were also made available on Queen's official website, with a competition guaranteed to whet the appetites of aspiring bedroom sound engineers: fans who submitted alternate mixes of the song got the chance to meet Roger and have his or her submission professionally mixed in his home studio. Unfortunately for those involved, the competition came and went without a winner, either indicating Roger's ambivalence toward it, or nobody submitted a good enough mix.

Roger obviously favored the song, and, in a neat bit of synchronicity, used a new recording as the opening track on *Fun On Earth* – much like Queen had closed *Queen II*, and then opened *Sheer Heart Attack*, with a snippet of 'I Do Like To Be Beside The Seaside', *Electric Fire* closes with Roger shouting "One night stand!", and his very next solo album opens with it. The re-recording updates the familiar recording with live drums, a newly-written first verse ("Politicians wanna be in the palace / Priests wanna be in the choir / Just got one simple need / My heart's desire"), and a double-time outro, but still retains all the grit of the original.

ONE RAINY WISH *(Hendrix)*
• Compilation (Brian): *In From The Storm* • Album (Brian): *World*

Jimi Hendrix had long been a source of inspiration to both Freddie and Brian. In Freddie's case, it was the guitarist's experimentation in stereo that opened the vocalist's eyes to production methods and taking full advantage of the studio, while Brian admired him as a guitarist and lyricist. In 1994, he was asked if he wanted to contribute a track to a Hendrix tribute album arranged by the late guitarist's former producer, Eddie Kramer; Brian agreed and chose a rather unorthodox song, 'One Rainy Wish', originally from Hendrix's 1967 album *Axis: Bold As Love*.

"Somebody asked me to do a tribute to Hendrix," Brian explained in a contemporary interview for *Another World*, "and I think they asked me to do something like 'Burning The Midnight Lamp' or something, and I thought, 'Oh please – how can I possibly do it when it's been done perfectly by the master?' So I said, 'Can I choose my own track?' and they said okay. So I chose 'One Rainy Wish' because I think it was done really quickly by Jimi Hendrix – it's something he put down in ten minutes, and the lyric, I think, is genuinely a dream. That's the way I hear it. I've written stuff from dreams before, and I think Hendrix had this dream. And you know it sounds like 'golden rose'? Everybody thinks it's a golden rose, like a rose made of gold, but there's a little scrap of paper which is in one of the Hendrix biographies, where he's

written down his dream, and he says, 'Gold and rose, the colour of the dream I had'.

"So I thought, 'That's what it's about,' you know, it's about these colours, and it always sends shivers up my spine, 'cos it's so real – it's like he drifts off into his dream, so I wanted to recreate that, and make it a bit more spacey, in the modern way you can do, with production. So I just really enjoyed doing it, and it's a big challenge doing a Hendrix song. Me and Freddie used to listen to Hendrix albums, and sort of go round to the speaker here, and say 'Well, a piece of guitar appears over here, and then it sort of comes over here.' You know, all these little secret things that you don't realize at first. And there'd be a bit of backwards guitar and a backwards vocal and if you played your record backwards it would say something different."

While the result is inspiring and worthy of inclusion on *In From The Storm*, it certainly doesn't capture the magic and innocence of the original. Further remixed for *Another World*, the song sits more comfortably among the other songs, though as a remnant of the abandoned *Heroes* project, it would have been better consigned as a non-album B-side.

ONE VISION *(Queen)*
• A-side: 11/85 [7] • Album: *AKOM* • CD Single: 11/88
• Bonus: *AKOM* • Live: *Magic, Wembley, Budapest*
• Compilation: *Hits2, Classic* • Live (Q+PR): *Ukraine*

After Live Aid, Queen discovered a renewed enthusiasm for the music industry – John later said, "It was the one day I was proud to be involved in the music business; a lot of days you certainly don't feel that!" – and for each other. Their initial plan was to take the remainder of 1985 and all of 1986 off, and possibly come back with a new album and tour in 1987. Instead, after a six-week break, the band reconvened at Musicland Studios in Munich at the beginning of September with the intent of creating their first song since 'Thank God It's Christmas' more than a year before.

"Freddie was on the phone and he wanted to go back into the studio and do some more recording," John explained in 1985. "So in the end we went back into the studio and we actually recorded another single. It was his idea, really, that we could go in and actually write a song together. In fact, I was late getting to the recording sessions because I was on holiday at the time, but it's credited as a Queen composition, but to be honest, I would say it was mainly Roger, Brian and Freddie that did most of the writing for it."

'One Vision' was the result of those sessions, and was a welcome return to form: crunching guitars, idealistic lyrics and a grandiose approach to production and performance. Opening with swirling synths, played by Freddie and Brian, the song also features slowed-down vocals – not heard since the days of 'Bring Back That Leroy Brown' and 'Lazing On A Sunday Afternoon' – saying "God works in mysterious ways" and then just "mysterious ways" (Freddie 'sang' the first line and Brian provided the second) before leading into a catchy guitar riff. The original words were courtesy of Roger, who provided a world-weary look at the state of society in the mid-1980s, with "visions of one sweet union." The lyrics were tweaked by Freddie and Brian, and several of Roger's original lines – including "one God damned religion" and "just one politician" – either didn't scan properly or were deemed too controversial and toned down.

Roger said in a 1986 interview, "The original words were actually about Martin Luther King Jr and now I haven't got a clue what it's about! Somebody said it was about Bob Geldof, but I don't think it is." When asked if he knew the meaning of the original lyrics, he retorted, "No, not any more! Well, they changed my words!" adding, when asked who did the changing, "That rotter Freddie!"

It wasn't the first time that Freddie would step in and take control of a song, nor would it be the last, but the band felt such a collaborative energy that it became a four-way composition instead of a Taylor-only. "I like to capture a song very quickly so that it's fresh and you can work on it afterwards," the vocalist said in 1986. "But I hate trying to write a song, and if it's not coming – 'Oh, come on, let's try this' – it either comes quickly, and then you have it, like the basic skeleton, and then I say, 'Yes, we have a song,' then we can start putting in all the clever bits. But if the song's not happening, I normally say, 'Oh forget it, let's try something else'."

The song featured an interesting programmed drum sequence which would later be extracted for use as the single's B-side, 'Blurred Vision'. Brian mysteriously said, "There's a lot of influences on here: the drum solo on here is just an opportunity to do strange, psychedelic things." Roger elaborated: "It was basically my lyric with the others putting in the odd line. It was a good collaboration on that song."

"Sometimes, people take videos too seriously," Freddie said in 1985. "If I write a song and put it on a video, I don't want to create a very specific image, because you ruin peoples' perception of it. Every time you hear a song, you have your own image of what it's like. Sometimes the best thing to do with a video is to keep it very open; that way, the person who's listening to it doesn't suddenly say, 'My God, he's destroyed the image that I wanted the song to be!'" It was with that in mind that the band did something out of the ordinary. "We made a very rare decision to have documentary cameras in there while we were recording," Brian said of the sessions in 2003, "but the documentary cameras actually ruined the whole thing, because I think everyone was so conscious of them being there – everyone sort of played to the cameras. And when I watch any pieces of that now, I think it's totally false." Roger concurred, saying, "I thought they'd never bloody go away, to be honest."

Rudi Dolezal and Hannes Rossacher, or The Torpedo Twins, were an Austrian producer-director team who had worked on the Austrian television show *Hier und jetzt* in the early 1980s and had met the band while they were on tour in Austria in 1982. Dolezal conducted interviews with Freddie, Roger and Brian (seen on the bonus disc of *On Fire At The Bowl*) and a friendship started; in mid-1985, the Torpedo Twins expressed an interest in creating a documentary about Queen, which would eventually surface two years later as *The Magic Years*. Their first order of business was to film a promotional video for 'One Vision' and they received the band's permission to film the recording sessions, the only time the band were professionally filmed during recording sessions. (Other videos, like 'Somebody To Love', 'Flash', or 'Headlong', were filmed well after the songs had been recorded.)

The video finds the band at work and play in Musicland, stripping away the need for concepts and costumes. However, what does capture the imagination is the 'In The Studio' portion of *The Magic Years* (subsequently released on the *Greatest Video Hits 2* DVD) which shows the genesis of the song, from birth to completion. There are fluffed notes, arguments and general camaraderie (several lines for the song, deleted or not even considered, have been collected onto various bootlegs as 'Fun Vision', including the hilarious improvisation, "One dump, one turd, two tits, John Deacon!"), as well as a fascinating segment of Roger, Brian and Freddie mulling over the lyric to get it just right. The best footage was pulled together to form the promotional video, and several of the out-takes appeared in the 'Extended Vision' cut of the video, featured on the second disc of *Greatest Video Hits 2*. To coincide with the tenth anniversary of the release of 'Bohemian Rhapsody', the introduction featured the iconic pose of the four heads looking moodily at the camera before giving way to the band, ten years on, fading into the first sequence as Roger and John look over at each other, bewildered.

The single was released in November 1985 and would be the band's only single release that year. However, it showed that Live Aid had signalled a commercial rebirth when the single peaked at No. 7 in the UK, though it reached a dismal No. 61 in the US. (Considering the lack of promotion Queen were giving their American releases, it's surprising they still had an audience at all.) Several different versions of the song were released on various formats: the 'Extended Vision' version added an extra 90 seconds of the programmed drum sequence; the single version ran at 4'02, while the full-length version, including a longer intro and outro, clocked in at 5'10. A US promo also surfaced, featuring a 3'46 edit, though this has yet to be officially released on any format. An extended remix, running at 6'23, appeared on 12" versions of the single, and was also featured as an 'extra magical ingredient' on CD versions of A Kind Of Magic.

The accompanying press release for the single, which explained that the song was inspired by Live Aid, was misinterpreted in the press as being a cash-in on the event, which could not have been further from the truth. "I was absolutely devastated when I saw that in the press," Roger lamented shortly afterwards. "It was a terrible mistake and I was really annoyed about it. Some public relations person got hold of the wrong end of the stick. I went absolutely bananas when I saw that."

"We do a lot of stuff for charities," Brian explained, "but 'One Vision' was a way of getting back to what we're doing. And if we didn't run ourselves as a business we wouldn't be around for the next Live Aid. We're not in the full-time business of charity at all. We're in the business of making music, which is a good enough end in itself."

The band were contacted by director Russell Mulcahy shortly before the 'One Vision' sessions with an offer to provide the soundtrack to a film project of his called Highlander. The band agreed and started work on this song, but, strangely, didn't contribute it to Mulcahy's project. Instead, 'One Vision' featured in Sidney J Furie's Top Gun-wannabe Iron Eagle, though the film was a critical and commercial bomb, and the song gained more notice from its accompanying album and tour, where it served as the perfect concert opener for the Magic tour. The song was brought out of

mothballs in June 2008, when Queen + Paul Rodgers used it as a concert opener at the Hyde Park 46664 concert; the song was retained as the opener for the first four dates of the Rock the Cosmos tour, before being dropped in favor of 'Surf's Up . . . School's Out !'. The song returned to the set list full time on the Queen + Adam Lambert tour in 2015, once again serving as the atmospheric show opener.

ONE VOICE (Moody)

• Digital Download: 4/15 • Album (Brian & Kerry): Golden

First recorded by The Wailin' Jennys in 2004, 'One Voice' was covered by Brian and Kerry on Golden Days, and features the guitarist gorgeously backing up Kerry throughout. Another mid-tempo ballad, 'One Voice' is a highlight of Golden Days, and, like 'It's Gonna Be Alright (The Panic Attack Song)', a light of hope in a world turned dark.

ONE YEAR OF LOVE (Deacon)

• Album: AKOM

Rarely had Queen strayed so dangerously near to the sickly-sweet, but they came close with John's sole contribution to A Kind Of Magic, 'One Year Of Love'. Unorthodox, in that the main instruments are the synthesizer and a sappy orchestra (arranged by Lynton Naiff), the song plods along at a slow pace as Freddie disconcertingly screeches a set of lyrics that claim the protagonist will never fall in love again.

Brian rather mordantly described the song in 1986, saying, "There's a song called 'One Year Of Love', which John wrote, and that was written around a different romantic interest. It's about the Highlander as he is in the 20th century when he's just about to fall in love again, even though he said he wouldn't – ha-ha! That's a romantic song, too."

Perhaps the guitarist's caustic remarks stemmed from the lack of any guitar work on the song (the band's only other notable guitar-free tracks being 'Seaside Rendezvous' and 'My Melancholy Blues'). Instead of a guitar solo, John drafted Steve Gregory to deliver a saxophone solo, reminiscent of his own throaty contribution to George Michael's 1984 single 'Careless Whisper'. John would later guest on Gregory's 1994 debut solo album, Bushfire. An early version of the song, recorded 25 January 1986 at Musicland Studios, featured the keyboard-driven backing track, without the orchestra, and, apart from being slightly rearranged, also boasted a simplistic guitar solo, though this was likely performed by John instead of Brian.

A drastically different, and more melancholy, performance of the song appeared in the *Highlander* film, which omitted the schmaltzy background altogether and replaced it with a tasteful piano backing and a more restrained vocal performance from Freddie. As an added bonus, for the *Highlander* commemorative DVD re-release, an extended mix of the song was included, though it's not known whether this mix is an officially commissioned one.

The song was chosen as a single release in October 1986 in European and Australasian countries, with 'Don't Lose Your Head' as the B-side; a video was created by DoRo for the 1992 US video compilation *Classic Queen*, which blended arbitrary clips of the band with more appropriate moments from *Highlander*.

ONLY MAKE BELIEVE (*Twitty/Nance*)
• CD single (Brian): 9/98

Conway Twitty's original version of 'It's Only Make Believe' was released in November 1958 and reached No. 1 in the charts, thus making it a perfect contender for Brian's *Heroes* project (for more information, see the entry for *Another World* in Part Two). Although that project was abandoned, the recording was included on the September 1998 single release of 'Why Don't We Try Again'. With a powerful lead vocal and superb background harmonies from Brian, as well as a great instrumental backing from Brian's full band, the song is worth repeated listens, and would have been a great inclusion on *Another World* in lieu of 'Slow Down'.

The song was also included on the Japanese *Red Special* and American *Retro Rock* mini-albums, and was performed live throughout Brian's 1998 Another World tour as the opening number, although he took on a different guise: instead of performing the song as himself, he came out in full 1950s regalia, with a Brylcreemed wig and garish sideburns, as T E Conway, Conway Twitty's 'cousin'.

OTRO LUGAR: *see* ANOTHER WORLD

OUR LITTLE RENDEZVOUS (*Berry*)

This rarely covered Chuck Berry song was performed live by 1984.

OVERTURE PICCANTE (*Mercury/Moran*)
• Album (Freddie): *Barcelona* • B-side (Freddie): 1/89 [95]

Closing *Barcelona* in a glorious manner, 'Overture Piccante' is a six-minute recap of the album, with segments from 'Barcelona', 'Guide Me Home', 'The Fallen Priest', 'La Japonaise', 'The Golden Boy', and 'When This Tired Old Body Wants To Sing' mixed together to create a unique song. (That latter title, with a fast piano backing and chanted vocals of "Sing it, sing it", remained a mystery until its release on *The Solo Collection* in 2000.) Though it would have been more appropriate to have ended with the delicate 'How Can I Go On', only seven usable tracks were recorded during the sessions, so 'Overture Piccante' was created to boost the running time of the album to just over 40 minutes.

PAIN IS SO CLOSE TO PLEASURE (*Mercury/Deacon*)
• Album: *AKOM*

'Pain Is So Close To Pleasure', the obligatory funk-disco amalgamation that graced every Queen album since *News Of The World*, is a delightful collaboration between John and Freddie that, oddly, wasn't destined for the *Highlander* film. Written as an upbeat cousin of 'Cool Cat', the song features an astounding bass line, a soaring guitar solo, and absolutely soulful falsetto vocals from Freddie. "That's really sort of a Motown sounding track," Brian explained in a 1986 radio interview, "very unusual for us."

Initially written by John, the song features him not only on bass, but rhythm guitar, electric piano, and drum programming. According to Peter Freestone, Freddie's contributions in arranging the song were so significant that John insisted that he be given co-credit, marking the third official collaboration between the two.

In keeping with Capitol's arbitrary singles selections from *A Kind Of Magic* (the only single from that album that was similar between EMI and Capitol was the title track), 'Pain Is So Close To Pleasure' was issued as the final US single selection from the album in August 1986. To its credit, the record company issued a superior single mix (remixed by Mack after the conclusion of the Magic tour) with snappier production and additional programmed drums which were absent from the album version. The extended remix, present on 12" versions of the single, brought the running time to nearly seven minutes. Housed in perhaps one of Queen's finest single sleeve covers,

'Pain Is So Close To Pleasure' failed to chart in the US, though it peaked at No. 26 in the Dutch charts, hence its inclusion on *The Singles Collection – Volume 3* in 2010.

PARISIENNE WALKWAYS *(Lynott/Moore)*
• Album (Brian & Kerry): *Golden*

Released as a single by former Thin Lizzy guitarist Gary Moore, 'Parisienne Walkways' reached No. 8 in the UK charts in 1979, and was a favorite of Brian's, having added it to his *Air Guitar Compilation* in November 2016. On *Golden Days*, the song is Brian's requisite showcase for The Red Special, with Kerry appearing only infrequently, answering Brian's licks beautifully.

PARTY *(Queen)*
• Album: *Miracle*

This playful track, awash in programmed drums and synthesizers, served as the all-important opener for Queen's first album in three years. Inspired by Freddie's extravagant parties, the song is nothing if not energetic, with plenty of screaming guitars and a committed vocal from Freddie, but the parts don't add up to the whole, resulting in an uninspired start to *The Miracle*.

PASSION FOR TRASH *(Macrae)*
• Album (The Cross): *MBADTK*

Joshua J Macrae's first song written for The Cross, 'Passion For Trash' is a surprisingly good rock song, with the best moments within the first few seconds when the guitars mesh with the drums and bass. Yet another song about sex, this time the dirty, trashy kind, the song is short and sweet, with a well-used stop-and-go rhythm that showcases Roger's best rocker voice. The keyboards are mixed to the background here until the climax, and the guitar solo is inspired, contributing to what is an overall strong composition. An early version was recorded in December 1989 at Jam Studios, and features its author on lead vocals. This version was later released in 2013 on Roger's nearly all-encompassing box set, *The Lot*.

PEACHES: *see* NOW I'M HERE

PENETRATION GURU *(Moss)*
• Album (The Cross): *MBADTK*

A punkish song written by Clayton Moss and taken at a breakneck pace, 'Penetration Guru' is, as its title suggests, a thinly veiled double entendre relating to the joys of sex; it may also be the first song to ever use the word 'bandaloop'. This song is a disappointment considering that it came from the same person who wrote 'Better Things', but the guitars and tempo help reaffirm the fact that The Cross, despite the occasional set of dumb lyrics, were just a really good, old-fashioned rock band.

PEOPLE ON STREETS *(Taylor)*
• B-side (Roger): 9/98 [45] • Album (Roger): *Electric*

Not to be confused with the first version of 'Under Pressure' before David Bowie became involved, 'People On Streets' is one of the few songs on the *Electric Fire* album performed almost exclusively by Roger, who contributes drums, bass and keyboards (along with Jonathan Perkins on the latter); only Jason Falloon contributes the occasional guitar lick. The song features a mysterious vocal performance from 'Arty' (a phonetic spelling of RT, Roger's initials, which he would return to in 2006 on the collaborative Felix + Arty single 'Woman You're So Beautiful (But Still A Pain In The Ass)'), and is a slight misstep on an otherwise faultless album. The lyrics, surprisingly, aren't about the downside, the faux-concern of celebrities (and, yes, politicians) for the poverty-stricken, but instead feature Roger imploring those who weild that kind of power to actually do something about it and fix it.

A 'mashed' version was included on the 'Pressure On' single as well as the Japanese CD version of *Electric Fire*, with some of the lyrics replaced by an anonymous rapper and with a darker musical approach. Not surprisingly, the song wasn't a mainstay in the set list, and was only performed a few times on Roger's 1999 Electric Fire tour before being dropped.

PHONE *(May)*
• Soundtrack (Brian): *Furia*

This is a short, atmospheric keyboard piece, with the main theme performed by flute and doubled by keyboards.

PLAY THE GAME (Mercury)

• A-side: 5/80 [14] • Album: *Game* • Live: *On Fire, Montreal*

By the time *The Game* was released, Freddie's songs had started to focus mainly on the pursuit of love and happiness, and most of his lyrics took a more literal approach. The lead-off track from Queen's eighth studio album, 'Play The Game' is a straightforward plea, wearied by lust and mindless sex, for love and romance. "I don't really sympathize with [the] lyrics," Roger said in 1980. "It was suggested that we call the album *Play The Game*, and I don't like the idea of that; basically, that means, in English, let's go along with the Establishment. I don't particularly sympathize with that view."

Roger appeared to have misinterpreted the song's meaning; according to Peter "Phoebe" Freestone, Freddie's personal assistant, the song was written about Freddie's then-lover Tony Bastin, who wasn't following Freddie's arbitrary rules of love at the time, and was summarily given a gift of a Rolex watch – the singer's "going away present" for lovers. Constructed as a languid piano ballad, written in the same vein as earlier tracks like 'Jealousy' and 'You Take My Breath Away', 'Play The Game' is brought to extraordinary heights by Brian's solo, and Freddie's piano is excellent. The problem is the presence of a synthesizer, which creates a sheet of noise instead of enhancing the textures, achieving what Brian could have easily done instead and with better results. However, the band was determined to evolve, and instead of using the synthesizer as an atmospheric addition (as on 'Sail Away Sweet Sister' and 'Save Me'), on 'Play The Game' it's just there to be there. In 2014, a slightly edited version was released on the *Queen Forever* compilation, which lopped off the introductory synthetic swoops, presenting it more in the style as it was when performed live.

The Official International Fan Club spring 1980 magazine reported that an alternate version was recorded: "Staying at the same hotel [as Queen] in Germany were Andy Gibb and Leif [Garrett] and so the boys invited them to visit the studio during the recording. The band were putting the finishing touches to a backing track when Freddie insisted that Andy Gibb sing with them. The track, as yet untitled, is one of Freddie's compositions and he was very impressed with Andy's voice and was heard to remark how good it was." Gibb, the youngest brother of the brothers Gibb (who formed the Bee Gees in 1958), was at that time enjoying his status as a teenage heart-throb and solo artist. This recording has been denied by those "in the know", but this party line has been thrown about before with other songs, so time will only tell whether or not this actually, definitively exists.

Released as the third single from *The Game* in May 1980, the song, backed with Roger's non-album 'A Human Body', peaked at a respectable No. 14 in the UK, but stumbled to a dismal No. 42 in the US. The music video, shot at Trillian Studios and directed by Brian Grant, implements green screen technology (footage of roaring fires and zooming stars play behind the mostly stoic band) to liven up what is an otherwise straightforward performance video. Much like the synthesizer that is so prevalent in the song, this technology might have been groundbreaking at the time, but it hasn't aged well at all, and remains an unimpressive addition to the band's catalog of music videos. The highlight of the video is an amusing exchange between Freddie and Brian, where the former snatches the latter's guitar – *not* The Red Special, as Brian refused his precious instrument to be subjected to such abuse, but a cheap Fender Stratocaster knock-off – and runs away with it, only to toss it back to the guitarist in time for his solo.

The song translated better to the live setting, where it was a mainstay in the set between 1980 and 1982 (the song was also rehearsed for the 1984 Queen Works! tour, but didn't make it into the set list). Because the band wouldn't incorporate synthesizers into their live performances until later in 1980, with the release of the *Flash Gordon* soundtrack, Brian was taken to task to fill out the sound, which he did with aplomb. An especially spirited live version was released on *Queen Rock Montreal*, while a rendition with Morgan Fisher assisting on synthesizers was released on *Queen On Fire: Live At The Bowl*.

The song was brought out of mothballs for Queen + Adam Lambert's spring/summer 2016 festival tour throughout Europe, serving as an introduction to 'Killer Queen', and again as a full performance on the 2018 summer tour.

POLAR BEAR (May)

• Compilation (Smile): *Ghost Of A Smile*

Written by Brian in 1968, 'Polar Bear' is a sublime ballad, an unorthodox genre for an aspiring three-piece rock band to write. The lyric compares a forgotten man to a stuffed polar bear in a store window, witnessing the world going by in front of his helpless eyes, declaring of a lovely girl that "I see her as I'd see a star / Love her from where you are." Featuring an especially beautiful acoustic guitar solo, the highlight of the song is the delicate harmonies of Brian, Roger and Tim Staffell. Recorded in September 1969 at De Lane Lea Studios and produced by Fritz Freyer, the song was later issued on *Gettin' Smile* in 1982 and *Ghost Of A Smile* in 1998. "Brian wrote 'Polar Bear' and sings lead," Tim remembered. "It was a gentle song about … a polar bear! It was a bit out of character, I suppose. Although, it was in that sense that Smile wanted to be dynamic, meaning we could be sensitive when called upon."

'Polar Bear' was recorded by Queen during sessions for the debut album in 1972. Though rumors circulated that it was Barry Mitchell on bass, which would fix the recording date at 1970, a reliable collector has revealed recently that no material was recorded with Mitchell, and that the song actually features John Deacon. More definitively, Mitchell himself, in an impromptu online Q&A on noted fan site queenzone.com, confirmed both points.

The technical quality of the song would lead the listener to believe that the performance is little more than a demo, but Freddie's vocal delivery is clearly the highlight. Because the song is written in a higher register, the vocalist is forced into a falsetto for the chorus, which is executed beautifully. While it's easy to see why 'Polar Bear' wasn't included on the first album – it was far too delicate and downbeat among the other rock-oriented tracks, and 'The Night Comes Down' filled that niche perfectly – it still deserves to be heard.

POWER TO LOVE (*Macrae/Noone/Moss*)
• Album (The Cross): *MBADTK* • A-side (The Cross): 4/90 [85] • Live (The Cross): *Bootleg, Germany*

The songwriting on *Mad: Bad: And Dangerous To Know* was surprisingly strong, and while most fans argue that *Blue Rock* is The Cross' strongest album released, their sophomore effort had its moments, too. Witness 'Power To Love', which at first listen is more typical of the mid-1980s power metal ballads, but is actually a strong composition with obvious roots in Roger's work with Queen. Taken at a heavy tempo, dominated mostly by drums and root notes on the guitar, the focus is on Roger's voice, with occasional embellishments on slide guitar from Clayton Moss.

Not surprisingly, considering all the strong material

on the album, 'Power To Love' was chosen as the first (and only) UK single from the album. Backed by Joshua J Macrae's 'Passion For Trash', the single performed abysmally, peaking at No. 85, thus becoming the proverbial final nail in the coffin of The Cross' homegrown success. From here on, all their singles (and their final album) would be continental-exclusive, becoming a minor sensation in Germany. This would also mark the first time that a single by The Cross didn't feature at least a collaboration credit for Roger.

A video directed by the Torpedo Twins was prepared for the single and is one of their finest and most elaborate. Imagine all the raunch of 'Body Language' with the pomp and circumstance of 'It's A Hard Life': the band perform on stage in full gear (with Roger hamming it up for the cameras, more interested in mugging than in focusing on his mimed guitar parts), completely oblivious to the Renaissance debauchery taking place above them as dozens of well-endowed women and bewigged men engage in a good old-fashioned orgy. As with any good orgy, food is also served, and string cheese and grapes are held and rubbed suggestively; the power to love, indeed.

PRESSURE ON (*Taylor*)
• A-side (Roger): 9/98 [45] • Album (Roger): *Electric*

Kicking off *Electric Fire*, Roger's fourth proper solo album, with an infectious groove, 'Pressure On' may arguably be his finest single choice in years. Expanding on the moods previously explored on *Happiness?*, the song is "just sort of the typical day-to-day pressures which everybody sort of has," said Roger, adding dryly that it was 'Under Pressure Mark II', though that downplays its effectiveness as a song by comparing it to a more popular one.

While it's true that the lyrics deal with everyday pressures, Roger has honed his songwriting abilities and not only comes up with some memorable lines ("Analysts here, therapists there / You ain't getting me sitting in your chair") but avoids the cringe-inducing couplets that hamper some of his other major works.

'Pressure On' features a lovely melody, with a repetitive guitar motif as Roger delivers an understated vocal performance, using his natural voice instead of shouting or screeching in the rock'n'roll mode he'd used for most of his career. The band he assembled for the sessions – Keith Prior on drums, Jason Falloon on guitars, Steve Barnacle on bass, Mike Crossley on keyboards and the underused Treana Morris on backing vocals – is tight and on good form, leaving Roger to contribute only vocals, one of the rare instances when he doesn't perform anything instrumental on one of his own tracks.

Chosen as the first single from *Electric Fire* in September 1998, the single mix of 'Pressure On', with a 'mashed' version of 'People On Streets' and a 'Dub Sangria' mix of 'Tonight' on one disc, and 'Dear Mr Murdoch' and the non-album 'Keep A-Knockin'' on a second disc, peaked at only No. 45 in the UK, despite a fair amount of promotion and a prominent position in the live setting.

PRINCES OF THE UNIVERSE *(Mercury)*
• Album: *AKOM*

It had been quite some time since Freddie had written a hard rock song, instead preferring to dabble in funk and requisite piano-based ballads, but 'Princes Of The Universe' would prove to be one of the last he would write in his lifetime; but what a track to go out on.

When viewed in context with the *Highlander* movie (which the song was written for, being promoted to the status of main theme because of its anthemic sound), 'Princes Of The Universe' is a celebration of immortality and of defending one's honor to the death. In conjunction with Queen's history, it's a cry of defiance, and it wouldn't be far-fetched to suggest that Freddie was subconsciously insinuating that the band were the princes. Indeed, 1986 was a banner year for the band: they would prove that, for the brief two months they were on the road, they could still sell out packed stadia across Europe and the UK, and it's not surprising that, with all the extra exposure that Live Aid, *Highlander* and 'A Kind Of Magic' – both single and album – afforded them, they were regarded as the hottest ticket of the year.

It's understandable that Freddie was gloating, especially if it meant that more songs would be written and recorded in this style. Unfortunately, hard rock would be the exception rather than the rule: after this, the band rarely ventured down this path again, revisiting it only occasionally on the next two albums. However, a lot is crammed into the song and several phases of Queen's career are revisited; the heavy drum beat and vocal harmonies of 'Fat Bottomed Girls' forms the basis of the song, with a guitar riff that sounds like a variant of the earlier album track 'Gimme The Prize (Kurgan's Theme)'. This is no ordinary rock song – 'Princes Of The Universe' twists and turns through many tricky passages

and time signatures similar to 'Bicycle Race', with the pomp and bombast turned up to 11.

It was perhaps for this reason that the song was not aired in the live setting, which may be one of Queen's most erroneous omissions, but, when viewed in this light, is entirely understandable. Perhaps because it was released as a single only in America and Japan, the song remains virtually unknown, although a video was filmed in New York in April 1986, which shows the band on the set of *Highlander* amid explosions, wind machines, and a walk-on cameo from Christophe "Connor MacLeod" Lambert. This would be one of the few instances when any other country besides Britain received a promotional video for a single, but unfortunately it did little to boost sales. 'Princes Of The Universe' failed to chart in America, but enjoyed a new lease of life when it was used as the theme song for the long-running television adaptation of *Highlander*.

PROCESSION *(May)*
• Album: *Queen2* • Live: *Rainbow* • Compilation: *On Air*

Opening *Queen II* in a dirge-like manner, Brian's guitar extraordinaire 'Procession' is an exquisite orchestration, with the Red Special seamlessly leading into the opening arpeggios of 'Father To Son'.

Brian explained in 1998, "That's this Deakey amp. It's a little one-watt amp that John Deacon built and brought into the studio one day. I had done 'Procession' with [Vox] AC30s and it sounded just a little bit too smooth. I wanted it to sound more violin-like and orchestral. So I double-tracked some of the layers using that little amp. Incredible. I've used it ever since on anything where there's a real orchestral-type sound. And depending where you put the microphone in front of the amp, you can really tune the sound. It's very directional. It's a germanium transistor amp, which is a transformer coupled – unlike things these days; that isn't really done any more – with silicon transistors. There's this guy Dave Peters, who is one of the designers of the AC30 and a real expert on valve electronics and the early days of transistors. I'm working with him trying to reproduce the Deakey amp. Maybe we'll put it on the market. I have to talk to John about it, as it happens. Because John made the thing. And he's very kindly allowed me to use it ever since. It's pretty magical."

'Procession' was played over the PA system as the opening number every night between September 1973 and May 1975 (reprised for the band's Earl's Court Arena concerts in June 1977), serving as a perfect, atmospheric introduction to Queen's shows. Thirty-seven years later, the song resurfaced as the introductory number for the Queen + Adam Lambert tour.

THE PROPHET'S SONG (May)

• Album: *Opera*

While Freddie was spending most of his time laboring over 'Bohemian Rhapsody', taking the band into uncharted waters, Brian was pouring all his energy into 'The Prophet's Song' (originally titled 'People Of The Earth' and divided into four parts), certainly Queen's most epic number to date and about as adventurous as Freddie's excursion into opera. Starting off the second side of *A Night At The Opera* in an ominous fashion, a gust of wind washes across the speakers, revealing the faint strains of a toy koto, an instrument which Brian had picked up during the band's tour of Japan in April 1975. Eventually giving way to a full band performance, 'The Prophet's Song' is a raging rocker which starts and ends slowly but, somewhere in the middle, builds to proportions far greater than anything the band had explored prior.

Lyrically, the song contains slightly religious overtones, though not overbearingly so (and certainly not as much as Freddie's early compositions). Brian paints an atmospheric picture of a prophet in a dream "on a moonlight stair", predicting the end of the world to shocked listeners "summoned by [their] own hand." The seer concludes by preaching that "love is still the answer", though Brian revealed that the song was not meant to give answers, only ask questions.

In an uncharacteristic move, he explained the song fairly in-depth, justifiably proud of what may be his finest set of lyrics: "I had a dream about what seemed like revenge on people, and I couldn't really work out in the dream what it was that people had done wrong. It was something like a flood. Things had gone much too far and, as a kind of reparation, the whole thing had to start again. In the dream, people were walking on the streets trying to touch each other's hands, desperate to try to make some sign that they were caring about other people. I felt that the trouble must be – and this is one of my obsessions, anyway – that people don't make enough contact with each other.

"A feeling that runs through a lot of the songs I write is, that if there is a direction to mankind, it ought to be a coming together, and at the moment, it doesn't seem to be happening very well. I worry about it a lot. I worry about not doing anything about it. Things seem to be getting worse. But I wasn't trying to preach in the song at all. I was just trying to put across the questions which are in my mind, rather than the answers, which I don't believe I have. The only answer I can see is to be aware of things like that and to sort of try to put yourself to rights. There is an overseer in the song, though, whose cry to the multitudes is to 'listen to the warning of the seer'. In the song is this guy who also appeared in the dream. I don't really know whether he was a prophet or an impostor, but anyway, he's standing up there and saying, 'Look, you've got to mend your ways.' I still don't know whether he's the man who thinks he's sent from God or whether he isn't."

Freddie was equally vocal about the track, telling Kenny Everett shortly before *A Night At The Opera*'s release, "Brian has an outrageous mammoth epic track which is one of our heaviest numbers to date. He's got his guitar extravaganza on it. You see, Brian has acquired a new guitar specially built so he can almost make it speak. It will *talk* on this track." Funny that Freddie failed to mention his two and a half minute vocal showcase inserted in the middle of the song. Consisting mainly of "la la" overdubbed numerous times, the sequence is a relentless yet fascinating interplay in stereo and studio techniques, which can only fully be appreciated on the 2002 DVD-A release of *A Night At The Opera*. Freddie's voice bounces from speaker to speaker, creating a dizzying yet breathtaking effect that is still impressive over 30 years on.

Unfortunately, 'The Prophet's Song' has been unfairly overshadowed by 'Bohemian Rhapsody'. Brian's composition is arguably the superior cut, which may be blasphemy to some, but 'The Prophet's Song' deserves accolades for pushing the boundaries that Queen had been tiptoeing around on their first three albums. There's no doubt that, had 'Bohemian Rhapsody' not been written, 'The Prophet's Song' would be considered Queen's biggest groundbreaker. Unusually, Brian later mentioned that 'The Prophet's Song' was briefly mooted as the single release instead of 'Bohemian Rhapsody', but considering EMI baulked at a six-minute cod-opera track being released without any editing, it's difficult to imagine them okaying the release of this eight-minute epic without considerable editing.

The song was performed live between 1975 and 1978, usually in its own right, until 1977, when the vocal segment was interpolated into 'White Man'. Once Queen started to steer their music away from progressive rock, 'The Prophet's Song' was dropped from the set list, never to return.

PSYCHO LEGS: *see*
'DEATH ON TWO LEGS (DEDICATED TO......'

PURSUIT *(May)*
• Soundtrack (Brian): *Furia*

The first upbeat original piece of music on the *Furia* soundtrack, 'Pursuit' is a lengthy composition, running just over three minutes, and consists mostly of programmed drums and keyboard blasts, ending with the sound of a gunshot and disposed shell.

PUT IT ALL DOWN TO LOVE *(Edney)*
• Album (The Cross): *Blue* • German CD single (The Cross): 10/91

Written by Spike Edney, 'Put It All Down To Love' is an energetic rocker from *Blue Rock*, one of three tracks the keyboardist would submit for the album. With a snarling guitar line and strangely Queen-like vocal harmonies, the song is lyrically inconsequential; its strength lies in the musical performance, unsurprisingly strong, especially by *Blue Rock* standards. The song was released as part of the 'Life Changes' CD single in a slightly edited form, with the concluding guitar solo from the previous track, 'Millionaire', serving as the introduction to 'Put It All Down To Love'.

PUT OUT THE FIRE *(May)*
• Album: *Space*

Politically, Queen weren't outspoken, satisfied with spreading the message of love, peace and understanding instead of preaching to the masses. However, there were times when a band member felt so moved by an event that he would channel his feelings into a song, and the results were generally mixed. 'Put Out The Fire' was Brian's indirect tribute to John Lennon, who had been slain by a deranged 'fan' on 8 December 1980.

The song is one of the few rock tracks presented on *Hot Space*, opening up the second side with a deliberately crunchy guitar riff and a powerful vocal from Freddie. The guitar solo was recorded one drunken night in Munich; Brian always intended to re-record it, but maintained it sounded good enough on its own account, complementing the anger and rage in the lyrics. "That wasn't a first take," Brian told *On The Record* in 1983. "I had done a lot of solos for that – hated every one of them. And then we came back from a club where we used to go to have some drinks. I think

I was well on the way – you know, we were all plucked out and slightly inebriated – and we had a ridiculous echo effect which Mack was putting back through the cans. I said, 'That sounds unbelievable! I want to put it on every track.' He said, 'Okay, try 'Put Out The Fire'.' So we put it on the machine, and I just played through it. That was what we used. It was inspiring, like these huge stereo echo sounds coming from all over the place. I could hardly hear what I was doing, but it was sounding so good and I was so drunk. To be honest, I don't think it's that good a solo. It's got a sort of plodding thing going behind it; I never felt totally happy with it."

Released as the B-side of the US issue of 'Calling All Girls' in July 1982, the song was performed during the Rock 'n' America and Hot Space Japanese tours as an interpolation during 'Now I'm Here', leading into 'Dragon Attack'. 'Put Out The Fire' was never performed in its entirety, and was dropped from the set list by the time of the 1984 Queen Works! tours, though it had been rehearsed.

QUALITY STREET *(Taylor)*
• Album (Roger): *Earth*

Most of the songs on *Fun On Earth* deal with Roger's newfound love, Sarina; apart from the energetic blasts of 'One Night Stand!' and 'I Am The Drummer (In A Rock n' Roll Band)', or the sociopolitical posturing of 'The Unblinking Eye (Everything Is Broken)' and 'Say It's Not True', the album is rife with love songs and messages to Sarina, promising a better life in the twilight of his age. 'Quality Street' continues with the laidback, down-to-earth mission statement found elsewhere on *Fun On Earth*, with Roger once again delivering the words in a breathy sigh, though he becomes more impassioned as the song goes on, as the tempo picks up pace and the performance becomes more aggressive.

QUEEN TALKS
• CD Single: 10/91 [16]

A curious inclusion in a database of Queen songs is this short extract from an interview, running less than two minutes and featuring a multitude of common snippets from interviews conducted through the years. Released on the 12" and CD single versions of 'The Show Must Go On' in October 1991, 'Queen Talks' is utterly pointless.

QUE SERA, SERA: *see*
EXTRACTS FROM GARDEN LODGE

RACHMANINOV'S REVENGE: *see*
THE FALLEN PRIEST

RACING IN THE STREET *(Springsteen)*
• Album (Roger): *Frontier*

Unusually for Roger, *Strange Frontier* contained two cover songs: an electronic update of Bob Dylan's 'Masters Of War' and a strong rendition of Bruce Springsteen's 1978 track 'Racing In The Street'. "I've always loved that song," Roger told *Modern Drummer* in 1984. "I did it kind of mid-tempo, hopefully the way he would have done it if he would have decided to do it mid-tempo. His version, of course, is very slow." Roger's arrangement is reminiscent of The Boss' style, with an uplifting piano melody and ringing acoustic guitar chords (one of the few tracks on the album to feature the instrument so prominently), and Roger delivers the words and sentiments convincingly, but it's out of place among an album rife with threats of nuclear holocaust.

RADIO GA GA *(Taylor)*
• A-side: 1/84 [2] • Album: *Works* • CD Single: 11/88
• Live: *Magic, Wembley, 46664, Budapest*
• Bonus: *Works* • Live (Q+PR): *Return*

It had taken Queen nearly four years to create some new sounds that were not only memorable but also innovative and creative. *Hot Space* had been a misstep, and the band paid dearly for it: the resulting lack of success in the charts reinforced the idea that the world was not ready for disco courtesy of Queen. It was time to rethink their strategy and work on creating something more in their style.

During recording sessions for the follow-up to *Hot Space* in August 1983, which saw the band recording for the first (and only) time in North America – Los Angeles, specifically The Record Plant, the same studio in which Brian had recorded his mini-EP *Star Fleet Project* earlier in the year – a chord sequence came to Roger while he was fooling around with a synthesizer: "The song came after I'd locked myself in a studio for three days with a synthesizer and a drum-machine." By the end of those three days, he had produced a fairly complex demo of what may be Queen's finest single of the 1980s.

'Radio Ga Ga' is a carefully constructed excursion into pop-rock, combining elements of disco and funk without being overbearing about it. With a bubbling synthesizer backing and a cracking drum-machine pattern, the song chugs along at a medium pace as the funky bassline percolates in the background, and is doubled by a synth bass part courtesy of Fred Mandel. As a matter of fact, synthesizers largely dominate the song – no wonder, since Mandel is augmented by Freddie and Roger on keyboards – and Brian's parts are limited to a soaring slide guitar solo before the final chorus.

If that is the song's only downfall, then it's a minor quibble; by 1984, programming and synthesizers had advanced far beyond the primitive squeaks and honks that artists such as Stevie Wonder and Pete Townshend had pioneered back in the 1970s. The band weren't willing to revisit the ill-advised noises on 'Play The Game', nor were they ever again going to feature synthesizers as a main instrument. Keep in mind that many of the hottest bands released synthesizer-dominated albums in 1984: The Cars' *Heartbeat City*, for example, was constructed entirely of programmed instruments.

"I'm an instinctive musician," Roger explained in 1984. "I can play keyboards, guitar and drums, and I can write songs. I have a facility for writing music, but I don't want to know anything particularly technical – like what the chords are called. Even in 'Radio Ga Ga' there are some very difficult chords. I don't know what they're called, but it doesn't matter. I'm a much better guitarist than I am a keyboard player, but now I find melodically it's much easier to write on [a] keyboard. 'Radio Ga Ga' was a completely keyboard-written song. I defy anyone to write that on the guitar because you wouldn't find the chords, they wouldn't come naturally to any guitar player I know."

Lyrically, the song is similar to the 1980 Buggles single 'Video Killed the Radio Star' in addressing the decline of radio as a medium and bemoaning the overnight sensation of video. A bit surprising perhaps, coming from the band who had popularized the advent of music videos with 'Bohemian Rhapsody'. "I was desperate for inspiration!" he told *Sounds* in 1984. "One day the radio came on in our house, and my three-year-old son Felix came out with 'Radio Poo Poo'! I thought that sounded good, so I changed it around a bit and came up with 'Radio Ga Ga'." Originally, the song was titled 'Radio Ka Ka' (it remained this way even during the recording of the track: according to Roger, if you listen carefully to the chorus, the band are actually singing "All we hear is radio ka ka"), but the others were nervous about the reception a song with that title would receive from disc jockeys worldwide and chose the safe way instead. Capitol Records, Queen's new home in North America, was nervous as well; having spent an exorbitant sum on signing Queen, they weren't best pleased that the first record to come from the band was about the downfall of radio. In a telex dated 26 October 1983, Capitol's president Jim Mazza wrote to Jim Beach, "Here are some new lyrical changes for 'Radio Ga Ga'. These are by no means professional lyrics, only ideas, and do in fact change the sentiment of the song to one of a supportive endorsement of radio's future, rather than a prediction of its demise. Pls [sic] understand that the American radio community is extremely concerned over the impact video music is having on their listenership, thus our concern and recommended lyrical changes." The suggested changes, indeed, are far from professional; if what was eventually released was polished up from Mazza's changes, then, intriguingly, what were Roger's original lyrics?

"I liked the title, and I wrote the lyric afterwards," Roger explained in a contemporary interview. "It happened in that order, which is a bit strange. The song is a bit mixed up as far as what I wanted to say. It deals with how important radio used to be, historically speaking, before television, and how important it was to me as a kid. It was the first place I heard rock'n'roll. I used to hear a lot of Doris Day, but a few times each day I'd also hear a Bill Haley record or an Elvis Presley song. Today it seems that video, the visual side of rock'n'roll, has become more important than the music itself – too much so, really. I mean, music is supposed to be an experience for the ears more than the eyes."

"I seem to participate more on John's or Roger's tracks," Freddie said in 1984. "They let me help them and suggest more things. Brian's got his own sort of writing ideas and they are very strong to start with anyway. I don't seem to be able to get into his ideas so much. But in a way that's quite good. I'd rather leave it to him, and it doesn't mean I just stay out of it altogether. I let him sort of do a lot of it. Whereas with John's songs or Roger's songs, I'm sort of getting there at the early stage. They don't mind me sort of tearing it apart and then piecing it back together again. Every way. Sometimes I'll take the whole song over. Like 'Radio Ga Ga'. I just instantly felt that there was something, there was going to be something in there.

You could build that into a really good, strong, saleable commodity. And I think Roger was just thinking about it as just another track. And I just said, 'No, I think it needs...' So I virtually took it over. And he went on a holiday skiing for about a week … and he said 'Okay, you do what you want'."

Roger was adamant that the song become a single, and the others agreed with him. Released as a forerunner to *The Works* in January 1984, 'Radio Ga Ga', backed with the non-album 'I Go Crazy', brought Queen back to the upper strata of the UK charts, and became their first Top Ten hit since 'Under Pressure' in October 1981, ultimately reaching No. 2. An extended remix, clocking in at 6'54, surfaced on the 12" issues of the single, but offered nothing revelatory except for the extension of some of the instrumental and vocal a cappella sections. The US issue, which also featured an edited promo version (chopped from 5'48 to 4'23), came a month later and was also fairly successful, reaching a modest No. 16 in the charts; unfortunately, this made it their last Top 20 single in Freddie's lifetime.

The press weren't enthusiastic about the single. *NME* said, "Displays a lack of substance, intention, cohesion or spirit. Arrogant nonsense, it quite upset my afternoon," while *Record Mirror* was slightly less caustic: "After a long absence, Queen come bouncing back. All we're going to hear from our radios for the next few weeks is 'Radio ga ga, radio goo goo'."

It's ironic that a song criticizing the emphasis placed on music videos should receive one of its own; even more ironic is that it turned out to be Queen's finest video. The year before, Freddie had been approached by Giorgio Moroder, who asked if Freddie would be interested in contributing some music to his restructure of Fritz Lang's *Metropolis*. 'Love Kills' was that song, and when it came time to shoot a video for 'Radio Ga Ga' in November 1983, the band asked Moroder if they could obtain a few clips from the original film to use in their video. They had to go through the German government first, but were ultimately able to purchase the necessary clips.

Filming for the video took place on 23 and 24 November 1983, showing black and white footage of the band flying around in a futuristic car, with scenes of *Metropolis* in the background, while Roger navigates and Freddie sings. (Roger revealed, "I seem to remember that we had a vodka and tonic hidden somewhere in that car," while Brian said, "I don't think we look particularly comfortable in this car – I know I don't, I don't think John does. Roger's got a job to do, driving the thing, so he was lucky, and Freddie had a job to do, and that was singing.") The video then cuts to a view of the band, now in full color, raising their arms in salute as their legions of followers (in actuality, lucky members of the fan club), dressed in suits and bowler hats, imitate their heroes.

"In my mind, this was the best video we were ever responsible for," Brian said in 2003. "It shows the fact that there was a lot of thought put into it before we even opened the coffers to pay for the thing and get going on it. It was great that we were able to lay our hands on this original footage from Fritz Lang's fantastic *Metropolis* movie ... David Mallet filmed this really beautiful period footage, and also some lovely black and white stuff which dovetailed quite well into the original Fritz Lang stuff. And here we have us in a car which is zooming around in the original *Metropolis* landscape ... It always staggers me that some people either don't get it," he continued, "or pretend not to get it: when we get to the part where it's totalitarian and everyone's got their arms in the air, people think that we didn't know that was the case, but obviously this song is about the kind of recognition that things are getting very mechanized and meaningless and people are becoming robots. So obviously, there's a sort of irony to the whole thing which is built in, and people didn't get it, and I'm still shocked! People thought we were really trying to be dictators."

Roger was impressed with the end result, saying, "Beautifully done by David Mallet, one of his best pieces of work, and really one of our best videos, although I must admit that I find the polystyrene car a little comical." He continued, saying, "It was fun: we had three days and it was a monumental effort. A lot of time splicing it together afterwards. Even in those days this was one of our over-the-top ones. I think it worked. Of course, the song was a hit, which was sort of gratifying, especially for me, I suppose, being the writer."

Brian held similar opinions about the video: "One of Mallet's great contributions is – when the chorus comes, you get a handclap. It was repeated electronically on the record, and so it sounds like a double handclap, and Mallet seized upon it and made it a double handclap done by the audience ... I think it became the first great proof of the power of television. The first time we played this to a non-Queen audience at Live Aid, everybody knew what to do at that point. Astonishing, really. It just had to be the power of the video; there was no other way they would have known to put their hands in the air and do this double handclap thing!"

The song became an instant live favorite: first performed in Brussels on 24 August 1984, it remained in the set list until the last Queen performance on 9 August 1986. Queen had also 'performed' the song during two mimed festivals in 1984: the first at the San Remo Festival on 3 February and the second on 12 May at the Montreux Golden Rose Festival, which saw Brian and John both miming along to the synthesizer parts. (Incidentally, they were the only two members not to play synth on the actual recording.) Roger later incorporated it into his solo gigs, including the September 1993 performance at Cowdray Park, and it was performed in most post-Queen events, notably at the Concert For Life on 20 April 1992, with Paul Young on lead vocals. The song was later incorporated into the 2005 Queen + Paul Rodgers tour, with Roger running to the front of the stage to sing the opening verses while a drum-machine played the intro; the subsequent verses would be sung by Paul, while Roger would resume his more familiar place behind the drums. Unsurprisingly, the song was revived for live dates with Queen + Adam Lambert.

RAIN *(Lennon/McCartney)*
• Compilation (Freddie): *Solo Collection*

Originally released as the B-side of The Beatles' 1966 'Paperback Writer' single, 'Rain' was a perennial favorite of Freddie's and was performed regularly by Ibex in the live setting. It remained the only officially released track from the 9 September 1969 show at The Sink Club in Liverpool, appearing in 2000 on *The Solo Collection*; why the other eight tracks from this concert weren't included is anyone's guess, though the official reason was that the quality was too poor. Having listened to the full concert, I can assure you that the quality remains constant throughout, and if they were able to clean up this version for release, the other songs would have been no problem either.

RAIN MUST FALL *(Queen)*
• Album: *Miracle*

Oftentimes, the margins of Queen's albums resulted in some of their more adventurous songs, unfairly neglected by the hit parade but containing just as many delights as the mainstream singles. 'Rain Must Fall' pairs a set of optimistic lyrics and a vaguely Caribbean beat for a satisfying album track; bouncy and peppy in its approach, the mood conjures up a sunny summer's day. Written mostly by John with assistance from Freddie, the song contains many layers of programmed drums (which Roger later ruefully revealed he had to tone back, so as to leave room for other instruments) and a percolating bassline, with a melody borrowed – perhaps unconsciously – by Candi Staton's 1976 single 'Young Hearts Run Free'. Freddie sings a superb vocal, as always, and Brian turns in a scorching guitar solo, and while 'Rain Must Fall' would never be a serious candidate for single release, it's a refreshing breather on an album recorded by a band who knew their singer was running on borrowed time.

REACHING OUT (Hill/Black)
• Live (Q+PR): Return

Recorded by a makeshift band called Rock Therapy in April 1996, 'Reaching Out' was donated to the Nordoff-Robbins Music Therapy Centre, another charity event that Brian involved himself in. The song featured several star contributions, including Charlie Watts (drums), Jeff Beck and Andy Fairweather-Low (guitars), Lulu and Shara Nelson (backing vocals), Sam Brown (keyboards), Pure Strings (orchestrations) and Paul Rodgers on lead vocals.

Produced by Andy Hill, who co-wrote the song with Don Black, and recorded at Comfort's Place Studio in Surrey, the track was released as a single in June 1996 yet failed to chart, despite its strength as a song. It became one of the few recorded musical collaborations between Brian and Paul Rodgers, and was therefore performed as the opening song on the 2005 Queen + Paul Rodgers tour.

RED HOUSE (Hendrix)

Despite the US leg of the 2006 Queen + Paul Rodgers tour boasting only a few surprises (and not being the "rolling set list" that Roger had promised fans), Jimi Hendrix's blues extravaganza 'Red House' was performed live on the final night in Vancouver.

REGGAE: 'BIRD IN HAND' (Perry)
• Soundtrack (Brian): Furia

Written by Lee Perry and performed by The Upsetters, 'Reggae: 'Bird In Hand'' features no involvement whatsoever from Brian, other than the fact that it was included on the Furia soundtrack.

RESPECT (Redding)

Otis Redding's well-known single, best covered by Aretha Franklin, was a surprising choice for 1984 to perform live; not all that surprising was the fact that The Reaction covered it, too.

RESURRECTION (May/Powell/Page)
• Album (Brian): BTTL • A-side (Brian): 6/93 [33]
• Live (Brian): Brixton

In the late 1980s, Cozy Powell was starting to work on a new album, his fourth as a solo artist. The long and prestigious career of this influential drummer started in 1965, when he joined a band called The Sorcerers, though success didn't come until 1971 when he hooked up with the Jeff Beck group, replacing Mickey Waller. The group recorded two albums and promptly folded, with Beck forging his own musical career in jazz-fusion. Powell also went solo, releasing 'Dance With The Devil' as a single in 1973, before joining forces with former Deep Purple guitarist Ritchie Blackmore – thus, Rainbow was born. When that group dissolved, Powell spent most of the 1980s working with such luminaries as Keith Emerson and Greg Lake, Black Sabbath, and Whitesnake.

It was inevitable that, at some point, Cozy and Brian would start working together. The two met in the early 1970s, with Brian often in the audience at Jeff Beck's gigs and Cozy turning up to Queen's concerts. The two became friendly over the years, and developed a musical kinship when Brian would occasionally jam with Black Sabbath. In 1991, after a horse he was riding suffered from a heart attack and collapsed on top of him, shattering his pelvis, Cozy spent six months rehabilitating himself and writing material for a solo album, The Drums Are Back. 'Ride To Win', written by Powell and Jamie Page, was a relentless performance, sounding like the apocalypse with Cozy's thunderous drums. "Brian heard some of [the tracks I wrote], liked what he heard, and said, 'Could I use a couple for my album? We'll rearrange 'em, and I'll write some lyrics,'" Cozy told Rip magazine in 1993. "We ended up working on a couple of those tracks, which then ended up on Back To The Light."

"For me, ['Resurrection'] reminds me of an era that is almost gone from my memory," Brian explained on his website in 2014, "when I was convinced, following the loss of Freddie, that my destiny out there was as some kind of singing guitar hero. I poured a massive amount of energy into the track … inspired by the work of the fabulous Cozy Powell, who had thrown in his support in a massive way, propelling me forward, out of the dark place I'd found myself in after Freddie passed away."

With Brian on guitars, bass and keyboards and Cozy on drums (Don Airey, who had been in Cozy Powell's Hammer in 1974, later laid down additional keyboards), the duo put together an even terser version, as close to heavy metal as Brian would ever get on a solo album. The lyrics feature few references to organized religion, being of a more personal nature: as elsewhere on *Back To The Light*, Brian channels his confusion of life without Freddie into song, cheerleading himself to break through his depression and "rise". The strength of the track is in the instrumentation, and it's essentially a showcase for Cozy. Brian was so impressed with his performance that the track was billed as 'Featuring Cozy Powell', and joined Brian on his 1992/1993 Back To The Light world tour; suitably, 'Resurrection' became a regular in the live set list at the time, allowing Cozy to show off his talents with an extended drum solo. Also featured was the '1812 Overture', performed by Spike Edney on keyboards with accompaniment from Cozy, leading into the concluding, hard rock finale of 'Bohemian Rhapsody'. The song was included in the 1998 set list, with a drum solo performed by Eric Singer, and was performed out of respect for Cozy, who died in a car accident on 5 April 1998, right before the Another World tour was due to start.

'Resurrection' was chosen as the fourth single from *Back To The Light*. A bold move, the song was edited from its lengthy 5'24 running time to a more palatable 4'38, with a five-minute promo edit also appearing, and reached No. 33 in the charts. A promotional video, directed by Eric Zimmermann and shot by Swell Pictures, Inc., was created for the single, and while there's a certain level of cheesiness to it, Brian later recalled the shoot with fondness. "The video is really a separate vision," he recalled. "I collaborated with the H-Gun team, to make a clip which took the track into a different universe … for fun and entertainment, and perhaps to tear myself further away from the real underlying pain which gave birth to the song. Cozy and I spent a day surrounded by chemical bonfires, in a film studio in LA - being hooligans and heroes and having great fun." In 2014, the video was remastered and cleaned up and was uploaded to Brian's personal YouTube account, indicating he was inspired by Roger's nearly all-encompassing box set *The Lot* and was gearing up to release his own retrospective collection. As of this writing (spring 2018), this welcome project has yet to materialize.

REVELATIONS *(Taylor)*
• Album (Roger): *Happiness?* • B-side: 11/17

Sandwiched nicely between 'Happiness?' and 'Touch The Sky', 'Revelations' is an up-tempo rocker, the like of which was mostly absent on *Happiness?*. Starting off with programmed percussion and a funky bass line from Phil Spalding, the song kicks into high gear with some of Roger's most propulsive drumming and aggressive guitar work from Jason Falloon. Lyrically, Roger again sings of the problems affecting the world, and it's at times such as these that one appreciates Freddie's talent for editing the written word. While the lyrics to 'Revelations' aren't the worst Roger has ever written, they certainly do border on cringe-inducing, especially the first verse. In a bizarre twist of foreshadowing, Roger predicted the criticism of his shortcomings as a lyricist: "Now you can label me stupid or naïve with this song / But when children are starving / I know what's right and what's wrong."

The song, like the rest of the *Happiness?* album (except for 'Freedom Train'), was performed live on the 1994-1995 tour, but wasn't revisited for Roger's next solo outing. A remix, subtitled 'The Hungry Mix' (and pointlessly – or perhaps erroneously – dropping the 's' in the title), was released on the November 2017 'Journey's End' 10" EP; it's marginally interesting, but one listen will suffice.

REVOLUTION *(Lennon/McCartney)*

Originally issued as the B-side to The Beatles' 'Hey Jude' in 1968, 'Revolution' was performed live by The Cross at the Gosport Festival on 30 July 1992.

RIDE THE WILD WIND *(Queen)*
• Album: *Innuendo* • B-side (Roger): 11/94 [32]
• Bonus: *Innuendo*

Closing the first side of *Innuendo* is this up-tempo rocker, whose lyrics beg the main character's girl to throw caution to the wind and "live life on the razor's edge." The words are sung in a hushed tone by Freddie, with prominent backing and secondary vocals from Roger. A powerful rhythm section is built up, with John's bassline complementing the song well and Roger overlaying a combination of programmed and real drums. An early version, recorded with Roger on lead vocals, was released on the 2011 bonus disc of *Innuendo*, and is a fascinating insight into what latter-day tracks would have worked well with the song's composer, instead of Freddie, on lead vocals.

Brian, as usual, contributes a wonderful guitar solo, which was often the saving grace on many of Queen's dodgier recordings. However, 'Ride The Wild Wind' is an ace song, with the lyrics recalling images of Roger's video for his 1984 single, 'Strange Frontier' (the video was a throwback to the James Dean film, *Rebel Without A Cause*), and it would have been an ideal single if not for the other, more obviously chart-friendly, songs presented on *Innuendo*. That didn't stop it from becoming a single in Poland after Freddie's death in 1992, where it went to No. 1.

THE RING (HYPNOTIC SEDUCTION OF DALE) (Mercury)
• Album: *Flash*

Lasting only 57 seconds, 'The Ring (Hypnotic Seduction Of Dale)' leads in from Freddie's prior track, 'Ming's Theme (In The Court Of Ming The Merciless)' and consists of a piercing synthesizer riff underscoring suggestive moaning from Dale Arden.

RIP IT UP (Blackwell/Marascaico)

Little Richard's 1956 No. 17 hit single was performed live by The Cross during their inaugural 1988 German tour as the final number of the concert, just before the encore performance of 'Stand Up For Love'.

RIVER OF WORDS

This out-take from *The Miracle* consists of little else than Brian futzing around on the guitar with some programmed drums choogling away behind him. Premiered at an unknown Queen convention, with the infamous "Property of Queen Productions" watermark imposing itself every few seconds or so, and leaked onto YouTube in April 2016, the most interesting thing about the track is the title. Whether it was developed any further is not known.

ROBBERY

From the same batch of demos as 'Self-Made Man' and 'My Secret Fantasy', 'Robbery' is a fast-paced

rocker similar to 'Headlong' or 'The Hitman', and it's likely that, due to such a comparison, the song wasn't completed. The lyrics are largely improvised, and authorship claims for the song vary between Roger and Brian.

ROCK-A-BYE DIXIE: *see* EXTRACTS FROM GARDEN LODGE

ROCK AND ROLL FANTASY (Rodgers)

Written by Paul Rodgers and taken from Bad Company's 1979 album *Desolation Angels*, 'Rock And Roll Fantasy' was a suitable choice to be played live by the Queen + Paul Rodgers band, though it only appeared three times in the set list. It made its debut in Aruba, and was included in the two stateside shows in 2005. It's a surprising omission, since the song was a hit single in 1979, reaching No. 13, and also earned a rightful place on US album rock radio, helping Bad Company to remain in the limelight for many years.

ROCK IN RIO BLUES (Queen)
• CD Single: 12/95 [6] • Bonus: *Heaven*

For years, Queen's live sets often included well-rehearsed impromptu pieces (that terminology is an oxymoron; however, given the tight structure of a typical Queen show, complete improvisation was generally kept to a minimum) which would often be based on a sole piano line, turning into a tour de force by the song's conclusion with nonsensical vocalizations from Freddie (a good example of this is on the *Live At Wembley Stadium* CD).

When the band appeared at the Rock In Rio Festival in January 1985, they rehearsed a special version of the improvisation which featured a unique set of 'lyrics' to the already customary backing. This presentation, officially titled 'Rock In Rio Blues', was released on the CD single of 'A Winter's Tale' in December 1995 and as the B-side of the US issue of 'Too Much Love Will Kill You' in January 1996, but the song is largely superfluous next to any other live improvisation and should be considered for completists only.

ROCK IT (PRIME JIVE) (Taylor)
• Album: *Game*

"'Rock It (Prime Jive)' is totally elemental," Roger explained in a 1980 *Sounds* interview. "It's the most basic song ever that just says you can enjoy rock and roll. That's all." An apt description for what may be one of the drummer's most underrated songs, opening up the second side of *The Game* with a deceptively rudimentary set of guitar arpeggios as Freddie croons, "When I hear that rock and roll / It gets down to my soul." The song then explodes into life as Roger assumes the vocal responsibilities.

Sounding like an out-take from Roger's *Fun In Space* album, the song glides along at a raucous clip with a tight rhythm section and some soaring guitar, including an especially jarring solo. Oddly, the real star of the show is the synthesizer, which adds interesting, spacey flourishes to the recording; co-producer Mack recently revealed that they were added because there was too much empty space between verses.

Two versions of the song were recorded: one with Freddie on lead vocals throughout, and the other with Roger on vocals. Freddie and Brian agreed that the former was superior, but John, Roger and Mack fought for the latter, since it added to the diversity of the album. A compromise was struck, and Mack joined together the introduction from Freddie's version with the main vocals from Roger's.

It mattered little in concert, since Freddie took the reins. It was played sparsely, though, receiving only a handful of airings between 1980 and 1981, then resurfacing as the opening number on the 1982 Rock 'n' America tour and three of the six Japanese Hot Space shows.

ROLLIN' OVER *(Marriot/Lane)*
• Album (Brian): *BTTL*

Originally recorded by The Small Faces in 1968 for their concept album *Ogden's Nut Gone Flake*, 'Rollin' Over', in its original state, was a mid-tempo rocker lasting less than two minutes, albeit with some fine vocals by the song's writers, Steve Marriot and Ronnie Lane. In Brian's hands, however, the song becomes a scorching tour de force of guitar riffs and exploding drums, turning into what might as well be an out-take from one of Queen's earlier albums (indeed, Smile played it in their touring days).

Unfortunately, the song has received little in the way of fan appreciation, most regarding it as too weak a song to close such a pivotal album, Brian's first. Considering the sombre route Brian took with 'Just One Life', the song that precedes 'Rollin' Over', it's perhaps best that he closed the album with an all-out

rave-up, as if to say that, despite his personal issues at the time, he can still find solace in good old-fashioned rock'n'roll.

With Chris Thompson assisting Brian on vocals, ably backed up by Miriam Stockley and Maggie Ryder, the song opens with the tinkling of Mike Moran's piano before striking out fully courtesy of the rhythm section of Gary Tibbs on bass and Geoff Dugmore on drums. Brian takes any opportunity possible to steer the song back in his direction, soloing after most of the verses, and even throwing in a lick of The Beatles' 'Day Tripper'. It's quite possibly Brian's most enjoyable cover, second only to 'All The Way From Memphis'.

'Rollin' Over' was played live by The Brian May Band in Buenos Aires and Santiago in November 1992, but was dropped after the first two dates, never to be performed again.

ROLL WITH YOU *(May/Ellis)*
• Digital Download: 2/16 • Album (Brian & Kerry): *Golden*

Just like 'Dangerland' had been a surprisingly tough rock song from *Anthems*, Brian and Kerry Ellis deliver another scorcher with 'Roll With You'. There's still a theatrical bent to the song, making it perfect for the stage, but Brian's guitar helps keep it from straying too far into parody.

ROUGH JUSTICE *(Taylor)*
• B-side (The Cross): 1/88 [84] • Album (The Cross): *Shove*

Roger's third solo project was a hit-or-miss affair, but 'Rough Justice' was one of the better songs to come out of the sessions, closing the patchy *Shove It* album in the way it deserves: with a good old-fashioned rocking finale. Recorded entirely by Roger and Spike Edney, the song is set to a merciless, driving rhythm that comes to a quick conclusion.

'Rough Justice' was released as the B-side of 'Shove It' in January 1988 and was performed regularly by The Cross over the years. The version that concludes the US version of the album features a brief, 50-second reprise of 'Shove It'.

RUNAWAY *(Shannon/Crook)*
• Download (Q+PR): *Cosmos*

Brian vaguely alluded to "toying with including a

cover song from the 1950s" on *The Cosmos Rocks* in a June 2008 interview in *Classic Rock Magazine*, and this was proudly trumpeted on the press release as being the first time Queen ever recorded a cover song for an album. (Not entirely true: 'Jailhouse Rock' was recorded for the debut album, and 'New York, New York' was intended for the *Highlander* soundtrack.) As with most things Queen-related, these plans changed, and nothing but original material was released on *The Cosmos Rocks*, leaving 'Runaway' – written and first recorded by Del Shannon in 1961 (not the 1950s), then covered by Lawrence Welk, The Small Faces, and Bonnie Raitt – on the cutting room floor. Which is a shame, because the performance is exuberant, with a lively rhythm and searing guitar licks, as the band clearly relish singing the "wah-wah-wah-wonder" falsetto backing vocals. The song was released as a bonus track on the iTunes-only release of *The Cosmos Rocks*, a deserved position, though it would have also been well-suited as a non-album B-side of 'C-Lebrity'.

SAIL AWAY SWEET SISTER *(May)*
• Album: *Game* • Bonus: *Game*

An underrated highlight from *The Game*, Brian's delicate 'Sail Away Sweet Sister' is subtitled on the lyric sleeve as "To The Sister I Never Had", finding the guitarist offering up advice to his absent sister. Brian takes the lead vocal, the last time he would do so on a Queen song until 1991's 'Lost Opportunity', over a carefully constructed backing track consisting of bass, drums and piano (often thought to be performed by Brian, but recently revealed to be the work of Freddie). The first take, erroneously labeled as being recorded in February 1980, with Brian on guide vocals (and doing little more than mumbling his way through lyrics that had yet to be finalized), was released on the 2011 reissue of *The Game*.

Brian's vocal performance is touching, with Freddie interjecting in the bridge, turning in a gorgeous four lines. The guitarist later expressed regret that he hadn't pushed for the song to be released as a single, before conceding that its prevention from candidacy was because he, not Freddie, sang the lead vocals. Worse still, the song was never performed live – a shame since it would have worked perfectly alongside 'Save Me', which was recorded at the same session in the summer of 1979 – but Brian finally gave it its debut on his 1998 Another World tour.

SANDBOX

This spirited out-take from a 1979 Musicland jam session for *The Game* features Freddie on piano and shouted interjections, Roger on drums, and John on what can only be described as lead bass. (Brian is completely absent from the recording, hence John's increased role.) Queen archivist Greg Brooks played the recording at a 2003 Queen Fan Club convention, and hinted that it was a predecessor of 'Coming Soon', but there's nothing to suggest the connection in its performance or structure.

SATURDAY NIGHT'S ALRIGHT FOR FIGHTING
(John/Taupin)

Elton John's 1973 classic first made its first appearance in the Queen Lizzy tour in 1977, and was performed only a handful of times during that year before being dropped indefinitely. It was then performed again between 1982 and 1985, generally on Saturday nights, though it usually amounted to little more than an instrumental version. Some renditions do feature Roger and Freddie duetting on the words, and the band would always turn in an enjoyable performance.

SAVE ME *(May)*
• Album: 1/80 [11] • Album: *Game* • Live: *On Fire, Montreal* • Bonus: *Game*

More popular yet equally as emotive as Brian's 'Sail Away Sweet Sister', 'Save Me' closes *The Game* beautifully. Another piano ballad, exploding with a memorable chorus, the song finds the main character in the midst of a broken relationship. "We actually wrote very separately in those days," Brian told Redbeard on the syndicated North American radio series *In The Studio*, "and we never really talked about what the songs meant. I think we were quite shy about what we were trying to say in them. We tend to talk about things more now ... I wrote ['Save Me'] – to cut a long story short – I wrote it about a friend, someone who was going through a bad time, and I imagined myself in their shoes, kind of telling the story. Someone whose relationship is totally fucked up and how sad that person was."

Recorded in the summer of 1979 in Munich, 'Save Me' was performed during the same concerts that introduced 'Crazy Little Thing Called Love'; it was retained in the live setting, with Brian on piano, until the conclusion of the 1982 Hot Space tours. It was also released as the second single from *The Game* in January 1980, although only as a UK single, peaking at No. 11.

A video was filmed at Alexandra Palace on 22 December 1979, directed by Keith McMillan and using animation in a Queen video for the first time. With a storyboard by Brian and animated by a Japanese company called Cucumber, the video was subsequently issued on the *Greatest Flix* video in 1981, and was restored for the 2002 *Greatest Video Hits 1* DVD.

SAY IT'S NOT TRUE *(Taylor)*
• Live: *46664* • Download/CD Single: 12/07 [90]
• Album (Q+PR): *Cosmos* • Live (Q+PR): *Return, Ukraine* • Album (Roger): *Earth*

Written and recorded for the 46664 project in 2003, Roger's stunning 'Say It's Not True' was performed at the charity concert held in Cape Town, South Africa, on 29 November 2003. With Dave Stewart and Brian on acoustic guitars front stage, and a hidden accordion player, Roger sang the lead vocals of a song gently chastising ignorance and naïveté; the result was an early highlight of the show, even though it was incorporated merely to allow a set change from Bob Geldof to Paul Oakenfold. This live version was released on the 46664 companion album, *Part One: African Prayer*, with "Magic potions for lives" changed to "Magic cocktails". The song was retained for the 2005 Queen + Paul Rodgers tour, with Roger taking lead vocals center stage accompanied by Danny Miranda and Jamie Moses on acoustic guitars and Spike Edney on keyboards. A live acoustic version was released on *Return Of The Champions*, though it lacks the spontaneous energy of the live 46664 version.

While the 2003 studio version has yet to be released, the song was returned to in 2007 during sessions for *The Cosmos Rocks*. As the first official single to be released from the sessions, expectations were high for a return to form, and with critics (and vocal fan opponents) ready to lambaste the song should it underperform. Replacing the delicate acoustic guitar bed with a synthetic drone, the first verse and chorus are sung by Roger, with Brian joining in for the second verse, before the two founding members of Queen duetting beautifully on the second chorus. The song, driven by a simple acoustic guitar melody and subdued drums, then kicks into high gear for the final chorus, with the Red Special screaming alongside Paul's arresting vocal delivery, turning the song into a

full-fledged power ballad.

Fans and critics were placated for the time being, raising expectations even further for the full album, which wouldn't be released until nine months later. 'Say It's Not True' was released as a free download-only single on World AIDS Day, 1 December 2007, with a physical CD single (due to popular demand) released at the end of the month. Unfortunately, the reception to the song had softened by that point: those who wanted the song already had it, and the CD single offered nothing else new to entice fans to purchase it (despite the promise of all proceeds going to the 46664 project), and so the single stalled at an abysmal No. 90 in the UK charts.

The song was performed live throughout the 2008 Rock The Cosmos tour, one of the three mainstays from *The Cosmos Rocks* in the set (the others were 'Cosmos Rockin'' and 'C-lebrity'), this time in the arrangement of the 2007 studio version. A touching and slightly out-of-breath rendition was duly released in June 2009 on *Live In Ukraine*.

Roger was justifiably proud of the song, and would, in his increasingly rarer solo live performances after the Rock The Cosmos tour, incorporate the song into his set lists whenever he could. On 25 May 2013, Roger appeared at the Rock Against Cancer benefit concert in All Cannings, performing a four song set that included 'A Kind Of Magic', 'Under Pressure', Jimi Hendrix's 'Little Wing', and 'Say It's Not True'. Legendary guitar virtuoso Jeff Beck assisted Roger on guitar on 'Say It's Not True', adding some truly beautiful, electrifying licks. A rehearsal recording was duly added to *Fun On Earth*, with some studio trickery added to make it sound not quite like a rehearsal recording. While this marks the fifth time the song was released, it doesn't quite match the simplistic power of the initial live 46664 acoustic rendition, nor does it reach the stratospheric heights of the 2007 re-recording with Paul Rodgers, yet Beck's presence gives it a new slant to the heightened emotions that lie at the core of the song.

SCANDAL *(Queen)*
• Album: *Miracle* • A-side: 10/89 [25] • Bonus: *Miracle*

A rare highlight on the second side of *The Miracle*, 'Scandal' is a vicious attack on the tabloids of which Brian and Freddie (and, to a lesser extent, Roger) were victims. Written in 1988, around the time that Brian's first marriage was falling apart, tabloid reporters published photographs of Brian and his new girlfriend,

Anita Dobson. Brian, typically, was outraged and disappointed that his children had to hear of private matters through the press.

"It's something which has affected us, individually, as members of the group recently," Brian told *Hard 'n' Heavy* in 1989. "It's very strange, 'cause we were fairly famous for a long time in England, you know, the last fifteen years or whatever, but we didn't become a prey to these kind of scummy papers until recently. And it's not related to what you are doing, you know. They are not interested what music you play, or anything. They just want the dirt, and if they can't find any they'll invent it if they choose to pick on you. So we were all going through a lot of changes in our lives and suddenly it became a big problem, you know, in a similar way... you've heard about what they did to Elton, you know? These stories about Elton, and everything, which he sued them for and got a million quid off 'em. You know, great. Well they did very similar things to me particularly, and to a certain extent to Roger, and Freddie also had been through it a little while before. But this thing is total... you know, steam in and destroy someone's life. They really are the scum of the earth. You can't exaggerate it too much."

Though the song doesn't make as powerful a statement as its songwriter would have liked, it's a powerful rocker with a bubbling synthesizer and some great guitar work from Brian. Released as the fourth single from *The Miracle*, it was the least successful release from that album, peaking at No. 25 in the UK, despite the inclusion of John's non-album 'My Life Has Been Saved' as the flipside. In the US, it became the second single release but failed to make any impact on the charts. An extended remix, adding nearly two minutes to the original running time, was released on 12" versions of the single as well as on CD versions of *The Miracle*, with a completely new intro.

A video, filmed in October 1989 by Rudi Dolezal and Hannes Rossascher at Pinewood Studios, turned out to be less than stellar. The band basically ran through the song on a soundstage with newspaper clippings plastered randomly, and with a big painted banner in the background declaring, "We Want It All!" "I don't think it's totally successful, this video, as a portrayal of what's in the song," Brian explained. "It's a kind of brave attempt, but it's a little cold, and you don't really see the band interacting as a band. It's a bit stagey. But at least it makes you think of what the song's really about." Unspectacular at best, the single's lack of success accounted for its exclusion from

Greatest Hits II (as well as its counterpart, *Greatest Flix II*), but nothing could justify its exclusion from the third instalment. The video was eventually released on *Greatest Video Hits 2* in 2003.

SEAGULL *(Ralphs/Rodgers)*
• Live (Q+PR): *Ukraine*

The closing track from Bad Company's 1974 self-titled debut album was performed on the 2005 Queen + Paul Rodgers tour, with Paul on acoustic guitar and vocals and Roger accompanying him on conga drums. While the song was removed from the set after a few performances, it was returned to on the 2008 Rock The Cosmos tour, gaining a permanent spot in the repertoire and, subsequently, on *Live In Ukraine*.

SEASIDE RENDEZVOUS *(Mercury)*
• Album: *Opera*

Closing the first side of *A Night At The Opera* in tongue-in-cheek manner, Freddie's delightful 'Seaside Rendezvous' shows the vocalist's love of music hall as he sings about a romantic getaway for two by the water. Driven by piano, and containing no guitar whatsoever, the most intriguing features of the song are the orchestrations of brass and woodwind, as vocalized by Roger and Freddie respectively. The songwriter rather coyly told *NME* in 1975 that "[It] has a 1920s feel to it, and Roger does a tuba and clarinet on it vocally, if you see what I mean. I'm going to make him tap dance too; I'll have to buy him some Ginger Rogers tap shoes." In actuality, the tapping was done by the drummer with thimbles on a washboard.

SEE WHAT A FOOL I'VE BEEN *(May)*
• B-side: 2/74 [10] • CD Single: 11/88 • Bonus: *Queen2*
• Live: *Rainbow, Odeon* • Compilation: *On Air*

Written by Brian in the late 1960s and included in Smile's set lists at the time, this blues pastiche was dusted off and polished up for inclusion in early Queen set lists. The song was first recorded at Trident Studios during sessions for the first album in 1972 but remained unreleased; a second version was recorded the following August while the band was recording *Queen II*, and was released as the B-side of 'Seven Seas Of Rhye' in February 1974.

Live versions would include alternate lyrics, but the studio version features a camped-up vocal performance by Freddie. Upon first listen, this can be a bit off-putting, but the result is a fine slice of blues that the band would never attempt again. 'See What A Fool I've Been' was performed between 1970 and 1976, and revisited in 1977 during Queen's improvised gig for the fans who attended the 'We Are The Champions' video shoot. Live versions were released in 2014 and 2015 on *Live At The Rainbow '74* and *A Night At The Odeon*, respectively, while a version recorded for the BBC was released on the 2011 deluxe edition of *Queen II*, resurfacing five years later on the expansive *On Air* compilation.

Though the song was derived from 'That's How I Feel' by Sonny Terry and Brownie McGhee, it was credited solely to Brian since it's an entirely traditional blues scale – the Terry/McGhee version is hardly unique.

SELF-MADE MAN

At the 2000 Fan Club Convention, Greg Brooks unveiled a slew of previously unreleased and unknown Queen tracks. Though he played tracks mainly from the *Miracle/Innuendo* sessions, Brooks showed that the band had then been at a songwriting peak. A perfect example is 'Self-Made Man', appearing in demo form with Brian providing the lead vocals while Freddie sings the bridge (similar to 'Sail Away Sweet Sister'). An exemplary track, the demo appears to be nearly complete and would have been an ideal inclusion on *Innuendo*, during sessions for which the song was recorded. Had it been released, it would have been credited to Queen though the song was written mostly by Brian.

SEVEN SEAS OF RHYE (Mercury)

• A-side: 2/74 [10] • Album: *Queen2* • Live: *Magic, Wembley, Budapest, Rainbow, Odeon* • CD Single: 11/88
• Bonus: *Queen2* • CD Single: 10/95 [2]

Queen's breakthrough hit began life as a slower instrumental on the debut album (see next song entry) but what finally emerged in February 1974 was a delicious slice of glam rock that summed up Freddie's early writing style perfectly. With a mesmerizing piano intro, sped up for effect, the band give the song everything they've got – even now, over 30 years after its original release, the band still sound as if they're trying to prove something to the world. What was eventually proven, of course, was Freddie's mastery of words, and everyone else's difficulty in interpreting and analyzing them. The words for 'Seven Seas Of Rhye' are ambiguous and defy any explanation; Roger

himself told *Mojo* in 1999, "I never understood a word of it, and I don't think Freddie did either, but it was just sort of gestures really, but it was a fine song." The words work well together and create an aural painting of mythology, something which fascinated Freddie at this time (consider his other compositions, especially from the first three albums). Freddie himself later said in a 1977 BBC Radio One documentary, "My lyrics are basically for people's interpretations, really. I've forgotten what they were all about. It's really factitious, I know it's like bowing out or the easy way out, but that's what it is. It's just a figment of your imagination. It all depends on what kind of song really. At that time I was learning about a lot of things. Like song structure and as far as lyrics go, they're very difficult as far as I'm concerned. I find them quite a task and my strongest point is actually melody content. I concentrate on that first; melody, then the song structure, then the lyrics come after actually."

The song was recorded during sessions for *Queen II* in August 1973 at Trident Studios, but wasn't included in the set list until it became a bona-fide hit the following year. It stayed in the set list until 1975, then was revived in 1984 for the Queen Works! tour and remained in the live setting until 1986. An absurd dance remix of the song was included as a bonus track on the 1991 remaster of *Queen II*; while this may represent the dregs of the remix and remaster programme kick-started by Hollywood Records, rumor has it that the song's original composer was fairly smitten with the new recording.

As well as bearing the distinction of being Queen's first true hit, peaking at No. 10 in the UK in February 1974, the song is also noted for being Queen's first appearance on *Top Of The Pops* that same month. When David Bowie, riding high on the success of 'Rebel, Rebel', had to bow out of an appearance, Queen were approached, even though they hadn't technically had a hit single yet. The band were duly shuffled into Pete Townshend's Eel Pie Studios (ostensibly to record a new backing but actually pretending to do so to pacify the Musician Union representative) the day before their appearance, which marked the first time the band were seen on British television. This footage was long believed to have been destroyed, until second generation copies showed up in 2007, ultimately appearing on YouTube and related video sites.

SEVEN SEAS OF RHYE... (Mercury)
• Album: *Queen*

A taster of what went on to become Queen's first true hit in February 1974, 'Seven Seas Of Rhye...' (note the ellipsis) is taken at a slower pace and is devoid of any lyrics. Closing the debut album, the song's presence is questionable, and doesn't offer too much insight into what would eventually become a completed song. And, at a mere 1'15, it fades out just as it gets going.

Roger said in 1977, "I think Freddie had half written the song and we thought it was a nice 'tail out' to the first album, with the idea of starting the second album with the song."

SEX SHOW

On the commentary track on the 2007 DVD *Queen Rock Montreal*, Brian mentions this title as one that Freddie was working on during the summer 1981 recording sessions in Montreux. Freddie improvises some words just prior to the proper start of 'Keep Yourself Alive' ("Ooh, ha ha / We're gonna shake it out / Shake it out"), but whether this was a completed song or just a fragment rightfully abandoned in its early stages remains to be seen.

SHA-LA-LA-LA-LEE *(Lynch/Shuman)*

This is another Small Faces hit performed live by 1984.

SHAG OUT: *see* HANGMAN

SHAKE *(Cooke)*

Sam Cooke's 'Shake' was performed live by 1984.

SHAKE, RATTLE & ROLL *(Turner)*

Originally recorded by Joe Turner, 'Shake, Rattle & Roll' became more well known as recorded by Bill Haley and His Comets in 1954. Between 1970 and 1976, Queen incorporated their own interpretation into the set list as a lasting number in the Rock 'n' Roll Medley.

SHE BLOWS HOT AND COLD *(Mercury)*
• B-side (Freddie): 7/85 [57] • B-side (Freddie): 11/92 [8] • Compilation (Freddie): *Solo Collection*

Another enjoyable rocker from the *Mr Bad Guy* sessions, 'She Blows Hot And Cold' sounds like it was largely an improvisation. With a rollicking piano performed by Fred Mandel (including a terrific solo

midway through), the song could be the cousin of 'Man On The Prowl'; indeed, it sounds like a Queen cast-off, especially with the Brian May-inspired guitar solo by Paul Vincent. Perhaps realizing the parallel, Freddie asked Brian to play on the song, with a terrific out-take appearing on the Freddie Mercury box set; it may have been this take that Paul Vincent used as a template for his own performance, much to Brian's later annoyance.

Released as the B-side of 'Made In Heaven' in July 1985, an extended version was created for the release, including several unused segments of the song. The original version was part of the 'In My Defence' single reissue in November 1992, though the version that is commonly available now excises a 12-second introductory segment comprised of faintly heard voices and an extended drum intro.

SHE MAKES ME (STORMTROOPER IN STILETTOES) *(May)*
• Album: *SHA*

Marking Brian's second appearance as lead vocalist on a Queen song, the penultimate track on *Sheer Heart Attack* is a dense, mid-paced rocker, and totally at odds with his other three compositions on the album. Often the subject of derision among Queen fans, the song was written during a period in Brian's life where he wasn't exactly sure of his future in a rock band, as 1974 hadn't been his best year: he was given a tetanus shot earlier in the year and developed gangrene in his right arm, and it was thought for some time that amputation would be necessary; then, while on Queen's first US tour in support of Mott the Hoople, he contracted hepatitis, and the band were forced to withdraw from the tour and focus instead on their third album; to top it off, midway through the sessions, Brian developed an ulcer, often interrupting sessions so that he could run to the nearest studio toilet and vomit.

'She Makes Me (Stormtrooper In Stilettoes)' focuses on a theme of self-doubt and uncertainty; 'she' can be seen as a metaphor for Queen, and Brian's ultimate decision to stick to his guns. The result is remarkable, since a clearly ailing Brian allows some of his suffering to bleed over into his vocal performance. The song, driven by some rudimentary acoustic guitar work from Brian, incorporates some nifty guitar orchestrations, concluding with the sound of Brian's heavy breathing and the sound of an ambulance's wail. In 2011, the subtitle, penned by Roger due to the song's insistent rhythm ("It was actually Roger's idea in the beginning to put this subtitle on because he said, 'Look, I really like this song, it has a great beat and everything but I don't like this title,'" Brian later told QueenOnline. com. "This is in 1975 [sic] or something. He said, 'You should call it "Stormtroopers in Stilettoes" if it has this big beat,' and I said, 'OK, you can call it that as well if you want.' So we put 'She Makes Me', and in brackets, 'Stormtroopers in Stilettoes'."), was also the name of an all-encompassing photo exhibit of Queen's early years, held at the East End's Old Truman Brewery.

SHE'S GONE (Crudup)

Arthur 'Big Boy' Crudup's blues standard 'She's Gone' was performed live by 1984.

SHEER HEART ATTACK (Taylor)
• Album: NOTW • B-side: 2/78 [34] • Live: Killers, On Fire, Montreal • Bonus: NOTW

Originally written for the album of the same name but held back for a more appropriate time, 'Sheer Heart Attack' is the band's first excursion into punk, and it's not surprising to learn that Roger was responsible. With some raucous rhythm guitar played by the drummer, the song mocks the punks' attitude towards music and society, with a particularly scathing "I feel so – inar-inar-inar-inarticulate" parodying the stuttering and incoherence of certain punk records.

However, Queen were not a punk band, which is evident in their skilled performance on this track (even though Roger, who also plays bass and drums, and Brian, who plays only a squealing guitar solo, were the only musicians); they never truly regarded punk as an insurgent genre, treating it instead as a passing fad. "It sounds like a punk, or 'new wave' song," Brian told Circus in 1978, "but it was written at the same time as the Sheer Heart Attack LP. [Roger] played it to us then but it wasn't quite finished and he didn't have time to complete it before we started recording. That was three years ago and now almost all these records you hear are like that period." Roger, meanwhile, wasn't as diplomatic with punk music: "At the moment [punk is] suffering from all the worst symptoms of hype and the oldest plagues of the business possible. It's so much crap right now. I like raw rock'n'roll, mind you, and I like the Sex Pistols' album but…there's nothing new, it doesn't mean much at the moment."

"We came up with the title for the Sheer Heart Attack album," Roger explained in 1999, "and it was a song that I had an idea for, but I hadn't actually finished the song yet. By the time I had finished the song we were two albums later, so it just struggled out on the News Of The World album. It's quite interesting because we were making an album next door to ... the Sex Pistols, and it really fit into that punk explosion that was happening at the time."

The song quickly became a live favorite, and was performed as the show closer between November 1977 and May 1978, before becoming a first encore number thereafter. Still, it would often replace 'We Will Rock You' and 'We Are The Champions' as a closing number in 1980, and was even performed as the opening number on a few dates in 1982. 'Sheer Heart Attack' would allow the band to let loose on stage, with Brian providing some excellent guitar work as Freddie ran around the stage, bashing amps and monitors with his microphone stand (nb, it is Freddie, not Roger, who sings lead vocals on the song). The song was played at virtually every show between 1977 and 1982, and was included on a handful of shows in 1984 before being dropped indefinitely. It also appeared as the B-side of 'Spread Your Wings' (in the UK) and 'It's Late' (in the US and Japan) in 1978, and if a version from the Sheer Heart Attack sessions exists, it would be a revelation to hear how the song was handled in 1974, since it's next to impossible to imagine it on any album but News Of The World.

An early instrumental version, featuring some additional raucous guitar by Roger at the beginning and a proper ending, was released in 2017 on the 40th anniversary box set of News Of The World.

SHOOTING STAR (Rodgers)
• Live (Q+PR): Ukraine

First released on Bad Company's 1975 album Straight Shooter, 'Shooting Star', unusually, wasn't released as a single but gained prominence on US radio's AM waves and album-oriented rock channels, which favored album tracks over hit singles. The song, with its rags-to-riches story of a kid discovering The Beatles and vowing to become a rock legend, and a hard-hitting chorus, remains a staple of rock radio, making it a perfect inclusion in Queen + Paul Rodgers' set list. Yet it wasn't until the 2008 Rock The Cosmos tour that 'Shooting Star' debuted, with a performance duly released on Live In Ukraine the following year.

THE SHORES OF FORMENTERA *(Taylor)*

This upbeat, atmospheric track was recorded during sessions for *Fun On Earth* but ultimately didn't make the cut. Its most obvious home would have been on *The Lot*, but, frustratingly, it was kept off and instead used as background music for Roger's recently-revamped official website.

SHOVE IT *(Taylor)*
• A-side (The Cross): 1/88 [84] • Album (The Cross): *Shove* • Bonus (The Cross): *Shove*

The 1980s aren't remembered fondly for their musical output and nothing sums up the decade better than 'Shove It', one of the strangest and most unwelcome Queen-related tracks. Recorded in the summer of 1987 at Mountain Studios, the song has a danceable beat overlaid with nasty trick-shot percussion. The only redeeming factor is the grungey guitar performance, while the most offensive aspect is the unnecessary use of sampling. Clips from several of Queen's older songs, notably 'Fat Bottomed Girls', 'Bohemian Rhapsody' and 'Flash', were inserted throughout the song, creating an uncomfortable listening experience.

One would hope that the lyrics would at least be up to par, but Roger essentially raps a set of the worst lyrics ever committed to paper, as he tells certain posh groups – VIPs, royalty, etc – to do as the title suggests. What makes the sentiments hard to swallow is the fact that Roger was himself living a life of luxury, making the mood and message of the song all the more hypocritical.

Oddly, 'Shove It' was chosen not only as the title of the album but also as the second single released by The Cross, though it was, in all but name, a Roger Taylor solo song. Backed by 'Rough Justice' (which would have been a far superior choice as the lead track), the song fared poorly in the UK, reaching an abysmal No. 84 in the charts, the worst chart performance of any track released from the album. Several alternate versions also surfaced, including an extended mix (bringing the running time up to five minutes, well beyond tolerable) and a 'Metropolix Mix', which sped up the song and made the percussion even louder. The most bizarre variation of 'Shove It' came in the form of 'The 2nd Shelf Mix', which was essentially an extended version of the extended version, released as a bonus track on the UK CD of the album. All versions of the song were mercilessly included on Roger's 2013 box

set, *The Lot*. A video was filmed by VDO Productions during November 1987 at Crazy Larry's Club in Chelsea, with the band "asking" the crowd what's "in" and what can be "shoved"; quite a concept.

Special mention must be given to the sleeve of the single, which is one of the more creative artistic decisions made in Queen's career. Drawn in the style of a Warner Bros cartoon, a gloved hand, looking suspiciously like its owner was Bugs Bunny, is shown giving the middle finger, while other trademarks of the cartoons are featured, including a desert background (recalling Wile E Coyote and Roadrunner) and a curtain similar to the one Porky Pig pokes his head out of at the conclusion of 'Loony Toon'. Imaginative and offensive at the same time, which is twice as much as can be said about the song itself.

THE SHOW MUST GO ON *(Queen)*
• Album: *Innuendo* • A-side: 10/91 [16] • Compilation: *Hits3* • Live: *46664* • Live (Q+PR): *Return, Ukraine*

By the time the band started work on *Innuendo*, they knew they were existing on borrowed time. As has been so often stated, especially by Brian, Freddie demanded that the band continue to write songs and give them to him; his soul, energy and passion were still there, even if his physical presence was fading away. It must have been particularly disturbing for the vocalist, then, to sing 'The Show Must Go On', a song so blatantly influenced by him that people have often thought it was also written by him. Brian, however, wrote the song: he was going through a particularly difficult period in his life, and watching one of his closest friends withering away in front of him was heartbreaking.

Quite simply, 'The Show Must Go On' is one of Queen's finest songs and looks at the conclusion of a chapter of someone's life through the eyes of an ageing actor: "Inside my heart is breaking / My make-up may be flaking / But my smile still stays on." Opening with a particularly mournful organ intro, the song is a veritable tour de force of emotions, brilliantly captured in both vocal and instrumental performance.

"'The Show Must Go On' came from Roger and John playing the sequence and I started to put things down," Brian told *Guitarist* in 1994. "At the beginning it was just this chord sequence but I had this strange feeling that it could be somehow important and I got very impassioned and went and beavered away at it. I sat down with Freddie and we decided what the theme should be and wrote the first verse. It's a long story, that song, but I always felt it would be important because we were dealing with things that were hard to talk about at the time, but in the world of music you could do it."

The overall performance is tight and well-structured, with plenty of freedom for Brian's guitar to roam, and while the arrangement may be typically overblown in the unique Queen manner, there's a certain feeling about the track that allows all the instruments to breathe properly. The middle eight of the song, concluding with "I can fly, my friends," provides the perfect epitaph for Freddie. Vocal harmonies are sparse; when they are present, they're used either to complement a certain lyric or to add more backing to the chorus. The star of the show, then, is Freddie, who reportedly recorded the vocal in one take.

"It's my favourite song on the album, now," Brian told *Guitar World* in 1991, shortly after *Innuendo* came out, obviously trying not to reveal too much about the song itself. "It's got that kind of sadness, but it's hopeful." Roger concurred in 1993, saying, "Typical Queen, sort of a closing track, metaphorical in a way." Brian told *Vox* that "I very much like the last track on the album, which is called 'The Show Must Go On'. It's one of those things which evolved, and there's bits of all of us in it. It has a little bit of retrospective stuff and it has a little bit of forward looking stuff. There was a point where I looked into it and got a vision of it, and put down a few things; and felt it meant something special, so I'm pretty fond of that one. Sometimes these tracks have a life of their own and no matter what you do they have a certain sound to them. [It] has a very broad and lush sound to it, which I like." Ten years after its release, Brian told *Goldmine*, "For some reason, John and Freddie and Roger had been playing around with things in the studio and I heard one of the sequences they had come up with, and I could just hear the whole thing descending from the skies ... almost in the form, sound-wise, that it ended up. It's something that came as a gift from heaven, I suppose. I did some demos, chopped things up, did some singing demos and some guitar and got it to a point where I could play it to the guys, and they all thought it was something worth pursuing. Then Freddie and I sat down, and I got out my scribblings and said, 'What do you think of all this?' It was a very strange and memorable moment really, because what I'd done was come up with something which I thought was the world viewed through his eyes. We didn't talk

about it as such. We talked about in terms of the story ... it was very poignant at the time, but strange, not precious in any sense. It was just a song and we just loved the idea of it. I was very pleased with the way it came out, especially the way Freddie pushed his voice to ridiculous heights. Some of that stuff I mapped out in falsetto for him, and I remember saying, 'I really don't know if this is asking way too much...' And he went, 'Oh darling, not a problem. I'll have a couple of vodkas then go ahead and do it.' And he did."

It was fitting, then, that the song was chosen as the final proper single from *Innuendo*, released in October 1991 to minimal fanfare. Backed by Queen's first single, 'Keep Yourself Alive', the synchronization of the situation is clearer with hindsight: the band were aware that the end of their career was coming, and it made sense to put their first single as the flipside of their last single. The single peaked no higher than No. 16 in the UK charts, but was coupled with the reissue of 'Bohemian Rhapsody' in the US when released in January 1992, promptly shooting up the charts to No. 2, their highest position there (and first Top Ten single) since 'Another One Bites The Dust' in 1980.

Since Freddie was too ill to film a video for the single (he had already made his final film performance in May 1991 with 'These Are The Days Of Our Lives'), the band left the task of assembling one in the hands of The Torpedo Twins, who constructed a touching remembrance of Queen over the years, pulling clips from all the officially released videos as well as a few previously unissued moments. This video was later issued on the *Greatest Flix II* and *Classic Queen* videos in the UK and US respectively.

Live performances of the song were initially limited to two with Brian, Roger and John, both of them with Elton John on lead vocals. The flamboyant vocalist/pianist, a close friend of Freddie's, declared at the Concert for Life in April 1992 that the song was his favorite from *Innuendo*, and proceeded to hoarsely deliver his own touching performance, which may have been one of the highlights of the evening. Elton later included the song in subsequent solo performances as a memorial for his friend, and even made it a part of his 1992 video release, *Elton John – Live World Tour 1992*. The second performance came in January 1997 at the Bejart Ballet for Life in Paris, France, which was inexplicably issued on *Greatest Hits III* and *Greatest Flix III* in 1999.

Brian included the song in his 1998 set lists, and Roger and Brian performed the song in several *We*

Will Rock You musical one-offs, the most notable being at the 30 April 2002 concert in Amsterdam, as well as the 46664 concert in Cape Town in November 2003. Most recently, the song was incorporated into the 2005/2006 Queen + Paul Rodgers tour, and again on the 2008 Rock The Cosmos tour, with stirring renditions issued on *Return Of The Champions* and *Live In Ukraine*; however, none of the live versions can match the drama and passion the band produced on the studio version. The song was later returned to on Queen + Adam Lambert tours.

SILVER SALMON

Long rumored to not exist, 'Silver Salmon' is a raucous, Black Sabbath-style rocker originating from the 1977 sessions for *News Of The World* – not, as had long been assumed, from the 1972 debut album sessions (the drums, including timbales, and Freddie's vocal strength are the main arguing points). The song was apparently written by Tim Staffell, though Queen give it a different treatment than may have originally been intended. With explosive drum fills and a crunching guitar riff, Freddie practically screams the lyrics over the din, though there appear to be times when the band are unsure in which direction to take the song. Nevertheless, it's a curious recording and, for the casual fan, a revelation.

SINCE YOU'VE BEEN GONE *(Ballard)*
• Live (Brian): *Brixton*

In 1975, following the break-up of Deep Purple, guitarist Ritchie Blackmore formed the rock group Rainbow, which employed a revolving cast of musicians. The following year, Cozy Powell joined the group and remained its drummer until 1980; their most well-known album came in 1979 with *Down To Earth*. Easily ranking as one of the best rock albums of the late 1970s, one of its two hit singles was 'Since You've Been Gone', written by Russ Ballard, charting at No. 6 in September 1979.

When forming his touring band for the upcoming Back To The Light world tour in 1992, Brian asked Cozy Powell to be the drummer in the group, and duly inserted 'Since You've Been Gone' into the set list. A live version appeared on the 1994 album *Live At The Brixton Academy*, and is a particularly hard-rocking track, with Brian attempting to mimic the vocals of Graham Bonnet. While it may have been

more interesting to have heard an obscure Queen track, it's an enjoyable performance, though it comes nowhere near surpassing the original. The song was later incorporated into the 1998 Another World tour, this time as a tribute to Cozy, who had died in a car accident on 5 April of that year.

SISTER BLUE *(Noone)*
• Album (The Cross): *MBADTK* • Live: *Bootleg*

Written by Peter Noone, 'Sister Blue' is a rollicking rocker from *Mad: Bad: And Dangerous To Know*, and ties with 'Liar' as the highlight of Noone's three contributions to the album. While the lyric matter is ambiguous, Roger turns in a fine vocal delivery, imploring the main character to "lose that ball and chain, shake it loose" as The Cross form a dense backing, full of chugging guitars and thick drums. The song was performed live during the 1990 tour in support of the album, with a live version appearing on the fan club-only album, *The Official Bootleg*, in early 1991.

SLEEPING ON THE SIDEWALK *(May)*
• Album: *NOTW* • Bonus: *NOTW*

Opening side two of the *News Of The World* album, Brian's excursion into cool blues comes as a surprise, especially considering that the last blues track to be recorded was 'See What A Fool I've Been' in 1973. However, with the eclectic diversions on *News Of The World*, it's a welcome addition, allowing the guitarist a second opportunity to sing lead vocals.

Continuing Brian's discomfort with becoming successful too quickly (see also 'Good Company', 'Long Away' and 'Leaving Home Ain't Easy'), he changes the story up, allowing a bit of humor as he relates his fame to a trumpeter in a jazz band. Coerced into numerous contracts allowing him everything his heart desires, the protagonist enjoys his life on the road until he realizes that he's not only become yesterday's news, but that it's also not all it's cracked up to be, ultimately deciding that he prefers life on the sidewalk instead of in the spotlight.

Brian told BBC's Radio One in 1983, "That was the quickest song I ever wrote in my life, I just wrote it down. It's funny because it's one of the ones I'm quite pleased with as well. It's not trying too hard, it's not highly subtle but I think it leaves me with quite a good feeling. It was sort of a one-take thing as well. Although I messed around with the take a lot and chopped it about and rearranged it, it was basically the first take, which we used. So it has that kind of sloppy feel that I think works with the song. Which we never would have dreamed [of doing] with the previous albums. We always used to work on the backing tracks until they were a million per cent perfect and if they weren't we would splice together two which were. We'd go to great lengths, but for this album we wanted to get that spontaneity back in." A legend was built up over the years that the band were recorded unaware that the tape was rolling, which Brian debunked in 2008 on his Soapbox: "We were fully aware that the tape was rolling – stories get a little modified over the years, I guess."

'Sleeping On The Sidewalk' was played a handful of times on the News Of The World US tour, but was dropped because it didn't work as well as planned. Rumors abounded for decades that this was one of the few Queen tracks to have been performed live but never been recorded; in 2017, a live version, cryptically described simply as "Live In The USA" on the sleeve notes, finally emerged on the *News Of The World* 40th anniversary box set, and featured Freddie on slightly campy lead vocals. Brian, meanwhile, maintained affection for the song, performing it on his 1998 solo tours, and even reviving it at some of the *We Will Rock You* musical after-parties.

SLEEPY BLUES

Though the origins of 'Sleepy Blues' (also known as 'Drunken Blues') are unknown, the song is a bit of a curio in that it features Brian recording an idea for a song, undoubtedly intended for *Back To The Light*, but features no instruments whatsoever. Instead, Brian provides vocal approximations of the instruments he envisions on the final version, which was apparently never recorded. Brian introduces the song by saying, "Right. Now, this is a song, some blues for the session upcoming, dated the fifth of March or something. Due for some sessions soon for my solo album ... This is a blues song." Understandably, the demo remained unreleased, though it's worth checking out for Brian's distinctive 'harmonica' solo.

SLOW DOWN (Williams)
• Album (Brian): *World*

Originally written and recorded by Larry Williams in the late 1950s, 'Slow Down' was later popularized by

The Beatles, who were aficionados of his work and covered several of his songs in their career. As recorded by The Brian May Band – indeed, the only track on all of *Another World* to feature a full band arrangement – the song is strong enough but comes off as filler, sounding like it was more fun to record than it is to listen to.

"The only track we really recorded live is 'Slow Down', which I have played with my old band," Brian explained, though what old band he was referring to is anyone's guess; Queen never performed the song live. "Otherwise I had a plan, a frame to which people should play. I found a friend and a fiend in the computer. It is a friend because you can write wonderfully with it. For the album I spent most of the time programming a good drum track. The track had, of course, not been used but instead of describing to Cozy Powell what he should play, he heard it directly. But a computer can also be terrible because you can become obsessed and spend your whole life with it."

The song, originally part of Brian's *Heroes* project (see the entry for *Another World* in Part Two for more information), was recorded in 1996 but would have been better suited as a non-album track. Surprisingly, given its obviously spontaneous recorded performance, the song was only performed twice during the Another World tour: the first time in Hamburg on 3 October 1998, with a second and final performance in Birmingham on 28 October.

SMALL (Taylor)
• Album (Q+PR): *Cosmos* • Album (Roger): *Earth*

Roger's songwriting on *The Cosmos Rocks* was a surprise to fans; not only was it consistently strong, with clever arrangements and a diversity of styles, but the lyrics were mostly decent, with only a few true Rogerisms ("I've got a criminal urge to twist and shout", "Some may say I'm lackadasical", "There's a rock'n'roll fever in every place / Next thing you know they'll be rockin' out in space") thrown in for good measure. But Roger has a tendency to surprise the listener with a beautiful, reflective song that is so at odds with his usual style that, upon first listen, one would be forgiven for mistaking it as someone else's song – 'These Are The Days Of Our Lives', for example. Such was the case with 'Small', a sublime acoustic rocker that seemingly had Brian's fingerprints all over it, but was actually largely the work of Roger.

With a superficial message of the joys of relaxing in the country, there's an introspective and philosophical sense that this simple escape be allowed to everyone when the pressures and stresses of reality become too much. When surrounded by nature, these problems appear insignificant compared to the majesty of the environment. While Paul was given a fair amount of questionable lyrics to sing on *The Cosmos Rocks* (some his own fault), he sounds comfortable on 'Small', with a nod to Free's 'Lying In The Sunshine' – which also explores similar sentiments to this song ("I'd rather sit right here and think about the world", "If you could only feel the same / Your world would be a peaceful place") – not going unnoticed. While most of the album would be mired in either fun but meaningless songs or bloated sociopolitical statements, 'Small' is a true highlight, and an indicator that, beneath the sarcastic diatribes and questionable rhyming schemes, Roger could still deliver the goods.

When Nick Weymouth, webmaster for Queenonline, asked Roger on the Official Queen Podcast if any material from *The Cosmos Rocks* would wind up on *Fun On Earth*, Roger confirmed there was: "It's a sort of... proper, acoustic version of a song called 'Small', which I did on the album, and then it got very much taken away from the original idea of it, so I tried to take it back to how I originally thought of it... It's a very home-by-the-fire version." Indeed, the *Fun On Earth* re-recording strips the song back to its acoustic basics, with the occasional accoutrement (electric guitar, bass guitar, keyboards, glockenspiel) introduced during the choruses to add a bit of flavor.

SMALL (REPRISE) *(Taylor/May/Rodgers)*
• Album (Q+PR): *Cosmos*

This brief, two minute reprise of standout track 'Small' is, like most reprises, nice but inessential listening. But after the manic rush of 'Surf's Up . . . School's Out !', 'Small (reprise)' is a perfect way to bow out, the vocal harmonies and Red Special gently breaking against seagull caws.

SMILE *(Taylor)*
• Album (Roger): *Earth*

This delicate ballad, opening with multi-tracked Rogers representing an angelic chorus before giving way to a lovely piano melody, closes *Fun On Earth* in a suitably reflective mood, with Roger recommending an optimistic view toward life's little setbacks. 'Smile' is one of the oldest known tracks on *Fun On Earth*,

having been premiered at the 2010 Queen Fan Club convention, and then played again the following year, now segueing into 'I Am The Drummer (In a Rock n' Roll Band)', though this sequencing was dropped for the final album release.

SO SAD *(Everly)*

The Everly Brothers' 'So Sad' was performed live by 1984.

SO SWEET

Authorship of this track is unknown, but it's a fairly standard blues rocker, with the unofficial title of 'So Sweet (Got To Get Away)'. An Ibex recording from The Sink Club, Liverpool on 9 September 1969 exists, albeit of poor quality.

SOMEBODY TO LOVE *(Mercury)*
• A-side: 11/76 [2] • Album: *Races* • CD Single: 11/88
• Bonus: *Races* • A-side: 4/93 [1] • CD Single: 12/95 [6]
• Compilation: *Hits3* • Live: *On Fire, Montreal*

Queen, and Freddie particularly, were feeling adventurous. After proving they could tackle opera with 'Bohemian Rhapsody', it was anyone's guess what they would attempt next. It came as no surprise, then, when 'Somebody To Love' was released as the precursor to *A Day At The Races*. The band's first excursion into gospel, incorporating the backing vocals of Brian, Freddie and Roger as a gospel choir, was a success upon its release as a single in November 1976, peaking at No. 2 in the UK and No. 13 in the US.

Freddie writes about an issue on which he was very vocal, allowing little room for misinterpretation. The entire performance is impressive, with a strong rhythm section laid down by piano, bass and drums, giving the song a chance to breathe and affording Brian the freedom to add his own parts as he saw fit. The result can be heart-wrenching: the pain and longing in Freddie's voice is evident, especially in the opening line.

"[It's] Aretha Franklin-influenced," Roger told *Circus* in 1977. "Freddie's very much into that. We tried to keep the track in a loose, gospel-type feel. I think it's the loosest track we've ever done." With that in mind, it became one of the band's most performed songs, and a highlight of any show between 1977 and 1985 (the song was omitted from most 1980 and 1982 US and Japanese set lists). For years, however, it eluded any live album release, being left off the *Live Killers* album in lieu of several inferior tracks. A powerful version from the June 1982 Milton Keynes Bowl performance was finally issued in 2004 on the *Queen On Fire: Live At The Bowl* CD and DVD, and is an early highlight of a spectacular show. (This version was re-released in 2011 on the bonus EP of the *A Day At The Races* reissue.) A remix was presented for the 1991 reissue of *A Day At The Races*, which attempted to recreate the live version – especially the vocal breakdown and stark drum passages – but nothing can compare to a decent live rendition, of which there are several.

The song was reissued in April 1993 with George Michael on vocals, extracted from his performance at the Concert For Life on 20 April 1992. Clearly, Michael knows his stuff, and the performance was unanimously voted the finest of the night, causing rumous to form that he would become lead singer of the band. While Roger and Brian may have entertained the thought, especially as late as 1997, they ultimately decided against it, with the guitarist saying, "You know, we're very good friends with George, and he did a wonderful job at the tribute. But at the moment it wouldn't suit either him or us to team up in some way. I think we have our separate ideas about our careers. That doesn't mean that we never want to work with him, I think he's fantastic, but the rumors were not true, he was never joining Queen."

His rendition of 'Somebody To Love' earned the single a deserving No. 1 placement in the UK, while the extended play disc it was issued on in the US reached No. 30, even receiving airplay, which by that time was something of a feat for a new Queen single. This version was subsequently issued on the insipid *Greatest Hits III* album in 1999.

While the song was ignored during Queen + Paul Rodgers' time, it was revived with Adam Lambert in 2012, and became an undoubted highlight of each show at which it was performed.

SOME DAY, ONE DAY *(May)*
• Album: *Queen2*

Coming between the more well-known 'White Queen (As It Began)' and Roger's raucous 'The Loser In The End', Brian's 'Some Day, One Day' unfortunately fell mostly on deaf ears. Despite being a gorgeous song which evokes images of kings and castles from the middle ages, the song received scant attention upon release, due mostly to the lack of an appearance in the

live setting. Driven by a beautiful acoustic guitar line and incorporating breathtaking guitar orchestrations, Brian sings (his first lead vocal appearance on a Queen record) about a love that has never been, but could be, with its songwriter later explaining, "[It] was born of my sadness that a relationship seemingly couldn't be perfect on earth, and I was visualizing a place in eternity where things would be different ... the acoustic 'tickling' and the overlaid smooth sustained electric guitars were intended to paint a picture of that world."

SOME THINGS THAT GLITTER *(May/Taylor/Rodgers)*
• Album (Q+PR): *Cosmos*

On 'We Believe' and 'Still Burnin'', Brian sounds like he's going through the motions, delivering rote, by-numbers material as if he was trying to convince not only Paul and Roger that he was interested in *The Cosmos Rocks*, but himself. Not so on 'Some Things That Glitter', an utterly gorgeous piano ballad that, yes, Brian is known to deliver, but when he delivers, the result is astounding. Addressing an awkward girl blossoming into an intellectual and confident person, with a gentle admonishment of arbitrary societal standards, the song is reminiscent of 'Sail Away Sweet Sister' and 'Why Don't We Try Again', with some lovely vocal harmonies and a soaring guitar solo. Paul certainly liked the song, telling the *Halesowen News*, "Some of the songs on the album are different; some are very natural and organic, like 'Voodoo', but there are others that are beautifully produced, too: 'All That Glitters' *[sic]*, for example."

It's useless to ponder the "what if"s of the world, but with 'Some Things That Glitter', it's difficult not to: not only would it have made a fine follow-up single to 'C-Lebrity', thus guaranteeing it a position in the set list, it would have also been stunning to have heard Brian sing lead vocals instead of Paul. Brian certainly had faith in the song, submitting it to sessions for Kerry Ellis's *Anthems* album, a version of which was duly released on that album, albeit pointlessly retitled to 'I Loved A Butterfly'.

SON AND DAUGHTER *(May)*
• B-side: 7/73 • Album: *Queen* • Compilation: *BBC, On Air* • Live: *Rainbow, Odeon*

One of the band's first real attempts at blues, a genre in which they didn't find much extended success, 'Son And Daughter' is likely the song that garnered the most comparisons to Led Zeppelin. With interesting subject matter (instead of a single parent having to do the work of two parents, the song features a child who has to please his parents by accepting the roles of both son and daughter), it worked far better in the live setting than on record, where it was reduced to a three-minute song devoid of the improvisational sections that made so many live performances spectacular. The song was performed as early as 1970, but was eventually dropped in favor of newer material by 1976; vastly different live versions, all interpolating magnificent guitar solos, were released in 2014 and 2015 on *Live At The Rainbow '74* and *A Night At The Odeon*, respectively.

Two BBC versions exist. The first, recorded on 25 July 1973, is an enjoyable but perfunctory run-through, with the band only just starting to expand the track through improvisation. The second, recorded on 3 December and issued on *Queen At The Beeb*, is an exciting, seven-minute excursion that is far superior to the album version. It allowed Brian the chance to showcase his guitar techniques, incorporating a solo that would later be worked into 'Brighton Rock'. Both versions recorded for the BBC were subsequently released on the 2016 compilation *On Air*.

SON OF STAR FLEET *(May)*
• B-side (Brian): 10/83 [65]

Essentially a re-edited mix of 'Star Fleet', 'Son Of Star Fleet' features all the instrumental bits of the original song in a convenient, four-minute piece, thus earning Brian even more royalties. As of this writing, the song has yet to appear on compact disc.

SOUL BROTHER *(Queen)*
• B-side: 10/81 [1] • CD Single: 11/88 • Compilation: *Vision* • Bonus: *Space*

Recorded during sessions for *The Game*, 'Soul Brother' was credited as a Queen composition presumably because of the numerous references to previous song titles: 'You're My Best Friend', 'We Will Rock You' and 'Somebody To Love' are among the many titles mentioned. The song, which glides along at an easy, soul-based pace, was released as the B-side of 'Under Pressure' in October 1981, and then on the US 'Heaven For Everyone' single in June 1996. The song was given wider exposure on the 2009 box set *The Singles Collection – Volume 2* and then two years later on the *Hot Space* reissue. "Freddie told me one day he had

a surprise for me," Brian later said of the song. "He said, 'I've written a song about you, but it needs your touch on it!' I think, curiously, we were both working on songs separately which referred to each other. Can't remember which one of mine it was, since a lot of my songs were obliquely aimed at him (as well as to be sung by him!). Anyway we got in the studio and he played this song. Now whether it was really about me I don't know. But I thought it was fab. I know he wrote it in about 15 minutes! As to why not on an album – well, Freddie deliberately wrote it as a B-side to fill a gap, so I imagine the album was already sewn up."

SOUL (SEE YOU IN HULL) *(Falloon)*

Performed on Roger's 1994/1995 Happiness? tour, little is known about 'Soul (See You In Hull)' except that it was written and sung by Jason Falloon, Roger's guitarist of choice for *Happiness?* and *Electric Fire* and the two supporting tours.

SOUVENIR *(McCartney)*

In May 2001, the Fan Club reported that Brian, Roger and possibly John had been asked by Paul McCartney to contribute to a tribute album for Linda McCartney, who had been Paul's wife for nearly 30 years when she died in 1998 of breast cancer. 'Souvenir', a track from McCartney's recently released *Flaming Pie* album, was named as their contribution, but, for whatever reason, the project either didn't go ahead or Queen's contribution wasn't used; it's not even known if the song was recorded or not.

SPACE *(May)*
• Album (Brian): *World*

Just as *Back To The Light* starts off with a short keyboard introduction, so does *Another World*. 'Space' can hardly be considered a song, but it sets a mood for the album to follow, indicating that all is not going to be bright and happy. Brian said of the piece, "I just wanted to put that little fragment on as an introduction to the album – it's nice to sort of tease in that way, I think. And for me, I wanted something just to set up the big heavy opening track, and just set the mood of where the album's going."

SPREAD YOUR WINGS *(Deacon)*
• Album: *NOTW* • A-side: 2/78 [34] • CD Single: 11/88
• CD Single: 2/96 [15] • Live: *Killers* • Bonus: *NOTW*
• Compilation: *On Air*

John's standout track from *News Of The World* is one of the few connections between Queen past and Queen future: a piano rocker with a memorable chorus, as well as some remarkable guitar and drum work. Written about a drifter named Sammy who's done nothing with his life, the song drives home a poignant message of expanding one's comfort zone and searching for more in life than sweeping up a bar.

The song was issued as a single in February 1978, peaking at a disappointing No. 34 in the UK. In the US, Elektra mistakenly assumed the song wasn't commercial enough and instead issued 'It's Late'. The song was included in the set list between 1977 and 1979, but was dropped before the start of the 1980 Game tour. The introduction was reprised on a few occasions throughout the 1982 and 1984 tours, but never progressed beyond a rendition of the chorus.

A far superior BBC take was recorded on 28 October 1977, taken at a slightly faster pace with a more aggressive guitar sound, and including a raucous up-tempo ending that was unfortunately not attempted on the album version. This arrangement was performed on the 1977 News Of The World North American tour, but the band reverted to the standard performance for the 1978 European leg of that tour, simply because the song had been released as a single there and so the band wanted to present it as faithfully as possible. The BBC version was finally released on the 2011 double-disc edition of *News Of The World*, and again in 2016 on the BBC retrospective *On Air*. A markedly different alternate take, running nearly five minutes, was unearthed for the 40th anniversary box set of *News Of The World*, while the song was performed live for the first time in 38 years by Queen + Adam Lambert, though the band were seemingly unhappy with the arrangement (or the reception), and dropped it after a handful of performances.

STAND UP FOR LOVE *(Taylor)*
• Album (The Cross): *Shove* • B-side: 7/88

One of the better tracks from *Shove It*, 'Stand Up For Love' features a tenacious guitar riff and a prominent Hammond organ, played by Spike Edney, and contains fairly typical lyrics in which Roger proclaims the benefits of love. The song is raucous and rollicking, and if it hadn't been for the typical late-1980s production, it may have become a hit. Unusually, female backing vocalists are featured in a call-and-response chorus, but the women are not credited; the same can be said of the mystery saxophone player, who adds embellishments throughout, including a disjointed solo.

'Stand Up For Love' became the closing track of The Cross' 1988 tour, and was resurrected in 1992 for the series of festivals and parties at which The Cross performed, the most notable being at the December 1992 Christmas shows at The Marquee Club.

STAR FLEET *(Bliss/May)*
• A-side (Brian): 10/83 [65] • Album (Brian): *Starfleet*
• CD single (Brian): 11/92 [19]

"I used to get up with my little boy [Jimmy] and watch it religiously every Saturday morning," Brian said of the original *Star Fleet* television series. "And he said, 'Daddy, you should play that!', and I thought, 'Actually, that's a rather good piece of music!'" Opening with Eddie Van Halen's trademark finger-picked guitar, with Brian providing the lead in the background, the musicians take a few moments to come together. However, once Eddie and Brian lock into that crucial guitar riff nearly 30 seconds in, the band (also including bassist Phil Chen, drummer Alan Gratzer and keyboardist Fred Mandel) is down to serious business.

Though the synthesizer dominates for the most part, Brian found a way to incorporate the instrument in a way that *Hot Space* couldn't: instead of being so reliant on the instrument and featuring it prominently, it takes a backseat, though at times it almost sounds as if Brian is duelling with the synth. Truly an inspired decision, and there's no doubt that had *Hot Space* sounded like this track, it would have been far better received.

The words, which are not Brian's, are spread out so far between instrumental interludes that the song would have survived without them. However, Brian interprets them well, and his vocal performance on this song is commendable. "'Star Fleet' is the theme tune for a superb TV sci-fi series broadcast in England for kids of all ages; Japanese visuals and a British soundtrack including music by Paul Bliss," Brian explained in the liner notes for the *Star Fleet Project* EP. "The heroes pilot space vehicles which can assemble into a giant robot for land battles. The aliens fly fantastic insect-like craft which spawn similar fighting machines, all intent on possession of the secret of F Zero One –

having been introduced to all this by my small boy, I became equally obsessed by it, and formed the idea of making a hard rock version of the title theme.

"In 'Star Fleet', recorded on the first day, you can hear a kind of nervous exhilaration," he continued. "The new situation [of recording with the four new musicians] produced a strange and different kind of energy ... I've attempted to hone [the song] into something like a 'proper record' – my thanks to Roger for helping me with the chorus vocals. But I haven't messed one scrap with the tracking done on the day. The rest is simply mixed 'naked'."

The song comes to a premature conclusion five minutes in, but Brian and Eddie clearly aren't ready to end the party: the band continue jamming for a further three minutes, though the synth is now no longer part of the equation. The song comes to a definite close, followed by a snippet of undoubtedly good-natured, albeit incomprehensible, dialog, and one of the most satisfyingly bizarre compositions related to Queen is over. It would be hard to imagine anyone within Queen taking the song seriously, but it's a fun little excursion that deserves more attention than it's been given over the years. Strangely, it lived on – at the conclusion of 'One Vision' on the 1986 Magic tour, the band launched into the ascending false conclusion before leading into 'Tie Your Mother Down'.

Despite only three songs appearing on the mini-album, EMI and Elektra nevertheless extracted a single, and the title track was clearly the most commercial of the bunch. To make it even more appealing, various edits were created: the first and standard edit ran 4'25 and featured a new keyboard introduction (it was this version that was released as the single in the UK), while the second and lesser-known edit ran only 3'03, albeit pitched slightly higher than normal, and was released as the US single. Both of these versions contained a leaner edit with less instrumental space between verses; perhaps due to realizing the strength of the instrumental segments, a separate edit was created and released as the B-side, titled 'Son Of Star Fleet'. The single, released towards the end of October 1983, went on to peak at an unsurprising No. 65 in the UK, not charting at all in the US. Perhaps recognizing that *Star Fleet Project* had been out of print for nearly a decade, this song, along with 'Let Me Out', was placed on the first CD single issue of 'Back To The Light' in November 1992. A demo was recorded by Brian shortly before the sessions commenced in order to give the musicians a guide to the structure; this hasn't yet surfaced in the

collector's circle.

A video was created for the single, and has gone down in Queen folklore as being simultaneously the strangest and scariest video created. With the decapitated head of Brian floating around periodically, lip-synching to the words, segments of the original cartoon series were also inserted, making for an unsettling viewing experience. Still, much like Brian's other videos, it remains unfairly obscure, and deserves to be seen if only for its kitsch value.

STATE OF SHOCK

One of three tracks recorded with Michael Jackson in early 1983 at his home studio, 'State Of Shock' was later re-recorded with Mick Jagger on vocals and released as a single from The Jackson 5's *Victory* album in 1984, but the original, unreleased version is great fun and deserves to be heard. With a strident guitar riff and a poppy drum-machine backing, the song sounds like an extension of 'Staying Power' in terms of lyrical matter, and wouldn't sound out of place on either *Mr Bad Guy* or Michael Jackson's own *Thriller* album.

Along with 'Victory', this track was rumored to have been included on a 2002 Michael Jackson compilation, but, unfortunately, this never happened. These two songs were further worked on by Brian and Roger for the 2014 *Queen Forever* compilation, but were set aside in favor of a William Orbit remix of 'There Must Be More To Life Than This'. Considering the tight reins that Jackson's estate holds over his music, it's unlikely that these recordings will ever be released.

STAYING POWER (Mercury)
• Album: *Space* • B-side: 8/82 [40] • Live: *On Fire*
• Bonus: *Space*

The opening track of *Hot Space* is an upbeat excursion into funk that wears its Michael Jackson influence proudly on its sleeve. Featuring a hot brass section (arranged by Arif Mardin in Los Angeles) and synthesizer flourishes in place of Brian's guitar, the song is slightly let down by the lyrics, a declaration of Freddie's sexual prowess and, ahem, 'staying power'. (The original title was the more obscene 'Fucking Power'; considering Freddie's other songs at the time consisted of 'Body Language' and the unreleased 'Sex Show', this era undoubtedly marked the climax of the vocalist's lust for lust.)

Live, the song featured Morgan Fisher (or Fred

Mandel, depending on the tour) playing synth bass while John took over rhythm guitar, allowing Brian to concentrate on solos and inject a rock feel into the song. The song was a mainstay of the 1982 Hot Space tour, and was even the only *Hot Space* song to remain in the set list beyond that tour, being performed on the first half of the 1984 Queen Works! European tour.

Elektra issued the song as the final *Hot Space* single in the US in November 1982, more than two months after the Rock 'n' America tour had concluded. Unsurprisingly, the single didn't chart, but was unique in that it offered the first extended remixes of the song and its B-side, John's more commercial 'Back Chat'. (The pairing was flipped in the UK, and released in August 1982.) An extended remix was also created by John Luongo, which turned the song into a full-scale disco workout. Inexplicably, this remix wasn't released on the 2011 reissue of *Hot Space*; in its stead was a live version from the Milton Keynes Bowl.

THE STEALER *(Rodgers/Fraser/Kossoff)*

First recorded by Free and released on their 1970 album *Highway*, 'The Stealer' was a staple of AM radio, and a favorite of the Faces, who incorporated it into their set lists at the time. The same couldn't be said of Queen + Paul Rodgers, who performed it live only once on the 2008 Rock The Cosmos tour, in Zürich on 29 September.

STEALIN' *(Queen)*
• B-side: 6/89 [7]

An interesting leftover from the *Miracle* sessions, 'Stealin'' evolved from a jam dominated largely by Freddie. The original recording ran at a lengthy 12 minutes, and contained an amusing interchange between several multi-tracked Freddies, and at times it sounds as if he's arguing with himself. Mostly a throwaway, but still a compelling listen, four minutes were chopped off that version and re-edited for official use, when it appeared as the B-side of 'Breakthru' in June 1989. While not the strongest track ever written by Queen, it certainly would have made for a nice diversion on *The Miracle*, if only for its prominent use of 12-string acoustic guitar.

STEP ON ME *(May/Staffell)*
• Compilation (Smile): *Ghost Of A Smile*

Recorded during the June 1969 sessions at Trident Studios, with future Queen one-time co-producer John Anthony at the controls, 'Step On Me' is one of the most Queen-like tracks to be written and recorded by Smile. That's no surprise, since it was largely written by Brian, even featuring the guitarist on complex harmonies and piano. ("The tune and most of the words were written by Brian," Tim Staffell later recalled. "I contributed to the words.") Telling the story of a manipulative girlfriend, 'Step On Me' is a jaunty and enjoyable track with great vocals and arrangements, and may be the highlight of the sessions. Chosen as the B-side to 'Earth' in August 1969, the song was performed semi-regularly in the live set list, but the studio version remained unreleased until the 1982 *Gettin' Smile* album and again in 1998 on the *Ghost Of A Smile* compilation.

STILL BURNIN' *(May/Rodgers/Taylor)*
• Album (Q+PR): *Cosmos*

In the years following Brian's semi-retirement from a solo career, he immersed himself in a variety of projects that were as far removed from music as could be: he rekindled an interest in stereo photography, compiling a book of photographs by T. R. Williams as *A Village Lost And Found: Scenes In Our Village*; finished his PhD degree by publishing his astrophysics thesis, *A Survey Of Radial Velocities In The Zodiacal Dust Cloud*, and an all-encompassing book, *Bang! The Complete History Of The Universe*; and became a social activist, joining Nelson Mandela's 46664 AIDS awareness campaign and later forming his own, Save Me, to protect all animals against cruel and unnecessary treatment. He somehow was also able to work on the *We Will Rock You* musical, appearing at each country's opening nights since it started in 2002, and produce Kerry Ellis's debut EP, *Wicked In Rock*, and her first album, *Anthems*, all while preserving and producing Queen's back catalog. The farthest thing from his mind was to be an active musician again, evident in his reluctance to tour and paucity of newly-written songs, which can be counted on one hand since the beginning of the 2000s.

So it's surprising that Brian would be the instigator of 'Still Burnin'', a flacid blues stomper that extols the wonder of creativity in a performer. The precious opening moments, where Roger's drums kick up some dust and Brian gets the feel of the sound before locking into the groove, intimates the song's spontaneity, but when it finally does get moving, the results are underwhelming. "Music lights this flame in me," Paul bellows, before reassuring listeners, "Don't think for a moment that my heart went cold," but it all rings hollow. Brian may indeed have felt reinvigorated by his association with Paul Rodgers, but it doesn't show in his three contributions to the album; only on 'Some Things That Glitter' does the traditional May spark ignite, but by then the impact is gone. With an expected burst of 'We Will Rock You' – the message of which is either to remind everyone that Queen has a musical, or that Brian is keen on relying on past glories – following a gritty, wah-wah'd guitar solo, 'Still Burnin'' doesn't so much rage as it does fan the cooling embers.

STONE COLD CRAZY (May/Mercury/Taylor/Deacon)
• Album: SHA • B-side: 11/89 [21] • Bonus: SHA • Live: Rainbow • Compilation: On Air

Originally written by Freddie in 1969 during his tenure as the lead singer of Wreckage, 'Stone Cold Crazy' was one of the first songs performed by Queen the following year, and underwent a series of transformations until it became the blistering rocker presented on Sheer Heart Attack. Credited to the entire band since nobody could remember who wrote which parts, this would become the only four-way collaboration the band would undertake until 'Soul Brother' in 1980.

Lyrically, the song continues with the 1920s feel presented on 'Bring Back That Leroy Brown' as Freddie finds himself "dreaming [he] was Al Capone." The lyrics are jumbled together, with three verses and choruses crammed into two minutes of raucous thrashing, still allowing for several manic guitar solos after each verse. It's a perfect example of the band's musical diversity in different types of rock, and can also be viewed as a forerunner of Queen's brief excursion into punk. The song was covered by Metallica in 1991, where it became a hit for that band and even earned them a Grammy. Industrial rocker Trent Reznor, frontman and genius behind Nine Inch Nails, remixed the song in 1991 for a promo single; sadly, this was passed up in favor of a more straightforward remix for the remastered release of Sheer Heart Attack. For those who want a new twist on the song, Reznor's rendition is highly recommended.

'Stone Cold Crazy' was performed by the band with James Hetfield on lead vocals at the 1992 Concert For Life, but had been performed by Queen between 1970 and 1977, then resurrected for the Queen Works!

tours in 1984. A live version from the 1974 Rainbow performance was issued as the B-side to 'The Miracle' in November 1989 and previously on the Rare Live video. A version recorded at the BBC on 16 October 1974 was released as a bonus track on the 2011 Sheer Heart Attack deluxe reissue, and again five years later on the On Air BBC retrospective.

STONE FREE (Hendrix)

Originally released by The Jimi Hendrix Experience in 1967, 'Stone Free' was performed by Ibex at The Sink Club, Liverpool on 9 September 1969 but lasted barely a minute. The song was erroneously listed as 'Rock Me Baby', though it's likely that The Yardbirds track was also performed by Ibex at some point. Not entirely by coincidence, 1984 also included the song in their set list.

STOP ALL THE FIGHTING (Mercury)
• B-side (Freddie): 4/85 [11] • B-side (Freddie): 1/93 [29] • Compilation (Freddie): Solo Collection

Recorded during sessions for Mr Bad Guy, 'Stop All The Fighting' is an energetic rocker, sounding like an out-take from one of the numerous new wave rockers emerging at the time. The lyrics are nothing spectacular, almost mirroring the sentiments of 'Is This The World We Created...?' but far more aggressively. Strangely, Freddie nearly snarls the lyrics, and it's easy to see why this song wasn't included on the album. Instead, it was issued as the B-side of 'I Was Born To Love You' in April 1985, with an extended mix created especially for the release. This version could technically be considered the B-side of the extended version of 'Love Kills', since it was released on a separate bonus disc, albeit as a double-pack with 'I Was Born To Love You'. The song was later issued as the B-side of the reissued 'The Great Pretender' single in January 1993.

STORM (May)
• Soundtrack (Brian): Furia

Suitably opening with the sound of a storm breaking, 'Storm' is an extension of 'First Kiss' but performed on keyboards, though the orchestra is introduced midway through for accompaniment. The remaining 30 seconds of the piece consist of dialog from the film.

STORY OF A HEART (Andersson/Ulvaeus)
• Album (Brian & Kerry): Golden

QUEEN – COMPLETE WORKS

Written and recorded by former ABBA band member Benny Andersson, 'Story Of A Heart' is a lovely, delicate ballad, with a ticking clock (or heartbeat) providing the rhythm, before the song explodes to life momentarily, settling down for the conclusion. Bookended by Kerry intoning "This is the story, a story of a heart, and all of it mine ... And now you've heard my story," the song is a gorgeous interlude, serving as a chaser to the mainstream pop of 'The Kissing Me Song'.

STRANGE FRONTIER *(Taylor)*
• Album (Roger): *Frontier* • A-side (Roger): 7/84 [98]

Starting with an atmospheric synthesizer-drum duet before kicking into high gear with an accelerated drum roll, the title track to Roger's second solo album is strong and solid, with a heavy bass line bouncing throughout, and occasional blasts of marimba coloring the song and keeping things interesting. This was the second time Roger had used the instrument on one of his songs, though by this time it had entered the pop mainstream via the Thompson Twins' 'Hold Me Now' and, later, David Bowie's 'Blue Jean'.

Effectively telling the story of a nuclear holocaust, a major threat in the early to mid-1980s, the song contains some of Roger's most biting lyrics, though the final verse, surging into overdrive thanks to the introduction of some elaborate choral backing vocals, is particularly poignant: "Someday soon they'll drop the big one / No more dad and no more mum."

When asked by famed Los Angeles disc jockey Jim Ladd if he'd ever been involved with the 'No Nukes' movement, Roger responded in the affirmative, saying, "I'm involved in the English version ... it's called the CND [Campaign For Nuclear Disarmament]. And I'm a member of it and I contribute and I believe what they're doing is right, and, basically, a lot of the songs on [*Strange Frontier*] are directly or undirectly [sic] about that, because I think that's the most important issue of the age, and that's what I wanted to write about."

'Strange Frontier', backed with a remixed version of 'I Cry For You (Love, Hope & Confusion)', was issued as the second single from the album in July 1984. Unfortunately, interest in the album and its related singles had started to wane, and the single barely limped into the Top 100, peaking at a dismal No. 98 in the UK. Not even one of Roger's better videos could help. Directed by George Bloom and filmed in Malibu, California in July 1984, the video is an almost scene-perfect reproduction of James Dean's classic *Rebel Without A Cause*, in which

Roger races up the side of a mountain to an inconclusive finale, all for the attention of a girl.

The song made a welcome appearance in both The Cross' various set lists and during Roger's 1999 Electric Fire tour, and was well-received by the crowds. Surprisingly, it made a few other appearances, notably in 2000 at a gig with the SAS Band and at the tenth anniversary tribute concert for Freddie on 24 November 2001, with Brian guesting on guitar.

STUPID CUPID *(Sedaka)*
• Live: *Rainbow, Odeon*

Another favorite of Freddie's, he would occasionally throw a few lines of this Neil Sedaka song, made popular by Connie Francis in 1958, into the Rock 'n' Roll Medley up until 1977. A live version from 11 December of that year was included on the 1989 video anthology, *Rare Live*.

SUBSTITUTE *(Townshend)*

Arguably The Who's finest pop single, 'Substitute' was performed live by 1984, and was later performed by The Cross at the fan club's first Christmas show at the Marquee, along with special guest Roger Daltrey on lead vocals.

SUMMERTIME BLUES *(Cochran/Capehart)*

Originally recorded by Eddie Cochran but later covered to devastating effect by Blue Cheer and The Who in the late 1960s, 'Summertime Blues' was performed live by The Cross at the Gosport Festival on 30 July 1992.

SUNNY DAY *(Taylor)*
• Album (Roger): *Earth*

This reimagining of 'Woman You're So Beautiful (But Still A Pain In The Ass)' turns the delightful, reggae-infused original into a lovely ballad. The song still retains all of the charm of the original, but the new twist turns it into something a little more conventional albeit more in line with the laid-back feel of *Fun On Earth*. Featuring one of the few full band performances on the album – elsewhere, Roger plays most of the instruments, though old stalwarts Spike Edney, Jason Falloon, and Jonathan Perkins are on 'Sunny Day' – the song is a treat, updating the mood of the quirky original to be more of an all-out love song.

While the only official single to have been released from the album was 'The Unblinking Eye (Everything Is Broken)', and that was four years prior to the release of *Fun On Earth*, 'Sunny Day' was used for the promotional rounds, with a disc pressed for radio use. ('Up' and 'Be With You' also received this distinction much later, by which time the album was out of the charts.) A video was made, with Roger perched on the balcony of his stately Surrey mansion singing the words, while illustrations from the album's sleeve, drawn by son Felix, and choice lyrics, penned in Roger's handwriting, fly around him. Apart from some gratuitous studio shots of Roger drumming and Jason Falloon playing the guitar solo, this is a largely homemade affair, a perfect snapshot into Roger's frame of mind – and the beautiful countryside behind him doesn't hurt, either.

SURF'S UP . . . SCHOOL'S OUT ! *(Taylor/Rodgers/May)*
• Album (Q+PR): *Cosmos*

For fans and casual observers alike, reading through the song titles of *The Cosmos Rocks* would be cause to sue Queen + Paul Rodgers for injuries due to whiplash: with a mishmash of fairly straightforward ('Some Things That Glitter', 'Through The Night', 'Small') and ludicrous ('Cosmos Rockin'', 'C-Lebrity'), nothing conjures up an image far better than 'Surf's Up . . . School's Out !', though what kind of image this evokes is up to the listener. By slamming together two titles from The Beach Boys and Alice Cooper, the very nature of the song is thrown into question, with a hybrid of shock theatrical surf rock making for an alarming first impression. The reality is slightly more tame, if not as thrilling: 'Surf's Up . . . School's Out !' is an epic rocker that throws all of the elements that the band didn't employ on the first 12 tracks into one gigantic soup of experimentation. For this reason alone, the song is a success, with Paul finally perfecting the balance between tongue-in-cheek and straightforward deliveries, while Brian especially appears to have been rocked from his indifference, turning in an electrifying, over-the-top guitar performance. Roger is especially on top form, not only contributing thunderous drums and rollicking timpani but prominent vocals, to the point that he's practically duetting with Paul. Twisting and turning through contrasting rhythms and arrangements, with a wailing harmonica and distorted bass added for good measure, the song brings *The Cosmos Rocks* to a bombastic close. It's just a shame that the rest of the album couldn't have been this left field,

for the cheeky humor that often graced Queen's albums was sorely missing up until now.

The song was a natural for the live setting, and yet the band didn't perform it until 21 September 2008, when it replaced 'One Vision' as a rightful show opener, where it remained for nine further performances. Unfortunately, Brian was less than thrilled with its prominent position, and insisted it be moved further back in the set, where it followed 'C-Lebrity' and preceded 'Seagull', and even then it was truncated further to excise the bridge.

SURRENDER *(Taylor)*
• Album (Roger): *Electric* • A-side (Roger): 3/99 [38]
• CD single (Roger): 3/99 [38]

'Surrender' starts off innocently enough, with Roger introducing the back-story of an abusive man ("He wants a punchbag / Not a wife"), after which Treana Morris takes the lead in the role of the battered wife. Roger said of the song on *Retro Countdown* with Mark Dennison, "'Surrender' is all about domestic violence. And it's really sung from the woman's point of view, the sort of point of view, I suppose, of the battered wife or girlfriend. Which is quite a poignant point of view. And I suppose it's quite depressing, really! I think it's a subject which is hardly touched, and it is a subject which does affect a lot of people all over the world, is rarely talked about and is very hard to deal with." When *The Times* noted that the lyrics were largely autobiographical, the question was raised whether 'Surrender' was based on personal experience, to which Roger quietly responded, "I experienced some of that in my formative years, yes."

Chosen as the second single release from *Electric Fire*, albeit six months after 'Pressure On', 'Surrender' (with an exclamation point added for its single release) nevertheless performed better, reaching No. 38 in the UK, due to its prominence in the set list. A radio remix rearranged the track slightly, while two live versions were presented on the second CD single of the release. Both were taken from the Cyberbarn performance, with the audio version preserving the full performance and the video version an edited take of the same rendition.

SURRENDER TO THE CITY: *see* DEEP RIDGE

SWEET LADY *(May)*

• Album: *Opera*

Sheer Heart Attack had drawn a definitive line between the formative years of Queen and the path they would take on subsequent albums: their first two albums were drawn heavily from the epic swagger and extraterrestrial mysticism of Led Zeppelin, while their third album was more focused on shorter pop songs, with the occasional rock tune thrown in to remind fans that they hadn't been entirely ensconced by the hit parade. While Freddie would chase his indulgences in various genres, John had his finger on the pulse of pop, and Roger could be counted on to deliver a zag with his contributions, Brian was the only one who would make sure their rock roots never totally faded; the guitarist's songs on *A Night At The Opera* were varied, but none flew the flag of rock higher than 'Sweet Lady', an unpretentious rocker in 3/4 time that was the most basic of performances on an otherwise extravagant album.

"'Sweet Lady' musically came from a riff and I was fascinated with the idea of a heavy riff in 3/4 time rather than 4/4," Brian later explained. "Because 3/4 is the time of the waltz, traditionally it's a very gentle sound. People used to dance to it and whatever. So the fact that I could find this riff in 3/4 which seemed to have an urgency and heaviness to it was a fascinating thing for me. And I think in your head, you kind of refuse to hear it in 3/4, which is why it's still powerful I think. Well, it's my theory anyway. And lyrically, as a lot of my stuff it's about relationships and what I saw in my own relationships and the relationships of people around me which I still really feel is the fundamental building material of our lives. I'm not very good on politics on a grand scale but I'm intrigued by what happens one to one between people. I think some of those are the strongest forces in our lives and so that's what the song's about."

The song was one of three songs from *A Night At The Opera* to be performed live on the 1975 tour (the others were 'Bohemian Rhapsody' and 'The Prophet's Song'), and 'Sweet Lady' remained in the set list until June 1977, by which time it was dropped in favor of newer material. A particularly energetic version from the 1976 Hyde Park concert was included as a bonus video on the 30th anniversary edition of *A Night At The Opera*.

TAKE ANOTHER LITTLE PIECE OF MY HEART:
see **LET ME LIVE**

TAKE LOVE *(Rodgers)*

The 2006 Queen + Paul Rodgers tour brought two new additions to the set list: the first was a revival of 'Dragon Attack', which hadn't been played live since 1985, and the second was a brand-new song, titled 'Take Love'. Written by Paul, the song was a live favorite on the US tour, and this led to speculation that it would be recorded on *The Cosmos Rocks*; yet, when the running order was revealed in the summer of 2008, 'Take Love' was nowhere to be found. The official reasoning was that, while the song was recorded during sessions, the band felt that it didn't gel properly, and was dropped in a half-finished state.

TANGO: 'CUESTA ABAJO' *(Gardel)*

• Soundtrack (Brian): *Furia*

Performed by Manuel Cedron and featuring no involvement whatsoever from Brian, this is a jaunty, upbeat piece in the tango style (obviously) with plenty of piano and accordion.

TAVASZI SZÉL VIZET ÁRASZT

(trad. arr. Mercury/May)

• Bonus: *Wembley* • Live: *Budapest*

Midway through their acoustic set at the Nepstadion in Budapest on 27 July 1986, Brian and Freddie took a lighthearted break to perform a specially rehearsed interpretation of the Hungarian national anthem. Keen on connecting with the audience, who were seeing their first-ever Queen concert, Freddie sang the song in its native tongue; not an easy task, yet he took careful precautions and scrawled the lyrics phonetically on his hand. "I'm over the moon!" he beamed to the audience at the song's conclusion.

First released in 1987 on the video cassette *Queen In Budapest*, the song appeared as a bonus track on the 2003 reissue of *Live At Wembley Stadium*, before being given its proper release on the 2012 live album *Hungarian Rhapsody: Queen Live In Budapest*.

TEAR IT UP *(May)*

• Album: *Works* • B-side: 9/84 [13] • Live: *Wembley, Budapest*

The response to *Hot Space* had affected the band so deeply that, following the supporting tour's conclusion in November 1982, they took some much needed time off to ponder the future of the band. While Freddie and Roger embarked on solo careers, and John relaxed with his family, Brian spent a great deal of time co-producing, with Mack, Heavy Petting's debut record, *Lettin' Loose*. Touted as the Scottish equivalent of Def Leppard, Brian was influenced by the heavy metal band, which reaffirmed his ideals as a guitar god, and he would implement a heavier sound from this point forward, preferring to write louder material to counteract the more mainstream songs his bandmates would write.

'Tear It Up' was one of the first songs Brian wrote for *The Works*, and can be seen as an attempt to rekindle the flame of rock'n'roll that had nearly burned out on the band's previous rhythmic-inspired albums. Though it doesn't say much lyrically, the band are clearly having a ball, with Brian delivering a crunching guitar riff (and some suitable scorching lines here and there) and Roger offering a variant on the 'We Will Rock You' footstomps and handclaps. Freddie sounds as committed as ever, planting his tongue firmly in cheek at times with some of the lines ("I love you for your mind, baby, gimme your body" and "I gotta tell you baby you're driving me gaga!"), though 'Tear It Up' is obviously a good-time throwaway rocker, devoid of a deeper message, and simply serves as proof that Queen hadn't lost their ability to rock.

The song was issued as the B-side of 'Hammer To Fall' in September 1984, and was performed as the first proper opening song on the 1984 and 1985 Works! tours, albeit in a heavily truncated fashion. It was later incorporated into the medley for the 1986 Magic tour, but the song, in its entirety, has yet to be performed live.

A demo version with Brian on lead vocals exists, but has yet to see the light of day.

TEEN DREAMS: *see* TENEMENT FUNSTER

TENEMENT FUNSTER *(Taylor)*
• Album: *SHA* • EP: *First EP* • CD Single: 11/88
• Bonus: *SHA* • Compilation: *On Air*

Roger's exquisitely dark rocker is an unexpected early highlight on the *Sheer Heart Attack* album, and shows the drummer's maturity as a songwriter. Even though the subject matter still centers around girls, cars and rock'n'roll, the song is exceptionally well-written and arranged. Eluding the live setting during Queen's career as a rock band, the song was finally introduced in 1994 during Roger's solo Happiness? tour.

The song sounds undeniably like a Marc Bolan rocker; even the title seems like a combination of T. Rex's 'Jeepster' and 'Tenement Lady'. The working title was 'Teen Dreams' (itself an unmistakable echo of Bolan's January 1974 hit 'Teenage Dream'), and not 'Tin Dreams' as has been widely reported, before it became known as 'You're Young And You're Crazy'. When the track appeared on *Queen's First EP* in May 1977, it finally featured a proper ending as opposed to the original segue into 'Flick Of The Wrist'. An alternate version, recorded on 16 October 1974 for the BBC, used the same backing track as the album version but with more aggressive vocals from Roger. This version was finally officially released in 2011 on the deluxe edition of *Sheer Heart Attack*, and again five years later on the BBC retrospective *On Air*.

TEO TORRIATTE (LET US CLING TOGETHER) *(May)*
• Album: *Races* • Bonus: *Races*

After Queen's first appearance in Japan in the spring of 1975, the band were touched by the country's civility and appreciation for everything Queen. Brian, in particular, was overjoyed at reaching a whole new level of Queen fans, especially considering that most of them didn't speak much English. Upon the band's return trip the following year, the guitarist was surprised to see that devotion for the band was still strong, so he wrote a song thanking the people of Japan. In 2007, he elaborated further: "[It] was the was the result of feeling 'untimely ripped' from our lovely Japanese fans. I had never experienced anything like the love that was showered upon on when we were a young Rock Group in Japan. So suddenly, I felt I wanted to say (on behalf of Queen) that I missed them, and we would not forget."

'Teo Torriatte (Let Us Cling Together)' is an exquisite piano ballad that closes *A Day At The Races* in magnificent style. Written entirely by Brian, with lyrical translation assistance from Chika Kujiraoka, the song is emotively delivered by Freddie, turning in a touching vocal that allowed plenty of singalong opportunities when performed live.

With Brian on acoustic piano, Vox electric piano and harmonium, the song is adventurous and features a poignant bridge and multi-tracked concluding chorus. The song was reserved for only Japanese tours, and it was performed in 1979, 1981 and 1982 (but not, suspiciously, in 1985), and also issued as a Japanese-only single, shorn of the album's closing

"Escher guitar staircase", in March 1977, with 'Good Old-Fashioned Lover Boy' as the flipside. The song was remixed in 2005 for the Japanese compilation album *Jewels II*, while, more significantly, it was released on the awareness album *Songs For Japan*, compiled as a response to the aftermath of the devastating 9.0 magnitude earthquake and tsunami that destroyed parts of Japan on 11 March 2011. Appropriately, the song was performed on Japanese tour dates by Queen + Paul Rodgers and Queen + Adam Lambert, sung by Brian and often heavily abridged.

THANK GOD IT'S CHRISTMAS *(Taylor/May)*
• A-side: 11/85 [21] • Compilation: *Vision, Hits3*
• B-side: 12/95 [6] • CD Single: 12/99 [6]

As if Queen hadn't done enough in 1984, they ended the year with their first (and only) attempt at a Christmas single. The idea was conceived by Brian and Roger, which accounts for the joint composition credit: "Roger and I both came up with an idea for a Christmas single around July of [1984]," Brian explained in 1997. "We went in and demo'd both of them, and we decided that Roger's was the best one. The other song, my one, became Anita's Christmas song a couple of years later, 'I Dream Of Christmas'." With a hypnotic drum loop and pulsating bass guitar, the song was recorded in London in July 1984, just before the Works! tour started, with the lead vocal overdubbed by Freddie in Montreux. Brian later explained that having to record the single in the summer was a necessity: "Well, the funny thing is that you have to make Christmas records in the summer, and you just don't feel like it. 'Cause if you start making them at Christmas, obviously it's all over before you've got it out."

Issued in November 1984, the single replaced the original plan to issue 'Man On The Prowl' and 'Keep Passing The Open Windows' as a single; instead, these two songs were placed on the B-side of 'Thank God It's Christmas'. It peaked at No. 21 in the UK but received no US release, and was finally issued on CD on the 1999 compilation *Greatest Hits III*. It also appeared as the B-side of 'A Winter's Tale' in 1995 and on the CD single of 'Under Pressure ('rah' mix)' in 1999.

THANK YOU *(Page/Plant)*

Shortly before Robert Plant's interpretation of 'Crazy Little Thing Called Love' at the Concert For Life, he and Brian appeared front stage to perform a touching one-verse acoustic rendition of his 1969 *Led Zeppelin II* track.

THERE MUST BE MORE TO LIFE THAN THIS *(Mercury)*
• Album (Freddie): *BadGuy* • Compilation (Freddie): *Solo Collection*

Despite surfacing on *Mr Bad Guy* in April 1985, 'There Must Be More To Life Than This' dates back to the *Hot Space* recording sessions in 1981, but was left on the chopping block until being revived in 1983 when it was planned as the closing track on *The Works*. When Brian and Freddie wrote 'Is This The World We Created...?', this song was given the boot once again and instead became an album track on *Mr Bad Guy*. A shame, since this song is a highlight of *Mr Bad Guy* and shows Freddie's concern with a world falling apart, predating the pacifist attitudes expressed in such songs as 'Do They Know It's Christmas?' and the whole Live Aid experience in 1985.

"Basically, it's just a song about people," Freddie told Rudi Dolezal in 1985. "It's basically another love song, but it's hard to call it that ... It's all to do with the fighting and basically it's a love and peace song. But I really don't like to write message songs, but this one just came out and it's very generic. It's all to do with, why do people get themselves into so many problems? It's basically that, but I don't want to dwell on that too much. It's just one of those songs that I had for a while."

An instrumental version was created for the box set in 2000, while an early take, recorded on 25 May 1984, has Freddie trying to make his way through several takes of the piano introduction. While not essential listening, it's still interesting to hear the difficulty that Freddie had in getting the song right. It was also reported in 1996 that John Deacon had remixed the track for inclusion on a potential box set; to date, this version remains unreleased.

Before it was considered for his solo album, Freddie brought the song to an impromptu session with Michael Jackson in the summer of 1983 at Jackson's Neverland Ranch, along with 'State Of Shock' and 'Victory', the latter a song reportedly recorded by Queen during sessions for *Hot Space*. Jackson was a self-professed fan of Queen, especially their dancier material, and Freddie's 'Staying Power' could have been mistaken as an *Off The Wall* out-take; the mutual respect and admiration for each other made for an interesting time in the studio, though reports surfaced years later that there was a great deal of tension during the six-hour session. Depending on who you believe, the collaboration fell apart either due to Freddie's apparent discomfort with the studio environment (Jim Beach later recalled, "They got on well except for the fact that I suddenly got a call from Freddie, saying, 'Miami [Freddie's nickname for Jim], dear, can you get on over here … You've got to get me out of here, I'm recording with a llama … I've had enough and I want to get out") or because Jackson was uncomfortable with Freddie's liberal use of cocaine during the sessions, but the simple fact of the matter was that the two friends drifted apart, which Freddie later regretfully explained: "We would actually go out and have dinner, but now he just stays at home, he doesn't like coming out at all … I think one of the tracks would have been on the *Thriller* album if I had finished it, but I missed out."

Queen's 1981 take on the song was rescued from mothballs in 2011, where Brian, absent from the original session, added some guitar before it was passed on to producer William Orbit, who had cut his teeth on Madonna's *Ray Of Light*, Blur's *13*, and Katie Melua's *The House*. Orbit added additional keyboards before blending the original recording with the duet vocals recorded, resulting in a pleasant if unremarkable meeting of two of the greatest vocalists of all time. (A version had been produced by Brian which was a little more adventurous and experimental, but was rejected by Michael Jackson's estate. This version, dubbed the "Gold Mix", leaked out onto the bootleg market late in 2015.) The battle between Queen Productions and Jackson's estate was like "wading through glue," according to Roger, who later commented that there were plans to include the other two collaborations, "but we could only have one track with Michael, which is a great shame."

THESE ARE THE DAYS OF OUR LIVES (Queen)
• Album: *Innuendo* • AA-side: 12/91 [1] • EP: *Five Live*
• Live (Q+PR): *Return*

Written by Roger for the *Innuendo* album, this delicate ballad is a heartfelt tribute to Freddie, a precursor of the 1994 Roger song 'Old Friends'. The song achieves poignancy in Freddie's exquisite vocal performance, which is largely a solo affair except for a harmony vocal (also from Freddie) on the choruses. Roger was not normally known for expressing nostagia, and the song is uncharacteristic yet appropriate. Whereas Brian immortalizes Freddie in most of his post-*Innuendo*

songs, Roger is able to sum it up perfectly in 'These Are The Days Of Our Lives'. Freddie was Roger's closest friend within the band, so it's no surprise that the drummer would offer something as gorgeous as this track.

Issued as a double A-sided single with 'Bohemian Rhapsody' in December 1991, the song went on to peak at No. 1 in the UK; it was also issued as a US single in September 1991, with 'Bijou' on the B-side, but failed to chart. 'These Are The Days Of Our Lives' is accompanied by a touching video, filmed on 30 May 1991, which was the last time Freddie appeared in front of a camera. The video is decidedly low-key, in keeping with the nature of the song, but because Brian was in Los Angeles at the time of filming, he had to be edited in later. The video was then given to Disney animation studios, where it acquired a gorgeous animated sequence of two young lovers growing old together. This version was issued on the 1992 VHS compilation *Classic Queen*, but the original version remained unreleased in the UK until 1999, when it appeared on *Greatest Flix III*.

The song was also performed by George Michael and Lisa Stansfield at the Concert For Life, and subsequently appeared on the 1993 EP *Five Live*. Roger also incorporated the song into his two major tours in support of *Happiness?* and *Electric Fire*, and it was performed on both the Queen + Paul Rodgers and Queen + Adam Lambert tours, both times with Roger on lead vocals.

'39 (May)
• Album: *Opera* • B-side: 5/76 [7] • Live: *Killers* • CD Single: 11/88 • Live (Brian): *Brixton* • Live (Q+PR): *Return*, *Ukraine* • Bonus: *Opera*

Brian's standout acoustic track from *A Night At The Opera* briefly turns Queen into a skiffle band, with a jaunty guitar intro giving way to John's upright bass and Roger's bass drum and tambourine. (Brian said he suggested the upright bass as a joke, but John took the instrument home and learned it.) Brian's melancholy vocals are contrasted nicely by backing vocals from Roger and Freddie, who reach the higher registers of their ranges almost perfectly.

""39' is a science fiction story about someone who goes away and leaves his family," Brian explained in 1975, "and because of the time-dilation effect, where the people on earth have aged a lot more than he has when he returns, he's aged a year and they've aged a hundred years. I felt that about my home at the time having been away and seen this vastly different world of rock music which was totally different from the way I was brought up."

Released as the B-side of 'You're My Best Friend' in May 1976, the song became a live favorite soon after, was performed at every concert during the acoustic segment throughout 1976 and 1979, and was resurrected on a few occasions by Brian and Freddie in 1984 and 1986. A recording from Earl's Court Arena on 7 June 1977 was released in 2011 on the deluxe edition of *A Night At The Opera*. The song was also performed by Brian, Roger, John and George Michael at the Concert For Life on 20 April 1992, and served as an introduction to 'Let Your Heart Rule Your Head' on Brian's 1993 tour; an example of the latter can be heard on *Live At The Brixton Academy*. The song was resurrected for the 2005/2006 Queen + Paul Rodgers tour, and Brian would perform it solo as a singalong with the audience during his acoustic segment, which also included 'Love Of My Life'. The song was returned to on the 2008 Rock The Cosmos tour, this time as a nearly full-band performance (Paul was absent during the number), with Roger once again returning to bass drum and tambourine, Spike Edney on accordion, Jamie Moses on acoustic guitar, Danny Miranda on upright electric bass, and all five on backing vocals. Brian returned to the simplistic, solo approach on the Queen + Adam Lambert tours, performing it as a lead-in to 'Love Of My Life'.

THROUGH THE NIGHT (Rodgers/May/Taylor)
• Album (Q+PR): *Cosmos*

While most of the songs on *The Cosmos Rocks* are lyrically suspect, they at least have a plot to ponder, even if the writers of the songs might have momentarily lost their own. Not so on 'Through The Night', a clodhopping piano ballad buried at the end of the album, out of sight and out of mind. That's not to say it's a bad song: the performance is strong, with a mournful guitar melody wailing away along with Paul's strong vocal delivery, but the words say a lot without actually saying anything at all. Much like the perplexed protagonist in the song, 'Through The Night' simply wanders, listlessly coming to a close without making an impact.

TIE YOUR MOTHER DOWN (May)
• Album: *Races* • A-side: 3/77 [31] • CD Single: 11/88
• Bonus: *Races* • CD Single: 1/98 [13] • Compilation:

WWRYHits • Live: *Killers, Magic, Wembley, On Fire, Montreal, Budapest* • Live (Brian): *Brixton* • Live (Q+PR): *Return, Ukraine*

Centered around a rousing guitar lick, 'Tie Your Mother Down' opens dramatically with a spiralling guitar crescendo that bookends the album. "It's an M C Escher painting," Brian commented. "It was supposed to be the musical equivalent of that ridiculous staircase going around four sides of a square, and it seems to always be going upwards ... every part is going up, and each part fades into an octave below. It's also backwards, because I played it all descending." This was edited off the single release, while the remainder of the song remains unchanged.

Misinterpreted as a song about unseemly parental bedroom activities, the song is really about teenage lust and throwing caution to the wind, even if it means going against your parents' wishes. Brian explained to Q in 1998 that "The genesis of the song goes back to when I was doing my Ph.D. in astronomy I spent a few months in Tenerife, and every day when the sun went down I'd go to the top of a mountain and just play a lovely Spanish guitar I had back then – which I've subsequently lost. And I came up with this riff, which stuck in my head. When I played that riff I used to sing the phrase 'Tie your mother down,' just as a joke, really. Years later when we finally came to record the song properly, I fully expected this to be changed, but Freddie believed it to be perfect. I thought it was a crap title, but Freddie said it meant something to him, so he knows the answer, and who am I to argue?

"Sometimes you get a little riff, and you just put some words with it, and then you don't even think about what they mean ... Musically the riff was heavily influenced by Rory Gallagher who was an inspiration to me as a musician and a person, and because of the title it came to represent teenage angst, somebody who really wanted to tie their parents down. And because it's so dramatic, it's always been a good way to open or close a set. In fact, I visualized smoke bombs and lighting changes in the studio. It was that sort of song."

The visual element of the song was included in the accompanying promotional video, filmed in New York during a soundcheck for the A Day At The Races US tour in February 1977. Directed by Bruce Gowers, the promo was strictly a performance video, with a suitably over-the-top explosion that blasted Roger off his stool during one of the takes. Perhaps a bit too raucous for the average singles buyer, the song was nevertheless issued in March 1977, where it peaked at No. 31 in the UK but at a disappointing No. 49 in the US.

The song was performed at every show between September 1976 and August 1986, as well as being played by Brian at almost every solo show. Brian and Roger have also played the song at most functions since Freddie's death, the most notable being at the Concert For Life, with Def Leppard vocalist Joe Elliot singing lead. The song rightly regained the coveted spot of the opening song on the 2005 Queen + Paul Rodgers tour, after the short intro of 'Reaching Out', and remained in the set the following year and again on the 2008 Rock The Cosmos tour. Unsurprisingly, the song once again made an appearance in the Queen + Adam Lambert tours, where its position changed frequently, often being performed later in the set.

TIME (Clark/Christie)
• Soundtrack (Freddie): Time • A-side (Freddie): 5/86 [32] • B-side (Freddie): 5/86 [32] • Compilations (Freddie): Pretender, FM Album, The Solo Collection

Along with 'In My Defence', Freddie was asked to provide vocals on the title track for Dave Clark's West End musical, premiering on 9 April 1986 at London's Dominion Theatre (which would later be home to Queen's own We Will Rock You musical). A third track, 'Born To Rock 'N' Roll', was recorded as a demo but was ultimately unused, since Dave had promised Cliff Richard that song. Three months after his first contribution was recorded, Freddie returned to Abbey Road Studios in January 1986 with Mike Moran in tow to lay down a backing track. With Mike on keyboards, Ray Russell on guitars, Brett Morgan on drums, Alan Jones on bass and John Christie (who also co-wrote the song with Dave Clark) and Freddie's friend Peter Straker on backing vocals, Freddie immaculately laid down one of his finest vocal performances of the period, second only to 'In My Defence'.

The lyrical matter wasn't quite as personal to Freddie as his earlier contribution, though it would prove to be an eerie portent: the repeated chorus backing vocals of "Time waits for no one" would soon come true for Freddie. Set to a slower, ballad-like arrangement, the words are a depressing reminder that no one is impervious to the ravages of time, but there is a thinly veiled optimism in Freddie's performance, substantiating Sir Laurence Olivier's exclamation that Freddie was a true actor.

Regarded as the most commercial song from the soundtrack album, 'Time' was released as a single in May 1986, just before Freddie joined the rest of Queen at rehearsals for their upcoming Magic tour. The single was backed with an instrumental version of the track, while two separate versions (essentially the main track split into two sections), titled 'Time' and 'Time (reprise)', were issued on the soundtrack. An extended version was also issued, adding nearly 40 seconds of additional material, including a saxophone solo by an uncredited musician. The extended version is superior to the single mix, though the 1992 remix, by Nile Rodgers and appearing on The Great Pretender and The Freddie Mercury Album compilations, remains the finest version, adding a new dimension to an already strong track.

A video was shot at the Dominion Theatre on 22 May 1986 at ten o'clock in the morning, an absurdly early yet necessary time to start filming. The theatre was booked for evening performances, and the film crew had until 3:00 pm to film the performance, which was done as economically as possible. For the first – but certainly not last – time, a group of youngsters was used as extras, adding a certain degree of sentiment and poignancy to the video, and it remains a wonderful, albeit little-seen, performance.

Later that night, Freddie attended the performance of the show at the Dominion, where he hatched up the crazy scheme to become a pre-show ice-cream vendor, giving rise to one of the more memorable Freddie legends. Decked out in the full uniform, he remained anonymous at first, dutifully handing out the ice creams, but started to grow impatient – not only that, he had no idea how much to charge – and started to throw the frozen treats into the audience until his supply ran out. Once the crowd had figured out who the prankster was, Freddie left to rapturous applause, paying for the freebies he had just given away.

TIME TO SHINE (Rodgers/May/Taylor)
• Album (Q+PR): Cosmos

When recording sessions began for The Cosmos Rocks, Paul came armed with a handful of songs he felt were worthy, though two of them had been written and performed on his 2007 UK solo tour. 'Time To Shine' was the first completely new song he submitted for The Cosmos Rocks, and, as Brian commented in Rolling Stone, "That … was the first time we thought, 'Ooh, we have a record here; this actually sounds like us.'" While Brian and Roger would write songs specifically for Paul's voice, attempting to suit his blues rock swagger, Paul wrote 'Time To Shine' as an attempt to ape Queen's style, and largely succeeds, despite its ricky-ticky U2 guitar riff. Roger agreed, telling *Rolling Stone*, "It was very suitable for us – quite grand and big."

Unfortunately, the words are to the detriment of the song, alluding to Paul's credit in *The Cosmos Rocks* booklet: "May the force be with you (seriously!)". 'Time To Shine' is a song of spiritual harmony, an urging to find one's inner peace and serenity through adversity, and comes off sounding cheesy and laughter-inducing in the process. What saves the song is a soaring instrumental backing and Paul's transcendental vocal delivery, eclipsing most of the other songs on *The Cosmos Rocks*.

The song was performed only once on the 2008 Rock the Cosmos tour, on 23 September in Antwerpen, but it failed to get moving after a mistimed cue into the first chorus, and what could have been a noteworthy inclusion into the set was removed the following night.

TOCCATA AND FUGUE IN D MINOR *(Bach)*

Johann Sebastian Bach's 'Toccata And Fugue In D Minor' was performed live by Smile in 1968 and 1969.

TONIGHT *(Taylor)*
• B-side (Roger): 9/98 [45] • Album (Roger): *Electric* • CD single (Roger): 3/99 [38] • B-side: 11/17

Upon first listen, 'Tonight' sounds like a simple love song, the only song from *Electric Fire* to feature an acoustic guitar so prominently. In fact, it's a celebration of love, be it platonic or romantic, and may contain an underlying tribute to Freddie. With a gorgeous melody, including an absolutely sublime acoustic guitar solo from Jason Falloon, 'Tonight' chugs away with the double-drum action of Roger (providing the rhythm) and Keith Prior (providing the brushed snare) and comes to a close by recalling the mood and feel of 'Who Needs You' from 1977.

The song was premiered at the Cyberbarn gig on 24 September 1998, and it was this version that appeared on the CD single of 'Surrender' in March 1999. An earlier remix, given the subtitle of 'Dub Sangria', emphasized the pseudo-Latin rhythm (excising most of the words to become a semi-instrumental) and was released as the B-side of 'Pressure On' in September 1998. Another remix, subtitled 'The Cocktail Mix', was released on the November 2017 'Journey's End' 10" vinyl EP; this version was more of a remix of the 'Dub Sangria' version, except

with full vocals. While the original is still a treat, this is a gorgeous alternative. 'Tonight' was also performed live on the 1999 Electric Fire tour, making little attempt to recreate the backing from the album, instead giving the song a more conventional approach that dulled its impact significantly.

TOO MUCH LOVE WILL KILL YOU
(May/Musker/Lamers)
• A-side (Brian): 8/92 [5] • Album (Brian): *BTTL*
• B-side (Brian): 6/93 [23] • Live (Brian): *Brixton*
• Album (Queen): *Heaven* • A-side (Queen): 2/96 [15]

The years between *A Kind Of Magic* and *The Miracle* were particularly difficult for Brian. Not only was his marriage with his wife Chrissy falling apart (the couple divorced in 1987), his father became ill and eventually passed away in the early summer of 1988. The band had also taken a temporary hiatus, with the prospect of future live work fading quickly.

Brian fell into a deep depression that he tried to cure by recording his first solo album, as well as jamming with his peers and young upstarts alike. He took on the task of producing Bad News, a parody hair metal band from the minds of UK's comedy troupe The Young Ones. He also contributed to the recording career of his post-divorce girlfriend, former *EastEnders* star Anita Dobson. Finally, Brian channeled his depression into a song that perfectly summed up his state of mind at the time.

'Too Much Love Will Kill You' was originally written and recorded for Brian's solo project in 1988, before being turned over to Queen and recorded for inclusion on *The Miracle*, but was ultimately rejected. (Freddie reportedly dismissed the song as being "good, but not *that* good.") Songwriting royalties were the main dispute: the song was co-credited to Frank Musker and Elizabeth Lamers, songwriting friends of Brian who also helped him record a personal demo earlier that year. Brian's version was later issued on his 1992 solo album *Back To The Light*, and issued as a single later that year, where it became his highest-charting solo single (and, up until that point, the highest-charting solo single by any band member), peaking at No. 5. He had performed the song unaccompanied except for his own piano at the Concert For Life, turning in an emotive yet understated performance.

"It was a big step to do it and I wanted to do it for

Freddie," Brian told *Guitarist* in 1992 of his Concert For Life performance. "It wasn't that the song had a particular relevance – it wasn't about AIDS – but it was a song that I felt was the best way of expressing myself and also the best thing I had to offer at the time. It was terrifying! It was in front of 72,000 people in the Stadium, half a billion people around the world and so it took an incredible amount of getting hold of myself to do it. As I was walking over to the piano I was thinking, 'Should I really be doing this?' So it was difficult, it really was. It's so easy to do in rehearsal and yet, when that moment comes, something happens to your throat. Plus it really brought me back in touch with what was going on; suddenly there was only me doing my personal little bit."

Equally beautiful was a guitar version, which was released as part of the CD single in August 1992, featuring The Red Special 'singing' the words instead of Brian, though this has become something of a rarity over the years, much like a live version that was released on the 'Resurrection' CD single from Los Angeles. A different live version, from the Brixton Academy, was released on Brian's sole live CD, *Live At The Brixton Academy*.

The 1988 recording was dusted off six years later and released as-is on *Made In Heaven*. (It had first been planned as a bonus track on the *Live At Wembley '86* CD, to capitalize on Brian's performance at the Concert For Life, but was removed at the last minute.) 'Too Much Love Will Kill You' was issued as the third single from the album in February 1996, reaching No. 15 in the UK charts (it was also issued as the first single from the album in the US a month earlier, climbing no higher than No. 118) and securing a well-deserved spot on the 1999 *Greatest Hits III* compilation.

TOO MUCH MONKEY BUSINESS *(Berry)*

This Chuck Berry song was played live by 1984.

TOP OF THE WORLD, MA *(The Cross)*
• Album (The Cross): *MBADTK* • Live (The Cross): *Bootleg* • Compilation (The Cross): *Lot*

One of two tracks written as a five-way split between The Cross, 'Top Of The World, Ma' is a great rocker, opening up *Mad: Bad: And Dangerous To Know* with a declaration of lust for a girl, with the protagonist prepared to shout it from the rooftops. The song features a great guitar solo from Clayton Moss, with

Spike's Hammond organ high in the mix, and gets The Cross' first proper collective album off to a rollicking start. 'Top Of The World, Ma' became the second song performed on the Mad: Bad: And Dangerous To Know tour, and was later shuffled in the set for the 1991 Blue Rock tour, becoming the closing number instead. A live version from 1990 was released on the fan club-only disc, *The Official Bootleg*. An extended remix was created for a potential single release, with 'Closer To You' as the A-side, though it remained unreleased until *The Lot* in 2013.

TOSS THE FEATHERS *(trad.)*

Performed by The Corrs on 29 November 2003 at the Cape Town 46664 concert, Roger was asked by Andrea Corr to play drums on this traditional Irish song, lively in execution even if it offers little room for Roger to showcase his talents.

TOUCH THE SKY *(Taylor)*
• Album (Roger): *Happiness?*

Blending in effortlessly from 'Revelations', 'Touch The Sky' is one of Roger's most delicate songs, and was written about Debbie Leng, Roger's then-girlfriend and mother of three of the drummer's children. The song features touching lyrics, almost an update of 'Breakthru' and 'Final Destination' (especially the line "and when you smile, you set the world alight"), though there are a few lines that are somewhat cringe-inducing. With Jason Falloon on guitar and Mike Crossley on keyboards, Roger provides the remainder, with his powerful drumming a particular highlight.

The song was performed live on the 1994/1995 Happiness? tour, complete with the lengthy keyboard-dominated introduction, but was not reprised for further live airings.

TRACK 13 *(Queen)*
• Bonus: *Heaven*

For those fans who accidentally left their CD players running after the final strains of 'It's A Beautiful Day (reprise)' concluded *Made In Heaven*, they were greeted with several unusual sounds. Those sounds have been confirmed by Brian to have been written about Freddie's journey into Heaven, and were constructed mainly by John, Roger and Brian along with David Richards.

"This was started by me having fun with the ASR10

sampler," Richards said in 2001. "I took the opening chords of 'It's A Beautiful Day' and made them loop forever. Then I added some of Freddie talking through strange echoes. Brian and Roger heard it and came in to add some effects of their own and we thought of it as a surreal Requiem. It was the end of the album and we all were feeling very emotional."

The piece runs at an astonishing 23 minutes, and was understandably included only on the CD versions of the album (the vinyl and cassette versions featured a pointless, seven-second edit). In this author's opinion, the piece, which has received the original official title of 'Track 13', is best listened to late at night with all the lights off.

TURN ON THE TV (Taylor)
• B-side (Roger): 8/77

The flipside of Roger's August 1977 debut solo single, 'Turn On The TV' borrows its title from the opening line of 'Sheer Heart Attack' and, like 'I Wanna Testify', is about as far away from punk or new wave as could be expected. Dealing with apathy and the summer doldrums, the song is like an upbeat rewrite of 'Drowse', set to a funky, disjointed rhythm. Roger handles all the instrumental duties here, but it's hard to escape the notion that 'Turn On The TV' is little more than filler.

TUTTI FRUTTI (Penniman/LaBostrie/Lubin)
• Live: Wembley, Budapest

A superb rendition of Little Richard's 1957 hit single was performed nightly as the centerpiece of the acoustic medley on the Magic tour, starting off with a terrific acoustic introduction, allowing plenty of interaction between Freddie and the audience, before giving way to a fiery electric finish. An edited version from Wembley Stadium appeared on the 1992 Live At Wembley '86, but was reinstated fully for the 2003 reissue, retitled Live At Wembley Stadium. A less polished but no less energetic version was released on Hungarian Rhapsody.

TWIST AND SHOUT (Medley/Russell)

Originally performed by The Isley Brothers in 1962 and made famous by The Beatles on their 1963 debut, Please Please Me, 'Twist And Shout' was performed as an encore number during Roger's 1994/1995 Happiness? tour.

TWO SHARP PENCILS (GET BAD) (Taylor)
• B-side (Roger): 7/84 • A-side (Roger): 7/17

A candidate for one of the strangest Queen-related tracks ever recorded, 'Two Sharp Pencils (Get Bad)' shows that Roger still had an ear cocked towards the funkier side of the charts. Unfortunately, everything here is programmed and dates the song to a specific week in the summer of 1984, becoming embarrassingly obsolete the second it hit the shops. The backing is terse and deviates little, and the words are sung by Roger with his voice electronically lowered to give the impression that he is soulful and funky. In all, 'Two Sharp Pencils (Get Bad)' should have remained unreleased, especially in favor of some of the stronger material recorded during the sessions, but it was issued instead on the 12" version of 'Strange Frontier'.

Unusually, the song was remixed by house musicians Anna Wall and Corbi, turning the song into a DJ's dream. Released on the Music For Freaks label in July 2017, four versions were created, all but the radio mix running close to seven minutes. Depending on your preference for house music, the remix is interesting, though it borders on the tedious for fans of the original.

THE UNBLINKING EYE (EVERYTHING IS BROKEN) (Taylor)
• Download (Roger): 11/09 • CD Single (Roger): 1/10
• Album (Roger): Earth

Just as he had done with 'Woman You're So Beautiful (But Still A Pain In The Ass)' following the 2006 North American leg of the Queen + Paul Rodgers tour, Roger went back into the studio after the 2008 Rock the Cosmos tour to work on some further solo material. With the creative juices flowing and the ideas abundant, Roger worked discontinuously at The Priory on songs throughout 2008 and 2009, before announcing the first fruits of his labors that November. Titled 'The Unblinking Eye (Everything Is Broken)', the song was touted as a protest song: "What happened to the protest song?" Roger mused in the press release. "Music is now so polished, shiny and predictable, we have forgotten to try and say something with it. I am getting old and like everyone, have the right to say something about the 'state of control' we live under – powerless to do anything about it."

With 'We Believe' marking the only foray into sociopolitical statements on The Cosmos Rocks, it was up to Roger to pick up the slack, and, while 'The Unblinking Eye' isn't as ham-fisted as Brian's power ballad, it's just as lyrically clumsy, taking over six minutes to say a lot that we already know: there are pointless wars dragging on, the government is increasingly exercising their power to spy on its citizens, and nations are left broken and unfixable while its people are being taxed higher and higher. "We are directionless," Roger seethed in the press release. "I'm pissed off – you should be, too."

But Roger doesn't *sound* pissed off; instead, he seems resigned, weary to constantly bleating on about the foibles and misdemeanors of government officials, and aware that he could write about it as much as he want, but corruption and greed will still exist. This works against the effectiveness of the song, an epic ballad that is masterfully performed by Roger (and including a Stylophone solo); if it had been married to an angrier arrangement, the song would have packed more of a punch, but as it stands, it's a lumbering, lugubrious, albeit well-intentioned, ballad that merely hints at the vexation Roger was trying to express.

Released in November 2009 as a download-only single, 'The Unblinking Eye (Everything Is Broken)' was well-received in the fan community, though it eluded a wider audience. Released the same week as the *Absolute Greatest* compilation, Roger duly mentioned his new single a few times in promotional rounds, promising a physical release "eventually". Unfortunately, the song was forgotten as quickly as it was released, and when it finally was released on CD in January 2010, not even the addition of a semi-instrumental mix and an in-the-studio video could entice the general public to purchase it. As a result, the single failed to chart, but if Roger was discouraged by its failure, he didn't let on, and continued with the recording of his next solo album. When *Fun On Earth* appeared in November 2013, 'The Unblinking Eye (Everything Is Broken)' was included, albeit as an abridged version, trimming the song to just under five minutes – incidentally, the hardest rocking section ("High street's full of holes") was omitted, thus losing the only anger the song truly possessed. Stick to the original.

UNDER AFRICAN SKIES

Brian mentioned this title as an unreleased song from the 46664 sessions from March 2003 on his soapbox, which he had hoped to continue work on after the sessions were completed. Soon after, Brian

was reminded about the 1986 Paul Simon track of the same name, and he sheepishly admitted to forgetting Simon's track existed. Whether the song will be completed remains to be seen.

UNDER DISPUTE: *see* BANANA BLUES

UNDER PRESSURE *(Queen/Bowie)*
• A-side: 10/81 [1] • Album: *Space* • Live: *Magic, Wembley, On Fire, Montreal, Budapest* • CD Single: 11/88 • Compilation: *Hits2, Classic, WWRYHits, On Air* • A-side: 12/99 [14]

In July of 1981, following their first shows in South America, Queen found some semblance of peace at Montreux Studios. They reluctantly started work on their follow-up to *The Game* but, because they had just spent so much time recording not only that album but also *Flash Gordon* in late 1980, and then toured the world several times over in such a short amount of time, there was no real rush to get any product out. Besides, they were planning on releasing their first compilation album, which would do nicely until they came up with some new sounds.

But that didn't stop them from getting a handful of songs in the can: skeleton versions of 'Back Chat', 'Life Is Real (Song For Lennon)', 'Cool Cat' and most likely 'Put Out The Fire' were started during preliminary sessions for the new album. Brian explained the story in the *Greatest Video Hits 2* commentary in 2003: "[It's] complex, really. We just happened to be in the studio, and David [Bowie] dropped in and we started jamming. We went out for some food and thought, 'Wouldn't it be great to do some original ideas.' John came up with the riff that started it all off, and we all got into it.

"Then it came to what is this song about? David came up with the idea of us all going in one after the other and singing what we thought the tune should be – I think he'd done that with some other people – but we did that and then we sat down and chose bits of everything. It was really done in an odd way. So that gave you the tune, and at that point David started to feel very strongly about what he felt the song was about, so he wrote a set of lyrics – first of all, it was called 'People On Streets', but he wanted to revise it and make it slightly more abstract, so it became 'Under Pressure'."

"That was through David Richards, the engineer at the studio," Bowie said of the collaboration. "David knew that I was in town and phoned me up and asked me to come down ... So I went down, and these things happen, you know. Suddenly you're writing something together, and it was totally spontaneous, it certainly wasn't planned. It was, er ... peculiar."

Bowie was working on 'Cat People (Putting Out Fire)' with Giorgio Moroder when he ran into David Richards, who had previously engineered *"Heroes"* in 1977 and would go on to work on several of Bowie's mid-1980s albums. The two struck up a conversation and Richards introduced Bowie to his new employers. The five musicians started jamming on old songs (Peter "Ratty" Hince recalled, "They were just jamming in the studio and it all got recorded – 'All the Young Dudes', 'All the Way from Memphis', and various rock classics") before it was suggested that they write their own. "Absolutely nothing was written," Roger said in 2002, "and, in fact, all that we were doing was jamming and David came in one night, and we were just playing other people's songs for fun and David said, 'This is stupid, why don't we just write one?' ... We took the multi-track tapes to New York and I spent all day there with David and mixed it that night. I remember we were fiddling about and we got the bassline, and then we went for a pizza! And when we got back, we couldn't remember it, and somebody thought of it ... John did, yes."

Prior to Bowie's arrival, the band were working on their own improvisation, which was titled 'Feel Like'; when Bowie showed up, they borrowed the piano line and came up with a completely new riff and lyrics. It's easy to hear who wrote what parts: the scat introduction can be seen as a foreshadowing of Freddie's 1985 single 'Living On My Own', while the "insanity laughs" section is more in the ambiguous vein of Bowie's early 1970s hits. The finale from the middle eight, in which Brian's guitar finally comes to the fore along with an astounding drum break, is pushed into heavy Queen territory, while the finger-clicking coda and "This is our last dance" recalls Bowie's early single, 'You've Got A Habit Of Leaving'.

It was a song that adhered to both artists' styles and the results were splendid. Roger revealed that "We'd never actually collaborated with anybody before, so certain egos were slightly bruised along the way," while Brian confirmed as much, saying, "To have his ego mixed with ours was a very volatile mixture ... it "made for a very hot time in the studio."

"He was quite difficult to work with," Brian reflected in 1982 in *International Musician & Recording World*, "because it was the meeting of two different methods of working. It was stimulating but, at the same time, almost impossible to resolve. We're very pigheaded and set in our ways and Mr Bowie is, too. In fact, he's probably as pigheaded as the four of us put together. I think it was a worthwhile thing to do. But after 'Under Pressure' was done, there were continual disagreements about how it should be put out or if it should even be put out at all. David wanted to redo the entire thing. I had given up by that time because it had gone a long way from what I would have liked to see. But there is still a lot of good stuff in the song. There was a compromise: Freddie, David and Mack actually sat down and produced a mix under a lot of strain. Roger was also along to keep the peace to some extent, because he and David are friends."

"David Bowie and Freddie and I have been friends for the past few years," Roger said at the time. "'Under Pressure' was a spontaneous collaboration." That spontaneity is obvious on the finished recording: the song sounds almost unfinished and is more of a rough mix state than a polished final recording. Bowie confirmed this: "It stands up better as a demo. It was done so quickly that some of [the lyric] makes me cringe a bit."

Crystal Taylor revealed, "On the first night of recording 'Pressure', at the end of the evening Brian and myself went on a bit of a binge and ended up back at the studio with David Richards for a jam session. Once again we were out of it and Brian wanted to play, with him on guitar, David on piano and yours truly drumming, and let me assure you that I am the world's worst drummer when I'm sober, so try to imagine this. David actually taped it, and years later we listened, and out of about an hour of playing there is actually ten minutes of good rock."

With the song completed, EMI embraced the recording and wanted to release it. Since nothing else had been recorded (except for additional Bowie backing vocals on Freddie and John's 'Cool Cat', a song Bowie asked them not to release), an out-take from *The Game* called 'Soul Brother' became the B-side and Queen were thefore accorded 'top billing'. When it came time to film a promotional video for the single, the band were more or less indifferent to the notion and Bowie was unavailable, so, through the latter's recommendation, director David Mallet was enlisted to come up with something suitable.

The result was both as haphazard and as special as the recording itself. With numerous scenes of pressure (traffic jams, buildings being blown up, unemployment, the stock market crashing and so forth) culled from old newsreel footage intercut with scenes from silent movies starring Greta Garbo, John Gilbert and even Max Screck's Nosferatu, the promo was a superb portrayal of the lyric and became Queen's first video not to feature them in any visual form. Unfortunately, scenes of an IRA car bombing had to be edited out in order for the video to be played on *Top Of The Pops*, but it was a small price to pay.

The single was released in October 1981 and became a smash, reaching No. 1 in the UK – Queen's first since 'Bohemian Rhapsody' and Bowie's first since 'Ashes To Ashes' the previous year – while peaking at a more modest No. 29 in the US. The song was re-released several times over the next two decades, never more famously than in November 1999 when a remix was included on the barrel-scraping *Greatest Hits III* album. Normally, remixes were something that fans tended to shy away from, but since this featured direct involvement from Brian and Roger (the latter was the prime mover in the remix), the results were more pleasing to the ear. Subtitled the 'rah' mix (which is what appears to be chanted following a brief, previously unreleased vocal improvisation from Bowie and Freddie about New York City), the song incorporated a more upbeat drum rhythm and some new guitar licks from Brian. Because its inclusion on the third greatest hits package was of little benefit, Parlophone reacted by releasing it as a single in support of the compilation, where it promptly reached No. 14 in the UK.

Notoriously, the song was sampled heavily by Vanilla Ice in 1990, who incorporated the bass riff and piano into his hit single 'Ice Ice Baby'. Brian said of the situation in 1991, "I first heard it in the fan club downstairs. I just thought, 'Interesting, but nobody will ever buy it because it's crap.' Turns out I was wrong. Next thing, my son's saying it's big here: 'And what are you going to do about it, Dad?' Actually, Hollywood [Records] are sorting it out because they don't want people pillaging what they've just paid so much money for. We don't want to get involved in litigation with other artists ourselves; that doesn't seem very cool, really. Anyway, now I think it's quite a good bit of work in its way." Vanilla Ice himself appeared to hold no grudges, but was bewildered as to why everyone was making a big fuss out of it. In a VH-1 special in the late 1990s, interview footage was shown from the time of the single's release in which he explained how the two songs were completely different merely because he threw an extra bass note and sampled cymbal splash into the riff.

'Under Pressure' became an instant crowd favorite, and was first performed at the November 1981 *We Will Rock You* video shoot in Montreal, remaining in the set until August 1986. While Bowie didn't incorporate the song into his own set list until 1995, the band embraced it, and it would often become one of the highlights of any given evening. The song would be given a rougher treatment, and the key lowered so that Freddie could sing both his own and Bowie's parts (Roger would have the task of performing the higher-pitched vocals, naturally). A live version was included on the CD single of the 'rah' remix in 1999, while a superb version sung by Bowie and former Eurythmics vocalist Annie Lennox was performed at the Concert for Life on 20 April 1992.

"It wasn't the best recording ever made," Roger stated contrarily in 2003, "but it was one of the best songs we ever did. It sort of endured quite well – I love the last section. I found it very invigorating and interesting – a successful collaboration."

UNIVERSAL THEME

Another unknown track, 'Universal Theme' was likely an original track by Wreckage, and was performed on 31 October 1969 at Ealing College Of Art.

UNTITLED

Written and recorded by Brian in 2001, this track, with the unofficial title of 'Untitled', is an anthemic doodle, with keyboards and the Red Special duelling nicely, on top of a bed of programmed drums and piano, though what destination Brian had in mind for this recording is unknown. The song was premiered in 2010 at the Queen Fan Club convention.

UP *(Taylor)*
• Album (Roger): *Earth*

With a percolating sequencer and some particularly jagged guitar work, 'Up' sounds like it could have been an out-take from *Strange Frontier*; instead, it's one of the highlights of *Fun On Earth*, its charging electricity sitting at odds with the more introspective and romantic moments, yet it still lyrically retains those sentiments: written as a mission statement to his girlfriend Sarina, Roger promises her a "house in the sky" and that "I'll make you a queen / I'll give you a crown / We'll live in our dreams / And never look down". 'Up' is one of those simplistic songs that can be expected of Roger, but oftentimes it's his most simplistic songs that are his best, and 'Up' is a latter-day highlight of Roger's discography that deserves more recognition than it will get.

VAGABOND OUTCAST

Much like 'So Sweet', authorship of 'Vagabond Outcast' is not known, although it's likely that it's an original written by Freddie. Indeed, on the only recorded performance of the song, coming from The Sink Club, Liverpool on 9 September 1969, Freddie introduces the song as "one of our own." It's an enjoyable, if slight, song; unfortunately, the quality of the tape leaves much to be desired, and the lyrics are indecipherable.

VICTORY

In early 1983, after concluding the final tour in support of *Hot Space*, Freddie and his assistant Peter Freestone stopped by old pal Michael Jackson's home, where the two vocalists recorded three tracks together: Freddie's 1981 composition 'There Must Be More To Life Than This' and two duets titled 'State Of Shock' and 'Victory'. The latter became the title of the 1984 album by The Jacksons, though it's not known if a version was recorded by them, and 'Victory' remains the only song recorded by Freddie and Michael that isn't regularly available on the bootleg market.

Apparently, a Queen version of 'Victory' exists, either from the 1982 *Hot Space* or 1983 *The Works* sessions, with, according to Greg Brooks, Roger and Brian contributing backing vocals.

VOODOO *(Rodgers/May/Taylor)*
• Album (Q+PR): *Cosmos*

With Paul Rodgers now teamed up with Brian and Roger, the possibilities for exploring new musical avenues were endless. The three musicians couldn't have come from more contrasting backgrounds: Brian and Roger were well-versed in a mélange of styles, each of their albums shifting lanes with each song – and sometimes within a song – while Paul earned a pedigree in gritty blues rock, his early albums with Free a more straightforward alternative to Led Zeppelin. While Brian and Roger went to extensive pains to reassure

fans and critics that Paul was one of Freddie's favorite singers (despite there being no mention whatsoever of the vocalist in any interviews prior to Freddie's death; even Paul was unconvinced, vaguely recalling that he maybe once ran into Freddie in the corridor of Peter Grant's offices), the reality was that they came from different schools of thought and approach, and it was this creative uncertainty that created the best results on *The Cosmos Rocks*.

Coming after the lightweight 'Call Me' is 'Voodoo', a song that, along with 'Warboys (A Prayer For Peace)', Paul had already written and performed on his 2007 solo tour, deeming it a worthy submission to the sessions. The three were messing around in the studio one day, jamming to 'House Of The Rising Sun' before they naturally progressed to 'Voodoo'. As Paul told the *Halesowen News*, "I picked up an acoustic guitar and played it, then Roger came in on the drums, Brian then joined in, and we played through it. We recorded the second or third take. It ended up being quite a sparse song with not much instrumentation on it, and, dare I say it, very bluesy, very loose. We didn't know what we were going to do or sound like, so we were just playing to see what came up." Its spontaneity is the most invigorating aspect of it, sounding like an off-the-cuff, uncalculated blues jam, with Paul spinning the seductions of a black magic woman while Brian channels his inner Carlos Santana.

In an attempt to expand the set list at a time when the Queen + Paul Rodgers association was coming to an end, 'Voodoo' was integrated into the repertoire on the 2008 Rock The Cosmos tour, only on a half dozen occasions throughout that November.

VOODOO CHILD (SLIGHT RETURN) *(Hendrix)*

Jimi Hendrix's 1968 track (not to be confused with the epic jam 'Voodoo Chile') was performed live by Roger Taylor throughout his 1994/1995 Happiness? tour. More tellingly, it was also rehearsed by Queen on 18 September 1970, the day Jimi Hendrix died.

VULTAN'S THEME (ATTACK OF THE HAWKMEN)
(Mercury)
• Album: *Flash*

A pulsating composition from the *Flash Gordon* album, this piece chronicles Vultan's attack on Ming and his henchmen in typical Queen fashion. Roger's pounding drums over a funky bassline form the basic track, while Freddie lays down an anthemic synthesizer riff, making the song a perfect lead-in for the equally anthemic 'Battle Theme'. 'Vultan's Theme (Attack Of The Hawkmen)' was performed as part of the Flash Medley at four of the five Japanese concerts in 1981.

WALKING THE DOG (Thomas)

This Rufus Thomas-penned track, covered by many artists including The Rolling Stones, was played live by 1984.

WALTZING MATILDA (trad)

Another traditional song, Brian threw a snippet of this (along with a further traditional Australian song, 'I Still Call Australia Home') into his nightly guitar solo while on tour in Australia in 1998.

WARBOYS (A PRAYER FOR PEACE)

(Rodgers/Taylor/May)
• Album (Q+PR): Cosmos

Written by Paul in 2006 after the tour with Brian and Roger came to an end, 'Warboys (A Prayer For Peace)' started off as a tense acoustic rocker, with a tentative version played on the tour that spawned Live In Glasgow the following year. "It's been on the back-burner for a long time, actually," Paul told Vintage Rock's Junkman. "And I never really got it finished. There's been a lot of wars, not just the current one. In between starting the writing of that song and its culmination right now, it just seems to be appropriate now. I was playing this for a wonderful lady friend of mine called Cynthia. And I was saying, 'You know, I've got this song, and it just needs a middle eight and goes something like this...' and I said, 'That's what it needs.' And the song was finished right there, you know."

When brought to the Cosmos Rocks sessions in 2007, the song was given a heavier treatment, with Roger being a prime mover in its arrangement. The terse acoustic backing was retained, with military tattoo drumming from Roger giving way to a more conventional rock performance. Battle sounds are overlaid for good measure, while a wah-wahed Red Special represents further conflict, and while it's a welcome rocker on The Cosmos Rocks, its message has been muddled, with Paul apparently under the belief that soldiers are little else than automata being used

for politicians' personal gains.

"I called 'Warboys' as a sub-title 'A Prayer To Peace' because I wanted people to understand that it is a prayer for peace; it's not a glorification of war in any way," Paul told Junkman. "I'm of the opinion, when you look back through the history of mankind, there always seems to have been hardwired into us this need for warfare. I wish, I really truly wish, we could transcend that. And live and work the earth as if it was a garden. You know what I mean? And share things. It would be so cool if we were more spiritually aware."

'Warboys (A Prayer For Peace)' was performed only three times on the 2008 Rock The Cosmos tour, beginning in Moscow on 16 September and removed after Berlin on 21 September.

WAS IT ALL WORTH IT? (Queen)
• Album: Miracle

Concluding The Miracle in a most grandiose and pompous manner, 'Was It All Worth It?' was, at the time, believed to have been Queen's swan song; so ill was Freddie during the sessions that his doctors were uncertain if he would live to see the album released. Hence the joy in Freddie's vocals, where he sings an autobiographical set of lyrics about Queen's rise to fame and fortune: this isn't a sad, melancholy reflection, but instead a celebration of a life (and career) well-lived.

While several songs from The Miracle were constructed from lengthy jams, and many of the songs pieced together disjointedly from separate bits, 'Was It All Worth It?' is a full-on masterpiece, deliberately created to be heard as a statement rather than as a menu of ideas. Recalling the bombast of Queen's earlier albums, the song starts off with some atmospheric synthesizers before Brian tears down the neck of his Red Special and the band join in for a truly epic story. David Richards recalled that Freddie was the originator of the song, but that the lyrics were a true collaboration between all four (Roger threw in the line, "So mystic / Surrealistic"), while the instrumental arrangement and structure is a collaboration between Freddie and Brian. Indeed, Brian's guitar is all over this song, but is balanced nicely by a sprightly piano line which echoes the riff and an atmospheric synthesizer drone in the backing, giving a nice structure to the steady rhythm that Roger and John lay down.

The orchestra in the middle of the song wasn't a live orchestra, but was programmed on the Kurzweil synthesizer, the same instrument Mike Moran used to create the musical backings for Freddie's *Barcelona* album. "[It's] all Emulator and synthesisers," David Richards told *Sound On Sound* magazine in 1989. "Originally the song didn't go like that at all, but the band wanted that section added and then moved around two or three times. Because it was virtually a live recording there was no click track, so I had to insert a space on the master, time it, add an equal space on the slave, and then add timecode. So some parts of the song go to about 10 generations of copying, but because we were working digitally there's no loss of quality." It was during these sessions that Brian created another idea that was ultimately unused, but stems from the same sort of arrangement; titled 'Chinese Torture', this composition was used as a bonus track on CD issues of *The Miracle*.

WE ARE THE CHAMPIONS *(Mercury)*
• A-side: 10/77 [2] • Album: *NOTW* • CD Single: 11/88
• B-side: 2/96 [15] • Live: *Killers, Magic, Wembley, 46664, On Fire, Montreal, Budapest* • Live (Q+PR): *Return, Ukraine* • Album: *NOTW*

"I was thinking about football when I wrote it. I wanted a participation song, something the fans could latch on to. It was aimed at the masses; I thought we'd see how they took it. It worked a treat. When we performed it at a private concert in London, the fans actually broke into a football chant between numbers. Of course, I've given it more theatrical subtlety than an ordinary football chant. You know me."

Freddie's explanation to *Circus* in 1978 of his (arguably) most well-known composition belies any of the numerous overanalyzed and wrongly interpreted accounts that have materialised over the years. While Dave Marsh, in a 1978 review of *Jazz* in *Rolling Stone*, absurdly called Queen the first fascist band due to this song, others have called it pigheaded and arrogant, while some have even considered it an admission of Freddie's sexuality. Of course, the last one is stretching it quite a bit, but the other descriptions all contribute to the legacy of a simple rock song that was intended to bring audience and band closer together.

The history of 'We Are The Champions' is sadly unreported, due to Freddie's insistence on not discussing his songs at length. The commonly accepted story is that, while Brian was off writing a football chant ('We Will Rock You'), Freddie was coming up with his own football chant, though it would eventually become more of a winner's song than anything. Freddie was notorious for being less-than-complimentary about the press around this time, but Freddie reacted against this in 1978, telling *Circus*, "I certainly wasn't thinking about the press when I wrote it. I never think about the British music press these days ... I suppose it could also be construed as my version of 'I Did It My Way': we have made it, and it certainly wasn't easy. No bed of roses as the song says. And it's still not easy."

The song is a classic case of starting off with a whisper and ending with a scream. Opening with a delicate and subdued piano and vocal introduction, the track quickly escalates into a boisterous singalong, praising not only the band for being champions, but the audience too. "You've brought me fame and fortune / And everything that goes with it / I thank you all!", Freddie sings, and, contrary to what more cynical journalists have said, he actually sounds genuinely thankful for his success. The song ends inconclusively, with the final "of the world" left unsung, but the message is clear: without the audience, Queen wouldn't exist.

"You know, songs aren't always about what the words say," Brian told *Circus* in 1978. "Messages in songs can appear different. I always see that as the difference between prose and poetry. Prose can mean exactly what it says, while poetry can mean the opposite. That goes for this song. Freddie's stuff is often tongue-in-cheek anyway, as you know. This song is very theatrical. Freddie is very close to his art. You could say he's married to his music, whether it's 'I Did It My Way' or his 'There's No Business Like Show Business'. I must say, when he first played it for us in the studio, we all fell on the floor with laughter. So many of the people in the press hate us because we've sidestepped them and got where we have without them.

"But there's no way the song says anything against our audiences. When the song says 'we', it means us and the fans. When we did that special concert [referring to the video shoot for 'We Are The Champions'], the fans were wonderful. They understood it so well. I know it sounds corny, but it brought tears to our eyes."

It's no surprise that the song was issued as the first single from *News Of The World* in October 1977. What isn't quite as well-known is that, in the UK, 'We Are The Champions' was the A-side, while Brian's 'We Will Rock You' appeared as the B-side; in the US, both songs were issued as a double A-side. The single peaked at an impressive No. 2 in Britain, despite the lack of a

British tour until May 1978; in America, it reached No. 4, their highest-charting US single ever, backed by an extensive North American tour and heavy promotion of the single, both on radio and in the live set. (A rough mix, extending the song to over four minutes and featuring some additional wild guitar work from Brian, was released in 2017 on the 40th anniversary edition of *News Of The World*, and is a treat.)

The video, directed by Derek Burbridge and filmed at the New London Theatre on 6 October 1977, shows Freddie dressed in a Nijinsky ballet suit, and is the visual depiction of the vocalist's original intent that band and audience be united as one. For the first, but certainly not the last, time, the band enlisted the assistance of Fan Club members to help with the video. With only four days' notice, some got their invitation too late, but that didn't stop over 800 fans from showing up and participating. As a thank you, the band performed a special, impromptu concert (see Part Three for more information). An alternate version of the video was shown in recent years on *Top Of The Pops 2*, with completely different editing and different guitar parts towards the song's conclusion; unfortunately, this version has not yet been released commercially.

Due to the massive success of the single (in France, it peaked at No. 1 for 12 weeks, at that time the maximum allotted time a single was allowed at the top; as a result, 'We Will Rock You' then became the A-side, and the single enjoyed a further 12 weeks at No. 1), the band performed the song at every live show between November 1977 and August 1986. Though it's customary to think of the song as the most obvious show closer, it didn't achieve that status until May 1978; until then, along with 'We Will Rock You', it was merely the first encore performance, and the show would end up closing with 'Jailhouse Rock' and 'Sheer Heart Attack'. Generally, though, the original coupling became the closer shortly after that (except for a few performances in 1980, as well as being split by 'Friends Will Be Friends' in 1986), since it was the most logical and appropriate way to end a Queen show.

At the Concert For Life on 20 April 1992, Brian introduced Freddie's favorite singer, Liza Minnelli, who came out to sing an interesting adaptation of the song. What was more heartfelt was the appearance of all the guest musicians coming out during the second chorus to provide backing vocals, a tactic which had been used at Live Aid in 1985 with 'Do They Know It's Christmas?'. Unsurprisingly, the song became a mainstay in both the Queen + Paul Rodgers and Queen + Adam Lambert tours, always as the final encore of the night, and allowing the band to provide a show-stopping finale while their lights and stage effects went into full force, always to the delight of the audience.

There were numerous reissues, thanks in no small part to the song's immediate adoption as a sports anthem, but perhaps the most controversial move came in 2001, when Brian and Roger re-recorded the song with Robbie Williams. The makeover was recorded for the film *A Knight's Tale* and was played during the credits. However, there was one person missing from the recording; John, who was originally invited to participate, declined, thus confirming his status of retirement. When the bassist heard the finished product, he blasted the song, saying it did no justice to the original and that Robbie wasn't fit to perform any of Queen's songs. It is a sentiment shared by many of Queen's fans; any rumors that Robbie would become the next vocalist for Queen have fallen by the wayside.

WE BELIEVE *(May/Rodgers/Taylor)*
• Album (Q+PR): *Cosmos* • Italian CD Promo (Q+PR): 11/08 [4]

The normally mild-mannered and reserved Brian May would channel his political and social beliefs into song, whenever he felt the occasion deserved it. Starting with 'White Man' in 1976, after researching the plight of Native Americans struggling to survive in North America while on tour there, Brian would only infrequently become incensed enough to write a song about his particular ire du jour; more often than not, these broadsides were clunky and maladroit, and while their messages were well-intended, the delivery left a lot to be desired. As good a songwriter as Brian is, his message songs fall flat-footed, as evident with the embarrassment that is '46664 (The Call)'.

This is true with 'We Believe', an epic power ballad that is firmly rooted in world-changing messages and a synthetic arrangement that would have been suitable in the late 1980s, but sounds horribly outdated in 2008. Astonishingly, in a preview article in *Classic Rock Magazine*, Brian called this a "fairly upbeat" song, but one glance at the words indicates the opposite: the song explores the evils of mankind and the lying, manipulative nature of politicians, with an optimistic bent that somewhere out there, someone can wave a magic wand and fix all of the world's problems. (If only it was that easy.) "This is very much Brian's song, that one, in which I think he sort of puts his views on everything, you know - on the state of everything according to him," Roger explained in a 2008 BBC Radio 2 interview. "It's very, it's very well meant, you know: 'There's no evil that we didn't have a hand in', I think is quite well put and, yeah, it's a sort of statement."

As with all of Brian's message songs, the intent is good in 'We Believe' but the delivery is its downfall, with a ponderous arrangement that brings its running time to just over six minutes, and well over the point of tolerability; there aren't any dynamics to engage listeners, and, apart from a searing guitar solo, the song fails to pick up. Whereas on some of the other songs on the album Paul sounds ill at ease with the subject matter, here he's most convincing, making the best of the lyrics and harnessing his vocal power into an emotional performance, thus becoming one of the few saving graces of this song.

'We Believe' was released as an Italian-only promotional single in November 2008, and was edited significantly to a more digestible three minutes, peaking at No. 4 in the Virgin Radio charts. At one point this song and 'Call Me' were in the running for the follow-up single to 'C-Lebrity' and, as it was in heavy rotation in the live repertoire at the time, 'We Believe' appeared to be headed for that honor; unfortunately, due to mounting tensions with the primary musicians, the single failed to materialize. When performed live, the song's arrangement varied between its album rendition, with Paul on all vocals, and an alternate approach, with Brian on lead vocals on the first verse.

WE WILL ROCK YOU *(May)*
• B-side: 10/77 [2] • Album: *NOTW* • CD Single: 11/88
• Bonus: *NOTW* • CD Single: 2/96 [15] • CD Single: 1/98 [13] • Live: *Killers, Magic, Wembley, 46664, On Fire, Montreal, Budapest* • A-side: 7/00 [1] • Live (Brian): *Brixton* • Live (Q+PR): *Return, Ukraine* • Bonus: *NOTW*
• Compilation: *On Air*

It's astonishing that a simple rock song with only a minimal stomp-stomp-clap backing and a short burst of guitar has gone on to become an anthem for every sports team on the planet. Even more amazing was the amount of success it garnered. Not only was it the lead-off track on *News Of The World*, but it was played extensively in concert, and has been released countless times in countless countries on countless singles and

compilations. More recently, it even became the title of Queen's foray into the world of stage musicals.

Of course, the track is 'We Will Rock You', a defiant response to the punks, critics and nay-sayers. More specifically, it's about a man going through the various stages of life – childhood, adulthood, and death – and falling on hard times ("You got mud on your face / Big disgrace"). The song was constructed as a counterpart to Freddie's more melodic 'We Are The Champions' and was inspired by the events of Queen's May 1977 UK tour, a brief trip that included Bristol, Southampton, Stafford, Glasgow, Liverpool and London, which was the band's most extensive tour of their homeland since December 1975. Fans in those cities were so excited that their favorite band had finally decided to return home that they gave the band a run for their money: they sang their hearts out to every song, which gave Freddie and Brian their own ideas for separate songs.

"That was a response to a particular phase in our career when the audience was becoming a bigger part of the show than we were," Brian explained to *Guitar World* in 1993. "They would sing all the songs. In a place like Birmingham, they'd be so vociferous that we'd have to stop the show and let them sing to us. So both Freddie and I thought it would be an interesting experiment to write songs with audience participation specifically in mind. My feeling was that everyone can stamp and clap and sing a simple motif. We did that record at Wessex, which is an old converted church that has a naturally good sound to it. There are no drums on there. It's just us, stamping on boards many times with many primitive delay machines and clapping. A bit of singing, a bit of guitar playing and that's it."

"It came very quickly," Brian told *Undercover* magazine in 1998. "It was after an experience we had with an audience. It was fairly early on in our history. We used to like people to sit and damn well listen to the songs, you know. We weren't a dance band or a sing along group. Then suddenly, people would start to sing along with the songs and they would sing everything. In the beginning we thought, 'Oh god, what are we going to do about this? It's annoying!' After a little while, we realized that that was how people felt and it kind of felt good if you actually conditioned yourself that way. One evening we finished a concert and we went off. It was actually in Birmingham, in England. And the audience sang to us a kind of a football song or whatever, you know. It was a very moving experience. Freddie and I looked at each other and thought, 'Something important has just happened here, and we should embrace it rather than fight it.' We both went away and starting writing with the idea that we would involve the audience deliberately. And Freddie wrote 'We Are the Champions' and I wrote 'We Will Rock You'. I think I woke up about three in the morning and I heard the initial beat in my head and I thought, 'That's what an audience could do. They could sing something along to it, something that was a kind of uniting feeling.' That's what happened. We did it very quickly in the studio. Roger thought it was a joke because there was no drums on it."

Roger confirmed this in a 1984 issue of *Modern Drummer*: "Everybody thinks that's drums, but it's not. It's feet. We sat on a piano and used out feet on an old drum podium. It's rather hard to explain in words what we did, but what you hear isn't drums. We must have recorded it, I don't know, 15 times or so. We put all sorts of different repeats on it to make it sound big. There's a catch though. When we do 'Rock You' live, I have to do it with drums, so everything is slightly delayed. Everything is to suit the song. To have just one way of working would result in the inability to change or adapt. A good drummer must be flexible. It's imperative."

Much like The Rolling Stones' 'Honky Tonk Women' and its original counterpart 'Country Honk', two different versions of 'We Will Rock You' exist: the first is the more famous stripped-back version, while the second is an actual band performance. Examples of this can be found on *Live Killers* and the 2011 double-disc reissue of *News Of The World* (taken from a November 1982 performance in Tokyo): the song starts off with a raucous guitar riff, a rarity in Queen's vast canon, and is kicked into high gear with a cavalcade of drums before falling into place with a driving rhythm section. The words are the same, but the performance is more energetic, even allowing a short snippet of a bass solo to sneak in during Brian's guitar solo. This version was only ever used during live performances between 1977 and 1982, where it served as the introductory number for practically every show.

A more reserved uptempo version was recorded for the band's sixth BBC session in October 1977, and remained unreleased until May 2002, when it was released as part of a promotional sequence for the musical of the same name, on a CD single featuring other versions of the song as part of a tie-in with British newspaper *The Sun* – the same paper that morbidly hounded Freddie in his dying days, incidentally, and which Roger lashed out against in 1994 with 'Dear Mr Murdoch', a vicious diatribe against its owner.

What's most interesting about the song is that it wasn't initially released as a UK single, only appearing as the B-side of 'We Are The Champions'. Of course, in the US it was a double A-side release with that song, and was also extracted from *Live Killers* as an Elektra-only single release in August 1979. In early 1978, the song was boosted to A-side status in France when 'We Are The Champions' ran its 12-week course (see the entry above for details), and while it appeared in many remixes over the next few years, most are too minute or monotonous to mention.

One that *should* be mentioned is a release that has caused upset among many Queen fans. In 1991, Hollywood Records started its massive re-release programme of the band's back catalog and included as a bonus track on *News Of The World* a remix of 'We Will Rock You', intriguingly subtitled 'Ruined by Rick Rubin'. Rubin had produced a plethora of major acts, including Red Hot Chili Peppers, Johnny Cash and System of a Down. This time, he deconstructed 'We Will Rock You', stripping it of almost everything except the vocals and rebuilding it around an urban-sounding drum-machine loop; he then called in Flea and Chad (bassist and drummer, respectively, from Red Hot Chili Peppers) to add some flavor to the remix. Rubin then sampled some of Brian's own guitar from 'Stone Cold Crazy' and added a recurring siren motif throughout as well as record scratches. The result is a glorious presentation of noise, but some fans were not receptive to the new approach and preferred not to acknowledge its existence.

A five-track promotional release came in mid-1991 of this version, along with four other mixes: Ruined Instrumental, Big Beat a Cappella, Effects a Cappella and Zulu Scratch a Cappella. Two other remixes were made but remain unreleased: Clap a Cappella and Effects Instrumental. While these other mixes become monotonous after a while, fans are urged to give the proper remix a chance; it may be an acquired taste, but it does contain some nice bits and does justice to the idea of updating the song for the 1990s.

If fans were outraged by the Rick Rubin remix, they must have been doubly so by two others. In 2000, Brian and Roger re-recorded the song with pop band 5ive, while in 2004, the duo re-recorded the song with Britney Spears, Beyoncé and Pink each taking a verse. This was done for a Pepsi advertisement, which also featured Brian and Roger as Roman kings while the three female singers are portrayed as gladiators in the

Coliseum. Oh yes, and there's a soda-based product in there somewhere, too.

The recording with 5ive was just as controversial, since it featured new lyrics 'rapped' by the pop band. Brian played guitar and bass in addition to co-producing with Richard Stannard and Julian Gallacher, and, when the single appeared in July 2000, ecstatic 5ive (and perhaps some reluctant Queen) fans snatched it up, and it became the first time the song reached No. 1 in the UK.

As for the original version, it reached a modest No. 4 in its US double-bill pairing with 'We Are The Champions', and didn't chart at all when released in its live format. The song took on a new life in the live setting: it was the fast-paced opener for many years, but as the second encore it carried an extra air of expectation. The audience knew by that point that the show was approaching its conclusion, but they still sang as vociferously as ever, while Freddie would let them take over the choruses as he pranced around the stage, working the crowd into a frenzy. "At concerts, I discovered, people tend to do three claps rather than two stamps and a clap," Brian told *Guitar World* in 1993. "The amazing thing is to go to football matches, or sports events in general, and hear people do it. It's very gratifying to find that it has become part of folklore, sort of. I'll die happy because of that." And it doesn't matter which sport, either – baseball, football, rugby, or soccer – as long as there's some sort of participatory vibe at the venue, the song (or even just the stomp-stomp-clap rhythm) is likely to emerge.

A video was constructed in January 1978 at Roger's mansion in Surrey. By that point, the members had become wealthy businessmen as well as musicians. They decided, then, that they need not be managed by an outsider any longer. Fortunately their current manager, John Reid, was also managing Elton John and had decided one megastar was enough. So, between takes for 'Spread Your Wings', the band rushed off in Freddie's Rolls-Royce and terminated their contract with Reid before going their separate, amicable ways. As a celebration of their freedom, they ran through 'We Will Rock You' for the cameras almost as an afterthought.

"It's really odd, but it wasn't really something we considered important at the time," Brian said of the low-budget, almost slapdash video constructed for the song, "and then, in the fullness of time, 'We Will Rock You' just became this incredible anthem which – along with 'We Are The Champions' – represented us all

over the world." In the commentary for the 2003 DVD *Greatest Video Hits 1*, Brian confirmed that "Yeah, I do feel very proud of it, really, in a sense. That's kind of my gravestone, I suppose."

WE'RE GOING HOME *(Lee)*

A variation of Ten Years After's track 'I'm Going Home' was performed by Ibex on 9 September 1969 at The Sink Club, Liverpool. This would be the final track of the standard set, with an encore coming shortly after. Unfortunately, the available tape cuts off prematurely so it's not known what songs made up the encore. Doubly unfortunate is the fact that Brian and Roger, then of Smile, joined Ibex on stage, making this the first known performance of the embryonic Queen.

WE'RE GOING WRONG *(Bruce)*

Originally released by Cream on their 1967 album *Disraeli Gears*, 'We're Going Wrong' was a regular in the Ibex set list, with a recording coming from The Sink Club, Liverpool on 9 September 1969.

THE WEDDING MARCH *(Wagner, arr. May)*
• Album: *Flash*

A suitably over-the-top rendition of the traditional marriage anthem, sounding like a perverse cross between Hendrix's interpretation of 'Star Spangled Banner' and Queen's own 'God Save The Queen'. Brian's guitar arrangement of Wagner's 'The Wedding March', lasting a little under one minute, appeared on *Flash Gordon* and appropriately accompanied the scene in which Ming and Dale are married.

"I make sure that the whole thing is planned and treated like you would give a score to an orchestra to do," Brian told BBC's Radio One in 1983. "It's a complete orchestration. So, it's a different kind of approach really but I enjoy doing those things. It's sort of indulgence really but, at the same time, I thought it would be funny for that 'Wedding March' to come out that way. Because all our people, who know our music, would recognize that immediately as one of our treatments and anyone else in the cinema would think of it as a strange 'Wedding March'. It's meant it to be a musical joke anyway, in the film, so it was just heightening that joke really."

WHAT ARE WE MADE OF *(May)*
• Album (Brian): *The Adventures of Pinocchio*

Of Brian's two contributions to *The Adventures Of Pinocchio* soundtrack in 1996, 'What Are We Made Of' is the most conventional. Written by Brian, the song features Norwegian singer Sissel duetting with Brian on a touching set of lyrics that are more universal than would normally be expected of a soundtrack composition. With orchestral arrangements by Lee Holdridge, the song was recorded at Allerton Hill and features a strong, ballad-like backing, performed almost exclusively by Brian (except for the drums, by Cozy Powell). But the emphasis is on the vocals. Brian's voice had matured greatly since the release of *Back To The Light*, and he's in fine form here, meshing beautifully with Sissel's angelic voice to truly poignant effect.

It's a shame, then, that the song didn't receive a higher-profile release: the soundtrack to the film wasn't exactly a hot seller, nor was the film all that popular at the box-office, and Brian's two contributions remained largely unheard. There were rumblings in contemporary Queen Fan Club magazines that the song was due to be released on Brian's *Another World*, and Brian even briefly flirted with the idea, but the song was kicked to the curb in lieu of, frankly, substandard material: 'What Are We Made Of' is a beautiful, latter-day classic, and deserved far more recognition than it was given.

WHATCHA GONNA DO 'BOUT IT? *(Potter/Samwell)*

The Small Faces' 1966 hit single was performed live by 1984 and The Reaction.

WHATEVER HAPPENED TO SATURDAY NIGHT?
(O'Brien)
• CD single (Brian): 9/98

Initially intended for Brian's *Heroes* project, 'Whatever Happened To Saturday Night?' was written by Richard O'Brien and recorded for the cult-classic film *The Rocky Horror Picture Show*. As originally performed by Meatloaf, the song absolutely rocks and is a highlight of the film, but in Brian's hands it's a different story. Though the backing of Cozy Powell on drums, Spike Edney on keyboards and brothers Andy and Steve Hamilton on saxophones is rollicking and faithful to the original, the vocals ultimately let it down. Brian is no Meatloaf, and is assisted by Madeline Bell, Gareth

Marx, Shelley Preston, Anita Dobson and Emily May on backing vocals in an attempt to beef things up. It's enjoyable enough, but its non-appearance on *Another World* (it was released on the US *Retro Rock* mini-album) was the right decision.

WHEN THIS OLD TIRED BODY WANTS TO SING (LATE NIGHT JAM)
• Compilation (Freddie): *Solo Collection*

A fast-paced jam between Freddie on vocals and Mike Moran on piano, 'When This Tired Old Body Wants To Sing' was recorded on 22 June 1987 and remained (largely) unreleased until the 2000 box set. The piano line that Mike is playing at the beginning of the jam, as well as the chanted "Sing it! Sing it!" vocals, was recycled into 'Overture Piccante' on *Barcelona*, but, with the full jam closing the second disc of rarities on the box set, it's more at home here. One does wonder just how much vodka Freddie had imbibed by the time the tape started rolling, though.

WHEN WE WERE YOUNG

In promotional materials for the impending release of *Fun On Earth*, 'When We Were Young' was listed as part of the track list, yet when the album was released in November 2013, it was nowhere to be found. Whether the song exists (rumors persist it started during sessions for *The Cosmos Rocks*) or was just somebody confusing a key line from 'These Are The Days Of Our Lives' as an entirely different song remains to be seen; the ever-reliable paragon of information, Wikipedia, states that the song was used in the film for *Solitary*, the soundtrack of which Roger provided, though as of this publishing, the song has yet to surface.

WHERE ARE YOU NOW? *(Taylor)*
• Album (Roger): *Electric*

Though the title sounds like a tribute to Freddie, 'Where Are You Now?' is a ponderous song in which Roger makes reference to God and the placement of religion in Roger's life. This might be looking a bit too deeply into the words, though with lines like "There must be more to life than this bum deal" and "Just trying to file a flight plan / Need some direction, need it now", this is not a difficult connection to make.

Set at a mid-tempo pace with dominant keyboards played by Roger and Mike Crossley (the latter provides a sublime piano solo where a guitar solo from the mighty Jason Falloon may have otherwise featured), the song breaks down in the middle, leaving only Roger's drums and vocals as the driving force, before each instrument is reintroduced. It's interesting that Jason Falloon's guitar melody recalls the opener's riff in 'Pressure On'. Perhaps it was this similarity that excluded the song from the live setting.

WHIPPING BOY

Not much is known about 'Whipping Boy' other than that it may have been recorded during sessions for *Hot Space* in 1982. Some collectors have insisted that it is an unreleased demo recording of a completely new song, while others have posited that it may be a working title for Brian's piano ballad 'My Boy', also recorded during the *Hot Space* sessions. The song was returned to in 1983 for sessions for *The Works*, and even ended up on the short-list of songs to appear on the album, but it was ultimately discarded.

THE WHISPERERS *(Taylor/Evans)*
• Album (Roger): *Electric*

In the press release for *Electric Fire*, it's stated that "Nicholas Evans provided the inspiration for the spiritually inclined 'The Whisperers' ... tell[ing] of the ancient art of training wild horses via softly spoken verbal commands, a more subtle approach than the harsh tradition of dominating the animals through force." Evans' *The Horse Whisperer* (which was the working title of the song but truncated for final release) was published in 1995 and features heavily in the lyric, so much so that Roger gave Evans a co-credit. It also happened to be turned into a major motion picture in 1998, starring Robert Redford.

"I read the book way before the movie came out, which I though was disappointing," Roger explained. "I thought it was a very elegantly written book and if I wanted a good ambient, wide-open spaces, Montana kind of feel to a song, I could not improve on that. I sent Nicholas Evans a copy of the song and he thought it was great and when I said would he like a credit on the song, I just lifted some of the words from the book."

Set to a mid-tempo, keyboard-dominated backing atypical of Roger, the song premiered at the 1998 Fan Club Convention along with 'No More Fun' and 'Tonight'. Unlike those two songs, 'The Whisperers' was doomed to obscurity, and was never attempted in the live setting.

WHITE MAN *(May)*
• B-side: 11/76 [2] • Album: *Races*

This forgotten rocker, 'White Man' (originally recorded in July 1976 as 'Simple Man') opens the second side of *A Day At The Races* in discordant style, with plenty of raw guitar and pounding drums that sound out of place on this album. The song takes a political stance, which was a rarity in Queen's songs and is ultimately the major downfall of the track: written about the Native Americans' plight caused by white explorers and the Westernization of the natural environment, the song, despite its best intentions, borders on preachy and is easily the weakest of the *A Day At The Races* tracks.

"'White Man' is the B-side," Freddie told *Circus* in 1977. "It's Brian's song, a very bluesy track. Gave me the opportunity to do raucous vocals. I think it'll be a great stage number." The song became a regular on the 1977 A Day At The Races and 1977/1978 News Of The World tours, interpolated into 'The Prophet's Song'.

WHITE QUEEN (AS IT BEGAN) *(May)*
• Album: *Queen2* • EP: *First EP* • CD Single: 11/88
• Bonus: *Queen2* • Live: *Rainbow, Odeon* • Compilation: *On Air*

Slowing the mood down on *Queen II* after the raucous finale of 'Father To Son', Brian's gorgeous 'White Queen (As It Began)' sneaks in with a hidden guitar introduction, as Freddie sings, virtually unaccompanied, his tale of the proverbial queen of his heart. Enriched by some of Brian's most beautiful lyrics, the song's delicacy transforms into a full-on assault as Brian, Roger and John launch into a fantastic instrumental section, showcasing the Red Special in all its glory.

"I wrote this at College, where I led a relatively sheltered life, even though the University on the whole was a pretty rampant pace!" Brian explained in 2004. "I had been reading *The White Goddess* by Robert Graves, which explored the role of the idealized Virgin/Mother/Queen figure in art through history, and the name for our group, decided just around that time, fitted in with this perfectly – which was one of the reasons I was convinced to go with the name. The personal side is bound up with a girl (of course!) whom I saw every day at College, and was to me the ultimate goddess. It's incredible in retrospect, but because I held her in such awe, in three years I never had the courage to speak to tell her, or even speak to her."

The song was included in the live setting between 1974 and early 1977, before being dropped for the News Of The World US tour, though it was reprised once in 1978. A version recorded for the BBC on 3 April 1974 surpasses the original's beauty thanks to a lovely piano-guitar duet that supplants the normal guitar orchestrations. This rendition was finally released in 2016 on *On Air*, while two live recordings, one from the band's November 1974 concert at the Rainbow Theatre and the other a year later at Hammersmith Odeon, were released in 2014 (*Live At The Rainbow '74*) and 2015 (*A Night At The Odeon*), respectively.

WHO NEEDS YOU *(Deacon)*
• Album: *NOTW* • Bonus: *NOTW*

A slightly comedic number, John's 'Who Needs You' introduced a new style into Queen's already expansive sound spectrum: Latin music. The instrumental line-up is interesting since it features Brian and John playing acoustic guitars, with the former also shaking maracas as Freddie taps a cowbell. The arrangement doesn't get much more complex than that, except for some subtle guitar harmonies from Brian, but the acoustic guitar solo is absolutely sublime, and had been the cause of much debate over the years regarding its performer; in 2014, Brian finally confirmed that it was he who played the solo. An early version, announced as Take 2 by Mike Stone, stripped the song down to its essentials, with John on acoustic guitar, Brian on maracas, and Freddie singing a set of unfinished lyrics, "la-la"ing along to the melody where the words had yet to be finalized. (There also appears to be some minimal bass, suggesting Roger might have deputized on the instrument.)

The words are vengeful, as Freddie sings of a sly girl who keeps the protagonist waiting until he can bear no longer, declaring that he doesn't need her any more. Not surprisingly, 'Who Needs You' wasn't performed live as it didn't suit the setting (it would be difficult to imagine the band performing the song in the expansive stadia they were dominating by this time), but it makes *News Of The World* that much more diverse.

WHO WANTS TO LIVE FOREVER *(May)*
• Album: *AKOM* • A-side: 9/86 [24] • Live: *Wembley, Budapest* • Compilation: *Hits2, Classic*

"The hero of [*Highlander*] discovers in his first battle that he can't die," Brian explained of his 1986 composition

'Who Wants To Live Forever', "and unfortunately he finds that he falls in love with this girl, and everybody tells him that it's a bad idea if they stay together because eventually she must grow old and die, and he won't. But nevertheless he does, he stays with her and she does grow old and she dies in his arms and she says, 'I never understood why you stayed with me,' and he says, 'I see you just the same as I saw you when I first met you', and she's old and she's dying. I was very moved by that and I wrote this song called 'Who Wants To Live Forever (When Love Must Die)'."

Brian's exquisite ballad was written in the backseat of his car after viewing a 20-minute rough-cut of the film; by the time he returned home, he had completed the melody by humming his ideas into a mini tape-recorder. "This is a very different era, of course," Brian said in 2003. "The song was written – I've documented this very well, I know – but what happened was we went to see the *Highlander* rushes with Russell Mulcahy, and that was our first experience in any way with *Highlander* – I hadn't read the script; I don't think any of us had – and it was very moving ... [It] kind of opened up a floodgate in me – I was dealing with a lot of tragedies in my life: the death of my father, the death of my marriage, and so forth. I could immediately hear this 'Who Wants To Live Forever' in my head, and it was almost complete in the car going home – I remember singing it to my manager as he drove me home, and he was pretty surprised. He said, 'Where did that come from?' and I said, 'I don't even know.'"

It's interesting, then, to hear what resulted from a few hummed lines, since 'Who Wants To Live Forever' turned into a traditional Queen power-anthem, backed by the Royal Philharmonic Orchestra. The song actually features only Brian on keyboards, guitars and vocals, with Freddie also on vocals; there is no bass guitar, and the percussion is a combination of programmed drums by Brian and David Richards and the percussion section from the Royal Philharmonic Orchestra. The orchestration, arranged by Brian and Michael Kamen, is gorgeous and suits the song perfectly, reaching a full climax by the time Brian's restrained guitar solo begins.

For the first time since 1980, Brian contributes lead vocals, though it's only sporadic: the opening verse, half of the bridge, and the closing line – the melancholy, "Who waits forever anyway?" – are all sung by Brian. For the film version, Freddie sings the entirety of the song, but it's the stark contrast of Brian's quiet, almost mumbled voice and Freddie's powerful performance that makes the song so haunting.

Released in September 1986 as the final single from *A Kind Of Magic*, 'Who Wants To Live Forever' was backed by 'Killer Queen' and issued as a UK-only single, reaching a disappointing No. 24 in the charts. The 12" version featured an instrumental reworking titled 'Forever' (see separate entry for that song), and all versions featured a four-minute edit of the title track, though the song's full power and beauty can be found only on the album cut, which is the definitive version. The song was performed live on the 1986 Magic tour, and featured Brian on keyboards during the first part but switching to guitar in time for his solo.

A video was shot on 16 September 1986 at the Tobacco Wharf in London, and was directed by David Mallet. The video shows Freddie, Brian and John dressed in formal wear with the Royal Philharmonic Orchestra and a 40-strong boys' choir accompanying the band. Roger is perched behind a pair of timpani and a bass drum, and is the only one dressed informally, which he humorously addressed: "Yeah, I got quite drunk doing this [video]. I couldn't remember my bits. I must've been drunk, because I'm dressed appallingly in some denim outfit. I must've fallen into a vat of bleach! This was a long, boring shoot, and it's all terribly serious. It looks a bit religious, so I can't say I'm very keen on that." Brian commented further, saying, "To my mind, I don't think the video does that much for the song, but it's nice to see Freddie very formal."

Roger agreed that the song worked well in the context of the movie: "I really love the song in the context of the *Highlander* film, with all the moving shots of the highlander and his wife, and she's getting old and it's all shot in the Highlands, and I thought that was very beautiful and very moving."

In 1989, to support the British Bone Marrow Donor Appeal, Brian arranged a session at Olympic Studios for a specially re-recorded version of the track, sung by two child vocalists, Ian Meeson and Belinda Gillett. Brian produced and played keyboards and guitar, while Roger assisted on drums and John on bass, with Michael Kamen adding string arrangements. The song was majestically recreated by pop star Seal at the Concert For Life, heightened by an emotional vocal performance, and was undoubtedly one of the most underrated renditions of the day.

The song was passed over for inclusion in the Queen + Paul Rodgers setlist, but became an undoubted highlight when it was introduced into the Queen + Adam Lambert tours, retaining a rightful spot in the repertoire at nearly every concert.

WHOLE HOUSE ROCKIN' *(Taylor)*
• Bonus (Roger): *Earth*

In interviews for *The Cosmos Rocks*, Brian mentioned that 'Cosmos Rockin'' had been submitted by Roger, and that its original working title was 'Whole House Rockin'', though the guitarist suggested the increasing venue size: first house, then town, then world, then universe, and, finally, the cosmos. While there's something special about the Queen + Paul Rodgers version, Roger's recording deconstructs the song to its barest bones, transforming it into a good-time boogie-woogie, as opposed to the tongue-in-cheek Status Quo tribute 'Cosmos Rockin'' became.

WHOLE LOTTA SHAKIN' GOIN' ON *(Williams)*

Jerry Lee Lewis' 1957 single was performed in Osaka on 24 October 1982 and on 15 May 1985 as encore numbers. The Cross also performed it with Brian on guitar and John on bass during their Fan Club Christmas party in December 1988, with Chris Thompson on vocals.

WHY DON'T WE TRY AGAIN *(May)*
• Album (Brian): *World* • A-side: 9/98 [44]

Reportedly written for a Queen project (it would be easy to assume that it was submitted for *Innuendo* or the sessions shortly thereafter, but Brian tended to sit on songs for a while), 'Why Don't We Try Again' is about Brian living on his own, which could be about his divorce from Chrissy in the late 1980s. Throughout the song, he questions whether his motives were right, suggesting that their "love was stronger than history" and that it "will never cease to be."

Set to a mid-tempo, keyboard-dominated backing, the instrumentation is never intrusive, with appropriate musical peaks and valleys accentuating the emotions and poignancy of the lyrics. Whereas Brian's voice sounded thin and weak on *Back To The Light*, by 1998 he had built up his confidence as a vocalist, and 'Why Don't We Try Again' features one of his finest vocal performances, confirming that he always sounds more at ease with the slower ballads than with the challenging rockers. While there aren't any drums, a drum-machine does keep the rhythm going, with Cozy Powell adding bursts of percussion and timpani. This author was quick to label it as an attempt to rewrite

'Too Much Love Will Kill You', but that does the song a huge and unfair disservice: while 'Why Don't We Try Again' can be categorized as, superficially, a ballad, the message is completely different, evoking the pain and despair brought upon by a disintegrating relationship, and is not only the highlight of *Another World*, but a major achievement in Brian's songwriting canon.

An edited version of 'Why Don't We Try Again' (reducing the running time from 5'22 to 4'06) was rightly chosen as the second UK single, peaking at No. 44 (seven places better than the lead-off single, 'Business'). The song was performed on only a few occasions during the 1998 Another World tour, which is probably for the best, since it would be nearly impossible to reach the notes Brian managed in the studio recording during a gruelling live set.

WILDERNESS (May)

• Album (Brian): *World*

Another World is a far more adventurous collection of songs than on *Back To The Light*, with Brian dabbling in both conventional ballads and rockers while feeding his creative drive for experimentation. Most of the time, the experimentations are well-intentioned but out of place; 'Cyborg', written for a computer game, sticks out the most, while 'China Belle' and 'The Guv'nor' border on the conventional but are instilled with an infectious joy that rise beyond the pale. How, then, to classify 'Wilderness'? On no other song on the album does Brian so successfully question "an outpouring of a confused brain" than he does on this, but the arrangement would have benefited from a more organic approach; as it is entirely self-performed, there's a synthetic sheen that sits mildly ill at the ease with the rest of the album. Regardless, it fits the theme of Brian's never-ending quest to find himself.

"'Wilderness' was a fusion of a lot of feelings I had at the time which were (and *are*) hard to express," Brian said of the song. "It was one of those songs which more or less wrote themselves. I had no confidence in it at the time, but Justin [Shirley-Smith] encouraged me to finish it. There is a lot of darkness in these songs from this period which I find hard to revisit even now. The upside is that they were part of a path which led me eventually to a good place, though not in a way I was expecting..."

A WINTER'S TALE (Queen)

• Album: *Heaven* • A-side: 12/95 [6] • Bonus: *Heaven*

After the *Innuendo* sessions finished in early 1991, Freddie insisted that the band return to Mountain Studios in Montreux to start work on another album. Freddie was so energized by the rush of recording that he already had several songs written that he wanted to get down on tape, among them the atmospheric 'A Winter's Tale'. According to Jim Hutton, the song had been written in the winter of 1990 in Montreux during a recording session, as Freddie sat on the porch of his rented home on Lake Geneva.

The words are of the observational type, which was unusual for Freddie but a welcome approach. The listener is almost placed into Freddie's lakeside seat as he sings about "smoking chimney tops" and "little girls scream[ing] and cry[ing]", set to an idyllic, laid-back instrumentation. As Freddie sings the lyrics, one gets a sense of sadness in the performance, as he acknowledges that all that surrounds him is "an extraordinary place", even referencing an older song ("there's a kind of magic in the air"), but there's still an optimistic, blissful bent to the words.

"I love the last song he wrote, 'A Winter's Tale'," Brian told the *Daily Mirror* in 2002. "It doesn't philosophize, it's just about how beautiful life is. He wrote it one morning, beside the lake and looking at the mountains." Brian later told *Classic Rock* magazine in 2011, "Freddie mainly used the piano for songwriting, but there were times when he'd get inspiration when he wasn't around his instrument. It could be any experience; a skate on the pond. One of the last songs he wrote, 'A Winter's Tale', was written purely sat looking out on the mountains from the other side of Lake Geneva. He could obviously hear it all in his head, although he didn't have any musical instruments with him. I remember him coming into the studio and saying, 'I've got this idea … just give me a few minutes.' Then he brought it to life. That's a beautiful track, actually."

The song was virtually completed during the post-*Innuendo* sessions, though it sounds as if Roger re-recorded his drum track and Brian and Roger added the vocal harmonies later. (A stripped-back mix, designated as the "Cosy Fireside Mix", moves Freddie's vocal higher up and reduces the keyboards somewhat; this version was released on the 2011 deluxe edition of *Made In Heaven*.) Chosen as the second single from *Made In Heaven* in December 1995, 'A Winter's Tale' was a perfect holiday choice; the band, too, recognized the opportunity, and coupled the song with their 1984 non-album single, 'Thank God It's Christmas'. Two CD singles were issued, the first using three remastered singles from the 1970s ('Now I'm Here', 'You're My Best Friend' and 'Somebody To Love'), while the second offered 'Thank God It's Christmas' along with the previously unissued 'Rock In Rio Blues' from 1985.

The single peaked at No. 6 in the charts (though it wasn't given a US release), and two videos were created for the release. The first was a standard cut-and-paste DoRo affair, though it added a special effect of the lyrics being 'written' on the screen in Freddie's handwriting. The more standard version was commissioned by the British Film Institute for the 1996 release, *Made In Heaven: The Videos* and was directed by Chris Rodley. Retitled 'Outside-In', the video shows the ecstasy of landscape as a man dreams his last few images of colour, texture, light and movement in the world. Heavy stuff, yet neither video, apart from the latter's inclusion on the aforementioned video anthology, has yet been released on any official Queen product; the song was also overlooked for inclusion on the 1999 *Greatest Hits III* compilation, though it was finally released in 2010 on the final *Singles Collection* box set.

WISHING WELL

(Bundrick/Kirke/Kossoff/Rodgers/Yamauchi)
• Live (Q+PR): *Return*

Released on Free's 1973 album *Heartbreaker*, 'Wishing Well' was written for departed guitarist Paul Kossoff, who left the band due to an escalating problem with drug addiction. The song, which apparently holds an equal amount of significance for Brian and Roger, was introduced to the live set list on 28 April 2005 in Hamburg. The song remained in the set on the 2008 Rock The Cosmos tour, but, curiously, wasn't released on *Live In Ukraine*.

WITHOUT YOU *(Bulsara)*

This original composition written by Freddie was performed on two occasions by Wreckage: first on 26 October 1969 and five days later, on 31 October, both at Ealing College Of Art.

WOMAN YOU'RE SO BEAUTIFUL (BUT STILL A PAIN IN THE ASS) *(Taylor)*
• Download: 8/06

In August 2006, a mystery website appeared on MySpace in the name of Felix & Arty, with a song titled 'Woman You're So Beautiful (But Still A Pain In The Ass)'. Fans on the online Queen community were puzzled by the song, pondering the identities of Felix & Arty, though the more resourceful listeners were able to surmise that the curious Arty moniker was a phonetic pronunciation of Roger Taylor's initials, and that the name itself had been credited on the *Electric Fire* track, 'People On Streets'. Felix, of course, is Roger's son. Born during sessions for *The Game* on 22 May 1980, he was known in Queendom for shouting "radio ka ka", thus initiating one of the band's biggest hits, as well as for appearing on the rear sleeve of *Electric Fire*.

Felix wrote a message on the website explaining the genesis of the song: "My dad wrote it a few months back and the first mix was cut with himself on vocals. We all thought it was pretty catchy and that he had done a good job all round. But, ever the perfectionist, he wasn't quite happy with what he had, and started tinkering with it, suggesting that I cut a vocal for it. Not being particularly experienced in this field, I was very chuffed to be asked, and gave it a go in the studio. I was pleased with the result, it sounded pretty good and was dead catchy (almost irritatingly so). My dad was happier with this cut too, so he thought he would try and hawk it to Transistor Project and Parlophone as a summer single. They took the bait and here we are!"

According to Felix, the song was written during the Queen + Paul Rodgers tour of Japan in October 2005 and first recorded in April 2006 at Roger's home studio, though work continued on the song into the next month, which was when Felix added his vocals. When asked if, like Paul Rodgers' 'Take Love', it was intended for the reported new album, Felix balked at the idea and claimed it was always intended as a solo single. In terms of the lyrical theme, Felix intimated that the song "started off as a sort of statement about how women are, paradoxically, both wonderful and incredibly annoying" and that it's "just a damn good, reggae-lite summer pop tune, with a killer chorus that stays in your head whether you like it or not." It's hard to disagree with him, and 'Woman You're So Beautiful' confirmed that the creative bug had bitten Roger once again.

WOOLLY HAT: *see* COOL CAT

WORKING CLASS HERO *(Lennon)*
• Album (Roger): *Electric*

"I am a big John Lennon fan, I could go on about him forever," Roger gushed in 1998. "I think the *Plastic Ono*

Band album wasn't a big hit when it was first released ... This song is probably not so well known by a whole generation so we decided to do a different kind of rock band variation on it."

There's something vaguely hypocritical about a multi-millionaire rock star like Roger covering John Lennon's 'Working Class Hero'; then again, by the time Lennon had written and recorded the song in 1970, he, too, was a multi-millionaire himself, which is just another of the perfect ironies that makes the world go round. Simply said, Roger's rendition of Lennon's diatribe against the upper classes is initially questionable, and the full-band performance of the originally acoustic solo recording muddles the song and makes the power of the lyrics less effective.

However, it should be remembered that *Electric Fire* is largely autobiographical, and that the song relates to some aspect of Roger's early life before he made it big as a rock star (this was an angle that contemporary reviews couldn't grasp). Despite the obvious flaws, the instrumental backing is hypnotic, with Keith Airey's guitar creating considerable feedback throughout most of the song. While it's an appreciated nod towards John Lennon, one would have preferred another original number from Roger, especially on such a personal album.

YEAH *(Queen)*
• Bonus: *Heaven*

Hardly constituting a track in its own right, 'Yeah' is a four-second snippet of Freddie saying exactly that, extracted from 'Don't Try Suicide'. Instead of counting this as the ending of 'It's A Beautiful Day (Reprise)', it is inserted between the former song and a 22-minute instrumental.

YELLOW BREEZES *(Mercury/Moran)*
• Compilation (Freddie): *Solo Collection*

One of the more interesting compositions to be released on *The Solo Collection*, 'Yellow Breezes' was recorded during sessions for *Barcelona* on 9 March 1987 at Townhouse Studios in London, but is the polar opposite of the sound Freddie was trying to achieve on that album. Largely improvised with Mike Moran on keyboards, David Richards providing the drum programming and Erdal Kizilkay on bass, the song is a showcase for Kizilkay, who features prominently. The song has a slight Caribbean tone (with Freddie making a reference to John Deacon's 1977 composition, 'Who

Needs You', with the line "Oh muchachos!"). Lasting over five minutes, the song is interesting though inconsequential, but is definitely worth a listen.

YOU AND I *(Deacon)*
• Album: *Races* • B-side: 3/77 [31]

John had a knack for writing deliberately chart-friendly pop songs but the best example of his pop sensibility comes in 'You And I', a superb song that strays from the bubblegum he was nearing on 'You're My Best Friend'. Another song written for his wife Veronica, the bassist's contribution to *A Day At The Races* is a highlight of the album, thanks to the perfect balance between piano, guitars and a tight rhythm section.

"That was a track by John Deacon, his contribution to this album," Freddie told Kenny Everett in 1976. "His songs are good and are getting better every time, actually. I'm getting a bit worried, actually. He's sort of quiet, loads of people think that. Don't underestimate him, he's got a fiery streak underneath all that. I talk so much anyway, he likes to let me do all the talking. But once people crack that thin ice, then he's alright."

"It's very John Deacon, with more raucous guitars," Freddie told *Circus* in 1977. "After I'd done the vocals, John put all these guitars in, and the mood has changed. I think it's his strongest song to date." No argument there, and there's no doubting 'You And I' would have been a far better choice for single release than 'Tie Your Mother Down' or 'Good Old-Fashioned Lover Boy'. However, John's song was featured only as the B-side of that single (and on the US release of 'Long Away' in June 1977), and was disregarded as a choice in the live setting.

YOU DON'T FOOL ME *(Queen)*
• Album: *Heaven* • A-side: 11/96 [17]

A sleek and sexy rocker tucked away on the *Made In Heaven* album, the origins of 'You Don't Fool Me' have been forever cast into doubt due to an ambiguous description on the *Greatest Hits III* sleeve notes: "Harking back to the early 80's and their disco-flavored *Hot Space* album, Queen wrote and recorded 'You Don't Fool Me' as a latter-day foray into dance music." Thus, fans have been under the impression that the song was an out-take from the *Hot Space* sessions, but it's easy to hear that the song is 1990s in sound and approach.

A collaboration between Roger and Freddie, 'You

Don't Fool Me' was written and recorded during the post-*Innuendo* sessions but left unfinished when Freddie died. Not an easy song to love upon first listening, it eventually grows in interest with repeated listens, and while it may bring back memories of 'Body Language' and 'Staying Power', the song is redeemed by real instrumentation and a stunning guitar solo from Brian. Released as a single in November 1996, the song may not have been the most ideal choice for the singles chart – certainly, 'Made In Heaven' or 'I Was Born To Love You' were far superior choices – though it did make it to No. 17.

Here's where the story gets a bit ludicrous. In an attempt to foster the belief that 'You Don't Fool Me' was a decent club single, the band commissioned various DJs to remix the song for various worldwide markets. The resulting 15 remixes are less than stellar – while there are a few diamonds in the rough, the majority of the releases are truly the nadir of Queen's singles output. Forget the bastardized 'Liar' in 1974 or 'It's Late' in 1978: the 'You Don't Fool Me' remixes transform Queen from a respectable rock band to an anonymous dance club act. When compiling a running order for *The Singles Collection* in the late 2000s, Greg Brook admitted that his intent was to have every single variation on there, but that Brian and Roger had vetoed inclusion of any remix of 'You Don't Fool Me'. While some fans would cry foul at this attempt at revisionism, in this instance, the right decision was made, and only the four minute single edit was released, along with the standard album version.

A video was commissioned by the British Multimedia Institute in 1996, directed by Mark Szaszy. The video is based on the concept of androgyny and the sexual code of appearance and identity separation between the sexes. This video was issued on the video compilations *Made In Heaven: The Films* and on the more commercially geared *Greatest Flix III*.

'YOU HAD TO BE THERE' *(Taylor)*
• Album (Roger): *Happiness?* • B-side (Roger): 9/94 [26]

Nestled away on the second side of *Happiness?* is this minor-key ballad, written about Freddie and Roger's relationship with him. The most touching verse is the second one, in which Roger briefly details the darker years following his friend's death, when "the night was hell", though he attempts to remain optimistic about "happy days that might come again", remaining hopeful that they will meet again. Roger plays all the instruments except for the soaring guitar solo, in which Jason Falloon extracts sounds from his guitar that resemble David Gilmour's style, and the whole song, all three minutes of it, is a poignant tribute to Freddie.

"You Had To Be There" was released as the B-side of 'Foreign Sand' in September 1994 and was also performed on the resulting world tour, and was one of the highlights of the show. As with most of *Happiness?*, the song was kept out of the set for subsequent tours.

YOU KEEP ME HANGING ON
(Holland/Dozier/Holland)

Originally performed by Diana Ross and the Supremes, 'You Keep Me Hanging On' was performed live by 1984.

YOU TAKE MY BREATH AWAY *(Mercury)*
• Album: *Races* • Bonus: *Races*

After the raucous opening of 'Tie Your Mother Down', the next song was designed to slow down the mood of *A Day at the Races*, and 'You Take My Breath Away' was the perfect choice. Written for Freddie's then-lover David Minns (not Mary Austin, as has long been rumored), the result is an unabashed love song that finds the vocalist wearing his heart on his sleeve. With Freddie only on multi-tracked vocals and piano, and an understated guitar solo from Brian, the song is spread out over a luxurious five minutes. 'You Take My Breath Away' was written after Queen's spring 1976 tour in Japan, where Freddie was inspired by both their culture and their music, and based the melody on the Japanese Pentatonic scale.

"This one I did myself, I multi-tracked myself," Freddie told Kenny Everett in 1976. "So the others weren't used on this for the voices. I played piano and basically, I don't know how we managed to stay this simple, you know, with all our overdubs and things. People seem to think that we're over-complex, and it's not true. It depends on the individual track really, if it needs it – we do it. So this is pretty sparse actually by Queen and our standards."

The song was one of the few to be premiered before its official release date, when it was performed at the four summer shows in 1976. With only Freddie on vocals and piano, he was amazed that it went off so well (it's breathtaking to listen to the performance from Hyde Park, despite audience members shouting for people to sit down). "'You Take My Breath Away' is a slow ballad with a new twist," Freddie explained to *Circus* in 1977. "That's another track I did at Hyde Park, with just me on the piano. It was very nerve-wracking, playing all by myself in front of 200,000 people. I didn't think my voice would come through; it's a very emotional, laid-back number."

The song remained in the set list until June 1977, when it was replaced by 'My Melancholy Blues'. The introductory a cappella vocal section was used as a lead-in to 'Who Wants To Live Forever' on the 2017 Queen + Adam Lambert tour.

YOU'RE MY BEST FRIEND *(Deacon)*
• Album: *Opera* • A-side: 5/76 [7] • Live: *Killers* • CD Single: 11/88 • Bonus: *Opera* • CD Single: 12/95 [6]

By 1975, John hadn't exactly established himself as a proficient songwriter. He had missed out on composing songs for the first two albums, and his first composition – 'Misfire' from *Sheer Heart Attack* – was an inoffensive but slight pop song that lacked substance. It's surprising, then, that 'You're My Best Friend' has become one of John's most well-known and endearing songs, and that it broke the tradition of Freddie- and Brian-only singles.

"I'm very pleased with that, actually," Freddie told *Rock Australia Magazine* in 1976. "John has really come into his own. Brian and myself have mostly written all the songs before, and he's been in the background; he's worked very hard, and his song's very good, isn't it? It's nice. It even adds to the versatility, y'know what I mean. It's nice that four people can write and they're all strong; if John or anyone else wrote a song that we thought was weak, it would never be on the album. So he has had to work really hard on it to keep up the standard."

Written for his wife Veronica (the two had been dating since 1971, and married in January 1975) and composed on an electric piano, which John also plays on the final cut, 'You're My Best Friend' is a simple love song with no hidden or deeper meanings: John is in love, and he wants the world to know. "Freddie didn't like the electric piano," John explained in a Christmas Eve 1977 BBC radio interview, "so I took it home and I started to learn on the electric piano and basically that's the song that came out of the thing when I was learning to play it. It was written on that instrument and it sounds best on that."

"John just came from nowhere with this song," Brian explained. "It was only the second song he'd written for the group and it was just this perfect pop song." The guitarist continued: "I think [the song] is amazing. He went out completely on a limb to do that. It's not the kind of thing we'd done before but he knew exactly what he wanted."

It was a huge risk to issue the song as the follow-up to 'Bohemian Rhapsody', since it was the complete opposite of that single. Unpretentious, short and sweet, it was nevertheless a Top Ten UK hit, reaching No. 7 in Britain and even reaching a respectable No. 16 in the US. A performance video, again directed by Bruce Gowers, was shot in April 1976 at Elstree Studios. It isn't as groundbreaking as its predecessor but conveys the mood nicely: the band are seated in a barn with the only natural light coming from hundreds of candles. The result, which is a rather subtle and deliberate downplaying of the previous single's eccentricities, is sentimental, which was shattered somewhat when Roger declared on the commentary track for the video on the *Greatest Hits 1* DVD in 2002 that the day was blisteringly hot and that the farmers had only recently moved the cows out, making the atmosphere all the more stifling.

'You're My Best Friend' was performed as part of the medley between September 1976 and September 1980, and almost every performance of the song in that time sounds strangely similar. The song was remixed in 1991 for the Hollywood Records reissue of *A Night At The Opera*, adding an echo to the drums but leaving the majority of the song untouched. Surprisingly, Brian performed an abbreviated solo acoustic version of the song, with vociferous audience participation, on the final night of the Queen + Adam Lambert tour at the Hammersmith Apollo on 14 July 2012.

(YOU'RE SO SQUARE) BABY I DON'T CARE
(Leiber/Stoller)
• Live: *Wembley, Budapest* • Compilation: *On Air*

Opening the rock'n'roll acoustic medley after 'Is This The World We Created...?' during the 1986 Magic tour was this hit by Elvis Presley. This song showed the band in high spirits, evident on the *Live At Wembley Stadium* DVD, in which Freddie cavorts around the stage in a policeman's hat.

YOU'RE THE ONLY ONE

An unreleased recording by Freddie dating from the *A Kind Of Magic* sessions, nothing is known about this song except the title and that it's a piano-based demo; it's unlikely that the band recorded this.

YOU'RE YOUNG AND YOU'RE CRAZY: *see* BANANA BLUES

YOUNG LOVE *(Taylor)*
• Album (Roger): *Frontier*

Languishing forgotten on the second side of *Strange Frontier* is this upbeat, jangly rocker, with a bed of acoustic and electric guitars dominating the arrangement that sits at odds with the rest of the album. With a "Wall of Sound" production style recalling Phil Spector's glory days, 'Young Love' is a kind of update of 'Tie Your Mother Down', with Roger imploring young lovers to "stick to your guns and show the world that you just don't care". Like other songs on *Strange Frontier*, 'Young Love' strikes an inspirational anthem, with a prolonged outro full of some lovely guitar and keyboard work.

YOUR KIND OF LOVER *(Mercury)*
• Album (Freddie): *BadGuy* • Compilations (Freddie): *Pretender, FM Album, The Solo Collection*

Starting off as a slow piano ballad, 'Your Kind Of Lover' quickly ascends into an explosive dance number, with a terrific piano performance from Fred Mandel. As with most of the songs on the album, the lyrics deal with Freddie's fascination with love, and while the words in this case aren't quite as consequential as the others, they still find the vocalist in an upbeat mood.

Two earlier versions eventually surfaced on *The Solo Collection*: the first, recorded in March 1984, features only piano and occasional drum overdubs, while the second, recorded two months later, features a more pronounced piano and slightly altered lyrics (including improvised scats where Freddie hadn't yet finalized the words). A remix by Steve Brown, with arrangements and instrumentation by Andrew Flashman and Andrew King, was issued on the 1992 compilations *The Great Pretender* in the US and *The Freddie Mercury Album* in the UK.

PART FOUR

QUEEN LIVE

Much has been said about Queen's live performances, and it would be foolish to attempt to expand upon what is already known and what has already been written. With that in mind, I recommend Queen Concerts (www. queenconcerts.com), a fantastically run website that offers details on virtually every Queen-related show from the pre-Queen years to the recent Kerry Ellis and Brian May tour. Bob Wegner's Queen Live Site (queenlive.ca) goes one step further and analyzes existing bootlegs and offers a huge database of previously unseen live photographs. Also notable is Queen Live: A Concert Documentary by Greg Brooks, which took the first step by introducing fans to the previously unexplored world of Queen in the live setting.

Consequently, this section serves only as a broad overview of Queen live. Each tour has been divided into a separate entry, with a general set list given. Remember that not every song was performed every night, but the songs listed in the following pages were performed throughout the respective tour, whether as a semi-regular addition or as a one-off. It should also be noted that the repertoire of Queen's earliest concerts between 1970 and 1972, and even into 1973, are not known. Only a handful of songs are known to have been performed, while – inevitably, yet regrettably – a more detailed dissection is not obtainable. With the known information, a general overview is the only option.

This section deals only with Queen's performances as a band between 1970 and 1986; further analyzes of pre-Queen bands and their performances can be found in Part One, while the Freddie Mercury Tribute Concert, solo concerts and the various Queen + partnerships are examined in Part Seven.

1970

27 JUNE TO 19 DECEMBER

Musicians: Brian May (guitar, vocals), Freddie Mercury (vocals, tambourine), Roger Taylor (drums, vocals), Mike Grose (bass guitar until 25 July), Barry Mitchell (bass guitar after 25 July)

Itinerary:
June 27: City Hall, Truro
July 12: Imperial College, London
July 18: Imperial College, London
July 25: PJ's Club, Truro
July 31: City Hall, Truro
August 23: Imperial College, London
September 4: Swiss Cottage Private School, London
October 16: College of Estate Management, London
October 30: College of Technology, St Helens
October 31: Cavern Club, Liverpool

November 14: Ballspark College, Hertford
December 5: Shoreditch College, Egham
December 18: College of Technology, St Helens
December 19: Congregational Church Hall, St Helens

Following weeks of rehearsals, Freddie Mercury, Brian May, Roger Taylor and Mike Grose (a friend of Roger's) made their stage debut in Truro, the home town of Roger and Mike, on 27 June 1970, albeit under the name Smile. This show had been organized by Roger's mother for a Red Cross charity event and, months earlier, Roger had agreed that Smile would make an appearance. With that band now defunct, and not wanting to let his mother or the charity down, Roger made good on his word and, instead, his new band performed. The band made £50 that night, a sizable sum (especially for a charity gig) in those days; still known as Smile, they made their way to the Imperial College in London, and the first official acknowledgment of the newly named band came on

18 July with an ad reading, "Queen invite you to a private showing at Imperial College."

While the band were well aware they had to overcome several hurdles in order to establish a following, their first obstacle came not with finding an audience, but with retaining band members: Mike Grose left the band after four concerts, informing the others after the PJ's Club gig that he was going to be staying in Truro. In a panic, the band held auditions at Imperial College for a replacement and found Barry Mitchell. Roger's friend, Roger Crossley, had encouraged him to check the bassist out. After one rehearsal, Barry was in, becoming the second known bass guitarist in Queen. Various accounts have Barry arriving either days after Mike's departure or in August 1970, so it's not known who, if anyone, filled in on bass in the interim.

The first known concert with Barry took place at Imperial College, though it would be his second gig with the band, held in a private school in north London with an audience of American children whose parents all worked for the American Embassy, that made an impression on the rising stars. The children were young, certainly years below the band's target audience, and weren't receptive to the music Queen offered.

On 18 September, Jimi Hendrix died – a tragic blow to Freddie, who considered Hendrix his musical hero and shut down the Kensington Market stall out of respect. During rehearsals later that evening, Freddie led the band through several Hendrix songs, including 'Voodoo Chile'. Later, at the College of Estate Management on 16 October, the missing element of Queen was in attendance; John Deacon later recalled that he was at this gig and remained nonplussed, saying, "They were all dressed in black, and the lights were very dim too, so all I could really see were four shadowy figures. They didn't make a lasting impression on me at the time."

The band's set consisted of several originals but was mostly comprised of cover versions of songs by The Who, The Rolling Stones, Jimi Hendrix, Buddy Holly, The Beatles, The Shadows, Elvis Presley, James Brown, Little Richard, The Everly Brothers, The Yardbirds, Gene Vincent, Ricky Nelson, The Spencer Davis Group and Led Zeppelin, among others. Three known original compositions were definitely written and performed around this time: 'Stone Cold Crazy' would usually open the band's sets; 'Liar' would be the closer; and 'Keep Yourself Alive' was reportedly the first song Queen

played with Mike Grose. Songs that had been written by various band members while in Smile, Wreckage and Ibex would generally round out the repertoire. At this point, Freddie remained a vocalist, and Barry Mitchell was later surprised when he was told that Freddie played piano as well as singing. Certainly, songs with piano wouldn't be performed on stage until at least 1974. Barry later confirmed more songs in the set list at the time in an impromptu online interview on Queenzone.com: 'Doing All Right', 'Great King Rat', 'Modern Times Rock 'n' Roll', and 'Hangman'.

1971

8 JANUARY TO 31 DECEMBER

Musicians: Brian May *(guitar, vocals)*, Freddie Mercury *(vocals, tambourine)*, Roger Taylor *(drums, vocals)*, Barry Mitchell *(bass guitar until 9 January)*, Doug Bogie *(bass guitar, 19 and 20 February)*, John Deacon *(bass guitar, 2 July onwards)*

Itinerary:
January 8: Marquee Club, London
January 9: Technical College, Ewell
February 19: Hornsey Town Hall, London
February 20: Kingston Polytechnic, London
July 2: Surrey College, Surrey
July 11: Imperial College, London
July 17: The Gardens, Penzance
July 19: Rugby Club, Hayle
July 24: Young Farmers Club, Wadebridge
July 29: The Gardens, Penzance
July 31: City Hall, Truro
August 2: Rugby Club, Hayle
August 9: Driftwood Spars, St Agnes
August 12: Tregye Hotel, Truro
August 14: NCO's Mess, RAF Culdrose
August 17: City Hall, Truro
August 21: Carnon Downs Festival, Tregye
October 6: Imperial College, London
December 9: Swimming Baths, Epsom
December 31: Rugby Club, Twickenham

The previous year had ended in turmoil for Queen: Barry Mitchell, who had become the band's permanent bass guitarist, informed Brian, Roger and Freddie that he would be leaving. He wanted to settle down and marry, and realized that raising a family on a struggling musician's salary wouldn't work. To put it more bluntly, he later stated, "Queen were an excellent band, but we were going nowhere fast." While Mary Austin, Freddie's girlfriend at the time, would make an attempt to convince Barry to stay, the others felt his time had passed and were ready to find someone else.

Barry's final concert was on 9 January 1971 at the Technical College in Ewell, where Queen supported Kevin Ayers and The Whole World Band, with Genesis also on the bill. Long-standing friend and roadie Ken Testi, who had worked with Brian and Roger while in Smile, recorded the set, and Barry was certain he had this copy in his possession, but closer inspection revealed it to be Queen's September 1973 Golder's Green Hippodrome radio broadcast.

The next member of the rhythm section was Doug Bogie, who had been hastily recruited but, according to legend, was fired as quickly as he had been hired. On the second and final night of his tenure within Queen, Doug became overzealous on stage and started to jump around in "a manner most incongruous", according to Brian in *As It Began*. But the reality was that Doug served as a fill-in bassist and, when he started to get serious about his studies again, was asked to make a decision between Queen or classes. He chose the latter, much to the annoyance of the other band members. "I thought that we have played two excellent and exciting gigs," Bogie later recalled. "However, in the back of the borrowed van after the Yes gig at Kingston Polytechnic, there was one of those taking everything apart discussions: 'so everything is terrible', 'it's a waste of time', and Freddie announces he doesn't want to continue. So, as the new boy who knows nothing of their past activities and relationships, I just accept that that is the end of the experiment! A shame, but not unusual with bands with creative members."

The band's hopes of finding a decent bass guitarist who wanted to become professional was quickly fading. In early 1971, John Deacon, with his friends Peter Stoddart and Christine Farnell, was introduced to two of Christine's friends, Brian May and Roger Taylor, while at a disco in Chelsea. Once the pleasantries were out of the way, Christine explained to John that Brian and Roger had been through many bass guitarists but had little success in holding on to one. John offered his services and, days later, turned up in a lecture hall at Imperial College to audition for Queen. He had a small bass amp (later dubbed the 'Deaky amp') that was initially a source of derision among the others but quickly became admired for the warm tones it produced. The band ran through 'Son And Daughter'

a few times and the long-suffering band members had finally found the vital addition that would complete the Queen line-up for over 20 years.

At the same time, Chris Dummett, who had previously worked with Freddie in Sour Milk Sea, also auditioned that day to become a second guitarist for Queen but had the misfortune of having to play on Brian's homemade guitar. The instrument was tailor-made for Brian's hands and was therefore difficult to play for anyone unaccustomed to it, and Chris later recalled that his fingers "slid all over it" and that little of what he played was in time or tune. Figuring that Queen could produce enough sound with just one guitar, Freddie and Chris parted ways for good.

The band's first concert with John Deacon was on 2 July in Surrey, though it got off to an inauspicious start when there was a disagreement between Freddie and John: the bassist had shown up to the gig wearing one of his favorite T-shirts, but Freddie was displeased with the outfit and insisted on lending John one of his own. On 17 July the band embarked upon their first proper tour, organized by Roger and based around his home county of Cornwall. The band were less than amused when some of the fliers advertised the band as 'Roger Taylor and Queen' or, in some cases, 'Legendary Cornish drummer Roger Taylor' in large letters with 'and his band Queen' beneath it in smaller letters.

Before the tour started, the band and their entourage – consisting of roadies Ken Testi and John Harris, various girlfriends, friends and hangers-on – set up base at Roger's mother's house, but when she expressed displeasure at having her home taken over, the group packed up their bags and rented a small three-bedroom cottage on the outskirts of Truro.

The tour progressed through Cornwall and was well received, though, at Driftwood Spars on 9 August, the band ran into an issue that was poorly handled. The owner of the pub ran onto the stage when the band started their set and demanded that they turn their amplifiers down, but the band refused. After the show, heated words were exchanged between band and owner, who threatened not to pay them, but the situation was ultimately smoothed over and the band were given their money. On the way back to their rented house, Roger's knowledge of the back roads of his home town helped the band avoid disaster: a group of local teenagers gave chase after the band's van, but they were able to escape their tormentors.

The final night was at Carnon Downs Festival in Tregye, where the band performed their first outdoor gig and were second from bottom on the bill, behind headliners Arthur Brown's Kingdom Come followed by Hawkwind, The Duster Bennett Band, Tea And Symphony, Brewer's Droop, Indian Summer, and Graphite. Barracuda was the only band to appear beneath Queen. Advertisements for the festival depicted a nude girl with a floppy summer hat playing a flute, with "Food, freaks, licensed bar, and lovely things" promised for those who attended.

Roadie Ken Testi had been taking classes in St Helen's while the band were out on the road and, when the Cornish tour ended, he secured time at De Lane Lea Studios for Queen to record a demo tape. While these recordings took place in December, all four band members continued their studies so they would have something to fall back on in case Queen didn't work out. Roger had signed up for a course at the North London Polytechnic with a focus on a biology degree back in July, though he had only done so because he was in need of extra cash and the course he chose earned him eligibility for a grant. Brian took up a teaching position at Stockwell Manor School, John continued studying for his degree in electronics, and Freddie continued to run his Kensington Market stall with Roger, though he would leave late in 1971.

With a demo tape in his hand, Ken Testi shopped the band around to record companies and attracted the attention of Paul Conroy, an employee of Charisma Records, who got Ken a meeting with the owner, Tony Stratton-Smith. The band were offered an advance of £20,000, which was tempting, but the offer was turned down and used as leverage for future offers from other record labels. Ken continued to work hard for Queen while the band themselves finished up the year with two shows: the first at the Swimming Baths in Epsom on 9 December, the second a New Year's Eve bash at the Twickenham Rugby Club. Fatefully, John Anthony, who then worked for Trident, and EMI Publishing's Ronnie Beck attended the Epsom show, with the latter meeting up with the band afterwards and offering them a publishing deal, despite the poor acoustics (the venue itself being in a swimming pool).

1972

28 JANUARY TO 20 DECEMBER

Musicians: John Deacon *(bass guitar)*, Brian May *(guitar, vocals)*, Freddie Mercury *(vocals, tambourine)*, Roger Taylor *(drums, vocals)*

Repertoire included: 'Son And Daughter', 'Great King Rat', 'Jesus', 'The Night Comes Down', 'Liar', 'Keep Yourself Alive', 'See What A Fool I've Been', 'Stone Cold Crazy', 'Hangman', 'Jailhouse Rock', 'Bama Lama Bama Loo', 'Doing All Right', 'Jailhouse Rock', 'Be Bop A Lula', 'Shake, Rattle & Roll', 'Stupid Cupid', 'Big Spender'

Itinerary:
January 28: Bedford College, London
March 10: Kings College Hospital Medical School, London
March 24: Forest Hill Hospital, London
November 6: Pheasantry Club, London
December 20: Marquee Club, London

The band performed only five known dates in 1972. Brian, Roger and John were still involved with their studies, which took precedence for much of the year. Nevertheless, the five gigs the band performed were memorable.

The first, on 28 January at Bedford College, was arranged by John and saw only six people show up; he later cited this as one of the most embarrassing experiences of his career. The second was organized by Ken Testi's two flatmates, Paul Conroy and Lyndsay Brown, who had been hassled by Ken for gigs relentlessly. Queen were given the support spot at King's College Hospital, and it was from this show that the earliest known set list of a Queen show has surfaced: 'Son And Daughter', 'Great King Rat', 'Jesus', 'The Night Comes Down', 'Liar', 'Keep Yourself Alive', 'See What A Fool I've Been', 'Stone Cold Crazy', 'Hangman', 'Jailhouse Rock' and 'Bama Lama Bama Loo' were all played that night.

After months of deliberation and negotiation, the band were signed to Trident in November 1972, though recording sessions for their first album had started over the summer. In September, Roger graduated from North London Polytechnic with a degree in biology while John received a degree in electronics from London University. Brian was still holding on to his teaching job, and his thesis had been drafted but not typed when he decided that music was to become his life. His professors balked at the idea and tried to convince him otherwise (one teacher asked him to consider the "prospects, security, and pension" of a doctorate) but Brian wouldn't budge; Queen was his passion.

The band played only two more gigs during the year: one at the Pheasantry Club in London and another at the Marquee Club on 20 December, where the set was recorded and is now owned by Queen Productions; 'Great King Rat', 'Son And Daughter', 'Jesus', 'Doing All Right', 'Ogre Battle', 'Keep Yourself Alive', 'Liar', 'Jailhouse Rock' and 'Bama Lama Bama Loo' made up the set list. These two shows were designed as showcases to drum up interest in a record deal (Trident wasn't a record company, but a management organization), though none was forthcoming.

1973

9 APRIL TO 2 NOVEMBER

Musicians: John Deacon *(bass guitar)*, Brian May *(guitar, vocals)*, Freddie Mercury *(vocals, tambourine)*, Roger Taylor *(drums, vocals)*

Repertoire: 'Procession', 'Father To Son', 'Son And Daughter', 'Ogre Battle', 'Hangman', 'Stone Cold Crazy', 'Keep Yourself Alive', 'Liar', 'See What A Fool I've Been', 'Jailhouse Rock' / 'Stupid Cupid' / 'Big Spender' / 'Bama Lama Bama Loo' / 'Jailhouse Rock' *(reprise)*

Itinerary:
April 9: Marquee Club, London
July 13: Queen Mary College, Basingstroke
September 13: Golders Green Hippodrome, London
October 13: Underground, Bonn-Bad Godesburg, Germany
October 14: Le Blow Up, Luxembourg, Luxembourg
October 20: Paris Theatre, London
October 26: Imperial College, London
November 2: Imperial College, London

Most of 1973 was spent putting finishing touches to Queen's debut album, and the band would perform only eight live shows between April and the beginning of November. Their first show of the year was at the Marquee Club for a third showcase gig, this time for Jac Holtzman at Elektra; he was so enamored with the band that he signed them directly after the show. EMI had signed the band for the UK the previous month and, after two years of slogging away on their debut album, the band finally had representation in the two dominant music industries.

Their next performance came on the same day the debut album was released, though the set list by this time started to represent music that would be incorporated onto their second and third albums: 'Father To Son' and 'Ogre Battle' would later surface on *Queen II*, while 'Stone Cold Crazy' was featured on *Sheer Heart Attack*, yet all three were concert favorites during this time.

The band were offered a live radio broadcast from the BBC's Golders Green Hippodrome in September, having just recorded their second album, but the BBC radio session would be their only gig for a month. Their 13 October performance in Bonn was their first show in a country other than England, and the next night they travelled to Luxembourg for a show to be broadcast on Radio Luxembourg's *In Concert*; the equipment reportedly failed, however, and nothing was recorded. Another Radio One *In Concert* gig was to take place on 20 October, but it appears that, once again, the equipment failed and nothing was transmitted. The last two shows before their first major tour were at Imperial College: their first appearance, on 26 October, was attended by Paul Watts, an EMI representative who had signed the band back in March; their second appearance on 2 November was a last-minute rehearsal for the upcoming tour.

Set lists for these eight concerts are, like earlier repertoires, unknown, but a good selection of new and old songs was performed. The set started to take a more structured form, with the *Queen II* instrumental, 'Procession', used as introductory music played over the PA before the band entered for 'Father To Son', which had become the new set opener. 'Jesus' and 'The Night Comes Down' were omitted, while 'Hangman' and 'See What A Fool I've Been' were retained and would be performed intermittently through 1975 and 1976 respectively.

The band weren't receiving much press in the early days, apart from a few interviews (the group held one in *Melody Maker* in July, while Brian got his own in *Guitar Magazine* the following month), and whatever press did come through was mostly non-committal praise. Rosemary Horide was an early champion of the band, and praised their November Imperial College concert in *Disc*: "Six months ago [at the Marquee in April], when I saw the band, they showed promise but weren't very together. This time they were very good ... The group were musically very good, their stage presence was excellent and when you consider that the material was all their own, it was a remarkable performance for a new group. The material was far above average, and it was obvious how hard the band worked at entertaining by the tremendous rapport that was established ... On the whole it was a very good night, and a highly creditable performance. If Queen are this good on the tour with Mott The Hoople (which they start next week) Mott had better watch out. Queen could turn out to be a bit more than just a support band."

MOTT THE HOOPLE UK TOUR:
12 NOVEMBER TO 14 DECEMBER 1973

Musicians: John Deacon (bass guitar), Brian May (guitar, vocals), Freddie Mercury (vocals, tambourine), Roger Taylor (drums, vocals)

Repertoire: 'Procession', 'Father To Son', 'Son And Daughter', 'Ogre Battle', 'Hangman', 'Great King Rat', 'Jailhouse Rock' / 'Shake, Rattle & Roll', 'Keep Yourself Alive', 'Liar', 'Big Spender', 'Modern Times Rock'n'Roll', 'See What A Fool I've Been'

Itinerary:
November 12: Town Hall, Leeds
November 13: St Georges, Blackburn
November 15: Gaumont, Worcester
November 16: Lancaster University, Lancaster
November 17: Liverpool Stadium, Liverpool
November 18: Victoria Hall, Hanley
November 19: Civic Hall, Wolverhampton
November 20: New Theatre, Oxford
November 21: Guildhall, Preston
November 22: City Hall, Newcastle
November 23: Apollo Theatre, Glasgow
November 25: Caley Cinema, Edinburgh
November 26: Opera House, Manchester
November 27: Town Hall, Birmingham
November 28: Brangwyn Hall, Swansea
November 29: Colston Hall, Bristol
November 30: Winter Gardens, Bournemouth
December 1: Kursaal, Southend
December 2: Central Hall, Chatham
December 6: Cheltenham College, Cheltenham
December 7: Shaftesbury Hall, London
December 8: Liverpool University, Liverpool
December 14: Hammersmith Odeon, London (afternoon and evening shows)

In September 1973, Queen's manager in America, Jack Nelson, contacted Bob Hirschmann, manager of Mott the Hoople, and asked if they would be interested in having Queen on board for their upcoming UK tour. Hirschmann, an acquaintance of Jack's, was hesitant at first until £3000 was offered to allow Queen to tour with Mott. An agreement was drawn up and the band were well on their way to beginning a structured tour, their first ever.

The itinerary was a rigorous one: 25 shows in five weeks, with few nights off between shows. The set was restricted to a minimum of a dozen songs, with 'Procession' serving as a taped introduction (as it would for every show until May 1975) and 'See What A Fool I've Been' occasionally performed in lieu of 'Hangman'. The set generally ended with 'Big Spender' and 'Modern Times Rock'n'Roll' (the latter Roger's first composition written for the band but with Freddie on lead vocals), the shows lasting between 40 and 45 minutes. Though press reaction was mixed (when it appeared: Queen were less than pleased that they weren't receiving as much press as they felt they should have), fans who had come to see Mott were impressed with Queen, and the word-of-mouth exposure helped build Queen's fan-base.

On 1 December, during Mott's customary encore of 'All The Young Dudes', the band were invited on stage to assist with backing vocals. Brian, Roger and Freddie excitedly complied (John, not being a singer, watched from the wings), though no audio recording of this performance has surfaced. The final gig of the tour took place at the revered Hammersmith Odeon, with both bands performing an afternoon and evening show; Brian's parents showed up to see his son in full flight for the first time within Queen. A humbled Harold May even signed an autograph for a rabid Queen fan who had discovered his identity.

Brian later reflected on this period in 1998: "Mott The Hoople was really our first experience of life on the road, and a pretty blinding experience it was, I must say. It's always remained close to my heart, 'cause we grew up on that tour. We had to. It was just insanity. And to survive you had to adapt; you had to become a rock'n'roll kind of animal and in the good sense of the word, you know. And, yeah, it was phenomenal. And I used to watch them do 'All The Way From Memphis' every night, and every night the place would erupt; it was like an earthquake. They really were a fantastic band live. Should have stayed together, I have to say."

The tour ended on 14 December, but the band still had further miscellaneous dates to fulfil that weren't part of the Mott the Hoople excursion. The latter had been lengthy, but it was an enjoyable experience and the band were now ready for their own headlining campaign.

15 TO 28 DECEMBER 1973

Musicians: John Deacon *(bass guitar)*, Brian May *(guitar, vocals)*, Freddie Mercury *(vocals, tambourine)*, Roger Taylor *(drums, vocals)*

Repertoire: 'Procession', 'Father To Son', 'Son And Daughter', 'Ogre Battle', 'Hangman', 'Great King Rat', 'Jailhouse Rock' / 'Shake, Rattle & Roll' / 'Stupid Cupid' / 'Jailhouse Rock' *(reprise)*, 'Keep Yourself Alive', 'Liar', 'Big Spender', 'Bama Lama Bama Loo'

Itinerary:
December 15: Leicester University, Leicester
December 21: County Hall, Taunton
December 22: Town Hall, Peterborough
December 28: Top Rank, Liverpool

Four additional shows were performed following the Mott the Hoople tour, with the gig at the Top Rank Suite in Liverpool reuniting the band with two old friends: second support group Great Day featured Mike Bersin, former Ibex guitarist and collaborator with Freddie, and Ken Testi, former Queen roadie and early band manager. Queen were second on the bill to 10cc at this gig, which would become their final supporting gig in the UK; they would support Mott the Hoople again in the spring of 1974, this time in North America.

1974

SUNBURY MUSIC FESTIVAL:
26/27 JANUARY 1974

Musicians: John Deacon *(bass guitar)*, Brian May *(guitar, vocals)*, Freddie Mercury *(vocals, tambourine)*, Roger Taylor *(drums, vocals)*

Repertoire: 'Procession', 'Father To Son', 'Son And Daughter', 'Ogre Battle', 'Hangman', 'Great King Rat', 'Jailhouse Rock' / 'Shake, Rattle And Roll' / 'Stupid Cupid' / 'Jailhouse Rock' *(reprise)*, 'Keep Yourself Alive', 'Liar', 'Big Spender', 'Modern Times Rock'n'Roll'

Australia's Woodstock, the Sunbury Pop Festival, held in Sunbury, Victoria, was a popular gathering from 1972 to 1975 that was held on a small, private farm and attracted that best bands the continent could offer. Inexplicably, Queen were booked as the headliners,

the first time a non-Australian band headed the show, which understandably drew some ire from inebriated fans, impatient journalists, and those involved in the festival. The band didn't earn any further brownie points with the local roadies when they showed up to the event in a hired limousine, and even their road crew received a good drubbing: the local crews who had been hired to assemble the lights were pushed aside in favor of Queen's own crew, and, understandably irate that they lost out on money and work, the Australian crew did everything they could to sabotage the band's set.

Additionally, Freddie and Brian were both feeling unwell, and with the band jet-lagged and Brian developing gangrene in his arm from an inocculation in London, their set was less than perfect, which only delighted the audience. Local DJ Jim Keays, who emceed the event, did the band no favors when he introduced them: "Well, we've got another load of limey bastards tonight. They're probably going to be useless, but let's give them something to think about!" Keays then dropped trou and mooned the crowd, walking off to cheers as he derisively called the band "stuck-up pommies". (Incidentally, Keays was a Scot who had emigrated to Australia.) After Queen's understandably lacklustre set, Keays returned and once again haraunged the band to the audience: "D'you want anymore from these pommie bastards, or do ya want an Aussie rock band? How about Madder Lake?" The response was most definitely not in Queen's favor, and so Keays had effectively whisked Queen's chance at an encore away from them. The band left the stage, tails tucked between their legs, though Freddie was overheard to have declared, "When we come back to Australia, Queen will be the biggest band in the world!"

Brian went into greater detail when speaking to Australian radio in 1977, by which time Queen were well on their way to becoming the biggest band in the world: "I got very ill on the flight because we got injections for smallpox, feeling really dead, apart from the journey, which is about 30 hours or something. And it was very hot. We just couldn't handle the heat, having come from English winter. We played the gig. Freddie had a lot of trouble with his ears. A lot of problems. It's very strange. He went swimming, and he completely went deaf. He couldn't understand what was happening. He was getting very worried. We did the first night, and lots of strange feelings on stage, a lot of animosity from not the Australian groups, but from the road crews, and they didn't want to move our gear. The didn't want to give us any help. We finally went on stage and played the set. There was an MC, I can't remember his name, who, before we went on, said 'Don't worry, you've got some Australian groups afterwards, but here they are anyway, Queen.' We couldn't believe it. In the beginning it was, we were all sort of looking and not sure what to make of it, I think, but after a couple numbers we went well, and we thought we got everybody going and everything. And we came off stage, and there's a lot of reaction, and the same guy went back on the stage and said, 'Well, that's all of them now', and they're kinda still going, saying, 'We want more', or whatever, and he says, 'Do you want to hear more Queen or do you want to hear Madder Lake?' So that was it, and he basically managed to kill the sort of reaction from us, which was quite amazing, yet he was on there about five minutes during this applause and eventually saying, 'Well, OK, we're gonna have Madder Lake now'. So we felt a little unhappy about that! The musicians we met were great. It was just these few people."

Despite the circumstances, the band still won over more than a few in the audience, with several fans who were there recalling that the reception was positive. (Incidentally, Madder Lake bassist Kerry McKenna recalled that the band redeemed themselves from the poor introduction.) However, the band were obviously unhappy, and pulled out of performing the following night, instead preferring to return home. The band would return to Australia only twice more, in 1976 and 1985, by which time they had become a massive success, and any hard feelings that may have been held were forgotten.

QUEEN II UK TOUR:

1 MARCH TO 2 APRIL 1974

Musicians: John Deacon (*bass guitar*), Brian May (*guitar, vocals*), Freddie Mercury (*vocals, piano, tambourine*), Roger Taylor (*drums, vocals*)

Repertoire: 'Procession', 'Father To Son', 'Ogre Battle', 'White Queen (As It Began)', 'Great King Rat', 'Hangman', 'Son And Daughter', 'Keep Yourself Alive', 'Liar', 'Jailhouse Rock' / 'Shake, Rattle And Roll' / 'Stupid Cupid' / 'Be Bop A Lula' / 'Jailhouse Rock' (*reprise*), 'Big Spender', 'Modern Times Rock'n'Roll', 'Great King Rat', 'The Fairy Feller's Master-Stroke', 'See What A Fool I've Been'

Itinerary:

March 1: Winter Gardens, Blackpool
March 2: Friars, Aylesbury
March 3: Guildhall, Plymouth
March 4: Festival Hall, Paignton
March 8: Locarno, Sunderland
March 9: Corn Exchange, Cambridge
March 10: Greyhound, Croydon
March 12: Roundhouse, Dagenham
March 14: Town Hall, Cheltenham
March 15: University, Glasgow
March 16: University, Stirling
March 19: Winter Gardens, Cleethorpes
March 20: University, Manchester
March 22: Civic Centre, Canvey Island
March 23: Links Pavilion, Cromer
March 24: Woods Leisure Centre, Colchester
March 26: Palace Lido, Douglas, Isle of Man
March 28: University, Aberystwyth
March 29: The Gardens, Penzance
March 30: Century Ballroom, Taunton
March 31: Rainbow Theatre, London
April 2: Barbarella's, Birmingham (*postponed from 17 March*)

Queen's second major tour of the UK was already planned by the time 'Seven Seas Of Rhye' was released as their second single, but the track's unexpected success helped make this tour their first sell-out. However, the first night in Blackpool got off to an inauspicious start when the van carrying their lighting rig was delayed, resulting in a late start.

The tour saw little change from the previous set list, though 'White Queen (As It Began)' and 'Seven Seas Of Rhye' were added, with Freddie perched at the piano for the first time. Occasional performances of 'Great King Rat' and even 'The Fairy Feller's Master-Stroke' adorned the set list, along with 'See What A Fool I've Been', the non-album B-side to Queen's then-current single. The Rock 'n' Roll Medley now appeared as an encore, with 'Big Spender' and 'Modern Times Rock'n'Roll' becoming the second and final encore; 'Liar' concluded the regular set. Nutz supported the band on this tour, and were well liked by Queen; when it became clear that Nutz's management hadn't booked proper hotels, instead having them stay in dingy bungalows, Freddie offered to let the band stay with Queen when space permitted.

It's rare that a flash of inspiration can be pinpointed to a specific time or place, but while the band were tuning up before their show in Plymouth, they overheard the audience singing 'God Save The Queen'. Appreciating the gesture, Brian and Roger would later record a version of the national anthem following sessions for *Sheer Heart Attack*, a track used to conclude almost every subsequent live performance.

While the band had always dressed up in outlandish fashions on previous tours, this was the first time that they would theme their outfits around an album, with black and white threads designed by Zandra Rhodes, chosen to mirror the *Queen II* album sides. Additionally, Freddie and Brian painted their fingernails with black and white nail polish, showing that every consideration, no matter how small, had gone into their presentation. Roger was less enamored with his own outfit, recalling in 2013 that he had worn his once at Friars in Aylesbury, "and I sweated so much I never wore it again."

The tour had been well-received up to this point, though press coverage was minimal. Unfortunately, the press was present for the show in Stirling, reporting that "When Queen failed to return to the stage after three encores, fights started. Two members of Queen's road crew were injured and taken to hospital. Sunday night's gig at Barbarella's, Birmingham, had to be canceled for Queen were without sufficient crew and also had to answer police inquiries at Stirling." That show was rescheduled to become the final night of the tour on 2 April. In light of the stress and aggravation, and the tedium of assembling and disassembling the lighting rig night after night, the lighting crew announced that they no longer wished to service the band any more. Trident duly arranged a replacement – James Dann – who would work for the band for many years.

At Friars Club in Aylesbury, a journalist noted that Brian's arm, which would develop gangrene from inocculations prior to the Sunbury Pop Festival, was starting to bother him: "At first there was a certain amount of doubt as to whether they were going to go on or not. Anyway they did and I'm beginning to wonder if that was a wise decision." The Glasgow show received a more complimentary review, despite multiple power failures: "Despite lights being brought down to a minimum, Queen had hardly played half a dozen bars before the first fuse blew – cutting out all sound. Apologies and two fuses later, the roadies were insisting that the set should end. The largest crowd the QM had seen in years kept their cool with only a few perfunctory whistles breaking the silences. Warnings

unheeded, Freddie Mercury continued to vibrate chainmail hips from Brian May's constructive guitar lead. The set, though drastically reduced in content, drama, and lighting, continued. Mercury's stance and occasionally his voice gave only the slightest clue that the anxious roadies running about at the side of the stage wanted to switch the whole thing off."

Further aggravation came in Manchester when the band's van was broken into while Queen were on stage; thieves stole John Deacon's suitcase, which contained many personal items, including photos taken in Australia. (Freddie was also a victim, this time of a drunken audience member, with a roadie recalling, "Queen had just taken the stage, and this bloke shouted to Freddie, 'You fucking poof'. Freddie demanded that the crew turn the spotlight on the crowd and find this fella. He then said to him, 'Say that again, darling', and the bloke didn't know what to do. I saw him literally shrink this six-foot bloke down to an inch.") Perhaps in an attempt to relieve pent-up frustration, the band started living the rock star lifestyle by having post-show parties back in the hotel which would carry on until all hours of the morning. Following their show on the Isle of Man, the band received word that *Queen II* had reached No. 7 in the UK, with their debut album finally reaching the charts as well, entering at No. 47. The band's elation resulted in the demolition of a hotel room, which would subsequently become a further part of their tradition.

The band were convinced they'd be unable to sell out the prestigious Rainbow Theatre in Finsbury Park; promoter Mel Bush assured them otherwise, confident in Queen's drawing power. He turned out to be correct when tickets for the show sold out within a week. The show wasn't without incident, however: during 'Liar', Brian broke a string and had to jump to his back-up guitar, a Fender Stratocaster. Forty years later, this concert was released, along with the two November dates, on *Live At The Rainbow '74*, and offered a fascinating insight into the live Queen experience at the time. The tour ended on 2 April with the rescheduled Birmingham concert, but not without incident: Roger had bet Dave Lloyd (the lead singer of Nutz) a bottle of champagne that he wouldn't strip naked and streak across the stage. Lloyd and members of the road crew surprised the band during 'Modern Times Rock'n'Roll' by accepting Roger's challenge; whether Lloyd ever got his bottle of champagne is unknown, though he certainly deserved it.

MOTT THE HOOPLE US TOUR:
16 APRIL TO 12 MAY 1974

Musicians: John Deacon *(bass guitar)*, Brian May *(guitar, vocals)*, Freddie Mercury *(vocals, piano, tambourine)*, Roger Taylor *(drums, vocals)*

Repertoire: 'Procession', 'Father To Son', 'Ogre Battle', 'White Queen (As It Began)', 'Doing All Right', 'Son And Daughter', 'Keep Yourself Alive', 'Seven Seas Of Rhye', 'Liar', 'Jailhouse Rock' / 'Shake, Rattle And Roll' / 'Stupid Cupid' / 'Be Bop A Lula' / 'Jailhouse Rock' *(reprise)*, 'Big Spender', 'Modern Times Rock'n'Roll', 'Great King Rat', 'Hangman', 'See What A Fool I've Been'

Itinerary:
April 16: Regis College, Denver, Colorado
April 17: Memorial Hall, Kansas City, Missouri
April 18: Keil Auditorium, St Louis, Missouri
April 19: Fairgrounds Appliance Building, Oklahoma City, Oklahoma
April 20: Mid-South Coliseum, Memphis, Tennessee
April 21: St Bernard Civic Auditorium, New Orleans, Louisiana
April 26: Orpheum Theater, Boston, Massachusetts (rescheduled from 27 April)
April 27: Palace Theater, Providence, Rhode Island
April 28: Exposition Hall, Portland, Maine
May 1: Farm Arena, Harrisburg, Pennsylvania
May 2: Agricultural Hall, Allentown, Pennsylvania
May 3: King's College, Wilkes-Barre, Pennsylvania
May 4: Palace Theater, Waterbury, Connecticut
May 7-12: Uris Theater, New York, New York

After the 1973 tour in support of Mott the Hoople, Queen were asked back for a North American tour in the spring of 1974. Realizing the potential of a breakthrough there, the band promptly agreed – it was too good an opportunity to pass up. An eight-week tour was booked throughout mid-April and early June, covering most of the larger markets of the country (especially New England, where 'Keep Yourself Alive' had received considerable promotion). As befits the dynamic between opening act and the main draw, Mott the Hoople received most of the press, and any reports that Queen got were mostly negative. John Rockwell wrote of the first night at Uris Theater, "Queen, another British band, opened the bill. This was its first New York performance, and the group made a mixed impression. It was enjoyable enough to listen

to, particularly Brian May's virtuostic guitar playing. But Freddie Mercury, the lead singer, is addicted to the toothy, unconvincing posturings, and the other three members just stand about limply, unable to provide much visual relief."

Still, the tour gave the band not only their first glimpse of America, but showed them the ropes of being a touring band. Brian would recall to contactmusic.com in 2011, "That was when we learned how to be rock stars. Just as you thought the day was over, one of Mott would burst into your room, loaded with bottles and whatever else, and off you'd go again. It was very, very full-on and very, very exciting." Roger concurred: "Mott were perfect for us. They had an open-minded, very rock 'n' roll, insane audience. They were liberated, colourful – not the normal rock crowd … The shows got bigger, but it was rough. [Freddie] wouldn't get out of the van some nights. He and Brian had black and white fingernails and literally wore dresses, but the tough audiences in Liverpool and Glasgow and Newcastle loved us."

The set list was largely the same as it had been during the UK tour, with 'Hangman', 'Great King Rat' and 'See What A Fool I've Been' performed only occasionally and 'Seven Seas Of Rhye' becoming the penultimate number of the main set. (Reportedly, 'Mad The Swine' was performed once during this tour, though no recorded performance exists.) The tour progressed without incident until Harrisburg, where Aerosmith and Queen were both booked as support. When arguments broke out between the members of the two bands as to who should go on first, Brian and Aerosmith lead guitarist Joe Perry finally got fed up with the quarrelling, becoming extremely "relaxed" over a bottle of Jack Daniels.

"We were so drunk we could hardly walk by the time the argument finished," Brian recalled to Jacky Smith in *As It Began*. "When we finally went on [an agreement was made that a local Harrisburg act would go on first, followed by Queen, then Aerosmith], I remember, through a haze, whacking the first chord and realizing that, among the echo, I couldn't hear a thing. I played the whole show from memory, and decided to compensate by giving it lots of action. Everyone thought it was wonderful! So I decided two things for the future: one, I would always 'give it action'; and two, I would never drink more than a pint before a show. I have since stuck by both of those resolutions."

When the touring entourage arrived in New

York on 6 May, Queen felt they had finally made it. Unfortunately, their triumph would be cut short: in New Orleans on 26 April, Brian had complained of pain, and worse was to come when the band moved on to Boston after six nights at New York's Uris Theater. "The first morning I woke up in the Parker House in Boston, I felt like my whole body was made of lead," Brian explained. "I tried to eat a grapefruit, which someone had said would make me feel better, then I dragged myself to the bathroom mirror, and saw that I was a deep shade of yellow." Freddie agreed, saying, "When he turned yellow, we thought he had food poisoning."

Brian had contracted hepatitis, which was aggravated by the inocculations given to the band prior to their Australian show earlier in the year, and vaccines were administered to everyone who had come into contact with Brian. Queen backed out of the 18 remaining dates, being hastily replaced by Kansas, which disappointed a large portion of the audience in Detroit: with no announcement being made and Kansas opening the show, the audience started booing and hissing during their set, prompting one of the members to seethe into the mic, "Queen's not here, so shut the fuck up!" A scheduled North American tour for September was postponed until the following year.

With his confidence in tatters, Brian was ordered to take six weeks of bed rest while his bandmates took advantage of the forced hiatus and, out of desperation, started work on their make-it-or-break-it album.

SHEER HEART ATTACK UK & EUROPEAN TOUR:
30 OCTOBER TO 13 DECEMBER 1974

Musicians: John Deacon *(bass guitar, triangle on 'Killer Queen'),* Brian May *(guitar, vocals, banjo on 'Bring Back That Leroy Brown'),* Freddie Mercury *(vocals, piano, tambourine),* Roger Taylor *(drums, vocals)*

Repertoire: 'Procession', 'Now I'm Here', 'Ogre Battle', 'Father To Son', 'White Queen (As It Began)', 'Flick Of The Wrist', 'In The Lap Of The Gods' / 'Killer Queen' / 'The March Of The Black Queen' / 'Bring Back That Leroy Brown', 'Son And Daughter', 'Keep Yourself Alive', 'Seven Seas Of Rhye', 'Stone Cold Crazy', 'Liar', 'In The Lap Of The Gods... Revisited', 'Big Spender', 'Modern Times Rock'n'Roll', 'Jailhouse Rock', 'God Save The Queen'

Itinerary:
October 30: Palace, Manchester
October 31: Victoria Hall, Hanley
November 1: Empire Theatre, Liverpool
November 2: University, Leeds
November 3: Theatre, Coventry
November 5: City Hall, Sheffield
November 6: St George's Hall, Bradford
November 7: City Hall, Newcastle
November 8: Apollo Theatre, Glasgow
November 9: University, Lancaster
November 10: Guildhall, Preston
November 12: Colston Hall, Bristol
November 13: Bournemouth, Winter Gardens
November 14: Gaumont, Southampton
November 15: Brangwyn Hall, Swansea
November 16: Town Hall, Birmingham
November 18: New Theatre, Oxford
November 19/20: Rainbow Theatre, London
November 23: Koncerthus, Gothenburg, Sweden
November 25: Helsingin Kulttuuritalo, Helsinki, Finland
November 27: Olympen, Lund, Sweden
December 2: Brienner Theatre, Munich, Germany
December 4: Jahrhunderthalle, Frankfurt, Germany
December 5: Musikhalle, Hamburg, Germany
December 6: Sartory Saal, Cologne, Germany
December 7: venue unknown, Singen, Germany
December 8: Congre Gebouw, Hague, Holland
December 10: 140 Theatre, Brussels, Belgium
December 13: Palacio de los Deportes, Barcelona, Spain

Adversity typically yields inspired results: Queen's third single, 'Killer Queen', was high in the charts by the time of their second UK tour of 1974, and its companion album, *Sheer Heart Attack*, was finalized for a November release. With Brian restored to health, Queen put the events of the year behind them and were ready to start afresh: their *Sheer Heart Attack* tour would not only take in the usual territories of England and North America, but it also marked the first time the band would undertake tours of Europe and Japan. The tour started in October 1974 and extended until May 1975; except for the occasional break, this time stretch was largely uninterrupted and would become Queen's longest tour to date.

The UK and European tour commenced on 30 October in Manchester and saw a completely restructured set list: incorporating a considerable amount of material from the *Sheer Heart Attack* album, this tour also saw the genesis of the medley. Though it would be fine-tuned over the years to include contemporary tracks that worked well together, the first medley consisted of 'In The Lap Of The Gods', 'Killer Queen', 'The March Of The Black Queen' (appearing for the first time on this tour) and 'Bring Back That Leroy Brown'. Strangely, another tradition – the Rock 'n' Roll Medley – was dropped during this tour: the first encore would commence with 'Big Spender', leading into 'Modern Times Rock'n'Roll', while the show would end proper with 'Jailhouse Rock', a re-recording of 'God Save The Queen' being played on the PA as the band left the stage.

The band took to the stage with renewed vigor, and it's no surprise that these shows have been regarded as their most exciting and consistent. The fans certainly thought so at the time: riots were starting to become common, breaking out on three different occasions in the early part of the tour. "Chaos hit Queen on the second night of their first headling tour at Liverpool Empire, when fans rushed the stage," *Melody Maker* reported. "And at Leeds University, as bouncers were hauling away fans, lead singer Freddie Mercury stopped the show and managed to calm the audience." One bouncer noticed a 16-year-old girl on the verge of being crushed, and grabbed her in time and gave her a new seat on top of John's amp.

NME's Tony Stewart hinted at the Liverpudlian frenzy: "Encountering 3,000 Liverpool looners going completely bonkers over a band is an occurence which does rather unbalance and astound this writer. Frankly, I hadn't expected it. Whether they deserve this acclaim is, of course, a different matter entirely; however, after seeing the Liverpool gig, I think they do. Musically, the band pull off an act that is both enjoyable and entertaining, shifting through apparent disparaties in style that encompass white heat energy rock, vaudeville knees-up, melodic sophistication, and high camp ... Not unexpectedly, stage presence played quite an important part in the act (though it was never used to disguise musical inadequacies. I must confess the sight of Mercury hurling his all across the stage proved to be a visual bonus to complement the exciting dynamics of their numbers ... The gig could have been better I'm sure, but it was still a hotsie."

Also in Leeds, Roger's on-stage monitor failed and, despite several attempts to signal his roadie, the problem was not resolved. Backstage, the drummer threw a temper tantrum and kicked an immobile object, causing considerable pain in his ankle and leading all to believe he had broken it. He was taken to Leeds Infirmary for X-rays, and it turned out – much to everyone's relief – he had only bruised it. The third riot, in Glasgow, was the most memorable: Freddie attempted to calm the crowd, but ventured a bit too close to the fracas and was dragged into the audience by his scarf. Security came to the rescue, and he promptly discarded the offending item for the remainder of the show, dismissing the incident as a "rather undignified affair." Despite the riots, Brian was especially complimentary of the tour, recalling to *Record Mirror* that December, "The tour was amazing, we can't believe it. People said we wouldn't sell out at this time of year because there were so many other tours around, but we were turning more away towards the end. The audience at the Apollo in Glasgow was amazing. In fact most of the gigs in the north were staggering, places like Bradford and Sheffield. They knew all the songs, even the words on the new album before it was out."

The tour progressed steadily through the UK before concluding on 19 and 20 November at the Rainbow, a return to the coveted venue just eight months after their first appearance there. This time, with an expanded set list, it was decided that both nights would be recorded and filmed for possible use as the band's cinematic feature, though the end result was vetoed. (In 1992, the concert was heavily edited and overdubbed for inclusion on the *Box Of Tricks* collection, while the full concert finally received release in 2014 on *Live At The Rainbow '74*.) Following the show, an end of tour party was held at the Swiss Cottage Holiday Inn in London, during which the band were presented with a brass plaque to commemorate a sell-out tour. Brian was a little more critical of their hometown shows: "We didn't enjoy the first Rainbow gig, though we'd had a hard day and we started changing things on stage, and there were the lights for the video to set up," Brian told *Record Mirror*, also indicating that the show had been filmed. "It was like Bertram Mills' Circus – there were so many things going on, we didn't feel too easy. London is very inhibited, you feel as though you're in a theatre, and since people seem to be tightening up on bouncers, you don't feel as though you can run around. We'd like to see a more subtle attitude from bouncers. It's not our wish that they should be heavy. The presence of bouncers probably provokes more violence anyway." Not that Roger helped keep things peaceful: frustrated with the impeding film crew, at the conclusion of 'Jailhouse Rock' on the second night, he trashed his drum kit.

After a brief rest, the band flew to Sweden to begin their first European tour. Brian was hesitant to admit defeat after Mott The Hoople and Faces had performed poorly-received gigs there: "I've got a slight feeling that Europe is not as bad as people think. In Germany, tickets are selling well and we're pretty confident." Lynyrd Skynyrd supported them on this tour, which didn't sit well with some of the band. "They were awful," Roger cuttingly recalled 30 years later. "They were southern rednecks and they couldn't believe it when they saw the four of us caked in make-up and dressed like women. They were outraged, confused and a little frightened, because four nancy boys were giving them a run for their money. In fact, there were actually people from their record company who would stand in the audience holding up banners that said things like 'Shit' and 'Queen Suck'. Things could be unbelievably petty back then – they paid people to heckle us! God, Lynyrd Skynyrd. They were arseholes, frankly. When they played that song, 'Free Bird', it seemed to go on for hours. As I remember, they had three lead guitarists. Hmm, well we only seemed to need one. Absolute arseholes."

The tour took an unexpected turn when, following the third show in Lund, a selection of dates had to be canceled due to the band's equipment truck breaking down; it is not known what cities or countries the band was due to perform in. The truck was repaired in time for the Munich show, though another problem arose when the driver negotiated too small a bridge and became stuck. Frustrated, the band called Edwin Shirley Trucking as a replacement, and were so appreciative of the crew's efforts that they employed them on every tour thereafter.

Overall, Europe didn't take kindly to Queen; *Record Mirror* reported that the audience, mostly American GIs, in Frankfurt were more responsive to Lynyrd Skynyrd than to the main act. "It was, said the tall and studious Brian May, like playing to a vacuum cleaner. 'We were just pouring it out and [the audience] were sucking it in, with nothing coming back. I tell you, for the first time in many months I felt like I'd done a hard day's work when I came off stage.' May, along with the rest of the band, is sitting in the diner of Frankfurt's Why Not club reflecting on Queen's second date in Germany. The mood is not bad, but there's an undercurrent of steely determination following the difficulties of that night's gig ... None of the boys seem

overly worried and the general feeling in their road party – and among the visiting journalists – is one of disdain for the Frankfurt crowd. A crowd of dopers into boogie rock is hardly likely to appreciate futuristic guitar pyrotechnics and 1975 flash a la Mercury. 'Still,' muses May, now installed at the night spot, 'they could have returned something. The more an audience feed back, the better we play – naturally – but there I just felt like I was wasting my time.'"

Dutch magazine *Oor* was slightly more positive: "On 8 December I decided to visit the 'Big Music Day' in The Hague. And I must say, I do not regret my decision ... But, it was possible to deliver an even more professional show, especially in terms of stage presentation. Queen gave away a rousing show. A truly royal spectacle, which amused me a lot. Carefully put together, the show was convincing almost in its entirety. It is a band full of ideas, both musically and visually. Singer Freddie Mercury moved across the stage as if he was The Queen herself. And surprisingly, on stage the band succeeded in putting across their often complex music very well ... A highly entertaining and varying evening of modern rock 'n' roll, on which I enjoyed myself a lot. Queen's huge popularity in the UK is completely logical."

Consequently, the band wouldn't return to Europe until May 1977, instead focusing on conquering America after an embarrassing false start.

1975

SHEER HEART ATTACK NORTH AMERICAN TOUR:
5 FEBRUARY TO 6 APRIL 1975

Musicians: John Deacon (*bass guitar, triangle on 'Killer Queen'*), Brian May (*guitar, vocals, banjo on 'Bring Back That Leroy Brown'*), Freddie Mercury (*vocals, piano, tambourine*), Roger Taylor (*drums, vocals*)

Repertoire: 'Procession', 'Now I'm Here', 'Ogre Battle', 'Father To Son', 'White Queen (As It Began)', 'Flick Of The Wrist', 'In The Lap Of The Gods' / 'Killer Queen' / 'The March Of The Black Queen' / 'Bring Back That Leroy Brown', 'Son And Daughter', 'Keep Yourself Alive', 'Seven Seas Of Rhye', 'Stone Cold Crazy', 'Liar', 'In The Lap Of The Gods... Revisited', 'Big Spender', 'Modern Times Rock'n'Roll', 'Jailhouse Rock', 'God Save The Queen'

Itinerary:

February 5: Agora, Columbus, Ohio

February 7: Palace Theater, Dayton, Ohio

February 8: Music Hall, Cleveland, Ohio *(afternoon and evening shows)*

February 9: Morris Civic Auditorium, South Bend, Indiana

February 10: Ford Auditorium, Detroit, Michigan

February 11: Student Union Auditorium, Toledo, Ohio

February 14: Palace Theater, Waterbury, Connecticut

February 15: Orpheum Theater, Boston, Massachusetts *(afternoon and evening shows)*

February 16: Avery Fisher Hall, New York, New York *(afternoon and evening shows)*

February 17: War Memorial, Trenton, New Jersey

February 19: Armory, Lewiston, New York

February 21: Capitol Theater, Passaic, New Jersey

February 22: Farm Arena, Harrisburg, Pennsylvania

February 23: Erlinger Theater, Philadelphia, Pennsylvania *(afternoon and evening shows)*

February 24: Kennedy Center, Washington, D.C.

March 5: Mary E Sawyer Auditorium, La Crosse, Wisconsin

March 6: Dane County Coliseum, Madison, Wisconsin

March 7: Uptown Theater, Milwaukee, Wisconsin

March 8: Aragon Ballroom, Chicago, Illinois

March 9: Keil Auditorium, St Louis, Missouri

March 10: Coliseum, Fort Wayne, Indiana

March 12: Municipal Auditorium, Atlanta, Georgia

March 13: Civic Auditorium, Charleston, South Carolina

March 14: Marina, Miami, Florida

March 18: St Bernard Civic Auditorium, New Orleans, Louisiana

March 20: Municipal Hall, San Antonio, Texas

March 23: McFarlin Auditorium, Dallas, Texas

March 25: Municipal Theater, Tulsa, Oklahoma

March 29: Santa Monica Civic Auditorium, Los Angeles, California *(afternoon and evening shows)*

March 30: Winterland, San Francisco, California

April 2: Kindmens Fieldhouse, Edmonton, Alberta

April 3: Corral, Calgary, Alberta

April 6: venue unknown, Seattle, Washington

With their sights set on conquering America on their own, Queen flew to the Beacon Theater in New York City on 31 January 1975 to tighten their set list for the upcoming tour. (The set remained largely the same as last year's, though a *Circus* magazine spotlight revealed that the band rehearsed 'Nevermore', which sadly didn't make it into the set list.) They had been given a six-week break, which was used to their advantage: US tours are generally longer than most tours, since there's more ground to cover, and Queen's two-month tour would involve 38 shows at 30 different venues. To provide further promotion, the band would give at least two radio interviews in each city, which became a source of irritation among the band, especially Roger, who later commented that he was often hungover during the interviews, and his threshold for answering the same tedious questions was considerably lower than usual.

Queen's main support band for this tour was Kansas – the same band that had replaced them on the Mott The Hoople tour the previous year – though Mahogany Rush and Styx would occasionally fill in instead. Kansas lead singer Steve Walsh recalled years later in an interview with classicbands.com that Queen "were fantastic. Real nice people, except Freddie … He was an asshole. But everybody else was great … He was a prima donna. Diva, if you will. That word was not meant to be a compliment, although a lot of people consider it to be. That's bullshit. That's having an ego bigger than you are talented, bigger than you deserved. That's what being a diva is. That's what a prima donna is and that's what Freddie was."

Unfortunately for Queen, the tour was marred by further health problems. Because of the demanding itinerary, Freddie's voice gave out completely after the second show in Philadelphia. A throat specialist from the University of Pennsylvania Hospital was called, diagnosing two suspected throat nodules and recommending the vocalist refrain from singing, and even speaking, for three months. Not wanting to disappoint the band or the fans, Freddie decided to test out his voice on one more show (Washington, D.C.), which didn't see any drastic change for the better. The others hadn't been informed of Freddie's condition until before the Washington show, when they were told that it would be their last for at least three months. Freddie sought a second opinion, with a local specialist again called in; the vocalist was informed he had severe swelling but that nodules weren't the cause and only one or two weeks' rest was necessary. Relieved, Queen canceled six concerts, recommencing the tour in Wisconsin on 5 March.

The tour continued largely without incident, though Freddie still had problems with his voice; consequently, some dates were postponed to give him more time to relax, with the final show in Portland on 7 April being canceled altogether. Not all problems were related to health: during the evening concert in Los Angeles, John split his trousers early in the show, which caused Freddie to exclaim, "Bass guitarist John Deacon, oh he's there. He's split his trousers! Have a look! A little nice bit of fun." The embarrassed bassist was able to slink off and change during Brian's guitar solo. On a more significant note, the band witnessed Led Zeppelin's epic 27 March concert at the Los Angeles Forum, and Brian later commented that his dream was to appear there with Queen. (Freddie, meanwhile, shrugged the show off, saying it was far too loud for his liking.) "We thought if we played the Rainbow in London we'd made it," Brian recalled. "Then we saw Zeppelin at the Forum and thought, 'Jesus Christ, if we ever make this kind of thing' … Our manager was there and he said, 'Couple of years' time, you'll be doing this'." They would do so less than two years later.

While the audience reception to the tour was wild, critical notices were decidedly mixed. *The Boston Globe* wrote that Queen's nemeses, Lynyrd Skynyrd, were once again the opening act at the afternoon show at the Orpheum, but they declined to appear for the evening show. "Credit Mr. May for Queen's distinctively sophisticated electronic sound which explores new musical frontiers without resorting to the use of synthesizers. His carefully controlled echo effects provide a perfect background for the exaggerated histrionics of lead singer Freddie Mercury. Bedecked in a skin-tight white satin suit, fingernails painted black and flashing the toothiest grin you've ever seen, Mercury is very much the center of attention in Queen's stage show. Prancing back and forth with both grace and a hint of naughtiness, he is in total command of his audience. And this audience loved every minute of it." Another review was more constructive: "One of the group's strong points – the dynamic interplay between and within songs and the juxtaposition of heavy, bashing numbers with lighter, relatively frail pop tunes – is, in its absence, one of the major complaints that can be leveled against Queen's live show. Perhaps it was because their concert a week ago last Saturday at the Orpheum was their first appearance in Boston … but one of the unsettling undercurrents which kept an immensely enjoyable concert from being categorized as great was a feeling that Queen was simply trying too hard … Nevertheless, such complaining is virtual quibbling when considering just how far above the current standard of rock music Queen stands."

Lisa Robinson's review of the New York show was more sarcastic in its tone: "Smoke is coming out at the audience and I turn to Lee Childers to ask what the name of this song is. 'What's the name of this? Are you kidding? "Smoke Gets In Your Eyes", darling.' Oh. It actually sounds like 'Flick Of The Wrist' or 'Tenement Funster' – one of those from *Sheer Heart Attack* that remind me of Bowie – but I could be wrong. Anyway, the sound is good – the entire stage production looked dramatically effective … and Freddie Mercury's stage presence is simply overwhelming … All of a sudden it is apparent that the dry ice/smoke machine is not working properly. A mixture of smoke and dry ice comes rolling over the stage and nearly asphyxiates the front three rows, the rows I might add, in which all journalists have been placed. I think it is a riot. A boy in front of me puts up an umbrella. I also notice that a boy on the aisle to my left is totally nodded out; head slumped over the arm of the chair."

The New York Times was especially vicious of Queen's popularity and headlining stature: "Its last time here, six months ago, it was at the bottom of the bill in a Broadway rock season. And yet it's difficult to see why Queen deserves this fervor. The music, falling into the heavy metal variety, full of ponderous chord and dramatic pause, is scarcely superoriginal, and its instrumental technique has been heard before – Brian May, guitarist, is heavily into feedback, occasionally to the point of regurgitation. Even the singing and stage mannerisms of Freddie Mercury glitter in the reflections of others." Chris Charlesworth wasn't impressed either, and indicated the critical disconnect from fan appreciation: "Queen's music, to me, was tedious, and their on-stage presence (an essential quality if you choose to run the heavy-rock-with-glitter-overtones race) was an almost laughably bizarre mish-mash of every other more successful band of their genre … It is only fair to point out that my view of the concert appeared to be that of the minority and the majority went home satisfied."

SHEER HEART ATTACK JAPANESE TOUR:
19 APRIL TO 1 MAY 1975

Musicians: John Deacon *(bass guitar, triangle on 'Killer Queen')*, Brian May *(guitar, vocals, banjo on 'Bring Back That Leroy Brown')*, Freddie Mercury *(vocals, piano, tambourine)*, Roger Taylor *(drums, vocals)*

Repertoire: 'Procession', 'Now I'm Here', 'Ogre Battle', 'Father To Son', 'White Queen (As It Began)', 'Flick Of

The Wrist', 'Hangman', 'Great King Rat', 'In The Lap Of The Gods' / 'Killer Queen' / 'The March Of The Black Queen' / 'Bring Back That Leroy Brown', 'Son And Daughter', 'Doing All Right', 'Keep Yourself Alive', 'Seven Seas Of Rhye', 'Stone Cold Crazy', 'Liar', 'In The Lap Of The Gods... Revisited', 'Big Spender', 'Modern Times Rock'n'Roll', 'Jailhouse Rock', 'See What A Fool I've Been', 'God Save The Queen'

Itinerary:
April 19: Budokan Hall, Tokyo
April 22: Aichi Taiikukan, Nagoya
April 23: Nokusai Taikan, Kobe
April 25: Kyuden Taiikukan, Fukuoka
April 28: Taiikukan, Okayama
April 29: Yamaha Tsumagoi Hall, Shizuoka
April 30: Bunkan Taiikukan, Yokohama
May 1: Budokan Hall, Tokyo

Following Queen's successful North American tour, the band flew to Kawai in Hawaii for a short break before venturing to Japan. Arriving at Haneda Airport on 17 April, they were surprised to discover over 3000 screaming fans greeting them as they walked off the plane. They were then whisked off to a press reception and presented with awards for high record sales for *Sheer Heart Attack* and 'Killer Queen'. Their reception was equated to the Beatlemania of a decade before, and would be reprised every time Queen visited the country. Roger later recalled with amusement that when he entered a store, the owner recognized him and repeated "Ah, you Queen!" while he took pictures of the bemused drummer for 10 minutes.

The tour started on 19 April at the Budokan Arena, which was immediately sold out. The excitement of the 10,000-strong crowd was so great that, when the band appeared, a pack of fans rushed the stage and Freddie stopped the show to retain order. Luckily for the band, local promoters had employed sumo wrestlers as a means of security. The reception throughout the tour only intensified, and the band played off this energy by delivering not only a high octane set every night, but also delivering a few rarities: both 'Great King Rat' and 'See What A Fool I've Been' were rotated in periodically, while 'Hangman' was performed on the final night.

John later commented that when the audiences were screaming during the band's set, it seemed as if the arena walls were shaking, making for a scary yet exhilarating experience. Queen were touched at the warmth the locals exuded: Freddie, especially, fell in love with the country, and would make special trips there for shopping excursions or to just enjoy the culture and the people. Brian's friend Chris Smith visited the guitarist after the tour, and found a dejected guitarist: "He said, 'I was just in The Beatles. We got this amazing reception, even at the airport. Now I've gone from that to this'," as he gestured at his bathroom wall covered in fungus. The band made a collective decision: Trident had to go, and a proposed return to North America in September was canceled, as was a US-only single release of a re-recorded 'Keep Yourself Alive'. They would spend the better part of the summer and autumn battling their management while recording their fourth album.

A NIGHT AT THE OPERA UK TOUR:
14 NOVEMBER TO 24 DECEMBER 1975

Musicians: John Deacon (*bass guitar, triangle on 'Killer Queen'*), Brian May (*guitar, vocals, banjo on 'Bring Back That Leroy Brown'*), Freddie Mercury (*vocals, piano, tambourine*), Roger Taylor (*drums, vocals*)

Repertoire: 'Bohemian Rhapsody' (*taped intro*), 'Ogre Battle', 'Sweet Lady', 'White Queen (As It Began)', 'Flick Of The Wrist', 'Bohemian Rhapsody' / 'Killer Queen' / 'The March Of The Black Queen' / 'Bohemian Rhapsody' (*reprise*) / 'Bring Back That Leroy Brown', 'Son And Daughter', 'The Prophet's Song', 'Stone Cold Crazy', 'Doing All Right', 'Keep Yourself Alive', 'Seven Seas Of Rhye', 'Liar', 'In The Lap Of The Gods... Revisited', 'Now I'm Here', 'Big Spender', 'Jailhouse Rock', 'God Save The Queen', 'Modern Times Rock 'n' Roll', 'See What A Fool I've Been', 'Hangman', 'Shake, Rattle & Roll', 'Stupid Cupid', 'Be Bop A Lula', 'Saturday Night's Alright For Fighting', 'Father To Son'

Itinerary:
November 14/15: Empire Theatre, Liverpool
November 16: Theatre, Coventry
November 17/18: Colston Hall, Bristol
November 19: Capitol, Cardiff
November 21: Odeon, Taunton
November 23: Winter Gardens, Bournemouth
November 24: Gaumont, Southampton
November 26: Free Trade Hall, Manchester (afternoon and evening shows)
November 29-December 2: Hammersmith Odeon, London

December 7: Civic Hall, Wolverhampton
December 8: Guildhall, Preston
December 9/10: Odeon, Birmingham
December 11: City Hall, Newcastle
December 13: Caird Hall, Dundee
December 14: Capitol, Aberdeen
December 15/16: Apollo Theatre, Glasgow
December 24: Hammersmith Odeon, London

On the strength of the 'Bohemian Rhapsody' single, Queen's 1975 UK tour became a supremely hot ticket. This would be the last tour in which the band were able to perform in the intimate settings their relative obscurity before 'Bohemian Rhapsody' had afforded them. The largest venue this time around was the Hammersmith Odeon, with a four-night sell-out in the middle of the tour and a fifth appearance there at the end of the itinerary.

In addition to filming the video for 'Bohemian Rhapsody' at Elstree Studios, the band also conducted rehearsals there, significantly reorganizing their set list. Gone was the 'Procession' intro, and the medley was given a minor reshuffle in order to introduce segments of music previously unheard. Perhaps most startling was the promotion of 'Now I'm Here' from concert opener to first encore performance: while the song was a natural to serve as an introduction to a Queen concert, it received greater prominence in the encore, becoming a storming rendition on any given night.

An article with *Record Mirror* indicated that the tour was hastily arranged, with Freddie telling the magazine, "It's all been such a rush. We only had two days to rehearse before the tour." With such a dearth of time, the tour got off to a rocky start: "He's slightly piqued because shortage of time has made it possible for only three numbers frm the new album to be included in the show and one of them ('The Prophet's Song') is 'but a mere skeleton of what it should be.' In answer to reassurances that it sounded very good, he snaps: 'Yes of course it does, but it should be better. It's not all there. This tour has been thrown together, my dears,' he says finally. 'Thrown together' … The perfectionist Mr. Mercury may be far from satisfied yet, but if Queen's show was 'thrown together', it was done so marvellously well. Visually it was stunning, largely because it was the best-lit concert I've ever seen … Musically, the show more than matches its trappings. Freddie's voice is in amazing good shape, Brian's playing is just heavenly and the rhythm department is everything one would expect of it – and more."

Most intriguingly, each concert started with a taped intro of 'Bohemian Rhapsody', constructed by Kenny Everett. In a panic, Freddie had contacted his DJ friend the night before the tour started, asking for assistance in creating a worthwhile overture; the result started off with Kenny intoning exaltedly, "Ladies and gentlemen … *A Night At The Opera*", followed by a snippet of 'Ogre Battle' and leading into the opera section of 'Bohemian Rhapsody', by the conclusion of which the band would enter stage left and finish the song, excising the final verse, instead jumping directly into 'Ogre Battle'. From the new album, which wouldn't be released until 21 November, only 'Sweet Lady' and 'The Prophet's Song' would be performed in full; the ending of the latter was arranged to feature a tape recording of the outro sound effects, and would speed up several keys, effectively leading into 'Stone Cold Crazy'. 'Bohemian Rhapsody' now book-ended the medley; all the other songs from the album, except for 'Seaside Rendezvous' and 'Good Company', would be introduced into the set on subsequent tours.

The tour started in Liverpool (originally, the 15 November date was the starting point, but another show was added the day before to accomodate demand) with Oxford-based band Mr Big as support, and reception was unsurprisingly warm. This was Queen's first UK tour in nearly a year, and the audience wanted to show just how much they supported the band. Freddie had taken to wearing a silk kimono (a souvenir from Japan) during the encore, and one night, as he put it, "I did the impromptu strip. I took the belt off and thought, 'I'll dangle the sash.' I dropped it. Then I thought, 'Can I get it back?' Of course I couldn't. Then I spotted this girl obviously after my kimono. I thought, 'No way, dearie.' I flung it to safety off stage."

In Southampton in the last week of November, the band received news that 'Bohemian Rhapsody' had reached No. 1, and spirits remained high throughout the remainder of the tour.After a show in Newcastle on 11 December, the band were stopped by police and escorted to the station to be searched for drugs. The lead vocalist of Mr Big later explained that the strongest drug on the bus consumed that night was a bottle or two of Southern Comfort; some suspicious-looking pills were later discovered to be aspirin. (A far cry from what the band would get into on later tours!)

After the tour's conclusion in Aberdeen and Glasgow, the band performed a special Christmas Eve concert at Hammersmith Odeon that was broadcast live on Radio One and BBC2's *The Old Grey Whistle*

Test, and repeated several times thereafter. Similar to the Rainbow show from last year, Brian especially was frustrated with the show, as reported in *Sounds*: "Both Fred and Brian felt the show was fantastic while they were doing it but were horrified when they saw a videotape immediately afterwards. 'It's not up to you anymore. It's up to the cameras, the lighting people. You can't help getting Mycroft images (those colored lines that dominated the screen half the time) when the cameras got that close to me. I knew that was going to happen. It's also very hard to decide what audience to cater for. The people in front of you have paid money to see you but at the same time you're doing a prestigious concert and you have to try to make sure you come across on TV.' Both Fred and Brian felt they failed in that respect. But then, the show did come in the middle of business meetings delayed by their recent tour and preparations for four months in America, the far east and Australia. They had two days to 'perfect the repertoire: what do you choose and what do you leave out? Also we were used to pacing ourselves for an hour and a half. I wouldn't want to do live TV again. Film is much better because you have control over it.'"

Regardless of the band's criticisms, the tour was well-received in the press. Phil Sutcliffe in *Sounds* wrote of the earlier Hammersmith shows, "[They] exuded the same exhilarating mixture of heavy, grandiose, beautiful and sheer extravagant silliness encapsulated in their superb No. 1 ['Bohemian Rhapsody']. And to spend an awful lot of time smiling with sheer pleasure at a rock show can be no bad thing. The inch-perfection of every movement, calculated for effect and co-ordinated to the lights is one entertaining feature, 'artistic' in the showbiz sense and at the same time amusing you with the absurdity of taking so much trouble over ephemera." The show was finally released on disc and video in 2015 as *A Night At The Odeon: Hammersmith 1975*.

1976

A NIGHT AT THE OPERA NORTH AMERICAN TOUR:
27 JANUARY TO 13 MARCH 1976

Musicians: John Deacon *(bass guitar, triangle on 'Killer Queen')*, Brian May *(guitar, vocals, banjo on 'Bring Back That Leroy Brown')*, Freddie Mercury *(vocals, piano, tambourine)*, Roger Taylor *(drums, vocals)*
Repertoire: 'Bohemian Rhapsody' *(taped intro)*, 'Ogre

Battle', 'Sweet Lady', 'White Queen (As It Began)', 'Flick Of The Wrist', 'Bohemian Rhapsody' / 'Killer Queen' / 'The March Of The Black Queen' / 'Bohemian Rhapsody' *(reprise)* / 'Bring Back That Leroy Brown', 'Son And Daughter', 'The Prophet's Song', 'Stone Cold Crazy', 'Doing All Right', 'Lazing On A Sunday Afternoon', 'Keep Yourself Alive', 'Seven Seas Of Rhye', 'Liar', 'In The Lap Of The Gods… Revisited', 'Now I'm Here', 'Big Spender', 'Jailhouse Rock', 'God Save The Queen', 'Modern Times Rock 'n' Roll', 'See What A Fool I've Been', 'Hangman', 'Shake, Rattle & Roll', 'Stupid Cupid', 'Be Bop A Lula', 'Saturday Night's Alright For Fighting'

Itinerary:
January 27: Palace Theater, Waterbury, Connecticut
January 29/30: Music Hall, Boston, Massachusetts
January 31-February 2: Tower Theater, Philadelphia, Pennsylvania
February 5-8: Beacon Theater, New York, New York
February 11/12: Masonic Temple, Detroit, Michigan
February 13: Riverfront Coliseum, Cincinnati, Ohio
February 14: Public Hall, Cleveland, Ohio
February 15: Sports Arena, Toledo, Ohio
February 18: Civic Centre, Saginaw, Michigan
February 19: Veterans Memorial Auditorium, Columbus, Ohio
February 20: Syrian Mosque, Pittsburgh, Pennsylvania
February 22/23: Auditorium Theater, Chicago, Illinois
February 26: Keil Auditorium, St Louis, Missouri
February 27: Convention Center, Indianapolis, Indiana
February 28: Dane County Coliseum, Madison, Wisconsin
February 29: Coliseum, Fort Wayne, Indiana
March 1: Auditorium, Milwaukee, Wisconsin
March 3: St Paul's Auditorium, Minneapolis, Minnesota
March 7: Berkeley Community, Berkeley, California
March 9-12: Santa Monica Civic Auditorium, Los Angeles, California (afternoon and evening shows on the 9th)
March 13: Sports Arena, San Diego, California

After Queen's triumphant jaunt across the UK, they took three weeks off before flying to New York on 20 January 1976 to commence rehearsals for their upcoming US tour. Support acts were both Elektra artists, and varied depending on the legs of the tour: The Cate Brothers, a southern soul duo, discovered by Levon Helm, who had just released their eponymous debut album, and Bob Seger And The Silver Bullet Band; both were far removed from the regal rock of Queen. The set list remained similar to that presented on the UK leg, with only 'Lazing On A Sunday Afternoon' shoehorned awkwardly between 'Doing All Right' and 'Keep Yourself Alive'. The audience's reception to the song throughout the tour was averagely lukewarm, which affected the band's confidence in it; it would be out of the set by the end of the year. As the tour progressed, the band would drop 'Lazing On A Sunday Afternoon' and replace it with either 'Hangman' or 'Modern Times Rock 'n' Roll' – or, in some cases, both.

New to the Queen entourage for this tour was Gerry Stickells, who had previously been a roadie-cum-tour manager for Jimi Hendrix and was engaged in the absence of Jack Nelson. The band's third tour of the US (and second headlining tour) began in Connecticut at the end of January 1976, almost coming to a premature end in New York when three over-zealous female fans fought viciously for Freddie's scarf, oblivious to the fact that it was still round his neck.

The tour wound its way through all the major hotspots of Queen popularity. The band even sold out the Beacon Theater in New York, resulting in a four-night residency, though the original plan was for only three nights. It was only because of intense ticket demands that a fourth night was hastily added. There were also five shows at the Santa Monica Civic Auditorium in Los Angeles prior to the tour wrapping up in San Diego.

While the audiences were all rabid with their appreciation, most reviews were lukewarm or cautiously complimentary. "On the Music Hall stage Thursday night, the members of Queen proved themselves worthy of their hype only up to a point," opined *The Boston Globe*. "What they lose outside the technical cocoon of the recording studio, they only partially make up for with dynamic, crowd-pleasing theatrics." *The New York Times* was also damning with faint praise: "The music is sharply and tensely constructed, switching abruptly from mood to mood, blending styles into a febrile collage ... If one really liked the results – and the sold-out house Thursday was demonstrative in its enthusiasm – one might talk of an extension of Beatles complexity by post-Who basics. Except that for this observer, the end result is too often calculated and precious. Mr. Mercury is a good singer, and he has improved his stage presence, but he is still self-consciously posturing. And for all the skill and invention elsewhere, the music sounds hollow at the core."

However, California fully accepted the band, with reviews that were positively glowing. "For those who keep a social history of rock, there was a concert/ceremony of special interest and importance Tuesday night at Santa Monica Civic Auditorium," *The Los Angeles Times* purred. "A major new force in rock was officially crowned. The band's name, quite appropriately, was Queen. It's a group with the power, ambition and, crucially, the swagger to be a superstar attraction ... Though Queen's debut last year [at the same venue] was well-received, the band's performance and material (thanks to songs from its new, finely-honed *A Night At The Opera* album) was more consistent and impressive this time. Indeed, the evening's chief disappointment was the group's not using more songs from its new album ... Queen needs greater sociological identification with its audience to be a maximum force in rock, but it has enough exciting, appealing attributes – musical and visual – to be a far more attractive subject of rock stardom (as measured by the ability to fill 18,000-20,000 seat halls) than most bands that have it to that level in recent years."

It was this tour that convinced Brian that they were finally making it in North America. "It's finally really happening for us over there," he said to *Record Collector* later that year. "We really reached towards our peak with [*A Night At The Opera*] and it was great to see it break into the US charts. It's always hard to get accepted over there – especially on the West Coast. But we were having sell outs everywhere. There's a different kind of response between British and American audiences. Here the fans are more reserved until they have reached a point where they can explode. In the States they are ready to explode at the beginning. They will give you anything you want ... once you gain their favour."

A NIGHT AT THE OPERA JAPANESE TOUR:
22 MARCH TO 4 APRIL 1976

Musicians: John Deacon (*bass guitar, triangle on 'Killer Queen'*), Brian May (*guitar, vocals, banjo on 'Bring Back That Leroy Brown'*), Freddie Mercury (*vocals, piano, tambourine*), Roger Taylor (*drums, vocals*)

Repertoire: 'Bohemian Rhapsody' (*taped intro*), 'Ogre Battle', 'Sweet Lady', 'White Queen (As It Began)', 'Flick Of The Wrist', 'Bohemian Rhapsody' / 'Killer Queen' / 'The March Of The Black Queen' / 'Bohemian Rhapsody' (*reprise*) / 'Bring Back That Leroy Brown', 'Son And

Daughter', 'The Prophet's Song, 'Stone Cold Crazy', 'Doing All Right', 'Keep Yourself Alive', 'Seven Seas Of Rhye', 'Liar', 'In The Lap Of The Gods... Revisited', 'Now I'm Here', 'Big Spender', 'Jailhouse Rock', 'God Save The Queen', 'Lazing On A Sunday Afternoon', 'Modern Times Rock 'n' Roll', 'See What A Fool I've Been', 'Hangman', 'Father To Son', 'Shake, Rattle & Roll', 'Stupid Cupid', 'Be Bop A Lula', 'Saturday Night's Alright For Fighting', 'Whole Lotta Shakin' Goin' On'

Itinerary:
March 22: Budokan Hall, Tokyo
March 23: Aichi Ken Gymnasium, Nagoya
March 24: Kosei Kaikan, Himeji City
March 26: Kyuden Gymnasium, Fukuoka (afternoon and evening shows)
March 29: Kosei Nenkin Kaikan, Osaka (afternoon and evening shows)
March 31/April 1: Budokan Hall, Tokyo
April 2: Miyagi-Ken Sports Centre, Sendai
April 4: Nichidai Kodo, Tokyo

Considering the overwhelming response Queen received in Japan the previous year, it was no surprise that they agreed to return, with 'Bohemian Rhapsody' and *A Night At The Opera* making waves worldwide. This time, the Japanese tour was more adventurous, taking in more cities and featuring, on two occasions, both afternoon and evening shows, though this would wreak havoc on Freddie, and most of the shows from this leg found his voice in rough shape. The set list also was a little more varied, with the band pulling out two old favorites they hadn't played in a while, and, indeed, would never play again: 'Hangman' and 'Father To Son'. The shows went over extremely well, with the audience often whipping themselves into a frenzy, and it was this reception that influenced Brian to write 'Teo Torriatte (Let Us Cling Together)', recorded and released later in the year on *A Day At The Races*.

A NIGHT AT THE OPERA AUSTRALIAN TOUR:

11 TO 22 APRIL 1976

Musicians: John Deacon *(bass guitar, triangle on 'Killer Queen')*, Brian May *(guitar, vocals, banjo on 'Bring Back That Leroy Brown')*, Freddie Mercury *(vocals, piano, tambourine)*, Roger Taylor *(drums, vocals)*

Repertoire: 'Bohemian Rhapsody' *(taped intro)*, 'Ogre Battle', 'Sweet Lady', 'White Queen (As It Began)',

'Flick Of The Wrist', 'Bohemian Rhapsody' / 'Killer Queen' / 'The March Of The Black Queen' / 'Bohemian Rhapsody' *(reprise)* / 'Bring Back That Leroy Brown', 'Son And Daughter', 'The Prophet's Song', 'Stone Cold Crazy', 'Doing All Right', 'Keep Yourself Alive', 'Seven Seas Of Rhye', 'Liar', 'In The Lap Of The Gods... Revisited', 'Now I'm Here', 'Big Spender', 'Jailhouse Rock', 'God Save The Queen', 'Modern Times Rock 'n' Roll', 'See What A Fool I've Been', 'Shake, Rattle & Roll', 'Stupid Cupid', 'Be Bop A Lula', 'Saturday Night's Alright For Fighting'

Itinerary:
April 11: Entertainment Centre, Perth
April 14/15: Apollo Stadium, Adelaide
April 17/18: Horden Pavilion, Sydney
April 19/20: Festival Hall, Melbourne
April 22: Festival Hall, Brisbane

Despite the poor experience the band had at the Sunbury Pop Festival in January 1974, Queen had vowed to return there, realizing that the fans weren't the problem, and it would've been a shame to have deprived them of their updated concert experience. Plans had been set in motion to return in 1975, but it wouldn't be until April 1976 that they finally graced Australia's shores, and the reception was far more positive this time, thanks to the success of 'Bohemian Rhapsody' and *A Night At The Opera*. The set list remained largely unchanged, though the band would throw in occasional performances of 'Modern Times Rock 'n' Roll' and 'See What A Fool I've Been' and a handful of covers, including 'Shake, Rattle & Roll', 'Stupid Cupid', 'Be Bop A Lula', and 'Saturday Night's Alright For Fighting'.

Reviews were far more complimentary this time, giving the band the confidence they needed to want to return (which they wouldn't do for nearly a decade): "Frenzied fans of the British rock group Queen were dragged from the stage at the end of a Festival Hall concert last night," one review read. "Bouncers had their hands full as young girls tried to leap onto the stage at lead singer Freddie Mercury. At the end of the show, Mercury stripped to a pair of red and white hot pants and threw roses to the audience. The crowd – mainly teenyboppers – went wild. The four-man group stunned the capacity crowd with explosions and flooded the stage with smoke." Another read, "Queen spewed blinding light, colour, sand, smoke, explosives and roses on to its capacity audience at Festival Hall last night. Their rough blend of hard rock and theatrics almost approached the 'feelies' of Huxley's *Brave New World* for audience participation."

SUMMER UK TOUR:

1 TO 18 SEPTEMBER 1976

Musicians: John Deacon *(bass guitar, triangle on 'Killer Queen')*, Brian May *(guitar, vocals, banjo on 'Bring Back That Leroy Brown', acoustic guitar on "39')*, Freddie Mercury *(vocals, piano, tambourine)*, Roger Taylor *(drums, vocals, bass drum and tambourine on "39')*

Repertoire: 'Bohemian Rhapsody' *(taped intro)*, 'Ogre Battle', 'Sweet Lady', 'White Queen (As It Began)', 'Flick Of The Wrist', 'You're My Best Friend' / 'Bohemian Rhapsody' / 'Killer Queen' / 'The March Of The Black Queen' / 'Bohemian Rhapsody' *(reprise)* / 'Bring Back That Leroy Brown', 'Brighton Rock', 'Son And Daughter' *(reprise)*, "39', 'You Take My Breath Away', 'The Prophet's Song', 'Stone Cold Crazy', 'Doing All Right', 'Lazing On A Sunday Afternoon', 'Tie Your Mother Down', 'Keep Yourself Alive', 'Liar', 'In The Lap Of The Gods... Revisited', 'Now I'm Here', 'Big Spender', 'Jailhouse Rock', 'God Save The Queen'

Itinerary:
September 1/2: Playhouse Theatre, Edinburgh
September 10: Cardiff Castle, Cardiff
September 18: Hyde Park, London

After Queen returned home from their lengthy *A Night At The Opera* world tour, they deliberately allowed themselves a rest from both live and studio work. In July, they started work on *A Day At The Races* but quickly realized that work was taking longer than anticipated, meaning that an extensive tour during the remainder of the year would be impossible. The band duly scheduled four shows in September, smack-dab in the middle of the sessions, which also saw a bit of a shake-up to repertoire: 'Tie Your Mother Down' and 'You Take My Breath Away' from the new album were added, as were both sides of Queen's then-current single, 'You're My Best Friend' and "39'. These concerts would be among the few occasions when Queen introduced new, unreleased material into a live show.

The mini-tour kicked off on 1 and 2 September (originally planned for 20 and 21 August, according to *Melody Maker*) in Edinburgh as part of the Scottish Festival of Popular Music, and Queen appeared on the bill alongside Elton John, John Miles, Rainbow and comedian Billy Connolly. The third date at Cardiff Castle was also a multi-billed festival, with Queen headlining and Manfred Mann, Andy Fairweather-Low and Frankie Miller's Full House appearing as support. This concert was marred by excessive rain, which Roger later wrote about in the autumn 1976 issue of the Queen fan club magazine: "The sight of the rain pouring down through the spotlights on everybody, and of Freddie splashing his way through pools of water at the front of the stage will remain indelibly printed on our memories forever. The fact that people stayed on and enjoyed themselves right to the end made it quite a moving occasion for us. In fact, I was so overcome I just had to wreck me drum kit at the end, which reduced Crystal, my roadie, to floods of tears rivalling the rain (it was a brand new kit too!). Anyway if you were there thanks for being our bravest audience ever and I hope the pneumonia cleared up."

The fourth and final date, eight days after the Cardiff appearance (which, in turn, had been eight days after the Scottish dates), was a free concert in Hyde Park held on the sixth anniversary of Jimi Hendrix's death. This was designed as a homecoming for Queen, as well as a token of appreciation (hence no admission charge) to their British fans for their support. Queen's support comprised Steve Hillage, Kiki Dee, and Supercharge. This concert, on a stage built for The Rolling Stones' concert nearly a month prior, featured a set list shake-up: due to time constraints, 'Doing All Right', 'Lazing On A Sunday Afternoon', 'Tie Your Mother Down' and all songs including 'Now I'm Here' and beyond were not performed. The band had been allowed an hour to perform by the local police and, when their set over-ran by 20 minutes, the band were threatened with jail if they attempted to return to the stage. Freddie in particular had little desire to be hauled away in a white leotard, so duly complied. Bob Harris, who compered the event, had the unenviable task of informing the crowd of 150,000 to 200,000 people that, despite their cries of "We want Queen!", the band's set was over.

Record Mirror wrote of Queen's Edinburg gigs, "After four months rehearsing new material, [they] bounced back into concert with an explosive one-and-a-half hour set at the Playhouse, which earned them a standing ovation. They oozed class, and seemed to be having a ball on stage after their lay-off. They were visually stunning, the lighting effects synchronizing with the sounds, and their musicianship was impressive." *NME*, meanwhile, ripped the band to shreds: "Basically, it's rubbish, a theatrical synthesis of the grossest lumps of regimented noise the sometime power trio can contrive. As they thunder away, Mercury emerges from the wings once more, looking like a frog in a balletic white skintight catsuit, and magesterially conjures up giant flashes that erupt deafeningly out of the stage. The audience do likewise from their serried seats." *Record Mirror* was more (reluctantly) positive of their Hyde Park gig, drawing attention to the synchronicity of the band's deliberate performance on the sixth anniversary of Jimi Hendrix's death (even calling Brian a "silver winged angel"): "Queen aren't Hendrix, they're Queen. Or, to put it another way, they're Freddie Mercury. He's an overt poser, a slick precision-like and ultimately professional entertainer who has found his way into that small gang of people we call stars. His performance before 250,000 people in Hyde Park on Saturday was proof that he could stand beside Jagger, Bowie and a handful of Americans."

Queen had once again decided to film the show for fans who hadn't been able to attend – or perhaps couldn't see the band from such a distance. Roger mentioned in the autumn 1976 fan club magazine that the film was due to be broadcast on TV soon, but only 'Sweet Lady' would be broadcast, on 14 December 1976 on *The Old Grey Whistle Test*. (The same footage was repeated on Don Kirshner's *Rock Concert* programme on 8 February 1977.) Rumors and speculation that the show was filmed in its entirey have persisted for years, though Jacky Smith revealed in 2001 that "the quality is very very bad and they cannot 'rescue' it as it was filmed on 16mm and not stored properly." However, a complete, pro-shot video was eventually leaked to collectors, and while it's indeed rough, it's still a spectacular performance; footage over the years has since been cleaned up and trickled out onto documentaries, lending credence to the hope that someday this concert will be released.

The show had an effect on both Queen's fans and the band themselves, with Brian later recalling, "I think that Hyde Park was one of the most significant gigs in our career. There was a great affection because we'd kind of made it in a lot of countries by that time, but England was still, you know, we weren't really sure if we were really acceptable here. So it was a wonderful feeling to come back and see that crowd and get that response."

1977

QUEEN LIZZY NORTH AMERICAN TOUR:
13 JANUARY TO 18 MARCH 1977

Musicians: John Deacon (*bass guitar, triangle on 'Killer Queen'*), Brian May (*guitar, vocals, banjo on 'Bring Back That Leroy Brown', acoustic guitar on "39'*), Freddie Mercury (*vocals, piano, tambourine*), Roger Taylor (*drums, vocals, bass drum and tambourine on "39'*)

Repertoire: 'Intro', 'Tie Your Mother Down', 'Ogre Battle', 'White Queen (As It Began)', 'Somebody To Love', 'Killer Queen' / 'The Millionaire Waltz' / 'You're My Best Friend' / 'Bring Back That Leroy Brown', 'Sweet Lady', 'Brighton Rock', "39', 'You Take My Breath Away', 'White Man', 'The Prophet's Song', 'Bohemian Rhapsody', 'Stone Cold Crazy', 'Keep Yourself Alive', 'Liar', 'In The Lap Of The Gods... Revisited', 'Now I'm Here', 'Big Spender', 'Jailhouse Rock', 'God Save The Queen', 'Saturday Night's Alright For Fighting', 'Stupid Cupid', 'Be Bop A Lula'

Itinerary:
January 13: Auditorium, Milwaukee, Wisconsin
January 14: Dane County Coliseum, Madison, Wisconsin
January 15: Gardens, Columbus, Ohio
January 16: Convention Center, Indianapolis, Indiana
January 18: Cobo Hall, Detroit, Michigan
January 20: Civic Center, Saginaw, Michigan
January 21: Elliot Hall of Music, Louisville, Kentucky
January 22: Wings Stadium, Kalamazoo, Michigan
January 23: Richfield Coliseum, Cleveland, Ohio
January 25: Central Canadian Exhibition Center, Ottawa, Ontario
January 26: The Forum, Montreal, Quebec
January 28: Stadium, Chicago, Illinois
January 30: St John's Arena, Toledo, Ohio
February 1: Maple Leaf Gardens, Toronto, Ontario
February 3: Civic Center, Springfield, Illinois
February 4: University of Maryland, College Park, Maryland
February 5: Madison Square Garden, New York, New York
February 6: Nassau Coliseum, Long Island, New York
February 8: War Memorial Auditorium, Syracuse, New York
February 9: Boston Gardens, Boston, Massachusetts
February 10: Civic Center, Providence, Rhode Island

February 11: Civic Center, Philadelphia, Pennsylvania
February 19: Sportatorium, Miami, Florida
February 20: Civic Center, Lakeland, Florida
February 21: Fox Theater, Atlanta, Georgia
February 22: Auditorium, Birmingham, Alabama
February 24: Keil Auditorium, St Louis, Missouri
February 25: Lloyd Noble Center, Norman, Oklahoma
February 26: Moody Coliseum, Dallas, Texas
February 27: Sam Houston Arena, Houston, Texas
March 1: Coliseum, Phoenix, Arizona
March 3/4: The Forum, Los Angeles, California
March 5: Sports Arena, San Diego, California
March 6: Winterland, San Francisco, California
March 11: PNE Coliseum, Vancouver, British Columbia
March 12: Paramount, Portland, Oregon
March 13: Arena, Seattle, Washington
March 16/17: Jubilee Auditorium, Calgary, Alberta
March 18: Northlands Arena, Edmonton, Alberta

When *A Day At The Races* was finally completed in November 1976, the band made the radical decision to not tour the album right away. Even so, 1977 would prove one of their busiest years. The band flew to Boston in the first week of January to commence ten days of rehearsals for their upcoming American tour. The set list was significantly restructured to accommodate new material: 'The March Of The Black Queen' was dropped, as was the 'Bohemian Rhapsody' taped intro; in its stead was the guitar intro of *A Day At The Races*, while the now-departed opener would be performed in its entirety later in the set, though the operatic section would be played from the studio version over the PA, leaving dry ice and lights to do the heavy lifting. In addition, 'Somebody To Love', 'The Millionaire Waltz' and 'White Man' were all added to the set, ('Long Away' was also rehearsed, presumably with Freddie on lead vocals, though it was ultimately not performed), though it was the first number, Queen's current single, that would cause some concern for Roger: "'Somebody To Love' was hard to do because there are so many voices on the record that I didn't know if we'd be able to do it. I enjoy playing it now, but when we first started the tour, we were dreading it when it came round in the set." The mid-set medley also saw a shake-up, with 'Killer Queen' becoming the opening number, followed by 'The Millionaire Waltz', 'You're My Best Friend' and 'Bring Back That Leroy Brown'. Less frequent performances of 'Saturday Night's Alright For Fighting', 'Stupid Cupid' and 'Be Bop A Lula' occasionally peppered the sets, depending

on the band's collective mood and the audience reception.

What was most significant about this tour was the support act. Queen soon discovered that Thin Lizzy, fronted by Phil Lynott, had every intention of upstaging them, though the reviews were usually in Queen's favor. A rivalry was cooked up in the press, but Lizzy's guitarist, Scott Gorham, maintained it was a friendly rivalry: "A lot of bands get paranoid about not letting the support act upstage them, and to keep you down they won't give you a soundcheck, etc. But we didn't get any of that from Queen. They said right away, 'Here's the PA. Now you'll need soundchecks and lights, and what else?' Together we had the attitude that we would set out as a British attack to conquer America. Of course we were two very different bands. Lizzy was a sort of punk band with street cred, whereas Queen were very polished and sophisticated, so you see there was no competitiveness on that score." Appropriately, considering that 1977 marked Queen Elizabeth II's Silver Jubilee, the tour was called the Queen Lizzy (geddit?) North American tour, though this wouldn't happen until later: Cheap Trick and Head East were the support acts for the first few dates.

Unfortunately, Queen were touring during one of the coldest winters North America had ever encountered. Following the Chicago show, the band were due to perform at Hara Arena in Dayton, Ohio on 29 January, but the tankers transporting fuel to heat the arena were stranded with frozen diesel tanks. Ever the consummate professionals, Queen offered to play regardless, but officials decided to cancel the show. Brian later recalled, "We were very lucky, actually. We had a very good crew, and they managed to truck the stuff around through all the worst weather, and we only lost one gig in all that bad weather. And that wasn't because we weren't there. It's because they would not allow us to use the power because they had a fuel shortage. That was pretty frustrating, but we managed to fulfill all the contracts, which is great." Two other dates – in Sacramento and Fresno, on 8 and 9 March respectively – were canceled, reportedly due to problems with Freddie's voice.

This tour saw Queen playing to larger audiences, though the transfer from concert halls to arenas and stadia wouldn't come into full effect until later in the year. The band did get to perform at the legendary Madison Square Garden during this tour, the first – and certainly not the last – time they would appear there. Not every night was a massive success, though:

due to the frigid temperatures, audiences were often a little more riled up than usual; in Chicago, they were downright irate. During 'The Millionaire Waltz', a dozen eggs were thrown on stage, resulting in Brian slipping and injuring his tailbone. The band stopped mid-performance and left the stage, conferring to continue regardless of the disruption, and came back on 15 minutes later. Freddie angrily admonished the audience ("Listen, you motherfuckers, we don't have to play for you if we don't want to! But for the other 99% of you who want to see the show, we'll continue.") and the band picked up where they left off. Brian was in considerable pain, though, and the only encore of the night was 'Now I'm Here'.

Queen fulfilled one of their dreams by playing at Madison Square Garden on this tour. It was at this concert that Brian flew his father, Harold, over (on a Concorde jet, no less; Harold was a technical civil servant and had actually designed the blind landing equipment), and Brian later remembered with particular emotion at the pride he felt in his father witnessing his trade, which Harold didn't necessarily approve of: "[He] understood the force and the fulfillment there was for me. He said, 'I'm so envious because I shut that part of me out of my life. You've achieved more in your life than I ever will'. It was a terrible moment. I felt very sad and thought about it for a long time. So I went back and had another conversation with him, explaining that his life had enabled me to do what I was doing. It wasn't long before he died, so it was important to straighten that stuff out. I only realise now how much pain I caused my dad."

As usual, reviews of the tour were mixed, and while the audience reaction was always wild, critical notices weren't. A reviewer in Dallas missed the point entirely: "Considering that Queen is one of the most popular shows around – and you certainly couldn't argue with the enthusiasm of the crowd at Moody Coliseum last Friday – it seemed odd that the best this third-generation rock band could come up with was an array of rock cliches from the first generation ... [This] could be easily forgiven, of course, if the performers indicated it was all in fun like, say, Kiss does. On the contrary, Queen not only took themselves dead seriously, but appeared to mock the crowd for doing likewise." *The Montreal Gazette* was downright savage. "Queen's sound was even more offensive because the group has been hyped as something more dynamic. One sensed that the only way their 'music' is to be

performed night after night is by sheer memorization. The changes of tempo are so quick – and so facile. There was nothing there but mundane technique, the kind that can be rehearsed and repeated ad nauseum ... Queen is propelled by the sound of its own success. Thus there is flashing, blinking lighting, phoney smoke and all the easily purchased gimmicks one comes to expect from a 'glitter rock' ensemble ... Audiences are baited to be carried away by the clockwork energy of performance which is why it hardly matters whether Queen turns it on or not."

The New York Times was complimentary, albeit reluctantly: "If commerciality is your criterion, it's hard to complain; Queen has sold a lot of records. But live, the group rocks out in a more direct manner, and the virtue of on-the-spot wizardry to recommend them. Within the not always congenial context of this kind of artsified progressive rock, Queen gives a good show, slick and solidly crafted." Boston's *The Tech* also had kind words: "Queen showed a sell out crowd at the Boston Garden Wednesday night that their concerts can be as amusing and elegant as their studio work. From the first rush of fog to 'God Save The Queen', their show was an impressive combination of technical wizardry and wryly sophisticated theatrics."

Typically, the West Coast was the most impressed with Queen's show, with the *LA Times* raving, "The band's lavishly-designed, strikingly executed show confirmed its place at the forefront of the third wave of the English rock groups. Queen has more power than the Electric Light Orchestra, more accessibility than Genesis, more range than Bad Company ... Queen has the basic rock stylebook down so pat that it has even picked up some of the pretentiousness and excesses of other bands. But none of the familiar patterns has kept the band from asserting its own identity. The group may lean on various proven styles, but it always gives the music a distinctive touch." In Seattle, the reviewer was positively overjoyed with the show: "It was majestic. It was regal, full of pomp and circumstance. And it was gaudy, mad and make-believe. Which is as it should have been, for last night at the Arena a capacity audience was in the court of Queen, the delightfully clever but slightly balmy British rock group. The group is known for its high energy, wall-of-sound, full-force performances and last night it delivered. It was a lot like other Queen shows here but stronger, more forceful than before. It was full tilt rock 'n' roll, 90 minutes of intense, draining, hard-driving music."

Queen were so taken with the reception that they

would return to the States for a second full-length tour in November, this time with a completely different show.

A DAY AT THE RACES EUROPEAN TOUR:
8 TO 19 MAY 1977

Musicians: John Deacon *(bass guitar, triangle on 'Killer Queen'),* Brian May *(guitar, vocals, banjo on 'Bring Back That Leroy Brown', acoustic guitar on "39'),* Freddie Mercury *(vocals, piano, tambourine),* Roger Taylor *(drums, vocals, bass drum and tambourine on "39')*

Repertoire: 'Intro', 'Tie Your Mother Down', 'Ogre Battle', 'White Queen (As It Began)', 'Somebody To Love', 'Killer Queen' / 'Good Old-Fashioned Lover Boy' / 'The Millionaire Waltz' / 'You're My Best Friend' / 'Bring Back That Leroy Brown', 'Death On Two Legs (Dedicated to......', 'Sweet Lady', 'Brighton Rock', "39', 'You Take My Breath Away', 'White Man', 'The Prophet's Song', 'Bohemian Rhapsody', 'Stone Cold Crazy', 'Keep Yourself Alive', 'In The Lap Of The Gods... Revisited', 'Now I'm Here', 'Liar', 'Jailhouse Rock', 'God Save The Queen', 'Saturday Night's Alright For Fighting', 'Stupid Cupid', 'Be Bop A Lula', 'Doing All Right'

Itinerary:
May 8: Ice Stadium, Stockholm, Sweden
May 10: Scandinavium, Gothenburg, Sweden
May 12: Broendby Hall, Copenhagen, Denmark
May 13: Congresscentrum, Hamburg, Germany
May 14: Jahrunderhalle, Frankfurt, Germany
May 16: Philipshalle, Düsseldorf, Germany
May 17: Ahoy Hall, Rotterdam, Holland
May 19: Sporthalle, Basle, Switzerland

Queen hadn't toured Europe since December 1974, and a lot had changed in the intervening two-and-a-half years. In order to ensure decent ticket sales, the band scheduled a brief tour through Sweden, Denmark, Germany, Holland and Switzerland, performing eight shows in eight cities over a two-week period. The set list remained largely unchanged except for the additions of 'Good Old-Fashioned Lover Boy' to the medley and 'Death On Two Legs (Dedicated to......' following it, though John Deacon had reported in the spring 1977 issue of the Queen fan club magazine that "we hope to include material from our forthcoming album, if we have time to rehearse it well enough before we hit the road."

The band were relieved when tickets for the eight shows sold out reasonably quickly, with the penultimate show in Rotterdam (their second ever appearance in Holland) selling out within an hour of going on sale. Following the show, the band appeared at an EMI reception held aboard a boat in which Queen were rewarded with 38 silver, gold and platinum discs for record sales in the country. The tour concluded in Basle on 19 May, and the band had only a brief period in which to relax before moving on to a tour of their home country.

A DAY AT THE RACES UK TOUR:
23 MAY TO 7 JUNE 1977

Musicians: John Deacon *(bass guitar, triangle on 'Killer Queen'),* Brian May *(guitar, vocals, banjo on 'Bring Back That Leroy Brown', acoustic guitar on "39'),* Freddie Mercury *(vocals, piano, tambourine),* Roger Taylor *(drums, vocals, bass drum and tambourine on "39')*

Repertoire: 'Intro', 'Tie Your Mother Down', 'Ogre Battle', 'White Queen (As It Began)', 'Somebody To Love', 'Killer Queen' / 'Good Old-Fashioned Lover Boy' / 'The Millionaire Waltz' / 'You're My Best Friend' / 'Bring Back That Leroy Brown', 'Death On Two Legs (Dedicated to......', 'Sweet Lady', 'Brighton Rock', "39', 'You Take My Breath Away', 'White Man', 'The Prophet's Song', 'Bohemian Rhapsody', 'Stone Cold Crazy', 'Keep Yourself Alive', 'In The Lap Of The Gods... Revisited', 'Now I'm Here', 'Liar', 'Jailhouse Rock', 'God Save The Queen', 'Saturday Night's Alright For Fighting', 'Stupid Cupid', 'Be Bop A Lula', 'Doing All Right', 'I'm A Man', 'Mannish Boy', 'Lucille', 'Procession'

Itinerary:
May 23/24: Hippodrome, Bristol
May 26/27: Gaumont, Southampton
May 29: Bingley Hall, Stafford
May 30/31: Apollo Theatre, Glasgow
June 2/3: Empire Theatre, Liverpool
June 6/7: Earl's Court Arena, London

The set list for Queen's first tour in the UK since September 1976 hadn't changed from the European leg, though 'I'm A Man', 'Mannish Boy' and 'Lucille' all made rare appearances; the *Queen II* track 'Procession' replaced the *A Day At The Races* guitar intro as the opening music played on the PA system for the two Earl's Court Arena shows. In Greg Brooks' *Queen Live:*

A Concert Documentary, he states that 'Mull Of Kintyre' was performed during the Liverpool concerts in June, but this is improbable, given that Paul McCartney and Denny Laine wouldn't even write the song until August.

This tour saw Queen, and especially Freddie, at their most regal, obviously taking pride in being back on home turf after travelling to all corners of the world. The two final dates at Earl's Court Arena were treated as the band's true homecoming: Led Zeppelin had sold out five nights there two years earlier, and it was seen at the time as *the* place for a band to play. They pulled out all the stops for the last night of their UK tour, with a brand new lighting rig in the shape of a crown – an appropriate gesture, considering it was Queen Elizabeth II's Silver Jubilee that year. Realizing the significance, the band recorded and filmed both shows with the intention of releasing the result as their first live album and video, but the idea was dropped, ostensibly so that Queen could work on *News Of The World* instead.

This marked the height of Queen's total disconnect from the press. With punk and New Wave displacing the old wave, one-time supporters of Queen suddenly became detractors, and took every opportunity to rake the band over the coals. At least *Record Mirror*'s review of the Southampton show was positive: "As stage super egos go, [Freddie's] must be one of the largest – but why not? He's got a great voice and he's one of the very best rock pianists around ... After kicking off with 'Tie Your Mother Down', Queen trod a little uncertainly at first with some dangerous lapses in the show's pace and mood. Happily, about two-thirds of the way through the two hour show they went into 'Bohemian Rhapsody' and suddenly everything clicked. From then on the atmosphere was electric. The concert had crossed that invisible barrier that separates the good from the great and became the kind of evening no one would forget for a long time." The Earl's Court review, too, from the same magazine was positive: "Mercury, his face one minute angelic and sweet, the next evil and dark, spits the lyrics [to 'Stone Cold Crazy'] out at you. Dry ice billows over the stage floor as they move into overdrive for 'In The Lap Of The Gods' and the place is filled with May's guitar work as he displays his supersonic style. Mercury moves to the front of the stage tossing red and white carnations out to the tentacles of hands that plead for them and him. Then with one more almighty flash, the stage is left empty – they've gone! More, more, more, more and hand clapping gathers momentum, screams and shouts echo around the gigantic hall as they step back on to the stage. Launching into 'Liar', May, his face streaming sweat, pushes out a guitar solo that many a person would be envious of."

Not all was rosy, though. *Melody Maker* was especially vicious of the band's performance at the Bristol Hippodrome: "On the evidence of this gig, at least, there was little to suggest that [the band] still tackled their set with any serious degree of commitment or genuine enthusiasm, with the result that their much-vaunted effects seemed wholly excessive, and their music hollow and wimpish. A case of innumerable layers of gloss and veneer wrapped around a band doing little more than going through the motions, an experience that's about as entertaining as a knee in the groin." *The Times* was dismissive of Earl's Court: "I had hoped to fly in the face of fashion and give last night's concert an enthusiastic notice. It turned out to be one of those events that justify the emergence of the new wave bands, the triumph of technology over music. Queen have long been accused of being mere technicians and certainly their exploitation of a phenomenal barrage of equipment was quite breathtaking ... But, as befits our national condition, everything was over inflated. The lighting, although magnificently timed and controlled, began to take over the music; the barrage of smoke bombs, Freddie Mercury's costume changes, including one that must have been a Shirley Bassey reject, and his cavorting round the stage, all seemed imposed on the songs to make them more entertaining ... Through all the noise, which for this hall was reasonably good, and all the superficial excitement, I felt there was a coldness on stage, not to the performance, but to the music itself, as if this was just another way to fill an evening."

While their critical appreciation was at an all-time low, the fans couldn't have been more enthusiastic. In Stafford, the band were stunned to hear the audience singing 'You'll Never Walk Alone' in the interim between the regular set and the encore. Written by Rodgers and Hammerstein and from the 1945 musical *Carousel*, the song was adapted by fans of the Liverpool Football Club in the early 1960s, and was immediately synonymous with staunch loyalty. "The audience was responding hugely, and they were singing along with everything we did," an emotional Brian later recalled. "I remember talking to Freddie about it, and I said, 'Obviously, we can no longer fight this. This has to be something which is part of our show and we have to embrace it,' the fact that people want to participate – and, in fact, everything becomes a two-way process now. And we sort of looked at each other and went, 'Hmm. How interesting'." The two responded to this by writing the ultimate audience participation anthems: 'We Will Rock You' and 'We Are The Champions'.

'WE ARE THE CHAMPIONS' VIDEO SHOOT:
6 OCTOBER 1977

Musicians: John Deacon *(bass guitar)*, Brian May *(guitar, vocals)*, Freddie Mercury *(vocals, piano, tambourine)*, Roger Taylor *(drums, vocals)*

Repertoire: 'Tie Your Mother Down', 'Keep Yourself Alive', 'Somebody To Love', 'White Man', 'The Prophet's Song', 'Liar', 'Bohemian Rhapsody' / 'Now I'm Here', 'Jailhouse Rock', 'See What A Fool I've Been'

In anticipation of the single release of 'We Are The Champions', the Queen fan club sent out a notice to members that they were invited to attend the filming of their promotional video at New London Theatre in Drury Lane. Despite the last-minute invitation, 900 fans showed up and displayed their enthusiasm for five takes of the video; as a thank you, the band performed a special 10-song mini-concert, featuring the rare inclusion of 'See What A Fool I've Been' as the final song.

Bob Harris and his film crew were on hand to shoot some footage for a proposed documentary, which remained unreleased for 40 years, before being assembled and edited into a spectacular feature on the deluxe box set edition of *News Of The World*, released in 2017. The band were more relaxed and loose than they had ever been before, with the intimacy of the setting harkening back to their up-and-coming years earlier in the decade. A truly unique medley of 'Bohemian Rhapsody' and 'Now I'm Here' was played, due to the absence of backing tapes: following Brian's guitar solo, and just before the operatic section, the band launched right into the *Sheer Heart Attack* number. Given that Queen were between tours, they turned in an absolutely spectacular performance, one that's just crying out for release in some form.

NEWS OF THE WORLD NORTH AMERICAN TOUR:
11 NOVEMBER TO 22 DECEMBER 1977

Musicians: John Deacon *(bass guitar, fretless bass on "39' and 'My Melancholy Blues', triangle on 'Killer Queen')*, Brian May *(guitar, vocals, acoustic guitar on 'Love Of My Life' and "39')*, Freddie Mercury *(vocals, piano, tambourine)*, Roger Taylor *(drums, vocals, lead vocals on 'I'm In Love With My Car', bass drum and tambourine on "39')*

Repertoire: 'We Will Rock You' (slow/fast), 'Brighton Rock', 'Somebody To Love', 'Death On Two Legs (Dedicated to......' / 'Killer Queen' / 'Good Old-Fashioned Lover Boy' / 'I'm In Love With My Car' / 'Get Down, Make Love' / 'The Millionaire Waltz' / 'You're My Best Friend', 'Spread Your Wings', 'It's Late', 'Liar', 'Love Of My Life', "39', 'My Melancholy Blues', 'White Man', 'Instrumental Inferno', 'The Prophet's Song', 'Now I'm Here', 'Stone Cold Crazy', 'Bohemian Rhapsody', 'Tie Your Mother Down', 'We Will Rock You', 'We Are The Champions', 'Sheer Heart Attack', 'Jailhouse Rock', 'God Save The Queen', 'Keep Yourself Alive', 'Doing All Right', 'Ogre Battle', 'Sleeping On The Sidewalk', 'White Christmas'

Itinerary:
November 11: Cumberland County Civic Center, Portland, Maine
November 12: Boston Gardens, Boston, Massachusetts
November 13: Civic Center, Springfield, Massachusetts
November 15: Civic Center, Providence, Rhode Island
November 16: Memorial Coliseum, New Haven, Connecticut
November 18/19: Cobo Hall, Detroit, Michigan
November 21: Maple Leaf Gardens, Toronto, Ontario
November 23/24: The Spectrum, Philadelphia, Pennsylvania
November 25: Scope Arena, Norfolk, Virginia
November 27: Richfield Coliseum, Cleveland, Ohio
November 29: Capitol Center, Washington, D.C.
December 1/2: Madison Square Garden, New York, New York
December 4: University Arena, Dayton, Ohio
December 5: Chicago Stadium, Chicago, Illinois
December 8: The Omni, Atlanta, Georgia
December 10: Tarrant County Convention Center, Fort Worth, Texas
December 12: The Summit, Houston, Texas
December 15: Aladdin Center, Las Vegas, Nevada
December 16: Sports Arena, San Diego, California
December 17: County Coliseum, Oakland, California
December 20/21: Long Beach Arena, Long Beach, California
December 22: Inglewood Forum, Los Angeles, California

The musical climate had shifted dramatically in 1977, with punk and new wave suddenly competing for attention in the hit parade. This stylistic sea change affected Queen only marginally, though they were aware that they couldn't keep doing the bombastic, overly-produced albums they had been famous for. *News Of The World* was their response to the stripped-back *modus operandi* of the year, and, in an effort to prevent themselves from waffling on too much in the studio, they booked a six-week North American tour for November 1977. Once the new album was completed, the band started rehearsals during the last week of October at Shepperton Studios with a completely revised set list. Gone was 'Tie Your Mother Down' as the opener (instead becoming the final performance before the encores), while 'White Queen (As It Began)', 'Ogre Battle' and 'Sweet Lady' were all dropped permanently. Instead, the band added an exciting new rendition of 'We Will Rock You', restructured from the stripped back original into a blazing rock performance, opened the shows, while other *News Of The World* tracks – 'Get Down, Make Love', 'Spread Your Wings', 'It's Late', 'My Melancholy Blues', 'Sheer Heart Attack' and 'We Are The Champions' – were sprinkled liberally throughout the set, offering a good representation of the new stylistic changes on their latest release.

The medley, too, benefited from a minor shake-up, with Roger's 'I'm In Love With My Car' added, marking the first time that Roger provided lead vocals on his own composition, and would become a live favorite for the next four years. While Brian and Roger would continue to sing their own compositions on *Jazz* and *The Game*, Roger would be the only member of the band to get a solo vocal spot in the live shows. Lucky for Brian, then, that his solo came in the form of a nightly guitar showcase, which showed no signs of exiting the set at any time. Strangely, 'Brighton Rock' would become the second performance of the night, and only then would it be performed almost exactly as it was on *Sheer Heart Attack*. Brian's solo would come later in the show, following 'White Man', and would make extensive use of the band's massive lights set-up. Unusually, 'We Will Rock You' and 'We Are The Champions' did not conclude the shows; instead, 'Sheer Heart Attack' and 'Jailhouse Rock' would be the final songs, remaining so until May 1978, though the band would occasionally change the order around on subsequent tours.

After rehearsals concluded, the band flew to New Haven, Connecticut, taking over the Metro Coliseum

for final preparations. Their equipment list by now totalled a massive 60 tons, with a specially modified lighting rig resembling a crown that had been premiered at Earl's Court Arena in June. The stage had expanded to include three catwalks and two raised platforms flanking the main stage, a layout the band would use to good effect not only on this tour but on subsequent tours as well.

The band's image had started to change drastically by this point. Freddie hadn't quite yet abandoned the skintight suits, though leather was starting to make its way into his wardrobe; he would generally enter the stage wearing black-and-white diamond-patterned tights beneath an oversized, black leather jacket. The transformation from tights to leather would take place by the time of the *Jazz* tour the following year. Roger and Brian's look hardly changed, with both preferring comfortable clothing as opposed to Freddie's flashier threads. John, too, had abandoned the overalls he had worn on the previous tour for a more subdued appearance, though his hair had changed dramatically: some time before the *News Of The World* sessions started in July, he had chosen to crop his hair severely, causing both band and crew to refer to him as The Birdman (of Alcatraz).

The tour started on 11 November in Portland, Maine and was notable for the first of two known performances of Brian's 'Sleeping On The Sidewalk', with Freddie on vocals (a live rendition was finally released on the 2017 deluxe box set edition of *News Of The World*); the song would be performed infrequently during the first few dates of the tour before being retired permanently. One of the other new additions was far more successful and stuck around for many years: Freddie's *A Night At The Opera* masterpiece, 'Love Of My Life', was premiered at this show as well, and was performed differently from the album version. Brian and Freddie would be perched on stools front and center, with Brian on an acoustic guitar and Freddie singing lead vocals; at this stage, it hadn't yet become common for the fans to take over the singing of this song.

Following Portland, the tour wound its way through north-eastern America, though Queen were travelling in style this time around: they had been able to afford their own private jet, which was agreed to with some slight resistance since commercial flights were considered to be a far safer alternative. The band flew to Norfolk, Virginia after their performance at The Spectrum in Philadelphia on 24 November to attend a showing of artist Frank Kelly Freas, who had painted the reworking of the *News Of The World* album sleeve.

The following week saw their first appearance of the tour at Madison Square Garden, and it proved to be a momentous performance. When he bounded on stage for the first encore of 'We Will Rock You' and 'We Are The Champions', Freddie donned a jacket and hat with New York Yankees logos, much to the appreciation of the audience. That baseball team had just won the World Series and had adopted 'We Are The Champions' as their team song; Freddie's gesture was all too appropriate, and the band's first encore was suitably extended to allow for more audience participation.

Because the tour dates were taking place in late November and early December, the climate was unpredictable in the northern states, many concerts coming close to cancelation as a result. One interesting example occurred at the University Of Dayton in Ohio on 4 December. University officials deemed the weather too dangerous and duly canceled, but the band insisted on performing anyway. The band went on to play to 2000 appreciative fans, just 800 short of capacity.

On 8 December 8, the BBC's 'Whispering' Bob Harris arrived in Texas (while the band were in Atlanta) with a film crew to cover Queen's two shows in the Lonestar State: one at the Tarrant County Convention Center in Fort Worth on 10 December, another the following evening at The Summit in Houston. The resulting footage was intended for a documentary that was apparently never completed; while the Houston show was filmed and would later be shown at Fan Club conventions over the years, the closest any of the material came to official release would be on the 1989 *Rare Live* video collection. The performance at The Summit has often been regarded as not only Queen's finest show of the tour, but of their entire career. Though that judgment doesn't take into account a multitude of guitar problems, the band were definitely on top form that night, and it remains a shame that the show has yet to be officially released.

Unfortunately, the backlash against Queen had taken control of the American press, and this tour didn't find favor with many critics. *The Tech* wrote of their Boston show, "It took very little to please the largely high-school-aged crowd, and Queen complied by putting out a mediocre effort ... As Mercury took his final bow, he announced, 'It's been a pleasure doing business with you all'. And a poor business it was. Technically, the concert was marred by poor sound quality, and awful lighting work from the spotlight crew. The group's choice of songs was also poor, favoring the newer, campier Mercury-authored tunes instead of the tighter solid rockers. After the concert had ended, someone in the audience remarked, 'Queen's hard rock days are gone'." *The Hartford Courant* was equally unimpressed: "Queen, the British rock quartet, attacked a packed New Haven Coliseum Wednesday night with a barrage of ear-splitting guitar blasts and vibrant vocal squeals. But between the heavy-metal assaults the group also found time for the ricky-tick piano ditties and pop hymns that are its claims to fame ... Except for a couple of lapses into too-loud guitar crunching, Queen performed admirably – even without the lush sound of their records." "While it rained steadily outside, inside Queen reigned unsteadily over the Capital Centre in a solo concert that, in addition to beginning 45 minutes late, was more glitter than gold," *The Washington Post* sneered. "The concert ranged from the musically humdrum to the theatrically manic. Enthroned beneath a silver and black crown, 20 by 54 feet by 46 feet, their music too often became an irrelevancy. Their manic energy seemed forced; their flamboyance lacked finesse." *The LA Times*, however, walked away pleased: "The rock concert scene may have started sluggishly in '77, but it's ending with a stir. There was Aerosmith's snarl last month, Rod Stewart's rejoice last week and now: Queen. Already hailed as the best of the mid-'70s British arrivals, Queen is back with its most spectacularly staged and finely honed show yet. Coupled with its stylish new *News Of The World* album, the tour should push the classy foursome even further into forefront of contemporary rock bands ... Freddie Mercury, the band's flashy lead singer and occasional pianist, sang and moved with more confidence and dynamics than ever. Wearing a black and white Harlequin outfit open to the waist, Mercury pranced around the stage in a way that gave the band's already dramatic numbers even added lure and punch. When he sings potent, upbeat tunes like 'Liar', there are few in rock who can match Mercury's vocal bit. But he's equally satisfying on softer, more tender numbers."

With only four concerts left, a tipsy John shoved his right hand through a plate-glass window at the after-show party; despite 19 stitches and a bulky bandage, he was still able to perform the remaining shows with no cancelations or rescheduling necessary. On 22 December, the final date of the 1977 US tour and only three days before Christmas, the band treated the audience to something special: during the acoustic segment, Freddie told the audience, "We've kind of cooked up something in the dressing room we've never ever done before." Brian and Freddie then performed an acoustic rendition of 'White Christmas', truly a one-off as the band would never perform any other holiday songs live; even 'Thank God It's Christmas' wouldn't be attempted. A recording of this performance finally surfaced in 2017, and it's truly a beautiful and heartfelt rendition.

To add to the festive mood, 5000 balloons were released into the audience, though the real surprise came at the conclusion of the night. For the second encore, the band's bodyguard, dressed as Father Christmas, walked onto the stage with a huge sack slung round his shoulder, out of which jumped Freddie to lead the band through 'Sheer Heart Attack' and 'Jailhouse Rock'. Also joining the band on stage were the director of EMI as a gingerbread man, John Reid as an elf, three professional dancers, and members of the road crew as an assortment of festive characters, including reindeer, clowns, and walking Christmas trees – a suitable way to end one of Queen's most successful years.

1978

NEWS OF THE WORLD EUROPEAN & UK TOUR:
12 APRIL TO 13 MAY 1978

Musicians: John Deacon *(bass guitar, fretless bass on ''39' and 'My Melancholy Blues', triangle on 'Killer Queen')*, Brian May *(guitar, vocals, acoustic guitar on 'Love Of My Life' and ''39')*, Freddie Mercury *(vocals, piano, tambourine)*, Roger Taylor *(drums, vocals, lead vocals on 'I'm In Love With My Car', bass drum and tambourine on ''39')*

Repertoire: 'We Will Rock You' (slow/fast), 'Brighton Rock', 'Somebody To Love', 'Death On Two Legs (Dedicated to......' / 'Killer Queen' / 'Good Old-Fashioned Lover Boy' / 'I'm In Love With My Car' / 'Get Down, Make Love' / 'The Millionaire Waltz' / 'You're My Best Friend', 'Spread Your Wings', 'It's Late', 'Liar', 'Love Of My Life', ''39', 'My Melancholy Blues', 'White Man', 'Instrumental Inferno', 'The Prophet's Song', 'Now I'm Here', 'Stone Cold Crazy', 'Bohemian Rhapsody', 'Tie Your Mother Down', 'We Will Rock You', 'We Are The Champions', 'Sheer Heart Attack', 'Jailhouse Rock', 'God Save The Queen', 'Big Spender', 'White Queen (As It Began)'

Itinerary:
April 12: Ice Stadium, Stockholm, Sweden
April 13: Falkoner Theatre, Copenhagen, Denmark
April 14: Ernst Merck Halle, Hamburg, Germany
April 16/17: Forêt Nationale, Brussels, Belgium
April 19/20: Ahoy Hall, Rotterdam, Holland
April 21: Forêt Nationale, Brussels, Belgium
April 23/24: Pavillion de Paris, Paris, France
April 26: Westfallenhalle, Dortmund, Germany
April 28: Deutschlandhalle, Berlin, Germany
April 30: Hallenstadion, Zurich, Switzerland
May 2: Stadthalle, Vienna, Austria
May 3: Olympiahalle, Munich, Germany
May 6/7: New Bingley Hall, Stafford
May 11-13: Empire Pool, London

The band flew home to their families on 24 December 1977 and, after such an exhausting year, had a few months to themselves. Indeed, Queen would perform no concerts until 12 April, their longest break from touring since their formation. When they did finally take to the stage again in Stockholm, the set list hadn't changed since the North American tour, though both 'Spread Your Wings' and 'It's Late' were a permanent part of the set list and the order was shuffled only marginally, depending on the night.

In Copenhagen, the band's massive lighting rig was unable to be used at the Falkoner Theatre, so they had to make do with only the basic lights. A similar situation would arise in Hamburg the following night, but the rig was back to its full glory for the remainder of the tour. In Brussels, while the crown was rising, two of the switches used to lift the rig failed, resulting in a false start that forced the band to leave the stage and the effect to start over. Brian recalled in 2012, "We had, at the time, this huge lighting rig in the shape of a crown, because we were Queen, right? At the beginning of the show it was down on the deck. It's down on the stage as a sort of introduction to the show. We played with a sort of intro tape or whatever, and lots of smoke came out and it lifted off like a rocket from the stage. At this point we're underneath it because we're getting ready to play. It's powered by these chain hoist things; it's not actually rocket powered, you know. So on this particular occasion they wired up the chain hoists wrong, and I was on the side that went down and I was like, 'Oh, fuck! Let's get out of here real quick'. Looking back on it, it was amusing, but at the time it was a little scary. It's a definite Spinal Tap moment." He later likened the moment to the sinking Titanic: "We went, 'Do we preserve our dignity or our lives here?' It turned out to be one of those things, as often happens, which was special and very nice, because when we eventually get back on and do it properly there was this great bond between us and the audience, because they realized that we're human and stuff can go wrong. It was one of the greater nights that I remember. It was a really good night."

A third date was added in Brussels on 21 April, with the band returning to the Forêt Nationale since it was the largest concert hall in the city and the first two shows had sold out so quickly that the promoters needed to meet the demand. However, Queen's biggest coup would come two days later, when they made their debut in France. That country hadn't initially been receptive to the band, but when 'We Are The Champions' was released there the previous year, it (coupled with its flip, 'We Will Rock You') stayed at the top spot for a mighty 24 weeks in all. It was this boost of confidence that made the Parisian concerts so memorable, and the band would return on several occasions thereafter, though not as frequently as they would to Germany and Belgium.

The tour wound its way through Germany, Switzerland, Austria (for the first time, to a rapturous response) and back through Germany again before the last five concerts of the tour, which took place in Stafford and London. These would be the band's only British shows of the year, and they wouldn't return to their home field until November 1979. During the first night's performance in Bingley of 'Love Of My Life', Freddie stopped singing and let the vociferous audience take over, inaugurating a tradition that would stay in place for the remainder of Queen's live career. The last three shows in London were reportedly recorded for a potential live release, but the material went unused. A shame, considering 'White Queen (As It Began)' was brought out of mothballs, and the band finally decided to switch around the encores, beginning the tradition of ending shows with 'We Will Rock You' and 'We Are The Champions'.

Reviews were rather vicious, with the only positive one coming from *The Birmingham Evening Mail*: "Their highnesses deigned to give audience to their adoring subjects 35 minutes late. But what's that to the converted thousands, many of whom have been queuing since the previous day? Their arrival, accompanied by majestic music of the spheres and a fair representation of a spaceship take-off, transforms what should be a pop concert into more of a rock mass

… The regal quartet have style and swagger, and the skill to accompany it, as they pulsate their way through their rhythmic hymnal. The show is ostentatious, exciting and the only lull as they skip from heavy, to light and fantastic, is during indulgent guitar and vocal solos which are electronic exercises rather than music." Freddie was less than pleased with the British press, dedicating 'Death On Two Legs' to them with a few rather unsavory words: "[They've taken] a lot of beating the last couple of nights from us," he noted, calling them "fucking wankers" and that they "eat shit in the bath." *Record Mirror* called this out in their review of the Wembley Arena show: "Oooh, he just couldn't stand it anymore. It was hot on stage and those tight trousers were probably killing him. Queen have been working tremendously hard and all they've been getting from the press is a selection of slag offs. So Fred just had to stamp his little feet and say something. But horrors, such vitriol from somebody normally so refined. We can't print what he actually said, but he used the slang word for intercourse and a word ruder than *masturbation*. Queen have been reeling from more than a few punches over the past year. It started with a gentle slap about the face, then a few blows to the chest before a full heated blow to the groin. To write nice things about Queen is considered positively passé. But it's true Queen aren't moving on, they're still relying on the golden oldies to get the crowd going. But the fans are still dedicated – the chaff having been discarded for a hardcore following. For the time being Queen can afford to put on a show that was largely similar to last year's but in 12 months they're going to have to rethink and the next album could be make or break time."

JAZZ NORTH AMERICAN TOUR:
28 OCTOBER TO 20 DECEMBER 1978

Musicians: John Deacon (*bass guitar, fretless bass on "39'* *and 'My Melancholy Blues'*), Brian May (*guitar, vocals, acoustic guitar on 'Love Of My Life' and "39'*), Freddie Mercury (*vocals, piano, tambourine*), Roger Taylor (*drums, vocals, lead vocals on 'I'm In Love With My Car', bass drum and tambourine on "39'*)

Repertoire: 'We Will Rock You' (*fast*), 'Let Me Entertain You', 'Somebody To Love', 'If You Can't Beat Them', 'Death On Two Legs (Dedicated to......' / 'Killer Queen' / 'Bicycle Race' / 'I'm In Love With My Car' / 'Get Down, Make Love' / 'You're My Best Friend', 'Now I'm Here',

'Spread Your Wings', 'Dreamers Ball', 'Love Of My Life', "39", 'It's Late', 'Brighton Rock', 'Fat Bottomed Girls', 'Fun It' *(intro)* / 'Keep Yourself Alive', 'Bohemian Rhapsody', 'Tie Your Mother Down', 'Sheer Heart Attack', 'We Will Rock You', 'We Are The Champions', 'God Save The Queen', 'Jailhouse Rock', 'Big Spender'

Itinerary:
October 28: Convention Center, Dallas, Texas
October 29: Mid-South Coliseum, Memphis, Tennessee
October 31: Civic Auditorium, New Orleans, Louisiana
November 3: Sportorium, Miami, Florida
November 4: Civic Center, Lakeland, Florida
November 6: Capitol Center, Washington, D.C.
November 7: New Haven Coliseum, New Haven, Connecticut
November 9/10: Cobo Arena, Detroit, Michigan
November 11: Wings Stadium, Kalamazoo, Michigan
November 13: Boston Gardens, Boston, Massachusetts
November 14: Civic Center, Providence, Rhode Island
November 16/17: Madison Square Garden, New York, New York
November 19: Nassau Coliseum, Uniondale, Long Island, New York
November 20: The Spectrum, Philadelphia, Pennsylvania
November 22: Nashville Auditorium, Nashville, Tennessee
November 23: Checkerdome, St Louis, Missouri
November 25: Richfield Coliseum, Cleveland, Ohio
November 26: Riverfront Coliseum, Cincinnati, Ohio
November 28: War Memorial Auditorium, Buffalo, New York
November 30: Central Canadian Exhibition Center, Ottawa, Ontario
December 1: The Forum, Montreal, Quebec
December 3/4: Maple Leaf Garden, Toronto, Ontario
December 6: Dane County Coliseum, Madison, Wisconsin
December 7: Chicago Stadium, Chicago, Illinois
December 8: Kemper Arena, Kansas City, Missouri
December 12: Seattle Coliseum, Seattle, Washington
December 13: Portland Coliseum, Portland, Oregon
December 14: PNE Coliseum, Vancouver, British Columbia
December 16: Oakland Coliseum, Oakland, California
December 18-20: Inglewood Forum, Los Angeles, California

With *Jazz* in the can and ready to be released, Queen embarked on another lengthy trek of North America in October 1978, with the band once again restructuring their set list and delivering a new lighting rig that was a far cry from the massive "crown" of the previous tour: rows of green and red lights now hovered close to the stage before rising when the band made their entrance, which earned the affectionate nickname of The Pizza Oven due to the tremendous heat it gave off. The band incorporated several new songs from the yet-to-be-released *Jazz* album ('Let Me Entertain You', 'Bicycle Race', 'If You Can't Beat Them', 'Dreamers Ball' and 'Fat Bottomed Girls'), but by this point in their career their popularity had increased to the point that they had to cater to the average singles-buyer instead of their die-hard fans; gone were the quirkier songs of yesteryear, as well as anything from *Queen II* (though fans were heard to shout for 'Ogre Battle', 'Flick Of The Wrist', and even 'Jesus') and instead was a fast-paced rock show, with Freddie taking the words of 'Let Me Entertain You' to heart, turning a concert into a spectacle.

The years of playing live together had paid off in dividends, and the band became a more confident unit, with the already-tight rhythm section of Roger and John becoming so connected to one another that they would freely bounce off one another's groove, which allowed Brian the freedom to experiment musically without worrying about the rhythm tapering off. The band would often stretch songs out well beyond their breaking point, and both Brian and Freddie would extemporize on guitar and vocals during their respective showcases. The set may have lost some of the idosyncratic songs that defined the band's earlier repertoire, but Freddie became more of a natural entertainer, and the band played off of that in exciting ways.

The tour opened in Dallas on 28 October, and introduced not only the new lighting rig, but also a smaller stage – a precursor of what is now known as the B-stage – that was lowered from above, with a bare-bones drum set and three stools; the band would perform 'Dreamers Ball', 'Love Of My Life', and "39" in this intimate setting, though the concept wouldn't stick around past the following year's Japanese tour. Roger also insisted on not only a short drum solo during 'Brighton Rock', but also a timpani showcase directly afterward, an indulgence that would be represented on *Live Killers* the following year, and would remain a staple until 1981.

The set remained fairly static, with only 'Jailhouse Rock' inserted as an encore number in Memphis in honour of Elvis Presley, who had died the previous August. During this tour, Queen's excesses became legendary: during their concert in New Orleans on Halloween, Freddie was in a particularly licentious mood, quipping before 'Love Of My Life' that he was going to go backstage for a rest, "Maybe get a blow-job." Elsewhere, 'Spread Your Wings' was routinely introduced as 'Spread Your Legs', and 'Fat Bottomed Girls' was dedicated to girls – and guys, on the rare occasion – with prodigious posteriors. The Halloween show became the stuff of legend, not necessarily because of the performance itself (which was rather hurried, presumably because the band knew what was to come), but for the aftershow party, which has gone down in Queen lore as one of the most debaucherous nights in their history. (See Part 2 for more information, and decide for yourself what is fact and what is fiction.)

The debauchery only intensified in New York, when the band hit upon a good idea. The poster of 65 nude female cyclists had been withheld from the US issue of *Jazz* due to a public outcry from enraged parents and feminist groups. Having dutifully removed the poster, Roger and members of the road crew scoured local strip clubs to offer the real thing to the audience: as Freddie gleefully howled "Get on your bikes and ride!" during 'Fat Bottomed Girls', five well-endowed strippers came on stage astride their bicycles. Roger later recalled of the spectacle, "We wanted people to think we were having fun and being silly. But there was also a lot of hard work. Trouble is, we got better and better at having a good time."

The Sentinel Star was disappointed with Queen's show: "It is always a bit of a disappointment to go to a rock concert and hear canned music. Even if Queen can't match their lush and complete studio sound in concert, the least the group do is not walk off stage and change clothes while the tape recorder plays 'Bohemian Rhapsody'. Despite the tape, the Saturday night concert at the Lakeland Civic Centre was not all a disappointment ... The computerized lighting system above the stage had 15 rows of lights, with 20 lights per row, that made the stage look alternately like a light-flooded football field and an exotic discotheque. There were nine light men positioned around the auditorium and they had the aim of champion marksmen, never missing an opportunity to enlighten Freddie Mercury, who danced and jumped and pranced around the stage with lightning-fast robot moves that would have made C3PO jealous ... But the show did not get raunchy. The group played three songs from their upcoming album, *Jazz*. Only one of the songs sounded as if it might feel comfortable in New Orleans. The group is much better at rock with intricate electronic sounds than it is at jazz."

The New York Times was equally unimpressed, perhaps because they missed out on the bevy of bicycle-riding beauties. "Queen, which played Madison Square Garden for the first of two consecutive nights on Thursday, is a classic case of a band adored by its fans that is still not a consistently, massively successful group on commercial terms, and not very impressive from a critical – or at least this critical – standpoint, either ... It's hard to care much. Lyrically, Queen's songs manage to be pretentious and irrelevant. Musically, for all the virtuosity – though it was cheating a bit to turn over the complex middle portion of their 'Bohemian Rhapsody' to a taped version, with empty stage and flashing lights – the songs still sound mostly pretty empty, all flash and calculation."

1979

JAZZ EUROPEAN TOUR:
17 JANUARY TO 1 MARCH 1979

Musicians: John Deacon (*bass guitar, fretless bass on "39'* and *'My Melancholy Blues'*), Brian May (*guitar, vocals, acoustic guitar on 'Love Of My Life' and "39'*), Freddie Mercury (*vocals, piano, tambourine*), Roger Taylor (*drums, vocals, lead vocals on 'I'm In Love With My Car', bass drum and tambourine on "39'*)

Repertoire: 'We Will Rock You' *(fast)*, 'Let Me Entertain You', 'Somebody To Love', 'If You Can't Beat Them', 'Death On Two Legs (Dedicated to......)' / 'Killer Queen' / 'Bicycle Race' / 'I'm In Love With My Car' / 'Get Down, Make Love' / 'You're My Best Friend', 'Now I'm Here', 'Don't Stop Me Now', 'Spread Your Wings', 'Dreamers Ball', 'Love Of My Life', ''39', 'It's Late', 'Brighton Rock', 'Keep Yourself Alive', 'Bohemian Rhapsody', 'Tie Your Mother Down', 'Sheer Heart Attack', 'We Will Rock You', 'We Are The Champions', 'God Save The Queen', 'Fat Bottomed Girls', 'Mustapha' *(intro)*, 'Jailhouse Rock', 'Big Spender'

Itinerary:
January 17: Ernst Merckhalle, Hamburg, Germany
January 18: Ostee Hall, Kiel, Germany
January 20: Stadthalle, Bremen, Germany

January 21: Westfallenhalle, Dortmund, Germany
January 23: Messesportspalace, Hannover, Germany
January 24: Deutschlandhalle, Berlin, Germany
January 26/27: Forêt Nationale, Brussels, Belgium
January 29/30: Ahoy Hall, Rotterdam, Holland
February 1: Sportshalle, Cologne, Germany
February 2: Festhalle, Frankfurt, Germany
February 4: Hallenstadium, Zurich, Switzerland
February 6: Dom Sportova, Zagreb, Yugoslavia
February 7: Tivoli Halle, Ljubljana, Yugoslavia
February 10/11: Basketball Halle, Munich, Germany
February 13: Sporthalle Boeblingen, Stuttgart, Germany
February 15: Saalandhalle, Saarbrücken, Germany
February 17: Palais de Sport, Lyon, France
February 19-21: Palacio de Deportef, Barcelona, Spain
February 23: Pabellon del Real Madrid, Madrid, Spain
February 25: Les Arenas, Potiers, France
February 27-March 1: Pavillion de Paris, Paris, France

Jazz hadn't exactly continued with the same amount of success that the band had enjoyed in the first half of the decade, and Queen made a conscious decision to suspend any recording of a new album until they felt comfortable enough to do so, provided the environment proved suitable. As it was, they were preoccupied with the European and Japanese leg of the *Jazz* tour, before which they decided to record enough shows to release their first, long-overdue live album.

In the middle of January, Queen flew to Hamburg to rehearse and shake off the dust, introducing some more material from *Jazz*, notably album opener 'Mustapha' (which would be released as a European-only single due to audience demand) and their current single, 'Don't Stop Me Now'. The tour opened in Hamburg on 17 January, and despite the preparations, Freddie's voice wasn't in its best shape, though he would often laugh it off during the call-and-response vocal section of 'Now I'm Here'. (It would only get more unpredictable over the years, when he took up smoking, more as an affectation than for the habit.) Regardless, the audience was still ecstatic and if they noticed anything was amiss with Freddie's voice, they didn't let on; besides, so boisterous were they that they inevitably drowned out any errors with their singing.

Though the tour focused heavily on Germany, the band still made some debuts, notably in Yugoslavia, and they returned to France, Belgium, Holland, Switzerland, and Spain. Still, the band were firing on

all cylinders on the 2 February concert in Frankfurt, with many of the performances being culled for the upcoming *Live Killers* album. The focus was less on spectacle, as the shows were being recorded and not filmed, though the band reprised the buxom beauties on bicycles routine from Madison Square Garden in Munich, with four local strippers appearing onstage at the conclusion of 'Fat Bottomed Girls'; not everyone was pleased, with local authorities demanding that the naked girls be clothed should the spectacle be repeated the following night. (It was, and they were.)

The Barcelona gig, while enjoyable for fans, wasn't as positively received by the band, with Brian commenting, "I thought last night was not as good as it should've been, for various reasons, and I think tonight will be a lot better. We had very high expectations of last night, but it didn't quite live up to it for us. We had some technical problems and sound problems, and there was a certain untogetherness which we all knew was there but we couldn't really do anything about, you know? We just looked at each other and said, 'Hey, it's not quite clicking'. I don't know, it just seemed a little quiet. The whole thing was a little low key. We're putting a lot of energy into it but it didn't actually seem to come out as big as it should've done. I have to be honest, because I always enjoy playing, and it's always a buzz to play, and yet sometimes you feel that you didn't quite pull it off as you wanted to. When you come off stage you know." Freddie agreed: "I felt they were a bit restrained last night. Maybe they expected something more, because they were reading all the New Orleans stories. They could've been looser, but maybe we're spoiled as well because we've had German and French audiences going absolutely berserk."

The shows in Paris, which wrapped up the tour, were a relative party, with the band pulling out all the stops and letting their hair down. It was here that a faction of fans was dubbed The Royal Family by Freddie; these loyal members would follow the band on this and the Crazy Tours, and while Freddie eventually became irritated at their presence (seeing the same faces in the front row wasn't exactly pleasing, and occasionally the fans would overstep their bounds by threatening the band if they didn't play certain songs they wanted to hear), there was still an air of jocularity at these shows. It also helped that the three concerts were filmed, possibly with the intention of having a visual aspect to the upcoming live album, though the footage was scrapped and wouldn't have made for good cinematic viewing anyway: the first night was filmed by a single camera, though a few more would be made available for the following two nights. This footage was played over many years at Queen fan club conventions, and fans have since clamored for its release, though it will likely remain in Queen's vaults for the foreseeable future.

JAZZ JAPANESE TOUR:
13 APRIL TO 6 MAY 1979

Musicians: John Deacon *(bass guitar, fretless bass on "39'* *and 'My Melancholy Blues'),* Brian May *(guitar, vocals, acoustic guitar on 'Love Of My Life' and "39'),* Freddie Mercury *(vocals, piano, tambourine),* Roger Taylor *(drums, vocals, lead vocals on 'I'm In Love With My Car', bass drum and tambourine on "39')*

Repertoire: 'We Will Rock You' *(fast),* 'Let Me Entertain You', 'Somebody To Love', 'If You Can't Beat Them', 'Death On Two Legs (Dedicated to......' / 'Killer Queen' / 'Bicycle Race' / 'I'm In Love With My Car' / 'Get Down, Make Love' / 'You're My Best Friend', 'Now I'm Here', 'Teo Torriatte (Let Us Cling Together)', 'Don't Stop Me Now', 'Spread Your Wings', 'Dreamers Ball', 'Love Of My Life', "39', 'It's Late', 'Brighton Rock', 'Keep Yourself Alive', 'Bohemian Rhapsody', 'Tie Your Mother Down', 'Sheer Heart Attack', 'We Will Rock You', 'We Are The Champions', 'God Save The Queen', 'Fat Bottomed Girls', 'Mustapha' *(intro),* 'Jailhouse Rock', 'Big Spender'

Itinerary:
April 13/14: Budokan Hall, Tokyo
April 19/20: Festival Hall, Osaka
April 21: Practica Ethics Commemoration Hall, Kanazawa
April 23-25: Budokan Hall, Tokyo
April 27: Central International Display, Kobe
April 28: International Display, Nagoya
April 30/May 1: Kyuden Athletic Association, Fukuoka
May 2: Prefectural Athletic Association, Yamaguchi
May 5/6: Makomani Ice Arena, Sapporo
After putting the finishing touches on *Live Killers* throughout the remainder of March, Queen flew off to Tokyo the following month to begin their longest tour to date of Japan. While the beginning of the tour would find Freddie in stellar voice, he would soon fall victim to a lack of preservation, with the back half of the tour resulting in some of his roughest vocals to date, meaning that not only was some of the more

demanding material omitted, but he had to get a little creative with his phrasing, which makes for some interesting listening.

The set list remained largely the same, with the obvious addition of 'Teo Torriatte (Let Us Cling Together)' to the repertoire (with Brian on piano); this was the band's first opportunity to perform the song live in the country that had inspired it, and the audience predictably loves it. The band opening changed slightly, this time with the slow/fast combination of 'We Will Rock You', as they had done in 1977 on the *News Of The World* tour, because Japan had not been on the itinerary when Queen were touring that album.

Despite Freddie's ailing voice, the band still turned in 15 highly enjoyable performances throughout this tour, and with the adventurous set list containing a handful of tracks that hadn't been released on *Live Killers*, recordings from this show are often in superb quality (due to advanced recording equipment) and are a treat to listen to. The final night, with Freddie's voice as rested as it could be, featured the vocalist giving thanks to Queen's road crew at various points; they returned the appreciation by appearing onstage in the band's spare stage outfits, wielding tambourines and any other percussive instruments they could find, and dancing as the band played 'Don't Stop Me Now', thus bringing the meaning of "having a ball" to a whole new level.

SAARBRÜKEN FESTIVAL:
18 AUGUST 1979

Musicians: John Deacon *(bass guitar),* Brian May *(guitar, vocals, acoustic guitar on 'Love Of My Life'),* Freddie Mercury *(vocals, piano, maracas, tambourine),* Roger Taylor *(drums, vocals, lead vocals on 'I'm In Love With My Car')*

Repertoire: 'We Will Rock You' *(fast),* 'Let Me Entertain You', 'If You Can't Beat Them', 'Mustapha' / 'Death On Two Legs' / 'Killer Queen' / 'I'm In Love With My Car' / 'Get Down, Make Love' / 'You're My Best Friend', 'Now I'm Here', 'Somebody To Love', 'Spread Your Wings', 'Love Of My Life', 'Keep Yourself Alive', Drum Solo / Guitar Solo, 'Bohemian Rhapsody', 'Tie Your Mother Down', 'Sheer Heart Attack', 'Jailhouse Rock', 'We Will Rock You', 'We Are The Champions', 'God Save The Queen'

Queen weren't known for playing festivals, preferring to stick to extensive tours where the musical performance and quality were at a peak instead of one-offs that were inevitably unpredictable, at best. Surprisingly, they accepted an invitation to be headliners at the August 1979 Saarbrüken Festival over such artists as Rory Gallagher, Red Baron, Molly Hatchet, Albert Lee and Ten Years After, Lake, Voyager, and The Commodores, and with 30,000 people in attendance, they realized that such a show would be good for their profile in Germany.

Unfortunately, it wasn't one of their best gigs: the set was riddled with technical difficulties that finally caused Roger to destroy his drum set at the conclusion of the show. As if that wasn't enough, he had also attempted to bleach his hair earlier in the day, but had applied too much and seen his hair turn bright green. The set list was adjusted slightly, with 'Fat Bottomed Girls', 'Dreamers Ball', and 'Don't Stop Me Now' being unfortunate casualties, but 'Mustapha' was performed as the first song of the medley, albeit truncated somewhat. The band revived 'Jailhouse Rock' for this performance, and had asked Rory Gallagher if he would like to join them for the song, but he declined.

CRAZY TOUR:
22 NOVEMBER TO 22 DECEMBER 1979

Musicians: John Deacon (*bass guitar, fretless bass on "39"*), Brian May (*guitar, vocals, acoustic guitar on 'Love Of My Life', "39", and 'Crazy Little Thing Called Love', piano on 'Save Me'*), Freddie Mercury (*vocals, piano, tambourine, maracas, acoustic guitar on 'Crazy Little Thing Called Love'*), Roger Taylor (*drums, vocals, lead vocals on 'I'm In Love With My Car', bass drum and tambourine on "39"*)

Repertoire: 'Jailhouse Rock', 'We Will Rock You' (*fast*), 'Let Me Entertain You', 'If You Can't Beat Them', 'Fat Bottomed Girls', 'Somebody To Love', 'Mustapha' / 'Death On Two Legs' / 'Killer Queen' / 'I'm In Love With My Car' / 'Get Down, Make Love' / 'You're My Best Friend', 'Save Me', 'Now I'm Here', 'Don't Stop Me Now', 'Spread Your Wings', 'Love Of My Life', "39", 'Keep Yourself Alive' / Drum Solo / Guitar Solo / 'Brighton Rock' (*reprise*), 'Crazy Little Thing Called Love', 'Bohemian Rhapsody', 'Tie Your Mother Down', 'Sheer Heart Attack', 'We Will Rock You', 'We Are The Champions', 'God Save The Queen'

Itinerary:
November 22: Royal Dublin Society Hall, Dublin, Eire
November 24: National Exhibition Centre, Birmingham
November 26/27: Apollo Theatre, Manchester
November 30/December 1: Apollo Theatre, Glasgow
December 3/4: City Hall, Newcastle-Upon-Tyne
December 6/7: Empire Theatre, Liverpool
December 9: Hippodrome, Bristol
December 10/11: Brighton Centre, Brighton
December 13: Lyceum Ballroom, London
December 14: Rainbow Theatre, London
December 17: Tiffany's, Purley, London
December 19: Tottenham Mayfair, London
December 20: Lewisham Odeon, London
December 22: Alexandra Palace, London

The last time Queen had toured England was in May 1978, with a meagre five-date run that hardly left their fans satisfied. In an effort to reconnect with their estranged fellow countryfans, Queen dispatched Gerry Stickells to find suitable venues in which the band could perform, with only one caveat: there was to be none of the expansive arenas the band had filled over the past three years, but more intimate settings that a band of their stature would normally avoid.

"We had played the big places," Brian explained, "and although we loved them and felt it was good that more and more people could come and see us, we also felt we were losing touch with the audience. Our whole show was about audience contact: we felt close to them, they felt close to us. But with those big places they were so far away, so distant. So we got Gerry Stickells to find some small, silly venues for us. We didn't want just ordinary little theatres; we wanted places that were different. We played the medium-sized places first, then the daft ones. We called it the Crazy Tour and thoroughly enjoyed it!"

Due to the size of the venues, the band's Pizza Oven lighting rig had to be scaled back considerably; at venues like the Lyceum Ballroom and Tottenham Mayfair, holes had to be drilled into the ceiling to accommodate the rig, or, in the case of the latter, be abandoned completely, instead relying on spotlights and a circle of lights around Roger's gong, which afforded a certain intimacy to the show that sat at odds with Queen's megastar status at the time.

The Crazy Tour, a cheeky *double entendre* indicating not only the eccentricity of going back to smaller venues but also the recent success of the 'Crazy Little

Thing Called Love' single, started on 22 November 1979 with Queen's first concert in Ireland – though it was supposed to start two days earlier in Cork, this was canceled for reasons unknown. The songs performed hadn't changed much, though the order was frequently switched, as there were often multiple shows in one city and the band wanted to offer a different show for fans who might have been traveling a bit. The fast version of 'We Will Rock You' was moved to second place in the set, and was replaced by 'Let Me Entertain You' for a handful of shows. 'Jailhouse Rock' was also introduced as a set opener for a few shows, and 'Tie Your Mother Down' was occasionally moved from late in the set to the second song performed. Two new songs, 'Crazy Little Thing Called Love' and the newly recorded yet still unreleased 'Save Me', were also introduced. The former featured Freddie strumming away on an acoustic guitar for the first time, while the latter featured Brian on piano, the first time that British fans would see Brian playing the instrument.

The opening night in Dublin was one of the rare occasions when 'God Save The Queen' was not performed over the PA system; instead, the show ended with 'We Are The Champions', though a specially rehearsed rendition of 'Danny Boy' was performed before 'Crazy Little Thing Called Love' during the first encore. The tour also saw the reappearance of The Royal Family, a loyal clan of fans who had travelled around Europe all year to see Queen play live, and they showed their loyalty by starting a conga line during 'Don't Stop Me Now' in Birmingham. Later in Glasgow, they left a note backstage that asked for 'Liar' to be performed, or else the band wouldn't make it out of the city alive. In keeping with the spontaneous nature of the tour – and perhaps fearing for their lives a little – the debut album track was brought out of mothballs.

Also in Glasgow, an embarrassing moment came when Roger, despite having sung 'I'm In Love With My Car' nightly since November 1977, had a mental block and completely forgot the words to his own song. What followed was a semi-instrumental version that featured the drummer repeatedly singing the only line he could remember before Freddie jumped in to save the performance with some equally dodgy lyrics. In Liverpool, Brian and Freddie performed a brief, off-the-cuff rendition of Wings' 'Mull Of Kintyre', with Freddie quipping that he'll be Linda McCartney. Wings, also on their own tour of the UK, had just performed in Liverpool the week before.

On 19 December, the band played in one of the smallest venues of the tour – a venue in Tottenham so small that they were unable to fit their already stripped-back lighting rig onto the stage and had to play with the venue's lights instead; interestingly, the same problem had been encountered at the Lyceum on the 13th, forcing the crew to drill two holes in the ceiling. More startlingly, Gerry Stickells, who had been on tour with Queen as their manager for three years, had collapsed backstage due to exhaustion earlier in the tour and was rushed to a local hospital. "The doctors told me to take it easy for a while," he explained, "but none of them have ever been on the road with Queen. That advice is almost impossible to take. The tour might have been small in venue size, but it was a hassle. Some of the places were so tiny that trying to cram in a band the size of Queen was nigh on impossible. But that's what they pay me for, working miracles."

The critics approached the band's return to smaller venues with surprisingly open minds. Following Queen's first-ever show in Ireland, *The Dublin Evening Press* offered more of a career retrospective than an actual review, though the writer was clearly impressed: "Queen in concert is a theatrical experience, a complete show. There's the excellence of the band's music, a heritage which goes back over eight enormously successful albums, several box office breaking world tours and smash singles … The blurbs will tell you that their show is two hours of Queen in direct contact with their audience, and that's exactly how it is." *The Birmingham Evening Mail* was complimentary: "The range and versatility that have elevated Queen to supergroup status was all there. But the outfit were forced to pump out such volume to fill the [NEC Hall] that the distortion of the sound ruined the effect … I didn't think the intricate recordings that Queen delight in would be possible to recreate live. And they weren't quite, but they came so close you couldn't complain." *Sounds*, meanwhile, had to be won over: "Ever considered Queen's songs seriously? Ever really listened to them? I haven't. I've been far too busy listening to that old chunkachunka dub to really take any notice of this bunch of shrink-wrapped unit shifters. But consider for me the moment the total absurdity of a song called 'Fat Bottomed Girls'. A messy, meandering, annoying tune that shows absolutely no direction at all. Useless mocking lyrics that refuse to vacate your mind. You end up wondering just what kind of genius makes you sing along to such rubbish … The fans sang along, ecstatic and carefree, and once more I wonder why. Why were they singing such empty lyrics? What could these words possibly mean to them, and yet, every line had been memorized and was chanted with almost religious fervor. Perhaps it's the Queen method of filling in the empty lifestyles of their supporters. Pure fantasy. A musical James Bond movie. Queen are exceptionally important and must be admired, despite the fact that they will never be considered hip again. I left the Apollo in a state of absolute amazement. The realization that I'd actually enjoyed every second of a credibility-blowing Queen gig was beginning to burn away at my confused mind. There is no hope for me now."

The tour wound up at Alexandra Palace on 22 December with the filming of the promotional video for 'Save Me'. At the same show, Freddie walked on stage during the second encore of 'We Will Rock You' in his silver lurex suit with a bunch of bananas, throwing them into the audience for reasons known only to him. Perhaps the bananas were a metaphor for Queen's craziest idea for a tour yet – while Alexandra Palace held 3,000 people, some of the smallest venues on the tour were clubs with a capacity of a few hundred. From this point forward, Queen would never be able to pull off a stunt like this again.

CONCERTS FOR THE PEOPLE OF KAMPUCHEA:
26 DECEMBER 1979

Musicians: John Deacon *(bass guitar, fretless bass on "39'),* Brian May *(guitar, vocals, acoustic guitar on 'Love Of My Life', "39', and 'Crazy Little Thing Called Love', piano on 'Save Me'),* Freddie Mercury *(vocals, piano, tambourine, maracas, acoustic guitar on 'Crazy Little Thing Called Love'),* Roger Taylor *(drums, vocals, lead vocals on 'I'm In Love With My Car', bass drum and tambourine on "39')*

Repertoire: 'Jailhouse Rock', 'We Will Rock You' *(fast),* 'Let Me Entertain You', 'Somebody To Love', 'If You Can't Beat Them', 'Mustapha' / 'Death On Two Legs (Dedicated to......)' / 'Killer Queen' / 'I'm In Love With My Car' / 'Get Down, Make Love' / 'You're My Best Friend', 'Save Me', 'Now I'm Here', 'Don't Stop Me Now', 'Spread Your Wings', 'Love Of My Life', "39', 'Keep Yourself Alive', 'Brighton Rock', 'Crazy Little Thing Called Love', 'Bohemian Rhapsody', 'Tie Your Mother Down', 'Sheer Heart Attack', 'We Will Rock You', 'We Are The Champions', 'God Save The Queen'

In July 1979, just as Queen were finishing recording sessions in Munich, they were approached by Paul McCartney, asking if they would be interested in taking part in a series of concerts to raise money for the people of Kampuchea. The band agreed and were given the coveted time slot of performing as the sole band on the first night, 26 December. Other bands on the bill consisted mostly of the kind of acts who had helped confer 'dinosaur' status on Queen (and McCartney): The Clash, Ian Dury and The Blockheads, The Pretenders, Rockpile, The Specials, and Elvis Costello and The Attractions were all invited to perform, while only Queen, Paul McCartney and Wings, and a newly reformed The Who were part of the 'old guard'. The bill also included a specially formed supergroup called Rockestra.

The band didn't offer any changes to their standard repertoire, running through their well-rehearsed set with the recently added 'Save Me' and 'Crazy Little Thing Called Love' thrown in. In fact, at the conclusion of the latter, the audience started to sing the latter song on their own, causing the band to come back in with a reprise.

Musically, the band were tight, delivering a terrific set that closely mirrored the *Live Killers* album, but with enough additional material – especially a soaring 'Somebody To Love' and superb 'If You Can't Beat Them', both absent from that album – to make the experience unique. 'Save Me' had yet to attain its status as a Queen classic – its single release would come the next month, thanks to the positive audience response on the Crazy Tour – but 'Now I'm Here' was always a powerhouse of a track; fittingly, the latter was the only Queen song included on the live compilation album of these concerts, released the following year. 'Don't Stop Me Now', 'If You Can't Beat Them', "39', and 'Spread Your Wings', meanwhile, received their last-ever performances at this event.

NME was caustic about Queen's appearance. "If my equations are right, this gig alone – the first in a sold-out series of four dedicated to Kampuchea – should raise a healthy 20 grand. Who knows, Queen may be feeding the 10,000 with their loaf of royal bran after all. But apart from the Unicef posters and Brian May briefly mentioning the cause, this was just another Queen techno-flash dry-iced affair ... Mercury still treats each precious song like a magnum opus and the audience like a cast of extras in the Cecil B. de Mille production of the Ten Commandments. (No prize for guessing Mercury's role.) ... I don't admire Queen's music but their gesture was unerringly sound (though it can't be any big deal for a mega-band to donate one night's earnings). Altogether, it's a very long way from the Hammy Odeon to Kampuchea, but help is on the way."

Queen's entire set was filmed but has yet to surface anywhere officially apart from some footage thrown into the documentaries *The Magic Years* and *Champions Of The World*, usually seen with Peter Ustinov introducing the band, which he did for the 1980 re-broadcast.

1980

THE GAME NORTH AMERICAN TOUR:

30 JUNE TO 30 SEPTEMBER 1980

Musicians: John Deacon *(bass guitar)*, Brian May *(guitar, vocals, acoustic guitar on 'Love Of My Life' and 'Crazy Little Thing Called Love', piano on 'Save Me')*, Freddie Mercury *(vocals, piano, tambourine, acoustic guitar on 'Crazy Little Thing Called Love')*, Roger Taylor *(drums, vocals, timpani, lead vocals on 'I'm In Love With My Car')*

Repertoire: 'Jailhouse Rock', 'We Will Rock You' *(fast)*, 'Let Me Entertain You', 'Play The Game', 'Mustapha' / 'Death On Two Legs (Dedicated to......' / 'Killer Queen' / 'I'm In Love With My Car' / 'Get Down, Make Love', 'Save Me', 'Now I'm Here' / 'Dragon Attack' / 'Now I'm Here' *(reprise)*, 'Fat Bottomed Girls', 'Love Of My Life', 'Keep Yourself Alive', 'Instrumental Inferno', 'Brighton Rock' *(reprise)*, 'Crazy Little Thing Called Love', 'Bohemian Rhapsody', 'Tie Your Mother Down', 'Another One Bites The Dust', 'Sheer Heart Attack', 'We Will Rock You', 'We Are The Champions', 'God Save The Queen', 'You're My Best Friend', 'Need Your Loving Tonight', 'Somebody To Love', 'Rock It (Prime Jive)'

Itinerary:
June 30: PNE Coliseum, Vancouver, British Columbia
July 1: Coliseum, Seattle, Washington
July 2: Coliseum, Portland, Oregon
July 5: Sports Arena, San Diego, California
July 6: Compton Terrace, Phoenix, Arizona
July 8/9, 11/12: The Forum, Los Angeles, California
July 13/14: Coliseum, Oakland, California
August 5: Mid-South Coliseum, Memphis, Tennessee
August 6: Riverside Centroplex, Baton Rouge, Louisiana
August 8: City Myriad, Oklahoma City, Oklahoma
August 9: The Reunion, Dallas, Texas
August 10: The Summit, Houston, Texas
August 12: The Omni, Atlanta, Georgia
August 13: Coliseum, Charlotte, North Carolina
August 14: Coliseum, Greensboro, North Carolina

August 16: Civic Center, Charleston, South Carolina
August 17: Market Square Arena, Indianapolis, Indiana
August 20: Civic Center, Hartford, Connecticut (rescheduled from 24 August)
August 22: The Spectrum, Philadelphia, Pennsylvania (rescheduled from 27 August)
August 23: Civic Center, Baltimore, Maryland (rescheduled from 26 August)
August 24: Civic Center, Pittsburgh, Pennsylvania (rescheduled from 31 August)
August 26: Civic Center, Providence, Rhode Island
August 27: The Spectrum, Portland, Maine
August 29: The Forum, Montreal, Quebec
August 30: CNE Grandstand, Toronto, Quebec
August 31: Convention Center, Rochester, New York
September 10: Mecca, Milwaukee, Wisconsin
September 11: Market Square Arena, Indianapolis, Indiana
September 13: Civic Center, Omaha, Nebraska
September 14: St Paul Civic Center, Minneapolis, Minnesota
September 16: Kemper Arena, Kansas City, Missouri
September 17: Checkerdome, St Louis, Missouri
September 19: The Horizon, Chicago, Illinois
September 20: Joe Louis Arena, Detroit, Michigan
September 21: Coliseum, Cleveland, Ohio
September 23: Veteran's Memorial Coliseum, New Haven, Connecticut
September 24: War Memorial, Syracuse, New York
September 26: Boston Gardens, Boston, Massachusetts
September 28-30: Madison Square Garden, New York, New York

Having earned their first *Billboard* No. 1 single with 'Crazy Little Thing Called Love', Queen booked a lengthy campaign of North America for the summer of 1980, which would afford them their first No. 1 album, and another No. 1 single with 'Another One Bites The Dust'. If any year proved Queen's Stateside staying power, it would be 1980, though the success would be short-lived.

The band flew to Los Angeles on 19 June to begin preparations for their 44-date tour, with the set list more closely mirroring that of last year's Crazy Tour, albeit with more songs from *The Game* added: 'Crazy Little Thing Called Love' and 'Save Me' were already mainstays, as was Queen's latest single, 'Play The Game'; both 'Need Your Loving Tonight' and 'Rock It (Prime Jive)' were staples, albeit on alternating nights, while 'Dragon Attack' and, surprisingly, 'Another

One Bites The Dust' had yet to be introduced to the repertoire. Wisely, the band broke up the tour into three legs, with three weeks separating the first and the second, and two weeks dividing the second and third. Not only was this done to preserve Freddie's voice, especially on such a gruelling and lengthy tour, but also to allow the band to return to England to record the soundtrack for *Flash Gordon* (and for Roger to record his debut solo album, *Fun In Space*).

The stage show was marginally stripped back, with a lighting rig, known alternately as the Fly Swatter or the Bic Razor, featuring seven sets of moveable lights, each controlled by one person. Speaking of Bic razors, Freddie had done the audacious and grown a mustache – itself a result of his embracing the "gay clone" look his coterie was adapting – which outraged fans; some of the more outspoken ones went the extra mile and pelted the stage with disposable razors, much to Freddie's amusement. Over 30 years later, Roger still couldn't fathom the negative reaction Freddie got to growing a cookie duster: "We got more publicity out of him growing that than if we'd all ridden naked down Oxford Street on an open-top bus."

The band were clearly riding a massive high on this tour, and the critics took note. "Freddie Mercury continues to be the visual focal point of the act," one wrote of their Inglewood show "strutting around the stage with considerable dramatic flair. The showman – and the ham – in Mercury had its fullest expression when he returned for the second encore dressed in short shorts, sitting on the shoulders of Darth Vader and singing 'We Will Rock You'." *The Chicago Tribune* offered a pretty scathing take-down of Freddie's push-broom, but was otherwise pleased with the show: "The emphasis this time is on the harder rock that Queen has been coming up with of late in the interests of self-preservation. Mercury's affected posturings of the past, as well as his grandiose and lush-textured turns at the keyboard, have been cut back considerably [not so – he played piano on 12 out of 30 songs performed throughout this tour, the most he would play on any tour], and the results are a far more powerful performance. Some of the band's more 'arty' material, such as the 1975 hit 'Bohemian Rhapsody', with its operatic approach and taped segments, and the Moroccan-influenced 'Mustapha', are still in the set, to be sure. But there are a lot more things along the lines of 'Jailhouse Rock', the old Elvis Presley hit that opened the show, and the band's recent hit, 'Another One Bites The Dust'. With Mercury spending less time

at the piano these days, the softer numbers seem to be at a minimum though guitarist Brian May had a nice solo segment and later teamed up with Mercury for a quieter acoustic ballad. It was a nice change of pace that went over with the bored and babbling audience about as well as the mustache."

THE GAME EUROPEAN & UK TOUR:
23 NOVEMBER TO 18 DECEMBER 1980

Musicians: John Deacon *(bass guitar)*, Brian May *(guitar, vocals, acoustic guitar on 'Love Of My Life' and 'Crazy Little Thing Called Love', piano on 'Save Me', piano and synthesizer on 'Flash's Theme')*, Freddie Mercury *(vocals, piano, tambourine, acoustic guitar on 'Crazy Little Thing Called Love')*, Roger Taylor *(drums, vocals, timpani, lead vocals on 'I'm In Love With My Car')*

Repertoire: 'Jailhouse Rock', 'We Will Rock You' *(fast)*, 'Let Me Entertain You', 'Play The Game', 'Mustapha' / 'Death On Two Legs (Dedicated to......' / 'Killer Queen' / 'I'm In Love With My Car' / 'Get Down, Make Love', 'Save Me', 'Now I'm Here' / 'Dragon Attack' / 'Now I'm Here' *(reprise)*, 'Fat Bottomed Girls', 'Love Of My Life', 'Keep Yourself Alive', 'Instrumental Inferno', 'Flash's Theme', 'The Hero', 'Brighton Rock' *(reprise)*, 'Crazy Little Thing Called Love', 'Bohemian Rhapsody', 'Tie Your Mother Down', 'Another One Bites The Dust', 'Sheer Heart Attack', 'We Will Rock You', 'We Are The Champions', 'God Save The Queen', 'Battle Theme', 'Need Your Loving Tonight', 'Imagine'

Itinerary:
November 23: Hallenstadio, Zurich, Switzerland
November 25: Le Bourget La Retonde, Paris, France
November 26: Sportshalle, Cologne, Germany
November 27: Groenoordhalle, Leiden, Holland
November 29: Gurgahalle, Essen, Germany
November 30: Deutschlandhalle, Berlin, Germany
December 1: Stadhalle, Bremen, Germany
December 5: NEC, Birmingham
December 8-10: Wembley Arena, London
December 12/13: Forêt Nationale, Brussels, Belgium
December 14: Festhalle, Frankfurt, Germany
December 16: Hall Rheus, Strasbourg, France
December 18: Olympiahalle, Munich, Germany

The band's banner year continued in November 1980 with the commencement of their European and UK tour, ostensibly to promote *The Game* though their soundtrack to the *Flash Gordon* film was released towards the end of the tour, and so the band duly added three of the more live-friendly numbers – 'Flash's Theme', 'Battle Theme', and 'The Hero' – to their already expansive repertoire. In an effort to give freshness to the set list, the band would occasionally end the main set with 'We Will Rock You' and 'We Are The Champions', before returning for their encores with 'Another One Bites The Dust', 'Sheer Heart Attack', and 'Tie Your Mother Down'. Uniquely, the band also incorporated a synthesizer into their arsenal of musical instruments, with Brian gamely playing it on 'Flash's Theme', which also featured him on piano.

Sadly, one of the more interesting cover versions on the tour came about through tragic circumstances: on 8 December, John Lennon was murdered by a crazed fanatic, and an emotional Queen incorporated a hastily-rehearsed rendition of 'Imagine' into the set. The song would return for the remainder of the tour starting with the second night in Brussels. More mundanely, Roger and John celebrated the end of the tour by demolishing their instruments onstage – not surprising for the drummer, who trashed his drum set on more than one occasion, but witnessing the mild-mannered John heaving his Fender bass into his amps must have been a sight to behold.

Just to prove that Queen's commercial success with *The Game* and its singles hadn't changed critics' assessments of them and the transition from rock band to pop band, *Record Mirror* dragged them across the coals, criticizing the precision of their show in Paris: "Clearly [Queen are] just in it for the money. Cynical? You should have heard what Freddie had to say to the kids who'd mortgaged an arm and a leg to be there: 'It's very nice to see you all in this shithole tonight. What the fuck are we doing here?' Indeed, Freddie, what? Your usual pre-gig huddle with accountants, managers and promoters revealed that only 6,000 out of a possible 15,000 tickets had been sold for the first-ever show in this Le Bourget aircraft hangar. That's still a bob or two, Fred, but I don't suppose those lights come cheap, not that they could even rescue this distressing debacle." *Sounds* was more complimentary: "Almost too perfect was the timing, too seemingly effortless the delivery of a set which covered the entire span of Queen's output to date, from 'Keep Yourself Alive' to *Flash Gordon* … Undoubtedly the sovereign of UK pomp rock, Freddie strutted, posed and preened himself through two hours of it, helped along by a spectacular light show and a few carefully placed pyrotechnics."

1981

THE GAME JAPANESE DATES:
12 TO 18 FEBRUARY 1981

Musicians: John Deacon *(bass guitar)*, Brian May *(guitar, vocals, acoustic guitar on 'Love Of My Life' and 'Crazy Little Thing Called Love', piano on 'Save Me', piano and synthesizer on 'Flash's Theme')*, Freddie Mercury *(vocals, piano, tambourine, acoustic guitar on 'Crazy Little Thing Called Love', synthesizer on 'Vultan's Theme (Attack Of The Hawkmen)')*, Roger Taylor *(drums, vocals, timpani, lead vocals on 'I'm In Love With My Car')*

Repertoire: 'Jailhouse Rock', 'We Will Rock You' *(fast)*, 'Let Me Entertain You', 'Play The Game', 'Mustapha' / 'Death On Two Legs (Dedicated to……)' / 'Killer Queen' / 'I'm In Love With My Car' / 'Get Down, Make Love', 'Save Me', 'Now I'm Here' / 'Dragon Attack' / 'Now I'm Here' *(reprise)*, 'Fat Bottomed Girls', 'Love Of My Life', 'Keep Yourself Alive', 'Instrumental Inferno', 'Battle Theme', 'Flash's Theme', 'The Hero', 'Crazy Little Thing Called Love', 'Bohemian Rhapsody', 'Tie Your Mother Down', 'Another One Bites The Dust', 'Sheer Heart Attack', 'We Will Rock You', 'We Are The Champions', 'Teo Torriatte (Let Us Cling Together)', 'God Save The Queen', 'Vultan's Theme (Attack Of The Hawkmen)', 'Need Your Loving Tonight', 'Rock It (Prime Jive)'

Itinerary:
February 12/13, 16-18: Budokan Hall, Tokyo

This mini-tour of Japan was scheduled as a warm-up of Queen's upcoming South American tour, with the band performing five shows over the span of a week at the Budokan in Tokyo. The set remained the same, with the obvious addition of 'Teo Torriatte (Let Us Cling Together)', occasionally performed as a third encore, and with 'Need Your Loving Tonight' and 'Rock It (Prime Jive)' swapping places on alternate nights, though the biggest surprise was 'Vultan's Theme (Attack Of The Hawkmen)', performed as part of a *Flash Gordon* medley with Freddie playing synthesizer.

The band were clearly pleased with these five dates. "It's the best tour we've done there," Brian recalled later that year, "and we've done four tours, and it was clearly hysterical. Our audience is changing a bit from a kind of teeny-bop audience into a more rock audience in Japan. Japan was one of the few places where we had a young audience, but now it's more in line with how it is in the States and Europe."

SOUTH AMERICA BITES THE DUST TOUR:
28 FEBRUARY TO 21 MARCH 1981

Musicians: John Deacon *(bass guitar)*, Brian May *(guitar, vocals, acoustic guitar on 'Love Of My Life' and 'Crazy Little Thing Called Love', piano on 'Save Me' and 'Flash's Theme')*, Freddie Mercury *(vocals, piano, tambourine, acoustic guitar on 'Crazy Little Thing Called Love')*, Roger Taylor *(drums, vocals, timpani, lead vocals on 'I'm In Love With My Car')*

Repertoire: 'We Will Rock You' *(fast)*, 'Let Me Entertain You', 'Play The Game', 'Somebody To Love', 'Mustapha' / 'Death On Two Legs (Dedicated to......' / 'Killer Queen' / 'I'm In Love With My Car' / 'Get Down, Make Love', 'Need Your Loving Tonight', 'Save Me', 'Now I'm Here' / 'Dragon Attack' / 'Now I'm Here' *(reprise)*, 'Fat Bottomed Girls', 'Love Of My Life', 'Keep Yourself Alive', 'Instrumental Inferno', 'Flash' / 'The Hero', 'Crazy Little Thing Called Love', 'Bohemian Rhapsody', 'Tie Your Mother Down', 'Another One Bites The Dust', 'Sheer Heart Attack', 'We Will Rock You', 'We Are The Champions', 'God Save The Queen', 'Rock It (Prime Jive)', 'Jailhouse Rock'

Itinerary:
February 28/March 1: Estadio José Amalfitani, Buenos Aires, Argentina
March 4: Estadio José María Minella, Mar del Plata, Argentina
March 6: Estadio Mundialista Gigante de Arroyito, Rosario, Argentina
March 8: Estadio José Amalfitani, Buenos Aires, Argentina
March 20/21: Estádio Cícero Pompeu de Toledo, Sao Paolo, Brazil

Queen were always open to performing in new countries, with South America proving an attractive proposition given that the live version of 'Love Of My Life' had been in the singles chart there for over 12 months. When the itinerary was announced, fans and critics alike were shocked: bands as big as Queen didn't travel to South America (though The Rolling Stones came close in 1975) due to the logistical nightmares involved. Promoter José Rota, for example, was approached by the Argentinean intelligence service and presented with various hypothetical situations, one of which involved a terrorist strolling on stage, holding a gun to Freddie's head and ordering him to say "Viva Perón." Rota replied with an impassioned speech lamenting the fact that thousands of Queen fans couldn't come together for a few hours just to enjoy a rock concert. His ruse worked, and the tour went ahead.

While the band was in Japan, Jim Beach flew over to Rio de Janeiro with Gerry Stickells to organize everything. "There was no one at all in South America who had the experience to promote anything as huge as a Queen tour," Beach explained in *As It Began*, "so I personally flew down to Rio and set up a temporary production office at the Rio Sheraton Hotel for three months. From there I could easily commute to Buenos Aires to keep an eye on the proceedings." The band's production manager, Chris Lamb, flew into Argentina in February and duly had his cases searched at customs. The passes for the tour were discovered: two naked young ladies, one Japanese and one South American, sharing a banana in a suggestive pose. Lamb had to spend the next few hours covering the women's chests with a black marker.

There were also equipment problems: to fly 20 tons of gear from Tokyo to Buenos Aires was exorbitant in price and also lengthy (nearly 36 hours). Additionally, 40 tons of equipment were flown in from Miami as well as additional artificial turf to cover the countries' coveted football fields, plus 16 tons of stage scaffolding from Los Angeles and five tons of lights. In the bustle of transportation, an oversized, 40-foot container fell from its truck and remained in the street for 48 hours before a crane large enough to accommodate the container's size could be located.

When Queen arrived in Argentina on 23 February, the country virtually exploded in a frenzy: when the band emerged from their plane, the airport's sound system broadcast Queen music non-stop, and the band's every move was transmitted on local television. Never before had a country embraced Queen so warmly, with the possible exception of Japan. On the first night of the tour at the Velez Sarfield in Buenos Aires, the band went down a storm, though special mention should be given to the audience who sang so vociferously that Freddie willingly stopped singing to let them carry on. No one was prepared for the performance of 'Love Of My Life', though: the opening chords were obscured by the din of the 54,000-strong audience cheering and applauding, which quickly died down in time for the vocals so that every fan could sing each word perfectly.

The set list for this tour changed little from the previous one, though 'Somebody To Love' had been rightly reinstated: only occasional performances of 'Rock It (Prime Jive)' and 'Jailhouse Rock' peppered the set list, while 'Need Your Loving Tonight' was common to all seven shows. The show on 1 March was broadcast live on national television, bringing in 35 million viewers in both Argentina and Brazil; the show on 8 March was also transmitted live.

In common with shows booked for Cordoba on 4 March and Rio de Janeiro on the 27th, a concert scheduled for Porto Alegre on the 13th was canceled, giving the band nearly two weeks of rest. They were invited to meet General Viola, President Designate of Argentina, an offer accepted by everyone except Roger. "I didn't want to meet him because that would have been playing into their hands," he explained. "We were playing for the people. We didn't go there with the wool pulled over our eyes. We know fully what the [political] situation is like in some of those countries. But for a time we made thousands of people happy. Surely that must count for something?"

While the band performed for several thousands of ecstatic fans, it was the two dates in Brazil that saw them playing to their largest audiences there, with a capacity of 130,000 fans each night. All shows on this tour were either recorded for radio or filmed for television (or both), broadcast to fans who couldn't make it to the shows – including a canceled gig in Rio on 19 March. A video and audio document of this tour is long overdue.

GLUTTONS FOR PUNISHMENT TOUR:
25 SEPTEMBER TO 18 OCTOBER 1981

Musicians: John Deacon *(bass guitar)*, Brian May *(guitar, vocals, acoustic guitar on 'Love Of My Life' and 'Crazy Little Thing Called Love', piano on 'Save Me' and 'Flash's Theme')*, Freddie Mercury *(vocals, piano, tambourine, acoustic guitar on 'Crazy Little Thing Called Love')*, Roger Taylor *(drums, vocals, timpani, lead vocals on 'I'm In Love With My Car')*

Repertoire: 'We Will Rock You' *(fast)*, 'Let Me Entertain You', 'Play The Game', 'Somebody To Love', 'Killer Queen' / 'I'm In Love With My Car' / 'Get Down, Make Love', 'Save Me', 'Now I'm Here' / 'Dragon Attack' / 'Now I'm Here' *(reprise)*, 'Fat Bottomed Girls', 'Love Of My Life', 'Keep Yourself Alive', 'Instrumental Inferno', 'Flash' / 'The Hero', 'Crazy Little Thing Called Love', 'Bohemian Rhapsody', 'Tie Your Mother Down', 'Another One Bites The Dust', 'Sheer Heart Attack', 'We Will Rock You', 'We Are The Champions', 'God Save The Queen', 'Need Your Loving Tonight', 'Jailhouse Rock', 'Battle Theme'

Itinerary:
September 25-27: Poliedro de Caracas, Caracas, Venezuela
October 9: Estadio Universitaro de Monterrey, Monterrey, Mexico
October 17/18: Estadio Olimpico de beisbol Ignacio Zaragoza, Puebla, Mexico

Having achieved a collective goal that was both exhausting and rewarding with the South America Bites The Dust Tour, Queen continued charting new territories in the autumn of 1981 with six dates in Mexico and Venezuela (a Pacific Rim trek was also in the works, but ultimately scrapped). The band flew to New Orleans on 15 September to start rehearsals before departing for Caracas six days later, where they turned in three increasingly uneasy and tense shows at the Poliedro de Caracas. Both South America and Mexico were still unfamiliar with rock concert protocol, and a rock concert was seemingly an excuse to go absolutely wild, which also meant the band were often dodging projectiles being launched at the stage. On the final night in Caracas, Freddie was visibly and audibly irritated with the audience, with his parting words being a terse, "Let's go home and get fucked! Ciao!"

The Venezuelan dates were initially going to run until 30 September, but when it was announced that former president Rómulo Betancourt had died, the country was thrown into a period of chaos and mourning. It couldn't have happened at a worse time for the band: Brian, Roger, and John had agreed to appear on RCTV's Fantastic, hosted by Guillermo "Fantástico" González, (Venezuela's equivalent of *Top Of The Pops*; Freddie had declined to appear), and were in the midst of a truly zany appearance when an announcer rushed onstage to declare Betancourt's death. With a two-minute silence called for, the band couldn't understand what was going on, and were none the wiser when a counter-announcement was made to the effect that Betancourt hadn't died after all. The next two concerts were canceled when Betancourt eventually did pass away; Venezuela essentially shut down in a state of mourning, including the airports. The band and road crew had to bribe their way out of the country in order to escape to Miami for a period of rest before the trio of Mexican dates.

The misfortune continued for the road crew as they decamped to Loredo, Texas, to cross the border into Mexico. "Under normal circumstances you can visit Mexico on a US driver's license," Peter "Ratty" Hince recalled. (Perhaps in 1981, but certainly not anymore.) "But the crew were told that we all needed visas." Not only that, only six visas would be approved per day, and with a 18-member crew and time of the essence, Gerry Stickells greased some palms and the crew was allowed to cross into no-man's land outside the border … where they were ordered to wait. Several hours later, and with some more cash exchanging hands, the relieved crew were released, only to be stopped 60 miles down the road before they reached another checkpoint, and were … ordered to wait, before even more money was produced. "The official line on the visas was that we were 'assisting Mexican technicians'," Hince recalled to Mark Blake. "I still have the visa application and there was some unbelievable stuff on there: a mugshot, a profile picture, fingerprints, mother's maiden name, shape of eyes … it was just an excuse for someone to get some cash."

At least the concert itself went off mostly without a hitch; the band turned in a memorable performance, with John sneaking in a bit of the embryonic 'Back Chat' riff into 'Another One Bites The Dust', while the band jammed briefly on 'Under Pressure' during 'Now I'm Here'. However, a bridge outside the stadium collapsed as the audience was departing; there weren't any fatalities, but there were many injuries, forcing the police to lock the stadium gates and refusing anyone from the Queen crew to leave. Stickells once again to the rescue…

The band were so exhausted, and the crew so feared for their lives (the Kentucky Fried Chicken they had been provided wasn't chicken at all, but actually rodent), that the second night was canceled, as were three dates in Guadalajara at Estadio Jalisco, planned for 14, 15, and 16 October. The band instead went their separate ways, Brian and John to Los Angeles, and Roger and Freddie to Dallas, where they would unknowingly be resting up for the most challenging two dates they would perhaps ever play.

The itinerary originally had Mexico City on the schedule, with the band fully expecting to play there, until the government and organizers switched the venue to Estadio Olimpico de beisbol Ignacio Zaragoza at the last minute without alerting anyone. The reason for the switch was simply to avoid the larger crowds of Mexico City, but general incompetence and corruption resulted in a thoroughly pissed-off band, who only channeled their aggression into their performance. Additionally, the stadium, which had been built for the Olympics in 1952, had fallen into disrepair, with the crew alarmed to discover it was literally falling apart. Some tiers collapsed during the show, with many fans seriously injured, sustaining broken arms and legs.

Fans were searched thoroughly and batteries were confiscated from those who were going to record the show, but once inside, those same fans could rebuy their batteries from the police at astronomical cost. Once the show started, the audience was already rowdy, drunk, and out of their heads in general: the crowd started to throw rubbish – shoes, bottles, their precious batteries, etc. – at the band during their performance. Brian was nailed with dirt during his guitar solo, and Freddie concluded the performance with an aggravated "Adios amigos, you motherfuckers!" and "Take your shoes back!" Roger was even more irritated, trashing a few cymbals and stands when it came time for the final bow. Unfortunately for personal manager Paul Prenter, a fan scored a direct hit with a battery on his head, knocking the roadie on his back and bringing about a loud cheer from the other crew members. Once the show ended, only one door was open for fans to leave through, and with 150,000 fans exiting at once, the police lost their patience and engaged in brute force towards line jumpers, leaving them bleeding and battered on the ground. The chaos spread to backstage, with the band ushered into a small underground room (John, a claustrophobic, understandably did not enjoy this experience), ostensibly for their safety, but also to force the band to sign a binding document guaranteeing they would return the following night. They did, and it mostly went off without a hitch, though the band still made sure to get out of Dodge after the second night, canceling all remaining shows and returning to Munich to recuperate.

At the end of the tour, John summed up the year in words that mirrored the feelings of his bandmates: "It's always very exciting to play in a country for the first time, and 1981 has really been our year for discovering new audiences we didn't even know existed." Roger was less diplomatic, writing in the winter 1981 Queen fan club magazine: "Glad to be back from Mexico – it was hell! – well, difficult to say the least – nasty authorities, corrupt officials & food poisoning, plus risk of death, etc. Apart from that it was wonderful!"

WE WILL ROCK YOU VIDEO SHOOT:

24 & 25 NOVEMBER 1981

Musicians: John Deacon *(bass guitar)*, Brian May *(guitar, vocals, acoustic guitar on 'Love Of My Life' and 'Crazy Little Thing Called Love', piano on 'Save Me' and 'Flash's Theme')*, Freddie Mercury *(vocals, piano, tambourine, acoustic guitar on 'Crazy Little Thing Called Love')*, Roger Taylor *(drums, vocals, timpani, lead vocals on 'I'm In Love With My Car')*

Repertoire: 'We Will Rock You' *(fast)*, 'Let Me Entertain You', 'Play The Game', 'Somebody To Love', 'Killer Queen' / 'I'm In Love With My Car' / 'Get Down, Make Love', 'Save Me', 'Now I'm Here' / 'Dragon Attack' / 'Now I'm Here' *(reprise)*, 'Love Of My Life', 'Under Pressure', 'Keep Yourself Alive', Drum Solo, Guitar Solo, 'Instrumental Inferno', 'Flash' / 'The Hero', 'Crazy Little Thing Called Love', 'Bohemian Rhapsody', 'Tie Your Mother Down', 'Another One Bites The Dust', 'Sheer Heart Attack', 'Jailhouse Rock', 'We Will Rock You', 'We Are The Champions', 'God Save The Queen'

These Canadian shows (both at The Forum in Montreal) were specially filmed for use as Queen's first concert video. Though distinct from the band's recent tours, the set list remained virtually unchanged; 'Under Pressure' was incorporated for the first time, and 'Need Your Loving Tonight' was omitted. While there remained some confusion about Queen's set, with reports ultimately erroneously reporting that the latter was performed, the release of *Queen Rock Montreal* in 2007 – and the unearthing of several bootlegs – confirmed the set. Brian threw in references to 'Back Chat' during the instrumental inferno, and Freddie also sang lyrics from an unreleased – possibly unrecorded – song called 'Sex Show'.

The intent of the filming was to take the film on the road, with Mobilevision's original goal to be a traveling theatre. Fans in every city would then "be" at the concert, hence why the original release featured the audience mixed so low, initiating the false pretense that the Quebecoise audience was muted and unresponsive. Quite the opposite, in fact; bootlegs and the *Queen Rock Montreal* DVD confirm that the audience was just as wild as it had been in the past, and that the band's foul mood stemmed from the presence of director Saul Swimmer and his film crew. Brian later spoke about the band's mood that night at the DVD's London premiere on 16 October 2007:

"What you will see in this film is a very edgy, angry band, carving out a performance in a rather uncomfortable situation. But it does mean it's very high energy, real, and raw. In addition, although the actual quality of the film was great, you will see camera work from camera men who did not remotely know the show, directed by a director who didn't know the show either. The subsequent editing was consequently chaotic. They cobbled together bits of both shows visually, choosing the bits where the cameras had found the right person at the right time. They then matched up the sound as best they could, but there were many bits where you were hearing sound from one night, but watching the visuals from the other. Still, the film went out, and was seen by a lot of people in a 'live' situation."

Freddie was especially miffed when Swimmer insisted that he perform the same moves and wear the same outfits both nights. Brian continued his explanation of the show: "For a start, we were not on tour, so all the sound and lights and production and crew had to be reassembled just for this occasion, and we had to rehearse ourselves up to speed. Plus, we didn't get on with Mr. Saul Swimmer at all. Freddie in particular took an instant dislike to the man, and this turned to something like hatred, when we discovered on the first night that Swimmer had put up his own lights on the audience, changed the colors in our lights, and had cameras all over the stage. Obviously we were not going to be able to treat it like a normal gig. It got worse on the second night, when Saul Swimmer demanded that Freddie wear the same clothes as the first night, and make the same moves. This guy had no idea that the show wasn't choreographed. We basically did what we liked, so tempers flared – and it shows."

1982

HOT SPACE EUROPEAN & UK TOUR:

9 APRIL TO 5 JUNE 1982

Musicians: John Deacon *(bass guitar, rhythm guitar on 'Staying Power')*, Brian May *(guitars, vocals, piano on 'Save Me', acoustic guitar on 'Love Of My Life' and 'Crazy Little Thing Called Love')*, Freddie Mercury *(vocals, piano, acoustic rhythm guitar on 'Crazy Little Thing Called Love')*, Roger Taylor *(drums, vocals, Syndrums, co-lead vocals on 'Action This Day')*, Morgan Fisher *(piano, keyboards, synthesizer)*

Repertoire: 'Flash' *(taped intro)* / 'The Hero', 'Tie Your Mother Down', 'Action This Day', 'Play The Game',

'Staying Power', 'Somebody To Love', 'Get Down, Make Love', 'Instrumental Inferno', 'Under Pressure', 'Love Of My Life', 'Save Me', 'Fat Bottomed Girls', 'Crazy Little Thing Called Love', 'Bohemian Rhapsody', 'Now I'm Here', 'Dragon Attack', 'Now I'm Here' (reprise), 'Another One Bites The Dust', 'Sheer Heart Attack', 'We Will Rock You', 'We Are The Champions', 'God Save The Queen', 'We Will Rock You' (fast), 'Back Chat', 'Body Language', 'Liar'

Itinerary:

April 9: Scandinavium, Gothenburg, Sweden
April 10: Ice Stadium, Stockholm, Sweden
April 12: Drammenshallen, Oslo, Norway
April 16/17: Hallenstadion, Zurich, Switzerland
April 19/20: Palis de Sport, Paris, France
April 22/23: Forêt Nationale, Brussels, Belgium
April 24/25: Groenoordhalle, Leiden, Holland
April 28: Festhalle, Frankfurt, Germany
May 1: Westfallenhalle, Dortmund, Germany
May 3: Palais de Sport, Paris, France
May 5: Eilenriedehalle, Hannover, Germany
May 6/7: Sportshalle, Cologne, Germany
May 9: Carl-Diem Halle, Würzburg, Germany
May 10: Sporthalle Boeblingen, Stuttgart, Germany
May 12/13: Stadhalle, Vienna, Austria
May 15: Waldbuehne, Berlin, Germany
May 16: Ernst Merck Halle, Hamburg, Germany
May 18: Eisspdorthalle, Kassel, Germany
May 21: Olympiahalle, Munich, Germany
May 29: Elland Road Football Stadium, Leeds
June 1/2: Ingliston Showground, Edinburgh
June 5: Milton Keynes Bowl, Buckinghamshire

Following the completion of their *Hot Space* album in March 1982, Queen reconvened later that month to commence rehearsals for their upcoming European tour. The band took the opportunity to refurbish their set list, which had remained constant since 1979; gone was the medley consisting of 'Killer Queen', 'I'm In Love With My Car', and 'Get Down, Make Love', as well as the fast version of 'We Will Rock You'. Instead, the band opened with an atmospheric taped introduction ('Flash') which segued into a raucous rendition of 'The Hero'.

From there, the set reached extraordinary new heights while the band introduced several tracks from the new album; in the process, they eliminated several of their older songs. Of the new items, 'Action This Day' and 'Staying Power' were regulars in the set, with the latter featuring John on electric rhythm guitar; keyboardist

Morgan Fisher provided the bassline on synthesizer.

Fisher was a new addition to the line-up, marking the first – but certainly not the last – time that an outside musician would join the band. In 1970, the keyboardist formed Morgan with Bob Sapsed on bass, Maurice Bacon on drums, and none other than Tim Staffell on vocals and acoustic guitar. They released an album, *Nova Solis*, in 1972, though critical success eluded them and they broke up shortly thereafter. Fisher would later work with Mott The Hoople and continue to release solo albums. The addition of a keyboardist was a last-minute decision, and the band spent a few days rehearsing with Morgan just before travelling to Gothenburg on 8 April.

Apart from 'Action This Day', 'Staying Power' and 'Under Pressure' (which had been introduced during the Canadian shows in 1981), the band would also occasionally perform 'Back Chat' and 'Body Language', with 'Liar' as the most surprising addition for the early dates of the tour. The first actual number, apart from 'The Hero' which served merely as an introduction, would generally be 'Tie Your Mother Down', though – as with previous tours – the band would switch the set list around at times, bringing back the fast version of 'We Will Rock You' or introducing 'Sheer Heart Attack' as the first actual song performed. 'Las Palabras De Amor (The Words Of Love)' was rehearsed for the Leeds show on 29 May but went unperformed. References to 'Spread Your Wings', 'I Go Crazy', and, surprisingly, 'My Fairy King' were also made throughout the tour, and showed the relative spontaneity that the band were exhibiting this year. By the middle of the tour, the set would become more static, and all of the shuffling around would return to a set similar to the previous year's.

The band hadn't toured Europe since December 1980, so it's no surprise that the four were nervous about embarking on this tour. They needn't have worried – they were received rapturously at every show, though most of the new *Hot Space* material wasn't. During the introduction of 'Staying Power' in Frankfurt, a section of the audience started to boo, causing Freddie to snap, "If you don't wanna hear it, fuckin' go home!" Otherwise, he would maintain his cool, memorably stating during the Milton Keynes concert that "People get so excited about these things. It's only a bloody record!"

It wasn't just the *Hot Space* material that irked the audience. Queen had chosen new wave group Bow Wow Wow as their support act, but the crowds made it quite clear how they felt about the band by pelting them with bottles. Bow Wow Wow pulled out of the tour, with their final date performed on 25 April. Teenage vocalist Annabella Lwin said, "The fans were extremely hostile. We decided to come home before one of us got badly hurt. There was no point in carrying on, really." Brian added: "We liked [Bow Wow Wow] very much. There was a certain section in the audience that found them very modern. Our audience, it's a sad comment, is perhaps a little narrow-minded in that way. It's only a small percentage. Most people gave them a very good hearing, but there were a few people who went so far as to throw things at them, which to be honest I was pretty disgusted at. Unfortunately, Bow Wow Wow decided to throw them back, as a matter of policy. On a couple of nights in particular it just snowballed into a big fight, which became very silly." After The Fire were hastily brought in as Bow Wow Wow's replacement on 28 April.

The tour wound its way through most of Europe (with two concerts at Frankfurt's Festhalle on 28 and 29 April reduced to just one on the 28th), ending on 21 May in Munich, the day *Hot Space* was released. Eight days later, Queen started a short, four-date UK tour, though the band had apparently intended it to be longer: applications were made for shows at both Manchester United (Old Trafford) and Arsenal (Highbury) football grounds, but turned down for the sole reason that Pope John Paul II was on his own 'tour' round England and all the portable toilets had been booked for his appearances. The two dates were replaced with those in Leeds and Milton Keynes, though the tour was supposed to end with a performance at the Albert Hall; Queen's proposal was denied because officials feared the band's massive lighting rig created safety risks.

Instead, the tour ended at Milton Keynes Bowl in Buckinghamshire on 5 June, which became one of Queen's most well-known performances. It was filmed by Gavin Taylor and broadcast on 4 January 1983 on The Tube, receiving its American premiere on the fledgling MTV network on 20 August. The performance was finally released on both DVD and CD in October 2004 as *Queen On Fire: Live At The Bowl*.

ROCK 'N' AMERICA TOUR:
21 JULY TO 15 SEPTEMBER 1982

Musicians: John Deacon *(bass guitar, rhythm guitar on 'Staying Power')*, Brian May *(guitars, vocals, piano on 'Save Me', acoustic guitar on 'Crazy Little Thing Called Love')*, Freddie Mercury *(vocals, piano, acoustic rhythm guitar*

on *'Crazy Little Thing Called Love')*, Roger Taylor *(drums, vocals, Syndrums, co-lead vocals on 'Action This Day')*, Fred Mandel *(piano, keyboards, synthesizer)*

Repertoire: 'Flash' *(taped intro)* / 'Rock It (Prime Jive)', 'We Will Rock You' *(fast)*, 'Action This Day', 'Play The Game', 'Now I'm Here', 'Dragon Attack', 'Now I'm Here' *(reprise)*, 'Save Me', 'Calling All Girls', 'Back Chat', 'Get Down, Make Love', 'Instrumental Inferno', 'Body Language', 'Under Pressure', 'Fat Bottomed Girls', 'Crazy Little Thing Called Love', 'Bohemian Rhapsody', 'Tie Your Mother Down', 'Another One Bites The Dust', 'We Will Rock You', 'We Are The Champions', 'God Save The Queen', 'Somebody To Love', 'Life Is Real (Song For Lennon)', 'Staying Power', 'Saturday Night's Alright For Fighting'

Itinerary:
July 21: The Forum, Montreal, Quebec
July 23: Boston Gardens, Boston, Massachusetts
July 24: The Spectrum, Philadelphia, Pennsylvania
July 25: Capitol Center, Washington, D.C.
July 27/28: Madison Square Garden, New York, New York
July 31: Richland Coliseum, Cleveland, Ohio
August 2/3: Maple Leaf Gardens, Toronto, Ontario
August 5: Mark Square Arena, Indianapolis, Indiana
August 6: Joe Louis Arena, Detroit, Michigan
August 7: Riverfront Coliseum, Cincinnati, Ohio
August 9: Meadowlands Arena, East Rutherford, New Jersey
August 10: New Haven Coliseum, New Haven, Connecticut
August 13/14: Poplar Creek, Chicago, Illinois
August 15: Civic Center Arena, St Paul, Minnesota
August 19: Civic Center, Biloxi, Mississippi
August 20: The Summit, Houston, Texas
August 21: The Reunion, Dallas, Texas
August 24: The Omni, Atlanta, Georgia
August 27: City Myriad, Oklahoma City, Oklahoma
August 28: Kemper Arena, Kansas City, Missouri
August 30: McNichols Arena, Denver, Colorado
September 2: Portland Coliseum, Portland, Oregon
September 3: Seattle Coliseum, Seattle, Washington
September 4: PNE Coliseum, Vancouver, British Columbia
September 7: Oakland Coliseum, Oakland, California
September 10: ASU Arena, Temple, Texas
September 11/12: Irving Meadows, Irving, Texas
September 14/15: Inglewood Forum, Los Angeles, California

After a lengthy summer break, the band flew to Montreal on 18 July to set up camp and make final adjustments to the set list. Several of the newer songs from *Hot Space* were introduced: 'Life Is Real (Song For Lennon)' made its live debut, while 'Calling All Girls' and 'Body Language' became mainstays in the set and 'Somebody To Love' and 'Staying Power' made less frequent appearances. 'The Hero' was replaced entirely by 'Rock It (Prime Jive)', a startling opening number since it wasn't as concise as its predecessor and tended to meander at times. Surprisingly, for the first time since its debut in November 1977, 'Love Of My Life' was dropped altogether; this may have been done to create the illusion that Queen were still a rock band at heart, and omitting the popular ballad was one way to reinforce that image.

The tour started on 21 July at The Forum in Montreal, with support by Billy Squier, and any theories that *Hot Space* had damaged ticket sales were quickly dispelled. While their American fans hadn't reacted favorably to the new album, they were relieved to find that Queen still knew how to rock, and were surprised when songs like 'Calling All Girls', 'Action This Day', 'Back Chat' and 'Staying Power' (on the rare occasions that it was performed) sounded fresher than on the album. The band, too, worked hard to reassure their audience they hadn't lost their edge, blazing through their set with aplomb and maintaining a steady schedule of tour dates to make sure they remained on top of their game.

There were some personnel changes: Morgan Fisher hadn't been asked back as the keyboardist. He told the Italian Queen Fan Club in 2009, "I had been accustomed to rock the way Mott played it. It was rougher, wilder, more spontaneous than Queen, who were very perfectionist in their approach. Plus by that time I had changed my lifestyle and was not the funny hard-drinking guy Queen had known during their tours with Mott. I think the timing was wrong – I didn't feel so comfortable with Queen in 1982, and I think they sensed it. During a break between the Europe tour and the forthcoming US tour, they sent me a telegram to say that they had decided they didn't need a keyboard player any more. Perhaps they were a bit embarrassed to tell me that actually they didn't feel comfortable with me either – they soon found another keyboard player for their US tour." Fred Mandel was instead drafted, and with a resumé including Alice Cooper's Alice Cooper Show and Flush The Fashion and Pink Floyd's The Wall, he instantly added a new energy to Queen's songs. Mandel would

later work on Star Fleet Project and Mr Bad Guy after the *Hot Space* tour ended, and Queen would also ask him to assist with synthesizers and arrangements on *The Works*. Sadly, Mandel's tenure with Queen was short-lived: when the tour ended in November, he was offered a job by Elton John and worked on most of the flamboyant pianist's mid-1980s albums.

At the tour's second stop in Boston, the city declared 23 July an official Queen Day, with the band present for a short speech and to receive the keys to the city. This, of course, helped solidify Queen's confidence in their American reception, and the Boston gig became an early highlight of the tour. Most of the dates passed without incident, though a scheduled concert in Memphis on 25 August was canceled. Earlier, at the Meadowlands in New Jersey on the 9th, one of The Red Special's strings snapped mid-solo, exactly the same thing happening to its replacement only moments later. In an uncharacteristic display of vexation, Brian threw the offending guitar over a bank of Vox amplifiers into the darkness.

The tour ended in LA, as most of their previous ones had, with a two-night stand at the Inglewood Forum. (An early itinerary indicated that a gig in Hawaii was planned on 26 September, but the band opted to perform on national television instead.) The band were in high spirits, with Billy Squier joining them on stage during 'Jailhouse Rock'. After their appearance on *Saturday Night Live* on 25 September (playing 'Crazy Little Thing Called Love' and 'Under Pressure' to rapturous applause, despite Freddie's strained voice), the band flew home for a few days' rest before their Japanese dates.

Just to prove that *Hot Space* hadn't permanently damaged Queen's reputation, the critics took note of the new energy in the set. "The concert was a sellout, with fans applauding wildly for all of the band's older hits and its stunning light show, which features scores of aircraft landing lights," the *Indiana Gazette* reported. "But the response was no more than polite when the group launched into several of its thumping, rhythm and blues tunes off the new album, including the first single, 'Body Language'. Deacon conceded that after three dancehall singles in a row – 'Another One Bites The Dust', 'Under Pressure' with David Bowie, and 'Body Language' – the band may have disillusioned many of its long-time fans. 'Yes, I think we have possibly lost some of the rock fans,' he said when asked about the muted audience reaction to the new tunes. 'It's something we are aware of and will bear in mind when we make our next album.'"

The New York Times was still cautious. "Although a visitor was duly impressed by the band's dynamic control, the clarity of its sound and the intricacy of its arrangements at Tuesday's concert, the emotional atmosphere on stage was closer to a military pageant than to a rock concert." The Washington Post, however, was especially complimentary. "Although some of Queen's newer songs have yet to attain the comfort of familiarity, there is a spectacular energy at the heart of its repertoire. Freddie Mercury, looking as if he'd been outfitted on the set of A Clockwork Orange, is an appropriately mercurial front man, energetic and appealing and possessed of a convincing and clear rock tenor … Queen's blatant disco hits – including 'Bus' [sic], 'Body Language', and 'Hot Space' [sic] – were overwhelming but not particularly convincing as funk, making Mercury come across as a plugged-in George Chakiris. Still, with remarkable sound and light systems to back them, Queen was a model of crunching efficiency and polished professionalism seldom matched in the rock arena."

The Elyria Chronicle opined, "There were no slow spots in the two-hour-plus concert. Mercury does not slack up on his voice. He constantly grimaces and plays to the audience, especially to seat-dancing girls. The show seemed especially well-planned but the secret may be in the ten-year bond between the members of the group. They know each other well and play easily." Meanwhile, The Toronto Sun positively dripped with praise: "While the funk-chic Hot Space album is facing a certain amount of radio programmer reluctance, it is providing their live show with a visceral immediacy it has not had in years. Shifting the foreground burden more towards the rhythm section has brought back the feeling of a band with four inseparable parts. Roger Taylor was set up with several pithy, punchy drum solos near the beginning, and John Deacon's impeccable basswork offered inescapable momentum. Atop that is all the visual and sonic flair we have come to expect of the flashiest band of our time … A superbly-paced stream of sensuous consciousness was maintained for two hours of electrifying togetherness." An ironic statement, considering the band was slowly splintering during this time. Indeed, the Japanese leg of the tour was performed as if the band was racing down the final stretch, with the finishing line just in sight.

HOT SPACE JAPAN TOUR:
19 OCTOBER TO 3 NOVEMBER 1982

Musicians: John Deacon *(bass guitar)*, Brian May *(guitars, vocals, piano on 'Save Me', acoustic guitar on 'Love Of My Life' and 'Crazy Little Thing Called Love')*, Freddie Mercury *(vocals, piano, acoustic rhythm guitar on 'Crazy Little Thing Called Love')*, Roger Taylor *(drums, vocals, Syndrums, co-lead vocals on 'Action This Day')*, Fred Mandel *(piano, keyboards, synthesizer)*

Repertoire: 'Flash' *(taped intro)* / 'The Hero', 'We Will Rock You' *(fast)*, 'Action This Day', 'Somebody To Love', 'Play The Game', 'Calling All Girls', 'Now I'm Here', 'Put Out The Fire', 'Dragon Attack', 'Now I'm Here' *(reprise)*, 'Love Of My Life', 'Save Me', 'Back Chat', 'Get Down, Make Love', 'Instrumental Inferno', 'Body Language', 'Under Pressure', 'Fat Bottomed Girls', 'Crazy Little Thing Called Love', 'Bohemian Rhapsody', 'Tie Your Mother Down', 'Teo Torriatte (Let Us Cling Together)', 'Another One Bites The Dust', 'We Will Rock You', 'We Are The Champions', 'God Save The Queen', 'Rock It (Prime Jive)', 'Jailhouse Rock', 'Saturday Night's Alright For Fighting', 'Whole Lotta Shakin' Goin' On'

Itinerary:
October 19/20: Kyuden Auditorium, Fukuoka
October 24: Hankyu Nishinomiyakyujo, Osaka
October 26: Kokusai Tenjijo, Nagoya
October 29: Hokkaidoritso Sangyo Kyoshinajaijo, Sapporo
November 3: Seibu Lions Stadium, Tokyo

For Queen's final tour dates of 1982, the band returned to Japan to perform six nights at five venues. The set list more closely resembled the one used on the European tour, with 'The Hero' and 'Rock It (Prime Jive)' alternating as the opening song, and 'Love Of My Life' reinstated; 'Calling All Girls' and 'Body Language' remained, with 'Put Out The Fire' added during the 'Now I'm Here' medley. Obviously, 'Teo Torriatte (Let Us Cling Together)' was also performed, though three covers – 'Jailhouse Rock', 'Saturday Night's Alright For Fighting' and 'Whole Lotta Shakin' Goin' On' – were also played at least once. The set lists were still unpredictable and fresh, which is a lot more than can be said for the static sets that would be played on their 1984 and 1986 tours.

However, as fresh as the sets were, the band were at odds with each other: the *Hot Space* tour had been lengthy and gruelling, and each band member was becoming weary of touring. Even Brian, who would sympathize with fans in later years over Queen's lack of live shows, had become fed up; all were looking forward to a well-deserved break.

The final night was filmed for future use, with an abridged version released the following year on the Japan-only release *Live In Japan*. 'Flash', 'The Hero', 'Now I'm Here', 'Put Out The Fire', 'Dragon Attack', the 'Now I'm Here' reprise, 'Crazy Little Thing Called Love' and 'Teo Torriatte (Let Us Cling Together)' were eventually released worldwide as extras on the 2004 *Queen On Fire: Live At The Bowl* DVD release.

Brian and John flew home on 4 November to spend time with their families, while Roger travelled to Hong Kong, Bangkok and Thailand for a short holiday. (He would return to Surrey by the 13th, premiering the *We Will Rock You* film at his home for friends of the band.) Freddie stayed on in Japan for an undetermined time to explore the finest boutiques the country had to offer; a fitting end to a trying year.

1983

CANCELED SOUTH AMERICAN TOUR:
OCTOBER/NOVEMBER 1983

Itinerary (all dates canceled):
October: Stadium, Belo Horizonte, Brazil
October: Maracana Stadium, Rio de Janeiro, Brazil
October: Morumbi Stadium, Sao Paulo, Brazil
October: Stadium, Curitiba, Brazil
October: Olympico, Porte Allegro, Brazil
November 23: Estadio Centenario, Montevideo, Uruguay

In the spring of 1983, it was announced that Queen intended to return to South America to play bigger stadiums (including Maracana Stadium in Rio de Janeiro, which could hold 206,000 people and was the largest stadium in the world). An itinerary was drafted for a series of five dates in October 1983, with all dates in Brazil, and a date in Montevideo on 23 November. Unfortunately, in a repeat of the band's first trek there in 1981, the planned tour was plagued with problems from the start: promoters, money and equipment all contributed to the endless hassle and, after discussions with Jim Beach and Gerry Stickells, the band decided to cancel the tour altogether and instead focus on their follow-up to *Hot Space*. The band would not tour in

South America again, although they would play at the Rock In Rio Festival in January 1985.

1984

SAN REMO FESTIVAL:
3 FEBRUARY 1984

Musicians: John Deacon *(bass guitar)*, Brian May *(guitar, vocals)*, Freddie Mercury *(vocals)*, Roger Taylor *(drums, vocals)*

Repertoire: 'Radio Ga Ga'

Queen were asked to appear at the San Remo Festival, marking the band's first time performing in Italy. Unfortunately for the 2000 assembled fans, Queen's set – along with those of Paul Young, Bonnie Tyler and Culture Club – was mimed and reduced to just one song, 'Radio Ga Ga', performed twice for the cameras. However, the audience didn't seem to mind, nor did the 30 million people who tuned in across Europe to watch the event.

MONTREUX GOLDEN ROSE POP FESTIVAL:
12 MAY 1984

Musicians: John Deacon *(bass guitar)*, Brian May *(guitar, vocals)*, Freddie Mercury *(vocals)*, Roger Taylor *(drums, vocals)*

Repertoire: 'Radio Ga Ga', 'Tear It Up', 'It's A Hard Life', 'I Want To Break Free'

The Golden Rose Pop Festival was a four-day event that took place in idyllic Montreux. Considering Queen owned a studio in the city, it was no surprise that they were asked to appear. On the third night of the festival, the band took the stage to an ecstatic audience, miming to four songs from *The Works*. Though no advocates of mimed performance, the band figured that the exposure was too good to pass up, though Freddie made it particularly obvious that he wasn't singing live. Couple this with Brian and John's humorously unrealistic attempts to play along to the synth backings of 'Radio Ga Ga' and 'I Want To Break Free' and the result is one of the more unique Queen performances. The footage was released in 2003 on the *Greatest Video Hits 2* DVD.

QUEEN WORKS! EUROPEAN & UK TOUR:
24 AUGUST TO 30 SEPTEMBER 1984

Musicians: John Deacon *(bass guitar)*, Brian May *(guitar, vocals, acoustic guitar on 'Is This The World We Created...?', 'Love Of My Life', and 'Crazy Little Thing Called Love')*, Freddie Mercury *(vocals, piano, electric rhythm guitar on 'Crazy Little Thing Called Love')*, Roger Taylor *(drums, electronic drums, vocals)*, Spike Edney *(keyboards, piano, vocals, guitar on 'Hammer To Fall')*

Repertoire: 'Machines (Or "Back To Humans")' *(intro)*, 'Tear It Up', 'Tie Your Mother Down', 'Under Pressure', 'Somebody To Love' / 'Killer Queen' / 'Seven Seas Of Rhye' / 'Keep Yourself Alive' / 'Liar', Improvisation, 'It's A Hard Life', 'Dragon Attack' / 'Now I'm Here', 'Is This The World We Created...?', 'Love Of My Life', 'Stone Cold Crazy' / 'Great King Rat' / Keyboard Solo / Guitar Solo / 'Brighton Rock', 'Another One Bites The Dust', 'Hammer To Fall', 'Crazy Little Thing Called Love', 'Saturday Night's Alright For Fighting', 'Bohemian Rhapsody', 'Radio Ga Ga', 'I Want To Break Free', 'Jailhouse Rock', 'We Will Rock You', 'We Are The Champions', 'God Save The Queen', 'Staying Power', 'Sheer Heart Attack', 'Not Fade Away', 'Mustapha' *(intro)*, "39' *(intro)*

Itinerary:
August 24: Forêt Nationale, Brussels, Belgium
August 28/29: RDS Simmons Hall, Dublin, Eire
August 31-September 2: NEC, Birmingham
September 4/5, 7/8: Wembley Arena, London
September 11: Westfallenhalle, Dortmund, Germany
September 14/15: Sportspalace, Milan, Italy
September 16: Olympiahalle, Munich, Germany
September 18: Omnisports, Paris, France
September 20: Groenoordhalle, Leiden, Holland
September 21: Forêt Nationale, Brussels, Belgium
September 22: Europhalle, Hannover, Germany
September 24: Deutschlandhalle, Berlin, Germany
September 26: Festhalle, Frankfurt, Germany
September 27: Schleyerhalle, Stuttgart, Germany
September 29/30: Stadhalle, Vienna, Austria

With their confidence boosted with the success of *The Works* and its first three singles, all Top 10 hits in the UK, Queen went into their UK and European tour with a renewed enthusiasm after the tumultuous *Hot Space* tour. Rehearsals were held sporadically throughout the summer of 1984, and saw a drastic change in the chosen songs. Gone was the introductory fast version of 'We Will Rock You' (though it was rehearsed), as well as most of the *Hot Space* material. 'Staying Power' survived for the first half of the tour, as an abridged introduction to 'Dragon Attack', but the most tantalising segments of the show were three sets of medleys: the first included 'Somebody To Love', 'Killer Queen', 'Seven Seas Of Rhye', 'Keep Yourself Alive' and 'Liar'; the second consisted of the 'Mustapha' intro (depending on the date), 'Staying Power', 'Dragon Attack' and 'Now I'm Here'; the third, and most interesting, was 'Stone Cold Crazy', 'Great King Rat', keyboard and guitar solos from Spike and Brian respectively, and the conclusion of 'Brighton Rock'. Intriguingly, the band rehearsed 40 songs, which saw them digging even deeper into their discography; some that didn't make the cut included 'I'm In Love With My Car', 'Sweet Lady', 'White Man', 'Play The Game', 'Need Your Loving Tonight', 'Put Out The Fire', 'Las Palabras De Amor (The Words Of Love)', and two renditions of 'Life Is Real (Song For Lennon)', one solo by Freddie on vocals and piano, and the other as an acoustic duet by Freddie and Brian.

With Fred Mandel unavailable to tour, due to commitments with Supertramp and Elton John, the band had to recruit a new auxiliary keyboardist. Spike Edney was hired as informally as Mack had been as Queen's new producer in 1979, and when he arrived in Munich in August, a day before the beginning of rehearsals, he joined the others in partying throughout the night and ended up missing the first day; fearing for his job, he was relieved to discover everyone else had, too. "The next day, we all managed to get to it eventually, to the first rehearsal, and all the gear was set up. The stage was huge, and I thought, 'Oh well, here we go, then', and we got to the first song, and what I'd forgotten was that they hadn't actually played together for two years. So they said, 'OK, let's try one of the new songs', I think it was 'Radio Ga Ga', and we started playing it, and course, I knew it, I'd been studying it for weeks. You know, '1, 2, 3, 4,' and we start and we get about a minute into the song and the whole thing collapses. And they all look at each other, you know, very sheepishly, and they say, 'Anyone know how it goes?' and I say, 'Well, actually, I know. I know how it goes,' and they said, 'Ah'. And so I started showing them the chords and everything and Fred looked at me and said, 'You don't know the words, do you?' and 'Well, yeah I do, actually,' so then they all came round the piano and we spent the whole day just going through songs, and I thought, 'I'm gonna be all right here, this'll be OK'!"

The tour started on 24 August in Brussels, which was more or less a warm-up gig (and an opportunity to film the 'Hammer To Fall' promotional video), before winding its way through Eire, England, Germany, Italy (their first-ever live dates there) and Austria. The band were in good spirits throughout the tour, with very little of the debauchery that had affected the *Hot Space* tour, though Freddie's voice was increasingly suffering from the effects of his decadence, and vocal issues would plague him throughout the tour. Additionally, in Hannover, Freddie slipped during 'Hammer To Fall' and injured his knee, which he had already damaged in a Munich club mêlée ("Some cunt kicked me," he explained, "It might mean I'll have to cut down on some of my more elaborate gorgeous stage moves"), forcing the concert to come to a premature close, and for him to remain in plaster for the remainder of the tour.

Otherwise, the tour would prove to be one of the band's more successful, with Roger later calling it one of his favorites. At Queen's London shows, Brian's daughter Louisa was in attendance, witnessing her father in action for the very first time. He dedicated 'Love Of My Life' to her, and even played a snippet of Brahms' 'Lullaby' in the solo. The following night, Roger's son Felix was in the audience, and Brian once again addressed the youth: "I would like to dedicate this song to all the children in the audience ... of any age at all. And especially to young Felix because it's his first concert. He's gonna be the drummer in the band one day." (Not quite: Felix's brother, Rufus, would play with Brian on his 2011 tour with Kerry Ellis, and then become the auxiliary drummer in Queen + Adam Lambert, though Felix would sing vocals on his father's 'Woman You're So Beautiful (But Still A Pain In The Ass)' single in 2006.) Overall, the London shows were more of a party than a serious concert presentation, with the culmination being on 5 September, Freddie's 38th birthday. The audience were clearly having a ball, singing 'Happy Birthday' to the singer on several occasions: the first was before 'Staying Power', with the second coming before 'Love Of My Life'. However, Freddie was offstage at the time, leading Brian, who was waiting for the audience to cool down, to softly admit, "It's not my birthday ... I'm sorry, he's gone home. It's his birthday." Freddie returned to the stage in time for the second verse (on this tour, the audience would always sing the first verse), but before he could sing, he was handed a gift, which he innocently inquired, "What is it, a jock strap?" After completing

the second verse, he stopped once again when handed a birthday card: "Someone sent me a card. I gotta open it, so hang on a minute." (Leave it to Freddie to stop a concert, especially during one of the more poignant songs, to open a birthday card onstage.) Nevertheless, he read it to himself, then laughed: "I can't read *this*! It's even too filthy for me!" Wisely, the band had an off day the next day; they all celebrated quite liberally at Freddie's after-show birthday party, and it was from this point forward that Freddie's voice would gradually deteriorate, not fully recovering until the following year.

The British press were still on the attack, however: *Sounds*, reviewing the Birmingham gig, had a bone to pick with the fans: "The disciples are here in their thousands, and at a mere glimpse of their heroes they become so noisy, so full of joy, it's like they actually believe in this band; like their lives are fully dependent on them; it's almost as if they honestly look upon Queen as (sincere, respectufl [sic] tones) IMPORTANT. Freddie Mercury is aware of this, knows exactly how they feel, and agrees with them completely. An explosion of sound and light: the crowd gasps. So many important songs to come, so much serious 'quality' music to enjoy. There's 'Radio Ga Ga', there's 'I Want To Break Free', there's ... endless crap."

Melody Maker, in a typo-ridden and poorly-researched review, seethed viciously, "Naively hoping to hear a selection of the very best singles which this band have produced over the years, we were treated [sic] instead to the biggest grossout this side of Giant Haystacks' beergut. All horrible frenzied guitar breaks, forgettable album tracks, and no sign at all of the subtleties one might hope to expect from a band who have written something as glorious as 'Don't Stop Me Now'. And no, I'm being totally serious ... At the end of this very bad day for Freddie, only rescued from total distaster by trotting out the entire back catalog, a great 'Bohemian Rhapsody' included, two comparisons spring to mind. One, Queen are not unlike an all-male British ABBA, good enough when they stick to the hits but big on the crap factor when they are let loose in public. And Freddie has a far better bum of course. Two, for all his camp peacock and feathers posturing, Fred still manages to look something like a perverse cross between a veteran bullfighter and a part-time member of the RUC."

Kerrang! came off as an embarrassing but well-intentioned child witnessing a concert for the very first time. "I do not believe it! I am stunned, I am astounded! I have been in the presence of something that stretched beyond the boundaries of mortality and attained the heights of something quite inexpressibly wonderful. I have witnessed a concert that has re-established my faith in the power of the rock medium as a truly awe-inspiring force! Guys, guys, if only you'd been there, you'd have seen it and felt it and lived it too!" After three more full paragraphs of slobbering fanboyism, the reviewer finally gets onto the show, concluding, "When Freddie cries out: 'We Are The Champions Of The World!' can you doubt the truthfulness of the old tart's words? Not me, squire, cos this was quite simply rock'n'roll at its very, very best."

QUEEN WORKS! SOUTH AFRICAN TOUR:
5 TO 20 OCTOBER 1984

Musicians: John Deacon *(bass guitar)*, Brian May *(guitar, vocals, acoustic guitar on 'Is This The World We Created...?', 'Love Of My Life', and 'Crazy Little Thing Called Love')*, Freddie Mercury *(vocals, piano, electric rhythm guitar on 'Crazy Little Thing Called Love')*, Roger Taylor *(drums, electronic drums, vocals)*, Spike Edney *(keyboards, piano, vocals, guitar on 'Hammer To Fall')*

Repertoire: 'Machines (Or "Back To Humans")' *(intro)*, 'Tear It Up', 'Tie Your Mother Down', 'Under Pressure', 'Somebody To Love' / 'Killer Queen' / 'Seven Seas Of Rhye' / 'Keep Yourself Alive' / 'Liar', Improvisation, 'It's A Hard Life', 'Dragon Attack' / 'Now I'm Here', 'Is This The World We Created...?', 'Love Of My Life', 'Another One Bites The Dust', 'Hammer To Fall', 'Crazy Little Thing Called Love', 'Bohemian Rhapsody', 'Radio Ga Ga', 'I Want To Break Free', 'Jailhouse Rock', 'We Will Rock You', 'We Are The Champions', 'God Save The Queen'

Itinerary:
October 5/6/7, 12/13/14, 18/19/20: Super Bowl, Sun City, Bophuthatswana

The European leg of the Queen Works! tour concluded on 30 September, later moving onto the band's first shows in South Africa, which were a disaster from the word go. The band flew into Bophuthatswana to play at least seven dates at the Sun City Superbowl in the first week of October, with the first date set for the 5th. Eleven dates were scheduled, but only eight were fully fulfilled: at the third show, Freddie's voice gave out completely after 'Somebody To Love', and instead of risking further damage, the band decided

to end the show early, and canceled the dates on the 9th and 10th to allow him time to rest. (During the downtime, Brian traveled to Soweto, just outside the capital of Johannesburg, to present at the Black African Awards Show. The experience touched him deeply: "It was quite amazing. The whole atmosphere, the warmth, the great friendliness of the people ... It was a night I'll never forget. I promised those people that one day Queen would go back to Soweto and play the stadium for them.") The remainder of the shows went off without a hitch, with Freddie remaining a bit more conservative with his voice; he still had a bit of fun, with the second-to-last night seeing him referencing both 'The March Of The Black Queen' and 'My Fairy King' before 'Killer Queen'.

Deflecting the criticism surrounding Sun City – essentially a wealthy white man's casino resort surrounded by poverty-stricken black communities – by merely stating that they played where they were asked to, the band insisted that the audiences be mixed and that a portion of the tickets be given away for free. (The average price of the ticket was 26 Rand, about £52.) Brian especially was supportive of his band's decision to play: "We're totally against apartheid and all it stands for, but I feel we did a lot of bridge building. We actually met musicians of both colours. They all welcomed us with open arms. The only criticism we got was from outside of South Africa."

It was enough criticism for the band to seriously consider their future. Upon their return to England, the Musicians' Union fined the band for breaking their guidelines: Sun City was the one place in the world the Union banned their members from playing in due to its stance on apartheid. Queen weren't proponents of segregation in any form, and Brian appeared in front of the Musicians' Union General Committee to give a passionate speech in defence of Queen's decision. "The general reaction was, at least, 'Thanks for coming, we understand why you did it now'. But they fined us anyway because we'd broken the rules." The band were so despondent toward the end of the year that they privately agreed to finish out the remainder of the tour dates and call it a day for the foreseeable future.

1985

ROCK IN RIO FESTIVAL:
12 TO 19 JANUARY 1985

Musicians: John Deacon *(bass guitar)*, Brian May

(guitar, vocals, acoustic guitar on 'Is This The World We Created...?', 'Love Of My Life', and 'Crazy Little Thing Called Love'), Freddie Mercury *(vocals, piano, electric rhythm guitar on 'Crazy Little Thing Called Love')*, Roger Taylor *(drums, electronic drums, vocals)*, Spike Edney *(keyboards, piano, vocals, guitar on 'Hammer To Fall')*

Repertoire: 'Machines (Or "Back To Humans")' *(intro)*, 'Tear It Up', 'Tie Your Mother Down', 'Under Pressure', 'Somebody To Love' / 'Killer Queen' / 'Seven Seas Of Rhye' / 'Keep Yourself Alive' / 'Liar', 'Rock In Rio Blues' (second night only), Improvisation, 'It's A Hard Life', 'Dragon Attack' / 'Now I'm Here', 'Is This The World We Created...?', 'Love Of My Life', Guitar Solo, 'Brighton Rock', 'Another One Bites The Dust', 'Hammer To Fall', 'Crazy Little Thing Called Love', 'Bohemian Rhapsody', 'Radio Ga Ga', 'I Want To Break Free', 'Jailhouse Rock', 'We Will Rock You', 'We Are The Champions', 'God Save The Queen'

Arranged by Queen's longtime tour manager Gerry Stickells, the Rock In Rio Festival was held over an eight-day period, with the band closing the shows on the first and last nights. Other major bands involved, along with several local Brazilian groups, were AC/DC, Def Leppard, Iron Maiden, Yes, James Taylor, George Benson, and Ozzy Osbourne. Queen were asked to headline the event due to South America's love affair with them on their 1981 tour; the band readily agreed because they had felt such a connection with the audience the first time around.

Roger, Brian and John left from London on Sunday 6 January, with Freddie journeying from Munich via Paris due to bad weather. The set list was unchanged apart from a specially written 'improvisation' called 'Rock In Rio Blues', based on what was more commonly known as 'Instrumental Inferno' on prior tours. The venue was Barra da Tijuca, a specially built site with a capacity of 250,000 – this would turn out to be one of Queen's biggest audiences, and one of the reasons they agreed to play in the first place. Gerry had arranged with the local Brazilian television station, Globo, to televise the festival throughout South America, while the band started negotiations with Globo about acquiring the rights to their segments, which were enthusiastically granted.

The first night, the band took the stage at two in the morning, though the audience's enthusiasm hadn't waned. In an 'event' that was widely reported in the British press, Freddie was apparently bombarded

with rubbish when he appeared for the first encore performance of 'I Want To Break Free' in his usual wig, falsies and pink sweater; audio and video proof exists, however, confirming that such an occurrence did not happen. (He was, however, booed, and promptly discarded the offending items, and they wouldn't return for the following night.) Following the show, EMI held a party at the Copacabana, which was also televised all over South America. Having been thrown into the pool fully clothed, Brian got wind of the fact that hundreds of fans had gathered on the beach outside the hotel and spelled out 'Queen' in the sand with 1500 candles. The guitarist and his daughter went to see for themselves, mingling with the fans for several hours in preference to the glittering celebrity affair.

By the time of Queen's second appearance, Rio had experienced torrential downpours, which turned the stadium into a veritable swamp. This didn't dampen the spirits of the audience, though, and the band were touched by their enthusiasm. The difficulty of playing in the rain during the small hours shows in the band's performance, however; amazingly, the band agreed for the show to be released, with a heavily edited video performance appearing on 13 May 1985 and entitled Live In Rio.

The following month, Brian was a guest DJ on Capital Radio, and talked briefly of how Rock In Rio had affected him: "We never quite believed that it was going to happen and we were going to get quarter of a million people a night or whatever, and it just actually happened. They all rolled up and one night it was pouring with rain and they were still there until two in the morning from four in the afternoon. It was very well-organized and very well-lit which is unusual, so you could actually see the audience very well, all in pools of different colored lights. I think there is going to be a video of that some time and perhaps people will be able to see, but it was quite something, I must say. And there was the feeling of it being the first time, which it was, because there never was that much rock and roll in Rio. Now there is, mate, I tell you!"

QUEEN WORKS! AUSTRALASIAN & JAPANESE TOUR:
13 APRIL TO 15 MAY 1985

Musicians: John Deacon *(bass guitar)*, Brian May *(guitar, vocals, acoustic guitar on 'Is This The World We Created...?', 'Love Of My Life', and 'Crazy Little Thing*

Called Love'), Freddie Mercury (vocals, piano, electric rhythm guitar on 'Crazy Little Thing Called Love'), Roger Taylor (drums, electronic drums, vocals), Spike Edney (keyboards, piano, vocals, guitar on 'Hammer To Fall')

Repertoire: 'Machines (Or "Back To Humans")' (intro), 'Tear It Up', 'Tie Your Mother Down', 'Under Pressure', 'Somebody To Love' / 'Killer Queen' / 'Seven Seas Of Rhye' / 'Keep Yourself Alive' / 'Liar', Improvisation, 'It's A Hard Life', 'Dragon Attack' / 'Now I'm Here', 'Is This The World We Created...?', 'Love Of My Life', Guitar Solo, 'Brighton Rock', 'Another One Bites The Dust', 'Hammer To Fall', 'Crazy Little Thing Called Love', 'Bohemian Rhapsody', 'Radio Ga Ga', 'I Want To Break Free', 'Jailhouse Rock', 'We Will Rock You', 'We Are The Champions', 'God Save The Queen', 'Rock In Rio Blues', 'Saturday Night's Alright For Fighting', 'Whole Lotta Shakin' Goin' On'

Itinerary, Australiasian tour:
April 13: Mount Smart Stadium, Auckland, New Zealand
April 16/17, 19/20: Sports and Entertainment Centre, Melbourne, Australia
April 25/26, 28/29: Entertainment Centre, Sydney, Australia

Itinerary, Japanese tour:
May 8/9: Budokan Hall, Tokyo
May 11: Yogishi Swimming Pool Auditorium, Tokyo
May 13: Aichi Auditorium, Nagoya
May 15: Castle Hall, Osaka

After yet another lengthy break, which afforded Freddie enough time to complete his first solo album, the band flew to New Zealand on 5 April to start rehearsals for their first Australasian tour in nearly a decade. The band took a week to get acquainted with their surroundings since it was their first – and only – appearance in New Zealand. The tour was destined to start on 11 April at Hawks Bay in Tamoana, with a third date on 14 April at Queen Elizabeth II Park in Christchurch, but ticket sales were poor – the Auckland gig didn't even sell out.

The band's first show on 13 April was memorable: Tony Hadley from Spandau Ballet joined them on stage for a performance of 'Jailhouse Rock'. Before the show, Freddie and Tony imbibed a little too much, which was noticeable whenever Freddie addressed the crowd. His first words of the night were, "Hello

New Zealand, we're gonna have one motherfucker of a time!" When introducing 'Hammer To Fall', he yelled, "Here's one for all you heavy metal fans to have a good jerk-off to!" When Tony appeared for the first encore, the two messed up the words to 'Jailhouse Rock' by singing 'Tutti Frutti' instead. And, as luck would have it, this was the one Queen show that was broadcast all over the country.

The band moved on to Melbourne on 15 April to commence a four-night stand at the Sports and Entertainment Center there. The final night was dogged with technical problems: the lights gave out midway through the show and the sound fluctuated throughout as well, much to the audible annoyance of Freddie. Because the band had visited Phil Collins on their one night off (18 April), he duly repaid the compliment and later explained that, despite all the problems, the show was still enjoyable.

On 21 April, the band flew to Sydney, where they relaxed for a few days before another four-night residency. Brian took advantage of the break and flew to the Great Barrier Reef with his wife, where the two learned to scuba dive. On the 27th, Elton John and John Reid, Queen's former manager, were in Sydney during Elton's own Australian tour. Reid treated Brian and John to a night at the Sydney Opera House, while Freddie, Roger and Elton soaked up the local nightlife.

The set list for this tour changed little, though 'Rock In Rio Blues' stayed in (it was renamed 'Tokyo Blues' during the Japanese leg), and only two cover versions, 'Saturday Night's Alright For Fighting' and 'Whole Lotta Shakin' Goin' On', were performed. Freddie's voice was in a better state than it had been at the beginning of the Works! tour, perhaps because the schedule wasn't as rigorous as it had been the previous year - throughout the month that Queen were on the road, they only played 14 shows, compared to 29 the year before.

Nevertheless, the band soldiered on to Japan, where – surprise! – the set list remained exactly the same. The band failed to include 'Teo Torriatte (Let Us Cling Together)' for some reason, though Freddie once again played the 'My Fairy King' / 'The March Of The Black Queen' improvisation that had started in South Africa the previous year. After the brief, six-day Japanese tour concluded, the band had every intention of calling it quits (again). But they had agreed to appear at Live Aid, not realizing the impact it would have on their career.

LIVE AID:

13 JULY 1985

Musicians: John Deacon *(bass guitar)*, Brian May *(guitar, vocals, acoustic guitar on 'Crazy Little Thing Called Love' and 'Is This The World We Created…?')*, Freddie Mercury *(vocals, piano, electric rhythm guitar on 'Crazy Little Thing Called Love')*, Roger Taylor *(drums, electronic drums, vocals)*, Spike Edney *(keyboards, piano, vocals, guitar on 'Hammer To Fall')*

Repertoire: 'Bohemian Rhapsody' *(intro)*, 'Radio Ga Ga', 'Hammer To Fall', 'Crazy Little Thing Called Love', 'We Will Rock You', 'We Are The Champions', 'Is This The World We Created…?'

While on tour in Australia, Spike Edney was contacted by Bob Geldof (Spike had been an occasional trombonist in Geldof's band The Boomtown Rats), telling him he was setting up an event in July to raise money for famine relief in Africa and asking if Queen would like to be involved. The band, however, were fed up with touring and were planning on taking the rest of the year and the following year off, before possibly recording again in 1987. Spirits were at an all-time low, which Spike relayed to Bob.

Undeterred, Bob called the band directly in Japan, and tried to sell them on the idea. The band declined once again but, over a meal in their Japanese hotel, finally agreed to say yes. They started rehearsals for the Live Aid event at the Shaw Theatre on 10 July, treating it like a proper show and not a one-off gig, knowing quite well that a lot of people were going to be watching. "We've always had our quiet periods and comebacks," Brian said at the time. "Geldof called Live Aid a jukebox, so it seemed obvious to simply play the hits and get off."

On the day of the concert, the band were understandably nervous, but at 6.44 pm GMT, comedians Mel Smith and Griff Rhys Jones simply walked on stage and announced, "Her Majesty … Queen." Enter the band, and their total shock and wide-eyed wonder is apparent from the minute they are seen on camera. It was like a homecoming for them: they hadn't played London since September 1984, and the reception showed just how appreciated they were. After running around the stage for a few seconds, Freddie settled down at the piano and opened the set with 'Bohemian Rhapsody'. Playing only the first half up until the guitar solo (playback tapes were

not allowed, and there was no way Queen were going to attempt to sing the operatic section), the band then kicked into 'Radio Ga Ga' and 'Hammer To Fall'.

The performance was not without its problems: during Brian's solo in 'Crazy Little Thing Called Love', he was obscured by a piercing stab of feedback for the first half, with the rest of the solo sadly muted. (One of Geldof's other caveats had been that no band was allowed a soundcheck, which didn't sit too well with Queen, but it was one of the sacrifices they had to make.) 'We Will Rock You' and 'We Are The Champions' followed, and even the most reluctant of audience members found themselves singing along.

Three hours later, at 9.48 pm, after Wham!'s performance and just before Paul McCartney's moving finale, Brian and Freddie were perched on stools at the front of the stage to perform 'Is This The World We Created…?', which was met with applause despite being marred by the ever-present feedback. Later, Freddie appeared with other luminaries for a star-studded singalong of the previous year's hit single, 'Do They Know It's Christmas?'

It was momentous, and the general consensus was that Queen were the band of the day. Despite one minor timing issue in 'Hammer To Fall', in which Freddie called for the ending of the song too early, the band had risen to the challenge and did not disappoint. By November, a BBC poll named Queen's performance at Live Aid the greatest live gig of all time, beating out Jimi Hendrix's Woodstock performance and The Sex Pistols' concert at the Manchester Free Trade Hall in 1976.

The band would speak highly of Live Aid for years after. John said, "The day was fabulous – people forgot that element of [competition] … It was a good morale-booster for us too, because it showed us the strength of support we had in England, and it showed us what we had to offer as a band." Brian agreed, saying, "I think Live Aid proved we didn't need backdrops or [the] cover of darkness … I'll remember Live Aid till the day I die." With their enthusiasm apparently restored, the band recanted on their previous decision to pack it all in and became an even more cohesive unit than before.

1986

MONTREUX GOLDEN ROSE POP FESTIVAL:

11 MAY 1986

Musicians: John Deacon *(bass guitar)*, Brian May *(guitar,* vocals), Freddie Mercury *(vocals)*, Roger Taylor *(drums, vocals)*

Repertoire: 'One Vision', 'A Kind Of Magic', 'Friends Will Be Friends', 'Hammer To Fall'

Just as they had done in May 1984, Queen returned to the Montreux Golden Rose Pop Festival to mime to four songs: three from the new album *A Kind Of Magic* ('One Vision', the title track and 'Friends Will Be Friends'), and 'Hammer To Fall' from *The Works*. Like the first time, Freddie made it obvious that he was miming (though the others tried their hardest to make it appear real) by positioning his microphone as far away from his mouth as possible. This footage was later released on the 2003 DVD *Greatest Video Hits 2*.

MAGIC TOUR:

7 JUNE TO 9 AUGUST 1986

Musicians: John Deacon *(bass guitar)*, Brian May *(guitar, vocals, keyboards on 'Who Wants To Live Forever', acoustic guitar on 'Love Of My Life', 'Is This The World We Created…?', '(You're So Square) Baby I Don't Care', 'Hello Mary Lou (Goodbye Heart)', 'Tutti Frutti', and 'Crazy Little Thing Called Love')*, Freddie Mercury *(vocals, piano, electric rhythm guitar on 'Crazy Little Thing Called Love')*, Roger Taylor *(drums, vocals, tambourine on '(You're So Square) Baby I Don't Care', 'Hello Mary Lou (Goodbye Heart)', and 'Tutti Frutti', effects on 'A Kind Of Magic')*, Spike Edney *(piano, keyboards, rhythm guitar on 'Hammer To Fall')*

Repertoire: 'One Vision', 'Tie Your Mother Down', 'In The Lap Of The Gods… Revisited' / 'Seven Seas Of Rhye' / 'Tear It Up', 'A Kind Of Magic', Vocal Improvisation, 'Under Pressure', 'Another One Bites The Dust', 'Who Wants To Live Forever', 'I Want To Break Free', 'Impromptu', Guitar Solo, 'Now I'm Here', 'Love Of My Life', 'Is This The World We Created…?', '(You're So Square) Baby I Don't Care', 'Hello Mary Lou (Goodbye Heart)', 'Tutti Frutti', 'Bohemian Rhapsody', 'Hammer To Fall', 'Crazy Little Thing Called Love', 'Radio Ga Ga', 'We Will Rock You', 'Friends Will Be Friends', 'We Are The Champions', 'God Save The Queen', 'Big Spender', 'Saturday Night's Alright For Fighting', 'Immigrant Song', 'Gimme Some Lovin'', 'Tavaszi Szél Vizet Áraszt'

Itinerary:
June 7: Rasunda Fotbollstadion, Stockholm, Sweden

June 11/12: Groenoordhalle, Leiden, Holland
June 14: Hippodrome de Vincennes, Paris, France
June 17: Forêt Nationale, Brussels, Belgium
June 19: Groenoordhalle, Leiden, Holland
June 21: Maimarktgelände, Mannheim, Germany
June 26: Waldbuehne, Berlin, Germany
June 28/29: Olympiahalle, Munich, Germany
July 1/2: Hallenstadion, Zurich, Switzerland
July 5: Slane Castle, Dublin, Eire
July 9: St James Park, Newcastle
July 11/12: Wembley Stadium, London
July 16: Maine Road, Manchester
July 19: Müngersdorfer Stadion, Cologne, Germany
July 21/22: Stadthalle, Vienna, Austria
July 27: Nepstadion, Budapest, Hungary
July 30: Amphitheatre, Frejus, France *(rescheduled from Cannes, 29 August, and Nice, 30 August)*
August 1: Monumental Plaza de Toros, Barcelona, Spain *(rescheduled from 31 July)*
August 3: Estadio Rayo Vallecano, Madrid, Spain *(rescheduled from 2 August)*
August 5: Estadio Municipal, Marbella, Spain *(rescheduled from 4 August)*
August 9: Knebworth Park, Stevenage, Hertfordshire

By June 1986, it had been nearly a year, excluding the Montreux Golden Rose Pop Festival, since Queen last appeared on stage, and demand for the band to tour again was becoming overwhelming. Originally, 1986 was to be an off year, much as 1983 had been, because the Queen Works! tours hadn't been the rejuvenation the band needed after the stressful *Hot Space* tours of 1982. Live Aid changed everything, however, and the band became excited once again about performing to an audience. In addition, Queen had become one of the hottest tickets in Europe and the United Kingdom; when venues were announced and tickets went on sale, most shows sold out almost instantly.

As with every tour, the band restructured their set list to incorporate new material and generally reshuffle the old favorites. From the new album, only four of the nine songs were integrated ('One Vision', 'A Kind Of Magic', 'Who Wants To Live Forever' and 'Friends Will Be Friends'), while there were surprising inclusions of 'In The Lap Of The Gods…Revisited' (last performed in 1977) and a rock 'n' roll acoustic medley of '(You're So Square) Baby I Don't Care', 'Hello Mary Lou (Goodbye Heart)', and 'Tutti Frutti'. Gone were the older songs: 'Great King Rat', 'Stone Cold Crazy', 'Somebody To Love', 'Keep Yourself Alive', 'Killer

Queen', 'Brighton Rock' and 'Jailhouse Rock' were all omitted to make way for newer material, though 'Liar' was used as an instrumental link between 'Seven Seas Of Rhye' and 'Tear It Up'. The most surprising omission was 'Somebody To Love', which had been performed on almost every tour since 1977 and was a highlight of any given show. 'It's A Hard Life', too, wasn't considered for the tour, and it's been suggested by fans that Freddie wanted to spend more time entertaining the crowd rather than being stuck at a piano. For the first time in years, 'Now I'm Here' was performed straight, with no additional songs inserted to form a medley.

The band started rehearsals for the tour in May 1986 at JVC Studios, taking a day in the middle to film the promotional video for 'Friends Will Be Friends' and thereby offering a look at the stage the band would be using for the tour: 64 feet in length, with two 40-foot wings, giving Freddie nearly 6000 square feet to run around in.

Midway through the rehearsals, Roger sat down for an interview and hyped the upcoming tour effectively: "We are going to play on the biggest stage ever built at Wembley, with the greatest light show ever seen. I think we are probably the best live band in the world at the moment, and we are going to prove it. No one who comes to see us will be disappointed," adding humorously that the general effect would be "bigger than bigness itself. It'll make Ben-Hur look like The Muppets." It's hard to disagree with him: while tours by U2, The Rolling Stones and Pink Floyd in the later part of the 1980s would take excess to a whole new level and overshadow the Magic tour, Queen's final tour was the biggest of its day.

Unfortunately, America missed out on the tour yet again: sales of 'One Vision' and A Kind Of Magic hadn't been encouraging, and the band weren't willing to take such a massive stage set-up from coast to coast. Surprisingly, Japan was not included in the itinerary either, nor was Australia or New Zealand. There were rumors that the beginning of 1987 would see the band back on stages around the world, but there's considerable evidence that Freddie knew that the Knebworth concert would be his last. "I think it was somewhere in Spain," Brian explained in 2003, "there was a little argument that broke out, and John got quite iffy about something, and Freddie turned around and said, 'Well, I'm not going to be doing this forever, this is probably the last time', and that was a bit of a jolt. I didn't know if that was an instant response or if there

was something else on his mind … I think he really knew what he was going to be dealing with."

Support throughout the tour alternated between The Bangles, Fountainhead, Big Country, Chris Rea, Status Quo, The Alarm, Craaft, Gary Moore, Belouis Some, Level 42, INXS, and Marillion. (In Mannheim, Marillion's lead vocalist, Fish, joined Queen on stage during 'Tutti Frutti', providing additional vocals, while Brian repaid the compliment in Cologne by appearing during Marillion's set on 'Market Square Heroes'.) Fans, however, would grow impatient during any given support act's set and start throwing items at the stage in an attempt to speed up the process. Perhaps the most unique support band on the tour was Z'Zi Labour in Budapest, who performed a version of The Rolling Stones' 'Honky Tonk Women' backed by a chorus of women dressed in peasant costumes.

The tour started on 7 June in Stockholm and was received rapturously, though the set list was marginally different from how it would end up being: 'Bohemian Rhapsody' followed 'I Want To Break Free', and 'Friends Will Be Friends' wasn't yet performed. (It would be introduced in Holland and was given a full rendition for the first two performances there; the remainder of the tour featured a heavily abridged version.) For the remainder of the dates, the standard set list would be changed around little. Apart from occasional performances of 'Big Spender', 'Saturday Night's Alright For Fighting', 'Gimme Some Lovin'' – as well as one-offs in the form of Led Zeppelin's 'Immigrant Song' and the traditional Hungarian folk song 'Tavaszi Szél Vizet Áraszt' – the band played it safe and stayed the course. Surprisingly though, 'Jailhouse Rock', which had been performed on at least one date per tour in the past, wasn't performed at all this time.

The shows progressed through Europe during June and early July, hitting all the usual hot spots prior to playing Slane Castle in Dublin on 5 July. Unfortunately, during this first show back on home ground the band were forced to stop after 'Seven Seas Of Rhye' due to a drunken fight, causing Freddie to roar his disapproval at the crowd; Brian was later hit in the head with a beer can, almost refusing to perform the encore as a result. Thankfully, the following night's show in Newcastle-Upon-Tyne went better than expected, with the show sold out within an hour and all proceeds donated to the Save The Children Fund.

The next two dates were Queen's genuine homecoming, and have been regarded, perhaps through a veil of sentimentality, as the band's finest shows ever. These Wembley concerts almost had to be canceled, however: Queen's pre-built stage was so huge that it wasn't able to fit into the venue, but after a major reconstruction, the road crew were able to come up with an alternate design that worked more comfortably. For these two shows, during 'A Kind Of Magic', four oversized inflatable dummies were let loose into the stadium as an added effect. While Brian and Roger's dummies were dragged into the audience, John and Freddie's floated away to freedom, with the vocalist ending up in a bemused family's garden several miles away.

The first night was partially filmed as a camera test for the following night: Queen had decided to film and record both shows for a planned live video and album. (The video wouldn't be released until 1990, and the album would follow two years later, while 'Is This The World We Created…?' from the first night and 'Hammer To Fall' from the second were included on *Live Magic* in December 1986.) The second night was also broadcast as a radio and television simulcast on 25 October. The show, titled *Real Magic*, was watched by 3.5 million people and was even broadcast in America during Westwood One's Superstar Concert. After the second concert, the band appeared at Kensington Roof Gardens in London for an after-show party, giving an impromptu performance as Dicky Hart And The Pacemakers (with Samantha Fox and Gary Glitter assisting on additional vocals), providing rollicking renditions of at least 'Tutti Frutti' and 'Sweet Little Rock And Roller', though the full set is not known.

Following a date in Manchester, the band's UK concerts were finished for the tour (except for Knebworth, which was added in haste after tickets for the band's home country sold out quickly). They returned to Germany for a date in Cologne which marked Brian's 39th birthday; he therefore threw in a snippet of "39' before 'Love Of My Life'. 'Saturday Night's Alright For Fighting', a rare song to be played during the Magic tour, was also performed following 'Tutti Frutti', but, sadly, these songs, in addition to the remainder of the show, will never be seen as Janos Zsombolyai, director of the band's show in Budapest, overtaped it later because of the cost of VHS tapes.

This concert had originally been scheduled for 25 July, then moved to the 26th, finally taking place on the 27th. Footage of Queen and entourage arriving in Budapest by hydrofoil (via the Danube) was filmed and later released on Live In Budapest, along with additional video footage of each band member let loose in the city. The band were visibly overwhelmed at the positive reception they received; as a display of their appreciation, after 'Love Of My Life' Freddie joked, "Now comes the difficult bit…" Brian then played the introduction to a traditional Hungarian folk song, 'Tavaszi Szél Vizet Áraszt', with Freddie reading the words from his hand.

After leaving Hungary, the band then trekked to France and Spain, encountering scheduling conflicts in both countries. The band's first appearance in Barcelona was notable in that, during a television interview, Freddie claimed that his favorite vocalist was Montserrat Caballé and that he would love to record with her; someone in her camp was clearly watching, as this was the impetus for their collaboration, *Barcelona*, the next year.

The date in Marbella was due to be the final show of the tour but ticket requests in the UK were so strong that promoter Harvey Goldsmith added a date at Knebworth Park. The show was filmed and recorded; the majority of songs on Live Magic were taken from it, but it has never been released in its entirety. While the show was marred by the death of a Status Quo fan, who was stabbed and was unable to receive proper medical attention before bleeding to death; at the same concert, an expectant mother went into labor during the show and gave birth on the grounds in an ambulance on the way to St John's Hospital.

The show has been considered the best of the tour because of the sheer enthusiasm both band and audience exhibited, though some have speculated that Freddie may have known that this would be Queen's final tour and wanted to go out on top. "That was a fun tour, I remember it being particularly good," Roger said with the benefit of hindsight. "And it was nice, because we were doing very big places, which is quite hard in Europe: we were doing big outdoor stadiums in most places, and when they weren't available, we would do big indoor stadiums, and they were all full, which was great."

PART FIVE

COMPILATIONS AND COLLABORATIONS

A. COMPILATION ALBUMS

A number of Queen compilations have appeared over the years; instead of attempting to name every last one, what follows is a simple guide to the standard compilation albums. Promo albums and overseas albums have been ignored.

GREATEST HITS

EMI EMTV 30, November 1981 [1]
Elektra 5E-564, November 1981 [14]
EMI CDP 7 46033 2, 1986
Parlophone CDPCSD 141, 1994
Hollywood 7 2061-62475 2, October 2004 [42]

1981 UK track listing: 'Bohemian Rhapsody' (5'56), 'Another One Bites The Dust' (3'37), 'Killer Queen' (3'02), 'Fat Bottomed Girls' *(edit)* (3'26), 'Bicycle Race' (3'03), 'You're My Best Friend' (2'52), 'Don't Stop Me Now' (3'31), 'Save Me' (3'49), 'Crazy Little Thing Called Love' (2'45), 'Somebody To Love' (4'58), 'Now I'm Here' (4'15), 'Good Old Fashioned Lover Boy' (2'55), 'Play The Game' (3'32), 'Flash' *(edit)* (2'51), 'Seven Seas Of Rhye' (2'50), 'We Will Rock You' (2'02), 'We Are The Champions' (3'02)

Bonus tracks on 2004 US CD reissue: 'I'm In Love With My Car' *(edit)* (3'12), 'Under Pressure' *(live version, Milton Keynes Bowl, June 1982)* (3'39), 'Tie Your Mother Down' *(live version, Milton Keynes Bowl, June 1982)* (3'50)

1981 US track listing: 'Another One Bites The Dust' (3'37), 'Bohemian Rhapsody' (5'56), 'Crazy Little Thing Called Love' (2'45), 'Killer Queen' (3'02), 'Fat Bottomed Girls' *(edit)* (3'26), 'Bicycle Race' (3'03), 'Under Pressure' (4'01), 'We Will Rock You' (2'02), 'We Are The Champions' (3'02), 'Flash' *(edit)* (2'51), 'Somebody To Love' (4'58), 'You're My Best Friend' (2'52), 'Keep Yourself Alive' (3'47), 'Play The Game' (3'32)

Despite Brian's claim that "we're not a singles group; we don't stake our reputation on singles and we never have done," the first collection of Queen's hits up until 1981 is perhaps the finest compilation of the band's music that has ever been released. What's most successful about the package is that all the songs were legitimate singles and selected adhering to the proviso that only singles that had reached the Top 30 be included, with 'We Will Rock You' the only B-side admitted, for obvious reasons.

The band had so many different singles in so many different countries that to release a universal compilation of the same tracks worldwide would have been unfair. In the interest of brevity, the following is a list of the songs that were included on other countries' releases: the live version of 'Love Of My Life' was included on versions released in Argentina, Brazil, Mexico and Venezuela instead of 'Seven Seas Of Rhye'; 'Spread Your Wings' was included on Belgian and Spanish releases; Australia gained 'Tie Your Mother Down' and 'Keep Yourself Alive' but lost 'Don't Stop Me Now', 'Save Me', 'Now I'm Here', 'Good Old-Fashioned Lover Boy', and 'Seven Seas Of Rhye'; Japan obviously received 'Teo Torriatte (Let Us Cling Together)' instead of 'Bicycle Race' and 'Good Old-Fashioned Lover Boy'; 'Death On Two Legs (Dedicated to......)' and 'Sweet Lady' were included on Bulgarian issues; and 'Under Pressure' was released on versions in Austria, Canada, Germany, Israel and the Netherlands.

It's interesting to note that this was not the first Queen compilation to be released, although it was the first official, universal compilation. In 1976, a South

Korean anthology appeared titled *The Best Of Queen* and featured several unconnected tracks (only three had been UK singles) from *Queen II* through *A Night At The Opera* (curiously, nothing from the first album was represented): 'Bohemian Rhapsody', 'Killer Queen', 'Some Day One Day', 'The March Of The Black Queen', 'Tenement Funster', 'White Queen (As It Began)', 'She Makes Me (Stormtrooper In Stilettoes)', 'You're My Best Friend', ''39', 'Death On Two Legs (Dedicated to......' and 'Brighton Rock'. This was then reissued in 1980 with a completely different track listing: 'White Queen (As It Began)', 'Bohemian Rhapsody', 'You're My Best Friend', 'Some Day One Day', 'The March Of The Black Queen', 'Good Old-Fashioned Lover Boy', 'Crazy Little Thing Called Love', 'Mustapha', ''39', 'We Will Rock You', 'We Are The Champions' and 'God Save The Queen'.

A similarly titled Polish compilation also appeared in 1980, but featured a completely different track listing: 'Brighton Rock', 'Killer Queen', 'Now I'm Here', 'Somebody To Love', 'Tie Your Mother Down', 'I'm In Love With My Car', ''39', 'Bohemian Rhapsody', 'Don't Stop Me Now', 'We Are The Champions' and 'We Will Rock You'.

THE COMPLETE WORKS

EMI QBOX 1, December 1985

The Complete Works collected Queen's 11 studio albums and *Live Killers* onto LP for the first time, with a bonus disc of seven previously unavailable A and B-sides ('See What A Fool I've Been', 'A Human Body', 'Soul Brother', 'I Go Crazy', 'Thank God It's Christmas' and the then-newly released 'One Vision' and 'Blurred Vision'). Considering Queen's love of packaging at the time, *The Complete Works* was presented in an exquisite black box with an embossed Queen crest, with each album packaged similarly (except in white sleeves with a gold Roman numeral to indicate which album was which: *Queen* was 'I', *Queen II* was 'II', *Sheer Heart Attack* was 'III', and so on). The original artwork was presented in one of two booklets, while the other booklet featured a tour itinerary, equipment list for the 1984-1985 Queen Works! tour, and a discography loaded with errors. To emphasize the "champions of the world" aspect even further, a world map was included, showing where Queen had played; John was dissatisfied with this extra, arguing that it made the band seem hell-bent on world domination.

QUEEN AT THE BEEB

Band Of Joy BOJLP001, December 1989 [67]
Hollywood HR-62005-2, March 1995

'My Fairy King' (4'06), 'Keep Yourself Alive' (3'48), 'Doing Alright' (4'11), 'Liar' (6'28), 'Ogre Battle' (3'57), 'Great King Rat' (5'56), 'Modern Times Rock 'n' Roll' (2'00), 'Son And Daughter' (7'08)

Musicians: John Deacon *(bass guitar)*, Brian May *(guitars, vocals, piano on 'Doing Alright')*, Freddie Mercury *(vocals, piano)*, Roger Taylor *(drums, percussion, vocals)* Recorded: Langham 1 Studio, February 5, 1973 *('My Fairy King' through 'Liar')* and December 3, 1973 *('Ogre Battle' through 'Son And Daughter')* Producer: Bernie Andrews

In December 1989, independent label Band Of Joy issued *Queen At The Beeb*, an eight-track disc containing Queen's first and third BBC radio sessions. (Why those sessions were chosen is unknown, especially because the first session contained the familiar album backing tracks with new vocals and the occasional guitar overdub.) Initially released only in the UK, the album peaked at a disappointing No. 67 for one week before falling out of the charts altogether. In March 1995, Hollywood Records released its own version of the album, titled *Queen At The BBC*, which offered completely new packaging, albeit the same tracks. While it was rumored that the entirety of Queen's radio sessions would be released in 1996, with the second 'Let Me Live' CD single proclaiming that the three BBC tracks ('My Fairy King', 'Doing All Right', and 'Liar') were "taken from the forthcoming album *Queen At The BBC*", it wasn't until 20 years later that this box set was released as *On Air*; previously, a selection of tracks were released on deluxe editions of their respective albums in 2011.

GREATEST HITS II

Parlophone PMTV 2, October 1991 [1]
Parlophone CDPMTV 2, October 1991 [1]

'A Kind Of Magic' (4'22), 'Under Pressure' (3'56), 'Radio Ga Ga' (5'43), 'I Want It All' *(edit)* (4'01), 'I Want To Break Free' *(edit)* (4'18), 'Innuendo' (6'27), 'It's A Hard Life' (4'09), 'Breakthru' (4'09), 'Who Wants To Live Forever' (4'57), 'Headlong' (4'33), 'The Miracle' (4'54), 'I'm Going Slightly Mad' (4'08), 'The Invisible Man' (3'58), 'Hammer To Fall' *(edit)* (3'40),

'Friends Will Be Friends' (4'08), 'The Show Must Go On' (4'23), 'One Vision' *(edit)* (4'02)

Considering Queen's enormous success between 1981 (when their first greatest hits album was released) and 1991, it was inevitable that a second series would be issued. In the summer of 1989, the Official International Queen Fan Club reported that *Greatest Hits II* was in the pipeline for the end of the year, with a competition running for fans to predict the track list. However, the sales of *The Miracle* were still strong enough, and the band didn't want to compete with themselves in the charts, and so the release was quietly delayed and the competition canceled. The compilation wasn't mentioned again until the summer of 1991, with the fan club announcing a planned release for October 1991.

What emerged that month was heralded by fans and critics alike as a fine release, not only because it cropped out all the dross from the intervening ten-year period, but because it was beautifully sequenced, without a track out of place. The compilers were apparently not aiming for completeness, though, with several singles missing, and *Hot Space* is one of the victims. While these omissions are difficult to understand 20 years after the fact, it should be remembered that CD was overtaking vinyl as the primary format, and this medium was still relatively new – and thus relatively expensive, meaning that a double disc with *all* of Queen's UK Top 40 singles between 1981 and 1991 would have been pretty costly for the time. Jacky Smith, manager of the fan club, mentioned that the band were disappointed that the five UK singles not represented – 'Back Chat', 'Body Language', 'Las Palabras De Amor (The Words Of Love)', 'Thank God It's Christmas', and 'Scandal' – couldn't have been fit on somehow, but that the decision was purely economical and not based on song quality or chart performance.

Additionally, nearly every track on the compilation was edited in some way, although most songs lost only a second or two of running time. Parlophone had initially suggested removing a track entirely, but, because of the 17-track rule that the band imposed with their first compilation, the decision to trim some songs down was preferable. On most tracks, it's barely noticable; on others, like 'Who Wants To Live Forever', 'The Miracle', and 'I'm Going Slightly Mad', it's slightly jarring. (Incidentally, had the single version of 'Who Wants To Live Forever' been used, the trimming wouldn't have been as necessary.)

Unlike the first compilation, which had multiple running orders and varying songs selected based on the popularity of certain singles in certain countries, *Greatest Hits II* featured a universal track list, meaning that several non-UK singles ('Calling All Girls', 'Pain Is So Close To Pleasure', 'One Year Of Love', 'Princes Of The Universe') were missing. Not that it made any difference: the album easily entered the charts at No. 1, and while it nearly slipped out of the Top 10 in the middle of November 1991, Freddie's death returned it to the top for four consecutive weeks. A bittersweet success indeed.

CLASSIC QUEEN

Hollywood HR-61311-2, March 1992 [4]

'A Kind Of Magic' (4'22), 'Bohemian Rhapsody' (5'56), 'Under Pressure' (3'56), 'Hammer To Fall' *(edit)* (3'40), 'Stone Cold Crazy' (2'14), 'One Year Of Love' (4'28), 'Radio Ga Ga' (5'43), 'I'm Going Slightly Mad' (4'08), 'I Want It All' *(edit)* (4'01), 'Tie Your Mother Down' *(edit)* (3'46), 'The Miracle' *(edit)* (4'24), 'These Are The Days Of Our Lives' (4'15), 'One Vision' *(edit)* (4'38), 'Keep Yourself Alive' (3'47), 'Headlong' (4'33), 'Who Wants To Live Forever' *(edit)* (4'00), 'The Show Must Go On' (4'23)

Since Queen had fallen off the American record-buying public's radar after the ill-fated *Hot Space* album was issued in 1982, there was little hope for *Greatest Hits II* to be released there: except for 'Under Pressure', 'Body Language', and 'Radio Ga Ga', none of the other singles had performed that well in the charts. Happily, the success of 'Bohemian Rhapsody', released posthumously in January 1992, as well as that song's inclusion in the spring movie hit *Wayne's World*, helped get the wheels turning for a unique, American-only compilation. *Classic Queen* – not the same package issued as a promo disc in 1989 by Capitol Records, which features a completely different track listing – isn't strictly a hits compilation, instead collecting 17 of Queen's more radio-friendly US hits as well as some non-singles.

Some of the songs were of doubtful merit: 'Stone Cold Crazy' was featured only because Metallica had scored a Grammy award with the song the previous year, and 'One Year Of Love' was included because it featured in *Highlander*, then enjoying cult success as a US TV show (though its unofficial theme song, 'Princes Of The Universe', would have been a better choice). To its credit though, the album features the proper single mix of 'Who Wants To Live Forever', as well as the first appearance on any compilation of the single mix of 'Tie Your Mother Down'. As with *Greatest Hits II*, most of the songs are edited, though the edit of 'The Miracle' is closer to butchery since it completely re-arranges the song, excising the bass-driven introduction.

While *Greatest Hits II* is clearly the superior release as far as a basic introduction to Queen's reign in the UK charts during their most commercially successful period, *Classic Queen* is a superb taster for fans of what they were up to while Queen were ignoring – and being ignored by – North America. Its peak chart position at No. 4 indicated that Hollywood Records had done an admirable job of revitalizing Queen's image.

GREATEST HITS (1992 US)
Hollywood HR-61265-2, September 1992 [11]

'We Will Rock You' (2'02), 'We Are The Champions' (3'02), 'Another One Bites The Dust' (3'37), 'Killer Queen' (3'02), 'Somebody To Love' (4'58), 'Fat Bottomed Girls' (4'22), 'Bicycle Race' (3'03), 'You're My Best Friend' (2'52), 'Crazy Little Thing Called Love' (2'45), 'Now I'm Here' (4'15), 'Play The Game' (3'32), 'Seven Seas Of Rhye' (2'50), 'Body Language' (4'29), 'Save Me' (3'49), 'Don't Stop Me Now' (3'31), 'Good Old-Fashioned Lover Boy' (2'55), 'I Want To Break Free' *(edit)* (4'20)

Released as a counterpart to *Classic Queen*, *Greatest Hits* isn't a reissue of the original 1981 album in the strictest sense. While there are similarities to the original 14-track version, this release is markedly different and should be considered a completely new project instead of a reissue. The problem is that while the original version contained only 14 tracks, they were all specifically US hits; the reissue added several tracks that hadn't even been released as singles in the US. The reason they were included is that three of the tracks – 'Under Pressure', 'Bohemian Rhapsody' and 'Keep Yourself Alive' – were already released on *Classic Queen*, leaving only 11 of the original 14 tracks with which to compile a playlist. Unfortunately, instead of considering US-only singles such as 'Need Your Loving Tonight', 'Liar', 'Jealousy', 'It's Late', 'Long Away' or the fast live version of 'We Will Rock You', Hollywood Records decided to use 'Seven Seas Of Rhye', 'Body Language', 'I Want To Break Free', 'Now I'm Here', 'Save Me' and 'Good Old-Fashioned Lover Boy', with the last

three songs again unreleased as singles in the US. It was a fairly slapdash effort, but – historical objections aside – the new 17-track album, while not superior to the original UK release, certainly plays better than the original US release; the track listing also runs far more smoothly and closely mirrors the UK release.

THE BOX OF TRICKS
Parlophone CDQTEL 0001, 1992

The 12" Collection: 'Bohemian Rhapsody' (5'53), 'Radio Ga Ga' *(extended version)* (6'54), 'Machines (Or "Back To Humans")' *(instrumental)* (5'10), 'I Want To Break Free' *(extended version)* (7'14), 'It's A Hard Life' *(extended version)* (5'09), 'Hammer To Fall' *(Headbangers mix)* (5'21), 'Man On The Prowl' *(extended version)* (6'08), 'A Kind Of Magic' *(extended version)* (6'29), 'Pain Is So Close To Pleasure' *(extended remix)* (6'05), 'The Invisible Man' *(extended version)* (5'30), 'The Show Must Go On' (4'32)

Distributed throughout Europe in 1992 and available by mail order only, *The Box Of Tricks* was an intriguing release. It was a special edition which featured previously unreleased or unavailable material and was not a standard repackaging of *Greatest Hits* and *Greatest Hits II*. Instead, the album contained a heavily edited video of Queen's November 1974 Rainbow Theatre performance (titled *Live At The Rainbow 1974*), a CD or cassette of *The 12" Collection* (see below), a purple badge and a patch with the Queen crest emblazoned in gold, a black T-shirt (again, with the Queen crest in gold), a book compiled from *Greatest Pix I* and *Greatest Pix II*, and an impressive poster featuring virtually every known picture sleeve of Queen's singles and albums over the years. As with any special edition release of such interest, *The Box Of Tricks* exists no more, though used copies sell for around $100. *The 12" Collection* compiled nine of Queen's A- and B-sides that were extended for 12" vinyl release, along with the curious inclusions of 'Bohemian Rhapsody' and 'The Show Must Go On' serving as bookends (those two songs were never released in extended versions), and while some of the mixes would later be released as bonus tracks on the Hollywood Records CD campaign, this is still the only place to find the remixes of 'Machines (Or "Back To Humans")', 'It's A Hard Life', 'Man On The Prowl', 'A Kind Of Magic', and 'Pain Is So Close To Pleasure'.

THE QUEEN COLLECTION
Hollywood HR-61407-2, 1994

This long-deleted US-only package collected *Classic Queen* and the 1992 *Greatest Hits* albums together for the first time, with a third disc containing the entirety of Queen's 1989 BBC radio interview with Mike Read and a bonus track of 'Thank God It's Christmas'.

GREATEST HITS I & II
Parlophone CDPCSC 161, November 1994 [37]
Hollywood HR 62042-2, November 1995

Released first in the UK in November 1994 to combine the first and second instalments of *Greatest Hits*, *Greatest Hits I & II* was issued a year later in the US to capitalize on the release of *Made In Heaven*. Offering nothing new except for updated packaging, the CDs are wrapped in a classy gold sleeve with slightly updated liner notes giving the background of each single release. Though it may have been a cash-cow in the UK, it marked the first US release of either album; unfortunately, a lack of promotion led to little significant impact on the charts.

THE ULTIMATE QUEEN BOX SET
Parlophone QUEENBOX 20, November 1995

Collecting Queen's 15 studio and three live albums onto 20 discs, *The Ultimate Queen Box Set* is exactly that: a lavish, limited edition, wall-mounted box set with almost all of Queen's officially released output – not recommended for those on a tight budget. The release was limited to 15,000 worldwide and has become quite rare, often fetching figures in the upper hundreds on Internet auction sites.

QUEEN ROCKS
Parlophone 823 0911, November 1997 [7]
Parlophone 823 0912, November 1997 [7]
Hollywood HR-62132-2, November 1997

'We Will Rock You' (2'01), 'Tie Your Mother Down' *(edit)* (3'45), 'I Want It All' *(edit)* (4'30), 'Seven Seas Of Rhye' (2'45), 'I Can't Live With You' *(1997 retake)* (4'47), 'Hammer To Fall' (4'22), 'Stone Cold Crazy' (2'14), 'Now I'm Here' (4'12), 'Fat Bottomed Girls' (4'16), 'Keep Yourself Alive' (3'45), 'Tear it Up' (3'24), 'One Vision' (5'09), 'Sheer Heart Attack' (3'25), 'I'm In Love With My Car' *(edit)* (3'11), 'Put Out The Fire'

(3'18), 'Headlong' (4'38), 'It's Late' (6'27), 'No-One But You (Only The Good Die Young)' (4'14)

Despite Brian's skepticism regarding the innumerable Queen compilations, Queen Productions decided to add to the ever-growing list of anthologies with previously released material. In the summer of 1997, it was announced that *Queen Rocks* – not to be confused with the Hollywood Records promotional compact discs from the early 1990s – would be released that November, comprised of Queen's heavier tracks. "With *Queen Rocks*," Brian told *Q* in July 1998, "we had this feeling that some of those early Queen albums had got a bit lost and we wanted to remind people that we were always a rock band. But it had to have the hits on, some of which I know were on the greatest hits record; otherwise, it would have been obscure for the sake of it. Personally, I'd rather people just bought *Queen II*."

Brian said of the album on *Top Billing* in January 1998, "We thought it would be nice to give people what we never gave them, which is everything 'up'. Like an album was normally very full of light and shade, all our albums were like that, you would find something very strong and then something very gentle on purpose, you know, so that the album was very listenable, I suppose. But we thought it would be just great to have an album that you can just bung in your car or whatever and it rocks the whole way." Roger agreed, saying, "The last album – *Made In Heaven* – was quite, quite slow, quite down, quite a lot of ballads, lots of slow songs, and we thought it would be nice if we did release a compilation, releasing the hard rock songs of Queen ... this album represents a lot of the reasons why people liked us in the beginning."

After the announcement, the Fan Club posted an early track list on their website, and at that stage 'Tie Your Mother Down' had been reportedly remixed, with the potential to be released as the first single from the album, with the 'I Can't Live With You' retake to be the second single (eventually). However, the track list was altered considerably to include more well-known songs as well as a new song from Brian, Roger and John: 'No-One But You (Only The Good Die Young)' (for the history of that song, see its entry in Part Three). "There were actually a lot of tracks available," Brian stated to *Top Billing*, "I think probably twice as many tracks as we could get on the CD. So we were able to be very picky, and I think when you can be choosy, then you can make a good combination."

The concept behind the album was commendable

but the final execution leaves a lot to be desired. While it's true that Brian did write the more rock-oriented material, to have nearly three-quarters of the material on the album represented by him – with only two tracks by Roger, one by Freddie, and two genuine collaborations – is an affront to the others' abilities to rock out. "The songs were just chosen because they were rock songs really, like the hard rock end of what we do," Brian shrugged at the album's press conference. "It's just that Freddie mainly was writing different stuff, I suppose." At the time, a second compilation was planned for the near future, but this idea never progressed beyond the planning stage. Interestingly, a sister compilation, reportedly of ballads and love songs, was to be released simultaneously, with 'No-One But You (Only The Good Die Young)' being the logical home. Instead, that album was canceled, and the new song was tacked on at the end, and the remixed 'Tie Your Mother Down' was dropped entirely.

Nonetheless, there are several redeeming factors. Despite the preponderance of predictable rock hits, it's nice to see 'Stone Cold Crazy', 'Keep Yourself Alive', 'Sheer Heart Attack', 'I'm In Love With My Car', 'Put Out The Fire' and especially 'It's Late' appear on a compilation album. The most interesting inclusion is 'I Can't Live With You'. In its original state, the song fell a bit flat, but Brian and Roger both felt the song deserved another chance, and the duo went back into the studios to record new guitar and drum parts (it's unlikely that John was involved in the re-recording), transforming the song into a worthy rocker.

Some fans were disappointed by the cover art which featured the classic Queen logo (as designed by Freddie and re-illustrated by Richard Gray) exploding. "Shall we be honest?" Brian opined, contradictorily, at the press conference. "It was done in pretty much of a hurry and the concept behind it is the crest exploding. I think we all felt that perhaps it wasn't quite how we imagined it would be, but time was very short. But it's fabulous, yes." The booklet, instead of containing informative liner notes, featured lyrics for those who felt inclined to sing along, and was adorned with crude-looking pencil drawings of the mythical creatures from the front cover, with one of the lions absurdly sporting a pair of sunglasses. The cover wasn't without its controversy: the nude nymphs were considered offensive in Brazil and South Africa, and, reflecting the pearl clutching of the 'Bicycle Race' / 'Fat Bottomed Girls' single, were

clothed, and humanity was saved. Brian stated in the customary promotional rounds that the standard cover would be on limited release, with a significantly altered cover appearing later; that cover excised all but the bodiless phoenix and placed it over a significantly smaller explosion, and was not as impressive as the first version.

As it stands, Queen Rocks is a refreshing reminder that, despite all the excess and studio trickery, Queen were still, in essence, a rock band. One can't help but wonder why the promised second instalment hasn't yet materialized, though in an age of programmable CD players and burners, the need for an official Queen Rocks Volume 2 is not as urgent as it once seemed.

THE CROWN JEWELS
Hollywood 162200, November 1998

An eight-disc box set released only in the US, The Crown Jewels collected the first eight studio albums (up to and including The Game) in an exquisite, dark-blue velvet box with cardboard replica sleeves and a booklet featuring complete lyrics and liner notes courtesy of MTV VJ Matt Pinfield. While the release was appreciated, fans have been waiting for the next instalment, which should have collected the remaining seven studio albums and maybe a bonus disc of non-album B-sides; this long after its release, however, the concept of releasing a lavish box set of the basic albums with no extras is just as absurd as not releasing a follow-up.

GREATEST HITS III
Parlophone 523 4522, November 1999 [5]
Hollywood 7-2061-622502, November 1999

'The Show Must Go On' (live with Elton John) (4'35), 'Under Pressure' ('rah' mix) (with David Bowie) (4'08), 'Barcelona' (Freddie Mercury and Montserrat Caballé) (edit) (4'25), 'Too Much Love Will Kill You' (4'18), 'Somebody To Love' (live with George Michael) (5'07), 'You Don't Fool Me' (5'22), 'Heaven For Everyone' (edit) (4'37), 'Las Palabras De Amor (The Words Of Love)' (4'29), 'Driven By You' (Brian May) (4'09), 'Living On My Own' (Freddie Mercury) (3'37), 'Let Me Live' (4'45), 'The Great Pretender' (Freddie Mercury) (3'26), 'Princes Of The Universe' (3'31), 'Another One Bites The Dust' (with Wyclef Jean) (4'20), 'No-One But You (Only The Good Die Young)' (4'11), 'These Are The Days Of Our Lives' (4'22)

Bonus track: 'Thank God It's Christmas' (4'19)

In the summer of 1999, Brian penned a fan club letter, stating that a third instalment in the greatest hits canon was being prepared, along with a "secret project" he was working on with Roger at the drummer's home studio. The secret project turned out to be a remix of 'Under Pressure', with new drums and guitar work adorning the original, along with vocal out-takes from Freddie and David Bowie. Roger's autumn letter to the fan club noted that the album would be credited to "Queen +", an interesting and creative way to circumvent the apparent fact that there wasn't enough material to create a proper third greatest hits collection, thus necessitating the presence of solo material, collaborations, and remixes.

Unfortunately, what was released in November 1999 is a wholly undignified affair: the fact that several key UK singles ('Scandal', 'A Winter's Tale', 'Body Language', 'Back Chat', 'Tie Your Mother Down', and 'Spread Your Wings', all of which were Top 40 hits) were omitted in favor of solo singles and remixes is unforgivable, especially considering those released between 1981 and 1991 had been dropped from consideration on *Greatest Hits II*. Additionally, the band had always made it clear that there was a distinct line drawn between Queen and their solo careers, so even though 'Barcelona', 'Driven By You', 'Living On My Own', and 'The Great Pretender' were all Top 10 singles, they were Top 10 solo singles, not Top 10 Queen singles.

The only redeeming factors of the album are the singles that hadn't yet been released on any UK compilation, along with the first album appearance of 'Thank God It's Christmas'. The remix of 'Under Pressure' is pleasant if superfluous, though it hadn't yet appeared as a single; ironically, the remix was issued as a single after it appeared on the album, reaching No. 14 in the UK and thus justifying its inclusion. *Greatest Hits III* could have been so much better; it could have served as a home for many of Queen's lesser-known but charting singles, thus giving new fans a better taste of the margins of the hit parade that the band were aiming for. As it is, the album is a wasted opportunity, with its lowly status in the Queen canon confirmed in 2011, when the first two hits records were rereleased, while the third instalment was (rightly) forgotten entirely.

THE PLATINUM COLLECTION
Parlophone 529 8832, November 2000 [63]
Parlophone 529 8832, May 2002 [2]
Hollywood 7 2061-62360-2, October 2002 [48]

Featuring all three *Greatest Hits* compilations, *The Platinum Collection* was yet another cash-in, but this time it worked: although the initial November 2000 release reached only No. 63 in the UK charts, its May 2002 re-release, to tie in with the debut of *We Will Rock You: The Musical*, was an unqualified success, peaking at No. 2. In October of the same year, it headed to the US where it performed only modestly in the charts, peaking at No. 48, though considering that the last time the band were in the American charts was in 1995 with *Made In Heaven*, this was comparatively gratifying.

Interestingly, it was revealed in 2005 that Queen Productions had intended to release this collection with a VHS version of *Greatest Video Hits 2* as a box set for a German shopping channel, but Roger expressed disgust at the idea: "We don't sell things on shopping channels!" he exclaimed. Unfortunately, production had already started by the time the idea was vetoed, and the product sat in a warehouse for years until Brian came up with the idea of giving them away at the September 2005 Fan Club Convention, with the caveat that none of them appear on eBay. Though, of course, human nature being what it is, many of them did.

STONE COLD CLASSICS
Hollywood 7 2061-62606-2, April 2006 [45]

'Stone Cold Crazy' (2'17), 'Tie Your Mother Down' (3'46), 'Fat Bottomed Girls' (3'25), 'Another One Bites The Dust' (3'36), 'Crazy Little Thing Called Love' (2'44), 'We Will Rock You' (2'02), 'We Are The Champions' (3'01), 'Radio Ga Ga' (5'49), 'Bohemian Rhapsody' (5'55), 'The Show Must Go On' (4'33), 'These Are The Days Of Our Lives' (4'15), 'I Want It All' (4'31)

Bonus tracks performed by Queen + Paul Rodgers: 'All Right Now' (6'55), 'Feel Like Making Love' (6'21)

Released in April 2006 as a cash-in on the US Queen + Paul Rodgers tour (which was just about to finish by the time this compilation was released) and the *American Idol* Queen night. Brian and Roger appeared on that popular show to offer their feedback and assist the contestants with appropriate arrangements, though

Brian was heavily critical of the way the show portrayed him and later regretted his decision to appear. At one point, a contestant wanted to turn 'We Will Rock You' into a more urbanized variation with a different rhythm, which Brian scoffed at, saying, "You're not doing that to my song." Whether it was mean-spirited (which many *American Idol* fans claimed) or interpreted wrongly (which Brian claimed) is beside the point; for fans subjecting themselves to the torture of watching manufactured pop stars stumble their way through their beloved band's hits, Brian's mild outburst was a downright hoot.

Stone Cold Classics was instigated by Hollywood Records, and Brian and Roger felt no need to promote the album; despite this, the compilation limped its way to No. 45 in the US charts, and may have gained Queen (and Paul Rodgers) a few new fans along the way.

THE A–Z OF QUEEN, VOLUME 1

Hollywood Records D000049500, July 2007

'A Kind Of Magic' (4'25), 'Another One Bites The Dust' (3'38), 'Bohemian Rhapsody' (5'54), 'Bicycle Race' (3'04), 'I Want It All' (4'02), 'Crazy Little Thing Called Love' (2'45), 'Don't Stop Me Now' (3'29), 'Fat Bottomed Girls' *(edit)* (3'27), 'Flash' *(edit)* (2'52), 'Innuendo' (6'31), 'Good Old-Fashioned Lover Boy' (2'54)

Bonus DVD: 'A Kind Of Magic' *(promo video)*, 'Another One Bites The Dust' *(from* Queen On Fire At The Bowl*)*, 'Bohemian Rhapsody' *(promo video)*, 'I Want It All' *(from* Return Of The Champions*)*, 'Crazy Little Thing Called Love'*(from* Live At Wembley Stadium*)*, 'Don't Stop Me Now'*(promo video)*, 'Fat Bottomed Girls'*(from* Return Of The Champions*)*, 'Innuendo'*(promo video)*, Wembley Stadium concert interview *(from* Live At Wembley Stadium*)*

In the never-ending cycle of compilation release after compilation release, *The A-Z Of Queen, Volume 1* takes an old idea and puts a different spin on it. Instead of being ordered chronologically, the songs are presented alphabetically, though someone should have had the compiler take a remedial course in alphabetics. Pedantry aside, *The A-Z Of Queen, Volume 1* was an exclusive, Wal-Mart- and Amazon.com-only release, designed to cash in on nothing in particular. However, it did allow Queen a good amount of shelf life in the chain store conglomerate, though this didn't amount

to substantial sales. The bonus of a DVD mixing promotional videos and selections from their live releases made the package appealing, while, more significantly, the 'Innuendo' promotional video was released for the first time in the US, as well as for the first time on DVD. (Further bonus material included downloadable ringtones of 'Play The Game' and 'Good Old-Fashioned Lover Boy'.) Whatever Hollywood Records' intentions for future alphabetically-themed compilations seems to have stagnated, for further volumes never appeared.

THE SINGLES COLLECTION, VOLUMES 1 – 4

Volume 1: Parlophone 50999 243358 2 9, December 2008

Disc 1: 'Keep Yourself Alive' (3'48), 'Son And Daughter' (3'22); *Disc 2:* 'Seven Seas Of Rhye' (2'49), 'See What A Fool I've Been' (4'33); *Disc 3:* 'Killer Queen' (3'01), 'Flick Of The Wrist' *(single version)* (3'17); *Disc 4:* 'Now I'm Here' (4'14), 'Lily Of The Valley' *(single version)* (1'39); *Disc 5:* 'Bohemian Rhapsody' (5'54), 'I'm In Love With My Car' (3'05); *Disc 6:* 'You're My Best Friend' (2'52), ''39' (3'30); *Disc 7:* 'Somebody To Love' (4'58), 'White Man' (4'59); *Disc 8:* 'Tie Your Mother Down' *(single version)* (3'45), 'You And I' (3'27); *Disc 9:* 'Good Old-Fashioned Lover Boy' (2'54), 'Death On Two Legs (Dedicated to......' (3'44), 'Tenement Funster' *(single version)* (2'58), 'White Queen (As It Began)' (4'35); *Disc 10:* 'We Are The Champions' (3'03), 'We Will Rock You' (2'03); *Disc 11:* 'Spread Your Wings' (4'35), 'Sheer Heart Attack' (3'27); *Disc 12:* 'Bicycle Race' (3'04), 'Fat Bottomed Girls' *(single version)* (3'27); *Disc 13:* 'Don't Stop Me Now' (3'29), 'In Only Seven Days' (2'30)

Volume 2: Parlophone 50999 965497 2 8, June 2009

Disc 1: 'Love Of My Life' *(live)* (3'43), 'Now I'm Here' *(live)* (8'42); *Disc 2:* 'Crazy Little Thing Called Love' (2'45), 'We Will Rock You' *(fast live)* (3'08); *Disc 3:* 'Save Me' (3'50), 'Let Me Entertain You' *(live)* (3'14); *Disc 4:* 'Play The Game' (3'33), 'A Human Body' (3'43); *Disc 5:* 'Another One Bites The Dust' (3'36), 'Dragon Attack' (4'19); *Disc 6:* 'Flash' *(single edit)* (2'52), 'Football Fight' (1'29); *Disc 7:* 'Under Pressure' (4'07), 'Soul Brother' (3'39); *Disc 8:* 'Body Language' (4'34), 'Life Is Real (Song For Lennon)' (3'30); *Disc 9:* 'Las Palabras De Amor (The Words Of Love)' (4'32), 'Cool Cat' (3'29); *Disc 10:* 'Calling All Girls' (3'54), 'Put Out The Fire' (3'20); *Disc 11:* 'Back Chat' *(single* remix) (4'12), 'Staying Power' (4'12); Disc 12: 'Radio Ga Ga' (5'50), 'I Go Crazy' (3'43); Disc 13: 'I Want To Break Free' (single version) (4'26), 'Machines (Or 'Back To Humans')' (5'09)

Volume 3: Parlophone 50999 984839 2 0, May 2010

Disc 1: 'It's A Hard Life' (4'10), 'Is This The World We Created...?' (2'13); Disc 2: 'Hammer To Fall' (single edit) (3'41), 'Tear It Up' (3'26); Disc 3: 'Thank God It's Christmas' (4'23), 'Man On The Prowl' (3'29), 'Keep Passing The Open Windows' (5'23); Disc 4: 'One Vision' (single edit) (4'04), 'Blurred Vision' (4'42); Disc 5: 'A Kind Of Magic' (4'28), 'A Dozen Red Roses For My Darling' (4'45); Disc 6: 'Friends Will Be Friends' (4'08), 'Princes Of The Universe' (3'32); Disc 7: 'Pain Is So Close To Pleasure' (single remix) (4'01), 'Don't Lose Your Head' (4'39); Disc 8: 'Who Wants To Live Forever' (single edit) (4'04), 'Forever' (3'21); Disc 9: 'One Year Of Love' (4'29), 'Gimme The Prize (Kurgan's Theme)' (4'35); Disc 10: 'I Want It All' (single edit) (4'04), 'Hang On In There' (3'46); Disc 11: 'Breakthru' (4'11), 'Stealin'' (3'59); Disc 12: 'The Invisible Man' (3'59), 'Hijack My Heart' (4'12); Disc 13: 'Scandal' (4'45), 'My Life Has Been Saved' (3'16)

Volume 4: Parlophone 50999 909215 2 0, October 2010

Disc 1: 'The Miracle' (5'03), 'Stone Cold Crazy' (live) (2'10); Disc 2: 'Innuendo' (6'33), 'Bijou' (3'37); Disc 3: 'I'm Going Slightly Mad' (4'25), 'The Hitman' (4'57); Disc 4: 'Headlong' (4'36), 'All God's People' (4'22); Disc 5: 'The Show Must Go On' (4'32), 'Queen Talks' (1'44); Disc 6: 'Bohemian Rhapsody' (5'57), 'These Are The Days Of Our Lives' (4'16); Disc 7: 'Heaven For Everyone' (single edit) (4'46), 'It's A Beautiful Day' (single version) (3'58); Disc 8: 'A Winter's Tale' (3'54), 'Rock In Rio Blues' (4'35); Disc 9: 'Too Much Love Will Kill You' (4'22), 'I Was Born To Love You' (4'52); Disc 10: 'Let Me Live' (4'48), 'We Will Rock You' (live) (2'57), 'We Are The Champions' (live) (4'05); Disc 11: 'You Don't Fool Me' (single version) (3'56), 'You Don't Fool Me' (album version) (5'25); Disc 12: 'No-One But You (Only The Good Die Young)' (4'15), 'We Will Rock You' (Ruined by Rick Rubin) (5'02), 'Gimme The Prize (Kurgan's Theme)' (instrumental remix) (4'02); Disc 13: 'Under Pressure' (rah mix) (4'09), 'Under Pressure' (Mike Spencer remix) (3'55), 'Under Pressure' (Knebworth mix) (4'18)

With Queen's contract with Parlophone running out, and the band in no apparent hurry to re-sign with them (Universal Music Group was their only consideration, with which the band signed on 8 November 2010), the record label continued to ask the band for product to fulfill their contract. One of the ideas that had been floated around for years was a definitive box set of Queen's single releases, with Greg Brooks, Queen's archivist, assembling a prototype for Brian and Roger to consider. As Brooks later explained, this concept was to be a 10-disc set with every known single released throughout the world in a book-bound box a la The Solo Collection, but, as with all good ideas being subjected to committee, the project was nitpicked to the point that what was eventually released barely represented the original idea.

Four box sets were eventually released over the course of 22 months, each set containing 13 discs of A- and B-sides that Queen had released as singles between 1973 and 1999. The list of omissions is staggering: for instance, because Elektra had commissioned edits of both 'Liar' and 'It's Late' without the band's input or permission, Brian and Roger vetoed those singles' inclusions, while the many remixes of 'You Don't Fool Me' were deemed overkill. Additionally, any single that didn't hit the Top 40 anywhere in the world was excluded, meaning some of the fringe releases (like 'Teo Torriatte (Let Us Cling Together)', 'Long Away', 'Jealousy', 'Mustapha', and 'Need Your Loving Tonight') were nowhere to be found. Perhaps the most confounding decision was to not include extended remixes or extra CD single tracks, with the official reasoning being that the set was to mimic the 7" format (thus begging the question, why not release the set on vinyl?), but with the disc averaging seven minutes in length, that was a lot of wasted space on a format that can hold up to 79 minutes.

The packaging, too, left much to be desired, though the compilers went to great lengths to reproduce unique single sleeves that had appeared in other territories, often being much more attractive and interesting than standard UK or US sleeves. (The Hungarian sleeve of 'Bicycle Race' / 'Fat Bottomed Girls' is especially interesting, while the 1978 UK repressing of 'Bohemian Rhapsody', wrapped in a lavish purple sleeve, was a nice alternate to the familiar release.) But the box art itself was minimal, and the lack of sleeve notes was a huge detriment, with only a line of text indicating where the sleeve originated on the rear of each disc, and production notes printed on the disc itself.

The few positives that can be gleaned from these four boxes is that not only is the sound drastically improved, but several non-album B-sides and A-side remixes received their digital debut, notably the leaner remix of 'Back Chat', the drastically rearranged 'Pain Is So Close To Pleasure', and 'A Human Body'. But this is all small potatoes compared to what could have been, and whether the four boxes were Parlophone's decision or Queen's, or a compromise between the two, doesn't excuse this frankly disappointing treatment of the band's back catalog.

ABSOLUTE GREATEST

Parlophone 50999 686643 2 9, November 2009 [3]
Hollywood Records 050087154790, November 2009 [195]

'We Will Rock You' (2'02), 'We Are The Champions' (3'01), 'Radio Ga Ga' (5'48), 'Another One Bites The Dust' (3'34), 'I Want It All' *(single version)* (4'00), 'Crazy Little Thing Called Love' (2'44), 'A Kind Of Magic' (4'22), 'Under Pressure' (4'06), 'One Vision' *(single version)* (3'58), 'You're My Best Friend' (2'52), 'Don't Stop Me Now' (3'31), 'Killer Queen' (2'58), 'These Are The Days Of Our Lives' (4'16), 'Who Wants To Live Forever' *(edit)* (4'55), 'Seven Seas Of Rhye' (2'44), 'Heaven For Everyone' *(single version)* (4'37), 'Somebody To Love' (4'48), 'I Want To Break Free' *(single version)* (4'22), 'The Show Must Go On' (4'27), 'Bohemian Rhapsody' (5'56)

Bonus disc, live performances: 'White Queen (As It Began)' *(Rainbow Theatre, November 1974)*, 'Killer Queen' and 'You Take My Breath Away' *(Earl's Court Arena, June 1977)*, 'The Millionaire Waltz' and 'My Melancholy Blues' *(The Summit, December 1977)*, 'Dreamers Ball' *(Pavilion de Paris, March 1979)*, 'We Will Rock You' *(fast)* and 'Let Me Entertain You' *(Nippon Budokan, May 1979)*, 'I'm In Love With My Car' and 'Now I'm Here' *(Hammersmith Odeon, December 1979)*, 'Save Me' *(Montreal Forum, November 1981)*, 'Somebody To Love' *(Milton Keynes Bowl, June 1982)*, 'Tie Your Mother Down' and 'Love Of My Life' *(Rock In Rio Festival, January 1985)*, 'One Vision', 'In The Lap Of The Gods … Revisited' and 'We Are The Champions' *(Wembley Stadium, July 1986)*, 'We Will Rock You' *(Nepstadion, July 1986)*

Ever since the release of *Greatest Hits* in 1981, Queen's

compilations have been thorough examinations of particular periods of time, highlighting the successful singles while leaving the deeper album cuts to be explored by more adventurous music aficionados. And that's precisely the problem with the more commercial side of Queen: while the likes of 'Bohemian Rhapsody', 'We Will Rock You', 'I Want To Break Free', and 'A Kind Of Magic' may indeed be the most popular selections to the average punter, there are loads of other songs in Queen's catalog that are worth further exploration. Yet, to try to sell a disc of deeper cuts would be difficult (but not impossible, as evident with the respectable chart performances of the *Deep Cuts* trilogy), which is why Queen's singles are consistently rehashed and repackaged in different permutations, with a new cover thrown on for good measure. The music is the same, but it's familiar and comfortable to millions.

What is interesting, though, is that there hasn't been a single disc release that collects *all* of Queen's most popular singles and so, with the clock ticking on Queen's association with EMI/Parlophone, their record company proposed such a concept and was met with overwhelming approval. So while *The Singles Collection* plodded on pointlessly, with four disappointing boxes featurring too many rare tracks for the curious listener who heard 'Bohemian Rhapsody' on the radio and wanted to explore the hits further, yet featuring too few rare tracks for the hardcore fan who wants it all in one convenient package, Parlophone collected 20 tracks from Queen's past, starting with 'Seven Seas Of Rhye' in 1974 and finishing up with 'Heaven For Everyone' 21 years later.

In order to preserve some kind of interest for the fans, Queenonline.com ran a competition, where the one fan who correctly guessed the tracklist would be rewarded with a copy of the compilation. Far more substantial was the multitude of formats the album was available: *Absolute Greatest* was released on both single and double disc formats, as well as a 52-page book (with the two discs), digital download, and on 12" vinyl. The second disc was hinted at online as featuring something truly unique, and while fans salivated over the thought of some non-hits being included, maybe even with a previously unreleased song or two, the reality wasn't as exciting: Brian and Roger recorded a commentary track where each song was explained and stories told, but where audio commentary on a DVD is engaging for the viewer, audio commentary on a CD isn't. It doesn't help, either, that Brian and Roger are telling the same stories that have already been told, with the only exceptions being for the *Innuendo* and *Made In Heaven* tracks. But nothing new or particularly noteworthy is revealed, and as a bonus for fans, it's a cheap reward. Far more worthy were both the book, which featured printed lyrics (and, in some cases, the original handwritten lyrics) and rare photos, and additional content on the second disc: when inserted into a computer with Internet access, the listener was able to stream rare live videos from over the years, starting with 'White Queen (As It Began)' from the Rainbow all the way 'We Will Rock You' from Budapest. Why the audio equivalent couldn't have been included instead of the commentary disc is just baffling.

But *Absolute Greatest* did the trick; upon its release in November 2009, just in time for the highly-lucrative Christmas market, the compilation rocketed up to No. 3 in the UK, achieving double platinum status. Throughout the rest of the world, *Absolute Greatest* reached the Top 40, except for North America, where it just barely made the charts at No. 195. Considering Hollywood Records' apparent disinterest in their own client, the fact that *Absolute Greatest* was even released speaks volumes; that it somehow managed to chart is a miracle.

DEEP CUTS, VOLUME 1
Island Records 276 542-4, March 2011 [92]

'Ogre Battle' *(standalone edit)* (4'12), 'Stone Cold Crazy' (2'16), 'My Fairy King' (4'09), 'I'm In Love With My Car' (3'05), 'Keep Yourself Alive' (3'48), 'Long Away' (3'33), 'The Millionaire Waltz' (4'56), "39' (3'30), 'Tenement Funster' (2'47), 'Flick Of The Wrist' (3'17), 'Lily Of The Valley' (1'45), 'Good Company' (3'23), 'The March Of The Black Queen' *(standalone edit)* (6'35), 'In The Lap Of The Gods … Revisited' (3'45)

DEEP CUTS, VOLUME 2
Island Records 277 178 2, June 2011 [175]

'Mustapha' (3'02), 'Sheer Heart Attack' (3'27), 'Spread Your Wings' (4'35), 'Sleeping On The Sidewalk' (3'07), 'It's Late' (6'26), 'Rock It (Prime Jive)' (4'32), 'Dead On Time' (3'24), 'Sail Away Sweet Sister' (3'32), 'Dragon Attack' (4'19), 'Action This Day' (3'33), 'Put Out The Fire' (3'19), 'Staying Power' (4'12), 'Jealousy' (3'14), 'Battle Theme' (2'19)

DEEP CUTS, VOLUME 3
Island Records 278 002 9, September 2011 [155]

'Made In Heaven' (5'25), 'Machines (Or 'Back To Humans')' (5'11), 'Don't Try So Hard' (3'39), 'Tear It Up' (3'27), 'I Was Born To Love You' (4'50), 'A Winter's Tale' (3'49), 'Ride The Wild Wind' (4'42), 'Bijou' (3'37), 'Was It All Worth It' (5'46), 'One Year Of Love' (4'29), 'Khashoggi's Ship' *(standalone edit)* (2'52), 'Is This The World We Created...?' (2'17), 'The Hitman' (4'57), 'It's A Beautiful Day' *(reprise)* (3'01), 'Mother Love' (4'49)

Leave it to a new record label to finally give the fans something they've been yearning after for years. Since EMI (and, to a similar extent, Queen Productions) suffered from the misunderstanding that the only Queen songs that mattered were the ones that made the charts, Universal Records proposed a concept that iTunes implemented shortly after its popularity exploded: release a single-disc compilation of some of the deeper cuts from Queen's extensive catalog.

The three compilations released over the course of six months in 2011 dove into Queen's back catalog, pulling out much of the lesser-known songs that deserved far more attention than their sister singles received. The 43 songs on the three albums were superb selections, though, as ever, there were several baffling omissions, the most glaring being 'White Queen (As It Began)' and 'You And I', two of Queen's earliest songs that were both fan favorites and, in the case of the latter, the single that should have been. (Guest co-compiler Taylor Hawkins later expressed surprise that these two songs weren't included, indicating that they were certainly on his own list.) Additionally, John's songwriting is barely represented, with only 'Spread Your Wings' and 'One Year Of Love' making the cut, and while most of the latter-day songs he had written were often selected as singles, that at least two more of his songs couldn't have been included certainly raised some eyebrows among fans.

All told, the *Deep Cuts* compilations are flawed if not fascinating, showing that the band was finally willing to step outside the expected tedium of greatest hits compilations and deliver something a little more left-field.

QUEEN FOREVER
Virgin EMI Records 0602547040831 (single disc), November 2014 [5]
Virgin EMI Records 0602547040855 (double disc), November 2014 [5]
Hollywood Records D002119702, November 2014 [38]

Single disc edition: 'Let Me In Your Heart Again' (4'31), 'Love Kills – The Ballad' (4'12), 'There Must Be More To Life Than This' *(with Michael Jackson)* (3'20), 'It's A Hard Life' (4'06), 'You're My Best Friend' (2'52), 'Love Of My Life' (3'33), 'Drowse' (3'38), 'Long Away' (3'32), 'Lily Of The Valley' (1'39), 'Don't Try So Hard' (3'39), 'Bijou' (3'36), 'These Are The Days Of Our Lives' (4'14), 'Las Palabras De Amor (The Words Of Love)' (4'31), 'Who Wants To Live Forever' (5'15), 'A Winter's Tale' (3'48), 'Play The Game' (3'14), 'Save Me' (3'46), 'Somebody To Love' (4'52), 'Too Much Love Will Kill You' (4'19), 'Crazy Little Thing Called Love' (2'43), 'I Was Born To Love You' *(Japanese bonus track)* (4'49)

Double disc edition: 'Let Me In Your Heart Again' (4'31), 'Love Kills – The Ballad' (4'12), 'There Must Be More To Life Than This' *(with Michael Jackson)* (3'20), 'Play The Game' (3'14), 'Dear Friends' (1'08), 'You're My Best Friend' (2'52), 'Love Of My Life' (3;33), 'Drowse' (3'38), 'You Take My Breath Away' (4'38), 'Spread Your Wings' (4'30), 'Long Away' (3'32), 'Lily Of The Valley' (1'39), 'Don't Try So Hard' (3'39), 'Bijou' (3'36), 'These Are The Days Of Our Lives' (4'14), 'Nevermore' (1'18), 'Las Palabras De Amor (The Words Of Love)' (4'31), 'Who Wants To Live Forever' (5'15), 'I Was Born To Love You' (4'49), 'Somebody To Love' (4'52), 'Crazy Little Thing Called Love' (2'43), 'Friends Will Be Friends' (4'06), 'Jealousy' (3'13), 'One Year Of Love' (4'27), 'A Winter's Tale' (3'48), ''39' (3'30), 'Mother Love' (4'47), 'It's A Hard Life' (4'06), 'Save Me' (3'46), 'Made In Heaven' (5'25), 'Too Much Love Will Kill You' (4'19), 'Sail Away Sweet Sister' (3'33), 'The Miracle' (4'57), 'Is This The World We Created...?' (2'12), 'In The Lap Of The Gods...Revisited' (3'46), 'Forever' (3'21), 'Teo Torriatte (Let Us Cling Together)' *(Japanese bonus track)* (5'08)

Back in 1997, two separate compilation albums were planned: one was to have been a collection focusing on Queen's heavier, rock-oriented songs, while the other was to have centered on the band's slower ballads. While the first compilation was released as *Queen Rocks*, the second, provisionally titled *Queen Ballads*, was scrapped, though one new song intended for that project, 'No-One But You (Only The Good Die Young)', was awkwardly grafted to the end of *Queen Rocks*. Fourteen years later, with Queen now on a new record label (Universal), the ballads compilation was brought out of mothballs and retitled as *Queen Forever*. While the contents were unspecified and presumably nebulous,

fans were nevertheless intrigued, with many hoping it would be a follow-up, of sorts, to *Made In Heaven*. The project was then pushed aside until 2014, when the compilation was finally released to relative indifference.

While Brian was quick to point that the compilation collected songs that time had forgotten, the original concept seemed to have fallen by the wayside, instead becoming a disparate dumping ground of slower songs and anything that had the word "love" in the title (how could anybody possibly have forgotten 'Crazy Little Thing Called Love'?). The main attraction, of course, was the appearance of three new songs: 'Let Me In Your Heart Again' was the biggest surprise, while a slower reconstruction of 'Love Kills' and a hybrid recording of 'There Must Be More To Life Than This', pairing Queen's original 1981 instrumental backing with the 1983 vocal performances of Freddie and Michael Jackson, were interesting on paper but provided diminishing returns upon repeated listens.

'Love Kills' had been drastically rearranged, turning it into a moody, atmospheric ballad, something that Brian claimed in interviews he had always wanted to do. (Remember that Freddie's original is, in effect, a Queen song; the liner notes for *Queen Forever* credit John on additional guitar, which explains the synthesized bass on the original.) The biggest offense, however, was 'There Must Be More To Life Than This': remixed by producer William Orbit, who had cut his teeth on Madonna's *Ray Of Light*, Blur's *13*, and Katie Melua's *The House*, the song was focused too much on Michael's voice, effectively turning Freddie into a guest vocalist on his own song. (It didn't help that Brian, who wasn't present on the original recording, provided additional guitar that was more in line with his latter day tone instead of the sound on *Hot Space*, making the recording busy and cluttered.) A version had been produced by Brian which was a little more adventurous and experimental, but was rejected by Michael Jackson's estate. This version, dubbed the "Gold Mix", leaked out onto the bootleg market late in 2015.

Upon the release of the album, Brian and Roger did a fair amount of promotion, with most of the focus obviously being on the three new songs. However, they couldn't hide their frustration with the album, both venting their spleens to *Classic Rock* magazine: "Apart from [the three new songs] it is a rather odd mixture of our slower stuff, I didn't want the double-album version they've put out," Roger said. "It's an awful lot for people to take in, and it's bloody miserable.

I wouldn't call it an album either. It's a compilation with three new tracks. It's more of a record company confection. It's not a full-blooded Queen album." Brian agreed: "I can understand Roger's reticence. He's not really a ballad writer, so this album's not really representative of Roger Taylor. It actually wasn't our idea. If it had been down to me it would have been an EP of these new songs, but we'd already promised the record company some kind of compilation."

Despite its flaws, *Queen Forever* performed respectably on the strength of the three new songs, reaching No. 5 in the UK and No. 38 in the US. Remarkably, the new arrangement of 'Love Kills' was performed live by Queen + Adam Lambert on a handful of dates in 2014, before it was inexplicably taken out of the set list. A shame, because it was an interesting diversion from the greatest hits set they had been peddling for three years by that point.

STUDIO COLLECTION

Virgin EMI Records 00602547202888, September 2015
Hollywood Records D002232801, September 2015

This lavish box set collected all of Queen's studio albums, from their debut to *Made In Heaven*, with beautiful remastering and a book containing many previously unseen photographs, artefacts, and handwritten lyrics. (A limited edition featured a Rega turntable, stylized to feature the Queen logo.) Spread out over 18 discs – *Queen II* was spread out over two discs, with the reverse of each disc a picture sleeve – on heavyweight 180g coloured vinyl, and featuring the vinyl formats of *Innuendo* and *Made In Heaven*, the box is an opulent collector's dream, though the price was pretty hefty (upwards of £500). Unfortunately, there was the occasional pressing issue, with *The Game* featuring some superficial warping on both sides of the disc that didn't affect playback, and a bonus disc or two of B-sides would have been appreciated, but these quibbles don't stop the box from being a truly essential purchase.

QUEEN ON AIR: THE COMPLETE BBC SESSIONS

Virgin EMI Records 0602557082289, November 2016 *(double disc edition)*
Hollywood Records D002424002, November 2016 *(double disc edition)*
Virgin EMI Records 0602557082227/D002456801, November 2016 *(triple disc vinyl edition)*

Virgin EMI Records 0602557082319, November 2016 *(box set edition)*

Disc One, The BBC Sessions – Session 1, 5 February 1973: 'My Fairy King' (4'17), 'Keep Yourself Alive' (3'53), 'Doing All Right (4'18), 'Liar' (6'38); *Session 2, 25 July 1973:* 'See What A Fool I've Been' (4'28), 'Keep Yourself Alive' (3'56), 'Liar' (6'37), 'Son And Daughter' (6'15); *Session 3, 3 December 1973:* 'Ogre Battle' (4'49), 'Modern Times Rock'n'Roll' (2'06), 'Great King Rat' (5'57), 'Son And Daughter' (7'18)

Disc Two, The BBC Sessions – Session 4, 3 April 1974: 'Modern Times Rock'n'Roll' (2'53), 'Nevermore' (1'30), 'White Queen (As It Began)' (5'00); *Session 5, 16 October 1974:* 'Now I'm Here' (4'26), 'Stone Cold Crazy' (2'18), 'Flick Of The Wrist' (3'31), 'Tenement Funster' (3'16); *Session 6, 28 October 1977:* 'We Will Rock You' (1'36), 'We Will Rock You' *(fast)* (2'52), 'Spread Your Wings' (5'33), 'It's Late' (6'37), 'My Melancholy Blues' (3'15)

Disc Three, Live On Air – Golders Green Hippodrome, London, 13 September 1973: 'Procession' (1:42), 'Father To Son' (5:29), 'Son And Daughter' (3:45), 'Guitar Solo' (1:26), 'Son And Daughter' *(reprise)* (2:08), 'Ogre Battle' (5:22), 'Liar' (7:27), 'Jailhouse Rock' (1:07); *Estádio do Morumbi, São Paulo, Brazil, 20 March 1981:* 'Intro' (0:26), 'We Will Rock You' *(fast)* (3:03), 'Let Me Entertain You' (3:21), 'I'm In Love With My Car' (2:06), 'Alright Alright' (2:40), 'Dragon Attack' (3:28), 'Now I'm Here' *(reprise)* (1:46), 'Love Of My Life' (4:42); *Maimarktgelände, Mannheim, Germany, 21 June 1986:* 'A Kind Of Magic' (6:26), 'Vocal Improvisation' (1:03), 'Under Pressure' (3:38), 'Is This The World We Created...?' (2:49), '(You're So Square) Baby I Don't Care' (1:27), 'Hello Mary Lou (Goodbye Heart)' (1:40), 'Crazy Little Thing Called Love' (4:55), 'God Save The Queen' (1:24)

Disc Four, The Interviews, 1976–1980: Freddie with Kenny Everett (Capital Radio, November 1976) (15:45), Queen with Tom Browne (BBC Radio One, Christmas 1977) (38:20), Roger with Richard Skinner (BBC Radio One, June 1979) (4:32), Roger with Tommy Vance (BBC Radio One, December 1980) (5:53), Roy Thomas Baker (The Record Producers, BBC Radio One, date unknown) (10:37)

Disc Five, The Interviews, 1980–1986: John (BBC Radio

One, March 1981) (2:26), Brian with John Tobler (BBC Radio One, June 1982) (11:06), Brian on with Richard Skinner and Andy Foster (BBC Radio One, March 1984) (11:46), Freddie (BBC Radio One, August 1984) (2:34), Brian (BBC Radio One, September 1984) (2:47), Freddie on with Graham Neale (BBC Radio One, September 1984) (5:15), Freddie with Simon Bates (BBC Radio One, April 1985) (28:45), Brian with David "Kid" Jenson (Capital Radio, Wembley Stadium, July 1986) (4:40)

Disc Six, The Interviews, 1986–1992: Roger with Andy Peebles (BBC Radio One, May 1986) (24:45), "Queen for an Hour" with Mike Read (BBC Radio One, May 1989) (41:17), Brian with Simon Bates (BBC Radio Two, August 1992) (5:54), Brian with Johnnie Walker (BBC Radio Two, October 1992) (2:51)

Queen's BBC sessions first appeared as a limited edition release on an off-shoot label in 1989, with only the first and third sessions being deemed worthy of release. An update was planned in 1996, with the 'Let Me Live' CD single, featuring three of the first session's tracks ('My Fairy King', 'Doing All Right', and 'Liar'), containing a teaser that an expanded double-disc release was imminent, though this ultimately amounted to nothing, with Jim Beach's reasoning that they didn't want to saturate the market. And so the release sat dormant for 20 years, but when *Queen On Air: The Complete BBC Sessions* finally emerged in November 2016, it was worth the wait.

Of course, the set wasn't *truly* complete: missing was Session 4's 'The March Of The Black Queen', though its absence could be justified in that it was simply the album version, with the segue into 'Funny How Love Is' fading out; also the *Top Of The Pops* version of 'Good Old-Fashioned Lover Boy' was seemingly forgotten entirely. However, these two omissions don't detract

whatsoever from the set, and it's a joy to finally have the other four sessions finally released.

While the standard release was a double-disc or triple vinyl containing 24 tracks ('We Will Rock You' was divided into two, the slow version and the fast version, with the *Siddhartha* interstitial removed), the box set added four additional discs that were absolutely worth the purchase. *Live On Air* featured 23 performances from 1973's Golders Green Hippodrome, 1981's concert in Brazil, and 1986's Mannheim concert, all three of which had been heavily bootlegged over the years but had nonetheless been broadcast on BBC radio. Unfortunately, these three concerts are edited and are not complete, but there are some absolutely beautiful performances to be found, and the transformation from being essentially a little-known cult band in 1973 to a worldwide success at the end of their touring career in 1986 is staggering.

Additionally, the three discs of interviews are a revelation, ranging from little-known discussions about the *Live Killers*, *Flash Gordon*, *Hot Space*, and *The Works* albums, to the well-known Christmas 1977 and May 1989 interviews that featured all four band members talking about their latest albums and their future. Freddie's interview with Kenny Everett from November 1976 is a true delight, with the two friends completely at ease with each other, though one particularly hilarious moment comes when Everett puts Freddie on the spot, having him read the weather report from a clipboard, which the vocalist gamely attempts. Spanning three-and-a-half hours, these interviews are absolutely essential in order to understand how both the creative process and the adaptation of live performances worked. *Queen On Air* isn't simply the band's BBC sessions on disc; this is a journey, and while the sampler of the double-disc edition will satisfy fans of Queen's music, their power and personality is best enjoyed with the box set.

B. COLLABORATIONS

Over the years, in between Queen's regular activities as a touring and recording band, the members have found time to loan their talents to many up-and-coming stars, as well as some of their peers. This section, listed chronologically, *covers as many of these collaborations as possible; it comes as no surprise that Brian, being the most willing to jam or contribute musically to anything, comes out the leader in this section.*

AL STEWART: PAST, PRESENT, AND FUTURE

(Roger Taylor)
CBS 32036, 1973

In addition to percussion on 'Roads To Moscow', Roger reportedly contributed to another song from Al Stewart's *Past, Present, And Future* album.

EUGENE WALLACE: DANGEROUS *(Roger Taylor)*
EMI EMC 3067, 1975

Produced by Robin Geoffrey Cable (hence the connection) and Del Newman at Trident Studios, Roger contributed percussion on an unspecified track, though 'Dangerous' is very likely the song in question. The album, recorded during sessions for *Queen* in 1972, remained unreleased until 1975 and also featured Phil Chen, Phil Collins and Mike Moran (all of whom would work with a Queen member many years later).

FOXX: TAILS OF ILLUSION *(Roger Taylor)*
GTO GTLP 006, October 1975

Roger contributed backing vocals for Foxx's *Tails Of Illusion* track 'Survival'. The song was recorded at Sarm East Studios in August 1975, during sessions for *A Night At The Opera*.

EDDIE HOWELL: THE MAN FROM MANHATTAN

(Freddie Mercury and Brian May)
Warner Brothers WB 16701, 1976

During sessions for *A Night At The Opera* in August 1975, Eddie Howell was in Sarm Studios where he happened to run into Freddie and Mike Stone one day. The young vocalist asked the duo if they would help him produce a track that he was working on. Despite the workload that *A Night At The Opera* would inevitably bring, Freddie and Mike agreed, and sessions for the song began shortly thereafter.

It's easy to hear Freddie's fingerprints all over the song; it was transformed from Eddie's original vaudeville vision, with trombones and brass, into an unmistakable Queen soundalike. With Freddie on piano, Barry De Souza on drums and Jerome Rimson on bass, Eddie, on acoustic guitars and lead vocals, sings about a conniving young man from New York City, whose "enemies flee at the sight of me", shaking "at the sound of my name." As a favor to Freddie, Brian contributed a suitably 'Killer Queen'-like guitar solo, but Roger and John weren't asked to participate because Freddie wanted to shy away from a carbon copy Queen sound.

When released as a single in 1976, the song didn't chart, but it wouldn't be completely out of place alongside the more experimental, music hall numbers from *Sheer Heart Attack* or *A Night At The Opera*. Inexplicably, the song was issued on the 1998 Smile compilation *Ghost Of A Smile*, along with an unnecessary remix subtitled 'Back Again', and then again two years later on *The Solo Collection*.

TRAX *(John Deacon, Brian May, Freddie Mercury, Roger Taylor)*

Reportedly, all four members of Queen contributed to this unreleased and now-erased album by Trax, recorded at Trident Studios during the *A Night At The Opera* sessions in August 1975. In what capacity or what songs were recorded remains unknown; Norman Sheffield confirmed that the tapes were deleted.

IAN HUNTER: ALL AMERICAN ALIEN BOY *(Brian May, Freddie Mercury, Roger Taylor)*
CBS 81310, May 1976

The three vocalists – Brian, Freddie and Roger – contributed backing vocals to Ian Hunter's 'You Nearly Did Me In', released on *All American Alien Boy*. The song was recorded during a break in the US *A Night At The Opera* tour at Jimi Hendrix's Electric Ladyland

Studios in New York (a dream come true for the three self-professed Hendrix fans) and was produced by Roy Thomas Baker.

PETER STRAKER: THIS ONE'S ON ME
(Freddie Mercury)
EMI EMC 3204, October 1977

Freddie's actor friend Peter Straker was recording a solo album in 1977 and asked Freddie to produce some songs for him. *This One's On Me*, released in October 1977, was produced by Freddie and Roy Thomas Baker (which led to Baker's involvement on *Jazz*), and two singles – 'Ragtime Piano Joe' backed with 'The Saddest Clown', and 'Jackie' backed with 'I've Been To Hell And Back' – were released in September 1977 and February 1978 respectively. Several of these songs were included on bootleg albums over the years, erroneously credited as out-takes recorded by Freddie. In addition to the four tracks mentioned, the album included 'Ada', 'The Day The Talkies Came', 'Heart Be Still', 'Annual Penguin Show' and 'Vamp'.

LONNIE DONEGAN: PUTTIN' ON THE STYLE
(Brian May)
Chrysalis CHR 1158, February 1978 [51]

Brian was asked by Lonnie Donegan to contribute to the original skiffle musician's comeback album, *Puttin' On The Style*. Excited by the possibility to record with his hero, Brian provided guitar on 'Diggin' My Potatoes' and 'I'm Just A Rolling Stone', though only the former was released. The album was recorded at Wessex Studios between July and September 1977, was produced by Adam Faith, and also featured other notable contributions from Ronnie Wood, Elton John, Ringo Starr and Rory Gallagher.

HILARY HILARY: 'HOW COME YOU'RE SO DUMB' / 'RICH KID BLUES' *(Roger Taylor)*
Mainly Modern UA STP 2, 1980

Essentially a Roger Taylor solo recording – produced by Roger, he also co-wrote the A-side with vocalist Hilary Vance while providing keyboards, drums, guitars and bass on both songs – and recorded during sessions for *The Game* in June 1979, this single was released just before *Flash Gordon* came out. Roger explained, "I've known Hilary for years but I didn't know she could sing until an old girlfriend told me. She was singing with a band in pubs occasionally so I rang up to ask for a tape and thought it was awful, [though] her voice was really good. It's very deep-sounding. I wrote the song with some help from Hilary and did the instrumental parts but my name isn't all over the sleeve. I don't want to do a Paul McCartney!"

QUARTZ: 'CIRCLES' *(Brian May)*
MCA 642, 1980

Metal band Quartz cut their teeth supporting Black Sabbath and AC/DC in the mid-1970s, and their debut eponymous album, released in 1977, was produced by Brian's friend and Sabbath guitarist Tony Iommi. Brian was duly asked to contribute guitar to a potential album track, 'Circles', which also featured Sabbath frontman and latter-day reality TV star Ozzy Osbourne on backing vocals, though the song would remain unreleased for three years, before being released as a B-side to 'Stoking Up The Fires Of Hell', from Quartz's second album, *Stand Up And Fight*. The song was released as a bonus track on the 2004 deluxe edition of their debut album.

GARY NUMAN: DANCE *(Roger Taylor)*
Beggars Banquet Bega 28, September 1981 [3]

Roger contributed to the tracks 'Crash', 'You Are You Are' and 'Moral'.

MEL SMITH: 'JULIE ANDREWS' GREATEST HITS' / 'RICHARD AND JOEY' *(Roger Taylor)*
Mercury MEL 1, 1981

In addition to producing this single by UK comedian Mel Smith, Roger also provided backing vocals. The song was released in 1981 but failed to chart.

KANSAS: VINYL CONFESSIONS *(Roger Taylor)*
Kirshner Kir 85714, 1982

Roger contributed to the tracks 'Right Away', 'Diamonds And Pearls' and 'Play The Game Tonight'.

BILLY SQUIER: EMOTIONS IN MOTION *(Freddie Mercury and Roger Taylor)*
Capitol EST 12217, October 1982

Recorded in January 1982 during sessions for *Hot Space*, Billy Squier's *Emotions In Motion* featured

Freddie and Roger singing backing vocals on the title track. An edited version was later released as a single but didn't reach the charts.

HEAVY PETTIN: LETTIN' LOOSE *(Brian May)*
Polydor HEPLP1, 1983

Brian produced Heavy Pettin's 1983 release, *Lettin' Loose*, which was recorded at Townhouse Studios in May 1983. Three singles – an edited version of 'Rock Me', 'In And Out Of Love' and 'Love Times Love' – were released in support of the album. The other tracks were 'Broken Heart', 'Love On The Run', 'Victims Of The Night', 'Shout It Out', 'Devil In Her Eyes', 'Hell Is Beautiful' and 'Roll The Dice'.

UNRECORDED JAM SESSION *(John Deacon)*

In 1983, John and an assembled group of friends – including tennis players Vitas Gerulaitas and John McEnroe (who switched their rackets for guitars), Scott Gorham, Martin Chambers, Simon Kirke and Mick Ralphs – convened at a rehearsal studio for a jam session, though nothing was actually recorded.

MAN FRIDAY & JIVE JUNIOR: 'PICKIN' UP SOUNDS' *(John Deacon)*
Malaco MAL 1211, 1983

Written by John and Robert Ahwai, this would evidently lead to The Immortals, a sideband that John formed to record 'No Turning Back' for the film *Biggles* in 1986. This rap track featured prominent bass by John and was later released as a single but failed to chart.

JEFFREY OSBOURNE: STAY WITH ME TONIGHT
(Brian May)
A&M AMLX 64940, August 1983

Brian provided guitars on the tracks 'Stay With Me Tonight' and 'Two Wrongs Don't Make A Right', which were recorded at the Mad Hatter Studios in Los Angeles during April 1983, while Brian was in town to record *Star Fleet Project*. 'Stay With Me Tonight' was later released as a single.

BILLY SQUIER: SIGNS OF LIFE *(Brian May)*
Capitol EJ 2401921, September 1984

Brian appears on the track '(Another) 1984'.

SIDEWAYS LOOK *(Roger Taylor)*
unreleased, 1985

Around this time, the production team of Taylor/ Richards were approached by Virgin Records and asked if they could produce one of their new signings, a Scottish group called Sideways Look. Material was recorded in March before Queen's Australasian tour, with a potential single titled 'Bulletproof Heart', and hopes were high. Unfortunately, Virgin decided against the project and dropped it, much to Roger's annoyance.

JIMMY NAIL: TAKE IT OR LEAVE IT *(Roger Taylor)*
Virgin CD VIP 111, April 1985

Actor Jimmy Nail, who starred in the film *Morons From Outer Space* and the television show *Auf Wiedersehen, Pet*, released a cover of the Rose Royce single 'Love Don't Live Here Anymore', which was produced by Roger and David Richards. The song was released in May and, in addition to the standard single version, an extended version was also released on 12″ single. The song, also included on the album *Take It Or Leave It*, was backed with 'Night For Day' and reached No. 3 in the UK.

FEARGAL SHARKEY: 'LOVING YOU' *(Roger Taylor)*
Virgin VS 770, June 1985

Produced by Roger and David Richards, with Roger also providing drums and synthesizers, the single by former Undertones front man Feargal Sharkey reached No. 26 in the UK.

CAMY TODOROW: 'BURSTING AT THE SEAMS'
(Roger Taylor)
Virgin VS 816, September 1985

Recorded at Mountain Studios in the summer of 1985, Camy Todorow's 'Bursting At The Seams' was produced by Roger and David Richards and featured Roger on drums. Two additional mixes – a 'backroom version' and an instrumental one – were released on the 12″ vinyl single in September 1985.

ROGER DALTREY: UNDER A RAGING MOON
(Roger Taylor)
10 PIX 17, October 1985

Later released as a single in March 1986, Roger Daltrey's 'Under A Raging Moon' was the title track of his latest solo album and was a tribute to The Who's late drummer, Keith Moon. Roger Taylor, along with Martin Chambers, Cozy Powell, Stewart Copeland, Zak Starkey (who would later join The Who in 1996 as their permanent drummer), Carl Palmer and Mark Brzezicki, provided a brief drum solo during the song's finale.

ELTON JOHN: ICE ON FIRE
(Roger Taylor and John Deacon)
Phonogram HISPD 26, November 1985

At Sol Studios in London during September 1985, Roger and John recorded their contributions to two Elton John songs: 'Too Young', which was released on the *Ice On Fire* album in November 1985, and 'Angeline', which was held back until the follow-up, *Leather Jackets*, in October 1986.

DEBBIE BYRNE: THE PERSUADER *(Roger Taylor)*
EMI EMX 430032, 1985

Roger contributed to 'Fools Rush In'.

CHRIS THOMPSON: RADIO VOICES *(Brian May)*
Ultra Phone 6.25922, 1985

Brian is on parts 1 and 2 of 'A Shift In The Wind'.

VIRGINIA WOLF: VIRGINIA WOLF *(Roger Taylor)*
Atlantic 781 274-1, February 1986

Roger and David Richards produced Virginia Wolf's eponymous debut album, recorded at Eel Pie Studios in London during the autumn of 1985. 'Waiting For Your Love' was released as an edited single with 'Take A Chance' on the B-side, and a further, US-only single, 'It's In Your Eyes' backed with 'Don't Run Away', was also released. The remaining tracks were 'Are We Playing With Fire', 'Make It Tonight', 'Only Love', 'Livin' On A Knife Edge', 'For All We Know' and 'Goodbye Don't Mean Forever'.

BILLY SQUIER: ENOUGH IS ENOUGH
(Freddie Mercury)
Capitol 064 240629 1, September 1986

In 1986, while he was recording his *Enough Is Enough* album in London, Billy ran into Freddie and played

for him an early take of 'Love Is The Hero', which Freddie responded to enthusiastically. The two fleshed out further ideas at Garden Lodge, and when it was recorded at Sarm East Studios, Freddie contributed prominent backing vocals; on the extended version, he provided a superbly sung introduction.

During sessions, Freddie and Billy co-wrote a song, 'Lady With A Tenor Sax', issued on the same album, and while that version doesn't feature any vocals from Freddie, a work-in-progress version was issued on *The Solo Collection*, which is essentially a duet between the two songwriters. The song is not much to speak of, though it's a snarling rocker with a great guitar melody and occasional synthesizer blasts.

ELTON JOHN: LEATHER JACKETS
(Roger Taylor and John Deacon)
Phonogram EJ LP 1, October 1986

See previous Elton John entry above.

MAGNUM: VIGILANTE *(Roger Taylor)*
Polydor POLD 5198, October 1986

Produced by Roger and David Richards, Roger also provided backing vocals on 'Sometime Love' and 'When The World Comes Down' (which was also released as a single). The other tracks were 'Lonely Night', 'Need A Lot Of Love', 'Midnight (You Won't Be Sleeping)', 'Red On The Highway', 'Holy Rider', 'Vigilante' and 'Back Street Kid'.

MINAKO HONDA: CANCEL
(Brian May and John Deacon)
Eastworld WTP 90433, 1986

Minako Honda's album *Cancel*, released only in Japan in 1986, was produced by Brian and featured a Japanese version of John's 1986 solo track 'No Turning Back', retitled 'Roulette', which the bassist also played on.

RAMONCIN: LA VIDA EN EL FILO *(Brian May)*
EMI 7 98299 2, 1986

The track in question here is 'Como Un Susurro'.

ERROL BROWN: 'THIS IS YOUR TIME'
(John Deacon)

Recorded in 1986, Errol Brown's 'This Is Your Time'

was co-written with John, who also played bass guitar, but the song remained unreleased.

MINAKO HONDA: 'CRAZY NIGHTS' / 'GOLDEN DAYS' *(Brian May)*
Columbia DB 9153, May 1987

Brian wrote, produced and played guitars on Japanese musician Minako Honda's 'Crazy Nights' and 'Golden Days'. Minako died in 2006, and Brian expressed a plan to re-release the tracks to a wider listening public.

MEAT LOAF: 'A TIME FOR HEROES' *(Brian May)*
Orpheum 060 187, July 1987

Brian provided guitar on Meat Loaf's 1987 single, 'A Time For Heroes', recorded in February 1987 at West Lake Audio in Los Angeles and later becoming the Official Internation Summer Special Olympics theme that year. The song was produced and arranged by Jon Lyons.

BAD NEWS: BAD NEWS *(Brian May)*
EMI EMC 3535, October 1987 [69]

After appearing on stage with them in November 1986, Brian rejoined spoof heavy metal band Bad News (actually actors from the anarchic BBC comedy *The Young Ones*) at Sarm Studios in May 1987, there to produce an album for them. The album, *Bad News*, was released later that year after a controversial version of 'Bohemian Rhapsody' was issued as their debut single. The album appeared in the US in 1989 on CD, with additional tracks taken from Bad News' second album ('Bad Dreams', 'AGM', 'Double Entendre' and the single version of 'Cashing In On Christmas'). The original was re-released in 2004 with additional bonus tracks.

The track listing for the 1987 release was 'Hey Hey Bad News', "Vim Is Angry" *(dialog)*, 'Warriors Of Ghengis Khan', "Excalibur" *(dialog)*, 'Bohemian Rhapsody', "Dividing Up The Spoils" *(dialog)*, "Introducing The Band" *(dialog)*, 'Bad News', "Hey Mr Bassman" *(dialog)*, "Hey Mr Drummer" *(dialog)*, 'Masturbike', "Padding" *(dialog)*, "Trousers" *(dialog)* and 'Drink Till I Die'. The bonus tracks on 2004 reissue were: 'Pretty Woman', 'Life Of Brian', 'Bad Dreams', 'AGM', 'O Levels', 'Double Entendre', 'Cashing In On Christmas' *(dub)*, 'Cashing In On Christmas' *(single version)* and 'Bohemian Rhapsody' *(Take 1)*.

ANITA DOBSON: TALKING OF LOVE *(Brian May)*
Odeon ODN 1007, December 1987

While Queen were on tour in Holland, Brian booked time in a local studio to record two demos: one for Minako Honda (which later became 'Golden Days') and another for actress Anita Dobson. The latter had already had a single – 'Anyone Can Fall In Love' – released in 1986, reaching No. 4 in the UK, so it was inevitable that a full album would follow released. Anita asked Brian to produce the sessions (along with playing guitar and keyboards), which took place throughout 1986 and 1987 and included a selection of covers and songs written by Brian specifically for the album.

Two of Brian's songs – 'Let Me In (Your Heart Again)' and 'I Dream Of Christmas' – had been recorded during Queen sessions, the former during *The Works* and the latter in July 1984 at the same session that yielded 'Thank God It's Christmas', while the title track was written by Brian for Anita in June 1986. Two other original songs – 'Funny Old Life, Ain't It' (written by Brian and Anita) and 'Don't Fall In Love With Anybody Else' (written by Chris Thompson and Anne Dudley) – and three covers – 'The Last Time I Made Love', 'To Know Him Is To Love Him' and 'You Can't Stay The Night' – rounded out the album, with 'Anyone Can Fall In Love' added to ensure sales.

The first single was the title track, backed with 'Sweet Talkin'' (a variation of the A-side written by Brian and Anita), and reached No. 43 upon its release in July 1987. 'I Dream Of Christmas' and its B-side 'Silly Christmas' (like 'Sweet Talkin'', a variation of the A-side, again written by Brian and Anita) were released in December 1987, while a third single – 'To Know Him Is To Love Him' backed with the abysmal rap, 'Funny Old Life, Ain't It' – was released in October 1988, both failing to chart. A final single, recorded in 1988, was a cover of 'In One Of My Weaker Moments' with several instrumental remixes of the song serving as the B-side. Like the previous singles, 'In One Of My Weaker Moments' failed to chart, and Anita, realizing that her career as a pop star was coming to a close, focused on her acting instead.

HOLLY JOHNSON: BLAST *(Brian May)*
MCA DMCG 6042, January 1989 [4]

Brian is on 'Love Train'.

LIVING IN A BOX: GATECRASHING *(Brian May)*
Chrysalis DCDL 1676, February 1989

The Brian track here is 'Blow The House Down'.

SIGUE SIGUE SPUTNIK: 'DANCERAMA' / 'BARBARANDROID' *(Roger Taylor)*
EMI SSS 6, March 1989

Roger remixed the two tracks that made up Sigue Sigue Sputnik's 1989 single, which peaked at No. 50 in the UK.

BLACK SABBATH: HEADLESS CROSS *(Brian May)*
EIRSA 1002, April 1989 [31]

Brian contributed guitar to 'When Death Calls', which featured Cozy Powell on drums, leading to the two recording 'Ride To Win' and 'Somewhere In Time' in 1992 (released on *Back To The Light* as 'Resurrection' and 'Nothin' But Blue', respectively). The Black Sabbath song was recorded between August and November 1988 at Soundmill Studios in Woodcray.

FUZZBOX: BIG BANG *(Brian May)*
Geffen PRO CD 3688, August 1989 [2]

Brian contributed guitar to Fuzzbox's hit 1989 single 'Self', which was also released on *Big Bang* in August of that year. Recorded during February 1989 at Unit 3 Studios in North West London, the single also featured a re-recording of 'Bohemian Rhapsody' as the B-side, but featured no involvement from Brian or anyone from Queen.

MORRIS MAJOR AND THE MINORS: 'STUTTER RAP' AND 'THIS IS THE CHORUS' *(John Deacon)*

Unusually, John agreed to don a blue wig and appear in the videos to these songs – unusual because he didn't contribute anything to the original recordings, which were released in 1989.

ARTISTS UNITED FOR NATURE: 'YES WE CAN'
(Brian May)
Virgin 662 764, 1989

Released under the name Artists United For Nature, this charity single in aid of preserving rain forests was recorded at Sarm Studios between July and August 1989, with Brian joining Ian Anderson, Joe Cocker, Carol Decker, Harold Faltermeyer, Herbie Hancock, Tommy Johnson, Chaka Khan, Stevie Lange, Michael McDonald, Richard Page, Maggie Reilly, Jennifer Rush, Sandra, Chris Thompson and Stefan Zauner.

ROCK AID ARMENIA: 'SMOKE ON THE WATER'
(Brian May & Roger Taylor)
Armen T 001, December 1989 [39]

Released under the name Rock Aid Armenia, this charity single in aid of the December 1988 Armenian earthquake was a re-recording of Deep Purple's classic 'Smoke On The Water'. Brian contributed guitars and Roger provided drums, while other musicians included: Bryan Adams, Bruce Dickson, Ian Gillan and Paul Rodgers (the first time Brian and Roger would work with Paul) on vocals; Ritchie Blackmore, David Gilmour, Tony Iommi and Alex Lifeson on guitars; Geoff Beauchamp on rhythm guitar, and Keith Emerson and Geoff Downes on keyboards.

ROCK AGAINST REPATRIATION: 'SAILING'
(Brian May)
IRS EIRS CD 139, 1990

Released under the name Rock Against Repatriation, this charity single in aid of Vietnamese boat people, who had settled in Hong Kong but were being forced back to Vietnam, featured Brian on guitar and was recorded on 1 January 1990. Other musicians included Bonnie Tyler, Paul Carrack, Curt Smith, Mark King, Judie Tzuke, Steve Hogarth, Kevin Godley, Fish, Ian Sutherland, Jim Diamond and Justin Hayward on vocals; Tom Conti, Marillion, Steve Hackett, Paul Muggleton and Judie Tzuke on backing vocals; Steve Hackett, Phil Manzanera and Steve Rothery on guitars; Pino Palladino on bass; Howard Jones on piano; Simon Phillips on drums, and Nick Magnus on percussion.

HALE & PACE AND THE STONKERS: 'THE STONK'
(Brian May and Roger Taylor)
London 869 863 2, March 1991

While Queen were busy recording their post-*Innuendo* songs, Brian was approached by British comedy duo Hale and Pace, who asked him to produce a charity single for Comic Relief. Sessions for the resulting song – called 'The Stonk' – started in January 1991 at Metropolis Studios and featured a host of musicians: Tony Iommi and David Gilmour (guitars), Neil

Murray (bass guitar), Roger Taylor, Cozy Powell and Rowan Atkinson (drums – who knew that Atkinson, television's Mr Bean, could play drums?), Joe Griffiths and Mike Moran (keyboards), and Chris Thompson, Judie Tzuke, Mike Moran, Maggie Ryder, Miriam Stockley and Suzie O'List (backing vocals). In addition to production duties, Brian also played guitar and keyboards. The single was released in March 1991 and quickly rose to No. 1 in the UK, helping raise thousands of pounds and awareness for Comic Relief. A video was also made, with all the musicians, as well as several comedians, appearing.

D.ROK: OBLIVION *(Brian May)*
Warhammer 0874 6, August 1991

Brian guests on 'Red Planet Blues' and 'Get Out Of My Way'.

EXTREME: 'LOVE OF MY LIFE' *(Brian May)*
A&M AMCD 698, May 1992 [12]

Extreme's version of 'Love Of My Life' from the Freddie Mercury Tribute Concert was released as the B-side of their 'Song For Love' single in May 1992, and featured additional guitar from Brian. Royalties were donated to the Terence Higgins Trust.

COZY POWELL: THE DRUMS ARE BACK
(Brian May and John Deacon)
Electrola CDODN 1008, August 1992

For more information on 'Ride To Win' and 'Somewhere In Time', to which both Brian and John contributed, see 'Resurrection' and 'Nothin' But Blue' in Part Three.

JUDY TZUKE: WONDERLAND *(Brian May)*
Castle Communications ESS CD 184, September 1992

Brian appears on 'I Can Read Books'.

SHAKY: 'RADIO' *(Roger Taylor)*
Epic 658 436 2, October 1992

Roger played drums on this single, which reached No. 37 in the UK. An acoustic version was also recorded and released on the CD single.

HANK MARVIN: INTO THE LIGHT *(Brian May)*

Polydor 517 148 2, October 1992

Perhaps one of the strangest Queen-related collaborations featured Brian on guitar backing former Shadows guitarist Hank Marvin on a twanged-up version of 'We Are The Champions'. The song was released as a single in October 1992 and reached No. 66 in the UK.

TONY MARTIN: BACK WHERE I BELONG *(Brian May)*
Polydor 5135 182, 1992

Brian is on 'If There Is A Heaven'.

PHENOMENA: PHENOMENA III: INNER VISION
(Brian May)
Parachute CD PAR 002, 1992

Brian contributed guitar to 'A Whole Lot Of Love' and 'What About Love' by Phenomena, which were recorded in 1988 but remained unreleased until 1992.

THE LEFT HANDED MARRIAGE: CRAZY CHAIN
(Brian May)
LHM1, February 1993

Bill Richards, former guitarist of 1984 and good friend of Brian May's, formed a folk-rock band called The Left Handed Marriage in the summer of 1965. Eighteen months later, in January 1967, they released their first album, the privately pressed *On The Right Side Of The Left Handed Marriage*, and when the band were to enter AMC Sound in March to record their follow-up, Bill called upon Brian and asked him to help create a fuller sound by providing guitar and backing vocals on some songs. On 4 April, Brian contributed to four of the songs: 'Give Me Time' (which later became 'I Need Time' and was co-written by Brian and Bill), 'She Was Once My Friend', 'Sugar Lump Girl' and 'Yours Sincerely'.

The sessions went well, though further sessions were booked on 31 July at Regent Sound Studios to produce more material. 'She Was Once My Friend' and 'I Need Time' were both re-recorded, with a new song, titled 'Appointment', also submitted. The first title was selected as a potential single, though all was aborted later in the year when a new record deal was not forthcoming. The band dissolved, and the songs were left unreleased until 1993 when the band reformed to record an album titled *Crazy Chain*. The three tracks from the Regent Sound session were included as bonus tracks, and interest in the band was briefly rekindled thanks to a fantastic exposé by John S Stuart in *Record Collector* around the same time.

PAUL RODGERS: MUDDY WATER BLUES

(Brian May)
Victory Music 828 414 2, 1993

Brian contributed guitar to 'I'm Ready', which was recorded at Powerhouse Studios in London during January 1993 and marked the second collaboration between Paul and Brian, more than a decade before the Queen + Paul Rodgers project.

GREENPEACE: ALTERNATIVE NRG *(Brian May)*

Hollywood 74321 18091 2, 1993

Brian contributed guitar to Soundgarden's 'New Damage', which was recorded in April 1993 "using solar energy", according to the album's liner notes.

GORDON GILTRAP: MUSIC FOR THE SMALL SCREEN *(Brian May)*

Munchkin Records MRCD 1, June 1995

Brian provided guitar on 'Heartsong' by Gordon Giltrap, recorded between February and July 1993 at Redditch in the Midlands. Other musicians include Midge Ure, Neil Murray, Steve Howe and Rick Wakeman.

OS PARALAMAS DO SUCESSO: SEVERINO

(Brian May)
EMI 829405 2, January 1994

Brian is on the intriguingly titled 'El Vampiro bajo el sol'.

JENNIFER RUSH: OUT OF MY HANDS *(Brian May)*

Electrola 724303 112623, 1994

Brian is on 'Who Wants To Live Forever'.
IN FROM THE STORM *(Brian May)*

BMG Music 09026 68233 2, 1995

Here, Brian appears on 'One Rainy Wish'.

STEFAN ZAUNER: SOME OTHER LANGUAGE

(Brian May)
Columbia 4811742, 1995

Brian is a guest on 'Make My Dream Come True'.

CARMINE APPICE: GUITAR ZEUS *(Brian May)*

No Bull Records 34336 2, 1995

Brian provided guitar on Carmine Appice's 'Nobody Knew', and was also featured on two different mixes: the radio version and a 'Black White House' mix.

ROCKY HORROR PICTURE SHOW *(Brian May)*

Show CD 025, 1995

Brian is heard on 'Whatever Happened To Saturday Night' and 'Wild And Untamed Thing'.

STATUS QUO: DON'T STOP *(Brian May)*

Polygram 531 035 2, 1996

Brian provided guitar on Status Quo's 1996 track 'Raining In My Heart', and it was during these sessions that Brian, Rick Parfitt and Francis Rossi recorded the guitar tracks for 'FBI' (see that song's entry in Part Three for more information).

VARIOUS ARTISTS: TWANG! A TRIBUTE TO HANK MARVIN AND THE SHADOWS

(Brian May)
PANGAE 72438 33928 2 7, 1996

'FBI' (see above).

VARIOUS ARTISTS: MOTH POET HOTEL

(Brian May)
COCA 13627, 1996

Brian is on the Mott cover 'All The Way From Memphis'.

PINOCCHIO: ORIGINAL SOUNDTRACK

(Brian May)
London 452 740 2, 1996

For more information on the titles 'Il Colosso' and 'What Are We Made Of', see their respective entries in Part Three.

SAS BAND: THE SAS BAND *(Roger Taylor and John Deacon)*

1997

Roger and John are on 'That's The Way God Planned It'.

LULLABIES WITH A DIFFERENCE *(Brian May)*
BMG 74321 634972, 1998

Brian is on 'My Boy'.

NAKED SUSHI: 'CARNIVOROUS GIRL' *(Roger Taylor)*
1999

Roger sang backing vocals on Naked Sushi's 'Carnivorous Girl', released on the 'No Name' CD single with 'Love' and 'Feel My Groove' as the other tracks.

STEVE HACKETT: FEEDBACK '86 *(Brian May)*
CAMCD 21, 2000

Brian contributed guitar to former Genesis guitarist Steve Hackett's December 1986 sessions, though the songs weren't released until 1992's *Unauthorized Biography* (Virgin CDVM 9014), and later reissued on *Guitar Noir* (Viceroy VIC8008 2) and *Feedback '86*. Brian and Steve collaborated on words and music on 'Slot Machine', with Brian also featuring on 'Cassandra' and 'Don't Fall Away From Me'.

TONY IOMMI: IOMMI *(Brian May)*
Divine Recordings 72435 27857 2, October 2000

Brian contributed additonal guitar to the tracks 'Goodbye Lament' and 'Flame On' for Black Sabbath guitarist Tony Iommi's *Iommi* album.

BOB GELDOF: SEX, AGE & DEATH *(Roger Taylor)*
EAGCD187, 2001

Roger Taylor contributed to his good friend Bob Geldof's first album in nearly a decade, playing drums and singing backing vocals on 'One For Me', 'Mind In Pocket', 'Mudslide', and 'Scream In Vain'. The album was also recorded at Roger's Cosford Mill Studios between 1999 and 2001.

GOOD ROCKIN' TONIGHT: THE LEGACY OF SUN RECORDS *(Brian May)*
Sire WPCR 11170, 2002

Brian is on '(I Don't Want Nobody) Teasin' Around (With Me)'.

ORIGINAL SOUNDTRACK: MISSION: IMPOSSIBLE II *(Brian May)*
Hollywood Edel 0110302HWR, 2002

Brian provided lead guitar to Foo Fighters' re-recording of Pink Floyd's classic 'Have A Cigar'.

DON NIX: GOING DOWN – THE SONGS OF DON NIX *(Brian May)*
Evidence ECD 26125-2, October 2002

Brian contributed guitars to Don Nix's 'Going Down'.

PROCOL HARUM: THE WELL'S ON FIRE *(Roger Taylor)*
CD Eagle (Red) 20006, 2003

With a band featuring Gary Brooker (lead vocals, piano), Geoff Whitehorn (guitars), Matthew Fisher (organ), Matt Pegg (bass guitar) and Mark Brzezicki (drums), Roger contributed backing vocals to Procol Harum's 'Shadow Boxed', released on *The Well's On Fire* in 2003.

QUARTZ: STAND UP AND FIGHT *(Brian May)*
Majestic Rock MAJCD037, 2004

Brian contributed guitar to 'Circles', the B-side of little-known band Quartz's 1977 single 'Stoking The Fires Of Hell'. The song (featuring Ozzy Osbourne on backing vocals), which wasn't released on the original debut album release of *Stand Up And Fight*, was later issued on the re-released album in 2004, having gone unnoticed for nearly 25 years.

THE YARDBIRDS: BIRDLAND *(Brian May)*
UKCD FN22802, April 2003

Brian is on 'Mr, You're A Better Man Than I'.

TIM STAFFELL: aMIGO *(Brian May)*
aMIGO Records aMOO 1, 2003

For years, it had been rumored that Tim Staffell, erstwhile vocalist, bassist and songwriter with Smile who was now making a comfortable living as a commercials director and designer, was planning on making a solo album. In 2001, he confirmed the rumors by forming a new band, aMIGO, and stating that he was going to record an album. The impetus of the album came from Tim's son Andrew, a drummer who had suggested that father and son record some material together.

Once a core band was formed – featuring Tim on vocals and guitar, Andrew on drums, Richard Lightman on bass guitar and John Webster on keyboards – sessions began in January 2002 at Aftertouch Studios. Sessions continued into 2003, with guest musicians Snowy White (former auxiliary guitarist with Pink Floyd), Morgan Fisher (whom Tim had worked with in the 1970s), former one-time Smile keyboardist Chris Smith, and others like Peter Hammond, Dave O'Higgins, Corrina Silvester, Johnny Griggs, Rob Tolchard, Peter Hammerton, Martin Shaw and Keith Johnson.

Brian's contributions were recorded last. 'Doin' Alright' and 'Earth' had been early Smile favorites and, initially, Tim had wanted to drastically rearrange them; he quickly decided, however, to leave well alone and remain faithful to the original recordings. Brian duetted with Tim on both songs and provided additional guitar, and Tim later said that his former bandmate's contributions were the highpoints of the album.

SOUNDTRACK: SPIDERMAN 2 *(Brian May)*
Interscope Records, June 2004

Brian contributed lead guitar to Jimmy Gnecco's 'Someone To Die For', released on the soundtrack to *Spiderman 2*, and produced by Rick Rubin.

ZUCCHERO: ZUCCHERO & CO *(Brian May)*
Polydor 981990, 2004

Brian contributed guitar to two of Zucchero's songs: 'Il Mare Impetuoso Al Tramonoto Sali Sulla Luna E Dietro Una Tendina Di Stelle...' and 'Madre Dolcissima'.

PETER KAY: '(IS THIS THE WAY TO) AMARILLO?'
(Brian May and Roger Taylor)

During rehearsals for the Queen + Paul Rodgers tour, Brian and Roger took some time to appear in the video for British comedian Peter Kay's 2005 Comic Relief single, a cover of the 1971 single '(Is This The Way To) Amarillo?' Like the other stars of the video, Brian and Roger are seen running with Peter; the three were filmed in front of a green screen that showed footage of Buckingham Palace while giving a handclap similar to 'Radio Ga Ga', before the scene cuts to Peter with other

guests. Kay would later join the band at their May 2005 Manchester concert for a version of this song.

HANNAH JANE FOX: WE WILL ROCK YOU – AROUND THE WORLD *(Roger Taylor)*

Roger produced 'Stalker', released on the iTunes-only download EP *We Will Rock You: Around The World*.

MEAT LOAF: BAT OUT OF HELL III: THE MONSTER IS LOOSE *(Brian May)*
Virgin 0946 3 77737 2 7, October 2006

At the behest of his good friend Meat Loaf, Brian contributed some screaming guitar to 'Bad For Good' on Mr. Loaf's third instalment in the *Bat Out Of Hell* series, this time subtitled *The Monster Is Loose*.

CLIFF RICHARD: TWO'S COMPANY – THE DUETS
(Brian May)
EMI 0094637707227, October 2006

Brian played guitar on 'Move It', released on the star-studded album *Two's Company*.

DIANA ROSS: I LOVE YOU *(Brian May)*
Angel 094637681220, October 2006

'Crazy Little Thing Called Love' was recorded for Diana Ross's 2006 *I Love You* album, and Brian duly contributed a vastly different guitar solo, in addition to some rudimentary bass.

MOMO CORTES: CONSTANTE CONTRADICCION
(Brian May)
2007

Brian played guitar on 'Tanto Amor No Es Bueno', a Spanish re-recording of 'Too Much Love Will Kill You'. Cortes was the original Galileo in the Spanish production of *We Will Rock You: The Musical*.

LYNN CAREY SAYLOR: YOU LIKE IT CLEAN
(Brian May)
2007

Alongside Danny Miranda and Spike Edney, Brian played guitar and contributed vocals to this American singer-songwriter's debut album, *You Like It Clean*, specifically the tracks 'If We Believe' (an original composition and first released in 2002, with a portion of the proceeds going to the Mercury Phoenix Trust) and 'We Belong' (a cover of Pat Benetar's 1984 single).

BANDAGED TOGETHER: ALL YOU NEED IS LOVE
(Brian May)
TOGCD1, 2009

Recorded for the Children In Need charity, this updated recording of The Beatles' classic plea for peace during the Summer of Love features Brian on guitar, alongside a host of other star musicians: Hugh Cornwell, Sharon Corr, Cara Dillon, Andy Dinan, Troy Donockley, Ade Edmondson, Paloma Faith, Bryan Ferry, Finbar Furey, Peter Gabriel, Anthony Head, Red Hurley, Imelda May, Lee Mead, Beth Rowley, Heather Small, Clare Teal, Bailey Tzuke, Midge Ure, Hayley Westenra, and Terry Wogan (vocals), Terry Taylor (acoustic guitar), Nick Mason (drums), Bill Wyman (bass guitar), and Jason Rebello (piano).

CATHERINE PORTER: GEMS FOR RUBY *(Brian May)*
Nova B001RTYKPO, March 2009

Brian played guitar on Catherine Porter's re-recording of Queen's 1976 classic 'Somebody To Love'.

MEAT LOAF: HANG COOL TEDDY BEAR *(Brian May)*
Mercury 273 4097, April 2010

Brian, alongside Steve Vai and Rob Cavallo on guitars and Justin Hawkins on backing vocals, contributed guitar to Meat Loaf's 'Love Is Not Real (Next Time You Stab Me In The Back)'.

TAYLOR HAWKINS AND THE COATTAIL RIDERS: RED LIGHT FEVER *(Brian May and Roger Taylor)*
RCA 8897684982, April 2010

Both Brian and Roger contributed their respective instruments on Hawkins's second solo album outside of the Foo Fighters, *Red Light Fever*, though they weren't on the same tracks: Brian played on 'Way Down' and 'Don't Have To Speak', while Roger was on 'Your Shoes'.

KERRY ELLIS: ANTHEMS *(Brian May)*
Decca 2740128, September 2010

Brian was almost immediately smitten with Kerry Ellis's voice since she was cast as Meat in *We Will Rock You: The Musical*, and went to great lengths to secure her a record deal – not that her credentials as a West End favorite wouldn't have helped anyway. Starting in 2006, Brian and Kerry worked on her full-length debut, recording material only when the two of them were available to do so in between other commitments; what emerged in September 2010 was a unique blend of orchestral rock and musical theater. Brian acted as producer and arranger, and contributed guitars, bass, piano, keyboards, and backing vocals, while the few guest musicians were friends of Brian's: Roger played drums with Keith Prior on 'No-One But You (Only The Good Die Young)' (itself recorded in 2005 and taken from the *We Will Rock You: Around The World* EP), Taylor Hawkins on drums on 'Defying Gravity' and 'I'm Not That Girl', and Rufus Taylor, Roger's son, on drums on four of the songs.

Unsurprisingly, it wasn't to everyone's tastes, and while Brian's heavy-handed gushing over her talents and arrogant dismissal that anyone who disliked the album was small-minded, critics and fans alike cocked an eyebrow at the involvement. The album performed respectably enough, entering the UK charts at No. 15, before it fell the following week to No. 78, and then dropped out entirely. Two singles – 'I'm Not That Girl' from *Wicked*, backed with 'Dangerland', and 'Anthem' from *Chess* – were released in the fourth quarter of 2010, but both failed to chart.

However, the album was significant for two reasons: first, it got the normally songwriting shy Brian to write two new songs – 'Dangerland' and 'I Can't Be Your Friend', the latter title with Don Black – both of which could have fit in nicely on *The Cosmos Rocks* (intriguingly, he opined that 'Some Things That Glitter', here pointlessly retitled as 'I Loved A Butterfly', was written for Kerry's voice, and not Paul Rodgers's). Secondly, it riled him from his post-Queen + Paul Rodgers ennui, and changed his stance on touring: in May 2011, he set out for a month-long UK tour with Kerry, and appeared rejuvenated and thrilled to be on a stage again. For its faults, and countering any claims that the album was an ego trip for Brian, *Anthems* may have relit that musical spark in Brian, that had been lacking for several years – and who in their right mind would deny a man of his age a little fun every now and then?

BOB GELDOF: HOW TO COMPOSE POPULAR SONGS THAT WILL SELL *(Roger Taylor)*
Mercury 274 745-2, February 2011

Roger once again helped his old friend Bob Geldof out with the humorously titled *How To Compose Popular Songs That Will Sell Well*, providing drums and backing vocals; as with *Sex, Age & Death*, individual song credits weren't provided, but Roger almost certainly played and sang on 'Silly Pretty Thing' and 'Here's To You', as well as the non-album bonus tracks 'Just Get On', 'The Fields Of Spring', and 'Battersea Morning'.

TANGERINE DREAM: STARMUS – SONIC UNIVERSE *(Brian May)*
Eastgate 061 CD, April 2013

Recorded on 24 June 2011 at the Magma Arte and Congresos Concert Hall on the island of Tenerife at the Starmus Festival, *Starmus – Sonic Universe* is, essentially, a collaborative effort between Brian and prolific German ambient/electronic band Tangerine Dream. The Starmus Festival was to celebrate the 50th anniversary of Yuri Gagarin's first flight into space, with Neil Armstrong and Buzz Aldrin appearing as special guests. Brian features throughout Tangerine Dream's set, with opener 'Supernova (Real Star Sounds)' being the definite highlight; of course, Brian jams in 'Last Horizon' and the obligatory 'We Will Rock You', but elsewhere, this is some pretty spacey, beautiful stuff, and should absolutely be checked out by anyone desiring a change of pace.

LADY GAGA: BORN THIS WAY *(Brian May)*
Streamline/Interscope Records B0015373-02, May 2011

Brian contributed guitar to Lady Gaga's fourth single from her *Born This Way* album, 'Yoü And I', which sounds like it could have been a modern-day Queen song – it even sampled the footstomps and handclaps from 'We Will Rock You'.

STEVE CROPPER: DEDICATED – A TRIBUTE TO THE 5 ROYALES *(Brian May)*
429 Records FTN17832, August 2011
Brian sang lead and backing vocals and played guitar on 'I Do'.

DAPPY: BAD INTENTIONS *(Brian May)*
Island Records/Takeover Entertainment 3711533, October 2012

Brian played guitar on 'Rockstar', and a performance of 'We Will Rock You' from Radio 1's *Live Lounge Session*

was released on deluxe CD and digital editions of the album.

YO MA MA: SYMPTOMOLOGY/SHORTCUTS TO INFINITY *(Brian May)*
MsMusic Productions MUS-102-2, 2012

Brian played guitar on 'Out Of The Darkness'.

IAN PAICE: THE SUNFLOWER SUPERJAM
(Brian May)
The Sunflower Jam TOWNDVD77, 2013

Brian played guitar on both Alice Cooper's 'School's Out' and Bruce Dickinson's 'Black Night' and 'Since You've Been Gone', as well as the all-star finale of 'Smoke On The Water', recorded live at the Sunflower Superjam at the Royal Albert Hall, 16 September 2012. Brian and Kerry Ellis also performed 'Born Free' and 'I Loved A Butterfly' earlier in the evening.

ARTFUL BADGER: BADGER SWAGGER
(Brian May)
Download only, June 2013

Brian cowrote 'Badger Swagger' as a protest against the British government's proposed badger cull. He also played guitar and piano alongside other such luminaries as Slash, David Attenborough, Kerry Ellis, and Sonny Green. He also wrote the music to, and played keyboards on, the spoken-word poem 'The Badger', which was written by Richard Bonfield for Brian and read by Virginia McKenna.

BRIAN WILSON AND VARIOUS ARTISTS: GOD ONLY KNOWS *(Brian May)*
RCA/Sony Music 88875029482, October 2014

The Beach Boys' tortured genius Brian Wilson was approached by the BBC to record an updated rendition of 'God Only Knows' to raise money for the Children In Need charity. Alongside Wilson, Elton John, Chris Martin, Stevie Wonder, Dave Grohl, One Direction, Pharrell, Sam Smith, Kylie Minogue, Chrissie Hynde, Lorde, Florence Welch, and Jools Holland, Brian contributed guitar.

BAND AID 30: DO THEY KNOW IT'S CHRISTMAS?
(Roger Taylor)
Virgin EMI Records 4714842, November 2014

Recorded on 15 November 2014 and release two days later to raise funds to fight the Ebola virus in Western Africa, this re-recorded charity single featured a wide swath of musicians, including Bono, Chris Martin, Sinéad O'Connor, Ellie Goulding, One Direction, Ed Sheeran, and Sam Smith, with Roger providing drums and backing vocals.

PROTAFIELD: NEMESIS *(Roger Taylor)*
Devfire DEV002CD, 2014

Roger contributed drums to the track 'Wrath' on this alternative/industrial rock band's debut album.

ADAM LAMBERT: THE ORIGINAL HIGH *(Brian May)*
Warner Bros. Records 549641-2, June 2015

Brian played guitar on 'Lucy'.

MOTÖRHEAD: BAD MAGIC *(Brian May)*
UDR/Motörhead Music UDR 057P18, August 2015

Brian played guitar on 'The Devil'.

JON TIVEN AND STEPHEN KALINICH: EACH SOUL HAS A VOICE *(Brian May)*
MsMusic Productions MUS-106-1, 2015

Brian played guitar on 'Rude Awakenings'.

VARIOUS ARTISTS: ONE VOICE (FROM THE DOCUMENTARY A DOG NAMED GUCCI)
(Brian May)
MVD Audio MVD8181LP, April 2016

This all-star lineup of Norah Jones, Aimee Mann, Susanna Hoffs, and Neko Case recorded a rendition of 'One Voice' for North America's Record Store Day,

and was released on 16 April 2016. Brian contributed backing vocals and guitar, and would go on to record his own version with Kerry Ellis.

RICK WAKEMAN: STARMUS *(Brian May)*
RRAW MFGZ019DVD, September 2016

Brian appeared once again at the Starmus Festival at the Magma Art & Congree Centre in Tenerife on 26 September 2014, where he played 'Last Horizon' and a suitable guitar solo, before launching into "39'. Brian appeared later on a performance of Yes's 'Starship Trooper'.

CRAIG WEIR AND THE CABALISTIC CAVALRY: THE HIGHLAND ROAD
Download only, 2017

Brian contributed his voice to the final two lines of this poem.

ARTISTS FOR GRENFELL: BRIDGE OVER TROUBLED WATER *(Brian May)*
Download only, 2017

Brian played guitar on this charity recording of Simon and Garfunkel's 'Bridge Over Troubled Water' to benefit the victims of the Grenfell Tower fire in West London. Other musicians included James Blunt, Roger Daltrey, Tony Hadley, Geri Halliwell, Robbie Williams, Nile Rodgers, and Pete Townshend. Brian's part was recorded in Los Angeles during rehearsals for the North American leg of Queen + Adam Lambert's tour.

JAYCE LEWIS: MILLION PART 1 *(Brian May)*
Devfire Entertainment/Caroline International/Universal Music Group DEV004CD, October 2017

Brian played guitar on 'We Are One'.

PART SIX

OTHER MEDIA:
RADIO, VIDEO, INTERACTIVE, STAGE

A: BBC RADIO SESSIONS

Queen's BBC radio appearances weren't particularly frequent, given their long history: they recorded only six sessions proper between 1973 and 1977 (three each for Bob Harris and the late, great John Peel) and broadcast only a handful of specially performed live concert performances. Two of the studio sessions were released in December 1989 by independent label Band Of Joy on a record called Queen At The Beeb. This went out of print rather quickly, but Hollywood Records offered their own version in March 1995 titled Queen At The BBC, which included the same songs from the 1989 release. Both of these albums featured material recorded during the first and third sessions from 1973, but why these sessions were chosen (seemingly at random) is anybody's guess.

In 1996, rumors circulated that EMI and Hollywood were going to release a double disc set called Live At The BBC with all 24 performances; three remastered songs – 'My Fairy King', 'Doing All Right' and 'Liar' – were even released on the second CD single of 'Let Me Live' in June 1996, with a sticker proudly declaring "from the upcoming release, Live At The BBC." Unfortunately, EMI hadn't offered anything new – the three songs had actually been taken from the 1989/1995 BBC release – and the rumored album fell by the wayside. Given the success of other bands' BBC releases around this time (The Beatles, The Who, Led Zeppelin, The Kinks, Jimi Hendrix, Cream, and David Bowie, to name but a few), an updated release is badly needed to supplant the fans' current option: poor-quality downloads from the Internet.

Queen Productions started to rectify this issue in 2011, when they finally released some of the rarer and more interesting selections on the 2011 deluxe reissues of each respective album, hinting that a more complete set will be available in the not-too-distant future. Indeed, in 2016, Queen On Air: The Complete BBC Sessions was released in multiple formats, containing all six BBC sessions, along with selections from three concerts recorded by the BBC and a handful of interviews from throughout the years.

JOHN PEEL'S SOUNDS OF THE SEVENTIES (SESSION 1)

• Recorded: 5 February 1973 • Broadcast: 15 February 1973 • Venue: Langham 1 Studio • Producer: Bernie Andrews • Engineer: John Etchells

'My Fairy King' (4'06), 'Keep Yourself Alive' (3'48), 'Doing All Right (4'11), 'Liar' (6'28)

Queen's first radio session took place before they had established themselves as a household name; they hadn't even released a single yet. As the band were recording their debut album at the time, they were more concerned with finalizing the result instead of rushing out to record four fresh versions of songs they had painstakingly worked on for the past few months – though they knew that this kind of exposure would be exceptional. So, a compromise was drawn, with the band delivering the backing tracks of four songs, with new vocals recorded by Freddie (and Roger).

The result is underwhelming – though, at the time, these unheard of songs from Queen, especially 'My Fairy King' (which hadn't been performed live), were a real treat to the band's early fanbase. There's not much to praise here in hindsight though: Freddie's lead vocal isn't drastically different on any of the songs, excepting the odd ad-lib here and there, but the real treat of the session is to hear Roger sing lead vocal on the final verse of 'Doing All Right', an arrangement which hadn't been attempted by the band in either the studio or the live setting. Unfortunately for Queen fans, Band of Joy picked perhaps the least interesting session to release on *Queen At The Beeb*.

BOB HARRIS'S SOUNDS OF THE SEVENTIES (SESSION 2)

• *Recorded:* 25 July 1973 • *Broadcast:* 13 August 1973 (without 'Keep Yourself Alive') • *Repeat:* 24 September 1973 (with 'Keep Yourself Alive') • *Venue:* Langham 1 Studio • *Producer:* Jeff Griffin • *Engineers:* Chris Lycett and John Etchells

'See What A Fool I've Been' (4'21), 'Keep Yourself Alive' (3'41), 'Liar' (6'28), 'Son And Daughter' (6'00)

When the band returned to Langham 1 Studio to record another radio session, *Queen* had just been released and they appreciated as much exposure as possible. Another odd arrangement was struck up, in which the band brought two master tracks – 'Keep Yourself Alive' and 'Liar' – and recorded new lead vocals, and then performed two new renditions of 'See What A Fool I've Been' and 'Son And Daughter', which could be undertaken rather quickly as they were fairly standard blues numbers.

The appearance of 'See What A Fool I've Been' was interesting, as the band hadn't included it on their debut album despite the fact that it was an integral part of their live show, usually performed as an encore. 'Son And Daughter', more indicative of Queen's live show at the time, was extended to nearly twice the running time of the album version, allowing for plenty of improvisation from the three instrumentalists. Freddie altered the "a woman expects a man to buckle down and shovel shit" line to end with "shhh" the first time around, and changed it to just "it" when repeated. The improvisation featured plenty of feedback and was one of the first recorded appearances of the 'Brighton Rock' solo that had already become a favorite in the live setting.

Excepting the two pre-recorded songs, this session offered a tantalizing glimpse into Queen's live sound at the time, which would be explored more fully during the next radio session.

IN CONCERT (RADIO ONE)

• *Recorded:* 13 September 1973 • *Broadcast:* 13 September 1973 (without Rock 'n' Roll Medley)

• *Venue:* Golders Green Hippodrome • *Producer:* Jeff Griffin • *Engineers:* John Etchells and Paul Deley

'Procession' (1'26), 'Father To Son' (4'57), 'Son And Daughter' (6'44), 'See What A Fool I've Been' (4'20), 'Ogre Battle' (5'24), 'Liar' (6'56), Rock 'n' Roll Medley ('Jailhouse Rock', 'Shake, Rattle & Roll', 'Stupid Cupid', 'Be Bop A Lula', 'Bama Lama Bama Loo', 'Jailhouse Rock (reprise)') (3'47)

A good month before Queen's official European tour in support of their debut album, the band were approached by the BBC to perform a concert specifically for radio use. The band agreed and rehearsed diligently for about a week before the taping to ensure that things went smoothly. With a restructured set list, including three new compositions from the upcoming second album and a smattering of concert favorites and old hits, the band launched into a surprisingly raw and thrilling set with an opening salvo of 'Procession' (which was broadcast over the PA system) and 'Father To Son', distinctly rearranged and lacking the concluding "a word in your ear" coda.

The between song commentary from DJ Alan Black isn't particularly enlightening, though there's a moment when he introduces each band member, and, using the debut album's liner notes as a reference, calls John "Deacon John". Freddie is heard to remark on mic, "No, it's not."

The original broadcast lacked the concluding Rock 'n' Roll Medley, and rumors have circulated over the years (by no less than Greg Brooks in his book *Queen Live*) that 'Hangman', 'Stone Cold Crazy' and 'Keep Yourself Alive' were all performed after 'Ogre Battle', with 'See What A Fool I've Been' closing the first part of the set. If these songs were performed that night, they haven't yet seen the light of day. In addition, Black clearly stated that the band would not be performing "their first single", though, again, this might have just been added for broadcast purposes.

JOHN PEEL'S SOUNDS OF THE SEVENTIES (SESSION 3)

• *Recorded:* 3 December 1973 • *Broadcast:* 6 December 1973 • *Venue:* Langham 1 Studio • *Producer:* Bernie Andrews • *Engineers:* Mike Franks and Nick Griffiths

'Ogre Battle' (4'57), 'Great King Rat' (5'56), 'Modern Times Rock 'n' Roll' (2'00), 'Son And Daughter' (7'08)

Queen's third BBC radio session in 12 months wrapped up an eventful year. Broadcast three days after recording, the band offered four fresh new items: three from their debut album and one from their upcoming second release. This session shows the band in their rawest form yet, a surprisingly refreshing approach from a band that thrived on perfection. The session commenced with a rendition of 'Ogre Battle' (taken at a slightly slower pace than the album version) which had been featured prominently in the live setting, and had been performed during Queen's broadcast from the Golders Green Hippodrome.

'Great King Rat' deviates little from the original studio version but is a far more energetic performance, and contains an obvious guitar solo overdub as well as poor vocal double-tracking at some points. 'Modern Times Rock 'n' Roll' and 'Son And Daughter' are both extended past their normal playing times, the latter track more than doubled in length to allow the band plenty of room for improvisation (making it similar to the version from the second session).

This session was chosen to be released on the *Queen At The Beeb* album in 1989, although one edit was made: 'Ogre Battle' lost its introductory 60 seconds of guitar feedback and screaming due to a mangled master tape. This introduction often popped up in less than decent quality on bootlegs throughout the years, dubiously labelled as an alternate take, though it's now assumed that the original master has been damaged beyond repair and the introduction is lost for good.

BOB HARRIS'S SOUNDS OF THE SEVENTIES (SESSION 4)

• *Recorded:* 3 April 1974 • *Broadcast:* 15 April 1974 • *Venue:* Langham 1 Studio • *Producer:* Pete Ritzema • *Engineer:* unknown

'Modern Times Rock 'n' Roll' (2'37), 'Nevermore' (1'26), 'White Queen (As It Began)' (4'46), 'The March Of The Black Queen' (6'42)

An interesting session, this set saw the band perform two new numbers and rework an old favorite. 'Modern Times Rock 'n' Roll' is given its second BBC broadcast, taken at a slower tempo with suitably raucous vocals from Roger. Just as the first version had contained an appropriate "it's not that I'm bright, just happy-go-lucky" interjection from its author (delivered in a broad Cockney accent, no less), the new version was noteworthy in that it featured a weird whistle-blowing

as well as Freddie and Roger screaming "Rock and roll!" towards the conclusion of the song.

'Nevermore' and 'White Queen (As It Began)' are certainly the highlights of the session, as they feature some lovely ensemble playing, and it's in the simplicity of the arrangements that both succeed. The first is given a heavier treatment, with drums and guitar entering before the final verse, while the second features a breathtaking piano and guitar duet in place of the album version's acoustic guitar solo.

The only complaints lie with the selection of the introductory track (why not 'Seven Seas Of Rhye'? – an obvious choice, considering it had been released as a single six weeks before) and the disappointing inclusion of 'The March Of The Black Queen' – disappointing in that the band don't actually attempt to recreate this epic composition, but instead play the standard album version, fading out pointlessly as the strains of 'Funny How Love Is' are heard. Opinions have wavered over the actual version that was presented; Greg Brooks has stated that there were further guitar and percussion overdubs, and that it was officially a remix, though a more in-depth listen reveals that there were no overdubs administered.

BOB HARRIS'S SOUNDS OF THE SEVENTIES (SESSION 5)

• *Recorded:* 16 October 1974 • *Broadcast:* 4 November 1974 • *Venue:* Maida Vale 4 Studio • *Producer:* Jeff Griffin • *Engineer:* Jeff Griffin

'Now I'm Here' (4'13), 'Stone Cold Crazy' (2'13), 'Flick Of The Wrist' (3'12), 'Tenement Funster' (2'46)

A disappointing session, this penultimate set saw the band bring the master tapes of four tracks from *Sheer Heart Attack* to Maida Vale 4 and merely record new lead vocals. It is because of this different-but-not-different approach that many bootleggers have attempted to disguise these recordings as alternate or early takes. But a cursory listen reveals that the songs are identical to their original counterparts, excepting the vocals.

'Now I'm Here' and 'Stone Cold Crazy' are unspectacular for this reason alone, while 'Flick Of The Wrist' and 'Tenement Funster' (featuring a more aggressive vocal from Roger) are interesting in that they feature slightly different edits due to their appearance as part of a medley on *Sheer Heart Attack*. Instead of 'Tenement Funster' fading into 'Flick Of The Wrist', it instead finishes on a distinctive power chord, fading into nothingness (it was this edit to the backing track that was later used for the *Queen's First EP* release in 1977). 'Flick Of The Wrist' is faded in, instead of using a clean intro as on the 'Killer Queen' single, and ends with a flash of feedback from Brian's guitar. These two selections were released on the 2011 deluxe edition of *Sheer Heart Attack*. Along with the first session, session four is the most inessential one of all six...

JOHN PEEL'S SOUND OF THE SEVENTIES (SESSION 6)

• *Recorded:* 28 October 1977 • *Broadcast:* 14 November 1977 • *Venue:* Maida Vale 4 Studio • *Producer:* Jeff Griffin • *Engineers:* Mike Robinson

'Spread Your Wings' (5'20), 'It's Late' (6'31), 'My Melancholy Blues' (3'10), 'We Will Rock You' (4'19)

...while the sixth is the most satisfying BBC session Queen recorded. This final session presented four electrifying selections from their *News Of The World* album (released the same day the session was recorded) with nary a pre-recorded backing tape in sight, with the minor exception of the introductory foot stomps and handclaps of 'We Will Rock You'. It had also been over three years since the band recorded a specific session for the *Sounds Of The Seventies* programme, which unfortunately meant that no material from *A Night At The Opera* or *A Day At The Races* was ever attempted. In fact, the band's only direct BBC involvement had been on *Top Of The Pops* in order to promote 'Good Old-Fashioned Lover Boy', four months before this recording session.

'Spread Your Wings' starts off the proceedings, and is a drastic reworking of the subdued album version: taken at a marginally faster pace, the song is more stripped-down and concludes with an exciting, up-tempo finale that would unfortunately not be attempted on stage. Freddie's piano playing here is exciting and inspired, while Brian's guitar is more understated than usual, providing capable rhythm parts not present on the more familiar take. 'It's Late' is the least satisfying number, replacing the improvised-sounding middle section with a 'Get Down, Make Love'-type sequence with harmonizer and vocal effects that sit awkwardly in what is arguably Queen's finest rocker. 'My Melancholy Blues' follows, and in

its original form was a moment of sublime beauty; it's difficult to imagine how it could possibly be bettered. Brian is present this time around, and adds some tastefully appropriate guitar accompaniment, but Freddie is still the obvious star of the show. The concluding burst of laughter sends shivers down one's spine.

The session concludes with what starts out as a perfunctory rendition of 'We Will Rock You', the band finally launching into a full-on rock version of the song, turning it into something akin to 'Tie Your Mother Down'. The band was really in fine form here, with an amazing guitar riff and even a short bass solo. The concluding drum feature and Freddie's confident shout of "All right!" are merely the icing on the cake in what is undoubtedly Queen's finest BBC session.

The official party line of the strange reading that separates the slow and fast versions of 'We Will Rock You' is that it was a BBC recording of Herman Hesse's *Siddhartha* and, upon listening to the playback of the song, the band were amused to discover the short, accidental interjection and decided to keep it. However, keen-eared fans noted that this text wasn't written as such in *Siddhartha*, and that it may instead be from a BBC radio analysis on Hesse's novel.

Over the years, bootlegs of this session have been widely circulated as live versions. This is an easy mistake to make, as the session was originally broadcast with rather annoying audience overdubs (screaming, whistling, applauding and the like), not only as the songs start and conclude but during most of the performance as well. This mars what is inarguably Queen's best BBC session, one which has often been erroneously labelled as a show from Manchester in 1978 (they didn't play Manchester in 1978).

In 2002, as part of a marketing ploy for the *We Will Rock You* musical, *The Sun* issued a three-track promotional CD of the title track, editing out the "slow" version and presenting a standalone "fast" version instead. This remained the only song to have been officially released from these sessions for nearly a decade, when 'Spread Your Wings' and 'My Melancholy Blues' were released on the 2011 deluxe edition of *News Of The World*, and the entire session was (pointlessly) included on the 40th anniversary box set edition of the same album in 2017; considering all four songs had been released the previous year on *Queen On Air*, this was disappointingly superfluous.

B: VIDEO

Queen were justly renowned for embracing the rock video. For every major single release starting with 'Bohemian Rhapsody' in 1975 through to Freddie Mercury's final on-screen appearance for 'These Are The Days Of Our Lives' in 1991, Queen made sure to stress the importance of visuals in enhancing their music. Following Freddie's death in November 1991, Queen Productions have largely concentrated on upgrading the videos for every available format – be it VHS, laserdisc or DVD – for all generations of Queen fans to enjoy.

At the same time, Queen's concerts were always a visual spectacle, and their lighting rigs and pyrotechnics were an impressive display. Queen first toyed with releasing a live video in 1974, with their legendary Rainbow Theatre concert filmed for potential release; it, and another concert at Earl's Court Arena in 1977, was scrapped as the band's first live video release. It wouldn't be until 1984 that We Will Rock You (filmed in November 1981) served as Queen's introduction into the live rock video world. As the tours grew progressively larger and more grandiose, the band was sure to employ the finest directors to film their shows.

Individual videos are covered under the appropriate entries in Part Three; what follows is a guide to Queen's official video releases.

GREATEST FLIX

• 1981 (90 mins) • PMI MVP 99 1011 2 • *Directors:* Bruce Gowers, Dennis DeVallance, Rock Flicks, Derek Burbridge, Kliebenst, Brian Grant, Daniella Green, Keith McMillan, Don Norman

'Killer Queen' *(montage)*, 'Bohemian Rhapsody', 'You're My Best Friend', 'Somebody To Love', 'Tie Your Mother Down', 'We Are The Champions', 'We Will Rock You' *(slow)*, 'We Will Rock You' *(fast live)*, 'Spread Your Wings', 'Bicycle Race', 'Fat Bottomed Girls', 'Don't Stop Me Now', 'Love Of My Life' *(live)*, 'Crazy Little Thing Called Love', 'Save Me', 'Play The Game', 'Another One Bites The Dust', 'Flash'

To commemorate Queen's tenth year as an active live band, a trilogy of compilations appeared in November 1981: the familiar blockbuster, *Greatest Hits*, a 17-track onslaught of the band's greatest Top Thirty hits from 'Seven Seas Of Rhye' to 'Flash'; *Greatest Pix*, a 96-page photographic history from the band's first photo sessions to their triumphant South American concerts; and *Greatest Flix*, collecting the 17 official promotional videos so far onto one 90-minute videocassette, along with an introductory photo montage set to the tune of 'Killer Queen' (a precursor to the now-standard photo gallery on DVD releases).

Greatest Flix is an excellent collection, starting with the revolutionary 'Bohemian Rhapsody' and working its way chronologically through to the then most recent video, 'Flash'. There are some omissions: both versions of 'Keep Yourself Alive' and 'Liar', for whatever reason, were not included on the release, nor was the now commonly accepted promotional video of 'Killer Queen', filmed for *Top Of The Pops* in October 1974. One more grating aspect of the collection is that each video segues into one another, so the beginning and end of each video is cut off slightly. But these are easy to overlook since it was meant to be a complement to *Greatest Hits* and not to offer anything extraordinarily comprehensive; in that respect, *Greatest Flix* succeeds admirably.

Unfortunately, the video has been out of print for years in the US and was replaced by the well intentioned but ultimately inferior *Classic Queen* and *Greatest Hits* collections in 1992, while the video remained largely in print for many years in the UK. Now considered obsolete thanks to the DVD release of *Greatest Video Hits Volume 1* in 2002, *Greatest Flix* has become something of a collector's item, an intriguing curio from a time when Queen were still an active, working band.

LIVE IN JAPAN

• 1983 (85 mins) • Apollon APVG 4004

'Flash', 'The Hero', 'Now I'm Here', 'Put Out The Fire', 'Dragon Attack', 'Now I'm Here' *(reprise)*, 'Love Of My Life', 'Save Me', 'Guitar Solo', 'Under Pressure', 'Crazy Little Thing Called Love', 'Bohemian Rhapsody', 'Tie Your Mother Down', 'Teo Torriatte (Let Us Cling Together)', 'We Will Rock You', 'We Are The Champions', 'God Save The Queen'

Featuring a Brian May-dominated selection of songs (of the 17 featured, 12 were written or arranged by him), *Live In Japan* was released exclusively in Japan (no surprise there) in early 1983 and is just one of many video releases that has yet to see a revamped and expanded release. Filmed at the Seibu Lions Stadium in Tokyo on 3 November 1982, the video sees Queen trawling through a (heavily edited) set at the end of an exhausting tour, and it's easy to see that tensions are high among the four. There are some wonderful performances here: the 'Now I'm Here' medley is as high energy as it gets, while 'Crazy Little Thing Called Love' finally shows the band in good spirits, with Fred Mandel's piano accompaniment an absolute highlight and one of the reasons the band continued with the extended jam.

Also nice is the first-ever release of 'Teo Torriatte (Let Us Cling Together)', a song that was performed only in Japan and took on a more poignant slant when sung in perfect English by the natives in the audience. Because the video was filmed at the end of a seven-month trek round the world, Freddie's voice in particular struggles throughout, and the band look extremely weary and exhausted. But *Live In Japan* remains an unavailable (in the Western hemisphere, at least) release offering a rare glimpse into some of the less explored aspects of Queen's tours. Thankfully, eight of the 17 songs ('Flash' through the 'Now I'm Here' reprise, 'Crazy Little Thing Called Love' and 'Teo Torriatte') were released as bonus tracks on the 2004 *Queen On Fire: Live At The Bowl* DVD, along with the sound of this concert's previously unreleased 'Calling All Girls' set to a photo gallery from the 1982 Hot Space tour.

WE WILL ROCK YOU

• 1984 (90 mins) • Peppermint 6122 • *Director:* Saul Swimmer

'We Will Rock You' *(fast)*, 'Let Me Entertain You', 'Play The Game', 'Somebody To Love', 'Killer Queen', 'I'm In Love With My Car', 'Get Down, Make Love', 'Save Me', 'Now I'm Here', 'Dragon Attack', 'Now I'm Here' *(reprise)*, 'Love Of My Life', 'Under Pressure', 'Keep Yourself Alive' / Drum Solo / Guitar Solo, 'Crazy Little Thing Called Love', 'Jailhouse Rock', 'Bohemian Rhapsody', 'Tie Your Mother Down', 'Another One Bites The Dust', 'Sheer Heart Attack', 'We Will Rock You', 'We Are The Champions', 'God Save The Queen'

Though filmed in November 1981 at the end of a triumphant year for Queen, *We Will Rock You* didn't see release for nearly three years. The delay wasn't due to sound issues or problems with the band's performance; instead, financial wrangles plagued the film from the start, and the projected theatrical release for the summer of 1982 came and went. A premiere was scheduled for March 1983 at Daytona Beach in Florida, but issues with the outdoor screen (which kept blowing over due its the sheer size – 60 by 80 feet) delayed the event for well over a year. It was finally issued on videocassette on 10 September 1984, the same day that 'Hammer To Fall' was released.

Was it worth the wait? In short, yes. Filmed specially for the purpose of releasing it as Queen's first live concert, *We Will Rock You* shows the band in a familiar setting in Montreal – The Forum – blazing through 26 of their greatest hits and lesser-known album songs. However – and there's *always* a however – the audience sound subdued, and it's not certain whether or not they were like this on the night or if it's merely down to the sound mix. Tellingly, Freddie becomes audibly frustrated at times, shouting at the audience during 'Jailhouse Rock', "C'mon, move it, you fuckers!" But the audience shots (when there are any) show them reacting wildly. Major complaints can also be levelled at the picture, which is excruciatingly dark compared to the general standard of Queen's video releases.

Two versions of the film were originally issued: a 60-minute version, with (unknown) omissions, and a full 90-minute version. The film was restored to its full 90-minute running time for a 1997 US laserdisc release, being converted to DVD the following year. This release restored the sound somewhat, making it more listenable than before, but it wasn't until 2001 that the film was released with vastly improved picture and sound quality.

15 OF THE BEST

• *1984 (60 mins)* • *KTEL NU 3240*

Not much is known about the video companion to the 1984 US-only compilation *15 Of The Best*, but it's likely that it contains videos for the following (judging by the tracklist of the album): 'Crazy Little Thing Called Love', 'We Will Rock You', 'Bohemian Rhapsody', 'Killer Queen', 'Fat Bottomed Girls', 'Tie Your Mother Down', 'Somebody To Love', 'Another One Bites The Dust', 'Bicycle Race', 'We Are The Champions', 'Body Language', 'You're My Best Friend', 'Calling All Girls', 'Save Me' and 'Play The Game'. If so, this marks the first video appearance of the two *Hot Space* tracks, 'Body Language' and 'Calling All Girls'.

THE WORKS VIDEO EP

• 1984 (20 mins) • PMI MVT 99 0010 2 • *Directors:* David Mallet, Tim Pope

Queen's first video EP collected the four promos filmed for *The Works* – 'Radio Ga Ga', 'I Want To Break Free', 'It's A Hard Life' and 'Hammer To Fall' – and, despite its success, has since been rendered obsolete by the plethora of video collections available throughout the world.

LIVE IN RIO

• 1985 (90 mins) • PMI MVP 99 1079 2 • *Director:* Aloysio Legey

'Machines (Or 'Back To Humans')', 'Tie Your Mother Down', 'Seven Seas Of Rhye', 'Keep Yourself Alive', 'Liar', 'It's A Hard Life', 'Now I'm Here', 'Is This The World We Created...?', 'Love Of My Life', 'Brighton Rock', 'Hammer To Fall', 'Radio Ga Ga', 'I Want To Break Free', 'We Will Rock You', 'We Are The Champions', 'God Save The Queen'

On 19 January 1985, Queen took to the stage at the Rock In Rio Festival at approximately two in the morning, to play to a packed stadium of about a quarter million Brazilians. Their performance was dodgy and the band were clearly worn out, but the band felt such an affinity with the locals that they implored Jim Beach to purchase the rights to release the footage on video. One has to wonder why: Queen's performance was indeed ragged, but it sounds even worse here, with a synth-heavy mix and a severely edited song selection that does little justice to the extended set list present on the 1984-85 Queen Works! tour.

Live In Rio should be avoided at all costs, though there are two redeeming performances. Not only does it mark the first – and only – live appearance of 'It's A Hard Life' on any video compilation, it also allows for the poignant sight of a chorus of 250,000 people taking the lead on 'Love Of My Life', with Freddie visibly moved and more than willing to let them sing.

WHO WANTS TO LIVE FOREVER /
A KIND OF MAGIC

• 1986 (10 mins) • PMI MVW 990059 2

Instead of offering a video collection of Queen's *A Kind Of Magic* videos, Queen Productions released the first video *single*, containing Brian's mournful 'Who Wants

To Live Forever' and Roger's poppy 'A Kind Of Magic'. Obviously, these now appear on the 2003 *Greatest Video Hits 2* DVD, and the concept for a video single didn't stick around too much longer.

LIVE IN BUDAPEST

• 1987 (90 mins) • PMI MVN 991146 2 • *Director:* Janos Zsombolyai

'Tavaszi Szel Vizet Araszt', 'One Vision', 'Tie Your Mother Down', 'In The Lap Of The Gods... Revisited', 'Seven Seas Of Rhye', 'Tear It Up', 'A Kind Of Magic' / Freddie insert / 'Under Pressure', 'Who Wants To Live Forever', 'I Want To Break Free' / Brian insert – Guitar Solo / 'Now I'm Here', 'Love Of My Life', 'Tavaszi Szel Vizet Araszt', 'Is This The World We Created...?', 'Tutti Frutti' / John insert / 'Bohemian Rhapsody', 'Hammer To Fall', 'Crazy Little Thing Called Love' / Roger insert / 'Radio Ga Ga', 'We Will Rock You', 'Friends Will Be Friends', 'We Are The Champions', 'God Save The Queen'

Queen's performance at the Nepstadion in Budapest on 27 July 1986 was memorable in that it was a major rock band's first performance behind the Iron Curtain since The Rolling Stones toured there in 1967. Hungarian director Janos Zsombolyai was commissioned to film the show in Budapest, and the result is the beautifully shot *Live In Budapest*, which some consider to be superior to *Live At Wembley '86*. At the time when both videos were widely available (the early 1990s), the Budapest compilation had the slight edge for the inclusions of 'Now I'm Here', 'Love Of My Life', 'Tavaszi Szel Vizet Araszt', and the extras showing each band member moving around Budapest. The performance was updated and remastered in 2012, released as *Hungarian Rhapsody: Queen Live In Budapest* on DVD, Blu-Ray, and CD, and is an essential purchase.

THE MAGIC YEARS

• 1987 (300 mins) • PMI MVP 99 1157 2 • *Compiled by:* DoRo (Rudi Dolezal and Hannes Rossacher)

Following the conclusion of the Magic Tour in August 1986, Queen Productions commissioned Rudi Dolezal and Hannes Rossacher, who had first worked with the band on the video for 'One Vision', to compile a video anthology of Queen's history. The result was *The Magic Years*, a wonderful, often inaccurate but well-intentioned overview of the band. Instead of taking a linear approach and offering a narrative of the history thus far, the anthology is divided into segments, spread across three videos. Volume One was subtitled *The Foundations*, and focused on the origins of the band and the band's pioneering of video production, while offering a tantalizing look into the recording of 'One Vision' as the volume's conclusion. Volume Two, subtitled *Live Killers In The Making*, concentrated on Queen as a live band, and Volume Three, subtitled *Crowned In Glory*, recalled the glories of Live Aid and their triumphant Magic Tour.

There are interviews aplenty here, with many of Queen's peers (like Paul McCartney, Mick Jagger, Elton John, and so forth) and those who worked with the band over the years, offering their insight and opinions. It's entertaining, it's extravagant, it's exciting – and it's a shame that there are no plans to release the anthology on DVD.

BOHEMIAN RHAPSODY / CRAZY LITTLE THING CALLED LOVE
• 1988 (10 mins) • Gold Rushes PM0022

Repeating the formula of 1986's video single for 'Who Wants To Live Forever' and 'A Kind Of Magic', this was a re-release of sorts, no doubt issued to capitalize on the 3-inch CD single campaign plaguing the UK at the time.

RARE LIVE: A CONCERT THROUGH TIME AND SPACE
• 1989 (120 mins) • PMI MVP 99 1189 3 • *Compiled by:* DoRo (Rudi Dolezal and Hannes Rossacher)

'Intro', 'I Want It All', 'Crazy Little Thing Called Love', 'Liar', 'Now I'm Here', 'Another One Bites The Dust' / Rock 'n' Roll Medley: 'Big Spender' / 'Jailhouse Rock' / 'Stupid Cupid' / 'Be Bop A Lula' / 'Jailhouse Rock' *(reprise)*, 'My Melancholy Blues', 'Hammer To Fall', 'Killer Queen', 'We Will Rock You', 'Somebody To Love', 'Tie Your Mother Down', 'Keep Yourself Alive', 'Love Of My Life', 'Stone Cold Crazy', 'Radio Ga Ga', 'You Take My Breath Away', 'Sheer Heart Attack', 'We Are The Champions', 'God Save The Queen'

Following up on the success of *The Magic Years*, directors Rudi Dolezal and Hannes Rossacher were commissioned by Jim Beach to compile the best performances of Queen's filmed live career onto a two-hour videocassette. Titled *Rare Live: A Concert Through Time And Space*, the video is a good idea ruined by

poor execution. There are many wonderful snippets of Queen throughout, with some truly exceptional footage from the band's first concerts in South America, their last in Japan, and standard footage of the band on their home turf, at Wembley Stadium, Hammersmith Odeon and Earl's Court Arena. The key word, however, is 'snippets': most of the performances are severely edited, with two songs – 'You Take My Breath Away' and 'We Are The Champions' – lasting less than two minutes.

To make matters worse, the performances switch back and forth, seemingly without reason, from concert to concert, sometimes within a song more than once. The whole effect is like trying to watch a Queen video with someone continuously switching the channels, and becomes irritating pretty quickly. As if that wasn't enough, the information given is usually incorrect, with dates and venues often attributed erroneously. For example, 'Liar' is listed as a rehearsal, though it's actually the standard video version – hardly a rehearsal.

There are no redeeming qualities to *Rare Live: A Concert Through Time And Space*. Thankfully, it's almost guaranteed to be out of print, but it has trickled through online auction sites every now and then, only to anger and outrage the curious buyer who might think it would be worth the price. It's not.

THE MIRACLE VIDEO EP
• 1989 (20 mins) • PMI MVL 99 0084 3

As with the videos for *The Works*, *The Miracle Video EP* collected four of the five videos filmed in support of *The Miracle* (the title track had not yet been completed, indicating that the release date was some time during November 1989, no doubt in time for the lucrative holiday market) and was the only official home for the 'Scandal' video until the 2003 release of *Greatest Video Hits 2*. The other tracks are 'I Want It All', 'Breakthru' and 'The Invisible Man'.

LIVE AT WEMBLEY '86
• 1990 (60 mins) • PMI MVP 99 1259 3 • *Director:* Gavin Taylor

'Brighton Rock', 'One Vision', 'Tie Your Mother Down', 'In The Lap Of The Gods... Revisited', 'Seven Seas Of Rhye', 'A Kind Of Magic', 'Under Pressure', 'Another One Bites The Dust', 'Who Wants To Live Forever', 'I Want To Break Free', 'Is This The World We Created...?',

'Tutti Frutti', 'Bohemian Rhapsody', 'Hammer To Fall', 'Crazy Little Thing Called Love', 'Radio Ga Ga', 'We Will Rock You', 'Friends Will Be Friends', 'We Are The Champions', 'God Save The Queen'

Released in 1990 as Queen's sole video compilation of the year, *Live At Wembley '86* proved immensely popular. It was the first widely available live video release since *We Will Rock You* in 1984, and captured the band during the post-Live Aid period when their popularity was at an all-time high. Consequently, the band were on top form and, because the Wembley concerts were midway through a lengthy tour, their energy was at a peak, and the fact that they were playing to a home crowd definitely helped.

Live At Wembley '86 is an enjoyable, albeit heavily edited, video. Nine songs ('Tear It Up', 'Impromptu', 'Brighton Rock Solo', 'Now I'm Here', 'Love Of My Life', '(You're So Square) Baby I Don't Care', 'Hello Mary Lou (Goodbye Heart)', 'Gimme Some Lovin'' and 'Big Spender') were omitted, and most that were included employ some questionable computer graphics that may have been astounding at the time but haven't worn well. Director Gavin Taylor's work is beautiful, capturing all the right moments at all the right times (and with 15 cameras positioned around the stage, this comes as no surprise), so, apart from the aforementioned gripes, the video is a triumph.

A special introductory clip featuring animation and time-lapse photography of the stage construction at Wembley is set to a backing of the studio solo section of 'Brighton Rock', before the synth introduction of 'One Vision' kicks off the concert proper. Of course, in 2003, the VHS release (long obsolete by that point) was improved upon with an expanded and restored cut of the concert, and while *Live At Wembley '86* may hold sentimental value for those who grew up watching the video, the DVD is all the more worth it.

GREATEST FLIX II
• 1991 (90 mins) • PMI MVD 1326 3 • *Directors:* Russell Mulcahy, David Mallet, Rudi Dolezal, Hannes Rossacher, Tim Pope, Jerry Hibbert

'The Show Must Go On' *(intro)*, 'A Kind Of Magic', 'Under Pressure', 'Radio Ga Ga', 'I Want It All', 'I Want To Break Free', 'Innuendo', 'It's A Hard Life', 'Breakthru', 'Who Wants To Live Forever', 'Headlong', 'The Miracle', 'I'm Going Slightly Mad', 'The Invisible Man', 'Hammer To Fall', 'Friends Will Be Friends',

'The Show Must Go On', 'One Vision', 'God Save The Queen *(closing titles)*'

Ten years on, and another trio of anniversary releases: along with *Greatest Hits II* to mark the 20th anniversary of Queen, *Greatest Flix II* and *Greatest Pix II* were also issued to rabid fans, and it's the video release of *Greatest Flix II* that holds the most interest. Featuring 17 videos of Queen's produced between 1981 and 1991, the compilation shows the band at their most visually creative, and *Greatest Flix II* does not disappoint. From the simplest of concepts to Queen at their most grandiose, *Greatest Flix II* is a feast for the eyes, showing that Queen were the masters of indulgence.

The video was released only in the UK, and it's likely that there weren't any initial plans to issue it in the States; thankfully, *Wayne's World* helped catapult Queen back into the limelight, changing the minds of Hollywood Records, and *Classic Queen* was released accordingly. As it stands, *Greatest Flix II* was replaced by the *Greatest Video Hits 2* DVD in 2003, though the original VHS is the only place to (legally) view the superb video for 'Innuendo'.

CLASSIC QUEEN
• 1992 (90 mins) • HR 40143 3 • *Directors:* Bruce Gowers, Dennis DeVallance, Rock Flicks, Derek Burbridge, Kliebenst, Brian Grant, Daniella Green, Keith McMillan, Don Norman, Brian Grant, Rudi Dolezal, Hannes Rossacher, David Mallet

'The Show Must Go On' *(intro)*, 'A Kind Of Magic', 'Bohemian Rhapsody', 'Under Pressure', 'Hammer To Fall', 'Stone Cold Crazy', 'One Year Of Love', 'Radio Ga Ga', 'I'm Going Slightly Mad', 'I Want It All', 'Tie Your Mother Down', 'The Miracle', 'These Are The Days Of Our Lives', 'One Vision', 'Keep Yourself Alive', 'Headlong', 'Who Wants To Live Forever', 'The Show Must Go On'

A companion to the US album release of the same name, *Classic Queen* collects 17 videos shot between 1981 and 1991, presenting them in the same order as on the album. Keen-eyed fans may notice that two of those songs – 'Stone Cold Crazy' and 'One Year Of Love' – never had videos made for them; in those instances, The Torpedo Twins come to the rescue to deliver the typical cut-and-paste videos for which they had become known. While *Greatest Flix II* is the superior release, there are certain aspects of

Classic Queen that are unique. 'Bohemian Rhapsody' is presented in a special re-edit by Penelope Spheeris, director of Wayne's World and the instigator of Queen's sudden success in America, while 'These Are The Days Of Our Lives' is a special version commissioned by Hollywood Records, with the standard music video interpolated with animation sequences that are unavailable elsewhere.

Along with 'Stone Cold Crazy' and 'One Year Of Love', 'These Are The Days Of Our Lives' and 'Keep Yourself Alive' make their video debuts, though the UK would be denied a video release of these for a few years. (The first two tracks, because they were never UK singles, would not be released on any British video compilation, but the last two would finally be released in 1999 on Greatest Flix III and in 2002 on Greatest Video Hits 1, respectively.) The tracks from The Works, A Kind Of Magic and The Miracle were also released for the first time in the US; the video EPs and singles weren't considered to be lucrative enough for the American market and so were never released there. Classic Queen does miss out on several key tracks from Greatest Flix II ('It's A Hard Life', 'Innuendo', 'Breakthru', 'The Invisible Man' and 'Friends Will Be Friends'), though the focus wasn't on presenting the video hits of Queen; rather, it merely served as a visual equivalent.

GREATEST HITS
• 1992 (90 mins) • PMI MVP 99 1011 2 • Directors: Bruce Gowers, David Mallet, Rudi Dolezal, Hannes Rossacher

'We Will Rock You', 'We Are The Champions', 'Another One Bites The Dust', 'Killer Queen', 'Somebody To Love', 'Fat Bottomed Girls', 'Bicycle Race', 'You're My Best Friend', 'Crazy Little Thing Called Love', 'Now I'm Here', 'Play The Game', 'Seven Seas Of Rhye', 'Body Language', 'Save Me', 'Don't Stop Me Now', 'Good Old-Fashioned Lover Boy', 'I Want To Break Free', 'Bohemian Rhapsody'

Just like its sister compilation album, the US video release of Greatest Hits presented 17 corresponding videos of the songs presented on its audio equivalent, with the original version of 'Bohemian Rhapsody' tacked on for good measure. While the Classic Queen video might be of more interest to buyers for the elaborate productions (most of Queen's early videos were straightforward performance videos), Greatest Hits shows a band eager to pioneer what was still a

novel medium, since there wasn't much of an outlet for these videos. There are some songs missing: 'Flash' and 'Spread Your Wings' are conspicuously absent, with cut-and-paste compilation videos of 'Good Old-Fashioned Lover Boy', 'Seven Seas Of Rhye' and 'Now I'm Here' instead. The only major complaint comes with the inclusion of 'Body Language', which is entirely out of place, though the other songs available here are more than worth it. Greatest Hits remained the only US video release of Queen's early promotional videos until the 2002 Greatest Video Hits 1 DVD, rendering this collection obsolete.

FINAL LIVE IN JAPAN
• 1992 (90 mins) • BMG BVVP 79

'Machines (Or 'Back To Humans')', 'Tear It Up', 'Tie Your Mother Down', 'Under Pressure', 'Somebody To Love', 'Killer Queen', 'Seven Seas Of Rhye', 'Keep Yourself Alive', 'Liar', 'It's A Hard Life', 'Now I'm Here', 'Is This The World We Created...?', 'Love Of My Life', 'Another One Bites The Dust', 'Hammer To Fall', 'Crazy Little Thing Called Love', 'Bohemian Rhapsody', 'Radio Ga Ga', 'I Want To Break Free', 'Jailhouse Rock', 'We Will Rock You', 'We Are The Champions', 'God Save The Queen'

Filmed at Yogishi Swimming Pool Auditorium in Tokyo on 11 May 1985 (not, technically, Queen's final concert in Japan, but at least shot during their final Japanese tour), Final Live In Japan improves upon the Live In Rio video by offering a nearly complete film of the much-criticized Works! tour. Sadly, the video was available only in Japan, though it was finally reissued in 2004 on DVD (again, exclusive to Japan), causing casual fans to pass over this interesting relic – which includes many performances rarely seen on video: 'It's A Hard Life', 'Jailhouse Rock' and one of the last live renditions of 'Somebody To Love' – because of incompatible video players and inflated import prices.

A CONCERT FOR LIFE: THE FREDDIE MERCURY TRIBUTE CONCERT FOR AIDS AWARENESS
• 1992 (VHS: 180 mins; DVD: 120 mins) • PMI MVB 4910623 • Directors: David Mallet, Jim Beach

1992 VHS release: Insert 1, Queen Introduction, 'Enter Sandman', 'Sad But True', 'Nothing Else Matters', Insert 2, Queen Medley, Insert 3, 'Now I'm Here', Insert 4, 'Knockin' On Heaven's Door', 'Paradize City',

Elizabeth Taylor speech, Insert 5, 'Tie Your Mother Down', 'I Want It All', 'Hammer To Fall', 'Stone Cold Crazy', 'Thank You / Crazy Little Thing Called Love', 'Too Much Love Will Kill You', 'Radio Ga Ga', 'Who Wants To Live Forever', 'I Want To Break Free', 'Under Pressure', 'All The Young Dudes', '"Heroes"', The Lord's Prayer, "39', 'These Are The Days Of Our Lives', 'Somebody To Love', 'Bohemian Rhapsody', 'The Show Must Go On', 'We Will Rock You', 'We Are The Champions', 'God Save The Queen', Insert 6

2002 DVD release: Insert 1, Queen Introduction, 'Tie Your Mother Down', 'I Want It All', 'Las Palabras De Amor (The Words Of Love)', 'Hammer To Fall', 'Stone Cold Crazy', 'Thank You / Crazy Little Thing Called Love', 'Too Much Love Will Kill You', 'Radio Ga Ga', 'Who Wants To Live Forever', 'I Want To Break Free', 'Under Pressure', 'All The Young Dudes', '"Heroes"', The Lord's Prayer, "39', 'These Are The Days Of Our Lives', 'Somebody To Love', 'Bohemian Rhapsody', 'The Show Must Go On', 'We Will Rock You', 'We Are The Champions', 'God Save The Queen', Insert 6, 'These Are The Days Of Our Lives' *(rehearsal)*, 'Under Pressure' *(rehearsal)*, 'Somebody To Love' *(rehearsal)*, Inserts 1-6, The Freddie Mercury Tribute Concert TV Documentary, Photo Galleries, Elizabeth Taylor speech

The 1992 A Concert For Life was not just a suitably grandiose send-off for Freddie, it was also an event to promote awareness of AIDS and its effects. No surprise, then, that portions of the video were released merely seven months after the event (in the UK; the US release didn't come until April 1993), with proceeds going to the Mercury Phoenix Trust. The film is beautifully shot by David Mallet, with several video inserts of Freddie throughout, and, despite the high emotions of the day, Brian, Roger and John play superbly.

The original VHS release was slightly edited, with most of the omissions due to licensing issues or sub-par performances. (Robert Plant's version of 'Innuendo' falls into the latter category, while Extreme's rendition of 'Love Of My Life' and their own 'More Than Words', Bob Geldof's 'Too Late God', U2's satellite performance of 'Till The End Of The World', Spinal Tap's 'Majesties Of Rock', Mango Groove's 'Special Star' and Zucchero's rendition of 'Las Palabras De Amor (The Words Of Love)' fall into the former.) The DVD release, issued to mark the tenth anniversary of the event, completely edited out the first half of the concert, though a bonus disc of rehearsals and photo galleries make interesting viewing.

BOX OF FLIX

• 1992 (20 mins) • PMI MVB 99132343 • *Directors:* Bruce Gowers, Dennis DeVallance, Rock Flicks, Derek Burbridge, Kliebenst, Brian Grant, Daniella Green, Keith McMillan, Don Norman, Russell Mulcahy, David Mallet, Rudi Dolezal, Hannes Rossacher, Tim Pope

During the massive catalog reissue craze in the wake of Freddie's death, Queen Productions bundled together the two *Greatest Flix* videos, with the original 1981 VHS long out of print, and threw in the added incentive of four previously unreleased performances: 'Keep Yourself Alive', 'Liar' (the first version from August 1973), 'Killer Queen' (from *Top Of The Pops*) and 'Now I'm Here' (from the November 1974 Rainbow Theatre concert).

LIVE AT THE RAINBOW 1974

• 1992 (52 mins) • released as part of *The Box Of Tricks* • *Director:* Bruce Gowers • *Producers:* Roy Thomas Baker (original sound), Mike Stone (original sound), Arkadi de Rakoff

'Procession', 'Now I'm Here', 'Ogre Battle', 'White Queen (As It Began)', 'In The Lap Of The Gods', 'Killer Queen', 'The March Of The Black Queen', 'Bring Back That Leroy Brown', 'Son And Daughter', Guitar Solo, 'Father To Son', Drum Solo, 'Keep Yourself Alive', 'Liar', 'Son And Daughter' *(reprise)*, 'Stone Cold Crazy', 'In The Lap Of The Gods... Revisited', 'Jailhouse Rock', 'God Save The Queen'

Live At The Rainbow 1974 was released as part of *The Box Of Tricks* in 1992 and was presented in a heavily edited and overdubbed 52-minute video performance. The overdubbing may be considered heresy among Queen fans, but it should be remembered that the band had intentions of releasing this concert as their first live album and video. Brian wrote in the spring 1975 fan club letter that "we're working everyday and most nights on our film of the Rainbow concert, mixing and editing to a suitable form for the *Whistle Test* and such like – so you'll be able to see us while we're away in the USA and Japan these coming three months." Unfortunately, the appearance on *The Old Grey Whistle Test* never happened, though it was released as an opener for *Jaws* in some UK theatres in 1977, and in the US it was the opener for *The Song Remains The Same* in 1976.

Easily the best reason to track down *The Box Of*

Tricks, this concert performance features much for fans to rejoice in, not least the much-coveted first incarnation of the medley ('In The Lap Of The Gods' through 'Bring Back That Leroy Brown'), as well as a smattering of early concert favorites that would be omitted from the repertoire by the time the band became masters of the arena. Simply, *Live At The Rainbow 1974* is exciting, scintillating and awesome, undoubtedly Queen's definitive concert performance. However, the VHS is now obsolete with the release of the multi-format *Live At The Rainbow '74*, undoubtedly the definitive version of this concert.

CHAMPIONS OF THE WORLD
• 1995 (120 mins) • PMI MVD 4915053 • *Directors:* DoRo (Rudi Dolezal and Hannes Rossacher)

To coincide with the release of *Made In Heaven* came *Champions Of The World*, a two-hour video anthology attempting to cover Queen's expansive history. Originally intended as a fourth instalment of *The Magic Years* to cover the 1987-95 period, it was decided in the early stages of compilation that the result would be too sombre, instead giving way to a condensed overview of the years 1969 to 1995. While new interviews with Brian, Roger, David Richards, Jim Beach and others were conducted, there's a lot of recycled material from *The Magic Years*, with many inaccuracies along the way in terms of the dates of particular songs being performed.

While it's not as comprehensive as it could be, *Champions Of The World* is an entertaining and enthralling documentary, and should be sought out by completists and fans alike (though it's currently unavailable on DVD).

MADE IN HEAVEN: THE FILMS
• 1996 (60 mins) • Wienerworld WNR 2066 • *Directors:* Bernard Rudden, Jim Gillespie, Nichola Bruce, Richard Heslop, Simon Pummell, Mark Szaszy, Chris Rodley • *Producers:* Jim Beach and Ben Gibson

'I Was Born To Love You', 'Evolution' *('Heaven For Everyone')*, 'Heart-Ache' *('Too Much Love Will Kill You')*, 'O' *('My Life Has Been Saved')*, 'You Don't Fool Me', 'Outside-In' *('A Winter's Tale')*, 'Return Trip' *('Let Me Live')*, 'Mother Love', 'Made In Heaven' *(closing titles)*

While Freddie had been adamant that he keep recording until he was physically unable to in the post-*Innuendo* sessions, it was a different matter when it came to visuals. With the release of *Made In Heaven*, the Freddie-less Queen then had a difficult task: to promote their singles on music television without their frontman. So the British Film Institute was commissioned to come up with a slew of experimental videos, with the result released on VHS later in 1996. Fan reception has varied, with the consensus being that without the band appearing in it, it's decidedly uninteresting, though those with more open minds were able to appreciate that each video told a story, instead of merely being a straightforward performance. The result is like a mini art film, and is one of their more interesting and unique video releases.

The VHS was re-released in 2003 with a bonus video of the making of *We Will Rock You: The Musical*, included simply because the musical had debuted the year before and the powers that be decided that any exposure is good exposure, when in reality, the two totally unrelated projects sit awkwardly side-by-side.

QUEEN ROCKS
• 1998 (78 mins) • Toshiba EMI TOVW 3292 • *Compiled by:* DoRo (Rudi Dolezal and Hannes Rossacher)

'Tie Your Mother Down' *(Through The Years)*, 'It's Late', 'Headlong', 'Now I'm Here', 'I Want It All', 'Tear It Up' *(Making Videos)*, 'One Vision' *(Extended Version)*, 'I'm In Love With My Car', 'We Will Rock You', 'Seven Seas Of Rhye', 'Hammer To Fall', 'Keep Yourself Alive', 'Stone Cold Crazy', 'Put Out The Fire', 'Sheer Heart Attack', 'Fat Bottomed Girls', 'No-One But You (Only The Good Die Young)', 'I Can't Live With You' *(Closing Titles)*, 'No-One But You (Only The Good Die Young)' *(Making-Of Video)*

Almost every compilation in the US or UK markets since 1981's *Greatest Hits* came with a video equivalent, and *Queen Rocks* was no exception. Instead of providing the already released versions, however, many of the videos here were either montages or new edits altogether. Unfortunately, much like the *Rare Live* fiasco nearly a decade before, *Queen Rocks* suffers the same fate of poor editing and over-familiar footage. Some of the more dubious edits include flames laid over footage of Queen performing 'Put Out The Fire' from 1982, while 'I'm In Love With My Car' is an amalgamation of Roger singing his composition from a 1981 concert and footage of – get this – automobiles.

The sole interesting aspect of the release was the

video for 'No-One But You (Only The Good Die Young)', filmed in the summer of 1997, reuniting Roger, Brian and John in front of the cameras for the first time since Freddie's death. Though the video would later suffer under the montage-happy hands of DoRo, the original version is a subdued and suitable performance. Presented entirely in black and white, the three remaining members are shown performing the song, with Brian appearing on piano for the first time on a Queen video. Unfortunately, sepia-toned shots of Freddie in his heyday would later be inserted to visually reinforce the fact that the song is, in fact, a tribute to him (as if the casual fan couldn't have gathered that from the lyrics), and it's this edit that has become the standard version.

GREATEST FLIX III

• 1999 (90 mins) • Parlophone 7243 4 • *Directors:* Rudi Dolezal, Hannes Rossacher, David Mallet, Russell Mulcahy, Bernard Rudden, Mark Szaszy

'Under Pressure' *('rah' mix)*, 'These Are The Days Of Our Lives', 'Princes Of The Universe', 'Barcelona', 'Too Much Love Will Kill You', 'Somebody To Love' *(live with George Michael)*, 'The Great Pretender', 'Heaven For Everyone', 'Las Palabras De Amor (The Words Of Love)', 'Let Me Live', 'Living On My Own', 'You Don't Fool Me', 'Driven By You', 'No-One But You (Only The Good Die Young)', 'The Show Must Go On' *(live with Elton John)*, 'Thank God It's Christmas' *(closing titles)*

Unlike *Greatest Hits III*, that compilation's video companion is actually worthwhile: Queen's visuals in later years became more intricate and better planned, and there isn't a poor selection on this collection. It's unfair to compare the third *Greatest Flix* to the third *Greatest Hits*, since the video flows better and filters out the duff items (thankfully, the rap remix of 'Another One Bites The Dust' is absent), while presenting rarely seen videos of 'Princes Of The Universe', 'Las Palabras De Amor (The Words Of Love)', Brian's 'Driven By You' and alternative videos for 'Heaven For Everyone' and 'Too Much Love Will Kill You'.

While the other videos had been previously released, it was usually in slightly different variations: 'These Are The Days Of Our Lives' had been included on *Classic Queen* with animation interspersed, while this version was the full black and white rendition. Freddie's solo videos were released on several video EP releases; 'Somebody To Love' with George Michael was

issued on *A Concert For Life* in 1993; and the *Made In Heaven* videos had been released on *Made In Heaven: The Films* in 1996.

Yet that's not a criticism, for the videos do deserve to be seen again; most of their original releases had either been rarely seen or deleted by the time of this video's release. The collection is bookended by two new performances. The 'rah' remix of 'Under Pressure' was edited together from pre-existing footage of Freddie (from Wembley, 1986) and David Bowie (from the tribute concert, 1992, with Annie Lennox carefully removed) performing the song, making it appear as though the two had actually performed it together, while the live 1997 version of 'The Show Must Go On' with Elton John hadn't been released before; it may have been superfluous on *Greatest Hits III*, but it's justified here. For the record, 'Thank God It's Christmas' was never given a video performance; here, it is merely played as the credits roll.

Inclusions of 'Scandal', 'Back Chat', 'Calling All Girls', 'Body Language', 'Spread Your Wings', 'Keep Yourself Alive', 'Liar' or 'A Winter's Tale' would have been appreciated, but because they hadn't been included on the album release they weren't even considered for *Greatest Flix III*. The video was rendered obsolete shortly after its release because of its lack of a DVD release, with most of the videos appearing on *Greatest Video Hits 2*.

GREATEST VIDEO HITS 1

• 2002 (200 mins) • Hollywood Records 2061 69011 9 • *Directors:* Bruce Gowers, Dennis DeVallance, Rock Flicks, Derek Burbridge, Kliebenst, Brian Grant, Daniella Green, Keith McMillan, Don Norman • *Producers:* Simon Lupton and Rhys Thomas

'Bohemian Rhapsody', 'Another One Bites The Dust', 'Killer Queen', 'Fat Bottomed Girls', 'Bicycle Race', 'You're My Best Friend', 'Don't Stop Me Now', 'Save Me', 'Crazy Little Thing Called Love', 'Somebody To Love', 'Spread Your Wings', 'Play The Game', 'Flash', 'Tie Your Mother Down', 'We Will Rock You', 'We Are The Champions', 'Now I'm Here' *(live at the Rainbow)*, 'Good Old-Fashioned Lover Boy' *(Top Of The Pops version)*, 'Keep Yourself Alive', 'Liar', 'Love Of My Life' *(live)*, 'We Will Rock You' *(fast live version)*, Documentary: Inside The Rhapsody ('The Bo Rhap Story', 'Making The Video', 'Creating The Rhapsody', and 'The Greatest Song')

Easter Egg: 'Bohemian Rhapsody *(flame version)*'

In October 2002, with Queen's video catalog in dire need of an update, fans were given reason to rejoice: finally, the band joined the digital age with the release of *Greatest Video Hits 1*, the first instalment of many in 'The DVD Collection'. Presenting all 16 of Queen's official performance videos between 1975 and 1980, along with the *Top Of The Pops* version of 'Killer Queen', *Greatest Video Hits 1* also featured a second disc of six additional videos: 'Now I'm Here' (the audio now taken from a November 1974 Rainbow Theatre concert), Queen's 1977 *Top Of The Pops* appearance for 'Good Old-Fashioned Lover Boy', the original promo videos of 'Keep Yourself Alive' and 'Liar', and two live versions of 'Love Of My Life' and 'We Will Rock You', which had been released on the original 1981 *Greatest Flix*.

As if that wasn't enough, Brian and Roger recorded a full commentary for the first disc, with archival comments from Freddie and John where appropriate; Brian and Roger's stories are informative and sometimes hilarious. The most revealing bonus feature, though, is on the second disc, with a lengthy documentary devoted to 'Bohemian Rhapsody'. The first part sees Brian in the studio deconstructing the song, right down to its barest elements, explaining the recording process and isolating the most interesting parts of the original 24-track recording. The other parts comprise interviews with Brian and Roger, discussing the recording of the song and, later, the process of filming the iconic video. The final segment, subtitled 'The Greatest Song', is a featurette with Brian and Roger collecting the award for the Number One single of all time.

While the footage is occasionally grainy and dark, there are some major revelations, since the songs are presented in full with no segues as was the case on previous video anthologies. Of particular interest is the first proper video for 'Bicycle Race', which was re-edited by David Mallet from original footage, filmed in October 1978 and languishing unreleased for nearly 25 years; this video comes closest to reassembling the original vision. (On previous video releases, censored footage of the naked bicycle race was intercut with stills of the band in action.) The biggest revelation, though, is reserved for those with a 5.1 audio DVD system, with each song benefiting from Surround Sound mixes produced by Justin Shirley-Smith; 'Bohemian Rhapsody' and 'You're My Best Friend', taken from the 2002 DVD-A release of *A Night At The Opera*, were

produced by Roy Thomas Baker and Brian May, while 'Spread Your Wings' was produced by Justin Shirley-Smith and Tim Young. The results are truly spectacular.

LIVE AT WEMBLEY STADIUM
• 2003 (300 mins) • Hollywood Records 2061 62400 9 • *Director:* Gavin Taylor • *Producers:* Simon Lupton and Rhys Thomas

'One Vision', 'Tie Your Mother Down', 'In The Lap Of The Gods...Revisited', 'Seven Seas Of Rhye', 'Tear It Up', 'A Kind Of Magic', 'Under Pressure', 'Another One Bites The Dust', 'Who Wants To Live Forever', 'I Want To Break Free', 'Impromptu', 'Brighton Rock Solo', 'Now I'm Here', 'Love Of My Life', 'Is This The World We Created...?', '(You're So Square) Baby I Don't Care', 'Hello Mary Lou (Goodbye Heart)', 'Tutti Frutti', 'Gimme Some Lovin'', 'Bohemian Rhapsody', 'Hammer To Fall', 'Crazy Little Thing Called Love', 'Big Spender', 'Radio Ga Ga', 'We Will Rock You', 'Friends Will Be Friends', 'We Are The Champions', 'God Save The Queen', 'A Kind Of Magic' *(from Friday night concert)*, 'Another One Bites The Dust' *(from Friday night concert)*, 'Tutti Frutti' *(from Friday night concert)*, 'Crazy Little Thing Called Love' *(from Friday night concert)*, 'We Are The Champions' *(from Friday night concert)*, 'Tie Your Mother Down' *(rehearsal)*, 'Seven Seas Of Rhye' *(rehearsal)*, 'A Kind Of Magic' *(rehearsal)*, 'I Want To Break Free' *(rehearsal)*, 'Now I'm Here' *(rehearsal)*, 'Bohemian Rhapsody' *(rehearsal)*

Marking the first instalment in an ongoing programme of DVD releases of Queen's filmed live shows, *Live At Wembley Stadium* is a much-needed improvement on the 1990 VHS *Live At Wembley '86*. The aim of this release was to not only offer an updated account of the landmark 1986 concert, but also to restore it to its full running time, minus the dated camera effects of the original. It may not have been the best Queen live show ever, but it was the most widely seen upon its initial release, and it was only natural that this be the first true Queen DVD concert release.

What is presented is terrific: the full, uncut 120-minute concert with updated sound and visuals, with enough bonus material to please even the most cynical fans. Six songs – 'A Kind Of Magic', 'Another One Bites The Dust', 'Tutti Frutti', 'Crazy Little Thing Called Love' and the finale of 'We Are The Champions' – are from the Friday night concert, which was used as a dry run for the camera crew to prepare angles and shot composition, while another six titles from pre-tour rehearsals are included, the quality of which isn't stunning but is fascinating nonetheless. Perhaps the most interesting bonus feature is the 'Queen cam', which allows the viewer to switch between exclusive angles of Brian, Roger, John and Freddie on four songs: 'One Vision', 'Under Pressure', 'Now I'm Here' and 'We Are The Champions'. A picture gallery is interesting but mostly superfluous, though it does mark the first release of the original version of 'A Kind Of Magic', last heard over the credits of *Highlander* in 1986.

The only thing that prevents this from being a definitive release is the omission of highlights from other Magic Tour shows, which would have been a better alternative than the interviews and documentaries included on the second disc (one can only hope these will be released when *Live In Budapest* is given the DVD treatment). However, those omissions (and inclusions) detract little from the overall product, and *Live At Wembley Stadium* should be the template on which further live DVD releases are based. For anyone who grew up watching *Live At Wembley '86* in wide-eyed wonder, or for anyone who had seen Queen at Live Aid and wanted to know what the fuss was all about, or for a budding Queen fan who needs a place to start their obsession, *Live At Wembley Stadium* is the genuine article.

GREATEST VIDEO HITS 2

• 2003 (200 mins) • Hollywood Records 2061 69017 9 • *Directors:* Russell Mulcahy, David Mallet, Rudi Dolezal, Hannes Rossacher, Mike Hodges, Brian Grant, Tim Pope • *Producers:* Simon Lupton and Rhys Thomas

'A Kind Of Magic', 'I Want It All', 'Radio Ga Ga', 'I Want To Break Free', 'Breakthru', 'Under Pressure', 'Scandal', 'Who Wants To Live Forever', 'The Miracle', 'It's A Hard Life', 'The Invisible Man', 'Las Palabras De Amor (The Words Of Love)', 'Friends Will Be Friends', 'Body Language', 'Hammer To Fall', 'Princes Of The Universe', 'One Vision', 'Back Chat', 'Calling All Girls', 'Staying Power' *(live at Milton Keynes Bowl)*, 'One Vision' *(Extended Vision)*, Freddie Mercury interview ('A Musical Prostitute'), *The Works* interviews, *A Kind Of Magic* interviews, Documentary: The Making of 'One Vision', *The Miracle* interviews, Documentary: The Making of *The Miracle* videos ('I Want It All', 'Scandal', 'The Miracle', 'The Invisible Man', and 'Breakthru'), Montreux Golden Rose Pop Festivals (1984: 'Radio Ga Ga', 'Tear It Up', 'It's A Hard Life', 'I Want To Break

Free'; 1986: 'One Vision', 'A Kind Of Magic', 'Friends Will Be Friends', 'Hammer To Fall')

Easter Eggs: 'Who Wants To Live Forever' *(Highlander version)*, 'Who Wants To Live Forever' *(1989 Ian & Belinda version)*

In November 2003, a little over a year after the first compilation appeared, *Greatest Video Hits 2* was released, and was of more interest than its predecessor. Abandoning straightforward performance videos in favor of producing mini-epics, the videos included on *Greatest Video Hits 2* are much more appealing to casual and ardent fans alike. Of particular interest are the inclusions of some truly rare videos: 'Scandal', 'It's A Hard Life', 'The Invisible Man' and 'Friends Will Be Friends' had been previously unavailable in the US, and while 'Las Palabras De Amor (The Words Of Love)' and 'Princes Of The Universe' had been previously released on *Greatest Flix III*, their inclusion here is more than welcome considering the 1999 compilation was available only on VHS and was out of print by 2003. As before, Brian and Roger provide commentary for each video, though their remarks were recorded separately and edited together to suggest they were in the same room; while it's not detrimental to the release, the camaraderie and interplay between the two is missed.

While the bonus features don't feature anything as revelatory as 'Inside The Rhapsody', there is plenty to rejoice in. For the first time, rarely seen videos of 'Calling All Girls' and 'Back Chat' make their appearance, with a live rendition of 'Staying Power' from the June 1982 Milton Keynes performance and an extended edit of the 'One Vision' video also included. Along with these videos, four interview segments were compiled – three feature each band member talking separately about *The Works*, *A Kind Of Magic* and *The Miracle*, while the fourth is Freddie talking with Rudi Dolezal in 1984 and is called 'A Musical Prostitute'. There are also three documentaries, with one detailing the making of the album cover for *The Miracle*, a second showing the recording of 'One Vision' (this documentary had been released in 1987 on *The Magic Years*, but that video anthology has been out of print for years), and the third showing the making of the videos from *The Miracle*.

To cap it all, two performances of Queen at the Montreux Golden Rose Pop Festival (one in 1984, the other in 1986) are also present, though these are inconsequential considering both were mimed and not performed live. The only thing missing is Queen's videos for *Innuendo*, *Made In Heaven*, and 'No-One But You (Only The Good Die Young)'; though these were initially promised for a third instalment, *Greatest Video Hits 3* has been abandoned indefinitely, and a more comprehensive, double-disc overview of Queen's videography may be on deck instead.

46664: THE EVENT
• 2004 (377 mins) • Warner Music Vision B 0001DI51M
• *Director:* David Mallet • *Producers:* Simon Lupton, Jim Beach, Jean Francois Cecillon

'Say It's Not True', 'Invincible Hope', '46664: The Call', 'The Show Must Go On', 'Toss The Feathers', 'Is This The World We Created...?', 'Everybody's Got To Learn Sometime', 'Amandla', 'Bohemian Rhapsody', 'I Want It All', 'I Want To Break Free', 'Radio Ga Ga', 'We Will Rock You', 'We Are The Champions', '46664 Chant', Interviews

Queen's performance from the November 2003 Cape Town concert in support of Nelson Mandela's 46664 campaign to bring awareness of the AIDS virus contains the first appearances of new material ('Say It's Not True', 'Invincible Hope', '46664: The Call' and 'Amandla') on a commercial release since *Made In Heaven* in 1995. The DVD of *46664: The Event* features Brian and Roger's complete set (credited as Queen), along with other guest performances – Brian with Andrea Corr on 'Is This The World We Created...?' and Roger with The Corrs on 'Toss The Feathers', among others – and is not only worthwhile from a musical standpoint, but also as a charitable venture.

QUEEN ON FIRE: LIVE AT THE BOWL
• 2004 (200 mins) • Parlophone 7243 5 44187 9 2
• *Director:* Gavin Taylor • *Producers:* Simon Lupton and Rhys Thomas

'Flash' / 'The Hero', 'We Will Rock You' *(fast)*, 'Action This Day', 'Play The Game', 'Staying Power', 'Somebody To Love', 'Now I'm Here' / 'Dragon Attack' / 'Now I'm Here *(reprise)*', 'Love Of My Life', 'Save Me', 'Back Chat', 'Get Down, Make Love', Guitar Solo / Drum Solo, 'Under Pressure', 'Fat Bottomed Girls', 'Crazy Little Thing Called Love', 'Bohemian Rhapsody', 'Tie Your Mother Down', 'Another One Bites The Dust', 'Sheer Heart Attack', 'We Will Rock You', 'We Are The Champions', 'God Save The Queen', Selections from Tokyo, November 1982

('Flash' / 'The Hero', 'Now I'm Here' / 'Put Out The Fire' / 'Dragon Attack' / 'Now I'm Here' *(reprise)*', 'Crazy Little Thing Called Love', 'Teo Torriatte (Let Us Cling Together)'. Selections from Vienna, May 1982 ('Another One Bites The Dust', 'We Will Rock You', 'We Are The Champions', 'God Save The Queen')

Fans rejoiced at the DVD release of *Queen On Fire: Live At The Bowl*. Even though it had been filmed for and broadcast on TV in 1982, it was from an era of Queen's history that was unfairly maligned and now interesting to explore. *Hot Space* may have been a let-down, but the band's performance at Milton Keynes Bowl on 5 June 1982 saw them blazing through a wonderful set combining old favorites and new compositions. And it should be noted that the *Hot Space* tracks – 'Action This Day', 'Staying Power' and 'Back Chat' – sound much better live than on record.

The video is shot superbly, again by Gavin Taylor, and while some of the shots focus a bit too much on Brian and Freddie, it's a minor complaint. The second disc contains a smattering of extras, including live performances of some neglected tracks from concerts in Vienna and Tokyo; the latter concert features an absolutely scorching version of 'Crazy Little Thing Called Love' and a great rendition of 'Teo Torriatte (Let Us Cling Together)'. While all the Japanese footage had been released on *Live In Japan* in 1982, it was released here worldwide for the first time.

Interview footage is also included, though the questions revolve around the band's light show instead of anything worthwhile. Brian and Roger are interviewed together, both of them alternating between weariness and humor; Freddie appears alone and bounces back and forth between indifference and annoyance. Overall, the bonus features are nice (a photo gallery of the 1982 tour is also included, though the only thing of interest is the backing music: the slideshow is set to a previously unreleased live version of 'Calling All Girls', also from the Japanese concert), but the real attraction is the first disc, a reminder that when Queen were on fire, they were virtually unstoppable.

LIVE AID
• 2004 (10 hours) • WSM R2 970383 • *Producers:* Jill Sinclair, Bob Geldof, John Kennedy

'Bohemian Rhapsody', 'Radio Ga Ga', 'Hammer To Fall', 'Crazy Little Thing Called Love', 'We Will Rock You', 'We

Are The Champions', 'Is This The World We Created...?'

When Bob Geldof received word that bootleg DVDs of the July 1985 Live Aid performance were being traded and sold for exorbitant prices on the Internet, he was outraged and went against his original claim that the performance would be a one-off, never to be seen again. Instead of having greedy bootleggers receive the profits, an edited four-disc box set of the two simultaneous concerts was released in November 2004, with all proceeds going to famine relief.

It was inevitable that Queen's set, widely considered the best of the day, was included, and what a treat it is. Finally, fans who were mere toddlers or not even born at the time of the concert were able to see what the hype was all about, and why the band (but mostly Freddie) were held in such high regard. As with the other sets, the technical setbacks were edited as well as possible (Brian's solo during 'Crazy Little Thing Called Love' was marred by irritating feedback, which was almost entirely omitted) to provide the most accurate portrayal possible of that legendary day. Some fans have argued that too much attention was paid to Freddie, while the others only occasionally stroll into the camera's view, but Brian, Roger and John have all stated that Live Aid was Freddie's time to show the world who he was, and there's no better place to see this than here.

For those not wishing to purchase the four-disc box set (though it really is worth it), a single disc of highlights was released. Titled *Live Aid: 20 Years Ago Today*, Queen are the only act to feature a full song ('Radio Ga Ga' in its entirety), with others reduced to merely soundbites.

THE MAKING OF A NIGHT AT THE OPERA

• 2005 (141 mins) • Eagle Vision EREDV579 • *Director:* Matthew Longfellow • *Producers:* Terry Shland, Geoff Kempin, Jamie Rugge-Price, Nick de Grunwald, and Martin R Smith

To coincide with the 30th anniversary of *A Night At The Opera*, Eagle Vision commissioned a fascinating documentary into the making of each track from Queen's seminal fourth album. With a slew of new interviews with Brian, Roger, Roy Thomas Baker, Jac Holzman, Nicky Horne, and peers of Queen including Joe Perry, among many others, the documentary deconstructs the album and offers insight and knowledge of the recording process. This

is highly recommended, and one wishes Queen would commission these kinds of documentaries for all of their albums.

QUEEN ROCK MONTREAL (AND LIVE AID)

• 2007 (95 mins) • Eagle Vision EREDV666-P • *Director, Montreal:* Saul Swimmer • *Director, Live Aid:* John G. Smith • *Producers, Montreal:* Saul Swimmer, Jim Beach, Adrian Scrope, Mack, Roger Taylor, Brian May, Geoff Kempin, Terry Shand, Kris Fredrikkson, Justin Shirley-Smith, Joshua J. Macrae • *Producers, Live Aid:* Michael Appleton, Phil Chilvers, Justin Shirley-Smith

Montreal: "Intro', 'We Will Rock You' *(fast)*, 'Let Me Entertain You', 'Play The Game', 'Somebody To Love', 'Killer Queen', 'I'm In Love With My Car', 'Get Down, Make Love', 'Save Me', 'Now I'm Here', 'Dragon Attack', 'Now I'm Here', 'Love Of My Life', 'Under Pressure', 'Keep Yourself Alive', Drum Solo, Guitar Solo, 'Crazy Little Thing Called Love', 'Jailhouse Rock', 'Bohemian Rhapsody', 'Tie Your Mother Down', 'Another One Bites The Dust', 'Sheer Heart Attack', 'We Will Rock You', 'We Are The Champions', 'God Save The Queen'; *Live Aid:* 'Bohemian Rhapsody', 'Radio Ga Ga', Freddie Singalong, 'Hammer To Fall', 'Crazy Little Thing Called Love', 'We Will Rock You', 'We Are The Champions', 'Is This The World We Created...?', Live Aid rehearsal, TV interview

Another year, another opportunity to milk the November 1981 Montreal concert. But this time, instead of Saul Swimmer and Mobilevision doing so, Queen Productions finally purchased the rights to and released the definitive release of this concert. It may be familiar to every Queen fan, but the footage has been fixed considerably, and is fascinating in that it feels like the audience is right there with the band – not a coincidence, as this was the original intent of the concert. A commentary track, recorded by Brian and Roger, complements the footage, and many fascinating tidbits are discovered, though a lot of it centers around the band's dislike of Saul Swimmer and his production team and camera crew.

On his Soapbox, Brian had promised "exciting bonus features" for the DVD, leading many fans to salivate at the thought of footage from their spring 1981 tour across South America, but what materialized was only marginally exciting: the band's full set at Live Aid (already released on the 2004 box set, *Live Aid*) and footage of the band rehearsing for their big day. While *Queen Rock Montreal* is undeniably a major upgrade in both sound and visuals, it was a disappointing release, with little to entice the fan who had countless versions of *We Will Rock You.*

LIVE AT WEMBLEY STADIUM
• 2011 (275 minutes) • Bravado BGAMQN23 *(box set)*, Island Records 06025-2779570-6, Universal Music DVD Video 06025-2779570-6 *(double-disc DVD)*
• *Director:* Gavin Taylor • *Producers:* Simon Lupton, Rhys Thomas, Brian May, Roger Taylor, Jim Beach, Gavin Taylor, Justin Shirley-Smith, Kris Fredriksson and Joshua J Macrae

DVD 1, Saturday night concert: 'One Vision', 'Tie Your Mother Down', 'In The Lap Of The Gods...Revisited', 'Seven Seas Of Rhye', 'Tear It Up', 'A Kind Of Magic', 'Under Pressure', 'Another One Bites The Dust', 'Who Wants To Live Forever', 'I Want To Break Free', 'Impromptu', 'Brighton Rock Solo', 'Now I'm Here', 'Love Of My Life', 'Is This The World We Created...?', '(You're So Square) Baby I Don't Care', 'Hello Mary Lou (Goodbye Heart)', 'Tutti Frutti', 'Gimme Some Lovin'', 'Bohemian Rhapsody', 'Hammer To Fall', 'Crazy Little Thing Called Love', 'Big Spender', 'Radio Ga Ga', 'We Will Rock You', 'Friends Will Be Friends', 'We Are The Champions', 'God Save The Queen'

DVD 2, Friday night concert: 'One Vision', 'Tie Your Mother Down', 'In The Lap Of The Gods...Revisited', 'Seven Seas Of Rhye', 'Tear It Up', 'A Kind Of Magic', 'Under Pressure', 'Another One Bites The Dust', 'Who Wants To Live Forever', 'I Want To Break Free', 'Impromptu', 'Brighton Rock Solo', 'Now I'm Here', 'Love Of My Life', 'Is This The World We Created...?', '(You're So Square) Baby I Don't Care', 'Hello Mary Lou (Goodbye Heart)', 'Tutti Frutti', 'Bohemian Rhapsody', 'Hammer To Fall', 'Crazy Little Thing Called Love', 'Big Spender', 'Radio Ga Ga', 'We Will Rock You', 'Friends Will Be Friends', 'We Are The Champions', 'God Save The Queen'

DVD 2 bonus features: Documentaries: *The Final Tour, The Wembley Weekend, Rehearsal Footage*

Reissued in 2011 in a deluxe box set "flight case", containing a mini blow-up doll of Freddie (the more gigantic version had been let loose into the sky on the night of the Wembley concert), photo book, replica concert ticket, soccer scarf, and Gerry Stickells Hawaiian shirt, VIP passes, and a hand-drawn map of

the 1986 tour by Brian's father, Harold (he reportedly did this for every Queen tour), *Live At Wembley Stadium* added a further bonus of featuring the first night's filmed concert on a second DVD. While the band is obviously a little more nervous, playing to their biggest hometown audience in their career (and the venue of their landmark Live Aid gig nearly a year later to the day), they still put on a magnificent show. The footage is a little rough, as it was shot simply to test the cameras and positions for the following night, but it's still a treat: Freddie is especially having a blast, remarking several times throughout the concert about the rain, which had started as a drizzle but became a full-on downpour: "Is everybody nice and wet? It's the only way to be in England!"

The second disc also features an additional 38 minutes of footage in the form of two documentaries, with Brian and Roger ruminating on the concert and the tour itself, plus 15 minutes of rehearsal footage that had already been released on the 2003 DVD of the set. (It's still nice to have, regardless of being repeated.) The package also contained the 2003 reissue of the second night on CD, while more industrious and technologically-advanced fans were able to rip the music from the first night for their listening pleasure. While the ephemera that adorns the set may be of little worth to all but the most ardent of collectors (a standalone double-disc DVD was released simultaneously), this edition of Queen's landmark London concert is still worth picking up, especially to see the differences between the two nights.

DAYS OF OUR LIVES
• 2011 (170/229 minutes) • Universal Music Group/ Island Records Group VFD59512/0602527885148 *(Blu-Ray)*, Universal Music Group/Island Records Group 0602527885131/VED59512 *(DVD)*, Eagle Rock Entertainment EVB334079 *(Blu-Ray)*, Eagle Vision EV304009 *(DVD)* • *Director:* Matt O'Casey • *Producers:* Simon Lupton, Rhys Thomas, Justin Shirley-Smith, Joshua J Macrae, Kris Fredriksson, Andrew Winter, Adam Barker, Jim Beach, Lesley Douglas, Iain Funnell, Richard Cook

After years of well-intended but unsatisfactory attempts, Queen finally got the documentary treatment they deserved with *Days Of Our Lives.* Screened on BBC2 over two nights – 29 and 30 May 2011 – and later released on both DVD and Blu-Ray formats, *Days Of Our Lives* is a superb retelling of

Queen's history, overseen by the band's team – and self-professed fans – Matt O'Casey, Simon Lupton, and Rhys Thomas. Featuring archival interviews along with new footage of Brian, Roger, Jim Beach, and a plethora of Queen's crew, the documentary explores all facets of Queen's history, though some bits (*Flash Gordon* and *Highlander*) are overlooked entirely, while others (*A Kind Of Magic* and *Made In Heaven*) are touched upon only briefly. Still, this is as close as fans will get to knowing the full history of their professional and personal lives, with Brian and Roger especially more comfortable with discussing some of the more tawdry moments from their career.

There's also plenty of newly-discovered footage to keep die-hard fans interested: the band performing 'Seven Seas Of Rhye' on *Top Of The Pops*; footage from the *News Of The World* sessions that was later released on *The American Dream* in 2017; live performances from Hyde Park, the 1977 US tour, and São Paulo; and backstage footage and promo video out-takes of the band over the years. Additionally, their promotional videos are given a slight refresh, notably 'Somebody To Love', 'We Are The Champions', 'Crazy Little Thing Called Love', and 'Radio Ga Ga', with alternate angles and out-takes making for a delightful view. There are also bonus segments on the Blu-Ray and DVD that discuss the aforementioned portions of Queen's history that weren't on the TV version, sectioned into standalone segments that are an absolute treat – check out the *Scrabble* footage, which features Brian and Roger reminiscing on some of the words that Freddie created, and Brian's highest-ever win (168 points for the word "lacquers", itself part of a slogan that Freddie had to come up with at Ealing; Brian's delight at Roger remembering "Adds lacquer to your knackers" and "Adds luster to your cluster" can only be seen to be believed).

SOLO VIDEOS

THE BRIAN MAY BAND: LIVE AT BRIXTON ACADEMY
• 1994 (89 mins) • PMI MVN 4911873 • *Director:* Gavin Taylor • *Producer:* Jim Beach

'The Dark', 'Back To The Light', 'Driven By You', 'Tie Your Mother Down', 'Love Token', 'Headlong', 'Love Token' (*reprise*), 'Love Of My Life', '39' / 'Let Your Heart Rule Your Head', 'Too Much Love Will Kill You', Keyboards Solo, 'Since You've Been Gone', 'Now I'm

Here', 'Guitar Extravagance', 'Resurrection', Band Introduction, 'Last Horizon', 'We Will Rock You', 'Hammer To Fall'

The video equivalent of Brian's sole live album (his 1998 Royal Albert Hall show was originally planned to be issued in early 1999 as a video and album release, but was canceled for unknown reasons) is an enjoyable romp through former Queen hits and new solo songs as Brian does his best to replicate his past band's old glories. The video differs slightly from the album, with a longer running time and additional dialog. *Live At The Brixton Academy* has been deleted and is difficult to locate anywhere, but should be picked up for a reasonable price since it serves as the only official documentation of Brian's first post-Queen tour.

ROGER TAYLOR: LIVE AT THE CYBERBARN (THE MAKING OF A WORLD RECORD)
• 1998 (58 mins) • PMI QD010002NJ • *Directors:* Rudi Dolezal, Hannes Rossacher and Simon Witter
• *Producers:* Jim Beach and Tim Massey • *Sound producer:* Joshua J Macrae

Roger's first video release, available by mail order only, was a documentary that focused on his record-breaking Cyberbarn concert from 24 September 1998. Unfortunately, *Live At The Cyberbarn (The Making Of A World Record)*, certainly a contender for the most unwieldy title in the Queen oeuvre, suffers at the edit-happy hands of Dolezal and Rossacher. The video is essentially a cut-and-paste affair, with only excerpts of the songs appearing intertwined with interview footage – apparently, it was too difficult to feature the concert in full and follow it with the interviews. To make matters worse, the video is presented as if being viewed on a computer screen, making for a strange experience. The footage was later released, minus effects, on Roger's nearly all-encompassing box set *The Lot*.

FREDDIE MERCURY: THE FREDDIE MERCURY VIDEO COLLECTION
• 2000 (VHS: 53 mins; DVD: 96 mins) • Parlophone 7243 4 92443 9 9 • *Directors:* Gavin Taylor, David Mallet, Rudi Dolezal and Hannes Rossacher

'Barcelona' (*mimed*), 'The Great Pretender', 'I Was Born To Love You', 'Time', 'How Can I Go On' (*mimed*), 'Made In Heaven', 'Living On My Own', 'The Golden Boy' (*mimed*),

'The Great Pretender' *(extended version)*, 'Barcelona', 'In My Defence', 'Guide Me Home' *(closing titles)*

Also released as part of the mammoth *Solo Collection* release in October 2000, *The Freddie Mercury Video Collection* amassed 11 of Freddie's official promotional videos into a neat little package, the first time any of them had been released as a unit. While the tracklisting appears to have been chosen completely at random, each video is more elaborate than its predecessor, with live versions of three songs from *Barcelona* thrown in at intervals: the title track, 'How Can I Go On' and 'The Golden Boy'. An added bonus is the extended version of 'The Great Pretender', which shows Freddie, Roger and Peter Straker goofing off behind the scenes while getting into their outfits. Freddie may have only made seven true promotional videos – and each of them is brilliant, showing just how much detail Freddie demanded of his directors – the four extra videos are worthy inclusions. The real treat comes later, however: interviews with the directors of each video explain the process and give tidbits of information. Definitely a terrific addition to the Queen video catalog, though similar packages for Brian's and Roger's videos would also be welcome.

FREDDIE MERCURY: THE UNTOLD STORY

• 2000 (112 mins) • *Directors:* Rudi Dolezal and Hannes Rossacher

Released only as part of the *Solo Collection* box set in October 2000 (and reworked as a separate release in September 2006 as *Lover Of Life, Singer Of Songs*), *The Untold Story* is a documentary based on all aspects of Freddie's life: his childhood, college experience, forming Queen, the music he produced, his many love affairs, and his untimely death. It's a lengthy documentary, with undue emphasis on his sexuality, a topic many fans feel should be consigned to the tabloids rather than an officially sanctioned documentary.

Regardless, *The Untold Story* is an interesting documentary including interviews with people who had been associated with Freddie in various ways: his sister, Kashmira Cooke, and mother, Jer Bulsara; the headmaster of the boarding school Freddie attended; school friends and teachers; former band members from Ibex and Wreckage; Tim Staffell, Brian May, Roger Taylor, Mary Austin, Jim Hutton, Peter Freestone, Mick Rock, Ian Hunter, Peter Straker, and still others. Most are respectful of Freddie, his memory, and his

achievements, and it's clear that the documentary was a labor of love. With a soundtrack provided by French pianist Thierry Lang, *The Untold Story* remains the definitive word on Freddie's life, and is certainly worth checking out.

FREDDIE MERCURY: THE GREAT PRETENDER

• 2012 (104 mins) • Eagle Vision EREDV949 *(DVD)*, Eagle Rock Entertainment/Mercury Songs Ltd. ERBRD5163 *(Blu-Ray)*, Eagle Vision EV305589 *(DVD)*, Eagle Rock Entertainment EVB334269 *(Blu-Ray)*
• *Director:* Rhys Thomas • *Producers:* Jim Beach, Rhys Thomas, Joss Crowley

This excellent documentary, created at the same time as the *Days Of Our Lives* programme, focuses solely on Freddie and features archival interviews with Freddie, as well as new footage with Brian, Roger, Montserrat Caballé, Jim Beach, John Reid, Mack, David Richards, Mike Moran, Peter "Phoebe" Freestone, and a slew of other friends and family related to Queen and Freddie. It's mostly been told all before, but this focuses heavily on his music, balancing it precociously with his personal life ("Phoebe" is on hand here to talk heavily about that, though thankfully he avoids repeating the same lurid story about Freddie's prodigious, ah, manhood that he revealed in the disgusting TV gossip documentary, *Freddie's Loves*). The biggest focus is of course on *Mr. Bad Guy* and *Barcelona*, and features contemporaneous interviews with David Wigg on the former, and new interviews with Montserrat about the latter. *The Great Pretender* essentially replaces *The Untold Story* and is a definite recommendation, especially for fans who want to hear more about the man behind the music – plus, there are rare out-takes of 'Take Another Little Piece Of My Heart' from September 1983 and Freddie's collaboration with Michael Jackson.

QUEEN + PAUL RODGERS VIDEOS

RETURN OF THE CHAMPIONS

• 2005 (140 mins) • Hollywood 2061 62527 9
• *Directors:* David Mallet and Aubrey 'Po' Powell ('Imagine' only) • *Producers:* Brian May, Roger Taylor, Paul Rodgers, Simon Lupton, and Rhys Thomas

'Reaching Out' / 'Tie Your Mother Down', 'I Want To Break Free', 'Fat Bottomed Girls', 'Wishing Well', 'Another One Bites The Dust', 'Crazy Little Thing Called Love', 'Say It's Not True', "39', 'Love Of My

Life', 'Hammer To Fall' *(slow/fast)*, 'Feel Like Makin' Love', 'Let There Be Drums', 'I'm In Love With My Car', Guitar Solo, 'Last Horizon', 'These Are The Days Of Our Lives', 'Radio Ga Ga', 'Can't Get Enough', 'A Kind Of Magic', 'I Want It All', 'Bohemian Rhapsody', 'The Show Must Go On', 'All Right Now', 'We Will Rock You', 'We Are The Champions', 'God Save The Queen', 'It's A Beautiful Day', 'Imagine *(Hyde Park, July 2005)*'

Released along with the live audio equivalent of Queen + Paul Rodgers' 2005 concert in Sheffield, *Return Of The Champions* is a fascinating, beautifully filmed DVD release that certainly stands up superbly against Queen releases with Freddie. The full impact of the visuals was lost on the CD but can be appreciated here. The performances are similar to the CD, but the added bonus of 'Imagine' from the Hyde Park concert in July 2005 makes the DVD all the more worthwhile.

SUPER LIVE IN JAPAN

• 2006 (207 mins) • Toshiba TOBW-3296 • *Director:* Toru Uehara ('Backstage in Budapest' directed by Rudi Dolezal and Hannes Rossacher) • *Producers:* HIP, Fuji Television, Fujipacific Music, Jim Beach, Chris Crawford, Simon Lupton, Justin Shirley-Smith

'Lose Yourself *(intro)*' / 'Reaching Out' / 'Tie Your Mother Down', 'Fat Bottomed Girls', 'Another One Bites The Dust', 'Fire And Water', 'Crazy Little Thing Called Love', 'Say It's Not True', "39', 'Love Of My Life', 'Teo Torriatte (Let Us Cling Together)', 'Hammer To Fall' *(slow/fast)*, 'Feel Like Makin' Love', 'Let There Be Drums', 'I'm In Love With My Car', Guitar Solo, 'Last Horizon', 'These Are The Days Of Our Lives', 'Radio Ga Ga', 'Can't Get Enough', 'A Kind Of Magic', 'I Want It All', 'Bohemian Rhapsody', 'I Was Born To Love You', 'The Show Must Go On', 'All Right Now', 'We Will Rock You', 'We Are The Champions', 'God Save The Queen', Documentary: Backstage In Budapest

Released only in Japan in April 2006, *Super Live In Japan* (not one of the better titles for a Queen release) is superior to *Return Of The Champions* since it features a slew of material that wasn't performed during the UK leg of the 2005 tour. 'Fire And Water' and 'Teo Torriatte (Let Us Cling Together)' are two unsurprising (but certainly welcome) additions, while a rendition of 'I Was Born To Love You', as performed by Brian on acoustic guitar and Roger on lead vocals, is reason enough to buy an import of the DVD. Filmed at the

Saitama Super Arena in Tokyo on 27 October 2005, the band are in good spirits here, though they are all visibly weary, considering the concert was coming at the end of a lengthy tour. A second disc features a 25-minute documentary, filmed by the Torpedo Twins, from Queen + Paul Rodgers' concert in Budapest in the spring of 2005, with interviews from the touring band and various tour personnel as well as fans.

LIVE IN UKRAINE

• 2009 (121 mins) • Parlophone 9 64603 2 0
• *Director:* David Mallet • *Producers:* Rocky Oldham, Dione Orrom, Jim Beach, Elena Branchuk, Justin Shirley-Smith, Kris Fredriksson, Joshua J. Macrae

'Cosmos Rockin'' (intro) / 'One Vision', 'Tie Your Mother Down', 'The Show Must Go On', 'Fat Bottomed Girls', 'Another One Bites The Dust', 'Hammer To Fall', 'I Want It All', 'I Want To Break Free', 'Seagull', 'Love Of My Life', "39', Drum Solo, 'I'm In Love With My Car', 'Say It's Not True', 'Shooting Star', 'Bad Company', Guitar Solo, 'Bijou', 'Last Horizon', 'Crazy Little Thing Called Love', 'C-Lebrity', 'Feel Like Makin' Love', 'Bohemian Rhapsody', 'Cosmos Rockin'', 'All Right Now', 'We Will Rock You', 'We Are The Champions', 'God Save The Queen'

Filmed on the opening night of Queen + Paul Rodger's 2008 tour, *Live In Ukraine* was, like its predecessor *Return Of The Champions*, a bare-bones affair, with only a (slightly) edited presentation of the concert released on a single disc. It was bound with its audio equivalent – also with 'A Kind Of Magic', 'Radio Ga Ga', and 'Wishing Well' absent – in a CD/DVD package, and in a special collector's tin that also included a T-shirt (!), and, of course, in its own right. As a concert documentary, it's interesting, but its similiarities to *Return Of The Champions* are glaringly obvious: only three songs from *The Cosmos Rocks* were performed, and only a few new choices balance out a predictable and tired set list. The band are still in good spirits, which is encouraging, especially considering relations between the primaries would disintegrate quickly as the tour progressed. It's a good DVD, but unspectacular, and its release six months after Paul officially announced the end of his partnership with Brian and Roger, and a very small promotional push, resulted in disappointing sales.

QUEEN + ADAM LAMBERT VIDEOS

LIVE IN JAPAN

• 2016 (80 mins) • Ward Records/Eagle Vision/ Universal Music Group GQXS-90208 • *Directors:* Chikara Tanaka *a.k.a* Riki • *Producers:* Shino Hayasaka (WOWOW) and Kota Akutsu (Win's Moment) • *Executive Producers:* Kohshiro Yamashita (WOWOW), Geoff Kempin and Terry Shand (Eagle Rock) • *Music Production:* Justin Shirley-Smith and Joshua J. Macrae • *Additional Music Mix Production:* Kris Fredriksson • *Video Post Production Supervision:* Justin Shirley-Smith and Kris Fredriksson

'Procession', 'Now I'm Here', 'Stone Cold Crazy', 'Another One Bites The Dust', 'Fat Bottomed Girls', 'In The Lap Of The Gods...Revisited', 'Seven Seas Of Rhye', 'Killer Queen', 'I Want It All', 'Teo Torriatte (Let Us Cling Together)', 'Love Of My Life', 'These Are The Days Of Our Lives', 'Under Pressure', 'I Was Born To Love You', 'Radio Ga Ga', 'Crazy Little Thing Called Love', 'Bohemian Rhapsody', 'We Will Rock You', 'We Are The Champions', 'God Save The Queen'

Filmed and recorded at the Super Sonic Festival at the QVC Marine Field in Chiba, Tokyo, on 17 August 2014, *Live In Japan* was released exclusively for the Japanese market, and represents the first physical release of the Queen + Adam Lambert partnership. Issued on multiple formats, as has now become the norm – double vinyl with CD and Blu-Ray, double vinyl with CD and DVD-V, Blu-Ray, Blu-Ray with CD, DVD-V with CD, Blu-Ray with CD in a box set, and DVD-V with CD in a box set, but, frustratingly, not as a standalone CD – this is a fine release, with the band firing on all cylinders, and Adam proving his mettle not only as a vocalist, but as a frontman. The set list isn't as inspired as it had been on previous Queen + Adam Lambert tours, but considering this was a festival performance, some concessions had to be made, and so the band played it relatively safe, though the inclusions of 'Teo Torriatte (Let Us Cling Together)' and 'I Was Born To Love You' are welcome indeed.

C: INTERACTIVE

Queen skated on the cutting edge of technology from the start thanks to the experimental nature of each band member, ever-ready to push the limits, sometimes inspiring a positive reaction ('Bohemian Rhapsody') and sometimes a resoundingly negative one (Hot Space). One medium that Queen dabbled in, initially successfully, was the Internet, an ever-burgeoning hotspot marketed towards the youth of the new millennium. Queen's first foray into the worldwide web came with the release of Made In Heaven, where advertisements for the now-defunct address, http://queen-fip.com, were contained in the liner notes. With a futuristic front page depicting an almost Orwellian cityscape, Queen's fans were able to receive access to the most up-to-date information on their favorite band.

Unfortunately, there was a lack of enthusiasm from those in charge of the site and, with the boom of fan sites boasting literally up-to-the-minute information as well as even more features, the official Queen site quickly became obsolete. Perhaps realizing that Queen deserved a proper site, Jacky Smith, head of the fan club, started up her own website in which the news was updated daily, though this, too, became obsolete when it was discovered that it offered little more. Promises were made to include an online shop, which would have been an ideal addition had fans not been obliged to pay by post; an online payment facility was finally set up in 2005, but by that time fans had already lost interest.

Queen's official page was revamped in late 1999 to coincide with Greatest Hits III, with many assurances made regarding timely updates. Only in 2002, however, was there an all-out attempt to make the website a viable source of information, thanks to a renewed interest in the band based partly on the enthusiastic reception of the We Will Rock You musical in various countries and, subsequently, on the re-formation of Queen (now containing only Roger and Brian) with Paul Rodgers handling lead vocals. With the band more in the public eye than they had been for a long time, neglecting such an important method of information delivery would be self-defeating, so QueenOnline (http://www.queenonline.com) blossomed into an international source of news, rivaled only by the stellar fansite QueenZone (http://www.queenzone.com), both containing forums (or noticeboards) allowing fans to interact with each other.

At some time in the early part of the new millennium, an unofficial Brian May site somehow became the guitarist's official forum, transformed from a fan site into a regularly viewed source of information straight from the man himself. He was given his own corner for personal thoughts and ramblings ('Brian's Soapbox') and publishes, almost daily, stories about how certain songs were written or recorded, or about whatever else is on his mind; recently, he has started a campaign against animal cruelty, Save Me. Fans are also encouraged to write in to Brian and to email him their thoughts or questions which, if the fan is lucky enough, will be personally answered by Brian himself – and maybe even featured on the website.

Of course, the dawn of social media in the late 2000s meant that Queen had to jump on board the bandwagon, and by the early 2010s, Queen's Facebook page and Twitter account (@QueenWillRock) have amassed 28.5 million likes and 1.52 million followers, respectively. These accounts would prove to be a far more effective marketing tool than their website or message board. Brian eventually jumped into the fray of social media, too, after one too many fake accounts were started in his name; he's far more communicative on Twitter (@DrBrianMay), where he can reach his 750,000+ followers, though his fascination with stereo photography and social justice is best seen on his Instagram account (@brianmayforreal). Roger, of course, wants nothing to do with social media, though he still has a Twitter account, @OfficialRMT, that his team handles in order to get the occasional word out.

Apart from the Internet, Queen have also made a few other forays into the world of interactive electronics, though they were greeted with only measured amounts of success.

QUEEN: THE EYE
Electronic Arts, 1997

Disc One – The Arena Domain: 'Made In Heaven' (1'08); 'I Want It All' (4'43); 'Dragon Attack' (4'22); 'Fight From The Inside' (3'02); 'Hang On In There' (0'57); 'In The Lap Of The Gods...Revisited' (0'32)*; 'Modern Times Rock 'n' Roll' (1'43); 'More Of That Jazz' (4'29); 'We Will Rock You (live)' (0'58); 'Liar' (1'26); 'The

Night Comes Down' (0'47); 'Liar' (1'26); 'Chinese Torture' (1'44); 'I Want It All' (4'54)

Disc Two – The Works Domain: 'Mustapha' (0'25)*; 'Mother Love' (4'16); 'You Take My Breath Away' (3'14); 'One Vision' (0'32); 'Sweet Lady' (1'03)*; 'Was It All Worth It?' (1'57); 'Get Down, Make Love' (3'48); 'Heaven For Everyone' (5'36); 'Hammer To Fall' (4'22); 'Tie Your Mother Down *(intro)'* (0'40); 'One Vision' (2'27); 'It's Late' (1'08)*; 'Procession' (1'14); 'Made In Heaven' (5'24)

Disc Three – The Theatre Domain: 'It's A Beautiful Day (reprise)' (1'37); 'Don't Lose Your Head' (1'59); 'Princes Of The Universe' (1'08); 'A Kind Of Magic' (4'25); 'Gimme The Prize (Kurgan's Theme)' (4'03)*; 'Bring Back That Leroy Brown' (0'26)*; 'A Kind Of Magic' (0'06)*; 'You Don't Fool Me' (5'57); 'Let Me Entertain You' (0'49); 'Khashoggi's Ship' (1'36); 'Forever' (3'21); 'Don't Try So Hard' (1'34*); 'Was It All Worth It?' (0'37)

Disc Four – The Innuendo Domain: 'Brighton Rock' (0'12); 'I'm Going Slightly Mad' (2'40); 'Bijou' (1'25); 'Khashoggi's Ship' (1'37); 'The Show Must Go On' (4'25); 'The Hitman' (1'07); 'Too Much Love Will Kill You' (1'50)*; 'I Can't Live With You' (4'40); 'Love Of My Life' (0'04)

Disc Five – The Final Domain: 'Death On Two Legs (Dedicated to...... *(piano intro)'* (0'39); 'Death On Two Legs (Dedicated to...... *(remainder of song)'* (3'07); 'Ride The Wild Wind' (4'45); 'Headlong' (4'53); 'Breakthru' (2'06); 'Hammer To Fall' (4'32); 'Gimme The Prize (Kurgan's Theme)' (4'11); 'The Hitman' (2'39); 'Don't Lose Your Head' (4'40)*; 'Gimme The Prize (Kurgan's Theme)' (4'10)*

*Songs marked with an asterisk (*) feature vocals; all others are instrumentals.*

Rumblings among the Queen fan communities had long speculated that the band were about to enter into the realm of interactive computer games, and in 1997 the rumor was confirmed. The basic premise of *Queen: The eYe* mirrors the plot of the *We Will Rock You* musical, set in the future where the world is ruled by an Orwellian machine called 'The eYe', which has abolished every creative outlet through which a human was previously able to express himself or herself. The main character, Dubroc, stumbles across

a collection of rock music (provided, obviously, by Queen), is branded a traitor to The eYe's vision, and is duly sentenced to death. At this point, the player takes over and tries to destroy The eYe and emerge from the various domains alive.

Unfortunately, despite the considerable amount of work that went into the project, it was deemed a failure due to poor promotion and confusing gameplay. The graphics were inadequate, though that didn't prevent a book – *The Art Of The eYe* – from being published, featuring landscapes which were nevertheless intriguing and interesting. The single redeeming factor of the project was the music available on the five discs, considerably edited, remixed and rearranged to suit gameplay, thus creating a unique listening experience that could be played on any CD player. Containing mostly instrumental reworkings of songs (partly or fully stripped of vocals) that were generally lesser known to the casual Queen fan, the songs were also substantially remixed to bring aspects previously buried or unheard to the forefront.

Queen: The eYe is now hard to find, though it wasn't exactly in surplus during its initial release. Fans of the band have little reason to track it down other than for the alternate song versions, as it isn't compatible with a PC system above Windows 98, nor is it even playable on any Macintosh, making its appeal all the more limited. Unsurprisingly, Queen didn't venture back into the gaming world, though their focus would remain on creating a surreal future in a different format.

THE TOP 100 BOOTLEGS

Available 8 March 2005:
A Day At The Apollo (30/5/1977)
Action And More Action (26/10/1982)
Jazz Final (6/5/1979)
Last Stand (15/5/1985)
Life Is Real (9/8/1982)

Available 10 September 2005:
Cardiac Arrest (31/3/1974 and 24/12/1975)
Cry Argentina (24 and 25/11/1981, taken from the official *We Will Rock You* video; 13/9/1973; and one track from *Live Killers*)
In Concert '74 (6/12/1974)

Available 24 October 2005:
Bonsoir Paris (28/2/1979)

Crazy Tour (26/12/1979)
Done Under Pressure (21/6/1986)

Available 12 December 2005:
Live Alive USA (1982 Rock 'n' America tour)
Procession (29/11/1973)
Seven Seas Of Tsumagoi (29/4/1975)

Available 16 January 2006:
Killer Queen (23/4/1975)
Warehouse Copenhagen (12/5/1977)
Xmas At The Beeb (24/12/1975)

Available 13 February 2006:
Domo Arigato Osaka (24/10/1982)
Immigrant Magic Berlin (26/6/1986)
When You Don't Wanna Hear It Frankfurt (28/4/1982)

In theory, the Top 100 Bootlegs was an inspired idea: beat the bootleggers at their own game and offer official downloads of the best-known bootlegs in existence. Unfortunately, the execution left much to be desired, and angered most diehard fans: instead of offering cleaned-up live shows, Queen Productions unleashed onto the Internet untouched bootlegs of dubious origin and with absurdly incorrect information. It was a project that was greeted tepidly, and rightly so: had something new and exciting been offered – perhaps a raiding of the live vaults to release soundboard-quality concerts (no need to remaster them, as Pearl Jam and The Who have been offering soundboard recordings of every concert of theirs since at least 2002) – it would have been hailed as worthwhile. Instead, it just confirmed how inadequately Queen's back catalog was being handled.

STEMS & MULTITRACKS

'Another One Bites The Dust' *(2 versions)*, 'Bohemian Rhapsody' *(2 versions)*, 'Brighton Rock', 'C-Lebrity', 'Crazy Little Thing Called Love' *(2 versions)*, 'Fat Bottomed Girls' *(album and single versions)*, 'Get Down, Make Love', 'Hammer To Fall', 'I Want It All' *(3 versions)*, 'I Want To Break Free' *(2 versions)*, 'Keep Yourself Alive', 'Killer Queen' *(2 versions)*, 'Now I'm Here', 'One Vision' *(2 versions)*, 'Play The Game', 'Somebody To Love' *(2 versions)*, 'Stone Cold Crazy', 'Tenement Funster', 'Tie Your Mother Down', 'Under Pressure' *(3 versions)*, 'We Are The Champions' *(3 versions)*, 'We Will Rock You'

While it's not in this book's interest to condone material not officially sanctioned by Queen, the stems and multitracks that have leaked onto the Internet in recent years are a difficult grey area. It's true that Queen Productions didn't release these as an official release, though they were okayed for use on the wildly popular *Guitar Hero* and *Rock Band* video game series. As such, industrious fans collected the 'stems' (isolated tracks of each song) and leaked them out onto the Internet for bedroom remix enthusiasts to go to town. It's a fascinating listen, offering fans exquisite insight into the painstakingly detailed process that each 'track' is made up of.

Furthermore, the legitimate leaking of four multitracks – 'Bohemian Rhapsody', 'Brighton Rock', 'Get Down, Make Love' and 'Killer Queen' – is even more fascinating, with all 24 tracks separated and isolated into their own file. The casual fan would be absolutely baffled by these, uncertain with which computer program they could even be played in (for the record, it's Audacity, or other similar programs). For those patient fans who fancy a try at coming up with alternate approaches to Queen songs, the stems and multitracks weren't so much a leak as they were a revelation and unintentional Christmas gift rolled into one.

D: WE WILL ROCK YOU: THE MUSICAL

The genesis of We Will Rock You: The Musical *can be pinpointed, depending on whom you believe, at either 1986 or (more realistically) 1997, shortly after the Bejart Ballet that January. While Brian had indicated in the past that the idea for a musical was thrown about following the conclusion of the Magic Tour, it's possible that no actual work was started as the band became increasingly busy,* *with the next decade occupied by Queen albums, Freddie's death, Made In Heaven and various solo projects. Brian commented in March 2001, when official news first hit that such a project was becoming a reality, that "We've actually been working on this damn musical for about four years and been through various ideas, some of which were biographical, which in the end we didn't want to do."*

In December 1998, MTVnews.com reported that "The life of Queen frontman Freddie Mercury is the basis of a new Broadway musical scheduled to open late this year or in early 1999. The play, tentatively titled *Queen*, uses that group's music to tell Mercury's life story from childhood through his untimely death from AIDS in 1991. The other members of Queen are co-producing the show, which was written by Craig Lucas, the screenwriter of the Meg Ryan/Alec Baldwin movie *Prelude To A Kiss*. The show will be directed by Chris Renshaw, whose credits include the most recent Broadway revival of *The King And I*. No word yet on who's in the running for the starring role."

With the benefit of hindsight, this information, no matter how accurate it may have been at the time, turned out to be false: the autobiographical idea was dropped, with a more absurdist and humorous angle being taken by another writer. Enter Ben Elton, a renowned British humorist who had made a name for himself with the TV comedies *The Young Ones* and *Blackadder*. His television-writing career faltered after that, though he went on to write a series of novels that were well received. He was contacted late in 2000 about writing a musical for Queen and promptly accepted, thus beginning one of the most controversial periods of Queen's post-Freddie career.

While many have argued that Freddie would have loved it, initial criticism centered around the fact that Brian was too involved with the project; when word of such censure received Brian, he justified his involvement with the musical by arguing that he loved the script and concept so much that he wanted to immerse himself in it as he felt it was such a personal undertaking. Roger was initially supportive of the musical and became fairly involved, but pulled out after its premiere in May 2002 to concentrate on other aspects of his life, while John was not involved in any way except to offer his blessing, though he did attend the premiere.

"The rumor is that we're doing a musical, which is true," Brian confirmed in March 2001. "Ben Elton has written us a fantastic script ... [He] came up with this great idea, so we've been workshopping it privately and possibly by the end of this year or the beginning of next year we hope it'll be on in the West End."

The synopsis of *We Will Rock You* was vaguely Orwellian in tone: kids of the future subscribe to uniformity, enjoying their simple lives, with music programmed by computers and sung by puppets. A group of rebels discovers that musical instruments, which have been banned, may still lurk in the depths of Planet Mall and that the only way to save the children from their automaton lifestyle is to find the instruments and start their own rock band. Part science fiction and part biting satire, the plot of the musical is admittedly thin, but it suited Queen's music and Elton's sense of humor perfectly. As Bob Wegner, who played guitar in the Canadian residency and runs his own spectacular Queen website (http://queenlive.ca), stated, "It's Rush's *2112* except they win in the end."

In September 2001, Brian and Jim Beach attended auditions for the show. Towards the beginning of December, early reports of cast members surfaced, with former *Young Ones* star Nigel Planer cast as Pop, while the next month saw confirmation of Kerry Ellis as Meat. Also in January 2002, Tony Vincent confirmed on his website that he would be cast as Galileo, the lead in the musical. On the production side, Robert De Niro (of all people) was named as a producer in March 2002, with Tribeca, his personal production company, handling the promotional and distribution side.

Meanwhile, rehearsals were moving along well, with the cast getting ready for the public previews on 24 April at the Dominion Theatre, where the musical was planned to start its residency. A fan club voicemail message two weeks before the previews stated that "The musical is taking up everyone's time and Brian and Roger are throwing themselves into the technical and band rehearsals, which have now begun down at the Dominion, so lots going on down there, and we think Brian is taking his bed down there and sleeps there most of the time as well, poor chap." Unfortunately, the previews were postponed due to technical difficulties and slated to start two days later than intended, but last-minute script tweaks were needed too, so they were canceled completely.

In an effort to make up lost promotion, Brian, Roger and the musical band appeared on *Parkinson* on 2 May, performing 'Somebody To Love', 'We Will Rock You' and 'We Are The Champions'. The show finally opened on 14 May 2002 at the Dominion Theatre, with initially mixed reviews. *The Sun* ran a review reading "Queen's Musical Is A Kind Of Magic"; "What an evening – magnifico," it concluded. One of the more scathing reviews, in *The Observer*, ran with a title decrying the musical as "Very, Very Frightening".

"Queen's memorable songs," it went on, "may have been preposterously overblown – hence the coinage 'pomp rock' – but the point was that these guys (and their fans) were having gloriously indulgent, stadium-sized fun. They were bloody good at what they did and you either loved it or, if you had no sense of camp, loathed it. They weren't making absurd claims about 'meaning', they just did it. In the show's defence, the band play hell for leather and the cast have serious voices. Alex Hanson's wonderfully droll bad guy looks like Max Headroom in Armani ('actually it's Marks and Spencers' – the jokes are that good) and sings up a storm. Likewize Sharon D Clarke's lethal Killer Queen could raise the dead. Hannah Jane Fox's Scaramouche comes over as a young, stroppy Anita Dobson and sings like – and I mean this as a serious compliment – a young Lulu. When Tony Vincent's sincere Galileo opens his mouth to sing, the hairs go up on the back of your neck."

While the reviews were caustic, the fans enjoyed it and it became one of the top draws in the West End. In January 2003, not quite a year after its London premiere, the design concept for an Australian version was signed off, with auditions starting the next month, while tickets for a Madrid premiere went on sale later in February; the Australian premiere came on 7 August 2003, the Madrid one on 3 November. Further openings in Moscow and Brisbane occurred through 2004, while Las Vegas was the site of the show's US premiere on 8 September that year. Reviews were predictably mixed, but fan reception was positive and the show ran for a good year before closing down to make way for other musicals. Apart from these cities, Cologne, Tokyo and Johannesburg, with Zurich coming at the end of 2006, were also given their own productions, though Brian wasn't quite as involved in these as he had been in the others (mainly due to the Queen and Paul Rodgers concerts).

In November 2002, a CD of two London performances from 12 and 13 July was released to modest acclaim (but not exceptional sales); a Spanish version, from performances between 16 and 27 January 2004, followed in August that year. As if that wasn't enough, a book was also published, chronicling the series of events and featuring not only the complete script but some truly spectacular photographs as well.

Original London cast, principals:
Galileo: Tony Vincent (May 2002-November 2003), Mig Ayesa (November 2003-August 2005), Peter Johansson (August 2005-present), *Scaramouche:* Hannah Jane Fox (May 2002-February 2006), Jenna Lee-James (February 2006-present), *Killer Queen:* Sharon D Clarke (May 2002-April 2004), Mazz Murray (April 2004-present), *Khashoggi:* Alexander Hanson (May 2002-November 2002), Clive Carter (November 2002-April 2005), Alex Bourne (April 2005-present), *Britney:* Nigel Clauzel (May 2002-April 2005), Colin Charles (April 2005-present), *Meat:* Kerry Ellis (May 2002-April 2004), Jenna Lee-James (April 2004-February 2006), Rachael Wooding (February 2006-present), *Pop:* Nigel Planer (May 2002-April 2004), Mark Arden (April 2004-April 2005), Jeff Shankley (April 2005-present).

Original London cast, ensemble:
Mig Ayesa *(understudy Galileo and Pop)*, Luke Baxter *(Big Macca, understudy Khashoggi and Pop)*, Stuart Dawes, Clare Foster *(understudy Meat)*, Jye Frasca *(Cliff Richard, understudy Big Macca)*, Elaine Gee, Dalh Haynes, Chris Holland *(understudy Big Macca and Britney)*, Nic Ineeson, Cameron Jack *(understudy Khashoggi and Britney)*, Jodie Jacobs *(understudy Scaramouche)*, Alex Jessop *(understudy Galileo)*, Peter Johansson, Jenna Lee-James *(understudy Scaramouche and Meat)*, Rory Locke, Gemma Maclean *(understudy Meat)*, Adam Murray, Mazz Murray *(teacher and understudy Killer Queen)*, Jai Ramage, Tamara Wall, Enna Woods.

Original London cast, swings:
Giorgia Barberi, Bekki Carpenter, Nikki Dyer, Alex Forster, Matthew Hudson, Mark Marson, Sarah O'Gleby.

Original London band:
Mike Dixon *(musical director, piano)*, Andy Smith *(keyboards)*, Spike Edney *(keyboards)*, Jeff Leach *(keyboards, synthesizer programming)*, Laurie Wizefield *(guitar)*, Alan Darby *(guitar)*, Neil Murray *(bass guitar)*, Tony Bourke *(drums)*, Julian Poole *(percussion)*

OTHER PERFORMANCES

Since its premiere in May 2002, both Brian and Roger, separately and together, have appeared at numerous after-show parties and on-stage performances. The following is a brief list and run-down of songs performed:

AFTER-SHOW PARTY, DOMINION THEATRE, LONDON

15 May 2002
Repertoire: 'Tie Your Mother Down' *(vocals: Kerry Ellis)*, 'Guitar Man' *(vocals: Ben Elton)*, 'Hammer To Fall *(slow/ fast)*' *(vocals: Brian)*, 'Tutti Frutti' *(vocals: Gary Booker)*, 'A Whiter Shade Of Pale' *(vocals: Gary Booker)*, 'Rock And Roll' *(vocals: Roger)*, 'With A Little Help From My Friends' *(vocals: all)*, 'All The Way' *(vocals: all)*
Note: Brian provided guitar on all songs, while Roger provided drums on all except 'Rock And Roll'; Eric Singer played drums alongside Roger throughout the performance.

'PARKINSON' (TV APPEARANCE)

18 May 2002
Repertoire: 'Somebody To Love' *(vocals: Hannah Jane Fox)*, 'Hammer To Fall' *(instrumental)*, 'We Will Rock You' *(vocals: Tony Vincent)*, 'We Are The Champions' *(vocals: Tony Vincent)*

AFTER-SHOW PARTY, VENUE UNKNOWN, MELBOURNE, AUSTRALIA

7 August 2003
Repertoire: 'Tie Your Mother Down' *(vocals: Brian and Amanda Harrison)*, 'Whole Lotta Love' *(vocals: unknown)*, 'Rock And Roll' *(vocals: Roger)*
Note: Brian provided guitar on all songs, while Roger provided drums on all except 'Rock And Roll'; his son, Rufus Tiger, played drums on that song and performed a solo at its conclusion.

AFTER-SHOW PARTY, PARIS HOTEL, LAS VEGAS, NEVADA

8 September 2004
Musicians: Brian May *(guitars)*, Roger Taylor *(drums)*, Steve Vai *(guitars)*, Nuno Bettencourt *(guitars)*, Steve Lukather *(guitars)*, Paul Crook *(guitars)*, Chad Smith *(drums)*, Eric Singer *(drums)*, Simon Phillips *(drums)*
Repertoire: 'Tie Your Mother Down' *(vocals: Jason Wooten and Kacie Sheik)*, 'The Show Must Go On' *(vocals: Kacie Sheik)*, 'Don't Stop Me Now' *(vocals: Jason Wooten)*, 'Stone Cold Crazy' *(vocals: Glen Hughes)*, 'Rock And Roll' *(vocals: Roger)*, 'Johnny B. Goode' *(vocals: Meatloaf)*, 'With A Little Help From My Friends' *(vocals: Jason Wooten)*
Note: A surprising set list, with both 'Don't Stop Me Now' and 'Stone Cold Crazy' making rare appearances; the last times Brian and Roger had played these songs were in 1979 and 1992, respectively.

AFTER-SHOW PARTY, LYRIC THEATRE, SYDNEY, AUSTRALIA

9 October 2004
Repertoire: 'Tie Your Mother Down' *(vocals: Brian and Amanda Harrison)*, 'I'm In Love With My Car' *(vocals: Roger)*, 'Rock And Roll' *(vocals: Roger)*, 'Little Wing' *(vocals: Brian)*, 'Johnny B. Goode' *(vocals: Andrew Swann)*, 'With A Little Help From My Friends' *(vocals: Kate Hoolihan)*
Note: Brian's and Roger's appearances were during the second part of the aftershow party; the first and third parts were performed by the cast of *We Will Rock You* and featured no involvement from Brian or Roger.

MTV RUSSIA MUSIC AWARDS, MOSCOW

16 October 2004
Repertoire: 'We Will Rock You', 'We Are The Champions'
Note: Brian and Roger, along with the Russian *We Will Rock You* cast, were special guests of the RMA's and were introduced by Konstantin Habenskiy.

AFTER-SHOW PARTY, THE STATE KREMLIN PALACE, MOSCOW, RUSSIA

17 October 2004
Repertoire: 'Tie Your Mother Down' *(vocals: Brian)*, 'I'm In Love With My Car' *(vocals: Roger)*, 'The Show Must Go On' *(vocals: Zemfira)*, 'Sleeping On The Sidewalk' *(vocals: Brian)*, 'We Will Rock You' *(vocals: musical cast)*, 'Rock And Roll' *(vocals: Roger)*, 'Johnny B. Goode' *(vocals: Evgeniy Drier and Anthon Bizeev)*, 'With A Little Help From My Friends' *(vocals: musical cast)*

Note: Another surprising set list, including the first performance of 'Sleeping On The Sidewalk' by Brian since 1998. Jim Beach provided backing vocals on all songs a bit too 'boisterously'.

'WETTEN DASS', NÜRNBERG, GERMANY (TV APPEARANCE)

12 December 2004

Repertoire: 'We Will Rock You', 'We Are The Champions', 'We Will Rock You'

Note: the second performance of 'We Will Rock You' was improvised. Also, Brian announced that a tour with Paul Rodgers would be taking place the following year.

AFTER-SHOW PARTY, VENUE UNKNOWN, COLOGNE, GERMANY

12 December 2004

Repertoire: 'Tie Your Mother Down' *(vocals: Brian and Brigitte Oelke)*, 'I'm In Love With My Car' *(vocals: Roger)*, 'The Show Must Go On' *(vocals: Alex Melcher)*, 'Little Wing' *(vocals: Brian)*, 'Don't Stop Me Now' *(vocals: Michaela Kovarikova)*, 'Sleeping On The Sidewalk' *(vocals: Brian)*, 'Rock And Roll' *(vocals: Roger)*, 'With A Little Help From My Friends' *(vocals: musical cast)*

1000TH SHOW, DOMINION THEATRE, LONDON

13 January 2005

Repertoire: 'Bohemian Rhapsody', 'Tie Your Mother Down', 'The Show Must Go On'

Note: Brian and Roger appeared at the conclusion of the 1000th performance of the musical, with the guitarist sharing lead vocals on 'Tie Your Mother Down' with Mazz Murray. The full cast provided vocals on the other two tracks. Brian made his appearance through a trapdoor in the stage, while Roger was initially hidden, with his drum kit placed on one of the platforms at Tottenham Court Road tube station and rising up at the appropriate time.

FOURTH ANNIVERSARY, DOMINION THEATRE, LONDON

11 May 2006

Repertoire: 'Bohemian Rhapsody', 'The Show Must Go On'

Note: Brian, Roger, and Ben Elton were all in attendance for this show, with Brian providing guitar on the two songs mentioned above. Roger, suffering from a lung infection, did not play on any songs.

FREDDIE'S 60TH BIRTHDAY PARTY, DOMINION THEATRE, LONDON

5 September 2006

Repertoire: 'Bohemian Rhapsody', 'Love Of My Life' *(vocals: Brian)*, 'Say It's Not True' *(vocals: Roger)*, 'The Show Must Go On'

Note: Bubblegum pop band McFly performed 'Don't Stop Me Now' earlier.

PLANNED FINAL PERFORMANCE, DOMINION THEATRE, LONDON

7 October 2006

Repertoire: 'Bohemian Rhapsody'

Note: This was the planned final performance at the Dominion Theatre, but the show was extended through 2007. Brian appeared and played guitar during both matinee and evening shows. Roger was in the audience but did not perform.

FIFTH ANNIVERSARY, DOMINION THEATRE, LONDON

14 May 2007

Repertoire: 'Bohemian Rhapsody', 'The Show Must Go On'

Note: Both Brian and Roger appeared, playing guitar and drums, respectively.

PREMIERE, CANON THEATRE, TORONTO, ONTARIO

1 August 2007

Repertoire: 'Bohemian Rhapsody', 'The Show Must Go On'

Note: The Top 7 finalists from *Canadian Idol* provided backing vocals on 'The Show Must Go On'.

CAST CHANGE, DOMINION THEATRE, LONDON

29 September 2007

Repertoire: 'Bohemian Rhapsody'

DOMINION THEATRE, LONDON

29 December 2007

Repertoire: 'Bohemian Rhapsody'

Note: With nothing better to do and finding himself in London's West End, Brian strolled onstage and performed the 'Bohemian Rhapsody' solo.

PREMIERE, RAIMUND THEATRE, VIENNA, AUSTRIA

24 January 2008

Repertoire: 'Bohemian Rhapsody'

SIXTH ANNIVERSARY, DOMINION THEATRE, LONDON

21 May 2008

Repertoire: 'Don't Stop Me Now', 'Bohemian Rhapsody', 'The Show Must Go On'

Note: Brian appeared for the sixth-anniversary show. In a true Spinal Tap moment, Brian's entrance during the 'Bohemian Rhapsody' solo was delayed when the trap door he was supposed to emerge from didn't open – because the crew member couldn't find the switch in the dark. He was able to make his way to the stage in time for the head-banging part.

DOMINION THEATRE, LONDON

10 January 2009

Repertoire: 'Bohemian Rhapsody'

PREMIERE, PALACE THEATRE, MANCHESTER

25 March 2009

Repertoire: 'Bohemian Rhapsody'

SEVENTH ANNIVERSARY, DOMINION THEATRE, LONDON

18 May 2009

Repertoire: 'Bohemian Rhapsody', 'The Show Must Go On'

Note: Ben Elton joined Brian emerging through the trap door during the 'Bohemian Rhapsody' solo.

PREMIERE, EMPIRE THEATRE, SUNDERLAND

11 June 2009

Repertoire: 'Bohemian Rhapsody'

Note: Brian was in attendance at the actual premiere the prior night, but opted to perform 'Bohemian Rhapsody' this night instead.

PREMIERE, HIPPODROME, BIRMINGHAM

2 July 2009

Repertoire: 'Bohemian Rhapsody'

Note: Poor Brian. Roger's drum kit, on a platform and sliding its way toward the front, snagged Brian's leg and caused the guitarist to topple into the kit, dislodging a few drums, a cymbal, and a microphone. The two laughed it off, with Brian, in considerable pain, joking, "It took us ages to rehearse that fall. I'm not sure Roger's kit will ever be the same again." Ben Elton was then introduced, who also made light of the fall and Roger's rock-star image: "That's what happens when you wear your sunglasses indoors!"

CAST CHANGE, DOMINION THEATRE, LONDON

12 September 2009

Repertoire: 'Bohemian Rhapsody', 'The Show Must Go On'

HIPPODROME, BRISTOL

17 September 2009

Repertoire: 'Bohemian Rhapsody'

Note: Roger's son Rufus played drums, joining Brian onstage mid-song.

PRESS NIGHT, PLAYHOUSE THEATRE, EDINBURGH, SCOTLAND

9 November 2009

Repertoire: 'Bohemian Rhapsody'

FIRST ANNIVERSARY, APOLLO THEATRE, STUTTGART, GERMANY

12 November 2009 Apollo Theater, Stuttgart, Germany (WWRY musical (charity evening))

Repertoire: 'Bohemian Rhapsody', 'The Show Must Go On'

Note: This notable occasion also raised funds for the Ein Herz für Kinder (A Heart For Children) foundation.

PREMIERE, ALLIANZ TEATRO, MILAN, ITALY

4 December 2009

Repertoire: 'Bohemian Rhapsody'

O2 DUBLIN, DUBLIN, IRELAND

31 January 2010 O2 Dublin, Dublin, Ireland (WWRY musical)

Repertoire: 'Bohemian Rhapsody'

Note: On this final date of the Irish leg, Brian and Roger both gave speeches, and Brian played on 'Bohemian Rhapsody'.

EIGHTH ANNIVERSARY, DOMINION THEATRE, LONDON

10 May 2010

Repertoire: 'Bohemian Rhapsody'

PREMIERE, BEATRIX THEATRE, UTRECHT, HOLLAND

3 September 2010

Repertoire: 'Bohemian Rhapsody'

CAST CHANGE, DOMINION THEATRE, LONDON

4 September 2010

Repertoire: 'Bohemian Rhapsody'

PREMIERE, THEATRE DES WESTENS, BERLIN, GERMANY
21 October 2010
Repertoire: 'Bohemian Rhapsody'

HIPPODROME, BIRMINGHAM
7 July 2011
Repertoire: 'Bohemian Rhapsody'

DOMINION THEATRE, LONDON
20 August 2011
Repertoire: 'Bohemian Rhapsody'

DOMINION THEATRE, LONDON
13 September 2011
Repertoire: 'We Will Rock You', 'We Are The Champions'
Note: Mel C on vocals.

HIPPODROME, BRISTOL
13 October 2011
Repertoire: 'Bohemian Rhapsody'

PLAYHOUSE THEATRE, EDINBURGH
1 December 2011
Repertoire: 'Bohemian Rhapsody'

THE OLIVIER AWARDS, ROYAL OPERA HOUSE, LONDON
15 April 2012
Repertoire: 'Bohemian Rhapsody'
Note: Brian and Elaine Paige presented The Audience Award to *Les Miserables*.

DOMINION THEATRE, LONDON
14 May 2012
Repertoire: 'Bohemian Rhapsody', 'The Show Must Go On'
Note: The 10th anniversary performance saw Brian guesting on 'Bohemian Rhapsody' and 'The Show Must Go On', with Roger joining on the last minute on drums.

CAPITAL FM ARENA, NOTTINGHAM
27 March 2013
Repertoire: 'Bohemian Rhapsody'

DOMINION THEATRE, LONDON
5 October 2013
Repertoire: 'Bohemian Rhapsody'

PREMIERE, HIPPODROME THEATRE, BALTIMORE, MARYLAND
15 October 2013
Repertoire: 'Bohemian Rhapsody'

DOMINION THEATRE, LONDON
31 May 2014
Repertoire: 'Bohemian Rhapsody', 'The Show Must Go On'
Note: Brian and Roger closed out the final performance of *We Will Rock You: The Musical* in London at both matinee and evening shows.

PREMIERE, MEHR! THEATRE, HAMBURG, GERMANY
16 March 2015
Repertoire: 'Bohemian Rhapsody'

E: THE QUEEN EXTRAVAGANZA

While there are a multitude of Queen tribute bands out there – some of the more notable ones are One Night Of Queen, Almost Queen, and Kween, touted as Japan's best tribute band – it wasn't until 2011 that Roger decided to take the reigns and sanction the first officially-endorsed tribute band.

While there are a multitude of Queen tribute bands out there – some of the more notable ones are One Night Of Queen, Almost Queen, and Kween, touted as Japan's best tribute band – it wasn't until 2011 that Roger decided to take the reigns and sanction the first officially-endorsed tribute band. At the time, Queen + Adam Lambert was just a twinkle in Brian and Roger's eye, and the drummer wanted to get Queen's music out there as best as he could. And so he oversaw auditions featuring mostly American musicians ("It's a terrible generalization, I know, but they tend to have better technique," he later said), handpicking the finest musicians who applied: Nick Radcliffe, Tyler Warren, François-Olivier Doyon, Darren Reeves, Tristan Avakian, Yvan Pedneault, Jeff Scott Soto, Jennifer Espinoza, Brian Gresh, and Brandon Ethridge. One musician who caught his eye was Marc Martel, whose audition of a note-perfect rendition of 'Somebody To Love' made waves around the world, with many fans going as far to say as Martel should be the one fronting Queen, not a tribute band. "We were very lucky to find Marc Martel," Roger later said. "That voice. You listen, close your eyes and you think it's Freddie. It's really uncanny. But all the band are amazing. We have been very lucky."

"There are an awful lot of bands out there doing our old act," Roger later said. "An awful lot of fake moustaches and underwhelming performances. We just thought, 'Wouldn't it be great to have a tribute act that actually does Queen justice?'" The Queen Extravaganza did just that, performing a variety of songs that had long been absent, or even had never been performed live, from Queen's set list: 'The March Of The Black Queen', 'In The Lap Of The Gods', 'Bicycle Race', 'You Take My Breath Away', 'Don't Stop Me Now', 'Save Me', 'Stone Cold Crazy', 'Tenement Funster', 'Flick Of The Wrist', 'Lily Of The Valley', and, in 2015 and 2016, the entirety of *A Night At The Opera*.

Containing all the theatrics of Queen's live heyday, The Queen Extravaganza is a faithful reproduction of the band's abilities as live performers, with some truly outstanding performances that allowed older fans to relive their past while introducing new fans to the magic and wonder of Queen's music. Check them out if you haven't already – it's as close to the real thing as you could get, besides Queen + Adam Lambert.

F: BOHEMIAN RHAPSODY

The plan to get Freddie Mercury on the big screen had been in the works for quite a long time, with the wheels finally set in motion in 2010. At that time, Sacha Baron Cohen, known to the world as Ali G, Borat Sagdiyev, Brüno Gehard, and Admiral General Aladeen, was tapped to play Freddie, with Graham King, executive producer of *Ali*, as producer and Peter Morgan, screenwriter for *The Queen* and *Frost/Nixon*, writing the script. Production on the film finally went ahead in April 2011, though Brian expressed reservations about the way the direction the project would take; nothing more was heard about the film until July 2013, when Baron Cohen left production due to creative differences. The official reasoning was that the actor was "too well-known" as a prankster, and that his presence would be distracting, though Baron Cohen told Howard Stern in March 2016 that Brian and Roger weren't keen on touching on Freddie's more debaucherous side: "There are amazing stories about Freddie Mercury. The guy was wild. He was living an extreme lifestyle [of] debauchery. There are stories of little people with plates of cocaine on their heads walking around a party. It [becomes] a less interesting movie [without those stories], but you've got to remember that they want to protect their legacy as a band, and they want it to be about Queen. And I fully understand that ... [After] my first meeting, I should never have carried on because a member of the band – I won't say who – said, 'This is such a great movie, because such an amazing thing happens in the middle of the movie.' I go, 'What happens in the middle of the movie?' He goes, 'Freddie dies.' I go, 'So you mean it's a bit like *Pulp Fiction*' where the end is the middle and the middle is the end? That's interesting.' He goes, 'No no no.' So I said, 'Wait a minute. What happens in the second half of the movie?' And he said, 'Well, we see how the band carries on from strength to strength.' And I said, 'Listen, not one person is going to see a movie where the lead character dies from AIDS and then you carry on to see [what happens to the band]."

Brian and Roger have since denied this was the direction the back half of the film would take, but the damage had been done: while Baron Cohen remained on friendly terms with the two, the search continued for a replacement. Dexter Fletcher was now in as director, though he didn't last long, citing creative differences with King, while Baron Cohen's replacement, Ben Whishaw, withdrew in March 2015.

The film seemed to be spiraling into development hell, an industry term for a project that would remain in perpetual development, only to be quietly scrapped and forgotten. Finally, in November 2016, the stars aligned, with controversial director Bryan Singer (*The Usual Suspects*, *Apt Pupil*, and a trio of *X-Men* films) now serving as director, and *Mr. Robot* star Rami Malek cast as Freddie. The rest of the band was also cast: Ben Hardy as Roger, Gwilym Lee as Brian, Joseph Mazzello as John, Allen Leech as Paul Prenter, Lucy Boynton as Mary, Aaron McCusker as Jim Hutton, Aidan Gilllen as John Reid, and Tom Hollander as Jim Beach.

A shot of Malek from the day of Live Aid was revealed in the winter of 2017, at the same time that Singer was removed from the project as director. Speculation persisted on the true reasoning, with the party line being disagreements between Malek and a mystery absence, though Singer had been accused over previous years of sexual misconduct, and with the #MeToo movement rightfully gaining traction in Hollywood, his removal might have been as a result of that. Fletcher was once again reinstated as director within days, with filming finally wrapping up on 29 January 2018, with a release date of November 1, being pushed up from an initial Christmas Day release.

Questions persisted over how the music would be portrayed, with Malek revealing to *Entertainment Weekly*, "We're going to use Freddie as much as possible and use myself as much as posssible. I'm in Abbey Road right now, if that should say anything to you. I'm not working on my acting." Freddie's original voice, Malek's dubbing, and a soundalike performer will blend together to create what will be silver screen Freddie's vocals. Brian and Roger are serving as music producers, and Brian posted a photo on his website in early May 2018 featuring himself and former Smile vocalist/bassist Tim Staffell, as well as Nile Rodgers, leading fans to speculate what exactly is in the works.

The focus on the film will be a brief period between 1979 and 1985, with the climax culminating at Queen's grandstanding, legendary appearance at Live Aid, though Brian has insisted that the film will be as family-friendly and mainstream as possible – much at odds with Baron Cohen's original vision of an R-rated gritty biopic.

PART SEVEN

Post-Queen

This section covers live performances by John Deacon, Brian May, Freddie Mercury and Roger Taylor as solo artists, both during their tenure with Queen and following the dissolution of Queen. Also included in this section are the Freddie Mercury Tribute Concert from April 1992 and the successful Queen + Paul Rodgers venture, which began in December 2004. At the conclusion of this section is a list of guest performances in which various members of Queen took part over the years.

FREDDIE MERCURY

Despite Freddie's high-profile standing as a rock vocalist, he never considered his solo career to be more important than Queen, and it was because of his commitment to the band that he never undertook a solo tour. However, he did perform a handful of shows on his own: one with the Royal Ballet, one in the musical *Time* and two with Montserrat Caballé.

ROYAL BALLET PERFORMANCE
7 OCTOBER 1979

Repertoire: 'Crazy Little Thing Called Love', 'Bohemian Rhapsody'

Before Queen started their Crazy Tour in November 1979, the Royal Ballet asked Freddie if he would be interested in dancing a special piece for a charity performance in aid of the City of Westminster Society for Mentally Handicapped Children. Freddie's love of ballet was no secret; he had long been an admirer of The Royal Ballet and had attended many performances, befriending one of the principal dancers, Wayne Eagling.

Despite never having danced (except for his on stage antics, which were hardly practised steps), Freddie jumped at the opportunity and started rehearsals in late September 1979. (It's likely that Freddie's love of ballet inspired some of the choreography in 'Crazy Little Thing Called Love', filmed on 22 September.) Working closely with Wayne and another dancer, Derek Dane, the three arranged steps to accompany 'Bohemian Rhapsody' and the as-yet unreleased single 'Crazy Little Thing Called Love', which were to be played by the orchestra with Freddie providing live vocals.

On 7 October, two days after 'Crazy Little Thing Called Love' was released as a single, Freddie made his live debut as a dancer at the London Coliseum and, though he was initially nervous, he performed with skill and grace. Roger, who showed up for moral support, said of Freddie's first ballet performance, "I was more nervous than he was. I mean, I wouldn't do it. That's just not my scene. I'd like to see anyone else have the courage to do that, and carry it off as well as he did. He had a lot of balls to go on that stage. He loves all that stuff."

IBIZA 92 FESTIVAL
(WITH MONTSERRAT CABALLé)
29 MAY 1987

Repertoire: 'Barcelona'

When, in 1987, the island of Ibiza staged a massive festival at the Ku Klub to celebrate Spain's projected staging of the 1992 Olympics, Freddie was asked to be the guest of honor. What better way to celebrate than by performing his newly completed track, the aptly titled 'Barcelona'? Despite it being months away from release, Freddie and Montserrat mimed to the song in a performance that no doubt assisted the single into the Top Ten upon its release in October.

TIME (*THE MUSICAL*)
14 APRIL 1988

Repertoire: 'Born To Rock 'N' Roll', 'In My Defence', 'It's In Every One Of Us', 'Time'

The *Time* musical album featured vocal contributions from Freddie on both 'In My Defence' and the title track, though he had personally vowed not to appear on stage in a musical. Nevertheless, when he was asked to appear at a special charity show for AIDS awareness, he agreed and duly performed a rousing four-song set, with one item – 'It's In Every One Of Us' – a duet with Cliff Richard. He was in fine voice and, while rumors have circulated over the years about a soundboard recording, it was recently confirmed that both Cliff Richard and Dave Clark own the master tapes of the performance, and that Queen Productions hopes to release them on a definitive Freddie compilation.

LA NIT FESTIVAL
(*WITH MONTSERRAT CABALLé*)
8 OCTOBER 1988

Repertoire: 'Barcelona', 'The Golden Boy', 'How Can I Go On'

Freddie's final live performance was anything but. Miming to three of the standout *Barcelona* tracks with Montserrat Caballé, Freddie's appearance at the La Nit festival was nevertheless a visual and aural treat. Celebrating the start of the four-year Cultural Olympiad, the beginning of which signalled the arrival of the Olympic torch and flag in Barcelona, the festival was a great opportunity for Freddie to go to extremes; each chorus of 'Barcelona' was accompanied by water rockets and, at its conclusion, a massive fireworks display went off. It was also a chance to expose the Spanish audience to his *Barcelona* album, which was released two days later.

However, Freddie became agitated almost immediately when he realized that the tape was running fractionally slower than intended, though it was hardly noticeable to anyone else. Despite this, Freddie's final performance in front of an audience (with all proceeds going to the International Red Cross Association) was magical and spectacular; it was subsequently released in 2000 on *Freddie Mercury: The Video Collection*.

THE CROSS

Formed by Roger in 1987, The Cross performed three major tours in the UK and Europe between 1988 and 1991. No one who saw them imagined that The Cross were intended as the next Queen; instead, they were a hard-rocking club band without all the extravagance of a Queen show. Unfortunately, the band weren't able to hold onto a record contract and, once a potential fourth album was scrapped following Freddie's death in 1991, Roger disbanded The Cross (apart from a few one-offs following the Blue Rock tour) and instead focused on his solo career.

SHOVE IT UK AND GERMAN TOUR
19 FEBRUARY TO 24 APRIL 1988

Musicians: Roger Taylor (*vocals, rhythm guitar, drums, percussion*), Spike Edney (*keyboards, vocals*), Joshua J Macrae (*drums, vocals*), Clayton Moss (*guitars, vocals*), Peter Noone (*bass guitar, vocals*)

Repertoire: 'Love Lies Bleeding (She Was A Wicked, Wily Waitress)', 'Cowboys And Indians', 'Love On A Tightrope', 'Man On Fire', 'Heaven For Everyone', 'Feel The Force', 'I'm In Love With My Car', 'Laugh Or Cry', 'Manipulator', 'Let's Get Drunk', 'It's An Illusion', 'Contact', 'Shove It', 'Strange Frontier', 'Let's Get Crazy', 'Stand Up For Love', 'Rip It Up'

Itinerary:
February 19: University, Leeds
February 20: University, Glasgow
February 21: Polytechnic, Leicester
February 23: Polytechnic, Sheffield
February 24: Rock City, Nottingham
February 26: University, Manchester
February 27: University, Bradford
February 28: The Mayfair, Newcastle
March 1: Mayfair Suite, Southampton
March 2: University, Cardiff
March 4: UEA, Norwich
March 5: The Hummingbird, Birmingham
March 6: Polytechnic, Leeds
March 7: Bristol Studio, Bristol

March 9: Civic Hall, Guildford
March 10: Town & Country Club, London
April 10: Subway, Osnabrück, Germany
April 11: Modernes, Bremen, Germany
April 12: Markthalle, Hamburg, Germany
April 13: Metropol, Berlin, Germany
April 14: Theaterfabrik, Munich, Germany
April 16: E-Werk, Erlangen, Germany
April 17: Music Hall, Frankfurt, Germany
April 18: Capitol, Hannover, Germany
April 19: Club Music & Action, Esslingen, Germany
April 21: Tor 3, Düsseldorf, Germany
April 22: Capitol, Mannheim, Germany
April 23: Westfallenhalle II, Dortmund, Germany
April 24: Biskuithalle, Bonn, Germany

After the release of The Cross' *Shove It* and the resulting publicity push in the last few months of 1987, the band's first tour of the UK was planned for February 1988. With unknown band Ya Ya supporting them, The Cross started their tour on the 19th in Leeds, after considerable rehearsals during the first part of the month. The set list drew heavily from *Shove It* (only 'Rough Justice' wasn't performed live, though 'Feel The Force', released only on the US version of the album, was finally aired in the UK) with a new composition, 'Manipulator', also performed.

Perhaps most surprising was Roger's decision to include material from his first two solo albums, the first time any of those songs had been performed; 'Man On Fire', 'Let's Get Crazy' and 'It's An Illusion' were all seemingly designed for the live setting, while unexpected performances of 'Laugh Or Cry' and 'Strange Frontier' were most welcome. Only one Queen song, Roger's own 'I'm In Love With My Car' (which hadn't been performed live in seven years), made it into the set list, and a song titled 'Let's Get Drunk' was also included, and was sung by Peter Noone.

The tour was sparsely attended, due in no small part to Roger's insistence that the advertisements announce The Cross, with "featuring Roger Taylor" in smaller print, and not Roger Taylor and The Cross, which was what the promoters wanted. He got his way, but at a price: whereas most of the venues could hold up to 1000 people, the band would often be playing to one-fifth of that number. For the German dates in April, Roger finally relented and agreed to promoters' demands that Roger Taylor and The Cross would draw significant crowds, but the decision came too late; on the final date in Bonn, between 50 and 60 people

showed up to a venue that held 500. Despite this, The Cross' first tour was a boozy, unpretentious and enjoyable experience for both band and audience.

MONTREUX GOLDEN ROSE POP FESTIVAL
12 MAY 1988

Musicians: Roger Taylor *(vocals, rhythm guitar)*, Spike Edney *(keyboards, vocals)*, Joshua J Macrae *(drums, vocals)*, Clayton Moss *(guitars, vocals)*, Peter Noone *(bass guitar, vocals)*

Repertoire: 'Manipulator', 'Heaven For Everyone'

Though he had already started recording the new Queen album after the conclusion of The Cross' first tour, Roger had an obligation to fulfil in May 1988 at the Montreux Golden Rose Pop Festival. The Cross had agreed to appear but insisted they perform their set live; the acts that performed at the Pop Festival almost always mimed to a backing tape, making it easier for sound engineers and the crews. However, The Cross were adamant and, as Jim Beach was not only their co-manager but also involved in organizing the festival, the powers that be agreed to the request, albeit grudgingly. 'Manipulator', which had been heavily featured in the tour repertoire and was touted as The Cross' next single release, and 'Heaven For Everyone', which had been the band's previous single in April, were the chosen songs.

FAN CLUB PARTY
4 DECEMBER 1988

Musicians: Roger Taylor *(vocals, rhythm guitar)*, Joshua J Macrae *(drums, vocals)*, Clayton Moss *(guitars, vocals)*, Peter Noone *(bass guitar, vocals)*, Mike Moran *(keyboards)*, Brian May *(guitar on '(I Believe I'll) Dust My Broom', 'I'm In Love With My Car', 'Early Morning Blues', 'Whole Lotta Shakin' Goin' On', vocals on '(I Believe I'll) Dust My Broom' and 'Early Morning Blues')*, John Deacon *(bass guitar on '(I Believe I'll) Dust My Broom', 'I'm In Love With My Car', 'Early Morning Blues', 'Whole Lotta Shakin' Goin' On')*, Chris Thompson *(vocals on 'Whole Lotta Shakin' Goin' On')*

Repertoire: 'Love Lies Bleeding (She Was A Wicked, Wily Waitress)', 'Cowboys And Indians', 'Heaven For Everyone', 'It's An Illusion', 'Contact', 'Man On Fire', 'Strange Frontier', '(I Believe I'll) Dust My Broom', 'I'm

In Love With My Car', 'Early Morning Blues', 'Whole Lotta Shakin' Goin' On'

In 1988, the fans were in for a genuine surprise at the Official Queen Fan Club's Christmas party at London's Le Palais. After an abbreviated set by The Cross, Brian walked on as a special guest and started to play the intro chords of Robert Johnson's '(I Believe I'll) Dust My Broom' before stopping and saying, "OK, I guess we need a little more help. Ladies and gentlemen, Mr John Deacon." The now-expanded band went on to perform '(I Believe I'll) Dust My Broom', 'I'm In Love With My Car', 'Early Morning Blues' and 'Whole Lotta Shakin' Goin' On', with Chris Thompson singing lead vocals on the final number. Mike Moran substituted for Spike Edney, who was on tour with Duran Duran (featuring, incidentally, a different Roger Taylor).

MAD: BAD: AND DANGEROUS TO KNOW EUROPEAN TOUR
21 MAY TO 15 JUNE 1990

Musicians: Roger Taylor *(vocals, rhythm guitar, drums, percussion)*, Spike Edney *(keyboards, vocals)*, Joshua J Macrae *(drums, vocals)*, Clayton Moss *(guitars, vocals)*, Peter Noone *(bass guitar, vocals)*

Repertoire: 'In Charge Of My Heart', 'Top Of The World, Ma', 'Closer To You', 'Cowboys And Indians', 'Breakdown', 'Penetration Guru', 'Power To Love', 'Liar', 'Heaven For Everyone', 'Better Things', 'Man On Fire', 'Old Men (Lay Down)', 'Sister Blue', 'Strange Frontier', 'Foxy Lady', 'Final Destination', 'Shove It', 'I'm In Love With My Car', 'It's An Illusion', 'Passion For Trash'

Itinerary:
May 21: Capitol, Hannover, Germany
May 22: Biskuithalle, Bonn, Germany
May 23: Blickpunktstudios, Dortmund, Germany
May 24: Outpost, Göttingen, Germany
May 26: Docks, Hamburg, Germany
May 27: Max Music Hall, Kiel, Germany
May 28: Metropol, Berlin, Germany
May 29: De Melkweg, Amsterdam, Germany
May 30: Hugennottenhalle, Frankfurt, Germany
June 1: Ku Klub, Ibiza, Spain
June 2: Ku Klub, Ibiza, Spain
June 3: Westernhagen, St Wendel, Germany
June 4: Serenadenhof, Nürnberg, Germany
June 5: Akantz, Tuttlingen, Germany

June 6: Alte Feuerwache, Mannheim, Germany
June 7: PC 69, Bielefeld, Germany
June 8: Theaterhaus Wangen, Stuttgart, Germany
June 15: Donauinsel, Vienna, Austria

After the release of *Mad: Bad: And Dangerous To Know*, The Cross were in an unusual position: they had just released their sophomore album yet no one was interested. The single, 'Power To Love', made little impression on the charts, and the band's record company wasn't inclined to promote a tour without a hit record. Much to The Cross' relief, it was discovered that Germany had taken a liking to their recorded output, so a tour was booked for the spring of 1990.

The band varied their set list this time around, with all of the new album performed (though 'Passion For Trash' was played only occasionally) and a selection of previous hits scattered throughout: 'Man On Fire' was fast becoming a concert highlight, while 'Strange Frontier' and occasionally 'It's An Illusion' were also brought back from the previous tour, along with *Shove It* favorites 'Cowboys And Indians', 'Heaven For Everyone' and the title track. Of course, Roger's 'I'm In Love With My Car' remained in the set, promoted to concert closer this time.

The tour was a relatively short one, and when it concluded Roger was called back to Montreux to complete *Innuendo*; the other members of The Cross started writing material for a third album.

FAN CLUB PARTY
7 DECEMBER 1990

Musicians: Roger Taylor *(vocals, rhythm guitar, drums, percussion)*, Joshua J Macrae *(drums, vocals)*, Clayton Moss *(guitars, vocals)*, Peter Noone *(bass guitar, vocals)*, Mike Moran *(keyboards)*, Brian May *(guitar on 'I'm In Love With My Car', 'Let Me Out', 'Tie Your Mother Down', and 'Lucille', vocals on 'Let Me Out' and 'Tie Your Mother Down')*

Repertoire: 'Top Of The World, Ma', 'Love Lies Bleeding (She Was A Wicked, Wily Waitress)', 'Breakdown', 'Penetration Guru', 'Bad Attitude', 'Liar', 'Man On Fire', 'Sister Blue', 'Final Destination', 'Foxy Lady', 'I'm In Love With My Car', 'Let Me Out', 'Tie Your Mother Down', 'Lucille'

In 1990, in what was fast becoming a seasonal tradition, The Cross were asked to perform at another fan club party, this time at the Astoria Theatre in London. An abbreviated variation of their 1990 set, with 'Love Lies Bleeding (She Was A Wicked, Wily Waitress')' added, the show's four-song encore started with 'I'm In Love With My Car'. Again, Brian strolled out onto the stage to rapturous applause to help with Roger's 1975 composition. He then took the mic for his 1983 *Star Fleet Project* track, 'Let Me Out' (which hadn't been performed live before) and Queen's classic 'Tie Your Mother Down', which featured both Roger and Brian on vocals. The encore concluded with a rendition of Little Richard's 'Lucille'.

Mike Moran again guested on keyboards (Spike Edney was playing with Bob Geldof in Warsaw), and the concert was issued on cassette in early 1991 as *The Official Bootleg*, a release exclusive to fan club members.

BLUE ROCK EUROPEAN TOUR
3 TO 27 OCTOBER 1991

Musicians: Roger Taylor *(vocals, rhythm guitar, percussion)*, Spike Edney *(keyboards, vocals)*, Joshua J Macrae *(drums, vocals)*, Clayton Moss *(guitars, vocals)*, Peter Noone *(bass guitar, vocals)*

Repertoire: 'Bad Attitude', 'Millionaire', 'Ain't Put Nothing Down', 'New Dark Ages', 'Baby It's Alright', 'Dirty Mind', 'Man On Fire', 'Power To Love', 'Top Of The World, Ma', 'The Also Rans'

Itinerary:
October 3: Tavastia Club, Helsinki, Finland
October 5: Hagadal, Hultsfred, Sweden
October 7: Konserthuset, Gothenburg, Sweden
October 9: Music Hall, Hannover, Germany
October 10: Rock Heaven, Herford, Germany
October 11: Docks, Hamburg, Germany
October 12: Astoria, Bremen, Germany
October 13: Tempodrom, Berlin, Germany
October 14: Freiheitshalle, Hof, Germany
October 15: Circus Krone, Munich, Germany
October 16: Stadthalle, Memmingen, Germany
October 18: Volkshaus, Zürich, Switzerland
October 19: Schwarzwaldhalle, Appenweiher, Germany
October 20: Maintauberhalle, Wertheim, Germany
October 21: Stadthalle, Offenbach, Germany
October 22: Philipshalle, Düsseldorf, Germany
October 23: Stadthalle, Erlangen, Germany
October 25: Festhalle, Dietenheim, Germany
October 26: Sporthalle Birkelbach, Erntebrück, Germany

October 27: Forum, Ludwigsburg, Germany

The Cross' final tour was in support of Birmingham band Magnum, who were promoting their 1990 album, *Goodnight L.A.*, with a tour across Europe in the autumn of 1991. The set list for this tour was drastically changed, with the first six songs (and occasionally 'The Also Rans', which was performed after 'Power To Love' during some shows) drawn from The Cross' new album *Blue Rock*. The remaining three numbers were from Roger's *Strange Frontier* ('Man On Fire') and The Cross' previous album, *Mad: Bad: And Dangerous To Know* ('Power To Love' and 'Top Of The World, Ma'), and were the only three songs that survived from the 1990 tour.

Given Freddie's imminent death, Roger obviously had other things on his mind at this time; his performances throughout were subdued and he sounded exhausted and worn out. The performances were tight and to the point, but for a final full-scale tour were also something of an anticlimax.

GOSPORT FESTIVAL
30 JULY 1992

Musicians: Roger Taylor *(vocals, rhythm guitar, drums, percussion)*, Spike Edney *(keyboards, vocals)*, Joshua J Macrae *(drums, vocals)*, Clayton Moss *(guitars, vocals)*, Peter Noone *(bass guitar, vocals)*, Bob Geldof *(vocals on 'Honky Tonk Women')*

Repertoire: 'Top Of The World, Ma', 'Love Lies Bleeding (She Was A Wicked, Wily Waitress', 'Rock It (Prime Jive)' *(intro)* / 'Twist And Shout', 'Mr Tambourine Man', 'Power To Love', 'Ain't Put Nothing Down', 'New Dark Ages', 'Rock And Roll', 'I'm A Man', 'Summertime Blues', 'Honky Tonk Women', 'Money (That's What I Want)', 'Man On Fire', 'Revolution', 'Stand Up For Love', 'I'm In Love With My Car', 'These Are The Days Of Our Lives'

The Cross were asked to perform at the annual summer Gosport Festival and, with Roger still unsure about the future of the band, agreed. They delivered a blistering set, including songs by Roger, The Cross, and Queen (notably a gorgeous 'These Are The Days Of Our Lives', which served as the finale), together with covers of songs by Bob Dylan, The Everly Brothers, Led Zeppelin, Bo Diddley, Eddie Cochran, The Rolling Stones, Barret Strong and The Beatles. Bob Geldof came on for one song as guest vocalist.

CHRISTMAS SHOWS

21 AND 22 DECEMBER 1992

Musicians: Roger Taylor *(vocals, rhythm guitar, drums, percussion)*, Spike Edney *(keyboards, vocals)*, Joshua J Macrae *(drums, vocals)*, Clayton Moss *(guitars, vocals)*, Peter Noone *(bass guitar, vocals)*, Tim Staffell *(vocals and guitar on 'Earth' and 'If I Were A Carpenter', both nights)*, Brian May *(guitar on 'Earth' and 'If I Were A Carpenter', second night only, and guitar and vocals on 'Too Much Love Will Kill You' and 'Tie Your Mother Down')*, Roger Daltrey *(vocals on 'I Can't Explain', 'I'm A Man', 'Born On The Bayou' and 'Substitute')*

Repertoire, first night: 'In Charge Of My Heart', 'Top Of The World, Ma', 'Love Lies Bleeding (She Was A Wicked, Wily Waitress', 'Rock It (Prime Jive)' *(intro)* / 'Twist And Shout', 'Ain't Put Nothing Down', 'Power To Love', 'Mr Tambourine Man', 'New Dark Ages', 'Rock And Roll', 'Heaven For Everyone', 'Man On Fire', 'Stand Up For Love', 'Earth', 'If I Were A Carpenter', 'I Can't Explain', 'I'm A Man', 'Born On The Bayou', 'Substitute', 'Radio Ga Ga', 'Money (That's What I Want)', 'Happy Xmas (War Is Over)', 'These Are The Days Of Our Lives'

Repertoire, second night: 'In Charge Of My Heart', 'Top Of The World, Ma', 'Love Lies Bleeding (She Was A Wicked, Wily Waitress', 'Rock It (Prime Jive)' *(intro)* / 'Twist And Shout', 'Ain't Put Nothing Down', 'Power To Love', 'Mr Tambourine Man', 'New Dark Ages', 'Rock And Roll', 'Heaven For Everyone', 'Man On Fire', 'Earth', 'If I Were A Carpenter', 'Stand Up For Love', 'Too Much Love Will Kill You', 'Tie Your Mother Down', 'Money (That's What I Want)', 'Happy Xmas (War Is Over)', 'Radio Ga Ga', 'These Are The Days Of Our Lives'

Roger returned to the Marquee Club for the first time since 23 July 1973 to perform two Christmas parties with The Cross and a slew of special guests. The band ran through a lengthy set, identical to the one presented at the Gosport Festival that summer, with a few notable additions and omissions. 'In Charge Of My Heart' was back as the concert opener, and only 'Twist And Shout', 'Mr Tambourine Man', 'Rock And Roll', 'I'm A Man', and 'Money (That's What I Want)' survived as cover renditions. However, Roger Daltrey, lead vocalist of The Who, appeared on stage to sing vocals on his former band's singles 'I Can't Explain' and 'Substitute', Bo Diddley's 'I'm A Man' and Creedence Clearwater Revival's 'Born On The Bayou'.

Tim Staffell, who had been the vocalist and bassist of Smile many moons ago, made a guest appearance, performing Smile's only single, 'Earth', and an old live favorite, 'If I Were A Carpenter'.

Brian had been asked to perform on the second night, and it was only logical that he appeared with Tim and Roger, too; thus, the power trio of Smile was reunited (performing the same songs Tim and Roger had played on the first night). Both nights featured an emotional rendition of John Lennon's 'Happy Xmas (War Is Over)' before closing with 'Radio Ga Ga' and 'These Are The Days Of Our Lives'.

GOSPORT FESTIVAL

29 JULY 1993

Musicians: Roger Taylor *(vocals, rhythm guitar, drums, percussion)*, Spike Edney *(keyboards, vocals)*, Joshua J Macrae *(drums, vocals)*, Clayton Moss *(guitars, vocals)*, Peter Noone *(bass guitar, vocals)*

Repertoire: 'In Charge Of My Heart', 'Love Lies Bleeding (She Was A Wicked, Wily Waitress)', 'Ain't Put Nothing Down', 'A Kind Of Magic', 'Power To Love', 'Better Things', 'Hand Of Fools (Out Of Control)', 'Life Changes', 'Penetration Guru', 'All The Young Dudes', 'Cowboys And Indians', 'New Dark Ages', 'Sister Blue', 'Radio Ga Ga', 'We Will Rock You', 'Top Of The World, Ma', 'Kansas City', 'These Are The Days Of Our Lives', 'Final Destination'

The Cross performed their final concert with Roger Taylor on 29 July 1993 at the Gosport Festival. The set list was similar to the previous year's performances, with 'A Kind Of Magic' and a smattering of *Mad: Bad: And Dangerous To Know* and *Blue Rock* songs thrown in (including the live premieres of 'Hand Of Fools (Out Of Control)' and 'Life Changes'), together with Roger's first live rendition of 'We Will Rock You'. The concert concluded with 'These Are The Days Of Our Lives' and an emotional 'Final Destination', which, in hindsight, was an entirely appropriate finale. While the name The Cross would be used occasionally for subsequent performances, the band eventually morphed into the SAS Band (Spike's All-Star Band).

BRIAN MAY

As well as undertaking a curious US radio tour in support of *Innuendo,* in 1991 Brian was asked to organize the Expo '92 Guitar Festival in Seville, Spain. Taking place just before Freddie's death in November, the experience was therapeutic for Brian: he enjoyed it so much that he organized his own solo tour the following year, which many fans considered equivalent to seeing Queen. The Brian May Band featured a rotating cast of musicians, with the only original supporting members Spike Edney on keyboards and Neil Murray on bass guitar. Jamie Moses wouldn't join the band until February 1993 and, while Cozy Powell was always Brian's favorite drummer, his untimely death in April 1998 almost put an end to The Brian May Band. Regardless, Brian soldiered on with Eric Singer in Cozy's place, but it became clear that such lengthy jaunts around the world were becoming too much. To date, the final Brian May Band concert was in Brisbane on 28 November 1998, and it appears that Brian has no intention of reviving the band anytime soon.

INNUENDO RADIO TOUR
25 MARCH TO 10 JUNE 1991

Repertoire included: Guitar Solo, 'The Invisible Man', 'I Can't Live With You', 'Under Pressure', 'We Will Rock You', 'Tie Your Mother Down', 'Somebody To Love', 'Brighton Rock', 'Stone Cold Crazy', 'Killer Queen', 'Headlong', 'Crazy Little Thing Called Love'

Itinerary:
March 25: New York, New York
April 17: Los Angeles, California
May 28: Boston, Massachusetts
May 29: Philadelphia, Pennsylvania
May 31: Dallas, Texas
June 4: San Jose, California
June 10: Toronto, Ontario

In the absence of a live concert tour to support *Innuendo,* a radio tour was organized, but with a twist. Since Brian was the only one who was able to promote the new album (John was never one for promotional events; Roger was recording an album with The Cross; and an ailing Freddie was doing his best to stay out of the public eye), he would field questions from both the DJ and call-in listeners – inevitably, Brian was inundated with queries as to when Queen would

return to the live circuit in the States – and then perform new guitar tracks over Queen songs picked by the DJ. Amusingly, after the radio performances were taped, the 'new' versions with the overdubbed guitar solos would be released on bootlegs, claiming to be alternate takes from the original sessions.

BACK TO THE LIGHT SOUTH AMERICAN TOUR
1 TO 9 NOVEMBER 1992

Musicians: Brian May *(vocals, guitars),* Cozy Powell *(drums),* Neil Murray *(bass guitar),* Spike Edney *(piano, keyboards, vocals),* Mike Caswell *(guitars),* Maggie Ryder *(backing vocals),* Miriam Stockley *(backing vocals),* Chris Thompson *(backing vocals)*

Repertoire: 'The Dark', 'Tie Your Mother Down', 'Driven By You', 'Back To The Light', 'Love Token', 'Love Of My Life', 'Let Your Heart Rule Your Head', 'Too Much Love Will Kill You', 'Now I'm Here', Guitar Solo, 'Resurrection', 'Last Horizon', 'Hammer To Fall', 'Now I'm Here', 'Since You've Been Gone', 'Rollin' Over', 'Let Me Out'

Itinerary:
November 1: New York City Disco, Buenos Aires, Argentina
November 3: Pista Atletica, Santiago, Chile
November 5: Centenario Stadium, Montevideo, Uruguay
November 6: Velez Sarfield, Buenos Aires, Argentina
November 9: Imperator Club, Rio de Janiero, Brazil

The Brian May Band's only dates of 1992 were in South America, which Brian hadn't played since 1985, returning to Argentina and Brazil but playing Chile and Uruguay for the first time. The set list drew heavily from his new album: nine of the 12 songs were performed live, with Brian's rendition of The Small Faces' 1968 song 'Rollin' Over' (itself a raucous climax to *Back To The Light)* exclusive to these shows. After the taped intro of 'The Dark', the band launched into the one-two rock punch of 'Tie Your Mother Down' and 'Driven By You', followed by the first ballad of the night, 'Back To The Light'. (On subsequent tours, 'Tie Your Mother Down' and 'Back To The Light' would switch places.) There was a decent balance of rockers and ballads, drawn from both Brian's solo album and Queen's past. Of his former band's catalog, Brian performed only five select songs; the only non-May penned Queen tune was 'Love Of My Life', introduced on this tour as a song that "everybody in the world knows ... except for me."

Most surprising is not what was performed but what wasn't: 'We Will Rock You', itself a staple of Queen shows and most post-Queen shows from 1993 on, was absent for these five concerts, though Brian introduced the song for subsequent legs of the tour. Occasionally, 'Let Me Out' was performed – certainly not for the first time, though it was still a welcome addition – and a rollicking rendition of 'Since You've Been Gone' (originated by Rainbow, Cozy Powell's former band) was also inserted from time to time.

What's interesting about these five shows is that The Brian May Band was still in an embryonic phase. Instead of Jamie Moses on guitar, Mike Caswell deputized, while Maggie Ryder, Miriam Stockley and Chris Thompson all provided backing vocals. By the time the US leg started in February 1993, all four were out, with Moses on guitar and Cathy Porter and Shelley Preston on backing vocals.

BACK TO THE LIGHT NORTH AMERICAN TOUR, FIRST LEG
23 FEBRUARY TO 6 APRIL 1993

Musicians: Brian May *(vocals, guitars)*, Cozy Powell *(drums)*, Neil Murray *(bass guitar)*, Jamie Moses *(guitars, backing vocals)*, Spike Edney *(piano, keyboards, vocals)*, Cathy Porter *(backing vocals)*, Shelley Preston *(backing vocals)*

Repertoire as headline act: 'The Dark', 'Back To The Light', 'Driven By You', 'Tie Your Mother Down', 'Love Token', 'Love Of My Life', "39' *(intro)*, 'Let Your Heart Rule Your Head', 'Too Much Love Will Kill You', Keyboard Solo, 'Since You've Been Gone', 'Now I'm Here', 'Guitar Extravagance', 'Resurrection' / Drum Solo / 'Bohemian Rhapsody' *(reprise)* / 'Resurrection' *(reprise)*, 'Last Horizon', 'Hammer To Fall', 'Let Me Out'

Repertoire as support act: 'The Dark', 'Back To The Light', 'Driven By You', 'Hammer To Fall', 'Love Token', 'Too Much Love Will Kill You', 'Now I'm Here', 'Resurrection' / Drum Solo / 'Bohemian Rhapsody' *(reprise)* / 'Resurrection' *(reprise)*, 'We Will Rock You' *(slow/fast)*

Itinerary:
February 23: Erwin Center, Austin, Texas *(supporting)*
February 25: Jefferson Civic Center, Birmingham, Alabama *(supporting)*
February 28: Roxy Theater, Atlanta, Georgia *(headline)*
March 2: The Agora, Cleveland, Ohio *(headline)*
March 5: Hammerjacks, Baltimore, Maryland *(headline)*
March 6: Coliseum, New Haven, Connecticut *(supporting)*
March 8: Cumberland County Civic Center, Portland, Maine *(supporting)*
March 9: Civic Center, Hartford, Connecticut *(supporting)*
March 12: Copps Coliseum, Hamilton, Ontario *(supporting)*
March 14: Beacon Theater, New York, New York *(headline)*
March 16: Civic Center, Augusta, Maine *(supporting)*
March 17: Boston Gardens, Boston, Massachussetts *(supporting)*
March 20: Carver Hawkeye Arena, Iowa City, Iowa *(supporting)*
March 21: Fargo Dome, Fargo, North Dakota *(supporting)*
March 24: Winnipeg Arena, Winnipeg, Manitoba *(supporting)*
March 26: Saskatchewan Place, Saskatoon, Saskatchewan *(supporting)*
March 28: Northlands Coliseum, Edmonton, Alberta *(supporting)*
March 30: BC Stadium, Vancouver, British Columbia *(supporting)*
April 1: Coliseum, Portland, Oregon *(supporting)*
April 3: Arco Arena, Sacramento, California *(supporting)*
April 4: Lawlor Event Center, Reno, Nevada *(supporting)*
April 6: The Palace Theater, Los Angeles, California *(headline)*

Brian's first major headlining tour as a solo artist started in Austin, Texas on 23 February 1993, more than a decade after Queen's final US show. Not confident that he would be able to fill arenas and stadia on his name alone, Brian was drafted by Guns n'Roses to be their support act for many of the dates, a position he was more than happy to accept. The only downside was the lack of promotion given to the handful of shows in which Brian was the headline attraction, most of which were sparsely attended. The situation would be rectified (albeit too late) on his return in October;

in the meantime, on 5 April, Brian appeared on *The Tonight Show With Jay Leno*, giving a brief interview bookended by performances of a truncated (and somewhat wearied) 'Back To The Light' and a raucous 'Tie Your Mother Down', with Slash assisting on guitar.

The set list hadn't changed much since the South American shows, with Brian's headlining set remaining largely the same. His support set, however, was severely abbreviated, with only the essentials – six tracks from *Back To The Light* and three Queen tracks, including a slow/fast rendition of 'We Will Rock You', which hadn't been performed in that style since 1979 – making up the repertoire. These shows also established the format for future tours: solos by Jamie Moses, Spike Edney, Brian and Cozy Powell were all inserted into the set. The latter really came to the fore on 'Resurrection', performing a breathless solo that interpolated an anthemic rendition of the '1812 Overture' and concluded with the rock section of 'Bohemian Rhapsody', before leading back into 'Resurrection' for a stunning finale. No surprise, then, when things slowed down considerably after such a display with the more mellow 'Last Horizon'.

By the end of the tour, after performing in many unusual cities (Fargo, Iowa City and Saskatoon weren't strong territories for Queen even at the height of their US popularity), the band had constructed a tight set and were undoubtedly on fire. They then took six weeks off to prepare for their first European and UK tour.

BACK TO THE LIGHT EUROPEAN AND UK TOUR, FIRST LEG
22 MAY TO 13 JULY 1993

Musicians: Brian May *(vocals, guitars)*, Cozy Powell *(drums)*, Neil Murray *(bass guitar)*, Jamie Moses *(guitars, backing vocals)*, Spike Edney *(piano, keyboards, vocals)*, Cathy Porter *(backing vocals)*, Shelley Preston *(backing vocals)*

Repertoire as headline act: 'The Dark', 'Back To The Light', 'Driven By You', 'Tie Your Mother Down', 'Love Token', 'Headlong', 'Love Of My Life', "39' *(intro)*, 'Let Your Heart Rule Your Head', 'Too Much Love Will Kill You', Keyboard Solo, 'Since You've Been Gone', 'Now I'm Here', 'Guitar Extravagance', 'Resurrection' / Drum Solo / '1812 Overture' / 'Bohemian Rhapsody' *(reprise)* / 'Resurrection' *(reprise)*, 'Last Horizon', 'We Will Rock You' *(slow/fast)*, 'God (The Dream Is Over)', 'Hammer To Fall', 'Let Me Out'

Repertoire as support act: 'The Dark', 'Back To The Light', 'Driven By You', 'Tie Your Mother Down', 'Love Token', 'Headlong', 'Love Of My Life', "39' *(intro)*, 'Too Much Love Will Kill You', 'Since You've Been Gone', 'Now I'm Here', 'Guitar Extravagance', 'Resurrection' / Drum Solo / 'Bohemian Rhapsody' *(reprise)* / 'Resurrection' *(reprise)*, 'We Will Rock You' *(slow/fast)*

Itinerary:

May 22: Hayakron Park, Tel Aviv, Israel *(supporting)*
May 24: Olympic Stadium, Athens, Greece *(supporting)*
May 26: Inonu Stadium, Istanbul, Turkey *(supporting)*
May 29: Rock Am Ring, Cologne, Germany *(headline)*
May 30: Garedn Stadion, Hannover, Germany *(headline)*
May 31: Franke Stadion, Nuremberg, Germany *(headline)*
June 2: Le Grande Rex Theatre, Paris, France *(headline)*
June 4: Playhouse Theatre, Edinburgh, Scotland *(headline)*
June 5: Ice Rink, Whitley Bay *(headline)*
June 6: Barrowlands, Glasgow, Scotland *(headline)*
June 8: Apollo Theatre, Manchester *(headline)*
June 9: City Hall, Sheffield *(headline)*
June 11: Ice Rink, Cardiff, Wales *(headline)*
June 12: NEC, Birmingham *(headline)*
June 15: Brixton Academy, London *(headline)*
June 16: Hammersmith Apollo, London *(headline)*
June 19: International Centre, Bournemouth *(headline)*
June 21: Ahoy Sport Paleis, Rotterdam, Holland *(headline)*
June 22: Wildparkstadion, Frankfurt, Germany *(headline)*
June 25: Waldstadion, Frankfurt, Germany *(supporting)*
June 26: Olympiastadion, Munich, Germany *(headline)*
June 27: Kis Stadion, Budapest, Hungary *(headline)*
June 29/30: Stadio Bradioa, Modena, Italy *(supporting)*
July 5: Estadio Olympic, Barcelona, Spain *(supporting)*
July 6: Estadio Vicente Calderon, Madrid, Spain *(supporting)*
July 8: Zenith Carriere Soldly, Nancy, France *(supporting)*
July 9: La Halle Tony Garnier, Lyon, France *(supporting)*
July 11: Stadium Site, Werchter, Belgium *(supporting)*
July 13: Bercy, Paris, France *(supporting)*

For their first dates outside North and South America, The Brian May Band visited three countries that Queen had never been able to perform in: Israel, Greece and Turkey. The exotic locales were due to prior commitments with Guns n'Roses, with Brian also supporting them in Frankfurt on 25 June and for the final eight dates of the tour. After the three introductory concerts, Brian returned to a more conventional itinerary, with shows in Germany and France before moving on to Scotland and the UK for ten dates. Further shows in Holland, Germany, Hungary, Italy, Spain, France and Belgium rounded out the tour.

The set list continued to evolve, with 'Headlong' the first post-1986 Queen song to be performed, and an emotional restructuring of John Lennon's 1970 confessional, 'God (The Dream Is Over)', serving as the penultimate number of the set. 'Let Me Out' was the only rarity, and was scarcely performed anyway; sadly, this song wasn't captured on the night Brian decided to record and film the show. The resulting album, *Live At Brixton Academy*, was an almost complete set, with technical difficulties during 'Last Horizon' and the complete performance of 'God (The Dream Is Over)' omitted due to copyright issues.

After Brian's performance in Budapest, the band met up once again with Guns n'Roses to complete the predetermined itinerary, with the standard supporting set reinstated. Following the Paris show on 13 July (in which Brian joined Guns n'Roses for 'Knockin' On Heaven's Door'), The Brian May Band took a well-deserved break from the road for nearly two months.

WINTERTHURER FESTIVAL
12 SEPTEMBER 1993

Musicians: Brian May *(vocals, guitars)*, Cozy Powell *(drums)*, Neil Murray *(bass guitar)*, Jamie Moses *(guitars, backing vocals)*, Spike Edney *(piano, keyboards, vocals)*, Cathy Porter *(backing vocals)*, Shelley Preston *(backing vocals)*

Repertoire: 'The Dark', 'Back To The Light', 'Driven By You', 'Tie Your Mother Down', 'Love Token', 'Headlong', 'Love Of My Life', "39' *(intro)*, 'Let Your Heart Rule Your Head', 'Too Much Love Will Kill You', 'Since You've Been Gone', 'Now I'm Here', 'Resurrection' / Drum Solo / 'Bohemian Rhapsody' *(reprise)* / 'Resurrection' *(reprise)*, 'Last Horizon', 'We Will Rock You' *(slow/fast)*, 'God (The Dream Is Over)', 'Hammer To Fall'

When Brian was asked to appear at the Winterthurer Festival in Switzerland, held at the Steinberggasse in Winterthur, he agreed, despite the fact that the event was smack in the middle of a three-month break

from live appearances. Running through the standard headline set featured on the previous legs, the band turned in a typical performance before going back on break for the next few weeks.

BACK TO THE LIGHT NORTH AMERICAN TOUR, SECOND LEG
4 TO 18 OCTOBER 1993

Musicians: Brian May *(vocals, guitars)*, Cozy Powell *(drums)*, Neil Murray *(bass guitar)*, Jamie Moses *(guitars, backing vocals)*, Spike Edney *(piano, keyboards, vocals)*, Cathy Porter *(backing vocals)*, Shelley Preston *(backing vocals)*

Repertoire: 'The Dark', 'Back To The Light', 'Driven By You', 'Tie Your Mother Down', 'Love Token', 'Headlong', 'Love Of My Life', "39' *(intro)*, 'Let Your Heart Rule Your Head', 'Too Much Love Will Kill You', 'Since You've Been Gone', 'Now I'm Here', 'Resurrection' / Drum Solo / 'Bohemian Rhapsody' *(reprise)* / 'Resurrection' *(reprise)*, 'Last Horizon', 'We Will Rock You' *(slow/fast)*, 'God (The Dream Is Over)', 'Hammer To Fall'

Itinerary:
October 4: Metropolis, Montreal, Quebec
October 5: The Music Hall, Toronto, Ontario
October 7: Palace Theater, New Haven, Connecticut
October 8: The Strand, Providence, Rhode Island
October 10: The Vic Theater, Chicago, Illinois
October 12: Royal Oak Theater, Detroit, Michigan
October 13: Modjeska Theater, Milwaukee, Wisconsin
October 14: World Theater, Minneapolis, Minnesota
October 17: Majestic Theater, Dallas, Texas
October 18: Rockefellers West, Houston, Texas

Returning for a second North American leg, The Brian May Band performed a nine-date tour with a set list that remained static throughout, and this was little more than a warm-up before the Japanese, European and UK tours still to come in November and December. Tackling states and provinces that had been missed the first time round, this was the band's first full headlining US tour, and the reception did not live up to expectations. Except for a Chicago concert on 12 September 1998 to promote *Another World*, Brian would not return to the US for a major tour for nearly 13 years.

BACK TO THE LIGHT JAPANESE TOUR

4 TO 13 NOVEMBER 1993

Musicians: Brian May *(vocals, guitars)*, Cozy Powell *(drums)*, Neil Murray *(bass guitar)*, Jamie Moses *(guitars, backing vocals)*, Spike Edney *(piano, keyboards, vocals)*, Cathy Porter *(backing vocals)*, Shelley Preston *(backing vocals)*

Repertoire: 'The Dark', 'Back To The Light', 'Tie Your Mother Down', 'Love Token', 'Headlong', 'Love Of My Life', '39' *(intro)*, 'Let Your Heart Rule Your Head', 'Too Much Love Will Kill You', 'Since You've Been Gone', 'Now I'm Here', 'Resurrection' / Drum Solo / 'Bohemian Rhapsody' *(reprise)* / 'Resurrection' *(reprise)*, 'Teo Torriatte (Let Us Cling Together)', 'We Will Rock You' *(slow/fast)*, 'God (The Dream Is Over)', 'Hammer To Fall', 'Let Me Out', 'Driven By You'

Itinerary:
November 4/5: Kosei Nenkin Hall, Tokyo
November 7: Yubin Chokin Hall, Hiroshima
November 8: Kosei Nenkin Hall, Osaka
November 10: Denayoku Hall, Sendai
November 11: Kyoiku Bunka Kaikan, Kawasaki
November 13: NHK Hall, Tokyo Bay

The Brian May Band made their way to Japan in the first week of November 1993 to commence a seven-night, six-venue tour, the first time Brian had returned to the treasured country in eight years. If the reception on the previous leg had been lacklustre, Japan more than made up for it. The tour began in Tokyo, with the only change made to the set list the addition of 'Teo Torriatte (Let Us Cling Together)', though 'Driven By You' was dropped in Osaka, seemingly for good (Brian explained it was too difficult to sing). The only other major change was on the final night, when a lengthy, 11-minute version of 'Let Me Out' made its final appearance as the penultimate song in the set. The band left Japan on 14 November, returning home for a few days before beginning another lengthy leg that would wrap up the year nicely.

BACK TO THE LIGHT EUROPEAN AND UK TOUR, SECOND LEG

20 NOVEMBER TO 18 DECEMBER 1993

Musicians: Brian May *(vocals, guitars)*, Cozy Powell *(drums)*, Neil Murray *(bass guitar)*, Jamie Moses *(guitars,* backing vocals)*, Spike Edney *(piano, keyboards, vocals)*, Cathy Porter *(backing vocals)*, Shelley Preston *(backing vocals)*

Repertoire: 'The Dark', 'Back To The Light', 'Tie Your Mother Down', 'Love Token', 'Headlong', 'Love Of My Life', '39' *(intro)*, 'Let Your Heart Rule Your Head', 'Too Much Love Will Kill You', 'Since You've Been Gone', 'Now I'm Here', 'Resurrection' / Drum Solo / 'Bohemian Rhapsody' *(reprise)* / 'Resurrection' *(reprise)*, 'Last Horizon', 'We Will Rock You' *(slow/fast)*, 'God (The Dream Is Over)', 'Hammer To Fall', 'I Want To Hold Your Hand', 'Big Spender', 'Mustapha', 'Las Palabras De Amor (The Words Of Love)', 'We Are The Champions', 'Merry Christmas', 'Is This The World We Created...?', 'Chinese Torture'

Itinerary:
November 20: Terminal One, Munich, Germany
November 21: Jahrhunderthalle, Frankfurt, Germany
November 23: CCH1, Hamburg, Germany
November 24: Eissporthall, Halle, Germany
November 27: Huxley's Neue Welt, Berlin, Germany
November 29: Elysee Montmartre, Paris, France
November 30: Philipshalle, Düsseldorf, Germany
December 3: Royal Albert Hall, London
December 4: Royal Centre, Nottingham
December 5: Aston Villa Centre, Birmingham
December 7: Ulster Hall, Belfast, Northern Ireland
December 8: Point, Dublin, Eire
December 10: Royal Court, Liverpool
December 11: Pavilion, Plymouth
December 14: Zeleste, Barcelona, Spain
December 15: Aqualung, Madrid, Spain
December 17: Cascais Pavilion, Lisbon, Portugal
December 18: Boavista, Oporto, Portugal

The final leg of the lengthy Back To The Light tour started in Germany and continued through France, the UK, Ireland, Spain and Portugal, with support from Robby Valentine (for the first six dates), Nine Below Zero (the UK/Eire dates only), and – interestingly – Sweet Sister (the final European dates).

The set list remained similar to previous legs, with 'Driven By You' still out of the set, though the band threw in several surprises for the final dates. In Halle, perhaps to commemorate the second anniversary of Freddie's death, Brian performed a rousing rendition of 'Big Spender' as the encore, while the Paris show featured a French-language version of 'Too Much

Love Will Kill You'. 'Is This The World We Created...?' was performed as an intro to 'Love Of My Life' in Berlin, 'Chinese Torture' was inserted into the guitar solo in Düsseldorf, and The Beatles' 'I Want To Hold Your Hand' was (suitably) performed in Liverpool; 'Las Palabras De Amor (The Words Of Love)' was performed in Barcelona and Madrid, with the latter venue also featuring 'Mustapha'. Perhaps the most surprising addition was the vocal intro to 'We Are The Champions', sung by Cathy Porter, before 'Hammer To Fall' in Oporto, and 'Merry Christmas' was reportedly performed as the final song that night.

It had been a prosperous and rewarding year for Brian, though he was now ready for a lengthy break before heading into the studios to work on the final tracks recorded with Freddie in the winter and spring of 1991; consequently, Brian wouldn't go out on tour again for nearly five years.

ANOTHER WORLD PROMOTIONAL CONCERTS
MAY TO 12 SEPTEMBER 1998

Musicians: Brian May *(vocals, guitars)*, Neil Murray *(bass guitar)*, Jamie Moses *(guitars, backing vocals)*, Spike Edney *(piano, keyboards, vocals)*, Steve Ferrone *(drums)*, Suzi Webb *(backing vocals)*, Zoe Nicholas *(backing vocals)*

Repertoire, VH1 performance (May 1998): 'On My Way Up', 'Driven By You', 'Why Don't We Try Again', 'Only Make Believe', 'Tie Your Mother Down'

Repertoire, European performances: 'Only Make Believe', 'On My Way Up', 'Driven By You', 'Why Don't We Try Again', 'Tie Your Mother Down' *(slow)*, 'Let Your Heart Rule Your Head', 'Hammer To Fall' *(slow/fast)*

Repertoire, Chicago: 'Business', 'Since You've Been Gone', 'Fat Bottomed Girls' / 'Gimme The Prize (Kurgan's Theme)', 'I Want It All', 'Headlong', 'We Will Rock You', 'Tear It Up', 'Tie Your Mother Down', 'Chinese Torture' / 'China Belle', 'Hammer To Fall' *(slow/fast)*

Itinerary:
June 5: Big Mama Club, Rome, Italy
June 9: Le Reservoir, Paris, France
June 11: Virgin Megastore, Oxford Street, London
June 20: Gala Night, Monte Carlo, Monaco
September 12: New World Music Theater, Chicago, Illinois

Brian has stated that touring is his lifeblood, his reason for being a musician, so it came as no surprise that he was itching to get back on the road after the release of *Another World*. But, just prior to the commencement of rehearsals in April 1998, Cozy Powell, who had been a driving force on the new album, died in a car accident, forcing Brian to question going through with the tour.

Instead of launching into a full-scale itinerary, a series of promotional concerts was planned. A semi-acoustic set was filmed for VH1 Europe in May and broadcast on 16 June, while three European-only shows were performed. Both set lists featured a smattering of new (*Another World*), old (*Back To The Light*) and older (a selection of Brian's highlights from Queen's back catalog) songs, though the most revelatory inclusion was 'Hammer To Fall', performed in a slow, stripped-down fashion before erupting into the familiar full-throttle rock arrangement.

After the brief, four-date European promotional tour, Brian and band flew to Chicago to give their one and only North American concert. Evidently, this Chicago date was supposed to make up for the lack of a tour; up to 600 fans from around the country flew or drove in to see the concert, and Brian rewarded them with the most comprehensive repertoire thus far, premiering two new songs: 'Business' and 'China Belle'.

All the live performances prior to the start of the tour featured a new band: Neil Murray, Jamie Moses and Spike Edney were all retained from the previous line-up, while session drummer Steve Ferrone, who had played on 'Another World', deputized on drums. The backing vocalists had changed, reportedly because Cathy Porter and Shelley Preston were at loggerheads with each other. Vocal back-up came instead from Suzi Webb and Zoe Nicholas who, in their spare time, were in an ABBA tribute group called FABBA.

ANOTHER WORLD TOUR
15 SEPTEMBER TO 7 NOVEMBER 1998

Musicians: Brian May *(vocals, guitars)*, Neil Murray *(bass guitar)*, Jamie Moses *(guitars, backing vocals)*, Spike Edney *(piano, keyboards, vocals)*, Eric Singer *(drums)*, Suzi Webb *(backing vocals)*, Zoe Nicholas *(backing vocals)*

Repertoire: 'Dance With The Devil' *(taped intro)*, 'Only Make Believe' *(Brian as 'T E Conway')*, 'C'mon Babe' *(Brian as 'T E Conway')*, 'Space' *(taped intro)*, 'Since You've Been Gone', 'Business', Keyboard Solo, 'China

Belle', 'White Man' *(intro)* / 'Fat Bottomed Girls', 'I Want It All' / 'Headlong' / 'Tear It Up' / 'The Show Must Go On', Bass Solo, 'Last Horizon', 'Love Of My Life', 'Driven By You', 'On My Way Up', 'Hammer To Fall' *(slow/fast)*, Guitar Solo, 'Resurrection' / Drum Solo / 'Resurrection' *(reprise)*, 'We Will Rock You', 'Tie Your Mother Down', 'Another World', 'All The Way From Memphis', 'No-One But You (Only The Good Die Young)', 'Why Don't We Try Again', 'Otro Lugar', 'Sleeping On The Sidewalk', 'Dancing Queen', 'Hoochie Coochie Man', 'Let Your Heart Rule Your Head', 'Sail Away Sweet Sister', 'Slow Down', 'With A Little Help From My Friends', 'Mustapha' *(intro)*, 'Kalinka'

Itinerary:

September 15: Teatro Jovellanos, Gijon, Spain
September 17: Zeleste, Barcelona, Spain
September 18: Macumba, Madrid, Spain
September 20: Ancienne Belgique, Brussels, Belgium
September 22: La Cigall, Paris, France
September 23: Music Centre, Utrecht, Holland
September 24: E Halle, Groningen, Holland
September 28: Rockefella, Oslo, Norway
September 28: Circus, Stockholm, Sweden
September 30: Stodola, Warsaw, Poland
October 2: Columbiahalle, Berlin, Germany
October 3: Grosse Freiheit, Hamburg, Germany
October 5: E-Werk, Cologne, Germany
October 7: Beethovensaal, Stuttgart, Germany
October 8: Zirkus Krone, Munich, Germany
October 10: Rockhaus, Vienna, Austria
October 12: Petofi, Budapest, Hungary
October 13: Posthof, Linz, Austria
October 18: Rolling Stone, Milan, Italy
October 19: Volkshaus, Zurich, Switzerland
October 21: Capitol Theatre, Offenbach, Germany
October 22: Small Sportshall, Prague, Czech Republic
October 24: Royal Concert Hall, Nottingham
October 25: Royal Albert Hall, London
October 27: Colston Hall, Bristol
October 28: NIA Academy, Birmingham
October 30: City Hall, Newcastle
October 31: Apollo Theatre, Manchester
November 2: City Hall, Sheffield
November 3: Royal Concert Hall, Glasgow, Scotland
November 6: Oktiabrsky Hall, St Petersburg, Russia
November 7: MSA Luzhniki Arena, Moscow, Russia

The 1998 Another World tour saw many firsts for Brian. Not only did he employ a new backing band, including latterday KISS drummer Eric Singer, he also visited countries which he had never previously toured. Apart from the expected stops in Spain, Belgium, France, Holland, Austria, Switzerland and Germany (not to mention the UK), The Brian May Band made its live debut in Norway, Sweden, Poland, the Czech Republic and Russia.

The set list was shaken up considerably, with eight of the 12 songs from *Another World* performed (though only six with any regularity) and several Queen songs played. 'White Man' served as an introduction to 'Fat Bottomed Girls' (which also featured the guitar/'bagpipe' solo from 'Gimme The Prize (Kurgan's Theme)'), while 'I Want It All', 'Headlong' (previously played on the Back To The Light tour), 'Tear It Up' and 'The Show Must Go On' formed a mid-set medley. Of course, old standards like 'Love Of My Life', 'Hammer To Fall' (the restructured slow/fast version first premiered earlier in the year), 'We Will Rock You' and 'Tie Your Mother Down' were still present, while less frequent performances of 'Sleeping On The Sidewalk', 'Sail Away Sweet Sister' and – surprisingly – the vocal introduction of 'Mustapha' peppered an already diverse set list.

Concerts opened with a taped introduction of 'Dance With The Devil', chosen in memory of Cozy Powell, followed by an announcement that Brian would be late and that his cousin, T E Conway, would perform a short set. The T E moniker is a clever and light-hearted parody of Conway Twitty and originated from a December 1994 guest appearance with the SAS Band, where Brian performed rousing renditions of 'Only Make Believe' and a countrified 'Tie Your Mother Down'. As T E during the 1998 tour, he again reprised 'Only Make Believe', which then segued into 'C'mon Babe' (essentially an instrumental version of 'Slow Down'), allowing Brian to switch out of character and into 'Brian mode': he appeared bent over in the same position as on the *Another World* cover while 'Space' played over the PA. At that song's conclusion, Brian would address the crowd as the band launched into Rainbow's 'Since You've Been Gone', chosen as set opener as a tribute to Cozy.

The tour commenced on 15 September 1998 in Gijon, including a Spanish rendition of 'Another World', titled 'Otro Lugar', and 'Why Don't We Try Again'. 'Otro Lugar' would be performed on the other two Spanish gigs, while it would be translated into French for the Paris show on 22 September. While in Madrid, the audience was apparently desperate for 'Mustapha' to be played so, before the Queen medley, Brian sang the vocal introduction, which, predictably, went down a storm. 'Sleeping On The Sidewalk' was performed only twice on the tour – once in Groningen and again in Newcastle – while 'Dancing Queen' was given a rare one-off rendition in Stockholm, sung by backing vocalists Suzi Webb and Zoe Nicholas, whom Brian introduced under their professional name of FABBA.

Unfortunately, two shows had to be canceled – one in Grenoble on 15 October and another in Modena the following day – due to Brian coming down with the flu, affecting his voice considerably. The tour moved on to the United Kingdom for eight nights; the concert at the Royal Albert Hall, in which Brian returned to the venue for the first time in nearly 30 years, was recorded and filmed for a live album and video that never saw release. Surprisingly, 'Sail Away Sweet Sister' was introduced midway through the UK tours, with Brian explaining in Manchester that he'd "had a look on the website yesterday and this was the most-requested song there." The band also performed a rare version of 'Too Much Love Will Kill You' that night, which would only later be introduced in Australia.

A set of proposed South American dates never came to pass, but a couple of Russian ones did. The band arrived in St Petersburg on 5 November and performed a blistering set the following night. The tour then moved on to Moscow, where Brian introduced a traditional Russian folk song, 'Kalinka', into his guitar solo and also changed the words of 'All The Way From Memphis' to 'All The Way From Moscow'.

ANOTHER WORLD JAPANESE TOUR
10 TO 14 NOVEMBER 1998

Musicians: Brian May *(vocals, guitars)*, Neil Murray *(bass guitar)*, Jamie Moses *(guitars, backing vocals)*, Spike Edney *(piano, keyboards, vocals)*, Eric Singer *(drums)*, Suzi Webb *(backing vocals)*, Zoe Nicholas *(backing vocals)*

Repertoire: 'Dance With The Devil' *(taped intro)*, 'Only Make Believe' *(Brian as 'T E Conway')*, 'C'mon Babe' *(Brian as 'T E Conway')*, 'Space' *(taped intro)*, 'Since You've Been Gone', Keyboard Solo, 'China Belle', 'Sail Away Sweet Sister', 'White Man' *(intro)* / 'Fat Bottomed Girls', 'I Want It All' / 'Headlong' / 'Tear It Up' / 'The Show Must Go On', Bass Solo, 'Last Horizon', 'Love Of My Life', 'Driven By You', '39' / 'On My Way Up', 'Hammer To Fall' *(slow/fast)*, Guitar Solo, 'Resurrection' / Drum Solo / 'Resurrection' *(reprise)*, 'We Will Rock You', 'Tie Your Mother Down', 'Another World', 'All The Way From Memphis', 'Teo Torriatte (Let Us Cling Together)'

Itinerary:
November 10: Sun Plaza, Tokyo
November 11: Shibuya Kokaido, Tokyo
November 13: Bottom Line, Nagoya
November 14: IMP Hall, Osaka

The lengthy Another World tour wasn't yet over: though Brian had played 32 dates in 15 different countries, both Japan and Australia were still calling. First up was a trip to far-flung Tokyo on 10 November, where a slightly altered set list was introduced. 'Sail Away Sweet Sister' was now a permanent fixture, while "39' also served as an introduction to 'On My Way Up'. Not surprisingly, 'Teo Torriatte (Let Us Cling Together)' was also part of the set list, introduced as a second encore in lieu of 'No-One But You (Only The Good Die Young)'. The first night in Tokyo saw Nuno Bettencourt joining the band on stage for additional guitar on 'Tie Your Mother Down'. On the 15th, The Brian May Band flew to Perth to fulfil the last six dates of their tour in Australia, the first time Brian had been there since 1985.

ANOTHER WORLD AUSTRALIAN TOUR
20 TO 28 NOVEMBER 1998

Musicians: Brian May *(vocals, guitars)*, Neil Murray *(bass guitar)*, Jamie Moses *(guitars, backing vocals)*, Spike Edney *(piano, keyboards, vocals)*, Eric Singer *(drums)*, Suzi Webb *(backing vocals)*, Zoe Nicholas *(backing vocals)*

Repertoire: 'Dance With The Devil' *(taped intro)*, 'Only Make Believe' *(Brian as 'T E Conway')*, 'C'mon Babe' *(Brian as 'T E Conway')*, 'Space' *(taped intro)*, 'Since You've Been Gone', Keyboard Solo, 'China Belle', 'White Man' *(intro)* / 'Fat Bottomed Girls', 'I Want It All' / 'Headlong' / 'Tear It Up' / 'The Show Must Go On', Bass Solo, 'Last Horizon', 'Love Of My Life', 'Too Much Love Will Kill You', 'Driven By You', "39' / 'On My Way Up', 'Hammer To Fall' *(slow/fast)*, Guitar Solo / 'Waltzing Matilda', 'Resurrection' / Drum Solo / 'Resurrection' *(reprise)*, 'We Will Rock You', 'Tie Your Mother Down', 'Another World', 'All The Way From Memphis'

Itinerary:
November 20: Metropolis Concert, Perth
November 22: Heaven Nightclub, Adelaide
November 23: Palais Theatre, Melbourne
November 25: Capital Theatre, Sydney
November 26: Workers Club, Newcastle
November 28: Alexandra Hills Hotel, Brisbane

The six-date, six-city Australian tour started on 20 November, five days after the band had arrived in Perth; Brian was heard to forlornly mention at the soundcheck in Adelaide that he wasn't used to playing such small venues. His attitude changed for the better, however, and the tour was well received. Brian even incorporated 'Waltzing Matilda' (and, in Sydney, 'I Still Call Australia Home') into his guitar solo.

The set list remained generally the same, with the rare exception of 'Too Much Love Will Kill You' being performed during the acoustic set. The final number of the shows was either 'Another World' or 'All The Way From Memphis' – 'No-One But You (Only The Good Die Young)' was omitted from this leg – depending on the night. On 26 November, Suzi Webb received a warm birthday greeting from both band and audience, while her on-stage present was a birthday cake presented by two firemen in G-strings, undoubtedly reminding Brian of 'Fat Bottomed Girls' at Madison Square Garden back in 1978.

Brian's 1998 campaign finished in Brisbane on the 28th. Apart from several one-offs over the next few years, it eventually transpired that the Another World tour would be his final solo venture. He became enveloped instead in other projects, namely the *We Will Rock You* musical, the 46664 concerts and Queen + Paul Rodgers, leaving little time to focus on a solo career.

BRIAN MAY & KERRY ELLIS

Brian's appreciation for Kerry Ellis has been well-documented. Ever since she caught the guitarist's eye in a late 2001 performance of *My Fair Lady*, he has touted her consistently as the Next Big Thing, even telling *What's On Stage* in 2010, "From the moment I first heard [her] sing, I was entranced, and felt the conviction that I would one day make an album for her. That conviction never left me." *Anthems* was released in September 2010, and fulfilled a personal goal for Brian, even if it wasn't exactly a critical or commercial success. With his creative juices flowing once again – he wrote two songs specifically for the album, and later commented that 'Some Things That Glitter' from *The Cosmos Rocks* was written with her in mind – Brian agreed to embark on a tour with her, using his name to appeal to a wider audience.

ANTHEMS TOUR
1 MAY TO 16 JULY 2011

Musicians: Kerry Ellis (*vocals*), Brian May (*guitars, vocals*), Rufus Taylor (*drums*), Stuart Morley and Jeff Leach (*keyboards*), Jamie Humphries (*guitar*), Neil Fairclough (*bass guitar*), Kirstie Roberts and Niamh McNally (*backing vocals*)

Repertoire: 'Overture' / 'Dangerland', 'I'm Not That Girl', 'I Can't Be Your Friend', 'Diamonds Are Forever', 'Somebody To Love', 'Crazy Little Thing Called Love', 'Last Horizon', 'Love Of My Life', 'Some Things That Glitter', 'Save Me', 'No-One But You (Only The Good Die Young)', 'You Have To Be There', 'I Love It When You Call', 'Defying Gravity', 'We Will Rock You', 'We Are The Champions', 'Anthems', 'Tie Your Mother Down'

Itinerary:
May 1, Royal Albert Hall, London
May 3, Philharmonic Hall, Liverpool
May 5, The Sage, Gateshead
May 6, City Hall, Sheffield
May 8, Royal Centre, Nottingham
May 9, Symphony Hall, Birmingham
May 11, Festival Theatre, Edinburgh
May 12, Royal Concert Hall, Glasgow
May 14, St David's Hall, Cardiff
May 16, Bridgewater Hall, Manchester
May 18, Theatre, Milton Keynes
May 19, Pavilion, Southend Cliffs
May 21, Forum, Bath
June 1, Hampton Court Palace Festival, London
July 16, RAF Cranwell

The *Anthems* tour kicked off with a double charity performance (matinee and evening) at the Royal Albert Hall on 1 May 2011, with proceeds benefiting Leukemia & Lymphoma Research. From the start, this was meant to be a theatrical event instead of just a concert: Kerry made her appearance as part of a group of hooded monks, tearing off her robe dramatically for the 'Dangerland' opener. All of *Anthems* was performed, and Brian even took to the mic a few times to lead the audience through an acoustic rendition of 'Love Of My Life'. His perfunctory guitar solo was given a slight revamp, leading into 'Last Horizon', while Kerry performed 'No-One But You (Only The Good Die Young)' on her own. Unsurprisingly, 'We Will Rock You' and 'We Are The Champions' ended the set, while 'Anthem' and 'Defying Gravity' were encore performances. The charity concerts were well-received, and served as an auspicious start to the tour.

As the tour of the United Kingdom unfolded, the set became a little more adventurous, with 'Tie Your Mother Down' added as the final number and 'Crazy Little Thing Called Love' introduced in Glasgow. Brian was clearly having a ball, with Rufus Taylor serving as a fine substitute for his father and injecting a much-needed shot of energy. While Kerry's voice inevitably strayed toward the West End perfection musical singers are noted for, she also employed a fine rock voice on the Queen songs, prompting one critic to wax hyperbolic: "[She] quickly dispelled any doubts about her ability to step into Freddie Mercury's shoes." A bold statement, yes, and not one that all fans would agree with, but after the rough-hewn partnership with Paul Rodgers, Brian needed something more on familiar footing, and Kerry proved to be a most worthy muse.

THE BORN FREE UK TOUR
5 TO 19 NOVEMBER 2012

Musicians: Kerry Ellis *(vocals)*, Brian May *(guitars, vocals)*, Stuart Morley or Jeff Leach *(keyboards)*

Repertoire: 'Born Free', 'I Loved A Butterfly', 'I (Who Have Nothing)', 'Dust In The Wind', 'The Kissing Me Song', 'Somebody To Love', 'Nothing Really Has Changed', 'Life Is Real (Song For Lennon)', 'The Way We Were', 'Since You've Been Gone', ''39', 'Something', 'Love Of My Life', 'I'm Not That Girl', 'No-One But You (Only The Good Die Young)', 'Last Horizon', 'Tie Your Mother Down', 'I Can't Be Your Friend', 'Knockin' on Heaven's Door', 'We Will Rock You', 'We Are The

Champions', 'In the Bleak Midwinter', 'Born Free', 'Crazy Little Thing Called Love', 'Good Company', 'Cosi Celeste'

Itinerary:
5 November, The Apex, Bury St Edmunds
6 November, The Assembly Halls, Leamington Spa
7 November, Corby Cube, Corby
9 November, Assembly Hall Theatre, Tunbridge Wells
10 November, St Georges Church, Brighton
11 November, Union Chapel, London
12 November, Alban Arena, St Albans
15 November, The Hawth Theatre, Crawley
16 November, New Theatre Royal, Portsmouth
17 November, City Hall, Salisbury
19 November, Swan Theatre, High Wycombe

This brief tour was stripped back compared to the 2011 *Anthems* tour, featuring only Brian on guitar and Kerry on vocals, with keyboards provided by Stuart Morley or Jeff Leach, depending on the date. The entire tour was recorded, with the *Acoustic By Candlelight* album assembled from a handful of the shows. Stagelighting was provided by candlelight – hence the live album's name – and was mostly acoustically performed, though The Red Special made an appearance on 'In The Bleak Midwinter', while Brian dusted off 'Good Company' in Portsmouth, playing ukulele on the live debut of his *A Night At The Opera* deep cut. (This performance was reprised in High Wycombe on the final night of the tour.) Unusually, several songs that wouldn't normally have featured in an acoustic set list were performed, and with such a back catalog of more suitable songs, it's a shame that something like 'We Will Rock You' and 'Tie Your Mother Down' were featured.

THE BORN FREE UK/EUROPEAN TOUR
17 JUNE TO 21 JULY 2013

Musicians: Kerry Ellis *(vocals)*, Brian May *(guitars, vocals)*, Jeff Leach *(keyboards)*

Repertoire: 'I (Who Have Nothing)', 'I Loved A Butterfly', 'Dust In The Wind', 'Born Free', 'Somebody To Love', 'Tell Me What You See', 'Nothing Really Has Changed', 'Life Is Real (Song For Lennon)', 'The Way We Were', ''39', 'Something', 'I'm Not That Girl', 'If I Loved You', 'Last Horizon', 'Knockin' On Heaven's Door', 'Tie Your Mother Down', 'We Will Rock You', 'The Kissing Me

Song', 'No-One But You (Only The Good Die Young)', 'Crazy Little Thing Called Love', 'The Continuing Story Of Bungalow Bill', 'I Can't Be Your Friend', 'We Are The Champions', 'Love Of My Life', 'Can't Help Falling In Love', 'Fog On The Tyne', 'Cosi Celeste'

Itinerary:
17 June, St John's Evangelist Church, Oxford
18 June, Pavilion Theatre, Bournemouth
19 June, The Anvil, Basingstoke
21 June, The Royal And Derngate, Northampton
23 June, Philharmonic Hall, Liverpool
24 June, Town Hall, Birmingham
25 June, The Lowry, Manchester
26 June, The Sage Gateshead, Gateshead
28 June, Malvern Theatre, Malvern
29 June, Venue Cymru, Llandudno, Wales
30 June, Olympia Theatre, Dublin, Ireland
8 July, La Cigale, Paris, France
13 July, Piazza Matteotti, Sogliano al Rubicone, Italy
14 July, Teatro d'Annunzio, Pescara, Italy
15 July, Wörtherseebühne, Klagenfurt, Austria
16 July, Diga Nazario Sauro, Grado, Italy
17 July, Auditorium di Milano, Milan, Italy
19 July, Montreux Jazz Festival, Stravinski Auditorium, Montreux, Switzerland
21 July, Guitare en Scene Festival, Stade des Burgondes, Saint-Julien-en-Genevois, France

Essentially a continuation of the brief, 11-date Born Free tour from November 2012, Brian and Kerry were joined by Jeff Leach on keyboards once again for this stripped-back campaign, again adorned by candlelight as the only stagelight. The set began with a video introduction of 'Badger Swagger', the absolutely abhorrent 'Badger Badger Badger', and a piss-take on the political campaign video, called "Badger Boys (Vote For Brian May)". The set list was slightly updated, with The Beatles' 'Tell Me What You See' and 'The Continuing Story Of Bungalow Bill' added (the latter would be performed only on the first five dates), and 'If I Loved You' and 'The Kissing Me Song' performed for the first time, both of which would eventually be recorded and released in 2017 on *Golden Days*. In Pescara, Zucchero's daughter Irene Fornaciari joined Brian and Kerry on 'I (Who Have Nothing)', 'Cosi Celeste', and 'Crazy Little Thing Called Love', while the Montreux show was filmed and released on DVD and Blu-Ray the following year as *The Candlelight Concerts: Live At Montreux 2013*.

ACOUSTIC BY CANDLELIGHT UK/EUROPEAN TOUR
19 FEBRUARY TO 5 APRIL 2014

Musicians: Kerry Ellis *(vocals)*, Brian May *(guitars, vocals)*, Jeff Leach *(keyboards)*

Repertoire: 'I (Who Have Nothing)', 'I Loved A Butterfly', 'Dust In The Wind', 'Born Free', 'Somebody To Love', 'Tell Me What You See', 'Nothing Really Has Changed', 'The Way We Were', 'Something', 'So Sad (To Watch Good Love Go Bad)', ''39', 'The Kissing Me Song', 'I'm Not That Girl', 'If I Loved You', 'Last Horizon', 'Love Of My Life', 'Tie Your Mother Down', 'No-One But You (Only The Good Die Young)', 'We Will Rock You', 'Crazy Little Thing Called Love', 'Is This The World We Created...?', 'I Can't Be Your Friend', 'Life Is Real (Song For Lennon)', 'Scarborough Fair', 'Also Sprach Zarathustra', 'We Are The Champions'

Itinerary:
18 February, Gordon Craig Theatre, Stevenage
19 February, Opera House, Buxton
21 February, Scarborough Spa, Scarborough
22 February, Grantham Meres Leisure Centre, Grantham
23 February, Theatre Royal, Bath
25 February, Congress Theatre, Eastbourne
26 February, Cliffs Pavilion, Southend
16 March, Crocus City Hall, Moscow, Russia
18 March, The Arena Riga, Riga, Latvia
21 March, The Great Hall, Palace Of The Republic, Minsk, Belarus
5 April, St George's Square, Valletta, Malta

Nothing really has changed, indeed: the Acoustic By Candlelight tour continued into the first quarter of 2014 with a similar set list and a similar stage setting, adding only 'So Sad (To Watch Good Love Go Bad)' as a permanent fixture, though a handful of covers and originals were thrown in occasionally, the most welcome being 'Is This The World We Created...?'.

ONE VOICE EUROPEAN TOUR
21 FEBRUARY TO 16 MARCH 2016

Musicians: Kerry Ellis *(vocals)*, Brian May *(guitars, vocals)*, Jeff Leach *(keyboards)*

Repertoire: 'I (Who Have Nothing)', 'I Loved A Butterfly', 'Dust In The Wind', 'Born Free', 'Somebody To Love',

'Tell Me What You See', 'Nothing Really Has Changed', 'The Way We Were', 'Something', 'One Voice', 'Bye Bye Love', 'Life Is Real (Song For Lennon)', 'I'm Not That Girl', 'Last Horizon', 'Love Of My Life', "39', 'Roll With You', 'We Will Rock You', 'No-One But You (Only The Good Die Young)', 'Crazy Little Thing Called Love', 'Can't Help Falling In Love', 'Who Wants To Live Forever', 'Is This The World We Created...?', 'The Kissing Me Song', 'If I Loved You', 'Starman', 'Take It Easy', 'Amazing Grace', 'Tavaszi Szél Vizet Áraszt'

Itinerary:
21 February, Teatro Le Muse, Ancona, Italy
22 February, Gran Teatro Geox, Padova, Italy
24 February, Obihall, Firenze, Italy
25 February, Arcimboldi, Milan, Italy
27 February, Palabam, Mantova, Italy
28 February, Auditorium Parco della Musica, Rome, Italy
2 March, ICE Congress Centre, Krakow, Poland
3 March, Gong, Ostrava, Czech Republic
5 March, Congress Centre, Zlin, Czech Republic
6 March, Boby Centre, Brno, Czech Republic
8 March, Congress Centre, Prague, Czech Republic
9 March, Incheba Hall, Bratislava, Slovakia
11 March, Congress Centre, Budapest, Hungary
12 March, Congress Centre, Budapest, Hungary
14 March, Sala Palatului, Bucharest, Romania
16 March, National Palace Of Culture, Sofia, Bulgaria

This 16-date tour continued the tried-and-trusted formula established in 2012, with only a handful of additions ('One Voice', 'Bye Bye Love', 'Roll With You'), though the set became more adventurous periodically, with occasional performances of 'Can't Help Falling In Love', 'Who Wants To Live Forever', 'The Kissing Me Song', 'Is This The World We Created...?', and emotional readings of 'Starman', dedicated to David Bowie who had passed away on 11 January of cancer, and the Eagles' 'Take It Easy', dedicated to Glenn Frey, who died a week later. A Christmas tour of the UK was announced in July 2016, and was set to commence on 7 December in Dorking, but was unexpectedly canceled after Brian was battling a "persistent illness", which he seems to have recovered from as of this writing (2018).

ROGER TAYLOR

Although he was the first to issue a solo record and the first to branch out into live performances (with The Cross), Roger was, surprisingly, the last member of Queen to embark on a solo tour. Roger only performed two major, albeit brief, solo tours; it's likely that he had achieved all he needed to with The Cross in the late 1980s and early 1990s, and that he was happier with semi-retirement than being constantly on the road. Much like Brian, Roger ended his solo career once the Queen name started to make waves in the music industry again. His final concert was on 3 April 1999, though the creative rebirth of the Queen + Paul Rodgers union, which resulted in *The Cosmos Rock*, has inspired Roger to restart his solo career.

HAPPINESS? TOUR
28 JULY TO 29 JANUARY 1995

Musicians: Roger Taylor (*vocals, drums, percussion, guitar*), Stewart Bradley (*bass guitar*), Michael Crossley (*keyboards, vocals*), Jason Falloon (*guitars, vocals*), Joshua J Macrae (*drums*)

Repertoire: 'A Kind Of Magic', 'Touch The Sky', 'Everybody Hurts Sometime', 'Ride The Wild Wind', 'Tenement Funster', 'Man On Fire', "You Had To Be There", 'I Want To Break Free', 'Foreign Sand', 'Voodoo Chile', 'Soul (See You In Hull)', 'I'm In Love With My Car', 'Happiness?', 'The Key', 'Revelations', 'These Are The Days Of Our Lives', 'We Will Rock You', 'Radio Ga Ga', 'Nazis 1994', 'Old Friends', 'The Show Must Go On', 'Twist And Shout', 'A Hard Rain's A-Gonna Fall', 'Dear Mr Murdoch', 'Loneliness...'

Itinerary, 1994:
July 28: Walpole Park, Gosport Festival, Gosport
September 15: Shepherd's Bush Empire, London
September 26: Sun Plaza, Tokyo, Japan
September 28: Club Citta, Kawasaki, Japan
September 30: Kokusai Koryu Centre, Osaka, Japan

October 14: Presswerk, Cologne, Germany
October 24: City Square, Milan, Italy
November 19: Shepherd's Bush Empire, London
November 20: Junction, Cambridge
November 22: Rock City, Nottingham
November 23: Riverside, Newcastle
November 24: Irish Centre, Leeds
November 26: Royal Court, Liverpool
November 27: The Leadmill, Sheffield
November 29: The Garage, Glasgow
November 30: Bierkeller, Bristol
December 1: Forum Assago, Milan, Italy
December 2: City Hall, Truro
December 3: Manchester University, Manchester
December 4: Civic Hall, Wolverhampton
December 8: Europe 1 Studios, Paris, France *(afternoon & evening shows)*

Itinerary, 1995:
January 16: Hippodrome, Monfalcone, Italy
January 17: Palazetto, Schio, Italy
January 18: Teatro Verdi, Genova, Italy
January 20: Vidia, Cesena, Italy
January 21: Teatro Tenda, Firenze, Italy
January 22: Palladium, Rome, Italy
January 24: Teatro Nazionale, Valetta, Malta
January 25: Teatro Metropolitan, Palermo, Italy
January 26: Teatro Metropolitan, Catania, Italy
January 29: Havanna Club, Napoli, Italy

Roger's first proper solo tour coincided with the release of *Happiness?* in September 1994, with dates restricted to smaller venues around the UK, though the touring band also journeyed to Japan, Germany, Italy and France. The musicians Roger employed for the tour were all from the *Happiness?* album sessions except for newcomer Stewart Bradley on bass guitar; the shows were guaranteed to be tight yet raunchy, and no one walked away disappointed.

The set included several surprises, not least the fact that all but one of the 12 tracks from *Happiness?* were performed live. (Only 'Freedom Train' eluded the repertoire, though 'Dear Mr Murdoch' and 'Loneliness...' were performed infrequently.) Also, the Queen choices drew more from the band's latter period, the only 1970s songs being 'I'm In Love With My Car', 'We Will Rock You' and an exciting rendition of 'Tenement Funster', marking its debut in the live setting. 'Ride The Wild Wind' made its live bow during this tour and became a veritable tour de force, while

the only solo track not taken from the new album was 'Man On Fire'. There were covers aplenty as well, with Jimi Hendrix's 'Voodoo Chile' and The Isley Brothers' 'Twist And Shout' as mainstays, though less frequent renditions of Bob Dylan's 'A Hard Rain's A-Gonna Fall' were also included.

Joshua J Macrae was the regular drummer, with Roger preferring to stay front and center and focus on his singing (and occasional guitar playing on 'I'm In Love With My Car' and 'Happiness?'), though he did take to the drums for 'Ride The Wild Wind', 'Tenement Funster', "You Had To Be There", 'Revelations', 'We Will Rock You' and 'Nazis 1994'.

Following the UK leg, it was announced that Roger would continue the itinerary into January 1995 with a brief tour of Italy. With ten dates in ten cities, this was the most extensive Italian tour undertaken by any Queen member. Each show was well attended, and Roger and the band finished the tour in high spirits. It was a surprise, then, that he took nearly four years to go back on the road.

1998 CONCERTS
24 SEPTEMBER AND 14 OCTOBER 1998

Musicians: Roger Taylor *(vocals, drums, percussion, guitar)*, Steve Barnacle *(bass guitar)*, Michael Crossley *(keyboards, vocals)*, Mike Exelby *(guitars)*, Jason Falloon *(guitars, vocals)*, Keith Prior *(drums)*, Treana Morris *(vocals on 'Surrender')*, Jonathan Perkins *(vocals on 'Surrender' (October 14 only) and 'She's Rich')*, Bob Geldof *(vocals on 'Like A Rolling Stone')*

Cyberbarn gig (September 24): 'We Will Rock You', 'Pressure On', 'A Nation Of Haircuts', 'Believe In Yourself', 'People On Streets', 'No More Fun', 'Tonight', 'Surrender', 'These Are The Days Of Our Lives', 'Radio Ga Ga'

Shepherd's Bush Empire (October 14): 'We Will Rock You', 'Pressure On', 'A Nation Of Haircuts', 'Believe In Yourself', 'People On Streets', 'No More Fun', 'Tonight', 'Surrender', 'She's Rich', 'Like A Rolling Stone', 'London Town, C'mon Down', 'These Are The Days Of Our Lives', 'I'm In Love With My Car', 'Tenement Funster', 'Strange Frontier', 'A Kind Of Magic', 'Radio Ga Ga'

Initially, Roger only planned two concerts to promote *Electric Fire*, his fourth solo album. The first was on 24 September 1998 and was by far his most memorable.

With hopes of broadcasting live on the Internet to all corners of the world – "We wanted to make this concert accessible to people throughout the world, not just to people with access to major cities," Roger explained in a press release – the concert was broadcast from his Surrey studio (or Cyberbarn, as it was dubbed for the occasion) with a small audience. Having set a world record that year for the largest exclusive online concert (595,000 views overall), the video was later edited by DoRo and released as *Live At The Cyberbarn*.

The second promotional concert was on 14 October at the Shepherd's Bush Empire. Treana Morris was the support act, performing, among others, a version of The Beatles' 'Ticket To Ride' and Queen's own 'Sleeping On The Sidewalk'. However, Roger had a host of guests stop by. Jonathan Perkins, who had provided vocals on the album version of 'Surrender', reprised his role on that song, singing co-lead with Treana (Roger stood patiently in the wings until the song was over), and then provided a number of his own entitled 'She's Rich'. Bob Geldof also made a surprise appearance, performing a thundering rendition of Bob Dylan's 'Like A Rolling Stone'.

Roger premiered eight new songs during these two concerts (seven were performed at both, with 'London Town, C'mon Down' debuted at Shepherd's Bush only) and introduced a new set list, very different from his previous one. The only question remained was, would he tour or not?

ELECTRIC FIRE UK TOUR
15 MARCH TO 3 APRIL 1999

Musicians: Roger Taylor (*vocals, drums, percussion*), Steve Barnacle (*bass guitar*), Michael Crossley (*keyboards, vocals*), Mike Exelby (*guitars*), Jason Falloon (*guitars, vocals*), Keith Prior (*drums*), Treana Morris (*vocals on 'Surrender' and 'Under Pressure'*)

Repertoire: 'Interlude In Constantinople' (*intro*), 'We Will Rock You', 'Pressure On', 'A Nation Of Haircuts', 'Believe In Yourself', 'I Want To Break Free', 'No More Fun', 'Tonight', 'A Kind Of Magic', 'Surrender', 'These Are The Days Of Our Lives', 'Under Pressure', 'London Town, C'mon Down', 'I'm In Love With My Car', 'Tenement Funster', 'Strange Frontier', 'Happiness?', 'Radio Ga Ga', 'People On Streets', 'Rock And Roll'

Itinerary:
March 15: Guildhall, Gloucester

March 16: Coal Exchange, Cardiff
March 18: Truro Hall, Cornwall
March 19: The Stage, Stoke
March 20: Manchester University, Manchester
March 21: Leadmill, Sheffield
March 23: The Garage, Glasgow
March 24: Liquid Rooms, Edinburgh
March 25: Riverside, Newcastle
March 27: Liverpool L2, Liverpool
March 28: The Junction, Cambridge
March 29: The Waterfront, Norwich
March 30: Wulfrun Hall, Wolverhampton
March 31: Rock City, Nottingham
April 2: Pyramid Centre, Portsmouth
April 3: Astoria Theatre, London

Roger had given no indication that he would tour *Electric Fire* – even Jacky Smith, a constant source of information, was left in the dark. The perfect time to have made such an announcement would have been when he appeared on *TFI Friday* on 9 October 1998, but no such topic was brought up. Nothing more was heard until the new year, when it was announced that Roger was working on a remix of 'Surrender', to be released as a single in March, and – almost as an afterthought – that he would be performing a short UK tour.

The tour itself was an extension of the two promotional concerts Roger gave in 1998, with eight new songs and a smattering of latterday Queen hits ('I Want To Break Free', 'A Kind Of Magic', 'These Are The Days Of Our Lives', 'Under Pressure' and 'Radio Ga Ga'), though the most surprising inclusions were 'Strange Frontier', last performed with The Cross in 1990, and 'Interlude In Constantinople', used as a suitably atmospheric taped introduction to each concert. The only song in the set list that came from *Happiness?* was the title track, an encore performance again before 'Radio Ga Ga' concluded the show.

Dubbed The Free Radicals, the band differed only slightly from the 1994-95 personnel: Jason Falloon and Michael Crossley were still on hand, while Steve Barnacle, Mike Exelby and Keith Prior were recruited on bass, guitars and drums respectively. The most exciting addition was Treana Morris, who had made her debut on *Electric Fire*'s standout track, 'Surrender', and would later join The Wire Daisies. She would duet superbly with Roger on 'Under Pressure' and 'Surrender' as well as providing backing vocals throughout. As on the previous tour, Roger stood front and center occasionally slapping a tambourine (during 'I Want To Break Free', 'A Kind Of Magic' and 'Surrender'), though he played no guitar on this tour. His drumming was also minimal, confined to the introduction and finale of 'We Will Rock You', the intros of 'Pressure On' and 'Under Pressure', and the solo and conclusion of 'London Town, C'mon Down'.

The most striking concert by far was Wolverhampton, where various band members had intimated to fans before the show that it would "definitely be memorable." It was certainly that: Brian May strolled on stage just before 'Under Pressure', which had been moved back as an encore number, staying through 'Rock And Roll' and concluding with 'Radio Ga Ga'. After this, Roger's last ever date as a solo artist was on 3 April 1999 at the Astoria Theatre in London, where he performed to 2000 people, perhaps the largest audience of the tour.

OTHER EVENTS

A CONCERT FOR LIFE: FREDDIE MERCURY TRIBUTE CONCERT FOR AIDS AWARENESS

20 APRIL 1992

Musicians, second part only: John Deacon *(bass guitar)*, Brian May *(guitar, vocals, lead vocal and keyboards on 'Too Much Love Will Kill You', acoustic guitar on 'Thank You', 'Crazy Little Thing Called Love', and "39")*, Roger Taylor *(drums, vocals, bass drum and tambourine on "39")*, Spike Edney *(keyboards, vocals)*, Slash *(guitar on 'Tie Your Mother Down')*, Tony Iommi *(guitar)*, Mike Moran *(keyboards on 'Somebody To Love')*, Joshua J Macrae *(percussion on 'These Are The Days Of Our Lives')*, Maggie Ryder, Miriam Stockley, Chris Thompson and Peter Straker *(backing vocals)*, The London Community Gospel Choir *(chorus vocals on 'Somebody To Love')*, Mick Ronson *(guitar on 'All The Young Dudes')*

Repertoire, first part: Metallica: 'Enter Sandman', 'Sad But True', 'Nothing Else Matters'; Extreme: Queen Medley ('Bohemian Rhapsody' / 'Keep Yourself Alive' / 'I Want To Break Free' / 'Fat Bottomed Girls' / 'Bicycle Race' / 'Another One Bites The Dust' / 'We Will Rock You' / 'Stone Cold Crazy' / 'Radio Ga Ga' / 'Bohemian Rhapsody'), 'Love Of My Life', 'More Than Words'; Def Leppard: 'Animal', 'Let's Get Rocked', 'Now I'm Here' *(with Brian)*; Bob Geldof: 'Too Late God'; Spinal Tap: 'Majesties Of Rock'; U2 (via satellite): 'Till The End Of The World'; Guns n'Roses: 'Paradise City', 'Knockin' On Heaven's Door'; Mango Groove: 'Special Star'.

Repertoire, 2nd part: 'Tie Your Mother Down' *(vocals: Joe Elliot)*, 'Pinball Wizard' *(intro)*, 'I Want It All' *(vocals: Roger Daltrey)*, 'Las Palabras De Amor (The Words Of Love)' *(vocals: Zucchero)*, 'Hammer To Fall' *(vocals: Gary Cherone)*, 'Stone Cold Crazy' *(vocals: James Hetfield)*, 'Innuendo' *(vocals: Robert Plant)*, 'Thank You' *(intro)* *(vocals: Robert Plant)*, 'Crazy Little Thing Called Love' *(vocals: Robert Plant)*, 'Too Much Love Will Kill You', 'Radio Ga Ga' *(vocals: Paul Young)*, 'Who Wants To Live Forever' *(vocals: Seal)*, 'I Want To Break Free' *(vocals: Lisa Stansfield)*, 'Under Pressure' *(vocals: David Bowie and Annie Lennox)*, 'All The Young Dudes' *(vocals: Ian Hunter)*, '"Heroes"' *(vocals: David Bowie)*, "39" *(vocals: George Michael)*, 'These Are The Days Of Our Lives' *(vocals: George Michael and Lisa Stansfield)*, 'Somebody To Love' *(vocals: George Michael)*, 'Bohemian Rhapsody' *(vocals: Elton John and Axl Rose)*, 'The Show Must Go On' *(vocals: Elton John)*, 'We Will Rock You' *(vocals: Axl Rose)*, 'We Are The Champions' *(vocals: Liza Minnelli)*, 'God Save The Queen'

The day after Freddie Mercury lost his battle against AIDS, Roger Taylor, Brian May and John Deacon held a meeting with Jim Beach to discuss plans for a tribute event. Many ideas were suggested, though nothing concrete was decided at the time; there were other matters to attend to first. The week after Freddie's death, a visibly distraught Roger and Brian appeared on ITV's *TV-AM* to talk about their friend's brave fight. "We are thinking of doing something next year, some kind of event in his name, that will be positive and raise a lot of money [for AIDS]," Roger said.

In February 1992, Roger and Brian attended a ceremony at the Hammersmith Odeon to accept a British Music Industry Rock and Pop Award ('Brit' Award) for 'These Are The Days Of Our Lives', voted the best single of 1991. Both gave short speeches, with Brian speaking warmly of Freddie and Roger then mentioning there would be "a concert that would be a tribute to Freddie's life at Wembley Stadium on April the 20th." Shortly afterwards, offers to take part came in from many of rock's finest vocalists – from Roger Daltrey, Joe Elliot, Robert Plant, David Bowie and Elton John to Seal, George Michael, Gary Cherone and James Hetfield. Also touted were Madonna and Eric Clapton, though both had prior obligations and were unable to attend.

Rehearsals for the show began in the middle of March in Shepherd's Bush, with Brian, Roger and eventually John deciding which songs to perform themselves and which to delegate to others. (The bassist, who had been hit the hardest by Freddie's death, was hesitant to partake at first, and Neil Murray deputized on bass for a good portion of the rehearsals in case John decided against performing.) In addition to the guest vocalists, the band was augmented for the occasion by Spike Edney on keyboards, Tony Iommi on guitar, and a handful of backing vocalists. The rehearsals moved to Bray Studios in April, amid fears that the poor weather would cause the event to be canceled. Thankfully, the weather cleared up and the show went ahead as planned.

On 20 April, Brian, Roger and John strode out onto the stage of Wembley Stadium to a deafening roar from the audience. "We are here today to celebrate the life and work and dreams of one Freddie Mercury," announced Brian. "We're gonna give him the biggest send-off in history!" The first half of the show was devoted to other artists performing their own hits. Highlights included a Queen medley from Extreme, Brian joining Def Leppard on 'Now I'm Here', spoof metal band Spinal Tap (Christopher Guest, Harry Shearer, and Michael McKean) performing 'Majesties Of Rock' and paring their set from 25 songs to one ("Because Freddie would have wanted it that way"), Bob Geldof performing a song he announced as having been co-written with Freddie ('Too Late God'), and a concluding speech about safe sex from Elizabeth Taylor.

Video footage of Freddie performing the intro to 'Somebody To Love' from Milton Keynes in 1982 linked the two halves, and after he bellowed "Are you ready, brothers and sisters?!" the opening strains of 'Tie Your Mother Down' echoed through the stadium as Brian, Roger and John – plus supporting musicians – provided a lengthy intro to one of the band's best-loved songs. The intro was apparently unintentional; Joe Elliot, who was providing lead vocals, was delayed in making the stage, forcing Brian to sing the first verse. Roger Daltrey then performed 'I Want It All', Zucchero followed with the first ever live airing of 'Las Palabras De Amor (The Words Of Love)', Gary Cherone

hammed things up for 'Hammer To Fall' and James Hetfield came out to sing 'Stone Cold Crazy'; the last two were perhaps the weakest performances thus far. Robert Plant had the opportunity to redeem things with the mighty 'Innuendo' but botched the lyrics terribly; thankfully, his take on 'Crazy Little Thing Called Love' went far better, with a brief snatch of Led Zeppelin's 1969 track 'Thank You' as an introduction.

Brian then came out front for a highly emotional reading of 'Too Much Love Will Kill You', soon to be released as the first single from his debut solo album, and Paul Young's 'Radio Ga Ga' vied with Seal's 'Who Wants To Live Forever' as the weakest performances alongside the aforementioned Cherone and Hetfield renditions. Lisa Stansfield performed 'I Want To Break Free', David Bowie duetted with Annie Lennox on a moving rendition of 'Under Pressure', then introduced former Mott the Hoople vocalist Ian Hunter and former Bowie alumnus Mick Ronson for a glam reunion on 'All The Young Dudes'. The song, complete with inaudible saxophone from Bowie and camped-up vocals from Hunter, was an obvious highlight but paled in comparison to the following number, an anthemic rendition of Bowie's 1977 '"Heroes"' which must remain the song's definitive live performance. The song was cut short when Bowie dropped to one knee to awkwardly deliver the Lord's Prayer, which caught everyone off guard – especially the ever-diplomatic Brian, who remarked, "I remember thinking it would have been nice if he'd warned me about that."

After this, George Michael's '39' marked the song's first live performance since 1979, while his gorgeous duet with Lisa Stansfield on 'These Are The Days Of Our Lives' was followed by a soulful solo rendition of 'Somebody To Love' – easily the highlight of the night. (Michael's performance was so strong it started rumors that Brian, Roger, and John would perform with him as Queen.) Elton John then croaked his way through 'Bohemian Rhapsody' (with Axl Rose joining in for the rock section) and 'The Show Must Go On', which Elton introduced as his personal favorite from *Innuendo*, a fact reinforced by the song's inclusion in his 1992 solo set. Axl then came back for 'We Will Rock You' and Liza Minelli offered a camped-up reading of 'We Are The Champions' that Freddie would have loved.

All in all, the concert raised £12 million for the Terence Higgins Trust. Some fans criticized the Live Aid-derived 'global jukebox' style of the event; most would have preferred a more intimate tribute with Freddie's vocalist friends, like Billy Squier or Montserrat Caballé, performing the songs. More suitable tributes would be performed later, but the Concert for Life remains unrivaled for its combination of sincerity and a star-studded line-up.

BÉJART BALLET LAUSANNE
17 JANUARY 1997

Musicians: John Deacon *(bass guitar)*, Brian May *(guitar, vocals)*, Roger Taylor *(drums, vocals)*, Elton John *(vocals)*, Spike Edney *(keyboards)*

Repertoire: 'The Show Must Go On'

1997 saw the Paris premiere of a ballet, directed and choreographed by Maurice Béjart, by the name of *Le Presbytère n'a rien perdu de son charme ni le jardin de son éclat* – 'The presbytery lost nothing of its charm nor the garden its gleam', a line from Gaston Leroux's *The Haunted Armchair*.

The ballet was inspired by the life of Freddie Mercury and the music of Queen; the full repertoire comprised 'It's A Beautiful Day', 'Time', 'Let Me Live', 'Brighton Rock', 'Heaven For Everyone', 'I Was Born To Love You', *'Cosi fan tutte'*, 'A Kind Of Magic', *'Thamos'*, 'Get Down, Make Love', *'Concerto pour piano'*, 'Seaside Rendezvous', 'You Take My Breath Away', *'Musique funèbre maçonnique'*, 'Radio Ga Ga', 'A Winter's Tale', 'Interlude', 'The Millionaire Waltz', 'Love Of My Life', 'Brighton Rock', 'Bohemian Rhapsody', 'I Want To Break Free' and 'It's A Beautiful Day (reprise)'. It was also a powerful work about AIDS, not only as a tribute to Freddie but to Béjart's former principal dancer Jorge Donn, who had died of the disease almost a year after Freddie.

In hindsight, it seems obvious that a Queen performance would be forthcoming, but it was certainly a surprise at the time. In the press release, it was revealed that Brian, Roger and John would close the show with 'The Show Must Go On', Elton John providing lead vocals. It would become the final time that John appeared in public with Brian and Roger; though the performance inspired Brian to write 'No-One But You (Only The Good Die Young)', which featured John on bass, John himself decided that Queen without Freddie wasn't a possibility and therefore retired from the music industry for good.

The performance was a definite show-stopper, an emotional reading of Freddie's swan song that was later included on both *Greatest Hits III* and *Greatest Flix III*.

HALL OF FAME INDUCTION
11 NOVEMBER 2004

Musicians: Brian May *(guitar)*, Roger Taylor *(drums)*, Paul Rodgers *(vocals)*, Spike Edney *(keyboards)*, Jamie Moses *(guitar)*, Pino Palladino *(bass guitar)*, Treana Morris *(backing vocals)*, Polyphonic Spree *(backing vocals, 'All Right Now')*

Repertoire: 'We Will Rock You', 'We Are The Champions', 'All Right Now'

This was the event that initiated the Queen + Paul Rodgers tour. Queen were being inducted into the UK Hall Of Fame and were asked to close the event in person. Not feeling up to the task of singing vocals, Brian and Roger asked Paul Rodgers to help them out (as a token of their appreciation, they agreed to perform one of Paul's songs); he did so dutifully, despite messing up a few of the words on both 'We Will Rock You' and 'We Are The Champions'. The assembled band blazed through these and Paul's own 'All Right Now', and the vibe afterwards was a positive one. Brian addressed the situation the next day on his website, remarking that a collaboration with Paul in the future would not be out of the question. A month later, dates for the first Queen tour in nearly 20 years were announced.

46664 – LONG WALK TO FREEDOM

In March 2003 Brian and Roger flew to South Africa for a week to record with former Eurythmics founder Dave Stewart and local African musicians. The sessions took place between 5 and 8 March at Milestone Studios in Cape Town, and were immediately productive: the group recorded a slew of ideas, with the germ of an idea (presumably 'Amandla') being completed so quickly that no one had time to switch on the machines. Thankfully, one of the singers, Muddy, captured the groove (with Dave on acoustic guitar and Brian on piano) on mini-cassette, using the recording as a sample while Roger overdubbed drums and Dave keyboards, with Brian adding some finishing touches with The Red Special.

Officially, only three tracks were recorded during these sessions – 'Invincible Hope', written by Roger; '46664 – The Call', written by Brian; and the aforementioned 'Amandla'. It was later revealed, however, that 'Say It's Not True' was written for the project and performed at the first concert in Cape Town, though it's not known if a studio recording exists. A fifth song was mentioned by Brian on his website under the title 'Under African Skies', but no other information was revealed. It's likely that these songs won't be released as part of any Queen-related project; a 46664 studio album was planned at one time, but has now been shelved indefinitely.

A series of concerts was also performed between 2003 and 2006: the inaugural concert was on 29 November 2003 in Cape Town, and Brian and Roger (under the name Queen) were the stars of the show. The next such concert came in March 2005, again in South Africa, and marked the live debut of Queen + Paul Rodgers, while Brian performed a set in June 2006 in Norway as a solo artist. Queen + Paul Rodgers returned in June 2008 in Hyde Park, three months before the official start of their Rock The Cosmos tour.

GREEN POINT STADIUM, CAPE TOWN, SOUTH AFRICA
29 NOVEMBER 2003

Musicians: Brian May *(guitars, vocals)*, Roger Taylor *(drums, vocals)*, Dave Stewart *(guitars)*, Andrea Corr *(lead vocal on 'Is This The World We Created...?')*, Zucchero *(lead vocal on 'Everybody's Got To Learn Sometime' and 'I Want It All')*, Thandiswa 'Tandy' Mazwai *(lead vocal on 'I Want To Break Free')*, Soweto Gospel Choir *(gospel vocals on 'Bohemian Rhapsody')*, Anastacia *(lead vocal on 'We Will Rock You' and 'We Are The Champions')*, Spike Edney *(keyboards, vocals)*, Jamie Moses *(guitars, vocals)*, Steve Stroud *(bass guitar, vocals)*, Eric Singer *(drums)*, Chris Thompson *(backing vocals, lead vocal on 'The Show Must Go On')*, Treana Morris *(backing vocals)*, Zoe Nicholas *(backing vocals)*

Repertoire: 'Say It's Not True', 'Invincible Hope', '46664 – The Call', 'The Show Must Go On', 'Is This The World We Created...?', 'Everybody's Got To Learn Sometime', 'Amandla', 'Bohemian Rhapsody' / 'I Want It All' / 'I Want To Break Free' / 'Radio Ga Ga', 'We Will Rock You', 'We Are The Champions'

The inaugural 46664 concert in Cape Town was a star-studded event. Along with Brian and Roger appearing as Queen, Beyoncé, Bob Geldof, Paul Oakenfold, Shifty Shellshock, TC, Amampondo Drummers, Baaba Maal, Youssou N'Dour, Yusuf Islam (formerly known as Cat Stevens), Peter Gabriel, Angelique Kidjo, Bono, The Edge, Dave Stewart, Annie Lennox, Abdel Wright, Yvonne Chaka Chaka, Bongo Maffin, Johnny Clegg, Jimmy Cliff, The Corrs, Ladysmith Black Mambazo, Abdel Wright, Danny K, Watershed, Zucchero, Ms Dynamite, Anastacia, Andrews Bonsu, Thandiswa Mazwai, and the Soweto Gospel Choir and Cast made up a day that fused rock with traditional African and world music.

Staged as a variant of Live Aid in a packed stadium of 40,000, the concert was atypical in that no full band (except The Corrs) was featured. Instead, a host of musicians, usually from other bands, would back up the highlighted artist; for instance, Bono and The Edge from U2 performed with Brian, Roger, Dave Stewart, Anastacia and Andrews Bonsu on 'Amandla', and Roger provided drums on The Corrs' 'Toss The Feathers'.

Queen's set started with one of several new songs of the night, 'Say It's Not True', and was performed on a catwalk (during a set change) by Brian and Dave Stewart on acoustic guitars, with Roger providing lead vocals. The band then appeared later in the night after a speech by Nelson Mandela, performing a medley of 'Invincible Hope' (sung by backing vocalists Treana Morris, Zoe Nicholas and Chris Thompson), '46664 – The Call' (sung by Brian) and 'The Show Must Go On' (again, sung by the backing vocalists).

Brian and Roger would appear throughout the night on several other artists' performances: as mentioned, Roger played drums on 'Toss The Feathers', and Brian and Andrea Corr performed 'Is This The World We Created...?' Unsurprisingly, the show ended with a lengthy Queen medley of 'Bohemian Rhapsody', 'I Want It All', 'I Want To Break Free', 'Radio Ga Ga', 'We Will Rock You' and 'We Are The Champions' (the latter pair with Anastacia singing lead vocals).

The concert was a success, and Brian enthused about it on his website afterwards. The performance was released on both CD and DVD in 2004, with all proceeds donated to AIDS charities worldwide.

FANCOURT, GEORGE, SOUTH AFRICA
19 MARCH 2005

Musicians: Brian May *(guitars, vocals)*, Roger Taylor *(drums, vocals)*, Paul Rodgers *(vocals)*, Spike Edney *(piano, keyboards, vocals)*, Danny Miranda *(bass guitar)*, Jamie Moses *(guitars)*, Katie Melua *(lead vocal on 'Too Much Love Will Kill You')*, African Children's Choir *(backing vocals on 'We Will Rock You' and 'We Are The Champions')*

Repertoire: 'Tie Your Mother Down', 'Can't Get Enough', 'I Want To Break Free', 'Fat Bottomed Girls', 'Say It's Not True', 'Too Much Love Will Kill You', 'Hammer To Fall', 'A Kind Of Magic', 'Feel Like Making Love', 'Radio Ga Ga', 'Crazy Little Thing Called Love', 'The Show Must Go On', 'All Right Now', 'We Will Rock You', 'We Are The Champions'

Along with the confirmation of a European and UK tour for the spring of 2005, a second 46664 concert to be performed at Fancourt Country Club Resort was announced to draw attention to Nelson Mandela's AIDS awareness charities. After the controversy attached to their 1984 concerts, there was some trepidation as to the response, but times had clearly changed: apartheid legislation had been removed in the early 1990s, though most of the population still lived in poverty. The new band flew into George, South Africa on 17 March 2005, with final preparations taking place the following day (the band had rehearsed throughout most of February).

Fan response was generally positive, though many were quick to note that Paul was nervous and forgot more than a few lines; considering that only three songs of the 15 performed – 'Can't Get Enough',

'Feel Like Making Love' and 'All Right Now' – were from either Bad Company or Free, the odd flub was understandable and forgivable. A guest vocal on 'Too Much Love Will Kill You' from Katie Melua, who topped the British charts in 2003 with *Call Off The Search*, was a welcome surprise.

While the band was initially rusty and hesitant, it was still a positive experience for them, and they were enthusiastically received both by those in attendance on the night and those who were able to download from the Internet a short four-song clip of 'Tie Your Mother Down', 'Too Much Love Will Kill You', 'We Will Rock You' and 'We Are The Champions'.

FYLLINGEN, TROMOSO, NORWAY
11 JUNE 2005

Musicians: Brian May *(vocals, guitars)*, Spike Edney *(keyboards)*, Jamie Moses *(guitars)*, John Marte *(drums)*, Steve Stroud *(bass guitar)*, Jivan Gasparyan *(duduk on 'Theme From* The Gladiator' *and 'The Last Temptation Of Christ')*, Peter Gabriel *(vocals on 'The Last Temptation Of Christ')*, Zucchero *(vocals on 'Everybody's Got To Learn Sometime', 'Senza Una Donna', and 'Cosi Celeste')*, Sharon Corr *(vocals on 'Everybody's Got To Learn Sometime')*, Johnny Clegg *(vocals on 'Asimbonanga')*

Repertoire: 'Theme From *The Gladiator*', 'The Last Temptation Of Christ', 'Everybody's Got To Learn Sometime', 'Senza Una Donna', 'Cosi Celeste', 'Asimbonanga'

Brian appeared solo for this 46664 concert, and hinted on his website that he would be playing with Jivan Gasparyan, but that their set was still to be determined. Gasparyan, an Armenian musician and composer, is a professor at the Yerevan Conservatory where he instructs performers to professional levels in performance of the duduk (a double-reed instrument, cousin to the oboe). Brian and Jivan performed 'Theme From *The Gladiator*' and 'The Last Temptation Of Christ', with Peter Gabriel on lead vocals, before Brian returned on his own to play guitar on 'Everybody's Got To Learn Sometime', 'Senza Una Donna', 'Cosi Celeste' (singing one verse on this song, his only vocal performance of the night) and 'Asimbonanga'. As with the first 46664 concert, the house band consisted of Spike Edney on keyboards, Jamie Moses on guitars, John Marte on drums and Steve Stroud on bass.

HYDE PARK, LONDON

27 JUNE 2008

Musicians: Brian May *(guitars, vocals)*, Roger Taylor *(drums, vocals)*, Paul Rodgers *(vocals)*, Spike Edney *(piano, keyboards, vocals)*, Danny Miranda *(bass guitar, vocals)*, Jamie Moses *(guitars, vocals)*

Repertoire: 'Is This The World We Created...?' *(Brian and Andrea Corr)*, 'One Vision', 'Tie Your Mother Down', 'The Show Must Go On', 'We Will Rock You', 'We Are The Champions', 'All Right Now', 'Free Nelson Mandela' *(all-star finale)*

Three months before the Rock The Cosmos tour was due to start, Queen + Paul Rodgers interrupted the final recording sessions for *The Cosmos Rocks* to play at the Hyde Park concert for Nelson Mandela's 90th birthday celebration. Annie Lennox, Zucchero, The Corrs, Amy Winehouse, and Razorlight were on the bill (rumored appearances from U2 and Eminem failed to materialize), all compered by an enthusiastic Will Smith, and Brian likened the experience to 1985's

Live Aid. The sextet rehearsed extensively for the tour, trimming down six songs to 20 minutes, and offering up five Queen favorites and a rousing rendition of 'All Right Now'. There were some hiccups – Paul was clearly not fully prepared for the twists and turns of 'One Vision', starting to sing the bridge instead of the second verse – but they truly came alive with 'Tie Your Mother Down' and had the audience cheering wildly and singing along.

Earlier in the show, Brian appeared with Andrea Corr to sing an impassioned rendition of 'Is This The World We Created...?', and, much like Live Aid's 'Do They Know It's Christmas', an all-star finale helped out with Jerry Drammers' 'Free Nelson Mandela', recorded by The Special A.K.A. and produced by Elvis Costello in 1984. A barely coherent Amy Winehouse, teetering precariously on her feet, sang the opening verse, before a cast of a hundred bounced out onto the stage to bring the show to a close. Everyone was in high spirits, with Brian and Paul grinning wildly and clearly having a ball – a marked contrast from the spirits they would be in as the year came to an end.

QUEEN + PAUL RODGERS

EUROPEAN TOUR

28 MARCH TO 30 APRIL 2005

Musicians: Brian May *(guitars, vocals)*, Roger Taylor *(drums, vocals, congas)*, Paul Rodgers *(vocals, guitar)*, Spike Edney *(piano, keyboards, vocals)*, Danny Miranda *(bass guitar, vocals, guitar)*, Jamie Moses *(guitars, vocals)*

Repertoire: 'Reaching Out', 'Tie Your Mother Down', 'A Little Bit Of Love', 'I Want To Break Free', 'Fat Bottomed Girls', 'Wishing Well', 'Crazy Little Thing Called Love', 'Say It's Not True', ''39', 'Love Of My Life', 'Hammer To Fall', 'Feel Like Making Love', 'Let There Be Drums', 'I'm In Love With My Car', Guitar Solo, 'Last Horizon', 'These Are The Days Of Our Lives', 'Radio Ga Ga', 'Can't Get Enough', 'A Kind Of Magic', 'I Want It All', 'Bohemian Rhapsody', 'The Show Must Go On', 'All Right Now', 'We Will Rock You', 'We Are The Champions', 'God Save The Queen', 'Seagull', 'Long Away', 'Tavaszi Szel Vizet Araszt', 'Danube Waltz'

Itinerary:
March 28: Brixton Academy, London
March 30: Le Zenith, Paris, France
April 1: Palacio de los Deportes, Madrid, Spain
April 2: Palau Sant Jordi, Barcelona, Spain
April 4: Palalottomatica, Rome, Italy
April 5: Forum, Milan, Italy
April 7: Nelson Mandela Forum, Firenze, Italy
April 8: BPA Palas, Pesaro, Italy
April 10: St Jakob's Halle, Basel, Switzerland
April 13: Stadhalle, Vienna, Austria
April 14: Olympiahalle, Munich, Germany
April 16: Sazka Arena, Prague, Czech Republik
April 17: Arena, Leipzig, Germany
April 19: Festhalle, Frankfurt, Germany
April 20: Sportpaleis, Antwerpen, Belgium
April 23: Arena, Budapest, Hungary
April 25: Westfalenhalle, Dortmund, Germany
April 26: Ahoy, Rotterdam, Netherlands
April 28: Colour Line Arena, Hamburg, Germany
April 30: Globen, Stockholm, Sweden

It must be said that the 2005 touring band – consisting of Brian May, Roger Taylor, Paul Rodgers, former Blue Öyster Cult bassist Danny Miranda, and familiar stalwarts Jamie Moses and Spike Edney – is *not* the Queen we all know and love. "For years, I couldn't see the point of doing Queen again," Brian explained in 2005. "I couldn't visualise it. Then we performed some songs with Paul, and it was like a door opened in my mind. It suddenly occurred to me that we could do something which will give people a little bit of what they want but will also take it to a new place. I'm starting to wonder why we didn't think of it before."

Well, they *did* think of it before: rumors started to formulate shortly after the tribute concert in 1992 that George Michael would become Queen's new vocalist, and the same situation arose in 1997 after the Béjart Ballet event with Elton John. The closest the idea had previously come to fruition was in 2001, after Brian and Roger re-recorded 'We Are The Champions' with Robbie Williams for the film *A Knight's Tale*, but all parties cooled on the project and it wasn't pursued further. The 2004 UK Rock And Roll Hall Of Fame appearance with Paul Rodgers threw up the prospect of working with someone who wasn't like Freddie – flamboyant and over-the-top – and the first major tour utilizing the Queen name (with Paul Rodgers duly added on) kicked off on home turf at the Brixton Academy, nine days after the 46664 concert in South Africa.

Expanding upon the set presented during the Fancourt concerts, the new repertoire added a smattering of songs from both Paul Rodgers' and Queen's respective canon. In addition to the three songs performed in South Africa, Paul's 'A Little Bit Of Love', 'Wishing Well' and 'Seagull' were added, while, among others, hits like 'These Are The Days Of Our Lives', 'A Kind Of Magic', 'I Want It All' and – of course – 'Bohemian Rhapsody' were also included. An array of album material was brought out of mothballs: 'Love Of My Life' was inevitable, since it was perfect for audience participation and allowed Brian to conduct the crowd in his own way, while 'I'm In Love With My Car' made a welcome return after a 24-year absence from the Queen set list. Perhaps the most surprising inclusion was "39', which hadn't been performed by Queen since 1979. A brief, two-verse rendition from Brian was expanded later in the tour into a full performance, with the audience taking the lead for the most part.

The opening night at the Brixton Academy started off with a taped introduction of 'It's A Beautiful Day',

rejigged by Ross Robertson and DJ Koma into a techno mix that blended perfectly with the full (!) 23-minute 'Track 13' from *Made In Heaven*. Eminem's 'Lose Yourself' was heard next before Paul launcherd into the opening verse of 'Reaching Out', which had been recorded as a charity single featuring Brian and Paul back in 1996. Brian then appeared for the opening bars of 'Tie Your Mother Down', with the curtain dramatically parting to reveal the other four musicians. After the first four numbers, the set took an acoustic turn, with Bad Company's 'Seagull' (and later Roger's gorgeous 'Say It's Not True') as the introductory song and Brian taking over for "39' and 'Love Of My Life'.

The acoustic segment took place at the end of the catwalk, with a slightly larger platform (or B-stage) that placed the band right in the middle of the audience. After the acoustic segment concluded, 'Hammer To Fall' was drastically reworked in an arrangement similar to Brian's own rendition for his 1998 Another World tour; Brian would sing the first verse, with Paul joining him at the B-stage for the second. Brian's ever-evolving guitar solo became a showcase not only for his technique but also for the massive lighting rig, blending effortlessly into his own solo song, 'Last Horizon'. A pre-taped drum intro to 'These Are The Days Of Our Lives' followed, with Roger singing lead vocals at the B-stage, staying there for the introduction of 'Radio Ga Ga' before Paul took over.

The song that caused most concern to the band was 'Bohemian Rhapsody'; how could they tackle such an important song? The solution was simple: the video screen would show Freddie on piano singing the introduction (from the 1986 Wembley concert), with the band playing along until leaving the stage for the operatic bit, with images of Queen's past flashing on the screen. For the hard rock section, Paul would take over on lead vocals and, when the slow coda approached, both Freddie and Paul would duet on the closing lines. It was a neat homage to Freddie's memory and succeeded in integrating him into the show without it appearing hokey.

The subsequent tour wound its way through France and Spain without incident until the 2 April show in Barcelona: Pope John Paul II suffered a massive heart attack and the fate of the first show in Italy was thrown into doubt. He died two days later and, at the concert that night, the band's entrance was preceded by a minute's silence, Brian later dedicating 'Love Of My Life' to all the "great lost ones."

On 7 April, Paul was suffering a throat infection,

meaning that his time on stage was limited and the set list had to be restructured. He only sang on the first five songs before taking an extended break until 'Radio Ga Ga', 'Can't Get Enough' and 'A Kind Of Magic', having another rest until 'Bohemian Rhapsody', then staying for the remainder of the show. As a result, 'Seagull' was replaced with 'Say It's Not True', and Brian and Roger had to make the decision which songs to sing themselves. Roger took over lead vocals on the fast portion of 'Hammer To Fall', while Brian sang 'I Want It All' on his own.

At the final show in Italy, two additions to the set list were made: Brian threw in a snippet of 'Long Away' before ''39', while a cover of Sandy Nelson's 'Let There Be Drums' became the introduction to 'I'm In Love With My Car'. As Paul was still ill, the vocal arrangements of the previous night remained the same. The tour continued through Switzerland, Austria, Germany, the Czech Republik and Belgium before the band made a return visit to Hungary, with Brian performing the traditional folk song 'Tavaszi Szel Viszet Araszt' during his acoustic segment. The Budapest show was also filmed for a potential DVD release, though the preferred show in Sheffield on 9 May took precedence and was released as *Return Of The Champions* in October. The set list remained largely unchanged until 28 April in Hamburg, when Free's 'Wishing Well' was included after 'Fat Bottomed Girls', remaining in the set until the end of the year.

Critical reaction was surprisingly positive. The one dissenting voice was from Brixton's *Financial Times*, who opined that "The idea of Queen without Freddie Mercury is about as enticing as summer without sunshine ... This Brixton Academy show, performed for an audience drawn by lottery from the group's official fan club, was their first date. But neither the warmth of the welcome nor the evident bond between band and fans could make up for a sluggish evening of quasi-karaoke. Paul Rodgers was the singer given the thankless task of filling Mercury's shoes. Rodgers has an impressive rock pedigree – he was in the bands Free and Bad Company – but despite a number of Mercury-esque attributes (robust voice, leather trousers, facial hair), he could not hope to match the original's showmanship ... Endless Brian May guitar solos were scant consolation, and even a storming finale of 'We Will Rock You' and 'We Are the Champions' came too late to salvage the evening. This, I am afraid, is one show that should not go on."

The Daily Telegraph was more sympathetic: "The

first night of a 32-date European tour by Queen + Paul Rodgers proved a remarkable rock'n'roll experience, a daring and potentially disastrous experiment that, most of the time, worked brilliantly. This wasn't merely two of the three surviving members of Queen teaming up with a replacement vocalist. It was a rare, if not unique, marriage of pop legends." Even Stockholm's *The Local* was glowing. "'Irreplaceable' is a word to be used sparingly but it could almost have been Freddie Mercury's nickname. The flamboyant genius, the ultimate showman, the rocker with a voice of a nightingale – when Mercury died in 1991, mourning fans the world over understood the remaining band members' decision to put Queen on ice. Thirteen years later, Brian May and Roger Taylor, Queen's guitarist and drummer respectively, decided that they had at last found their man. Despite the cynicism of many, at least here in Stockholm, Paul Rodgers is not an unknown. Brian May describes him as 'one of the world's great vocalists' and anyone familiar with his work with Free and Bad Company will know that he is not a man to be daunted by a big stage. And so it proved. From the thunderous opener 'Tie Your Mother Down' to the traditional finale of 'We Are The Champions', Rodgers brought such vitality to Queen's catalogue that there was no room for sentimentality at Stockholm's Globen arena on Saturday night. Rodgers is canny enough – and Queen understand their fans well enough – not to try to replace Freddie Mercury. But with his powerful voice – less pure than Mercury's but more throaty, more bluesy – he doesn't so much claim the songs as his own as respectfully offer an interpretation. And that's good enough for Queen fans."

UK TOUR
3 TO 14 MAY 2005

Musicians: Brian May *(guitars, vocals)*, Roger Taylor *(drums, vocals)*, Paul Rodgers *(vocals, guitar)*, Spike Edney *(piano, keyboards, vocals)*, Danny Miranda *(bass guitar, vocals, guitar)*, Jamie Moses *(guitars, vocals)*

Repertoire: 'Reaching Out', 'Tie Your Mother Down', 'I Want To Break Free', 'Fat Bottomed Girls', 'Wishing Well', 'Crazy Little Thing Called Love', 'Say It's Not True', ''39', 'Love Of My Life', 'Hammer To Fall', 'Feel Like Making Love', 'Let There Be Drums', 'I'm In Love With My Car', Guitar Solo, 'Last Horizon', 'These Are The Days Of Our Lives', 'Radio Ga Ga', 'Can't Get Enough', 'A Kind Of Magic', 'I Want It All', 'Bohemian Rhapsody', 'The Show

Must Go On', 'All Right Now', 'We Will Rock You', 'We Are The Champions', 'God Save The Queen', 'Is This The Way To Amarillo?', 'Under Pressure', 'Another One Bites The Dust', 'Fire And Water'

Itinerary:
May 3: Metro, Newcastle
May 4: MEN-Arena, Manchester
May 6: NEC Arena, Birmingham
May 7: International, Cardiff
May 9: Hallam FM Arena, Sheffield
May 11: Wembley Pavilion, London
May 13: Odyssey, Belfast
May 14: The Point, Dublin

After a brief break, the Queen + Paul Rodgers touring band performed their first UK tour. The tour started on 3 May in Newcastle, though Paul's vocal problems persisted and both 'The Show Must Go On' and 'Feel Like Making Love' were temporarily dropped. Otherwise, the set list remained largely the same, though the second night in Manchester saw a unique encore: not only did 'Under Pressure' make its debut (mainly sung by Roger), but Peter Kay and Patrick McGuinness made an appearance to perform 'Is This The Way To Amarillo?' Brian and Roger had appeared in the video for Kay's Comic Relief charity single, which would be released a week after the final Queen + Paul Rodgers gig, and had duly asked Peter and Patrick to perform the song at their Manchester concert.

In Birmingham, 'Under Pressure' remained and 'Another One Bites The Dust' received its premiere performance, finally giving the absent John Deacon two songs in his former band's set list. In Cardiff the following night, 'The Show Must Go On' and 'Feel Like Making Love' returned, with 'Under Pressure' temporarily replaced by 'Another One Bites The Dust' as the first encore number. The Sheffield performance was filmed and recorded, eventually seeing release in October as the *Return Of The Champions* CD and DVD; 'Under Pressure' was brought back, though Brian announced that the song wouldn't be released and was just a personal bonus track for that night's audience.

Once again, the British press was positive, drawing attention to the absent friend but respectfully conceding that Paul was a suitable stand-in. Sheffield's *The Star* wrote, "As the lights went down the original members of the line-up took to the stage – drummer Roger Taylor and lead guitarist Brian May, complete with trademark perm. The crowd went wild but if it was dark-clad, long

straggly-haired rock types you were expecting in the packed audience you would have been disappointed. From 10-year-olds sitting on their dads' shoulders to 30-somethings, 40-somethings, even pensioners, there were all sorts singing along to Mercury's lyrics. Just as the audience reflected the band's wide appeal, Rodgers intentionally set out not to try and be the new Freddie Mercury. But he did an excellent job with his voice – sexy, husky and strong, stepping out of the limelight for almost half the set which was performed by May and Taylor." Birmingham's *Evening Telegraph* opined, "Queen without Freddie Mercury might seem, on paper, a brazen case of Hamlet without the prince, but they conjured up a truly majestic kind of magic for a packed-to-the-rafters NEC. The concept worked because, rather than trying to act as a replacement or a substitute for the great showman, Paul Rodgers provided a triumphant alternative. He might not boast Mercury's charisma and theatricality, but he proved that he is a superb rock vocalist in his own right as he wove some of his own hits ('Feel Like Making Love', 'Wishing Well') into the Queen back catalogue … May – one of the very few men in the world who can look cool wearing bubble-curls and a big girl's blouse – was in supreme form, reminding us that his unique, gloriously fluid guitar was a key component in Queen's success. And Taylor, too, clearly revelled in the occasion, especially when introducing the one new song, poignant AIDS warning 'Say It's Not True'. It remains to be seen whether this project will produce more fresh material but as they led an ecstatic audience through encore choruses of 'All Right Now', 'We Will Rock You' and 'We Are The Champions', it was difficult to imagine that they won't be back with more of the same. You can't have it all, but when some of the greatest rock music ever written is recreated so brilliantly, you've got more than most of us could dared to have dreamed of."

OPEN AIR TOUR
2 TO 15 JULY 2005

Musicians: Brian May *(guitars, vocals)*, Roger Taylor *(drums, vocals)*, Paul Rodgers *(vocals, guitar)*, Spike Edney *(piano, keyboards, vocals)*, Danny Miranda *(bass guitar, vocals, guitar)*, Jamie Moses *(guitars, vocals)*

Repertoire: 'Reaching Out', 'Tie Your Mother Down', 'I Want To Break Free', 'Fat Bottomed Girls', 'Wishing Well', 'Another One Bites The Dust', 'Crazy Little Thing Called Love', 'Say It's Not True', "39', 'Love Of My Life',

'Hammer To Fall', 'Feel Like Making Love', 'Let There Be Drums', 'I'm In Love With My Car', Guitar Solo, 'Last Horizon', 'These Are The Days Of Our Lives', 'Radio Ga Ga', 'Can't Get Enough', 'A Kind Of Magic', 'I Want It All', 'Bohemian Rhapsody', 'The Show Must Go On', 'All Right Now', 'We Will Rock You', 'We Are The Champions', 'God Save The Queen', 'Imagine'

Itinerary:

July 2: Estadio Restelo, Lisbon, Portugal
July 6: Rhein-Energie Stadion, Cologne, Germany
July 10: Gelredome, Arnhem, Netherlands
July 15: Hyde Park, Parade Ground, London
    (rescheduled from 8 July)

The Queen + Paul Rodgers band proceeded to a four-city open-air itinerary that offered them bigger audiences than the indoor venues had permitted. Brian was ill during the Cologne show but, apart from messing up the guitar intro of 'I Want To Break Free', was in a good mood to match that of the audience, who were in high spirits despite getting drenched before the show even started. (Paul duly threw in a line from 'Singin' In The Rain' following 'Feel Like Makin' Love'.) In particular, there was a rousing reception given to 'We Will Rock You' and 'We Are The Champions' when the cast of the *We Will Rock You* musical joined the band on stage.

A proposed concert at Hyde Park on 8 July, reprising the original Queen's triumphant 1976 free concert there and with The Darkness scheduled to join the band for a song or two, was postponed for a week as a mark of respect; the day before, London had been the target of a series of terrorist bombings, claiming 52 lives. The rescheduled Hyde Park gig therefore included a resonant, semi-acoustic rendition of John Lennon's 'Imagine', with Brian, Roger and Paul each taking a verse at the end of the catwalk, later regrouping on the main stage for a full-band coda.

The Independent was pleased with the Hyde Park show. "On the evidence of this concert, one has to ask where on earth has [Paul Rodgers] been for the last two and a half decades? It is a mini mystery of rock, like the riddle of why John Deacon, Queen's original bassist, is not on the tour and seems to have been written out of the script. The linking of guitarist Brian May and drummer Roger Taylor of Queen with Rodgers is both inspired and odd. Inspired because the voice is so great, and he retains a stage presence. He swings a microphone stand in the same way as Mercury, even if he hasn't got the same swagger and panache, and even

if he and the rest of Queen cannot remotely play an audience in the way that Freddie did. But the pairing is odd because Rodgers in his heyday was to some degree the antithesis of Mercury and Queen. Free were a band for the sweaty university circuit. The fans of their heavy, driving rock and intense ballads, were the 'heads', the post-hippies who were, frankly, unlikely to be playing 'Bohemian Rhapsody' in their bedrooms. Freddie Mercury was camp; Paul Rodgers, whose sexuality was traditional rock star hetero, was never, ever camp. This oddity was well illustrated at Friday's concert when Queen's 'Fat Bottomed Girls' was immediately followed by Free's 'Wishing Well'. The first is typically cheeky (excuse the pun), the second moody and contemplative. Yet, somehow it worked. Rodgers did justice to Queen's classics and resurrected his own, with as many people singing along to Free's 'All Right Now' as to Queen's 'We Will Rock You'. And, it was a joy to be reminded that 'Radio Ga Ga' is one of the best singalong stadium anthems ever."

ARUBA & US SHOWS
8 TO 22 OCTOBER 2005

Musicians: Brian May *(guitars, vocals)*, Roger Taylor *(drums, vocals)*, Paul Rodgers *(vocals, guitar, piano)*, Spike Edney *(piano, keyboards, vocals)*, Danny Miranda *(bass guitar, vocals, guitar)*, Jamie Moses *(guitars, vocals)*

Repertoire: 'Reaching Out', 'Tie Your Mother Down', 'Fat Bottomed Girls', 'Another One Bites The Dust', 'Crazy Little Thing Called Love', 'Bad Company', 'Say It's Not True', "39', 'Love Of My Life', 'Hammer To Fall', 'Feel Like Making Love', 'Let There Be Drums', 'I'm In Love With My Car', Guitar Solo, 'Last Horizon', 'These Are The Days Of Our Lives', 'Radio Ga Ga', 'Can't Get Enough', 'Rock 'n' Roll Fantasy', 'A Kind Of Magic', 'I Want It All', 'Bohemian Rhapsody', 'The Show Must Go On', 'All Right Now', 'We Will Rock You', 'We Are The Champions', 'God Save The Queen', "39'

Itinerary:

October 8: Aruba Entertainment Center, Oranjestad, Aruba
October 16: Continental Airlines Arena, East Rutherford, New Jersey
October 22: Hollywood Bowl, Los Angeles, California

The Queen + Paul Rodgers band continued their 2005 campaign with three shows in October, each spaced about a week apart. The first was in Aruba, a surprising choice of locale, though the concert sold out fairly quickly and the band played to a packed house. The second and third shows marked the first time Brian and Roger had visited the United States under the Queen banner since 1982. The two concerts, one in East Rutherford and the other in Los Angeles, were seen as tests: if the shows were successful, there was the possibility of a full-scale US tour the following year. Thankfully, both shows were sold out and the band performed to enthusiastic audiences.

The sets differed slightly from previous legs. 'I Want To Break Free' and 'A Kind Of Magic' were dropped in favor of 'Bad Company' (with Paul on piano) and 'Rock 'n' Roll Fantasy', the first time either song was performed that year. In LA, Guns N' Roses guitarist Slash joined the band on stage during 'Can't Get Enough', causing uproar among the audience.

JAPANESE TOUR
26 OCTOBER TO 3 NOVEMBER 2005

Musicians: Brian May *(guitars, vocals)*, Roger Taylor *(drums, vocals)*, Paul Rodgers *(vocals, guitar, piano)*, Spike Edney *(piano, keyboards, vocals)*, Danny Miranda *(bass guitar, vocals, guitar)*, Jamie Moses *(guitars, vocals)*

Repertoire: 'Reaching Out', 'Tie Your Mother Down', 'Fat Bottomed Girls', 'Another One Bites The Dust', 'Fire And Water', 'Crazy Little Thing Called Love', 'Bad Company', 'Say It's Not True', "39', 'Love Of My Life', 'Teo Torriatte (Let Us Cling Together)', 'Hammer To Fall', 'Feel Like Making Love', 'Let There Be Drums', 'I'm In Love With My Car', Guitar Solo, 'Last Horizon', 'These Are The Days Of Our Lives', 'Radio Ga Ga', 'Can't Get Enough', 'A Kind Of Magic', 'Wishing Well', 'I Want It All', 'I Was Born To Love You', 'Bohemian Rhapsody', 'The Show Must Go On', 'All Right Now', 'We Will Rock You', 'We Are The Champions', 'God Save The Queen', 'Long Away', 'I Want To Break Free'

Itinerary:
October 26/27: Saitama Arena, Tokyo
October 29/30: Yokohama Arena, Yokohama
November 1: Nagoya Dome, Nagoya
November 3: Fukuoka Dome, Fukuoka

While the Aruba and North American shows in October were successful and enjoyable for Queen + Paul Rodgers, they merely served as a warm-up for the

band's first full-scale tour of Japan since 1985. 'Teo Torriatte (Let Us Cling Together)', a song reserved for Japanese audiences, was included, while 'Wishing Well' was brought back in place of 'Rock 'n' Roll Fantasy'. Even more surprising, following 'I Want It All' Roger and Brian, acoustic guitar in hand, strolled out to the end of the catwalk and duetted on Freddie's 1985 solo track 'I Was Born To Love You'. In its re-recorded state as released on *Made In Heaven*, the song, issued as a single in both 1996 and 2004, had become to Japan what 'Love Of My Life' was to South America.

The band played to capacity crowds each night, though, on his website, Brian would cite the "spaced-out" European itinerary and "highly intensive" Japanese schedule as mental and physical hindrances, also mentioning that he didn't feel on top form during the US gigs either. He affirmed his determination, however, to perform better for the Stateside crowds in future, suggesting that plans were already afoot to bring Queen + Paul Rodgers to American soil.

NORTH AMERICAN TOUR
3 MARCH TO 13 APRIL 2006

Musicians: Brian May *(guitars, vocals)*, Roger Taylor *(drums, vocals)*, Paul Rodgers *(vocals, guitar, piano)*, Spike Edney *(piano, keyboards, vocals)*, Danny Miranda *(bass guitar, vocals)*, Jamie Moses *(guitars, vocals)*

Repertoire: 'Reaching Out', 'Tie Your Mother Down', 'Fat Bottomed Girls', 'Can't Get Enough', 'Take Love', 'Crazy Little Thing Called Love', 'Love Of My Life', 'Hammer To Fall', 'Feel Like Making Love', 'Let There Be Drums', 'I'm In Love With My Car', Guitar Solo, 'Last Horizon', 'Bad Company', 'Another One Bites The Dust', 'Dragon Attack', 'These Are The Days Of Our Lives', 'Radio Ga Ga', 'Under Pressure', 'The Show Must Go On', 'Bohemian Rhapsody', 'We Will Rock You', 'All Right Now', 'We Are The Champions', 'God Save The Queen', 'I Want To Break Free', "39', 'Say It's Not True', 'Under Pressure', 'Red House'

Itinerary:
March 3: American Airlines Arena, Miami, Florida
March 5: Veterans Memorial Arena, Jacksonville, Florida
March 7: Gwinett Center, Duluth, Georgia
March 9: MCI Center, Washington, D.C.
March 10: DCU Center, Worcester, Massachussets
March 12: Nassau Coliseum, New York, New York

March 14: Wachovia Spectrum, Philadelphia, Pennsylvania

March 16: Air Canada Centre, Toronto, Ontario

March 17: HSBC Arena, Buffalo, New York

March 20: Mellon Arena, Pittsburgh, Pennsylvania

March 21: Quicken Loans Arena, Cleveland, Ohio

March 23: Allstate Arena, Rosemont, Illinois

March 24: Palace of Auburn Hills, Detroit, Michigan

March 26: Xcel Energy Center, St Paul, Minnesota

March 27: Bradley Center, Milwaukee, Wisconsin

March 31: Glendale Arena, Glendale, Arizona

April 1: State University's Cox Arena, San Diego, California

April 3: Arrowhead Pond, Anaheim, California

April 5: HP Pavilion, San Jose, California

April 7: MGM Garden Arena, Las Vegas, Nevada

April 10: Key Arena, Seattle, Washington

April 11: Rose Garden, Portland, Oregon

April 13: Pacific Coliseum, Vancouver, British Columbia

Rehearsals for the band's first major US tour began in February 2006 and, though little attempt was made to update the set list, a few surprises were in store. 'Dragon Attack' was resurrected for the first time since 1985, and 'Bad Company' was retained, having not had a single performance during the European leg. The most surprising addition was 'Take Love', a new song written by Paul for the union's first studio album.

Apart from performances of 'I Want To Break Free', ''39' and 'Say It's Not True' during the first few shows (plus Jimi Hendrix's 'Red House' at the final concert in Vancouver), the set list remained static, though songs were occasionally moved around to keep the band on their toes. Dissenters were quick to point out that some shows performed to less than capacity; while it was true that the band enjoyed only four sold-out shows (Toronto, Detroit, Las Vegas and Vancouver), they hardly experienced the kind of half-full arenas the nay-sayers indicated. Unfortunately, promotion for the tour was scant. The larger cities ran radio ads and special promotions, but areas that had never been Queen-friendly (Florida, Georgia and Arizona) were accorded a minimum of publicity.

While Queen had rarely attracted positive notices in the US, some reviews raked Brian and Roger over the coals for even daring to go out on tour without Freddie. The Boston Globe wrote, "It was much trumpeted as a Queen reunion, but no matter how much you squinted as the awkwardly named Queen + Paul Rodgers combo

pounded out beloved classic rock anthems at the DCU Center on Friday night, it just wasn't anything close … The most haunting moment came when the video screen displayed 1970s footage of Queen: skinny, sexy kids with cool haircuts and endless possibilities. Before an encore of 'We Will Rock You', Free's 'All Right Now', and 'We Are the Champions' came the audacious 'Bohemian Rhapsody'. As Taylor and May played their parts, a video screen displayed footage of the late Freddie Mercury singing and playing piano. For a while the pair were actually backing a tape of themselves. Eventually the band moved in, with Rodgers voicing the song's more rocking parts. Superstar karaoke." Chicago's Daily Herald was equally unimpressed: "Imagine if the staples of 1970s arena rock – leather pants, fog, levitating pianos, drum solos, strobes – went through a modern day makeover that now included tanning, teeth whitening, expert designer duds and intermittent video footage that, like Oprah's makeover specials, illustrated how then was scraggly and now is shiny. The result would be much like what arrived at the Allstate Arena Thursday, a tour that crossbred Queen and Bad Company, two bands from the classic rock years that previously had nothing in common other than they shared airplay in the glory years of FM radio … The longer than two-hour show featured many usual Queen hits, but because Mercury, one of the most distinctive personalities in rock, also happens to be dead, the set list was padded with songs where that niggling little fact wouldn't be so noticeable. Which meant too much time for Roger Taylor's C-level power ballads ('The Days of Our Lives'), a new song from Rodgers ('Take Love') and forgotten Queen songs like 'Dragon Attack' that were never missed in the first place. Devoting time to such limp material, when many of Queen's classics were ignored, was like showing up to Symphony Center to hear the Chicago Symphony Orchestra play 'Chopsticks'."

Still, the critical response was, just like the 2005 leg, mostly positive. Miami's South Florida Sun-Sentinel was overly apologetic for the low turn-out on the first night: "One would think that a venue as massive as the AmericanAirlines Arena and a band as monumental as Queen would be ideally suited for each other. Sadly, though, on the opening night of the legendary '70s rock group's first major tour since the death of their lead singer, the arena was full of empty seats and half-hearted fans. Until the final 60 minutes and the band's awe-inspiring encore, even those in the front rows stood placidly, awaiting a call to action from their aging idols." Duluth's *Forsyth County News* praised to Paul but wrote that "the highlight of the show was seeing Brian May play live. May plays the guitar the way an expert marksman would shoot a rifle, taking out one incredible riff at a time. I had no idea how unique his playing style was until I saw him live. He hits every note with melodic precision, and then without warning he would switch from rifle to machine gun and absolutely blow the crowd away. As impressive as Mercury's writing and singing was, it turns out that the styling of May's guitar is as equally defining as the heart of Queen. Roger Taylor's casual drumming style is equally as unique and it was great to see the two Queen veterans back in the limelight … It will be interesting to see if the band decides to write together and we can see what happens when operatic rock and roll meets the dirty South." *The Philadelphia Inquirer* wrote, "Having the bluesy belter from Bad Company replace the campy, operatic Mercury was akin to replacing the cast of *Desperate Housewives* with guys from *The Sopranos*. Yet the audience that sold out the Wachovia Spectrum on Tuesday night found it could be done. Sonically, Queen is the same as it ever was. Guitarist May's towering glissandos and drummer Taylor's chunky rhythms were in place. May rather touchingly sang 'Love Of My Life', which he called 'Freddie's love song.' Taylor did his creepy smash, 'I'm in Love With My Car', as well as Mercury's synth-slick 'Radio Ga Ga' … Oddly, Rodgers' own material – like his soul-metal 'Bad Company' – fit right in with Queen's sleekly crunchy harangue. While Rodgers upped the gruffness, Queen turned 'Feel Like Makin' Love' from casually cool to shuck-jiving."

Milwaukee's *Journal Sentinel* reported a tender moment: "About halfway through, May took the front of the stage alone to sing Freddie's ballad 'Love of My Life'. Before he could begin, he had to wait for a prolonged wave of applause to subside. 'People of Milwaukee,' he told the crowd, 'I wasn't feeling very glam tonight, so you've given me a lift.' Clearly, the feeling was reciprocal." Anaheim's *Orange County Register* offered a warm welcome: "As steadfast Queen devotees who trekked out to the Hollywood Bowl last October know, this wasn't the re-established outfit's first or even sole chance at re-proving itself. Perhaps that's why Monday night's heartier return, at the Pond, didn't come close to selling out. When you charge people $200 a ticket for what's billed as one of just two North American dates – and the only one in the Western half of the U.S. – they tend not to turn out

when you come back a little more than five months later on a full-fledged tour. Yet here's the real stinker for those who went then but not now: You missed the better, more rocking show … A new tune, which I'll guess is titled 'Take Love Where You Find It', suggests there's more life left to this mash-up – and that Queen's singular sonics could add girth to Rodgers' melodies. But even if it remains nothing more than a tribute act, it deserves a continued run. In an era of misguided revivals – I've heard the New Cars, and you shouldn't – this reconstituted Queen is that rare attraction worth seeing more than once."

The final night, as reported in the *Vancouver Sun*, was *the* show to see: "It was a thrill to see the big presence that is the long, curly haired May, who shared the spotlight with Rodgers almost throughout. May is one of rock'n'roll's greatest guitarists after all, and Rodgers knows what it's like to work with the best. As promised, he's too great a musician to want to attempt an impersonation of Freddie Mercury, who died in 1991. Unlike the Doors of the 21st Century show that played at the same venue last summer, Queen with Paul Rodgers is not a case of a veteran band needing to replace its frontman with a look-alike that sounds-alike. Rodgers doesn't look or sound like Queen's famous frontman Freddie Mercury, which was just fine with the mixed ages audience. Nobody would have come expecting a straight ahead Queen concert. This version is really a supergroup, a retrospective combo of Queen and Rodgers' legendary Bad Company and Free … So great was the shared feeling for the power of musically pure, tastefully revisited old rock'n'roll, that it may go down in history as the night that arena rock officially made its comeback. At least for those of us who didn't experience it the first time around."

ROCK THE COSMOS TOUR
12 SEPTEMBER TO 29 NOVEMBER 2008

Musicians: Brian May *(guitars, vocals)*, Roger Taylor *(drums, vocals)*, Paul Rodgers *(vocals, guitar, piano)*, Spike Edney *(piano, keyboards, keytar, vocals)*, Danny Miranda *(bass guitar, vocals)*, Jamie Moses *(guitars, vocals)*

Repertoire: 'Cosmos Rockin' *(intro tape)* / 'Surf's Up . . . School's Out !' *(intro tape)*, 'Hammer To Fall', 'Tie Your Mother Down', 'Fat Bottomed Girls', 'Another One Bites The Dust', 'I Want It All', 'I Want To Break Free', 'C-lebrity', 'Surf's Up . . . School's Out !', 'Seagull', 'Love

Of My Life', "39', Bass Solo / Drum Solo, 'I'm In Love With My Car', 'A Kind Of Magic', 'Say It's Not True', 'Bad Company', 'We Believe', Guitar Solo, 'Bijou', 'Last Horizon', 'Radio Ga Ga', 'Crazy Little Thing Called Love', 'The Show Must Go On', 'Bohemian Rhapsody', 'Cosmos Rockin'', 'All Right Now', 'We Will Rock You', 'We Are The Champions', 'God Save The Queen', 'Shooting Star', 'One Vision', 'Wishing Well', 'Warboys (A Prayer For Peace)', 'Feel Like Makin' Love', 'Time To Shine', 'The Stealer', 'Las Palabras De Amor (The Words Of Love)', 'Tavaszi Szél Vizet Áraszt', 'Blue Danube Waltz', 'Voodoo', 'Maybe It's Because I'm A Londoner', 'Under Pressure'

Itinerary:

12 September, Freedom Square, Kharkov, Ukraine
15 September, Olympic Sports Complex, Moscow, Russia
16 September, Olympic Sports Complex, Moscow, Russia
19 September, Arena, Riga, Latvia
21 September, Velodrom, Berlin, Germany
23 September, Sportpaleis, Antwerp, Belgium
24 September, Bercy, Paris, France
26 September, Palalottomatica, Rome, Italy
28 September, Arena, Milan, Italy
29 September, Hallenstadion, Zurich, Switzerland
1 October, Olympiahalle, Munich, Germany
2 October, SAP Arena, Mannheim, Germany
4 October, TUI Arena, Hannover, Germany
5 October, Color Line Arena, Hamburg, Germany
7 October, Ahoy, Rotterdam, Holland
8 October, Rockhal, Esch-sur-Alzette, Luxembourg
10 October, Arena, Nottingham
11 October, SECC, Glasgow, Scotland
13 October, O2 Arena, London
14 October, Arena, Cardiff, Wales
16 October, NIA, Birmingham
18 October, Echo Arena, Liverpool
19 October, Arena, Sheffield
22 October, Palau Sant Jordi, Barcelona, Spain
24 October, Estadio de Futbol "La Condomina", Murcia, Spain
25 October, Palacio de Deportes, Madrid, Spain
28 October, Arena, Budapest, Hungary
29 October, Belgrade Arena, Belgrade, Serbia
31 October, O2 Arena, Prague, Czech Republic
1 November, Stadthalle, Vienna, Austria
4 November, Arena, Newcastle
5 November, MEN Arena, Manchester
7 November, O2 Arena, London
8 November, Wembley Arena, London
14 November, Festival City, Dubai, UAE
19 November, San Carlos de Apoquindo, Santiago de Chile, Chile
21 November, Estadio Velez Sarsfield, Buenos Aires, Argentina
26 November, Via Funchal, Sao Paulo, Brazil
27 November, Via Funchal, Sao Paulo, Brazil
29 November, HSBC Arena, Rio De Janeiro, Brazil

With the 2005/2006 Return Of The Champions tour over and done with, Brian, Roger, and Paul came to a general consensus that the partnership shouldn't end just yet. "It was amazing how seamlessly our different styles fit together," Paul told *Rolling Stone* in May 2008. "We came offstage really buzzed about it and said, 'Let's do some more.'" Throughout 2007 and 2008, the trio worked on songs for their debut album, but the elation of the tour still lingered on. "We didn't know we were doing the right thing until the tour started in earnest," Roger said in *Classic Rock Magazine*. "Then it got better and better, and by the time the American dates ended that decision had been vindicated." Brian agreed: "Reaction-wise there were nights when I thought, 'Gosh, this is the equal of anything in the past'. It was utterly ecstatic."

Sessions for *The Cosmos Rocks* took up most of the band's creative time, but by March 2008, plans had been solidified for an extensive world tour to begin in September in the Ukraine, with further dates in Europe, the UK, and Latin America, with a trek to the US planned for early 2009. Because of his high-profile website, where fans can easily write in, Brian was inundated with complaints by irate fans of the selected venues, with an Irish fan named Jim getting under the guitarist's skin by calling it a "disgrace" that Queen + Paul Rodgers didn't book anything in Ireland. Shocked at this reaction, Brian wrote a tongue-in-cheek entry on his website that apologized to the collective countries from selected "arm-chair" fans, before joking that the whole thing be called off. This was brought up in a *Classic Rock Magazine* interview, which Brian laughingly shrugged off: "People don't realise that you can't always get the halls you want. And of course, the fans can also travel. We're doing our fair share of that."

A crass statement, perhaps, especially considering the economic crunch that fans were already feeling with the worldwide collapse of the banks in the autumn of 2008. But in the band's defence, they were indeed traveling to new and exciting places: the tour kicked off in Kharkov, with first-time performances in Moscow, Latvia, Serbia, Prague, and Dubai. South American dates were planned tentatively for the end of November, and Hollywood Records was confident that a North American leg would occur in the early part of 2009. Of course, the expected venues in Paris, Madrid, Berlin, Rome, and Zürich, as well as a handful of "hometown" cities (Birmingham, Sheffield, Manchester, and London), were also planned, and Brian expressed enthusiasm for the upcoming tour on his website, overjoyed that he was finally going to be mix new music with the hits for the first time in 10 years. Roger and Paul, meanwhile, hit the print presses, drumming up interest well before the band hit the road.

"I don't want us to feel just like old guys playing the hits," Roger told *Rolling Stone* that May. "Hopefully [this new album] will be a creative rebirth for us." Paul agreed in an interview with Australia's *The Courier Mail* in September, but was a bit more cautious for the band's long-term goals: "The reason I came together with Brian and Roger is because it feels good musically and I'll only do it, I will only do this for as long as it feels good. We're only committed to the end of this tour and there are no commitments beyond that so it will remain to be seen if we even continue after that." The singer also felt compelled to reaffirm his status as a singer, and that he had no intent on mimicking Freddie: "It had to work on a musical level for me. I'm a musician. I'm a singer and a songwriter. I have great respect for what Freddie did, he was flamboyant, he was a showman, a great frontman, very entertaining and people loved him, and it was great for magazines too because it was great copy. But you see, that's not who I am. The only way I could do this was to actually just be myself, which is much more down to earth. Sorry. Perhaps I'm a little boring, but I'm just me."

The tour began on 12 September in Kharkov, at a concert organized weeks before it was performed, with the well-intentioned message: "Don't Let AIDS Ruin Your Life". Unusually, this was recorded and filmed professionally by David Mallet, marking the first instance by Queen that the kick-off date of a tour was to be released publically. This was a bold move, considering the set list hadn't been finalized yet, and followed a little too closely to the 2005/2006 tour. Indeed, as the tour hit its stride throughout the coming weeks, the band would become more adventurous, with new and some previously unplayed songs introduced as the band's confidence grew.

Unfortunately, there was a sameness with the previous tour's set, with most of the same songs retained, and only a few swapped out for new ones. But what was new was interesting: 'One Vision' made a return to the set as an abbreviated opener, and 'Bijou' was given its live premiere in a unique tribute to Freddie: while Brian played the mournful guitar live, Freddie's studio vocals were pumped through the massive sound system as visions of the singer flashed on the screen above the stage. 'Bohemian Rhapsody', too, was performed similar to the 2005/2006 tour, with Freddie's vocals this time taken from the *Queen Rock Montreal* DVD. '39' was performed as a half duo, half full band arrangement: after 'Love Of My Life', a bass drum was placed next to Brian on the B-stage, and Roger ran down the catwalk to join his friend. After one verse and chorus, Brian would stop the song as roadies set up additional microphones behind him, and the guitarist would call the rest of the band down to assist with vocal harmonies and instruments. Roger's drum solo was different, too: instead of 'Let There Be Drums', Roger would start off with a bass and snare drum, and as he pounded away, roadies would assemble a kit around him, and as it came to a thundering conclusion, the band would launch into 'I'm In Love With My Car' – which clearly made Roger breathless on more than one occasion.

By the time the band got to Berlin, 'One Vision' was dropped permanently in favor of 'Surf's Up . . . School's Out !', a most appropriate – and daring – opener. 'Time To Shine' was added in Antwerp, but out as quickly as it was introduced due to a mistimed cue into the first chorus. 'Seagull', always a favorite of Paul's, was replaced in Zurich in favor of 'The Stealer', and 'Warboys (A Prayer For Peace)' was performed only three times early on in the tour. 'Wishing Well' and 'Shooting Star' were also early casualties, and both 'Hammer To Fall' and 'Feel Like Makin' Love' were frequently in and out of the set. It seemed that the band had little clue exactly how they wanted the new set to be prepared, and with only three constant new songs – 'C-Lebrity', 'Say It's Not True', and 'Cosmos Rockin'' – the new album was severely underrepresented. Only as the tour progressed did 'Surf's Up . . . School's Out !', 'We Believe', and 'Voodoo' start to make more frequent appearances.

The tour lumbered on throughout October, and on the 13th, Danny Miranda was hospitalized. By noon the next day the Cardiff gig was in serious jeopardy of being canceled, but Neil Murray was hastily recruited and a quick rehearsal was held. 'We Believe' was dropped in favor of 'Feel Like Makin' Love', as Neil admitted that would be the one song he would be bound to make mistakes in, though he felt confident enough in his abilities for it to be reinstated the following night. By Liverpool, Danny was back on his bass duties, and ready and eager to assist Roger in his nightly upright electric bass solo. (In his absence, Jamie played the bass during Roger's solo.)

As South America had been neglected on the 2005/2006 tour, five dates were tacked onto the end of the schedule, and fans were predictably rabid. At press conferences, the exhausted primary musicians were interviewed by overeager journalists, but the focus was clearly pointed on Brian and Roger, with many mentions – and fond remembrances – of Freddie made. Paul simply stood awkwardly, forgotten and ignored, as it was clear that as long as he sang with Brian and Roger, he would always be in Freddie's shadow. The South American leg saw both 'Under Pressure' and 'Las Palabras De Amor (The Words Of Love)' added, though the latter had received its live debut a month prior in Madrid. The Buenos Aires gig was filmed for a potential DVD release, and was also televised across the country. By the time the tour wrapped up in Rio de Janeiro, fans were clamoring for news of the tour to continue into 2009.

The Rock The Cosmos tour had seen vast improvements – despite the set being too similar (and the always lovely 'These Are The Days Of Our Lives' inexplicably not performed even once) to the 2005/2006 tour, journalists were, on the whole, pleased. While Freddie's absence was inevitable, it was especially surprising that critics, after years of vilifying him, suddenly praised him. Glasgow's *The Herald* wrote, "Nobody could ever have filled the ballet slippers of Freddie Mercury and Paul Rodgers makes no attempt to do so. He has nothing to prove to anybody and sings Queen's songs his way. And for the most part, it works beautifully." Nottingham's *Telegraph* made note of Paul's awkwardness and commended Brian on picking up the slack: "It was May who took the limelight, strutting around with his big, bouncy hair, firing off little solos as the band – including three supporting players on bass, guitar and keyboards – warmed up with 'Hammer To Fall' and 'Tie Your Mother Down'. His assurance was in contrast with Rodgers, who looked frankly a bit awkward and exposed; he strikes me as a singer who is happiest behind a microphone stand rather than parading and preening."

Apart from a tired dig at Brian's hair, the Wharf.

co.uk review of the London O2 show was positive: "The veteran rockers made a triumphant return to London proving once again there's no substitute for great songs and well-honed stage-craft ... No major surprises perhaps, but one of the best shows you're likely to see this or any other year." *The Birmingham Post* praised Paul: "It could be argued that Queen without Freddie Mercury is like a bacon butty without brown sauce, yet the stinging guitar of Brian May was always as much a part of their sound as their late frontman's voice ... With Paul Rodgers, the pocket-sized powerhouse from Free and Bad Company, they have found a kindred spirit." *The Journal Live* also took note of Paul's increasing confidence: "[Rodgers] had the crowd eating out of his hand – only one man could take his limelight: a certain Brian May. Looking effortlessly cool churning out electric riffs that worked the crowd into frenzy and then just as comfortable sitting on the edge of the runway stage singing the softly anthemic 'Love of My Life', with a 10,000-strong backing choir." *The Birmingham Mail* summed up the fans' general opinon of the tour thusly: "With a back catalogue so rich in treasures it would be criminal not to continue sharing the joys of a Queen concert, so thank you, Brian May and Roger Taylor, for ensuring the show goes on."

Sadly, the show was just about to end. The slapdash manner of the construction of the repertoire was unusual for such perfectionists as Brian and Roger, and only after the tour concluded was it made unofficially public (through sources, hence its unofficial status) that not all was rosy behind the scenes. Reports varied over the tension, but Brian was clearly displeased with 'Surf's Up ... School's Out !' as the opener; when 'Hammer To Fall' returned to the set in Nottingham, it was as the first number, and its displaced opener was performed right before the acoustic set. Furthermore, the increasing omissions of Paul's solo material, and the general similarities to the preceding tour, made it clear that the band hadn't rehearsed a whole lot of new material. There was some tension reported between Paul and Brian: the vocalist wanted to rehearse more songs, while the guitarist was content with the hits show the set had become. By the end of October, Brian had ceased writing about the tour on his Soapbox; he had started off as prolific as before, but there wasn't any mention of the tour throughout November. By the time the tour ended, he had written a cryptic note on his site: "Tonight ... the very end of a long voyage." Four days later, Brian addressed a fan who asked if the band were splitting up, responding that nothing concrete had been decided for their future. When asked of plans for a release of the South American gigs, Brian went on the defensive, protesting that he was more interested in working in the "now" than on the "past"; that gigs that took place less than a month prior could be considered in the past was a telling statement.

There was no further mention of the tour into 2009, with Brian remaining tight-lipped on the future, though he did talk at length of animal rights and his new protégée, Kerry Ellis. There was no mention of Paul Rodgers anywhere, and the vocalist finally broke radio silence in May by announcing a tour with a reformed Bad Company. As to the future of Queen + Paul Rodgers? "At this point we're gonna sit back from this," Paul told Billboard. "My arrangement with [Brian and Roger] was similar to my arrangement with Jimmy (Page) in The Firm in that it was never meant to be a permanent arrangement ... It's kind of an open book, really. If they approach me to do something for charity,

for instance, or something like that ... I'd be very much into doing that, for sure." He was more blunt with VH1: "We did a world tour, we did a second tour of Europe and the Far East and Eastern Europe and a studio album, and I think we're kind of leaving it there gently ... It's out there for us to do things in the future if there's something – a huge charity, say, like Nelson Mandela – but I think we are pretty much done." Indeed, that same month, Brian and Roger appeared on American Idol, backing silver medalist Adam Lambert on 'We Are The Champions'. The guitarist enthused to Rolling Stone shortly thereafter, "[We] are definitely hoping to have a meaningful conversation with [Adam] at some point. It's not like we, as Queen, would rush into coalescing with another singer just like that. It isn't that easy. But I'd certainly like to work with Adam. That is one amazing instrument he has there." After a suitable recuperation period, Brian and Roger made overtures to Adam to work together; in 2012, a new chapter of the Queen + saga began.

QUEEN + ADAM LAMBERT

Your mileage may vary when it comes to Brian and Roger's continued use of the Queen brand name. Whether the variety of artists to follow the "+" since 1999 is to your liking or not, there's one argument every ardent supporter will use: at least they're still out there, selling the brand and, occasionally, creating new music. The Cosmos Rocks, despite its underwhelming chart performance and frequently questionable lyrical subject matter, was a step in a direction; the pairing of Roger and Brian with Paul Rodgers was enough to get the creative juices flowing, something that can't be said of any of the other collaborations over the years. Yet the pairing ended prematurely: Rodgers was likely frustrated with being compared to Freddie Mercury at every turn, and Brian must have sensed that the end was near, fighting for a static set list as the Queen + Paul Rodgers Rock the Cosmos tour wound its way through Europe and South America. Whatever went on behind the scenes is up to conjecture, and Brian was at least gracious enough to not mention if any bad blood had spilled between the three primaries, but it became apparent that all was not well as the tour ended.

The guitarist distanced himself from continuous live performances, occasionally appearing here and

there at the We Will Rock You musical or jumping on stage with musical protege Kerry Ellis, but it wasn't until May 2011 that he finally embarked on another tour. With Ellis' Anthems set for a September 2011 release, the duo performed an intimate 16-date tour across England that earned rave reviews from fans and critics alike. But there was no hint of any kind of Queen + collaboration in the pipeline, with Brian seemingly thrilled to have his life return to some kind of normalcy. That all changed in November 2011, when Brian and Roger teamed up with Adam Lambert to accept the Global Icon Award at the MTV European Music Awards, where they performed a predictable but nonetheless exciting medley of 'The Show Must Go On', 'Under Pressure', 'We Will Rock You', and 'We Are The Champions'. Afterwards, the trio were interviewed by the BBC, and the electricity in the air was evident: "We're just delighted to still be around; so many of our friends aren't," Roger said. "And it's great to be here and actually to be appreciated – and to have our brilliant, genius, friend, singer, Adam Lambert here. Well, what a voice. One in a hundred million." Adam paid respect to Freddie: "It was such an honor to be asked to sing with Queen and they're obviously one of my favourite rock bands of all time. I mean, Freddie Mercury has influenced me vocally, performance-wise, so much, and the music that they created together, it broke the mould of what rock music was. It definitely inspires me on a day to day basis when I'm creating music. And also Freddie, you know, Freddie and I have a lot of other things … in common and, you know, I think that's something that speaks of a great deal progression that's happening in our society, and we're moving forward. We can be honest and open about who we are, and I think Freddie's spirit lives on."

The following year, the sparks that flew clearly hadn't burned out, and before long, a tour was announced for that July. "Judging by my incoming mail, this decision will make a lot of people very happy," Brian rather cavalierly exclaimed. "It's a worthy challenge for us, and I'm sure Adam would meet with Freddie's approval!" Adam also couldn't hide his excitement: "I'm completely in awe of the Queen phenomenon. The thought of sharing the stage for a full set is so beautifully surreal. I'm honoured to be able to pay my respects to Freddie's memory. He's a personal hero of mine and I am deeply grateful for the chance to sing such powerful music for fans of this legendary band. I know the evening will be a huge milestone for me, and with the support of Brian, Roger and the rest of the band I know magic will be on display."

Magic truly was on display, not only for the first dates of their inaugural tour, but for every show thereafter: Adam jumped into his role with aplomb, and while no one can argue that Paul Rodgers is a fantastic vocalist, the younger singer was able to command a crowd in a way that Paul just couldn't. Besides Adam's amazing charisma and charm, he was also more of a theatrical singer, allowing the band to perform songs they either wouldn't have been able to with Paul, or pull some more adventurous material out of their hats. (Paul likely wouldn't have been caught dead riding around on a pink tricycle to the strains of 'Bicycle Race'.)

Older and more conservative fans cried foul at a c-lebrity now fronting Queen, though those who saw the band in action were eventually (begrudgingly) won over. There's no doubt that Adam had earned his ermine robe and crown, and while Queen + Adam Lambert still delights audiences around the world, playing to cities and countries that Queen had been unable to play in their heyday, talk of a studio album still persists, though the trio remain noncommittal

on the idea, preferring to take their show on the road instead of laboring over ideas in the studio. Based on the lukewarm reception to *The Cosmos Rocks*, it seems that Brian and Roger aren't in any hurry to travel down that path again: while Brian agreed that the album had some "good material and we worked damn hard for months on end … nobody cared. It just disappeared. We sort of got the message, rightly or wrongly, that people just wanted to hear Queen with Freddie on record." Judging by the reception Queen + Adam Lambert has gotten, that message seems to have changed entirely.

EUROPEAN TOUR:
30 JUNE TO 14 JULY 2012

Musicians: Brian May *(guitars, vocals)*, Roger Taylor *(drums, vocals)*, Adam Lambert *(vocals)*, Spike Edney *(keyboards, vocals)*, Rufus Taylor *(drums, percussion)*, Neil Fairclough *(bass guitar, vocals)*

Repertoire: 'Flash's Theme' *(taped intro)* / 'The Hero', 'Seven Seas Of Rhye', 'Keep Yourself Alive', 'We Will Rock You' *(fast)*, 'Fat Bottomed Girls', 'Don't Stop Me Now', 'Under Pressure', 'I Want It All', 'Who Wants To Live Forever', 'A Kind Of Magic', 'These Are The Days Of Our Lives', 'Love Of My Life', "39", 'Dragon Attack' / Drum Solo / 'Last Horizon' / Guitar Solo, 'I Want To Break Free', 'Another One Bites The Dust', 'Radio Ga Ga', 'Somebody To Love', 'Crazy Little Thing Called Love', 'The Show Must Go On', 'Bohemian Rhapsody', 'Tie Your Mother Down', 'We Will Rock You', 'We Are The Champions', 'God Save The Queen', 'Life Is Real (Song For Lennon)', 'You're My Best Friend'

Itinerary:
June 30: Maidan Nezalezhnosti, Kiev, Ukraine
July 3: Olympijskiy Stadium, Moscow, Russia
July 7: Stadion Miejski, Wrocław, Poland
July 11/12/14: HMV Hammersmith Apollo, London, England

Queen + Adam Lambert kicked off their first proper shows together with a six-date mini tour in June 2012, with a trio of shows in Eastern Europe and three more on homeground at the Hammersmith Apollo. The first date, in Kiev, was a charity concert that also featured Elton John: titled "Your Life Is Not A Game – Let's Stop AIDS Together!", this was the coming-out party for the newly-minted band, who delivered a rousing set list that was far more adventurous and career-spanning than the Queen + Paul Rodgers gigs ever saw. Indeed, several songs were brought out of mothballs for these dates, which quickly grew into concert favorites and set list staples: 'The Hero', 'Seven Seas Of Rhye', 'Keep Yourself Alive', the fast version of 'We Will Rock You', 'Don't Stop Me Now', 'Who Wants To Live Forever', and 'Somebody To Love' were all dusted off for these shows, while further rare acoustic performances of 'Life Is Real (Song For Lennon)', 'You're My Best Friend', and 'The Show Must Go On' were given a bash in London.

The 3 July concert in Moscow was meant to be a warm-up gig to the Sonisphere Festival to be held at Knebworth between 6 and 8 July, with the band headlining on the 7th, but the Festival was later canceled due to logistical nightmares. (Sonisphere would return in 2014, but was canceled indefinitely the following year.) The band's first shows in London were received as a triumph, with reviews excitedly heralding the return of the band – while also pointing out that Adam was a better fit than Paul Rodgers. *The Independent* noted, "With his spiked diamante epaulettes, high heels and tight leather trousers which eventually split under his exertions, Lambert looks the part, hits the notes with ease, and if he doesn't quite have Freddie's voracious, imperious strut, you at least believe he means it when, before 'Fat Bottomed Girls', he demands to 'see some ass'. The set list relies too heavily on saccharine Eighties gloop – 'Who Wants To Live Forever', 'A Kind Of Magic' and 'These Are The Days Of Our Lives' is a particularly trying sequence – and an utterly pointless drum battle between Roger Taylor and his son Rufus, and guitar exhibition from May, have you looking at your watch. But there's no arguing with hard-rocking early numbers such as 'Seven Seas Of Rhye', 'Tie Your Mother Down' and 'We Will Rock You', a song so good they play it twice. Nor with the grin-inducing 'Flash' intro, *Shaun Of The Dead* classic 'Don't Stop Me Now', the Chic-inspired 'Another One Bites The Dust', or the ersatz rockabilly of 'Crazy Little Thing Called Love', which prompts a deafening 'Ready, Freddie!' from the crowd. Mercury is a Banquo-like presence, frequently appearing on nostalgic footage, singing 'Love Of My Life' from beyond the grave, and, in a pyrotechnics-packed 'Bohemian Rhapsody', effectively duetting with Adam Lambert." *The Guardian* gave the band's Hammersmith run four out of five stars, opining that the show was "a spectacle of such overblown majesty that, somewhere, Freddie Mercury must have been chuckling approvingly. It's no insult

to Lambert, a theatrical pop star in his own right, to say he lacks Mercury's magisterial authority. The late singer still inhabits every one of Queen's songs, and the best Lambert could do was sing them with verve. While vocally equal to the crescendos and curlicues, he was unable to compete with Mercury's memory – something vividly proved during 'Love Of My Life', when 1980s footage of Mercury unexpectedly flashed on screen. The crowd's gasp spoke volumes. In any case, Lambert was frequently off stage, leaving guitarist Brian May and drummer Roger Taylor to perform a tranche of hits as a duo. They dispatched 'One Vision', 'A Kind Of Magic' and 'These Are The Days Of Our Lives', with Taylor introducing the last as 'a song about looking back and reminiscing'. That also defined the evening itself: this gig commemorated marching shoulder-to-shoulder for 40 years, the last Queen men standing. Lambert was back for the big, primal stompers, audibly growing in confidence as he worked through 'Radio Ga Ga', 'We Are The Champions' and 'We Will Rock You'. The fireworks and lasers that came with the finale, 'Bohemian Rhapsody', were appropriately grandiose – how else to finish a terrific show in which no gesture was too overwrought?" *The Telegraph* wasn't convinced: "This has to go down as one of the strangest gigs I have ever seen. At one point, during 'Bohemian Rhapsody', the whole band leave the stage for a pre-recorded operatic section by their younger selves, returning to perform the finale with Lambert duetting with video footage of the late Freddie Mercury. This was effectively Queen paying tribute to themselves, with a young, gay American pop singer standing in for their legendary frontman. Whatever happened to rock and roll? To be fair, Queen were always a peculiar band, musically and theatrically, straddling heavy rock, pop, folk, disco and music hall. It took the charisma of their extravagantly talented frontman to hold it all together. Those are big boots to fill, and tottering around on a pair of black platforms in a black leather and brocade outfit, it takes the *American Idol* star a while to find his feet. While Mercury's camp machismo manifested as a kind of strutting bravura, Lambert seems merely camp, like an over-excited cast member from *We Will Rock You*. Hand-picked by guitarist Brian May, Lambert can certainly handle the vocal range of Queen's songs although he sings in a softer, more soulful, modern pop style, without Mercury's rock grit or operatic bombast ... The fans loved it but it left me feeling slightly queasy, watching another great band turn into a pastiche of themselves.

You can't begrudge old musicians wanting to play their own hits. With his white ringlets and a wizardy cloak, May looks increasingly like a rock Gandalf. He remains a phenomenal guitarist, though, and a solo spot in which he plays off his own echoing rhythm makes you wonder why he thinks he needs a band at all. Roger Taylor impresses too with an extended solo, drumming up a storm in a family duel with son Rufus on percussion. But individual set pieces couldn't quite cohere into something unified or transcendent. The other session musicians hug the edge of the stage as if trying to make themselves invisible. They deliver the hits with crowd pleasing gusto but it never really feels like a band. It's a Queen show. But it's not Queen."

iHEARTRADIO MUSIC FESTIVAL 2013
MGM GRAND GARDEN ARENA,
LAS VEGAS, NEVADA
20 SEPTEMBER 2013

Musicians: Brian May *(guitars, vocals)*, Roger Taylor *(drums, vocals)*, Adam Lambert *(vocals)*, Spike Edney *(keyboards, vocals)*, Rufus Taylor *(drums, percussion)*, Neil Fairclough *(bass guitar, vocals)*

Repertoire: 'Bohemian Rhapsody', 'Another One Bites The Dust', 'Crazy Little Thing Called Love', 'Who Wants To Live Forever', 'Somebody To Love', 'Fat Bottomed Girls', 'Dragon Attack', 'We Will Rock You', 'We Are The Champions'

This brief concert, Queen + Adam Lambert's first in North America, would be their only live show of the year, and while it was an extremely shortened set as part of the iHeartRadio Music Festival, the band still turned in a rousing concert. Intriguingly, 'Somebody To Love' was performed with the band fun. (Brian had been asked to perform with the band at their Grammy Awards appearance earlier that year, but the guitarist had to bow out due to knee problems), and lead vocalist Nate Ruess duetted with Adam on 'Fat Bottomed Girls'. *Rolling Stone* was complimentary: "Lambert astounded the audience on songs like 'We Will Rock You' and the closing 'We Are The Champions' and 'Crazy Little Thing Called Love'. He frequently worked in unison with May, the two sharing the front of the stage as the guitarist reminded everyone of his considerable prowess by bringing his parts in 'Bohemian Rhapsody' to life." *Hollywood Reporter* also raved, "Right before

a closing duet of the classically campy anthem, 'Fat Bottomed Girls', fun. leader Nate Ruess described Lambert as 'the best singer I know'. Lambert proved that statement to the fullest during the band's medley-heavy set. Strutting to Roger Taylor's thunderous back beat and clearly enjoying his time in the spotlight, Lambert graciously traded licks with Ruess, who sang three songs as Queen's special guest … Lambert was a commanding presence throughout, belting such arena anthems as 'Bohemian Rhapsody', 'We Will Rock You' and 'We Are The Champions' with his signature wail and sick range, and was equally captivating as he dialed it down for the pensive 'Who Wants To Live Forever'. That ballad, in particular, elicited a rousing applause from the diverse audience of music fans young and old."

ONCE IN A LIFETIME NORTH AMERICAN TOUR:
19 JUNE TO 28 JULY 2014

Musicians: Brian May *(guitars, vocals)*, Roger Taylor *(drums, vocals)*, Adam Lambert *(vocals)*, Spike Edney *(keyboards, vocals)*, Rufus Taylor *(drums, percussion)*, Neil Fairclough *(bass guitar, vocals)*

Repertoire: 'Procession' / 'Now I'm Here', 'Stone Cold Crazy', 'Another One Bites The Dust', 'Fat Bottomed Girls', 'In The Lap Of The Gods...Revisited', 'Seven Seas Of Rhye', 'Killer Queen', 'Somebody To Love', 'I Want It All', 'Love Of My Life', "39', 'These Are The Days Of Our Lives', Drum Battle, 'Under Pressure', 'Love Kills', 'Who Wants To Live Forever', 'Last Horizon' / Guitar Solo, 'Tie Your Mother Down', 'Radio Ga Ga', 'Don't Stop Me Now', 'Crazy Little Thing Called Love', 'The Show Must Go On', 'Bohemian Rhapsody', 'We Will Rock You', 'We Are the Champions', 'God Save The Queen'

Itinerary:
June 19: United Center, Chicago, Illinois
June 21: MTS Centre, Winnipeg
June 23: Credit Union Centre, Saskatoon
June 24: Rexall Place, Edmonton
June 26: Scotiabank Saddledome, Calgary, Alberta
June 28: Pepsi Live at Rogers Arena, Vancouver, British Columbia
July 1: SAP Center, San Jose, California
July 3: The Forum, Los Angeles, California
July 5/6: The Joint, Las Vegas, Nevada
July 9: Toyota Center, Houston, Texas

July 10: American Airlines Center, Dallas, Texas
July 12: The Palace at Auburn Hills, Detroit, Michigan
July 13: Air Canada Centre, Toronto, Ontario
July 14: Bell Centre, Montreal, Quebec
July 16: Wells Fargo Center, Philadelphia, Pennsylvania
July 17: Madison Square Garden, New York, New York
July 19: Mohegan Sun Arena, Uncasville, Connecticut
July 20: Merriweather Post Pavilion, Washington, D.C.
July 22: TD Garden, Boston, Massachusetts
July 23: Izod Center, East Rutherford, New Jersey
July 25: Mohegan Sun Arena, Uncasville, Connecticut
July 26: Boardwalk Hall, Atlantic City, New Jersey
July 28: Air Canada Centre, Toronto, Ontario

Having dipped their toes in the water with a brief, six-date tour in 2012, and a one-off festival appearance the following year, Queen + Adam Lambert embarked on their first full-length tour of North America on 19 June 2014, performing a 24-date tour over six weeks. The band certainly returned to more of a fanfare than they had the last time they were Stateside, in March and April 2006 with Paul Rodgers: press previews were ecstatic, with one-time enemy *Rolling Stone* writing eloquent, fawning notices.

The stage and lights had also changed quite a bit, in order to give North America a true wowing, the likes of which hadn't been seen at a Queen concert since perhaps the late 1970s: a massive curtain, emblazoned with the Queen logo, shields the audience from viewing the stage, but once the pre-recorded tape of 'Procession' finished with a fanfare, the band launched into 'Now I'm Here', with the curtain dropping once the song got going. Adam also channeled Freddie's theatrical side, singing the entirety of 'Killer Queen' from a giant purple couch, before chugging from a bottle of Armand de Brignac Brut Gold champagne and playfully spitting some into the audience.

The set list was updated slightly, with the opening gambit of 'Procession' and 'Now I'm Here' serving as a more appropriate introduction, while 'Stone Cold Crazy', 'In The Lap Of The Gods…Revisited', and 'Killer Queen' were new additions. The biggest surprise was performed only a handful of times, but it was certainly one of the most interesting performances of the tour: the reworked "ballad" version of 'Love Kills', which had been rearranged for the upcoming *Queen Forever* compilation, was given a rare live airing before its release. While the original version was beautifully performed and sung by Freddie, this rearrangement was successful mostly due to the strength of Adam's voice,

who commanded the song with relative ease. That it was later dropped from the set list was a terrific shame.

The reviews were almost universally glowing, a far cry from the tepid response that Queen + Paul Rodgers received. "Lambert managed to be both respectful in his approach to the material – all of which dated from Mercury's tenure – and confident as he worked a catwalk that curved around from behind the drum riser and out through the first several rows," *The Baltimore Sun* wrote. "And while Lambert's voice is neither as full nor as rich as Mercury's – he wouldn't have been onstage if his predecessor had been available – it does cut with a contemporary R&B edge that had the effect of updating the band's sound." *The Chicago Tribune* was pleased: "The chemistry among the trio was evident: Lambert grooved to Taylor's beats on the drum platform, May and Lambert's respective guitar and vocal gymnastics interlaced effortlessly … Lambert's role was not to be underestimated, though. He brought spine-tingling prowess to the epic 'Who Wants To Live Forever' and 'Somebody To Love', campiness to 'Killer Queen', rockabilly dance poses to 'Crazy Little Thing Called Love' and respect during 'Bohemian Rhapsody', where he traded vocals with Mercury on screen as the band and audience harmonized along." "Having previously toured and recorded with Paul Rodgers during the mid-2000s to mixed reviews, Queen has found the ideal frontman in Adam Lambert," *The Orange County Register* opined. "The *American Idol* runner-up initially performed with the group in the '09 season finale and then did half a dozen European dates with the band. May recently told *Rolling Stone*, 'This [American tour] is the closest you'll ever get to see Queen as it was in our golden days.' Indeed. Lambert, 32, has a strikingly similar sense of panache when compared with Mercury, plus an impressive vocal range. Each was on full display in Inglewood amid a spectacular show rife with classic rock bombast (i.e. the requisite drum and guitar solos) that clocked in at just over two hours … All told, the band still sounded great. Here's hoping Lambert continues with them for awhile."

Some, however, were not convinced, with *The New York Times* being at least fair in its assessment: "Mr. Lambert, who, like other *American Idol* contestants, is a student and mimic of pop idols past, has clearly decided how he wants to approach his alliance with Queen. He's no longer the goth-styled, crotch-grabbing character he was while touring for his solo albums. Now he's deferential, boyish and trying to update Queen — an English band whose heyday was in the

1970s and early 1980s — with a touch of American R&B in his voice and with hip-hop stage patter. Neither is a winning strategy. His voice loses fullness as it ascends, his R&B melismata are whiny, and his patter is embarrassing. Trying to lead an audience chant of 'Bite it!' during Queen's gleefully murderous 'Another One Bites The Dust' and spitting something he drank from a Champagne bottle onto nearby fans were the lowest points ... Unfortunately, the band indulged itself with long solos reminiscent of bloated 1970s shows; really, there was no need for a bass solo by Mr. Fairclough, even if Mr. Taylor joined him to drum on the bass strings near the end. There were also stretches when Mr. May and Mr. Taylor sang or shared lead vocals, including the most open tributes to Mercury; they were only adequate. They were featured during a long, sagging midconcert stretch of unaccompanied solos, and it took the show some time to recover momentum afterward." *The Houston Press* was also unimpressed: "Now, admittedly, the decision to do this tour with Lambert is the one that in theory should make the most sense. And sometimes it actually makes more than sense; on songs like 'Killer Queen' and 'I Want It All' they actually do manage to make some magic, and it's quite impressive. The problem is that these magic moments are few and far between. Adam Lambert is probably the best choice to front Queen if you need a warm body to fill that position; he's miles ahead of Paul Rodgers and a much better contemporary choice than, say, Lady Gaga. The problem is that just because he's the best choice doesn't mean he's a good choice. Again, there's no doubt that he can sing. Seeing him live will give you a greater appreciation of his skills as a singer; he is multitudes more impressive than he seems on TV. But while his voice may be amazing, it doesn't really fit into the type of music that Queen plays, even though all signs point toward the idea that he should ... Here's the real mind-bender for you though: Lambert is the one that's getting the short end of the stick here. All the people who believe the problem here is that Lambert can't fill Mercury's shoes have it all wrong; the problem is that Adam Lambert is too talented to vamp on stage while Brian May works his way through yet another (admittedly impressive) guitar solo ... Adam Lambert needs to find someone to write the right song that shows off his voice and his charisma. Queen needs to give up the ghost and just fucking use Mercury's vocal tracks for all the songs that need them if they're going to tour."

ONCE IN A LIFETIME FESTIVAL DATES:
30 JUNE TO 14 JULY 2012

Musicians: Brian May *(guitars, vocals)*, Roger Taylor *(drums, vocals)*, Adam Lambert *(vocals)*, Spike Edney *(keyboards, vocals)*, Rufus Taylor *(drums, percussion)*, Neil Fairclough *(bass guitar, vocals)*

Repertoire: 'Procession' / 'Now I'm Here', 'Stone Cold Crazy', 'Another One Bites The Dust', 'Fat Bottomed Girls', 'In The Lap Of The Gods...Revisited', 'Seven Seas Of Rhye', 'Killer Queen', 'Somebody To Love', 'I Want It All', 'Teo Torriatte (Let Us Cling Together)', 'Love Of My Life', '39', 'These Are The Days Of Our Lives', Drum Battle, 'Under Pressure', 'Dragon Attack', 'I Was Born To Love You', 'Who Wants To Live Forever', 'Last Horizon' / Guitar Solo, 'Tie Your Mother Down', 'Radio Ga Ga', 'Crazy Little Thing Called Love', 'Bohemian Rhapsody', 'We Will Rock You', 'We Are The Champions', 'God Save The Queen'

Itinerary:
August 14: Supersonic Festival, Olympic Park, Seoul, South Korea
August 16: Summer Sonic Festival, Maishima Sports Island, Osaka, Japan
August 17: Summer Sonic Festival, Chiba Marine Stadium & Makuhari Messe, Chiba, Japan

This brief, three-date tour saw Queen + Adam Lambert performing festival shows in South Korea (the first time Queen played live there) and Japan. Unsurprisingly, 'I Was Born To Love You' was performed live in lieu of 'Love Kills', which had been dropped two dates from the conclusion of the North American tour; unlike previous tours with Queen + Paul Rodgers, where it was performed acoustically by Brian and Roger, Adam sang lead vocals and the entire band served up a rousing rendition. In Japan, the set list was truncated heavily, with only 18 songs performed, though 'Teo Torriatte (Let Us Cling Together)' was added for obvious reasons. *The Japan Times* was pleased with Queen + Adam Lambert's show at the Summer Sonic Festival in Chiba: "No act better summed up what Summer Sonic 2014 aimed for than Queen + Adam Lambert – a veteran act with a new twist. Forty-four years since forming, only two original members (Brian May and Roger Taylor) chug along under the Queen name. Nobody in the stadium seemed concerned about that, though, they danced and sang along to classics like 'Under Pressure' and 'Radio Ga Ga'. Lambert, best known as runner-up from the 2009 edition of *American Idol*, was no Freddie Mercury, but impressed nonetheless. 'What do you think of the new man?' guitarist May asked, to loud cheers."

ONCE IN A LIFETIME DOWN UNDER TOUR:
22 AUGUST TO 4 SEPTEMBER 2014

Musicians: Brian May *(guitars, vocals)*, Roger Taylor *(drums, vocals)*, Adam Lambert *(vocals)*, Spike Edney *(keyboards, vocals)*, Rufus Taylor *(drums, percussion)*, Neil Fairclough *(bass guitar, vocals)*

Repertoire: 'Procession' / 'Now I'm Here', 'Stone Cold Crazy', 'Another One Bites The Dust', 'Fat Bottomed Girls', 'In The Lap Of The Gods…Revisited', 'Seven Seas Of Rhye', 'Killer Queen', 'Somebody To Love', 'I Want It All', 'Love Of My Life', "39', 'These Are The Days Of Our Lives', Bass Solo, Drum Battle, 'Under Pressure', 'Dragon Attack', 'Who Wants To Live Forever', Guitar Solo, 'Tie Your Mother Down', Vocal Solo, 'I Want To Break Free', 'Radio Ga Ga', 'Crazy Little Thing Called Love', 'Bohemian Rhapsody', 'We Will Rock You', 'We Are The Champions', 'God Save The Queen', 'A Kind Of Magic', 'The Show Must Go On', 'Waltzing Matilda', 'Don't Dream It's Over'

Itinerary:
August 22: Perth Arena, Perth, WA, Australia
August 26/27: Allphones Arena, Sydney, Australia
August 29/30: Rod Laver Arena, Melbourne, Australia
September 1: Brisbane Entertainment Centre, Brisbane, Australia
September 3/4: Vector Arena, Auckland, New Zealand

The Once In A Lifetime tour continued on to Australia and New Zealand, with the band taking their well-worn set down under for the first time since 1985. (Of course, Brian had visited Australia on his own solo tours, but Queen + Paul Rodgers missed out during their run.) Not much changed from the North American tour, with 'I Want To Break Free' becoming a mainstay, while 'A Kind Of Magic' rotated spots with 'These Are The Days Of Our Lives'. On 27 August, Lady Gaga, in town for her own concert, joined the band onstage to duet with Adam on 'Another One Bites The Dust', while Brian performed the perennial unofficial national anthem of Australia, 'Waltzing Matilda', on the final night of the tour. The tour then wound its way

to Auckland for two shows at the Vector Arena, where Brian played a snippet of Crowded House's 'Don't Dream It's Over' before 'Love Of My Life'.

The Sydney Morning Herald was happy to have seen Queen again: "Lambert, bringing Mercury by way of George Michael from the minute he stepped out in studded and glittered leather, in a sense was on a hiding to nothing. As good as his voice is, as flamboyant as his stage persona is, as many outfits as he could change into (five, if you're wondering), he was not going to really measure up against the legend as much as the reality of one of the best front men ever. On the other hand, Lambert had little to lose as everyone expected him to not measure up and some probably expected him to mess up. Therefore he could impress with a wide and expansive voice that only sometimes tipped over into excessively florid but never missed a (high, low or mid) note. And he could entertain with a sense of the theatrical which was in the spirit, if never as natural (I blame the performance schools and talent shows), as Queen's original. That said, I'm not sure Freddie Mercury would have given a shout out to 'all my fat-assed bitches out there'." *The Herald Sun* opined, "Thanks to social media, we have seen a lot of people really bothered by Queen continuing to exist, now with guest singer Adam Lambert. None of those people were in the sold out Rod Laver Arena last night … Within minutes you focus less on who isn't there rather who is – May is one of the all time rock guitar heroes whose work is instantly identifiable and nothing has changed. And Lambert plugs into Queen perfectly, if anything dialling down his theatricality … slightly. He may be having the most fun of all; reviving Queen's catalog in a huge arena with decadent production is an incredible and challenging gift for any singer. While he's got unmistakable Mercury in his performer DNA, Lambert puts just enough of himself in these songs to stop it being the world's most musically accurate Queen tribute act. 'Thank you for suspending your disbelief and letting me sing these amazing songs', Lambert tells the crowd, which include plenty of his own fans. 'I'm just up here trying to make Freddie proud.'" *The New Zealand Herald* was also complimentary: "Lambert proved he had plenty stage presence along with a winning personality and very busy costume department. But vocally, it sounded as if his strengths are up top. Still, his takes on many of the songs did – as they say in *Idol* land – make them his own. That's whether it was his Michael Jackson-like tilt at 'Another One Bites The Dust' or his Elvis lip-curl on the rockabilly of 'Crazy Little Thing Called Love' near the end. And the more theatrical numbers and challenging melodies like 'Killer Queen', which had him propped upon a purple chaise longue at the end of the stage runway, proved his forte more than the straight rockers … While witnessing a Queen live show without Mercury might never quite feel like the genuine article, seeing May fire off another raygun solo over the heads of a very happy Vector crowd made this feel anything but a group becoming a cover band of itself. More a reminder of who invented this stadium rock stuff in the first place. Yes, Queen + Adam Lambert = the sum of their very good parts."

QUEEN + ADAM LAMBERT ROCK BIG BEN LIVE
31 DECEMBER 2014

Musicians: Brian May *(guitars, vocals)*, Roger Taylor *(drums, vocals)*, Adam Lambert *(vocals)*, Spike Edney *(keyboards, vocals)*, Rufus Taylor *(drums, percussion)*, Neil Fairclough *(bass guitar, vocals)*

Repertoire: 'Don't Stop Me Now', 'I Want To Break Free', 'Somebody To Love', 'Another One Bites The Dust', 'Under Pressure', 'Fat Bottomed Girls', 'Radio Ga Ga', 'I Want It All', 'Crazy Little Thing Called Love', 'The Show Must Go On', 'Bohemian Rhapsody' / 'Killer Queen' / 'Bohemian Rhapsody' *(reprise)*, 'We Will Rock You', 'We Are The Champions'

Filmed on New Year's Eve 2014 for BBC1, this show was performed live in Westminster Cathedral's Central Hall, in the shadow of Big Ben, not only in front of 2,000 ecstatic fans, but across the globe on a webstream. Queen + Adam Lambert pulled out some big surprises: at the start of 'We Will Rock You', bagpipes from John Jamieson were featured, while 'Don't Stop Me Now' was an unexpected concert opener. Additionally, 'Killer Queen' replaced the operatic section of 'Bohemian Rhapsody' (which was the first number played after midnight struck), making for a unique performance that recalled the medley concept from 1975. The concert was an unparalleled success, with 5.83 million viewers tuning in for the first part, while the second part received double those numbers. However, the most astonishing part of the night remained in rehearsal: 'Drowse' was performed, though, given its obscurity, it was understandably not played during the concert.

UK/EUROPEAN TOUR:
13 JANUARY TO 27 FEBRUARY 2015

Musicians: Brian May *(guitars, vocals)*, Roger Taylor *(drums, vocals)*, Adam Lambert *(vocals)*, Spike Edney *(keyboards, vocals)*, Rufus Taylor *(drums, percussion)*, Neil Fairclough *(bass guitar, vocals)*

Repertoire: 'One Vision', 'Stone Cold Crazy', 'Another One Bites The Dust', 'Fat Bottomed Girls', 'In The Lap Of The Gods…Revisited', 'Seven Seas Of Rhye', 'Killer Queen', 'I Want To Break Free', 'Don't Stop Me Now', 'Somebody To Love', 'Love Of My Life', ''39', 'These Are The Days Of Our Lives', Bass Solo, Drum Battle, 'Under Pressure', 'Save Me', 'Who Wants To Live Forever', Guitar Solo, 'Tie Your Mother Down', Vocal Solo, 'I Want It All', 'Radio Ga Ga', 'Crazy Little Thing Called Love', 'Bohemian Rhapsody', 'We Will Rock You', 'We Are The Champions', 'God Save The Queen', 'Dragon Attack', 'A Kind Of Magic', 'The Show Must Go On'

Itinerary:
January 13: Metro Radio Arena, Newcastle
January 14: The SSE Hydro, Glasgow, Scotland
January 17/18: O2 Arena, London
January 20: First Direct Arena, Leeds
January 21: Phones 4u Arena, Manchester
January 23: Barclaycard Arena, Birmingham
January 24: Capital FM Arena, Nottingham
January 26: Zénith de Paris, Paris, France
January 29: Lanxess Arena, Cologne, Germany
January 30: Ziggo Dome, Amsterdam, Netherlands
February 1: Wiener Stadthalle, Vienna, Austria
February 2: Olympiahalle, Munich, Germany
February 4: O2 World, Berlin, Germany
February 5: O2 World, Hamburg, Germany
February 7: Festhalle, Frankfurt, Germany
February 10: Mediolanum Forum, Milan, Italy
February 13: Schleyerhalle, Stuttgart, Germany
February 15: Jyske Bank Boxen, Herning, Denmark
February 17: O2 Arena, Prague, Czech Republic
February 19: Hallenstadion, Zurich, Switzerland
February 21: Tauron Arena Krakow, Krakow, Poland
February 24: Wembley SSE Arena, London
February 26: Liverpool Echo Arena, Liverpool
February 27: Motorpoint Arena, Sheffield

Queen + Adam Lambert set off on a lengthy, 26-date tour of the UK, Europe, and Eastern Europe in January 2015, rejigging their set list slightly: the concert opener became the rather predictable 'One Vision', while 'A Kind Of Magic' became a semi-permanent regular, though the biggest surprise was the addition of 'Save Me', performed for the first time since 1982. In Scotland, the bagpipe arrangement during the intro of 'We Will Rock You' was reprised, with a young Craig Weir joining the band onstage: "When I got an email from Brian May asking me to play with them I thought it was a wind-up," Craig told *The Evening Times*. "But it soon became clear it really was him and he really was asking me to play with them at their Scots show. When I was confirmed for the gig I instantly got the shakes. I couldn't believe it. To say I've stood on stage and played with Queen is more than a little ridiculous!"

Unfortunately, illnesses plagued the band throughout the tour, with Brian suffering from the flu in Cologne, while a gig in Brussels on 8 February had to be canceled due to Adam suffering from acute bronchitis. As a result, the set list was shuffled around a bit to remove some of the more demanding material ('Stone Cold Crazy', 'The Show Must Go On', 'Who Wants To Live Forever', and Adam's vocal solo), but Brian's spirits weren't entirely dampened: he threw in little snippets of 'The Blue Danube', 'I (Who Have Nothing)', 'Maybe It's Because I'm A Londoner', 'You've Got To Hide Your Love Away', and 'Plaisir d'amour' at various shows, just prior to 'Love Of My Life'. Once Adam had regained his health, 'Dragon Attack', a personal favorite of his, was performed on several occasions on the back half of the tour.

Once again, the tour received rave reviews, with the UK press more favorable of Adam than they had been of Paul Rodgers. *The Liverpool Echo* wrote, "Freddie Mercury had a rare and unusual gift. He managed to make us all magnificent for five minutes. His songs brought out the strutting peacock in the mildest mannered of music fans. In a couple of decades, Queen wrote more hits than most musicians do in a lifetime, and performed them around the world to adoring fans. And then, suddenly and seemingly so unfairly, Freddie was stolen from us by a cruel illness and the music stopped. It has carried on, of course, in many forms. Original band members Brian may and Rodger Taylor re-united, with the help of Free and Bad Company singer Paul Rodgers, for a series of gigs. But that was more a meeting of bands, a guest performance. It has taken Adam Lambert, the former American Idol star who was just nine years old when Freddie died, to truly re-create that magic. He has an arena-filling charisma and an effortless soaring voice, but there

the comparisons stop. He's not much like Freddie in the way he sings or the way he looks but somehow it works. It's not *Stars In Their Eyes* and it doesn't feel like a tribute show. Somehow they make it seem new and fresh and strangely credible … From 'Under Pressure' through 'Fat Bottomed Girls', 'Killer Queen', 'Don't Stop Me Now' and 'Somebody To Love', the American Idol gave a performance that was somehow all his own, and yet fitted perfectly with the rest of the band. Add in the bombastic 'I Want It All', a clap-along 'Radio Ga Ga' and the naughtiest delivery of 'Crazy Little Thing Called Love' anyone could hope for and Adam Lambert held the ECHO arena crowd in the palm of his jewel-encrusted hand." *The Express* gave the Wembley SSE Arena show four out of five stars: "Unfairly accused by some of cynically cashing in on Mercury's legacy while bassist John Deacon opted for a quiet retirement, the duo have existed as a band for considerably longer without their flamboyant frontman than with him … Lambert certainly has the soaring, effortless vocal ability and flamboyant stage presence for the job and, nearing the completion of this European tour, appears supremely confident. Pouting, thrusting and flirting his way through the two-hour live seat, his bucketless energy and enthusiasm for Queen's back catalog is clear. The man who could be Mercury's young apprentice is having the time of his life – as are May and Taylor, who are clearly enjoying the injection of energy Lambert brings to proceedings … Lambert isn't apologetic for not being Freddie Mercury – he's clearly aware that even after so long, the moustached maestro's shadow looms large. What do we think of the new guy? We approve. And we get the feeling Freddie would have done, too."

DON'T STOP THEM NOW SOUTH AMERICAN TOUR:
16 TO 30 SEPTEMBER 2015

Musicians: Brian May *(guitars, vocals)*, Roger Taylor *(drums, vocals)*, Adam Lambert *(vocals)*, Spike Edney *(keyboards, vocals)*, Rufus Taylor *(drums, percussion)*, Neil Fairclough *(bass guitar, vocals)*

Repertoire: 'One Vision', 'Stone Cold Crazy', 'Another One Bites The Dust', 'Fat Bottomed Girls', 'In The Lap Of The Gods…Revisited', 'Seven Seas Of Rhye', 'Killer Queen', 'Don't Stop Me Now', 'I Want To Break Free', 'Somebody To Love', 'Love Of My Life', "39', 'These Are The Days Of Our Lives', Bass Solo, Drum Battle,

'Under Pressure', 'Save Me', 'Ghost Town', 'Who Wants To Live Forever', Guitar Solo, 'Tie Your Mother Down', 'I Want It All', 'Radio Ga Ga', 'Crazy Little Thing Called Love', 'The Show Must Go On', 'Bohemian Rhapsody', 'We Will Rock You', 'We Are The Champions', 'God Save The Queen', 'Las Palabras De Amor (The Words Of Love)'

Itinerary:

September 16: Ginásio do Ibirapuera, São Paulo, Brazil

September 18: Rock in Rio Brazil 2015, City of Rock, Rio de Janeiro, Brazil

September 21: Gigantinho, Porto Alegre, Rio Grande do Sul, Brazil

September 25: Estadio GEBA, Buenos Aires, Argentina

September 27: Orfeo Superdomo, Córdoba, Argentina

September 30: Pista Atlética, Estadio Nacional Julio Martínez Prádanos, Santiago, Chile

After a seven month break, Queen + Adam Lambert returned to the live circuit, this time embarking on a South American trek that saw them perform six dates over two weeks. The set list remained largely the same, except for the addition of Adam's 'Ghost Town', released on his *The Original High* album and here restructured as a rock song. This performance of Adam's solo material was a treat, considering he didn't have as much of an output as Paul Rodgers had, and the band performed the song admirably, resulting in a handful of his songs being incorporated over the next few tours. *Billboard* weighed in on the welcome change: "Freddie Mercury remains irreplaceable, but Queen fans hungry to see the surviving band members live in the 21st century owe Adam Lambert a healthy debt of gratitude for bringing the British band's classic material back to the stage with style, aplomb and an incredible set of pipes. So it's about time that Queen returned the favor and lent their majestic stadium rock touch to one of Lambert's solo tracks. Playing São Paulo on 16 September, Queen + Adam Lambert performed the latter's 'Ghost Town' live for the first time together. The eerie whistle hook from *The Original High* original is replaced by Brian May's guitar, giving the Max Martin-produced track a hard rock recasting. The song is surprisingly durable – it wouldn't sound out of place on a live double LP set from the '70s."

The São Paulo gig served as a warm-up for the Rock In Rio Festival, where Queen returned 30 years after they last appeared, serving as the headliner on the first

night. The concert was broadcast live on television and streamed online, while the band played to 85,000 enthusiastic fans in the stadium. The concert was filmed in full HD, leaving fans hoping that perhaps a Blu-Ray release will be imminent.

FESTIVAL DATES:
20 MAY TO 12 SEPTEMBER 2016

Musicians: Brian May *(guitars, vocals)*, Roger Taylor *(drums, vocals)*, Adam Lambert *(vocals)*, Spike Edney *(keyboards, vocals)*, Rufus Taylor *(drums, percussion)*, Neil Fairclough *(bass guitar, vocals)*

Repertoire: 'Flash' *(taped intro)*, 'The Hero', 'Hammer To Fall', 'Seven Seas Of Rhye', 'Stone Cold Crazy', 'Fat Bottomed Girls', 'Play The Game', 'Killer Queen', 'I Want To Break Free', 'Somebody To Love', 'Love Of My Life', 'These Are The Days Of Our Lives', Drum Battle, 'Under Pressure', 'Crazy Little Thing Called Love', 'Don't Stop Me Now', 'Another One Bites The Dust', 'I Want It All', 'Who Wants To Live Forever', 'Last Horizon' / Guitar Solo, 'Tie Your Mother Down', 'The Show Must Go On', 'Bohemian Rhapsody', 'Radio Ga Ga', 'We Will Rock You', 'We Are The Champions', 'God Save The Queen', 'One Vision', 'A Kind Of Magic', 'Keep Yourself Alive', 'Dragon Attack'

Itinerary:

May 20: Rock in Rio Lisboa 2016, Parque da Bela Vista, Lisbon, Portugal

May 22: Palau Sant Jordi, Barcelona, Spain

May 25: Steel City Festival 2016, Linzer Stadium, Linz, Austria

May 27: RheinEnergieStadion, Cologne, Germany

May 29: Jelling Musikfestival 2016, Festivalpladsen, Jelling, Denmark

June 3: Kaisaniemen puisto, Helsinki, Finland

June 5: Song Festival Ground, Tallinn, Estonia

June 9: Sweden Rock Festival 2016, Norje Havsbad, Norje, Sweden

June 12: Isle of Wight 2016, Seaclose Park, Newport, England

June 15: Palais 12, Brussels, Belgium

June 17: Rock the Ring 2016, Autobahnkreisel, Hinwil, Switzerland

June 19: Stadion MOSiR, Oswiecim, Poland

June 21: Piata Constitutiei, Bucharest, Romania

June 23: Arena Muzika 2016, Georgi Asparuhov Stadium, Sofia, Bulgaria

June 25: Hydrogen Festival 2016, Anfiteatro Camerini, Padua, Italy
September 12: Park HaYarkon, Tel Aviv, Israel

The band once again hit the road in May 2016, playing at 16 festivals over the course of a month (with another festival, in Tel Aviv, popping up in September). Once again, the set list was restructured, with opening numbers alternating between the atmospheric 'Flash' / 'The Hero' and 'One Vision', while 'Hammer To Fall' became the second number of the night to be performed. The biggest addition was 'Play The Game', receiving its first performances since 1982, albeit in an abridged form, serving as an intro to 'Killer Queen'. Elsewhere, Brian threw in snippets of 'Barcelona', 'Eine kleine nachtmusik', 'Hubava si moya goro', 'O Sole mio', and 'Hava Nagila' into his nightly guitar solo, depending on the night and the city.

"Queen's legendary lead singer may have gone on to the great stage in the sky, but his spirit pervaded Tel Aviv's Yarkon Park on Monday as his band electrified the more than 50,000 fans who had come from all over the country to hear some of the greatest hits the 1970s and 1980s produced," *The Times Of Israel* wrote. "Not that half-Jewish American singer Adam Lambert didn't give a rocking rendition of hits ranging from 'Fat Bottomed Girls' to 'Don't Stop Me Now' and 'Killer Queen'. He even managed a few words of Yiddish, light-heartedly complaining, "Oy vey iz mir, oy gevald, it's hot here!" … May told the crowd he'd heard that 'in Israel, you sing quite well', before launching into a haunting solo of the ballad 'Love Of My Life' and encouraging the crowd to accompany him 'for Freddie'."

ASIAN TOUR:
17 TO 30 SEPTEMBER 2016

Musicians: Brian May (*guitars, vocals*), Roger Taylor (*drums, vocals*), Adam Lambert (*vocals*), Spike Edney (*keyboards, vocals*), Rufus Taylor (*drums, percussion*), Neil Fairclough (*bass guitar, vocals*)

Repertoire: 'Seven Seas Of Rhye', 'Hammer To Fall', 'Stone Cold Crazy', 'Fat Bottomed Girls', 'Don't Stop Me Now', 'Killer Queen', 'Somebody To Love', 'Love Of My Life', 'These Are The Days Of Our Lives', Drum Battle, 'Under Pressure', 'Crazy Little Thing Called Love', 'Another One Bites The Dust', 'I Want It All', 'Last Horizon', 'Who Wants To Live Forever', 'The Show Must Go On', 'Tie Your Mother Down', 'I Want To

Break Free', 'Bohemian Rhapsody', 'Radio Ga Ga', 'We Will Rock You', 'We Are The Champions', 'God Save The Queen', 'Teo Torriatte (Let Us Cling Together)', 'I Was Born To Love You'

Itinerary:
September 17: Formula 1 Singapore Grand Prix 2016, The Padang, Singapore, Singapore
September 19: TWTC Nangang Exhibition Hall, Taipei, Taiwan
September 21/22/23: Nippon Budokan, Tokyo, Japan
September 26: Mercedes-Benz Arena, Shanghai, China
September 28: AsiaWorld-Arena, Hong Kong, China
September 30: Impact Arena, Bangkok, Thailand

Queen + Adam Lambert embarked on their first Asian tour, returning to Japan but also playing gigs in Singapore, Taipei, Shanghai, Hong Kong, and Bangkok. The set list didn't change much, apart from the obvious inclusions of 'Teo Torriatte (Let Us Cling Together)' and 'I Was Born To Love You', though the opener was now 'Seven Seas Of Rhye', a surprisingly effective concert starter, though 'Play The Game' hadn't survived from the festival dates from earlier in the year.

NORTH AMERICAN TOUR:
23 JUNE TO 5 AUGUST 2017

Musicians: Brian May (*guitars, vocals*), Roger Taylor (*drums, vocals*), Adam Lambert (*vocals*), Spike Edney (*keyboards, vocals*), Neil Fairclough (*bass guitar, vocals*), Tyler Warren (*percussion, drums, vocals*)

Repertoire: 'We Will Rock You' (*taped intro*), 'Hammer To Fall', 'Stone Cold Crazy', 'Tie Your Mother Down', 'Another One Bites The Dust', 'Fat Bottomed Girls', 'Killer Queen', 'Two Fux', 'Don't Stop Me Now', 'Bicycle Race', 'I'm In Love With My Car', 'Get Down, Make Love', 'I Want It All', 'Love Of My Life', 'Somebody To Love', 'Crazy Little Thing Called Love', Drum Battle, 'Under Pressure', 'I Want To Break Free', 'You Take My Breath Away' (*taped intro*), 'Who Wants To Live Forever', Guitar Solo, 'Radio Ga Ga', 'Bohemian Rhapsody', Day-O (*taped Freddie vocal improvisation, from Wembley*), 'We Will Rock You', 'We Are The Champions', 'God Save The Queen', 'TwoFux', 'It's Late', 'Spread Your Wings'

Itinerary:
June 23: Gila River Arena, Glendale, California
June 24: T-Mobile Arena, Las Vegas, Nevada

June 26/27: Hollywood Bowl, Los Angeles, California
June 29: SAP Center at San Jose, San Jose, California
July 1: KeyArena, Seattle, Washington
July 2: Rogers Arena, Vancouver, British Columbia
July 4: Rogers Place, Edmonton, Alberta
July 6: Pepsi Center, Denver, Colorado
July 8: CenturyLink Center Omaha, Omaha, Nebraska
July 9: Sprint Center, Kansas City, Missouri
July 13: United Center, Chicago, Illinois
July 14: Xcel Energy Center, Saint Paul, Minnesota
July 17: Bell Centre, Montreal, Quebec
July 18: Air Canada Centre, Toronto, Ontario
July 20: The Palace of Auburn Hills, Auburn Hills, Michigan
July 21: Quicken Loans Arena, Cleveland, Ohio
July 23: Mohegan Sun Arena, Uncasville, Connecticut
July 25: TD Garden, Boston, Massachusetts
July 26: Prudential Center, Newark, New Jersey
July 28: Barclays Center, Brooklyn, New York
July 30: Wells Fargo Center, Philadelphia, Pennsylvania
July 31: Capital One Arena, Washington, D.C.
August 2: Bridgestone Arena, Nashville, Tennessee
August 4: American Airlines Center, Dallas, Texas
August 5: Toyota Center, Houston, Texas

With interest in Queen reaching new heights, thanks not only to the ongoing treks Queen + Adam Lambert embarked on, but with the 40th anniversary box set commemorating *News Of The World* imminent, a 25-city tour was booked for the summer of 2017, finding the band touring North America once again. Tickets went on sale in January; due to overwhelming demand, a UK and European leg was announced in April for the late autumn, with further dates for Oceania and a second UK/European tour announced the following February. Rufus Taylor announced that he would not be partaking in the tour, due to commitments with The Darkness; in his stead was Queen Extravaganza's drummer Tyler Warren.

The set list was once again restructured, with a heavier focus on *News Of The World*: much to fans' delight, this meant that 'Get Down, Make Love', 'It's Late', and 'Spread Your Wings'; much to fans' chagrin and anger, however, the latter two titles, appearing in the set list for the first time since 1979, were removed after a handful of performances. 'Bicycle Race' was also brought out of mothballs for the first time since 1979, and featured Adam riding a glammed-up tricycle around the stage, while the vocalist's own new song, 'Two Fux', was given an admirable Queen-type

treatment. The stage also changed drastically: Frank, the robot that adorned the cover of *News Of The World*, was given great prominence, bursting his hand through the enveloping screen around the stage before lifting it up to reveal the band.

The reviews were once again ecstatic. *Variety* wrote of their Newark show, "Five songs into a killer Queen show Wednesday night at the Prudential Center in Newark, NJ, Adam Lambert stopped to ask a question. 'Is this the real life? Or is it just fantasy?' Lambert's quip, referencing the opening lines of 'Bohemian Rhapsody', may have been tongue-in-cheek, but it's also reality for the *American Idol* season eight runner-up, who had the good fortune of being chosen to front Queen ... It's a big job, as Lambert went on to explain, namely because singer Freddie Mercury died tragically in 1991. 'Let's be honest, there is only one Freddie Mercury,' the 35-year-old said from the stage. 'I'm a fan just like you guys. I'm just up here in a really expensive seat.' And it's a spot that Lambert has earned, as evidenced by the two-hour rock 'n' roll laser light spectacle that he led ... Lambert – careful not to mimic Mercury – brought his own artistry and interpretation to the music. Specifically, his emotive interpretation of 'Who Wants To Live Forever' as well as handling Mercury's vocals in a duet of 'Under Pressure' with Taylor induced goosebumps. It was simply that magnificent." *The Washington Times* was also pleased: "It's still very hard to imagine Queen without Mercury orchestrating the proceedings as the band began a 22-song set by launching into 'We Will Rock You' and quickly into Mr. May's crunching power chords on 'Hammer To Fall'. The overtly flamboyant Mr. Lambert made it clear early on that he would never attempt to fill Mercury's shoes, even explaining that he was just a lucky fan, and there will be 'only one Freddie Mercury'. Keeping the music alive was Mr. Lambert's goal, and he offered throughout the concert a potent vocal range and style with a clear passion for the source material ... I know this is not about a competition, but Mr. Lambert still has some vocal growl growing to do for the rock genre. He sounded a bit too Broadway at times especially in his version of 'Killer Queen' while sitting atop the robot head mascot (featured on the 1977 album art for *News Of The World*) – and wearing a pink suit and in platform shoes no less. He is certainly able to carry the notes, but Mercury's comparative, meatier delivery on a tune such as 'Somebody To Love' would often cause an outbreak of goosebumps ... If great music was not enough for an audience loaded with families and millennials, the visual presentation was outstanding in nearly every song.

A massive mirrored disco ball rotated light beams for 'I Want To Break Free'; confetti cannons exploded for 'We Are The Champions'; waves of multicolored lasers layered the arena for 'You Take My Breath Away' and 'Who Wants To Live Forever'; all of the original, younger members' video presence appeared in 'Bohemian Rhapsody'; and a massive projection of the robot mascot clapped along to 'Radio Ga Ga'. The pinnacle of effects was Mr. May's slightly indulgent solo. The maestro mixed those orchestrated layering of chords and notes as he seemingly floated in the cosmos, perched high above the audience. The multimedia accompanying him was an impressive mix of a star-filled and planet-rotating diorama display with even a robot hand guiding him to the heavens."

"Adam Lambert wants to get one thing out of the way," USA Today wrote. "'I know what some of you diehard fans are saying: "He's no Freddie Mercury"', Lambert said early into Queen's dazzling concert at Brooklyn's Barclays Center Friday night. 'No shit'. It was the first of many nods to the late Mercury, whose singular voice and boundless charisma helped Queen become one of the most popular bands of the 20th century. Lambert, 35, clearly felt the weight of expectation going into Friday's performance, despite having sang with the English rockers' current lineup (which includes original members Brian May and Roger Taylor) since 2011. But the former American Idol contestant needn't have worried. On Queen's current North American tour – which continues Sunday in Philadelphia and wraps 5 August in Houston – Lambert is a more than competent Mercury stand-in, bringing pop-punk snarl and a superhuman vocal range to fan favorites such as 'We Are The Champions', 'I Want It All' and 'Who Wants To Live Forever', an emotional evening highlight that, like 'Under Pressure' before it, left many concertgoers dewy-eyed. Lambert also emulated Mercury's flamboyant style, rocking a multitude of costume changes throughout the two-hour set that included glittery high-heeled boots, tight leather vests, and one particularly memorable hot-pink, flower-embroidered ensemble, which he happily declared 'the gayest suit you've ever seen'. Slinking down the guitar-shaped catwalk, gyrating across the stage and pedaling on a rose-covered bike for – you guessed it – 'Bicycle Race', Lambert exuded raw energy and dynamic showmanship, even when his self-confessed 'dad jokes' earned more groans than guffaws ... The arena concert was bolstered by flashy production values, including massive, rotating lighting rigs, confetti canons and a giant robot's head that rose up from under the stage. But it was the reverence to Queen's past, along with Lambert's generosity and magnetism, that ultimately made it such a satisfying evening for the band's longtime fans."

Billboard, meanwhile, suggested the obvious: "The Queen + Adam Lambert experiment – which began tentatively in 2012, three years after the legendary UK band joined the American Idol finalist on stage during the show's season finale, and has been touring the globe for much of the half-decade since – has now been fine-tuned, to the point where it should really be a permanent partnership. This isn't to say Lambert doesn't deserve his own career. But fronting Queen should probably be the pop star's full-time gig: perhaps not since Mick Fleetwood stumbled upon the Buckingham Nicks duo at Sound City 43 years ago – leading to a lineup change that would turn Fleetwood Mac into one of the biggest bands of all time – has there been a more serendipitous fusion of two established recording acts ... 'These two gentlemen are legends of rock 'n' roll', Lambert said on stage Monday night while introducing Queen's founding members, drummer Roger Taylor, 67, and guitarist May, who will turn 70 next month. 'Every time I take the stage with them, it blows my mind at what an honor this is – to be singing the music of Queen'. This came about five songs in, after Lambert, 35. had ridden in on a 3-D skull (modeled after the sci-fi album cover of Queen's '77 set News Of The World), singing a glorious 'Killer Queen', decked in a shiny pink suit and high-heels. The song was a showcase for his theatrically trained vocals, one of several during which he put his stamp on things in a way that was faithful to the band's past, but kept it all in the now ... When [the show] was over Lambert and May embraced, walking arm in arm toward the other band members (including Spike Edney on keyboards and Tyler Warren on percussion) for their final bows. The moment was one of many during which the two men appeared happy and very connected on stage. A classic guitarist and his muse, carrying on."

UK/EUROPEAN TOUR:
1 NOVEMBER TO 16 DECEMBER 2017

Musicians: Brian May *(guitars, vocals)*, Roger Taylor *(drums, vocals)*, Adam Lambert *(vocals)*, Spike Edney *(keyboards, vocals)*, Neil Fairclough *(bass guitar, vocals)*, Tyler Warren *(percussion, drums, vocals)*
Repertoire: 'We Will Rock You' *(taped intro)*, 'Hammer

To Fall', 'Stone Cold Crazy', 'Tie Your Mother Down', 'Another One Bites The Dust', 'Fat Bottomed Girls', 'Killer Queen', 'Don't Stop Me Now', 'Bicycle Race', 'I'm In Love With My Car', 'Get Down, Make Love', 'I Want It All', 'Love Of My Life', 'Somebody To Love', 'Crazy Little Thing Called Love', Drum Battle, 'Under Pressure', 'I Want To Break Free', 'Whataya Want From Me', 'You Take My Breath Away' *(taped intro)*, 'Who Wants To Live Forever', Guitar Solo, 'Radio Ga Ga', 'Bohemian Rhapsody', Day-O *(taped Freddie vocal improvisation, from Wembley)*, 'We Will Rock You', 'We Are The Champions', 'God Save The Queen', 'A Kind Of Magic', 'These Are The Days Of Our Lives', 'Tavaszi Szél Vizet Áraszt', 'You've Got To Hide Your Love Away', 'Leaning On A Lamppost'

Itinerary:

November 1: O2 Arena, Prague, Czech Republic
November 2: Olympiahalle, Munich, Germany
November 4: Papp László Budapest Sportaréna, Budapest, Hungary
November 6: Atlas Arena, Łódz, Poland
November 8: Wiener Stadthalle, Vienna, Austria
November 10: Unipol Arena, Bologna, Italy
November 12: Galaxie Amnéville, Amnéville, France
November 13: Ziggo Dome, Amsterdam, Netherlands
November 17: Žalgiris Arena, Kaunas, Lithuania
November 19: Hartwall Arena, Helsinki, Finland
November 21: Friends Arena, Stockholm, Sweden
November 22: Royal Arena, Copenhagen, Denmark
November 25: 3Arena, Dublin, Ireland
November 26: SSE Arena Belfast, Belfast, Northern Ireland
November 28: Echo Arena Liverpool, Liverpool
November 30: Arena Birmingham, Birmingham
December 1: Metro Radio Arena, Newcastle
December 3: SSE Hydro, Glasgow, Scotland
December 5: Motorpoint Arena Nottingham, Nottingham
December 6: First Direct Arena, Leeds
December 8: Sheffield Arena, Sheffield
December 9: Manchester Arena, Manchester
December 12/13: The O2, London
December 15: Wembley Arena, London
December 16: Arena Birmingham, Birmingham

The Queen + Adam Lambert touring machine continued onto the UK and Europe in November 2017, with a 26-date trek that offered up much of the same set list and many of the same spectacular theatrics that

North American fans had witnessed. Out was Adam's campy 'Two Fux', replaced with his breakout, P!nk-written hit, 'Whataya Want From Me', while 'A Kind Of Magic' and 'These Are The Days Of Our Lives' often rotated with each other. *Birmingham Live* wrote, "Let's cut to the quick – this show was dynamite with laser beam after laser beam. And in all the colours of the rainbow, too … This Arena Birmingham gig was like watching a rocket blasting off ready for a spectacular tour of Queen's "supersonic" rock and pop universe. Its payload included one of the best nights of special effects you could ever wish to see. Never once, though, did the show look set to burn up on re-entry because, while the stage hydraulics, the lighting and big screen visuals were all world class, the crystal-clear sound was always even better." *Manchester Evening News* was also impressed: "Queen are a band that created something so incredibly good that generations have fallen under the spell decades after the loss of the sun at the center of its universe – Rest in Peace Freddie. I feel bold saying it, but after five years of allowing Adam Lambert the unbelievable honour of taking the mic while Brian May and Roger Taylor drive out their formidable repertoire, I think the galaxy is back in motion. He is a massive shining star. Just like Freddie. Not Freddie. But my goodness, with all the best bits … We have seen a frontman [Adam] with no shortage of ego, who is both in wonder at how he has managed to get to where he is, but also two old boys of rock, who have stumbled upon someone fitting to let them share this beautiful catalog of songs with both the original generation of fans and those that came after."

"With his chunky good looks, trimmed black beard, swept-back blow-dried quiff and penchant for giant sunglasses, [Adam is] actually more of a George Michael lookalike," *The Telegraph* wrote in a four-out-of-five star review. "Only, unlike Michael (in his superstar years) and Mercury himself, Lambert is open about his sexuality, and more flamboyant even than Freddie.

"'I'm up here in the gayest suit you'll ever see in your life', he proudly announced at London's O2 Arena, flaunting about in a shiny pink, floral brocaded, shirtless three-piece ensemble accessorised with ludicrously high-heeled black and red platform boots. It was one of 10 costume changes, this one worn to accompany comically camp renditions of 'Killer Queen', 'Don't Stop Me Now' and 'Bicycle Race', during the latter of which he pedalled about the guitar-shaped stage on a pink tricycle, tossing out flowers to admirers … Freddie Mercury's presence is maintained in brief snatches of vocal and a sweet video duet with Brian May playing live on 'Love Of My Life'. But there is no sense of settling for second best when Lambert takes to the stage in gold cloak and crown. Absolutely powering through 'We Will Rock You' and leading a mass singalong of 'We Are The Champions', Lambert is the man who would be Queen."

OCEANIA TOUR:

17 FEBRUARY TO 6 MARCH 2018

Musicians: Brian May *(guitars, vocals)*, Roger Taylor *(drums, vocals)*, Adam Lambert *(vocals)*, Spike Edney *(keyboards, vocals)*, Neil Fairclough *(bass guitar, vocals)*, Tyler Warren *(percussion, drums, vocals)*

Repertoire: 'We Will Rock You' *(taped intro)*, 'Hammer To Fall', 'Stone Cold Crazy', 'Tie Your Mother Down', 'Another One Bites The Dust', 'Fat Bottomed Girls', 'Killer Queen', 'Don't Stop Me Now', 'Bicycle Race', 'I'm In Love With My Car', 'Get Down, Make Love', 'I Want It All', 'Love Of My Life', 'Somebody To Love', 'Crazy Little Thing Called Love', Drum Battle, 'Under Pressure', 'A Kind Of Magic', 'These Are The Days Of Our Lives', 'Whatya Want From Me', 'I Want To Break Free', 'You Take My Breath Away' *(taped intro)*, 'Who Wants To Live Forever', 'Last Horizon', Guitar Solo, 'Radio Ga Ga', 'Bohemian Rhapsody', Day-O *(taped Freddie vocal improvisation, from Wembley)*, 'We Will Rock You', 'We Are The Champions', 'God Save The Queen', 'Highway To Hell', 'Down Under', 'Waltzing Matilda'

Itinerary:
February 17/18: Spark Arena, Auckland, New Zealand
February 21/22: Qudos Bank Arena, Sydney
February 24: Brisbane Entertainment Centre, Brisbane
February 27/28: Adelaide Entertainment Centre, Adelaide
March 2/3: Rod Laver Arena, Melbourne
March 6: Perth Arena, Perth

Following a brief break, Queen + Adam Lambert took their tour onto Australia and New Zealand, once again presenting the same set list and the same presentation, with Brian offering a few snippets of 'Highway To Hell' and 'Waltzing Matilda' at various Australian dates, and 'Down Under' in Auckland. "Adam Lambert was up to costume change number seven or eight in one of the more extravagantly staged indoor concerts to ever hit these shores when I jotted down in my note

pad, 'Why shouldn't Queen still be playing live?'" *The New Zealand Herald* wrote. "The elastic-throated 21st Century front-man of one of the 20th Century's most wildly successful bands was towards the end of a two-hour, sold out Spark Arena gig that he was absolutely nailing and for some reason I still felt a little defensive. As if there were non-believers left to convert. Truth is, maybe all Queen fans are already worshipping at the altar of the collaboration that is these days billed as Queen + Adam Lambert. I sure am. Feeling like picking an argument with a Queen fan who may no longer even exist, Queen + Adam Lambert is such a victory both tonally and in substance that it probably surprises even the most diehard fans of both acts. This is, after all, a 48-year old band led by a 36-year old *American Idol* finalist who was born seven years after 'Bohemian Rhapsody' first topped the charts. He's had his own hits and his own chart-topping albums and there's little doubt Lambert is a star in his own right. But capable of filling Freddie Mercury's white Adidas sneakers? Yes. Crucially, because since first stepping into the role in 2012, Adam Lambert has never once tried to be Freddie Mercury. 'There will only be one rock god named Freddie Mercury,' he announced to cheers, and given he'd moments earlier also sought applause for 'the two rock 'n' roll legends I'm sharing the stage with tonight,' it was clear to any sceptic that this is a performer who understands perfectly his role."

In Australia, the reviews were equally ecstatic: "Not only did [Adam] have a commanding stage presence, his vocals effortlessly captured the range, power and spirit of Mercury's; something that cannot be claimed lightly … The lights display and strange antics were appropriately audacious. Massive rock endings, cocky struts from Lambert, lasers, moving screens, disco balls, and even a bike that rose up out of the stage which Lambert rode around while singing. Costume and outfit changes were plentiful, with Brian May's Gucci glitter sneakers being of particular note. Speaking of May – the man can really do no wrong. The show was just as much as a tribute to him and his talents as it was to Queen's legacy. Each song had a searing solo, and there were several moments of the show where May was the sole focus; either on a raised platform putting David Gilmour to shame, or having a quiet acoustic moment with the crowd, putting Bob Dylan to shame. May and Roger Taylor – the two performing members of the original line up – are in their seventies and late sixties respectively and could be forgiven for not providing the stamina that would be expected of such a show. However this was far from the case, and, if anything, the group grew more energised as the gig went on. Taylor in particular seemed sluggish at first, then started to hold his own. It wasn't until a drum solo and then a drum battle with the on-stage percussionist that Taylor really proved he still had the moves. The night closed on 'We Are The Champions' and an explosion of confetti, with May and Lambert walking down the stage runway, arms slung in camaraderie.

While an aura of authenticity was certainly lacking – and it did feel very much like a tribute show – the reality is that the performers weren't trying to make it anything more than that. Rather than recreate the past, the group wanted to put on a killer show and, in Lambert's own words, have everyone 'celebrate the life of Freddie.' And every single person in that arena, including the band, did exactly that."

GUEST APPEARANCES

Not surprisingly, Brian was the Queen member most willing to jump onto a stage and jam with any band he appreciated, though Roger wasn't too far behind (most were with the SAS Band or for charity) – even John and Freddie made the occasional guest appearance. This is a brief overview of when and where a certain band member jammed with whom, and, where possible, what songs were played.

BRIAN MAY: HAMMERSMITH ODEON, LONDON (*BLACK SABBATH*)

21 JANUARY 1981
Repertoire: 'Paranoid', 'Children Of The Grave'

FREDDIE MERCURY: HOGS GRUNT PUB, CRICKLEWOOD (*TAXI*)

8 JANUARY 1982
Repertoire: 'Jailhouse Rock'

FREDDIE MERCURY: VENUE UNKNOWN, MANCHESTER (*ELTON JOHN*)

19 NOVEMBER 1982
Repertoire: 'Whole Lotta Shakin' Goin' On', 'I Saw Her Standing There', 'Twist And Shout'

ROGER TAYLOR: THE TUBE (ROBERT PLANT)

22 JUNE 1983 [TV SEGMENT, NOT BROADCAST]
Musicians: Robert Plant *(vocals)*, Roger Taylor *(drums, backing vocals)*, Paul Martinez *(bass guitar)*, Bob Mayo *(guitar, synthesizers)*, J. Boodruffer *(keyboards)*, Robbie Blunt *(guitar)*
Repertoire: 'Little Sister', 'Treat Her Right', 'Sea Of Love', 'Pledge Pin', 'Other Arms', 'In The Mood', 'Big Log', 'Like I've Never Been Gone', 'Worse Than Detroit', 'Other Arms', 'In The Mood', Drum Intro / 'Big Log', 'Fat Lip', 'Burning Down One Side'

BRIAN MAY: THE FORUM, LOS ANGELES (*DEF LEPPARD*)

11 SEPTEMBER 1983
Repertoire: 'Travellin' Band'

BRIAN MAY: CAPITAL RADIO GUITAR MASTERCLASS

20 NOVEMBER 1983
Repertoire: Introduction, 'Pavan' *(2 takes)*, Guitar Improvisation, 'Love Of My Life'

While Queen were in Munich recording *The Works*, Brian was approached by Capital Radio to take part in an event called Rock School; Brian's set was augmented by two guitarists from the audience whom Brian would teach on stage. It took place at the Duke of York's Theatre in London and comprised two takes of a traditional song called 'Pavan', a brief guitar solo and a rendition of 'Love Of My Life'. This performance was broadcast live on radio and was later released on cassette.

BRIAN MAY: ROCK IN RIO FESTIVAL (PARALAMAS DO SUCCESSO)

16 JANUARY 1985
Repertoire unknown

BRIAN MAY: UNKNOWN VENUE, LONDON (*REO SPEEDWAGON*)

29 MAY 1985
Repertoire: 'Johnny B. Goode'

BRIAN MAY: UNKNOWN VENUE, NEW ORLEANS (*WITH EDDIE VAN HALEN & JOHN ENTWISTLE*)

22 JUNE 1985
Repertoire unknown

BRIAN MAY: HAMMERSMITH ODEON, LONDON (*BAD NEWS, WITH JIMMY PAGE*)

9 NOVEMBER 1986

Repertoire: 'Drink Till I Die', 'Masturbike', 'Warriors Of Ghengis Khan', 'Hey Hey Bad News', Guitar Duel', 'Bad News'

BRIAN MAY: READING ROCK FESTIVAL (*BAD NEWS*)

29 AUGUST 1987

Repertoire: 'Bohemian Rhapsody', 'Warriors Of Ghengis Khan', 'Hey Hey Bad News', 'Bad News', 'Life With Brian'

BRIAN MAY: HAMMERSMITH ODEON, LONDON (*DEF LEPPARD*)

9 SEPTEMBER 1987

Repertoire: 'Now I'm Here'

BRIAN MAY: HAMMERSMITH ODEON, LONDON (*BAD NEWS*)

5 NOVEMBER 1987

Repertoire: Guitar Solo, 'Hey Hey Bad News', 'Mama Weer All Crazee Now'

BRIAN MAY & JOHN DEACON: PRINCE'S TRUST CONCERT

5 JUNE 1988

Repertoire: 'Dancing With Tears In My Eyes' *(vocals: Midge Ure)*, 'What Is Love?' *(vocals: Howard Jones)*, 'Never Gonna Give You Up' *(vocals: Rick Astley)*, 'Wonderful Life' *(vocals: Colin Vearcombe)*, 'You Can't Hurry Love' *(vocals: Phil Collins)*, 'The Letter' *(vocals: Joe Cocker)*, 'You Win Again' *(vocals: The Bee Gees)*, 'Sledgehammer' *(vocals: Peter Gabriel)*, 'With A Little Help From My Friends' *(vocals: Joe Cocker & Marti Pellow)*

Brian played guitar on all songs, while John performed bass only on 'The Letter'. This concert was later issued on VHS and DVD.

BRIAN MAY: WEMBLEY ARENA, LONDON (*BON JOVI, ELTON JOHN, RICK ALLEN, LITA FORD*)

12 DECEMBER 1988

Repertoire: 'Get Back', 'Travellin' Band'

BRIAN MAY: MARQUEE CLUB, LONDON (*BAD NEWS, WITH JIMMY PAGE*)

16 AND 17 DECEMBER 1988

Repertoire unknown

BRIAN MAY: HAMMERSMITH ODEON, LONDON (*JERRY LEE LEWIS*)

21 NOVEMBER 1989

Repertoire: 'High School Confidential', 'Rockin' My Life Away', 'Johnny B. Goode', 'Whole Lotta Shakin' Goin' On', 'Great Balls Of Fire', 'Good Golly Miss Molly', 'Tutti Frutti', 'Mexicali Rose', 'Wild One'

Brian was invited to perform at this show, but when the notoriously unreliable Jerry Lee Lewis didn't show up for the planned rehearsals two weeks beforehand, there was some concern that the show would be canceled. Thankfully, Jerry Lee finally showed up, and the concert was filmed for a potential VHS release.

BRIAN MAY: HAMMERSMITH ODEON, LONDON (*MOTT THE HOOPLE*)

16 FEBRUARY 1990

Repertoire: 'All The Way From Memphis'

BRIAN MAY: HAMMERSMITH ODEON, LONDON (*BLACK SABBATH*)

8 SEPTEMBER 1990

Repertoire: 'Heaven And Hell', 'Paranoid', 'Heaven And Hell' *(reprise)*

BRIAN MAY: UNKNOWN VENUE, NEW YORK (*LES PAUL*)

25 MARCH 1991

Repertoire: 'Early Morning Blues', Improvisation

BRIAN MAY: EXPO '92 GUITAR FESTIVAL

19 OCTOBER 1991

Repertoire: 'Big Bad Moon', 'Liberty', 'Last Horizon', 'Driven By You', Guitar Solo, 'Tie Your Mother Down', 'Amazing Grace', 'Funk No. 49', 'Rocky Mountain Way', 'Can't Get Enough', 'Feel Like Makin' Love', 'All Right Now', 'Now I'm Here', 'Hey Joe'

In August 1991, Brian was asked by Tribute Productions to be the musical director of their guitar festival in Seville, Spain. Brian assembled a quality backing band: Cozy Powell and Steve Ferrone on drums, Neil Murray and Nathan East on bass guitars, Rick Wakeman and Mike Moran on keyboards. As it was a guitar festival, the world's top guitarists were also invited along: Joe Satriani, Steve Vai, Nuno Bettencourt and Joe Walsh were all asked to participate, while vocalists Gary Cherone and Paul Rodgers lent their voices to the repertoire. Brian's set included two unreleased tracks from his upcoming solo album – 'Last Horizon' and 'Driven By You' – as well as the obligatory guitar solo and 'Tie Your Mother Down', a crowd favorite.

The repertoire listed above only includes songs that Brian performed on: 'Big Bad Moon' was part of Joe Satriani's set, while 'Liberty' was part of 'Steve Vai's. 'Funk No. 49' and 'Rocky Mountain Way' were both performed by Joe Walsh, and 'Can't Get Enough', 'Feel Like Makin' Love' and 'All Right Now' were all sung by Paul Rodgers, who also sang the concluding number, 'Hey Joe'. American band Extreme was also involved, performing 'More Than Words' and 'Get The Funk Out', and vocalist Gary Cherone returned for a rousing rendition of 'Now I'm Here'. The concert lasted more than two hours and was broadcast worldwide. The audience reception was ecstatic, which inspired Brian to organize his first live tour a little over a year later.

BRIAN MAY: WEMBLEY STADIUM, LONDON (GUNS N' ROSES)

13 JUNE 1992
Repertoire: 'Tie Your Mother Down', 'We Will Rock You' *(slow/fast)*

BRIAN MAY: UNKNOWN VENUE, MODENA (PAVAROTTI & FRIENDS)

27 SEPTEMBER 1992
Repertoire: 'Too Much Love Will Kill You' *(Brian on vocals and guitar)*, 'La Donna e Mobile' *(Brian on triangle)*

BRIAN MAY: GROSVENOR HOUSE HOTEL, LONDON (WATER RATS' BALL)

NOVEMBER 1992
Repertoire unknown

Brian played with Phil Collins, Dec Cluskey, Joe Brown, Lonnie Donegan and Bert Weedon.

BRIAN MAY AND ROGER TAYLOR: DORO PARTY, VIENNA

19 NOVEMBER 1992
Repertoire: 'Money (That's What I Want)', 'Twist And Shout', 'Lucille', 'Long Tall Sally'

At a 1992 party in honor of the Torpedo Twins, Rudi Dolezal and Hannes Rossacher, Roger sang vocals on 'Money (That's What I Want)' and played drums on all songs, while Brian played guitar throughout. Campino and Nina Hagen sang 'Twist And Shout', with Nina

singing 'Lucille' next, and Klaus Meine from The Scorpions sang 'Long Tall Sally'.

BRIAN MAY: WEMBLEY ARENA, LONDON (EXTREME)

23 DECEMBER 1992
Repertoire: 'I Want To Break Free', 'Tie Your Mother Down'

BRIAN MAY: UNKNOWN VENUE, LONDON (PAUL RODGERS)

9 FEBRUARY 1993
Repertoire unknown

BRIAN MAY: BRIT AWARDS, LONDON (BON JOVI)

14 February 1993
Repertoire unknown

BRIAN MAY: PALAIS OMNISPORTS DE BERCY, PARIS (GUNS N' ROSES)

13 JULY 1993
Repertoire: 'Knockin' On Heaven's Door'

JOHN DEACON AND ROGER TAYLOR: COWDRAY RUINS CONCERT

18 SEPTEMBER 1993
Musicians: John Deacon *(bass guitar)*, Roger Taylor *(vocals, drums, guitar)*, Joshua J Macrae *(drums)*, Jason Falloon *(guitars)*, Adrian Milne *(keyboards)*, Paul Young *(vocals on 'Another One Bites The Dust')*
Repertoire: 'A Kind Of Magic', 'I Want To Break Free', 'We Will Rock You', 'Another One Bites The Dust', 'These Are The Days Of Our Lives', 'Radio Ga Ga'

Sponsored by Virgin Radio, this celebrity charity event was designed to raise £200,000 for the King Edward VII Hospital, with tickets costing between £80 and £140. John and Roger appeared as Queen and ran through a perfunctory set with Paul Young providing vocals on 'Another One Bites The Dust'. Because Roger was midway through sessions for his *Happiness?* album, Jason Falloon was asked to play guitar. Following Roger and John's set, Roger took the stage with Genesis to play drums on 'Turn It On Again', 'Hold On My Heart', 'I Can't Dance', 'Tonight Tonight Tonight' and 'Invisible Touch', then performed 'Stone Free' and 'Old Love' with Eric Clapton. He then returned for the All Star Finale on 'Gimme Some Lovin'', 'Ain't That Peculiar' and 'Can I Get A Witness?'

BRIAN MAY: THE FORUM, LONDON (*PAUL RODGERS*)

9 FEBRUARY 1994

Repertoire: 'I'm Ready', 'Fire And Water', 'Mr Big', 'Feel Like Makin' Love', 'A Little Bit Of Love', 'Stone Free', 'The Hunter', 'Bad Company', 'All Right Now', 'Crossroads'

BRIAN MAY: BRIT AWARDS, LONDON (*BON JOVI*)

15 FEBRUARY 1994

Repertoire: 'I'll Sleep When I'm Dead'

ROGER TAYLOR: MICK RONSON TRIBUTE CONCERT

29 APRIL 1994

Musicians: Roger Taylor *(drums, vocals on 'A Kind Of Magic')*, Jason Falloon, Simon Townshend, Phil Collen, Robbie Alter *(guitars)*, Peter Noone *(bass guitar)*, Spike Edney, Morgan Fisher *(keyboards)*, Steve Harley *(vocals on '(Come Up And See Me) Make Me Smile')*, Ian Hunter *(vocals on 'Once Bitten, Twice Shy', 'Resurrection Mary', 'Michael Picasso', and 'All The Young Dudes')*, Roger Daltrey *(vocals on 'Baba O'Riley' and 'Summertime Blues')* *Repertoire:* '(Come Up And See Me) Make Me Smile', 'A Kind Of Magic', 'Once Bitten, Twice Shy', 'Resurrection Mary', 'Baba O'Riley', 'Summertime Blues', 'Michael Picasso', 'All The Young Dudes'

After Mick Ronson died of liver failure on 29 April 1993, Ian Hunter organized a tribute concert in his honor at the Hammersmith Apollo, performed exactly a year after Ronson's death. Roger provided drums on eight songs, with his vocal spotlight being 'A Kind Of Magic' (incidentally, a song that he had been unable to perform at Freddie's tribute concert). Roger's contributions were ultimately issued on the audio and video releases of *The Mick Ronson Memorial Concert*, with 'Baba O'Riley' later featured on the 2005 compilation, *Roger Daltrey: Moonlighting*.

ROGER TAYLOR: THE GREAT MUSIC EXPERIENCE (*HOTEI, YOSHIKI, TOSHINORI KONDO, BON JOVI*)

22 AND 23 MAY 1994

Repertoire: 'Foreign Sand', 'Living On A Prayer', 'Bed Of Roses', 'Wanted: Dead Or Alive', 'Fly Into Your Dream'

BRIAN MAY: NIGHT OF ONE HUNDRED GUITARS (*PAUL RODGERS*)

26 JUNE 1994

Repertoire: 'Good Morning Little Schoolgirl', 'A Little Bit Of Love', 'Mr Big', 'Let Me Love You Baby' *(with Slash)*, 'The Hunter', 'Bad Company', 'All Right Now', 'Crossroads'

BRIAN MAY: MONTREUX JAZZ FESTIVAL (*PAUL RODGERS*)

6 JULY 1994

Repertoire: 'A Little Bit Of Love', 'All Right Now', 'Crossroads', 'Hoochie Coochie Man'

BRIAN MAY: WEMBLEY ARENA, LONDON (*MEAT LOAF*)

15 DECEMBER 1994

Repertoire: 'We Will Rock You', 'Roll Over Beethoven'

ROGER TAYLOR: GOSPORT FESTIVAL (*SAS BAND*)

16 DECEMBER 1994

Repertoire: 'Money (That's What I Want)'

BRIAN MAY: UNKNOWN VENUE, LONDON (*SAS BAND*)

17 DECEMBER 1994

Repertoire: 'Only Make Believe', 'Tie Your Mother Down'

Brian appeared as T E Conway for the first time here, performing Conway Twitty's 'Only Make Believe' and a country version of 'Tie Your Mother Down'. Brian would later appear as T E Conway in 1998 as the 'support act' on his own Another World tour.

ROGER TAYLOR: ROCK AGAINST HATE (*SAS BAND*)

17 JUNE 1995

Repertoire: 'Nazis 1994', 'Radio Ga Ga', 'Rock And Roll'

JOHN DEACON: SHEPHERD'S BUSH EMPIRE, LONDON (*SAS BAND*)

1 JULY 1995

Repertoire: 'My Girl', '634-5789', 'Crazy Little Thing Called Love'

BRIAN MAY: UNKNOWN VENUE, BOLOGNA (*ZUCCHERO*)

22 SEPTEMBER 1995

Repertoire: 'A Whiter Shade Of Pale', 'Madre Dolcissima (Mama)'

BRIAN MAY: UNKNOWN VENUE, LOS ANGELES (*PAUL RODGERS*)

[UNKNOWN DATE] 1996
Repertoire: 'Feel Like Makin' Love', 'All Right Now', 'Crossroads', 'Hoochie Coochie Man'

BRIAN MAY: BRIXTON ACADEMY, LONDON (STatus quo)

28 January 1996
Repertoire: 'FBI', Rock 'n' Roll Medley

Brian appeared at the video shoot for Status Quo's 'Raining In My Heart' and then performed an impromptu set for the audience, including 'FBI' and a brief rock 'n' roll medley.

BRIAN MAY: MONTREUX JAZZ FESTIVAL (*ZUCCHERO*)

12 JULY 1996
Repertoire: 'Madre Dolcissima (Mama)'

ROGER TAYLOR: INDIAN AWARDS (*ROBERT PLANT AND JIMMY PAGE*)

30 NOVEMBER 1996
Repertoire (mimed): 'Rock And Roll'

ROGER TAYLOR: UNKNOWN VENUE, CHIDDINGFOLD (*SAS BAND*)

13 DECEMBER 1996
Repertoire: 'Rock And Roll', 'That's The Way God Planned It'

ROGER TAYLOR: SHEPHERD'S BUSH EMPIRE, LONDON (*IAN HUNTER*)

14 MAY 1997
Repertoire: 'All The Young Dudes'

BRIAN MAY: UNKNOWN VENUE, LONDON (*ZUCCHERO*)

22 MAY 1997
Repertoire: 'Madre Dolcissima (Mama)'

BRIAN MAY: SHEPHERDS BUSH EMPIRE, LONDON (*JOE SATRIANI AND STEVE VAI*)

4 AND 5 JUNE 1997
Repertoire: 'Liberty', 'Going Down', 'My Guitar Wants To Kill Your Mama', 'Red House'

BRIAN MAY: BRIAN'S 50TH BIRTHDAY PARTY, SURREY

19 JULY 1997
Repertoire: 'All Right Now', 'All The Young Dudes', 'Tie Your Mother Down', 'Rock And Roll', 'Route 66'

At the party for Brian's 50th birthday, he assembled a group of his musician friends (including Spike Edney on keyboards, Jamie Moses on guitar, Neil Murray on bass, Geoff Dugmore on drums and Roger on drums and vocals; a notable absentee was John Deacon) to perform a brief, five-song concert for the partygoers. All the songs were sung by Brian, except 'Rock And Roll', which was sung by Roger.

ROGER TAYLOR: WEMBLEY ARENA, LONDON (*DANA GILLESPIE*)

5 OCTOBER 1997
Repertoire unknown

ROGER TAYLOR: SHEPHERD'S BUSH EMPIRE, LONDON (*FOO FIGHTERS*)

13 DECEMBER 1997
Repertoire: 'Sheer Heart Attack'

BRIAN MAY: DORO PARTY, PURKERSDORF

7 FEBRUARY 1998
Repertoire: 'Twist And Shout', 'Honky Tonk Women'

ROGER TAYLOR: ALTON, HAMPSHIRE (*SAS BAND*)

22 FEBRUARY 1998
Repertoire: 'Rock And Roll'

BRIAN MAY: WEMBLEY ARENA, LONDON (JOE SATRIANI, MICHAEL SCHENKER, ULI JON ROTH)

19 MAY 1998
Repertoire: 'The Thrill Is Gone', 'Voodoo Chile'

ROGER TAYLOR: WINTERSHALL ESTATE, SURREY

5 SEPTEMBER 1998
Repertoire: 'A Kind Of Magic', 'I Want To Break Free', 'These Are The Days Of Our Lives', 'We Will Rock You', 'Radio Ga Ga', 'Crucify Me' *(vocals: Bob Geldof)*, 'Working Class Hero' *(vocals: Bob Geldof)*, 'Like A Rolling Stone' *(vocals: Bob Geldof)*

BRIAN MAY: UNKNOWN VENUE, CHIDDINGFOLD (*SAS BAND*)

12 DECEMBER 1998

Repertoire: 'Only Make Believe', 'You're So Square (Baby I Don't Care)', 'Tie Your Mother Down', 'With A Little Help From My Friends', 'You're The Voice', 'Rudolph The Red-Nosed Reindeer'

BRIAN MAY: COZY POWELL TRIBUTE CONCERT

1 MAY 1999

Musicians: Brian May *(guitars, vocals),* Chris Thompson *(vocals),* Spike Edney *(keyboards, vocals),* Clayton Moss *(guitar),* John Marter *(drums),* Neil Murray *(bass guitar),* Suzi Webb *(backing vocals),* Zoe Nicholas *(backing vocals)*

Repertoire (Brian only): 'Since You've Been Gone', 'Tie Your Mother Down', 'Hammer To Fall', 'All The Young Dudes', 'With A Little Help From My Friends', 'You're The Voice'

A little over a year after Cozy Powell's untimely death, a tribute concert was organized by Spike Edney at the Buxton Opera House. After a lengthy set by the SAS Band, Brian joined in with a thundering version of 'Since You've Been Gone' and two other favorites. Brian then helped close the show with 'All The Young Dudes', 'With A Little Help From My Friends', and 'You're The Voice', all with Chris Thompson on vocals.

ROGER TAYLOR: CAFÉ DE PARIS, LONDON (*JIMMY PAGE, STEVEN TYLER, JOE PERRY, THE STEREOPHONICS, THE BLACK CROWES*)

27 JUNE 1999

Repertoire: 'Radio Ga Ga', 'A Kind Of Magic', 'Under Pressure' *(with Treana Morris),* 'Rock And Roll'

ROGER TAYLOR: ROGER'S 50TH BIRTHDAY PARTY, CORNWALL

26 JULY 1999

Repertoire: 'We Will Rock You', Jam Session, 'Rock And Roll'

BRIAN MAY: READING ROCK FESTIVAL (*SAS BAND*)

4 SEPTEMBER 1999

Repertoire: 'Since You've Been Gone', 'Last Horizon', 'Hammer To Fall' *(slow/fast),* 'Dragon Attack' *(vocals: Jeff Scott Soto),* 'Tie Your Mother Down', 'In The Lap Of The Gods... Revisited'

Brian sang vocals on all songs except as noted.

ROGER TAYLOR: UNKNOWN VENUE, STUTTGART (*SAS BAND*)

8 NOVEMBER 1999

Repertoire: 'Twist And Shout', 'I Want To Break Free', 'Radio Ga Ga', 'Rock And Roll', 'All The Young Dudes', 'We Are The Champions'

BRIAN MAY & ROGER TAYLOR: UNKNOWN VENUE, LONDON (*FOO FIGHTERS*)

25 November 1999

Repertoire: 'We Will Rock You' *(intro)* / 'Now I'm Here'

BRIAN MAY: WEMBLEY EXHIBITION CENTRE, LONDON

28 NOVEMBER 1999

Repertoire: Guitar Solo, 'We Will Rock You' *(solo only),* Jam Session

Much like the Capital Radio Guitar Session in 1983, Brian was asked to participate in the National Music Show. The guitar solo was essentially Brian dissecting his showcase, explaining delays and harmonies and the features of his guitar, while 'We Will Rock You' was only the distorted guitar solo. A jam session then followed with Chad Smith, the drummer of Red Hot Chili Peppers.

ROGER TAYLOR: SHEPHERD'S BUSH EMPIRE, LONDON (SAS BAND)

19 FEBRUARY 2000

Repertoire: 'Magic Is Loose', 'Radio Ga Ga'

BRIAN MAY AND ROGER TAYLOR: HYDE PARK, LONDON (*5IVE*)

9 JULY 2000

Repertoire: 'We Will Rock You', 'Tie Your Mother Down', 'With A Little Help From My Friends'

BRIAN MAY: CAT CLUB, LOS ANGELES (*GILBY CLARKE, ERIC SINGER, OTHERS*)

14 SEPTEMBER 2000

Repertoire: 'The Thrill Is Gone'

BRIAN MAY AND ROGER TAYLOR: MILLENIUM DOME, LONDON (*5IVE*)

27 SEPTEMBER 2000

Repertoire: 'We Will Rock You'

BRIAN MAY: BRIXTON ACADEMY, LONDON (*MOTORHEAD*)

22 OCTOBER 2000
Repertoire: 'Overkill'

ROGER TAYLOR: USHER HALL, EDINBURGH (*SAS BAND*)

14 DECEMBER 2000
Repertoire: 'A Kind Of Magic', 'Radio Ga Ga', 'Strange Frontier', 'With A Little Help From My Friends' *(vocals: Fish)*

ROGER TAYLOR: UNKNOWN VENUE, MANCHESTER (*SAS BAND*)

15 DECEMBER 2000
Repertoire: 'A Kind Of Magic', 'I Want To Break Free', 'Radio Ga Ga'

BRIAN MAY AND ROGER TAYLOR: WALDORF ASTORIA, NEW YORK

19 MARCH 2001
Repertoire: 'We Will Rock You', 'Tie Your Mother Down', 'Do It Again', 'Johnnie's Boogie', 'Everybody Needs Somebody To Love'

Queen were introduced into the prestigious Rock & Roll Hall Of Fame in 2001, and Brian and Roger appeared to represent the band (Jer Bulsara, Freddie's mother, gave a short speech on Freddie's behalf), performing 'We Will Rock You' and 'Tie Your Mother Down', with both performances augmented by Spike Edney on keyboards and Steve Barnacle on bass guitar; Dave Grohl and Taylor Hawkins inducted the band and later joined them on 'Tie Your Mother Down'. Brian later returned for the concluding all-star jam.

BRIAN MAY: MONTREUX JAZZ FESTIVAL

7 JULY 2001
Musicians: Brian May *(vocals, guitars)*, Jon Cleary *(piano)*, Chris Spedding *(guitar)*, John Hatton *(bass guitar)*, Bernie Dresel *(drums)*, Ray Herrmann *(saxophone)*, Charlie Peterson *(trumpet)*, Emily May *(backing vocals)*, Jimmy May *(backing vocals)*, Anita Dobson *(backing vocals)*
Repertoire: '(I Don't Want Nobody) Teasin' Around (With Me)', 'Let Me Out', 'Tie Your Mother Down', 'Whole Lotta Shakin' Goin' On'

This concert saw the only live performance of '(I Don't Want Nobody) Teasin' Around (With Me)', a standout track that was omitted from the *Good Rockin' Tonight: A Tribute To Sun Records* album (though it did appear as a bonus track in Japan). With his family – daughter Emily, son Jimmy and wife Anita – assisting on backing vocals, Brian then led the band into 'Let Me Out' and 'Tie Your Mother Down', before returning for 'Whole Lotta Shakin' Goin' On'. The previous night, Brian had appeared with Steve Lukather and Larry Carlton on 'Luke's Blues'.

ROGER TAYLOR: GOSPORT FESTIVAL (*SAS BAND*)

11 AUGUST 2001
Repertoire: 'Radio Ga Ga', 'I Want To Break Free', 'A Kind Of Magic', 'Rock And Roll', 'The Show Must Go On' *(vocals: Chris Thompson)*, 'We Will Rock You' *(vocals: Tony Hadley, Leo Sayer, and Mark Shaw)*, 'With A Little Help From My Friends' *(vocals: Fish)*, 'You're The Voice', 'All The Way'

BRIAN MAY: CAMBRIDGE UNION

9 OCTOBER 2001
Repertoire: 'With God On Our Side', 'We Will Rock You'

BRIAN MAY AND ROGER TAYLOR: FREDDIE MERCURY MEMORIAL

24 NOVEMBER 2001
Repertoire: 'Radio Ga Ga' *(vocals: Roger)*, 'Since You've Been Gone' *(vocals: Brian)*, 'Under Pressure' *(vocals: Roger and Treana Morris)*, 'Strange Frontier' *(vocals: Roger)*, 'Tie Your Mother Down' *(vocals: Brian)*, 'No-One But You (Only The Good Die Young)' *(vocals: Brian and Roger)*

A memorial concert was held at the Ocean Club in London to commemorate the tenth anniversary of Freddie's death, with the SAS Band as the main act. Brian and Roger then joined the band for the conclusion of the set, which saw many surprising additions: 'Under Pressure' with Treana Morris, Roger's 1984 solo song 'Strange Frontier', and an emotional rendition of 'No-One But You (Only The Good Die Young)' bringing the show to a poignant close.

BRIAN MAY: CAT CLUB, LOS ANGELES (*ERIC SINGER*)

18 JANUARY 2002
Repertoire: 'The Thrill Is Gone', 'Sympathy For The Devil'

BRIAN MAY: LIZA MINNELLI'S WEDDING

16 MARCH 2002

Repertoire: 'We Are The Champions', 'Tie Your Mother Down'

BRIAN MAY AND ROGER TAYLOR: MUSEUM SQUARE, AMSTERDAM

30 APRIL 2002

Repertoire: 'Radio Ga Ga' *(vocals: Roger)*, 'Tie Your Mother Down' *(vocals: Brian)*, 'Another One Bites The Dust' *(vocals: Patti Russo)*, 'Under Pressure' *(vocals: Roger and Patti Russo)*, 'Hammer To Fall' *(slow/fast)* *(vocals: Brian)*, 'The Show Must Go On' *(vocals: Patti Russo)*, 'No-One But You (Only The Good Die Young)' *(vocals: Brian and Roger)*, 'We Will Rock You' *(vocals: Brian)*, 'We Are The Champions' *(vocals: Trijntje Oosterhuis)*

Designed to celebrate the Dutch Queen's birthday, this was a special one-off performance that remained a secret until the day of the concert.

BRIAN MAY AND ROGER TAYLOR: BUCKINGHAM PALACE, QUEEN'S JUBILEE

3 JUNE 2002

Repertoire: 'God Save The Queen', 'Radio Ga Ga' *(vocals: Roger)*, 'We Will Rock You' *(vocals: Brian)*, 'We Are The Champions' *(vocals: Will Young)*, 'Bohemian Rhapsody' *(vocals: We Will Rock You cast)*, 'Move It' *(vocals: Cliff Richard and S Club 7)*, 'With A Little Help From My Friends' *(vocals: Joe Cocker)*, 'All You Need Is Love', 'Hey Jude'

This performance saw the iconic rendition of 'God Save The Queen', with Brian on guitar standing atop Buckingham Palace while the orchestra (including Roger on timpani) performed below him in the palace grounds. Brian and Roger then performed a brief set, introducing the *We Will Rock You* cast for 'Bohemian Rhapsody', after which Brian joined the all-star cast for 'Move It' and 'With A Little Help From My Friends'. Roger then came out to perform drums on 'All You Need Is Love' and 'Hey Jude'.

ROGER TAYLOR: COWDRAY PARK (*DAVID GIL-MOUR, RINGO STARR, BOB GELDOF, OTHERS*)

21 JUNE 2002

Repertoire: 'I Feel Fine', 'Jealous Guy', 'I Am The Walrus', 'My Sweet Lord'

ROGER TAYLOR: HEROES SQUARE, BUDAPEST (*F1 WITH V10*)

16 JULY 2002

Repertoire: 'Lust For Life', 'For Fuck's Sake', 'Pump It Up', 'Rock And Roll', 'Gloria', '"Heroes"', 'Let's Stick Together'

BRIAN MAY AND ROGER TAYLOR: WALK OF FAME AFTERPARTY

18 OCTOBER 2002

Repertoire: 'Tie Your Mother Down' *(vocals: Brian)*, 'Under Pressure' *(vocals: Roger and Patti Russo)*, 'Another One Bites The Dust' *(vocals: Patti Russo)*, 'Sleeping On The Sidewalk' *(vocals: Brian)*, 'I'm In Love With My Car' *(vocals: Roger)*, 'Stone Cold Crazy' *(vocals: Jeff Scott Soto)*, 'Crazy Little Thing Called Love', 'Hammer To Fall' *(slow/fast)* *(vocals: Brian)*, 'We Will Rock You', 'We Are The Champions' *(vocals: Roger and Brian)*, 'Rock And Roll' *(vocals: Roger)*

After being inducted into the Hollywood Walk Of Fame (Queen received a star on the famous sidewalk), Brian and Roger performed a set in the city with the SAS Band, with several guests stopping by: Nuno Bettencourt played guitar on 'Tie Your Mother Down', Fred Mandel provided keyboards on 'Crazy Little Thing Called Love' and 'Rock And Roll' featured Steve Vai on guitar and Carmine Appice on drums.

BRIAN MAY: DIAN FOSSEY GORILLA FUND CON-CERT

10 NOVEMBER 2002

Repertoire: 'Is This The World We Created...?' *(vocals: Brian)*, 'I'll Do My Crying In The Rain' *(vocals: Bryan Adams and Brian)*, 'Run To You' *(vocals: Bryan Adams)*, 'Crazy Little Thing Called Love' *(vocals: Bryan Adams)*

ROGER TAYLOR: IN SESSION (*SAS BAND*)

29 APRIL 2003

Repertoire: 'A Kind Of Magic', 'Jealous Guy', 'Radio Ga Ga', 'Rock And Roll', 'You're The Voice', 'All The Way'

BRIAN MAY: LONNIE DONEGAN MEMORIAL SER-VICE

8 MAY 2003

Repertoire: 'I'm Just A Rolling Stone', 'Have A Drink On Me'

BRIAN MAY AND ROGER TAYLOR: ARK CHARITY CONCERT (SAS BAND)

14 MAY 2003

Repertoire: 'I Want To Break Free', 'A Kind Of Magic', 'Radio Ga Ga', 'The Kids Are Alright' *(vocals: Bob Geldof)*, 'We Will Rock You' *(vocals: Brian)*, 'Tie Your Mother Down' *(vocals: Brian)*, 'Rock And Roll', 'Wish It Could Be Christmas Every Day'

Brian appeared only on 'We Will Rock You', 'Tie Your Mother Down' and 'Wish It Could Be Christmas Every Day'. Roger sang on the first three songs and 'Rock And Roll', and played drums on 'The Kids Are Alright', 'We Will Rock You', 'Tie Your Mother Down' and 'Wish It Could Be Christmas Every Day'.

BRIAN MAY AND ROGER TAYLOR: UNKNOWN VENUE, MODENA (PAVAROTTI & FRIENDS)

27 MAY 2003

Repertoire: 'We Will Rock You' *(vocals: Brian)*, 'Radio Ga Ga' *(vocals: Roger)*, 'Too Much Love Will Kill You' *(vocals: Brian and Pavarotti)*, 'We Are The Champions' *(vocals: Brian and Zucchero)*

BRIAN MAY & ROGER TAYLOR: SONGWRITER'S HALL OF FAME

12 JUNE 2003

Repertoire: 'Crazy Little Thing Called Love' *(vocals: Wynonna Judd)*, 'We Will Rock You' *(vocals: Brian)*

BRIAN MAY: HAMMERSMITH APOLLO (DEF LEPPARD)

31 OCTOBER 2003

Repertoire: 'Tie Your Mother Down'

BRIAN MAY: HOUSE OF GUITARS, LONDON

8 JANUARY 2004

Repertoire: 'Amazing Grace', Guitar Solo, 'Chinese Torture'

BRIAN MAY: UNIVERSITY OF HERTFORDSHIRE, HATFIELD

9 JANUARY 2004

Repertoire: Guitar Solo, 'We Will Rock You', Guitar Solo, 'Amazing Grace', 'Puttin' On The Style', 'Rock Island Line'

BRIAN MAY: ROYAL ALBERT HALL, LONDON (ZUCCHERO)

6 MAY 2004

Repertoire: 'Madre Dolcissima (Mama)', 'Il Mare Impetuoso Al Tramonto'

BRIAN MAY: ASTORIA, LONDON (IAN HUNTER)

28 MAY 2004

Repertoire: 'All The Way From Memphis'

BRIAN MAY: FENDER STRATOCASTER ANNIVERSARY

24 SEPTEMBER 2004

Repertoire: 'Oh Boy!', 'Maybe Baby', 'Love You More Than I Can Say', 'Every Day', 'Peggy Sue', 'I Fought The Law (And The Law Won)', 'That'll Be The Day', 'All Right Now', 'Stay With Me'

Unusual that Brian would appear at an anniversary concert commemorating the Fender Stratocaster, but he strapped one on for this concert and provided guitar on all nine tracks (only on the last two did he use the Red Special), singing lead on 'Maybe Baby' and 'That'll Be The Day'. Sonny Curtis sang on all the other songs, except 'All Right Now' (Paul Rodgers) and 'Stay With Me' (Ronnie Wood).

ROGER TAYLOR: MICROSOFT IT FORUM, COPENHAGEN (SAS BAND)

18 NOVEMBER 2004

Repertoire: 'Radio Ga Ga', 'Under Pressure', 'Rock And Roll', 'The Boys Are Back In Town', 'We Will Rock You', 'We Are The Champions'

Roger sang lead vocals on the first three songs, with Chris Thompson on 'Under Pressure', and played drums on the remainder. Midge Ure sang vocals on 'The Boys Are Back In Town'.

ROGER TAYLOR: WINTERSHALL ESTATE, SURREY (GARY BROOKER'S BAND DU LAC)

11 JUNE 2005

Repertoire: 'Say It's Not True', 'These Are The Days Of Our Lives', 'I Want To Break Free', 'I Can't Dance'

Eric Clapton and Ringo Starr, among others, were part of Gary Brooker's all-star group, Band Du Lac.

ROGER TAYLOR: ANTONIS PAPADOPOULOS STADIUM, LARNACA (SAS BAND)

16 JUNE 2005

Repertoire: 'Radio Ga Ga', 'Say It's Not True', 'These Are The Days Of Our Lives', 'Rock And Roll', 'Under Pressure', 'The Show Must Go On', 'We Will Rock You', 'We Are The Champions', 'With A Little Help From My Friends'

Roger sang vocals on the first five songs, with Chris Thompson on 'Under Pressure', and played drums on the others. Chris also sang vocals on 'The Show Must Go On'.

BRIAN MAY: MANDALAY BAY EVENTS CENTER, LAS VEGAS (*DEF LEPPARD*)

25 MAY 2006
Repertoire: '20th Century Boy'

BRIAN MAY & ROGER TAYLOR: HYDE PARK, LONDON (*FOO FIGHTERS*)

17 JUNE 2006
Repertoire: 'We Will Rock You' *(intro and finale)* / 'Tie Your Mother Down' *(vocals: Taylor Hawkins)*

BRIAN MAY: NOVELLO THEATRE, LONDON (*A TRIBUTE TO DAN CRAWFORD*)

16 JULY 2006
Repertoire: 'Who Wants To Live Forever' *(vocals: Mazz Murray)*

BRIAN MAY AND ROGER TAYLOR: WEMBLEY ARENA, LONDON (*McFLY*)

22 SEPTEMBER 2006
Repertoire: 'Don't Stop Me Now', Guitar Improvisation, '5 Colours In Her Hair'

ROGER TAYLOR: ALEXANDRA PALACE, LONDON

14 NOVEMBER 2006
Repertoire: 'Golden Slumbers' / 'Carry The Weight' / 'The End'

Roger inducted Led Zeppelin into the UK Rock 'n' Roll Hall of Fame, then played drums on three songs from The Beatles' *Abbey Road* to honor George Martin.

ROGER TAYLOR: BISLEY PAVILLION, WOKING (*SAS BAND*)

8 DECEMBER 2006
Repertoire: 'Woman You're So Beautiful (But Still A Pain In The Ass)', 'Strange Frontier, 'Merry Xmas (War Is Over)' *(all-star finale)*

The live premiere of the Felix + Arty track, with the latter on guitar and both on vocals.

ROGER TAYLOR: BAIN & COMPANY, SORRENTO, ITALY (*SAS BAND*)

8 MAY 2007
Repertoire: 'I Want To Break Free', 'Radio Ga Ga', 'Under Pressure', 'We Will Rock You' *(all-star finale)*,

'We Are The Champions' *(all-star finale)*

Roger sang lead vocals on all songs, with Kiki Dee helping on 'Under Pressure'.

ROGER TAYLOR: WEMBLEY STADIUM, LONDON (*LIVE EARTH*)

7 JULY 2007

Roger opened Al Gore's Live Earth concert with Chad Smith and Taylor Hawkins, billed as the SOS Allstars, with a piece written specially by Roger and featuring 40 additional drummers.

BRIAN MAY AND ROGER TAYLOR: O2 ARENA, LONDON (*FOO FIGHTERS*)

17 NOVEMBER 2007
Repertoire: "39'

ROGER TAYLOR: GOODWOOD HOUSE, GOODWOOD (*FESTIVAL OF SPEED GALA DINNER*)

12 JULY 2008
Repertoire unknown

Similar to Live Earth a year prior, Roger, Nick Mason of Pink Floyd, and Kenney Jones of The Small Faces and The Who performed a percussive trio set.

BRIAN MAY: PALLADIUM, LONDON (*ROYAL VARIETY'S 80TH ANNIVERSARY CONCERT*)

11 DECEMBER 2008
Repertoire: 'Defying Gravity' *(vocals: Kerry Ellis)*

ROGER TAYLOR: INDIGO2, LONDON (*SAS BAND*)

24 JANUARY 2009
Repertoire: 'Under Pressure', 'Tenement Funster', 'A Kind Of Magic', 'Cosmos Rockin'', 'We Will Rock You', 'We Are The Champions'

Roger performed drums only on 'We Will Rock You' and 'We Are The Champions', and sang lead vocals on the first four songs, with Patti Russo joining on 'Under Pressure'. His son, Rufus, played drums on the first five songs. 'Cosmos Rockin'' got its one and only live performance outside of Queen + Paul Rodgers.

BRIAN MAY: LUTON HOO, LUTON (*MAZZ MURRAY'S WEDDING*)

18 JUNE 2009
Repertoire: 'Love Of My Life', 'Tie Your Mother Down'

BRIAN MAY: SHAW THEATRE, LONDON (*KERRY ELLIS*)

20, 21, 25, AND 26 JUNE 2009
Repertoire: 'Who Wants To Live Forever', 'Crazy Little Thing Called Love'

ROGER TAYLOR: LONGBOROUGH (*SAS BAND*)

4 JULY 2009
Repertoire unknown

This private party, held for Hugh Sloane's wife's birthday, also featured Roger Daltrey, the Sugababes, Patti Russo, and Jeff Scott Soto, though no set list is known.

BRIAN MAY: JOHN MOORES UNIVERSITY, LIVERPOOL

23 JULY 2009
Repertoire: Guitar improvisation

BRIAN MAY: ROYAL ALBERT HALL, LONDON (*WOMAN*)

1 NOVEMBER 2009
Repertoire: 'I'm A Woman', 'Tie Your Mother Down'

Woman was an ad hoc four-piece group of female vocalists – Mazz Murray, Kerry Ellis, Gina Murray, and Ajay Casey – formed for this charity concert, Pinktober, to raise awareness and funds for breast cancer research.

BRIAN MAY: ROYAL ALBERT HALL, LONDON (*KERRY ELLIS*)

2 MAY 2010
Repertoire: 'Who Wants To Live Forever' *(vocals: Kerry Ellis and Adam Pascal)*, 'We Are The Champions' *(vocals: Ricardo Alfonso)*

BRIAN MAY AND ROGER TAYLOR: SCALA, LONDON (*TAYLOR HAWKS AND THE COATTAIL RIDERS*)

11 MAY 2010
Repertoire: 'I'm In Love With My Car' *(vocals: Roger)*, 'Sleeping On The Sidewalk' *(vocals: Brian)*, 'Long Away' *(vocals: Brian)*, 'Tenement Funster' *(vocals: Roger)*, 'Way Down' *(only Brian on guitar)*

BRIAN MAY AND KERRY ELLIS: HYDE PARK, LONDON (*KERRY ELLIS*)

11 SEPTEMBER 2010
Repertoire: 'Dangerland', 'I'm Not That Girl', 'Anthem', 'We Will Rock You', 'We Are The Champions'

BRIAN MAY AND ROGER TAYLOR: ROGER'S GARDEN, SURREY (*ROGER'S WEDDING PARTY*)

25 SEPTEMBER 2010
Repertoire unknown

Roger and his girlfriend Sarina married on 25 September 2010. Following the ceremony at Roger's Surrey mansion, the groom and his close friends and family – Brian, Roger's sons Rufus and Felix, Joshua J. Macrae, Roger Daltrey, Bob Geldof, Joe Elliot of Def Leppard, Martin Chambers of The Pretenders, Mike Rutherford of Genesis, Nick Mason of Pink Floyd, Gary Brooker of Procul Harum, Nicky Clark and Holly Skelton of FABBA, Ryan Molloy and Jeff Scott Soto – performed an unknown set.

BRIAN MAY: ROYAL ALBERT HALL, LONDON (*BRITISH LEGION FESTIVAL OF REMEMBRANCE*)

13 NOVEMBER 2010
Repertoire: 'Anthem'

BRIAN MAY: ROYAL ALBERT HALL, LONDON (*PRINCE'S TRUST ROCK GALA*)

17 NOVEMBER 2010
Repertoire: 'These Are The Days Of Our Lives' *(vocals: Roger)*, 'Last Horizon', 'It's A Hard Life' *(vocals: Tom Chaplin)*, 'Seven Seas Of Rhye' *(vocals: Midge Ure)*, 'We Will Rock You' *(all-star finale)*

The highlight of the night was Tom Chaplin's rendition of 'It's A Hard Life' (which Brian erroneously introduced as never being performed before), leading many to champion for a Queen + Tom Chaplin union.

BRIAN MAY AND ROGER TAYLOR: BATTERSEA POWER STATION, LONDON (*COLLARS & COATS GALA BALL*)

25 NOVEMBER 2010
Repertoire: 'Hound Dog' *(vocals: Brian)*, 'Under Pressure' *(vocals: Roger and Patti Russo)*, 'I Want It All' *(vocals: Roger Daltrey)*, 'We Will Rock You' *(all-star finale; vocals: Roger)*, 'With A Little Help From My Friends' *(all-star finale; vocals: Roger)*

Brian later wrote that this event's schedule was poorly organized, and several songs – 'Fire' and '(I Don't Want Nobody) Teasin' Around (With Me)' – had to be omitted.

ROGER TAYLOR: WINTERSHALL ESTATE, SURREY (*BAND DU LAC*)

4 JUNE 2011

Repertoire: 'Radio Ga Ga', '"Heroes"', 'Fat Bottomed Girls ', 'Voodoo Chile', 'A Kind Of Magic', 'Say It's Not True', 'Manic Depression', 'People Get Ready', 'Nessun Dorma', 'Uptight', 'Shout'

Roger appeared at this charity concert not too far from his mansion, performing a killer set with his son Rufus on drums, Spike Edney on keyboards, Steve Stroud on bass, and Jason Falloon on guitar. Ronnie Wood played guitar on 'Voodoo Chile' and Jeff Beck joined the stage for 'Say It's Not True' through 'Nessun Dorma'. Roger then played drums on the last two songs.

BRIAN MAY & KERRY ELLIS: THE SAVOY, LONDON (*BORN FREE FOUNDATION GALA DINNER*)

17 JUNE 2011

Repertoire: 'Born Free', 'Happy Birthday To You'

ROGER TAYLOR: MILTON KEYNES BOWL, MILTON KEYES (*FOO FIGHTERS*)

2 JULY 2011

Repertoire: 'Cold Day In The Sun'

BRIAN MAY: GOODWOOD ESTATE, GOODWOOD (*FESTIVAL OF SPEED*)

3 JULY 2011

Repertoire: Introduction, 'Driven By You', 'One Vision', 'Don't Stop Me Now', 'The Chain'

BRIAN MAY & ROGER TAYLOR: CAMDEN'S ROUNDHOUSE, LONDON (*FOO FIGHTERS*)

11 JULY 2011

Repertoire: 'Tie Your Mother Down'

BRIAN MAY: LITTLE JOHN'S FARM, READING (*MY CHEMICAL ROMANCE*)

26 AUGUST 2011

Repertoire: 'We Will Rock You', 'Welcome To The Black Parade'

Brian joined My Chemical Romance at The Reading Festival.

BRIAN MAY: NOKIA THEATRE, LOS ANGELES, CALIFORNIA (*LADY GAGA*)

28 AUGUST 2011

Repertoire: 'Yoü and I'

Brian provided guitar on this performance of Lady Gaga's latest single at the MTV Music Video Awards.

BRIAN MAY & ROGER TAYLOR: THE SAVOY, LONDON (*FREDDIE FOR A DAY*)

5 SEPTEMBER 2011

Repertoire included: 'Love Of My Life', 'These Are The Days Of Our Lives', 'Under Pressure', 'Good Old-Fashioned Lover Boy', 'Don't Stop Me Now', 'Crazy Little Thing Called Love', 'Say It's Not True', 'It's A Hard Life', 'Tie Your Mother Down', 'The Show Must Go On', 'We Will Rock You'

The above set list is an educated guess by Martin Skála. Guests included Kerry Ellis, Matt Lucas, Patti Russo, David Armand, Mike Rutherford, Tom Chaplin, Jeff Beck, Rufus Taylor, and the cast of *We Will Rock You: The Musical*, with Spike on keyboards and Neil Fairclough on bass.

ROGER TAYLOR: DAVINGTON PRIOR, FAVERSHAM (*BOB GELDOF*)

1 OCTOBER 2011

Repertoire unknown

Roger appeared at his friend Bob Geldof's 60th birthday, and jammed on an unknown set with Bill Wyman on bass, Gary Kemp on guitar, and Bono and Bob on vocals.

ROGER TAYLOR: PAPPY & HARRIETT'S PIONEERTOWN PALACE, PIONEERTOWN, CALIFORNIA (*SAS BAND*)

16 OCTOBER 2011

Repertoire included: 'Rip It Up', 'Voodoo Chile', 'Rock And Roll'

Roger appeared at Spike's 60th birthday and sang the above songs, which Neil Murray confirmed.

BRIAN MAY: CLAPHAM GRAND, LONDON (*SAS BAND*)

25 NOVEMBER 2011

Repertoire: 'No-One But You (Only The Good Die Young)', 'Somebody To Love', 'Tie Your Mother Down'

Commemorating 20 years since Freddie died, The SAS Band performed a tribute concert at the Clapham Grand. (Roger was also supposed to perform, but his mother had passed away a few days prior.) Brian appeared at the beginning of the show, with Kerry Ellis providing vocals on 'Somebody To Love', but he had already committed to another gig, and left after three songs to go to…

BRIAN MAY: HAMMERSMITH APOLLO, LONDON (*THE DARKNESS*)

25 NOVEMBER 2011
Repertoire: 'Bareback', 'Tie Your Mother Down', 'I Believe In A Thing Called Love'

BRIAN MAY: SCALA, LONDON (*MEL C*)

9 DECEMBER 2011
Repertoire: 'One Vision'

ROGER TAYLOR: G LIVE, GUILDFORD (*SAS BAND*)

13 DECEMBER 2011
Repertoire: 'A Kind Of Magic', 'Voodoo Chile', '"Heroes"', 'The Show Must Go On', 'We Will Rock You', 'We Are The Champions', 'Happy Xmas (War Is Over)', 'Santa Claus Is Coming To Town'

BRIAN MAY & KERRY ELLIS: TEATRO ARISTON, SAN REMO, ITALY (*SAN REMO FESTIVAL*)

16 FEBRUARY 2012
Repertoire: 'I (Who Have Nothing)', 'We Will Rock You'

Brian and Kerry appeared with Zucchero's daughter Irene Fornaciari at the San Remo Festival.

BRIAN MAY & KERRY ELLIS: PRINCE OF WALES THEATRE, LONDON (*WHATSONSTAGE.COM AWARDS*)

19 FEBRUARY 2012
Repertoire: 'Defying Gravity'

BRIAN MAY: MAIDA VALE STUDIOS, LONDON (*BBC RADIO ONE LIVE LOUNGE*)

27 FEBRUARY 2012
Repertoire: 'Rockstar', 'We Will Rock You'

Brian appeared with Dappy to perform their collaboration single, 'Rockstar', as well as 'We Will Rock You'

ROGER TAYLOR: BUSH HOUSE, LONDON

1 MARCH 2012
Repertoire: 'Radio Ga Ga'

Roger appeared at a bash for the BBC's 80th year of operation, performing a special version of 'Radio Ga Ga' with William Orbit on guitar, Amadou and Miriam on vocals, Anoushka Shankar on sitar, Pirashanna Thevarajah on percussion, Rosey Chan and Spike on keyboards, Gus Isidore on guitar and vocals, and Neil Fairclough on bass and vocals.

ROGER TAYLOR: APRES SKI BAR, FARINET, VERBIER, SWITZERLAND (*WASTE*)

20 MARCH 2012
Repertoire: 'Lonely Boy'

Roger and Bob Geldof turned up unannounced to Richard Branson's ski resort; the proprietor and mogul asked Roger if he'd join the house band, Waste, to which Roger duly agreed.

BRIAN MAY & KERRY ELLIS: SHAMWARI GAME RESERVE, EASTERN CAPE, SOUTH AFRICA

24 MARCH 2012
Repertoire: 'Nothing Really Has Changed'

During the filming of the 'Born Free' video in South Africa, Brian and Kerry Ellis surprised the song's composer, Virginia McKenna, with a performance of 'Nothing Really Has Changed'.

BRIAN MAY & KERRY ELLIS: GRAND CAFÉ AND BEACH, GRANGER BAY, CAPE TOWN, SOUTH AFRICA (*PRIDE OF CAPE TOWN*)

27 MARCH 2012
Repertoire: 'Born Free', 'Crazy Little Thing Called Love', 'I Loved A Butterfly'

Brian and Kerry appeared at the Pride Of Cape Town public arts festival alongside 50 life-size lion sculptures to perform a brief three-song set.

BRIAN MAY & KERRY ELLIS: COLOSSEUM, WATFORD (*FRIDAY NIGHT IS MUSIC NIGHT*)

20 APRIL 2012
Repertoire: 'Love Of My Life', 'Born Free', 'Save Me'

BRIAN MAY & ROGER TAYLOR: NOKIA THEATRE, LOS ANGELES, CALIFORNIA (*AMERICAN IDOL*)

25 APRIL 2012
Repertoire: 'Fat Bottomed Girls', 'Another One Bites The Dust', 'We Will Rock You', 'We Are The Champions'

Brian and Roger returned to *American Idol* to perform a five-minute medley with the Top 6 finalists for the week.

BRIAN MAY & ROGER TAYLOR: NOKIA THEATRE, LOS ANGELES, CALIFORNIA (*AMERICAN IDOL*)

26 APRIL 2012
Repertoire: 'Somebody To Love'

Brian and Roger, once again on *American Idol*, performed with The Queen Extravaganza band.

BRIAN MAY & KERRY ELLIS: KINGS ARM, ALL CANNINGS (*SAS BAND*)

26 MAY 2012
Repertoire: 'I Loved A Butterfly', 'The Way We Were', 'Crazy Little Thing Called Love', 'Defying Gravity', 'We Will Rock You', 'We Are The Champions', 'With A little Help From My Friends'

Brian and Kerry appeared at this charity show for cancer organisations. Organized by John Callis, a sound engineer for Paul McCartney, the show saw the duo playing their own set, with Brian joining the SAS Band (sans Spike) for the finale.

BRIAN MAY & ROGER TAYLOR: OLYMPIC STADIUM, LONDON (*OLYMPIC GAMES CLOSING CEREMONY*)

12 AUGUST 2012
Repertoire: Guitar Solo, 'We Will Rock You'

The London 2012 Olympic Games Closing Ceremony featured a who's-who of British bands – headlined by The Who. Freddie was on-hand, on-screen to get the audience going with his vocal improvisation from Wembley 1986, with Brian then providing a guitar solo and then 'We Will Rock You', with Jessie J on vocals and Roger on drums and timpani.

BRIAN MAY: BRIAN'S HOME, SURREY

27 AUGUST 2012
Repertoire included: 'Crazy Little Thing Called Love', 'All Right Now'

A private party held at Brian's house included the two aforementioned songs, though the full set is not known.

BRIAN MAY & KERRY ELLIS: GUILDFORD CATHEDRAL, GUILDFORD (*WILDLIFE ROCKS*)

1 SEPTEMBER 2012
Repertoire: 'Born Free', 'I Loved A Butterfly', 'I (Who Have Nothing)', 'Life Is Real (Song For Lennon)',

'Puttin' On The Style', 'Crazy Little Thing Called Love'

Brian and Kerry appeared at Wildlife Rocks, a charity concert set up by Harper Asprey Wildlife Rescue.

BRIAN MAY & KERRY ELLIS: THE SAVOY, LONDON (*FREDDIE FOR A DAY*)

3 SEPTEMBER 2012
Repertoire: 'One Vision', 'Born Free', 'Life Is Real (Song For Lennon)', 'Since You've Been Gone', 'Bohemian Rhapsody', 'The Show Must Go On', 'One Night', 'We Will Rock You', 'We Are The Champions'

Brian appeared at the Freddie For A Day event in honor of what would have been Freddie's 66th birthday, appearing on the above tracks with guests including Alfie Boe, Tom Jones, Al Murray, Rachel Tucker, Brenda Edwards, Madeline Bell, Marc Martel, Rhys Thomas, Nancy Dell'Olio, and Princess Eugenie. Roger also appeared, but only to introduce Madeline Bell.

BRIAN MAY & KERRY ELLIS: ROYAL ALBERT HALL, LONDON (*THE SUNFLOWER JAM*)

16 SEPTEMBER 2012
Repertoire: 'Born Free', 'I Loved A Butterfly', 'Black Night', 'Since You've Been Gone', 'School's Out', 'Smoke On The Water'

Featuring a band including Bruce Dickinson, Ian Paice, John Paul Jones, Paul "Wix" Wickens, Alice Cooper, Micky Moody, Mark King, Alfie Boe, and Uli Jon Roth, Brian played a two-song set with Kerry Ellis and then jammed on the final four songs.

ROGER TAYLOR: GOTHENBURG, SWEDEN (*SAS BAND*)

15 OCTOBER 2012
Repertoire included: '"Heroes"'

Roger appeared at this private gig at the IFS World Conference, alongside Roger Daltrey, Jeff Scott Soto, and Patti Russo.

BRIAN MAY & KERRY ELLIS: HIPPODROME CASINO, LONDON

16 OCTOBER 2012
Repertoire: 'Born Free', 'I (Who Have Nothing)', 'Crazy Little Thing Called Love'

Brian was a special guest on Kerry's mini-tour at the

newly-refurbished Hippodrome Casino.

BRIAN MAY & KERRY ELLIS: THE DORCHESTER, LONDON

24 NOVEMBER 2012

Repertoire: 'Born Free', 'I (Who Have Nothing)', 'Life Is Real (Song For Lennon)', 'The Kissing Me Song', 'Crazy Little Thing Called Love'

ROGER TAYLOR: MIKE RUTHERFORD'S HOUSE, LOXWOOD

28 DECEMBER 2012

Repertoire included: Drum Duet

Roger duelled with Mike Rutherford's son Harry on drums at the Genesis founder's Christmas party.

BRIAN MAY: OXFORD UNION, OXFORD

27 FEBRUARY 2013

Repertoire unknown

BRIAN MAY & KERRY ELLIS: ST PANCRAS RAILWAY STATION, LONDON (*SAVE THE TIGER FUND*)

1 MARCH 2013

Repertoire: 'Born Free', 'Dust In The Wind', 'The Continuing Story Of Bungalow Bill', 'The Kissing Me Song', 'Knocking On Heaven's Door', 'Crazy Little Thing Called Love'

BRIAN MAY & KERRY ELLIS: SISTER RAY, LONDON (*RECORD STORE DAY*)

19 APRIL 2013

Repertoire: 'The Kissing Me Song', 'Crazy Little Thing Called Love'

BRIAN MAY & KERRY ELLIS: PALLADIUM, LONDON

12 MAY 2013

Repertoire: 'I (Who Have Nothing)', 'The Way We Were', 'Crazy Little Thing Called Love', 'No-One But You (Only The Good Die Young)', 'The Kissing Me Song'

ROGER TAYLOR: KING'S ARMS, ALL CANNINGS (*SAS BAND*)

25 MAY 2013

Repertoire: 'A Kind Of Magic', 'Under Pressure', 'Say It's Not True', 'Little Wing', 'Peter Gunn Theme', 'New Orleans', 'All The Way'

Roger performed this seven-song set at the SAS Band's appearance at Rock Against Cancer. Jeff Beck guested on 'Say It's Not True' and 'Peter Gunn Theme', Marc Martel sang 'Under Pressure', and Jamie Moses sang 'New Orleans'. A rehearsal of 'Say It's Not True' appeared on *Fun On Earth*.

BRIAN MAY & KERRY ELLIS: AUDITORIUM STRAVINSKI, MONTREUX, SWITZERLAND (*MONTREUX JAZZ FESTIVAL*)

19 JULY 2013

Repertoire: 'I (Who Have Nothing)', 'Dust In The Wind', 'Born Free', 'Somebody To Love', 'Nothing Really Has Changed', 'Life Is Real (Song For Lennon)', 'The Way We Were', ''39', 'Something', 'Last Horizon', 'Love Of My Life', 'The Kissing Me Song', 'Tie Your Mother Down', 'We Will Rock You', 'No-One But You (Only The Good Die Young)', 'Crazy Little Thing Called Love'

BRIAN MAY & KERRY ELLIS: STADE DES BURGONDES, SAINT-JULIEN-EN-GENEVOIS, FRANCE (*GUITARE EN SCENE FESTIVAL*)

21 JULY 2013

Repertoire: 'I (Who Have Nothing)', 'Dust In The Wind', 'Born Free', 'Somebody To Love', 'Tell Me What You See', 'Life Is Real (Song For Lennon)', 'The Way We Were', ''39', 'Something', 'Last Horizon', 'Love Of My Life', 'The Kissing Me Song', 'Tie Your Mother Down', 'We Will Rock You', 'No-One But You (Only The Good Die Young)', 'Crazy Little Thing Called Love'

BRIAN MAY: NATURAL HISTORY MUSEUM, LONDON

31 AUGUST 2013

Repertoire included: 'Johnny B. Goode'

Brian's daughter, Emily, got married on this day, and so the father of the bride was convinced to jump onstage with the wedding band, The Bluejays, to perform this old Chuck Berry chestnut.

BRIAN MAY & KERRY ELLIS: THE SAVOY, LONDON

27 SEPTEMBER 2013

Repertoire: 'I (Who Have Nothing)', 'Born Free', 'Dust In The Wind', 'Is This The World We Created...?', 'Nothing Really Has Changed', 'Crazy Little Thing Called Love'

BRIAN MAY & KERRY ELLIS: ROYAL FESTIVAL HALL, LONDON (*DON BLACK TRIBUTE*)

3 OCTOBER 2013
Repertoire: 'Born Free'

BRIAN MAY & KERRY ELLIS: ROYAL ALBERT HALL, LONDON (*CITY ROCKS*)

1 APRIL 2014
Repertoire: 'I (Who Have Nothing)', 'Dust In The Wind', 'Born Free', 'Tie Your Mother Down'

Brian and Kerry were joined by The Feeling for 'Tie Your Mother Down'

BRIAN MAY & KERRY ELLIS: GUILDFORD CATHEDRAL, GUILDFORD (*WILDLIFE ROCKS*)

5 May 2014
Repertoire: Guitar Intro, 'Wild Thing', 'Tie Your Mother Down', 'Born Free', 'I Loved A Butterfly', 'Dust In The Wind', 'Nothing Really Has Changed', 'Somebody To Love', 'Crazy Little Thing Called Love'

Brian appeared with The Troggs on 'Wild Thing', before Kerry joined for the remainder of the set.

BRIAN MAY: CENTURY CLUB, LONDON

1 OCTOBER 2014
Repertoire: Guitar Improvisation

Brian played a brief improvisation at the launch of *Brian May's Red Special: The Story Of The Home-Made Guitar That Rocked Queen And The World.*

BRIAN MAY & ADAM LAMBERT: ITV STUDIOS, LONDON (*X-FACTOR*)

30 NOVEMBER 2014
Repertoire: 'Somebody To Love'

BRIAN MAY & ADAM LAMBERT: VELODROM, BERLIN, GERMANY (*THE HELENE FISCHER SHOW*)

25 DECEMBER 2014
Repertoire: 'Who Wants To Live Forever', 'I Want It All'

Filmed on 12 December but broadcast on Christmas Day.

BRIAN MAY & KERRY ELLIS: ARENA DI VERONA, VERONA, ITALY (*LO SPETTACOLO STA PER INIZIARE*)

1 JUNE 2015
Repertoire: 'Who Wants To Live Forever', 'No-One But You (Only The Good Die Young)', 'Somebody To Love', 'We Will Rock You', 'Bohemian Rhapsody'

Brian and Kerry were joined by Vittorio Grigolo on vocals on 'Who Wants To Live Forever' and 'Bohemian Rhapsody'

BRIAN MAY & KERRY ELLIS: ROSEWOOD HOTEL, LONDON (*BORN FREE FOUNDATION PRIVATE GIG*)

10 JULY 2015
Repertoire: 'I (Who Have Nothing)', 'I Loved A Butterfly', 'Dust In The Wind', 'Born Free', 'Somebody To Love', 'The Way We Were', 'Nothing Really Has Changed', ''39', 'Is This The World We Created...?', 'One Voice', 'The Kissing Me Song', 'Crazy Little Thing Called Love', 'We Will Rock You'

BRIAN MAY & KERRY ELLIS: THE PHEASANTRY, LONDON

5 SEPTEMBER 2015
Repertoire: 'I (Who Have Nothing)', 'Born Free', 'Crazy Little Thing Called Love'

Brian was a surprise guest at this concert. The last song was dedicated to Freddie, as it would've been his 69th birthday.

ROGER TAYLOR: MILTON KEYES BOWL, MILTON KEYES (*FOO FIGHTERS*)

5 SEPTEMBER 2015
Repertoire: 'Under Pressure'

Roger joined the Foo Fighters and John Paul Jones on this rousing rendition of 'Under Pressure'.

BRIAN MAY & KERRY ELLIS: THE DORCHESTER, LONDON (*DAVID SHEPHERD WILDLIFE FOUNDATION*)

9 OCTOBER 2015
Repertoire: 'I (Who Have Nothing)', 'I Loved A Butterfly', 'Born Free', 'Crazy Little Thing Called Love'

ROGER TAYLOR: G LIVE, GUILDFORD (*SAS BAND*)

5 DECEMBER 2015
Repertoire: '"Heroes"', 'Sunny Day', 'Voodoo Chile', 'Radio Ga Ga', 'Rock And Roll', 'Happy Xmas (War Is Over)'

ROGER TAYLOR: GUILDHALL, PORTSMOUTH (*SAS BAND*)

8 DECEMBER 2015

Repertoire: '"Heroes"', 'Sunny Day', 'Voodoo Chile', 'Radio Ga Ga', 'Rock And Roll', 'Happy Xmas (War Is Over)'

BRIAN MAY & KERRY ELLIS: LEICESTER SQUARE THEATRE, LONDON (*AN EVENING WITH RUSS BALLARD*)

20 JANUARY 2016

Repertoire: 'Since You've Been Gone', 'God Gave Rock And Roll To You', 'We Will Rock You', 'Hold Your Head Up'

BRIAN MAY: AUDITORIO DE TENERIFE, SANTA CRUZ DE TENERIFE, SPAIN (*STARMUS FESTIVAL*)

1 JULY 2016

Repertoire: 'Time/Inception'

ROGER TAYLOR: WINTERSHALL ESTATE, SURREY (*WINTERSHALL CHARITY ROCK CONCERT*)

2 JULY 2016

Repertoire: 'A Kind Of Magic', 'Under Pressure', 'Radio Ga Ga', '"Heroes"', 'Remember (Walking In The Sand)', 'Goin' Down', 'Hi-Ho Silver Lining', 'Life On Mars?'

ROGER TAYLOR: FESTIVAL, WICKHAM (*WICKHAM FESTIVAL*)

6 AUGUST 2016

Repertoire: 'A Kind Of Magic', '"Heroes"', 'Remember (Walking In The Sand)', 'Radio Ga Ga', 'Life On Mars?'

ROGER TAYLOR: NECKER ISLAND, BRITISH VIRGIN ISLANDS

27 AUGUST 2016

Repertoire unknown

Roger attended Richard Branson's party and sat in on drums on an unknown set.

PART EIGHT
Singles Discography

A. QUEEN

With a myriad of books and websites that chronicle Queen's extensive singles discography, this section makes no attempt to offer anything comprehensive; rather, this discography serves as a basic reference to the songs listed in Part Three. Only 7" vinyl singles are mentioned, though, once Queen started to release 12" vinyl and CD singles, new mixes and additional B-sides were added for their desirability. These releases are listed only if they offer something new or previously unavailable on the standard 7" release. Where applicable, chart placements in the respective countries appear in brackets at the end of each entry.

The UK singles are listed first; it's important to note that all Queen's single releases, up to and including 'Who Wants To Live Forever', were distributed by EMI, with Parlophone distributing subsequent releases. The US singles follow, with all singles up to and including 'Staying Power' distributed by Elektra. Capitol distributed singles starting with 'Radio Ga Ga' and concluding with 'Scandal', with all subsequent releases distributed by Hollywood.

UK SINGLES

July 1973: 'Keep Yourself Alive' / 'Son And Daughter' (EMI 2036)

February 1974: 'Seven Seas Of Rhye' / 'See What A Fool I've Been' (EMI 2121) [10]

October 1974 (double A-side): 'Killer Queen' / 'Flick Of The Wrist' (edit) (EMI 2229) [2]

January 1975: 'Now I'm Here' / 'Lily Of The Valley' (edit) (EMI 2256) [11]

October 1975: 'Bohemian Rhapsody' / 'I'm In Love With My Car (EMI 2375) [1]

June 1976: 'You're My Best Friend' / ''39' (EMI 2494) [7]

November 1976: 'Somebody To Love' / 'White Man' (EMI 2565) [2]

March 1977: 'Tie Your Mother Down' (edit) / 'You And I' (EMI 2593) [31]

May 1977: Queen's First EP: 'Good Old-Fashioned Lover Boy' / 'Death On Two Legs (Dedicated to......' / 'Tenement Funster!' (edit) / 'White Queen (As It Began)' (EMI 2623) [17]

October 1977: 'We Are The Champions' / 'We Will Rock You' (EMI 2708) [2]

February 1978: 'Spread Your Wings' / 'Sheer Heart Attack' (EMI 2757) [34]

October 1978 (double A-side): 'Fat Bottomed Girls' (edit) / 'Bicycle Race' (EMI 2870) [11]

January 1979: 'Don't Stop Me Now' / 'In Only Seven Days' (EMI 2910) [9]

June 1979: 'Love Of My Life' (live edit) / 'Now I'm Here' (live) (EMI 2959) [63]

October 1979: 'Crazy Little Thing Called Love' / 'We Will Rock You' (fast live) (EMI 5001) [2]

January 1980: 'Save Me' / 'Let Me Entertain You' (live) (EMI 5022) [11]

May 1980: 'Play The Game' / 'A Human Body' (EMI 5076) [14]

August 1980: 'Another One Bites The Dust' / 'Dragon Attack' (EMI 5102) [7]

November 1980: 'Flash' (edit) / 'Football Fight' (EMI 5126) [10]

October 1981: 'Under Pressure' (Queen & David Bowie) / 'Soul Brother' (EMI 5250) [1]

April 1982: 'Body Language' / 'Life Is Real (Song For Lennon)' (EMI 5293) [25]

June 1982: 'Las Palabras De Amor (The Words Of Love)' / 'Cool Cat' (EMI 5316) [17]

August 1982: 'Back Chat' (remix) / 'Staying Power' (EMI 5325) [40]

August 1982 (12"): 'Back Chat' (extended) / 'Staying Power' (extended) (12EMI 5325) [40]

January 1984: 'Radio Ga Ga' / 'I Go Crazy' (QUEEN 1) [2]

January 1984 (12"): 'Radio Ga Ga' (extended) / 'Radio Ga Ga' (instrumental) / 'I Go Crazy' (12 QUEEN 1) [2]

April 1984: 'I Want To Break Free' (remix) / 'Machines (Or 'Back To Humans')' (QUEEN 2) [3]

April 1984 (12"): 'I Want To Break Free' (extended) / 'Machines (Or "Back To Humans")' (12 QUEEN 2) [3]

July 1984: 'It's A Hard Life' / 'Is This The World We Created...?' (QUEEN 3) [6]

July 1984 (12"): 'It's A Hard Life' (extended) / 'Is This The World We Created...?' (12 QUEEN 3) [6]

September 1984: 'Hammer To Fall' (edit) / 'Tear It Up' (QUEEN 4) [13]

September 1984 (12"): 'Hammer To Fall' (Headbangers mix) / 'Tear It Up' (12 QUEEN 4) [13]

November 1984 (withdrawn): 'Man On The Prowl' / 'Keep Passing The Open Windows' (QUEEN 5)

November 1984: 'Thank God It's Christmas' / 'Man On The Prowl' / 'Keep Passing The Open Windows' (QUEEN 5) [21]

November 1984 (12"): 'Thank God It's Christmas' / 'Man On The Prowl' (extended) / 'Keep Passing The Open Windows' (extended) (12 QUEEN 5) [21]

November 1985: 'One Vision' (edit) / 'Blurred Vision' (QUEEN 6) [7]

November 1985 (12"): 'One Vision' (extended) / 'Blurred Vision' (12 QUEEN 6) [7]

March 1986: 'A Kind Of Magic' / 'A Dozen Red Roses For My Darling' (QUEEN 7) [3]

March 1986 (12"): 'A Kind Of Magic' (extended) / 'A Dozen Red Roses For My Darling' (extended) (12 QUEEN 7) [3]

June 1986: 'Friends Will Be Friends' / 'Seven Seas Of Rhye' (QUEEN 8) [14]

June 1986: 'Friends Will Be Friends' (extended) / 'Friends Will Be Friends' / 'Seven Seas Of Rhye' (12 QUEEN 8) [14]

September 1986: 'Who Wants To Live Forever' (edit) / 'Killer Queen' (QUEEN 9) [24]

September 1986: 'Who Wants To Live Forever' (edit) / 'Killer Queen' / 'Who Wants To Live Forever' / 'Forever' (12 QUEEN 9) [24]

November 1988: 'Seven Seas Of Rhye' / 'See What A Fool I've Been' / 'Funny How Love Is' (edit) (QUECD1)

November 1988: 'Killer Queen' / 'Flick Of The Wrist' (edit) / 'Brighton Rock' (QUECD2)

November 1988: 'Bohemian Rhapsody' / 'I'm In Love With My Car' / 'You're My Best Friend' (QUECD3)

November 1988: 'Somebody To Love' / 'White Man' / 'Tie Your Mother Down' (QUECD4)

November 1988: 'Good Old-Fashioned Lover Boy' / 'Death On Two Legs (Dedicated to......' / 'Tenement Funster!' (edit) / 'White Queen (As It Began)' (QUECD5)

November 1988: 'We Are The Champions' / 'We Will Rock You' / 'Fat Bottomed Girls' (edit) (QUECD6)

November 1988: 'Crazy Little Thing Called Love' / 'Spread Your Wings' / 'Flash' (edit) (QUECD7)

November 1988: 'Another One Bites The Dust' / 'Dragon Attack' / 'Las Palabras De Amor (The Words Of Love)' (QUECD8)

November 1988: 'Under Pressure' (Queen & David Bowie) / 'Soul Brother' / 'Body Language' (QUECD9)

November 1988: 'Radio Ga Ga' / 'I Go Crazy' / 'Hammer To Fall' (edit) (QUECD10)

November 1988: 'I Want To Break Free' (edit) / 'Machines (Or "Back To Humans")' / 'It's A Hard Life' (QUECD11)

November 1988: 'A Kind Of Magic' / 'A Dozen Red Roses For My Darling' / 'One Vision' (edit) (QUECD12)

May 1989: 'I Want It All' (edit) / 'Hang On In There' (QUEEN 10) [3]

May 1989 (12"/CD): 'I Want It All' (edit) / 'Hang On In There' / 'I Want It All' (12/CD QUEEN 10) [3]

June 1989: 'Breakthru' / 'Stealin'' (QUEEN 11) [7]

June 1989 (12"/CD): 'Breakthru' (extended) / 'Stealin'' / 'Breakthru' (12/CD QUEEN 11) [7]

August 1989: 'The Invisible Man' / 'Hijack My Heart' (QUEEN 12) [12]

August 1989 (12"/CD): 'The Invisible Man' (extended) / 'Hijack My Heart' / 'The Invisible Man' (12/CD QUEEN 12) [12]

October 1989: 'Scandal' / 'My Life Has Been Saved' (QUEEN 14) [25]

October 1989 (12"/CD): 'Scandal' (extended) / 'My Life Has Been Saved' / 'Scandal' (12/CD QUEEN 14) [25]

November 1989: 'The Miracle' / 'Stone Cold Crazy' (live) (QUEEN 15) [21]

November 1989 (12″/CD): 'The Miracle' / 'Stone Cold Crazy' (live) / 'My Melancholy Blues' (live) (12/CD QUEEN 15) [21]

January 1991: 'Innuendo' / 'Bijou' (QUEEN 16) [1]

January 1991 (12″/CD): 'Innuendo' (explosive version) / 'Under Pressure' (Queen & David Bowie) / 'Bijou' (12/CD QUEEN 16) [1]

March 1991: 'I'm Going Slightly Mad' / 'The Hitman' (QUEEN 17) [22]

March 1991 (12″/CD): 'I'm Going Slightly Mad' / 'The Hitman' / 'Lost Opportunity' (12/CD QUEEN 17) [22]

May 1991: 'Headlong' / 'All God's People' (QUEEN 18) [14]

May 1991 (12″/CD): 'Headlong' / 'All God's People' / 'Mad The Swine' (12/CD QUEEN 18) [14]

October 1991: 'The Show Must Go On' / 'Keep Yourself Alive' (QUEEN 19) [16]

October 1991 (12″): 'The Show Must Go On' / 'Keep Yourself Alive' / 'Queen Talks' (12 QUEEN 19) [16]

October 1991 (CD): 'The Show Must Go On' / 'Keep Yourself Alive' / 'Queen Talks' / 'Body Language' (CD QUEEN 19) [16]

October 1991 (CD): 'The Show Must Go On' / 'Now I'm Here' / 'Fat Bottomed Girls' / 'Las Palabras De Amor (The Words Of Love)' (CD QUEENS 19) [16]

December 1991 (double A-side): 'Bohemian Rhapsody' / 'These Are The Days Of Our Lives' (QUEEN 20) [1]

October 1995 (cassette): 'Heaven For Everyone' (edit) / 'It's A Beautiful Day' (remix) (TC QUEEN 21) [2]

October 1995 (CD): 'Heaven For Everyone' (edit) / 'It's A Beautiful Day' (remix) / 'Heaven For Everyone' (CD QUEENS 21) [2]

October 1995 (CD): 'Heaven For Everyone' (edit) / 'Keep Yourself Alive' / 'Seven Seas Of Rhye' / 'Killer Queen' (CD QUEEN 21) [2]

December 1995 (cassette): 'A Winter's Tale' / 'Thank God It's Christmas' (TC QUEEN 22) [6]

December 1995 (CD): 'A Winter's Tale' / 'Thank God It's Christmas' / 'Rock In Rio Blues' (CD QUEENS 22) [6]

December 1995 (CD): 'A Winter's Tale' / 'Now I'm Here' / 'You're My Best Friend' / 'Somebody To Love' (CD QUEEN 22) [6]

February 1996: 'Too Much Love Will Kill You' / 'We Will Rock You' / 'We Are The Champions' (QUEEN 23) [15]

February 1996 (CD): 'Too Much Love Will Kill You' / 'We Will Rock You' / 'We Are The Champions' / 'Spread Your Wings' (CD QUEEN 23) [15]

June 1996: 'Let Me Live' / 'Fat Bottomed Girls' / 'Bicycle Race' (QUEEN PD 24) [9]

June 1996 (CD): 'Let Me Live' / 'Fat Bottomed Girls' / 'Bicycle Race' / 'Don't Stop Me Now' (CD QUEENS 24) [9]

June 1996 (CD): 'Let Me Live' / 'My Fairy King' (BBC) / 'Doing Alright' (BBC) / 'Liar' (BBC) (CD QUEEN 24) [9]

November 1996 (cassette): 'You Don't Fool Me' / 'You Don't Fool Me' (Dancing Divaz club mix) (TC QUEEN 25) [17]

November 1996 (12″/CD): 'You Don't Fool Me' / 'You Don't Fool Me' (Dancing Divaz club mix) / 'You Don't Fool Me' (Sexy club mix) / 'You Don't Fool Me' (Late mix) (12/CD QUEEN 25) [17]

January 1998 (withdrawn): 'No-One But You (Only The Good Die Young)' / 'Princes Of The Universe' (QUEEN 26)

January 1998 (double A-side): 'No-One But You (Only The Good Die Young)' / 'Tie Your Mother Down' (edit) / 'We Will Rock You' (Ruined by Rick Rubin) / 'Gimme The Prize (Kurgan's Theme)' (instrumental) (QUEEN PD 27) [13]

February 2011 (download): 'Keep Yourself Alive' (long lost retake) / 'Stone Cold Crazy'

April 2011: Stormtroopers In Stillettoes: 'Keep Yourself Alive' (long lost retake) / 'Stone Cold Crazy' (Island Records 2765780)

November 2014 (download): 'Let Me In Your Heart Again' (William Orbit remix)

October 2016 (download): 'We Will Rock You' (fast BBC version)

October 2017 (download): 'We Will Rock You' (Raw Sessions version)

October 2017 (download): 'We Are The Champions' (Raw Sessions version)

US SINGLES

October 1973: 'Keep Yourself Alive' / 'Son And Daughter' (EK45863)

February 1974: 'Liar' (edit) / 'Doing All Right' (EK45884)

June 1974: 'Seven Seas Of Rhye' / 'See What A Fool I've Been' (EK45891)

October 1974 (double A-side): 'Killer Queen' / 'Flick Of The Wrist' (edit) (E45226) [12]

July 1975: 'Keep Yourself Alive' (edit) / 'Lily Of The Valley' / 'God Save The Queen' (E45268)

December 1975: 'Bohemian Rhapsody' / 'I'm In Love With My Car' (E45297) [9]

June 1976: 'You're My Best Friend' / "39' (E45318) [16]

December 1976: 'Somebody To Love' / 'White Man' (E45362) [13]

March 1977: 'Tie Your Mother Down' (edit) / 'Drowse' (E45385) [49]

June 1977: 'Long Away' / 'You And I' (E45412)

October 1977 (double A-side): 'We Will Rock You' / 'We Are The Champions' (E45441) [4]

April 1978: 'It's Late' / 'Sheer Heart Attack' (E45478) [74]

October 1978 (double A-side): 'Bicycle Race' / 'Fat Bottomed Girls' (edit) (E45541) [24]

February 1979: 'Don't Stop Me Now' / 'More Of That Jazz' (E46008) [86]

April 1979: 'Jealousy' / 'Fun It' (E46039)

August 1979: 'We Will Rock You' (live) / 'Let Me Entertain You' (live) (E46532)

December 1979: 'Crazy Little Thing Called Love' / 'Spread Your Wings' (live) (E46579) [1]

June 1980: 'Play The Game' / 'A Human Body' (E46652) [42]

August 1980: 'Another One Bites The Dust' / 'Don't Try Suicide' (E47031) [1]

November 1980: 'Need Your Loving Tonight' / 'Rock It' (Prime Jive)' (E47086) [44]

January 1981: 'Flash' (edit) / 'Football Fight' (E47092) [42]

October 1981: 'Under Pressure' (Queen & David Bowie) / 'Soul Brother' (E47235) [29]

April 1982: 'Body Language' / 'Life Is Real (Song For Lennon)' (E47452) [11]

July 1982: 'Calling All Girls' / 'Put Out The Fire' (E69981) [60]

November 1982: 'Staying Power' / 'Back Chat' (E67975)

February 1984: 'Radio Ga Ga' / 'I Go Crazy' (B5317) [16]

April 1984: 'I Want To Break Free' (edit) / 'Machines (Or "Back To Humans")' (instrumental) (B5350) [45]

July 1984: 'It's A Hard Life' / 'Is This The World We Created...?' (B5372) [72]

October 1984: 'Hammer To Fall' (edit) / 'Tear It Up' (B5424)

November 1985: 'One Vision' (edit) / 'Blurred Vision' (B5530) [61]

November 1985 (12"): 'One Vision' (extended) / 'Blurred Vision' (V-15210) [61]

April 1986: 'Princes Of The Universe' / 'A Dozen Red Roses For My Darling' (B5568)

June 1986: 'A Kind Of Magic' / 'Gimme The Prize (Kurgan's Theme)' (B5590) [42]

June 1986 (12"): 'A Kind Of Magic' / 'Gimme The Prize (Kurgan's Theme)' (V-15232) [42]

August 1986: 'Pain Is So Close To Pleasure' (edit) / 'Don't Lose Your Head' (B5633)

August 1986 (12"): 'Pain Is So Close To Pleasure' (extended) / 'Don't Lose Your Head' (V-15260)

May 1989: 'I Want It All' (edit) / 'Hang On In There' (B44372) [50]

October 1989: 'Scandal' / 'My Life Has Been Saved' (B45771)
October 1989 (CD): 'Scandal' / 'My Life Has Been Saved' / 'Hijack My Heart' / 'Stealin'' (CDP 7 15514 2)

January 1991: 'Headlong' / 'Under Pressure' (Queen & David Bowie) (HR64920)

September 1991: 'These Are The Days Of Our Lives' / 'Bijou' (HR64868)

February 1992 (double A-side): 'Bohemian Rhapsody' / 'The Show Must Go On' (HR64794) [2]

May 1992 (CD): 'We Will Rock You' (ruined by Rick Rubin) / 'We Will Rock You' (ruined instrumental) / 'We Are The Champions' (ruined by Rick Rubin) / 'We Will Rock You' (big beat a cappella) / 'We Will Rock You' (Zulu scratch a cappella) (HB665732)

July 1992 (cassette): 'We Are The Champions' / 'We Will Rock You' / 'These Are The Days Of Our Lives' (HR659254) [52]

July 1992: 'We Are The Champions' / 'These Are The Days Of Our Lives' (HR659257) [52]

July 1992 (CD): 'We Are The Champions' / 'We Will Rock You' / 'We Are The Champions' (HR659252) [52]

January 1996: 'Too Much Love Will Kill You' (edit) / 'Rock In Rio Blues' (HR640052) [118]

January 1996 (CD): 'Too Much Love Will Kill You' (edit) / 'Rock In Rio Blues' (HR640054) [118]

June 1996: 'Heaven For Everyone' (edit) / 'Soul Brother' (HR640064)

June 1996 (CD): 'Heaven For Everyone' (edit) / 'Soul Brother' (HR640062)

November 1996 *(12")*: 'You Don't Fool Me' *(Freddie's Club mix)* / 'You Don't Fool Me' / 'You Don't Fool Me' *(Freddie's Revenge Dub)* / 'You Don't Fool Me' *(Queen For A Day mix)* (HR660030)

April 2011 *(7")*: 'Keep Yourself Alive' / 'Son And Daughter' (D001349621)

November 2017 *(7")*: 'We Are The Champions' / 'We Will Rock You' (D002697911)

B. QUEEN + ...

Since Freddie's death in 1991, Brian and Roger (and occasionally John) have collaborated with other musicians, or commissioned remixes of their songs, with the intent of releasing them as singles. More often than not the results have been of a questionable nature, but the desired effects were often achieved: a wider exposure to an *audience that otherwise wouldn't have been aware of Queen's songs, plus the placement of the band back in the charts. The following singles are the major singles (not promotional only) that have been credited as "Queen +".*

GEORGE MICHAEL:

April 1993: *Five Live EP:* 'Somebody To Love' / 'Killer' *(George Michael only)* / 'Papa Was A Rolling Stone' *(George Michael only)* / 'These Are The Days Of Our Lives' *(with Lisa Stansfield)* / 'Calling You' *(George Michael only)* (R6340) [1]

April 1993 *(CD)*: *Five Live EP:* 'Somebody To Love' / 'Killer' *(George Michael only)* / 'Papa Was A Rolling Stone' *(George Michael only)* / 'These Are The Days Of Our Lives' *(with Lisa Stansfield)* / 'Calling You' *(George Michael only)* / 'Dear Friends' *(Queen only)* (CDRS 6340) [1]

May 1993: *Five Live EP:* 'Somebody To Love' / 'Killer' *(George Michael only)* / 'Papa Was A Rolling Stone' *(George Michael only)* / 'These Are The Days Of Our Lives' *(with Lisa Stansfield)* / 'Calling You' *(George Michael only)* / 'Dear Friends' *(Queen only)* (HR614792)

WYCLEF JEAN:

November 1998 *(CD)*: 'Another One Bites The Dust' / 'Another One Bites The Dust' *(Team 1 Black Rock Star Main Pass Mix)* / 'Another One Bites The Dust' *(Team 1 Black Rock Star Radio Edit)* (DRM CD 22364) [5]

DAVID BOWIE:

December 1999: 'Under Pressure' *('rah' remix edit)* / 'Bohemian Rhapsody' (QUEEN PD 28) [14]

December 1999 *(CD)*: 'Under Pressure' *('rah' remix edit)* / 'Bohemian Rhapsody' / 'Thank God It's Christmas' (CD QUEEN 28) [14]

December 1999 *(CD)*: 'Under Pressure' *('rah' remix edit)* / 'Under Pressure' *(Knebworth mix)* / 'Under Pressure' *(Mike Spencer mix)* / *enhanced section* (CD QUEENS 28) [14]

5IVE:

July 2000: 'We Will Rock You' *(radio edit)* / '5ive Megamix' (Parlophone 774 032) [1]

VANGUARD:

March 2003 *(CD)*: 'Flash' *(radio mix)* / 'Flash Mix' / *enhanced section* (NEBCD 041) [15]

March 2003 *(12")*: 'Flash' *(extended mix)* / 'Flash' *(electro mix)* (NEBT 041) [15]

March 2003 *(12")*: 'Flash' *(Tomcraft mix)* / 'Flash' *(Christian Smith & John Selway mix)* (NEBTX 041) [15]

THE MIAMI PROJECT:

December 2006: 'Another One Bites The Dust' *(Cedric Gervais & Second Sun radio edit)* / 'Another One Bites The Dust' *(Queen version)* (7TIV250) [31]

December 2006 *(CD)*: 'Another One Bites The Dust' *(Cedric Gervais & Second Sun radio edit)* / 'Another One Bites The Dust' *(Cedric Gervais & Second Sun vocal mix)* / 'Another One Bites The Dust' *(Oliver Koletzki remix)* / 'Another One Bites The Dust' *(A Skillz remix)* / 'Another One Bites The Dust' *(Soul Avengerz remix)* / 'Another One Bites The Dust' *(DJ Pedro & Olivier Berger mix)* / *enhanced section* (CDTIVS250) [31]

December 2006 *(12")*: 'Another One Bites The Dust' *(Cedric Gervais & Second Sun vocal mix)* / 'Another One Bites The Dust' *(Oliver Koletzki remix)* / 'Another One Bites The Dust' *(A Skillz remix)* (12TIV250) [31]

PAUL RODGERS:

December 2007 *(download)*: 'Say It's Not True'

December 2007 *(CD)*: 'Say It's Not True' / 'Say It's Not True' *(video)* (46664) [90]

September 2008: 'C-Lebrity' / 'Fire And Water' *(live)* (2370097) [33]

September 2008 *(CD)*: 'C-lebrity' / 'C-Lebrity' *(video from* Al Murray's Happy Hour*)* (2370102) [33]

C. SOLO

Solo singles round out the section: Roger's singles were distributed by EMI until 'Strange Frontier' (all his UK singles with The Cross were also distributed by EMI), with subsequent releases starting with 'Nazis 1994' distributed by Parlophone. His sole US single release on Elektra was 'Let's Get Crazy', with the remaining singles distributed by Capitol. EMI in the UK and Capitol in the US distributed Brian's first single, 'Star Fleet'; Parlophone distributed subsequent UK releases, with his few US singles

distributed by Hollywood. Freddie's single releases become a little complex. 'Love Kills' through 'Love Me Like There's No Tomorrow' were distributed by CBS in the UK and Columbia in the US; 'Time' was distributed by EMI; 'The Great Pretender', 'In My Defence' and subsequent singles were distributed by Parlophone, and 'Barcelona' (both 1987 and 1992 releases), 'The Golden Boy' and 'How Can I Go On' were all distributed by Polydor. Any US singles from 1991 onwards were distributed by Hollywood.

SMILE

August 1969: 'Earth' / 'Step On Me' (Mercury 72977 1-45117/8; *USA only*)

LARRY LUREX

June 1973: 'I Can Hear Music' / 'Goin' Back' (EMI 2030)

July 1973: 'I Can Hear Music' / 'Goin' Back' (Anthem AN 204)

FREDDIE MERCURY

September 1984: 'Love Kills' / 'Rotwang's Party (Robot Dance)' *(note: B-side does not feature Freddie)* (CBS A 4735) [10]

September 1984 *(12")*: 'Love Kills' *(extended)* / 'Rotwang's Party (Robot Dance)' *(note: B-side does not feature Freddie)* (CBS TA 4735) [10]

September 1984: 'Love Kills' / 'Rotwang's Party (Robot Dance)' *(note: B-side does not feature Freddie)* (Columbia 38-04606) [69]

September 1984 *(12")*: 'Love Kills' *(extended)* / 'Rotwang's Party (Robot Dance)' *(note: B-side does not feature Freddie)* (Columbia 44-05098) [69]

April 1985: 'I Was Born To Love You' / 'Stop All The Fighting' (CBS A 6019) [11]

April 1985 *(12")*: 'I Was Born To Love You' *(extended)* / 'Stop All The Fighting' (CBS TA 6019) [11]

April 1985: 'I Was Born To Love You' / 'Stop All The Fighting' (Columbia 38-04869) [76]

April 1985 *(12")*: 'I Was Born To Love You' *(extended)* / 'Stop All The Fighting' (Columbia 44-05197) [76]

July 1985: 'Made In Heaven' / 'She Blows Hot And Cold' (CBS A 6413) [57]

July 1985 *(12")*: 'Made In Heaven' *(extended)* / 'She Blows Hot And Cold' (CBS TA 6413) [57]

September 1985: 'Living On My Own' / 'My Love Is Dangerous' (CBS A 6555) [50]

September 1985 *(12")*: 'Living On My Own' *(extended)* / 'My Love Is Dangerous' *(extended)* (CBS TA 6555) [50]

November 1985: 'Love Me Like There's No Tomorrow' / 'Let's Turn It On' (CBS A 6725) [76]

November 1985 *(12")*: 'Love Me Like There's No Tomorrow' *(extended)* / 'Let's Turn It On' *(extended)* (CBS TA 6725) [76]

November 1985 *(12")*: 'Love Me Like There's No Tomorrow' *(extended)* / 'Let's Turn It On' *(extended)* / 'Living On My Own' *(extended)* / 'My Love Is Dangerous' *(extended)* (CBS TA 6725/6555) [76]

May 1986: 'Time' / 'Time' *(instrumental)* (EMI 5559) [32]

May 1986 (12"): 'Time' (extended) / 'Time' / 'Time' (instrumental) (12EMI 5559) [32]

March 1987: 'The Great Pretender' / 'Exercises In Free Love' (R 6151) [4]

March 1987 (12"): 'The Great Pretender' (extended) / 'The Great Pretender' / 'Exercises In Free Love' (12R 6151) [4]

October 1987: 'Barcelona' / 'Exercises In Free Love' (POSP 887) [8]

October 1987 (12"): 'Barcelona' (extended) / 'Barcelona' / 'Exercises In Free Love' (POSPX 887) [8]

October 1987 (CD): 'Barcelona' (edit) / 'Exercises In Free Love' / 'Barcelona' (extended) (POCD 887) [8]

October 1988: 'The Golden Boy' / 'The Fallen Priest' (PO 23) [83]

October 1988 (12"): 'The Golden Boy' / 'The Fallen Priest' / 'The Golden Boy' (instrumental) (PZ 23) [83]

October 1988 (CD): 'The Golden Boy' / 'The Fallen Priest' / 'The Golden Boy' (instrumental) (PZCD 23) [83]

January 1989: 'How Can I Go On' / 'Overture Piccante' (PO 29) [95]

January 1989 (12"): 'Guide Me Home' / 'How Can I Go On' / 'Overture Piccante' (PZ 29) [95]

January 1989 (CD): 'Guide Me Home' / 'How Can I Go On' / 'Overture Piccante' (PZCD 29) [95]

July 1992: 'Barcelona' (edit) / 'Exercises In Free Love' / 'Barcelona' (TV edit) (PO 221) [2]

July 1992 (CD): 'Barcelona' / 'Exercises In Free Love' / 'Barcelona' (extended) / 'Barcelona' (TV edit) (PZCD 221) [2]

November 1992 (CD): 'How Can I Go On' / 'The Golden Boy' / 'The Fallen Priest' (PZCD 234)

December 1992: 'In My Defence' / 'Love Kills' (remix) (R 6331) [8]

December 1992 (CD): 'In My Defence' (remix) / 'Love Kills' (remix) / 'She Blows Hot And Cold' / 'In My Defence' (CDRS 6331) [8]

December 1992 (CD): 'In My Defence' (remix) / 'Love Kills' (remix) / 'Mr Bad Guy' / 'Living On My Own' (remix) (CDR 6331) [8]

February 1993: 'The Great Pretender' / 'Stop All The Fighting' (R 6336) [29]

February 1993 (CD): 'The Great Pretender' / 'Stop All The Fighting' / 'Exercises In Free Love' / 'The Great Pretender' (remix) (CDR6336) [29]

February 1993 (CD): 'The Great Pretender' / 'The Great Pretender' (film version) (PRCD-10202-2)

July 1993: 'Living On My Own' (No More Brothers remix) / 'Living On My Own' (remix) (R 6355) [1]

July 1993 (CD): 'Living On My Own' (radio mix) / 'Living On My Own' (extended mix) / 'Living On My Own' (club mix) / 'Living On My Own' (album mix) (CDR6355) [1]

July 1993 (CD): 'Living On My Own' (radio mix) / 'Living On My Own' (extended mix) / 'Living On My Own' (club mix) / 'Living On My Own' (album mix) (PRCD-10287-2)

BRIAN MAY

October 1983: 'Star Fleet' (edit) / 'Son Of Star Fleet' (EMI 5436) [65]

November 1983: 'Star Fleet' (edit) / 'Son Of Star Fleet' (SPRO-9009)

November 1991: 'Driven By You' / 'Just One Life' (R 6304) [6]

November 1991 (12"): 'Driven By You' / 'Just One Life' / 'Driven By You' (advert version) (12R 6304) [6]

November 1991 (CD): 'Driven By You' / 'Just One Life' / 'Just One Life' (guitar version) (CDR6304) [6]

December 1991: 'Driven By You' / 'Just One Life' (HR64642)

August 1992: 'Too Much Love Will Kill You' / 'I'm Scared' (edit) (R 6320) [5]

August 1992: 'Too Much Love Will Kill You' / 'I'm Scared' (edit) / 'Too Much Love Will Kill You' (guitar version) / 'Driven By You' (new version) (CDR6320) [5]

November 1992: 'Back To The Light' / 'Nothin' But Blue' (R 6329) [19]

November 1992 (CD): 'Back To The Light' / 'Nothin' But Blue' / 'Star Fleet' / 'Let Me Out' (CDRX6329) [19]

November 1992 (CD): 'Back To The Light' / 'Nothin' But Blue' / 'Blues Breaker' (CDR 6329) [19]

June 1993 (12"/CD): 'Resurrection' (edit) / 'Love Token' (edit) / 'Too Much Love Will Kill You' (live) (12RPD 6351/ CDRS 6351) [23]

June 1993 (CD): 'Resurrection' / 'Driven By You Two' / 'Back To The Light' (live on The Tonight Show) / 'Tie Your Mother Down' (live on The Tonight Show) (CDR 6351) [23]

December 1993: 'Last Horizon' (edit) / ''39' / Let Your Heart Rule Your Head' (live) (R 6371) [51]

December 1993 (CD): 'Last Horizon' (edit) / 'Last Horizon' (live) / 'We Will Rock You' (live) / 'Last Horizon' (CDR6371) [51]

March 1995 *(CD)*: 'The Amazing Spiderman' *(mastermix)* / 'The Amazing Spiderman' *(sad bit)* / 'The Amazing Spiderman' *(white trouser)* / 'The Amazing Spiderperson' *(brown trouser)* / 'The Amazing DJ Perk' *(favourite strings)* (CDR6404) [35]

March 1995 *(12")*: 'The Amazing Spiderman' *(mastermix)* / 'The Amazing Spiderman' *(sad bit)* / 'The Amazing Spiderman' *(white trouser)* (12RPD 6404) [35]

March 1995 *(cassette)*: 'The Amazing Spiderman' *(mastermix)* / 'The Amazing Spiderman' *(sad bit)* (TCR 6404) [35]

May 1998: 'The Business' *(Rock on Cozy mix)* / 'Maybe Baby' (R 6498) [51]

May 1998 *(CD)*: 'The Business' *(Rock on Cozy mix)* / 'Maybe Baby' / 'Brian Talks' / 'Enhanced Multimedia Section' (CDR6498) [51]

August 1998 *(7"/CD)*: 'Why Don't We Try Again?' / 'Only Make Believe' / 'F.B.I.' (8860587/CDR 6504) [44]

BRIAN MAY AND KERRY ELLIS

November 2012 *(12"/download)*: 'Born Free' / 'Born Free' *(acoustic version)* (Duck Productions Ltd. KEI2002)

April 2013 *(7"/download)*: 'The Kissing Me Song' *(full version)* / 'The Kissing Me Song' *(radio edit)* (Duck Productions Ltd. KEO 7001)

April 2015 *(download)*: 'One Voice"

February 2016 *(download)*: 'Roll With You'

April 2016 *(download)*: 'Amazing Grace'

June 2017 *(download)*: 'Panic Attack'

ROGER TAYLOR

August 1977: 'I Wanna Testify' / 'Turn On The TV' (EMI 2679)

April 1981: 'Future Management' / 'Laugh Or Cry' (EMI 5157) [49]

May 1981: 'Let's Get Crazy' / 'Laugh Or Cry' (E47 151; *USA only*)

June 1981: 'My Country' *(edit)* / 'Fun In Space' (EMI 5200)

June 1984: 'Man On Fire' / 'Killing Time' (EMI 5478) [66]

June 1984 *(12")*: 'Man On Fire' *(extended)* / 'Killing Time' (EMI 12EMI 5478) [66]

July 1984: 'Man On Fire' / 'Killing Time' (Capitol B-5364)

July 1984 *(12")*: 'Man On Fire' *(extended)* / 'I Cry For You (Love, Hope & Confusion)' / 'It's An Illusion' (SPRO 9149/50)

August 1984: 'Strange Frontier' / 'I Cry For You (Love, Hope & Confusion)' *(remix)* / 'Two Sharp Pencils (Get Bad)' *(12" only)* (EMI 5490)

August 1984 *(12")*: 'Strange Frontier' *(extended)* / 'I Cry For You (Love, Hope & Confusion)' *(extended)* / 'Two Sharp Pencils (Get Bad)' (EMI 12 EMI 5490) [98]

September 1984: 'Strange Frontier' / 'I Cry For You (Love, Hope & Confusion)' (B5420)

September 1984 *(12")*: 'Strange Frontier' / 'Strange Frontier' *(extended)* (SPRO 9258)

May 1994: 'Nazis 1994' / 'Nazis 1994' *(radio remix)* (R 6379) [22]

May 1994 *(12")*: 'Nazis 1994' *(edit)* / 'Nazis 1994' *(radio mix)* / 'Nazis 1994' *(Makita mix)* / 'Nazis 1994' *(Big Science mix)* (12RC 6379) [22]

May 1994 *(CD)*: 'Nazis 1994' *(edit)* / 'Nazis 1994' *(radio mix)* / 'Nazis 1994' *(kick mix)* / 'Nazis 1994' *(Schindler's

mix)* / 'Nazis 1994' *(Makita mix)* / 'Nazis 1994' *(Big Science mix)* (CDR 6379) [22]

October 1994: 'Foreign Sand' *(edit)* / "You Had To Be There" (R 6389) [26]

October 1994 *(12")*: 'Foreign Sand' *(edit)* / "You Had To Be There" / 'Foreign Sand' / 'Final Destination' (12R 6389) [26]

October 1994 *(CD)*: 'Foreign Sand' *(edit)* / "You Had To Be There" / 'Foreign Sand' / 'Final Destination' (CDR 6389) [26]

November 1994: 'Happiness?' / 'Ride The Wild Wind' *(live)* (R 6399) [32]

November 1994 *(12")*: 'Happiness?' / 'Dear Mr Murdoch' / 'Everybody Hurts Sometime' *(live)* / 'Old Friends' *(live)* (12R 6399) [32]

November 1994 *(CD)*: 'Happiness?' / 'Loneliness...' / 'Dear Mr Murdoch' / 'I Want To Break Free' *(live)* (CDR 6399) [32]

October 1998: 'Pressure On' *(edit)* / 'People On Streets' *(mashed)* / 'Tonight' *(Dub Sangria)* (R 6507) [45]

October 1998 *(CD)*: 'Pressure On' *(edit)* / 'People On Streets' *(mashed)* / 'Tonight' *(Dub Sangria)* (CDR 6507) [45]

October 1998 *(CD)*: 'Pressure On' *(edit)* / 'Dear Mr Murdoch' / 'Keep A Knockin" (CDRS 6507) [45]

April 1999: 'Surrender' *(radio mix)* / 'London Town, C'mon Down' [38]

April 1999 *(CD)*: 'Surrender' *(radio mix)* / 'A Nation Of Haircuts' *(club cut)* / 'London Town, C'mon Down' *(edit)* (CDR 6517) [38]

April 1999 *(CD)*: 'Surrender' *(live)* / 'No More Fun' *(live)* / 'Tonight' *(live)* / 'Surrender' *(enhanced live video)* (CDR 6517) [38]

November 2009 *(download)*: 'The Unblinking Eye (Everything Is Broken)'

January 2010 *(CD)*: 'The Unblinking Eye (Everything Is Broken)' / 'The Unblinking Eye (Everything Is Broken)' *(Almost Completely Nude mix)* / 'The Unblinking Eye (Everything Is Broken)' *(video)* (NJ1001)

July 2011 *(download)*: 'Dear Mr Murdoch' *(nude mix)*

May 2017 *(download)*: 'Journey's End'

July 2017 *(12″)*: 'Two Sharp Pencils (Get Bad)' *(Anna Wall & Corbi remix)* / 'Two Sharp Pencils (Get Bad)' *(Jamie 3:26 Punk Funk version)* (Music For Freaks MFFV15015)

November 2017 *(10″)*: 'Journey's End' / 'Tonight' *(Cocktail Mix)* / 'Journey's End' *(instrumental)* / 'Revelation' *(The Hungry Mix)* (Omnivore Recordings OVS10-245)

April 2018 *(10″)*: 'Journey's End' / 'Journey's End' *(instrumental)* (Nightjar Productions Ltd 0602567332435)

FELIX + ARTY

August 2006 *(download)*: 'Woman You're So Beautiful (But Still A Pain In The Ass)' *(main mix)* / 'Woman You're So Beautiful (But Still A Pain In The Ass)' *(dance mix)* / 'Woman You're So Beautiful (But Still A Pain In The Ass)' *(mad mix)*

THE CROSS

October 1987: 'Cowboys And Indians' *(edit)* / 'Love Lies Bleeding (She Was A Wicked, Wily Waitress) ' (VS 1007) [74]

October 1987 *(12″)*: 'Cowboys And Indians' / 'Love Lies Bleeding (She Was A Wicked, Wily Waitress) ' (VST 1007) [74]

October 1987 *(CD)*: 'Cowboys And Indians' / 'Cowboys And Indians' *(edit)* / 'Love Lies Bleeding (She Was A Wicked, Wily Waitress)' (Virgin CDEP 10) [74]

January 1988: 'Shove It!' / 'Rough Justice' (VS 1026) [82]

January 1988 *(12″)*: 'Shove It!' *(extended)* / 'Rough Justice' / 'Shove It'! *(Metropolix mix)* (VST 1026) [82]

January 1988 *(CD)*: 'Shove It!' / 'Rough Justice' / 'Cowboys And Indians' / 'Shove It!' *(extended)* (Virgin CDEP 20) [82]

February 1988: 'Shove It!' / 'Feel The Force' (Virgin USA 7 99327; *USA only*)

April 1988: 'Heaven For Everyone' / 'Love On A Tightrope (Like An Animal) ' (VS 1062) [84]

April 1988 *(12″)*: 'Heaven For Everyone' / 'Love On A Tightrope (Like An Animal) ' / 'Contact' (VST 1062) [84]

July 1988: 'Manipulator' / 'Stand Up For Love' (VS 1100)

July 1988 *(12″)*: 'Manipulator' *(extended)* / 'Stand Up For Love' / 'Manipulator' (VST 1100)

May 1990: 'Power To Love' / 'Passion For Trash' (R 6251) [83]

May 1990 *(12″)*: 'Power To Love' *(extended)* / 'Passion For Trash' / 'Power To Love' (R 6251) [83]

May 1990 *(CD)*: 'Power To Love' *(extended)* / 'Passion For Trash' *(Macrae)* / 'Power To Love' (CDR 6251) [83]

JOHN DEACON

March 1986: 'No Turning Back' / 'No Turning Back' *(Chocs Away mix)* (MCA 1057)

March 1986 *(12″)*: 'No Turning Back' / 'No Turning Back' *(Chocs Away mix)* / 'No Turning Back' *(Joystick mix)* (MCAT 1057)

GOT TO FOLLOW THAT DREAM

In the second edition of this book, which I finished in June 2011, I wrote that Queen are more prevalent than ever. Little did I know that their status could only have risen further in the ensuing seven years, and that they've once again firmly ensconced themselves in the upper echelon of legacy bands, the true rock 'n' roll dinosaurs who don't have to resort to playing at county fairs or other such seemingly undistinguished venues. Brian May and Roger Taylor have happily taken Queen's torch, which had been extinguished far too soon with the death of Freddie Mercury, and reignited it, with the addition of Adam Lambert as their newest vocalist. It may not be the Queen of their glory days, but to be able to see Brian and Roger onstage in the 21st century is something that only few could have predicted would have happened. The two survivors of one of rock's greatest and most successful bands couldn't even have predicted it themselves, and continue to express amazement that Queen still endures as both a legacy act and as an ongoing beast.

Despite the underwhelming response and promotion of the Queen + Paul Rodgers album, *The Cosmos Rocks*, and the tumultuous resulting tour, Brian has come through, relatively unscathed. Though he had to cancel all of his commitments in 2016 due to a persistent illness, he rebounded with more enthusiasm than he'd had in years prior. Whether that's due to teaming up with Adam Lambert or finding his songwriting muse once again with Kerry Ellis is uncertain, but his interests extend beyond that of a rock god: permanently interested in astronomy, he's also published books on stereo and 3D photography, and remains a tireless advocate for animal rights.

Roger, meanwhile, has embraced aging, and continues to write and record on his own terms, producing quality material that is on a par with his peers, and even occasionally equal to his band's greatest moments. He married his muse, Sarina Potgieter, in September 2010, and the two have enjoyed the jet-setting lifestyle that his success has afforded him.

For John Deacon, the unflinching, rock-steady bassist with a savvy business command, he couldn't perceive of Queen without Freddie, and effectively retired from the music industry in 1997, after contributing bass to 'No-One But You (Only The Good Die Young)'. Despite some fabricated jabs at his former bandmates and an unsurprising carnal interest in scantily-clad women, John has given his silent blessing to all that Brian and Roger do, preferring to spend his time on the golf course and with his children than on a stage or in a recording studio. Occasionally spotted at a *We Will Rock You* premiere, in the wedding party of one of his children, or strolling the streets of London near his home, John is healthy and happy to be away from the spotlight glare.

Freddie Mercury may be gone, but he's certainly not forgotten. With Queen + Adam Lambert continuing to sell out arenas everywhere they go, each concert is a special tribute to him, and his legacy still endures to this day. While he was taken from us far too soon, his work has been rediscovered in the past decade, leading to bands and showmen inspired by his sound, his theatrics, and his charisma – artists like The Darkness, Lady Gaga, Foo Fighters, and My Chemical Romance all have him to thank for laying the groundwork. The imminent release of *Bohemian Rhapsody*, the long-delayed biopic, will undoubtedly open the eyes of a whole new generation, just waiting to discover the majesty of the messenger of the gods.

I don't know if this will be the final edition of this book. It was a long and arduous seven years to keep up with the frenetic activity of their archival releases and their ongoing world tours, but as long as Brian and Roger keep up with it, and as long as new and old fans keep discovering – or rediscovering – the band, then there will always be a place somewhere to find out more about Queen. Long may they reign.

Select Bibliography

BOOKS

Blake, Mark: *Is This The Real Life? The Untold Story Of Queen* (Da Capo Press, 2010)

Brooks, Greg, *Queen Live: A Concert Documentary* (Omnibus Press, 1995; revised 2005)

Brooks, Greg, sleeve-notes for *The Freddie Mercury Collection* (EMI, 2000)

Dean, Ken, *Queen: The New Visual Documentary* (Omnibus Press, 1992)

Freestone, Peter with David Evans, *Freddie Mercury: An Intimate Memoir* (Omnibus Press, 1998)

Gunn, Jacky and Jim Jenkins, *Queen: As It Began* (Hyperion, 1992)

Hodkinson, Mark, *The Early Years* (Omnibus Press, 1995; revised 2004)

Hogan, Peter K, *The Complete Guide To The Music Of Queen* (Omnibus Press, 1994)

Jackson, Laura, *Queen and I: The Brian May Story* (Smith Gryphon, 1994)

Lewry, Peter and Nigel Goodall, *The Ultimate Queen* (Simon & Schuster, 1998)

Lowe, Jacques, *Queen's Greatest Pix* (Quartet Books, 1981)

Nester, Daniel, *God Save My Queen: A Tribute* (Soft Skull Press, 2003)

Nester, Daniel, *God Save My Queen II: The Show Must Go On* (Soft Skull Press, 2004)

Power, Martin, *Queen: The Complete Guide To Their Music* (Omnibus Press, 2006)

Rider, Stephen, *These Are The Days Of Our Lives: The Essential Queen Biography* (Castle Communications, 1993)

St Michael, Mick, *Queen: In Their Own Words* (Omnibus Press, 1992)

Sutcliffe, Phil, *The Ultimate Illustrated History Of The Crown Kings Of Rock* (Voyageur Press, 2009)

Over the years, many books have been published about Queen, but few have been able to expand on *As It Began*, written by Jacky Gunn (now Smith) and Jim Jenkins. Because it features an impartial look at Queen's career, usually downplaying the raunchier or more controversial events, it's still the place to start since it simply tells the story. Though, it doesn't dwell on Freddie's sexuality or final days, since it was written mainly in the late 1980s and early 1990s, shortly before the singer's death.

In 1995, two meticulously researched books were published with contrasting subject matter and offering something new: Mark Hodkinson's *The Early Years* and Greg Brooks' *Queen Live: A Concert Documentary*. The former was a fascinating tome chronicling the pre-'Bohemian Rhapsody' days, from each member's early bands to Queen's formative years, with enough information to overwhelm even the most ardent fan. The latter explored a subject that few had attempted before: Queen's live shows, which were always spectacles to behold. However, the book contained several errors that would be discovered only with the benefit of subsequent research – errors, unfortunately, not rectified in the book's 2005 update. Despite fans offering corrections and Brooks' subsequent experience as Queen's official archivist, only the concerts performed in 1979 were given a complete overhaul, even though fans such as Martin Skála, Bob Wegner, Erin and Pieter Cargill, and countless others on the Internet, devote time and energy to make sure such information is accurate and readily available.

For a firsthand account, Peter 'Phoebe' Freestone's *Freddie Mercury* is a superb read, with many insider stories on just what taking care of the man was like. Inevitably, it becomes sombre toward the end, but most of the time it's a lighthearted and often amusing book. Daniel Nester's two books, *God Save My Queen* and *God Save My Queen II*, are endearing, touching, and humorous hybrids of prose and memoir, chronicling the American fan's obsession (and latter-day frustration) with the band, their albums, and their absence from US airwaves and stages. A book devoted to Queen's discography is perpetually in the works, compiled by Greg Brooks and Brian May; Brian was evidently an avid collector of his own band's memorabilia, acquiring everything from standard single releases to curios like a replica of Frank, the robot from *News Of The World*. Tentatively titled *I Want It All!*, the book has been on and off the scheduled-to-be-released list since 2004, and, much like Gerry Stickells' *Roadworks* (a tell-all book of Queen's days on the road initially announced for a 1996 publication date, but pushed back and quietly forgotten about), this book seems to have been put on the backburner for now.

Two books appeared in anticipation of Queen's 40th anniversary, and both are excellent. Phil Sutcliffe's *The Ultimate Illustrated History Of The Crown Kings Of Rock*, awkward title notwithstanding, is an embarrassment of riches, with each page stuffed with text, rare images, and memorabilia, while Mark Blake's *Is This The Real Life?* is a warts-and-all account of Queen's history. Three more books followed in 2011: *40 Years Of Queen* (Goodman Books) by Harry Doherty is an expansive (and expensive) box set that includes reproduction memorabilia and was compiled with the full co-operation of the band, and *On Camera, Off Guard: 1969–1982* (Pavillion Books) by Mark Hayward is a compilation of rare and unpublished photos, with the photographers offering anecdotes and recollections of the images. Most impressive is Peter "Ratty" Hince's *Queen Unseen* (John Blake Publishing Ltd.), published in October 2011 and featuring the author's insight and photographic expertise.

INTERNET

With the Internet's booming popularity in the early 2000s, it's not surprising that several hundred Queen fan pages popped up, most of dubious quality or intent. Almost all sites allow for optimal interaction between fans, and I count myself as happy and proud to have discussed (and argued!) with some of the top Queen collectors and most enthusiastic and passionate Queen fans on some of these sites. The following are absolutely essential sites to visit for information, and should be bookmarked by casual and die-hard Queen fans alike.

QueenZone	www.queenzone.com
Queenpedia	www.queenpedia.com
Queen Archives	www.queenarchives.com
Queen Concerts	www.queenconcerts.com
Queen Live	queenlive.ca
Bechstein Debauchery	
	sebastian.queenconcerts.com
Queen Cuttings	www.queencuttings.com
Queen Vault	www.queenvault.com
Queen + Paul Rodgers Tour	
	www.queentour2005.wegotit.at
QueenOnline	www.queenonline.com
Brian May	www.brianmay.com
Roger Taylor	www.rogertaylorofficial.com
Freddie Mercury	www.freddiemercury.com

SOCIAL MEDIA

facebook.com/Queen
twitter.com/QueenWillRock
instagram.com/officialqueenmusic
youtube.com/Queen
twitter.com/DrBrianMay
instagram.com/brianmayforreal
twitter.com/officialrmt
facebook.com/freddiemercury
youtube.com/freddiemercurysolo
twitter.com/MercuryMOTG
twitter.com/oiqfc

Acknowledgements

I am grateful for the love and support of the following people, without whom I never would have started this project.

My thanks to Thijs Arends, Adam Baboolal, Walter Bazen, Ivor Biggun, Dan Corson, Joey Crawford, Pim Derks, Andy Ferguson, Flashman, Jeroen Geerts, Benn Kempster, Patrick Lemieux, Dan McCord, Barry O'Neil, Richard Orchard, Steve (Stav) Pickard, Jonathan Planner, Sergey I Radchenko, Ian Regan, Janet Baynes Repetsky, Scott Simpson, Cynthia A Stevens, Freya Valentine, Mike VanMaldegiam, Leonardo Venegas, Davie Wilson, Tomasz Wiznieweski, and Zeni, for invaluable audio and video references. Special thanks to Erin & Pieter Cargill for carrying the torch.

The following fans are some of the top Queen collectors in the world, each with their own specialty and area of focus, and I was honored to be asked to be a part of this brain trust of Queen fans. It's been a pleasure to pick their brains and exchange wisdom and information, and without their invaluable knowledge and encouragement, this book wouldn't have been as comprehensive as it is. So to Pablo Amieva, David Backhouse, Ron Buczko, Ferdinando Frega, Barbara Johann, Niek Lucassen, Rien van Nispen, Craig Piper, Simon Reeve, Olivier Ruth, Sebastian, Martin Skála, Alexander Smirnov, John S. Stuart, Peter Vanek, and Bob Wegner, take a bow – it's been a privilege and an honor to work with them and trade information, all for the greater good. Additional props to Bob for his superb live website and for double-checking my research.

Thanks also to Stanley Loeb for helpful advice in the initial stages. Also, many thanks to Richard Reynolds and Marcus Hearn for giving a first-time author a chance, and to Laura Price, Simon Ward, Ayoola Solarin, Natasha MacKenzie and Ali Scrivens at Titan Books for their consideration, kindness, enthusiasm, and patience.

A big thank you for their undying support goes to Alessa Abruzzo, Scott Armstrong (Sr. and Jr.), Patrice Babineau, Chelsea Bennett, Bob Bingaman, Betty Bluvshtein & Chris Hackney, Ellen Brennan, Raoul Caes, my brother and partner-in-crime Tom Castagna, Mark Costello, Mike Czawlytko & Julia Favorov, Sean Caldwell, Jacob Carpenter, Drew Cornwall, Cameron Cuming, Joe & Danielle DeCarolis, Anthony DeLuca, Nick, Nikki and Mia DiBuono, Alex & Sam Docherty, Rachael Edwards, Ken & Brittney Ehrenzeller, Liz Evans & Chris Rattray, Eileen Falchetta, Matt Gorzalski, Dave Grow & Michelle Scott, Julia Green & Phil DeBiasio, Mabel Harper & Cass Sadler, Jim, Louise & Penelope Kent, Scott Koenig, JD Korejko & Su-Shan Jessica Lai, Brandon Lapsley, Steph Larson, Dan Lawler, Brad McGinnis, Laurel Miller, Steph Mlot, David Moreau, Gabrielle Mosquera, Jeremy, Maria & Graham Nagle, Michael Nathan, Matte Noble, Steve Orenshaw, Jess Roth, Kyra Schwartz, Steve Sokolow, Eleni Solomos, John Dougherty & Valentina, Kyle, Christine & Lillian Swing, Erin Tennity & Randy Richard, Rob Troyan & Lizzie Terrell, Amy Young, and Eric Zerbe. (Oh, and I can't forget Marissa Edelman.) Incalculable thanks to Lori, Hugh, and Edward McGovern, as well as all members of the Hedrick, Purvis, Ransford, Zimmerman, and Noble families. Additional thanks to John Malhman for saving my bacon on more than one occasion, and to HRH Philip Brooks for advice and for getting me through some tough times. And boops and doots to Finn for keeping me company. Special thanks and love to Meredith Ann McGovern: "You've captured my love, stolen my heart, changed my life."

Finally, I am forever thankful to my father Georg, my mother Lynn and my sister Leah for their words of encouragement and support. Special additional thanks to mom for not only undertaking the unenviable task of making sense of what I'd written through a careful editing process, but also for starting my obsession with Queen in 1993 with a cassette of *News Of The World*. What a ride it's been.

About The Author

Georg Purvis is a writer, graphic designer, and avid music collector and enthusiast. In April 2007, with Pieter and Erin Cargill, he co-founded the website Queenpedia (www.queenpedia.com), an ever-evolving place to find information about the band. You can find out more about him at georgwrites.com and on Twitter: @georgwithoutane.

THE COMPLETE DAVID BOWIE
(REVISED AND UPDATED 2016 EDITION)

NICHOLAS PEGG

The ULTIMATE Edition– Expanded and updated with more than 70,000 words of new material!

Critically acclaimed in its previous editions, *The Complete David Bowie* is recognized as the foremost source of analysis and information on every facet of Bowie's work. The A-Z of songs and the day-by-day dateline are the most complete ever published. From his boyhood skiffle performance at the 18th Bromley Scouts' Summer Camp, to the majesty of his final masterpiece Blackstar, every aspect of David Bowie's extraordinary career is explored and dissected by Nicholas Pegg's unrivaled combination of in-depth knowledge and penetrating insight.

'All Bowie books must now be measured against The Complete David Bowie'
TIMES LITERARY SUPPLEMENT

'My go-to book for anything to do with Bowie'
GARY KEMP, SPANDAU BALLET

'Absolutely thorough, absolutely definitive and absolutely entertaining'
BBC RADIO 5 LIVE

'Nick Pegg is the one of the foremost minds in Bowie-ology'
Q

'The Complete David Bowie *certainly lives up to its title…Pegg's opinionated and witty prose turns it into that rare thing: a reference book that sparkles*'
MOJO

ISBN: 9781785653650